2018 CANADIAN ELECTRICAL CODE AND RELATED PRODUCTS

P9-EKS-326

In addition to the *2018 Canadian Electrical Code, Part I*, CSA Group offers a variety of related publications and resources designed to help keep people safe and maximize productivity.

UPDATED

2018 CE Code Handbook C22.1HB-18

Provides detailed rationale and background information behind the requirements in the *2018 CE Code, Part I*, and delivers an explanation of the rules in plain, easy-to-understand language.

NEW

2018 CE Code Integrated eBook Bundle

Combines the 2018 *CE Code* with the Handbook and Electrical Quick Reference guide in one powerful eBook bundle accessible on your tablet/mobile device, desktop and any web browser.

NEW

Commercial, Industrial & Institutional Construction – 2018 CE Code Training Course

Offered online, in-class or on-site at your location, this course is designed to help users understand and meet *CE Code* requirements in commercial, industrial and institutional construction projects.

NEW EDITION

CSA Z462 – Workplace Electrical Safety

Revised and updated for 2018, *CSA Z462* provides guidance for best practices for safely working on and around electrical equipment, guidance on due diligence in prevention of electrical injuries, and more.

Learn More

For more information or to purchase CE Code products:

✆ 1 800 463 6727 ⬚ csagroup.org/CECode

CSA GROUP™

csagroup.org

CE CODE TRAINING RESOURCES & TOOLS

From tools and practice exams, to in-depth training to get you up-to-speed on all the changes and revisions in the 2018 edition of the *Canadian Electrical Code, Part I*, CSA Group offers a comprehensive suite of solutions based on the 2018 edition and other related standards. Visit our website for the latest information on our training courses and learning tools available.

Training Courses

Detailed Overview of Changes – 2018 Canadian Electrical Code Update	Designed for *Canadian Electrical Code* users who need to know the latest changes to the newest version of the *CE Code, Part I*, this course provides a comprehensive and detailed review of key changes to the 2018 edition.
Commercial, Industrial & Institutional Construction – 2018 Canadian Electrical Code	Details *CE Code* requirements for commercial, industrial and institutional construction projects, and is ideal for *CE Code* users who use the code to install and assemble electrical equipment.
Non-Construction (Manufacturing, Design, Planning) **– 2018 Canadian Electrical Code**	Designed to help users understand and meet *CE Code* specifications related to designing, approving and planning electrical requirements.
Renewable Energy 2018 Canadian Electrical Code	Outlines the appropriate *CE Code* requirements for renewable energy, the different types of renewable energy systems, relevant system components, functions, maintenance, safety and operation.
Navigating the 2018 Canadian Electrical Code	Provides practical guidance on how to navigate and use the Code to easily locate the information you need, when you need it.
Grounding & Bonding 2018 Canadian Electrical Code	Provides detail on the grounding, bonding and equipotential bonding requirements of Section 10 of the *CE Code, Part I*.
Modularized Customized Canadian Electrical Code	Offers a flexible training approach where you control the content, timing and cost of your training session. Choose from 47 subject areas from the *CE Code, Part I* and other electrical topics.
Alberta Online Updates – Changes 2018 CE Code	Provides an overview of the provincial amendments for applying the Code in Alberta.
2018 Online Pre-Master Electrician Course	Designed to help electricians in preparing for their Master Electrician Examination.
Workplace Electrical Safety based on CSA Z462	Updated to reflect numerous changes in the 2018 edition of *CSA Z462*, this course can help you and your business become better equipped to deal with electrical hazards.
Maintenance of Electrical Systems based on CSA Z463	This 1-day training course focuses on strategies that aid in establishing an electrical maintenance program under the framework of *CSA Z463*.

Tools & Study Guides

Mobile Calculator 2018 Canadian Electrical Code	Mobile Calculator based on the *2018 CE Code, Part I*, containing 11 of the most important calculations for electrical projects.
Commercial, Industrial & Institutional Construction Handbook – 2018 Canadian Electrical Code	With a focus on sections that apply to just the commercial, industrial and institutional construction markets, this handbook explains Code requirements, how to apply them and interpret them.
Renewable Energy Guide – 2018 Canadian Electrical Code	This guide focuses on installation of renewable energy systems based on Section 64 of the *CE Code, Part I*. It explains Code requirements, how to apply them and interpret them.
2018 Canadian Electrical Practice Exam (CEPE)	Features nearly 1800 sample questions and covers each block, task and sub-task in the Red Seal Occupational Analysis to improve your chances of Red Seal exam success.

You Might Also Be Interested In

- Significant Changes – 2018 Canadian Electrical Code Update **WEBINAR**

- CE Code Part III Essentials – Guidelines for Overhead and Underground Systems

- Overview of SPE-1000 Model Code for the Field Evaluation of Electrical Equipment

Learn More

For more information or to purchase CE Code products:

☎ 1 800 463 6727   🖥 csagroup.org/CECode

Revision History

C22.1-18, Canadian Electrical Code, Part I

Errata — May 2020	Revision symbol (in margin)
Appendix B Note to Rule 12-3030	Ⓔ
Rules 2-138, 8-202, 12-112, 16-212, 62-114, and 62-402 Tables 19, 39, and 66 Index	

Errata — September 2018	Revision symbol (in margin)
Note: *The error in Subrule 86-300 2) appeared in the first print run of the 2018* CE Code, Part I. *It has been corrected in subsequent print runs.* Appendix B Notes to Rules 8-106 11), 18-050, 26-012 b), and 26-656 2) Rules 8-200, 8-202, 10-300, 12-910, 12-2320, 18-094, 24-104, and 86-300 Tables 1, 18, and 41 Index	Ⓔ

Standards Update Service

C22.1-18
January 2018

Title: *Canadian Electrical Code, Part I*

To register for e-mail notification about any updates to this publication
- go to **shop.csa.ca**
- click on **CSA Update Service**

The **List ID** that you will need to register for updates to this publication is **2425666**.

If you require assistance, please e-mail **techsupport@csagroup.org** or call 416-747-2233.

 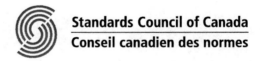

National Standard of Canada

C22.1-18
Canadian Electrical Code, Part I

Safety Standard for Electrical Installations
(Twenty-fourth edition)

- The *Canadian Electrical Code, Part I*, is a voluntary code for adoption and enforcement by regulatory authorities.
- The *Canadian Electrical Code, Part I*, meets the fundamental safety principles of International Standard IEC 60364-1, *Low-voltage electrical installations*.
- Consult with local authorities regarding regulations that adopt and/or amend this Code.

Published in January 2018 by CSA Group
A not-for-profit private sector organization
178 Rexdale Boulevard, Toronto, Ontario, Canada M9W 1R3

*To purchase standards and related publications, visit our Online Store at **shop.csa.ca***
or call toll-free 1-800-463-6727 or 416-747-4044.

ICS 29.020
ISBN 978-1-4883-1343-1

Contents

Committee on Canadian Electrical Code, Part I

(Membership list as of June 2017)

R.J. Kelly *(Chair)*	Government of Nunavut Community & Government Services, Iqaluit, Nunavut
S.W. Douglas *(Vice-Chair)*	International Association of Electrical Inspectors, Toronto, Ontario
T. Pope *(Senior Project Manager)*	CSA Group, Toronto, Ontario

Representing Provincial and Territorial Electrical Inspection Authorities

M.S. Anderson	SaskPower, Regina, Saskatchewan
C.C. Cormier	Alberta Municipal Affairs, Edmonton, Alberta
P. Daigle	New Brunswick Department of Public Safety, Miramichi, New Brunswick
R.T. Hiscock	Government of the Northwest Territories, Yellowknife, Northwest Territories
U. Janisch	Technical Safety BC, Langley, British Columbia
R.J. Kelly	Government of Nunavut Community & Government Services, Iqaluit, Nunavut
T. Kitson	Department of Communities, Lands and Environment, Charlottetown, Prince Edward Island
T.K. Kjartanson	Manitoba Hydro, Winnipeg, Manitoba
H. Lang	Government of Yukon, Whitehorse, Yukon
D.R.A. MacLeod	Nova Scotia Department of Labour and Advanced Education, Halifax, Nova Scotia
D. Mayne	Government of Newfoundland and Labrador, Human Resource Secretariat, St. John's, Newfoundland and Labrador
G. Montminy	Régie du bâtiment du Québec, Québec, Québec
T. Olechna	Electrical Safety Authority, Mississauga, Ontario

Representing Municipal Electrical Inspection Authorities

D. Hallock	City of Winnipeg, Winnipeg, Manitoba
S. Hoogenboom	City of Calgary, Calgary, Alberta
P. Corby	City of Victoria, Victoria, British Columbia

Representing Bahamas

D.B. King *(Associate)*	Ministry of Works and Transport, Nassau, Bahamas
Q.C. Knowles *(Associate)*	Flameless Electrical Contracting Ltd., Nassau, Bahamas

Representing Canada West Ski Areas Association

W. Sparks	Doppelmayr Canada Ltd., Kelowna, British Columbia

Representing Canadian Association of Fire Investigators

E. Randsalu *(Associate)*	Ontario Ministry of Community Safety & Correctional Services, Toronto, Ontario

Representing Canadian Association of Petroleum Producers

T.S. Driscoll   OBIEC Consulting Ltd., Calgary, Alberta

Representing Canadian Electrical Contractors Association

I. Laouini   Corporation des maîtres électriciens du Québec, Montréal, Québec

Representing Canadian Electricity Association

J. Côté   Hydro-Québec, Montréal, Québec
R. Pack   SaskPower, Saskatoon, Saskatchewan
A. Pottier   Nova Scotia Power Inc., Halifax, Nova Scotia

Representing Canadian Home Builders' Association and Canadian Manufactured Housing Institute

A. Chown *(Associate)*   Canadian Home Builders' Association, Ottawa, Ontario

Representing Committee on the Installation Code for Natural Gas and Propane Appliances

R. Charbonneau   Budget Propane, Valleyfield, Québec
(Associate)

Representing Committee on Use of Electricity in Mines

G. Lobay   CSA Consumer Network, Ottawa, Ontario

Representing Committee on Workplace Electrical Safety

D.T. Roberts   Schneider Electric Canada, Inc., Mississauga, Ontario

Representing Committees on the Canadian Electrical Code, Part II, Application of Electricity in Health Care, and Emergency Electrical Power Supply for Buildings

A.Z. Tsisserev   AES Engineering, Vancouver, British Columbia

Representing Communication Industry

S. Turcot   Bell Canada, Montréal, Québec

Representing Division of Building Research NRC

P. Rizcallah *(Associate)*   National Research Council Canada, Canadian Codes Centre, Ottawa, Ontario

Representing Education

K. Harrison   Northern Alberta Institute of Technology, Edmonton, Alberta
T. Simmons   British Columbia Institute of Technology, Burnaby, British Columbia

Representing Electro-Federation Canada

W.J. Bryans (Associate)	Electro-Federation Canada, Toronto, Ontario
R.P. de Lhorbe	Schneider Electric Canada, Inc., Richmond, British Columbia
P. Desilets	Leviton Manufacturing of Canada Limited, Pointe-Claire, Québec
V.V. Gagachev	Eaton, Burlington, Ontario
K.L. Rodel	Hubbell Canada LP, Pickering, Ontario
J. Singh (Associate)	Domtech Inc., Trenton, Ontario
M. Smith	Kitchener, Ontario

Representing Energy Industry Electrical Engineering Associates

D.G. Morlidge	Okotoks, Alberta

Representing Forest Products Association of Canada

T. Branch	PDR Technologies Inc., Oakville, Ontario

Representing Institute of Electrical and Electronics Engineers

B. Johnson (Associate)	Thermon, New Braunfels, Texas, USA

Representing Institute of Electrical and Electronics Engineers (Canada)

R. Leduc	Marex Canada Limited, Calgary, Alberta
J. Turner (Associate)	Swansea Consulting, Toronto, Ontario

Representing International Association of Electrical Inspectors

D.E. Clements (Associate)	International Association of Electrical Inspectors, Richardson, Texas, USA
S.W. Douglas	International Association of Electrical Inspectors, Toronto, Ontario

Representing Labour

L. Cronk	IBEW 1st District, Burnaby, British Columbia

Representing Mexico

M. Jimenez (Associate)	Associacion de Normalizacion y Certificacion AC, Del Gustavo A Madero, Mexico

Representing National Defence

J. Zulak	National Defence Headquarters, Ottawa, Ontario

Representing National Electrical Code Committees

M.W. Earley (Associate)	National Fire Protection Association, Quincy, Massachusetts, USA

Representing National Electrical Manufacturers Association

C.K. Hunter (Associate)	Cerro Wire LLC, Las Vegas, Nevada, USA

Representing National Elevator & Escalator Association

D. McColl   Otis Canada Inc., Mississauga, Ontario

Representing SCC Accredited Certification Organizations

R. Berman *(Associate)*   Underwriters Laboratories Inc., Northbrook, Illinois, USA
J.H. Morrison *(Associate)*   QPS Evaluation Services Inc., Toronto, Ontario
G. Paintal *(Associate)*   Underwriters Laboratories of Canada, Scarborough, Ontario
S. Paulsen *(Associate)*   CSA Group, Toronto, Ontario

Representing Wire and Cable Manufacturing

I. Müller   Nexans Canada Inc., Markham, Ontario

Ex Officio Members

N. Hanna   Electrical Safety Authority, Mississauga, Ontario

Former Members

In addition to the members of the Committee, the following former members made valuable contributions to the development of this Code:

D. Badry   Government of Yukon, Whitehorse, Yukon
L.R. Ferchoff   North Hill Engineering, Winnipeg, Manitoba
A. Kassabian   Ontario Ministry of Community Safety & Correctional Services, Toronto, Ontario
J. LeBlanc   New Brunswick Department of Public Safety, Moncton, New Brunswick
E. Low   TELUS, Burnaby, British Columbia
C. McLellan   Canadian Home Builders' Association, Ottawa, Ontario
S. Misyk   The Inspections Group Inc., Edmonton, Alberta
B.F. O'Connell   Tyco Thermal Controls (Canada) Ltd., Trenton, Ontario
I. Pye   British Columbia Safety Authority (BCSA), Nanaimo, British Columbia
E.M. Roberts   Canadian Electrical Contractors Association, Toronto, Ontario
J.B. Salmon   John B. Salmon Holdings Inc., Kitchener, Ontario
E. Sapnu   City of Winnipeg, Winnipeg, Manitoba
G.D. Sharp   Canadian Home Builders' Association, Ottawa, Ontario
M.K. Shea   AES Engineering, Victoria, British Columbia

Regulatory Authority Committee

T. Olechna *(Chair)*	Electrical Safety Authority, Mississauga, Ontario
D.R.A. MacLeod *(Vice-Chair)*	Nova Scotia Department of Labour and Advanced Education, Halifax, Nova Scotia
M.S. Anderson	SaskPower, Regina, Saskatchewan
P. Corby	City of Victoria, Victoria, British Columbia
C.C. Cormier	Alberta Municipal Affairs, Edmonton, Alberta
P. Daigle	New Brunswick Department of Public Safety, Miramichi, New Brunswick
D. Hallock	City of Winnipeg, Winnipeg, Manitoba
R.T. Hiscock	Government of the Northwest Territories, Yellowknife, Northwest Territories
S. Hoogenboom	City of Calgary, Calgary, Alberta
U. Janisch	Technical Safety BC, Langley, British Columbia
R.J. Kelly	Government of Nunavut Community & Government Services, Iqaluit, Nunavut
T. Kitson	Department of Communities, Lands and Environment, Charlottetown, Prince Edward Island
T.K. Kjartanson	Manitoba Hydro, Winnipeg, Manitoba
H. Lang	Government of Yukon, Whitehorse, Yukon
D. Mayne	Government of Newfoundland and Labrador, Human Resource Secretariat, St. John's, Newfoundland and Labrador
G. Montminy	Régie du bâtiment du Québec, Québec, Québec
T. Pope *(Senior Project Manager)*	CSA Group, Toronto, Ontario

Executive Committee

R.J. Kelly *(Chair)*	Government of Nunavut Community & Government Services, Iqaluit, Nunavut
S.W. Douglas *(Vice-Chair)*	International Association of Electrical Inspectors, Toronto, Ontario
P. Desilets	Leviton Manufacturing of Canada Limited, Pointe-Claire, Québec
G. Lobay	CSA Consumer Network, Ottawa, Ontario
G. Montminy	Régie du bâtiment du Québec, Québec, Québec
T. Olechna	Electrical Safety Authority, Mississauga, Ontario
A. Pottier	Nova Scotia Power Inc., Halifax, Nova Scotia
T. Simmons	British Columbia Institute of Technology, Burnaby, British Columbia
M. Smith	Kitchener, Ontario
A.Z. Tsisserev	AES Engineering, Vancouver, British Columbia
T. Pope *(Senior Project Manager)*	CSA Group, Toronto, Ontario

National Building Code/Canadian Electrical Code *Liaison Committee*

A.Z. Tsisserev *(Chair)*	AES Engineering, Vancouver, British Columbia
P. Rizcallah *(Vice-Chair)*	National Research Council Canada, Ottawa, Ontario
M.S. Anderson	SaskPower, Regina, Saskatchewan
G. Benjamin	Thomas & Betts Limited, Dorval, Québec
G. Dupont	Montréal, Québec
T. Fazzari	Mohawk College, Stoney Creek, Ontario
R.J. Kelly	Government of Nunavut Community & Government Services, Iqaluit, Nunavut
R.A. Nelson	CSA Group, Toronto, Ontario
S. Paulsen	CSA Group, Toronto, Ontario
T. Pope *(Senior Project Manager)*	CSA Group, Toronto, Ontario

Section Subcommittees

Section 0 — Object, scope, and definitions

G. Lobay *(Chair)*	CSA Consumer Network, Ottawa, Ontario
B.M. Baldwin	Baldwin Services Inc., Saskatoon, Saskatchewan
T.J. Burt	Fanshawe College Applied Science and Technology, London, Ontario
J. Côté	Hydro-Québec, Distribution, Montréal, Québec
D.J. Heron	Heron Electrical Consulting Inc., Worthington, Ontario
D. Lenasi	Philips Lighting North America, Langley, British Columbia
J.N. Martin	Electrical Safety Authority Field Evaluation (ESAFE), Ottawa, Ontario
P. McDonald	Underwriters Laboratories of Canada Inc., St. Albert, Alberta
S. Paulsen	CSA Group, Toronto, Ontario
D.T. Roberts	Schneider Electric Canada, Inc., Mississauga, Ontario
M.K. Shea	AES Engineering, Victoria, British Columbia *(Representing International Association of Electrical Inspectors)*
A.Z. Tsisserev	AES Engineering, Vancouver, British Columbia
T. Pope *(Senior Project Manager)*	CSA Group, Toronto, Ontario

Section 2 — General Rules

S.W. Douglas *(Chair)*	International Association of Electrical Inspectors, Toronto, Ontario
M. Smith *(Vice-Chair)*	Kitchener, Ontario
D. Beattie	Dan Beattie Electrical Inc., Spencerville, Ontario
L. Coulombe	Régie du bâtiment du Québec, Québec, Québec
G.W. Jones	Assiniboine Community College, Brandon, Manitoba
R.J. Kelly	Government of Nunavut Community & Government Services, Iqaluit, Nunavut
J.N. Martin	Electrical Safety Authority Field Evaluation (ESAFE), Ottawa, Ontario
D.G. Morlidge	Okotoks, Alberta
S. Paulsen	CSA Group, Toronto, Ontario
D.T. Roberts	Schneider Electric Canada, Inc., Mississauga, Ontario
R. Tuttle	City of Vancouver, Vancouver, British Columbia *(Representing International Association of Electrical Inspectors)*
T. Pope *(Senior Project Manager)*	CSA Group, Toronto, Ontario

Section 4 — Conductors

I. Müller *(Chair)*	Nexans Canada Inc., Markham, Ontario
A.Z. Tsisserev *(Vice-Chair)*	AES Engineering, Vancouver, British Columbia
G.R. Beer	Jay Electric & Enerscan Control, Brampton, Ontario
E. Cometa	CSA Group, Toronto, Ontario
R.P. de Lhorbe	Schneider Electric Canada, Inc., Richmond, British Columbia
T. Dinic	Electrical Safety Authority, Mississauga, Ontario
R. Drury	Pentair Thermal Management Canada Ltd., Trenton, Ontario
C.K. Hunter	Cerro Wire LLC, Las Vegas, Nevada, USA

S. Kelly	Electrical Safety Authority, Ottawa, Ontario *(Representing International Association of Electrical Inspectors)*
R. Kummer	Southwire Company, Carrollton, Georgia, USA
R.A. Nelson	CSA Group, Toronto, Ontario
J. Rowley	City of Vancouver, Vancouver, British Columbia
J. Singh	Domtech Inc., Trenton, Ontario
M. Staples	City of Victoria, Victoria, British Columbia
A. Popa *(Project Manager)*	CSA Group, Toronto, Ontario

Section 6 — Services and service equipment

R.J. Kelly *(Chair)*	Government of Nunavut Community & Government Services, Iqaluit, Nunavut
R.T. Hiscock *(Vice-Chair)*	RTH Electrical Consulting, Fort Steele, British Columbia
G. Benjamin	Thomas & Betts Limited, Dorval, Québec
W.J. Burr	Burr and Associates, Campbell River, British Columbia
J. Côté	Hydro-Québec Distribution, Montréal, Québec
P. Falzon	Electrical Safety Authority, Mississauga, Ontario
J.G. Gamble	C. Gamble Electric (1982) Ltd., Winnipeg, Manitoba
D. Letcher	Don Letcher (E.S.C.O.) Enterprises, Sherwood Park, Alberta *(Representing International Association of Electrical Inspectors)*
M. Mihaluk	Les installations électriques Auger inc., Montréal, Québec
S. Paulsen	CSA Group, Toronto, Ontario
E.J. Power	E.J. Power Engineering, Stanhope, Prince Edward Island
A.Z. Tsisserev	AES Engineering, Vancouver, British Columbia
T. Pope *(Senior Project Manager)*	CSA Group, Toronto, Ontario

Section 8 — Circuit loading and demand factors

A.Z. Tsisserev *(Chair)*	AES Engineering, Vancouver, British Columbia
S.W. Douglas *(Vice-Chair)*	International Association of Electrical Inspectors, Toronto, Ontario *(Representing International Association of Electrical Inspectors)*
Y. Boodram	Schneider Electric Canada, Inc., Mississauga, Ontario
J. Calabria	Smith + Andersen, Toronto, Ontario
C.C. Cormier	Alberta Municipal Affairs, Edmonton, Alberta
L. Coulombe	Régie du bâtiment du Québec, Québec, Québec
K. Forbes	City of Lethbridge, Lethbridge, Alberta
K.W. Harrison	St. Albert, Alberta
S. Jenken	City of Winnipeg, Winnipeg, Manitoba
G.W. Jones	Assiniboine Community College, Brandon, Manitoba
R.J. Kelly	Government of Nunavut Community & Government Services, Iqaluit, Nunavut
G. Kooner	Vancouver Airport Authority, Richmond, British Columbia
H. Park	Power Bus Way Ltd., Brampton, Ontario
S. Paulsen	CSA Group, Toronto, Ontario
R. Yousef	Electrical Safety Authority, Mississauga, Ontario
T. Pope *(Senior Project Manager)*	CSA Group, Toronto, Ontario

Section 10 — *Grounding and bonding*

R. Leduc *(Chair)*	Marex Canada Limited, Calgary, Alberta
M.K. Shea *(Vice-Chair)*	AES Engineering, Victoria, British Columbia *(Representing International Association of Electrical Inspectors)*
S.C. Bygrave	Stantec Consulting Ltd., Dartmouth, Nova Scotia
J. Calabrese	Electrical Safety Authority, Scarborough, Ontario
T. Dinic	Electrical Safety Authority, Mississauga, Ontario
N. LeForte	City of Surrey Planning Development Department, Surrey, British Columbia
C. LeGrandeur	Cenovus Energy Inc., Calgary, Alberta
G. Lobay	CSA Consumer Network, Ottawa, Ontario
M. Mihaluk	Les installations électriques Auger inc., Montréal, Québec
D.G. Morlidge	Okotoks, Alberta
C. Rueck	Southwire Canada, Burnaby, British Columbia
G. Sawyer	Marex Canada Limited, Calgary, Alberta
D. Zimmerman	SaskPower Electrical Inspections, Saskatoon, Saskatchewan
M. McEwen *(Project Manager)*	CSA Group, Toronto, Ontario

Section 12 — *Wiring methods*

S.W. Douglas *(Chair)*	International Association of Electrical Inspectors, Toronto, Ontario *(Representing International Association of Electrical Inspectors)*
I. Müller *(Vice-Chair)*	Nexans Canada Inc., Markham, Ontario
M.S. Anderson	SaskPower, Regina, Saskatchewan
G. Benjamin	Thomas & Betts Limited, Dorval, Québec
P. Daigle	New Brunswick Department of Public Safety, Miramichi, New Brunswick
B. Fuhr	DJA Engineering Services, Calgary, Alberta
T. Hamden	CSA Group, Toronto, Ontario
R.W. Horner	Atkore International (Allied Tube & Conduit Corporation), Harvey, Illinois, USA
C.K. Hunter	Cerro Wire LLC, Las Vegas, Nevada, USA
I. Laouini	Corporation des maîtres électriciens du Québec, Montréal, Québec
A. Nause	IPEX Management Inc., Oakville, Ontario
A. Pottier	Nova Scotia Power Inc., Halifax, Nova Scotia
K. Richards	BnZ Engineering, Burlington, Ontario
L. Letea *(Project Manager)*	CSA Group, Toronto, Ontario

Section 14 — *Protection and control*

R.P. de Lhorbe *(Chair)*	Schneider Electric Canada, Inc., Richmond, British Columbia
R.T. Hiscock *(Vice-Chair)*	RTH Electrical Consulting, Fort Steele, British Columbia
T. Branch	PDR Technologies Inc., Oakville, Ontario
S.C. Bygrave	Stantec Consulting Ltd., Dartmouth, Nova Scotia
L. Coulombe	Régie du bâtiment du Québec, Québec, Québec
S.G. Davies	KD Projects, DeWinton, Alberta
T. Evans	Underwriters Laboratories Inc., Toronto, Ontario
G.T. Gingara	Mosaic Potash, Esterhazy, Saskatchewan

D.J. Heron	Heron Electrical Consulting Inc., Worthington, Ontario
M. Lusk	CSA Group, Charlotte, North Carolina, USA
H.A. Masroor	Goodkey Weedmark and Associates Limited, Ottawa, Ontario
W.C. Rossmann	Jacobs Canada, Calgary, Alberta
L.G. Silecky	Mersen Canada Toronto Inc., Mississauga, Ontario *(Representing International Association of Electrical Inspectors)*
C. Thwaites	Mersen Canada Inc., Mississauga, Ontario
T. Pope *(Senior Project Manager)*	CSA Group, Toronto, Ontario

Section 16 — Class 1 and Class 2 circuits

T. Simmons *(Chair)*	British Columbia Institute of Technology, Burnaby, British Columbia
T.K. Kjartanson *(Vice-Chair)*	Manitoba Hydro, Winnipeg, Manitoba
P. Doucet	New Brunswick Department of Justice and Public Safety, Moncton, New Brunswick
R.J. Kelly	Government of Nunavut Community & Government Services, Iqaluit, Nunavut
D. Lenasi	Philips Lighting North America, Langley, British Columbia
N. Mashayekh	Eaton's Bussmann Business, Lachine, Québec
P. Olders	Ontario Electrical Industry Training Trust, Toronto, Ontario *(Representing International Association of Electrical Inspectors)*
S. Paulsen	CSA Group, Toronto, Ontario
W. Saworski	Concept Group, Saskatoon, Saskatchewan
G. Sawyer	Marex Canada Limited, Calgary, Alberta
A.Z. Tsisserev	AES Engineering, Vancouver, British Columbia
D. Zimmerman	SaskPower Electrical Inspections, Saskatoon, Saskatchewan
J. Mereuta *(Project Manager)*	CSA Group, Toronto, Ontario

Section 18 — Hazardous locations

T.S. Driscoll *(Chair)*	OBIEC Consulting Ltd., Calgary, Alberta
G. Lobay *(Vice-Chair)*	CSA Consumer Network, Ottawa, Ontario
D.S. Adams	QPS Evaluation Services Inc., Calgary, Alberta
A. Bozek	EngWorks Inc., Calgary, Alberta
M. Brown	Electrical Safety Authority, Cambridge, Ontario
M.T. Cole	Hubbell Canada LP, Pickering, Ontario
D.J. Heron	Heron Electrical Consulting Inc., Worthington, Ontario
B. Keane	Eaton, Mississauga, Ontario
R.R. Langlois	Stantec Consulting Ltd., Kitchener, Ontario
W.G. Lawrence	FM Approvals, LLC, Norwood, Massachusetts, USA
R. Leduc	Marex Canada Limited, Calgary, Alberta
D.G. Morlidge	Okotoks, Alberta
J.H. Morrison	QPS Evaluation Services Inc., Toronto, Ontario *(Representing International Association of Electrical Inspectors)*
V. Rowe	Marex Canada Limited, Nanaimo, British Columbia
B. Schneider	Intertek, Edmonton, Alberta

D. Stochitoiu	CSA Group, Toronto, Ontario
M. Throckmorton	Shell Canada Limited, Shell Upstream Americas, Calgary, Alberta
A. Hawley *(Project Manager)*	CSA Group, Toronto, Ontario

Section 20 — *Flammable liquid and gasoline dispensing, service stations, garages, bulk storage plants, finishing processes, and aircraft hangars*

T. Olechna *(Chair)*	Electrical Safety Authority, Mississauga, Ontario
V. Rowe *(Vice-Chair)*	Marex Canada Limited, Nanaimo, British Columbia
I. Barnes	AES Engineering, Victoria, British Columbia
M. Brown	Electrical Safety Authority, Cambridge, Ontario
R. Charbonneau	Budget Propane (1998) Inc., Valleyfield, Québec
L. Coulombe	Régie du bâtiment du Québec, Québec, Québec
G.J. Drew	Cenovus Energy Inc., Calgary, Alberta
G. Lobay	CSA Consumer Network, Ottawa, Ontario
A. Milivojevich	QPS Evaluation Services Inc., Toronto, Ontario *(Representing International Association of Electrical Inspectors)*
D.G. Morlidge	Okotoks, Alberta
E.J. Power	E.J. Power Engineering, Stanhope, Prince Edward Island
M.K. Shea	AES Engineering, Victoria, British Columbia
T. Pope *(Senior Project Manager)*	CSA Group, Toronto, Ontario

Section 22 — *Locations in which corrosive liquids, vapours, or excessive moisture are likely to be present*

N. Hanna *(Chair)*	Electrical Safety Authority, Mississauga, Ontario
R.J. Kelly *(Vice-Chair)*	Government of Nunavut Community & Government Services, Iqaluit, Nunavut
L. Cantelo	Electrical Industry Training Centres of Alberta, Sherwood Park, Alberta *(Representing International Association of Electrical Inspectors)*
G.T. Gingara	Mosaic Potash, Esterhazy, Saskatchewan
M. Khalid	R.V. Anderson Associates Limited, Toronto, Ontario
R.R. Langlois	Stantec Consulting Ltd., Kitchener, Ontario
G.T. Walker	Emery Electric, Shawnigan Lake, British Columbia
D. Wilson	Accredited Testing Services, Brandon, Manitoba
T. Pope *(Senior Project Manager)*	CSA Group, Toronto, Ontario

Section 24 — *Patient care areas*

A.Z. Tsisserev *(Chair)*	AES Engineering, Vancouver, British Columbia
N. Hanna *(Vice-Chair)*	Electrical Safety Authority, Mississauga, Ontario
M.S. Anderson	SaskPower, Regina, Saskatchewan
M. Brossoit	CSA Group, Pointe-Claire, Québec
R. Dodds	Vancouver General Hospital, Vancouver, British Columbia
L.R. Ferchoff	North Hill Engineering, Winnipeg, Manitoba
P.M. Gelinas	CIUSSS du Nord-de-L'île-de-Montréal Hôpital, Montréal, Québec

G. Hughes	University of New Brunswick, Department of Health, Fredericton, New Brunswick
S.H. Mallikarachchi	City of Winnipeg Planning, Property & Development, Winnipeg, Manitoba
M.B. Raber	M. B. Raber, P. Eng., Winnipeg, Manitoba
E. Smeltzer	Nova Scotia Power Inc., Lower Sackville, Nova Scotia *(Representing International Association of Electrical Inspectors)*
T. Pope *(Senior Project Manager)*	CSA Group, Toronto, Ontario

Section 26 — *Installation of electrical equipment*

T. Simmons *(Chair)*	British Columbia Institute of Technology, Burnaby, British Columbia
R. Leduc *(Vice-Chair)*	Marex Canada Limited, Calgary, Alberta
M. Brown	Electrical Safety Authority, Cambridge, Ontario
A. Chown	Canadian Home Builders' Association, Ottawa, Ontario
L. Coulombe	Régie du bâtiment du Québec, Québec, Québec
P. Desilets	Leviton Manufacturing of Canada Limited, Pointe-Claire, Québec
M.W. Earley	National Fire Protection Association, Quincy, Massachusetts, USA
V.V. Gagachev	Eaton, Burlington, Ontario
M. Mihaluk	Les installations électriques Auger inc., Montréal, Québec
R.A. Nelson	CSA Group, Toronto, Ontario
S. Paulsen	CSA Group, Toronto, Ontario
T.R. Titus	Electrical Safety Authority, New Hamburg, Ontario *(Representing International Association of Electrical Inspectors)*
A.Z. Tsisserev	AES Engineering, Vancouver, British Columbia
T. Pope *(Senior Project Manager)*	CSA Group, Toronto, Ontario

Section 28 — *Motors and generators*

M. Smith *(Chair)*	Kitchener, Ontario
V.V. Gagachev *(Vice-Chair)*	Eaton, Burlington, Ontario
M.S. Anderson	SaskPower, Regina, Saskatchewan
P. Baltazart	CIMA +, Edmonton, Alberta
D. Beattie	Dan Beattie Electrical Inc., Spencerville, Ontario
J.P. Boivin	CSA Group, Pointe-Claire, Québec
T. Branch	PDR Technologies Inc., Oakville, Ontario
S.G. Davies	KD Projects, DeWinton, Alberta
R.P. de Lhorbe	Schneider Electric Canada, Inc., Richmond, British Columbia
C. Fallon	City of St. John's Planning, Engineering & Regulatory Services, St. John's, Newfoundland and Labrador
S. Finnagan	St. Lawrence College, Kingston, Ontario
E.J. Friesen	E.J. Friesen and Associates Incorporated, Calgary, Alberta
L.G. Silecky	Mersen Canada Toronto Inc., Mississauga, Ontario *(Representing International Association of Electrical Inspectors)*
T. Pope *(Senior Project Manager)*	CSA Group, Toronto, Ontario

Section 30 — Installation of lighting equipment

P. Desilets *(Chair)*	Leviton Manufacturing of Canada Limited, Pointe-Claire, Québec
T. Dinic *(Vice-Chair)*	Electrical Safety Authority, Mississauga, Ontario
J.A. Davidson	JAD Consulting, Virden, Manitoba *(Representing International Association of Electrical Inspectors)*
B. Keane	Eaton, Mississauga, Ontario
Q.Y. Li	Mainland Technical Services Inc., Richmond, British Columbia
M. Mihaluk	Les installations électriques Auger inc., Montréal, Québec
D. Rittenhouse	Maple Ridge, British Columbia
M.K. Timmings	Binbrook, Ontario
A. Yearwood	CSA Group, Toronto, Ontario
J. Mereuta *(Project Manager)*	CSA Group, Toronto, Ontario

Section 32 — Fire alarm systems, smoke and carbon monoxide alarms, and fire pumps

M.S. Anderson *(Chair)*	SaskPower, Regina, Saskatchewan
A.Z. Tsisserev *(Vice-Chair)*	AES Engineering, Vancouver, British Columbia
S. Aspinwall	Smith + Andersen, Toronto, Ontario
A.N. Cavers	Underwriters Laboratories of Canada, Toronto, Ontario
R. Dodds	Vancouver General Hospital, Vancouver, British Columbia
D. Gnocchi	TornaTech Inc., St-Laurent, Québec
N. Hanna	Electrical Safety Authority, Mississauga, Ontario
S. Jenken	The City of Winnipeg, Winnipeg, Manitoba
R. MacKenzie	CSA Group, Toronto, Ontario
M. Paiement	SaskPower, Regina, Saskatchewan *(Representing International Association of Electrical Inspectors)*
V.R. Rochon	Fore Bears Forensic Science, King City, Ontario
D. Weber	Canadian Fire Alarm Association, Markham, Ontario
T. Pope *(Senior Project Manager)*	CSA Group, Toronto, Ontario

Section 34 — Signs and outline lighting

R. Pack *(Chair)*	SaskPower, Saskatoon, Saskatchewan
L. Cronk *(Vice-Chair)*	IBEW 1st District, Burnaby, British Columbia
L. Catton	Acme Design Service Ltd., Belle River, Ontario
F. Dabiet	Allanson International Inc., Toronto, Ontario
J.A. Davidson	JAD Consulting, Virden, Manitoba *(Representing International Association of Electrical Inspectors)*
D. Froese	Seventy-Seven Signs Limited, Saskatoon, Saskatchewan
E.J. Power	E.J. Power Engineering, Stanhope, Prince Edward Island
A. Yearwood	CSA Group, Toronto, Ontario
T. Pope *(Senior Project Manager)*	CSA Group, Toronto, Ontario

Section 36 — High-voltage installations

J. Côté *(Chair)*	Hydro-Québec, Distribution, Montréal, Québec
B. Lipson *(Vice-Chair)*	AES Engineering, Vancouver, British Columbia
R.M. Bartholomew	Electric Power Equipment Ltd., Vancouver, British Columbia
L. Coulombe	Régie du bâtiment du Québec, Québec, Québec
R.P. de Lhorbe	Schneider Electric Canada, Inc., Richmond, British Columbia
E.P. Dick	Electric Power Diagnostics, Toronto, Ontario
R. Head	Electrical Safety Authority, Cambridge, Ontario *(Representing International Association of Electrical Inspectors)*
D.J. Heron	Heron Electrical Consulting Inc., Worthington, Ontario
T. Tremblay	Electrical Safety Authority, Sudbury, Ontario
T. Pope *(Senior Project Manager)*	CSA Group, Toronto, Ontario

Section 38 — Elevators, dumbwaiters, material lifts, escalators, moving walks, lifts for persons with physical disabilities, and similar equipment

D. McColl *(Chair)*	Otis Canada, Inc., Mississauga, Ontario
K.C. Cheong	AES Engineering, Vancouver, British Columbia
U. Janisch	Technical Safety BC, Langley, British Columbia
D. Laguerre	Schindler Elevator Corporation, Toronto, Ontario
D. McLellan	Technical Standards & Safety Authority (TSSA), Toronto, Ontario
S. Mercier	Régie du bâtiment du Québec, Montréal, Québec
M. Mihai	Technical Standards & Safety Authority (TSSA), Toronto, Ontario
R. Mitchell	Electrical Safety Authority, Mississauga, Ontario *(Representing International Association of Electrical Inspectors)*
A. Rehman	Schindler Elevator Corporation, Morristown, New Jersey, USA
L. Yang	CSA Group, Toronto, Ontario
T. Pope *(Senior Project Manager)*	CSA Group, Toronto, Ontario

Section 40 — Electric cranes and hoists

M.S. Anderson *(Chair)*	SaskPower, Regina, Saskatchewan
D. Mayne *(Vice-Chair)*	Government of Newfoundland and Labrador, Human Resource Secretariat, St. John's, Newfoundland and Labrador
S. Bollito	RUETGERS Canada Inc., Hamilton, Ontario
M. Chumkovski	QPS Evaluation Services Inc., Toronto, Ontario *(Representing International Association of Electrical Inspectors)*
S.W. Douglas	International Association of Electrical Inspectors, Toronto, Ontario
K. Hood	Lloydminster, Alberta
T. Rodrigues	Technical Standards & Safety Authority (TSSA), Mississauga, Ontario
R. Rus	O'Brien Lifting Solutions, Burlington, Ontario
L. Uruski	Manitoba Labour, Winnipeg, Manitoba
L. Yang	CSA Group, Toronto, Ontario
T. Pope *(Senior Project Manager)*	CSA Group, Toronto, Ontario

Section 42 — Electric welders

A. Pottier *(Chair)*	Nova Scotia Power Inc., Halifax, Nova Scotia
R. May *(Vice-Chair)*	Surrey, British Columbia
J.P. Boivin	CSA Group, Pointe-Claire, Québec
F. Hegholz	Rostec Enterprises Inc., Rosalind, Alberta
D.A. Hisey	Canadian Welding Bureau, Fort Saskatchewan, Alberta
M. Mihaluk	Les installations électriques Auger inc., Montréal, Québec
L.G. Silecky	Mersen Canada Toronto Inc., Mississauga, Ontario *(Representing International Association of Electrical Inspectors)*
T. Pope *(Senior Project Manager)*	CSA Group, Toronto, Ontario

Section 44 — Theatre installations

G. Montminy *(Chair)*	Régie du bâtiment du Québec, Québec, Québec
I. Laouini *(Vice-Chair)*	Corporation des maîtres électriciens du Québec, Montréal, Québec
B. Bennett	Civic Theatres Toronto, Toronto, Ontario
J. Calabrese	Electrical Safety Authority, Scarborough, Ontario
K. Hood	Lloydminster, Alberta *(Representing International Association of Electrical Inspectors)*
M. Mihaluk	Les installations électriques Auger inc., Montréal, Québec
G.K. Rose	Pefferlaw, Ontario
K.E. Vannice	Portland, Oregon, USA
A. Yearwood	CSA Group, Toronto, Ontario
T. Pope *(Senior Project Manager)*	CSA Group, Toronto, Ontario

Section 46 — Emergency power supply, unit equipment, exit signs, and life safety systems

A.Z. Tsisserev *(Chair)*	AES Engineering, Vancouver, British Columbia
M.S. Anderson *(Vice-Chair)*	SaskPower, Regina, Saskatchewan
S. Aspinwall	Smith + Andersen, Toronto, Ontario
R.M. Bartholomew	Electric Power Equipment Ltd., Vancouver, British Columbia
S.C. Bygrave	Stantec Consulting Ltd., Dartmouth, Nova Scotia
P. Corby	City of Victoria, Victoria, British Columbia *(Representing International Association of Electrical Inspectors)*
R. Dodds	Vancouver General Hospital, Vancouver, British Columbia
T. Fazzari	Mohawk College, Stoney Creek, Ontario
N. Hanna	Electrical Safety Authority, Mississauga, Ontario
W.L. McAllister	City of Camrose, Camrose, Alberta
R.A. Nelson	CSA Group, Toronto, Ontario
M. Rendulic	Winnipeg School Division Building Department, Winnipeg, Manitoba
A. Yearwood	CSA Group, Toronto, Ontario
T. Pope *(Senior Project Manager)*	CSA Group, Toronto, Ontario

Section 52 — Diagnostic imaging installations

D.R.A. MacLeod *(Chair)*	Nova Scotia Department of Labour and Advanced Education, Halifax, Nova Scotia
M.B. Raber *(Vice-Chair)*	M. B. Raber, P. Eng., Winnipeg, Manitoba
M. Brossoit	CSA Group, Pointe-Claire, Québec
J.C. Einarson	Whitehorse, Yukon
W. Wetmore	QPS Evaluation Services Inc., Toronto, Ontario *(Representing International Association of Electrical Inspectors)*
T. Pope *(Senior Project Manager)*	CSA Group, Toronto, Ontario

Section 54 — Community antenna distribution and radio and television installations

S.M. Turcot *(Chair)*	Bell Canada, Montréal, Québec
J. Zulak *(Vice-Chair)*	Department of National Defence, Ottawa, Ontario
E. Chantigny	Standard Products Inc., St-Laurent, Québec
T. Chiu	Stantec Consulting Ltd., Vancouver, British Columbia
P. Olders	Ontario Electrical Industry Training Trust, Toronto, Ontario *(Representing International Association of Electrical Inspectors)*
T. Walker	TELUS, Calgary, Alberta
E. Yap	CSA Group, Toronto, Ontario
T. Pope *(Senior Project Manager)*	CSA Group, Toronto, Ontario

Section 56 — Optical fiber cables

S.M. Turcot *(Chair)*	Bell Canada, Montréal, Québec
J. Zulak *(Vice-Chair)*	Department of National Defence, Ottawa, Ontario
C.B. Chan	Coquitlam, British Columbia
S. Finnagan	St. Lawrence College, Kingston, Ontario
T. Hamden	CSA Group, Toronto, Ontario
P. Olders	Ontario Electrical Industry Training Trust, Toronto, Ontario *(Representing International Association of Electrical Inspectors)*
V. Rowe	Marex Canada Limited, Nanaimo, British Columbia
A.Z. Tsisserev	AES Engineering, Vancouver, British Columbia
T. Pope *(Senior Project Manager)*	CSA Group, Toronto, Ontario

Section 58 — Passenger ropeways and similar equipment

W. Sparks *(Chair)*	Doppelmayr Canada Ltd., Kelowna, British Columbia
U. Janisch *(Vice-Chair)*	Technical Safety BC, Langley, British Columbia
D. Bruce	Alberta Municipal Affairs, Edmonton, Alberta
M. Chumkovski	QPS Evaluation Services Inc., Toronto, Ontario *(Representing International Association of Electrical Inspectors)*
P. McDermott	Technical Standards & Safety Authority (TSSA), Toronto, Ontario
S. Mercier	Régie du bâtiment du Québec, Montréal, Québec
D. Uddenberg	Banff, Alberta

| T. Pope *(Senior Project Manager)* | CSA Group, Toronto, Ontario |

Section 60 — *Electrical communication systems*

S.M. Turcot *(Chair)*	Bell Canada, Montréal, Québec
J. Zulak *(Vice-Chair)*	Department of National Defence, Ottawa, Ontario
D.J. Andrews	DJA Engineering Services, Calgary, Alberta
S. Bent	Nova Scotia Power Inc., Kingston, Nova Scotia *(Representing International Association of Electrical Inspectors)*
C.B. Chan	Coquitlam, British Columbia
E. Chantigny	Standard Products Inc., St-Laurent, Québec
P. Desilets	Leviton Manufacturing of Canada Limited, Pointe-Claire, Québec
S. Finnagan	St. Lawrence College, Kingston, Ontario
W. Kwan	Industry Canada, Ottawa, Ontario
B. Lowe	CSA Group, Richmond, British Columbia
R.S. Smith	Riverview, New Brunswick
A.Z. Tsisserev	AES Engineering, Vancouver, British Columbia
T. Walker	TELUS, Calgary, Alberta
T. Pope *(Senior Project Manager)*	CSA Group, Toronto, Ontario

Section 62 — *Fixed electric heating systems*

T.S. Driscoll *(Chair)*	OBIEC Consulting Ltd., Calgary, Alberta
J. Turner *(Vice-Chair)*	Swansea Consulting, Toronto, Ontario
R. Barth	Thermon Inc., San Marcos, Texas, USA
J. Bradshaw	Pentair Thermal Management Canada, Edmonton, Alberta
J. Calabrese	Electrical Safety Authority, Scarborough, Ontario
T. De Francesco	Aeromation Inc., Vancouver, British Columbia
P.D. den Bakker	Shell Canada Ltd., Calgary, Alberta
G. Gagnon	Schluter Systems (Canada) Inc., Ste-Anne-de-Bellevue, Québec
T. Hamden	CSA Group, Toronto, Ontario
R. Loiselle	Suncor Energy Inc., Calgary, Alberta
D.W. McCallum	PCL Intracon Power, Vanscoy, Saskatchewan
R. Pack	SaskPower, Saskatoon, Saskatchewan *(Representing International Association of Electrical Inspectors)*
S. Pouliot	Stelpro Design Inc., St-Bruno, Québec
E.D. Stephens	EGS EasyHeat Ltd., Elmira, Ontario
M. Humphries *(Project Manager)*	CSA Group, Toronto, Ontario

Section 64 — *Renewable energy systems*

T. Simmons *(Chair)*	British Columbia Institute of Technology, Burnaby, British Columbia
S.W. Douglas *(Vice-Chair)*	International Association of Electrical Inspectors, Toronto, Ontario
T. Buchal	Intertek, Cortland, New York, USA
S. Eng	Enviro-Energy Technologies Inc., Markham, Ontario
T.K. Kjartanson	Manitoba Hydro, Winnipeg, Manitoba

S. Paulsen	CSA Group, Toronto, Ontario
J. Pinter	Pinter Electrical Consulting Inc., Lake Country, British Columbia
D.B. Pollock	Electrical Safety Authority, Ilderton, Ontario *(Representing International Association of Electrical Inspectors)*
A. Pottier	Nova Scotia Power Inc., Halifax, Nova Scotia
R. Yousef	Electrical Safety Authority, Mississauga, Ontario
T. Pope *(Senior Project Manager)*	CSA Group, Toronto, Ontario

Section 66 — *Amusement parks, midways, carnivals, film and TV sets, TV remote broadcasting locations, and travelling shows*

G. Montminy *(Chair)*	Régie du bâtiment du Québec, Québec, Québec
U. Janisch *(Vice-Chair)*	Technical Safety BC, Langley, British Columbia
J. Calabrese	Electrical Safety Authority, Scarborough, Ontario
R. Holden	Sim Lighting and Grip, Burnaby, British Columbia
K. Hood	Lloydminster, Alberta *(Representing International Association of Electrical Inspectors)*
S. Mercier	Régie du bâtiment du Québec, Montréal, Québec
S. Paulsen	CSA Group, Toronto, Ontario
J. Porter	Westbury National Show Systems Ltd., Scarborough, Ontario
A. Wanuch	KRE Electric Ltd., Mississauga, Ontario
W. White	City of Vancouver Development, Building and Licensing, Vancouver, British Columbia
K.S. Woods	IATSE Local 891, Port Moody, British Columbia
T. Pope *(Senior Project Manager)*	CSA Group, Toronto, Ontario

Section 68 — *Pools, tubs, and spas*

R. Pack *(Chair)*	SaskPower, Saskatoon, Saskatchewan
M.S. Anderson *(Vice-Chair)*	SaskPower, Regina, Saskatchewan
M. Brown	Electrical Safety Authority, Cambridge, Ontario
S.W. Douglas	International Association of Electrical Inspectors, Toronto, Ontario
W. Humphrey	Hayward Pool Products Canada Inc., Oakville, Ontario
D. Letcher	Don Letcher (E.S.C.O.) Enterprises, Sherwood Park, Alberta *(Representing International Association of Electrical Inspectors)*
T. Minna	EPI Electrical Contractors, Brampton, Ontario
L.B. Ross	New Market, Ontario
W.R. Wood	Pool & Hot Tub Council of Canada, Brampton, Ontario
A. Yearwood	CSA Group, Toronto, Ontario
T. Pope *(Senior Project Manager)*	CSA Group, Toronto, Ontario

Section 70 — *Electrical requirements for factory-built relocatable structures and non-relocatable structures*

| U. Janisch *(Chair)* | Technical Safety BC, Langley, British Columbia |
| H. Lang *(Vice-Chair)* | Government of Yukon, Whitehorse, Yukon |

M.S. Anderson	SaskPower, Regina, Saskatchewan
A. Chown	Canadian Home Builders' Association, Ottawa, Ontario
P. Daigle	New Brunswick Department of Public Safety, Miramichi, New Brunswick
J.C. Einarson	Whitehorse, Yukon
J. Hermary	Nickel Electric Ltd., Brandon, Manitoba
R.W. Morin	Grafton, Ontario *(Representing International Association of Electrical Inspectors)*
V. Thielmann	Nova 3 Engineering Limited, Winnipeg, Manitoba
T. Pope *(Senior Project Manager)*	CSA Group, Toronto, Ontario

Section 72 — *Mobile home and recreational vehicle parks*

R. Leduc *(Chair)*	Marex Canada Limited, Calgary, Alberta
D. Hallock *(Vice-Chair)*	City of Winnipeg, Winnipeg, Manitoba
M.S. Anderson	SaskPower, Regina, Saskatchewan
J. Baker	OPCA, Embro, Ontario
L. Coulombe	Régie du bâtiment du Québec, Québec, Québec
B. Cowley	Electrical Safety Authority, Ottawa, Ontario
P. Daigle	New Brunswick Department of Public Safety, Miramichi, New Brunswick
J.C. Einarson	Whitehorse, Yukon
K. Hood	Lloydminster, Alberta
U. Janisch	Technical Safety BC, Langley, British Columbia
D. Letcher	Don Letcher (E.S.C.O.) Enterprises, Sherwood Park, Alberta *(Representing International Association of Electrical Inspectors)*
T. Pope *(Senior Project Manager)*	CSA Group, Toronto, Ontario

Section 74 — *Airport installations*

C.C. Cormier *(Chair)*	Alberta Municipal Affairs, Edmonton, Alberta
S.W. Douglas *(Vice-Chair)*	International Association of Electrical Inspectors, Toronto, Ontario
E.J. Alf	Transport Canada — AARTAE, Ottawa, Ontario
G.W. Bradbury	B.T.E. Engineering Technology Services, St. Petersburg, Florida, USA *(Representing International Association of Electrical Inspectors)*
R. Chernish	Department of National Defence, Winnipeg, Manitoba
G.T. Gingara	Mosaic Potash, Esterhazy, Saskatchewan
D. Hallock	City of Winnipeg, Winnipeg, Manitoba
U. Janisch	Technical Safety BC, Langley, British Columbia
G. Kooner	Vancouver Airport Authority, Richmond, British Columbia
R. Larivée	Avia Rupta Solutions Inc., Montréal, Québec
S.H. Mallikarachchi	City of Winnipeg Planning, Property & Development, Winnipeg, Manitoba
T. Pope *(Senior Project Manager)*	CSA Group, Toronto, Ontario

Section 76 — *Temporary wiring*

| D.R.A. MacLeod *(Chair)* | Nova Scotia Department of Labour and Advanced Education, Halifax, Nova Scotia |

S.W. Douglas *(Vice-Chair)*	International Association of Electrical Inspectors, Toronto, Ontario *(Representing International Association of Electrical Inspectors)*
J. Calabrese	Electrical Safety Authority, Scarborough, Ontario
B. Doan	Sumner Electric London Ltd., Komoka, Ontario
T.K. Kjartanson	Manitoba Hydro, Winnipeg, Manitoba
S. Nair	WorkSafeBC, Richmond, British Columbia
B. O'Donnell	AC Powerline Construction, Pickering, Ontario
S. Paulsen	CSA Group, Toronto, Ontario
T. Pope *(Senior Project Manager)*	CSA Group, Toronto, Ontario

Section 78 — *Marine wharves, docking facilities, fixed and floating piers, and boathouses*

A. Pottier *(Chair)*	Nova Scotia Power Inc., Halifax, Nova Scotia
U. Janisch *(Vice-Chair)*	Technical Safety BC, Langley, British Columbia
W.J. Burr	Burr and Associates, Campbell River, British Columbia
P. Daigle	New Brunswick Department of Public Safety, Miramichi, New Brunswick
C.J. Estereicher	Merick Contractors Inc., Cochrane, Alberta
D.J. Heron	Heron Electrical Consulting Inc., Worthington, Ontario
D. Kalles	Industrial Electrical Contractors Limited, Toronto, Ontario
D. Keats	City of St. John's City Hall, St. John's, *(Representing International Association of Electrical Inspectors)*
T. Olechna	Electrical Safety Authority, Mississauga, Ontario
M.L. Vollmer	Michael Vollmer Yacht Design Inc., Burlington, Ontario
T. Pope *(Senior Project Manager)*	CSA Group, Toronto, Ontario

Section 80 — *Cathodic protection*

D.R.A. MacLeod *(Chair)*	Nova Scotia Department of Labour and Advanced Education, Halifax, Nova Scotia
H. Lang *(Vice-Chair)*	Government of Yukon, Whitehorse, Yukon
R.J. Maynard	Aurora Corrosion Control, a Division of Aurora Environmental Consulting Ltd., Calgary, Alberta
S. Paulsen	CSA Group, Toronto, Ontario
D. Schill	SaskPower, Regina, Saskatchewan *(Representing International Association of Electrical Inspectors)*
R. Stromer	RS Engineering Ltd., Calgary, Alberta
A.Z. Tsisserev	AES Engineering, Vancouver, British Columbia
R.G. Wakelin	Gull River Engineering Inc., Brooklin, Ontario
T. Pope *(Senior Project Manager)*	CSA Group, Toronto, Ontario

Section 84 — *Interconnection of electric power production sources*

A. Pottier *(Chair)*	Nova Scotia Power Inc., Halifax, Nova Scotia
M.S. Anderson	SaskPower, Regina, Saskatchewan
D. Desrosiers	CYME International T&D, St-Bruno, Québec
E.P. Dick	Electric Power Diagnostics, Toronto, Ontario

D.J. Heron	Heron Electrical Consulting Inc., Worthington, Ontario
B. Lipson	AES Engineering, Vancouver, British Columbia
A. Mak	WorleyParsons Canada, Edmonton, Alberta
D. Mascarenhas	Brampton, Ontario
S. Paulsen	CSA Group, Toronto, Ontario
J.C. Potts	QPS Evaluation Services Inc., Toronto, Ontario *(Representing International Association of Electrical Inspectors)*
V. Rowe	Marex Canada Limited, Nanaimo, British Columbia
T. Simmons	British Columbia Institute of Technology, Burnaby, British Columbia
T. Pope *(Senior Project Manager)*	CSA Group, Toronto, Ontario

Section 86 — Electric vehicle charging systems

P. Desilets *(Chair)*	Leviton Manufacturing of Canada Limited, Pointe-Claire, Québec
D. Mascarenhas *(Vice-Chair)*	Brampton, Ontario
D. Chandler	Vancouver Electric Vehicle Association, Vancouver, British Columbia
S. Dallas	Toronto Electric, Electric Mobility Canada, Toronto, Ontario
P.R. Hinse	University of Ontario Institute of Technology, Oshawa, Ontario
M. Mihaluk	Les installations électriques Auger inc., Montréal, Québec
T.W. Odell	Toronto Hydro-Electric System Ltd., Toronto, Ontario
J. Overton	City of Vancouver, Vancouver, British Columbia
S. Paulsen	CSA Group, Toronto, Ontario
J.C. Potts	QPS Evaluation Services Inc., Toronto, Ontario *(Representing International Association of Electrical Inspectors)*
J.E. Tarchinski	General Motors Company, Warren, Michigan, USA
A.Z. Tsisserev	AES Engineering, Vancouver, British Columbia
R. Yousef	Electrical Safety Authority, Mississauga, Ontario
P. Glowacki *(Project Manager)*	CSA Group, Toronto, Ontario

Appendix C

| R.J. Kelly *(Chair)* | Government of Nunavut Community & Government Services, Iqaluit, Nunavut |

Appendix D

| I. Müller *(Chair)* | Nexans Canada Inc., Markham, Ontario |

Appendix E

| T.S. Driscoll *(Chair)* | OBIEC Consulting Ltd., Calgary, Alberta |

Appendix F

| T.S. Driscoll *(Chair)* | OBIEC Consulting Ltd., Calgary, Alberta |

Appendix G

A.Z. Tsisserev *(Chair)*   AES Engineering, Vancouver, British Columbia

Appendix J — Annex J18

T.S. Driscoll *(Chair)*   OBIEC Consulting Ltd., Calgary, Alberta

Appendix J — Annex J20

T. Olechna   Electrical Safety Authority, Mississauga, Ontario

Appendix K

A.Z. Tsisserev *(Chair)*   AES Engineering, Vancouver, British Columbia

Appendix L

T.S. Driscoll *(Chair)*   OBIEC Consulting Ltd., Calgary, Alberta

Preface

This twenty-fourth edition of the *Canadian Electrical Code, Part I*, was approved by the Committee on the *Canadian Electrical Code, Part I*, and by the Regulatory Authority Committee at their June 2017 meetings in Halifax, Nova Scotia. This twenty-fourth edition supersedes the previous editions, published in 2015, 2012, 2009, 2006, 2002, 1998, 1994, 1990, 1986, 1982, 1978, 1975, 1972, 1969, 1966, 1962, 1958, 1953, 1947, 1939, 1935, 1930, and 1927.

This edition features important revisions to many Sections. Section 26 now mandates the use of tamper-resistant receptacles in additional areas where children may be present. Section 62 now requires ground fault circuit interrupter protection for heating devices and controls in proximity to tubs, sinks, and shower stalls.

Section 10 has been updated, reorganized, and significantly reduced in length. Requirements for power over ethernet systems have been added to Section 16, and requirements for marine wharves and similar facilities have been substantially updated and reorganized in Section 78.

To address the increasing use of electric vehicles, Section 8 now formally recognizes energy management systems as a method of reducing the load on building services. Because lighting control devices associated with energy management or home automation require power to operate, Section 4 now requires that an identified conductor be provided for all devices controlling permanently installed luminaires.

Other revisions in this edition include the following:
- in Section 26, Rules 26-400 to 26-726 have been reorganized and renumbered in order to group related concepts together and provide a more logical flow for the requirements;
- in many Sections, the redundant use of the term "approved" has been eliminated;
- clarification has been provided on arc-fault circuit interrupter protection for bathrooms, washrooms, existing circuits, and circuits supplying carbon monoxide or smoke alarms;
- requirements for dining area and refrigerator circuits have been clarified;
- the terms "jacketed", "insulated", and "covered" as applied to conductors have been clarified through a new definition of the term "jacket" and a revised definition of the term "conductor" in Section 0. As a result, the term "conductor" has been replaced with "insulated conductor" in many Sections of the Code;
- Section 82 has been deleted as it covered a technology that is no longer in use; and
- a new Appendix M containing French translations of markings has been added.

Many of the changes in this edition were developed by cross-functional working groups. Their work is gratefully acknowledged.

General arrangement

The Code is divided into numbered Sections, each covering some main division of the work. Sections 0 to 16 and 26 are considered general Sections, and the other Sections supplement or amend the general Sections. The Sections are divided into numbered Rules, with captions for easy reference, as follows:

a) **Numbering system** — With the exception of Section 38, even numbers have been used throughout to identify Sections and Rules. Rule numbers consist of the Section number separated by a hyphen from the 3- or 4-digit figure. The intention in general is that odd numbers may be used for new Rules required by interim revisions. Due to the introduction of some new Rules and the deletion of some existing Rules during the revision of each edition, the Rule numbers for any particular requirement are not always the same in successive editions.

b) **Subdivision of Rules** — Rules are subdivided in the manner illustrated by Rules 8-204 and 8-206, and the subdivisions are identified as follows:

00-000	Rule
1)	Subrule
a)	Item
i)	Item
A)	Item

c) **Reference to other Rules, etc.** — Where reference is made to two or more Rules (e.g., Rules 10-200 to 10-206), the first and last Rules mentioned are included in the reference. Where reference is made to a Subrule or Item in the same Rule, only the Subrule number and/or Item letter and the word "Subrule" or "Item" need be mentioned. If the reference is to another Rule or Section, then the Rule number and the word "Rule" shall be stated (e.g., "Rule 10-206 3)" and not "Subrule 3) of Rule 10-206").

The principal changes that have been made between the 2015 edition of the *Canadian Electrical Code, Part I*, and this new edition, published in 2018, are marked in the text of the Code by the symbol delta (Δ) in the margin. Users of the Code are advised that the change markers in the text are not intended to be all-inclusive and are provided as a convenience only; such markers cannot constitute a comprehensive guide to the reorganization or revision of the Code. Global revisions that improve the overall consistency and precision of Code language without affecting the interpretation of any specific Rule are not identified. Care must therefore be taken not to rely on the change markers to determine the current requirements of the Code. As always, users of the Code must consider the entire Code and any local amendments or interpretations.

This Standard has been developed in compliance with Standards Council of Canada requirements for National Standards of Canada. It has been published as a National Standard of Canada by CSA Group.

Acknowledgement
The use of material contained in the *National Electrical Code* is acknowledged.

The history and operation of the *Canadian Electrical Code, Part I*
The preliminary work in preparing the Canadian Electrical Code began in 1920 when a special committee, appointed by the main Committee of the Canadian Engineering Standards Association, recommended its development. A third meeting of this Committee was held in June 1927 with representatives from Nova Scotia, Québec, Ontario, Manitoba, Saskatchewan, and British Columbia in attendance. At this meeting, the revised draft, which had been discussed at the previous two meetings, was formally approved and it was resolved that it be printed as Part I of the *Canadian Electrical Code*.

The Committee on the *CE Code, Part I*, is composed of 41 members, with representation from inspection authorities, industry, utilities, and allied interests. The main Committee meets once a year and deals with reports that have been submitted by the Section Subcommittees, which work under the jurisdiction of the main Committee. Suggestions for changes to the Code may be made by any member of the Committee or anyone outside the Committee as outlined in Clause C6.

Notes:
1) *Although the intended primary application of this Standard is stated in its Scope, it is important to note that it remains the responsibility of the users of the Standard to judge its suitability for their particular purpose.*
2) *This Standard is subject to review within five years from the date of publication, and suggestions for its improvement will be referred to the appropriate committee.*
3) *All enquiries regarding this Standard should be addressed to CSA Group, 178 Rexdale Blvd., Toronto, Ontario, Canada M9W 1R3. Requests for interpretation should be worded in such a manner as to permit a specific "yes" or "no" answer based on the literal text of the requirement concerned. See Clause C9. Interpretations are available on the* Current Standards Activities *page at standardsactivities.csa.ca.*

Metric units

Symbols and conversion factors for SI units

Recognized symbols for SI units have been used in the *Canadian Electrical Code, Part I*. For the convenience of the user, these symbols and the units they represent have been listed in the following table; the table also gives a multiplying factor that may be used to convert the SI unit to the previously used unit.

Symbol	SI unit	Multiplying factor for conversion to previously used unit	Previously used unit
A	ampere(s)	1	ampere(s)
cm^3	cubic centimetre(s)	0.061	cubic inch(es)
°(s)	degree(s) (angle)	1	degree(s) (angle)
°C rise	degree(s) Celsius	1.8	degree(s) Fahrenheit
°C temperature	degree(s) Celsius	1.8 plus 32	degree(s) Fahrenheit
h	hour(s)	1	hour(s) (time)
Hz	hertz	1	cycles per second
J	joule(s)	0.7376	foot-pound(s)
kg	kilogram(s)	2.205	pound(s)
kJ	kilojoule(s)	737.6	foot-pound(s)
km	kilometre	0.621	mile(s)
kPa	kilopascal(s)	0.295	inch(es) of mercury
		0.334	feet of water
		0.145	pound(s) per square inch (psi)
kW	kilowatt	3415.179	BTU/h
lx	lux	0.093	foot-candle(s)
L	litre	0.220	gallon(s)
m	metre(s)	3.281	feet
m^2	square metre(s)	10.764	square feet
m^3	cubic metre(s)	35.315	cubic feet
MHz	megahertz	1	megacycles per second
min	minute(s)	1	minute(s)
mL	millilitre(s)	0.061	cubic inch(es)
mm	millimetre(s)	0.03937	inch(es)
mm^2	square millimetre(s)	0.00155	square inch(es)
N•m	newton•metre	8.85	pound-force inches
Ω	ohm(s)	1	ohm(s)

Symbol	SI unit	Multiplying factor for conversion to previously used unit	Previously used unit
Pa	pascal(s)	0.000295	inch(es) of mercury
		0.000334	feet of water
		0.000145	pounds per square inch (psi)
s	second(s)	1	second(s)
V	volt(s)	1	volt(s)
W	watt(s)	1	watt(s)
µF	microfarad(s)	1	microfarad(s)

Conduit sizes

Starting in the 2006 edition of the Code, the metric trade designator has been used exclusively to identify conduit size. The following table is provided for convenience only.

Conduit trade sizes

Inches	Metric designator
3/8	12
1/2	16
3/4	21
1	27
1-1/4	35
1-1/2	41
2	53
2-1/2	63
3	78
3-1/2	91
4	103
5	129
6	155
8	200

Reference publications

This Standard refers to the following publications, and the year dates shown indicate the latest editions available at the time the Standard was approved:

CSA Group

6.19-17
Residential carbon monoxide alarming devices

ASME A17.1-2013/CSA B44-13
Safety code for elevators and escalators

CSA B44.1-14/ASME A17.5-2014
Elevator and escalator electrical equipment

B52-13
Mechanical refrigeration code

CAN/CSA-B72-M87 (R2013)
Installation code for lightning protection systems

B108-14
Compressed natural gas fuelling stations installation code

B149.1-15
Natural gas and propane installation code

B149.2-15
Propane storage and handling code

B355-15
Lifts for persons with physical disabilities

CAN/CSA-B613-00 (withdrawn)
Private residence lifts for persons with physical disabilities

CAN/CSA-C22.2 No. 0-10 (R2015)
General requirements — Canadian Electrical Code, Part II

C22.2 No. 1-04 (withdrawn)
Audio, video, and similar electronic equipment

C22.2 No. 3-M1988 (withdrawn)
Electrical features of fuel-burning equipment

C22.2 No. 4-16
Enclosed and dead-front switches

C22.2 No. 5-16
Molded-case circuit breakers, molded-case switches, and circuit-breaker enclosures

C22.2 No. 14-13
Industrial control equipment

C22.2 No. 18.1-13
Metallic outlet boxes

C22.2 No. 18.2-06 (R2016)
Nonmetallic outlet boxes

C22.2 No. 18.3-12 (R2017)
Conduit, tubing, and cable fittings

C22.2 No. 18.4-15
Hardware for the support of conduit, tubing, and cable

C22.2 No. 29-15
Panelboards and enclosed panelboards

C22.2 No. 35-09 (R2014)
Extra-low-voltage control circuit cable, low-energy control cable, and extra-low-voltage control cable

C22.2 No. 38-14
Thermoset-insulated wires and cables

C22.2 No. 41-13
Grounding and bonding equipment

C22.2 No. 42-10 (R2015)
General use receptacles, attachment plugs, and similar wiring devices

C22.2 No. 42.1-13
Cover plates for flush-mounted wiring devices

C22.2 No. 45.1-07 (R2017)
Electrical rigid metal conduit — Steel

C22.2 No. 46-13
Electric air-heaters

C22.2 No. 48-15
Nonmetallic sheathed cable

C22.2 No. 49-14
Flexible cords and cables

C22.2 No. 51-14
Armoured cables

C22.2 No. 52-15
Underground secondary and service-entrance cables

C22.2 No. 56-17
Flexible metal conduit and liquid-tight flexible metal conduit

C22.2 No. 64-10 (R2014)
Household cooking and liquid-heating appliances

C22.2 No. 65-13
Wire connectors

C22.2 No. 66.3-06 (R2015)
Low voltage transformers — Part 3: Class 2 and Class 3 transformers

C22.2 No. 75-17
Thermoplastic insulated wires and cables

C22.2 No. 77-14
Motors with inherent overheating protection

C22.2 No. 82-1969 (R2013)
Tubular support members and associated fittings for domestic and commercial service masts

C22.2 No. 83-M1985 (R2017)
Electrical metallic tubing

C22.2 No. 83.1-07 (R2017)
Electrical metallic tubing — Steel

C22.2 No. 85-14
Rigid PVC boxes and fittings

C22.2 No. 96-17
Portable power cables

C22.2 No. 100-14
Motors and generators

C22.2 No. 106-05 (R2014)
HRC-miscellaneous fuses

C22.2 No. 107.1-16
Power conversion equipment

C22.2 No. 111-10 (R2015)
General-use snap switches

C22.2 No. 123-16
Metal sheathed cables

C22.2 No. 124-16
Mineral-insulated cable

C22.2 No. 126.1-17
Metal cable tray systems

CAN/CSA-C22.2 No. 126.2-02 (R2017)
Nonmetallic cable tray systems

C22.2 No. 127-15
Equipment and lead wires

C22.2 No. 129-10 (R2014)
Neutral-supported cables

C22.2 No. 130-16
Requirements for electrical resistance trace heating and heating device sets

C22.2 No. 131-14
Type TECK 90 cable

C22.2 No. 141-15
Emergency lighting equipment

CAN/CSA-C22.2 No. 157-92 (R2016)
Intrinsically safe and non-incendive equipment for use in hazardous locations

C22.2 No. 174-M1984 (R2017)
Cables and cable glands for use in hazardous locations

C22.2 No. 178.1-14
Transfer switch equipment

C22.2 No. 179-09 (R2014)
Airport series lighting cables

C22.2 No. 208-14
Fire alarm and signal cable

C22.2 No. 211.0-03 (R2013)
General requirements and methods of testing for nonmetallic conduit

C22.2 No. 211.1-06 (R2016)
Rigid types EB1 and DB2/ES2 PVC conduit

C22.2 No. 211.2-06 (R2016)
Rigid PVC (unplasticized) conduit

C22.2 No. 211.3-96 (withdrawn)
Reinforced thermosetting resin conduit (RTRC) and fittings

C22.2 No. 213-16
Non-incendive electrical equipment for use in Class I and II, Division 2 and Class III, Divisions 1 and 2 hazardous (classified) locations

C22.2 No. 214-17
Communications cables

C22.2 No. 218.1-13
Spas, hot tubs, and associated equipment

C22.2 No. 223-15
Power supplies with extra-low-voltage Class 2 outputs

CAN/CSA-C22.2 No. 227.1-06 (R2016)
Electrical nonmetallic tubing

C22.2 No. 227.2.1-14
Liquid-tight flexible non-metallic conduit

C22.2 No. 239-17
Control and instrumentation cables

C22.2 No. 248 series
Low-voltage fuses

C22.2 No. 250.0-08 (R2013)
Luminaires

CAN/CSA-C22.2 No. 250.13-17
Light emitting diode (LED) equipment for lighting applications

CAN/CSA-C22.2 No. 257-06 (R2015)
Interconnecting inverter-based micro-distributed resources to distribution systems

C22.2 No. 269.1-17
Surge protective devices — Type 1 — Permanently connected

C22.2 No. 269.2-17
Surge protective devices — Type 2 — Permanently connected

C22.2 No. 269.3-17
Surge protective devices — Type 3 — Cord connected, direct plug-in, and receptacle type

C22.2 No. 269.4-17
Surge protective devices — Type 4 — Component assemblies

C22.2 No. 269.5-17
Surge protective devices — Type 5 — Components

C22.2 No. 271-11 (R2016)
Photovoltaic cables

C22.2 No. 272-14
Wind turbine electrical systems

C22.2 No. 273-14
Cablebus

C22.2 No. 327-16
HDPE conduit, conductors-in-conduit, and fittings

C22.2 No. 330-17
Photovoltaic rapid shutdown systems

CAN/CSA-C22.2 No. 60079-0:15
Explosive atmospheres — Part 0: Equipment — General requirements

CAN/CSA-C22.2 No. 60079-1:16
Explosive atmospheres — Part 1: Equipment protection by flameproof enclosures "d"

CAN/CSA-C22.2 No. 60079-2:16
Explosive atmospheres — Part 2: Equipment protection by pressurized enclosure "p"

CAN/CSA-C22.2 No. 60079-5:16
Explosive atmospheres — Part 5: Equipment protection by powder filling "q"

CAN/CSA-C22.2 No. 60079-6:17
Explosive atmospheres — Part 6: Equipment protection by liquid immersion "o"

CAN/CSA-C22.2 No. 60079-7:16
Explosive atmospheres — Part 7: Equipment protection by increased safety "e"

CAN/CSA-C22.2 No. 60079-11:14
Explosive atmospheres — Part 11: Equipment protection by intrinsic safety "i"

CAN/CSA-C22.2 No. 60079-15:16
Explosive atmospheres — Part 15: Equipment protection by type of protection "n"

CAN/CSA-C22.2 No. 60079-18:16
Explosive atmospheres — Part 18: Equipment protection by encapsulation "m"

CAN/CSA-C22.2 No. 60079-25:14
Explosive atmospheres — Part 25: Intrinsically safe electrical systems

CAN/CSA-C22.2 No. 60079-26:16
Explosive atmospheres — Part 26: Equipment with equipment protection level (EPL) Ga

CAN/CSA-C22.2 No. 60079-28:16
Explosive atmospheres — Part 28: Protection of equipment and transmission systems using optical radiation

CAN/CSA-C22.2 No. 60079-29-1:17
Explosive atmospheres — Part 29-1: Gas detectors — Performance requirements of detectors for flammable gases

CAN/CSA-C22.2 No. 60079-30-1:17
Explosive atmospheres — Part 30-1: Electrical resistance trace heating — General and testing requirements

CAN/CSA-C22.2 No. 60529:16
Degrees of protection provided by enclosures

CAN/CSA-C22.2 No. 60601 series
Medical electrical equipment

CAN/CSA-C22.2 No. 60950-1-07 (R2016)
Information technology equipment — Safety — Part 1: General requirements

CAN/CSA-C22.2 No. 61730-1:11 (R2016)
Photovoltaic (PV) module safety qualification — Part 1: Requirements for construction

CAN/CSA-C22.2 No. 61730-2:11 (R2016)
Photovoltaic (PV) module safety qualification — Part 2: Requirements for testing

CAN/CSA-C22.2 No. 62109-1:16
Safety of power converters for use in photovoltaic power systems — Part 1: General requirements

CAN/CSA-C22.2 No. 62275:16
Cable management systems — Cable ties for electrical installations

CAN/CSA-C22.2 No. 62368-1-14
Audio/video, information and communication technology equipment — Part 1: Safety requirements

C22.3 No. 1-15
Overhead systems

C22.3 No. 7-15
Underground systems

CAN/CSA-C68.5-13
Shielded and concentric neutral power cable for distribution utilities

C68.10-14
Shielded power cable for commercial and industrial applications, 5–46 kV

C83-96 (R2016)
Communication and power line hardware

CAN3-C235-83 (R2015)
Preferred voltage levels for ac systems, 0 to 50 000 V

C282-15
Emergency electrical power supply for buildings

CAN/CSA-C50052-99 (R2016)
Cast aluminium alloy enclosures for gas-filled high-voltage switchgear and controlgear

CAN/CSA-C50064-99 (R2016)
Wrought aluminium and aluminium alloy enclosures for gas-filled high-voltage switchgear and controlgear

CAN/CSA-C50068-99 (R2016)
Wrought steel enclosures for gas-filled high-voltage switchgear and controlgear

CAN/CSA-C50069-99 (R2016)
Welded composite enclosures of cast and wrought aluminium alloys for gas-filled high-voltage switchgear and controlgear

CAN/CSA-C50089-99 (R2016)
Cast resin partitions for metal-enclosed gas-filled high-voltage switchgear and controlgear

CAN/CSA-C62155:06 (R2015)
Hollow pressurized and unpressurized ceramic and glass insulators for use in electrical equipment with rated voltages greater than 1000 V

CAN/CSA-IEC 61400-24:12
Wind turbines — Part 24: Lightning protection

IEEE 844.1-2017/CSA C22.2 No. 293.1-17
Skin effect trace heating of pipelines, vessels, equipment, and structures — general, testing, marking, and documentation requirements

IEEE 844.2/CSA C293.2
Application guide for design, equipment selection and installation of skin effect trace heating systems

M421-16
Use of electricity in mines

PLUS 2203 (withdrawn)
Guide for the Design, Testing, Construction, and Installation of Equipment in Explosive Atmospheres by John A. Bossert, 3rd edition, 2001

S413-14
Parking structures

SPE-1000-13
Model code for the field evaluation of electrical equipment

Z32-15
Electrical safety and essential electrical systems in health care facilities

Z98-14
Passenger ropeways and passenger conveyors

CAN/CSA-Z240 MH Series-92 (withdrawn)
Mobile homes

CAN/CSA-Z240 RV Series-08 (R2013)
Recreational vehicles

Z240 RV Series-14
Recreational vehicles

CAN/CSA-Z241 Series-03 (R2013)
Park model trailers

CAN/CSA-Z267-00 (R2011)
Safety code for amusement rides and devices

Z462-15
Workplace electrical safety

CAN/CSA-Z662-15
Oil and gas pipeline systems

ANSI (American National Standards Institute)
B77.1-2017
Passenger Ropeways — Aerial Tramways, Aerial Lifts, Surface Lifts, Tows and Conveyors — Safety Standard

C84.1-2016
American National Standard for Electric Power Systems and Equipment—Voltage Ratings (60 Hz)

ANSI/ASME (American National Standards Institute/American Society of Mechanical Engineers)
B1.20.1-2013
Pipe Threads, General Purpose (Inch)

ANSI/IEEE (American National Standards Institute/Institute of Electrical and Electronics Engineers)
487-2015
IEEE Standard for the Electrical Protection of Communications Facilities Serving Electric Supply Locations — General Considerations

ANSI/ISA (American National Standards Institute/International Society of Automation)
12.27.01-2011
Requirements for Process Sealing Between Electrical Systems and Flammable or Combustible Process Fluids

60079-10-1 (12.24.01)-2014
Explosive Atmospheres – Part 10-1: Classification of areas – Explosive gas atmospheres

RP 12.06.01-2003
Recommended Practice for Wiring Methods for Hazardous (Classified) Locations — Instrumentation — Part 1: Intrinsic Safety

ANSI/NEMA (American National Standards Institute/National Electrical Manufacturers Association)
WD 6-2016
Wiring Devices — Dimensional Specifications

Z535.4-2011
Product Safety Signs and Labels

API (American Petroleum Institute)
RP 14F (2008; R2013)
Design, Installation, and Maintenance of Electrical Systems for Fixed and Floating Offshore Petroleum Facilities for Unclassified and Class 1, Division 1 and Division 2 Locations

RP 14FZ (2013)
Design and Installation of Electrical Systems for Fixed and Floating Offshore Petroleum Facilities for Unclassified and Class I, Zone 0, Zone 1 and Zone 2 Locations

RP 500 (2012)
Recommended Practice for Classification of Locations for Electrical Installations at Petroleum Facilities Classified as Class I, Division 1 and Division 2

RP 505 (1997; R2013)
Recommended Practice for Classification of Locations for Electrical Installations at Petroleum Facilities Classified as Class I, Zone 0, Zone 1, and Zone 2

RP 2216 (2003; R2015)
Ignition Risk of Hydrocarbon Liquids and Vapors by Hot Surfaces in the Open Air

PUBL 4589 (1993)
Fugitive Hydrocarbon Emissions from Oil and Gas Production Operations

PUBL 4615 (1995)
Emission Factors for Oil and Gas Production Operations

PUBL 4638 (1996)
Calculation Workbook for Oil and Gas Production Equipment Fugitive Emissions

ASABE (American Society of Agricultural and Biological Engineers)
EP473.2-2001 (R2015)
Equipotential Plane in Livestock Containment Areas

ASTM International

ASTM B117-16
Standard Practice for Operating Salt Spray (Fog) Apparatus

C1055-03 (2014)
Standard Guide for Heated System Surface Conditions that Produce Contact Burn Injuries

D2487-11
Standard Practice for Classification of Soils for Engineering Purposes (Unified Soil Classification System)

E11-17
Standard Specification for Woven Wire Test Sieve Cloth and Test Sieves

E1226-12a
Standard Test Method for Explosibility of Dust Clouds

BNQ (Bureau de normalisation du Québec)

CAN/BNQ 1784-000 (2007)
Canadian Hydrogen Installation Code

CEA (Canadian Electricity Association)*

249 D 541 (1989)
Simplified Rules for Grounding Customer-Owned High Voltage Substations

266 D 991 (1995)
Clearance Distances Between Swimming Pools and Underground Electrical Cables

CEA Standards are available through CEATI International (Centre for Energy Advancement through Technological Innovation).

DIN [Deutsches Institut für Normung (German Institute for Standardisation)]

DIN IEC 60079-20-2 (withdrawn)
Explosive Atmospheres — Part 20-2: Material Characteristics — Combustible Dusts Test Methods

Energy Institute

EI 15
Model code of safe practice Part 15: Area classification code for installations handling flammable fluids, 2015

IEC (International Electrotechnical Commission)

60079-10-1:2015
Explosive atmospheres — Part 10-1: Classification of areas — Explosive gas atmospheres

60079-10-2:2015
Explosive atmospheres — Part 10-2: Classification of areas — Explosive dust atmospheres

60079-13:2017
Explosive atmospheres — Part 13: Equipment protection by pressurized room "p" and artificially ventilated room "v"

60079-14:2013
Explosive atmospheres — Part 14: Electrical installations design, selection and erection

60079-17:2013
Explosive atmospheres — Part 17: Electrical installations inspection and maintenance

60079-19:2010
Explosive atmospheres — Part 19: Equipment repair, overhaul and reclamation

60079-20-1:2010
Explosive atmospheres — Part 20-1: Material characteristics for gas and vapour classification — Test methods and data

60079-25:2010
Explosive atmospheres — Part 25: Intrinsically safe electrical systems

60079-26:2014
Explosive atmospheres — Part 26: Equipment with equipment protection level (EPL) Ga

60079-29-2:2015
Explosive atmospheres — Part 29-2: Gas detectors — Selection, installation, use and maintenance of detectors for flammable gases and oxygen

60079-29-3:2014
Explosive atmospheres — Part 29-3: Gas detectors — Guidance on functional safety of fixed gas detection systems

60300 Series
Dependability management

60364-1:2005
Low-voltage electrical installations — Part 1: Fundamental principles, assessment of general characteristics, definitions

60781:1989 (withdrawn)
Application guide for calculation of short-circuit currents in low-voltage radial systems

61010-1:2010
Safety requirements for electrical equipment for measurement, control, and laboratory use — Part 1: General requirements

GUIDE 117 (edition 1.0, 2010-10-13)
Electrotechnical equipment — Temperatures of touchable hot surfaces

IEC/IEEE (International Electrotechnical Commission/Institute of Electrical and Electronics Engineers)
60079-30-1:2015
Explosive atmospheres — Part 30-1: Electrical resistance trace heating — General and testing requirements

60079-30-2:2015
Explosive atmospheres — Part 30-2: Electrical resistance trace heating — Application guide for design, installation and maintenance

IEEE (Institute of Electrical and Electronics Engineers)

45-2002
IEEE Recommended Practice for Electrical Installations on Shipboard

80-2013
IEEE Guide for Safety in AC Substation Grounding

484-2002
IEEE Recommended Practice for Installation Design and Installation of Vented Lead-Acid Batteries for Stationary Applications

802.3-2015
IEEE Standard for Ethernet

835-1994 (R2012)
IEEE Standard Power Cable Ampacity Tables

837-2014
IEEE Standard for Qualifying Permanent Connections Used in Substation Grounding

844-2000
Recommended Practice for Electrical Impedance, Induction, and Skin Effect Heating of Pipelines and Vessels

902-1998
IEEE Guide for Maintenance, Operation, and Safety of Industrial and Commercial Power Systems (Yellow Book)

1202-2006
IEEE Standard for Flame-Propagation Testing of Wire and Cable

1349-2011
IEEE Guide for Application of Electric Motors in Class I, Division 2 and Class I, Zone 2 Hazardous (Classified) Locations

1584-2002
IEEE Guide for Performing Arc Flash Hazard Calculations

1673-2015
IEEE Standard for Requirements for Conduit and Cable Seals for Field Connected Wiring to Equipment in Petroleum and Chemical Industry Exposed to Pressures above Atmospheric (1.5 kPa, 0.22 psi)

C62.41.1-2002
IEEE Guide on the Surge Environment in Low-Voltage (1000 V and less) AC Power Circuits

C62.41.2-2002
IEEE Recommended Practice on Characterization of Surges in Low-Voltage (1000 V and less) AC Power Circuits

P1020/D12 (October 2011)
IEEE Draft Guide for Control of Small (100 kVA to 5 MVA) Hydroelectric Power Plants

PCIC-97-04, P.S. Hamer; B.M. Wood; R.L. Doughty; R.L. Gravell; R.C. Hasty; S.E. Wallace; J.P. Tsao; and Chevron Res. & Technol. Co., "Flammable vapor ignition initiated by hot rotor surfaces within an induction motor — reality or not?" in *Petroleum and Chemical Industry Conference,* Record of Conference Papers. 1997; 2002.

ISA (International Society of Automation)
12.01.01-2013
Definitions and Information Pertaining to Electrical Equipment in Hazardous (Classified) Locations

12.04.04-2012
Pressurized Enclosures

12.10-1988
Area Classification in Hazardous (Classified) Dust Locations

12.12.03-2011
Standard for Portable Electronic Products Suitable for Use in Class I and II, Division 2, Class I Zone 2 and Class III, Division 1 and 2 Hazardous (Classified) Locations

12.13.04:2007 (R2014)
Performance Requirements for Open Path Combustible Gas Detectors

12.20.01-2009 (R2014)
General Requirements for Electrical Ignition Systems for Internal Combustion Engines in Class I, Division 2 or Zone 2, Hazardous (Classified) Locations

Magison, Ernest. *Electrical Instruments in Hazardous Locations,* 4th edition, 2007

RP12.02.02-1996
Recommendations for the Preparation, Content, and Organization of Intrinsic Safety Control Drawings

TR12.2-1995
Intrinsically Safe System Assessment Using the Entity Concept

TR12.12.04:2011
Electrical Equipment in a Class 1, Division 2/Zone 2 Hazardous Location

TR12.13.01–1999
Flammability Characteristics of Combustible Gases and Vapors

TR12.13.03-2009
Guide for Combustible Gas Detection as a Method of Protection

TR12.21.01:2004 (R2013)
Use of Fiber Optic Systems in Class 1 Hazardous (classified) Locations

ISO (International Organization for Standardization)

965-1:2013
ISO general-purpose metric screw threads — Tolerances — Part 1: Principles and basic data

965-3:1998
ISO general purpose metric screw threads —Tolerances — Part 3: Deviations for constructional screw threads

4225:1994
Air quality — General aspects — Vocabulary

6184-1:1985
Explosion protection systems — Part 1: Determination of explosion indices of combustible dusts in air

ISO/IEC (International Organization for Standardization /International Electrotechnical Commission)

FDIS 80079-20-1
Explosive atmospheres — Part 20-1: Material characteristics for gas and vapour classification — Test methods and data

80079-20-2:2016
Explosive atmospheres — Part 20-2: Material characteristics — Combustible dusts test methods

NEMA (National Electrical Manufacturers Association)

VE 1-2017
Metal Cable Tray Systems

NFPA (National Fire Protection Association)

20-2016
Standard for the Installation of Stationary Pumps for Fire Protection

30-2018
Flammable and Combustible Liquids Code

40-2016
Standard for the Storage and Handling of Cellulose Nitrate Film

51A-2012 (withdrawn)
Standard for Acetylene Cylinder Charging Plants

61-2017
Standard for the Prevention of Fires and Dust Explosions in Agricultural and Food Processing Facilities

68-2013
Standard on Explosion Protection by Deflagration Venting

70-2017
National Electrical Code

70B-2016
Recommended Practice for Electrical Equipment Maintenance

77-2014
Recommended Practice on Static Electricity

91-2015
Standard for Exhaust Systems for Air Conveying of Vapors, Gases, Mists, and Noncombustible Particulate Solids

96-2017
Standard for Ventilation Control and Fire Protection of Commercial Cooking Operations

484-2015
Standard for Combustible Metals

496-2017
Standard for Purged and Pressurized Enclosures for Electrical Equipment

497-2017
Recommended Practice for the Classification of Flammable Liquids, Gases, or Vapors and of Hazardous (Classified) Locations for Electrical Installations in Chemical Process Areas

499-2017
Recommended Practice for the Classification of Combustible Dusts and of Hazardous (Classified) Locations for Electrical Installations in Chemical Process Areas

505-2013
Fire Safety Standard for Powered Industrial Trucks Including Type Designations, Areas of Use, Conversions, Maintenance, and Operation

654-2017
Standard for the Prevention of Fire and Dust Explosions from the Manufacturing, Processing, and Handling of Combustible Particulate Solids

655-2017
Standard for Prevention of Sulfur Fires and Explosions

664-2017
Standard for the Prevention of Fires and Explosions in Wood Processing and Woodworking Facilities

820-2016
Standard for Fire Protection in Wastewater Treatment and Collection Facilities

HAZ 10
Fire Protection Guide to Hazardous Materials, 2010

NRCC (National Research Council Canada)
National Building Code of Canada, 2015

National Farm Building Code of Canada, 1995

National Fire Code of Canada, 2015

ULC (Underwriters Laboratories of Canada)
S139-17
Standard Method of Fire Test for Evaluation of Integrity of Electrical Power, Data, and Optical Fibre Cables

CAN/ULC-S524-14
Standard for the Installation of Fire Alarm Systems

CAN/ULC-S531-14
Standard for Smoke Alarms

CAN/ULC-S2577-13
Standard for Suspended Ceiling Grid Low Voltage Systems and Equipment

Other publications
Alberta Municipal Affairs, *Electrical STANDATA*

Canada — *Navigation Protection Act,* R.S.C. 1985, c. N-22

Environment Canada, *Canadian Climate Normals*

Natural Resources Canada, *Atlas of Canada*

Natural Resources Canada, *Micro-Hydropower Systems: A Buyer's Guide,* 2004

Section 0 — Object, scope, and definitions
(See Appendix G)

Object (see Appendix B)

The object of this Code is to establish safety standards for the installation and maintenance of electrical equipment. In its preparation, consideration has been given to the prevention of fire and shock hazards, as well as proper maintenance and operation.

The requirements in this Code address the fundamental principles of protection for safety contained in Section 131 of International Electrotechnical Commission Standard 60364-1, *Low-voltage electrical installations*. IEC 60364-1, Section 131, contains fundamental principles of protection for safety that encompass protection against electric shock, thermal effects, overcurrent, fault currents, and overvoltage. Therefore, compliance with the requirements of this Code and proper maintenance will ensure an essentially safe installation. Safe installations may be also achieved by alternatives to this Code, when such alternatives meet the fundamental safety principles of IEC 60364-1 (see Appendix K). These alternatives are intended to be used only in conjunction with acceptable means to assess compliance of these alternatives with the fundamental safety principles of IEC 60364-1 by the authorities enforcing this Code.

Wiring installations that do not make provision for the increasing use of electricity may be overloaded in the future, resulting in a hazardous condition. It is recommended that the initial installation have sufficient wiring capacity and that there be some provision made for wiring changes that might be required as a result of future load growth.

This Code is not intended as a design specification nor as an instruction manual for untrained persons.

Scope

This Code applies to all electrical work and electrical equipment operating or intended to operate at all voltages in electrical installations for buildings, structures, and premises, including factory-built relocatable and non-relocatable structures, and self-propelled marine vessels stationary for periods exceeding five months and connected to a shore supply of electricity continuously or from time to time, with the following exceptions:
a) installations or equipment employed by an electric, communication, or community antenna distribution system utility in the exercise of its function as a utility, as recognized by the regulatory authority having jurisdiction, and located outdoors or in buildings or sections of buildings used for that purpose;
b) equipment and facilities that are used in the operation of an electric railway and are supplied exclusively from circuits that supply the motive power;
c) installations or equipment used for railway signalling and railway communication purposes, and located outdoors or in buildings or sections of buildings used exclusively for such installations;
d) aircraft; and
e) electrical systems in ships that are regulated under Transport Canada.

For mines and quarry applications, see also CSA M421.

This Code and any standards referenced in it do not make or imply any assurance or guarantee by the authority adopting this Code with respect to life expectancy, durability, or operating performance of equipment and materials so referenced.

Definitions

For the purpose of correct interpretation, certain terms have been defined and where such terms or their derivatives appear throughout this Code they shall be understood to have the following meanings. The ordinary or dictionary meaning of terms shall be used for terms not specifically defined in this Code.

Acceptable — acceptable to the authority enforcing this Code.

Accessible (as applied to equipment) — admitting close approach because the equipment is not guarded by locked doors, elevation, or other effective means.

Accessible (as applied to wiring methods) —
a)   not permanently closed in by the structure or finish of the building; and
b)   capable of being removed without disturbing the building structure or finish.

Accredited certification organization — an organization that has been accredited by the Standards Council of Canada, in accordance with specific criteria, procedures, and requirements, to operate, on a continuing basis, a certification program for electrical equipment.

Δ   **Aluminum-sheathed cable** — a cable consisting of one or more conductors assembled into a core and covered with a liquid- and gas-tight sheath of aluminum or aluminum alloy.

Ampacity — the current-carrying capacity of electric conductors expressed in amperes.

Approved (as applied to electrical equipment) —
1)   equipment that has been certified by a certification organization accredited by the Standards Council of Canada in accordance with the requirements of
    a)   CSA Group Standards; or
    b)   other standards that have been developed by a standards development organization accredited by the Standards Council of Canada, or other recognized documents, where CSA Group Standards do not exist or are not applicable, provided that such other standards or other recognized documents
        i)   are correlated with provisions of the *CE Code, Part I*; and
        ii)   do not create duplication with standards already listed in Appendix A; or
2)   equipment that conforms to the requirements of the regulatory authority (see Appendix B).

Authorized person — a qualified person who, in his or her duties or occupation, is obliged to approach or handle electrical equipment; or a person who, having been warned of the hazards involved, has been instructed or authorized to do so by someone having authority to give the instruction or authorization.

Auxiliary gutter — a raceway consisting of a sheet metal enclosure used to supplement the wiring space of electrical equipment and to enclose interconnecting conductors.

AWG — the American (or Brown and Sharpe) Wire Gauge as applied to non-ferrous conductors and non-ferrous sheet metal.

Bathroom — a room containing bathing or showering facilities and that may also contain a wash basin(s) and/or water closet(s).

Bonding — a low impedance path obtained by permanently joining all non-current-carrying metal parts to ensure electrical continuity and having the capacity to conduct safely any current likely to be imposed on it.

Bonding conductor — a conductor that connects the non-current-carrying parts of electrical equipment, raceways, or enclosures to the service equipment or system grounding conductor.

Box connector — see **Connector**.

Branch circuit — see **Circuit**.

Building — a structure that stands alone or that is cut off from adjoining structures by firewalls, unpierced or with openings, protected by approved fire doors.

Bus — a conductor that serves as a common connection for the corresponding conductors of two or more circuits.

Busway — a raceway consisting of metal troughing (including elbows, tees, and crosses, in addition to straight runs) containing conductors that are supported on insulators.

Cabinet — an enclosure of adequate mechanical strength, composed entirely of non-combustible and absorption-resistant material, designed either for surface or flush mounting, and provided with a frame, mat, or trim, in which swinging doors are hung.

Δ   **Cable** — a complete manufactured assembly of one or more insulated conductors, which may also include optical fibers, fillers, strength members, and insulating and protective material, with a continuous overall covering providing electrical, mechanical, and environmental protection to the assembly.

Cable tray — a raceway consisting of troughing and fittings formed and constructed so that insulated conductors and cables may be readily installed or removed after the cable tray has been completely installed, without damage either to conductors or their covering.

> **Ladder cable tray** — a prefabricated structure consisting of two longitudinal side rails connected by individual transverse members, with openings exceeding 50 mm in a longitudinal direction (see Appendix B).

> **Non-ventilated cable tray** — a prefabricated structure without openings within the integral or separate longitudinal side rails.

> **Ventilated cable tray** — a prefabricated structure consisting of a ventilated bottom within integral longitudinal side rails, with no openings exceeding 50 mm in a longitudinal direction (see Appendix B).

Cablebus — an assembly of insulated conductors with fittings and conductor terminations in a completely enclosed, ventilated, or non-ventilated protective metal housing (see Appendix B).

Cell — one of the hollow spaces, suitable for use as a raceway, of a cellular metal or cellular concrete floor, the axis of the cell being parallel to the longitudinal axis of the floor members.

Cellular floor — an assembly of cellular metal or cellular concrete floor members, consisting of units with hollow spaces (cells) suitable for use as raceways and, in some cases, non-cellular units.

Circuit (see Appendix B) —

> **Branch circuit** — that portion of the wiring installation between the final overcurrent device protecting the circuit and the outlet(s).

Communication circuit — a circuit that is part of a communication system.

Control circuit — the circuit that carries the electric signals directing the performance of a control device, but that does not carry the power that the device controls.

Δ **Extra-low-voltage power circuit** — a circuit, such as a valve operator and similar circuits, that is neither a remote control circuit nor a signal circuit, but that operates at not more than 30 V and that is supplied from a transformer or other device restricted in its rated output to 1000 V•A, but in which the current is not limited in accordance with the requirements for a Class 2 circuit.

Low-energy power circuit — a circuit other than a remote control or signal circuit that has the power supply limited in accordance with the requirements for Class 2 remote control circuits.

Multi-wire branch circuit — a branch circuit consisting of two or more ungrounded conductors having a voltage difference between them and an identified grounded conductor having equal voltage between it and each ungrounded conductor, with this grounded conductor connected to the neutral conductor.

Non-incendive circuit — a circuit in which any spark or thermal effect that may occur under normal operating conditions or due to opening, shorting, or grounding of field wiring is incapable of causing an ignition of the prescribed flammable gas or vapour.

Remote control circuit — any electrical circuit that controls any other circuit through a relay or an equivalent device.

Signal circuit — any electrical circuit, other than a communication circuit, that supplies energy to a device that gives a recognizable signal, such as circuits for doorbells, buzzers, code-calling systems, signal lights, etc.

Circuit breaker — a device designed to open and close a circuit by non-automatic means and to open the circuit automatically on a predetermined overcurrent without damage to itself when properly applied within its ratings.

Instantaneous-trip circuit breaker — a circuit breaker designed to trip only under short-circuit conditions.

Communication circuit — see **Circuit**.

Communication system — see **System**.

Community antenna distribution system — see **System**.

Concealed — rendered permanently inaccessible by the structure or finish of the building.

Δ **Conductor** — a conductive material that is constructed for the purpose of carrying electric current.

Bare conductor — a conductor having no covering or electrical insulation.

Covered conductor — a conductor covered with a dielectric material having no rated dielectric strength.

Insulated conductor — a conductor covered with a dielectric material having a rated dielectric strength.

Conduit — a raceway of circular cross-section, other than electrical metallic tubing and electrical non-metallic tubing, into which it is intended that conductors be drawn.

> **Flexible metal conduit** — a metal conduit that may be easily bent without the use of tools.
>
> **Liquid-tight flexible conduit** —
> a)   a flexible metal conduit having an outer liquid-tight jacket; or
> b)   a flexible liquid-tight non-metallic conduit.
>
> **Rigid conduit** — a rigid conduit of metal or a non-metallic material.
>
> **Rigid metal conduit** — a rigid conduit of metal made to the same dimensions as standard pipe and suitable for threading with standard pipe threads.
>
> **Rigid non-metallic conduit** — a rigid conduit of non-metallic material that is not permitted to be threaded.
>
> **Rigid PVC conduit** — a rigid non-metallic conduit of unplasticized polyvinyl chloride.
>
> **Rigid RTRC conduit Type AG** — a rigid non-metallic conduit of reinforced thermoset material suitable for direct burial or encasement in concrete and for exposed or concealed work.
>
> **Rigid RTRC conduit Type BG** — a rigid non-metallic conduit of reinforced thermoset material suitable for direct burial or encasement in concrete.
>
> **Rigid Type DB2/ES2 PVC conduit** — a rigid non-metallic conduit of PVC for direct burial or encasement in concrete or masonry.
>
> **Rigid Type EB1 PVC conduit** — a rigid non-metallic conduit of PVC for encasement in concrete or masonry.

Connector —

> **Box connector** — a device for securing a cable, via its sheath or armour, where it enters an enclosure such as an outlet box.
>
> **Wire connector** — a device that connects two or more conductors together or one or more conductors to a terminal point for the purpose of connecting electrical circuits.

Continuous duty — see **Duty**.

Control circuit — see **Circuit**.

Controller — a device or a group of devices for controlling in some predetermined manner the electric power delivered to the apparatus to which it is connected.

Cord set — an assembly consisting of a suitable length of flexible cord or power supply cable provided with an attachment plug at one end and a cord connector at the other end.

Current-permit — written permission from the inspection department to a supply authority stating that electric energy may be supplied to a particular installation.

Cut-out box — an enclosure of adequate mechanical strength, composed entirely of non-combustible and absorption-resistant material, designed for surface mounting, and having swinging doors or covers secured directly to, and telescoping with, the walls of the box proper.

Damp location — see **Location**.

Dead (as applied to electrical equipment) — the current-carrying parts of electrical equipment are free from any electrical connection to a source of voltage and from electrical charge and do not have a voltage different from that of earth.

Dead front — without live parts exposed to a person on the operating side of the equipment.

Different systems — see **System**.

Disconnecting means — a device, group of devices, or other means whereby the conductors of a circuit can be disconnected from their source of supply.

Dry location — see **Location**.

Duplex receptacle — see **Receptacle**.

Dust-tight — an enclosure constructed so that dust cannot enter it.

Duty — a requirement of service that demands the degree of regularity of the load.

> **Continuous duty** — a requirement of service that demands operation at a substantially constant load for an indefinitely long time.
>
> **Intermittent duty** — a requirement of service that demands operation for definitely specified alternate intervals of
> a)   load and no-load;
> b)   load and rest; or
> c)   load, no-load, and rest.
>
> **Periodic duty** — a type of intermittent duty in which the load conditions are regularly recurrent.
>
> **Short-time duty** — a requirement of service that demands operation at a substantially constant load for a short and definitely specified time.
>
> **Varying duty** — a requirement of service that demands operation at loads and for intervals of time, both of which may be subject to wide variation.

Dwelling unit — one or more rooms for the use of one or more persons as a housekeeping unit with cooking, eating, living, and sleeping facilities.

Electrical contractor — any person, corporation, company, firm, organization, or partnership performing or engaging to perform, either for their or its own use or benefit, or for that of another, and with or without remuneration or gain, any work with respect to an electrical installation or any other work to which this Code applies.

Electrical equipment — any apparatus, appliance, device, instrument, fitting, fixture, luminaire, machinery, material, or thing used in or for, or capable of being used in or for, the generation, transformation, transmission, distribution, supply, or utilization of electric power or energy, and, without restricting the generality of the foregoing, includes any assemblage or combination of materials or things that is used, or is capable of being used or adapted, to serve or perform any particular purpose or function when connected to an electrical installation, notwithstanding that any of such materials or things may be mechanical, metallic, or non-electric in origin.

Electrical installation — the installation of any wiring in or upon any land, building, or premises from the point(s) where electric power or energy is delivered by the supply authority or from any other source of supply, to the point(s) where such power or energy can be used by any electrical equipment, and the installation includes the connection of any such wiring with any of the electrical equipment and any part of the wiring and also includes the maintenance, alteration, extension, and repair of such wiring.

Electrical metallic tubing — a raceway of metal having circular cross-section into which it is intended that conductors be drawn and that has a wall thinner than that of rigid metal conduit and an outside diameter sufficiently different from that of rigid conduit to render it impracticable for anyone to thread it with standard pipe thread.

Electrical non-metallic tubing — a pliable non-metallic corrugated raceway having a circular cross-section.

Elevator — a hoisting and lowering mechanism equipped with a car or platform that moves in guides in a substantially vertical direction but not including tiering or piling machines that operate within one storey, or endless belts, conveyors, chains, buckets, or similar devices used for the purpose of elevating materials.

> **Electric elevator** — an elevator in which the motion of the car is obtained through an electric motor directly applied to the elevator machinery.

Elevator machinery — the machinery and its equipment used in raising and lowering the elevator car or platform.

Emergency lighting — lighting required by the provisions of the *National Building Code of Canada* for the purpose of facilitating safe exit and access to exit in the event of fire or other emergency.

Energized — electrically connected to, or is, a source of voltage.

Energized part — an energized conductive component.

Explosion-proof — enclosed in a case that is capable of withstanding without damage any explosion that may occur within it of a specified gas or vapour and capable of preventing the ignition of a specified gas or vapour surrounding the enclosure from sparks, flashes, or explosion of the specified gas or vapour within the enclosure.

Exposed (as applied to live parts) — live parts that can be inadvertently touched or approached nearer than a safe distance by a person, and the term is applied to parts not suitably guarded, isolated, or insulated.

Exposed (as applied to wiring methods) — not concealed.

Extra-low voltage — see **Voltage**.

Extra-low-voltage power circuit — see **Circuit**.

Feeder — any portion of an electrical circuit between the service box or other source of supply and the branch circuit overcurrent devices.

Fire-resisting (when applied to a building) — constructed of masonry, reinforced concrete, or equivalent materials.

General-use switch — see **Switch**.

Ground — a connection to earth obtained by a grounding electrode.

Ground fault — an unintentional electrical path between a part operating normally at some potential to ground, and ground.

Ground fault circuit interrupter (GFCI) — a device that functions to interrupt a circuit or portion of a circuit, within a predetermined time, when a current to ground exceeds some predetermined value that is less than that required to operate the overcurrent protective device of the supply circuit.

Ground fault circuit interrupter, Class A (Class A GFCI) — a ground fault circuit interrupter that will interrupt the circuit to the load, within a predetermined time, when the ground fault current is 6 mA or more but not when the ground fault current is 4 mA or less (see Appendix B).

Ground fault detection — a means of detecting a ground fault (see Appendix B).

Ground fault protection — a means of detecting and interrupting a ground fault current at a level less than the current required to operate the circuit overcurrent device (see Appendix B).

Grounded — connected effectively with the general mass of the earth through a grounding path of sufficiently low impedance and having an ampacity sufficient at all times, under the most severe conditions liable to arise in practice, to prevent any current in the grounding conductor from causing a harmful voltage to exist
a)   between the grounding conductors and neighbouring exposed conducting surfaces that are in good contact with the earth; or
b)   between the grounding conductors and neighbouring surfaces of the earth itself.

Grounding — a permanent and continuous conductive path to the earth with sufficient ampacity to carry any fault current liable to be imposed on it, and of a sufficiently low impedance to limit the voltage rise above ground and to facilitate the operation of the protective devices in the circuit.

Grounding conductor — the conductor used to connect the service equipment or system to the grounding electrode (see Appendix B).

Grounding electrode — a buried metal water-piping system or metal object or device buried in, or driven into, the ground to which a grounding conductor is electrically and mechanically connected.

Grounding system — see **System**.

Guarded — covered, shielded, fenced, enclosed, or otherwise protected by means of suitable covers or casings, barriers, rails or screens, or mats or platforms to remove the liability of dangerous contact or approach by persons or objects.

Hazardous location — see **Location**.

Δ   **HDPE conductors-in-conduit** — a complete assembly of conductors or cables inside a continuous length of HDPE conduit.

Δ   **HDPE conduit** — a non-metallic, smooth wall conduit of high-density polyethylene for direct burial or encasement in concrete or masonry.

Header — a raceway for electrical conductors, associated with an underfloor raceway or cellular floor system, that provides access to predetermined raceways or cells.

High-voltage — see **Voltage**.

Hoistway — any shaftway, hatchway, well hole, or other vertical opening or space in which an elevator, escalator, or dumbwaiter operates or is intended to operate.

Identified —
a)   when applied to a conductor, signifies that the conductor has
   i)   a white or grey covering; or
   ii) a raised longitudinal ridge(s) on the surface of the extruded covering on certain flexible cords, either of which indicates that the conductor is a grounded conductor or a neutral; and
b)   when applied to other electrical equipment, signifies that the terminals to which grounded or neutral conductors are to be connected have been distinguished for identification by being tinned, nickel-plated, or otherwise suitably marked.

Inaccessible —
a)   when applied to a room or compartment, signifies that the room or compartment is sufficiently remote from access or placed or guarded so that unauthorized persons cannot inadvertently enter the room or compartment; and
b)   when applied to electrical equipment, signifies that the electrical equipment is covered by the structure or finish of the building in which it is installed or maintained, or is sufficiently remote from access or placed so that unauthorized persons cannot inadvertently touch or interfere with the equipment.

Indicating switch — see **Switch**.

Industrial establishment — a building or part of a building (other than office or exhibit space) or a part of the premises outside the building where persons are employed in manufacturing processes or in the handling of material, as distinguished from dwellings, offices, and similar occupancies.

Inspection department — an organization legally authorized to enforce this Code and having jurisdiction over specified territory.

Inspector — any person duly appointed by the inspection department for the purpose of enforcing this Code.

Insulated — separated from other conducting surfaces by a dielectric material or air space having a degree of resistance to the passage of current and to disruptive discharge sufficiently high for the condition of use.

Insulating (as applied to non-conducting substances) — capable of bringing about the condition defined as insulated.

Intermittent duty — see **Duty**.

Intrinsically safe — that any spark or thermal effect that may occur in normal use, or under any conditions of fault likely to occur in practice, is incapable of causing an ignition of the prescribed flammable gas, vapour, or dust.

Isolating switch — see **Switch**.

Δ   **Jacket** — a non-metallic covering on a cable that provides mechanical and environmental protection for the cable.

Ladder cable tray — see **Cable tray**.

Lampholder — a device constructed for the mechanical support of lamps and for connecting them to circuit conductors.

Liquid-tight flexible conduit — see **Conduit**.

Δ **Live** — see **Energized**.

Δ **Live parts** — energized conductive components.

Location —

Damp location — an exterior or interior location that is normally or periodically subject to condensation of moisture in, on, or adjacent to electrical equipment and includes partially protected locations under canopies, marquees, roofed open porches, and similar locations.

Dry location — a location not normally subject to dampness, but that may include a location subject to temporary dampness as in the case of a building under construction, provided that ventilation is adequate to prevent an accumulation of moisture.

Δ **Hazardous location** (see Appendix B) — premises, buildings, or parts thereof in which
a) an explosive gas atmosphere is present, or may be present, in the air in quantities that require special precautions for the construction, installation, and use of electrical equipment;
b) dusts are present, or may be present, in the form of clouds or layers in quantities to require special precautions for the construction, installation, and operation of electrical equipment.

Ordinary location — a dry location in which, at normal atmospheric pressure and under normal conditions or use, electrical equipment is not unduly exposed to damage from mechanical causes, excessive dust, moisture, or extreme temperatures, and in which electrical equipment is entirely free from the possibility of damage through corrosive, flammable, or explosive atmospheres.

Outdoor location — any location exposed to the weather (see Appendix B).

Wet location — a location in which liquids may drip, splash, or flow on or against electrical equipment.

Low-energy power circuit — see **Circuit**.

Low-voltage — see **Voltage**.

Low-voltage protection — a device that operates on the reduction or failure of voltage to cause and maintain the interruption of power to the main circuit.

Low-voltage release — a device that operates on the reduction or failure of voltage to cause interruption of power to the main circuit, but not to prevent its re-establishment on the return of voltage to a safe operating value.

Luminaire — a complete lighting unit designed to accommodate the lamp(s) and to connect the lamp(s) to circuit conductors.

Machine tool, metal cutting — a power-driven machine, not portable by hand, used to remove metal in the form of chips.

Machine tool, metal forming — a power-driven machine, not portable by hand, used to press, forge, emboss, hammer, blank, or shear metals.

Manufactured wiring system — a wiring system containing component parts that are assembled in the process of manufacture and cannot be disassembled at the building site without damage to or destruction of the assembly.

Mineral-insulated cable — a cable having a bare solid conductor(s) supported and insulated by a highly compressed refractory material enclosed in a liquid- and gas-tight metal tube sheathing; the term includes both the regular type (MI) and the lightweight type (LWMI) unless otherwise qualified.

Mobile home — a transportable dwelling unit constructed to be towed on its own chassis (see Appendix B).

Mobile industrial or commercial structure — a transportable structure, other than a mobile home, constructed to be towed on its own chassis (see Appendix B).

Motor-circuit switch — see **Switch**.

MSG — the Manufacturer's Standard Gauge for uncoated steel.

Multi-outlet assembly — a surface or flush enclosure carrying conductors for extending one 2-wire or multi-wire branch circuit to two or more receptacles of the grounding type that are attached to the enclosure.

Multiple-section mobile unit — a single structure composed of separate mobile units, each towable on its own chassis, which, when towed to the site, are coupled together mechanically and electrically to form a single structure.

Multi-winding motor — a motor having multiple and/or tapped windings, intended to be connected or reconnected in two or more configurations, for operation at any one of two or more speeds and/or voltages.

Multi-wire branch circuit — see **Circuit**.

Neutral — the conductor (when one exists) of a polyphase circuit or single-phase, 3-wire circuit that is intended to have a voltage such that the voltage differences between it and each of the other conductors are approximately equal in magnitude and are equally spaced in phase (see Appendix B).

Non-combustible construction — the type of construction in which a degree of fire safety is attained by the use of non-combustible materials for structural members and other building assemblies (see Appendix B).

Non-incendive circuit — see **Circuit**.

Non-relocatable structure — a factory-built unit for use on permanent foundations.

Non-ventilated cable tray — see **Cable tray**.

Open (as applied to electrical equipment) — moving parts, windings, or live parts are exposed to accidental contact.

Outdoor location — see **Location**.

Outlet — a point in the wiring installation at which current is taken to supply utilization equipment.

Outline lighting — an arrangement of incandescent lamps or electric-discharge tubing to outline or call attention to certain features such as the shape of a building or the decoration of a window.

Overcurrent device — any device capable of automatically opening an electric circuit, under both predetermined overload and short-circuit conditions, either by fusing of metal or by electromechanical means.

Overload device — a device affording protection from excess current, but not necessarily short-circuit protection, and capable of automatically opening an electric circuit.

Panelboard — an assembly of buses and connections, overcurrent devices and control apparatus with or without switches, or other equipment constructed for installation as a complete unit in a cabinet.

Panelboard, enclosed — an assembly of buses and connections, overcurrent devices and control apparatus with or without switches, or other equipment installed in a cabinet.

Park model trailer — a recreational vehicle having a gross floor area not exceeding 50 m^2 when set up (see Appendix B).

Part-winding start motor — a motor arranged for starting by first energizing part of its primary winding and, subsequently, energizing the remainder of this winding in one or more steps, both parts then carrying current.

Periodic duty — see **Duty**.

Permanently connected equipment — equipment that is electrically connected to the supply by means of connectors that can be accessed, loosened, or tightened only with the aid of a tool.

Permit — the official written permission of the inspection department, on a form provided for the purpose, authorizing work to be commenced on any electrical installation.

Plenum — a chamber associated with air-handling apparatus for distributing the processed air from the apparatus (supply plenum) to the supply ducts or for receiving air to be processed by the apparatus (return plenum).

Portable (as applied to electrical equipment) — the equipment is specifically designed not to be used in a fixed position and receives current through the medium of a flexible cord or cable and usually an attachment plug.

Portable ground fault circuit interrupter — a ground fault circuit interrupter that is either of the direct plug-in type or specifically designed to receive current by means of a flexible cord or cable and an attachment plug and that incorporates one or more receptacles for the connection of equipment that is provided with a flexible cord or cable and an attachment plug.

Power supply cord — an assembly consisting of a suitable length of flexible cord or power supply cable provided with an attachment plug at one end.

Protected (as applied mainly to electrical equipment) — such equipment is constructed so that the electrical parts are protected against damage from foreign objects entering the enclosure.

PVC conduit — see **Conduit**.

Qualified person — one familiar with the construction and operation of the apparatus and the hazards involved.

Raceway — any channel designed for holding wires, cables, or busbars, and, unless otherwise qualified in the Rules of this Code, the term includes conduit (rigid and flexible, metal and non-metallic), electrical metallic and non-metallic tubing, underfloor raceways, cellular floors, surface raceways, wireways, cable trays, busways, and auxiliary gutters.

Readily accessible — capable of being reached quickly for operation, renewal, or inspection, without requiring those to whom ready access is a requisite to climb over or remove obstacles or to resort to portable ladders, chairs, etc.

Receptacle — one or more groups of female contacts, each group arranged in a configuration, all groups mounted on the same yoke and in the same housing, installed at an outlet and intended for the connection of one or more attachment plugs of a mating configuration.

> **Duplex receptacle** — a receptacle with two groups of female contacts.

> **Single receptacle** — a receptacle with one group of female contacts.

> **Split receptacle** — a receptacle with two or more groups of female contacts, having terminals adapted for connection to one or more multi-wire branch circuits.

Recreational vehicle — a portable structure intended as a temporary accommodation for travel, vacation, or recreational use (see Appendix B).

Recreational vehicle park — an area of land designed to accommodate recreational vehicles and park model trailers.

Relocatable structure — a factory-built unit for use without a permanent foundation.

Remote control circuit — see **Circuit**.

Residential occupancy — the occupancy or use of a building or part of a building by persons for whom sleeping accommodation is provided but who are not harboured or detained to receive medical care or treatment or are not involuntarily detained.

Resistant [used as a suffix (e.g., absorption-resistant, moisture-resistant, etc.)] — material constructed, protected, or treated so that it will not be readily damaged when subjected to the specific material or condition.

Separate built-in cooking unit — a stationary cooking appliance, including its integral supply leads or terminals and consisting of one or more surface elements or ovens, or a combination of these, constructed so that the unit is permanently built into a counter or wall.

Δ **Service, consumer's** — all that portion of the consumer's installation from the service box or its equivalent up to and including the point at which connection is made to the supply service.

Service, supply — any one set of conductors run by a supply authority from its mains to a consumer's service.

Δ **Service box** — an assembly consisting of an enclosure that can be locked or sealed, containing either fuses and a switch, or a circuit breaker, and of such design that it is possible to operate either the switch or circuit breaker to the open position by manual means when the box is closed (see Appendix B).

Service room — a room or space provided in a building to accommodate building service equipment and constructed in accordance with the *National Building Code of Canada* or applicable local legislation (see Appendix B, Note to Rule 26-012).

Shockproof (as applied to X-ray and high-frequency equipment) — such equipment is guarded with grounded metal so that no person can come into contact with any live part.

Short-time duty — see **Duty**.

Signal circuit — see **Circuit**.

Single dwelling — a dwelling unit consisting of a detached house, one unit of row housing, or one unit of a semi-detached, duplex, triplex, or quadruplex house.

Single receptacle — see **Receptacle**.

Slow-burning (as applied to conductor insulation) — insulation with flame-retardant properties.

Soldered — a union of metal surfaces by the fusion of a metal alloy, usually of lead and tin.

Special permission — the written authority of the inspection department.

Split receptacle — see **Receptacle**.

Splitter — an enclosure containing terminal plates or busbars having main and branch connectors.

Starter — a controller for accelerating a motor from rest to normal speed and for stopping the motor; the term usually implies inclusion of overload protection.

Supply authority — any person, firm, corporation, company, commission, or other organization responsible for an electrical power distribution network that connects to a consumer's service (see Appendix B).

Surface raceway — a surface-mounted or pendant enclosure, consisting of one or more channels for the purpose of containing and protecting conductors and intended to accommodate associated fittings, wiring devices, luminaires, and accessories.

Switch — a device for making, breaking, or changing connection in a circuit.

> **General-use switch** — a switch intended for use in general distribution and branch circuits and that is rated in amperes and is capable of interrupting its rated current at rated voltage.

> **Indicating switch** — a switch of such design or marked so that whether it is on or off may be readily determined by inspection.

> **Isolating switch** — a switch intended for isolating either a circuit or some equipment from its source of supply and that is not intended either for establishing or interrupting the flow of current in any circuit.

> **Motor-circuit switch** — a fused or unfused switch, rated in horsepower or kilowatts, capable of interrupting the maximum operating overload current of a motor of the same horsepower or kilowatt rating as the switch at the rated voltage.

Switchboard — a panel or assembly of panels on which is mounted any combination of switching, measuring, controlling, and protective devices, buses, and connections, designed to successfully carry and rupture the maximum fault current encountered when controlling incoming and outgoing feeders.

System (see Appendix B) —

Communication system — an electrical system whereby voice, sound, or data may be received and/or transmitted and that includes telephone, telegraph, data communications, intercommunications, paging systems, wired music systems, and other systems of similar nature, but excludes alarm systems such as fire, smoke, or intrusion, radio and television broadcast communication equipment, closed circuit television, or community antenna television systems.

Community antenna distribution system — a distribution system of coaxial cable, together with any necessary amplifiers or other equipment, that is used to transmit television or radio frequency signals typical of a community antenna television (CATV) system.

Different systems — those that derive their energy from different transformers or from different banks of transformers, or from different generators or other sources.

Grounding system — all conductors, clamps, ground clips, ground plates or pipes, and grounding electrodes by means of which the electrical installation is grounded.

Theatre — a building, or any portion of a building, that is used for public, dramatic, operatic, motion picture, or other performances.

Thermal cut-out — a device affording protection from excessive current, but not necessarily short-circuit protection, and containing a heating element in addition to, and affecting, a fusible member that opens the circuit.

Underfloor raceway — a raceway suitable for use in the floor.

Utilization equipment — equipment that utilizes electrical energy for mechanical, chemical, heating, lighting, or similar useful purposes.

Varying duty — see **Duty**.

Vault (transformer vault or **electrical equipment vault)** — an isolated enclosure, either above or below ground, with fire-resisting walls, ceilings, and floors for the purpose of housing transformers and other electrical equipment.

Ventilated cable tray — see **Cable tray**.

Vessel — any ship or boat or any other description of vessel used or designed to be used in navigation.

Voltage —

Extra-low voltage — any voltage not exceeding 30 V.

High voltage — any voltage exceeding 750 V.

Low voltage — any voltage exceeding 30 V but not exceeding 750 V.

Voltage of a circuit — the greatest root-mean-square (effective) voltage between any two conductors of the circuit.

Voltage-to-ground — the voltage between any given live ungrounded part and any grounded part in the case of grounded circuits, or the greatest voltage existing in the circuit in the case of ungrounded circuits.

Washroom — a room that contains a wash basin(s) and that may contain a water closet(s) but without bathing or showering facilities.

Wet location — see **Location**.

Δ   **Wire** — see **Conductor**.

Wire connector — see **Connector**.

Wireway — a raceway consisting of a completely enclosing arrangement of metal troughing and fittings formed and constructed so that insulated conductors may be readily drawn in and withdrawn, or laid in and removed, after the wireway has been completely installed, without damage either to conductors or to their covering.

Section 2 — General Rules

Administrative

2-000 Authority for Rules
By virtue of the authority vested in the inspection department, this Code has been adopted and the inspection department hereby orders and directs its observance.

2-002 Special requirements
Sections devoted to Rules governing particular types of installations are not intended to embody all Rules governing these particular types of installations, but cover only those special Rules or regulations that add to or amend those prescribed in other sections covering installations under ordinary conditions.

2-004 Permit
Electrical contractors or others responsible for carrying out the work shall obtain a permit from the inspection department before commencing work with respect to installation, alteration, repair, or extension of any electrical equipment.

2-006 Application for inspection
An application for inspection shall be filed with the inspection department on a form provided by the latter at the time the permit is obtained.

2-008 Fees
Fees for the permit and inspection in accordance with the schedule prescribed by the inspection department shall be paid at the time the permit is obtained.

2-010 Posting of permit
A copy of the permit shall be posted in a conspicuous place at the work site and shall not be removed until the inspection is completed.

2-012 Notification of inspection
The inspection department shall be notified in writing by the electrical contractor that work is ready for inspection at such time(s) allowing inspection before any work or portion of work is concealed.

2-014 Plans and specifications
Plans and specifications in duplicate, or in greater number if required by the inspection department (one copy to be retained by the inspection department), shall be submitted by the owner or an agent to, and acceptance obtained from, the inspection department before work is commenced on
a) wiring installations of public buildings, industrial establishments, factories, and other buildings in which public safety is involved;
b) large light and power installations and the installation of apparatus such as generators, transformers, switchboards, large storage batteries, etc.; or
c) such other installations as may be prescribed by the inspection department.

2-016 Current-permits
Except as provided in Rule 2-018, no reconnection, installation, alteration, or addition shall be connected to any service or other source of electric energy by a supply authority, electrical contractor, or other person, until a current-permit authorizing the supply of electric energy has been obtained from the inspection department.

2-018 Reconnection
A supply authority shall not require a current-permit for reconnection in cases where the service has been cut off for non-payment of bills or a change of occupant, provided that there have been no alterations or additions subsequent to the issuance of the last current-permit.

2-020 Reinspection
The inspection department reserves the right to reinspect any installation if and when it considers such action to be necessary.

2-022 Renovation of existing installations

The inspection department may require such changes as may be necessary to be made to existing installations where, through hard usage, wear and tear, or as a result of alterations or extensions, dangerous conditions have developed.

2-024 Use of approved equipment (see Appendices A and B)

1) Electrical equipment used in electrical installations within the jurisdiction of the inspection department shall be approved and shall be of a kind or type and rating approved for the specific purpose for which it is to be employed.

2) Notwithstanding Subrule 1), equipment described in Rule 16-222 1) a) shall not be required to be approved.

2-026 Powers of rejection (see Appendix B)

Even though approval has previously been granted, the inspection department may reject, at any time, any electrical equipment under any of the following conditions:

a) the equipment is substandard with respect to the sample on which approval was granted;

b) the conditions of use indicate that the equipment is not suitable; or

c) the terms of the approval agreement are not being carried out.

2-028 Availability of work for inspection

No electrical work shall be rendered inaccessible by lathing, boarding, or other building construction until it has been accepted by the inspection department.

2-030 Deviation or postponement

In any case where deviation or postponement of these Rules and regulations is necessary, special permission shall be obtained before proceeding with the work, but this special permission shall apply only to the particular installation for which it is given.

2-032 Damage and interference

1) No person shall damage any electrical installation or component thereof.

2) No person shall interfere with any electrical installation or component thereof except that when, in the course of alterations or repairs to non-electrical equipment or structures, it may be necessary to disconnect or move components of an electrical installation, it shall be the responsibility of the person carrying out the alterations or repairs to ensure that the electrical installation is restored to a safe operating condition as soon as the progress of the alterations or repairs permits.

Technical

General

2-100 Marking of equipment (see Appendix B)

1) Each piece of electrical equipment shall bear those of the following markings necessary to identify the equipment and ensure that it is suitable for the particular installation:

    a) the maker's name, trademark, or other recognized symbol of identification;

    b) catalogue number or type;

    c) voltage;

    d) rated load amperes;

    e) watts, volt amperes, or horsepower;

    f) whether for ac, dc, or both;

    g) number of phases;

    h) frequency in hertz;

    i) rated load speed in revolutions per minute;

    j) designation of terminals;

    k) whether for continuous or intermittent duty;

Δ   l)   short-circuit current rating or withstand rating;

    m)   evidence of approval; or

    n)   other markings necessary to ensure safe and proper operation.

2)   At the time of installation, each service box shall be marked in a conspicuous, legible, and permanent manner, to indicate clearly the maximum rating of the overcurrent device that may be used for this installation.

3)   At each distribution point, circuit breakers, fuses, and switches shall be marked, adjacent thereto, in a conspicuous and legible manner to indicate clearly

    a)   which installation or portion of installation they protect or control; and

    b)   the maximum rating of overcurrent device that is permitted.

Δ 4)   Where the maximum continuous load allowed on a fused switch or circuit breaker as determined in accordance with Rule 8-104 5) and 6) is less than the continuous operating marking of the fused switch or circuit breaker, a permanent, legible caution marking shall be field applied adjacent to the fused switch or circuit breaker nameplate to indicate the maximum continuous loading permitted for connection to the fused switch or circuit breaker.

5)   The marking on electrical equipment shall not be added to, or changed, to indicate a use under this Code for which the equipment has not been approved.

2-102 Warning and caution markings

Field-installed warning and caution markings required by this Code shall be written in the language(s) mandated by the local authorities adopting and enforcing this Code.

Δ   ## 2-104 Electrical equipment ratings (see Appendix B)

1)   Where electrical equipment is marked with a short-circuit current rating or withstand rating, the equipment selected for installation shall have a rating sufficient for the voltage employed and for the fault current that is available at the equipment terminals.

2)   Electrical equipment marked with both line-to-line and line-to-ground voltage ratings, such as 125/250 V, 120/240 V, 208Y/120 V, 480Y/277 V, or 600Y/347 V, shall be permitted to be connected only in a circuit that is solidly grounded and where

    a)   the nominal voltage of any conductor to ground does not exceed the lower of the two values of the equipment voltage rating; and

    b)   the nominal voltage between any two conductors does not exceed the higher value of the electrical equipment voltage rating.

2-106 Rebuilt equipment (see Appendix B)

1)   Where any electrical machine or apparatus is rebuilt or rewound with any change in its rating or characteristics, it shall be provided with a nameplate giving the name of the person or firm by whom such change was made together with the new marking.

2)   Where the original nameplate is removed, the original manufacturer's name and any original identifying data, such as serial numbers, shall be added to the new nameplate.

3)   Except as provided for in Subrule 4), the appropriate requirements of the *Canadian Electrical Code, Part II*, that apply to new electrical equipment shall also apply to rebuilt and rewound equipment unless it is impracticable to comply with such requirements.

4)   Rebuilt or refurbished moulded case circuit breakers or moulded case switches shall not be considered to be approved for the purpose of Rule 2-024.

2-108 Substitution

Where electrical equipment of the exact size or rating is not procurable for a given purpose, equipment of a larger size or rating that is consistent with the purpose shall be used, except where use of equipment of a smaller size or rating complies with Rule 2-030.

Δ **2-110 Circuit voltage-to-ground — Dwelling units**

Branch circuits in dwelling units shall not have a voltage exceeding 150 volts-to-ground except that, where the calculated load on the service conductors of an apartment or similar building exceeds 250 kV•A and where qualified electrical maintenance personnel are available, higher voltages not exceeding the voltage-to-ground of a nominal system voltage of 600Y/347 V shall be permitted to be used in the dwelling unit to supply the following fixed (not portable) equipment:

a) space heating, provided that wall-mounted thermostats operate at a voltage not exceeding 300 volts-to-ground;

b) water heating; and

c) air conditioning.

2-112 Quality of work

The mechanical arrangement and execution of the work in connection with any electrical installation shall be acceptable.

2-114 Material for anchoring to masonry and concrete

Wood or other similar material shall not be used as an anchor into masonry or concrete for the support of any electrical equipment.

2-116 Corrosion protection for materials used in wiring

1) Metals used in wiring, such as raceways, cable sheaths and armour, boxes, and fittings, shall be suitably protected against corrosion for the environment in which they are to be used or shall be made of suitable corrosion-resistant material.

2) Where practicable, dissimilar metals shall not be used where there is a possibility of galvanic action.

2-118 Soldering fluxes

Fluxes used for soldering copper and its alloys shall be of types that are non-corrosive to copper.

2-120 AWG sizes of conductors

Where reference is made in this Code to AWG size, this shall mean the copper AWG size, unless otherwise specified.

2-122 Installation of electrical equipment (see Appendix G)

Electrical equipment shall be installed so as to ensure that after installation there is ready access to nameplates and access to parts requiring maintenance.

2-124 Installation of other than electrical equipment

Equipment or material of other than an electrical nature shall not be installed or placed so close to electrical equipment as to create a condition that is dangerous.

Δ **2-126 Use of thermal insulation**

1) Where the hollow spaces between studding, joists, or rafters of buildings are to be filled with thermal insulation, the following restrictions, as applicable, shall apply to the installation of electrical wiring in such spaces:

a) special care shall be taken to ensure that conductor insulation temperatures are not exceeded due either to mutual heating of adjacent insulated conductors or cables or to reduced heat dissipation through the thermal insulation;

b) if the space is to be filled with a loose or free-flowing material that is non-corrosive, fire-resisting, and non-conductive and that is in compliance with the *National Building Code of Canada*, any type of wiring system recognized by this Code shall be permitted to be used, but special care shall be taken to ensure that there will be no strain on the insulated conductors or cables due to the weight or pressure of the insulating material;

c) if the thermal insulation material, in the form of batts or rigid sheets, is installed prior to the installation of the wiring and secured in place so that there will be no undue pressure on the insulated conductors or cables, no special precaution need be observed;

d) if thermal insulation made of or faced with metal is installed, the wiring shall conform to the following:

  i) a 25 mm separation shall be provided between the thermal insulation and knob-and-tube wiring; and

  ii) non-metallic-sheathed cable shall be permitted to be in contact with the insulation; and

e) mineral-insulated cable, aluminum-sheathed cable, or copper-sheathed cable shall not be used with types of thermal insulation that are liable to have a corrosive action on the sheath.

2) Thermal insulation material shall not be sprayed or otherwise introduced into the interior of outlet boxes, junction boxes, or enclosures for other electrical equipment.

2-128 Fire spread (see Appendices B and G)

1) Electrical installations shall be made so that the probability of spread of fire through firestopped partitions, floors, hollow spaces, firewalls or fire partitions, vertical shafts, or ventilating or air-conditioning ducts is reduced to a minimum.

2) Where a fire separation is pierced by a raceway or cable, any openings around the raceway or cable shall be properly closed or sealed in compliance with the *National Building Code of Canada*.

Δ **2-130 Flame spread requirements for electrical wiring and cables** (see Appendices B and G)
Insulated conductors and cables installed in buildings shall meet the flame spread requirements of the *National Building Code of Canada* or local building legislation.

2-132 Flame spread requirements for totally enclosed non-metallic raceways (see Appendices B and G)
Totally enclosed non-metallic raceways installed in buildings shall meet the flame spread requirements of the *National Building Code of Canada*.

Δ **2-134 Sunlight resistance requirements** (see Appendix B)
Insulated conductors and cables and totally enclosed non-metallic raceways installed and used where exposed to direct rays of the sun shall be marked for the purpose.

2-136 Insulation integrity (see Appendix B)
All wiring shall be installed so that, when completed, the system will be free from short-circuits and from grounds except as permitted in Section 10.

2-138 Use of Class A ground fault circuit interrupters

Ⓔ Δ Class A ground fault circuit interrupters shall be permitted as supplementary protection from shock hazard but shall not be used as a substitute for insulation or grounding except as permitted by Rule 26-702 2).

Protection of persons and property

2-200 General
Electrical equipment shall be installed and guarded so that adequate provision is made for the safety of persons and property and for the protection of the electrical equipment from mechanical or other damage to which it is liable to be exposed.

2-202 Guarding of bare live parts

Δ 1) Bare live parts shall be guarded against accidental contact by means of suitable enclosures except where the bare live parts are
   a) located in a suitable room, vault, or similar enclosed area that is accessible only to qualified persons; or
   b) as permitted elsewhere by this Code.

2) Where electrical equipment has mounted on it, within 900 mm of bare live parts, non-electrical components that require servicing by unqualified persons, suitable barriers or covers shall be provided for the bare live parts.

3) Entrances to rooms and other guarded locations containing exposed bare live parts shall be marked with conspicuous warning signs forbidding entry to unqualified persons.

Maintenance and operation

2-300 General requirements for maintenance and operation

1) All operating electrical equipment shall be kept in safe and proper working condition.

2) Electrical equipment maintained for emergency service shall be periodically inspected and tested as necessary to ensure its fitness for service.

3) Infrequently used electrical equipment maintained for future service shall be thoroughly inspected before use in order to determine its fitness for service.

4) Defective equipment shall either be put in good order or permanently disconnected.

2-302 Maintenance in hazardous locations

All electrical equipment installed in hazardous locations shall comply with Rule 18-010.

2-304 Disconnection (see Appendix B)

1) No repairs or alterations shall be carried out on any live equipment except where complete disconnection of the equipment is not feasible.

2) Three-way or four-way switches shall not be considered as disconnecting means.

3) Adequate precautions, such as locks on circuit breakers or switches, warning notices, sentries, or other equally effective means, shall be taken to prevent electrical equipment from being electrically charged when work is being done.

2-306 Shock and arc flash protection (see Appendix B)

1) Electrical equipment such as switchboards, panelboards, industrial control panels, meter socket enclosures, and motor control centres that are installed in other than dwelling units and are likely to require examination, adjustment, servicing, or maintenance while energized shall be field marked to warn persons of potential electric shock and arc flash hazards.

2) The marking referred to in Subrule 1) shall be located so that it is clearly visible to persons before examination, adjustment, servicing, or maintenance of the equipment.

Δ 2-308 Working space around electrical equipment (see Appendix B)

1) A minimum working space of 1 m with secure footing shall be provided and maintained about electrical equipment that
   a) contains renewable parts, disconnecting means, or operating means; or
   b) requires examination, adjustment, operation, or maintenance.

2) The working space referred to in Subrule 1) shall not be required behind equipment where there are no renewable parts such as fuses or switches on the back and where all connections are accessible from locations other than the back.

3) The working space referred to in Subrule 1) shall be in addition to the space required for the operation of drawout-type equipment in either the connected, test, or fully disconnected position and shall be sufficient for the opening of enclosure doors and hinged panels to at least 90°.

4) Working space with secure footing not less than that specified in Table 56 shall be provided and maintained around electrical equipment such as switchboards, control panels, and motor control centres having exposed live parts.

5) The minimum headroom of working spaces around switchboards or motor control centres where bare live parts are exposed at any time shall be 2.2 m.

2-310 Entrance to, and exit from, working space (see Appendices B and G)

1) Each room containing electrical equipment and each working space around equipment shall have unobstructed means of egress in compliance with the *National Building Code of Canada*.

Δ 2) Where a room or space referred to in Subrule 1) contains equipment that has a rating on the equipment nameplate of 1200 A or more, or is rated over 750 V, such equipment shall be arranged so that, in the event of a failure in the equipment, it shall be possible to leave the room or space referred to in Subrule 1) without passing the failure point, except that where this cannot be done, the working space requirement of Rule 2-308 1) and 2) shall be not less than 1.5 m.

3) For the purposes of Subrule 2), the potential failure point shall be any point within or on the equipment.

4) Doors or gates shall be capable of being readily opened from the equipment side without the use of a key or tool.

Δ **2-312 Transformer working space**

Except as provided for in Rule 26-242 and notwithstanding Rules 2-308 and 2-310, for transformers rated greater than 50 kVA, a minimum horizontal working space of 1 m shall be provided and maintained on the sides of the transformer that provide access to conductor connections.

2-314 Accessibility for maintenance (see Appendix G)

Passageways and working space around electrical equipment shall not be used for storage and shall be kept clear of obstruction and arranged to give authorized persons ready access to all parts requiring attention.

2-316 Receptacles required for maintenance of equipment

Where heating, ventilating, air-conditioning, and similar equipment is installed on a rooftop other than at a dwelling unit, at least one receptacle shall be

a) provided for the maintenance of this equipment; and

b) installed in accordance with Rule 26-710.

2-318 Illumination of equipment

Adequate illumination shall be provided to allow for proper operation and maintenance of electrical equipment.

2-320 Flammable material near electrical equipment

Flammable material shall not be stored or placed in dangerous proximity to electrical equipment.

2-322 Ventilation (see Appendix B)

Adequate ventilation shall be provided to prevent the development around electrical equipment of ambient air temperatures in excess of those normally permissible for such equipment.

2-324 Drainage

Electrical equipment having provision for draining moisture shall be installed so that the drainage path is not impeded.

2-326 Electrical equipment near combustible gas equipment (see Appendix B)

The clearance distance between arc-producing electrical equipment and a combustible gas relief device or vent shall be in accordance with the requirements of CSA B149.1.

Enclosures

2-400 Enclosures, type designations, and use (see Appendix B)

1) For the purposes of this Code, the following designations of enclosures for electrical equipment other than motors and generators shall be recognized for the intended use as specified in Table 65 and as follows:
    a) Type 1 for use indoors in ordinary locations;
    b) Type 2 for use indoors where the enclosure may be subject to drops of falling liquid due to condensation or other causes;
    c) Type 3R for use outdoors;
    d) Type 4 for use where the enclosure may be subject to direct streams of water;
    e) Type 5 for use indoors where the atmosphere may contain settling non-hazardous dust, lint, fibres, or flyings; and
    f) general-purpose enclosures for use indoors in ordinary locations.
2) Other enclosure types tabulated in Table 65 shall be permitted to be substituted for those required in Subrule 1) provided that they
    a) offer a degree of protection at least equal to that required by Subrule 1) for the intended use, as indicated in Table 65; and
    b) are marked in accordance with Rule 2-402.
3) Enclosures for equipment for use in a hazardous location shall be designated in accordance with Rule 18-052.

2-402 Marking of enclosures

1) Except for general-purpose enclosures, all enclosures described in Table 65 shall be marked with a type or enclosure designation.
2) In addition to the type or enclosure designation specified in Subrule 1), enclosures shall be permitted to be marked with an ingress protection (IP) designation.

2-404 Marking of motors

1) Drip-proof, weatherproof, and totally enclosed motors for use in non-hazardous locations shall be marked as follows:
    a) if a drip-proof motor, with the word "Drip-proof" or the code letters "DP";
    b) if a weatherproof motor, with the word "Weatherproof" or the code letters "WP"; and
    c) if a totally enclosed motor, with the words "Totally Enclosed" or the code letters "TE".
2) Notwithstanding Subrule 1), special-purpose motors that are intended to be used only as components of specific equipment need not be so marked.

Section 4 — Conductors

Δ **4-000 Scope** (see Appendix B)
1) This Section applies to conductors for services, feeders, branch circuits, and photovoltaic circuits with regard to
   a) the determination of maximum allowable conductor ampacity;
   b) the determination of maximum conductor termination temperature;
   c) the selection of neutral conductors;
   d) the selection of a conductor type for a specific condition of use; and
   e) conductor identification.
2) This Section does not apply to other conductors except where specifically referenced in other Sections of this Code.

4-002 Size of conductors
Except for flexible cord, equipment wire, control circuit insulated conductors, and cable, insulated conductors shall be not smaller than No. 14 AWG when made of copper and not smaller than No. 12 AWG when made of aluminum.

4-004 Ampacity of wires and cables (see Appendix B)
1) The maximum current that a copper conductor of a given size and insulation is permitted to carry shall be as follows:
   a) single-conductor and single-conductor metal-sheathed or armoured cable, in a free air run, with a cable spacing not less than 100% of the largest cable diameter, as specified in Table 1;
   b) one, two, or three conductors in a run of raceway, or 2- or 3-conductor cable, except as indicated in Item d), as specified in Table 2;
   c) four or more conductors in a run of raceway or cable, as specified in Table 2 with the correction factors applied as specified in Table 5C;
   d) single-conductor and 2-, 3-, and 4-conductor cables and single-conductor and 2-, 3-, and 4-conductor metal-armoured and metal-sheathed cables, unshielded and rated not more than 5 kV, in conductor sizes No. 1/0 AWG and larger, installed in accordance with configurations described in Diagrams D8 to D11 in an underground run, directly buried or in a raceway, as specified in Tables D8A to D11B or as calculated by the IEEE 835 calculation method;
   e) underground configurations not specified in Item d), in conductor sizes No. 1/0 AWG and larger, as calculated by the IEEE 835 calculation method;
   f) underground configurations in conductor sizes smaller than No. 1/0 AWG, as specified in Item b) or as calculated by the IEEE 835 calculation method; and
   g) shielded cables rated 5 kV to 46 kV in sizes No. 2 AWG to 1000 kcmil, as specified in Tables D17A to D17N for the configurations described therein and the conditions described in Table D17, or as calculated by the IEEE 835 calculation method.
2) The maximum current that an aluminum conductor of a given size and insulation is permitted to carry shall be as follows:
   a) single-conductor and single-conductor metal-sheathed or armoured cable, in a free air run, with a cable spacing not less than 100% of the largest cable diameter, as specified in Table 3;
   b) one, two, or three conductors in a run of raceway, or 2- or 3-conductor cable, except as indicated in Item d), as specified in Table 4;
   c) four or more conductors in a run of raceway or cable, as specified in Table 4 with the correction factors applied as specified in Table 5C;
   d) single-conductor and 2-, 3-, and 4-conductor cables and single-conductor and 2-, 3-, and 4-conductor metal-armoured and metal-sheathed cables, unshielded and rated not more than 5 kV, in conductor sizes No. 1/0 AWG and larger, installed in accordance with configurations

described in Diagrams D8 to D11 in an underground run, directly buried or in a raceway, as specified in Tables D8A to D11B or as calculated by the IEEE 835 calculation method;

e) underground configurations not specified in Item d), in conductor sizes No. 1/0 AWG and larger, as calculated by the IEEE 835 calculation method;

f) underground configurations in conductor sizes smaller than No. 1/0 AWG, as specified in Item b) or as calculated by the IEEE 835 calculation method; and

g) shielded cables rated 5 kV to 46 kV in sizes No. 2 AWG to 1000 kcmil, as specified in Tables D17A to D17N for the configurations described therein and the conditions described in Table D17, or as calculated by the IEEE 835 calculation method.

3) A neutral conductor that carries only the unbalanced current from other conductors, as in the case of normally balanced circuits of three or more conductors, shall not be counted in determining ampacities as provided for in Subrules 1) and 2).

4) When a load is connected between a single-phase conductor and the neutral, or between each of two phase conductors and the neutral, of a three-phase, 4-wire system, the common conductor carries a current comparable to that in the phase conductors and shall be counted in determining the ampacities as provided for in Subrules 1) and 2).

5) The maximum allowable ampacity of neutral supported cable shall be as specified in Tables 36A and 36B.

6) A bonding conductor shall not be counted in determining the ampacities as provided for in Subrules 1) and 2).

Δ 7) The correction factors specified in this Rule

a) shall not apply to conductors installed in auxiliary gutters containing 30 conductors or less; and

b) shall apply only to power and lighting conductors as follows:

i) the ampacity correction factors of Table 5A, where conductors are installed in an ambient temperature exceeding or anticipated to exceed 30 °C;

ii) the ampacity correction factors of Table 5B, where single-conductor cables are installed in free air in accordance with Subrule 9);

iii) the ampacity correction factors of Table 5C, where single-conductor cables are installed in free air, single conductors are installed in totally enclosed non-ventilated raceways, or multi-conductor cables are installed in ventilated and ladder-type cable trays or in non-ventilated cable trays in accordance with Subrule 1) c), 2) c), 11), 12), 13), 23), or 25), as applicable; and

iv) the ampacity correction factors of Table 5D, where single-conductor cables are installed in free air or single-conductor or multi-conductor cables are installed in ventilated and ladder-type cable trays in accordance with Subrule 8) or 24), as applicable.

8) Where the free air spacing between adjacent single-conductor cables is maintained at not less than 25% nor more than 100% of the diameter of the largest cable, the ampacity shall be obtained from Subrules 1) a) and 2) a) for copper and aluminum conductors respectively, multiplied by the correction factor from Table 5D.

9) Where up to and including four single-conductor cables in free air are spaced at less than 25% of the diameter of the largest conductor or cable, the ampacity shall be the same as that obtained from Subrules 1) a) and 2) a) for copper and aluminum conductors respectively, multiplied by the correction factor from Table 5B.

10) Notwithstanding Subrule 9), where not more than four non-jacketed single-conductor mineral-insulated cables are grouped together in conformance with Rule 4-008 3) and are installed on a messenger or as open runs with a maintained free air space of not less than 2.15 times the diameter of the largest cable contained within the group and adjacent groups or cables, the

ampacity of each conductor in the group shall be permitted to be determined in accordance with Subrule 1) a) without applying the correction factors of Table 5B.

11) More than four single-conductor cables in free air, when spaced at less than 25% of the largest cable diameter, shall have an ampacity obtained from Tables 2 and 4 for copper and aluminum conductors respectively, multiplied by the correction factor from Table 5C based on the total number of conductors.

12) Notwithstanding Subrule 11), when the length of a single-conductor cable run spaced at less than 25% of the largest cable diameter is less than 600 mm, the correction factor from Table 5C shall not apply.

13) Where multi-conductor cables are run in contact for distances greater than 600 mm, the ampacity of the conductors shall be corrected by applying the correction factors from Table 5C based on the total number of conductors in the cables.

14) The ampacity of conductors of different temperature ratings installed in the same raceway shall be determined on the basis of the conductor having the lowest temperature rating.

15) The ampacity of conductors added to a raceway and the ampacity of the conductors already in the raceway shall be determined in accordance with the applicable Subrules.

16) Where more than one ampacity could apply for a given circuit of single-conductor or multi-conductor cables as a consequence of a transition from an underground portion to a portion above ground, the lower value shall apply except as permitted in Subrule 17).

17) Where the lower ampacity portion of a cable installation consisting of not more than four conductors in total does not exceed 10% of the circuit length or 3 m, whichever is less, the higher ampacity shall be permitted.

18) When the load factor of the load is less than 1.00 and is known or can be supported by documentation, the ampacity of conductors derived from Subrules 1) d) and 2) d) shall be permitted to be increased by application of that load factor in the calculation of the ampacity.

19) In consideration of the increased ampacity of any conductor derived in accordance with Subrule 18), no further factors based on load diversity shall be permitted.

20) The ampacity of nickel or nickel-clad conductors shall be calculated using the method described in IEEE 835.

21) The maximum allowable ampacity of bare or covered conductors in free air shall be as specified in Table 66.

Δ 22) Notwithstanding Rules 4-006 and 8-200 1) b), 3-wire 120/240 V and 120/208 V service conductors for single dwellings and feeder conductors supplying single dwelling units of row housing, apartment, or similar buildings and terminating on equipment having a conductor termination temperature of not less than 75 °C shall be permitted to be sized in accordance with Table 39, and a permanent, legible caution marking shall be field applied adjacent to the fused switch or circuit breaker nameplate on the equipment to indicate the maximum calculated load from Table 39.

Δ 23) In ventilated and ladder-type cable trays, where the air space between adjacent insulated conductors or cables or both is maintained at greater than 100% of the diameter of the largest conductor or cable, the ampacity of the conductors or cables shall be as follows:
   a) for single insulated conductors, single-conductor cable, single-conductor metal-sheathed or armoured cable, and single-conductor mineral-insulated cable, the value as specified in Tables 1 and 3; and
   b) for multi-conductor cables, the value as specified in Tables 2 and 4 multiplied by the correction factor from Table 5C for the number of conductors in each cable.

Δ 24) In ventilated and ladder-type cable trays, where the air space between adjacent insulated conductors or cables or both is maintained at not less than 25% nor more than 100% of the diameter of the largest conductor or cable, the ampacity of the conductors or cables shall be the value specified in Subrule 23) multiplied by the correction factor specified in Table 5D for the arrangement and number of conductors or cables involved, unless a deviation permitting the use of other correction factors has been allowed in accordance with Rule 2-030.

Δ 25) In ventilated and ladder-type cable trays, where the air space between adjacent insulated conductors or cables or both is less than 25% of the diameter of the largest conductor or cable, and for any spacing in a non-ventilated cable tray, the ampacity of the conductors or cables shall be the value as specified in Table 2 or 4 multiplied by the correction factor specified in Table 5C for the total number of conductors in the cable tray.

Δ 26) Where cablebus is installed in a location with an ambient temperature exceeding or anticipated to exceed 30 °C, the ampacity correction factors of Table 5A shall be applied to the cablebus allowable conductor ampacities marked on the cablebus nameplate.

4-006 Temperature limitations (see Appendix B)

1) Where equipment is marked with a maximum conductor termination temperature, the minimum size of conductor used shall be based on the allowable ampacity in the temperature column in Table 1, 2, 3, or 4, with all relevant correction factors being applied as required by Rule 4-004, corresponding to the maximum termination temperature marked on the equipment.

2) For the purpose of Subrule 1), and except as provided for by other Rules of this Code, where the maximum conductor termination temperature for equipment is not marked, the maximum conductor termination temperature shall be considered to be
   a) 60 °C for equipment
       i)   rated not more than 100 A; or
       ii) marked for use with No. 1 AWG or smaller conductors; and
   b) 75 °C for equipment
       i)   rated more than 100 A; or
       ii) marked for use with conductors larger than No. 1 AWG.

3) Notwithstanding Subrule 2), for high-voltage equipment where conductor termination temperatures are not marked, it shall be permitted to consult the manufacturer to establish the permitted termination temperature.

4) Subrules 1) and 2) shall apply only to the first 1.2 m of conductor length measured from the point of termination on the equipment.

5) Where a cable transition is made to meet the requirements of Subrule 1) or 2), the length of a conductor terminating on equipment shall be not less than 1.2 m.

Δ 6) Where the conductor ampacity is selected from Tables D8A to D11B, Tables D17A to D17N, or Table 12E, Subrules 1) and 2) shall apply.

4-008 Induced voltages and currents in metal armour or sheaths of single-conductor cables (see Appendix B)

1) Where sheath currents in single-conductor cables having continuous sheaths of lead, aluminum, stainless steel, or copper are likely to cause the insulation of the conductors to be subjected to temperatures in excess of the insulation ratings, the cables shall be
   a) derated to 70% of the current-carrying rating that would otherwise apply;
   b) derated in accordance with the manufacturer's recommendations and in compliance with Rule 2-030; or
   c) installed in a manner that prevents the flow of sheath currents.

2) Circulating currents in single-conductor armoured cable shall be treated in the same manner as sheath currents in Subrule 1).

3) Single-conductor cables and single insulated conductors carrying more than 200 A shall not enter ferrous metal boxes through individual openings.

4) Where single-conductor cables and single insulated conductors carrying more than 200 A enter ferrous metal boxes, precautions shall be taken to prevent overheating of the wall of the box by induction.

5) Precautions to be taken to prevent overheating of the metal shall include the use of non-ferrous or non-metallic box connectors or cable glands, locknuts, bushings, and ground bushings.

6) All cables and insulated conductors making up a circuit shall enter the box through one common non-ferrous or insulating plate having a minimum thickness of 6.0 mm unless a deviation is allowed in accordance with Rule 2-030.

7) Where single-conductor mineral-insulated cables are used, all current-carrying conductors shall be grouped together to minimize induced voltage on the sheath.

4-010 Sizes of flexible cord
Flexible cord shall be not smaller than a No. 18 AWG copper conductor except for
a) tinsel cord, which shall be permitted to be No. 27 AWG copper; and
b) cords for use with specific devices, which shall be permitted to be No. 20 AWG copper.

4-012 Ampacity of flexible cords
1) The maximum current that two or more insulated copper conductors of a given size contained in a flexible cord are permitted to carry shall be as follows:
a) 2 or 3 insulated conductors, as specified in Table 12;
b) 4, 5, or 6 insulated conductors, 80% of that specified in Table 12;
c) 7 to 24 insulated conductors, 70% of that specified in Table 12;
d) 25 to 42 insulated conductors, 60% of that specified in Table 12; and
e) 43 or more insulated conductors, 50% of that specified in Table 12.

2) Conductors used for bonding equipment to ground and a conductor used as a neutral conductor that carries only the unbalanced current from other conductors as in the case of a normally balanced circuit of three or more conductors, are not counted in determining ampacities.

4-014 Equipment wire
The maximum current that an equipment wire of a given size is permitted to carry shall be as specified in Table 12.

4-016 Insulation of neutral conductors
1) Except as permitted by Rules 6-302, 6-308, 12-302, and 12-318, neutral conductors shall be insulated.
2) Where insulated neutrals are used, the insulation on the neutral conductors shall have a temperature rating not less than the temperature rating of the insulation on the ungrounded conductors.

4-018 Size of neutral conductor (see Appendix B)
1) The neutral conductor shall have sufficient ampacity to carry the unbalanced load.
2) The maximum unbalanced load shall be the maximum connected load between the neutral and any one ungrounded conductor as determined by Section 8 but subject to the following:
a) there shall be no reduction in the size of the neutral for that portion of the load that consists of
i) electric-discharge lighting; or
ii) non-linear loads supplied from a three-phase, 4-wire system; and
b) except as required otherwise by Item a), a demand factor of 70% shall be permitted to be applied to that portion of the unbalanced load in excess of 200 A.
3) The size of a service neutral shall be not smaller than the size of a neutral selected in accordance with Subrule 1) and shall
a) be not smaller than No. 10 AWG copper or No. 8 AWG aluminum; and

b) be sized not smaller than a grounded conductor as required by Rule 10-210 b), except in service entrance cable or where the service conductors are No. 10 AWG copper or No. 8 AWG aluminum.

4) In determining the ampacity of an uninsulated neutral conductor run in a raceway, it shall be considered to be insulated with insulation having a temperature rating not higher than that of the adjacent circuit conductors.

4-020 Common neutral conductor

Provided that when in metal enclosures all conductors of feeder circuits employing a common neutral are contained within the same enclosure, a common neutral shall be permitted to be employed for

a) two or three sets of 3-wire, single-phase feeders; or

b) two sets of 4-wire, three-phase feeders.

Δ **4-022 Installation of identified conductor** (see Appendix B)

1) Where a service, feeder, or branch circuit requires an identified conductor, it shall be installed
   a) in all separately enclosed switches and circuit breakers;
   b) in all centres of distribution associated with the circuit;
   c) with all connections to the identified conductor being made in the enclosures and centres; and
   d) in such a manner that any identified conductor can be disconnected without disconnecting any other identified conductor.

2) The identified conductor shall be installed at each location of a manual or automatic control device for the control of permanently installed luminaires at a branch circuit outlet.

4-024 Identification of insulated neutral conductors up to and including No. 2 AWG copper or aluminum

1) Except as permitted in Subrules 2), 3), and 4), all insulated neutral conductors up to and including No. 2 AWG copper or aluminum, and the conductors of flexible cords that are permanently connected to such neutral conductors, shall be identified by a white or grey covering or by three continuous white stripes along the entire length of the conductor.

2) Where conductors of different systems are installed in the same raceway, box, or other type of enclosure and the identified circuit conductor of one system is coloured by a white or grey covering, each identified circuit conductor of the other system, if present, shall be provided with a specific identification, and the identification shall be permitted to be an outer covering of white with an identifiable coloured stripe (not green) running along the insulation.

3) The covering of the other conductor or conductors shall show a continuous colour contrasting with that of an identified conductor; however, in the case of those flexible cords where the identified conductor is identified by a raised longitudinal ridge(s), the other conductors shall have no ridges.

4) For multi-conductor cable, the insulated neutral conductor shall be permitted to be permanently marked as the identified conductor by painting or other suitable means at every point where the separate conductors have been rendered accessible and visible by removal of the outer covering of the cable, and the painting or other suitable means of marking the identified conductor shall not render illegible the manufacturer's numbering of the conductor.

4-026 Identification of insulated neutral conductors larger than No. 2 AWG copper or aluminum

For insulated neutral conductors other than those mentioned in Rule 4-024 1), identification shall either be continuous, as for No. 2 AWG and smaller, or else each continuous length of conductor insulation shall be suitably labelled or otherwise clearly marked at each end at the time of installation, so that it can be readily identified.

4-028 Identification of Type MI neutral conductors

Where mineral-insulated cable is used for neutral conductors and where continuous identification of this type of conductor is, at present, technically impossible in manufacture, each continuous length of conductor shall be permanently and clearly marked at each end at the time of installation, so that it can be readily identified.

4-030 Use of identified conductors

1) An identified conductor shall not be used as a conductor for which identification is not required by these Rules; however, in armoured cable, aluminum-sheathed cable, copper-sheathed cable, and non-metallic-sheathed cable work, the identified conductor shall be permitted to be rendered permanently unidentifiable by painting or other suitable means at every point where the separate insulated conductors have been rendered accessible and visible by removal of the outer covering of the cable.

2) Where armoured cable, aluminum-sheathed cable, copper-sheathed cable, or non-metallic-sheathed cable containing an identified conductor is used for single-pole, three-way, or four-way switch loops, it shall not be necessary to render the identified conductor permanently unidentified at the switch if the connections are made so that an unidentified conductor is the return conductor from the switch to the outlet.

3) Where armoured cable, aluminum-sheathed cable, copper-sheathed cable, or non-metallic-sheathed cable is used so that the identified conductor forms no part of the circuit, the identified conductor shall be cut off short or other suitable means shall be employed to indicate clearly that the identified conductor does not form part of the circuit; this shall be done at every point where the separate conductors have been rendered accessible and visible by removal of the outer covering of the cable.

4) Where conductors of a multi-wire branch circuit are installed, employing an identified conductor, the continuity of the identified conductor shall be independent of device connections, such as connections for lampholders, receptacles, ballasts, etc., so that the devices can be disconnected without interrupting the continuity of the identified conductor.

4-032 Identification of insulated conductors

1) Insulated grounding or bonding conductors shall
   a) have a continuous outer finish that is either green or green with one or more yellow stripes; or
   b) if larger than No. 2 AWG, be permitted to be suitably labelled or marked in a permanent manner with a green colour or green with one or more yellow stripes at each end and at each point where the conductor insulation is accessible.

2) Insulated conductors coloured or marked in accordance with Subrule 1) shall be used only as grounding or bonding conductors.

3) Where colour-coded circuits are required, the following colour coding shall be used, except in the case of service entrance cable and when Rules 4-026, 4-028, and 6-308 modify these requirements:
   a) 1-phase ac or dc (2-wire) — 1 black and 1 red or 1 black and 1 white*† (where an identified conductor is required);
   b) 1-phase ac or dc (3-wire) — 1 black, 1 red, and 1 white*†; and
   c) 3-phase ac — 1 red (phase A), 1 black (phase B), 1 blue (phase C), and 1 white* (where a neutral is required).

   Or grey.
   † Or white with a coloured stripe (see Rule 4-024).

4) Where the midpoint of one phase of a 4-wire delta-connected secondary is grounded to supply lighting and similar loads, the conductor insulation shall be colour-coded in accordance with Subrule 3) and the phase A insulated conductor shall be the insulated conductor having the higher voltage-to-ground.

5) Where a panelboard is supplied from a 4-wire delta-connected system,
   a) the panelboard shall be manufactured with a barriered compartment to accommodate single-phase connections to the grounded conductor referred to in Subrule 4); and
   b) the phase conductor having the higher voltage-to-ground shall be separated from the barriered compartment.

4-034 Ampacity of portable power cable
1) The maximum current that one or more copper conductors of a given size contained in a portable power cable are permitted to carry shall be as specified in Table 12A.
2) When Type DLO cable is used as fixed wiring in cable tray in accordance with Rule 12-406 4), its ampacity shall be determined in accordance with Table 12E and Rule 4-004.
3) Conductors used for bonding equipment to ground, and a conductor used as a neutral that carries only the unbalanced current from other conductors as in the case of a normally balanced circuit of three or more conductors, are not counted in determining ampacities.

4

Section 6 — Services and service equipment

Scope

6-000 Scope
This Section applies to services, service equipment, and metering equipment for
a)   installations operating at voltages of 750 V or less; and
b)   installations operating at voltages in excess of 750 V except as modified by the requirements of Section 36.

General

6-100 Special terminology
In this Section, the following definition shall apply:

Transformer rated meter mounting device — a meter mounting device with current transformers and with or without test switches mounted in the same enclosure.

6-102 Number of supply services permitted (see Appendix B)
1)   Two or more supply services of the same voltage shall not be run to any building, except that additional supply services shall be permitted for supplying
   a)   fire pumps in accordance with Rule 32-304 1);
   b)   industrial establishments and other complex structures; or
   c)   completely self-contained occupancies where the occupancies
      i)   are not located one above the other; and
      ii)   have a separate entrance with direct access to ground level.
2)   When two or more supply services are installed to a building, all service boxes associated with the various consumer's services shall be grouped, where practicable.
3)   When two or more service boxes installed in accordance with Subrule 2) are not grouped together, a permanent diagram shall be posted on or near each service box indicating the location of all the other service boxes supplying power to the building.

6-104 Number of consumer's services permitted in or on a building
The number of consumer's services of the same voltage and characteristics, terminating at any one supply service, run to, on, or in any building, shall not exceed four, unless there is a deviation allowed in accordance with Rule 2-030.

6-106 Current supply from more than one system
Where an installation, or part of an installation, is to be supplied with current from two or more different systems, the switching equipment controlling the various supplies shall be constructed or arranged so that it will be impossible to accidentally switch on power from one source before power from another has been cut off.

6-108 Supply service from an electric railway system
A supply service shall not be run to a building from an electric railway system using a ground return, unless the building is connected with the operation of an electric railway.

6-110 Three-wire consumer's services
A 3-wire consumer's service shall be provided in all cases where more than two 120 V branch circuits are installed, unless such supply is not available from the supply authority.

6-112 Support for the attachment of overhead supply or consumer's service conductors or cables (see Appendix B)
1)   A means of attachment shall be provided for all supply or consumer's service conductors.
Δ   2)   The point of attachment shall be
   a)   on the same side of the building as the consumer's service head or equivalent;

b) solidly anchored to the structure or service mast;

c) in a position that allows the overhead service conductors or cables to have an angle away from the structure; and

d) in compliance with the requirements of the supply authority.

3) The point of attachment of supply or consumer's service conductors or cables shall not exceed 9 m above grade or sidewalk and shall be located such that the clearance of supply conductors or cables at any point above finished grade shall be not less than the following:

a) across highways, streets, lanes, and alleys: 5.5 m;

b) across driveways to residential garages: 4 m;

c) across driveways to commercial and industrial premises: 5 m; and

d) across ground normally accessible to pedestrians only: 3.5 m.

4) Exposed service conductors or cables that are not higher than windows, doors, and porches shall have a clearance of not less than 1 m from the windows, doors, or porches.

5) Where service masts are used, they shall be of metal and assembled from components suitable for service mast use.

6) Rigid steel conduit of a minimum nominal size of 63 trade size shall be permitted to be used for the purpose of Subrule 5), provided that all other requirements for a service mast are complied with.

Δ 7) Bolts shall be used for securing the means of attachment at the point of attachment, and if attached to wooden structural members, the latter shall be not less than 38 mm in any dimension.

8) The supply or consumer's service conductor support shall not be attached to the roof of a structure, except as permitted in Subrule 9).

9) Notwithstanding Subrule 8), it shall be permitted to fasten the upper service mast support and the eye bolt, to which a guy wire is attached, to a main structural member of the roof, such as a roof rafter, a roof truss, or the equivalent.

6-114 Methods of terminating conductors or cables at consumer's service

1) The supply end of a consumer's service shall be equipped with a service head that is suitable for use in a wet location, except as provided for in Subrules 2) and 3).

2) Where service cables are employed and are continuous from the supply service to the service equipment, the service head required by Subrule 1) shall be permitted to be omitted.

3) Where single- or multi-conductor cables are employed, the service head required by Subrule 1) shall be permitted to be omitted, provided that

a) the cable terminates in a cable termination suitable for exposure to the weather, or the cable ends are sealed with self-sealing weather-resistant thermoplastic tape or heat-shrinkable tubing;

b) both single- and multi-conductor cables are bent as necessary so that the conductors emerging from the sealed point of the cable termination point downwards; and

c) the cables are held securely in place by a clamp, fitting, or cable termination.

4) Conductors of different polarity shall be brought out through separately bushed holes of the service head.

5) Consumer's service conductors shall be installed as specified in Rule 6-302 3).

6) The overhead supply service conductors or cables and the consumer's service conductors shall be arranged according to the requirements of Rule 6-116 to prevent moisture and water from entering service raceways, cables, or equipment.

6-116 Consumer's service head location

The consumer's service head or equivalent shall be installed

a) in compliance with the requirements of the supply authority; and

Δ b) in such a position that the point of emergence of the conductors from the consumer's service head or equivalent is
   i) a minimum of 150 mm and a maximum of 300 mm above; and
   ii) a maximum of 600 mm horizontally from
       the support for attachment of the overhead service conductors or cables.

Control and protective equipment

6-200 Service equipment
1) Except as provided in Subrule 2), each consumer's service shall be provided with a single service box.
2) More than one service box shall be permitted to be connected to a single consumer's service, provided that
   a) the subdivision is made in a multiple or dual lug meter mounting device rated at not more than 600 A and 150 volts-to-ground; and
   b) the meter mounting device is located outdoors.
3) For the application of Rule 6-104, each subdivision of the meter mounting device shall be considered a consumer's service.

6-202 Subdivision of main consumer's service
In multiple occupancy and in single occupancy multi-rate service, each subdivision of the main consumer's service shall be provided with a separate service box, or equivalent multi-service equipment shall be used, unless there is a deviation allowed in accordance with Rule 2-030 for single occupancy multi-rate services only; where the main consumer's service overcurrent devices adequately protect any subdivision of the main consumer's service, the separate service box for the subdivision so protected shall be permitted to be omitted.

6-204 Fuse enclosure on service boxes
If a service box embodies one or more fuseholders, access to which may be had without opening the door, such fuseholders and their fuses shall be completely enclosed by a separate door, spring-closed or with a substantial catch.

6-206 Consumer's service equipment location (see Appendices B and G)
1) Service boxes or other consumer's service equipment shall be
   a) installed in a location that complies with the requirements of the supply authority;
   b) readily accessible or have the means of operation readily accessible; and
   c) except as provided for by Subrule 3), placed within the building being served as close as practicable to the point where the consumer's service conductors enter the building and not be located in
      i) coal bins, clothes closets, bathrooms, and stairways;
      ii) rooms where the ambient temperature exceeds 30 °C under normal conditions;
      iii) dangerous or hazardous locations;
      iv) locations where the headroom clearance is less than 2 m; or
      v) in any similar undesirable places.
2) Notwithstanding Subrule 1) b), where subject to unauthorized operation, the service disconnecting means shall be permitted to be rendered inaccessible by
   a) an integral locking device;
   b) an external lockable cover; or
   c) location of the service box inside a separate building, room, or enclosure.
3) The service disconnecting means shall be permitted to be placed on the outside of the building or on a pole provided that it is
Δ a) installed in an enclosure for use in outdoor locations or protected against the weather; and
   b) protected against mechanical damage if it is located less than 2 m above ground.

6-208 Consumer's service conductors location

1) Raceways or cables containing consumer's service conductors shall be located outside buildings unless they are

    a) embedded in and encircled by not less than 50 mm of concrete or masonry where permitted by Section 12;

    b) directly buried in accordance with Rule 6-300 and located beneath a concrete slab not less than 50 mm thick; or

    c) run in a crawl space located underneath a structure, provided that such a crawl space

        i) does not exceed 1.8 m in height between the lowest part of the floor assembly and the ground or other surface below it;

        ii) is of non-combustible construction; and

        iii) is not used for the storage of combustible material.

2) Notwithstanding Subrule 1), raceways or cables containing consumer's service conductors shall be permitted to enter the building for connection to a service box.

6-210 Oil switches and oil circuit breakers used as consumer's service switches

1) Isolating switches shall be installed on the supply side and interlocked with oil switches and oil circuit breakers except in the case of metal clad equipment, where the primary isolating device shall be considered to be the equivalent of an isolating switch or link.

2) Where overcurrent trip coils are used for breakers, one shall be installed on each ungrounded conductor of the circuit; however, if the capacity of the transformers and the extent of the network supplying the service is sufficiently small, and a deviation has been allowed in accordance with Rule 2-030, two trip coils, one in each phase of a 4-wire, two-phase ungrounded service, shall be permitted to be used.

6-212 Wiring space in enclosures

1) Enclosures for circuit breakers and externally operated switches shall not be used as junction boxes, troughs, or raceways for conductors feeding through or tapping off to other apparatus.

2) Notwithstanding Subrule 1), service equipment designed for accommodating current monitoring devices shall be permitted.

Δ 3) Consumer's service conductors that enter a service box that is not equipped with a barrier between the line and load sides shall

    a) enter the service box as close as possible to the line terminals of the main switch or circuit breaker; and

    b) not come into contact with or cross conductors connected to the load terminals of the main switch or circuit breaker.

6-214 Marking of service boxes

If there is more than one service box, each box shall be labelled in a conspicuous, legible, and permanent manner to indicate clearly which installation or portion of an installation it controls.

Wiring methods

6-300 Installation of underground consumer's service conductors

1) Except where a deviation has been allowed in accordance with Rule 2-030, consumer's service conductors that are located underground shall be

    a) installed in rigid conduit, or electrical non-metallic tubing permitted only for the underground portion of the tubing run, and be of a type for use in wet locations in accordance with Rule 12-102 3); or

    b) a single- or multi-conductor cable for service entrance use below ground in accordance with Rule 12-102 3), provided that

        i) the installation is in accordance with Rule 12-012; and

    ii)   the cable is without splice or joint except

        A)   in metering equipment located on the line side of the service box; or

        B)   where a cable transition is made to meet the requirements of Rule 4-006.

2)   Notwithstanding Subrule 1) b) ii), joints in the underground portion of a consumer's service shall be permitted where such joints are made in accordance with Rule 12-112 5) and are required to repair damage to the original installation or to accommodate a pole or service relocation.

3)   Raceways entering a building and forming part of an underground service shall be sealed and shall

    a)   enter the building above ground where practicable;

    b)   be suitably drained; or

    c)   be installed in such a way that moisture and gas will not enter the building.

4)   Consumer's service conduit connected to an underground supply system shall be sealed with a suitable compound to prevent the entrance of moisture or gases.

6-302 Installation of overhead consumer's service conductors

1)   Conductors of a consumer's service that are located above ground, at any point, on a building or other structure shall be installed in one of the following ways:

    a)   rigid conduit;

    b)   busway;

    c)   steel electrical metallic tubing;

    d)   flexible metal conduit, with lead-sheathed conductors;

    e)   mineral-insulated cable other than the lightweight type;

    f)   aluminum-sheathed cable or copper-sheathed cable;

    g)   Type ACWU75 or Type ACWU90 cable;

    h)   Type AC90 cable; or

    i)   Type TECK90 cable.

2)   That portion of the consumer's service conductors on the supply side of the consumer's service head that is run between buildings or structures or on the outside walls of buildings, crossing over or installed on a building roof, shall be permitted to be run as exposed wiring in accordance with Rules 12-302 to 12-318.

3)   The length of consumer's service conductors beyond the service head shall be adequate to enable connection to the supply service conductors or to the conductors referred to in Subrule 2) with a minimum length of 750 mm, and the conductors shall be provided with drip loops.

4)   Consumer's service conductors shall be not less than No. 10 AWG copper wire, nor less than No. 8 AWG aluminum wire.

5)   The insulation on consumer's service conductors shall be suitable for the temperatures that can be experienced in the particular locality.

6-304 Use of mineral-insulated cable and aluminum-sheathed cable

1)   Mineral-insulated cable, aluminum-sheathed cable, and copper-sheathed cable shall be permitted to be used for consumer's services, as specified in Rule 6-302,

    a)   in multi-conductor construction; or

    b)   in single-conductor construction in sizes larger than No. 4 AWG copper or aluminum.

2)   Mineral-insulated cable, aluminum-sheathed cable, and copper-sheathed cable shall be permitted to be exposed and secured directly to the surface over which it is run, but subject to protection as specified in Rule 6-306 b).

6-306 Consumer's service raceways

Consumer's service raceways shall

a)   contain only the consumer's service conductors, and except where a deviation has been allowed in accordance with Rule 2-030, only the conductors of one consumer's service;

b)   be protected against mechanical damage as required by Rule 12-934; and

c)   if of circular cross-section, have a minimum nominal trade size of 21.

6-308 Use of bare neutral in consumer's service
The neutral conductor of a consumer's service shall be permitted to be bare if this conductor is
a)   made of copper and is run in a raceway;
b)   made of aluminum and is run above ground in a non-metallic or an aluminum raceway;
c)   part of a busway or of a service entrance cable; or
d)   part of a neutral supported cable used in accordance with Rule 6-302 2).

6-310 Use of joints in consumer's service neutral conductors
The neutral or identified conductor of a consumer's service shall be without joints between the point of connection and the service box or equivalent consumer's service equipment, except that a joint shall be permitted where it is made
a)   by means of a clamp or bolted connection in a meter mounting device or at the service head if exposed wiring is used in accordance with Rule 6-302 2);
b)   by a joint underground in accordance with Rule 12-112 5), where such a joint is required to repair damage to the original installation or to accommodate a pole or service relocation; or
c)   where a cable transition is made to meet the requirements of Rule 4-006.

6-312 Condensation in consumer's service raceway
1)   The consumer's service raceway entering a building shall be sealed and shall be suitably drained where it enters the building above grade level.
2)   The consumer's service raceway shall not be terminated on top of the service box except where drained outdoors.

Metering equipment

6-400 Metering equipment
Metering equipment includes any current and potential (voltage) transformers as well as the associated measuring instruments.

6-402 Method of installing meter loops (see Appendix B)
1)   Meter loops shall be installed so that
a)   conductors between the service box and the meter are inaccessible to unauthorized persons;
b)   the wiring method is rigid conduit, flexible metal conduit, electrical metallic tubing, aluminum-sheathed cable, or armoured cable, except where equivalent protection is provided;
c)   spare conductors not less than 450 mm in length are provided at meter or current transformer connection points; and
d)   a suitable fitting, or service box with meter backplate, is provided.
2)   Metering equipment shall be connected on the load side of the service box, except that it shall be permitted to be connected on the supply side where
a)   no live parts or wiring are exposed;
b)   the supply is ac and the voltage does not exceed 300 V between conductors; and
c)   the rating of the consumer's service does not exceed
i)   200 A for a meter mounting device;
ii)   320 A for a meter mounting device equipped with a bypass means; or
iii) 600 A for a transformer rated meter mounting device located outdoors.

6-404 Enclosures for instrument transformers
1)   Instrument transformers used in conjunction with meters shall be installed in metal enclosures, except where access is to authorized persons only.
2)   The size of enclosures for instrument transformers shall comply with the requirements of the supply authority.

3) Enclosures for current transformers shall be installed on all consumer's services rated in excess of 200 A, except where
   a) current transformers are an integral part of consumer's service switchgear; or
   b) the supply authority uses meters that do not require current transformers.
4) Enclosures for instrument transformers shall have provision for securing of the transformers to the enclosures.

6-406 Disconnecting provisions for meters

In multiple occupancy and in single occupancy multi-rate service where individual metering is required, the conductors to each meter shall be provided with one of the following:
a) a separate service box or service equipment; or
b) a sealable meter fitting.

6-408 Location of meters

1) Meters and metering equipment shall be
   a) located as near as practicable to the service box except as provided for in Subrule 2);
   b) grouped where practicable;
   c) readily accessible;
   d) not located in coal bins, clothes closets, bathrooms, stairways, high ambient rooms, dangerous or hazardous locations, nor in any similar undesirable places;
   e) if mounted outdoors, of weatherproof construction or in weatherproof enclosures; and
   f) in compliance with the requirements of the supply authority.
2) Instrument transformers shall be permitted to be outside the consumer's premises and the meter inside the premises, provided that the secondary leads between the instrument transformers and the meter terminal box or test links are continuous and are installed in the same manner as consumer's service conductors, with the exception that a service box with disconnecting switch is not required.

6-410 Space required for meters

The space provided for meters shall comply with the requirements of the supply authority.

6-412 Metering requirements for impedance grounded systems

1) Equipment and wiring for supply authority metering on impedance grounded systems shall comply with the requirements of the supply authority.
2) Where a neutral point reference conductor is required for metering on impedance grounded systems, the reference conductor shall be
   a) insulated for the nominal system voltage;
   b) isolated from ground throughout its entire length; and
   c) permitted to be in the same raceway or cable assembly as the consumer's service conductors and to be carried through or extended from the consumer's service box to the metering equipment.

Section 8 — Circuit loading and demand factors

Scope

Δ **8-000 Scope**
This Section applies to
a)   maximum circuit loading;
b)   calculated loads for consumer's services, feeders, and branch circuits;
c)   use of demand factors;
d)   branch circuit positions required for dwelling units; and
e)   heater receptacles for vehicles.

8-002 Special terminology (see Appendix B)
In this Section, the following definitions shall apply:

Basic load — the load of lighting and receptacle circuits, based on the outside dimensions of a specific area of building occupancy, as listed in Table 14.

Calculated load — the load calculated in accordance with the applicable requirements of this Section.

Demonstrated load — historical maximum demand watt information recorded over at least a 24-month period for the same type of facility as the one in question, equated to watts per m^2.

Δ **Electric vehicle energy management system** — a means used to control electric vehicle supply equipment loads through the process of connecting, disconnecting, increasing, or reducing electric power to the loads and consisting of any of the following: a monitor(s), communications equipment, a controller(s), a timer(s), and other applicable device(s).

General

8-100 Current calculations
When calculating currents that will result from loads, expressed in watts or volt amperes, to be supplied by a low-voltage ac system, the voltage divisors to be used shall be 120, 208, 240, 277, 347, 416, 480, or 600 as applicable.

8-102 Voltage drop (see Appendices B and D)
1)   The voltage drop in an installation shall be based on the connected load of the feeder or branch circuit if known; otherwise it shall be based on 80% of the rating of the overload or overcurrent device protecting the branch circuit or feeder, and not exceed
a)   3% in a feeder or branch circuit; and
b)   5% from the supply side of the consumer's service (or equivalent) to the point of utilization.
2)   Notwithstanding Subrule 1), where overcurrent devices are selected in accordance with other Sections of this Code, the voltage drop shall be based on the calculated demand load of the feeder or branch circuit.
3)   Notwithstanding Subrule 1), wiring for general-use branch circuits rated at not more than 120 V or 20 A in dwelling units, with the insulated conductor length measured from the supply side of the consumer's service to the furthest point of utilization in accordance with the values in Table 68, shall be acceptable.
4)   Notwithstanding Subrule 1), at industrial establishments where conditions of maintenance and supervision ensure use by qualified persons, the design shall ensure that the voltage at the point of utilization is within the rating or voltage tolerance of the connected device(s).

8-104 Maximum circuit loading (see Appendix B)

1) The ampere rating of a consumer's service, feeder, or branch circuit shall be the ampere rating of the overcurrent device protecting the circuit or the ampacity of the conductors, whichever is less.

2) The calculated load in a circuit shall not exceed the ampere rating of the circuit.

3) The calculated load in a consumer's service, feeder, or branch circuit shall be considered a continuous load unless it can be shown that in normal operation it will not persist for
   a) a total of more than 1 h in any 2 h period if the load does not exceed 225 A; or
   b) a total of more than 3 h in any 6 h period if the load exceeds 225 A.

4) A load of a cyclic or intermittent nature shall be classified as continuous unless it meets the requirements of Subrule 3).

Δ 5) Where a fused switch or circuit breaker is marked for continuous operation at 100% of the ampere rating of its overcurrent devices, the continuous load as determined from the calculated load shall not exceed the continuous operation marking on the fused switch or circuit breaker and
   a) except as required by Item b), shall not exceed 100% of the allowable ampacities of conductors selected in accordance with Section 4; or
   b) shall not exceed 85% of the allowable ampacities of single conductors selected in accordance with Section 4.

Δ 6) Where a fused switch or circuit breaker is marked for continuous operation at 80% of the ampere rating of its overcurrent devices, the continuous load as determined from the calculated load shall not exceed the continuous operation marking on the fused switch or circuit breaker and
   a) except as required by Item b), shall not exceed 80% of the allowable ampacities of conductors selected in accordance with Section 4; or
   b) shall not exceed 70% of the allowable ampacities of single conductors selected in accordance with Section 4.

Δ 7) The continuous load as determined from the calculated load connected to a cablebus shall not exceed the values specified in Subrule 5) or 6).

Δ 8-106 Use of demand factors (see Appendix B)

1) In any case other than a service calculated in accordance with Rules 8-200 and 8-202, where the design of an installation is based on requirements in excess of those given in this Section, the service and feeder capacities shall be increased accordingly.

2) Where two or more loads are installed so that only one can be used at any one time, the one providing the greatest demand shall be used in determining the calculated demand.

3) Where it is known that electric space-heating and air-conditioning loads are installed and will not be used simultaneously, whichever is the greater load shall be used in calculating the demand.

4) Where a feeder supplies loads of a cyclic or similar nature such that the maximum connected load will not be supplied at the same time, the ampacity of the feeder conductors shall be permitted to be based on the maximum load that may be connected at any one time.

5) Where a feeder or service supplies motor or air-conditioning loads, a demand factor as determined by a qualified person shall be permitted to be applied to these loads, provided that a deviation has been allowed in accordance with Rule 2-030.

6) The ampacity of conductors of feeders or branch circuits shall be in accordance with the Section(s) dealing with the respective equipment being supplied.

7) Notwithstanding the requirements of this Section, the ampacity of the conductors of a feeder or branch circuit need not exceed the ampacity of the conductors of the service or of the feeder from which they are supplied.

8) Where additional loads are to be added to an existing service or feeder, the augmented load shall be permitted to be calculated by adding the sum of the additional loads, with demand factors as

permitted by this Code, to the maximum demand load of the existing installation as measured over the most recent 12-month period, but the new calculated load shall be subject to Rule 8-104 5) and 6).

9) For loads other than those calculated in accordance with Rules 8-200 and 8-202, feeder and service load calculations shall be permitted to be based on demonstrated loads, provided that such calculations are performed by a qualified person, as determined by the regulatory authority having jurisdiction.

10) Where electric vehicle supply equipment loads are controlled by an electric vehicle energy management system, the demand load for the electric vehicle supply equipment shall be equal to the maximum load allowed by the electric vehicle energy management system.

11) For the purposes of Rules 8-200 1) a) vi), 8-202 3) d), 8-204 1) d), 8-206 1) d), 8-208 1) d), and 8-210 c), where an electric vehicle energy management system as described in Subrule 10) monitors the consumer's service and feeders and controls the electric vehicle supply equipment loads in accordance with Rule 8-500, the demand load for the electric vehicle supply equipment shall not be required to be considered in the determination of the calculated load.

8-108 Number of branch circuit positions

1) For a single dwelling, the panelboard shall provide space for at least the equivalent of the following number of 120 V branch circuit overcurrent devices, including space for two 35 A double-pole overcurrent devices:
   a) 16 — of which at least half shall be double-pole, where the required ampacity of the service or feeder conductors does not exceed 60 A;
   b) 24 — of which at least half shall be double-pole
      i) where the required ampacity of the service or feeder conductors exceeds 60 A but does not exceed 100 A; or
      ii) where the required ampacity of the service or feeder conductors exceeds 100 A but does not exceed 125 A and provision is made for a central electric furnace;
   c) 30 — of which at least half shall be double-pole
      i) where the required ampacity of the service or feeder conductors exceeds 100 A but does not exceed 125 A; or
      ii) where the required ampacity of the service or feeder conductors exceeds 125 A but does not exceed 200 A and provision is made for a central electric furnace; and
   d) 40 — of which at least half shall be double-pole, where the required ampacity of the service or feeder conductors exceeds 125 A and the dwelling is not heated by a central electric furnace.

2) Notwithstanding Subrule 1), sufficient spaces for overcurrent devices shall be provided in the panelboard for the two 35 A double-pole overcurrent devices and for all other overcurrent devices, and at least two additional spaces shall be left for future overcurrent devices.

3) For a dwelling unit in an apartment or similar building, the panelboard shall provide space for at least the equivalent of the following number of 120 V branch circuit overcurrent devices, including space for one 35 A double-pole overcurrent device:
   a) 8 — where the required ampacity of the feeder conductors supplying the dwelling unit does not exceed 60 A; and
   b) 12 — where the required ampacity of the feeder conductors supplying the dwelling unit exceeds 60 A.

8-110 Determination of areas

The living area designated in Rules 8-200 and 8-202 shall be determined from inside dimensions and include the sum of
a) 100% of the area on the ground floor;

Δ b)   100% of any areas above the ground floor used for living purposes; and

Δ c)   75% of the area below the ground floor.

Δ

Calculated load for services and feeders

8-200 Single dwellings (see Appendix B)

Δ 1)   The calculated load for the service or feeder supplying a single dwelling shall be based on the greater of Item a) or b):

a)

    i)   a basic load of 5000 W for the first 90 m² of living area (see Rule 8-110); plus

    ii)   an additional 1000 W for each 90 m² or portion thereof in excess of 90 m²; plus

Ⓔ   iii)   any electric space-heating loads provided for with demand factors as permitted in Section 62 plus any air-conditioning loads with a demand factor of 100%, subject to Rule 8-106 3); plus

    iv)   any electric range load provided for as follows: 6000 W for a single range plus 40% of any amount by which the rating of the range exceeds 12 kW; plus

    v)   any electric tankless water heaters or electric water heaters for steamers, swimming pools, hot tubs, or spas with a demand factor of 100%; plus

    vi)   except as permitted by Rule 8-106 11), any electric vehicle supply equipment loads with a demand factor of 100%; plus

    vii)   any loads provided for that have a rating in excess of 1500 W, in addition to those outlined in Items i) to vi), at

        A)   25% of the rating of each load, if an electric range has been provided for; or

        B)   100% of the combined load up to 6000 W, plus 25% of the combined load that exceeds 6000 W, if an electric range has not been provided for; or

b)

    i)   24 000 W where the floor area, exclusive of the basement floor area, is 80 m² or more; or

    ii)   14 400 W where the floor area, exclusive of the basement floor area, is less than 80 m².

Δ 2)   The calculated load for the consumer's service or feeder conductors supplying two or more dwelling units of row housing shall be based on

a)   the calculated load in the dwelling unit, as determined in accordance with Subrule 1), excluding any electric space-heating loads and any air-conditioning loads, with application of demand factors to the calculated loads as required by Rule 8-202 3) a) i) to v); plus

b)   the requirements of Rule 8-202 3) b) to e).

3)   Notwithstanding Rule 86-302, the total load calculated in accordance with either Subrule 1) or 2) shall not be considered to be a continuous load for application of Rule 8-104.

8-202 Apartment and similar buildings (see Appendix B)

Δ 1)   The calculated load for the service or feeder from a main service supplying loads in dwelling units shall be the greater of Item a) or b):

a)

    i)   a basic load of 3500 W for the first 45 m² of living area (see Rule 8-110); plus

    ii)   an additional 1500 W for the second 45 m² or portion thereof; plus

    iii)   an additional 1000 W for each additional 90 m² or portion thereof in excess of the initial 90 m²; plus

Ⓔ   iv)   any electric space-heating loads provided for with demand factors as permitted in Section 62 plus any air-conditioning loads with a demand factor of 100%, subject to Rule 8-106 3); plus

    v)   any electric range load provided for as follows: 6000 W for a single range plus 40% of any amount by which the rating of the range exceeds 12 kW; plus

          vi)   any electric tankless water heaters or electric water heaters for steamers, swimming pools, hot tubs, or spas with a demand factor of 100%; plus

          vii)   any loads provided for, in addition to those outlined in Items i) to vi), at

               A)   25% of the rating of each load with a rating in excess of 1500 W, if an electric range has been provided for; or

               B)   25% of the rating of each load with a rating in excess of 1500 W plus 6000 W, if an electric range has not been provided for; or

    b)   60 A.

2)   The total load calculated in accordance with Subrule 1) and Subrule 3) a), b), and c) shall not be considered to be a continuous load for the application of Rule 8-104.

Δ   3)   The calculated load for the consumer's service or feeder supplying two or more dwelling units shall be based on the calculated load obtained from Subrule 1) a) and the following:

    a)   excluding any electric space-heating loads and any air-conditioning loads, the load shall be considered to be

          i)   100% of the calculated load in the unit having the heaviest load; plus

          ii)   65% of the sum of the calculated loads in the next 2 units having the same or next smaller loads to those specified in Item i); plus

          iii)   40% of the sum of the calculated loads in the next 2 units having the same or next smaller loads to those specified in Item ii); plus

          iv)   25% of the sum of the calculated loads in the next 15 units having the same or next smaller loads to those specified in Item iii); plus

          v)   10% of the sum of the calculated loads in the remaining units;

Ⓔ   b)   if electric space heating is used, the sum of all the space-heating loads as determined in accordance with the requirements of Section 62 shall be added to the load determined in accordance with Item a), subject to Rule 8-106 3);

Ⓔ   c)   if air conditioning is used, the sum of all the air-conditioning loads shall be added, with a demand factor of 100%, to the load determined in accordance with Items a) and b), subject to Rule 8-106 3);

    d)   except as permitted by Rule 8-106 11), any electric vehicle supply equipment loads not located in dwelling units shall be added with a demand factor as specified in Table 38; and

    e)   in addition, any lighting, heating, and power loads not located in dwelling units shall be added with a demand factor of 75%.

4)   The ampacity of feeder conductors from a service supplying loads not located in dwelling units shall be not less than the rating of the equipment installed with demand factors as permitted by this Code.

8-204 Schools

Δ   1)   The calculated load for the service or feeder shall be based on the following:

    a)   a basic load of 50 W/m² of classroom area; plus

    b)   10 W/m² of the remaining area of the building based on the outside dimensions; plus

    c)   electric space-heating, air-conditioning, and total loads of other permanently connected equipment based on the rating of the equipment installed; plus

    d)   except as permitted by Rule 8-106 11), any electric vehicle supply equipment loads with a demand factor as specified in Table 38; plus

    e)   cord-connected equipment intended for connection to receptacles rated more than 125 V or 20 A based on

          i)   80% of the rating of the receptacle; or

          ii)   the rating of the equipment intended for connection to the receptacle.

2) Demand factors shall be permitted to be applied as follows:
    a) for a building with an area up to and including 900 m² based on the outside dimensions:
        i) as permitted in Section 62 for any electric space-heating loads provided for; and
        ii) 75% for the balance of the load; and
    b) for a building with an area exceeding 900 m² based on the outside dimensions:
        i) as permitted in Section 62 for any electric space-heating loads provided for; and
        ii) the balance of the load shall be divided by the number of square metres to obtain a load-per-square-metre rating and the demand load may be considered to be the sum of
            A) 75% of the load per square metre multiplied by 900; and
            B) 50% of the load per square metre multiplied by the area of the building in excess of 900 m².

8-206 Hospitals

Δ 1) The calculated load for the service or feeder shall be based on the following:
    a) a basic load of 20 W/m² of the area of the building based on the outside dimensions; plus
    b) 100 W/m² for high-intensity areas such as operating rooms; plus
    c) electric space-heating, air-conditioning, and total loads of other permanently connected equipment based on the rating of the equipment installed; plus
    d) except as permitted by Rule 8-106 11), any electric vehicle supply equipment loads with a demand factor as specified in Table 38; plus
    e) cord-connected equipment intended for connection to receptacles rated more than 125 V or 20 A based on
        i) 80% of the rating of the receptacle; or
        ii) the rating of the equipment intended for connection to the receptacle.

2) Demand factors shall be permitted to be applied as follows:
    a) for a building with an area up to and including 900 m² based on the outside dimensions:
        i) as permitted in Section 62 for any electric space-heating loads provided for; and
        ii) 80% for the balance of the load; and
    b) for a building with an area exceeding 900 m² based on the outside dimensions:
        i) as permitted in Section 62 for any electric space-heating loads provided for; and
        ii) the balance of the load shall be divided by the number of square metres to obtain a load-per-square-metre rating and the demand load may be considered to be the sum of
            A) 80% of the load per square metre multiplied by 900; and
            B) 65% of the load per square metre multiplied by the area of the building in excess of 900 m².

8-208 Hotels, motels, dormitories, and buildings of similar occupancy (see Appendix B)

Δ 1) The calculated load for the service or feeder shall be based on the following:
    a) a basic load of 20 W/m² of the area of the building, based on the outside dimensions; plus
    b) lighting loads for special areas such as ballrooms, based on the rating of the equipment installed; plus
    c) electric space-heating, air-conditioning, and total loads of other permanently connected equipment based on the rating of the equipment installed; plus
    d) except as permitted by Rule 8-106 11), any electric vehicle supply equipment loads with a demand factor as specified in Table 38; plus
    e) cord-connected equipment intended for connection to receptacles rated more than 125 V or 20 A based on
        i) 80% of the rating of the receptacle; or
        ii) the rating of the equipment intended for connection to the receptacle.

2) Demand factors shall be permitted to be applied as follows:
   a) for a building with an area up to and including 900 m² based on the outside dimensions:
      i) as permitted in Section 62 for any electric space-heating loads provided for; and
      ii) 80% for the balance of the load; and
   b) for a building with an area exceeding 900 m² based on the outside dimensions:
      i) as permitted in Section 62 for any electric space-heating loads provided for; and
      ii) the balance of the load shall be divided by the number of square metres to obtain a load-per-square-metre rating and the demand load may be considered to be the sum of
         A) 80% of the load per square metre multiplied by 900; and
         B) 65% of the load per square metre multiplied by the area of the building in excess of 900 m².

Δ **8-210 Other types of occupancy**
The calculated load for the service or feeder for the types of occupancies listed in Table 14 shall be based on

a) a basic load in watts per square metre as required by Table 14 for the area of the occupancy served based on the outside dimensions of the occupancy, with application of demand factors as indicated in Table 14; plus
b) special loads such as electric space-heating, air-conditioning, motor loads, show window lighting, stage lighting, etc., based on the rating of the equipment installed with demand factors permitted by this Code; plus
c) except as permitted by Rule 8-106 11), any electric vehicle supply equipment loads with a demand factor as specified in Table 38.

8-212 Exit sign, emergency lighting, and show window loads
1) Where a panel is supplying specific types of lighting, such as exit signs or emergency lighting, which may be located throughout a building such that it is impossible to calculate the area served, the connected load of the circuits involved shall be used in determining a feeder size.
2) For show window lighting installations, the demand load shall be determined on the assumption that not less than 650 W/m will be required measured along the base of the window(s), except that a lower figure shall be permitted where a deviation has been allowed in accordance with Rule 2-030.

Branch circuits

8-300 Branch circuits supplying electric ranges
1) Conductors of a branch circuit supplying a range in a dwelling unit shall be considered as having a demand of
   a) 8 kW where the rating of the range does not exceed 12 kW; or
   b) 8 kW plus 40% of the amount by which the rating of the range exceeds 12 kW.
2) For the purpose of Subrule 1), two or more separate built-in cooking units shall be permitted to be considered as one range.
3) For ranges or cooking units installed in commercial, industrial, and institutional establishments, the demand shall be considered as not less than the rating.
4) The demand loads given in this Rule shall not apply to cord-connected hotplates, rangettes, or other appliances.

8-302 Branch circuits supplying data processing equipment
The total connected load of a branch circuit supplying one or more units of data processing equipment shall be considered to be a continuous load for the application of Rule 8-104.

8-304 Maximum number of outlets per circuit

1) There shall be not more than 12 outlets on any 2-wire branch circuit, except as permitted by other Rules of this Code.
2) Such outlets shall be considered to be rated at not less than 1 A per outlet, except as permitted by Subrule 3).
3) Where the connected load is known, the number of outlets shall be permitted to exceed 12, provided that the load current does not exceed 80% of the rating of the overcurrent device protecting the circuit.
4) Where fixed multi-outlet assemblies are used, each 1.5 m or fraction thereof of each separate and continuous length shall be counted as one outlet, but in locations where a number of electrical appliances are likely to be used simultaneously, each 300 mm or fraction thereof shall be counted as one outlet.

Heater receptacles for vehicles powered by flammable or combustible fuels

8-400 Branch circuits and feeders supplying heater receptacles for vehicles powered by flammable or combustible fuels

1) In the application of this Rule, the following definitions shall apply:

   Controlled — power to the receptacle is cycled by other than a manual operation.

   Restricted — pertaining to the block heater only and where the use of an in-vehicle heater or other vehicle heating device is not permitted.

2) At least one branch circuit protected by an overcurrent device rated or set at not more than 20 A shall be provided for each duplex receptacle or for every two single receptacles referred to in Rule 26-700 2).
3) Where the loading in each parking space or stall is not restricted or controlled, a separate branch circuit shall be provided for each parking space or stall and the feeder or service conductor shall be considered as having a demand load as follows:

Number of vehicle spaces or stalls	Demand load per space or stall, W	
	15 A circuit	**20 A circuit**
First 30	1200	1800
Next 30	1000	1500
All over 60	800	1200

4) Where branch circuits are provided for parking spaces or stalls in which the loading is restricted or controlled, the feeder or service conductors shall be considered as having a demand load as follows:

Number of vehicle spaces or stalls	Demand load per space or stall, W	
	15 A circuit	**20 A circuit**
First 30	650	975
Next 30	550	825
All over 60	450	675

5) Parking lots that may be fully occupied under normal usage shall be assigned a greater demand load per space or stall.

Δ
Electric vehicle energy management systems

8-500 Electric vehicle energy management systems
1) Electric vehicle energy management systems shall be permitted to monitor electrical loads and to control electric vehicle supply equipment loads.
2) An electric vehicle energy management system shall not cause the load of a branch circuit, feeder, or service to exceed the requirements of Rule 8-104 5) or 6).
3) An electric vehicle energy management system shall be permitted to control electrical power by remote means.

8

Δ

Section 10 — Grounding and bonding
Scope, object, and special terminology

10-000 Scope (see Appendix B)

This Section applies to

a)   grounding, as follows:
    i)   solidly grounded systems;
    ii)   impedance grounded systems; and
    iii) ungrounded systems;

b)   bonding; and

c)   equipotential bonding.

10-002 Object (see Appendix B)

The overall objective for grounding and bonding is to minimize the likelihood and severity of electric shock by establishing equipotentiality between exposed non-current-carrying conductive surfaces and nearby surfaces of the earth and to prevent damage to property during a fault, as follows:

a)   the objective of solidly grounding an electrical system and bonding its associated equipment is to establish a low impedance connection between the grounded conductor and the non-current-carrying conductive parts of the system to stabilize system voltage;

b)   the objective of grounding an electrical system through an impedance is to
    i)   limit the magnitude of ground fault currents;
    ii)   minimize the damage to equipment resulting from a single ground fault; and
    iii) stabilize system voltage;

c)   the objective of an ungrounded system is to
    i)   limit the magnitude of ground fault currents resulting from a single ground fault; and
    ii)   minimize the damage to equipment on the occurrence of a single ground fault;

d)   the objective of bonding is to interconnect the non-current-carrying conductive parts of electrical equipment and the system grounded point, where one exists, with sufficiently low impedance to
    i)   facilitate the operation of protective devices; and
    ii)   establish equipotentiality; and

e)   the objective of equipotential bonding is to establish equipotentiality.

10-004 Special terminology (see Appendix B)

In this section, the following definitions shall apply:

Equipotentiality — the state in which conductive parts are at a substantially equal electric potential.

Grounded conductor — in an electrical system, the conductor that is intentionally grounded.

Impedance grounded system — an electrical system in which a point (normally the midpoint or neutral) is connected through an impedance device

a)   to an impedance system bonding jumper; and

b)   by a grounding conductor, to a grounding electrode or to a conductive body that extends the ground connection.

Impedance system bonding jumper — a connection between the grounded side of an impedance grounding device and the non-current-carrying conductive parts of an electrical system.

Separately derived system — an electrical system in which the circuit conductors have no direct connection to the circuit conductors of a supply authority system other than those established by grounding and bonding connections.

Solidly grounded system — an electrical system in which a point is connected, without inserting an impedance grounding device,

a)   to a system bonding jumper; and

b)   by a grounding conductor, to a grounding electrode or to a conductive body that extends the ground connection.

System bonding jumper — a connection between the system grounded point and the non-current-carrying conductive parts of an electrical system to establish a solidly grounded system.

Ungrounded system — an electrical system in which no point of the system is intentionally grounded.

Grounding

Grounding — General

10-100 Current over grounding conductors (see Appendix B)

There shall be no objectionable passage of current over a grounding conductor.

10-102 Grounding electrodes (see Appendix B)

1)   Grounding electrodes shall consist of
a)   manufactured grounding electrodes;
b)   field-assembled grounding electrodes; or
c)   in-situ grounding electrodes forming part of existing infrastructure.

2)   Manufactured grounding electrodes shall
a)   in the case of a rod grounding electrode, consist of two rod electrodes
i)   spaced not less than 3 m apart;
ii)   interconnected with a grounding conductor sized as prescribed for grounding conductors; and
iii) driven to the full length of the rod;
b)   in the case of a chemically charged rod electrode, be installed to the full length of the rod; or
c)   in the case of a plate electrode, be
i)   in direct contact with exterior soil at not less than 600 mm below grade level; or
ii)   encased within the bottom 50 mm of a concrete foundation footing in direct contact with the earth at not less than 600 mm below finished grade.

3)   A field-assembled grounding electrode shall consist of
a)   a bare copper conductor not less than 6 m in length, sized in accordance with Table 43 and encased within the bottom 50 mm of a concrete foundation footing in direct contact with the earth at not less than 600 mm below finished grade; or
b)   a bare copper conductor not less than 6 m in length, sized in accordance with Table 43 and directly buried in earth at least 600 mm below finished grade.

4)   For the purposes of Rule 2-024, an in-situ grounding electrode shall not be considered electrical equipment and shall provide, at 600 mm or more below finished grade, a surface area exposure to earth equivalent to that of a similar manufactured grounding electrode.

5)   Where a local condition such as rock or permafrost prevents a grounding electrode from being installed at the required burial depth, a lesser acceptable depth shall be permitted.

10-104 Spacing and interconnection of grounding electrodes (see Appendix B)

Where there are multiple grounding electrodes at a building, they shall be

a)   separated by at least 2 m from each other;

b)   interconnected with a conductor
i)   made of material prescribed for grounding conductors;
ii)   sized as prescribed for grounding conductors; and

10

iii) protected from mechanical damage as required for grounding conductors; and

c) in the case of lightning protection systems, interconnected in accordance with Item b) at or below ground level.

10-106 Railway track as grounding electrodes (see Appendix B)

Railway track shall be permitted to be used as a grounding electrode only for railway lightning arresters and for the railway circuit itself.

10-108 Lightning protection system down conductors and grounding electrodes (see Appendices B and G)

1) Down conductors shall not be used for grounding electrical systems or electrical equipment.

2) The grounding electrode for a lightning protection system shall be dedicated for use solely by the lightning protection system.

10-110 Continuity of grounding conductors

No automatic cut-out or switch shall be installed in the grounding conductor unless the opening of the cut-out or switch disconnects all sources of energy.

10-112 Material for grounding conductors (see Appendix B)

1) The grounding conductor shall be
   a) of copper, aluminum, or other acceptable material; and
   b) permitted to be insulated or bare.

2) Grounding conductors shall be resistant to any corrosive condition existing at the installation or shall be protected against corrosion.

10-114 Grounding conductor size (see Appendix B)

1) Except as permitted by Subrule 2), the grounding conductor shall be sized not smaller than
   a) No. 6 AWG if of copper; or
   b) No. 4 AWG if of aluminum.

2) The grounding conductor shall be permitted to be sized smaller than prescribed in Subrule 1), provided that it is not smaller than the current-carrying conductor(s) of the system being grounded.

10-116 Installation of grounding conductors (see Appendix B)

1) The grounding conductor shall be electrically continuous throughout its length.

2) Where necessary, devices to control the effects of stray earth current shall be permitted to be connected in series with the grounding conductor.

3) A grounding conductor shall be protected from damage
   a) mechanically; or
   b) by location.

4) Raceways or sleeves constructed of magnetic materials used to enclose grounding conductors shall be connected to the grounding conductor at both ends.

5) A grounding conductor installed in the same raceway with service conductors shall be insulated, except that an uninsulated grounding conductor shall be permitted where the length of the raceway
   a) does not exceed 15 m between pull points; and
   b) does not contain more than the equivalent of two 90° bends between pull points.

10-118 Grounding conductor connection to grounding electrodes (see Appendix B)

1) The grounding conductor shall be connected to the grounding electrode at a point that will assure a permanent ground by means of
   a) a bolted clamp;
   b) copper welding by a fusion welding process;
   c) brazing;

d)   silver solder; or

e)   other equally substantial means.

2)   Where practicable, the connection to a grounding electrode shall be accessible.

Solidly grounded systems

10-200 DC systems required to be solidly grounded

DC systems shall be solidly grounded unless they meet the requirements for

a)   ungrounded systems; or

b)   impedance grounded systems.

10-202 Conductor of a dc system to be grounded (see Appendix B)

The conductor of a dc system to be grounded shall be

a)   one conductor of a 2-wire system; or

b)   the common conductor of a 3-wire system.

10-204 Grounding connections for dc systems

DC systems that are to be solidly grounded shall have the grounding connections made at a single point as close as practicable to the supply source.

10-206 AC systems required to be solidly grounded

1)   AC systems exceeding extra-low voltage shall be solidly grounded if

    a)   by doing so, their maximum voltage-to-ground does not exceed 150 V; or

    b)   the system incorporates a neutral conductor.

2)   AC systems exceeding the value prescribed by Subrule 1) a) shall be permitted to be ungrounded or impedance grounded, provided that they meet the requirements for

    a)   ungrounded systems; or

    b)   impedance grounded systems.

3)   Extra-low-voltage ac systems shall be solidly grounded where

    a)   run overhead outside;

    b)   supplied by transformers energized from systems of more than 150 volts-to-ground; or

    c)   supplied by transformers energized from ungrounded systems.

10-208 Conductor of an ac system to be grounded (see Appendix B)

1)   The conductor of an ac system to be grounded shall be

    a)   one conductor of a single-phase, 2-wire system — the identified conductor;

    b)   the mid-phase conductor of a single-phase, 3-wire system — the identified neutral conductor;

    c)   the mid-phase conductor of a multi-phase system having one wire common to all phases — the identified neutral conductor;

    d)   one conductor of a multi-phase system having one phase grounded — the identified conductor; and

    e)   the mid-phase conductor of one phase of a multi-phase system — the identified conductor.

2)   For the multi-phase system referred to in Subrule 1) e), only one phase shall be permitted to be grounded.

10-210 Grounding connections for solidly grounded ac systems supplied by the supply authority (see Appendix B)

The grounded conductor of a solidly grounded ac system supplied by the supply authority shall

a)   be connected to a grounding conductor at one point only at the consumer's service;

b)   have a minimum size as specified

    i)   for a bonding conductor; and

    ii)   for a neutral conductor when the grounded conductor also serves as a neutral;

c)   be connected to the equipment bonding terminal by a system bonding jumper; and

d) have no other connection to the non-current-carrying conductive parts of electrical equipment on the supply side or the load side of the grounding connection.

10-212 Grounding connections for solidly grounded separately derived ac systems (see Appendix B)

1) Except as permitted by Subrule 2), the grounded conductor of a solidly grounded separately derived ac system shall
   a) be connected to the equipment bonding terminal by a system bonding jumper
      i) at the source;
      ii) at the first switch controlling the system; or
      iii) at the tie point, where two or more systems terminate at a tie point;
   b) be connected to a grounding conductor at the same point on the separately derived system where the system bonding jumper is connected; and
   c) have no other connection to the non-current-carrying conductive parts of electrical equipment on the supply side or the load side of the grounding connection.

2) A separately derived ac system operating at 750 V or less shall be permitted to be grounded by the system bonding jumper that is connected to the bonding conductor included in the primary supply.

10-214 Grounding connections for portable generator assemblies and vehicle-mounted or mobile generators (see Appendix B)

1) A portable generator assembly shall not be required to be connected to a grounding electrode if the generator has the neutral bonded to the frame.

2) A mobile or vehicle-mounted generator shall not be required to be connected to a grounding electrode under the following conditions:
   a) the generator does not exceed a low-voltage rated output;
   b) the generator has the neutral bonded to the frame;
   c) the conductive frame of the generator is connected to the conductive frame of the vehicle by an equipotential bonding conductor;
   d) the generator supplies only
      i) electrical equipment installed on the vehicle;
      ii) electrical equipment that is cord-and-plug connected through receptacles mounted on the vehicle or on the generator; or
      iii) any combination of the equipment specified in Items i) and ii); and
   e) the non-current-carrying conductive parts of the electrical equipment referred to in Item d) are supplied by a circuit incorporating a bonding conductor.

Impedance grounded systems

Ⓔ **10-300 Qualified persons** (see Appendix B)
Where an electrical system is connected to an impedance grounding device, the system shall be maintained by a qualified person.

10-302 Use (see Appendix B)

1) Ungrounded conductors of an impedance grounded system shall be insulated to the nominal line-to-line voltage of the system.

2) The integrity of an impedance grounded system shall be monitored, and the system shall have an audible or visual alarm that corresponds to the occurrence of
   a) a ground fault on current-carrying conductors, including the neutral conductor where line-to-neutral loads are served;
   b) a ground fault on the conductor connecting the impedance grounding device to the source; and

   c)   a loss of continuity of the impedance grounding circuit from the system source through the impedance grounding device to the grounded non-current-carrying conductive parts of the electrical system.

3)   The alarm required by Subrule 2), and any extra (i.e., redundant) alarms if installed, shall
   a)   be clearly labelled as to their purpose;
   b)   clearly annunciate the status of the system to persons monitoring it; and
   c)   continue signalling until the condition is corrected.

4)   On the occurrence of any of the conditions described in Subrule 2), an impedance grounded system shall be automatically and immediately de-energized except as permitted by Subrule 5).

5)   On detection of a ground fault on the ungrounded conductors, an impedance grounded system shall be permitted to remain energized if
   a)   the system is operating at 5 kV or less;
   b)   the system serves no neutral loads;
   c)   the ground fault current is controlled at 10 A or less; and
   d)   the impedance grounding device is rated for continuous use.

10-304 Impedance grounding devices

1)   Impedance grounding devices not having a continuous rating shall be permitted where
   a)   provision is made to automatically de-energize the system without intentional delay on the detection of a ground fault; and
   b)   the time rating of the device is coordinated with the time-current rating of the protective devices of the system.

2)   Impedance grounding devices shall have an insulation voltage rating at least equal to the system line-to-neutral voltage.

10-306 Location of impedance grounding device warning signs (see Appendix B)

Where impedance grounding devices are used, warning signs indicating that the system is impedance grounded and the maximum voltage at which the neutral may be operating relative to ground shall be placed at
a)   the supply source;
b)   the consumer's service box or equivalent; and
c)   the supply authority's metering equipment.

10-308 Conductors used with impedance grounding devices (see Appendix B)

1)   The conductor connecting the impedance grounding device to the system source shall
   a)   be insulated for the nominal system voltage;
   b)   be identified white or grey;
   c)   be routed as directly as practicable;
   d)   not be grounded;
   e)   be sized to conduct the rated current of the impedance grounding device, and in no case less than
     i)   No. 12 AWG if of copper; or
     ii)   No. 10 AWG if of aluminum; and
   f)   be protected from damage
     i)   mechanically; or
     ii)   by location.

2)   The grounded side of the impedance grounding device shall be connected to the non-current-carrying parts of the electrical equipment by an impedance system bonding jumper sized to conduct the rated current of the impedance grounding device, and in no case less than
   a)   No. 12 AWG if of copper; or
   b)   No. 10 AWG if of aluminum.

Ungrounded systems

10-400 Ungrounded systems (see Appendix B)

1) DC or AC systems shall be permitted to be ungrounded, provided that the system is
   a) equipped with suitable ground fault detection; and
   b) maintained by qualified persons.
2) On the occurrence of a ground fault, the ground fault detection shall activate a visual or audible alarm to indicate the presence of the ground fault.
3) The alarm required by Subrule 2), and any extra (i.e., redundant) alarms if installed, shall
   a) be clearly labelled as to their purpose;
   b) clearly annunciate the status of the system to persons monitoring it; and
   c) continue signalling until the condition has been corrected.
4) Extra-low-voltage dc or ac systems shall be permitted to be ungrounded without having to comply with the ground fault detection requirements specified in Subrules 1) to 3).

10-402 Grounding connections for equipment in an ungrounded system (see Appendix B)

1) There shall be no connection between the grounding conductor and the system neutral where one is present.
2) The grounding conductor shall connect the grounding electrode to the non-current-carrying conductive enclosure of
   a) the supply source equipment of separately derived systems; or
   b) the service box.

Bonding

Bonding — General

10-500 Current over bonding conductors (see Appendix B)

There shall be no objectionable passage of current over a bonding conductor.

10-502 Clean surfaces (see Appendix B)

Where a non-conductive protective coating such as paint or enamel is used on conductive equipment, conduit, couplings, or fittings, such coating shall be removed from threads and other contact surfaces, or penetrated, to ensure a good electrical connection at the point of bonding.

10-504 Dissimilar metals

Where dissimilar metals that are not compatible cannot be avoided at bonding connections, connections shall be made using methods or material that will minimize deterioration from galvanic action.

10-506 Continuity of bonding conductors

No automatic cut-out or switch shall be installed in the bonding conductor of a wiring system unless the opening of the cut-out or switch disconnects all sources of energy.

Equipment bonding

10-600 Bonding for fixed electrical equipment

1) Except as permitted by Subrule 2), non-current-carrying conductive parts of electrical equipment shall be connected to a bonding conductor.
2) Non-current-carrying conductive parts of extra-low-voltage electrical equipment shall not be required to be connected to a bonding conductor.

10-602 Conductors in parallel runs

Where conductors are installed in parallel in separate cables, raceways, or bus, a bonding conductor shall be installed with each group of parallel conductors.

10-604 Bonding continuity for service equipment (see Appendix B)

1) The bonding continuity for service raceways, cable armour, cable sheaths, and all service equipment enclosures containing service conductors, including meter fittings, boxes, or the like, shall be assured by
   a) threaded couplings and threaded connections to the conductive enclosures, with joints made up tight where rigid metal conduit is used;
   b) couplings and connectors made up tight where electrical metallic tubing is used; and
   c) bonding bushings supplemented with a bonding conductor where the connection to the enclosure is made using standard locknuts.
2) Notwithstanding Subrule 1) c), a bonding bushing shall not be required for cable assemblies incorporating an internal bonding conductor in continuous contact with the cable armour, provided that the internal bonding conductor extends from the cable and connects to the service equipment.

10-606 Bonding continuity at other than service equipment (see Appendix B)

1) Bonding continuity of metal raceway, metal-sheathed cable, or armoured cable shall be assured by one of the methods specified in Rule 10-604 1), or by using
   a) standard box connectors made up tight;
   b) two locknuts, one inside and one outside of boxes and cabinets; or
   c) one locknut and a metal conduit bushing, provided that the bushing can be installed so that it is mechanically secure and makes positive contact with the inside surface of the box or cabinet.
2) Reducing washers shall not be used to maintain the bonding continuity of the wiring system.

10-608 Loosely jointed metal raceways

Where a metal raceway serves as the bonding conductor, and expansion joints and telescoping sections are installed, the electrical continuity of the raceways shall be assured with a bonding conductor.

10-610 Bonding means — Fixed equipment (see Appendix B)

1) The bonding means for fixed equipment shall consist of one of the following:
   a) an effective metallic interconnection between fixed equipment, consisting of metal raceway, metal sheath, or cable armour except
      i) armour as specified in Subrules 2) and 3);
      ii) the sheath of mineral-insulated cable when not of copper or aluminum, as specified in Subrule 4); or
      iii) where the raceway or cables are
         A) run underground;
         B) run in locations coming within the scope of Section 22; or
         C) otherwise subject to corrosion;
   b) a bonding conductor that is run with circuit conductors as a part of a cable; or
   c) a bonding conductor that is run with circuit conductors installed in raceways.
2) The armour of armoured cables incorporating a bonding conductor shall not be deemed to fulfill the requirements of a bonding conductor except where both the armour and the bonding conductor are in continuous electrical contact.
3) Unless otherwise marked, the armour of flexible metal conduit and liquid-tight flexible metal conduit shall not be deemed to fulfill the requirements of a bonding conductor, and a bonding conductor shall be run within the conduit.
4) The sheath of mineral-insulated cable, when not of copper or aluminum, shall not be deemed to fulfill the requirements of the bonding conductor, and bonding shall be by the method specified in Subrule 1) b).

5) When single-conductor cables are used for fixed equipment, and the metal armour or sheath of the cable has been isolated from the equipment at one end in accordance with Rule 4-008, a separate bonding conductor shall be installed for the fixed equipment.

10-612 Bonding conductor connection to electrical equipment

1) The bonding conductor to conduits, cabinets, equipment, and the like shall be attached by means of lugs, pressure connectors, clamps, or other equally substantial means.
2) Connections that depend on solder shall not be used.
3) A bonding connection shall be made at every non-metallic outlet box for any fitting or device that requires connection to a bonding conductor.
4) Where the connections between the branch circuit and the internal conductors of fixed equipment pass through an access cover, the bonding conductor connection shall remain continuous when the cover is removed.
5) In the case of metal-enclosed systems where bonding is provided by the metal enclosure, and a device attached to the enclosure has a bonding terminal, a bonding conductor shall be installed to bond the device to the enclosure.
6) A bonding conductor connection to the bonding terminal of a device shall be installed such that disconnection or removal of the device will not interfere with, or interrupt, the continuity of the bonding conductor.

10-614 Size of system bonding jumper or bonding conductor (see Appendix B)

1) The size of a field-installed system bonding jumper shall not be less than that determined in accordance with Table 16 based on the ampere rating or setting of the overcurrent device protecting the ungrounded conductors.
2) The size of a bonding conductor installed in accordance with Rule 10-604 at service equipment shall not be less than that determined in accordance with Table 16 based on the allowable ampacity of the largest ungrounded conductor.
3) The size of a field-installed bonding conductor installed at other than service equipment shall not be less than that determined in accordance with Table 16 based on
   a) the overcurrent device protecting the ungrounded conductors; or
   b) the allowable ampacity of the largest ungrounded conductor for installations where the size of the circuit conductors is increased to compensate for voltage drop.
4) The size of a field-installed bonding conductor installed with each group of parallel conductors run in separate raceways or cables shall be in accordance with Subrule 3) divided by the number of groups of parallel conductors.
5) Notwithstanding Subrules 2), 3), and 4), the bonding conductor shall not be required to be larger than the current-carrying conductors.
6) A metal raceway that is permitted to be used as a bonding conductor shall be considered to meet the requirements of this Rule.
7) A bonding means that is integral to a cable assembly shall be considered to meet the requirements of this Rule.

Equipotential bonding

10-700 Equipotential bonding of non-electrical equipment (see Appendix B)

The following parts of non-electrical equipment shall be made equipotential with the non-current-carrying conductive parts of electrical equipment:
a) the continuous metal water piping system of a building supplied with electric power;
b) the continuous metal waste water piping system of a building supplied with electric power;
c) the continuous metal gas piping system of a building supplied with electric power;
d) raised floors of conductive material with electrical wiring under the raised floor;

e)   the conductive metal parts of structures that livestock access; and

f)   metal tower and station structures of passenger ropeways, passenger conveyors, or material ropeways.

10-702 Installation

1)   Conductors for equipotential bonding shall be permitted to be installed as open wiring, provided that they are adequately secured.

2)   Where installed in structural members, conductors for equipotential bonding shall be installed in the same manner as non-metallic sheathed cable, except that they do not require bushed holes where run through metal studs.

10-704 Material for equipotential bonding conductors

Equipotential bonding conductors shall be of materials permitted for grounding conductors or for bonding means.

10-706 Equipotential bonding connections to non-electrical equipment (see Appendix B)

Equipotential bonding connections to non-electrical materials shall be made mechanically secure and be suitable for the condition(s) to which they are subjected.

10-708 Equipotential bonding conductor size

1)   Except as permitted by Subrule 2), the size of an equipotential bonding conductor shall be not smaller than

a)   No. 6 AWG if of copper; or

b)   No. 4 AWG if of aluminum.

2)   The size of an equipotential bonding conductor installed as concealed wiring and mechanically protected shall be permitted to be a minimum No. 10 AWG copper or No. 8 AWG aluminum.

10

Section 12 — Wiring methods

Scope

12-000 Scope (see Appendix B)
1) The provisions of Section 12 apply to all wiring installations operating at 750 V or less, except for

Δ   a)   Class 2 circuits unless otherwise specified in Rules 12-2300 to 12-2320 and Section 16;
   b)   community antenna distribution and radio and television circuits unless otherwise specified in Section 54;
   c)   optical fiber cables unless otherwise specified in Section 56;
   d)   communication circuit conductors unless otherwise specified in Section 60; and
   e)   conductors that form an integral part of factory-built equipment.

2) The provisions of this Section apply also to installations operating at voltages in excess of 750 V, except as modified by the requirements of Section 36.

General requirements

12-010 Wiring in ducts and plenum chambers

Δ   1)   No electrical equipment of any type, unless marked for the purpose, shall be installed in ducts used to transport dust, loose stock, or flammable vapours.

Δ   2)   No electrical equipment, unless marked for the purpose, shall be installed
   a)   in any duct used for vapour removal or for ventilation of commercial-type cooking equipment; or
   b)   in any shaft that is required by regulation to contain only such ducts.

3) Where cables are installed in ducts, plenums, or hollow spaces that are used to transport or move air as part of an environmental air system or in a duct or plenum chamber to connect to an integral fan system, the cables shall be in accordance with the requirements of Rules 2-130 and 12-100.

4) Notwithstanding Subrule 3), where a plenum or hollow space is created by a suspended ceiling having lay-in panels or tiles, flexible cord not exceeding 3 m in length and terminated with an attachment plug shall be permitted to supply pole-type multi-outlet assemblies, provided that the flexible cord is listed in Table 11 for hard usage and the supply voltage does not exceed 300 V.

5) Where a furnace cold-air return duct is formed by boxing in between joists, wiring methods specified in this Section for use in the particular location shall be permitted to be used.

12-012 Underground installations (see Appendix B)
1) Direct buried cables or raceways shall be installed to meet the minimum cover requirements of Table 53.

2) The minimum cover requirements shall be permitted to be reduced by 150 mm where mechanical protection is placed in the trench over the underground installation.

3) Mechanical protection shall consist of one of the following and, when in flat form, shall be wide enough to extend at least 50 mm beyond the cables or raceways on each side:
   a)   treated planking at least 38 mm thick;
   b)   poured concrete at least 50 mm thick;
   c)   concrete slabs at least 50 mm thick;
   d)   concrete encasement at least 50 mm thick; or
   e)   other suitable material.

4) Direct buried cables shall be installed so that they run adjacent to each other and do not cross over each other and with a layer of screened sand with a maximum particle size of 4.75 mm or screened earth at least 75 mm deep both above and below the conductors.

5) Where cables rise for terminations or splices or where access is otherwise required, they shall be protected from mechanical damage by location or by rigid conduit terminated vertically in the

trench and including a bushing or bell end fitting, or other acceptable protection, at the bottom end from 300 mm above the bottom of the trench to at least 2 m above finished grade, and beyond that as may be required by other Rules of the Code, and with sufficient slack provided in the cables at the bottom end of the conduit so that the cables enter the conduit from a vertical position.

Δ 6) Where a deviation has been allowed in accordance with Rule 2-030, cables buried directly in earth shall be permitted to be spliced or tapped in trenches without the use of splice boxes.

7) Raceways or cables, if located in rock, shall be permitted to be installed at a lesser depth entrenched into the rock in a trench not less than 150 mm deep and grouted with concrete to the level of the rock surface.

Δ 8) Raceways and armoured or metal-sheathed cables suitable for direct burial shall be permitted to be installed directly beneath a concrete slab at grade level, provided that the concrete slab is not less than a nominal 100 mm in thickness, the location and depth of the underground installation is marked in a conspicuous, legible, and permanent manner, and the raceway or cable is not subject to damage during or after installation.

9) Any form of mechanical protection that may adversely affect the cable shall not be used.

10) Backfill containing large rocks, paving materials, cinders, large or sharply angular substances, or corrosive material shall not be placed in an excavation where such materials may damage cables, raceways, or other substructures, prevent adequate compaction of fill, or contribute to corrosion of cables, raceways, or other substructures.

11) The initial installation shall be provided with a suitable marking tape buried approximately halfway between the installation and grade level, or adequate marking in a conspicuous location to indicate the location and depth of the underground installation.

12) Where underground raceways or cables are subject to movement by settlement or frost, provision shall be made for the prevention of damage to the conductors, conductor insulation, or the electrical equipment.

13) For installations not covered by the foregoing requirements of this Rule, the requirements of CSA C22.3 No. 7, or the applicable standard, whichever is more stringent, shall apply.

12-014 Conductors in hoistways

1) Where a deviation has been allowed in accordance with Rule 2-030, and where conductors other than those used to furnish energy to the elevator or dumbwaiter are installed in hoistways, they shall be mineral-insulated cable, aluminum-sheathed cable, copper-sheathed cable, or armoured cable or be run in rigid metal conduit, flexible metal conduit, or electrical metallic tubing.

2) The cable, conduit, or tubing referred to in Subrule 1) shall be
   a) securely fastened to the hoistway construction; and
   b) arranged so that terminal, outlet, or junction boxes open outside the hoistway, except that pull boxes shall be permitted to be installed in long runs for the purpose of supporting or pulling in conductors.

12-016 Lightning down conductors

Where lightning down conductors are installed, electrical wiring shall, where practicable, be kept at least 2 m from such conductors, except where bonding is provided in accordance with Rule 10-104.

12-018 Entry of raceways and cables into buildings

Holes in outer walls or roofs of buildings through which raceways or cables pass shall be filled to prevent infiltration of moisture.

12-020 Wiring under raised floors for data processing and similar systems

1) Flexible cords or cables, liquid-tight flexible conduit, and appliance wiring material with a jacket or overall covering to connect and interconnect data processing and similar systems shall be permitted to be installed under raised floors, provided that

   a) the raised floor is of non-combustible construction and, if of conductive material, is bonded to ground in accordance with Rules 10-700 to 10-708; and

   b) the cords or cables terminate in attachment plugs that have configurations in accordance with Diagram 2 or that are classified as industrial-type, special-use attachment plugs, receptacles, or connectors.

2) Branch circuit conductors installed under raised floors to supply receptacles shall be installed in rigid conduit, electrical metallic tubing, flexible metal conduit, armoured cable, or metal-sheathed cable, including mineral-insulated cable other than the lightweight type.

Conductors

General

12-100 Types of insulated conductors and cables (see Appendix B)

Insulated conductors and cables installed in any location shall be suitable for the condition of use as indicated in Table 19 for the particular location involved and with respect to, but not limited to

a) moisture, if any;

b) corrosive action, if any;

c) temperature;

d) degree of enclosure; and

e) mechanical protection.

Δ 12-102 Insulated conductors (see Appendix B)

1) Insulated conductors shall not be handled or installed when the ambient temperature is sufficiently low as to be liable to cause damage to the insulation.

2) Such insulated conductors shall not be installed so as to permit flexing or movement of the conductors after installation if the ambient temperature is liable to become low enough to damage the insulation during flexing or movement.

3) Except as provided for by Rules 12-122, 12-400, and 12-406, or as otherwise required by other Sections of this Code, insulated conductors and cables shall be of the types specified in Table 19 for the specific condition of use and shall be suitable for the particular location involved with respect to, but not limited to

   a) moisture;

   b) corrosive action;

   c) temperature;

   d) degree of enclosure; and

   e) exposure to mechanical damage.

4) Where harmful condensed vapours or liquids of either an acid or alkaline nature, or organic solvents such as hydrocarbons, ketones, esters, alcohols, or their liquid derivatives, can collect on or come in contact with the insulation, jacket, or covering on conductors or cables, such insulation, jacket, or covering shall be of a type resistant to these substances, or the insulation shall be protected by a sheath of lead or by other material impervious to the corrosive element.

12-104 Flame-tested coverings

Where the insulation on a conductor has a flame-tested covering, the covering shall be removed sufficiently at terminals and splices to prevent creepage of current over it.

12-106 Multi- and single-conductor cables (see Appendix B)

1) Where multi-conductor cable is used, all conductors of a circuit shall be contained in the same multi-conductor cable except that, where it is necessary to run conductors in parallel due to the capacity of an ac circuit, additional cables shall be permitted to be used, provided that any one such cable

   a) includes an equal number of conductors from each phase and the neutral; and

   b) is in accordance with Rule 12-108.

Δ 2) Insulated conductors in a cable shall not be used for connection to different power or distribution transformers or other different sources of voltage, except where

   a) the conductors are used for the supply and/or control of remote devices;

   b) the conductors are insulated for the voltage of the circuit having the highest voltage; and

   c) none of the conductors of the circuits of lower voltages is directly connected to a lighting branch circuit.

3) Where single-conductor cables are used, all single-conductor cables of a circuit shall be of the same type and temperature rating and, if run in parallel, shall be in accordance with Rule 12-108.

4) Single-conductor armoured cable used as a current-carrying conductor shall be of a type having non-magnetic armour.

5) A single-conductor cable carrying a current over 200 A shall be run and supported in such a manner that the cable is not encircled by magnetic material.

12-108 Conductors in parallel (see Appendix B)

1) Ungrounded and grounded circuit conductors of similar conductivity in sizes No. 1/0 AWG and larger, copper or aluminum, shall be permitted to be installed in parallel sets provided that each parallel phase or grounded conductor set individually consists of conductors that

   a) are free of splices throughout the total length;

   b) have the same circular mil area;

   c) have the same type of insulation;

   d) are terminated in the same manner;

   e) are of the same conductor material; and

   f) are the same length.

Δ 2) Notwithstanding Subrule 1) a), a single splice shall be permitted at each termination point

   a) to meet the requirements of Rule 4-006; and

   b) where spliced in the same manner.

3) In parallel sets, insulated conductors of one phase, polarity, or grounded circuit conductor shall not be required to have the same characteristics as those of another phase, polarity, or grounded circuit conductor.

4) The orientation of single-conductor cables in parallel, with respect to each other and to those in other phases, shall be such as to minimize the difference in inductive reactance and the unequal division of current.

5) Conductors of similar conductivity in sizes smaller than No. 1/0 AWG copper shall be permitted in parallel to supply control power to indicating instruments and devices, contactors, relays, solenoids, and similar control devices, provided that

   a) they are contained within one cable;

   b) the ampacity of each individual conductor is sufficient to carry the entire load current shared by the parallel conductors; and

   c) the overcurrent protection is such that the ampacity of each individual conductor will not be exceeded if one or more of the parallel conductors becomes inadvertently disconnected.

6) Where parallel conductors include grounded circuit conductors, each parallel set shall have a separate grounded circuit conductor.

12

7) Where the size of neutral conductors is reduced in conformance with Rule 4-018, neutral conductors smaller than No. 1/0 AWG shall be permitted in circuits run in parallel, provided that they are installed in conformance with all the requirements of Subrule 1).

12-110 Radii of bends in insulated conductors and cables
The radii of bends in insulated conductors and cables shall be sufficiently large to ensure that no damage is done to the conductors or cables or to their insulation, covering, or sheathing.

12-112 Conductor joints and splices
Ⓔ Δ 1) Conductors shall be spliced or joined with splicing devices or by brazing, welding, or soldering with a fusible metal or alloy.

2) Soldered splices shall first be spliced or joined so as to be mechanically and electrically secure without solder and then be soldered.

3) Joints or splices shall be covered with an insulation equivalent to that on the conductors being joined.

4) Joints or splices in conductors and cables shall be accessible.

5) Splices in underground runs of cable, if required due to damage to the original installation, shall be permitted to be made
   a) in junction boxes suitably protected from mechanical damage that are located at least 1 m above grade and secured to buildings or to stub poles; or
   b) notwithstanding the requirements of Subrule 4), by means of splicing devices or materials (kits) for direct earth burial.

12-114 Ends of insulated conductors
When the ends of insulated conductors at switches, outlets, and in similar places are not in use, they shall be insulated in the manner prescribed for joints and splices.

12-116 Termination of conductors (see Appendix B)
1) Connection of conductors to terminal parts shall be made by means of pressure connectors, solder lugs, or splices to flexible leads.

Δ 2) The portion of stranded conductors to be held by binding-screw terminals or solderless wire connectors shall have the strands confined so that there will be no stray strands to cause either short-circuits or grounds.

3) Stranded and solid conductors No. 10 AWG and smaller shall be permitted to be connected by means of binding-screw terminals or studs and nuts that have upturned lugs or the equivalent.

4) Stranded and solid conductors larger than No. 10 AWG shall be terminated in solderless conductor connectors or shall be permitted to be soldered into conductor connectors suitable for the purpose, except where prohibited by Section 10.

12-118 Termination and splicing of aluminum conductors
1) Adequate precautions shall be taken in the termination and splicing of aluminum conductors, including the removal of insulation and separators, the cleaning (wire brushing) of stranded conductors, and the compatibility and installation of fittings.

Δ 2) A joint compound, capable of penetrating the oxide film and preventing its reforming, shall be used for terminating or splicing all sizes of stranded aluminum conductors, unless the termination or splice is marked for use without compound.

Δ 3) Equipment connected to aluminum conductors shall be marked for the purpose, except
   a) where the equipment has only leads for connection to the supply; and
   b) equipment such as outlet boxes having only grounding terminals.

4) Aluminum conductors shall not be terminated or spliced in wet locations unless the termination or splice is adequately protected against corrosion.

5) Field-assembled connections between aluminum lugs and aluminum or copper busbars or lugs, involving bolts or studs 9.5 mm in diameter or larger, shall include as part of the joint any of the following means of allowing for expansion of the parts:
   a) a conical spring washer;
   b) a helical spring washer of the heavy series, provided that a flat steel washer of a thickness not less than one-sixth of the nominal diameter of the bolt or stud is interposed between the helical washer and any aluminum surface against which it would bear; or
   c) aluminum bolts or studs, provided that all the elements in the assembled connection are of aluminum.

Δ 6) Connection of aluminum conductors to wiring devices having binding-screw terminals around which conductors can be looped under the head of the screw shall be made by forming the conductor in a clockwise direction around the screw into three-fourths of a complete loop, and only one conductor shall be connected to any one screw.

12-120 Supporting of conductors (see Appendix B)
1) Conductors shall be supported so that no damaging strain is imposed on the terminals of any electrical apparatus or devices or on joints or taps.
2) Conductors in vertical raceways shall be supported independently of the terminal connections and at intervals not exceeding those specified in Table 21, and such supports shall maintain the continuity of the raceway system without damage to the conductors or their covering.
3) Conductors in raceways shall not hang over the edges of bushings, bends, or fittings of any kind in such a manner that the insulation may be damaged.
4) Vertical runs of armoured or sheathed cable such as TECK90, RA90, RC90, AC90, and ACWU90 shall have the internal conductor assembly supported at intervals not exceeding those specified in Table 21, or by
   a) incorporating a bend or bends equivalent to a total of not less than 90° at intervals not exceeding the distances specified in Table 21;
   b) installation of a horizontal run of the cable not less than the length of the vertical run; or
   c) use of cable that is specifically designed for vertical runs.

Δ **12-122 Equipment wire** (see Appendix B)
1) Equipment wire shall be of the types specified in Table 11 for the specific condition of use and shall be suitable for the particular location involved with respect to, but not limited to
   a) moisture;
   b) corrosive action;
   c) temperature;
   d) degree of enclosure; and
   e) exposure to mechanical damage.
2) Equipment wire used as luminaire wiring shall be not smaller than a No. 18 AWG copper conductor.
3) Equipment wire, including its assemblies for applications other than that given in Subrule 2), shall be not smaller than No. 26 AWG copper when rated 300 V and not smaller than No. 24 AWG copper when rated 600 V.

Open wiring

12-200 Open wiring Rules
Rules 12-202 to 12-224 apply only to single insulated conductors run as open wiring.

12-202 Types of insulated conductors
insulated conductors shall be of the types specified in Rules 12-100 and 12-102.

12-204 Spacing of insulated conductors

1) Spacings between insulated conductors and between insulated conductors and adjacent surfaces shall, except as otherwise provided for in this Rule, comply with the following:
   a) for normally dry locations, the spacings shall be not less than those specified in Table 20;
   b) where circuits of different voltages are run parallel to each other, the separation between adjacent insulated conductors of the different circuits shall be not less than that specified in Table 20 for insulated conductors of the circuit having the higher voltage; and
   c) in damp locations, a separation of at least 25 mm shall be maintained between insulated conductors and adjacent surfaces.
2) In all locations, a separation of at least 25 mm shall be maintained between insulated conductors and adjacent metal piping or conducting materials.
3) Where insulated conductors are run across the open faces of joists, studs, or timber, the separation between insulated conductors shall be as specified in Rule 12-212.
4) At connections to fittings and devices or in other cases where it is not practical to maintain the spacing specified in Subrules 1), 2), and 3), the insulated conductors shall be installed in raceways or insulating tubing.

12-206 Insulated conductor supports

1) Insulated conductors shall be supported rigidly on non-combustible, absorption-resisting insulators.
2) Split knobs shall not be used to support insulated conductors larger than No. 8 AWG copper or aluminum.
3) Conductors supported on solid knobs shall be securely tied to the knobs by tie-wires having insulation of the same type as that on the conductors that they secure.
4) Where used on metal surfaces, thermoplastic-insulated conductors shall not be mounted in split knobs or cleats.

12-208 Insulated conductors on flat surfaces

Where insulated conductors are run on flat surfaces, they shall be supported rigidly at intervals of not more than 1.5 m.

12-210 Material for attachment of insulated conductor supports

Knobs and cleats shall be fastened securely with screws.

12-212 Protection from mechanical damage

1) Where insulated conductors are supported on or run across the open faces of joists, wall studs, or other timber or on walls where exposed to mechanical damage, they shall be protected by running-boards, guard-strips, wooden boxing, or sleeves of iron pipe.
2) Where insulated conductors are not exposed to mechanical damage, they shall be permitted to be run directly from timber to timber but shall be
   a) of not less than No. 8 AWG copper or aluminum;
   b) separated from each other by not less than 150 mm; and
   c) supported at each timber.
3) Open wiring shall not be run across the tops of ceiling joists in unfinished attics or similar places.

12-214 Material for running-boards, guard-strips, and boxing

1) Material for running-boards, guard-strips, and boxing shall be at least 19 mm thick and the edges of running-boards shall project at least 12 mm beyond the insulators on both sides.
2) Guard-strips shall be at least as high as the insulators and placed as close to the insulated conductors as Table 20 permits.
3) In wooden boxing, there shall be a clear space of at least 25 mm between insulated conductors and adjacent surfaces, and the ends of boxing not abutting on the structure of the building shall be closed.

12-216 Ends of insulated conductors
1) Insulated conductors shall not be brought to a dead-end at any fitting distant more than 300 mm from the last supporting insulator.
2) Where insulated conductors of No. 8 AWG copper or aluminum or larger are run as open wiring, solid knobs or strain insulators shall be used at the ends of the run.

12-218 Insulated conductors passing through walls or floors
Where insulated conductors pass through walls, floors, timbers, or partitions, they shall be installed in raceways or insulating tubing.

12-220 Maintaining clearances
Sub-bases shall be installed under all surface-mounted switches and receptacles unless adequate clearances are otherwise maintained.

12-222 Where open wiring connects to other systems of wiring
Where open wiring is connected to conductors in raceways, armoured cable, or non-metallic-sheathed cable, the junction shall be made in a box, or at, or in, a fitting having a separately bushed hole for each conductor.

12-224 Provision for bonding
Where open wiring is used, provision for bonding to ground shall be made in accordance with Section 10.

Exposed wiring on exteriors of buildings and between buildings on the same premises

12-300 Exterior exposed wiring Rules
Rules 12-302 to 12-318 apply only to exposed wiring run on the exterior surfaces of buildings or between buildings on the same premises.

12-302 Types of insulated conductors and cables
Insulated conductors and cables shall be of types suitable for exposure to the weather as indicated in Table 19.

12-304 Location of insulated conductors and cables
1) Subject to the provisions of Rule 6-112, where the insulated conductors and cables are supported on or in close proximity to the exterior surfaces of buildings, they shall be installed and protected so that they shall not be a hazard to persons or be exposed to mechanical damage, and they shall not be less than 4.5 m from the ground unless a deviation has been allowed in accordance with Rule 2-030.
2) Where the insulated conductors and cables are exposed to mechanical damage from awnings, swinging signs, shutters, or other movable objects, they shall be run in rigid conduit made watertight.

12-306 Insulated conductor and cable supports
1) Insulated conductors and cables on the exterior surfaces of buildings shall be supported by brackets, racks, or insulators at intervals of not more than 3 m, and the individual insulated conductors and cables shall be a distance of at least 150 mm from one another and at least 50 mm from the adjacent surfaces.
2) Where petticoat insulators are used, they shall be installed at intervals of not more than 4.5 m under normal conditions and at smaller intervals where the insulated conductors and cables are subject to disturbance and shall be located so as to hold the individual insulated conductors and cables at least 300 mm apart and at least 50 mm from adjacent surfaces.
3) Where the insulated conductors and cables are not exposed to the weather, they shall be permitted to be supported on glass or porcelain knobs placed at intervals of not more than 1.5 m and holding the insulated conductors and cables at least 25 mm from adjacent surfaces.

4) Where insulated conductors and cables connected to a voltage of 300 V or less are located in proximity to insulated conductors and cables of a higher voltage not exceeding 750 V, the insulated conductors and cables of the higher voltage shall be mounted above and kept at least 300 mm away from the insulated conductors and cables of the lower voltage.

12-308 Minimum size of overhead conductors

Single conductors run aerially between buildings or supports on the same premises in spans exceeding 4.5 m shall be not smaller than

a) No. 10 AWG copper or No. 6 AWG aluminum for spans of more than 4.5 m but not more than 15 m;

b) No. 8 AWG copper or No. 4 AWG aluminum for spans of more than 15 m but not more than 30 m; and

c) No. 6 AWG copper or No. 3 AWG aluminum for spans of more than 30 m but not more than 40 m.

12-310 Clearance of insulated conductors and cables

Insulated conductors and cables shall be located or guarded so that they cannot be reached by a person standing on a fire escape, flat roof, or other portion of a building, and they shall be at least 2.5 m above the highest point of a flat roof or a roof that can be readily walked upon and at least 1 m above peaked roofs or the highest point of roofs that cannot be readily walked upon, except that where a deviation has been allowed in accordance with Rule 2-030, they shall be permitted to be less than 2.5 m but not less than 2 m above the highest point of a flat roof or roofs that can be readily walked upon.

12-312 Conductors over buildings

Conductors shall not be installed over buildings unless a deviation has been allowed in accordance with Rule 2-030.

12-314 Conductors on trestles

Where conductors pass over buildings, they shall, where practicable, be supported on structures not connected to the building but, where not practicable, they shall be supported on and secured to trestles constructed to bear the mechanical force of the conductors.

12-316 Power supply insulated conductors and cables

The insulated conductors and cables of a power supply system attached to the exterior surfaces of buildings shall be at least 300 mm from the cables of a communication system, unless one system is in conduit or is permanently separated from other systems by a continuous fixed non-conductor other than the insulation on the conductors.

12-318 Use of neutral supported cables

When neutral supported cables are used, the following requirements shall apply:

a) they shall not be mounted directly on any surface;

b) they shall be secured so that they will be not less than

   i) 1 m from a building in the case of Types NS75 and NS90; or

   ii) 50 mm from a building in the case of Types NS75 and NS90, marked FT1;

c) they shall be supported in spans of not more than 38 m in length;

d) the insulated conductors shall be secured to the messenger at all terminations; and

e) the bare neutral (messenger) when used as a neutral conductor forming part of an electrical circuit shall be

   i) supplied from a grounded ac system;

   ii) attached to an insulator at points of support and at terminations; and

   iii) not connected to or in contact with any grounded surface except as permitted by other Rules of this Code.

Δ

Flexible cables

12-400 Flexible cord Rules
Rules 12-402 to 12-406 apply only to the installation of flexible cord.

12-402 Uses of flexible cord (see Appendix B)
1) Flexible cord shall be of the types specified in Table 11 for the specific condition of use and shall be suitable for the particular location involved with respect to, but not limited to
   a) moisture;
   b) corrosive action;
   c) temperature;
   d) degree of enclosure; and
   e) exposure to mechanical damage.
2) Flexible cord shall be permitted to be used for
   a) electrical equipment for household or similar use that is intended to be
      i) moved from place to place; or
      ii) detachably connected according to a *Canadian Electrical Code, Part II* Standard;
   b) electrical equipment for industrial use that must be capable of being moved from place to place for operation;
   c) pendants;
   d) wiring of cranes, hoists, passenger ropeways, and passenger conveyors;
   e) the connection of stationary equipment to facilitate its interchange, where a deviation is allowed in accordance with Rule 2-030;
   f) the prevention of transmission of noise and vibration;
   g) the connection of electrical components between which relative motion is necessary;
   h) the connection of appliances such as ranges and clothes dryers; and
   i) both the connection, using an attachment plug, and the interconnection of data processing systems, provided that the cord is of the extra-hard-usage type.
3) Flexible cord and cord sets shall not be used
   a) as a substitute for the fixed wiring of structures and shall not be
      i) permanently secured to any structural member;
      ii) run through holes in walls, ceilings, or floors; or
      iii) run through doorways, windows, or similar openings;
   b) at temperatures above the temperature rating of the cord or at temperatures sufficiently low as to be liable to result in damage to the insulation or overall covering; and
   c) for the suspension of any device weighing more than 2.3 kg, unless the cord and device assembly are marked as capable of supporting a weight up to 11 kg.
4) Flexible cord shall be protected against mechanical damage by an insulating bushing or some other effective means where it enters or passes through the enclosure wall or the partitioning of a device or enters a lampholder.
5) Where a flexible cord is used as an extension cord or to plug into an appliance or other device, no live parts shall be exposed when one end is connected to a source of supply and the other end is free.

12-404 Flexible cord used in show windows or show cases
1) Flexible cord used in show windows or show cases shall, except for chain-type luminaires, be of at least hard-usage types.
2) The use of flexible cord to supply current to portable lamps and other devices for exhibition purposes shall be permitted.

12

12-406 Uses of portable power cable (see Appendix B)

1) Portable power cables shall be of the types specified in Table 11 for the specific condition of use and shall be suitable for the particular location involved with respect to, but not limited to
   a) moisture;
   b) corrosive action;
   c) temperature;
   d) degree of enclosure; and
   e) exposure to mechanical damage.

2) Portable power cables shall be permitted to be used for
   a) electrical equipment that is intended to be
      i) moved from place to place; or
      ii) detachably connected according to a *Canadian Electrical Code, Part II* Standard;
   b) wiring of cranes and hoists;
   c) the connection of stationary equipment to facilitate its interchange;
   d) the connection of electrical components between which relative motion is necessary; and
   e) the connection of equipment used in conjunction with travelling amusement rides.

3) Portable power cable shall not be used
   a) as a substitute for the fixed wiring of structures and shall not be
      i) permanently secured to any structural member;
      ii) run through holes in walls, ceilings, or floors of permanent structures; or
      iii) run through doorways, windows, or similar openings of permanent structures; or
   b) at a temperature above the temperature rating of the cable or at a temperature sufficiently low as to be liable to result in damage to the insulation or overall covering.

4) Notwithstanding Subrule 3) a), Type DLO cable in sizes 1/0 or larger shall be permitted to be used in permanent installations in cable tray, provided that the cable
   a) is marked as Type TC cable;
   b) conforms with the conditions of use for Type TC cable in accordance with Rule 12-2202 and as listed in Table 19;
   c) terminates in connectors marked for use with fine-strand cables; and
   d) has an ampacity rating as described in Table 12E and Rule 4-004.

5) Where portable power cable enters or passes through the wall of an enclosure or fitting, it shall be protected in accordance with Rule 12-3022.

6) Where a single-conductor Type DLO cable is installed in accordance with Subrule 4), installation shall comply with Rule 4-008 3) to 6).

Non-metallic-sheathed cable

12-500 Non-metallic-sheathed cable Rules

Rules 12-502 to 12-526 apply only to conductors run as non-metallic-sheathed cable.

12-502 Maximum voltage

Non-metallic-sheathed cable shall not be used where the voltage exceeds 300 V between any two conductors.

12-504 Use of non-metallic-sheathed cable (see Appendix B)

Non-metallic-sheathed cable shall be permitted in or on buildings of combustible construction and in or on other types of construction where acceptable.

12-506 Method of installation (see Appendices B and G)

1) The cable shall be run in continuous lengths between outlet boxes, junction boxes, and panel boxes as a loop system and the joints, splices, and taps shall be made in the boxes.

2) Where concealed wiring is connected to non-metallic-sheathed cable, the junction shall be made in a box.

3) Where open wiring is connected to non-metallic-sheathed cable, the junction shall be made in a box or at, or in, a fitting having a separately bushed hole for each conductor.

4) Where non-metallic-sheathed cable is run in proximity to heating sources, transfer of heat to the cable shall be minimized by means of an air space of at least
   a) 25 mm between the cable and heating ducts and piping;
   b) 50 mm between the cable and masonry or concrete chimneys; or
   c) 150 mm between the cable and chimney and flue cleanouts.

5) Notwithstanding Subrule 4), a thermal barrier conforming to the requirements of the *National Building Code of Canada* or local building legislation shall be permitted to be installed between the cable and heating sources to maintain the ambient temperature of the cable at not more than 30 °C.

6) Two-conductor cable shall not be stapled on edge.

12-508 Bending and stapling of cable (see Appendix G)
The cable shall not be bent, handled, or stapled in such a way that the insulated conductors or outer covering is damaged.

12-510 Running of cable between boxes and fittings (see Appendices B and G)
Δ 1) Where the cable is run between boxes and fittings, it shall be supported by straps, Type 2S or 21S cable ties, or other devices located
   a) within 300 mm of every box or fitting; and
   b) at intervals of not more than 1.5 m throughout the run.

2) Cables run through holes in joists or studs shall be considered to be supported.

3) Notwithstanding Subrules 1) and 2), where the cable is run as concealed wiring such that it is impracticable to support it, and where metal sheeting or cladding, metal joists, metal top or bottom plates, or metal studs are not used, the cable shall be permitted to be fished and need not be supported between boxes and fittings.

Δ 4) Notwithstanding Subrule 1) a), where cable is run to a switch or a receptacle with an integral enclosure incorporating an integral cable clamp, the cable shall be supported by straps, Type 2S or 21S cable ties, or other devices located within 300 mm of the switch or receptacle wall opening, and there shall be at least a 300 mm loop of unbroken cable or 150 mm of a cable end available on the interior side of the finished wall to permit replacement.

12-512 Not to be embedded (see Appendix G)
The cable shall not be buried in plaster, cement, or similar finish.

12-514 Protection on joists and rafters (see Appendix G)
Cables shall not be run on or across
a) the upper faces of ceiling joists or the lower faces of rafters in attic or roof spaces, where the vertical distance between the joists and the rafters exceeds 1 m; or
b) the lower faces of basement joists, unless suitably protected from mechanical damage.

Δ 12-516 Protection for cable in concealed installations (see Appendices B and G)
1) Where the cable is run through studs, joists, or similar members, the outer surfaces of the cable shall be kept a distance of at least 32 mm from the edges of the members, or the cable shall be protected from mechanical damage by
   a) a protector plate covering the width of the member; or
   b) a cylindrical bushing sized for the hole through the member, and extending a minimum of 13 mm beyond both sides of the member.

2) Where the cable is run through or along metal studs, joists, sheathing, or cladding, it shall be
   a) located so as to be effectively protected from mechanical damage both during and after installation; and
   b) protected where it passes through a member by an insert adequately secured in place.
3) Where the cable is installed immediately behind a baseboard, it shall be effectively protected from mechanical damage from driven nails.

12-518 Protection for cable in exposed installations (see Appendix G)
Cable used in exposed wiring shall be adequately protected against mechanical damage where it passes through a floor, where it is less than 1.5 m above a floor, or where it is exposed to mechanical damage.

12-520 Fished cable installation
Where the cable is used in concealed wiring and it is impracticable to provide the supports required by Rule 12-510, and where metal sheeting or cladding, metal joists, metal top or bottom plates, or metal studs are not used, the cable shall be permitted to be fished.

12-522 Where outlet boxes are not required
1) Where the cable is exposed, switch, outlet, and tap devices of insulating material shall be permitted to be used without boxes.
2) The openings in the devices shall fit closely around the outer covering of the cable.
3) The device shall fully enclose any part of the cable from which any part of the covering has been removed.
4) Where the conductors are connected to the devices by binding-screw terminals, there shall be as many screws as there are conductors, unless the cables are clamped within the device.

12-524 Types of boxes and fittings
1) Boxes and fittings shall be of a type for use with non-metallic-sheathed cable.
2) Where grounded metal boxes are not required by these Rules, outlet and switch boxes shall be permitted to be of fire-resisting moulded composition insulating material, furnished with a cover of the same material.

12-526 Provision for bonding
Where non-metallic-sheathed cable is used, provision for bonding to ground shall be made in accordance with Section 10.

Armoured cable

Δ ### 12-600 Armoured cable Rules
Rules 12-602 to 12-618 apply only to armoured cable installations.

12-602 Use (see Appendix B)
1) Armoured cable shall be permitted to be installed in or on buildings or portions of buildings of either combustible or non-combustible construction.
2) Armoured cable shall be of the type listed in Table 19 as suitable for direct burial if used
   a) for underground runs;
   b) for circuits in masonry or concrete, provided that the cable is encased or embedded in at least 50 mm of the masonry or concrete; or
   c) in locations where it will be exposed to weather, continuous moisture, excessive humidity, or to oil or other substances having a deteriorating effect on the insulation.
3) Notwithstanding Subrule 2), armoured cable in which the armouring is made wholly or in part of aluminum shall not be embedded in concrete containing reinforcing steel, unless
   a) the concrete is known to contain no chloride additives; or

b) the armour has been treated with a bituminous base of paint or other means to prevent galvanic corrosion of the aluminum.

4) Where armoured cables are laid in or under cinders or cinder concrete, they shall be protected from corrosive action by a grouting of non-cinder concrete at least 25 mm thick entirely surrounding them unless they are 450 mm or more under the cinders or cinder concrete.

5) In buildings of non-combustible construction, armoured cables having conductors not larger than No. 10 AWG copper or aluminum shall be permitted to be laid on the face of the masonry or other material of which the walls and ceiling are constructed and shall be permitted to be buried in the plaster finish for extensions from existing outlets only.

6) Armoured cable with overall jacket shall be permitted for use in a raceway when it is installed in accordance with Rule 12-902 2).

12-604 Protection for armoured cables in lanes
If subject to mechanical damage and unless otherwise protected, steel guards of not less than No. 10 MSG, adequately secured, shall be installed to protect armoured cables less than 2 m above grade in lanes and driveways.

12-606 Use of thermoplastic-covered armoured cable
Armoured cable of the type listed in Table 19 as suitable for direct earth burial and having a thermoplastic outer covering shall be used only where the outer covering will not be subjected to mechanical damage.

12-608 Continuity of armoured cable
Armoured cable shall be run in a manner such that the mechanical and electrical continuity of the armour is maintained throughout the run, and the armour of cables shall be mechanically and electrically secured to all equipment to which it is attached.

12-610 Terminating armoured cable (see Appendix B)
1) Where conductors issue from armour, they shall be protected from abrasion by
   a) an insulating bushing or equivalent protection installed between the conductors and the armour; or
   b) the inner jacket of an armoured cable, provided that the inner jacket is left protruding a minimum of 5 mm beyond the armour.
2) Where conductors are No. 8 AWG or larger, copper or aluminum, such protection shall consist of
   a) insulated-type bushings, unless the equipment is equipped with a hub having a smoothly rounded throat; or
   b) insulating material fastened securely in place that will separate the conductors from the armoured cable fittings and afford adequate resistance to mechanical damage.
3) Where armoured cable is fastened to equipment, the connector or clamp shall be of such design as to leave the insulating bushing or its equivalent visible for inspection.
4) Where conductors connected to open wiring issue from the ends of armouring, they shall be protected with boxes or with fittings having a separately bushed hole for each conductor.

12-612 Proximity to knob-and-tube and non-metallic-sheathed cable systems
Where armoured cable is used in a building in which concealed knob-and-tube wiring or concealed non-metallic-sheathed cable wiring is installed, the cable shall not be fished if there is a possibility of damage to the existing wiring.

12-614 Radii of bends in armoured cables
1) Where armoured cables are bent during installation, the radius of the curve of the inner edge of the bends shall be at least 6 times the external diameter of the armoured cable.
2) Bends shall be made without undue distortion of the armour and without damage to its inner or outer surfaces.

12

3) Where armoured cables are installed as described in Rule 12-602 6), the minimum bending radii measured at the innermost surface of the conduit or tubing shall be not less than
   a) 10.5 times the diameter of the cable for low-voltage cable;
   b) 18 times the diameter of the cable for high-voltage cable; or
   c) those specified by the cable manufacturer.

12-616 Concealed armoured cable installation

1) Where armoured cable is run through studs, joists, or other members, it shall be
   a) located so that its outer circumference is at least 32 mm from the nearest edge of the members; or
   b) protected from mechanical damage where it passes through the holes in the members.
2) Where armoured cable is installed immediately behind baseboards, it shall be protected from mechanical damage from driven nails.

12-618 Running of cable between boxes, etc.

Armoured cable shall be supported between boxes and fittings in accordance with Rule 12-510.

Mineral-insulated cable, aluminum-sheathed cable, and copper-sheathed cable

12-700 Mineral-insulated cable, aluminum-sheathed cable, and copper-sheathed cable Rules

Rules 12-702 to 12-716 cover the installation of mineral-insulated cable, aluminum-sheathed cable, and copper-sheathed cable and amend the other Rules of this Code where they apply.

12-702 Use

1) Mineral-insulated cable, aluminum-sheathed cable, and copper-sheathed cable shall be permitted to be installed in or on buildings or portions of buildings of either combustible or non-combustible construction.
2) Lightweight mineral-insulated cable shall be used only in multi-conductor assemblies.

12-704 Use when embedded

1) Mineral-insulated cable, round aluminum-sheathed cable, and copper-sheathed cable, except as noted in Subrule 3), shall be permitted to be used for underplaster extensions from existing outlets only or when encased or embedded in at least 50 mm of masonry or poured concrete.
2) Except as noted in Subrule 3), flat two-conductor aluminum-sheathed cable shall be permitted to be used for underplaster extensions from existing outlets only or, where a deviation has been allowed in accordance with Rule 2-030, embedded in masonry or concrete.
3) Cable having an aluminum sheath shall not be embedded in concrete containing reinforcing steel, unless
   a) the concrete is known to contain no chloride additives; or
   b) the sheath has been treated with a bituminous base paint or other means to prevent galvanic corrosion of the aluminum.

12-706 Method of supporting (see Appendix B)

Δ 1) Mineral-insulated cable, aluminum-sheathed cable, and copper-sheathed cable shall be securely supported by staples, straps, hangers, Type 2S or 21S cable ties, or similar fittings in such a manner as not to
   a) damage the sheath of the cable; or
   b) subject the cable or its termination fittings to undue strain.
2) Mineral-insulated cable, aluminum-sheathed cable, and copper-sheathed cable shall be secured at intervals not exceeding 2 m, except where the cable is fished and adequate supports are installed, if needed, adjacent to termination fittings.

3) When settlement of a structure may occur due to weight of contents, as in certain grain storage occupancies, provision shall be made so that mineral-insulated cable, aluminum-sheathed cable, and copper-sheathed cable runs, including their termination fittings, will not be subjected to undue strain.

4) Mineral-insulated cable, aluminum-sheathed cable, and copper-sheathed cable shall be permitted to be run on the surface of walls, partitions, or ceilings, or on or across structural members, subject to the applicable requirements of Rule 12-710.

Δ 12-708 Direct earth burial
Mineral-insulated cable having an aluminum outer sheath and aluminum-sheathed cable in direct contact with the earth shall be provided with a jacket or other corrosion-resisting covering.

12-710 Mechanical protection
1) Where subject to mechanical damage, mineral-insulated cable, aluminum-sheathed cable, and copper-sheathed cable shall be suitably protected.

2) Where mineral-insulated cable, aluminum-sheathed cable, or copper-sheathed cable is installed on the face of a wall, partition, ceiling, or structural member within 1.5 m of the floor, and in all locations where subject to mechanical damage, as for instance from industrial tractors, other vehicles, equipment, stockpiling, or excessive vibration, a suitable safeguard against such damage shall be provided.

3) Mineral-insulated cable, aluminum-sheathed cable, or copper-sheathed cable shall be protected, located, or arranged so that a 2-1/2 inch common nail cannot be driven into it, where the cable is
   a) run through bored or notched holes or grooves in wooden structural members;
   b) secured directly to the underside of wooden flooring; or
   c) located behind baseboards or casings.

4) In order to comply with Subrule 3), the hole, groove, or supporting strap containing the cable shall be permitted to be sufficiently oversized to permit the cable to move a distance equal to at least the radius of the cable.

5) Where mineral-insulated cable, aluminum-sheathed cable, or copper-sheathed cable passes from a point above grade to direct earth burial and is not otherwise protected against mechanical damage, a suitable pipe stub-up shall be arranged to encase the cable to a point, where practicable, at least 300 mm above grade and, in locations where frost heaving may occur, the encasement shall slide freely on the cable so as to avoid damage.

12-712 Radii of bends
1) The radius of the curve on the inner edge of bends made on mineral-insulated cable shall be not less than 6 times the external diameter of the sheath and shall be made so as not to damage the outer sheath.

2) The radius of the curve on the inner edge of bends made on smooth aluminum-sheathed cable shall be not less than
   a) 10 times the external diameter of the sheath for cable not more than 19 mm in external diameter;
   b) 12 times the external diameter of the sheath for cable more than 19 mm but not more than 38 mm in external diameter; and
   c) 15 times the external diameter of the sheath for cable more than 38 mm in external diameter.

3) The radius of the curve on the inner edge of bends made on corrugated aluminum-sheathed cable or corrugated copper-sheathed cable shall be not less than 9 times the external diameter of the sheath.

12-714 Termination of mineral-insulated cable (see Appendix B)
At all points where mineral-insulated cable terminates,

a) the end of the cable shall be sealed immediately after stripping to prevent entrance of moisture to the insulation;

b) each conductor extended beyond the sheath shall be provided with the proper insulation; and

c) mineral-insulated cable box connectors shall be used.

12-716 Connection to other forms of wiring
Where mineral-insulated cable, aluminum-sheathed cable, or copper-sheathed cable is connected to other forms of wiring, the junction shall be made in a box or at, or in, a fitting having a separately bushed hole for each conductor.

Flat conductor cable Type FCC

12-800 Type FCC under-carpet wiring system Rules
Rules 12-802 to 12-824 apply only to the installation of Type FCC under-carpet wiring systems.

12-802 Special terminology (see Appendix B)
In this Subsection, the following definitions shall apply:

Bottom shield — a protective layer that is between the floor and the Type FCC cable to protect the cable from physical damage.

Insulating end — an insulator designed to electrically insulate the exposed ends of Type FCC cables.

Metal tape — a metal overlay to prevent physical damage to the Type FCC system.

Top shield — an electrically conductive covering for under-carpet components of a Type FCC system that provides a degree of protection against physical damage and electric shock and may or may not be incorporated as an integral part of a Type FCC cable assembly.

Δ   **Transition assembly** — an assembly connecting a Type FCC system to other types of wiring systems.

Type FCC cable — a cable consisting of three or more flat separated conductors laid flat and parallel in the same plane and enclosed within an insulating assembly.

Type FCC cable connector — a device used for joining Type FCC cables, with or without the use of a junction box.

Type FCC system — a complete wiring system for installation only under carpet squares and that includes cable and associated fittings.

12-804 Use permitted
Type FCC systems shall be permitted to be used only for the extension of general-purpose and appliance branch circuits

a) in dry or damp locations;

b) on hard, smooth, continuous floor surfaces made of concrete, ceramic, composition flooring, wood, or similar materials; and

c) on floors heated in excess of 30 °C when the FCC system is marked for the purpose.

12-806 Use prohibited
Type FCC systems shall not be used

a) outdoors or in wet locations;

b) where subject to corrosive vapours or liquids;

c) in dwelling units;

d) in schools, hospitals, or institutional buildings except in office areas;

e)   on walls except where entering transition assemblies;

f)   under permanent-type partitions or walls;

g)   where the voltage exceeds 150 volts-to-ground or 300 V between any two conductors; or

h)   for branch circuits exceeding 30 A.

12-808 Floor covering

Floor-mounted Type FCC cable with associated steel tape, shielding cable connections, and insulating ends shall be covered with carpet squares not exceeding 750 mm and any adhesive used shall be of the release type.

12-810 Connections and terminations

1)   Type FCC cable connections shall be installed so that electrical continuity, insulation, and sealing against dampness and liquid spillage are provided.

2)   Bare ends shall be insulated and sealed by the use of insulating ends.

12-812 Shields

1)   Type FCC systems shall include a bottom shield.

2)   A metal top shield shall be installed over floor-mounted Type FCC cable, connectors, and insulating ends.

12-814 Enclosure and shield continuity (see Appendix B)

Metal shields, tapes, boxes, receptacle housings, and self-contained devices shall be electrically continuous and bonded to ground.

12-816 Connection to other systems

Power feed, bonding, and shield system connections between the Type FCC system and other wiring systems shall be accomplished in a transition assembly intended for surface or recessed mounting.

12-818 Anchoring

Type FCC system components shall be firmly secured to floors and walls by means of

a)   an adhesive in the case of cables; and

b)   mechanical fasteners in the case of associated fittings such as outlet boxes and transition assemblies.

12-820 Crossings

A Type FCC cable run shall be permitted to cross over or under another Type FCC cable run or communication flat cable, provided that there is a layer of metal shielding between each of the cables.

12-822 Mechanical protection

1)   All Type FCC systems installed under carpet squares shall be protected from physical damage by a metal tape completely covering the Type FCC cable and connections.

2)   Where surface or recessed wall mounting of the Type FCC cable is required to enter transition assemblies, additional mechanical protection shall be provided to prevent damage from items such as nails and screws.

Δ   ### 12-824 System height

Except as permitted by Rule 12-820, stacked runs of Type FCC cable shall not be permitted.

Raceways

General

12-900 Raceway Rules

Rules 12-902 to 12-944 apply to raceways and to insulated conductors and bare conductors run in raceways.

12-902 Types of insulated conductors and cables (see Appendix B)
1) Insulated conductors and cables shall be of types suitable for use in raceways as indicated in Table 19.
2) Notwithstanding Subrule 1), armoured cables as described in Rule 12-602 6) shall be permitted to be installed in a conduit or tubing, provided that
    a) the installation will not result in a greater fill than that specified in Table 8; and
    b) the installation conforms to one of the following conditions:
        i) the length of cable pulled into the conduit or tubing does not result in the calculated maximum pulling tension or the calculated maximum sidewall bearing pressure being exceeded; or
        ii) the run of conduit or tubing between draw-in points does not have more than the equivalent of two 90° bends with minimum radii of not less than 0.944 m for cable rated 1000 V or less and 1.524 m for cable rated in excess of 1000 V, and is limited to a maximum of
            A) 15 m for a three-conductor copper cable;
            B) 45 m for a single-conductor copper cable;
            C) 35 m for a three-conductor aluminum cable; or
            D) 100 m for a single-conductor aluminum cable.

12-904 Conductors in raceways (see Appendix B)
1) Where conductors are placed in metal raceways, all insulated conductors of a circuit shall be contained in the same raceway or in the same channel of a multiple-channel raceway except that, where it is necessary to run conductors in parallel due to the capacity of an ac circuit, additional enclosures shall be permitted to be used, provided that
    a) the conductors are installed in accordance with Rule 12-108 1);
    b) each enclosure includes an equal number of conductors from each phase and the neutral; and
    c) each enclosure or cable sheath is of the same material and has the same physical characteristics.
2) Except for cable tray, no raceway or compartment of a multiple-channel raceway shall contain conductors that are connected to different power or distribution transformers or other different sources of voltage, except where the conductors

Δ   a) are separated by the metal armour or metal sheath of a cable type listed in Table 19;
    b) are separated by a barrier of sheet steel not less than 1.34 mm (No. 16 MSG) thick or a flame-retardant non-metallic insulating material not less than 1.5 mm in thickness; or
    c) are used for the supply and/or control of remote devices, are insulated for at least the same voltage as that of the circuit having the highest voltage, and none of the conductors of the circuits of lower voltages is directly connected to a lighting branch circuit.

12-906 Protection of insulated conductors at ends of raceways
1) Bushings or equivalent means shall be used to protect insulated conductors from abrasion where they issue from raceways.
2) Where insulated conductors are No. 8 AWG or larger, copper or aluminum, such protection shall consist of
    a) insulated-type bushings, unless the equipment is equipped with a hub having a smoothly rounded throat; or
    b) insulating material fastened securely in place that will separate the insulated conductors from the raceway fittings and afford adequate resistance to mechanical damage.

12-908 Inserting insulated conductors in raceways

1) Cleaning agents or lubricants of an electrical conducting nature or that might have a deleterious effect on insulated conductor coverings shall not be used when inserting insulated conductors in raceways.

2) Lubricants used when inserting insulated conductors in raceways shall be either insulated conductor pulling compound, talc, or soapstone.

12-910 Conductors and cables in conduit and tubing (see Appendix B)

1) Conduit and tubing shall be of sufficient size to permit the conductors to be drawn in and withdrawn without damage to the conductors or conductor insulation.

2) Subrules 3), 4), and 5) shall apply only to complete systems and not to short sections of conduit and tubing used for the protection of portions of open wiring that would otherwise be exposed to mechanical damage.

3) The maximum number of conductors in one conduit or tubing shall not exceed 200.

4) The maximum number of insulated conductors or multi-conductor cables in one conduit or tubing shall be such that the insulated conductors or cables and their coverings will not result in a greater fill than that specified in Table 8, and in this determination,

   a) the interior cross-sectional area for various sizes of conduit and tubing shall be as specified in Tables 9A to 9P;

   b) notwithstanding Item a), the interior cross-section of raceways shall be permitted to be derived from their measured internal dimensions or from the manufacturer's listed specifications;

   c) the diameters and cross-sectional areas of single-conductor bare and insulated conductors and multi-conductor cables shall be obtained by measurement; and

   d) notwithstanding Item c), the dimensions of single conductors shall be permitted to be obtained from Tables 10A to 10D for the constructions identified in those Tables.

5) Notwithstanding Subrule 4), the maximum permitted number of conductors of the same size in one conduit shall be permitted to be determined from Tables 6A to 6K for single insulated conductors of the appropriate construction as listed in those Tables.

6) Tables 6A to 6K shall not be used to determine the maximum permitted number of insulated conductors of the same size in one HDPE conduit.

12-912 Joints or splices within raceways

There shall be no joints or splices in conductors or cables within raceways, except in the case of busways, wireways, cable trays, and surface raceways with removable covers.

12-914 Stranding of conductors

Except in the case of conductors used as busbars and mineral-insulated cables, single- or multi-conductor cables No. 8 AWG or larger, copper or aluminum, when installed in raceways, shall be stranded.

12-916 Electrical continuity of raceways

Metal raceways shall be electrically continuous throughout and electrically secured to all equipment to which they are attached.

12-918 Mechanical continuity of raceways

Raceways shall be mechanically continuous throughout and mechanically secured to all equipment to which they are attached.

12-920 Support of raceways

Raceways shall be supported independently of equipment forming part of the raceway system.

12-922 Removal of fins and burrs of raceways

Fins and burrs shall be removed from the ends of raceways.

12-924 Radii of bends in raceways

1) Where insulated conductors are drawn into a raceway, the radius of the curve to the centreline of any bend shall be not less than as shown in Table 7.
2) Bends shall be made without undue distortion of the raceway and without damage to its inner or outer surfaces.

12-926 Junction of open wiring and raceways

Where conductors connected to open wiring issue from the ends of raceways, they shall be protected with boxes or with fittings having a separately bushed hole for each conductor.

12-928 Entry of underground conduits into buildings

Where a conduit enters a building from an underground distribution system, the end of the conduit within the building shall be sealed with a suitable compound to prevent the entrance of moisture and gases.

12-930 Raceways installed underground or where moisture may accumulate

1) The requirements for Category 1 locations as specified in Section 22 shall be complied with where raceways are installed
   a) underground;
   b) in concrete slabs or other masonry in direct contact with moist earth; or
   c) in other locations where the conductors are subject to moisture.
2) Where lead-sheathed cables are used in such locations, a pothead or equivalent device shall be used to protect them from moisture and mechanical damage at their point of issue from the lead sheathing.

12-932 Metal raceways in plaster

In buildings of non-combustible construction where circuits run in metal raceways have conductors not larger than No. 10 AWG copper or aluminum, the circuits shall be permitted to be laid on the face of the masonry or other material of which the walls and ceiling are constructed and shall be permitted to be buried in the plaster finish.

Δ ## 12-934 Protection for raceways

Raceways installed less than 2 m above grade in an area where they are subject to mechanical damage shall be
a) of the rigid steel type;
b) protected by location; or
c) protected by steel guards of not less than No. 10 MSG, adequately secured in place.

12-936 Raceways installed in concrete, cinder concrete, and cinder fill (see Appendix B)

1) Raceways made wholly or in part of aluminum shall not be embedded in concrete containing reinforcing steel unless
   a) the concrete is known to contain no chloride additives; or
   b) the raceway has been treated with a bituminous base paint or other means to prevent galvanic corrosion of the aluminum.
2) Where metal raceways are laid in or under cinders or cinder concrete, they shall be protected from corrosive action by a grouting of non-cinder concrete at least 25 mm thick entirely surrounding them unless they are 450 mm or more under the cinders or cinder concrete.

12-938 Raceway completely installed before insulated conductors or cables are installed

Δ 1) Except for HDPE conductors-in-conduit, raceways shall be installed as a complete system before the insulated conductors or cables are installed in them.

2) Insulated conductors or cables shall not be drawn into or laid in raceways in a building under construction until the raceway fittings and insulated conductors are reasonably safe from damage due to construction operations.

12-940 Capping of unused raceways
Spare or unused raceways that terminate in enclosures shall be capped.

12-942 Maximum number of bends in raceways
Where it is intended that insulated conductors are to be drawn into a raceway, a run of raceway between outlets or draw-in points shall not have more than the equivalent of four 90° bends, including the bends located at an outlet or fitting.

12-944 Metal raceways (see Appendix B)
Electrical metal raceways embedded in parking lot slabs or pavement, road beds, and similar areas subject to vehicular traffic shall comply with the requirements of Rule 2-116 1).

Rigid and flexible metal conduit

12-1000 Rigid and flexible metal conduit Rules
Rules 12-1002 to 12-1014 apply only to the installation of rigid and flexible metal conduit.

12-1002 Use
1) Rigid and flexible metal conduit shall be permitted to be installed in or on buildings or portions of buildings of either combustible or non-combustible construction.
2) Rigid metal conduit used in damp or wet locations shall be threaded, and the joints and fittings shall be made watertight.

12-1004 Minimum size of conduits
No conduits having an internal diameter of less than 16 trade size shall be used, except that
a) 12 trade size flexible metal conduit shall be permitted to be used for runs of not more than 1.5 m for the connection of equipment; and
b) 12 trade size liquid-tight flexible conduit may be used as permitted by this Code.

12-1006 Conduit threads (see Appendix B)
1) Threads of rigid metal conduit shall be tapered.
2) External threads performed in the field shall comply with Table 40, using a standard chaser with a taper of 1 to 16.
3) Running threads shall not be permitted.
4) Notwithstanding Subrule 3), where rigid metal conduit protrudes through the enclosure wall and there are not sufficient threads to accommodate a bushing in accordance with Rule 12-906 1), additional threading shall be permitted on the conduit as a continuation of the tapered thread beyond those dimensions specified in Table 40.

12-1008 Thread engagement
The wall thickness of boxes to be drilled and tapped in the field shall be sufficient to ensure thread engagement of at least three complete threads.

12-1010 Maximum spacing of conduit supports (see Appendix B)
1) All rigid metal conduit of one size shall be securely attached to hangers or to a solid surface with the maximum spacings of the points of support not greater than
   a) 1.5 m for 16 and 21 trade size conduit;
   b) 2 m for 27 and 35 trade size conduit; and
   c) 3 m for 41 trade size conduit and larger.
2) Where rigid metal conduits of mixed sizes are run in a group, the conduit supports shall be arranged so that the maximum support spacing will be that given in Subrule 1) for the smallest conduit.

Δ 3) When flexible metal conduit is installed, it shall be secured by straps, Type 2S or 21S cable ties, or other devices at intervals not exceeding 1.5 m and within 300 mm on each side of every outlet box or fitting, except

   a) where flexible metal conduit is fished; and

   b) for lengths not over 900 mm at terminals where flexibility is necessary.

12-1012 Expansion and contraction of conduit (see Appendix B)

1) In locations subject to extreme temperature changes, provision shall be made for expansion and contraction in long runs of rigid conduit in the form of

Δ a) expansion joints; or

   b) in the case of surface-mounted rigid metal conduit only, two 90° bends in the conduit run.

2) If expansion joints are used with metal raceways, bonding jumpers shall be provided in accordance with Rule 10-608.

12-1014 Insulated conductors and cables in conduit

Insulated conductors and cables installed in metal conduits and flexible metal conduits shall be in accordance with Rule 12-910.

Rigid PVC conduit

12-1100 Use

1) Rigid PVC conduit shall be permitted for exposed and concealed work above and below ground in accordance with the Rules for threaded rigid metal conduit subject to the provisions of Rules 2-132 and 12-1102 to 12-1122.

2) Rigid PVC conduit shall be permitted in cinders or cinder concrete without the grouting referred to in Rule 12-936 2) being required.

12-1102 Restrictions on use

Rigid PVC conduit shall not be used where enclosed in thermal insulation.

12-1104 Temperature limitations (see Appendix B)

1) Rigid PVC conduit shall not be used where normal conditions are such that any part of the conduit is subjected to a temperature in excess of 75 °C.

2) Subrule 1) shall not prevent the use of insulated conductors having temperature ratings in excess of 75 °C, but such insulated conductors shall not have ampacities exceeding those of 90 °C insulated conductors, regardless of their temperature rating.

12-1106 Mechanical protection

Rigid PVC conduit shall be protected where exposed to mechanical damage either during installation or afterwards.

12-1108 Field bends (see Appendix B)

1) Rigid PVC conduit shall be permitted to be bent in the field, provided that bending equipment specifically intended for the purpose is used.

2) The minimum bending radius shall comply with Rule 12-924.

12-1110 Support of luminaires

Rigid PVC boxes shall not be used for the support of luminaires unless they are marked as being suitable for the purpose.

12-1112 Fittings

1) Rigid PVC conduit, including elbows and bends, shall not be threaded but shall be used with adapters and couplings, which shall be applied with solvent cement.

2) Female threaded PVC adapters shall be used together with a metal conduit nipple to terminate at threaded conduit entries in metal enclosures.

12-1114 Maximum spacing of conduit supports

1) All rigid PVC conduit of one size shall be securely attached to hangers or to a solid surface with the maximum spacing of the points of supports not greater than
   a) 750 mm for 16, 21, and 27 trade size conduit;
   b) 1.2 m for 35 and 41 trade size conduit;
   c) 1.5 m for 53 trade size conduit;
   d) 1.8 m for 63 and 78 trade size conduit;
   e) 2.1 m for 91, 103, and 129 trade size conduit; and
   f) 2.5 m for 155 trade size conduit.
2) Where conduits of mixed sizes are run in a group, the conduit supports shall be arranged so that the maximum support spacing will be that given in Subrule 1) for the smallest conduit.
3) Except where encased or embedded in at least 50 mm of masonry or poured concrete, conduit shall not be clamped tightly but shall be supported in such a manner as to permit adequate lineal movement to allow for expansion and contraction due to temperature change.

12-1116 Support of equipment

Rigid PVC conduit shall not be used to support electrical equipment, except as permitted by Rule 12-3012 2).

12-1118 Expansion joints (see Appendix B)

Unless the conduit is grouted in concrete, at least one expansion joint shall be installed in any conduit run where the expansion of the conduit due to the maximum probable temperature change during and after installation will exceed 45 mm.

12-1120 Maximum number of conductors

The maximum number of insulated conductors and bare conductors in rigid PVC conduit shall be determined in accordance with Rule 12-910.

12-1122 Provision for bonding continuity

1) A separate bonding conductor shall be installed in rigid PVC conduit in compliance with Rule 10-612.
Δ 2) Notwithstanding Subrule 1), where rigid PVC conduit is used as a consumer's service raceway between the service head and a meter-mounting device or service box, a separate bonding conductor shall not be required unless specifically mandated in other Sections of this Code.

12-1124 Split straight conduit

In existing installations, it shall be permitted to use split straight conduit to repair a damaged portion of raceway, provided that
a) both halves of each split conduit length are made with notches or grooves to ensure the integrity of the raceway and are properly matched together to form a close-fitting joint using PVC solvent cement;
b) when one end of the assembly is not equipped with an integral bell adapter, it is fixed with split couplings that shall be applied with PVC solvent cement;
c) each length of split straight conduit and each split coupling is tightly clamped at both ends, with additional clamps spaced not more than 500 mm apart;
d) non-removable band clamps made of stainless steel are used; and
e) the insulation of conductors in the raceway is not damaged.

Rigid Types EB1 and DB2/ES2 PVC conduit

12-1150 Use permitted (see Appendix B)
Rigid Types EB1 and DB2/ES2 PVC conduit and fittings shall be permitted to be used

a)   for installation underground in accordance with Rule 12-930, except that Type EB1 conduit shall be laid with its entire length encased or embedded in at least a 50 mm envelope of masonry or poured concrete; or

b)   in walls, floors, and ceilings where encased or embedded in at least 50 mm of masonry or poured concrete.

12-1152 Restrictions on use
Rigid Types EB1 and DB2/ES2 conduit and fittings shall not be used above ground except as permitted by Rule 12-1150 b).

12-1154 Temperature limitations (see Appendix B)
Temperature limitations shall comply with Rule 12-1104.

12-1156 Field bends (see Appendix B)
Field bends shall comply with Rule 12-1108.

12-1158 Fittings (see Appendix B)

1)   Rigid Types EB1 and DB2/ES2 PVC conduit, including elbows, bends, and other fittings fabricated from rigid Type EB1 and DB2/ES2 PVC conduit, shall not be threaded.

2)   Notwithstanding Subrule 1), threaded adapters acceptable for use in making threaded connections when properly attached to the conduit shall be permitted to be used.

12-1160 Maximum number of conductors
The maximum number of insulated conductors and bare conductors in rigid Types EB1 and DB2/ES2 PVC conduit shall be in accordance with Rule 12-910.

12-1162 Method of installation

1)   All cut edges shall be trimmed to remove rough edges.

2)   All joints between conduit lengths and between conduit lengths and bends, adapters, or separate couplings shall be made by a method specified for the purpose.

3)   Rigid Types EB1 and DB2/ES2 PVC conduit shall be secured mechanically to prevent disturbance of their alignment during construction.

12-1164 Split straight conduit
In existing underground or concrete embedded installations only, raceways shall be permitted to be formed using split straight conduit, provided that

a)   both halves of each conduit length are properly matched and clamped together to form a close-fitting concrete-tight joint;

b)   each length of conduit is tightly clamped at each end, with additional clamps spaced not more than 900 mm apart; and

c)   clamps made of stainless steel or other corrosion-resistant material are used when not embedded in concrete.

12-1166 Provision for bonding continuity
A separate bonding conductor shall be installed in rigid Types EB1 and DB2/ES2 conduit in compliance with Rule 10-612.

Rigid RTRC conduit

12-1200 Scope
Rules 12-1202 to 12-1220 apply only to the installation of rigid RTRC conduit Types AG, BG, and XW.

12-1202 Use
1) Rigid RTRC conduit Types AG, BG, and XW shall be permitted to be installed
   a) underground in accordance with Rule 12-012; and
   b) in walls, floors, and ceilings where encased or embedded in at least 50 mm of masonry or poured concrete.
2) Rigid RTRC conduit Types AG and XW shall, in addition to the locations permitted in Subrule 1), be permitted for installation in exposed and concealed locations.

12-1204 Restrictions on use (see Appendix B)
Rigid RTRC conduit shall not be used in buildings required to be of non-combustible construction, unless it has a flame spread rating and smoke developed classification as specified in the *National Building Code of Canada*.

12-1206 Mechanical protection
Rigid RTRC conduit shall be provided with mechanical protection where exposed to damage either during installation or afterwards.

12-1208 Field bends
Rigid RTRC conduit shall not be bent in the field.

12-1210 Temperature limitations
Rigid RTRC conduit shall not be used where normal conditions are such that any part of the conduit is subjected to a temperature in excess of 110 °C.

12-1212 Fittings
Rigid RTRC conduit shall not be threaded but shall be used with adapters and couplings specifically designed for the purpose.

12-1214 Expansion joints (see Appendix B)
Except where encased in concrete, at least one expansion joint shall be installed in any conduit run where the expansion of the conduit due to the maximum probable temperature change during and after installation will exceed 45 mm.

12-1216 Conduit supports
Where rigid RTRC conduit Type AG or XW is run in accordance with Rule 12-1202 2), it shall be supported with hangers or clamps
a) in such a manner as to permit adequate linear movement to allow for expansion and contraction due to temperature change; and
b) with the spacings of the supports not greater than those permitted in Rule 12-1010.

12-1218 Maximum number of conductors
The maximum number of insulated conductors and bare conductors in rigid RTRC conduit shall be determined in accordance with Rule 12-910.

12-1220 Provision for bonding
A separate bonding conductor shall be installed in rigid RTRC conduit in compliance with Rule 10-612.

Δ # High-density polyethylene (HDPE) conduit and HDPE conductors-in-conduit

12-1250 Use permitted
HDPE conduit, HDPE conductors-in-conduit, and fittings shall be permitted to be used
a) for installation underground in accordance with Rule 12-930; or
b) where encased or embedded in at least 50 mm of masonry or poured concrete.

12-1252 Restrictions on use
HDPE conduit, HDPE conductors-in-conduit, and fittings shall not be used above ground except as permitted by Rule 12-1250 b).

12-1254 Method of installation (see Appendix B)

1) All cut edges shall be trimmed to remove rough edges.

2) All joints between conduit lengths and between conduit lengths and bends, adapters, or separate couplings shall be made by a method specified for the purpose.

3) HDPE conduit and HDPE conductors-in-conduit shall be secured mechanically to prevent disturbance of their alignment during construction.

4) Fusion methods that result in an internal lip shall not be permitted.

5) HDPE conduit and HDPE conductors-in-conduit shall be permitted to be installed by horizontal directional drilling and plow-trenching, provided that the following requirements are met:
   a) a breakaway device shall be installed set to the maximum pulling tension of the conduit;
   b) conduit walls shall be dimension ratio 11 or thicker unless thinner conduit walls are allowed by assessment;
   c) installation shall be performed on continuous runs without the use of couplings or joints; and
   d) pipe elongation shall be compensated for before cutting the conduit.

6) HDPE conduit and HDPE conductors-in-conduit for direct burial installations shall be placed directly on the base materials.

12-1256 Temperature limitations

HDPE conduit and HDPE conductors-in-conduit shall not be used where normal conditions are such that any part of the conduit is subjected to a temperature in excess of its marked continuous operating temperature.

12-1258 Field bends

Where HDPE conduit or HDPE conductors-in-conduit are bent during installation, the radius of the curve shall be

a) not less than that specified by the HDPE conduit manufacturer; or

b) if not specified, at least 12 times the external diameter of the HDPE conduit or HDPE conductors-in-conduit.

12-1260 Fittings

HDPE conduit and HDPE conductors-in-conduit shall not be threaded.

12-1262 Expansion joints

Unless the conduit is grouted in concrete, at least one expansion joint shall be installed in any conduit run where the expansion of the conduit due to the maximum probable temperature change during and after installation will exceed 45 mm.

12-1264 Maximum number of conductors

The maximum number of conductors in HDPE conduit shall be in accordance with Rule 12-910.

12-1266 Split straight conduit

In existing underground or concrete embedded installations only, raceways shall be permitted to be formed using split straight conduit to repair a damaged portion of raceway, provided that

a) both halves of each conduit length are properly matched and clamped together to form a close-fitting concrete-tight joint;

b) each length of split straight conduit is tightly clamped at each end, with additional clamps spaced not more than 900 mm apart;

c) non-removable band clamps made of stainless steel or other corrosion-resistant material are used when not embedded in concrete; and

d) the insulation of conductors in the raceway is not damaged.

12-1268 Provision for bonding continuity

A separate bonding conductor shall be installed in HDPE conduit in compliance with Rule 10-612

Liquid-tight flexible conduit

12-1300 Scope
Rules 12-1302 to 12-1308 apply only to liquid-tight flexible conduit.

Δ ## 12-1302 Use of liquid-tight flexible metal and non-metallic conduit
1) Liquid-tight flexible conduit shall be permitted where a flexible connection is required in dry, damp, or wet locations and where permitted by other Sections of this Code.
2) Runs of not more than 1.5 m of 12 trade size liquid-tight flexible conduit shall be permitted for the connection of equipment.
3) Liquid-tight flexible conduit shall not be used
   a) where subject to mechanical damage;
   b) where exposed to gasoline or similar light petroleum solvents, corrosive liquids, or vapours having a damaging effect on the outer liquid-tight flexible conduit jacket;
   c) under conditions such that the temperature will exceed 60 °C unless marked for a higher temperature; or
   d) where flexing at low temperatures may cause damage.
4) Liquid-tight flexible conduit shall be permitted for direct burial in accordance with Rule 12-012 where marked for the purpose.
5) Liquid-tight flexible conduit installed in a building shall comply with Rule 2-132.

12-1304 Maximum number of conductors
1) The maximum number of insulated conductors and bare conductors in liquid-tight flexible conduit shall be in accordance with Rule 12-910.
2) For the purposes of Subrule 1), the cross-sectional area of 12 trade size shall be considered as 118 mm².

12-1306 Provisions for bonding
A separate bonding conductor shall be installed in liquid-tight flexible conduit in accordance with Section 10.

12-1308 Supports (see Appendix B)
Δ 1) Liquid-tight flexible conduit shall be supported by straps, Type 2S or 21S cable ties, or other devices
   a) within 300 mm of every outlet box, junction box, cabinet, or fitting; and
   b) with spacing between supports of not more than 1.5 m.
2) Notwithstanding Subrule 1) b), where liquid-tight flexible conduit is concealed and it is impracticable to provide supports, the liquid-tight flexible conduit shall be permitted to be fished.

Electrical metallic tubing

12-1400 Electrical metallic tubing Rules
Rules 12-1402 to 12-1414 apply only to electrical metallic tubing.

12-1402 Use
1) Electrical metallic tubing shall be permitted to be used
   a) for exposed work;
   b) for concealed work;
   c) in wet locations;
   d) in outdoor locations; and
   e) in or on buildings or portions of buildings of either combustible or non-combustible construction.
2) In addition to Subrule 1), electrical metallic tubing of the steel type shall be permitted to be used in concrete or masonry slabs in contact with the earth.

12-1404 Restrictions on use
Electrical metallic tubing shall not be used
a)   where it will be subject to mechanical damage either during installation or afterwards;
b)   where exposed to corrosive vapour except as permitted by Rule 2-116; or
c)   for direct earth burial.

Δ   ### 12-1406 Supports
Electrical metallic tubing shall be installed as a complete system and shall be securely fastened in place within 1 m of each outlet box, junction box, cabinet, or fitting, and the spacing between supports shall be in accordance with Rule 12-1010.

12-1408 Minimum tubing size
Electrical metallic tubing shall have an inside diameter of not less than 16 trade size tubing.

12-1410 Maximum number of conductors
Electrical metallic tubing shall not contain more insulated conductors and bare conductors of a given size than are specified in Rule 12-910.

12-1412 Connections and couplings
Where lengths of electrical metallic tubing are coupled together or connected to boxes, fittings, or cabinets, fittings shall be
a)   of the concrete-tight type for installation in poured concrete or in masonry block walls in which cores are filled with concrete or grout;
b)   of the wet location type for installation in wet or outdoor locations; or
c)   of the standard, concrete-tight, or wet location type for installation in ordinary locations or buried in plaster or masonry block walls.

12-1414 Provision for bonding continuity
1)   Where bonding is required by Section 10, a separate insulated bonding conductor shall be installed in electrical metallic tubing that is installed in
    a)   concrete or masonry slabs in contact with the earth;
    b)   a wet location; or
    c)   an outdoor location.

Δ   2)   Notwithstanding Subrule 1), where electrical metallic tubing is used as a consumer's service raceway between the service head and a meter-mounting device or service box, bonding shall be in accordance with Rule 10-604, unless a separate bonding conductor is specifically mandated in other Sections of this Code.

Electrical non-metallic tubing

12-1500 Use
Subject to the provisions of Rules 2-128 and 12-1502 to 12-1514, the installation of electrical non-metallic tubing shall be permitted
a)   underground in accordance with Rule 12-012; and
b)   in exposed or concealed locations.

12-1502 Restriction on use
Electrical non-metallic tubing shall not be used unless provided with mechanical protection where subject to damage either during or after construction.

Δ **12-1504 Supports** (see Appendix B)

Electrical non-metallic tubing shall be securely fastened in place by straps, Type 2S or 21S cable ties, or other devices within 1 m of each outlet box, junction box, cabinet, coupling, or fitting, and the spacing between supports shall be not more than 1 m.

12-1506 Maximum number of conductors

Electrical non-metallic tubing shall not contain more insulated conductors and bare conductors of a given size than are specified in Rule 12-910.

12-1508 Temperature limitations (see Appendix B)

1) Electrical non-metallic tubing shall not be used where normal conditions are such that any part of the tubing is subjected to a temperature in excess of 75 °C.
2) Subrule 1) shall not prevent the use of insulated conductors having temperature ratings in excess of 75 °C, but such insulated conductors shall not have ampacities exceeding those of 90 °C insulated conductors regardless of their temperature rating.

12-1510 Connections and couplings

1) Where lengths of electrical non-metallic tubing are coupled together or connected to boxes, fittings, or cabinets, fittings designed for the purpose shall be used.
2) Where lengths of electrical non-metallic tubing are coupled together underground, the couplings shall be applied using a solvent cement suitable for the purpose.

12-1512 Support of equipment

Electrical non-metallic tubing shall not be used to support electrical equipment.

12-1514 Provision for bonding continuity

A separate bonding conductor shall be installed in electrical non-metallic tubing in compliance with Rule 10-612.

Surface raceways

12-1600 Scope

Rules 12-1602 to 12-1614 apply only to surface raceways.

12-1602 Use of surface raceways (see Appendix B)

1) Surface raceways shall be permitted only for exposed surface installation in dry locations.
2) Notwithstanding Subrule 1), surface raceways shall be permitted to extend through walls, partitions, and floors, provided that
   a) the raceways are in unbroken lengths where passing through; and
   b) provision is made for removing the caps or covers on all exposed portions.
3) Surface raceways shall not be used where subject to mechanical damage.
4) Non-metallic surface raceways shall conform with Rule 2-132.

12-1604 Temperature limitations

1) Surface raceways shall not be used where subject to ambient temperatures in excess of 50 °C unless marked for a higher temperature.
2) Subrule 1) shall not prevent the use of insulated conductors having temperature ratings in excess of 75 °C, but such insulated conductors shall not have ampacities exceeding those of 75 °C insulated conductors regardless of their temperature ratings.

12-1606 Conductors in surface raceways (see Appendix B)

1) Insulated conductors shall be of the types indicated in Table 19 as being suitable for use in raceways.
2) The aggregate cross-sectional area of the installed insulated conductors and bare conductors shall not exceed 40% of the minimum available cross-sectional area of the raceway.

3) The cross-sectional area for insulated conductors and bare conductors specified in Subrule 2) shall be determined in accordance with Rule 12-910 4).

12-1608 Maximum voltage

The voltage between conductors contained in surface raceways shall not exceed 300 V unless the raceways are marked for a higher voltage.

12-1610 Joints and splices

Joints and splices shall be permitted in surface raceways having a removable cover that is accessible after installation and shall not fill the raceway to more than 75% of its area at that point.

12-1612 Provisions for bonding

A separate bonding conductor shall be installed in non-metallic surface raceways in compliance with Rule 10-612.

12-1614 Flat cable systems

1) Flat cables consisting of parallel conductors and side wings formed with integral insulation specifically designed for field installation in metal surface raceways with tap fittings and end cap devices shall be used only
   a) in branch circuits; and
   b) in horizontal runs with the conductors uppermost in the raceway.
2) Metal surface raceways, when used with flat cables, shall be permitted to have covers on the underside omitted when installed out of reach.

Underfloor raceways

12-1700 Where underfloor raceways are permitted

1) Underfloor raceways shall be permitted to be installed under the surface of concrete or other flooring material, but not below the floor.
2) Underfloor raceways shall not be used
   a) where they will be exposed to corrosive vapours;
   b) in commercial garages;
   c) in storage-battery rooms; or
   d) on the underside of the floor.

12-1702 Method of installing underfloor raceways

1) Underfloor raceways shall be installed in accordance with the manufacturer's instructions in addition to the other requirements of this Rule.
2) Underfloor raceways shall be laid so that their centreline coincides with a straight line drawn between the centres of successive junction boxes.
3) The raceways shall be mechanically secured to prevent disturbance of the alignment during construction.
4) The joints along the edges of the raceways and between the raceways, couplings, and junction boxes, and between the junction box cover plates and cover-rings, shall be filled with waterproof cement.
5) The raceways shall be arranged so that there are no low points or traps at the fittings or in the raceway run, and crossings shall be avoided where possible.

12-1704 Fittings for underfloor raceways

1) Where underfloor raceways are run at other than right angles, special fittings shall be provided if required.
2) The raceways shall be connected to distribution centre and wall outlets by conduit or fittings.
3) Dead-ends of the raceways shall terminate in junction boxes or other fittings.

12-1706 Taps and splices in underfloor raceways
Taps and splices in underfloor raceways shall be made only in header access units or in junction boxes.

12-1708 Inserts and junction boxes for underfloor raceways
1) Inserts and outlets in underfloor raceways shall be made electrically and mechanically secure.
2) Inserts other than the preset type shall be attached to the raceways and, where they are not made mechanically secure by being grouted in separately, they shall not be set until the floor is laid.
3) Inserts and junction boxes shall be levelled to the grade of the floor and sealed with watertight plugs.

12-1710 Setting of inserts
When setting inserts or cutting through the walls of underfloor raceways, adequate precautions shall be taken to prevent chips and dirt from falling into the raceway, and special tools designed for the purpose that cannot enter the raceway and damage the insulated conductors shall be used.

12-1712 Discontinued outlets in underfloor raceways
Where an outlet in an underfloor raceway is discontinued, the insulated conductors supplying the outlet shall be removed from the underfloor raceway.

12-1714 Area of conductors in underfloor raceways
1) The aggregate cross-sectional area of the insulated conductors and bare conductors and their insulation in an underfloor raceway shall not exceed 40% of the interior cross-sectional area of the raceway.
2) Subrule 1) shall not apply where the raceway contains only mineral-insulated cable, aluminum-sheathed cable, copper-sheathed cable, armoured cable, or non-metallic-sheathed cable.
3) The cross-sectional area for conductors specified in Subrule 1) shall be determined in accordance with Rule 12-910.

12-1716 Underfloor raceway junction boxes
Junction boxes shall not be used as outlet boxes in underfloor raceways.

12-1718 Inserts in post- and pre-stressed concrete floors
1) Where underfloor distribution raceways are used with post-stressed or pre-stressed poured-in-place floors, they shall be supplied with preset inserts.
2) After-set inserts or after-set access units shall not be placed into systems as described in Subrule 1) unless the resulting floor is in compliance with the performance requirements of the *National Building Code of Canada*.

Cellular floors

12-1800 Installation
Cellular floors shall be installed in accordance with the manufacturer's instructions.

12-1802 Conductors in cellular floors
1) Insulated conductors and bare conductors shall not be installed in a cellular floor
   a) where they will be exposed to corrosive vapour;
   b) in commercial garages; or
   c) in storage-battery rooms.
2) Insulated conductors and bare conductors shall not be installed in any cell or header that contains a pipe for steam, water, air, gas, drainage, or other non-electrical service.
3) Where the cell or header contains non-electrical services as described in Subrule 2), it shall be sealed, where practicable.
4) All conductors of a circuit shall be contained in the same cell of a cellular floor and, except as permitted by Rule 12-3030, the circuits of different systems shall not be contained therein.

12-1804 Maximum conductor size in cellular floors

No insulated conductor or bare conductor larger than No. 0 AWG copper or aluminum shall be installed in a cellular floor unless a deviation has been allowed in accordance with Rule 2-030.

12-1806 Cross-sectional area of cellular floors

1) Where a cellular floor contains other than mineral-insulated cable, aluminum-sheathed cable, copper-sheathed cable, armoured cable, or non-metallic-sheathed cable, the aggregate cross-sectional area of the insulated conductors, bare conductors, and cables shall not exceed 40% of the interior area of the header feeding the individual cells.

2) The cross-sectional area for insulated conductors, bare conductors, and cables specified in Subrule 1) shall be determined in accordance with Rule 12-910.

12-1808 Taps and splices in cellular floors

Taps and splices in cellular floors shall be made only in header access units or in junction boxes.

12-1810 Cellular floor markers

Where cellular floors are used, a suitable number of markers shall be installed for the future location of cells and for system identification, and the markers shall extend through the floor.

12-1812 Cellular floor junction boxes

1) Junction boxes used in cellular floors shall be levelled to floor grade and sealed against the entrance of water.

2) The junction boxes shall be constructed of metal and shall be electrically continuous with the headers.

3) Electrical continuity of cellular metal-floor members shall be obtained by spot welding or other equivalent means.

4) Spot welding shall be done in open spaces between cells and not to the cell walls.

Δ   ## 12-1814 Provision for bonding

1) A separate bonding conductor shall be installed in electrical cells and headers and shall be sized in accordance with Table 16.

2) Metal headers, cells, and fittings shall be bonded to ground in accordance with Section 10.

12-1816 Cellular floor inserts

1) Inserts in cellular floors shall be levelled to floor grade and sealed against the entrance of water.

2) Inserts shall be made of metal and shall be electrically continuous with the cellular metal-floor members.

Δ   3) When setting inserts or cutting through cell walls, adequate precautions shall be taken to prevent chips and dirt from falling into the cell and for preventing tools from entering the cells and damaging the conductor insulation within.

12-1818 Cellular floor extensions

Connections from cellular floors to cabinets and extensions from cells to outlets shall be made by means of rigid conduit, flexible metal conduit, or fittings.

12-1820 Cellular floor discontinued outlets

Where an outlet is discontinued, the insulated conductors supplying the outlet shall be removed from the cellular floor.

Auxiliary gutters

12-1900 Where auxiliary gutters are used to supplement wiring spaces

1) Where auxiliary gutters are used to supplement wiring spaces at meter centres, distribution centres, switchboards, and similar points in interior wiring systems, the gutters shall be permitted

to enclose insulated conductors, bare conductors, and cables, but they shall not be used to enclose busbars, switches, overcurrent devices, or other appliances or apparatus.

2) The auxiliary gutters shall not extend more than 6 m beyond the equipment that they supplement, and thereafter the insulated conductors, bare conductors, and cables shall be permitted to be contained in wireways or busways.

12-1902 Auxiliary gutter supports
Auxiliary gutters shall be securely supported throughout their entire length at intervals of not more than 1.5 m unless the gutter is plainly marked to indicate a greater distance.

12-1904 Auxiliary gutter cross-sectional area
1) The aggregate cross-sectional area of the insulated conductors and their insulation at a cross-section of an auxiliary gutter shall not exceed 20% of the cross-sectional area of the gutter at that point.

2) A single compartment of an auxiliary gutter shall not contain more than 200 insulated conductors at a cross-section.

3) The cross-sectional area for conductors specified in Subrule 1) shall be determined in accordance with Rule 12-910.

Busways and splitters

12-2000 Use
1) Busways and splitters shall be permitted to be used only for exposed work except as permitted in Subrules 5) and 7).

Δ 2) Busways and splitters shall not be installed outdoors or in wet or damp locations, unless marked for use in such locations.

3) Busways, splitters, and fittings shall not be placed
   a) where subject to mechanical damage;
   b) where subject to corrosive vapours;
   c) in hoistways; or
   d) in storage-battery rooms.

4) Busways shall be permitted to be used as risers in buildings of non-combustible construction when provided with fire stops in accordance with Rule 2-128.

5) Busways shall be permitted in false ceiling spaces, where a deviation has been allowed in accordance with Rule 2-030, provided that
   a) ventilation is adequate to prevent development of ambient temperatures in excess of 30 °C; otherwise the rating of the busway shall be reduced to 82%, 71%, and 58% for ambients of 40 °C, 45 °C, or 50 °C respectively, but in no case shall the ambient be higher than 50 °C;
   b) any take-off devices located in the false ceiling do not contain overcurrent protection;
   c) adequate working space exists between the busway and other services or structural parts;
   d) the busway is of the totally enclosed type, except that the ventilated type shall be permitted to be used provided that, in addition,
      i) the busbars are insulated for their full length, including joints between sections, unless provision is made that effectively fully encloses the bare busbars;
      ii) the false ceiling is not combustible; and
      iii) no combustible material is located within 150 mm of the busway; and
   e) if installed in areas used for the building ventilation system, the busway is of the totally enclosed type.

6) A splitter with a separate screw or stud for each connection shall be installed, in an accessible location, where two or more conductors are connected to a conductor larger than No. 6 AWG copper or No. 4 AWG aluminum.

7) Splitters shall be permitted to be installed flush in a wall, provided that they are accessible by removable covers.

12-2002 Extensions from busways and splitters

Rigid conduit, flexible metal conduit, surface raceways, cable trays, electrical metallic tubing, armoured cable, metal-sheathed cable, or, where necessary, hard-usage cord assemblies shall be used in extensions from busways and splitters and shall be connected to the busway or splitter in a manner appropriate to the material used in accordance with Rule 12-3022.

12-2004 AC circuits in busways and splitters

Where alternating current is used, all insulated conductors of a circuit shall be placed within the same busway, splitter, or section thereof, if the busway, splitter, or section is made of magnetic material.

12-2006 Busway and splitter supports

1) Busways installed horizontally shall be supported at intervals not greater than 1.5 m unless marked as being suitable for support at greater intervals.
2) Busways installed vertically shall be marked as being suitable for vertical installation.
3) Busways installed vertically shall be supported at each floor and at intervals not greater than 1.5 m unless marked as being suitable for support at greater intervals.
4) Busways shall be installed so that supports and joints are accessible for maintenance purposes after installation.
5) Splitters shall be supported at intervals not greater than 1.5 m unless marked as being suitable for support at greater intervals.

12-2008 Method of installation of busways

1) Where busways extend transversely through dry walls or partitions, they shall pass through the walls or partitions in unbroken lengths and shall be totally enclosed where passing through walls or partitions constructed of combustible material or masonry walls containing voids at the point where the busway passes through.
2) Busways shall be permitted to extend vertically through floors in dry locations if they are
   a) totally enclosed where passing through the floor and for the first 300 mm above the floor; and
   b) provided with fire stops in accordance with Rule 2-128.
3) Busways shall be provided with adequate protection against mechanical damage and personal contact with live parts for a distance of 2 m above any floor in an area accessible to other than qualified persons.
4) Dead-ends of busways shall be closed by fittings.
5) Busways installed outdoors or in parking areas and that are accessible to other than authorized persons shall be of the totally enclosed type.

12-2010 Plug-in devices for busways

When busways supply machine tools, a switch need not be furnished on the machine tool if
a) a plug-in device having a horsepower rating is used; and
b) the means of operating the plug-in device is readily within reach of the operator.

12-2012 Reduction in size of busways

Overcurrent protection shall be permitted to be omitted at points where busways are reduced in size, provided that the smaller busway
a) does not extend more than 15 m;
b) has a current rating at least equal to one-third the rating or setting of the overcurrent devices next back on the line;
c) is free from contact with combustible material; and
d) has an ampacity adequate for the intended load.

12-2014 Length of busways used as branch circuits

1) Busways that are used as branch circuits, and that are designed so that loads can be connected at any point, shall be limited to lengths such that the circuits will not be overloaded in normal use.

2) In general, the length of such a run in metres should not exceed the ampere rating of the branch circuit.

12-2016 Manufacturer's identification on busways and splitters

Busways and splitters shall be marked so that the manufacturer's name, trademark, or other recognized symbol of identification shall be readily legible when the installation is completed.

12-2018 Taps in splitters

Taps from busbars or terminal blocks in splitters shall issue from the box on the side thereof nearest to the terminal connections, and the insulated conductors shall not be brought into contact with uninsulated current-carrying parts of opposite polarity.

12-2020 Circuit restrictions in splitters

Splitters shall be used only for the purpose of making connections to the busbars or terminal blocks and shall not be used as a pull box for the insulated conductors of other circuits not connected to the main distribution terminals within the box.

Wireways

12-2100 Where wireways may be used

Δ 1) Wireways shall be permitted to be used only for exposed work and shall not be installed outdoors or in wet or damp locations, unless marked for use in such locations.

2) Wireways and fittings shall not be placed
   a) where subject to mechanical damage;
   b) where subject to corrosive vapours;
   c) in hoistways; or
   d) in storage-battery rooms.

3) Wireways shall be permitted to be used as risers in buildings of non-combustible construction when provided with fire stops in accordance with Rule 2-128.

12-2102 Method of installation of wireways

1) Where wireways extend transversely through dry walls or partitions, they shall pass through the walls or partitions in unbroken lengths.

2) Wireways shall be securely supported at intervals of not more than 1.5 m, unless they are plainly marked to indicate greater distances.

3) Dead-ends of wireways shall be closed by fittings.

4) Wireways shall be provided with adequate protection against mechanical damage for a distance of 2 m above any floor in an area accessible to other than qualified persons.

12-2104 Conductors in wireways

1) Conductors used in wireways shall be of the insulated types indicated in Table 19 as being suitable for use in raceways.

2) Except as permitted in Subrule 4), wireways and each compartment of divided wireways shall contain not more than 200 insulated conductors and bare conductors, and the aggregate cross-sectional area of the conductors and their insulation shall not exceed 20% of the interior cross-sectional area of the wireway or of each compartment of divided wireways.

3) No insulated conductor larger than 500 kcmil copper or 750 kcmil aluminum shall be installed in any wireway.

4) Wireways containing only signal and control conductors shall be permitted to contain any number of insulated conductors, but the aggregate cross-sectional area of the conductors and their insulation shall not exceed 40% of the interior cross-sectional area of the wireway.

5) The cross-sectional area for conductors specified in Subrules 2) and 4) shall be determined in accordance with Rule 12-910 4).

12-2106 Taps and splices in wireways

Where taps and splices are made on feeders or branch circuits within wireways, the connection shall be insulated and shall be accessible.

12-2108 Extensions from wireways

Rigid conduit, flexible metal conduit, surface raceways, cable trays, electrical metallic tubing, armoured cable, metal-sheathed cable, or, where necessary, hard-usage cord assemblies shall be used in extensions from wireways and shall be connected to the wireway in a manner appropriate to the material used in accordance with Rule 12-3022.

12-2110 AC circuits in wireways

Where alternating current is used, all insulated conductors of a circuit shall be placed within the same wireway, or section thereof, if the wireway is made of magnetic material.

12-2112 Manufacturer's identification on wireways

Wireways shall be marked so that the manufacturer's name, trademark, or other recognized symbol of identification shall be readily legible when the installation is completed.

Cable trays

12-2200 Method of installation (see Appendix B)

1) Cable trays shall be installed as a complete system using fittings or other means to provide adequate cable support and bending radius before the insulated conductors or cables are installed.
2) The maximum design load and associated support spacing shall not exceed the load/span ratings of the cable tray.
3) Cable trays shall not pass through walls except where the walls are constructed of non-combustible material.
4) Cable trays shall be permitted to extend vertically through floors in dry locations, if provided with fire stops in accordance with Rule 2-128 and if totally enclosed where passing through and for a minimum distance of 2 m above the floor to provide adequate protection from mechanical damage.
5) Cable trays shall be adequately supported by non-combustible supports.
6) The minimum clearances for cable trays shall be
   a) 150 mm vertical clearance, excluding the depth of the cable trays, between cable trays installed in tiers except that, where cables of 50 mm diameter or greater may be installed, the clearance shall be 300 mm;
   b) 300 mm vertical clearance from the top of the cable tray to all ceilings, heating ducts, and heating equipment and 150 mm for short length obstructions;
   c) 600 mm horizontal clearance on one side of cable trays mounted adjacent to one another or to walls or other obstructions, where the width of the cable tray installation does not exceed 1 m; and
   d) 600 mm horizontal clearance on each side of cable trays mounted adjacent to one another, where the width of the cable tray installation exceeds 1 m.
7) Notwithstanding Subrule 6), cable trays shall be permitted to have reduced clearances through chases, under gratings and process pipes, and around other such obstructions.
8) At least one expansion joint shall be installed in any cable tray run where the expansion of the cable tray due to the maximum probable temperature change during and after installation could damage the cable tray.

Δ **12-2202 Insulated conductors and cables in cable trays** (see Appendix B)
1) Insulated conductors and cables for use in cable trays shall be as listed in Table 19 and, except as permitted in Subrules 2) to 4), shall have a continuous metal sheath or interlocking armour.
2) Type TC tray cable shall be permitted in cable trays in areas of industrial establishments that are inaccessible to the public, provided that the cable is
   a) installed in conduit, other suitable raceway, or direct buried, when not in cable tray;
   b) provided with mechanical protection where subject to damage either during or after installation;
   c) no smaller than No. 1/0 AWG if a single-conductor cable is used; and
   d) installed only where qualified persons service the installation.
3) Notwithstanding Subrule 2) a) and b), Type TC-ER tray cable, where not subject to damage during or after installation, shall be permitted to transition between cable trays, and between cable trays and utilization equipment or devices, for a distance not exceeding
   a) 1.5 m without continuous support; and
   b) 7.5 m where continuously supported.
4) Conductors having moisture-resistant insulation and flame-tested non-metal coverings or sheaths of a type listed in Table 19 shall be permitted in ventilated or non-ventilated cable trays where not subject to damage during or after installation in
   a) electrical equipment vaults and service rooms; and
   b) other locations that are inaccessible to the public and are constructed as a service room where a deviation has been allowed in accordance with Rule 2-030.
5) Conductors and cables installed in cable tray shall be fastened by straps, cable ties, or other devices located at intervals of not more than 1.5 m throughout the run where
   a) excessive movement may be caused by fault current magnetic forces; and
   b) consistent minimum spacing requirements between insulated conductors and cables are required, to ensure that ampacity values are maintained for their designed application.
6) Where single insulated conductors and single-conductor cables are fastened to cable trays, precautions shall be taken to prevent overheating of the insulated conductors or cables at the fastener locations due to induction.

12-2204 Joints and splices within cable trays
Where joints and splices are made on feeders or branch circuits within cable trays, the connectors shall be insulated and shall be accessible.

12-2206 Connection to other wiring methods
Where cable trays are connected to other wiring methods, the arrangement shall be such that the insulated conductors and cables will not be subject to mechanical damage or abrasion, and such that effective bonding will be maintained.

12-2208 Provisions for bonding (see Appendix M)
1) Except as provided for in Subrules 2) and 3), metal cable tray shall be bonded at intervals not exceeding 15 m and the size of bonding conductors shall be based on the ampacity of the largest ungrounded conductor as specified in Rule 10-614 in the circuits carried by the cable tray.
2) Where metal supports for metal cable trays are bolted to the tray and are in good electrical contact with the grounded structural metal frame of a building, the tray shall be deemed to be bonded to ground.
3) Notwithstanding Rule 12-2200 1) and Section 10, metal cable tray shall not be required to be bonded to ground where all of the cables contained within the tray
   a) have an interlocking metal armour; or
   b) have a continuous metal sheath that is permitted to be used as a bonding method.

4) All metal cable tray that is not bonded, as permitted by Subrule 3), shall have a permanent, legible warning notice carrying the wording "INTERLOCKING METAL ARMOUR CABLES OR CONTINUOUS METAL SHEATH CABLES ONLY", or equivalent, placed in a conspicuous position, with the maximum spacing of warning notices not to exceed 10 m.

Cablebus

12-2250 Scope (see Appendix B)
Rules 12-2252 to 12-2258 apply only to the installation of cablebus as a complete system.

12-2252 Use of cablebus (see Appendix B)
1) Class A cablebus shall be permitted for installations
    a) accessible to the public; or
    b) where Class B cablebus is permitted.
2) Class B cablebus shall be permitted only for installations
    a) accessible only to authorized persons;
    b) isolated by elevation or by barriers; and
    c) serviced by qualified electrical maintenance personnel.

12-2254 Methods of installation (see Appendix B)
1) Cablebus shall be installed as a complete system using fittings or other means to provide adequate insulated conductor and cable support and bending radius as specified by the manufacturer.
2) The maximum design and support spacing shall not exceed the ratings specified by the manufacturer.
3) Cablebus shall be adequately supported by non-combustible supports.
4) The minimum clearances for cablebus shall be
    a) 150 mm vertical clearance, excluding depth of cablebus, between cablebus installed in tiers except that, where cables of 50 mm diameter or greater are installed inside the cablebus, the clearance shall be 300 mm;
    b) 300 mm vertical clearance from the top of the cablebus to all ceilings, heating ducts, and heating equipment and 150 mm for short length obstructions;
    c) 600 mm horizontal clearance on one side of cablebus mounted adjacent to one another or to walls or other obstructions, where the width of the cablebus enclosure installation does not exceed 1 m; and
    d) 600 mm horizontal clearance on each side of cablebus mounted adjacent to one another, where the width of the cablebus enclosure installation exceeds 1 m.
5) At least one expansion joint shall be installed in any cablebus run where the expansion of the cablebus due to the maximum probable temperature change during and after installation could damage the cablebus.
6) Cablebus shall be securely supported at intervals not exceeding 3.7 m.
7) Notwithstanding Subrule 6), where spans longer than 3.7 m are required, the structure shall be specifically designed for the required span length.
8) Cablebus shall not pass through walls except where the walls are constructed of non-combustible material.
9) Cablebus shall be permitted to extend transversely through partitions or walls, other than fire walls, provided that the section within the wall is continuous, protected against physical damage, and unventilated.
10) Cablebus shall be permitted to extend vertically through floors in dry locations where it is
    a) sealed at the penetration by a fire stop system that has a rating not less than the fire resistance rating for the fire separation in conformance with Rule 2-128;
    b) totally enclosed where passing through the floor; and

c) totally enclosed for a minimum distance of 2 m above the floor to provide adequate protection from mechanical damage except that in areas accessible only to qualified persons, ventilation above the floor shall be permitted.

11) Cablebus shall be permitted to extend vertically through dry floors and platforms, provided that the cablebus is totally enclosed at the point where it passes through the floor or platform and for a distance of 2 m above the floor or platform.

12) Cablebus shall be permitted to extend vertically through floors and platforms in wet locations where

a) there are curbs or other suitable means to prevent waterflow through the floor or platform opening; and

b) the cablebus is totally enclosed at the point where it passes through the floor or platform and for a distance of 2 m above the floor or platform.

13) Cablebus shall be provided with fire stops in accordance with Rule 2-128.

12-2256 Connection to other wiring methods

Where cablebus is connected to other wiring methods, the arrangement shall be such that the insulated conductors and cables will not be subject to mechanical damage or abrasion, and such that effective bonding will be maintained.

12-2258 Provisions for bonding (see Appendix B)

1) Where metal supports for metal cablebus are bolted to the cablebus enclosure and are in good electrical contact with the grounded structural metal frame of a building, the cablebus enclosure shall be deemed to be bonded to ground.

2) Where the conditions of Subrule 1) do not apply, the metal cablebus shall be adequately bonded

a) at intervals not exceeding 15 m, and the size of bonding conductors shall be based on the allowable ampacity as specified in Rule 10-614; or

Δ
Δ
b) at both ends, where the cablebus enclosure is marked for use as a bonding conductor.

Extra-low-voltage suspended ceiling power distribution systems

12-2300 Scope (see Appendix B)

Rules 12-2302 to 12-2320 apply only to the installation of extra-low-voltage suspended ceiling power distribution systems.

12-2302 Special terminology (see Appendix B)

In this Subsection, the following definitions shall apply:

Busbar — a non-insulated conductor electrically connected to the source of supply, physically supported on an insulator, and providing a power rail for connection to utilization equipment.

Busbar support — an insulator that runs the length of a section of suspended ceiling bus rail and serves to support and isolate the busbars from the suspended grid rail.

Connector — an electro-mechanical fitting made with insulating material compatible with the busbar.

Load connector — an electro-mechanical connector used to supply power from the busbar to utilization equipment.

Pendant connector — an electro-mechanical or mechanical connector used to suspend extra-low-voltage luminaire or utilization equipment below the grid rail and to supply power from the busbar to the luminaire or utilization equipment.

Power feed connector — an electro-mechanical connector used to connect

a) the output from a Class 2 power supply to a power distribution cable;

b) the output from a Class 2 power supply directly to the busbar; or

c) a power distribution cable to the busbar.

Rail-to-rail connector — an electro-mechanical connector used to interconnect busbars from one ceiling grid rail to another ceiling grid rail.

Extra-low-voltage suspended ceiling power distribution system — an extra-low-voltage system that serves as a support for a finished ceiling surface and consists of a busbar and busbar support system to distribute power to utilization equipment supplied by a Class 2 power supply.

Grid bus rail — a combination of the busbar, busbar support, and structural suspended ceiling grid system.

Rail — the structural support for a suspended ceiling system, typically forming the ceiling grid supporting the ceiling tile and utilization equipment such as sensors, actuators, audio/video devices, extra-low-voltage luminaires, and similar electrical equipment.

Reverse polarity protection (back-feed protection) — a system that prevents two interconnected power supplies connected positive to negative from passing current from one power source into a second power source.

Suspended ceiling grid — a system that serves as a support for a finished ceiling surface and utilization equipment.

12-2304 General
1) An extra-low-voltage suspended ceiling power distribution system shall be a complete system, with the utilization equipment, Class 2 power supply, and fittings as part of the same identified system.
2) Notwithstanding Subrule 1), an extra-low-voltage suspended ceiling power distribution system shall be permitted to supply extra-low-voltage utilization equipment not identified as part of the same system.

12-2306 Use permitted
Extra-low-voltage suspended ceiling power distribution systems shall be permanently connected and shall be permitted for use
a) with extra-low-voltage Class 2 circuits;
b) in dry locations;
c) in residential, commercial, and industrial applications; and
d) in other spaces used for environmental air where a duct, plenum, or hollow space is created by the suspended ceiling having lay-in panels or tiles, provided that
   i) electrical equipment having a metal enclosure or a non-metallic enclosure and fittings is suitable for use within an air-handling space; and
   ii) the system complies with the requirements of Rules 2-130 and 12-100.

12-2308 Use prohibited
Extra-low-voltage suspended ceiling power distribution systems shall not be installed
a) in damp or wet locations;
b) where subject to corrosive fumes or vapours, such as in storage-battery rooms;
c) where subject to physical damage;
d) in concealed locations;
e) in patient care areas as defined in Section 24;
f) in hazardous locations; or
g) as part of a fire-rated assembly, unless designed for use as part of the assembly.

12-2310 Class 2 circuit conductors

Insulated circuit conductors and cables shall
a)   meet the requirements of Rule 16-210; and
b)   be installed in accordance with Section 16.

12-2312 Disconnecting means

1)   To allow for servicing or maintenance of extra-low-voltage suspended ceiling power distribution systems, a disconnecting means shall be provided for the Class 2 power supply and shall be accessible and within sight of the Class 2 power supply.
2)   A disconnecting means that is connected to a multi-wire branch circuit shall safely and simultaneously disconnect all ungrounded conductors from the Class 2 power supply.

12-2314 Securing and supporting (see Appendix B)

1)   An extra-low-voltage suspended ceiling power distribution system shall be secured to the mounting surface of the building structure in accordance with the system installation and operating instructions.
2)   The individual power grid rails shall be mechanically secured to the overall suspended ceiling grid assembly.

12-2316 Connectors (see Appendix B)

1)   Connections to busbars, cables, and conductors shall be accessible after installation.
2)   The following connectors shall be permitted to be used as connection or interconnection devices:
    a)   load connectors;
    b)   pendant connectors;
    c)   power feed connectors; and
    d)   rail-to-rail connectors.

12-2318 Output connections and reverse polarity protection (back-feed protection)

1)   Class 2 power supplies shall not have the output connections paralleled or otherwise interconnected.
2)   An extra-low-voltage suspended ceiling power distribution system with Class 2 dc circuits shall be
    a)   installed as a complete system, including the power supply; or
    b)   provided with reverse polarity protection (back-feed protection) as part of the grid rail busbar or as part of the power feed connector, if the Class 2 power supply is not provided as part of a complete system.

Ⓔ ### 12-2320 System grounding

Class 2 load side circuits for extra-low-voltage suspended ceiling power distribution systems shall not be grounded.

Manufactured wiring systems

12-2500 Uses permitted

1)   A manufactured wiring system shall be permitted to be installed
    a)   in accessible and dry locations; and
Δ   b)   in spaces for environmental air when marked for the application and installed in accordance with Rule 12-010.
2)   Notwithstanding Subrule 1) a), a manufactured wiring system shall be permitted to extend into walls for connection to switch and outlet points.

12-2502 Installation

A manufactured wiring system shall be installed in accordance with Rules 12-602 to 12-618.

Bare busbars and risers

12-2600 Where bare busbars are permitted to be used
Bare conductors shall not be used as main risers or feeders in buildings unless a deviation has been obtained in accordance with Rule 2-030, and
a)   the building is of non-combustible construction;
b)   the conductors are placed in a chase, channel, or shaft located or guarded so that the conductors are inaccessible;
c)   suitable cut-offs to protect against the vertical spread of fire are provided where floors are pierced;
d)   the mechanical and electrical features of the installation and the conductor supports are suitable and the following specific requirements are met in the case of busbars rated 1200 A or less:
   i)   where flat busbars 6.35 mm or less in thickness are used, the continuous current rating shall not exceed 1000 A per 645 mm^2 of cross-sectional area of copper busbar or 700 A in the case of aluminum busbars; and
   ii)   busbar supports shall be spaced not more than 750 mm apart, with minimum clearance across insulating surfaces between bars of opposite polarity of not less than 50 mm, and 25 mm between busbars and any grounded surface; and
e)   the resulting installation is acceptable.

Installation of boxes, cabinets, outlets, and terminal fittings

12-3000 Outlet boxes (see Appendix B)
1)   A box or an equivalent device shall be installed at every point of outlet, switch, or junction of conduit, raceways, armoured cable, or non-metallic-sheathed cable.
2)   Non-metallic outlet boxes shall not be used in wiring methods using metal raceways or armoured or metal-sheathed cable, except where the boxes are provided with bonding connections between all cable entry openings.
3)   Where metal fittings are used to terminate a non-metallic wiring method to a non-metallic outlet box, the metal fittings shall be bonded to ground.
4)   Metal boxes embedded in parking lot slabs or pavement, road beds, and similar areas subject to vehicular traffic shall comply with the requirements of Rule 2-116 1).
5)   The box shall be provided with a cover or luminaire canopy.
6)   At least 150 mm of free insulated conductor shall be left at each outlet for making of joints or the connection of electrical equipment, unless the insulated conductors are intended to loop through lampholders, receptacles, or similar devices without joints.
Δ 7)   Notwithstanding the requirements of Subrule 1), an outlet box shall not be required where provision for connection is integral to the equipment.
8)   Notwithstanding the requirements of Subrule 1), an outlet box shall not be required for a switch or a receptacle conforming to Rule 12-3010 7).
Δ 9)   Where a pendant ceiling fan and all possible accessories weigh less than 16 kg and are intended to be supported by a ceiling outlet box, the outlet box shall be marked for fan support.
10)   Floor boxes shall be installed in accordance with the manufacturer's installation instructions for the type of floor intended.

12-3002 Outlet box covers (see Appendix B)
1)   Cover plates installed on flush-mounted boxes and surface-mounted outlet boxes shall be of a type for which each is designed.
Δ 2)   Flush-mounted floor box covers shall be suitable for the type of floor.

12-3004 Terminal fittings
1)   Where insulated conductors and bare conductors are run from the ends of conduit, armoured cable, surface raceways, or non-metallic-sheathed cable to appliances or open wiring, an outlet

fitting or terminal fitting shall be permitted to be used instead of the box required by Rule 12-3000, and the insulated conductors and bare conductors shall be run without splice, tap, or joint within the fitting.

2) The fitting shall have a separately bushed hole for each insulated conductor and bare conductor.

3) The fittings shall not be used at outlets for luminaires.

12-3006 Terminal fittings behind switchboards

Where insulated conductors issue from conduit behind a switchboard or more than eight insulated conductors issue from a conduit at control apparatus or a similar location, an insulating bushing shall be permitted to be used instead of the box required by Rule 12-3000.

12-3008 Boxes in concrete construction

1) Where used in concrete slab construction, ceiling outlet boxes shall have knockouts spaced above the free or lower edge of the boxes a distance of at least twice the diameter of the steel reinforcing bars so that conduit entering the knockouts shall clear the bars without offsetting.

2) Sectional boxes shall not be used embedded in concrete or masonry construction.

3) Boxes made wholly or in part of aluminum shall not be embedded in concrete containing reinforcing steel unless
   a) the concrete is known to contain no chloride additives; or
   b) the box has been treated with a bituminous base paint or other means to prevent galvanic corrosion of the aluminum.

12-3010 Outlet box supports (see Appendix B)

1) Except as permitted by Subrule 6), boxes and fittings shall be firmly secured to studs, joists, or similar fixed structural units other than wooden, metal, or composition lath, in accordance with this Rule.

2) Where ganged sectional boxes are used, they shall be secured to metal supports or to wooden boards at least 19 mm thick that are rigidly secured to the structural units.

3) Where boxes having any dimension greater than 100 mm are used, they shall be secured on at least two sides or shall be secured to metal supports or to wooden boards at least 19 mm thick that are rigidly secured to the structural units.

4) Where boxes are mounted on metal studs, additional support shall be provided to prevent movement of the box after the drywall is installed.

5) Mounting nails or screws shall not project into nor pass through the interior of an outlet box unless
   a) the nails or screws are located so as not to be more than 6.4 mm from the back or ends of the box; and
   b) the nails or screws are located so that they will not interfere with insulated conductors or connectors.

6) This Rule shall not apply to boxes and fittings installed after the studs, joists, or structural units have been concealed.

Δ 7) This Rule shall not apply to a switch or a receptacle with an integral enclosure for use with non-metallic-sheathed cable and having brackets that securely fasten the integral enclosure to walls or ceilings of conventional construction.

8) Where a ceiling outlet box marked for fan support is installed, the outlet box shall be
   a) securely attached directly to the building structure; or
   b) attached by a bar hanger securely attached directly to the building structure.

9) A pendant ceiling fan and all possible accessories weighing 16 kg or more shall be supported independently of the outlet box.

12-3012 Boxes, cabinets, and fitting supports

1) Boxes, cabinets, and fittings shall be fastened securely in place.

2) Boxes and fittings having a volume of less than 1640 mL shall be permitted to be attached to a firmly secured exposed raceway by threading or other equally substantial means.

12-3014 Accessibility of junction boxes

1) Pull-in, junction, and outlet boxes, cabinets and gutters, and joints in conductors and cables shall be accessible.

2) A vertical space of 900 mm or more shall be required to provide ready access.

12-3016 Outlet boxes, cabinets, and fittings (see Appendix B)

1) The front edges of boxes, cabinets, and fittings installed in walls or ceilings shall not be set in more than 6 mm from the finished surface and, where the walls or ceilings are of wood or other combustible material, shall be flush with the finished surface or shall project from the surface.

2) Gaps or open spaces in plaster surfaces of walls or ceilings shall be filled in around the front edges of boxes, cabinets, and fittings.

3) Outlet boxes requiring wet location cover plates shall be installed in a manner that the intended seal between the outlet box and the cover is ensured.

4) Flush boxes, cabinets, and fittings shall be of a type suitable for the intended location of installation.

12-3018 Outlet boxes attached to existing plaster work

Where outlet boxes installed as additions to existing work are mounted directly upon existing plaster surfaces, they shall be fastened securely in place.

12-3020 Outlet boxes, etc., in damp places

Where boxes, cabinets, and fittings are installed in damp places, they shall be placed or constructed so as to prevent moisture from entering and accumulating in them.

12-3022 Entrance of cables into boxes, cabinets, and fittings

1) Where cables pass through the walls of boxes, cabinets, or fittings, provision shall be made to
   a) protect the insulation on the conductors from damage;
   b) protect terminal connections from external strain;
   Δ c) provide electrical continuity between a metal box, cabinet, or fitting and conduit, armour, or metal sheathing of cables, whether or not the armour or metal sheathing is to be used as a bonding conductor;
   d) prevent damage to a non-metallic sheath applied over armour or metal sheathing for protection against moisture or corrosion; and
   e) close the openings through which the cables pass in such a manner that any remaining opening will not permit entrance of a test rod 6.75 mm in diameter.

2) Where insulated conductors run as open wiring enter a box, cabinet, or fitting, they shall pass through insulating bushings or be installed in raceways or insulating tubing.

Δ 3) Where non-metallic-sheathed cable or tray cable enters a box, cabinet, or fitting, a box connector, either as a separate device designed for use with such cable or as part of the box, cabinet, or fitting, shall be used to secure the cable in place adequately and without damage to the cable jacket or conductor insulation.

4) Where rigid or flexible metal conduit, electrical metallic tubing, or armoured cable enters boxes, cabinets, or fittings, it shall be secured in place in accordance with the requirements of Section 10.

Δ 5) Where metal-sheathed cables enter boxes, cabinets, or fittings, the box connector shall be installed in a manner that will meet the requirements of Section 10 without damage to the cable jacket or conductor insulation and shall be of a type for use with the cable.

6) Where liquid-tight flexible metal conduit, flexible metal conduit, armoured cable, or metal-sheathed cable of a type having a non-metallic sheath over the armour or metal sheath enters a box, cabinet, or fitting, the box connector shall ensure electrical continuity without damage to the non-metallic sheath unless the point of connection is in a dry location free from corrosive

atmosphere, where the non-metallic sheath shall be permitted to be stripped back a sufficient distance.

Δ 7) Where single-conductor cables or insulated single conductors enter metal boxes through separate openings, precautions shall be taken in accordance with the requirements of Rule 4-008.

12-3024 Unused openings in boxes, cabinets, and fittings
Unused openings in boxes, cabinets, and fittings shall be effectively closed by plugs or plates affording protection substantially equivalent to that of the wall of the box, cabinet, or fitting.

12-3026 Extensions from existing outlets
1) Where a surface extension is made from an existing outlet of concealed wiring, a box or an extension-ring shall be mounted over the original box and electrically and mechanically secured to it.
2) The extension shall then be connected to the box or extension-ring in the manner prescribed by this Section for the method of wiring employed in making the extension.

12-3028 Multi-outlet assemblies
1) Multi-outlet assemblies shall be used only in normally dry locations as extensions to wiring systems.
2) Multi-outlet assemblies shall not be used in any bathroom, kitchen, or any place where the assembly would be subject to mechanical damage.
3) Multi-outlet assemblies shall be permitted to be carried through but not run within dry partitions, provided that
   a) no outlet falls within the partition;
   b) the removal of any cap or cover necessary for proper installation is not prevented; and
   c) the assembly is of metal or, if not of metal, is surrounded by metal or the equivalent.
4) Multi-outlet assemblies shall not be concealed within the building finish, but
   a) the back and sides of metal assemblies shall be permitted to be set in plaster applied after the assembly is in place; or
   b) the back and sides of non-metallic assemblies shall be permitted to be set in a preformed recess in the building finish; and
   c) shall be permitted to be recessed in a baseboard or other wood trim member.

12-3030 Insulated conductors in boxes, cabinets, or fittings (see Appendix B)
1) Insulated conductors that are connected to different power or distribution transformers or other different sources of voltage shall not be installed in the same box, cabinet, or fitting unless
   a) a barrier of sheet steel not less than 1.3 mm thick or a flame-retardant, non-metallic insulating material not less than 1.6 mm in thickness is used to divide the space into separate compartments for the insulated conductors of each system;
   b) the insulated conductors are used for the supply and/or control of remote devices and are insulated for at least the same voltage as that of the circuit having the highest voltage and none of the insulated conductors of the circuits of lower voltages is directly connected to a lighting branch circuit; or
   c) the insulated conductors are used for the supply of a double-throw switch in an emergency lighting system.
2) Where a barrier is used, it shall be fastened rigidly to the box, cabinet, or fitting, or a device assuring positive separation of the insulated conductors shall be used.

12-3032 Wiring space in enclosures (see Appendix B)
1) Enclosures for overcurrent devices, controllers, and externally operated switches shall not be used as junction boxes, troughs, or raceways for insulated conductors feeding through to other apparatus.

2) Notwithstanding Subrule 1),
- a) enclosures for overcurrent devices, controllers, and externally operated switches shall be permitted to be used as junction boxes
  - i) for all installations where a single feeder supplying another enclosure is tapped from it and the connectors used each provide an independent clamping means for each conductor and each clamping means is independently accessible for tightening or inspection; or
  - ii) where wiring is being added to an enclosure forming part of an existing installation and the insulated conductors, bare conductors, splices, and taps do not fill the wiring space at any cross-section to more than 75% of the cross-sectional area of the space; and
- b) enclosures for overcurrent devices, controllers, and externally operated switches shall be permitted to be used as raceways where the insulated conductors are being added to enclosures forming part of an existing installation, and all the insulated conductors and bare conductors present do not fill the wiring space at any cross-section to more than 40% of the cross-sectional area of the space.
3) Insulated conductors entering enclosures shall enter such enclosures as near as practicable to their terminal fittings.
4) Notwithstanding Subrule 1), enclosures for overcurrent devices, controllers, and externally operated switches shall be permitted to be used as raceways for wiring associated with instrument transformers and energy usage metering devices, provided that
- Δ a) each such enclosure is designed to house instrument transformers and energy usage metering devices; and
- b) the wiring does not fill the wiring space at any cross-section to more than 75% of the cross-sectional area of the space.

Δ **12-3034 Maximum number of insulated conductors in a box** (see Appendix B)
1) Boxes shall be of sufficient size to provide usable space for all insulated conductors contained in the box, subject to the following:
- a) an insulated conductor running through a box with no connection therein shall be considered as one insulated conductor;
- b) each insulated conductor entering or leaving a box and connected to a terminal or connector within the box shall be considered as one insulated conductor;
- c) an insulated conductor of which no part leaves the box shall not be counted; and
- d) No. 18 and No. 16 AWG fixture-wires supplying a luminaire mounted on the box containing the fixture-wires shall not be counted.
2) Except as specified in Subrule 3) and subject to the details given in Subrule 1), boxes of the nominal dimensions given in Table 23 shall not contain more insulated conductors of a given size than permitted by the Table, and the number of conductors shall be reduced for each of the following conditions as applicable:
- a) one insulated conductor if the box contains one or more fixture studs or hickeys;
- b) one insulated conductor for every pair of conductor connectors with insulating caps (no deduction for one conductor connector, deduct one insulated conductor for 2 or 3 conductor connectors, two insulated conductors for 4 or 5 conductor connectors, etc.); or
- c) two insulated conductors if the box contains one or more flush devices mounted on a single strap.
3) Where a box contains a device having a dimension greater than 2.54 cm between the mounting strap and the back of the device, the total usable space shall be reduced by the space occupied by the device, calculated as 32 cm³ multiplied by the depth of the device in centimetres.

4) Subject to the details given in Subrules 1) and 3), boxes having nominal dimensions or volume other than those shown in Table 23, or any box containing insulated conductors of different sizes, shall have the amount of usable space per insulated conductor as specified in Table 22, but the number of insulated conductors so calculated shall be reduced for each of the conditions of Subrule 2) as applicable with the exception of Subrule 2 b), provided that such exception is based on the size of the largest insulated conductor that is included with every pair of conductor connectors.

5) The total usable space in a box considered under Table 22 shall be considered to be the internal volume of the box and shall disregard any space occupied by locknuts, bushings, box connectors, or clamps.

6) Where sectional boxes are ganged, or where plaster rings, extension rings, or raised covers are used in conjunction with boxes, ganged or otherwise, and are marked with their volume measurement, the space in the box shall be the total volume of the assembled sections.

12-3036 Pull box or junction box sizes

1) For the purposes of Subrule 2), the equivalent cable to trade size of raceway shall be the minimum trade size raceway that would be required for the number and size of conductors in the cable.

2) Where a pull or junction box is used with raceways containing insulated conductors of No. 4 AWG or larger, or with cables containing insulated conductors No. 4 AWG or larger, the box shall
   a) for a raceway or cable entering the wall of a box opposite to a removable cover, have a distance from the wall to the cover not less than the trade diameter of the largest raceway or equivalent cable plus 6 times the diameter of the largest insulated conductor;
   b) for straight pulls or runs of cable, have a length of at least eight times the trade diameter of the largest raceway or equivalent cable; and
   c) for angle and U pulls or runs of cable,
      i) have a distance between each raceway or cable entry inside the box and the opposite wall of the box of at least six times the trade diameter of the largest raceway or equivalent cable, plus the sum of the trade diameters of all other raceways or equivalent cables on the same wall of the box; and
      ii) have a distance, as measured in a straight line, between the nearest edges of each raceway or cable entry enclosing the same insulated conductor of at least
         A) six times the trade diameter of the raceway or equivalent cable; or
         B) six times the trade diameter of the larger raceway or equivalent cable if they are of different sizes.

12

Section 14 — Protection and control

Scope

Δ **14-000 Scope** (see Appendix B)

This Section applies to the protection and control of electrical circuits and apparatus installed in accordance with the requirements of this Section and other Sections of this Code.

General requirements

14-010 Protective and control devices required

Except as otherwise provided for in this Section or in other Sections dealing with specific equipment, electrical apparatus and ungrounded conductors shall be provided with

a) devices for the purpose of automatically opening the electrical circuit thereto,
   i) if the current reaches a value that will produce a dangerous temperature in the apparatus or conductor; and
   ii) in the event of a ground fault, in accordance with Rule 14-102;

b) manually operable control devices that will safely disconnect all ungrounded conductors of the circuit at the point of supply simultaneously, except for multi-wire branch circuits that supply only fixed lighting loads or non-split receptacles, and that have each lighting load or receptacle connected to the neutral and one ungrounded conductor; and

c) devices that, when necessary, will open the electrical circuit thereto in the event of failure of voltage in such a circuit.

14-012 Ratings of protective and control equipment (see Appendix B)

In circuits of 750 V and less,

a) electrical equipment required to interrupt fault currents shall have ratings sufficient for the voltage employed and for the fault current that is available at the terminals; and

b) electrical equipment required to interrupt current at other than fault levels shall have ratings sufficient for the voltage employed and for the current it must interrupt.

14-014 Series rated combinations (see Appendix B)

Notwithstanding Rule 14-012 a), a moulded case circuit breaker shall be permitted to be installed in a circuit having an available fault current higher than its rating, provided that

Δ a) the circuit breaker is a recognized component of a series rated combination;

b) it is installed on the load side of an overcurrent device that has an interrupting rating at least equal to the available fault current;

c) the overcurrent device on the line side of the lower rated circuit breaker is as specified on the equipment in which the lower rated circuit breaker is installed;

d) the equipment in which the lower rated circuit breaker is installed is marked with a series combination interrupting rating at least equal to the available fault current; and

e) the overcurrent devices installed in a series rated combination are marked at the time of installation in a conspicuous and legible manner to indicate that they must be replaced only with components of the same type and rating.

14-016 Connection of devices

Devices required by this Section shall not be connected in any grounded conductors except where

a) the devices simultaneously or previously disconnect all ungrounded conductors;

b) an overcurrent device is in a 2-wire circuit having one grounded conductor and where there is a possibility that the grounded conductor may assume a voltage difference between itself and ground, due to unreliable grounding conditions of sufficient magnitude to create a dangerous condition; or

c) overcurrent devices are located in that part of a circuit that is connected by a 2-pole polarized or unpolarized attachment plug, provided that the circuit is rated 15 A, 125 V or less.

Protective devices

General

14-100 Overcurrent protection of conductors (see Appendix B)

Each ungrounded conductor shall be protected by an overcurrent device at the point where it receives its supply of current and at each point where the size of conductor is decreased, except that such protection shall be permitted to be omitted in each of the following cases:

a) where the overcurrent device in a larger conductor properly protects the smaller conductor;

b) where the smaller conductor
   i) has an ampacity not less than the combined computed loads of the circuits supplied by the smaller conductor and not less than the ampere rating of the switchboard, panelboard, or control device supplied by the smaller conductor;
   ii) is not over 3 m long;
   iii) does not extend beyond the switchboard, panelboard, or control device that it supplies; and
   iv) is enclosed in non-ventilated raceways, armoured cable, or metal-sheathed cable when not part of the wiring in the switchboard, panelboard, or other control devices;

c) where the smaller conductor
   i) has an ampacity not less than one-third that of the larger conductor from which it is supplied; and
   ii) is suitably protected from mechanical damage, is not more than 7.5 m long, and terminates in a single overcurrent device rated or set at a value not exceeding the ampacity of the conductor, but beyond the single overcurrent device the conductor shall be permitted to supply any number of overcurrent devices;

d) where the conductor
   i) forms part of the only circuit supplied from a power or distribution transformer rated over 750 V with primary protection in accordance with Rule 26-250 1), 2), and 3) and that supplies only that circuit;
   ii) terminates at a single overcurrent device with a rating not exceeding the ampacity of the conductor(s) in the circuit; and
   iii) is protected from mechanical damage;

e) where the smaller conductor is No. 14 AWG or larger, is in a control circuit, and is located external to the control equipment enclosure, and
   i) the rating or setting of the branch circuit overcurrent device is not more than 300% of the ampacity of the control circuit conductor; or
   ii) the opening of the control circuit would create a hazard;

f) where the smaller conductor supplies a transformer, and
   i) the conductor supplying the primary of the transformer has an ampacity not less than one-third that of the larger conductor;
   ii) the conductor supplied by the secondary of the transformer has an ampacity not less than the ampacity of the primary conductor multiplied by the ratio of the primary to the secondary voltage;
   iii) the total length of one primary plus one secondary conductor (the longest, if more than one winding), excluding any portion of the primary conductor that is protected at its own ampacity, does not exceed 7.5 m;
   iv) the primary and secondary conductors are protected from mechanical damage; and

v)   the secondary conductor terminates in a single overcurrent device rated or set at a value not exceeding its ampacity; or

g)   where the smaller conductor

    i)   is supplied by a circuit at not more than 750 V;

    ii)   is supplied from an overhead or underground circuit and is run overhead or underground except where it enters a building;

    iii)   is installed in accordance with the requirements of Section 6; and

    iv)   terminates in service equipment in accordance with Section 6.

14-102 Ground fault protection (see Appendix B)

1)   Ground fault protection shall be provided to de-energize all normally ungrounded conductors of a faulted circuit that are downstream from the point or points marked with an asterisk in Diagram 3 in the event of a ground fault in those conductors as follows:

    a)   for circuits of solidly grounded systems rated more than 150 volts-to-ground, less than 750 V phase-to-phase, and 1000 A or more; and

    b)   for circuits of solidly grounded systems rated 150 V or less to ground and 2000 A or more.

2)   Except as permitted by Subrule 8), the maximum setting of the ground fault protection shall be 1200 A and the maximum time delay shall be 1 s for ground fault currents equal to or greater than 3000 A.

3)   The ampere rating of the circuits referred to in Subrule 1) shall be considered to be

    a)   the rating of the largest fuse that can be installed in a fusible disconnecting device;

    b)   the highest trip setting for which the actual overcurrent device installed in a circuit breaker is rated or can be adjusted; or

    c)   the ampacity of the main conductor feeding the devices located at points marked with an asterisk in Item 2 of Diagram 3, in the case where no main disconnecting device is provided.

4)   This protection shall be provided by

    a)   an overcurrent device that incorporates ground fault protection;

    b)   a ground fault tripping system consisting of a sensor(s), relay, and auxiliary tripping mechanism; or

    c)   other means.

5)   The sensor(s) referred to in Subrule 4) shall be

    a)   sensors that vectorially totalize the currents in all conductors of the circuit, including the grounded circuit conductor, where one is provided, but excluding any current flowing in the ground fault return current path;

    b)   sensors that sense ground fault current flowing from the fault to the supply end of the system through the ground return path; or

    c)   a combination of these two types of sensors.

6)   Sensors referred to in Subrule 5) a) shall be permitted to be installed at any point between the supply transformer and the downstream side of the disconnecting means marked with an asterisk in Diagram 3, but if located downstream from this disconnecting means, the sensors shall be placed as close as practicable to its load terminals.

7)   Sensors referred to in Subrule 5) b) shall be located on each connection between neutral and ground; however, where the neutral is grounded both at the supply transformer and at the switching centre, the sensor at the transformer shall not be required, provided that the maximum pickup setting of the ground fault relay does not exceed 1000 A.

8)   In ground fault schemes where two or more protective devices in series are used for ground fault coordination, the upstream protective device settings shall be permitted to exceed those specified in Subrule 2) where necessary to obtain the desired coordination, provided that the final downstream ground fault protective device in each circuit required to be protected conforms to the requirements of Subrule 2).

14-104 Rating of overcurrent devices (see Appendix B)

1) The rating or setting of overcurrent devices shall not exceed the allowable ampacity of the conductors that they protect, except

Δ a) where a fuse or circuit breaker having a rating or setting of the same value as the ampacity of the conductor is not available, and the maximum calculated or known load is in accordance with the Rules of Section 8, the ratings or settings given in Table 13 shall be permitted to be used within the maximum value of 800 A;

b) in the case of equipment wire, flexible cord in sizes Nos. 16, 18, and 20 AWG copper, and tinsel cord, which are considered protected by 15 A overcurrent devices; or

c) as provided for by other Rules of this Code.

2) Except as provided for by Subrule 1) c), the rating of overcurrent protection shall not exceed

a) 15 A for No. 14 AWG copper conductors;

b) 20 A for No. 12 AWG copper conductors;

c) 30 A for No. 10 AWG copper conductors;

d) 15 A for No. 12 AWG aluminum conductors; and

e) 25 A for No. 10 AWG aluminum conductors.

14-106 Location and grouping

Overcurrent devices shall be located in readily accessible places, except as provided for elsewhere in this Code, and shall be grouped where practicable.

Δ **14-108 Enclosure of overcurrent devices** (see Appendix B)

1) Overcurrent devices shall be enclosed in cut-out boxes or cabinets unless they form a part of an assembly that affords equivalent protection, or unless mounted as part of switchboards, panelboards, or controllers located in rooms or enclosures free from easily ignitable material and dampness, and accessible only to authorized persons.

2) Operating handles of circuit breakers shall be made accessible without opening any door or cover giving access to live parts.

14-110 Grouping of protective devices at distribution centre

1) Where the number of lighting branch circuits originating from a common enclosure exceeds

a) two, in a single-phase, 3-wire system; or

b) three, in a three-phase, 4-wire system,

overcurrent devices protecting such circuits shall be contained in a panelboard.

2) Where a panelboard is not required, and a fusible switch is used, all overcurrent devices shall have the same rating.

3) For the purposes of this Rule, each ungrounded conductor of a multi-wire branch circuit shall be counted as a separate circuit.

14-112 Overcurrent devices in parallel

1) Overcurrent devices shall not be connected in parallel in circuits of 750 V or less.

2) Notwithstanding Subrule 1), semiconductor fuses having interrupting ratings of 100 000 A and more, 750 V and less, and circuit breakers rated 750 V and less shall be permitted to be connected in parallel provided that they are factory assembled in parallel as a single unit.

14-114 Application of supplementary protectors (see Appendix B)

Supplementary overcurrent protection shall not be used as a substitute for branch circuit overcurrent devices or in place of branch circuit protective devices specified in this Section.

Fuses

14-200 Time-delay and low-melting-point fuses
1) Plug and cartridge fuses of the low-melting-point types, including time-delay fuses that also have low melting points, shall be marked so as to be readily distinguishable.
2) The marking referred to in Subrule 1) shall be the letter "P" for low-melting-point types that do not have time-delay characteristics and the letter "D" for time-delay fuses.

14-202 Use of plug fuses
Plug fuses and fuseholders shall not be used in circuits exceeding 125 V between conductors, except in circuits supplied from a system having a grounded neutral and having no conductor operating at more than 150 volts-to-ground.

14-204 Non-interchangeable fuses (see Appendix B)
1) Where plug fuses are used in branch circuits, they shall be of such a type and installed so that they are non-interchangeable with a fuse of larger rating.
2) Where any alterations or additions are made to an existing fusible panelboard, all the plug fuses in the panelboard shall be made to comply with the requirements of Subrule 1), where practicable.

14-206 Fuseholders for plug fuses
Fuseholders for plug fuses shall be of the so-called "covered" type where readily accessible to unauthorized persons.

14-208 Rating of fuses
1) Plug fuses shall be rated at not more than 30 A.
2) Standard cartridge fuses shall not be used in capacities larger than 600 A or in circuits at more than 600 V.
3) The fuses referred to in Rule 14-212 b), c), and d) that are used in circuits rated at 750 V or less are not limited in current rating.
4) Fuses for use in circuits of more than 750 V are not limited in current or voltage rating.

14-210 Fuses and fuseholders
Only fuses and fuseholders of proper rating shall be used, and no bridging or short-circuiting of either component shall be permitted.

14-212 Use of fuses (see Appendix B)
Class C, CA, CB, CC, G, H, J, K, L, R, T, HRCI-MISC, and HRCII-MISC fuses shall be permitted to be used as follows:
a) Class H fuses, where a standard interrupting rating of 10 000 A symmetrical or less is required;
b) Class CA, CB, CC, G, J, K, L, R, T, or HRCI-MISC, which have a higher interrupting rating, shall be permitted to be used instead of Class H fuses;
c) Class C and HRCII-MISC fuses shall be permitted to be used for overcurrent protection only where circuit overload protection is provided by other means; and
d) Class C and HRCII-MISC fuses shall be permitted to be used in those applications where this Code permits the installation of fuses greater than the ampere rating of the load, provided that the rating of the Class C or HRCII-MISC fuses does not exceed 85% of the maximum permitted rating.

Circuit breakers

14-300 Circuit breakers, general
1) Circuit breakers shall be of the trip-free type.
2) Indications shall be provided at the circuit breaker and at the point of operation to show whether the circuit breaker is open or closed.

14-302 Construction of circuit breakers (see Appendix B)

Where circuit breakers are provided for the protection of apparatus or ungrounded conductors, or both, they shall open the circuit in all ungrounded conductors by the manual operation of a single handle and by the action of overcurrent, except

a) where single-pole circuit breakers are permitted by Rule 14-010 b); or

b) in branch circuits derived from a 3-wire grounded neutral system, two single-pole manually operable circuit breakers shall be permitted to be used instead of a 2-pole circuit breaker, provided that

i) their handles are interlocked with a device as provided by the manufacturer so that all ungrounded conductors will be opened by the manual operation of any handle; and

ii) each circuit breaker has voltage ratings not less than that of the multi-wire branch circuit.

14-304 Non-tamperable circuit breakers

Branch circuit breakers, unless accessible only to authorized persons, shall be designed so that any alteration by the user of either tripping current or time will be difficult.

14-306 Tripping elements for circuit breakers

Circuit breakers shall be equipped with tripping elements as specified in Table 25.

14-308 Battery control power for circuit breakers

1) When power for operating the overcurrent element of a circuit breaker is derived from a battery, the battery voltage shall be continuously monitored.

2) If the battery voltage drops to a value insufficient to operate the circuit breaker overcurrent element

a) the circuit breaker shall automatically trip; or

b) an alarm shall operate continuously until the battery voltage is restored.

3) A suitable warning notice shall be placed on or adjacent to the circuit breaker indicating that battery control power must be available before the circuit breaker is closed.

Control devices

General

14-400 Rating of control devices

Control devices shall have ratings suitable for the connected load of the circuits that they control and, with the exception of isolating switches, shall be capable of safely establishing and interrupting such loads.

14-402 Disconnecting means required for fused circuits (see Appendix B)

Circuits protected by fuses shall be equipped with disconnecting means, integral with or adjacent to the fuseholders, whereby all live parts for mounting fuses can be readily and safely made dead; however, such disconnecting means shall be permitted to be omitted in any one of the following cases:

a) instrument and control circuits on switchboards where the voltage does not exceed 250 V;

b) primary circuits of voltage transformers having a primary voltage of 750 V or less, on switchboards; and

c) a circuit having only one ungrounded conductor where a plug fuse is used.

14-404 Control devices ahead of overcurrent devices

Control devices used in combination with overcurrent devices or overload devices for the control of circuits or apparatus shall be connected so that the overcurrent or overload devices will be dead when the control device is in the open position, except where this is impracticable.

14-406 Location of control devices

1) Control devices, with the exception of isolating switches, shall be readily accessible.

2) Remotely controlled devices shall be considered to be readily accessible if the means of controlling them are readily accessible.

14-408 Indication of control device positions
Manually operable control devices shall indicate the ON and OFF positions, unless the application of the devices makes this requirement unnecessary.

14-410 Enclosure of control devices
Control devices, unless they are located or guarded in a way that renders them inaccessible to unauthorized persons and prevents fire hazards, shall have all current-carrying parts in enclosures of metal or other fire-resisting material.

14-412 Grouping of control devices
Control devices controlling feeders and branch circuits shall be grouped where practicable.

14-414 Connection to different circuits
1) Where electrical equipment is supplied by two or more different transformers or other different sources of voltage, then
   a) a single disconnecting means that will effectively isolate all ungrounded conductors supplying the equipment shall be provided integral with or adjacent to the equipment; or
   b) each supply circuit shall be provided with a disconnecting means integral with or adjacent to the equipment, and the disconnecting means shall be grouped together.
2) Notwithstanding Subrule 1), disconnecting means integral with or adjacent to equipment need not be provided for control circuits originating beyond the equipment and not exceeding 150 volts-to-ground, provided that all associated bare live parts are protected against inadvertent contact by means of barriers.
3) Where multiple disconnecting means as in Subrule 1) b) are provided, suitable warning signs shall be placed on or adjacent to each disconnecting means so that all of the disconnecting means must be opened to ensure complete de-energization of the equipment.
4) Where barriers are used as required in Subrule 2), a suitable warning sign shall be placed on or adjacent to the equipment, or on the barriers, indicating that there is more than one source of supply to the equipment.

14-416 Control devices used only for switching
Except as permitted by other Rules in this Code, control devices that perform only switching functions shall disconnect all ungrounded conductors of the controlled circuit when in the OFF position.

Switches

14-500 Operation of switches
Knife switches and other control devices, unless located or guarded in a way that renders them inaccessible to unauthorized persons, shall be constructed so that they can be switched to the OFF position without exposing live parts.

14-502 Mounting of knife switches
1) Single-throw knife switches shall be mounted with their bases in a vertical plane.
2) Single-throw knife switches shall be mounted so that gravity will not tend to close them.
3) Double-throw knife switches shall be permitted to be mounted so that the throw will be either vertical or horizontal but, if the throw is vertical, a positive locking device or stop shall be provided to ensure that the blades remain in the open position when so set, unless the switch is not intended to be left in the open position.

14-504 Maximum rating of switches
Unless of special design, knife switches rated at more than 600 A at 750 V or less shall be used only as isolating switches.

14-506 Connection of switches

Manual single-throw switches, circuit breakers, or magnetic switches shall be connected so that the blades or moving contacts will be dead when the device is in the open position, except that the following need not comply:

a) branch-circuit breakers that have all live parts other than terminals sealed and that are constructed so that the line and load connections can be interchanged;

b) switchgear that is provided for sectionalizing purposes and has a suitable caution notice attached to the assembly;

c) switches that are immersed in a liquid and have a suitable caution notice attached to the outside of the enclosure;

d) switches that are designed so that all live parts are inaccessible when the device is in the open position; and

e) magnetic switches, when preceded by a circuit breaker or manual switch that is located in the same enclosure or immediately adjacent and is marked to indicate that it controls the circuit to the magnetic switch, unless this is obvious.

14-508 Rating of general-use ac/dc switches (see Appendix B)

AC/DC switches shall be rated as follows:

a) for non-inductive loads other than tungsten-filament lamps, switches shall have an ampere rating not less than the ampere rating of the load;

b) for tungsten-filament lamp loads, and for combined tungsten-filament and non-inductive loads, switches shall be "T" rated, except where

   i) the switches are used in branch circuit wiring systems in dwelling units; in private hospital or hotel rooms; or in similar locations, but not in public rooms or places of assembly;

   ii) the switch controls permanently connected luminaires or lighting outlets in one room only, or in one continuous hallway where luminaires may be located at different levels or in attics or basements not used for assembly purposes; and

   iii) the switch is rated at not less than 10 A, 125 V; 5 A, 250 V; or for the four-way types, 5 A, 125 V; 2 A, 250 V;

c) canopy switches controlling a tungsten-filament lamp load shall be "T" rated or shall have an ampere rating at least three times the ampere rating of the load; and

d) for inductive loads, switches shall have an ampere rating of twice the ampere rating of the load.

Δ 14-510 Use and rating of manually operated general-use ac switches (see Appendix B)

1) Manually operated general-use switches intended for ac systems shall have an ampere rating not less than the current rating of the load when they are installed in branch circuits supplying

   a) tungsten-filament lamp loads at 120 V maximum;

   b) non-inductive loads; or

   c) inductive loads at not less than 75% power factor lag.

2) The current rating of the switches shall be not less than 15 A in conjunction with a voltage rating of 120 or 277 V.

3) Switches shall be adapted for mounting in flush-device boxes, surface-type boxes, or special boxes or have complete self-enclosures.

14-512 Manually operated general-use 347 V ac switches (see Appendix B)

1) Manually operated general-use 347 V ac switches shall be used only for the control of non-inductive loads other than tungsten-filament lamps and for inductive loads where the power factor is not less than 75% lagging.

2) The current rating of the switches shall be not less than 15 A in conjunction with a voltage rating of 347 V.

14

3) The switches designed for mounting in boxes shall not be readily interchangeable with the switches referred to in Rules 14-508 and 14-510.

14-514 Manually operated switches in circuits exceeding 300 volts-to-ground

When controlling circuits exceeding 300 volts-to-ground, the switches referred to in Rules 14-508 and 14-512 shall not be ganged or grouped in the same enclosure unless the enclosure provides permanently installed barriers.

Protection and control of miscellaneous apparatus

14-600 Protection of receptacles

Receptacles shall not be connected to a branch circuit having overcurrent protection rated or set at more than the ampere rating of the receptacle, except as permitted by other Sections of this Code.

14-602 Additional control devices not necessary

Portable appliances need not be equipped with additional control devices where the appliances are
a) rated at not more than 1500 W; and
b) provided with cord connectors, attachment plugs, or other means by which they can be disconnected readily from the circuits.

14-604 Outlet control from more than one point

Where switches are used to control an outlet or outlets from more than one point, the switches shall be connected so that all switching is done only in the ungrounded circuit conductor.

14-606 Panelboard overcurrent protection

1) Except for panelboards where more than 90% of the overcurrent devices supply feeders or motor branch circuits, every panelboard shall be protected on the supply side by overcurrent devices having a rating not greater than that of the panelboard.
2) The overcurrent protection required by Subrule 1) shall be permitted to be in the primary of a transformer supplying the panelboard, provided that the panelboard rating in amperes is not less than the overcurrent rating in amperes multiplied by the ratio of the primary to the secondary voltage.

14-608 Remote control circuits

Remote control circuits of remotely controlled apparatus shall be arranged so that they can be conveniently disconnected from their source of supply at the controller, but as an alternative the disconnecting of the apparatus from the supply circuit shall be permitted to be arranged so that it also disconnects the remote control circuit from the supply circuit.

14-610 Protection of circuits supplying cycling loads

Where fuses protect circuits in which more than 50% of the circuit rating is a cycling load, such as thermostatically controlled electric space heaters, clothes dryers, or water heaters, they shall be time-delay or low-melting-point fuses of the type referred to in Rule 14-200 or fuses as referred to in Rule 14-212 b); however, in dwelling units, the fuses referred to in Rule 14-212 b) shall have the same low-melting-point characteristics as those referred to in Rule 14-200.

14-612 Transfer equipment for standby power systems

Transfer equipment for standby power systems shall prevent the inadvertent interconnection of normal and standby sources of supply in any operation of the transfer equipment.

Solid-state devices

14-700 Restriction of use

Solid-state devices shall not be used as isolating switches or as disconnecting means.

14-702 Disconnecting means required

1) Supplementary disconnecting means shall be provided where failure of or leakage through a solid-state device could result in transfer of energy between two or more power sources.

2) The disconnecting means referred to in Subrule 1) shall be connected into the circuit in such a way that, when opened, it will prevent transfer of energy between the different power sources, and shall be

a) provided as an integral part of the solid-state device; or

b) installed as close as practicable to, and in sight of, the solid-state device.

14-704 Warning notices required

Suitable warning notices shall be placed

a) on the supplementary disconnecting means required by Rule 14-702 so that

i) this disconnecting means shall be opened in the event of a failure of any of the power sources or in the event of servicing of any component in the circuits of the other power sources; and

ii) both line and load terminals may be energized when the disconnecting means is open; and

b) on all other upstream disconnecting means so that an alternative power source(s) exists in the circuit and that the supplementary disconnecting means must also be opened to prevent the possibility of feedback from the alternative source(s).

14

Section 16 — Class 1 and Class 2 circuits

General

Δ **16-000 Scope** (see Appendix B)
1) This Section applies to
   a) Class 1 and Class 2 remote control circuits;
   b) Class 1 and Class 2 signal circuits;
   c) Class 1 extra-low-voltage power circuits;
   d) Class 2 low-energy power circuits; and
   e) Class 2 power and data communication circuits connecting power sourcing equipment and powered devices.
2) This Section does not apply to
   a) communication circuits as specified in Section 60; and
   b) circuits forming an integral part of a device.

16-002 Classifications
Circuits covered by this Section are that portion of the wiring system between the load side of the overcurrent device or the power-limited supply and all connected equipment, and shall be classified as follows:
a) Class 1 — circuits that are supplied from sources having limitations in accordance with Rule 16-100; and
b) Class 2 — circuits that are supplied from sources having limitations in accordance with Rule 16-200.

16-004 Class 1 extra-low-voltage power circuits
Circuits that are neither remote control circuits nor signal circuits but that operate at not more than 30 V, where the current is not limited in accordance with Rule 16-200 and that are supplied from a transformer or other device restricted in its rated output to 1000 V•A, shall be classed as extra-low-voltage power circuits and shall be considered Class 1 circuits.

16-006 Class 2 low-energy power circuits
Circuits that are neither remote control circuits nor signal circuits but in which the current is limited in accordance with Rule 16-200 shall be classed as low-energy power circuits and shall be considered Class 2 circuits.

16-008 Hazardous locations
Where the circuits or apparatus within the scope of this Section are installed in hazardous locations, they shall also comply with the applicable Rules of Section 18.

16-010 Circuits to safety control devices
Where the failure to operate of a remote control circuit to a safety control device will introduce a direct fire or life hazard, the remote control circuit shall be deemed to be a Class 1 circuit.

16-012 Circuits in communication cables
1) Class 1 circuits shall not be run in the same cable with communication circuits.
2) Class 2 remote control and signal circuits or their parts that use conductors in a cable assembly with other conductors forming parts of communication circuits are, for the purposes of this Code, deemed to be communication circuits and shall conform to the applicable Rules of Section 60.
Δ 3) Class 2 power and data communication circuits shall comply with Rules 16-300 to 16-350.

Class 1 circuits

16-100 Limitations of Class 1 circuits
1) Class 1 extra-low-voltage power circuits shall be supplied from a source having a rated output of not more than 30 V and 1000 V•A.

2) Class 1 remote control and signal circuits shall be supplied by a source not exceeding 600 V.

16-102 Methods of installation for Class 1 circuits

The equipment and conductors of Class 1 circuits shall be installed in accordance with the requirements of other appropriate Sections of this Code, except as provided for in Rules 16-104 to 16-118.

16-104 Overcurrent protection of Class 1 circuits

1) Conductors of Class 1 circuits shall be protected against overcurrent in accordance with Section 14 of this Code, except
   a) where other Rules of this Code specifically permit or require other overcurrent protection; or
   b) where the conductors are of No. 18 or No. 16 AWG copper and extend beyond the equipment enclosure, they shall be protected by overcurrent devices rated at a maximum of 5 A and 10 A respectively.
2) Where overcurrent protection is installed at the secondary terminals of the transformer and the transformer is suitably enclosed, overcurrent protection shall not be required on the primary side other than the normal overcurrent protection of the branch circuit supplying the transformer.

16-106 Location of overcurrent devices in Class 1 circuits

1) In Class 1 circuits, the overcurrent devices shall be located at the point where the conductor to be protected receives its supply.
2) The overcurrent device shall be permitted to be an integral part of the power supply.

16-108 Class 1 extra-low-voltage power circuit sources including transformers

To comply with the 1000 V•A limitation, Class 1 extra-low-voltage power circuit sources including transformers shall not exceed a maximum power output of 2500 V•A, and the product of the maximum current and maximum voltage shall not exceed 10 000 V•A with the overcurrent protection bypassed.

16-110 Conductor material and sizes

1) Copper conductors smaller than No. 14 AWG shall be permitted to be used in Class 1 circuits if
   a) installed in a raceway;
   b) installed in a cable assembly; or
   c) within a flexible cord in accordance with Rule 12-402.
2) Subject to the conditions specified in Subrule 1), conductors shall be not smaller than
   a) No. 16 AWG for individual conductors pulled in raceways;
   b) No. 18 AWG for individual conductors laid in raceways; and
   c) No. 18 AWG for an integral assembly of two or more conductors.

16-112 Insulated conductors for Class 1 wiring

1) Where conductors larger than No. 16 AWG copper are used in a Class 1 circuit, they shall be of any type selected in accordance with Rule 12-102 3).
2) Where conductors of No. 18 or No. 16 AWG copper are used in a Class 1 circuit, they shall be equipment wire of the type suitable for such use as selected in accordance with Rule 12-122 1).

16-114 Conductors of different circuits in the same enclosure, cable, or raceway

1) Different Class 1 circuits shall be permitted to occupy the same enclosure, cable, or raceway without regard to whether the individual circuits are ac or dc, provided that all conductors are insulated for the maximum voltage of any conductor in the enclosure, cable, or raceway.
2) Power supply conductors and Class 1 circuit conductors shall not be permitted in the same enclosure, cable, or raceway except when connected to the same equipment, and all conductors are insulated for the maximum voltage of any conductor in the enclosure, cable, or raceway.

16-116 Mechanical protection of remote control circuits

Where mechanical damage to a remote control circuit would result in a hazardous condition as outlined in Rule 16-010, all conductors of such remote control circuits shall be installed in conduit or electrical

16

metallic tubing or be otherwise suitably protected from mechanical damage or other harmful conditions such as moisture, excessive heat, or corrosive action.

16-118 Class 1 circuits extending aerially beyond a building
Class 1 circuits that extend aerially beyond a building shall comply with Rules 12-300 to 12-318.

Class 2 circuits

Δ **16-200 Limitations of Class 2 circuits** (see Appendix B)
1) Class 2 circuits, depending on the voltage, shall have the current limited as follows:
   a) **0 to 20 V** — circuits in which the open-circuit voltage does not exceed 20 V shall have an overcurrent protection rating not exceeding 5 A, except that overcurrent protection shall not be required where the current is supplied from
      i) primary batteries that under short-circuit will not supply a current exceeding 7.5 A after 1 min;
      ii) a transformer or other power supply device having a Class 2 output; or
      iii) a device having characteristics that, under normal operating conditions or under fault conditions, limits the output current to a value not exceeding 5 A and the output volt amperes to a value not exceeding 5 A multiplied by the open-circuit voltage;
   b) **over 20 V but not exceeding 30 V** — circuits in which the open-circuit voltage exceeds 20 V but does not exceed 30 V shall have an overcurrent protection rating in amperes not exceeding 100 V•A divided by the open-circuit voltage, except that the overcurrent protection shall not be required where the current is supplied from
      i) primary batteries that under short-circuit will not supply a current exceeding 5 A after 1 min;
      ii) a transformer or other power supply device having a Class 2 output; or
      iii) a device having characteristics that, under normal operating conditions or under fault conditions, limit the output current to a value in amperes not exceeding 100 V•A divided by the open-circuit voltage;
   c) **over 30 V but not exceeding 60 V** — circuits in which the open-circuit voltage exceeds 30 V but does not exceed 60 V shall have an overcurrent protection rating in amperes not exceeding 100 V•A divided by the open-circuit voltage, except that the overcurrent protection shall not be required where the current is supplied from
      i) a transformer or other power supply device having a Class 2 output; or
      ii) a device having characteristics that, under normal operating conditions or under fault conditions, limit the output current to a value in amperes not exceeding 100 V•A divided by the open-circuit voltage;
   d) **over 60 V but not exceeding 150 V** — circuits in which the open-circuit voltage exceeds 60 V but does not exceed 150 V shall have an overcurrent protection rating in amperes not exceeding 100 V•A divided by the open-circuit voltage, and in addition shall be equipped with current-limiting means other than overcurrent protection that, under normal operating conditions or under fault conditions, limit the output current to a value in amperes not exceeding 100 V•A divided by the open-circuit voltage.
2) A device having energy-limiting characteristics shall be permitted to consist of a series resistor of suitable rating or other similar device.
3) A Class 2 power supply shall not be connected in series or parallel with another Class 2 power source.
4) A device having a Class 2 output shall be permitted for use as a device having energy-limiting characteristics, provided that it is marked as being suitable for the purpose.

Δ **16-202 Methods of installation on the supply side of overcurrent protection, transformers, or devices having Class 2 outputs**

In Class 2 circuits, the conductors and equipment on the supply side of overcurrent protection, transformers, or devices having Class 2 outputs shall be installed in accordance with the requirements of other appropriate Sections of this Code.

Δ **16-204 Marking**

A Class 2 power supply unit shall have permanent markings that are readily visible after installation to indicate

a)   the class of supply and its electrical rating; and

b)   suitability for wet locations when intended for wet locations.

16-206 Overcurrent protection for Class 2 circuits

1)   Overcurrent protection of different ratings shall not be of an interchangeable type.

2)   The overcurrent protection shall be permitted to be an integral part of a transformer or other power supply device.

16-208 Location of overcurrent devices

Overcurrent devices shall be located at the point where the conductor to be protected receives its supply.

16-210 Conductors for Class 2 circuit wiring (see Appendix B)

1)   Conductors for use in Class 2 circuits shall be of the type suitable for the application as selected in accordance with Rule 12-102 3) except that where conductors smaller than No. 14 AWG are permitted, equipment wire Types REW, SEW-1, SEWF-1, TEW, and TEWN shall be permitted, provided that the equipment wires are installed in raceways.

2)   Type ELC conductors shall be limited in use to

a)   Class 2 circuits operating at 30 V or less;

b)   dwelling units in buildings of combustible construction;

c)   dry locations; and

d)   where concealed or exposed, locations where the conductors are not subject to mechanical damage.

3)   Type ELC conductors shall not be permitted for the wiring of heating control circuits or fire safety circuits such as fire alarm or smoke alarm devices.

4)   Conductors shall be of copper and shall not be smaller than

a)   No. 16 AWG for individual conductors pulled into raceways;

b)   No. 19 AWG for individual conductors laid in raceways;

c)   No. 19 AWG for an integral assembly of two or more conductors;

d)   No. 22 AWG for an integral assembly of four or more conductors;

e)   No. 24 AWG for an integral assembly of six or more conductors; and

f)   No. 26 AWG for an integral assembly of ten or more conductors.

5)   Notwithstanding Subrule 4) d), No. 22 AWG Type ELC copper wire shall be permitted in an integral assembly of two or more conductors where the conductors are not pulled into raceways.

6)   The maximum allowable current shall be as listed in Table 57 for sizes No. 16 AWG and smaller, but in no case shall exceed the current limitations of Rule 16-200.

Δ 7)   Notwithstanding Subrules 4) and 6), eight-conductor cables for Class 2 power and data communication circuits shall be permitted for use in accordance with Table 60.

16-212 Separation of Class 2 circuit conductors from other circuits

1)   Conductors of Class 2 circuits shall be separated at least 50 mm from insulated conductors of electric lighting, power, or Class 1 circuits operating at 300 V or less, and shall be separated at least

600 mm from any insulated conductors of electric lighting, power, or Class 1 circuits operating at more than 300 V, unless for both conditions effective separation is afforded by use of

a) metal raceways for the Class 2 circuits or for the electric lighting, power, and Class 1 circuits, subject to the metal raceway being bonded to ground;

b) metal-sheathed or armoured cable for the electric lighting, power, and Class 1 circuit conductors, subject to the sheath or armour being bonded to ground;

c) non-metallic-sheathed cable for the electric lighting, power, and Class 1 circuits operating at 300 V or less; or

d) non-metallic conduit, electrical non-metallic tubing, insulated tubing, or equivalent, in addition to the insulation on the Class 2 circuit conductors or the electric lighting, power, and Class 1 circuit conductors.

2) Where the electric lighting or power conductors are bare, all Class 2 circuit conductors in the same room or space shall be enclosed in a metal raceway that is bonded to ground, and no opening, such as an outlet box, shall be permitted to be located within 2 m of the bare conductors if up to and including 15 kV or within 3 m of bare conductors above 15 kV.

3) Unless the conductors of the Class 2 circuits are separated from the conductors of electric lighting, power, and Class 1 circuits by an acceptable barrier, the conductors in Class 2 circuits shall not be placed in any raceway, compartment, outlet box, junction box, or similar fitting with the conductors of electric lighting, power, or Class 1 circuits.

4) Subrule 3) shall not apply where the conductors of a power circuit are in the raceway, compartment, outlet box, junction box, or similar fitting for the sole purpose of supplying power to the Class 2 circuits, and all conductors are insulated for the maximum voltage of any conductor in the enclosure, cable, or raceway, except that no Class 2 conductor installed in a raceway, compartment, outlet box, junction box, or similar fitting with such conductors of a power circuit shall show a green-coloured insulation, unless the Class 2 conductor is completely contained within a sheathed or jacketed cable assembly throughout the length that is present in such a raceway or enclosure.

Ⓔ Δ 5) Notwithstanding Subrule 3), electric lighting, power, and Class 1 circuit conductors shall be permitted to be used in a cable that contains Class 2 circuit conductors, provided that the cable is marked as being suitable for applications of Class 2 circuit conductors that are

a) intended for the supply or control, or both, of remote devices associated with the non-Class 2 conductors; and

b) insulated for the maximum voltage of any conductor in the cable.

16-214 Conductors of different Class 2 circuits in the same cable, enclosure, or raceway
Conductors of two or more Class 2 circuits shall be permitted within the same cable, enclosure, or raceway, provided that all conductors in the cable, enclosure, or raceway are insulated for the maximum voltage of any conductor.

16-216 Penetration of a fire separation
Conductors of a Class 2 circuit extending through a fire separation shall be installed so as to limit fire spread in accordance with Rule 2-128.

16-218 Conductors in vertical shafts and hoistways
Class 2 conductors and cables installed in a vertical shaft or hoistway shall meet the requirements of Rules 2-128 and 2-130.

16-220 Class 2 conductors and equipment in ducts and plenum chambers
Class 2 conductors and equipment shall not be placed in ducts or plenum chambers except as permitted by Rules 2-130 and 12-010.

Δ **16-222 Equipment located on the load side of overcurrent protection, transformers, or devices having Class 2 outputs** (see Appendix B)

1) Equipment located on the load side of overcurrent protection, transformers, or devices having Class 2 outputs shall
   a) for Class 2 circuits operating at not more than 42.4 V peak, be acceptable for the particular application; and
   b) for Class 2 circuits operating at more than 42.4 V peak, comply with Rule 2-024 1).

2) Notwithstanding Subrule 1) a), lighting products, electromedical equipment, equipment for hazardous locations, and thermostats incorporating heat anticipators shall comply with Rule 2-024 1).

3) The operating voltage of the equipment referred to in Subrule 1) shall not exceed
   a) for dry or damp locations
      i) 30 V rms for sinusoidal ac;
      ii) 42.4 V peak for other waveforms (nonsinusoidal ac);
      iii) 60 V continuous dc; and
      iv) 24.8 V peak for interrupted dc (square wave dc at a rate of 10 to 200 Hz); and
   b) for wet locations (not including immersion)
      i) 15 V rms for sinusoidal ac;
      ii) 21.2 V peak for nonsinusoidal ac;
      iii) 30 V for continuous dc; and
      iv) 12.4 V peak for interrupted dc (square wave dc at a rate of 10 to 200 Hz).

16-224 Class 2 circuits extending beyond a building

Where Class 2 circuits extend beyond a building and are run in such a manner as to be subject to accidental contact with lighting or power conductors operating at a voltage exceeding 300 V between conductors, the conductors of the Class 2 circuits shall also meet the requirements of Section 60.

16-226 Underground installations

1) Underground installations of Class 2 circuits shall be installed in accordance with Rule 12-012.
2) Direct buried Class 2 circuits shall maintain a minimum horizontal separation of 300 mm from other underground systems except when installed in accordance with Subrule 3).
3) Direct buried Class 2 circuits shall be permitted to be placed at random separation in a common trench with power circuits that are for the sole purpose of supplying power to the Class 2 circuits, provided that
   a) the Class 2 circuit is in a metal-sheathed cable, with the sheath bonded to ground;
   b) the power circuit operates at 750 V or less; and
   c) all conductors are insulated for the maximum voltage of any conductor in the trench.

Δ
Class 2 power and data communication circuits

16-300 Scope (see Appendix B)

Rules 16-300 to 16-350 apply to Class 2 power and data communication circuits.

16-310 Special terminology (see Appendix B)

In this Subsection, the following definitions shall apply:

Cable bundle — two or more cables that are tied together or in contact with one another in a closely packed configuration for a length of at least 1 m.

Class 2 power and data communication circuit — a Class 2 circuit in which the conductors transmit power or data, or both.

16

Power sourcing equipment — equipment that supplies power to powered devices and that may be capable of communicating data.

Powered device — equipment supplied with power from power sourcing equipment and that may be capable of communicating data.

16-320 Equipment output limitations
A Class 2 power and data communication circuit shall be supplied from power sourcing equipment with an output limited to 100 V•A and 60 V dc.

16-330 Cables and conductor ampacity (see Appendix B)
1) Conductors for Class 2 power and data communication circuits shall be suitable for the application in accordance with Rule 12-102 3).
2) Where communication cable marked with the suffix "-LP" is used
   a) the maximum current that each insulated conductor is permitted to carry shall be limited to the current rating marked on the cable; and
   b) ampacities for conductors smaller than No. 26 AWG, or for conductors in cable bundles of more than 192 cables, shall be permitted to be determined by a qualified person, as recognized by the regulatory authority having jurisdiction, provided that a deviation has been allowed in accordance with Rule 2-030.
3) Where communication cable not marked with the suffix "-LP" is used
   a) the maximum current that each insulated conductor shall be permitted to carry shall be as specified in Table 60, based on
      i) the size of the conductor;
      ii) the cable temperature rating;
      iii) the number of cables in a cable bundle in contact with each other; and
      iv) the smallest conductor size and lowest temperature rating of any cable in the cable bundle;
   b) not more than 192 cables shall be permitted to be bundled together; and
   c) where not more than four conductors in each cable are used to transmit power, the maximum current that each conductor shall be permitted to carry shall be permitted to be calculated by multiplying the values listed in Table 60 multiplied by 1.4.
4) The maximum current permitted in a Class 2 power and data communication circuit shall not exceed the rating of the connectors or components used in the circuit.
5) The correction factors of Table 5A shall apply where Class 2 power and data communication circuit cables are installed in an ambient temperature exceeding 30 °C.
6) Notwithstanding Rule 8-102 1), for Class 2 power and data communication circuits, the circuit length shall ensure that the voltage at the point of utilization is within the rating or voltage tolerance of the connected powered device(s).
7) Where more than one cable bundle is installed in a ventilated and ladder-type cable tray, cable bundles shall be spaced at not less than 25 mm.
8) Notwithstanding Subrules 2) and 3), where communication equipment rated at 60 W or less is powered by a communications cable having a minimum conductor size of No. 24 AWG, such communications cable shall not be required to comply with bundling requirements.
9) Where the maximum conductor termination temperature for equipment is not marked, it shall be considered to be 60 °C.

16-340 Wiring method
1) Conductors for Class 2 power and data communication circuits shall be used only when such conductors are part of a common cable assembly marked as being suitable for the application.
2) Conductors for Class 2 power and data communication circuits extending beyond a building shall be installed in accordance with Rule 16-224.

3) Underground installations of conductors for Class 2 power and data communication circuits shall comply with Rule 12-012.

4) Conductors for a Class 2 power and data communication circuit shall not be connected in series or parallel with other conductors for Class 2 power and data communication circuits.

16-350 Marking

Markings to indicate the class of supply and the electrical rating of power sourcing equipment shall be permanent and readily visible for inspection after installation.

Section 18 — Hazardous locations

Scope and introduction

18-000 Scope (see Appendices B, F, and J)

1) This Section applies to locations in which electrical equipment and wiring are subject to the conditions indicated by the following classifications.

2) This Section supplements or amends the general requirements of this Code.

3) For additions, modifications, renovations to, or operation and maintenance of existing facilities employing the Division system of classification, the continued use of the Division system of classification shall be permitted.

4) Where the Division system of classification is used as permitted by Subrule 3), the Rules for Class I, II, and III locations found in Annex J18 of Appendix J shall apply.

18-002 Special terminology (see Appendix B)

In this Section, the following definitions shall apply:

Cable gland — a device or combination of devices intended to provide a means of entry for a cable or flexible cord into an enclosure situated in a hazardous location and that also provides strain relief and shall be permitted to provide sealing characteristics where required, either by an integral means or when combined with a separate sealing fitting.

Cable seal — a seal that is installed at a cable termination to prevent the release of an explosion from an explosion-proof enclosure and that minimizes the passage of gases or vapours at atmospheric pressure.

Conduit seal — a seal that is installed in a conduit to prevent the passage of an explosion from one portion of the conduit system to another and that minimizes the passage of gases or vapours at atmospheric pressure.

Degree of protection — the measures applied to the enclosures of electrical apparatus to ensure

a) the protection of persons against contact with live or moving parts inside the enclosure and protection of apparatus against the ingress of solid foreign bodies; and

b) the protection of apparatus against ingress of liquids.

Δ **Descriptive system document** (see Appendix F) — a document in which the items of electrical apparatus, their electrical parameters, and those of the interconnecting wiring are specified.

Dust — generic term including both combustible dust and combustible flyings.

> **Combustible dust** — dust particles that are 500 μm or smaller (material passing a No. 35 standard sieve as defined in ASTM E11) and present a fire or explosion hazard when dispersed and ignited in air.

>> **Conductive dust** — combustible metal dust.

>> **Non-conductive dust** — combustible dust other than combustible metal dust.

> **Combustible flyings** — solid particles, including fibres, greater than 500 μm in nominal size that may be suspended in air and can settle out of the atmosphere under their own weight.

Equipment protection level (EPL) — the level of protection assigned to equipment based on its likelihood of becoming a source of ignition and distinguishing the differences between explosive gas atmospheres, explosive dust atmospheres, and the explosive atmospheres in mines susceptible to firedamp.

> **EPL Da** — equipment for explosive dust atmospheres, having a "very high" level of protection, that is not a source of ignition in normal operation, during expected malfunctions, or during rare malfunctions.

> **EPL Db** — equipment for explosive dust atmospheres, having a "high" level of protection, that is not a source of ignition in normal operation or during expected malfunctions.

> **EPL Dc** — equipment for explosive dust atmospheres, having an "enhanced" level of protection, that is not a source of ignition in normal operation and may have some additional protection to ensure that it remains inactive as an ignition source in the case of regular, expected occurrences (e.g., failure of a lamp).

> **EPL Ga** — equipment for explosive gas atmospheres, having a "very high" level of protection, that is not a source of ignition in normal operation, during expected malfunctions, or during rare malfunctions.

> **EPL Gb** — equipment for explosive gas atmospheres, having a "high" level of protection, that is not a source of ignition in normal operation or during expected malfunctions.

> **EPL Gc** — equipment for explosive gas atmospheres, having an "enhanced" level of protection, that is not a source of ignition in normal operation and that may have some additional protection to ensure that it remains inactive as an ignition source in the case of regular, expected occurrences (e.g., failure of a lamp).

Explosive atmosphere — a mixture with air, under atmospheric conditions, of flammable substances in the form of gas, vapour, dust, fibres, or flyings that, after ignition, permits self-sustaining propagation.

Explosive dust atmosphere — a mixture with air, under atmospheric conditions, of flammable substances in the form of dust, fibres, or flyings that, after ignition, permits self-sustaining propagation.

Δ **Explosive gas atmosphere** — a mixture with air, under atmospheric conditions, of flammable substances in the form of gas or vapour that, after ignition, permits self-sustaining flame propagation.

Δ **Flammable limits** — the lower and upper percentage by volume of concentration of flammable gas or vapour in air that will form an ignitable mixture.

> **LFL** — lower flammable limit.

> **UFL** — upper flammable limit.

Fluid — a substance in the form of gas, vapour, or liquid.

Hazardous location — see **Location** in Section 0.

Δ **Hazardous location cable** — a cable that bears an "HL" marking.

Δ **Intrinsically safe circuit** — a circuit in which any spark or thermal effect produced under prescribed conditions, which include normal operation and specified fault conditions, is not capable of causing ignition of a given explosive atmosphere.

18

Δ **Intrinsically safe electrical system** — an assembly of interconnected items of electrical equipment, described in a descriptive system document, in which the circuits or parts of circuits intended to be used in a hazardous location are intrinsically safe.

Δ **Non-incendive field wiring circuit** — a circuit, described in a descriptive system document, in which any spark or thermal effect that may occur under normal operating conditions or due to opening, shorting, or grounding of field wiring is not capable of causing an ignition of a given explosive atmosphere.

Normal operation — the situation in which the plant or equipment is operating within its design parameters.

Primary seal — a seal that isolates process fluids from an electrical system and that has one side of the seal in contact with the process fluid.

Protective gas — the gas used to maintain pressurization or to dilute a flammable gas or vapour.

Secondary seal — a seal that is designed to prevent the passage of process fluids at the pressure it will be subjected to upon failure of the primary seal.

Type of protection — a defined method to reduce the risk of ignition of explosive atmospheres.

Zone 0 — a location in which explosive gas atmospheres are present continuously or are present for long periods.

Zone 1 — a location in which
a) explosive gas atmospheres are likely to occur in normal operation; or
b) the location is adjacent to a Zone 0 location, from which explosive gas atmospheres could be communicated.

Zone 2 — a location in which
a) explosive gas atmospheres are not likely to occur in normal operation and, if they do occur, they will exist for a short time only; or
b) the location is adjacent to a Zone 1 location, from which explosive gas atmospheres could be communicated, unless such communication is prevented by adequate positive-pressure ventilation from a source of clean air, and effective safeguards against ventilation failure are provided.

Zone 20 — a location in which an explosive dust atmosphere, in the form of a cloud of dust in air, is present continuously, or for long periods, or frequently.

Zone 21 — a location in which an explosive dust atmosphere, in the form of a cloud of dust in air, is likely to occur in normal operation occasionally.

Zone 22 — a location in which an explosive dust atmosphere, in the form of a cloud of dust in air, is not likely to occur in normal operation but, if it does occur, will persist for a short period only.

Δ **18-004 Classification of hazardous locations** (see Appendices B, J, and L)
1) Hazardous locations shall be classified according to the nature of the hazard, as follows:
   a) explosive gas atmospheres; or
   b) explosive dust atmospheres.
2) Hazardous location classification shall be carried out and documented by qualified persons.
3) The hazardous location classification required by Subrule 2) shall be authenticated by the person assuming responsibility for the classification.

4) Notwithstanding Subrules 2) and 3), installations within the Scope of Section 20 shall be permitted to be classified in accordance with Section 20.

Δ **18-006 Locations containing an explosive gas atmosphere** (see Appendices B and L)
Locations containing explosive gas atmospheres shall be divided into Zones 0, 1, and 2 based on frequency of occurrence and duration of an explosive gas atmosphere.

Δ **18-008 Locations containing an explosive dust atmosphere** (see Appendices B and L)
Locations containing explosive dust atmospheres shall be divided into Zones 20, 21, and 22 based on frequency of occurrence and duration of an explosive dust atmosphere.

18-010 Maintenance (see Appendix B)
Special precautions shall be observed as follows:
a) unauthorized repairs or alterations shall not be made to live equipment; and
b) electrical equipment shall be maintained in its original safe condition.

General

Δ **18-050 Electrical equipment** (see Appendices B and J)
1) Electrical equipment for use in hazardous locations shall be suitable for the specific explosive atmosphere that will be present.
2) Equipment with a type of protection permitted in a Zone 0, Zone 1, or Zone 2 location shall be suitable for one of the following:
   a) **Group IIC**, consisting of atmospheres containing acetylene, carbon disulphide, or hydrogen, or other gases or vapours of equivalent hazard;
   b) **Group IIB**, consisting of atmospheres containing acrylonitrile, butadiene, diethyl ether, ethylene, ethylene oxide, hydrogen sulphide, propylene oxide, or unsymmetrical dimethyl hydrazine (UDMH), or other gases or vapours of equivalent hazard;
   c) **Group IIA**, consisting of atmospheres containing acetaldehyde, acetone, cyclopropane, alcohol, ammonia, benzine, benzol, butane, ethylene dichloride, gasoline, hexane, isoprene, lacquer solvent vapours, naphtha, natural gas, propane, propylene, styrene, vinyl acetate, vinyl chloride, xylenes, or other gases or vapours of equivalent hazard; or
   d) **XXXXX**, where XXXXX is a chemical formula or chemical name suitable for that specific gas or vapour.
3) Equipment marked Group "IIC" shall be permitted to be used for applications where Group IIA or Group IIB equipment is required.
4) Equipment marked Group "IIB" shall be permitted to be used for applications where Group IIA equipment is required.
5) Equipment marked for a specific gas or vapour shall be permitted for applications where the specific gas or vapour may be encountered.
6) Equipment with a type of protection permitted in a Zone 20, Zone 21, or Zone 22 location shall be suitable for one of the following:
   a) **Group IIIC**, combustible metal dusts;
   b) **Group IIIB**, combustible dust other than combustible metal dust; or
   c) **Group IIIA**, solid particles, including fibres, greater than 500 μm in nominal size, that may be suspended in air and could settle out of the atmosphere under their own weight.

18

Δ **18-052 Marking** (see Appendices B and J)

Electrical equipment installed in hazardous locations shall have markings that are suitable for the Zone in which the equipment is installed.

Δ **18-054 Temperature** (see Appendix B)

1) In Zone 0, 1, and 2 locations, the maximum surface temperature rating, if marked on equipment, shall not exceed the minimum ignition temperature determined for the hazardous location in which the equipment is installed.

2) If no maximum surface temperature rating is marked on equipment installed in Zone 0, 1, and 2 locations, the maximum surface temperature rating shall be deemed to be 100 °C.

3) In Zone 20, 21, and 22 locations, the maximum external surface temperature rating, as marked on equipment, shall not exceed the lower of the dust cloud or dust layer ignition temperature determined for the hazardous location in which the equipment is installed.

4) Equipment installed in accordance with Rule 18-150 2) or 3) shall have surface temperatures at any point on the equipment that may be exposed to an explosive gas atmosphere that do not exceed the minimum ignition temperature determined for the hazardous location in which the equipment is installed.

18-056 Rooms, sections, or areas

Each room, section, or area, including motor and generator rooms and rooms for the enclosure of control equipment, shall be considered a separate location for the purpose of determining the classification of the hazard.

18-058 Equipment rooms

1) Where walls, partitions, floors, or ceilings are used to form hazard-free rooms or sections, they shall be
   a) of substantial construction;
   b) built of or lined with non-combustible material; and
   c) such that the rooms or sections will remain free from hazards.

2) Where a non-hazardous location within a building communicates with a Zone 2 location or an explosive dust atmosphere, the locations shall be separated by close-fitting, self-closing fire doors.

3) Communication from a Zone 1 location shall be a Zone 2 location unless ventilation and safeguards from ventilation failure are provided as described in Item b) of the definition of Zone 2 given in Rule 18-002.

18-060 Metal-covered cable (see Appendix B)

1) Where exposed overhead conductors supply mineral-insulated cable in a hazardous location, surge arresters shall be installed to limit the surge voltage level on the cable to 5 kV.

2) Where single-conductor metal-covered cable is used in hazardous locations, it shall be installed so as to prevent sparking between cable sheaths or between cable sheaths and metal bonded to ground, and the cables in the circuit shall
   a) be clipped or strapped together in a manner that will ensure good electrical contact between metal coverings, at intervals of not more than 1.8 m, and the metal coverings shall be bonded to ground; or
   b) have the metal coverings continuously covered with insulating material and bonded to ground at the point of termination in the hazardous location only.

18-062 Pressurized equipment or rooms (see Appendix B)

Electrical equipment and associated wiring in locations containing explosive atmospheres shall be permitted to be located in enclosures or rooms constructed and arranged so that a protective gas pressure is effectively maintained, in which case the provisions of Rules 18-100 to 18-158 shall not be required.

Δ **18-064 Intrinsically safe and non-incendive electrical equipment and wiring** (see Appendices B and F)
1) Where an intrinsically safe electrical system or non-incendive field wiring circuit is installed in a hazardous location, a descriptive system document shall be provided.
2) Intrinsically safe electrical systems and non-incendive field wiring circuits shall be installed in accordance with the descriptive system document.
3) Except as permitted by Subrule 4), no raceway, compartment, enclosure, outlet, junction box, or similar fitting, excluding cable tray, shall contain insulated conductors of intrinsically safe or non-incendive field wiring circuits and insulated conductors of any other circuit unless the conductors are separated by
   a) not less than 50 mm;
   b) the metal armour or sheath of cable assemblies;
   c) a grounded metal barrier not less than 1.34 mm (No. 16 MSG) thick; or
   d) a non-metallic insulating material not less than 1.5 mm in thickness.
4) Insulated conductors of different intrinsically safe or non-incendive field wiring circuits shall be permitted in the same raceway, compartment, outlet, junction box, or multi-conductor cable, provided that
   a) the insulated conductors of each circuit are within grounded electrically conductive shields, braids, or sheaths; or
   b) the insulated conductors of each circuit have insulation with a minimum thickness of 0.25 mm.
5) Raceways or cable systems for wiring of intrinsically safe or non-incendive equipment in explosive atmospheres shall be installed to minimize migration of flammable fluids to other locations.
6) All apparatus forming part of an intrinsically safe or non-incendive system shall be identified as being part of an intrinsically safe or non-incendive system.
7) Intrinsically safe and non-incendive field wiring circuits shall be identified at terminal and junction locations.
8) Wiring methods for intrinsically safe or non-incendive field wiring circuits shall be
   a) identified with permanently affixed labels; or
   b) colour coded light blue where no other cables or insulated conductors coloured light blue are used.

18-066 Cable trays in explosive dust atmospheres
Cable trays in explosive dust atmospheres shall be installed to minimize the buildup of dust or fibre on the cables.

18-068 Combustible gas detection (see Appendices B and H)
Electrical equipment suitable for non-hazardous locations shall be permitted to be installed in a Zone 2 location, and electrical equipment suitable for Zone 2 locations shall be permitted to be installed in a Zone 1 location, provided that
a) no specific equipment suitable for the purpose is available;
b) the equipment, during its normal operation, does not produce arcs, sparks, or hot surfaces capable of igniting an explosive gas atmosphere; and
Δ c) the location is continuously monitored by a combustible gas detection system that will
   i) activate an alarm when the gas concentration reaches 20% of the lower flammable limit;

18

    ii)   activate ventilating equipment or other means designed to prevent the concentration of gas from reaching the lower flammable limit when the gas concentration reaches 20% of the lower flammable limit, where such ventilating equipment or other means is provided;

    iii) automatically de-energize the electrical equipment being protected when the gas concentration reaches 40% of the lower flammable limit, where the ventilating equipment or other means referred to in Item ii) is provided;

    iv) automatically de-energize the electrical equipment being protected when the gas concentration reaches 20% of the lower flammable limit, where the ventilating equipment or other means referred to in Item ii) cannot be provided; and

    v)   automatically de-energize the electrical equipment being protected upon failure of the gas detection instrument.

18-070 Flammable fluid seals (see Appendix B)

1)   Electrical equipment with a primary seal in contact with flammable fluids shall be
    a)   constructed or installed so as to prevent migration of flammable fluid through the wiring system; and
    b)   used at pressures lower than the marked maximum working pressure (MWP).

2)   Where Subrule 1) is met through the installation of secondary seals, the possibility of primary seal failure shall be indicated by
    a)   design features that will make the occurrence of a primary seal failure obvious; or
    b)   acceptable marking means indicating that the enclosure may contain flammable fluid under pressure.

18-072 Bonding in hazardous locations

1)   Exposed non-current-carrying metal parts of electrical equipment, including the frames or metal exteriors of motors, fixed or portable lamps or other utilization equipment, luminaires, cabinets, cases, and conduit, shall be bonded to ground using
    a)   bonding conductors sized in accordance with Rule 10-614; or
    b)   rigid metal conduit with threaded couplings and threaded bosses on enclosures with joints made up tight.

2)   Notwithstanding Subrule 1), where raceways or cables incorporate an internal bonding conductor, box connectors with standard locknuts shall be permitted to bond the metallic armour or raceway.

18-074 Uninsulated exposed parts

There shall be no uninsulated exposed parts of an electrical installation or of electrical equipment such as electrical conductors, buses, terminals, or components unless they are
a)   additionally protected by type of protection "ia", "ib", "ic", or "nA" as suitable for the location and operate at less than
    i)   15 V in wet locations; and
    ii)   30 V in other than wet locations; or
b)   installed as provided for in Rule 18-250 2) for electric cranes, hoists, and similar equipment in a Zone 22 location.

Explosive gas atmospheres

Installations in Zone 0 locations

Δ   **18-090 Equipment, Zone 0 locations** (see Appendices B and F)

Electrical equipment installed in a Zone 0 location shall be in accordance with Table 18.

Δ **18-092 Wiring methods, Zone 0** (see Appendix B)
1) The wiring method for connection of equipment shall be intrinsically safe.
2) A cable marked "HL" that contains one or more circuits that are not intrinsically safe shall be permitted to pass through a Zone 0 location, provided that
   a) it passes completely through the Zone 0 area with no fittings or connections less than 300 mm beyond each boundary; and
   b) it is protected from mechanical damage by a raceway or other effective means within the Zone 0 area.

18-094 Sealing, Zone 0
1) Seals shall be provided where conduit leaves a Zone 0 location with no box, coupling, or fitting in the conduit run between the seal and the point at which the conduit leaves the location, except that a rigid unbroken conduit that passes completely through a Zone 0 area, with no fittings less than 300 mm beyond each boundary, need not be sealed, provided that the termination points of the unbroken conduit are in non-hazardous areas.
2) Seals shall be provided on cables at the first point of termination after entry into the Zone 0 location.
Ⓔ 3) Seals as specified in Subrules 1) and 2) shall not be required to be explosion-proof or flameproof "d" but shall be identified for the purpose of minimizing the passage of gases, vapours, or dusts under normal operating conditions and shall be accessible.

Installations in Zone 1 locations

Δ **18-100 Equipment, Zone 1 locations** (see Appendices B and F)
Electrical equipment installed in a Zone 1 location shall be in accordance with Table 18.

18-102 Wiring methods, Zone 1 (see Appendix B)
1) The wiring method shall be threaded rigid metal conduit or hazardous location cables with associated cable glands suitable for the application.
2) Explosion-proof or flameproof "d" boxes, fittings, and joints shall be threaded for connection to conduit and cable glands.
3) Threaded joints that are required to be explosion-proof or flameproof "d" shall be permitted to be either tapered or straight and shall comply with the following:
   a) tapered threads shall have at least 4-1/2 fully engaged threads, and running threads shall not be used; and
   b) metric straight threads shall have a tolerance class 6g/6H and shall have at least 5 fully engaged threads.
4) Where thread forms differ between the equipment and the wiring system, suitable adapters shall be used.
5) Conduit and cable entries into increased safety "e" enclosures shall be made so as to maintain the degree of protection provided by the enclosure.
6) Cables shall be installed and supported so as to avoid tensile stress at the cable glands.
Δ 7) Wiring methods for intrinsically safe equipment and associated circuits designed and installed as "ia", "ib", or intrinsically safe for Class I locations shall be permitted to be exempt from the requirements of Subrules 1) to 4).

18-104 Sealing, Zone 1 (see Appendix B)
1) Conduit seals shall be provided in conduit systems where
   a) the conduit enters an explosion-proof or flameproof "d" enclosure containing devices that may produce arcs, sparks, or high temperatures, and shall be located as close as practicable to

the enclosure, or as marked on the enclosure, but not further than 450 mm from the enclosure;

b) the conduit is 53 trade size or larger and enters an explosion-proof or flameproof "d" enclosure housing terminals, splices, or taps, and shall be located no further than 450 mm from the enclosure; or

c) the conduit leaves the Zone 1 location with no box, coupling, or fitting in the conduit run between the seal and the point at which the conduit leaves the location, except that a rigid unbroken conduit that passes completely through a Zone 1 area, with no fittings less than 300 mm beyond each boundary, need not be sealed, provided that the termination points of the unbroken conduit are in non-hazardous areas.

2) Only explosion-proof or flameproof "d" unions, couplings, reducers, and elbows that are not larger than the trade size of the conduit shall be permitted between the sealing fitting and an explosion-proof or flameproof "d" enclosure.

3) Cable seals shall be provided in a cable system where
   a) the cable enters an enclosure required to be explosion-proof or flameproof "d"; or
   b) the cable first terminates after entering the Zone 1 area.

4) Where secondary seals, cable seals, or conduit seals are required, they shall conform to the following:
   a) the seal shall be accessible after installation;
   b) splices and taps shall not be made in fittings intended only for sealing with compound, nor shall other fittings in which splices or taps are made be filled with compound;
   c) where there is a probability that liquid or other condensed vapour may be trapped within enclosures for control equipment or at any point in the raceway system, acceptable means shall be provided to prevent accumulation or to permit periodic draining of such liquid or condensed vapour; and
   d) where there is a probability that liquid or condensed vapour may accumulate within motors or generators, joints and conduit systems shall be arranged to minimize entrance of liquid, but if means to prevent accumulation or to permit periodic draining are judged necessary, such means shall be provided at the time of manufacture and shall be deemed an integral part of the machine.

5) Runs of cables, each having a continuous sheath, either metal or non-metal, shall be permitted to pass through a Zone 1 location without seals.

6) Cables that do not have a continuous sheath, either metal or non-metal, shall be sealed at the boundary of the Zone 1 location.

18-106 Motors and generators, Zone 1 (see Appendix B)
Increased safety "e" motor installations shall meet the requirement for thermal protection of cage induction motors given in IEC 60079-14.

18-108 Luminaires, Zone 1
1) Each luminaire shall be protected by a suitable guard or by location.
2) Pendant luminaires suspended by and supplied through threaded rigid conduit stems and threaded joints shall
   a) be provided with set screws or other effective means to prevent loosening; and
   b) for stems longer than 300 mm, be provided with
      i) permanent and effective bracing against lateral displacement at a level not more than 300 mm above the lower end of the stem; or
      ii) flexibility in the form of a fitting or flexible connector suitable for the purpose and for the location not more than 300 mm from the point of attachment to the supporting box or fitting.

18-110 Flexible cords, Zone 1

1) Flexible cords shall be permitted to be used for connection between a portable lamp, or other portable utilization equipment, and the fixed portion of its supply circuit and, where used, shall
   a) be of the extra-hard-usage type;
   b) contain, in addition to the insulated conductors of the circuit, a bonding conductor;
   c) be provided with a sealing gland where the flexible cord enters a box, fitting, or enclosure that is required to be explosion-proof or flameproof "d"; and
   d) where entering an increased safety "e" enclosure, be terminated with a suitable increased safety "e" cord connector.

2) Flexible cord shall also be permitted for that portion of the circuit where fixed wiring methods cannot provide the necessary degree of movement for fixed and mobile electrical utilization equipment and, where used, shall
   a) meet all the requirements of Subrule 1); and
   b) be protected from damage by location or by a suitable guard.

Installations in Zone 2 locations

18-150 Equipment, Zone 2 locations (see Appendices B and F)

Δ 1) Electrical equipment installed in a Zone 2 location shall be in accordance with Table 18.

Δ 2) Notwithstanding Subrule 1) and Rule 18-052, the following shall be permitted:
   a) transformers, capacitors, solenoids, and other windings that do not incorporate sliding or make-and-break contacts, heat-producing resistance devices, and arcing or spark-producing components;
   b) conduit and cables as specified in Rule 18-152 1);
   c) non-explosion-proof or non-flameproof enclosures housing
      i) non-arcing connections and connecting devices such as joints, splices, terminals, and terminal blocks;
      ii) switches, controllers, and circuit breakers meeting the requirements of Subrule 1);
      iii) unfused isolating switches that are interlocked with their associated current-interrupting devices such that they cannot be opened under load; or
      iv) not more than
         A) ten sets of enclosed fuses; or
         B) ten circuit breakers that are not used as switches for the normal operation of the lamps for the protection of a branch circuit or a feeder circuit that supplies fixed lighting;
   d) for the protection of motors, appliances, and luminaires,
      i) a standard plug or cartridge fuse, provided that it is placed within an explosion-proof or flameproof "d" enclosure;
      ii) a fuse installed within a non-explosion-proof or non-flameproof enclosure, provided that the operating element of the fuse is
         A) immersed in oil or other suitable liquid; or
         B) enclosed within a hermetically sealed chamber; or
      iii) a fuse installed within a non-explosion-proof or non-flameproof enclosure, provided that the fuse is
         A) of a non-indicating, filled, current-limiting type; or
         B) of an indicating, filled, current-limiting type constructed in a manner such that the blown fuse indication does not cause the fuse body to be penetrated; or

18

e) motors, generators, and other rotating electrical machines of the open or non-explosion-proof type that
    i) except as permitted by Subrule 3), do not incorporate arcing, sparking, or heat-producing components; or
Δ   ii) incorporate arcing, sparking, or heat-producing components that comply with the requirements of Rule 18-100.

3) The machines referred to in Subrule 2) e) i) shall be permitted to contain anti-condensation heaters suitable for non-hazardous locations, provided that they
    a) do not use arcing or sparking components;
    b) do not use temperature-limiting controls;
    c) comply with the requirements of Rule 18-054 under normal operating conditions; and
Δ   d) are marked on a separate nameplate on the machine with
        i) the maximum surface temperature of the heater in degrees Celsius; or
        ii) a temperature code that indicates the maximum surface temperature.

Δ **18-152 Wiring methods, Zone 2** (see Appendix B)
1) The wiring method shall be
    a) threaded metal conduit;
    b) hazardous location cables;
    c) Type TC cable, installed in cable tray in accordance with Rule 12-2202;
    d) armoured cable with overall non-metallic jacket, such as TECK90, ACWU90, copper-sheathed RC90, or aluminum-sheathed RA90;
    e) control and instrumentation cables with an interlocking metallic armour and a continuous jacket in control circuits (Type ACIC);
    f) Type CIC cable (non-armoured control and instrumentation cable) installed in cable tray in accordance with the installation requirements of Rule 12-2202 2), where
        i) the voltage rating of the cable is not less than 300 V;
        ii) the circuit voltage is 150 V or less; and
        iii) the circuit current is 5 A or less;
    g) rigid RTRC conduit Type XW, provided that
        i) boxes, fittings, and joints are marked with the suffix "-XW"; and
        ii) installation is performed in industrial establishments that are not accessible to the public and where only qualified persons service the installation; or
Δ   h) liquid-tight flexible metal conduit and connectors, marked for heavy duty.
2) Explosion-proof or flameproof "d" boxes, fittings, and joints shall be threaded for connection to conduit and cable glands.
3) Threaded joints that are required to be explosion-proof shall be permitted to be either tapered or straight and shall comply with the following:
    a) tapered threads shall have at least 4-1/2 fully engaged threads, and running threads shall not be used; and
    b) metric straight threads shall have a tolerance class 6g/6H and shall have at least 5 fully engaged threads.
4) Where thread forms differ between the equipment and the wiring system, suitable adapters shall be used.
5) Cables shall be installed and supported so as to avoid tensile stress at the cable glands.
6) Boxes, fittings, and joints need not be explosion-proof or flameproof "d", except as required by the Rules in this Section.

7) Cable glands shall be compatible with the degree of protection and explosion protection provided by the enclosure that the cable enters, where the area classification and environmental conditions require these degrees of protection.

8) Wiring methods for intrinsically safe equipment and associated circuits designed and installed as "ia", "ib", "ic", intrinsically safe for Class I locations, or non-incendive shall be permitted to be exempt from the requirements of Subrules 1) to 4).

18-154 Sealing, Zone 2 (see Appendix B)

1) Conduit seals shall be provided in a conduit system where
   a) the conduit enters an enclosure that is required to be explosion-proof or flameproof "d", and shall be located as close as practicable to the enclosure, or as marked on the enclosure, but not farther than 450 mm from the enclosure;
   b) the conduit leaves the Zone 2 location with no box, coupling, or fitting in the conduit run between the seal and the point at which the conduit leaves the location, except that a rigid unbroken conduit that passes completely through a Zone 2 area, with no fittings less than 300 mm beyond each boundary, need not be sealed, provided that the termination points of the unbroken conduit are in non-hazardous areas; or
   c) the conduit leaves a Zone 2 location outdoors, in which case the seal shall be permitted to be located more than 300 mm beyond the Zone 2 boundary, provided that it is located on the conduit before the conduit enters an enclosure or building.

2) Only explosion-proof or flameproof "d" unions, couplings, reducers, and elbows that are not larger than the trade size of the conduit shall be permitted between the sealing fitting and an explosion-proof or flameproof "d" enclosure.

3) Cable seals shall be provided in a cable system where
   a) the cable enters an enclosure required to be explosion-proof or flameproof "d"; or
   b) the cable enters an enclosure not required to be explosion-proof or flameproof "d", and the other end of the cable terminates in a non-hazardous location in which a negative atmospheric pressure greater than 0.2 kPa exists.

4) Where a run of conduit enters an enclosure that is required to be explosion-proof or flameproof "d", every part of the conduit from the seal to that enclosure shall comply with Rule 18-102.

5) Runs of cables, each having a continuous sheath, either metal or non-metal, shall be permitted to pass through a Zone 2 location without seals.

6) Cables that do not have a continuous sheath, either metal or non-metal, shall be sealed at the boundary of the Zone 2 location.

7) Where seals are required, Rule 18-104 4) shall apply.

18-156 Luminaires and portable lamps, Zone 2

1) Each luminaire shall be protected, by suitable guards or by location, against physical damage that would invalidate the type of protection.

Δ 2) Pendant luminaires shall be suspended by threaded rigid conduit stems or by other means as specified by the manufacturer.

3) Where pendant luminaires are suspended by threaded rigid conduit stems longer than 300 mm, they shall be provided with
   a) permanent and effective bracing against lateral displacement at a level not more than 300 mm above the lower end of the stem; or
   b) flexibility in the form of a fitting or flexible connector suitable for the purpose and for the location not more than 300 mm from the point of attachment to the supporting box or fitting.

4) Portable lamps shall comply with Rule 18-108.

18

18-158 Flexible cords, Zone 2

1) Flexible cords shall be permitted to be used only for connection between permanently mounted luminaires, portable lamps, or other portable utilization equipment and the fixed portion of supply circuits and, where used, shall

    a) be of the extra-hard-usage type;

    b) contain, in addition to the insulated conductors of the circuit, a bonding conductor;

    c) be provided with a sealing gland where the flexible cord enters a box, fitting, or enclosure that is required to be explosion-proof or flameproof "d"; and

    d) be provided with an increased safety "e" cord connector where the flexible cord enters an increased safety "e" fitting or enclosure.

2) Flexible cord shall also be permitted for that portion of the circuit where fixed wiring methods cannot provide the necessary degree of movement for fixed and mobile electrical utilization equipment and, where used, shall

    a) meet all the requirements of Subrule 1); and

    b) be protected from damage by location or by a suitable guard.

Explosive dust atmospheres

Installations in Zone 20 locations

Δ **18-190 Equipment, Zone 20 locations** (see Appendix B)

Electrical equipment installed in a Zone 20 location shall be in accordance with Table 18.

18-192 Wiring methods, Zone 20 (see Appendix B)

1) The wiring method shall be

    a) threaded rigid metal conduit; or

    b) hazardous location cables.

2) Cables shall be installed and supported so as to avoid tensile stress at the cable glands.

Δ 3) Where flexible connections are necessary, they shall be provided by

    a) liquid-tight flexible metal conduit and connectors, marked for heavy duty; or

    b) extra-hard-usage flexible cord and hazardous location cable glands.

4) Where flexible connections are subject to oil or other corrosive conditions, the insulation of the conductors shall be suitable for the condition or shall be protected by means of a suitable sheath.

Δ 5) Wiring methods for intrinsically safe equipment and associated circuits designed and installed as "ia" or intrinsically safe for Class II or Class III locations shall be permitted to be exempt from the requirements of Subrule 1).

18-194 Sealing, Zone 20

Where a raceway provides communication between an enclosure that is required to be dust-tight and one that is not, the entrance of dust into the dust-tight enclosure through the raceway shall be prevented by

a) a permanent and effective seal;

b) a horizontal section not less than 3 m long in the raceway; or

c) a vertical section of raceway not less than 1.5 m long and extending downward from the dust-tight enclosure.

18-196 Flexible cords, Zone 20

Flexible cords shall be extra-hard-usage cord with cable glands suitable for the application.

Installations in Zone 21 locations

Δ **18-200 Equipment, Zone 21 locations** (see Appendix B)
Electrical equipment installed in a Zone 21 location shall be in accordance with Table 18.

18-202 Wiring methods, Zone 21 (see Appendix B)
1) The wiring method shall be
   a) threaded rigid metal conduit; or
   b) hazardous location cables.
2) Boxes, fittings, and joints shall be threaded for connection to conduit or cable glands, and boxes and fittings shall be suitable for use in Zone 21 locations.
3) Cables shall be installed and supported so as to avoid tensile stress at the cable glands.
Δ 4) Where flexible connections are necessary, they shall be provided by
   a) liquid-tight flexible metal conduit and connectors, marked for heavy duty; or
   b) extra-hard-usage flexible cord and hazardous location cable glands.
5) Where flexible connections are subject to oil or other corrosive conditions, the insulation of the conductors shall be suitable for the condition of use or shall be protected by means of a suitable sheath.
Δ 6) Wiring methods for intrinsically safe equipment and associated circuits, designed and installed as "ia" or "ib" or intrinsically safe for Class II or Class III locations, shall be permitted to be exempt from the requirements of Subrules 1) and 2).

18-204 Sealing, Zone 21
Where a raceway provides communication between an enclosure that is required to be dust-tight and one that is not, the entrance of dust into the dust-tight enclosure through the raceway shall be prevented by
a) a permanent and effective seal;
b) a horizontal section not less than 3 m long in the raceway; or
c) a vertical section of raceway not less than 1.5 m long and extending downward from the dust-tight enclosure.

Installations in Zone 22 locations

18-250 Equipment, Zone 22 locations
Δ 1) Electrical equipment installed in a Zone 22 location shall be in accordance with Table 18.
2) Where installed in Zone 22, Group IIIA locations, travelling cranes and hoists for material handling, travelling cleaners for textile machinery, and similar equipment shall conform to the following:
   a) the power supply to contact conductors shall be isolated from all other systems, ungrounded, and equipped with
      i) recording ground detection that will give an alarm and will automatically de-energize the contact conductors in case of a fault to ground; or
      ii) ground fault detection that will give a visual and audible alarm and maintain the alarm as long as power is supplied to the system and the ground fault remains;
   b) contact conductors shall be located or guarded so as to be inaccessible to other than authorized persons and shall be protected against accidental contact with foreign objects; and
   c) current collectors shall conform to the following:
      i) they shall be arranged or guarded to confine normal sparking and to prevent escape of sparks or hot particles;
      ii) to reduce sparking, two or more separate surfaces of contact shall be provided for each contact conductor;

18

    iii)   reliable means shall be provided to keep contact conductors and current collectors free of accumulations of lint or flyings; and

    iv)   control equipment shall be suitable for Zone 22.

18-252 Wiring methods, Zone 22 (see Appendix B)

1) The wiring method shall be
   a) threaded metal conduit;
   b) hazardous location cables;
   c) Type TC cable installed in cable tray in accordance with Rule 12-2202 and enclosed in rigid conduit or another acceptable wiring method wherever it leaves the cable tray;
   d) armoured cable with overall non-metallic jacket, such as TECK90, ACWU90, copper-sheathed RC90, or aluminum-sheathed RA90;
   e) control and instrumentation cables with an interlocking metallic armour and a continuous jacket in control circuits (Type ACIC);
   f) Type CIC cable (non-armoured control and instrumentation cable) installed in cable tray in accordance with the installation requirements of Rule 12-2202 2), where
      i) the voltage rating of the cable is not less than 300 V;
      ii) the circuit voltage is 150 V or less; and
      iii) the circuit current is 5 A or less;
   g) rigid RTRC conduit Type XW, provided that
   Δ   i) boxes, fittings, and joints are marked with the suffix "-XW"; and
      ii) installation is performed in industrial establishments that are not accessible to the public and where only qualified persons service the installation; or
   Δ h) liquid-tight flexible metal conduit and connectors, marked for heavy duty.
2) Boxes and fittings in which taps, joints, or terminal connections are made shall be either an Enclosure Type 4 or 5, or
   a) be provided with telescoping or close-fitting covers or other effective means to prevent the escape of sparks or burning material; and
   b) have no openings, such as holes for attachment screws, through which, after installation, sparks or burning material might escape, or through which exterior accumulations of dust or adjacent combustible material might be ignited.
3) Cables shall be installed and supported so as to avoid tensile stress at the cable glands.
Δ 4) Where it is necessary to use flexible connections, the provisions of Rule 18-202 4) b) and 5) shall apply.
Δ 5) Wiring methods for intrinsically safe equipment and associated circuits designed and installed as "ia", "ib", "ic", intrinsically safe for Class II or Class III locations, or non-incendive shall be permitted to be exempt from the requirements of Subrules 1) and 2).

18-254 Sealing, Zone 22

Sealing of raceways shall conform to Rule 18-204.

C22.1-18

Section 20
Flammable liquid and gasoline dispensing, service stations, garages, bulk storage
plants, finishing processes, and aircraft hangars

Section 20 — Flammable liquid and gasoline dispensing, service stations, garages, bulk storage plants, finishing processes, and aircraft hangars

20-000 Scope (see Appendices G and J)

1) This Section supplements or amends the general requirements of this Code and applies to installations as follows:
   a) gasoline dispensing and service stations — Rules 20-002 to 20-014;
   b) propane dispensing, container filling, and storage — Rules 20-030 to 20-042;
   c) compressed natural gas refuelling stations, compressors, and storage facilities — Rules 20-060 to 20-070;
   d) commercial repair garages — Rules 20-100 to 20-112;
   e) bulk storage plants — Rules 20-200 to 20-212;
   f) finishing processes — Rules 20-300 to 20-314; and
   g) aircraft hangars — Rules 20-400 to 20-422.

2) For additions, modifications, or renovations to, or operation and maintenance of, existing facilities employing the Division system of classification for Class I locations, the continued use of the Division system of classification shall be permitted.

3) Where the Division system of classification is used for Class I locations, as permitted by Subrule 2), the Rules for Class I locations found in Annex J20 of Appendix J shall apply.

4) The definitions stated in Rule 18-002 shall also apply to Section 20.

Gasoline dispensing and service stations

20-002 General

1) Rules 20-004 to 20-014 apply to electrical apparatus and wiring installed in gasoline dispensing and service stations and other locations where gasoline or other similar volatile flammable liquids are dispensed or transferred to the fuel tanks of self-propelled vehicles.

2) Other areas used as lubritoriums, service rooms, repair rooms, offices, salesrooms, compressor rooms, and similar locations shall conform to Rules 20-100 to 20-112 with respect to electrical wiring and equipment.

Δ **20-004 Hazardous areas** (see Appendix B)

1) Except as provided for in Subrule 3), the space within a dispenser enclosure up to 1.2 m vertically above its base, including the space below the dispenser that may contain electrical wiring and equipment, shall be a Zone 1 location.

2) The space within a nozzle boot of a dispenser shall be a Zone 0 location.

3) The space within a dispenser enclosure above the Zone 1 location as specified in Subrule 1) or spaces within a dispenser enclosure isolated from the Zone 1 location by a solid vapour-tight partition or by a solid nozzle boot but not completely surrounded by a Zone 1 location shall be a Zone 2 location.

4) The space within 450 mm horizontally from the Zone 1 location within the dispenser enclosure as specified in Subrule 1) shall be a Zone 1 location.

5) The space outside the dispenser within 450 mm horizontally from the opening of a solid nozzle boot located above the vapour-tight partition shall be a Zone 2 location, except that the classified area need not extend beyond the plane in which the boot is located.

6) In an outside location, any area beyond the Zone 1 area (and in buildings not suitably cut off) within 6 m horizontally from the exterior enclosure of any dispenser shall be a Zone 2 location that extends to a level 450 mm above driveway or ground level.

20

C22.1-18

Section 20
Flammable liquid and gasoline dispensing, service stations, garages, bulk storage plants, finishing processes, and aircraft hangars

7) In an outside location, any area beyond the Zone 1 location (and in buildings not suitably cut off) within 3 m horizontally from any tank fill-pipe shall be a Zone 2 location that extends upward to a level 450 mm above driveway or ground level.

8) Electrical wiring and equipment, any portion of which is below the surface of areas defined as Zone 1 or Zone 2 in Subrule 1), 4), 6), or 7), shall be considered to be within a Zone 1 location that extends at least to the point of emergence above grade.

9) Areas within the vicinity of tank vent pipes shall be classified as follows:

a) the spherical volume within a 900 mm radius from the point of discharge of any tank vent pipe shall be considered a Zone 1 location and the volume between the 900 mm radius and the 1.5 m radius from the point of discharge of a vent shall be considered a Zone 2 location;

b) for any vent that does not discharge upward, the cylindrical volume below both the Zone 1 and Zone 2 locations extending to the ground shall be considered a Zone 2 location; and

c) the hazardous area shall not be considered to extend beyond an unpierced wall.

10) Areas within lubrication rooms shall be classified as follows:

a) the area within any pit or space below grade or floor level in a lubrication room shall be considered a Zone 1 location, unless the pit or space below grade is beyond the hazardous areas specified in Subrules 6), 7), and 9), in which case the pit or space below grade shall be considered a Zone 2 location;

b) notwithstanding Item a), for each floor below grade that is located beyond the hazardous area specified in Subrules 6), 7), and 9) and where adequate ventilation is provided, a Zone 2 location shall extend up to a level of only 50 mm above each such floor; and

c) the area within the entire lubrication room up to 50 mm above the floor or grade, whichever is higher, and the area within 900 mm measured in any direction from the dispensing point of a hand-operated unit dispensing volatile flammable liquids shall be considered a Zone 2 location.

20-006 Wiring and equipment within hazardous areas

1) Electrical wiring and equipment within the hazardous areas defined in Rule 20-004 shall conform to Section 18 requirements.

2) Where dispensers are supplied by rigid metal conduit, a union and a flexible fitting shall be installed between the conduit and the dispenser junction box in addition to any sealing fittings required by Section 18.

3) The flexible metal fitting required by Subrule 2) shall be installed in a manner that allows relative movement of the conduit and the dispenser.

Δ 4) Where dispensers are supplied by a cable, provision shall be made to separate the cable from the dispenser junction box without rendering ineffective the explosion-proof cable seal.

20-008 Wiring and equipment above hazardous areas

Wiring and equipment above hazardous areas shall conform to Rules 20-106 and 20-110.

20-010 Circuit disconnects

Each circuit leading to or through a dispensing pump shall be provided with a switching means that will disconnect simultaneously all ungrounded conductors of the circuit from the source of supply.

20-012 Sealing

1) Seals as required by Section 18 shall be provided in each conduit run entering or leaving a dispenser or any cavities or enclosures in direct communication with a dispenser.

2) Additional seals shall be provided in conformance with Rules 18-104 and 18-154, and the requirements of Rules 18-104 1) c) and 18-154 1) b) shall include horizontal and vertical boundaries.

C22.1-18

Section 20
Flammable liquid and gasoline dispensing, service stations, garages, bulk storage
plants, finishing processes, and aircraft hangars

20-014 Bonding
All non-current-carrying metal parts of dispensing pumps, metal raceways, and other electrical equipment shall be bonded to ground in accordance with Section 10.

Propane dispensing, container filling, and storage

20-030 Scope (see Appendix B)
Rules 20-032 to 20-042 apply to locations in which propane is dispensed or transferred to the fuel tanks of self-propelled vehicles or to portable containers and to locations in which propane is stored or transferred from rail cars or tanker vehicles to storage containers.

20-032 Special terminology
In this Subsection, the following definitions shall apply:

Container refill centre — a facility such as a propane service station that is open to the public and at which propane is dispensed into containers or the fuel tanks of motor vehicles and that consists of propane storage containers, piping, and pertinent equipment, including pumps and dispensing devices.

Filling plant — a facility such as a bulk propane plant, the primary purpose of which is the distribution of propane, that receives propane in tank car or truck transport for storage and/or distribution in portable containers or tank trucks, that has bulk storage, and that usually has container filling and truck loading facilities on the premises.

Propane — any material that is composed predominantly of the following hydrocarbons either by themselves or as mixtures: propane, propylene, butane (normal butane or iso-butane), and butylene.

20-034 Hazardous areas
In container refill centres and in filling plants, the hazardous areas shall be classified as listed in Table 63.

20-036 Wiring and equipment in hazardous areas
1) All electrical wiring and equipment in the hazardous areas referred to in Rule 20-034 shall conform to the requirements of Section 18.
2) Where dispensing devices are supplied by rigid metal conduit, the requirements of Rule 20-006 2) and 3) shall be met.

20-038 Sealing
1) Seals shall be installed as required by Section 18 and the requirements shall be applied to horizontal as well as vertical boundaries of the defined hazardous locations.
2) Seals for dispensing devices shall be provided as required by Rule 20-012.

20-040 Circuit disconnects
Each circuit leading to or through a propane dispensing device or pump shall be provided with a switching means that will disconnect simultaneously all ungrounded conductors of the circuit from the source of supply.

20-042 Bonding
All non-current-carrying metal parts of equipment and raceways shall be bonded to ground in accordance with Section 10.

Compressed natural gas refuelling stations, compressors, and storage facilities

20-060 Scope (see Appendix B)
1) Rules 20-062 to 20-070 apply to locations in which compressed natural gas is dispensed to the fuel tanks of self-propelled vehicles and to associated compressors and storage facilities.

20

C22.1-18

Section 20
Flammable liquid and gasoline dispensing, service stations, garages, bulk storage
plants, finishing processes, and aircraft hangars

2) The Rules in this Subsection do not apply to vehicle refuelling appliances installed in accordance with CSA B149.1 that do not have storage facilities.

20-062 Hazardous areas

Compressed natural gas refuelling stations, compressors, and storage facilities shall be classified as shown in Table 64.

20-064 Wiring and equipment in hazardous areas

1) All electrical wiring and equipment in the hazardous areas defined in Rule 20-062 shall comply with the requirements of Section 18.

2) Where dispensing devices are supplied by rigid metal conduit, the requirements of Rule 20-006 2) and 3) shall be met.

20-066 Sealing

1) Seals shall be installed as required by Section 18, and the requirements shall be applied to horizontal as well as vertical boundaries of the defined hazardous locations.

2) Seals for dispensing devices shall be provided as required by Rule 20-012.

20-068 Circuit disconnects

Each circuit leading to a compressor or a dispensing device shall be provided with a switching means that will disconnect simultaneously all ungrounded conductors of the circuit from the source of supply.

20-070 Bonding

All non-current-carrying metal parts of equipment and raceways shall be bonded to ground in accordance with Section 10.

Commercial repair garages

20-100 Scope (see Appendix B)

Rules 20-102 to 20-112 apply to commercial garages where vehicles powered by gasoline, propane, or other flammable fuels are serviced or repaired.

Δ ### 20-102 Hazardous areas

1) For each floor at or above grade, the entire area up to a level 50 mm above the floor shall be a Zone 2 location except that adjacent areas shall not be classified as hazardous locations, provided that they are
   a) elevated from a service and repair area by at least 50 mm; or
   b) separated from a service and repair area by tight-fitting barriers such as curbs, ramps, or partitions at least 50 mm high.

2) For each floor below grade, the entire area up to a level 50 mm above the bottom of outside doors or other openings that are at, or above, grade level shall be a Zone 2 location except that, where adequate ventilation is provided, the hazardous location shall extend up to a level of only 50 mm above each such floor.

3) Any pit or depression below floor level shall be a Zone 2 location that extends up to 50 mm above the floor level.

20-104 Wiring and equipment in hazardous areas

Within hazardous areas as defined in Rule 20-102, wiring and equipment shall conform to the applicable requirements of Section 18.

20-106 Wiring above hazardous areas

1) All fixed wiring above hazardous areas shall be in accordance with Section 12 and suitable for the type of building and occupancy.

2) For pendants, flexible cord of the hard-usage type shall be used.

C22.1-18

Section 20
Flammable liquid and gasoline dispensing, service stations, garages, bulk storage
plants, finishing processes, and aircraft hangars

3) For connection of portable luminaires, portable motors, or other portable utilization equipment, flexible cord of the hard-usage type shall be used.

20-108 Sealing

1) Seals shall be installed as required by Section 18, and the requirements of Rule 18-154 1) b) shall include horizontal and vertical boundaries.

2) Raceways embedded in a floor or buried beneath a floor shall be considered to be within the hazardous area above the floor if any connections or extensions lead into or through such an area.

20-110 Equipment above hazardous areas

1) Fixed equipment that is less than 3.6 m above floor level and that may produce arcs, sparks, or particles of hot metal, such as cut-outs, switches, charging panels, generators, motors, or other equipment (excluding receptacles and luminaires) having make-and-break or sliding contacts, shall be of the totally enclosed type or constructed to prevent escape of sparks or hot metal particles.

2) Permanently installed luminaires that are located over lanes through which vehicles are commonly driven shall be permitted to be suitable for non-hazardous locations and shall be
   a) located not less than 3.6 m above floor level; or
   b) protected from mechanical damage by a guard or by location.

3) Portable luminaires shall
   a) be of the totally enclosed gasketted type, equipped with a handle, lampholder, hook, and substantial guard attached to the lampholder or handle, and all exterior surfaces that may come in contact with battery terminals, wiring terminals, or other objects shall be of non-conducting materials or shall be effectively protected with an insulating jacket;
   b) be of the unswitched type; and
   c) not be provided with receptacles for attachment plugs.

20-112 Battery charging equipment

Battery chargers and their control equipment, and batteries being charged, shall not be located within the hazardous areas classified in Rule 20-102.

Bulk storage plants

20-200 Scope

Rules 20-202 to 20-212 apply to locations where gasoline or other similar volatile flammable liquids are stored in tanks having an aggregate capacity of one carload or more, and from which such products are distributed (usually by tank truck).

Δ ## 20-202 Hazardous areas

Hazardous locations at bulk storage plants shall be classified as shown in Table 69.

20-204 Wiring and equipment in hazardous areas

All electrical wiring and equipment in the hazardous areas defined in Rule 20-202 shall conform to the requirements of Section 18.

20-206 Wiring and equipment above hazardous areas

1) Wiring installed above a hazardous location shall conform to the requirements of Section 12 and be suitable for the type of building and the occupancy.

2) Fixed equipment that may produce arcs, sparks, or particles of hot metal, such as lamps and lampholders, cut-outs, switches, receptacles, motors, or other equipment having make-and-break or sliding contacts, shall be of the totally enclosed type or constructed to prevent the escape of sparks or hot metal particles.

3) Portable lamps or utilization equipment and the flexible cords supplying them shall conform to the requirements of Section 18 for the class of location above which they are connected or used.

20

C22.1-18

Section 20
Flammable liquid and gasoline dispensing, service stations, garages, bulk storage
plants, finishing processes, and aircraft hangars

20-208 Sealing

1) Seals shall be installed in accordance with Section 18 and shall be applied to horizontal as well as vertical boundaries of the defined hazardous locations.

2) Buried raceways under defined hazardous areas shall be considered to be within such areas.

20-210 Gasoline dispensing

Where gasoline dispensing is carried on in conjunction with bulk station operations, the applicable provisions of Rules 20-002 to 20-014 shall apply.

20-212 Bonding

All non-current-carrying metal parts of equipment and raceways shall be bonded to ground in accordance with Section 10.

Finishing processes

20-300 Scope

Rules 20-302 to 20-314 apply where paints, lacquers, or other flammable finishes are regularly or frequently applied by spraying, dipping, brushing, or by other means, and where volatile flammable solvents or thinners are used or where readily ignitable deposits or residues from such paints, lacquers, or finishes may occur.

Δ **20-302 Hazardous locations**

1) The following areas shall be Zone 1 locations:
   a) where adequate ventilation is provided, the interiors of spray booths and their exhaust ducts;
   b) all space within 6 m horizontally in any direction, extending to a height of 1 m above the goods to be painted, from spraying operations more extensive than touch-up spraying and not conducted within the spray booth, and as otherwise shown in Diagram 5;
   c) all space within 6 m horizontally in any direction from dip tanks and their drain boards with the space extending to a height of 1 m above the dip tank and drain board; and
   d) all other spaces where hazardous concentrations of flammable vapours are likely to occur.

2) For spraying operations within an open-face spray booth, the extent of the Zone 2 location shall extend not less than 1.5 m from the open face of the spray booth, and as otherwise shown in Diagram 4.

3) For spraying operations confined within a closed spray booth or room or for rooms where hazardous concentrations of flammable vapours are likely to occur, such as paint mixing rooms, and as otherwise shown in Diagram 10, the space within 1 m in all directions from any openings in the booth or room shall be a Zone 2 location.

4) All space within the room but beyond the limits for Zone 1 as classified in Subrule 1) for extensive open spraying, and as otherwise shown in Diagram 5 for dip tanks and drain boards and for other hazardous operations, shall be Zone 2 locations.

5) Adjacent areas that are cut off from the defined hazardous area by tight partitions without communicating openings, and within which hazardous vapours are not likely to be released, shall be permitted to be classed as non-hazardous.

6) Drying and baking areas provided with adequate ventilation and effective interlocks to de-energize all electrical equipment not meeting the requirements for the classified area in case the ventilating equipment is inoperative shall be permitted to be classed as non-hazardous.

7) Notwithstanding the requirements of Subrule 1) b), where adequate ventilation with effective interlocks is provided at floor level, and as otherwise shown in Diagram 6,
   a) the space within 1 m horizontally in any direction from the goods to be painted and such space extending to a height of 1 m above the goods to be painted shall be a Zone 1 location; and

C22.1-18

Section 20
Flammable liquid and gasoline dispensing, service stations, garages, bulk storage
plants, finishing processes, and aircraft hangars

b) all space between a 1 m and a 1.5 m distance above the goods to be painted and all space within 6 m horizontally in any direction beyond the limits for the Zone 1 location shall be a Zone 2 location.

8) Notwithstanding the requirements of Subrule 2), where a baffle of sheet metal of not less than No. 18 MSG is installed vertically above the front face of an open-face spray booth to a height of 1 m or to the ceiling, whichever is less, and extending back on the side edges a distance of 1.5 m, the space behind this baffle shall be a non-hazardous location.

9) Notwithstanding the requirements of Subrule 3), where a baffle of sheet metal of not less than No. 18 MSG is installed vertically above an opening in a closed spray booth or room to a height of 1 m or to the ceiling, whichever is less, and extends horizontally a distance of 1 m beyond each side of the opening, the space behind the baffle shall be a non-hazardous location.

20-304 Ventilation and spraying equipment interlock
The spraying equipment for a spray booth shall be interlocked with the spray booth ventilation system so that the spraying equipment is made inoperable when the ventilation system is not in operation.

20-306 Wiring and equipment in hazardous areas
1) All electrical wiring and equipment within the hazardous areas as defined in Rule 20-302 shall conform to the requirements of Section 18.

Δ 2) Unless designed for use in both areas with readily ignitable deposits and areas with flammable vapour, no electrical equipment shall be installed or used where it may be subject to a hazardous accumulation of readily ignitable deposits or residue.

3) Illumination of readily ignitable areas through panels of glass or other transparent or translucent materials shall be permitted only where
   a) fixed lighting units are used as the source of illumination;
   b) the panel is non-combustible and effectively isolates the hazardous area from the area in which the lighting unit is located;
   c) the panel is of a material or is protected so that breakage is unlikely; and
   d) the arrangement is such that normal accumulations of hazardous residue on the surface of the panel will not be raised to a dangerous temperature by radiation or conduction from the source of illumination.

4) Portable electric lamps or other utilization equipment shall
   a) not be used within a hazardous area during operation of the finishing process; and
Δ b) meet the requirements for Zone 2 locations when used during cleaning or repairing operations.

5) Notwithstanding Subrule 2),
   a) totally enclosed and gasketted lighting shall be permitted to be used on the ceiling of a spray room where adequate ventilation is provided; and
   b) infrared paint drying units shall be permitted to be used in a spray room if the controls are interlocked with those of the spraying equipment so that both operations cannot be performed simultaneously, and if portable, the paint drying unit shall not be brought into the spray room until spraying operations have ceased.

20-308 Fixed electrostatic equipment
Electrostatic spraying and detearing equipment shall conform to the following:
Δ a) no transformers, power packs, control apparatus, or other electrical portions of the equipment except high-voltage grids and their connections shall be installed in any of the hazardous areas defined in Rule 20-302, unless they meet the requirements for the classified area;
   b) high-voltage grids or electrodes shall be
      i) located in suitable non-combustible booths or enclosures provided with adequate ventilation;
      ii) rigidly supported and of substantial construction; and

20

C22.1-18

Section 20
Flammable liquid and gasoline dispensing, service stations, garages, bulk storage
plants, finishing processes, and aircraft hangars

       iii)   effectively insulated from ground by means of non-porous, non-combustible insulators;

c)   high-voltage leads shall be

       i)   effectively and permanently supported on suitable insulators;

       ii)   effectively guarded against accidental contact or grounding; and

       iii)   provided with automatic means for discharging any residual charge to ground when the supply voltage is interrupted;

d)   where goods are being processed,

       i)   they shall be supported on conveyors in such a manner that the minimum clearance between goods and high-voltage grids or conductors cannot be less than twice the sparking distance; and

       ii)   a conspicuous sign indicating the sparking distance shall be permanently posted near the equipment;

e)   automatic controls shall be provided that will operate without time delay to disconnect the power supply and to signal the operator in the event of

       i)   stoppage of ventilating fans;

       ii)   failure of ventilating equipment;

       iii)   stoppage of the conveyor carrying goods through the high-voltage field;

       iv)   occurrence of a ground or of an imminent ground at any point on the high-voltage system; or

       v)   reduction of clearance below that specified in Item d); and

f)   adequate fencing, railings, or guards that are electrically conducting and effectively bonded to ground shall be provided for safe isolation of the process, and signs shall be permanently posted designating the process area as dangerous because of high voltage.

20-310 Electrostatic hand spraying equipment

Electrostatic hand spray apparatus and devices used with such apparatus shall conform to the following:

a)   the high-voltage circuits shall be intrinsically safe and not produce a spark of sufficient intensity to ignite any vapour-air mixtures, nor result in an appreciable shock hazard to anyone coming in contact with a grounded object;

b)   the electrostatically charged exposed elements of the hand gun shall be capable of being energized only by a switch that also controls the paint supply;

c)   transformers, power packs, control apparatus, and all other electrical portions of the equipment, with the exception of the hand gun itself and its connections to the power supply, shall be located outside the hazardous area;

d)   the handle of the spray gun shall be bonded to ground by a metallic connection and be constructed such that the operator in normal operating position is in intimate electrical contact with the handle in order to prevent buildup of a static charge on the operator's body;

e)   all electrically conductive objects in the spraying area shall be bonded to ground and the equipment shall carry a prominent, permanently installed warning regarding the necessity for this bonding feature;

f)   precautions shall be taken to ensure that objects being painted are maintained in metallic contact with the conveyor or other grounded support, and these precautions shall include the following:

       i)   hooks shall be regularly cleaned;

       ii)   areas of contact shall be sharp points or knife edges; and

       iii)   points of support of the object shall be concealed from random spray where feasible and, where the objects being sprayed are supported from a conveyor, the point of attachment to the conveyor shall be located so as to not collect spray material during normal operation; and

g)   the spraying operation shall take place within a spray area that is adequately ventilated to remove solvent vapours released from the operation, and the electrical equipment shall be interlocked with the ventilation of the spraying area so that the equipment cannot be operated unless the ventilation system is in operation.

Section 20

C22.1-18

Flammable liquid and gasoline dispensing, service stations, garages, bulk storage plants, finishing processes, and aircraft hangars

20-312 Wiring and equipment above hazardous areas

1) All fixed wiring above hazardous areas shall conform to Section 12.

2) Equipment that may produce arcs, sparks, or particles of hot metal, such as lamps and lampholders for fixed lighting, cut-outs, switches, receptacles, motors, or other equipment having make-and-break or sliding contacts, where installed above a hazardous area or above an area where freshly finished goods are handled, shall be of the totally enclosed type or constructed to prevent the escape of sparks or hot metal particles.

20-314 Bonding

All metal raceways and all non-current-carrying metal portions of fixed or portable equipment, regardless of voltage, shall be bonded to ground in accordance with Section 10.

Aircraft hangars

20-400 Scope

Rules 20-402 to 20-422 apply to locations used for storage or servicing of aircraft in which gasoline, jet fuels or other volatile flammable liquids, or flammable gases are used, but shall not include those locations used exclusively for aircraft that have never contained such liquids or gases, or that have been drained and properly purged.

Δ ## 20-402 Hazardous areas

1) Any pit or depression below the level of the hangar floor shall be a Zone 1 location that shall extend up to the floor level.

2) The entire area of the hangar, including any adjacent and communicating areas not suitably cut off from the hangar, shall be a Zone 2 location up to a level 450 mm above the floor.

3) The area within 1.5 m horizontally from aircraft power plants, aircraft fuel tanks, or aircraft structures containing fuel shall be a Zone 2 location that extends upward from the floor to a level 1.5 m above the upper surface of wings and of engine enclosures.

4) Adjacent areas in which hazardous vapours are not likely to be released, such as stock rooms, electrical control rooms, and other similar locations, shall be permitted to be classed as non-hazardous when adequately ventilated and when effectively cut off from the hangar itself in accordance with Rule 18-058.

20-404 Wiring and equipment in hazardous areas

1) All fixed and portable wiring and equipment that is or may be installed or operated within any of the hazardous locations defined in Rule 20-402 shall conform to the requirements of Section 18.

Δ 2) All wiring installed in or under the hangar floor shall conform to the requirements for Zone 1 locations.

3) Wiring systems installed in pits, or other spaces in or under the hangar floor, shall be provided with adequate drainage and shall not be placed in the same compartment with any other service except piped compressed air.

4) Attachment plugs and receptacles in hazardous locations shall be explosion-proof, or shall be designed so that they cannot be energized while the connections are being made or broken.

20-406 Wiring not within hazardous areas

1) All fixed wiring in a hangar not within a hazardous area as defined in Rule 20-402 shall be installed in metal raceways or shall be armoured cable, Type MI cable, aluminum-sheathed cable, or copper-sheathed cable, except that wiring in a non-hazardous location as set out in Rule 20-402 4) shall be permitted to be of any type recognized in Section 12 as suitable for the type of building and the occupancy.

2) For pendants, flexible cord of the hard-usage type and containing a separate bonding conductor shall be used.

20

C22.1-18

Section 20
Flammable liquid and gasoline dispensing, service stations, garages, bulk storage
plants, finishing processes, and aircraft hangars

Δ 3) For portable utilization equipment and lamps, flexible cord of the hard-usage type and containing a separate bonding conductor shall be used.

4) Suitable means shall be provided for maintaining continuity and adequacy of the bonding between the fixed wiring system and the non-current-carrying metal portions of pendant luminaires, portable lamps, and other portable utilization equipment.

20-408 Equipment not within hazardous areas

1) In locations other than those described in Rule 20-402, equipment that is less than 3 m above wings and engine enclosures of aircraft and that may produce arcs, sparks, or particles of hot metal, such as lamps and lampholders for fixed lighting, cut-outs, switches, receptacles, charging panels, generators, motors, or other equipment having make-and-break or sliding contacts, shall be of the totally enclosed type or constructed to prevent the escape of sparks or hot metal particles, except that equipment in areas described in Rule 20-402 4) shall be permitted to be of the general-purpose type.

2) Lampholders of the metal shell, fibre-lined type shall not be used for fixed lighting.

3) Portable lamps that are used within a hangar shall comply with Rule 18-100.

Δ 4) Portable utilization equipment that is, or may be, used within a hangar shall be of a type suitable for use in Zone 2 locations.

20-410 Stanchions, rostrums, and docks

Δ 1) Electric wiring, outlets, and equipment, including lamps on, or attached to, stanchions, rostrums, or docks that are located, or likely to be located, in a hazardous area as defined in Rule 20-402 3), shall conform to the requirements for Zone 2 locations.

2) Where stanchions, rostrums, and docks are not located, or are not likely to be located, in a hazardous area as defined in Rule 20-402 3), wiring and equipment shall conform to Rules 20-406 and 20-408, except for the following:

   a) receptacles and attachment plugs shall be of the locking type that will not break apart readily; and

   b) wiring and equipment not more than 450 mm above the floor in any position shall conform to Subrule 1).

3) Mobile stanchions with electrical equipment conforming to Subrule 2) shall carry at least one permanently affixed warning sign, to the effect that the stanchions are to be kept 1.5 m clear of aircraft engines and fuel tank areas.

20-412 Sealing

1) Seals shall be installed in accordance with Section 18 and shall apply to horizontal as well as to vertical boundaries of the defined hazardous areas.

2) Raceways embedded in a masonry floor or buried beneath a floor shall be considered to be within the hazardous area above the floor when any connections or extensions lead into or through the hazardous area.

20-414 Aircraft electrical systems

Aircraft electrical systems shall be de-energized when the aircraft is stored in a hangar and, whenever possible, while the aircraft is undergoing maintenance.

20-416 Aircraft battery charging and equipment

1) Aircraft batteries shall not be charged when installed in an aircraft located inside or partially inside a hangar.

2) Battery chargers and their control equipment shall not be located or operated within any of the hazardous areas defined in Rule 20-402 but shall be permitted to be located or operated in a separate building or in an area complying with Rule 20-402 4).

3) Mobile chargers shall carry at least one permanently affixed warning sign stating that the chargers are to be kept 1.5 m clear of aircraft engines and fuel tank areas.

C22.1-18

Section 20
Flammable liquid and gasoline dispensing, service stations, garages, bulk storage
plants, finishing processes, and aircraft hangars

4) Tables, racks, trays, and wiring shall not be located within a hazardous area, and shall conform to the provisions of Section 26 pertaining to storage batteries.

20-418 External power sources for energizing aircraft

1) Aircraft energizers shall be designed and mounted so that all electrical equipment and fixed wiring are at least 450 mm above floor level, and they shall not be operated in a hazardous area as defined in Rule 20-402 3).

2) Mobile energizers shall carry at least one permanently affixed sign stating that the energizers are to be kept 1.5 m clear of aircraft engines and fuel tank areas.

3) Aircraft energizers shall be equipped with polarized external power plugs and with automatic controls to isolate the ground power unit electrically from the aircraft in case excessive voltage is generated by the ground power unit.

4) Flexible cords for aircraft energizers and ground support equipment shall be of the extra-hard-usage type and shall include a bonding conductor.

20-420 Mobile servicing equipment with electrical components

Δ 1) Mobile servicing equipment such as vacuum cleaners, air compressors, air movers, etc., having electrical wiring and equipment not suitable for Zone 2 locations shall
   a) be designed and mounted so that all such wiring and equipment is at least 450 mm above the floor;
   b) not be operated within the hazardous areas defined in Rule 20-402 3); and
   c) carry at least one permanently affixed warning sign stating that the equipment is to be kept 1.5 m clear of aircraft engines and fuel tank areas.

2) Flexible cords used for mobile equipment shall be of the extra-hard-usage type and shall include a bonding conductor.

3) Attachment plugs and receptacles shall provide for the connection of the bonding conductor to the raceway system.

Δ 4) Equipment shall not be operated in areas where maintenance operations likely to release hazardous vapours are in progress, unless the equipment is at least suitable for use in a Zone 2 location.

20-422 Bonding

All metal raceways, and all non-current-carrying metal portions of fixed or portable equipment, regardless of voltage, shall be bonded to ground in accordance with Section 10.

20

Section 22 — Locations in which corrosive liquids, vapours, or excessive moisture are likely to be present

General

22-000 Scope
This Section applies to electrical equipment and installations in locations in which corrosive liquids, vapours, or excessive moisture are likely to be present, and supplements or amends the general requirements of this Code.

22-002 Category definitions (see Appendix B)
Locations covered in this Section shall be classified as follows:

a) **Category 1** — the location is one in which moisture in the form of vapour or liquid is present in quantities that are liable to interfere with the normal operation of electrical equipment, whether the moisture is caused by condensation, the dripping or splashing of liquid, or otherwise; and

b) **Category 2** — the location is one in which corrosive liquids or vapours are likely to be present in quantities that are likely to interfere with the normal operation of electrical equipment.

22-004 Application of category definitions
Where the expressions "Category 1" or "Category 2" do not appear in any Rule in this Section, the Rule shall apply to both categories.

Equipment

22-100 Essential equipment only (see Appendix B)
1) Only electrical equipment that is essential for the processes being carried on in a room or section of a building shall be installed in Category 1 and Category 2 locations.
2) Service equipment, motors, panelboards, switchboards, and other electrical equipment shall, where practicable, be installed in rooms or sections of the building that are not Category 1 or Category 2 locations.
3) Enclosures containing moulded case circuit breakers shall not be located in a Category 2 location unless marked as suitable for the application.

22-102 Type of construction
1) Where the electrical equipment is, or is likely to be, partially or wholly submerged, it shall be of a submersible type of construction.
2) Where the electrical equipment is, or is likely to be, subjected to direct streams of liquid under pressure, it shall be of a watertight type of construction.
3) Where the electrical equipment is, or is likely to be, exposed to corrosive vapours, it shall be of a corrosion-resistant type of construction.
4) Where the electrical equipment is, or is likely to be, exposed to splashing of water, it shall be of a weatherproof or watertight type of construction.
5) Where the electrical equipment is, or is likely to be, exposed only to the falling or condensing of moisture, it shall be of a drip-proof, weatherproof, or watertight type of construction.
6) Where a protective coating on electrical equipment is, or may be, exposed to corrosive liquids or vapour, the coating shall be suitable for the corrosive condition.

22-104 Pendant lampholders
1) Pendant lampholders shall be of the weatherproof type and hung from insulated stranded copper conductors of not less than No. 14 AWG.
2) Where the pendant insulated conductors exceed 900 mm in length, they shall be twisted together.

22-106 Luminaires

1) Every luminaire in a Category 1 location shall be constructed so that water cannot enter or accumulate within the luminaire.

2) Every luminaire in a Category 2 location shall be totally enclosed, gasketted, and of a corrosion-resistant type of construction.

22-108 Receptacles, plugs, and cords for portable equipment

1) Every receptacle and attachment plug for portable equipment shall be
   a) of the weatherproof type; and
   b) provided with grounding terminals and conductors properly bonded to ground.

2) Flexible cords or power supply cables for portable equipment shall contain a bonding conductor and be of the outdoor type suitable for hard usage as selected in accordance with Rules 12-402 1) and 12-406 1).

Wiring

22-200 Wiring method in Category 1 locations

1) Where insulated conductors or cables are exposed to moisture in a Category 1 location, they shall
   a) if used in exposed wiring, be of the types selected in accordance with Rule 12-102 3) and rated
      i) for exposed wiring in wet locations; or
      ii) for exposed wiring where exposed to the weather, provided that they are located more than 1.5 m horizontally or 2.5 m vertically from floors, decks, balconies, or stairs; and

Δ   b) if used in a raceway, be of the types selected in accordance with Rule 12-102 3) for use in raceways in wet locations.

2) Non-metallic-sheathed cable of the NMW or NMWU type shall be permitted to be used in a Category 1 location.

3) Armoured cable, aluminum-sheathed cable, and copper-sheathed cable installed in a Category 1 location shall be of the type selected in accordance with Rule 12-102 3) for direct earth burial.

4) Split knobs or cleats shall not be used in a Category 1 location.

5) Mineral-insulated cable shall be permitted to be used in a Category 1 location, but if the cable is secured to walls, it shall be spaced at least 6 mm from the wall at each point of support.

6) Aluminum conductors shall not be used in Category 1 locations unless the termination or joint is adequately sealed against ingress of moisture.

22-202 Wiring method in Category 2 locations

1) Where insulated conductors or cables are exposed to corrosive liquids or vapours in a Category 2 location, they shall
   a) if used in exposed wiring, be of a type with corrosion-resistant protection and be located more than 1.5 m horizontally or 2.5 m vertically from floors, decks, balconies, or stairs; and
   b) if used in conduit, be of a type with corrosion-resistant protection.

2) Non-metallic-sheathed cable of the NMW or NMWU type shall be permitted to be used in a Category 2 location.

3) Surface metal raceways, underfloor raceways, bare conductors, armoured cable except where permitted in Table 19 for exposure to corrosive action, wireways, busways, and split knobs shall not be used in Category 2 locations.

4) Mineral-insulated cable shall be permitted to be used in a Category 2 location if the corrosive action is not of such a nature as to cause deterioration of the outer sheath.

5) Aluminum-sheathed cable and copper-sheathed cable shall be permitted to be used in a Category 2 location, provided that they have suitable corrosion-resistant protection where necessary.

22

6) Aluminum conductors shall not be used in Category 2 locations unless the termination or joint is adequately sealed against ingress of corrosive liquids or vapours.

22-204 Wiring methods in buildings housing livestock or poultry (see Appendix B)

1) Wiring in buildings housing livestock or poultry shall be of the type selected in accordance with Rule 12-102 3) for wet locations.

2) Where non-metallic-sheathed cable is used in buildings housing livestock and poultry, it shall be of the NMW or NMWU type.

3) Notwithstanding Subrules 1) and 2), wiring selected in accordance with Rule 12-102 3) for damp locations shall be permitted in buildings housing livestock or poultry when provided with adequate ventilation.

4) Aluminum conductors shall not be used in buildings housing livestock or poultry.

5) Non-metallic-sheathed cable shall be provided with mechanical protection, in the form of rigid steel or rigid non-metallic conduit or other suitable material to protect against damage from rodents, when
   a) installed in exposed locations less than 300 mm above any horizontal surface;
   b) installed in exposed locations on the side of floor joists or other structural members less than 100 mm below the upper surface of the floor joists or other structural members;
   c) run in attics; or
   d) run in concealed spaces.

22-206 Rinks

1) Insulated conductors run as open wiring in accordance with Rules 12-200 to 12-224 shall be permitted to be used for the lighting of curling or skating rink areas that are subject to condensation, provided that the insulated conductors are suitable for wet locations as selected in accordance with Rule 12-102 3).

2) The wiring method used in waiting rooms and other portions of rinks shall be in accordance with Section 12 based on the area and moisture conditions involved.

3) Rink areas that are provided with positive mechanical ventilation capable of changing the air at least three times per hour shall be permitted to be regarded as dry locations.

Drainage, sealing, and exclusion of moisture and corrosive vapour

22-300 Drip loops

Where exposed insulated conductors or non-metallic-sheathed cables enter into or issue from a Category 1 or Category 2 location, the insulated conductors or cables shall pass through the wall of the location in an upward direction from the Category 1 or Category 2 location, and in the case of exposed insulated conductors or cables, shall be in non-combustible, non-absorptive insulating tubes.

22-302 Drainage, sealing, and exclusion of moisture

1) Where conduit is used, it shall be
   a) arranged to drain at frequent intervals to suitable locations;
   Δ b) equipped with fittings that permit the moisture to drain out of the system;
   c) installed to give 12 mm clearance from the supporting surface when either the conduit or supporting surface is metallic; and
   d) sealed to prevent the migration of corrosive vapour where, due to the location of equipment, such migration is considered possible.

2) Where a conduit, aluminum-sheathed cable, or copper-sheathed cable leaves a warm room and enters a cooler atmosphere, it shall be sealed off to prevent breathing and subsequent condensation and shall be sealed in such a manner that condensate will not be trapped at the seal.

3) Every joint in a conduit in a Category 1 location shall be watertight.

4) Every cabinet and fitting in a Category 1 location shall be
    a) of splash-proof or drip-proof construction;
    b) placed so as to prevent moisture or water from entering and accumulating within; and
    c) mounted to give at least 12 mm clearance from the supporting surface when either the
        enclosure or supporting surface is metallic.

Circuit control

22-400 Circuit control
Every circuit in a Category 1 or Category 2 location shall, where practicable, be arranged so that the
current-carrying conductors can be entirely cut off from the supply of electrical power or energy at a
convenient point outside the location.

Materials

22-500 Corrosion-resistant material
All conduits, metal enclosures, and fittings, including every bolt and screw used to secure electrical
equipment, shall be protected by or be of material resistant to the specific corrosive environment.

Bonding

22-600 Exposed, non-current-carrying metal parts
Exposed, non-current-carrying metal parts of fixed or portable equipment shall be bonded to ground in
accordance with Section 10.

Sewage lift and treatment plants

22-700 Scope
1) Rules 22-702 to 22-710 apply to the installation of electrical facilities in sewage lift and pumping
    stations, and in primary and secondary sewage treatment plants where the environment could
    contain multiple hazards, such as moisture, corrosion, explosions, fire, and atmospheric poisoning.
2) Rules 22-702 to 22-710 do not apply to methane generation facilities associated with some
    treatment facilities.

22-702 Special terminology
In this Subsection, the following definitions shall apply:

Continuous positive pressure ventilation — a ventilation system capable of maintaining a positive
pressure in a room or area and of changing the air in the room or area at least six times an hour with
means for detecting ventilation failure.

Dry well — the location below ground designed to accommodate equipment associated with waste
water pumping and isolated from the wet well location to prevent the migration of gases and vapours
into the dry well.

Suitably cut off — an area rendered impermeable and cut off from an adjoining area with no means of
liquid, gas, or vapour communication between the areas at atmospheric pressure.

Wet well — the location below ground where the raw sewage is collected and temporarily stored
before passing through the lift pumps or being processed in a treatment plant.

22-704 Classification of areas (see Appendix B)
1) Sewage lift and treatment plants shall be classified for
    a) hazardous areas in accordance with Section 18; and
    b) corrosive liquids, vapours, or moisture in accordance with this Section.

22

Δ 2) Wet wells provided with adequate continuous positive pressure ventilation shall be considered Zone 2.

3) Except as permitted by Subrule 5) c), all locations below ground suitably cut off from locations in which sewage gases may be present shall be considered Category 1.

4) All locations in which sewage gases may be present in explosive concentrations shall be considered hazardous areas and Category 2.

5) The following areas shall be permitted to be classified as ordinary locations:

a) all locations suitably cut off from a Category 2 location and not classified as a Category 1 location;

b) all locations not suitably cut off from a Category 2 location but with adequate continuous positive pressure ventilation; and

c) dry well locations below ground where adequate heating and adequate continuous positive pressure ventilation is installed.

22-706 Wiring methods

1) Wiring methods within hazardous areas shall be in accordance with Section 18.

2) Wiring methods in a Category 1 or a dry Category 2 location shall be in accordance with Rules 22-200 and 22-202, respectively.

3) Wiring methods in a wet or damp Category 2 location shall be in accordance with Rule 22-202, with the following exceptions:

a) rigid steel conduit and electrical metallic tubing shall not be used;

b) armoured cable, mineral-insulated cable, aluminum-sheathed cable, and copper-sheathed cable shall be permitted to be used, provided that the cable is spaced from walls by at least 12 mm, has a corrosion-resistant jacket, and the cable connectors are adequately sealed against ingress of corrosive liquids or vapours; and

c) grounding and bonding conductors shall be insulated or otherwise protected from corrosion, and the point of connection to ground, if exposed to a corrosive atmosphere, shall be protected from corrosion or be of a material resistant to the specific corrosive environment.

4) Conduits installed from the wet well to an electrical enclosure shall be sealed with a suitable compound to prevent the entrance of moisture, vapour, or gases into the enclosure.

22-708 Electrical equipment

1) Electrical equipment installed in hazardous areas shall be in accordance with Section 18.

2) Electrical equipment installed in a Category 1 or a dry Category 2 location shall be in accordance with the applicable requirements of this Code.

3) Electrical equipment installed in a wet or damp Category 2 location shall be in accordance with the applicable requirements of this Code, with the following exceptions:

a) receptacles shall be fitted with self-closing covers and, if of the duplex type, have individual covers over each half of the receptacle;

b) lighting switches shall have weatherproof covers;

c) unit emergency lighting equipment and emergency lighting control units, other than remote lamps, shall not be located in such locations;

Δ d) heating equipment shall be marked for use in such locations or installed outside the corrosive location;

e) motors shall be totally enclosed and fan cooled and shall not incorporate dissimilar metals relative to the motor frame and connection box; and

f) electrical equipment in wet well areas shall not contain devices that will cause an open arc or spark during normal operation.

4) Ventilation fans shall not be located within the wet well, and fan blades shall be of spark-resistant material.

Δ   5)   Areas provided with continuous positive pressure ventilation shall be interlocked to de-energize all electrical equipment not marked for use in an explosive gas atmosphere in case the ventilating equipment is inoperative.

22-710 Grounding of structural steel
Structural steel below ground in contact with the surrounding earth shall be bonded to the system ground.

Section 24 — Patient care areas

24-000 Scope (see Appendix B)
1)   This Section applies to the installation of
   a)   electrical wiring and equipment within patient care areas of health care facilities; and
   b)   the portions of the electrical systems of health care facilities designated as essential electrical systems.
2)   Except as noted in Rules 24-104 7) and 24-108, this Section does not apply to installations of electrical communication systems as covered in Section 60, nor to radio and television installations as covered in Section 54.
3)   This Section supplements or amends the general requirements of this Code.

24-002 Special terminology (see Appendix B)
In this Section, the following definitions shall apply:

Anaesthetizing location — any area of a health care facility where the induction and maintenance of general anaesthesia are routinely carried out in the course of the examination or treatment of patients.

Applied part — the part or parts of medical electrical equipment, including the patient leads, that come intentionally into contact with the patient to be examined or treated.

Basic care area — a patient care area where body contact between a patient and medical electrical equipment is neither frequent nor usual.

Body contact — an intentional contact at the skin surface or internally, but no direct contact to the heart.

Cardiac contact — an intentional contact directly to the heart by means of an invasive procedure.

Casual contact — contact by voluntary action with a device that has no applied part and is not intended to be connected to a patient.

Conditional branch — the portion of an essential electrical system in which circuits require power restoration by emergency service within 24 h, depending on special circumstances such as environmental or climatic conditions.

Critical care area — a patient care area that is an anaesthetizing location, or in which cardiac contact between a patient and medical electrical equipment is frequent or normal.

Delayed vital branch — the portion of an essential electrical system in which the circuits require power restoration within 2 min.

Emergency power system — a power system that is supplied from an emergency supply and connected to feed essential systems.

Emergency supply — one or more in-house generators of electricity intended to be available in the event of a failure of all other supplies and capable of supplying all the essential loads.

Essential electrical system — an electrical system that has the capability of restoring and sustaining a supply of electrical energy to specified loads in the event of a loss of the normal supply of energy.

Hazard index — for a given set of conditions in an isolated power system, the current, expressed in milliamperes and consisting of resistive and capacitive leakage and fault currents, that would flow through a low impedance if the low impedance were to be connected between either isolated conductor and ground.

Health care facility — a set of physical infrastructure elements that are intended to support the delivery of specific health-related services.

Δ **Health care facility administration** — the unit responsible for planning, organizing, directing, and controlling the health care facility in accordance with the policies of the health care facility and government statutes.

Intermediate care area — a patient care area in which body contact between a patient and medical electrical equipment is frequent or normal.

Isolated system — an electrical distribution system in which no circuit conductor is connected directly to ground.

Line isolation monitor — a device that measures and displays the total hazard index of an isolated electrical system and provides warning when the index reaches a preset limit.

Normal supply — the main electrical supply into a building or a building complex; it may consist of one or more consumer services capable of supplying all loads in the building or building complex.

Patient — a person undergoing medical investigation or treatment.

Patient care area — an area intended primarily for the provision of diagnosis, therapy, or care.

Patient care environment — a zone in a patient care area that has been pre-selected for the accommodation of a patient bed, table, or other supporting mechanism, and for the accommodation of equipment involved in patient treatment, and that includes the space within the room 1.5 m beyond the perimeter of the bed, table, or other supporting mechanism in its normal location and to within 2.3 m of the floor.

Patient care environment bonding point — a common bus, in a patient care environment, that is bonded to ground, and that serves as a common point to which equipment and other bonding connections can be made by means of a group of jacks.

Total hazard index — the hazard index of a given isolated system with all appliances, including the line isolation monitor, connected.

Vital branch — the portion of an essential electrical system in which the circuits require power restoration within 10 s.

Patient care areas

24-100 Rules for patient care areas (see Appendix B)
Rules 24-102 to 24-116 shall apply to those patient care areas that have been designated as
a)   basic care areas;
b)   intermediate care areas; or
c)   critical care areas.

24-102 Circuits in basic care areas (see Appendix B)
1)   The branch circuits supplying receptacles or permanently connected equipment in basic care areas shall be supplied from a grounded distribution system.

2) Branch circuit insulated conductors shall be copper and shall be sized not smaller than No. 12 AWG.

Δ 3) Except as permitted by Subrule 4), branch circuits that supply receptacles or permanently connected medical electrical equipment within a patient care environment shall supply only loads within that patient care environment.

Δ 4) A branch circuit described as in Subrule 3) shall be permitted to be extended to supply loads within one additional patient care environment, provided that the two patient care environments are adjacent to each other.

Δ 5) Where an electrical system in a health care facility includes loads that are designated as essential in accordance with Subrule 24-302 1), each patient care environment described in Subrule 3), or pair of patient care environments described in Subrule 4), shall be supplied by at least one branch circuit from a panelboard that is part of an essential electrical system.

6) Branch circuits shall be supplied at not more than 150 volts-to-ground, unless designated for special-purpose use (e.g., to supply mobile X-ray, laser, and similar equipment) or for permanently connected equipment.

7) A branch circuit that supplies receptacles or permanently connected electrical equipment as described in Rule 24-300 shall not supply receptacles or permanently connected equipment that is not part of the essential electrical system.

8) A circuit consisting of conductors connected to communication or nurse call equipment that is installed within a patient care area shall be deemed a Class 1 circuit in accordance with the applicable Rules of Section 16.

24-104 Bonding to ground in basic care areas (see Appendix B)

1) Bonding conductors shall be insulated unless they are
   a) installed in non-metallic conduit; or

Δ   b) incorporated into a cable that is constructed in such a manner that contact between any metal shield or armour, if it is present, and a bare bonding conductor is not possible.

Ⓔ Δ 2) All receptacles and other permanently connected equipment shall be bonded to ground by copper equipment bonding conductors, sized in accordance with Table 16 but in no case smaller than No. 12 AWG, installed in accordance with Rule 10-612 and run with the circuit conductors in accordance with the following:
   a) each multi-wire branch circuit shall be provided with its own equipment bonding conductor;
   b) except as permitted by Items c) and d), each 2-wire branch circuit supplying a receptacle in a patient care environment shall be provided with its own equipment bonding conductor;
   c) when the receptacles in a patient care environment are supplied from two 2-wire branch circuits in the same raceway, a single equipment bonding conductor shall be permitted to be shared by the two circuits; or
   d) when receptacles intended for a pair of adjacent patient care environments are supplied by three 2-wire branch circuits and one of the circuits is intended to be shared by both environments, the three circuits shall be permitted to share two equipment bonding conductors.

3) Utilization equipment bonding conductors required by Subrules 2), 6), and 7) shall terminate either at the panelboard supplying the branch circuits to the patient care environment from which they arise or on a separately installed busbar that is bonded to that panelboard.

Δ 4) Where branch circuits for a patient care environment are supplied from more than one panelboard, the panelboards shall be bonded together with a single copper equipment bonding conductor sized in accordance with Table 16, but in no case smaller than a No. 6 AWG.

Δ 5) Each panelboard supplying branch circuits as described in Rule 24-102 3) shall be bonded to ground by a copper utilization equipment bonding conductor that is
   a) installed in the same raceway as the circuit conductors supplying that panelboard or installed in accordance with Rule 10-612, and sized in accordance with Table 16; or
   b) incorporated into the assembly of the cable supplying that panelboard.

6) Each item of three-phase equipment shall be bonded to ground with a copper equipment bonding conductor that is
   a) sized in accordance with Table 16, but is in no case smaller than No. 12 AWG; and
   b) connected to its own terminal at the equipment and the panelboard.

7) If they could become energized, exposed non-current-carrying metal parts of communication, radio, or television equipment, other than telephone sets, in a patient care environment shall be bonded to ground using a copper equipment bonding conductor sized in accordance with Subrule 6), by
   a) connection to the bonding screw in the communication section of a barriered and ganged metal outlet box that serves a patient care environment; or
   b) connection to an equipment bonding conductor or bonding busbar for that patient care environment as identified in Subrule 3).

8) If they could become energized, exposed non-current-carrying metal parts of non-electrical equipment, in a patient care environment, shall be bonded to ground using a copper equipment bonding conductor sized in accordance with Subrule 6) by connection to an equipment bonding conductor or bonding busbar for that patient care environment as identified in Subrule 3).

Δ 9) Notwithstanding Subrules 1) and 2), recessed and surface-mounted luminaires located more than 2.3 m above floor level, and their associated switches located outside a patient care environment, shall be permitted to be bonded in accordance with Section 10.

24-106 Receptacles in basic care areas (see Appendix B)
1) Receptacles intended for a given patient care environment shall be located to minimize the likelihood of their inadvertent use for a patient care environment for which they are not intended.
2) Receptacles located in areas that are routinely cleaned using liquids that normally splash against the walls shall be installed not less than 300 mm above the floor.
3) Receptacles located in bathrooms or washrooms shall be located
   a) within 1.5 m of the wash basin; and
   b) outside of any bathtub enclosure or shower stall.
4) Receptacles intended for housekeeping equipment and other non-medical loads shall be so identified.
5) Except for receptacles as described in Subrule 3), all 15 A and 20 A non-locking receptacles shall be hospital grade.
6) All receptacles that are supplied from circuits in an essential electrical system as described in Rule 24-302 shall be coloured red, and no other receptacles shall be so coloured.
7) Receptacles shall not be of the isolated ground type.

24-108 Other equipment in basic care areas
Notwithstanding the requirements of Rule 60-400, emergency signalling and similar equipment manufactured in conformance with the additional watertightness requirements of the CAN/CSA-C22.2 No. 60601 series of standards, and intended for use in shower stalls and bathtub enclosures, shall be permitted to be installed at normal heights within such stalls and enclosures.

24-110 Circuits in intermediate and critical care areas (see Appendix B)
The branch circuits supplying receptacles or other permanently connected equipment in intermediate or critical care areas shall be supplied from either a grounded system meeting the requirements of Rule 24-102 or an isolated system meeting the requirements of Rule 24-200, except that all branch

24

circuits supplying loads within patient care environments, other than those supplying multi-phase equipment, shall be 2-wire circuits.

24-112 Bonding to ground in intermediate and critical care areas (see Appendix B)

1) Bonding to ground in intermediate and critical care areas shall conform to Rule 24-104 whether the supply is derived from a grounded or an isolated system.

2) If a patient care environment bonding point is provided, it shall be bonded to the panelboard serving the patient care environment with which it is associated by either
   a) a bonding jumper connecting it to the bonding terminal in an enclosure that accommodates the bonding point along with receptacles for a patient care environment; or
   b) a copper conductor that is installed for that purpose and is run in the same raceway as the equipment bonding conductors serving that patient care environment.

24-114 Receptacles in intermediate and critical care areas (see Appendix B)

Receptacles in intermediate and critical care areas shall
a) meet the requirements of Rule 24-106; and
b) where supplied from an isolated system, be identified as such.

24-116 Receptacles subject to standing fluids on the floor or drenching of the work area (see Appendix B)

All receptacles in areas subject to standing fluids on the floor or drenching of the work area shall be
a) protected by a ground fault circuit interrupter of the Class A type; or
b) supplied by an isolated system conforming to Rule 24-200.

Isolated systems

24-200 Rules for isolated systems (see Appendix B)

1) Rules 24-202 to 24-208 shall apply to isolated systems installed under the provisions of Rules 24-110 and 24-116.

2) In a patient care environment supplied by an isolated system, branch circuits supplying only fixed luminaires and permanently connected medical electrical equipment shall be permitted to be supplied by a conventional grounded system, provided that wiring for grounded and isolated circuits does not occupy the same raceway.

24-202 Sources of supply (see Appendix B)

1) The means of supply to an isolated system shall be
   a) the secondary of one or more isolating transformers having no direct electrical connection between primary and secondary windings;
   b) a motor-generator set; or
   c) a suitably isolated, battery-powered inverter supply.

2) Where more than one single-phase isolated power system serves a single patient care environment, the grounding buses of all of these systems shall be bonded together with a copper bonding conductor
   a) having a total impedance not greater than 0.2 Ω; and
   b) sized not smaller than that permitted by Table 16.

24-204 Single-phase isolated circuits (see Appendix B)

1) Except where Rule 24-206 applies, isolated circuits shall meet the requirements of Subrules 2) to 7).

Δ 2) Isolated circuits shall
   a) not be deliberately grounded, except through the impedance of an isolation-sensing device (e.g., an isolation monitor);

b) have insulated circuit conductors of one of the following types:
   i) RW75 EP;
   ii) RW75 XLPE;
   iii) RW90 EP; or
   iv) RW90 XLPE;
c) have the insulation of one circuit conductor coloured orange and the other coloured brown;
d) have the orange-insulated conductor connected to the nickel screw of receptacles; and
e) have overcurrent devices that will open all ungrounded conductors simultaneously.

3) Any disconnecting means controlling an isolated circuit shall safely and simultaneously disconnect all ungrounded conductors.

4) Single-phase isolated circuits shall be 2-wire circuits with copper equipment bonding conductors, operating at voltages (rms) between conductors not exceeding
   a) 300 V for special-use receptacles and for permanently connected equipment; and
   b) 150 V for other receptacles.

5) A single-phase isolated system shall include automatic means (a line isolation monitor), with an indicator located where visible to persons using the system, to monitor the impedance-to-ground of the system together with any loads connected to it.

Δ 6) At the time of installation the total impedance (capacitive and resistive) between ground and each energized conductor of a single-phase isolated system shall exceed 200 000 Ω without utilization equipment or the line isolation monitor connected.

7) Where a single-phase isolated system is employed, it shall supply
   a) general-purpose receptacles in
      i) a single anaesthetizing location;
      ii) one or more patient care environments in a single room; or
      iii) a maximum of two patient care environments in separate but adjacent rooms, provided that the alarm indicator clearly identifies the patient care environments affected by the fault; or
   b) special-purpose receptacles at different locations or in different patient care environments, provided that the system is used only for one purpose and is arranged so that only one receptacle can be energized at a time.

24-206 Individually isolated branch circuits (see Appendix B)
A single-phase isolated system that supplies only a single load via a single branch circuit shall meet the requirements of Rule 24-204 2) to 6), except that
a) overcurrent devices need not be installed in the isolated circuit; and
b) the use of a line isolation monitor shall be optional.

24-208 Three-phase isolated systems (see Appendix B)
A three-phase isolated system shall
a) supply
   i) permanently connected medical equipment; or
   ii) special-purpose receptacles in one or more anaesthetizing locations or patient care environments, provided that the system is used only for the one purpose and is arranged so that only one receptacle can be energized at a time;
b) meet the requirements of Rule 24-204 2) a), b), and e);
c) have its insulated circuit conductors identified as follows:
   i) isolated conductor No. A — orange;
   ii) isolated conductor No. B — brown; and
   iii) isolated conductor No. C — yellow; and
d) meet the requirements of Rule 24-204 3).

24

Essential electrical systems

24-300 Rules for essential electrical systems (see Appendix B)

Rules 24-302 to 24-306 shall apply to those portions of a health care facility electrical system in which the interruption of a normal supply of power would jeopardize the effective and safe care of patients, with the object of reducing hazards that might arise from such an interruption.

24-302 Circuits in essential electrical systems (see Appendix B)

Δ 1) An essential electrical system shall consist of circuits that supply loads designated by the health care facility administration as being essential for
   a) life safety in accordance with Section 46;
   b) care of the patient; and
   c) effective operation of the health care facility.

2) An essential electrical system shall consist of at the minimum a vital branch and may also include a delayed vital branch or a conditional branch, or both.

3) The wiring of the essential electrical system shall be kept entirely independent of all other wiring and equipment and shall not enter a luminaire, raceway, box, or cabinet occupied by other wiring except where necessary
   a) in transfer switches; and
   b) in emergency lights supplied from two sources.

Δ 4) Where the essential electrical system includes conductors as specified in Rule 46-108 1), the wiring separation requirements of Rule 46-108 4) and 5) shall not apply, provided that
   a) all overcurrent devices of the essential electrical system are selectively coordinated; or
   b) the vital branch and delayed vital branch of the essential electrical system are kept entirely separate from the conditional branch.

24-304 Transfer switches (see Appendix B)

1) All transfer switches shall comply with the requirements of the supply authority.

2) Automatic transfer switches used in essential electrical systems shall conform to the requirements of CSA C22.2 No. 178.1 and, in addition, shall
   a) be electrically operated and mechanically held; and
   b) include means for safe manual operation.

3) Manual transfer switches shall conform to the following:
   a) the switching means shall be mechanically held and the operation shall be by direct manual control or by electrical remote manual control utilizing control power from the supply to which the load is being transferred;
   b) a manual transfer switch that is operated by electrical remote manual control shall include a means for safe manual mechanical operation;
   c) reliable mechanical interlocking (and, in the case of a switch operated by electrical remote manual control, electrical interlocking) to prevent interconnection of the normal and the emergency supplies of power shall be inherent in the design of a manual transfer switch; and
   d) a manual transfer switch shall include a readily visible mechanical indicator showing the switch position.

4) The vital and delayed vital branches shall be connected to the emergency power supply by means of one or more automatic transfer switches.

5) The conditional branch shall be connected to the emergency power supply by either a manual or an automatic transfer switch.

Δ   **24-306 Emergency supply**

An emergency supply shall be

a)   one or more generator sets in accordance with CSA Z32; and

b)   located on the health care facility premises and installed in a service room or enclosure in accordance with CSA C282.

24

Section 26 — Installation of electrical equipment

General

26-000 — *Reserved for future use.*

26-002 Connection to identified terminals or leads

Wherever a device having an identified terminal or lead is connected in a circuit having an identified conductor, the identified conductor shall be connected to the identified terminal or lead.

26-004 Equipment over combustible surfaces (see Appendix B)

Where there is a combustible surface directly under stationary or fixed electrical equipment, that surface shall be covered with a steel plate at least 1.6 mm thick that shall extend not less than 150 mm beyond the equipment on all sides, if

a) the equipment is marked to require such protection; or

b) the equipment is open on the bottom.

26-006 Installation of ventilated enclosures

Ventilated enclosures shall be installed in a manner that does not restrict ventilation.

26-008 Sprinklered equipment (see Appendix B)

Where electrical equipment vaults or electrical equipment rooms are sprinklered, the electrical equipment contained in such vaults or rooms shall be protected where needed by non-combustible hoods or shields arranged to minimize interference with the sprinkler protection.

26-010 Outdoor installations

1) Outdoor installations of apparatus, unless housed in suitable enclosures, shall be surrounded by suitable fencing in accordance with Rules 26-300 to 26-324.

2) Outdoor equipment shall be bonded to ground.

26-012 Dielectric liquid-filled equipment — Indoors (see Appendices B and G)

Δ 1) Except as permitted in Subrule 5), dielectric liquid-filled electrical equipment containing more than 23 L of liquid in one tank, or more than 69 L in a group of tanks, shall be located in an electrical equipment vault.

2) Except as permitted in Subrule 4), dielectric liquid-filled electrical equipment containing 23 L of liquid or less in one tank, or 69 L or less in a group of tanks, shall be

    a) installed in a service room conforming to the requirements of the *National Building Code of Canada*;

    b) provided with a metal pan or concrete curbing capable of collecting and retaining all the liquid of the tank or tanks;

    c) isolated from other apparatus by fire-resisting barriers, with metal-enclosed equipment considered as providing segregation and isolation; and

    d) separated from other dielectric liquid-filled electrical equipment by such a distance that, if the liquid in such equipment were spread at a density of 12 L/m^2, the areas so covered would not overlap; these areas being deemed to be circular if the tank (or group of tanks) is in an open area, semi-circular if the tank is against a wall, and quarter-sector if the tank is in a corner.

3) Notwithstanding Subrules 1) and 2), motor starters shall be permitted to have these quantities of liquids doubled.

Δ 4) Capacitors filled with flammable liquids of 14 L or less in each tank shall not be required to be installed in a service room, provided that

    a) a metal pan or concrete curbing that is capable of collecting and retaining all the liquid of the tank or tanks is installed;

    b) no other dielectric liquid-filled electrical equipment nor any combustible surface or material is within 4.5 m unless segregated by fire-resisting barriers, with metal-enclosed equipment considered as providing segregation; and

    c)   each capacitor tank is provided with overcurrent protection to minimize rupture of the case.

Δ 5)   Dielectric liquid-filled equipment containing more than 23 L of liquid in one tank, or more than 69 L in a group of tanks, shall be permitted to be installed in accordance with Subrule 2), provided that the following additional conditions are met:

    a)   the equipment is protected from mechanical damage either by location or guarding;

    b)   the equipment contains a non-propagating liquid having a flash point of 275 °C or higher;

    c)   equipment other than transformers is provided with

        i)   a means of absorbing gases generated by arcing inside the case; or

        ii)   a pressure relief device;

    d)   transformers with ratings exceeding 25 kV•A at 25 Hz or 37.5 kV•A at 60 Hz are provided with

        i)   a means of absorbing gases generated by arcing inside the tank; or

        ii)   a pressure relief vent; and

    e)   where the transformers referred to in Item d) are rated at 15 000 V or more, the service room is accessible only to authorized persons.

26-014 Dielectric liquid-filled equipment — Outdoors (see Appendix B)

  1)   Except as permitted by Subrule 3), dielectric liquid-filled electrical equipment containing more than 46 L in one tank, or 137 L in a group of tanks, and installed outdoors shall not be located within 6 m of

    a)   any combustible surfaces or material on a building;

    b)   any door or window; or

    c)   any ventilation inlet or outlet.

  2)   The dimension referred to in Subrule 1) shall be the shortest line-of-sight distance from the face of the container containing the liquid to the building or part of the building in question.

  3)   Notwithstanding the requirements of Subrule 1), the equipment shall be permitted to be installed within 6 m of any item listed in Subrule 1), provided that a wall or barrier with non-combustible surfaces or material is constructed between the equipment and that item.

  4)   Where dielectric liquid-filled electrical equipment containing more than 46 L in one tank, or 137 L in a group of tanks, is installed outdoors, it shall

    a)   be inaccessible to unauthorized persons;

    b)   not obstruct firefighting operations;

    c)   if installed at ground level, be located on a concrete pad draining away from structures or be in a curbed area filled with coarse crushed stone; and

    d)   not have open drains for the disposal of the liquid in proximity to combustible construction or materials.

Isolating switches

26-100 Location of isolating switches

  1)   Isolating switches shall be permitted to be located so that a hook stick is required to operate them.

  2)   Isolating switches shall be plainly marked to minimize the chance that they will be opened under load, unless

    a)   they are located or guarded so that they are inaccessible to unauthorized persons; or

    b)   they are interlocked so that they cannot normally be opened under load.

Circuit breakers

26-120 Indoor installation of circuit breakers

  1)   Dielectric liquid-filled circuit breakers installed indoors shall be installed in accordance with Rule 26-012.

26

2) Circuit breakers installed in electrical equipment vaults shall be operable without opening the door of the vault.

Fuses and fusible equipment

26-140 Installation of fuses
Fuses shall be located so that
a)   their operation will not result in injury to persons or damage to property or other equipment; and
b)   they can be readily inserted or removed.

26-142 Fusible equipment
Fusible equipment shall employ low-melting-point fuses of the type referred to in Rule 14-200 or fuses as referred to in Rule 14-212 b) when connected to conductors whose ampacity is based on Table 1 or 3 or on Column 4 of Table 2 or 4, unless equipment using other types of fuses is marked as being suitable for such use.

Capacitors

26-200 Capacitors exempted
The requirements of Rules 26-202 to 26-222 shall not apply to capacitors that form component parts of factory-assembled electrical equipment nor to surge protective capacitors.

26-202 Capacitors installed indoors
Dielectric liquid-filled capacitors located indoors shall be installed in accordance with Rule 26-012.

26-204 Guarding of capacitors
All live parts of capacitors shall be inaccessible to unauthorized persons.

26-206 Grounding of capacitors
Non-current-carrying metal parts of capacitors shall be bonded to ground.

26-208 Conductor size for capacitors
1)   The ampacity of capacitor feeder circuits and branch circuits shall be not less than 135% of the rated current of the capacitor.
2)   Where a branch circuit supplies two or more capacitors, the overcurrent device protecting the conductors of the branch circuit shall be considered as protecting the taps made thereto to supply single capacitors, provided that
a)   the tap is not more than 7.5 m long; and
b)   its conductors comply with Subrule 1) and also have an ampacity not less than one-third that of the branch circuit conductors from which they are supplied.

26-210 Overcurrent protection (see Appendix B)
An overcurrent device, rated or set as low as practicable without causing unnecessary opening of the circuit, but not exceeding 250% of the rated current of the capacitor, shall be provided in each ungrounded conductor of a capacitor feeder or branch circuit, unless a deviation has been allowed in accordance with Rule 2-030.

26-212 Disconnecting means for capacitor feeders or branch circuits
1)   A disconnecting means shall be provided in each ungrounded conductor connected to each capacitor bank in order that the capacitors can be made dead without having to disconnect other loads.
2)   The disconnecting means shall be within sight of and not more than 9 m from the capacitor unless the disconnecting means can be locked in the open position.
3)   A warning notice shall be affixed to the disconnecting means used on circuits having capacitors only, stating that
a)   the circuit has capacitors; and

b) a waiting period of 5 min is necessary when the circuit is opened, after which the capacitors shall be discharged before handling.

26-214 Rating of the disconnecting means for capacitor feeders or branch circuits
The disconnecting means for a capacitor feeder or branch circuit shall be rated not less than 135% of the rated current of the capacitor.

26-216 Rating of contactors for capacitor feeders or branch circuits
Contactors used for the switching of capacitors shall have a current rating not less than the following percentage of the rated capacitor current:
a) open-type contactor: 135%; and
b) enclosed-type contactor: 150%.

26-218 Special provisions for motor circuit capacitors
1) Where a capacitor is connected on the load side of a motor circuit disconnecting means
   a) individual disconnecting means for the capacitor need not be provided;
   b) the rating of the disconnecting means, the overcurrent device, and the size of the motor circuit conductors need not be greater than would be required without the capacitor; and
   c) the ampacity of the conductors connecting the capacitor to the motor circuit shall be in accordance with Rule 26-208 and shall be not less than one-third that of the motor circuit conductors.
2) Where a capacitor is connected on the load side of a motor controller
   a) the rating of the capacitor shall not exceed the value required to raise the no-load power factor of the motor to unity;
   b) the rating or setting of the overload device shall be reduced to a value corresponding to the current obtained with the improved power factor;
   c) individual overcurrent protection for the capacitor need not be provided;
   d) the motor shall not be subject to star-delta starting, auto-transformer starting, or switching service such as plugging, rapid reversals, reclosings, jogging, or other similar operations that generate overvoltages and overtorques; and
   e) time-delay devices shall be installed in the motor control circuit of motors driving high inertia loads, so that the motor cannot be restarted until the residual voltage is reduced to 10% of the nominal value.

26-220 Transformers supplying capacitors
The volt-ampere rating of a transformer supplying a capacitor shall not be less than 135% of the capacitor volt-ampere rating.

26-222 Drainage of stored charge of capacitors
1) Capacitors shall be provided with a means of draining the stored charge.
2) The draining means shall be such that the residual voltage will be reduced to 50 V or less after the capacitor is disconnected from the source of supply
   a) within 1 min in the case of capacitors rated at 750 V or less; and
   b) within 5 min in the case of capacitors rated at more than 750 V.
3) The discharge circuit shall be
   a) permanently connected to the terminals of the capacitor bank; or
   b) provided with automatic means of connecting it on removal of voltage from the line.
4) The discharge circuit shall not be switched or connected by manual means.
5) Motors, transformers, or other electrical equipment capable of constituting a suitable discharge path, connected directly to capacitors without the interposition of a switch or overcurrent device, shall be considered to constitute a suitable discharge path.

26

Transformers

Δ **26-240 Transformers — General** (see Appendix B)

1) In this Subsection,
   a) "transformer" shall mean a single-phase transformer, a polyphase transformer, or a bank of two or three single-phase transformers connected to operate as a polyphase transformer; and
   b) "unit substation" shall mean an integrated unit consisting of one or more transformers, disconnecting means, overcurrent devices, and other associated equipment, each contained in a suitable enclosure designed and constructed to restrict access to live parts.

2) Transformers shall be constructed so that all live parts are enclosed unless they are installed to be inaccessible to unauthorized persons.

3) Conductors and cables used for connection to air-cooled (dry-type) transformers shall be permitted to enter a transformer enclosure through the top only where the transformer is marked to permit such entry.

4) Transformers shall be protected from mechanical damage.

5) Dielectric liquid-filled transformers shall be mounted so that there is an air space of 150 mm between transformers, and between transformers and adjacent surfaces of combustible material except the plane on which the transformer is mounted.

Δ **26-242 Outdoor transformer and unit substation installations**

1) Except as permitted by Subrule 2), where transformers or unit substations, including their conductors, cables, and control and protective equipment, are installed outdoors, they shall
   a) be installed in accordance with Rule 26-014 if they are dielectric liquid-filled;
   b) have the bottom of their platform not less than 3.6 m above ground if they are isolated by elevation;
   c) have the entire installation surrounded by a suitable fence in accordance with Rules 26-300 to 26-324 if they are not isolated by elevation or not housed in suitable enclosures; and
   d) have conspicuously posted, suitable warning signs indicating the highest voltage employed except where there is no exposed live part.

2) Dielectric liquid-filled, pad-mounted distribution transformers, either independently installed or forming part of a unit substation, shall be installed at least 3 m from any combustible surface or material on a building and at least 6 m from any window, door, or ventilation inlet or outlet on a building, except where
   a) a wall or barrier with non-combustible surfaces or material is constructed between the transformer and any door, window, ventilation opening, or combustible surface; or
   b) the transformer is protected by an internal current-limiting fuse and equipped with a pressure relief device, with working spaces around the transformer of at least 3 m on the access side and on all other sides, as follows:
      i) 1 m for three-phase transformers; and
      ii) 0.6 m for single-phase transformers.

26-244 Transformers mounted on roofs (see Appendix B)

1) Except as permitted by Subrule 2), dielectric liquid-filled transformers installed on the roof of a building shall be located in an electrical equipment vault in accordance with Rules 26-350 to 26-356 and adequately supported by means of non-combustible construction.

2) Transformers containing a non-propagating liquid, suitable for the purpose and having a flash point not less than 275 °C, that are installed on the roof of a building need not be located in an electrical

equipment vault but shall not be placed adjacent to doors or windows, nor within 4.5 m of discharge vents for flammable fumes or combustible or electrically conductive dusts.

26-246 Dry-core, open-ventilated-type transformers

1) Transformers of the dry-core, open-ventilated type shall be mounted so that there is an air space of not less than 150 mm between transformer enclosures and between a transformer enclosure and any adjacent surface except floors.

2) Notwithstanding Subrule 1), where the adjacent surface is a combustible material, the minimum permissible separation between the transformer enclosure and the adjacent surface shall be 300 mm.

3) Notwithstanding Subrule 1), where the adjacent surface is the wall on which the transformer is mounted, the minimum permissible separation between the enclosure and the mounting wall shall be 6 mm if the adjacent surface is made of
   a) non-combustible material;
   b) combustible material adequately protected by non-combustible heat insulating material other than sheet metal; or
   c) combustible material shielded by grounded sheet metal with an air space of not less than 50 mm between the sheet metal and the combustible material.

4) Dry-type transformers not of the sealed type shall not be installed below grade level unless adequate provision is made to prevent flooding.

5) Dry-type transformers not of the sealed type shall be installed in such a manner that water or other liquids cannot fall onto the windings.

26-248 Disconnecting means for transformers

A disconnecting means shall be installed in the primary circuit of each power and distribution transformer.

26-250 Overcurrent protection for power and distribution transformer circuits rated over 750 V

1) Except as permitted in Subrules 2), 3), and 4), each ungrounded conductor of the transformer feeder or branch circuit supplying the transformer shall be provided with overcurrent protection
   a) rated at not more than 150% of the rated primary current of the transformer in the case of fuses; and
   b) rated or set at not more than 300% of the rated primary current of the transformer in the case of breakers.

2) Where 150% of the rated primary current of the transformer does not correspond to a standard rating of a fuse, the next higher standard rating shall be permitted.

3) An individual overcurrent device shall not be required where the feeder or branch circuit overcurrent device provides the protection specified in this Rule.

4) A transformer having an overcurrent device on the secondary side rated or set at not more than the values in Table 50 or a transformer equipped with coordinated thermal overload protection by the manufacturer shall not be required to have an individual overcurrent device on the primary side, provided that the primary feeder overcurrent device is rated or set at not more than the values in Table 50.

26-252 Overcurrent protection for power and distribution transformer circuits rated 750 V or less, other than dry-type transformers

1) Except as permitted in Subrules 2) to 6), each ungrounded conductor of the transformer feeder or branch circuit supplying the transformer shall be provided with overcurrent protection rated or set at not more than 150% of the rated primary current of the transformer.

26

2) Where the rated primary current of a transformer is
   a) 9 A or more, and 150% of this current does not correspond to a standard rating of a fuse or non-adjustable circuit breaker, the next higher standard rating shall be permitted; or
   b) less than 9 A, an overcurrent device rated or set at not more than 167% of the rated primary current shall be permitted, except that where the rated primary current is less than 2 A, an overcurrent device rated or set at not more than 300% of the rated primary current shall be permitted.

3) An individual overcurrent device shall not be required where the feeder or branch circuit overcurrent device provides the protection specified in this Rule.

4) A transformer having an overcurrent device on the secondary side rated or set at not more than 125% of the rated secondary current of the transformer shall not be required to have an individual overcurrent device on the primary side, provided that the primary feeder overcurrent device is rated or set at not more than 300% of the rated primary current of the transformer.

5) Notwithstanding Subrule 4), where the rated secondary current of a transformer is
   a) 9 A or more, and 125% of this current does not correspond to a standard rating of a fuse or non-adjustable circuit breaker, the next higher standard rating shall be permitted; or
   b) less than 9 A, an overcurrent device rated or set at not more than 167% of the rated secondary current shall be permitted.

6) A transformer equipped with coordinated thermal overload protection by the manufacturer and arranged to interrupt the primary current shall not be required to have an individual overcurrent device on the primary side if the primary feeder overcurrent device is rated or set at a value
   a) not more than 6 times the rated current of the transformer for a transformer having not more than 7.5% impedance; or
   b) not more than 4 times the rated current of the transformer for a transformer having more than 7.5% but not more than 10% impedance.

26-254 Overcurrent protection for dry-type transformer circuits rated 750 V or less (see Appendix B)

1) Except as permitted in Subrule 2), each ungrounded conductor of the transformer feeder or branch circuit supplying the transformer shall be provided with overcurrent protection rated or set at not more than 125% of the rated primary current of the transformer, and this primary overcurrent device shall be considered as protecting secondary conductors rated at 125% or more of the rated secondary current.

2) Notwithstanding Subrule 1), a transformer having an overcurrent device on the secondary side set at not more than 125% of the rated secondary current of the transformer shall not be required to have an individual overcurrent device on the primary side, provided that the primary feeder overcurrent device is set at not more than 300% of the rated primary current of the transformer.

3) Where a value not exceeding 125% of the rated primary current of the transformer as specified in Subrule 1) does not correspond to the standard rating of the overcurrent device, the next higher standard rating shall be permitted.

Δ **26-256 Conductor size for transformers** (see Appendix B)

1) The conductors supplying transformers shall have an ampacity rating
   a) not less than 125% of the rated primary current of the transformer for a single transformer; or
   b) not less than the sum of the rated primary currents of all transformers plus 25% of the rated primary current of the largest transformer for a group of transformers operated in parallel or on a common feeder.

2) The secondary conductors connected to transformers shall have an ampacity rating
    a) not less than 125% of the rated secondary current of the transformer for a single transformer; or
    b) not less than 125% of the sum of the rated secondary currents of all the transformers operated in parallel.
3) Notwithstanding Subrules 1) and 2), primary and secondary conductors shall be permitted to have an ampacity rating not less than that required by the demand load, provided that they are protected in accordance with Rules 14-100 and 14-104.
4) Where the transformer overcurrent protection is selected in accordance with Rule 26-250 1) or 2) or 26-254 3), the primary and secondary conductors connected to the transformer shall be protected in accordance with Rules 14-100 and 14-104.
5) Where multi-rating transformers are used, the primary and secondary conductors shall have an ampacity rating not less than 125% of the rated primary and secondary current of the transformer at the utilization voltage.

26-258 Transformer continuous load (see Appendix B)

For the purpose of transformer overcurrent protection and conductor sizes selected in accordance with Rules 26-250 to 26-256, the continuous load as determined from the calculated load connected to the transformer secondary shall not exceed the values specified in Rule 8-104 5) or 6).

26-260 Overcurrent protection of instrument voltage transformers (see Appendix B)

1) Except under the conditions of Subrules 2) and 3), instrument voltage transformers shall have primary fuses rated not more than
    a) 10 A for low-voltage circuits; and
    b) 3 A for high-voltage circuits.
2) Primary fuses shall not be installed where they would be connected in the grounded primary neutral connection of "Y" or "Open Y" connected voltage transformers.
3) Primary fuses shall be permitted to be omitted
    a) where the transformers are protected by adequate power fuses or other adequate protective devices for clearing equipment failure, and convenient means are provided for disconnecting the transformers on the primary side;
    b) where voltage transformers and meters, operating at low voltage and installed in suitable enclosures, are used in place of self-contained meters; or
    c) where both voltage and current transformers are supplied by the manufacturer in a single enclosure filled with an insulating medium, which may be air for use on low-voltage circuits if the enclosure is non-combustible, and where
        i)   the primary terminals outside the enclosure are common to both voltage and current transformers; and
        ii) the enclosures are installed outdoors, if filled with an insulating medium that will burn in air.

26-262 Marking of transformers

Each transformer shall be provided with a nameplate bearing the following marking:
a) manufacturer's name;
b) rating in kilovolt amperes;
c) rated full load temperature rise;
d) primary and secondary voltage ratings;
e) frequency in hertz;
f) liquid capacity, if of the liquid-filled type;
g) type of liquid to be used;
h) rated impedance, if of the power or distribution type; and

26

i)   basic impulse insulation level (BIL) for transformers rated 2.5 kV voltage class and higher.

26-264 Auto-transformers

1)   For the purposes of this Rule, "auto-transformers" shall mean transformers in which part of the turns are common to both primary and secondary ac circuits.

2)   Auto-transformers shall not be connected to interior wiring systems, other than a wiring system or circuit used wholly for motor purposes, unless
   a)   the system supplied contains an identified grounded conductor solidly connected to a similar identified grounded conductor of the system supplying the auto-transformer;
   b)   the auto-transformer is used for starting or controlling an induction motor; or
   c)   the auto-transformer supplies a circuit wholly within the apparatus that contains the auto-transformer.

3)   Where an auto-transformer is used for starting or controlling an induction motor, it shall be permitted to be included in a starter case or installed as a separate unit.

4)   Notwithstanding Subrule 2), auto-transformers shall be permitted for fixed voltage transformation in circuits not incorporating a grounded circuit conductor.

26-266 Zero sequence filters (see Appendix B)

1)   For the purposes of this Rule, a "zero sequence filter" shall mean a zig-zag or otherwise wound transformer installed to reduce unbalanced current in a three-phase, 4-wire circuit.

2)   Ampacities of conductors supplying zero sequence filters in conformance with Rule 4-004 shall be based on the neutral conductor being a current-carrying conductor.

3)   Phase conductors shall have an ampacity of at least 125% of the rated primary current.

4)   The neutral conductor shall have an ampacity equal to at least 125% of the neutral current rating.

5)   Overcurrent protection for the filter shall not exceed 125% of the rated primary current.

6)   The overcurrent protection required by Subrule 5) shall be equipped with an integral device arranged to activate a warning signal or alarm when operation of the overcurrent protection occurs.

Fences

26-300 General

Rules 26-302 to 26-324 apply to fences for guarding electrical equipment, especially transformers, located outdoors.

26-302 Clearance of equipment

1)   The minimum clearance between the fence and unguarded live parts shall be in accordance with Table 33.

2)   The minimum clearance between the fence and enclosures containing live parts shall be 1.1 m.

3)   The clearance shall provide adequate working space around the equipment, taking into consideration the space required for draw-out types of equipment and the opening of enclosure doors.

26-304 Height of fence

The fence, excluding barbed wire, shall be not less than 1.8 m high.

26-306 Barbed wire

The fence shall be topped with not less than three strands of barbed wire.

26-308 Setting of posts

1)   Posts shall be set at a depth of 1.1 m for end, gate, and corner posts and 1 m for intermediate posts wherever ground conditions permit.

2)   Where ground conditions do not permit the depth specified in Subrule 1), extra bracing or concrete footings shall be provided.

3) Concrete footings may be required for metal posts in any case.
4) The spacing between posts shall be 3 m maximum.
5) End, gate, and corner posts shall be adequately braced against strain.

26-310 Gates

1) Gates shall open outwardly wherever possible but, if it is necessary that they open inwardly, they shall not, when open, come into contact with the frame or enclosure of any electrical equipment.
2) Gates shall be adequately braced as necessary, and double gates shall be used where the width of the opening exceeds 1.5 m.
3) Centre stops shall be provided for double gates.
4) Gates shall have provision for securing with padlocks.

26-312 Chain link fabric

1) Chain link fabric shall be securely attached to all posts and gate frames.
2) Chain link fabric shall be reinforced as necessary at top and bottom to prevent distortion.
3) Chain link fabric shall extend to within 50 mm of the ground.
4) Chain link fabric shall
   Δ
   a) be made of galvanized steel not less than 3.6 mm in diameter;
   b) have a mesh not greater than 50 mm; and
   c) be not less than 1.8 m in width.

26-314 Use of wood

Where wood slats are acceptable, they shall
a) extend to within 50 mm of the ground;
b) be placed on the outside of the stringers; and
c) be spaced not more than 40 mm apart, except that where the frame or enclosure of any electrical equipment is less than 2 m from the fence, there shall be no spacing permitted.

26-316 Posts

1) Metal posts shall be
   a) made of galvanized steel;
   b) 88.9 mm specified outside diameter nominal pipe size (11.31 kg/m) for corner, end, and gate posts; and
   c) 60.3 mm specified outside diameter nominal pipe size (5.44 kg/m) for intermediate posts.
2) Wood posts shall be not less than 140 × 140 mm and shall be suitably protected against decay.

26-318 Top rails

Top rails shall
a) be made of galvanized steel;
b) have a 42.2 mm specified outside diameter nominal pipe size (3.35 kg/m); and
c) be provided with suitable expansion joints where necessary.

26-320 Wood stringers

Wood stringers shall be not less than 38 × 140 mm nominal size if two are used and not less than 38 × 89 mm nominal size if three are used.

26-322 Wood slats

Wood slats shall be not less than 19 × 89 mm nominal size.

26-324 Preservative treatment

1) Steel or iron parts shall be either hot dip galvanized or electroplated with non-ferrous metal.
2) Wood shall be impregnated, treated, or well painted before assembly and, where in contact with the earth or concrete, shall be impregnated or otherwise suitably treated against decay.

26

Electrical equipment vaults

26-350 General
1) For the purposes of Rules pertaining to the construction of electrical equipment vaults, the single word "vault(s)" shall be understood to have the same meaning as "electrical equipment vault(s)".
2) Vaults shall not be used for storage purposes.

26-352 Vault size
Vaults shall be of such dimensions as to accommodate the installed equipment with at least the minimum clearances specified in the pertinent Sections of this Code.

26-354 Electrical equipment vault construction (see Appendices B and G)
Every electrical equipment vault, including the doors, ventilation, and drainage, shall be constructed in accordance with the applicable requirements of the *National Building Code of Canada*.

26-356 Illumination
1) Each vault shall be provided with adequate lighting, controlled by one or more switches located near the entrance.
2) Luminaires shall be located so that they can be relamped without danger to personnel.
3) Each vault shall have a grounding-type receptacle installed in accordance with Rule 26-700 and located in a convenient location inside the vault and near the entrance.

Cellulose nitrate film storage

26-360 General
Rules 26-360 to 26-368 apply to any portion of a building in which cellulose nitrate film is stored.

26-362 Equipment in film-vaults
No electrical equipment other than that necessary for fixed lighting shall be installed in film-vaults.

26-364 Wiring methods in film-vaults (see Appendix B)
1) The wiring method in film-vaults shall comply with any of the methods specified in Rule 18-152 1) a), b), and d).
2) Conduit or cable shall not run directly from vault to vault, but only from the switch to the luminaire within the vault.
Δ 3) Conduit shall be sealed off near the switch enclosure with a fitting and compound.

26-366 Luminaires in film-vaults
Luminaires shall comply with Rule 18-150.

26-368 Circuits in film-vaults
1) Luminaires shall be controlled by a switch located outside the film-vault.
2) A red pilot light shall be provided to indicate when the switch is closed and shall be located outside the film-vault.
3) Wiring shall be arranged so that when the switch is open, all ungrounded conductors within the film-vault will be de-energized.

Lightning arresters

26-400 Use and location of lightning arresters
1) Lightning arresters shall be installed in every distributing substation in locations where lightning disturbances occur frequently and no other adequate protection is provided.
2) Lightning arresters installed for the protection of utilization equipment
    a) shall be permitted to be installed either inside or outside the building or enclosure containing the equipment to be protected; and
    b) shall be isolated by elevation, enclosed, or otherwise made inaccessible to unauthorized persons.

26-402 Indoor installations of lightning arresters

1) Where lightning arresters are installed in a building, they shall be located well away from all equipment other than that which they protect and from passageways and combustible parts of buildings.

2) Where lightning arresters containing oil are installed in a building, they shall be separated from other equipment by walls conforming to electrical equipment vault construction requirements in accordance with Rules 26-350 to 26-356.

26-404 Outdoor installations of lightning arresters

Where arresters containing oil are located outdoors, means of draining or absorbing oil shall be provided by

a) ditches or drains; or

b) paving the yard in which the arrester is contained with cinders or other absorbent material to an adequate depth.

26-406 Choke coils for lightning arresters

Where choke coils are used in connection with a lightning arrester, the coils shall be installed between the lightning arrester tap and the apparatus to be protected.

26-408 Connection of lightning arresters

The connection between arrester and line conductor shall be

a) made of a copper conductor not smaller than No. 6 AWG;

b) as short and as straight as practicable with a minimum of bends; and

c) free of sharp bends and turns.

26-410 Insulation of lightning arrester accessories

The insulation from ground and from other conductors for accessories such as gap electrodes and choke coils shall be at least equal to the insulation required at other points of the circuit.

Low-voltage surge protective devices

26-420 Low-voltage surge protectors (see Appendix B)

1) Except as provided for in Subrule 2), where low-voltage surge protective devices are to be connected to a consumer's service, they shall be installed outdoors at least 12.5 mm from combustible material

    a) at the service head supplying the consumer's service;

    b) at any supply point on the overhead distribution;

Δ   c) on the load side of a self-contained utility revenue meter socket, provided that the socket is fitted with lugs for the termination; or

    d) on any outdoor distribution enclosure supplied from underground distribution.

2) Low-voltage surge protective devices shall be permitted to be connected to an overcurrent device or to a branch circuit supplying utilization equipment in the building.

Storage batteries

26-500 Scope

1) Rules 26-502 to 26-512 apply to the installation of storage batteries.

2) Rule 26-514 applies to the installation of electrical equipment, other than storage batteries, in a battery room.

26-502 Special terminology

In this Subsection, the following definitions shall apply:

Sealed cell or **battery** — a storage battery that has no provision for the addition of water or electrolyte or for the external measurement of electrolyte specific gravity.

Storage battery — a battery consisting of more than one rechargeable cell of the lead-acid, alkaline, or other electrochemical type.

26-504 Location of storage batteries
Batteries with exposed live parts shall be kept in a room or enclosure accessible only to authorized personnel.

26-506 Ventilation of battery rooms or areas (see Appendix B)
1) Storage-battery rooms or areas shall be adequately ventilated.
2) Storage batteries shall not be subjected to ambient temperatures greater than 45 °C or less than the freezing point of the electrolyte.

26-508 Battery vents
1) Vented cells shall be equipped with flame arresters.
2) Sealed cells shall be equipped with pressure release vents.

26-510 Battery installation
1) Battery trays, racks, and other surfaces on which batteries are mounted shall be
   a) level;
   b) protected against corrosion from the battery electrolyte;
   c) except as permitted in Subrule 5), covered with an insulating material having a dielectric strength of at least 1500 V;
   d) of sufficient strength to carry the weight of the battery; and
   e) designed to withstand vibration and sway where appropriate.
2) Battery cells shall be spaced a minimum of 10 mm apart.
3) Battery cells having conductive containers shall be installed on non-conductive surfaces.
4) Sealed cells and multi-compartment sealed batteries having conductive containers shall have an insulating support if a voltage is present between the container and ground.
5) Cells and multi-compartment vented storage batteries, with covers sealed to containers of non-conductive, heat-resistant material, shall not require additional insulating support.
6) Batteries having a nominal voltage greater than 150 V and with cells in rubber or composition containers shall be sectionalized into groups of 150 V or less.

26-512 Wiring to batteries
1) The wiring between cells and batteries and between the batteries and other electrical equipment shall be
   a) bare conductors that shall not be taped;
   b) open wiring;
   c) a flexible cord;
   d) mineral-insulated cable, provided that it is adequately protected against corrosion where it may be in direct contact with acid or acid spray; or
   e) aluminum-sheathed cable or copper-sheathed cable, provided that it has suitable corrosion-resistant protection where necessary.
2) Where wiring is installed in rigid conduit or electrical metallic tubing
   a) the conduit or tubing shall be of corrosion-resistant material or other materials suitably protected from corrosion;
   b) the end of the raceway shall be tightly sealed with sealing compound, rubber tape, or other material to resist the entrance of electrolyte by spray or creeping;
   c) the conductor shall issue from the raceway through a substantial glazed insulating bushing;
   d) at least 300 mm of the conductor shall be free from the raceway where connected to a cell terminal; and
   e) the raceway exit shall be located at least 300 mm above the highest cell terminal to reduce electrolyte creepage or spillage entering the raceway.

26-514 Wiring methods and installation of equipment in battery rooms
The installation of wiring and equipment in a battery room shall be in accordance with the requirements for a dry location.

Resistance devices

26-550 Location of resistance devices
Resistance devices, including wiring to the resistance elements, shall be installed so that the danger of igniting adjacent combustible material is reduced to a minimum.

26-552 Conductors for resistance devices
Insulated conductors used for connection between resistance elements and controllers, unless used for infrequent motor starting,
    a)   shall be selected in accordance with Rule 12-102 3) as being suitable for the temperature involved and in no case less than 90 °C; and

Δ   b)   shall be permitted to be grouped where the voltage between any two insulated conductors in the group does not exceed a maximum of 75 V, provided that the insulated conductors have a flame-retardant insulation or jacket.

26-554 Use of incandescent lamps as resistance devices
1)   Incandescent lamps shall be permitted to be used
    a)   as protective resistors for automatic controllers; or
    b)   where a deviation has been allowed in accordance with Rule 2-030, as resistors in series with other devices, provided that the resulting installation is acceptable.
2)   Where incandescent lamps are used as resistors, they shall
    a)   be mounted in porcelain lampholders on non-combustible supports;
    b)   be arranged so that they cannot be subjected to a voltage greater than that for which they are rated;
    c)   be provided with a permanently attached nameplate showing the wattage and voltage of the lamp to be used in each lampholder;
    d)   not carry or control the main current; and
    e)   not constitute the regulating resistance of the device.

Panelboards

26-600 Location of panelboards (see Appendix G)
1)   Panelboards shall not be located in coal bins, clothes closets, bathrooms, stairways, high ambient rooms, dangerous or hazardous locations, nor in any similar undesirable places.
2)   Panelboards in dwelling units shall be installed as high as possible, with no overcurrent device operating handle positioned more than 1.7 m above the finished floor level.

26-602 Panelboards in dwelling units (see Appendix B)
1)   A panelboard shall be installed in every dwelling unit except for dwelling units in hotels and motels, and dwelling units that
    a)   are not individually metered for electrical power consumption; and
    b)   have been created by subdivision of a single dwelling.
2)   Every panelboard installed in accordance with Subrule 1) shall have a single supply protected by overcurrent devices, and this supply shall be capable of being disconnected without disconnecting the supply to any other dwelling unit.

Branch circuits

26-650 Special terminology
In this Subsection, the following definitions shall apply:

26

Arc-fault protection — a means of recognizing characteristics unique to both series and parallel arc-faults and de-energizing the circuit when an arc-fault is detected.

Combination-type arc-fault circuit interrupter — a device that provides both series and parallel arc-fault protection to the entire branch circuit wiring, including cord sets and power supply cords connected to the outlets, against the unwanted effects of arcing.

Outlet branch-circuit-type arc-fault circuit interrupter — a device that provides both series and parallel arc-fault protection to downstream branch circuit wiring, cord sets, and power supply cords against the unwanted effects of arcing and also provides series arc-fault protection to upstream branch circuit wiring.

26-652 Branch circuits for residential occupancies

Branch circuits for all residential occupancies (including dwelling units and single dwellings) shall meet the following requirements:

Δ a) receptacles installed for refrigerators in accordance with Rule 26-724 d) i) shall be supplied by at least one branch circuit that does not supply any other outlets, except a recessed clock receptacle intended for use with an electric clock;
b) at least one branch circuit shall be provided solely for receptacles installed in the laundry room or in a space where the complete plumbing is installed to accommodate a washing machine;
c) at least one branch circuit shall be provided solely for receptacles installed in the utility room;
d) each receptacle installed in a cupboard, wall cabinet, or enclosure for the use of a microwave oven in accordance with Rule 26-720 h) shall be supplied by a branch circuit that does not supply any other outlets, and this circuit shall not be considered as forming part of the circuits required under Rule 26-654 b);
e) a separate branch circuit shall be provided solely to supply power to each central vacuum system;
f) the ampere rating of the branch circuit wiring supplying receptacles with CSA configuration 5-20R shall be not less than 20 A; and
g) a separate branch circuit shall be provided solely to supply power to each receptacle described in Rule 26-720 n).

26-654 Branch circuits for dwelling units

Branch circuits for dwelling units (including single dwellings) shall meet the following requirements:

a) branch circuits from a panelboard installed in accordance with Rule 26-602 shall not be connected to outlets or electrical equipment in any other dwelling unit;
b) except as may be permitted by Items c) and d), at least two branch circuits shall be provided for receptacles (5-15R split or 5-20R) installed for kitchen counters of dwelling units in accordance with Rule 26-724 d) iii), iv), and v), and
    i) no more than two receptacles shall be connected to a branch circuit; and
    ii) no other outlets shall be connected to these circuits;
c) notwithstanding Item b), where the provisions of Rule 26-724 d) iii) require only one receptacle, only one branch circuit need be provided;
d) notwithstanding Item b) i), receptacles identified in Rule 26-720 d) shall be permitted to be connected to those receptacles required by Rule 26-724 d) iii), even though the circuit already supplies two receptacles;
e) outdoor receptacles readily accessible from ground level and installed in accordance with Rule 26-726 a) shall be supplied from at least one branch circuit dedicated for those outdoor receptacles; and
f) at least one branch circuit shall be provided solely for the receptacles in a carport or garage of a single dwelling, except that the luminaires and garage door operator for these areas shall be permitted to be connected to this circuit.

26-656 Arc fault protection of branch circuits for dwelling units (see Appendix B)

Arc-fault protection of branch circuits for dwelling units shall meet the following requirements:

1) Each branch circuit supplying 125 V receptacles rated 20 A or less shall be protected by a combination-type arc-fault circuit interrupter, except for branch circuits supplying

   a) receptacles installed in accordance with

Δ

      i) Rule 26-720 f), provided that no other receptacles are connected to these circuits; or

      ii) Rule 26-724 d) i), iii), iv), and v); and

   b) a single receptacle for a sump pump where

      i) the receptacle is labelled in a conspicuous, legible, and permanent manner identifying it as a sump pump receptacle; and

      ii) the branch circuit does not supply any other receptacles.

2) Notwithstanding Subrule 1), the entire branch circuit need not be provided with arc-fault protection where

   a) an outlet branch-circuit-type arc-fault circuit interrupter is installed at the first outlet on the branch circuit; and

   b) the wiring method for the portion of the branch circuit between the branch circuit overcurrent device and the first outlet consists of metal raceway, armoured cable, or non-metallic conduit or tubing.

Δ 3) Where one or more 125 V receptacles rated 20 A or less are added to an existing branch circuit that is not provided with arc-fault protection as required by this Rule, the entire branch circuit need not be provided with arc-fault protection where an outlet branch-circuit-type arc-fault circuit interrupter is installed at the first added receptacle to the existing branch circuit.

Receptacles

26-700 General (see Appendix B)

1) Receptacle configurations shall be in accordance with Diagrams 1 and 2, except

   a) for receptacles used on equipment solely for interconnection purposes;

   b) for receptacles for specific applications as required by other Rules of this Code; or

   c) where other configurations are suitable.

2) Except as provided for by other Rules of this Code, receptacles having configurations in accordance with Diagrams 1 and 2 shall be connected only to circuits having a nominal system voltage and ampere rating corresponding to the rating of the configurations.

3) Receptacles connected to circuits having different voltages, frequencies, or types of current (ac or dc) on the same premises shall be designed so that attachment plugs used on such circuits are not interchangeable.

4) Receptacles with exposed terminals shall be used only in fittings, metal troughs, and similar devices.

5) Receptacles located in floors shall be enclosed in floor boxes.

6) Receptacles rated 30 A or more and installed facing downward shall have provision for locking or latching to prevent unintentional detachment.

7) After installation,

   a) receptacle faces shall project a minimum of 0.4 mm from metal or conductive faceplates;

   b) any openings around the receptacle or cover shall be such that a rod 6.75 mm in diameter will not enter; and

Δ   c) receptacles, faceplates, and covers shall not prevent an attachment plug from being used in the manner in which it is intended to be used.

26

26-702 Bonding of receptacles (see Appendix B)

1) Where grounding-type receptacles are used in existing installations to replace the ungrounded type, the grounding terminal shall be effectively bonded to ground and one of the following methods shall be permitted to be used:
   a) connection to a metal raceway or cable sheath that is bonded to ground;
   b) connection to the system ground by means of a separate bonding conductor; or
   c) bonding to an adjacent grounded metal cold-water pipe.

Δ 2) Notwithstanding Subrule 1), at existing outlets where a bonding means does not exist in the outlet box, grounding-type receptacles shall be permitted to be installed, provided that each receptacle is protected by a ground fault circuit interrupter of the Class A type.

3) A bonding conductor shall not be extended from any receptacle protected by a ground fault circuit interrupter of the Class A type in accordance with Subrule 2) to any other outlet.

26-704 Protection of receptacles by a ground fault circuit interrupter of the Class A type (see Appendix B)

Receptacles having CSA configuration 5-15R or 5-20R installed within 1.5 m of sinks (wash basins complete with a drainpipe), bathtubs, or shower stalls shall be protected by a ground fault circuit interrupter of the Class A type, except where the receptacle is
a) intended for a stationary appliance designated for the location; and
b) located behind the stationary appliance such that it is inaccessible for use with general-purpose portable appliances.

26-706 Tamper-resistant receptacles (see Appendix B)

Δ 1) All receptacles of CSA configuration 5-15R and 5-20R installed in the following locations shall be tamper-resistant receptacles and shall be so marked:
   a) child care facilities;
   b) guest rooms and suites of hotels and motels;
   c) preschools and elementary education facilities; or
   d) dwelling units.

2) Notwithstanding Subrule 1), receptacles dedicated for stationary appliances such that the receptacle is rendered inaccessible and receptacles located above 2 m from the floor or finished grade shall not be required to be tamper resistant.

26-708 Receptacles exposed to the weather (see Appendix B)

1) Receptacles exposed to the weather shall be provided with wet location cover plates.

2) Receptacles of CSA configurations 5-15R, 5-20R, 5-20RA, 6-15R, 6-20R, and 6-20RA shall be provided with cover plates suitable for wet locations, whether or not a plug is inserted into the receptacle, and marked "Extra Duty".

3) Notwithstanding Subrules 1) and 2), cover plates marked "Wet Location Only When Cover Closed", or the equivalent, shall be permitted for receptacles
   a) installed facing downward at an angle of 45° or less from the horizontal; or
Δ   b) located at least 1 m above finished grade or floor level and not in a wet location.

4) Where receptacles exposed to the weather are installed in surface-mounted outlet boxes, the cover plates shall be held in place by four screws or by some other equivalent means.

5) Where receptacles exposed to the weather are installed in flush-mounted outlet boxes, the boxes shall be installed in accordance with Rule 12-3016 and the cover plates shall be fitted to make a proper weatherproof seal.

26-710 Receptacles for maintenance of equipment located on rooftops (see Appendix B)

Receptacles required by Rule 2-316 for maintenance of heating, ventilating, air-conditioning, and similar equipment located on a rooftop shall be
a) protected by a ground fault circuit interrupter of the Class A type;

b) supplied by a separate branch circuit that does not supply any other outlets or equipment;

c) of CSA configuration 5-20R;

d) located within 7.5 m of the rooftop electrical equipment;

e) located not less than 750 mm above the finished roof; and

f) protected from mechanical damage.

Receptacles for residential occupancies

26-720 General (see Appendices B and G)

Receptacles for all residential occupancies (including dwelling units and single dwellings) shall meet the following requirements:

a) for the purposes of this Rule, "finished wall" shall mean any wall finished to within 450 mm of the floor with drywall, wood panelling, or like material;

b) for the purposes of this Rule, all receptacles shall be CSA configuration 5-15R or 5-20R (see Diagram 1);

c) receptacles shall not be mounted facing up in the work surfaces or counters in the kitchen or dining area;

d) where receptacles (5-15R split or 5-20R) are installed on a side of a counter work surface in a kitchen designed for use by persons with disabilities, such receptacles shall not be considered as substituting for the receptacles required by Rule 26-724 d);

e) at least one duplex receptacle shall be provided
   i) in each space where the complete plumbing is installed to accommodate a washing machine;
   ii) in each laundry room, in addition to any receptacle specified in Item i);
   iii) in each utility room; and
   iv) in any unfinished basement area;

f) at least one receptacle shall be installed in each bathroom and washroom with a wash basin(s) and shall be located within 1 m of any one wash basin;

g) receptacles installed in bathrooms shall, where practicable, be located at least 1 m but in no case less than 500 mm from the bathtub or shower stall, this distance being measured horizontally between the receptacle and the bathtub or shower stall, without piercing a wall, partition, or similar obstacle;

h) a receptacle shall not be placed in a cupboard, cabinet, or similar enclosure, except where the receptacle is
   i) an integral part of a factory-built enclosure;
   ii) provided for use with an appliance that is suitable for installation within the enclosure;
   iii) intended only for a microwave oven;
   iv) intended only for a cord-connected range hood; or
   v) intended only for a cord-connected combination microwave oven/range hood fan;

i) except for cord-connected dishwashers, in-line water heaters, garbage disposal units, and other similar appliances, receptacles installed in cupboards, cabinets, or similar enclosures in accordance with Item h) ii) shall be de-energized unless the enclosure door is in the fully opened position;

j) any receptacle that is part of a luminaire or appliance, or that is located within cabinets or cupboards as permitted by Item h), or that is located more than 1.7 m above the floor shall not be considered as any of the receptacles required by this Rule;

k) where a switched duplex receptacle is used instead of a lighting outlet and luminaire, the receptacle shall be considered as one of the wall-mounted receptacles meeting the requirements of Rule 26-724 a), provided that only half of the receptacle is switched;

l) at least one receptacle shall be provided for each cord-connected central vacuum system, where the complete duct for such a central vacuum system is installed;

m)   public corridors and public stairways in buildings of residential occupancies shall have at least one duplex receptacle in each 10 m of length or fraction thereof; and

n)   where required by the *National Building Code of Canada*, receptacles for use with electric vehicle supply equipment as specified in Rule 86-306 shall be provided for car spaces in a garage or carport serving buildings of residential occupancies.

Δ **26-722 Protection of residential occupancy receptacles installed outdoors by a ground fault circuit interrupter of the Class A type** (see Appendix B)
Except for vehicle heater receptacles provided in conformance with Rule 8-400, all receptacles installed outdoors and within 2.5 m of finished grade shall be protected with a ground fault circuit interrupter of the Class A type.

26-724 Receptacles for dwelling units (see Appendices B and G)
Receptacles for dwelling units (including single dwellings) shall meet the following requirements:

a)   except as otherwise provided for in this Code, in dwelling units duplex receptacles shall be installed in the finished walls of every room or area, other than bathrooms, hallways, laundry rooms, water closet rooms, utility rooms, or closets, so that no point along the floor line of any usable wall space is more than 1.8 m horizontally from a receptacle in that or an adjoining space, such distance being measured along the floor line of the wall spaces involved;

b)   at least one duplex receptacle shall be provided in each area, such as a balcony or porch, that is not classified as a finished room or area in accordance with Item a);

c)   the usable wall space referred to in Item a) shall include a wall space 900 mm or more in width but shall not include doorways, areas occupied by a door when fully opened, windows that extend to the floor, fireplaces, or other permanent installations that would limit the use of the wall space;

d)   in dwelling units there shall be installed in each kitchen
   i)   one receptacle for each refrigerator;
   ii)   where a gas supply piping or a gas connection outlet has been provided for a free-standing gas range, one receptacle behind the intended gas range location not more than 130 mm from the floor and as near midpoint as is practicable, measured along the floor line of the wall space intended for the gas range;
   iii) a sufficient number of receptacles (5-15R split or 5-20R) along the wall at counter work surfaces (excluding sinks, built-in equipment, and isolated work surfaces less than 300 mm long at the wall line) so that no point along the wall line is more than 900 mm from a receptacle measured horizontally along the wall line;
   iv)   at least one receptacle (5-15R split or 5-20R) installed at each permanently fixed island counter space with a continuous long dimension of 600 mm or greater and a short dimension of 300 mm or greater;
   v)   at least one receptacle (5-15R split or 5-20R) installed at each peninsular counter space with a continuous long dimension of 600 mm or greater and a short dimension of 300 mm or greater; and
   vi)   a sufficient number of duplex receptacles installed on the remaining finished walls in accordance with Item a);

e)   the receptacles specified in Item d) shall not be located
   i)   on the area of the wall directly behind the kitchen sink; or
   ii)   on the area of the counter directly in front of the kitchen sink; and

f)   no point in a hallway within a dwelling unit shall be more than 4.5 m from a duplex receptacle as measured by the shortest path that the supply cord of an appliance connected to the receptacle would follow without passing through an opening fitted with a door.

26-726 Receptacles for single dwellings (see Appendices B and G)
Receptacles for single dwellings only shall meet the following requirements:

a)   for each single dwelling, at least one duplex receptacle shall be installed outdoors so as to be readily accessible from ground or grade level for the use of appliances that need to be used outdoors;

Δ b)   at least one duplex receptacle readily accessible from floor or grade level shall be provided for each car space in a garage or carport of a single dwelling; and

c)   one receptacle shall be provided in a garage for each cord-connected overhead garage door opener and shall be located within 1 m of the overhead door opener.

Electric heating and cooking appliances

26-740 Location of non-portable appliances
Non-portable electric heating and cooking appliances shall be installed so that the danger of igniting adjacent combustible material is reduced to a minimum.

26-742 Separate built-in cooking units
Tap conductors feeding individual built-in cooking units from a single branch circuit shall be permitted to be smaller than the branch circuit conductors, provided that the tap conductors

a)   are not more than 7.5 m in length;

b)   have an ampacity not less than the ampere rating of the built-in cooking unit they supply; and

c)   have an ampacity not less than one-third the ampere rating of the branch circuit overcurrent device.

Δ **26-744 Supply connections for appliances** (see Appendix B)

1)   Except as permitted in Subrule 10), all electric heating and cooking appliances shall have only one point of connection for supply.

2)   Where an electric clothes dryer having an input in excess of 1500 W at 115 V but not exceeding 30 A is intended to be installed in a dwelling unit, a receptacle of CSA configuration 14-30R, as shown in Diagram 1, shall be installed for the supply of energy to the appliance.

3)   An electric clothes dryer having an input in excess of 1500 W at 115 V but not exceeding 30 A, and used in a dwelling unit, shall be cord-connected by means of a cord and attachment plug of CSA configuration 14-30P to the receptacle referred to in Subrule 2).

4)   Where a free-standing electric range, having a calculated demand of 50 A or less, is intended to be installed in a dwelling unit, a receptacle of CSA configuration 14-50R, as shown in Diagram 1, shall be installed for the supply of electric energy to the appliance.

5)   The receptacle required by Subrule 4) shall be permitted to be connected to a branch circuit rated at not less than 40 A.

6)   The receptacle required by Subrule 4) shall be installed

a)   above the finished floor at a height not exceeding 130 mm to the centre of the receptacle;

b)   as near midpoint as is practicable, measured along the floor line of the wall space intended for the electric range; and

c)   with the U-ground slot oriented to either side.

7)   In a dwelling unit, a free-standing electric range having a calculated demand of 50 A or less shall be cord-connected by means of a cord and attachment plug of CSA configuration 14-50P.

8)   Appliances that are intended for connection by a wiring method as specified in Section 12 shall be permitted to be cord-connected using an attachment plug and receptacle.

9)   The receptacles required by Subrules 2) and 4) shall be flush-mounted wherever practicable.

26

10) A permanently connected electric heating and cooking appliance provided with multiple points of connection shall be permitted to be supplied from more than one branch circuit, provided that
    a) the appliance is marked accordingly; and
    b) connection to the different branch circuits conforms to Rule 14-414.

26-746 Appliances exceeding 1500 W

1) Every electric heating and cooking appliance rated at more than 1500 W shall be supplied from a branch circuit used solely for one appliance, except that more than one appliance shall be permitted to be connected to a single branch circuit, provided that the following is used:
    a) a multiple-throw manually operated device that will permit only one such appliance to be energized at one time; or
    b) an automatic device that will limit the total load to a value that will not cause operation of the overcurrent devices protecting the branch circuit.

2) Every electric heating and cooking appliance rated at more than 1500 W shall be controlled by an indicating switch that shall be permitted to be in the circuit or on the appliance, except that
    a) if the rating of the appliance does not exceed 30 A, an attachment plug and receptacle shall be permitted to be used instead of a switch; and
    b) if the appliance has more than one individual heating element, each controlled by a switch, no main switch need be provided.

3) For the purpose of this Rule, two or more separate built-in cooking units shall be considered as one appliance.

26-748 Signals for heated appliances

Where glue pots, soldering irons, or appliances intended to be applied to combustible materials are used in other than dwelling units,
a) each appliance or group of appliances shall be provided with an indicating switch and a red pilot light; or
b) each appliance shall be equipped with an integral temperature-limiting device, in which case the pilot light shall be permitted to be omitted where a deviation has been allowed in accordance with Rule 2-030.

26-750 Control of ventilation of commercial cooking equipment

Where a fan is used to ventilate commercial cooking equipment, the control for the fan motor shall be readily accessible, within reach of the cooking equipment, and external to the ventilation duct or hood.

Heating equipment

26-800 Scope

Rules 26-802 to 26-808 apply to circuits supplying power for the operation and control of non-portable heating equipment that uses solid, liquid, or gaseous fuel.

26-802 Mechanical protection of cables

Cables for all branch circuit or tap conductors within 1.5 m from the floor shall be adequately protected from mechanical damage.

26-804 Fuel burner safety controls (see Appendix B)

Fuel burner safety controls shall be installed in accordance with the requirements of CSA C22.2 No. 3.

26-806 Heating equipment rated 117 kW and less (see Appendix B)

1) Except as permitted by Subrule 3), all electric power for a heating unit and associated equipment operating in connection with it shall be obtained from a single branch circuit that shall be used for no other purpose.

2) For the purpose of this Rule, circulating pumps and similar equipment need not be considered as associated equipment, provided that such equipment is not essential for the safe operation of the heating unit.

3) Subrule 1) shall not apply to a water heater using a gaseous fuel.
4) The branch circuit shall be permitted to be tapped as necessary to supply the various pieces of associated equipment, but there shall be no overcurrent protection supplied in the tap to any piece of associated equipment the operation of which is essential to the proper operation of the heating unit, unless the control equipment is of such a nature that the heating unit will be shut down if the associated equipment fails to function due to the operation of the overcurrent device.
5) Suitable disconnecting means shall be provided for the branch circuit.
6) The disconnecting means shall be permitted to be a branch circuit breaker at the distribution panelboard, provided that the panelboard is located between the furnace and the point of entry to the area where the furnace is located.
7) Where a separate switch is required due to the unsuitable location of the branch circuit breaker, it shall
   a) not be located on the furnace nor in a location that can be reached only by passing close to the furnace; and
   b) be marked to indicate the equipment it controls.

26-808 Heating equipment rated at more than 117 kW
1) All electric power for the heating unit and associated equipment operating in connection with it shall be obtained from a single feeder or branch circuit that shall not be used for other purposes.
2) A suitable disconnecting means shall be provided for the feeder or branch circuit.

Pipe organs

26-900 Installation of electrically operated pipe organs
1) Organ blower motors, when located remote from the organ console, shall be provided with a pilot lamp located at the organ console.
2) A receptacle shall be provided in the organ loft to facilitate the use of a portable lamp.

Submersible pumps

26-950 Special terminology
In this Subsection, the following definitions shall apply:

Deep well submersible pump — a submersible pump intended for use in a well casing or similar protective enclosure that does not have provision for electrical connection by conduit.

Submersible pump — a pump-motor combination where the enclosed electrical equipment is intended to operate submerged in water.

26-952 General
Submersible pumps shall be installed in accordance with the manufacturer's instructions and Rule 26-954 or 26-956 as applicable.

26-954 Deep well submersible pumps installed in wells
Deep well submersible pumps installed in wells shall comply with the following:
a) the power supply cable run from the well head to the pump shall be
   i) Types RWU75, RWU90, TWU, or TWU75 single-conductor cables or twisted assemblies of these types, suitable for handling at −40 °C; or
   ii) Type SOW, G, G-GC, W, or the equivalent portable power cable;
b) the supply cables shall be suitably supported at intervals not exceeding 3 m to the discharge pipe;
c) the supply cables shall be run from the well head to the main distribution panelboard in accordance with the requirements of Section 12; and
d) pumps shall be bonded to ground in accordance with Section 10 except that when the discharge pipe is of metal and is continuous from the pump to the well head, the equipment bonding

26

conductor shall be permitted to be terminated by connection to a discharge pipe at the well head location.

26-956 Submersible pumps installed in bodies of water

1) Submersible pumps installed in bodies of water shall comply with the following:
   a) the voltage supplying the submersible pump shall not exceed 150 volts-to-ground;
   b) the pump motor shall be bonded to ground by a bonding conductor that
      i) is sized in accordance with Rule 10-614;
      ii) is integral with the supply cable or within the same protective enclosure as the power supply cables if single-conductor cables are used;
      iii) has the same type of insulation as the supply conductors; and
      iv) terminates adjacent to the location where the branch circuit conductors receive their supply;
   c) the wiring method to the pump shall be
      i) Type RWU75, RWU90, TWU, or TWU75 or equivalent single-conductor cables or twisted assemblies of these types, suitable for handling at −40 °C and enclosed in a plastic water pipe or in rigid PVC conduit; or
      ii) Type SOW, G, G-GC, W, or the equivalent portable power cable;
   d) ground fault protection shall be provided to de-energize all normally ungrounded conductors supplying the submersible pump, with a ground fault current trip setting adjusted to function as low as practicable to permit normal operations of the pump, but in no case shall the ground fault current setting be greater than 10 mA for an operating time period not exceeding 2.7 s; and
   e) the supply cables shall be run from an outdoor connection facility, above or below ground, to the main distribution panelboard in accordance with the requirements of Section 12.

2) Notwithstanding Item 1) a), submersible pumps installed in bodies of water shall be permitted to operate at voltages exceeding 150 volts-to-ground where
   a) a deviation has been allowed in accordance with Rule 2-030;
   b) the operating voltage does not exceed 5.5 kV;
   c) the electrical installation is maintained by qualified electrical maintenance staff; and
   d) the area around the submersible pump is protected from access by the public by fencing, cribbing, or isolation and so marked.

Data processing

26-1000 Permanently connected data processing units

Branch circuits supplying permanently connected data processing units shall not supply any other types of loads.

Section 28 — Motors and generators

Scope

28-000 Scope
This Section supplements or amends the general requirements of this Code and applies to the installation, wiring methods, conductors, protection, and control of electric motors and generators.

General

28-010 Special terminology
In this Section, the following definitions shall apply:

Locked rotor current rating — a current rating marked on electric equipment or, where not marked, deemed to be equal to six times the full load current rating from the nameplate of the equipment or from Table 44 or 45 as applicable.

Non-continuous duty motor — a motor having characteristics or ratings described in Section 0, Definitions, under **Duty**, as **Short-time duty**, **Intermittent duty**, **Periodic duty**, and **Varying duty**.

Rated load current (for a hermetic refrigerant motor-compressor) — a value marked on a hermetic refrigerant motor-compressor intended for use where applicable to ascertain wiring, protection, and control for the unit.

Δ **Refrigerant motor-compressor** — an appliance consisting of a refrigerant gas compressing section and a motor that may include a terminal box and cover and other electrical components, including starting and overload components, heaters, fans, or an electronic control.

> **Hermetic refrigerant motor-compressor** — a refrigerant motor-compressor in which the refrigerant gas compressing section and motor are enclosed in the same housing, permanently sealed by welding or brazing, with no external shaft seals, such that the motor operates in a refrigerant atmosphere with or without oil.

> **Semi-hermetic refrigerant motor-compressor** — a refrigerant motor-compressor in which the refrigerant gas compressing section and motor are each enclosed in separate housings that are secured together by gasketted joints and may include shaft seals, such that the motor does not operate in a refrigerant atmosphere.

Service —

> **Continuous duty service** — any application of a motor where the motor can operate continuously with load under any normal or abnormal condition of use.

> **Non-continuous duty service** — an application of a motor where the apparatus driven by the motor has the characteristics described in Section 0, Definitions, under **Duty**, as **Short-time duty**, **Intermittent duty**, **Periodic duty**, and **Varying duty**.

Service factor — a multiplier that, when applied to the rated horsepower of an ac motor, to the rated armature current of a dc motor, or to the rated output of a generator, indicates a permissible loading that may be carried continuously at rated voltage and frequency.

28-012 Guarding
Exposed live parts of motors and controllers operating at 50 V or more between terminals shall be guarded against accidental contact by means of enclosures or by location, except that stationary motors having commutators, collectors, and brush rigging located inside motor end brackets and not

28

conductively connected to supply circuits operating at more than 150 volts-to-ground shall be permitted to have live parts exposed.

28-014 Methods of guarding
Methods of guarding of motors having exposed live parts shall be by
a)   installation in a room or enclosure that is accessible only to authorized persons;
b)   installation on a suitable balcony, gallery, or platform elevated and arranged to exclude other than qualified persons;
c)   elevation by 2.5 m or more above the floor; or
d)   guard rails if the motor operates at 750 V or less.

28-016 Ventilation
1)   Adequate ventilation shall be provided to prevent the development around motors of ambient air temperatures exceeding 40 °C for integral horsepower motors and 30 °C for fractional horsepower motors.
2)   Notwithstanding Subrule 1), motors suitable for use in higher ambient temperatures shall be specifically marked for the temperatures in which they will operate.
3)   In locations where dust or flying material will collect in or on motors in quantities that interfere with the ventilating or cooling of motors, thereby causing dangerous temperatures, suitable types of enclosed motors that will not overheat under prevailing conditions shall be used.

Wiring methods

28-100 Stationary motors (see Appendix B)
The wiring method for stationary motors shall be in accordance with the applicable requirements of Sections 12 and 36.

28-102 Portable motors
Connections to portable motors shall be permitted using flexible cord that has a serviceability not less than that of Type S cord, unless the motor forms part of a motor-operated device.

Δ ### 28-104 Motor supply conductor insulation temperature rating and ampacity (see Appendix B)
1)   Supply conductors to a motor connection box shall have
a)   an insulation temperature rating equal to or greater than that required by Table 37, unless the motor is marked otherwise;
b)   the insulation temperature rating derived from Item a) increased by the difference between the maximum ambient temperature and 30 °C, where the ambient temperature is higher than 30 °C; and
c)   an ampacity based on a 75 °C conductor insulation rating.
2)   Notwithstanding Subrule 1) c), where a 90 °C insulated conductor is used as the supply conductor to a Class A motor, the conductor ampacity shall be permitted to be based on a 90 °C conductor insulation rating.
3)   Where Table 37 requires insulation temperature ratings in excess of 75 °C, the motor supply insulated conductors shall
a)   be not less than 1.2 m long; and
b)   terminate in a location not less than
i)   600 mm from any part of the motor, for motors rated less than 100 hp; or
ii)   1.2 m from any part of the motor, for motors rated 100 hp or larger.

28-106 Insulated conductors — Individual motors

1) The insulated conductors of a branch circuit supplying a motor for use on continuous duty service shall have an ampacity not less than 125% of the full load current rating of the motor.

2) The insulated conductors of a branch circuit supplying a motor for use on non-continuous duty service shall have an ampacity not less than the current value obtained by multiplying the full load current rating of the motor by the applicable percentage given in Table 27 for the duty involved, or for varying duty service where a deviation has been allowed in accordance with Rule 2-030 by a percentage less than that specified in Table 27.

3) Tap conductors supplying individual motors from a single set of branch circuit overcurrent devices supplying two or more motors shall have an ampacity at least equal to that of the branch circuit insulated conductors, except that where the tap conductors do not exceed 7.5 m in length, they shall be permitted to be sized in accordance with Subrule 1) or 2), provided that the ampacity so determined is not less than one-third of the ampacity of the branch circuit insulated conductors.

28-108 Insulated conductors — Two or more motors

1) Insulated conductors supplying a group of two or more motors shall have an ampacity not less than
   a) 125% of the full load current rating of the motor having the largest full load current rating plus the full load current ratings of all the other motors in the group, where all motors in the group are for use on continuous duty service;
   b) the total of the calculated currents determined in accordance with Rule 28-106 2) for each motor, where all motors in the group are for use on non-continuous duty service; or
   c) the total of the following, where the group consists of two or more motors for use on both continuous and non-continuous duty service:
      i) 125% of the current of the motor having the largest full load current rating for use on continuous duty service;
      ii) the full load current ratings of all other motors for use on continuous duty service; and
      iii) the calculated current determined in accordance with Rule 28-106 2) for motors for use on non-continuous duty service.

2) Where the circuitry is interlocked in order to prevent all motors of the group from running at the same time, the size of the conductors feeding the group shall be permitted to be determined for the motor, or group of motors operating at the same time, that has the largest rating selected as determined in Subrule 1).

3) Demand factors shall be permitted to be applied where the character of the motor loading justifies reduction of the ampacity of the insulated conductors to less than the ampacity specified in Subrule 1), provided that
   a) the insulated conductors have sufficient ampacity for the maximum demand load; and
   b) the rating or setting of the overcurrent devices protecting them is in accordance with Rule 28-204 4).

28-110 Feeder conductors

1) Where a feeder supplies both motor loads and other loads, the ampacity of the insulated conductors shall be calculated in accordance with Rules 28-106 and 28-108 plus the requirements of the other loads.

2) The ampacity of a tap from a feeder to a single set of overcurrent devices protecting a motor branch circuit shall be not less than that of the feeder, except that the ampacity of the tap shall be permitted to be calculated in accordance with Rules 28-106 and 28-108 if the tap does not exceed
   a) 3 m in length and is enclosed in metal; or
   b) 7.5 m in length, has an ampacity not less than one-third that of the feeder, and is suitably protected from mechanical damage.

28

28-112 Secondary insulated conductors

1) Insulated conductors connecting the secondaries of wound rotor motors to their controllers shall have an ampacity not less than
   a) 125% of the rated full load secondary current for motors used on continuous duty service; or
   b) the percentage of rated full load current specified in Table 27 for motors used on non-continuous duty service.
2) Ampacities of insulated conductors connecting secondary resistors to their controllers shall be not less than that determined by applying the appropriate percentage in Table 28 to the maximum current that the devices are required to carry.

Overcurrent protection

Δ **28-200 Branch circuit overcurrent protection** (see Appendix B)
1) Each ungrounded conductor of a motor branch circuit shall be protected by an overcurrent device in accordance with Subrules 2) to 5).
2) The overcurrent device required by Subrule 1) shall be
   a) a non-time-delay fuse;
   b) a time-delay fuse;
   c) an inverse-time circuit breaker;
   d) an instantaneous-trip (magnetic only) circuit interrupter applied in accordance with Rule 28-210; or
   e) a self-protected combination motor controller selected in accordance with Rule 28-500.
3) The rating of the overcurrent device required by Subrule 1) shall
   a) not exceed the values given in Table 29 using the rated full load current of the motor, except that an overcurrent device having a minimum rating or setting of 15 A shall be permitted even though it exceeds the values specified in Table 29; and
   b) for a branch circuit supplying two or more motors, not exceed the maximum value permitted by Rule 28-206.
4) Where an overcurrent device rated in accordance with Subrule 3) a) will not permit the motor to start, the rating or setting of the overcurrent device shall be permitted to be increased as follows:
   a) for a non-time-delay fuse, not more than
      i) 400% of the motor full load current, for fuses rated up to 600 A; or
      ii) 300% of the motor full load current, for fuses rated 601 to 6000 A;
   b) for a time-delay fuse, not more than 225% of the motor full load current; and
   c) for an inverse time circuit breaker, not more than
      i) 400% of the motor full load current, for circuit breakers rated up to 100 A; or
      ii) 300% of the motor full load current, for circuit breakers rated greater than 100 A.
5) Where the overcurrent device required by Subrule 1) is a thermal magnetic circuit breaker that has separate instantaneous-trip settings, the instantaneous-trip setting shall not be greater than that specified in Rule 28-210.

28-202 Overcurrent protection marked on equipment
Where branch circuit protective device characteristics and ratings or settings are specified in the marking of motor control equipment, they shall not be exceeded, notwithstanding any greater rating or setting permitted by Rule 28-200.

28-204 Feeder overcurrent protection
1) For a feeder supplying motor branch circuits only, the ratings or settings of the feeder overcurrent device shall not exceed the calculated value of the overcurrent device permitted by Rule 28-200 for the motor that is permitted the highest rated overcurrent devices of any motor supplied by the

feeder, plus the sum of the full load current ratings of all other motors that will be in operation at the same time.

Δ 2) Where a feeder supplies a group of motors, two or more of which are required to start simultaneously, and the feeder overcurrent devices as calculated in accordance with Subrule 1) are not sufficient to allow the motors to start, the rating or setting of the feeder overcurrent devices shall be permitted to be increased as necessary, to a maximum that does not exceed the rating permitted for a single motor having a full load current rating not less than the sum of the full load current ratings of the greatest number of motors that start simultaneously, plus the sum of the full load current ratings of all other motors that will be in operation at the same time, provided that this value does not exceed 300% of the ampacity of the feeder conductors.

3) Where a feeder supplies one or more motor branch circuits together with other loads, the overcurrent protection required shall be determined by calculating the overcurrent protection required for the motor circuits and adding to this value the requirements of the other loads supplied by the feeder.

4) Where a demand factor has been applied as permitted in Rule 28-108 3), the rating or setting of the overcurrent device(s) protecting a feeder shall not exceed the ampacity of the feeder, except as permitted by Rule 14-104 and Table 13.

28-206 Grouping of motors on a single branch circuit

Two or more motors shall be permitted to be grouped under the protection of a single set of branch circuit overcurrent devices having a rating or setting calculated in accordance with Rule 28-204 1), provided that the protection conforms to one of the following:

a) the rating or setting of the overcurrent devices does not exceed 15 A;

b) protection is provided for the control equipment of the motors by having the branch circuit overcurrent devices rated or set at
   i) values not in excess of those marked on the control equipment for the lowest rated motor of the group as suitable for the protection of that control equipment; or
   ii) in the absence of such markings, values not in excess of 400% of the full load current of the lowest rated motor;

c) the motors are used on a machine tool or woodworking machine under the following conditions:
   i) the control equipment is arranged so that all contacts that open motor primary circuits are in enclosures, either forming part of the machine base or for separate mounting, that have a wall thickness not less than 1.69 mm for steel, 2.4 mm for malleable cast iron, or 6.3 mm for other cast metal; that have hinged doors with substantial catches; and that have no openings to the floor or the foundation on which the machine rests; and
   ii) the rating or setting of the branch circuit overcurrent protection is not greater than that permitted by Table 29 for the full load current rating of the largest motor in the group, plus the sum of the full load current ratings of all other motors in the group that may be in operation at one time, but in no case more than 200 A at 250 V or less or 100 A at voltages from 251 to 750 V;

d) all the motors are operated by a single controller, as provided for in Rule 28-500 3) d);

e) where a deviation is allowed in accordance with Rule 2-030 for the group of motors that form part of the coordinated drive of a single machine or process, whereby the failure of one motor to operate creates a hazard unless all the other motors in the group are stopped; or

f) the motors are contained within and form part of refrigerant equipment on a 120 V branch circuit protected at not more than 20 A where each motor is rated not more than 1 hp and has a full load current rating of not more than 6 A.

28

28-208 Size of fuseholders
Where fuses are used for motor branch circuit or feeder protection, the fuseholders shall not be of a size smaller than those required to accommodate fuses of the maximum rating permitted by Table 29, except that fuseholders of a smaller size shall be permitted to be used
a) where Rule 28-202 is applicable;
b) where fuses having time delay appropriate for the starting characteristics of the motor are used, in which case the fuseholders shall be not smaller than those required to accommodate fuses rated at 125% of the full load current of the motor; or
c) in the case of a circuit supplying a group of motors, where the fuseholders accommodate fuses of a size calculated by taking 150% of the largest motor current and adding to this value the applicable full load currents of all other motors in the group that may be in operation at the same time.

Δ **28-210 Instantaneous-trip circuit breakers** (see Appendix B)
When used for branch circuit protection, instantaneous-trip circuit breakers shall be part of a combination motor starter or controller that also provides overload protection and
a) rated or adjusted, for an ac motor, to trip at not more than 1300% of the motor full load current or at not more than 215% of the motor locked rotor current, where given, except that ratings or settings for trip currents need not be less than 15 A; or
b) rated or adjusted, for a dc motor rated at 50 hp or less, to trip at not more than 250% of the motor full load current, or for a dc motor rated at more than 50 hp, to trip at not more than 200% of the motor full load current.

Δ **28-212 Semiconductor fuses** (see Appendix B)
Where power electronic devices are used in a solid-state motor controller system, semiconductor fuses integral to the controller shall be permitted in addition to the protection determined by Rule 28-200 1).

Overload and overheating protection

28-300 Overload protection required
The branch circuit conductors and control equipment of each motor shall have overload protection, except as permitted by Rule 28-308.

28-302 Types of overload protection
1) Overload devices shall be either
   a) a separate overload device that is responsive to motor current and that shall be permitted to combine the function of overload and overcurrent protection if it is capable of protecting the circuit and motor under both overload and short-circuit conditions; or
   b) a protective device, integral with the motor and responsive to motor current or to motor current and temperature, provided that such a device will protect the insulated circuit conductors and control equipment as well as the motor.
2) Fuses used as separate overload protection of motors shall be time-delay fuses of the type referred to in Rule 14-200.

28-304 Number and location of overload devices (see Appendix B)
1) The number and location of current-responsive devices shall, unless otherwise required, be as follows:
   a) if fuses are used, one in each ungrounded conductor; or
   b) if devices other than fuses are used, as specified in Table 25.

2) Unless a deviation has been allowed in accordance with Rule 2-030, where current-responsive devices are used for the overload protection of three-phase motors, such devices shall consist of three current-responsive elements that shall be permitted to be
   a) connected directly in the motor circuit insulated conductors as required by Subrule 1); or
   b) fed by two or three current transformers connected so that all three phases will be protected.

28-306 Rating or trip selection of overload devices (see Appendix B)
1) Overload devices responsive to motor current, if of the fixed type, shall be selected or rated or, if of the adjustable type, shall be set to trip at not more than the following:
   a) 125% of the full load current rating of a motor having a marked service factor of 1.15 or greater; or
   b) 115% of the full load current rating of a motor that does not have a marked service factor or where the marked service factor is less than 1.15.
2) Where a motor overload device is connected so that it does not carry the total current designated on the motor nameplate, such as for wye-delta starting, the percentage of motor nameplate current applying to the selection or setting of the overload device shall be clearly marked on the motor starter shown in the motor starter manufacturer's overload selection table.

28-308 Overload protection not required (see Appendix B)
Overload protection shall not be required for motors complying with any of the following:
a) a manually started motor rated at 1 hp or less that is continuously attended while in operation and is on
   i) a branch circuit having overcurrent protection rated or set at not more than 15 A; or
   ii) an individual branch circuit having overcurrent protection as required by Table 29 if it can be readily determined from the starting location that the motor is running;
b) an automatically started motor having a rating of 1 hp or less forming part of an assembly equipped with other safety controls that protect the motor from damage due to stalled rotor current and on which a nameplate, located so that it is visible after installation, indicates that such protection features are provided; or
c) a motor that conforms with CSA C22.2 No. 77.

28-310 Shunting of overload protection during starting
Overload protection shall be permitted to be shunted or cut out of the circuit during the starting period, provided that the device by which the protection is shunted or cut out cannot be left in the starting position and that the overcurrent device is in the motor circuit during the starting period.

28-312 Automatic restarting after overload
Where automatic restarting of a motor after a shutdown on overload could cause injury to persons, the overload or overheating devices protecting the motor shall be arranged so that automatic restarting cannot occur.

28-314 Overheating protection required (see Appendix B)
Each motor shall be provided with overheating protection, except as permitted by Rule 28-318.

28-316 Types of overheating protection (see Appendix B)
Where required by Rule 28-314, overheating protection shall be provided by devices integral with the motor and responsive to both motor current and temperature or to motor temperature only, and shall be arranged to cut off power to the motor or, where a deviation has been allowed in accordance with Rule 2-030, to activate a warning signal when the temperature exceeds the safe limit for the motor.

28-318 Overheating protection not required
Overheating protection shall not be required
a) where the motor circuit requires no overload protection under Rule 28-308; or

28

b) where overload protective devices required by Rule 28-302 adequately protect the motor against overheating due to excess current, and the motor is in a location where
   i)   ambient temperatures are not more than 10 °C higher than those at the location of the overload devices; and
   ii) dust or other conditions will not interfere with the normal dissipation of heat from the motor.

Undervoltage protection

28-400 Undervoltage protection required for motors (see Appendix B)
Motors shall be disconnected from the source of supply in case of undervoltage by one of the following means, unless it is evident that no hazard will be incurred through lack of such disconnection:
a) when automatic restarting is liable to create a hazard, the motor control device shall provide low-voltage protection; or
b) when it is necessary or desirable that a motor stop on failure or reduction of voltage and automatically restart on return of voltage, the motor control device shall provide low-voltage release.

Control

28-500 Control required
1) Except as permitted by Subrule 3), each motor shall be provided with a motor starter or controller for starting and stopping it that has a rating in horsepower not less than the rating of the motor it serves.
2) A motor controller need not open the circuit in all ungrounded conductors to a motor unless it also serves as a disconnecting means.
3) The motor starter or controller specified in Subrule 1) shall not be required for motors in the following applications:
   a) a single-phase portable motor rated at 1/3 hp or less connected by means of a receptacle and attachment plug rated not in excess of 15 A, 125 V;
   b) a motor controlled by a manually operated general-use switch complying with Rule 14-510 having an ampere rating not less than 125% of the full load current rating of the motor;
   c) a 2-wire portable ac or dc motor having a rating not in excess of 1/3 hp, 125 V controlled by a horsepower rated single-pole motor switch;
Δ d) two or more motors that are required to operate together shall be permitted to be operated from a single controller; or
Δ e) for a motor where the controller is specifically designed for use with that motor, it need not be rated in horsepower.

28-502 Control location
A motor controlled manually, either directly or by remote control of a motor starter, shall have the means to operate of the controller located as follows:
a) the controller shall be located such that safe operation of the motor and the machinery driven by it is assured, or the motor and the machinery shall be guarded or enclosed to prevent accidents due to contact of persons with live or moving parts; or
b) where compliance with Item a) is not practicable because of the type, size, or location of the motor or machinery and its parts, devices shall be provided at each point where the danger of accidents exists by which means the machine or parts of the machine may be stopped in an emergency.

28-504 Starters having different starting and running positions
1) Manual motor starters having different starting and running positions shall be constructed so that they cannot remain in the starting position.

2) Magnetic motor starters having different starting and running positions shall be constructed so that they cannot remain in the starting position under normal operating conditions.

28-506 Grounded control circuit

When power for a control circuit for a motor controller is obtained conductively from a grounded system, the control circuit shall be arranged so that an accidental ground in the wiring from the controller to any remote or signal device will not

a)   start the motor; or

b)   prevent the stopping of the motor by the normal operation of any control or safety device in the control circuit.

Disconnecting means

28-600 Disconnecting means required

1) Except as permitted by Subrules 2) and 3), a separate disconnecting means shall be provided for
   a)   each motor branch circuit;
   b)   each motor starter or controller; and
   c)   each motor.

2) A single disconnecting means shall be permitted to serve more than one of the functions described in Subrule 1).

3) A single disconnecting means shall be permitted to serve two or more motors and their associated starting and control equipment grouped on a single branch circuit.

28-602 Types and ratings of disconnecting means (see Appendix B)

1) A disconnecting means for a motor branch circuit shall be
   a)   a manually operable fused or unfused motor-circuit switch that complies with Rule 14-010 b) and has a horsepower rating not less than that of the motor it serves;
   b)   a moulded case switch or circuit breaker that complies with Rule 14-010 b) and has a current rating not less than 115% of the full load current rating of the motor it serves;
   c)   an instantaneous-trip circuit breaker that complies with Rules 14-010 b) and 28-210;
   d)   an equivalent device that opens all ungrounded conductors of the branch circuit simultaneously and is capable of safely making and interrupting the locked rotor current of the connected load;
   e)   a single plug fuse for a branch circuit having one grounded conductor feeding a 2-wire single-phase or dc motor rated at not more than 1/3 hp, provided that it is used only as an isolating means and is not used to interrupt current; or
   f)   the draw-out feature of a high-voltage motor starter or controller of the draw-out type that complies with Rule 14-010 b), provided that it is used only as an isolating means and is not used to interrupt current.

2) A disconnecting means serving a group of motors on a single branch circuit shall have
   a)   a current rating not less than 115% of the full load current rating of the largest motor in the group plus the sum of the full load current ratings of all the other motors in the group that may be in operation at the same time; and
   b)   a horsepower rating not less than that of the largest motor in the group if a motor-circuit switch is used.

3) A disconnecting means for a motor, motor starter, or controller shall comply with Subrule 1), except that
   a)   an isolating switch or a general-use switch used as an isolating switch, if lockable in the open position, marked as required by Rule 26-100 2), and having a current rating not less than 115%

28

of the full load current rating of the motor it serves, shall be permitted to serve as the disconnecting means for a motor or motor starter

     i)   rated at more than 100 hp if for three-phase operation; or

    ii)   rated at more than 50 hp if for other than three-phase operation;

  b) a manually operated across-the-line type of motor starter marked "Suitable for Motor Disconnect" shall be permitted to serve as both starter and disconnecting means for

     i)   a single motor, provided that it has a horsepower rating not less than the single motor it serves;

    ii)   a group of motors, provided that it has a horsepower rating not less than the largest motor in the group and a current rating not less than 115% of the full load current of the largest motor in the group plus the sum of the full load currents of all the other motors in the group that may be in operation at the same time; or

    iii) a motor or group of motors contained in equipment such as an air-conditioning, refrigeration, or heating unit, provided that

       A)   the equipment does not contain overcurrent protection; and

       B)   the starter is rated in accordance with Item i) for a single motor or Item ii) for a group of motors;

  c) an attachment plug shall be permitted to serve as a disconnecting means for a portable motor and its starting and control equipment, provided that

     i)   the attachment plug and receptacle have a current rating not less than the ampacity of the minimum size conductors permitted for the motor branch circuit or tap in which they are connected and are used only as an isolating means and not to interrupt current; or

    ii)   the attachment plug and receptacle are used as permitted by Rule 28-500 3);

  d) the draw-out feature of a high-voltage starter or controller of the draw-out type shall be permitted to serve as the disconnecting means for the motor or controller, provided that it is used only as an isolating means and is not used to interrupt current;

  e) a manually operated general-use ac switch complying with the requirements of Rule 14-510 that has a current rating not less than 125% of the full load current of the motor and that need not be horsepower rated shall be permitted to be used as a disconnecting means for a single-phase motor; and

  f) a fused or unfused motor-circuit switch shall be permitted to be used as a disconnecting means for a group of motors served from a single circuit and need not have a rating greater than that necessary to accommodate the proper rating of fuse required for the fused switch, provided that it has

     i)   a horsepower rating not less than that of the largest motor in the group; and

    ii)   a current rating not less than 115% of the full load current of the largest motor in the group plus the sum of the full load currents of all the other motors in the group that may be in operation at the same time.

4)   The disconnecting means shall not be of a type that is electrically operated either automatically or by remote control.

5)   An enclosure that contains the disconnecting means for an air-conditioning, refrigeration, or heating unit and that is located outdoors shall be suitable for the environment, and where conduit is used as part of the wiring to the disconnecting means located in the enclosure, the conduit shall be drained and sealed in accordance with Rule 22-302.

28-604 Location of disconnecting means

1)   The motor branch circuit disconnecting means described in Rule 28-602 1) a) to d) shall

  a) be located at the distribution centre from where the motor branch circuit originates; and

b) where intended to serve as a single disconnecting means for a motor branch circuit, motor, and controller or starter, also be

   i) located in accordance with Subrule 3); or

   ii) capable of being locked in the open position by a lock-off device and be clearly labelled to describe the load or loads connected.

2) The motor branch circuit disconnecting means described in Rule 28-602 1) f) shall be located in accordance with Subrule 3).

3) Except as required in Subrule 5), the motor and motor starter or controller disconnecting means shall be located

   a) within sight of and within 9 m of the motor and the machinery driven by it; and

   b) within sight of and within 9 m of the motor starter or controller.

4) Notwithstanding Subrule 3), where a motor or group of motors is fed from a single branch circuit in which the branch circuit disconnecting means is not capable of being acceptably locked in the open position and where the motor disconnecting means is a manually operable across-the-line type of motor starter, the motor disconnecting means shall be permitted to be located beyond the limits defined in Subrule 3), provided that

   a) it is capable of safely making and interrupting the locked rotor current of the connected load;

   b) it is capable of being locked in the open position; and

   c) it can be demonstrated that the location specified in Subrule 3) is clearly impracticable.

5) The motor disconnecting means for air-conditioning and refrigeration equipment shall be located within sight of and within 3 m of the equipment.

6) The disconnecting means shall be readily accessible or have the means for operating them readily accessible.

7) Motor-driven machinery of a movable or portable type for industrial use shall have a motor-circuit switch or circuit breaker mounted on the machine and accessible to the operator.

Refrigerant motor-compressors

28-700 Rules for refrigerant motor-compressors

Rules 28-702 to 28-714

a) apply to refrigerant motor-compressors, including hermetic refrigerant motor-compressors and semi-hermetic refrigerant motor-compressors, hereafter referred to as motor-compressors; and

b) supplement or amend the general Rules of this Section.

28-702 Marking

Motor-compressors, or equipment that incorporates them, shall be marked as required by Rule 2-100; specifically, the marking shall show the rated load current and the locked rotor current rating.

28-704 Horsepower rated equipment

1) Horsepower rated equipment used for the control of motor-compressors and not having a locked rotor current rating shall be given an equivalent locked rotor current rating equal to 6 times the full load current rating.

2) Where the full load current rating is not marked, an equivalent full load current rating shall be determined from the horsepower rating by referring to Table 44 or 45 as applicable.

28-706 Insulated conductor ampacity

The allowable ampacity of insulated conductors of a branch circuit supplying a motor-compressor, or equipment consisting of one or more motor-compressors and other loads, shall be based on the marked rated load current of the motor-compressor or equipment and shall comply with the general requirements of this Section.

28

28-708 Overcurrent protection

1) Except as permitted in Subrule 2), each ungrounded conductor of a branch circuit feeding a motor-compressor shall be protected by an overcurrent device rated or set at not more than 50% of the locked rotor current of the motor-compressor, unless such a device will not permit the motor-compressor to start, in which case the rating or setting shall be permitted to be increased to a value not exceeding 65% of the locked rotor current of the motor-compressor.

2) Subrule 1) shall not be deemed to require use of overcurrent devices rated or set at less than 15 A.

28-710 Overload protection

The branch circuit insulated conductors and control equipment for each motor-compressor shall be provided with overload protection complying with Rules 28-302 to 28-306, except that

a) the rating or setting of overload relays shall not exceed 140% of the marked rated load current of the motor-compressor;

b) the rating or setting of other overload devices, such as fuses, shall not exceed 125% of the marked rated load current of the motor-compressor; and

Δ c) assemblies consisting of one or more motor-compressors with or without other loads in combination shall be permitted to include the overload protection as part of the assembly.

28-712 Control equipment

1) Control equipment used for the control of motor-compressors shall have

   a) either a marked or an equivalent locked rotor current rating not less than that of the motor-compressor that it controls; and

   b) either a marked or an equivalent full load current rating not less than that of the rated load current of the motor-compressor that it controls.

2) In all other respects, control equipment for motor-compressors shall be in accordance with Rules 28-500, 28-502, and 28-506.

28-714 Disconnecting means

1) The disconnecting means serving a motor-compressor shall have

   a) a continuous duty current rating not less than 115% of the rated load current of the motor-compressor; and

   b) an interrupting capacity, or an equivalent locked rotor current rating as determined in accordance with Rule 28-704, that is not less than the locked rotor current rating of the motor-compressor.

2) Where one disconnecting means serves one or more motor-compressors together with other loads, the disconnecting means shall have

   a) a continuous duty current rating not less than 115% of the rated load current of the motor or motor-compressor having the largest rated load current plus the sum of the rated load currents and full load currents of all other loads that may be in operation at the same time; and

   b) an interrupting capacity, or equivalent locked rotor current rating as determined in accordance with Rule 28-704, that is not less than the locked rotor current rating of the motor or motor-compressor having the largest marked or equivalent locked rotor current rating plus the sum of the full load current rating of all other loads that may be in operation at the same time.

Multi-winding and part-winding-start motors

28-800 Rules for multi-winding and part-winding-start motors

Rules 28-802 to 28-812 apply to the installation of multi-winding and part-winding-start motors.

28-802 Permanent connection

Where a multi-winding motor is used with windings connected in a permanent configuration, it shall be treated as a single-winding motor with ratings corresponding to the winding configuration used.

28-804 Conductor sizes

1) The insulated circuit conductors on the supply side of the controller for a multi-winding or part-winding-start motor shall be of a size specified by Rule 28-106 for the largest full load current of any winding configuration provided by the controller as connected.

2) Each insulated conductor run from the controller to the motor shall be of the size specified by Rule 28-106 for the largest full load current of any winding or winding configuration that it must supply.

28-806 Overcurrent protection

1) Each ungrounded conductor on the supply side of the controller shall be protected by an overcurrent device rated or set in accordance with Rule 28-200 for the largest full load current rating of any winding configuration provided by the controller as connected.

2) Each ungrounded conductor run from the controller to the motor shall be protected by an overcurrent device rated or set in accordance with Rule 28-200 for the largest full load current of any winding configuration served by the insulated conductor so protected, unless the overcurrent device required by Subrule 1) adequately protects it.

3) Notwithstanding Subrules 1) and 2), if the motor is a part-winding-start motor, a single set of overcurrent devices on the supply side of the controller shall be permitted to protect both windings, and if a time-delay fuse is used, it shall be permitted to have a maximum rating of 150% of full load current.

28-808 Overload protection

1) Each winding or configuration shall be provided with overload protection in accordance with Rules 28-300 to 28-310, rated or set at not more than 125% of the full load current rating of the winding or configuration so protected.

2) For a part-winding-start motor, separate overload devices need not be supplied for each winding, provided that overload devices are
   a) located in the circuit, feeding the winding that is used for starting;
   b) arranged to de-energize both windings when an overload occurs; and
   c) selected in accordance with the motor or equipment manufacturer's recommendation.

28-810 Controls

Each multi-winding or part-winding-start motor shall be provided with starting and control equipment in accordance with Rules 28-500, 28-502, and 28-506, except that

Δ a) the controller shall be specifically designed for use with the motor that it controls;

   b) where separate control equipment is provided for each winding or configuration, the individual controllers shall be rated in horsepower (or locked rotor current) not less than the rating of the winding or configuration controlled by each, and interlocks shall be provided where necessary to prevent simultaneous operation of controllers not intended to be so operated; or

Δ c) the starting and control equipment for each primary winding of a part-winding-start motor shall have a horsepower (or locked rotor current) rating not less than that of the motor or be specifically designed for use with that motor and so marked.

28-812 Disconnecting means

Each multi-winding motor and its control equipment shall be provided with disconnecting means in accordance with Rules 28-600 to 28-604 except that, for the purpose of Rule 28-602, the horsepower (or locked rotor current) rating of the motor shall be that for the winding or configuration having the largest horsepower (or locked rotor current) rating, and the full load current rating of the motor shall be that for the winding or configuration having the largest full load current rating.

28

Protection and control of generators

28-900 Disconnecting means required for generators (see Appendix B)

1) Except as provided for in Subrule 3), a separate disconnecting means shall be provided for each generator and for each circuit supplying all protective devices and control apparatus required for operation of the generator.
2) The disconnecting means specified in Subrule 1) shall disconnect the generator and all protective devices and control apparatus from the circuits connected to the generator.
3) The disconnecting means specified in Subrule 1) need not be provided where the generator is
   a) constructed with an integral disconnecting means that disconnects the generator and all protective devices and control apparatus from the circuits connected to the generator; or
   b) provided with a disconnecting means in accordance with CSA C282.

28-902 Protection of constant-voltage generators

1) Constant-voltage generators, whether dc or ac, shall be protected from excess current by overcurrent devices, except that
   a) where the type of apparatus used and the nature of the system operated make protective devices inadvisable or unnecessary, the protective devices need not be provided; or
   b) where an ac generator and a transformer are located in the same building and are intended to operate as a unit for stepping up or stepping down voltage, the protective devices shall be permitted to be connected to the primary or the secondary of the transformer.
2) Subrule 1) shall not apply to exciters for ac machines.

28-904 Generator not driven by electricity

Where a generator not driven by electricity supplies a 2-wire grounded system, the protective device shall be capable of disconnecting the generator from both insulated conductors of the circuit.

28-906 Balancer sets

Where a 3-wire dc system is supplied by 2-wire generators operated in conjunction with a balancer set to obtain a neutral, the system shall be equipped with protective devices that disconnect the system in the event of an excessive unbalancing of voltages.

28-908 Three-wire dc generators

1) Three-wire dc generators, whether shunt or compound wound, shall be equipped with
   a) a 2-pole circuit breaker with two tripping elements; or
   b) a 4-pole circuit breaker connected in the main-and-equalizer leads and tripped by two tripping elements.
2) The circuit breaker shall be connected so that it is actuated by the entire armature current.
3) One tripping element shall be connected in each armature lead.

Section 30 — Installation of lighting equipment

30-000 Scope

This Section applies to the installation of lighting equipment and supplements or amends the general requirements of this Code.

30-002 Special terminology (see Appendix B)

In this Section, the following definitions shall apply:

Cabinet lighting system — a complete extra-low-voltage lighting assembly consisting of a plug-in power supply having a Class 2 output, luminaires, wiring harness, and connectors, intended for surface or recessed mounting under a shelf or similar structure or in an open or closed cabinet.

Cable lighting system — a permanently connected extra-low-voltage lighting system that comprises an isolating-type transformer with bare secondary conductors for connection to one or more luminaire heads.

Landscape lighting system — an extra-low-voltage lighting system consisting of an isolating-type power supply, luminaire assemblies, and fittings to provide flood or decorative lighting for gardens, walkways, patio areas, or similar outdoor locations and for specific indoor locations such as atriums and malls.

Recessed luminaire — a luminaire that is designed to be either wholly or partially recessed in a mounting surface.

Recessed luminaire, Type IC (intended for insulation contact) — a recessed luminaire designed for installation in a cavity filled with thermal insulation and permitted to be in direct contact with combustible materials and insulation.

Recessed luminaire, Type IC, inherently protected (intended for insulation contact) — a recessed luminaire that does not require a thermal protective device and cannot exceed the maximum allowable temperatures under all conceivable operating conditions.

Recessed luminaire, Type Non-IC (not intended for insulation contact) — a recessed luminaire designed for installation in a cavity with minimum dimensions and spacings to thermal insulation and combustible material.

Recessed luminaire, Type Non-IC, marked spacings (not intended for insulation contact) — a recessed luminaire designed for installation in a cavity where the clearances to combustible building members and thermal insulation are specified by the manufacturer.

Undercabinet lighting system — a complete extra-low-voltage lighting assembly consisting of a plug-in power supply having a Class 2 output, luminaires, wiring harness, and connectors, intended for surface mounting only under a shelf or similar structure or in an open or closed cabinet.

General

30-100 General

Rules 30-100 to 30-112 cover general requirements that apply to
a)   the installation of luminaires, lampholders, incandescent filament lamps, and electric-discharge lamps; and
b)   the wiring and electric equipment used in conjunction with this installation.

30-102 Voltage

1)   Branch circuit voltage shall not exceed 150 volts-to-ground in dwelling units.

2) Branch circuit voltage shall not exceed a nominal system voltage of 347/600Y in other than dwelling units.

30-104 Protection (see Appendix B)

Luminaires, lampholders, and lighting track shall not be connected to a branch circuit protected by overcurrent devices rated or set at more than

a) 15 A in dwelling units;

b) 15 A in other than dwelling units, where the input voltage exceeds 347 V nominal;

c) 20 A in other than dwelling units, where the input voltage does not exceed 347 V nominal; or

d) 40 A in other than dwelling units, where the load is from

  i) luminaires with lampholders of the incandescent mogul base type;

  ii) high-intensity discharge (HID) luminaires, with or without auxiliary lighting systems, where the input voltage does not exceed 120 V nominal;

  iii) tungsten halogen luminaires with double-ended lampholders, where the input voltage does not exceed 240 V nominal; or

  iv) luminaires provided with an integral overcurrent device rated at not more than 15 A, where the input voltage does not exceed 120 V nominal.

Δ **30-106 Overcurrent protection of high-intensity discharge lighting equipment**

Overcurrent protection shall not be provided in a high-intensity discharge luminaire or separate ballast box unless the combination is so marked.

Δ **30-108 Overcurrent protection for arc lamp luminaires**

An overcurrent device shall be provided for each arc lamp or series of lamps.

Δ **30-110 Polarization of luminaires**

The identified conductor shall be attached to the luminaire terminal or insulated conductor that has been distinguished for identification or otherwise suitably marked unless the luminaire is suitable for connection to line-to-line voltages.

30-112 Bonding of lighting equipment

Non-current-carrying metal parts of luminaires and associated equipment shall be bonded to ground in accordance with Section 10.

Location of lighting equipment

30-200 Near or over combustible material

Δ 1) Luminaires installed near or over combustible material shall be equipped with shades or guards to limit the temperature to which the combustible material may be subjected to a maximum of 90 °C.

2) Luminaires installed under the conditions of Subrule 1) shall be of the unswitched type.

3) Where luminaires are installed over readily combustible material, every luminaire shall be controlled by an individual wall switch, but a wall switch shall be permitted to control more than one luminaire if every luminaire is located at least 2.5 m above floor level, or located or guarded so that the lamps cannot be readily removed or damaged.

4) Switches and luminaires installed under the conditions of Subrule 1) shall have no exposed wiring.

30-202 In show windows

1) Except for luminaires installed in accordance with Rule 30-1206, or luminaires of the chain suspension type, no luminaire having exposed wiring shall be used in a show window.

2) No lampholder having a paper or fibre lining shall be used in a show window.

3) Exposed flexible cord or equipment wire shall not be used to supply permanently installed luminaires in show cases or wall cases.

30-204 In clothes closets

Δ 1) Every luminaire installed in a clothes closet shall be located on the ceiling or on the front wall above the door of the closet, unless suitable for mounting on the trim or sidewall of the doorway.

2) Lampholders and luminaires of the pendant or suspended type, and lampholders and luminaires of the bare lamp type, shall not be installed in clothes closets.

Installation of lighting equipment

30-300 Live parts

Luminaires, lampholders, and associated equipment shall be installed so that no live part is exposed to contact while they are in use.

30-302 Supports

1) Every luminaire shall be securely supported.

2) Where a luminaire weighs more than 2.7 kg or exceeds 400 mm in any dimension, it shall not be supported by the screwshell of the lampholder.

3) Where the weight of a luminaire does not exceed 13 kg, the luminaire shall be permitted to be supported by a wall outlet box attached directly to the building structure or by a wall outlet box attached to a bar hanger.

4) Where the weight of a luminaire does not exceed 23 kg, the luminaire shall be permitted to be supported by a ceiling outlet box attached directly to the building structure or by a ceiling outlet box attached to a bar hanger.

5) Where the weight of a luminaire prohibits the installation methods specified in Subrule 3) or 4), the luminaire shall be supported
   a) independently of the outlet box; or
   b) by a fixture hanger provided with an integral outlet box suitable for the purpose.

6) Rigid PVC boxes shall not be used for the support of luminaires unless they are marked as being suitable for the purpose.

30-304 Outlet boxes to be covered

Every outlet box used with lighting equipment shall be provided with a cover or covered by a luminaire-canopy, outlet-box-type luminaire, or other device.

30-306 Wiring space

1) Every luminaire-canopy and outlet box shall be installed so as to provide adequate space for insulated conductors and connections.

2) Every luminaire shall be constructed and installed so that insulated conductors in the luminaire and outlet box are not subjected to temperatures greater than those for which the insulated conductors are rated.

30-308 Circuit connections

1) Every luminaire shall be installed so that the connections between the luminaire insulated conductors and the branch circuit insulated conductors can be inspected without disconnecting any part of the wiring unless the connection employs a plug and receptacle.

2) Luminaires weighing more than 4.5 kg shall be installed so that the branch circuit wiring connections and the bonding connections will be accessible for inspection without removing the luminaire supports.

3) Branch circuit insulated conductors within 75 mm of a ballast within the ballast compartment shall have a maximum allowable insulated conductor temperature of not less than 90 °C.

30

Δ 4) The connection of branch circuit insulated conductors exceeding 150 volts-to-ground to the conductors of each luminaire utilizing double-ended lamps connected to a ballast or driver shall be made by
   a) means of mated separable conductor connectors that will safely disconnect all conductors of the luminaire from branch circuit conductors simultaneously, when the conductor connectors are separated;
   b) connecting the plug of a luminaire equipped with a power supply cord into a receptacle;
   c) inserting the female connector of a cord set into a luminaire equipped with an inlet; or
   d) permanently connecting the insulated branch circuit conductors to the terminals of a luminaire equipped with disconnecting means that will open simultaneously all conductors supplying the ballast(s) or driver(s) when access to the ballast or driver compartment is made.

30-310 Luminaire as a raceway
1) Insulated branch circuit conductors run through a luminaire shall be contained in a raceway that is an integral part of the luminaire and that meets the requirements for a surface raceway, except that the insulated conductors of a 2-wire, 3-wire, or 4-wire branch circuit supplying the luminaires shall be permitted to be carried through luminaires marked as suitable for continuous row mounting.
2) Ballasts located within the luminaires referred to in Subrule 1) shall be deemed to be sources of heat and the conductors supplying the luminaires shall
   a) have a voltage rating not less than 600 V;
   b) have an insulation temperature rating not less than 90 °C; and
   c) be of a type
      i) selected in accordance with Rule 12-102 3) as being suitable for use in raceways; or
      ii) selected in accordance with Rule 12-402 1) as being suitable for use in accordance with this Rule, provided that the insulated conductors are not smaller than No. 14 AWG and do not extend beyond the luminaires through raceways more than 2 m long.
3) Notwithstanding Subrule 2), non-metallic-sheathed cable shall be permitted to be used for supplying the luminaires, provided that it has a temperature rating of 90 °C.

30-312 Combustible shades and enclosures (see Appendix G)
Every luminaire having a combustible shade or enclosure shall be installed to provide an adequate air space between the lamps and the combustible shade or enclosure.

30-314 Minimum height of low luminaires (see Appendix G)
1) Where a rigid luminaire is located at a height of less than 2.1 m above the floor and is readily accessible, the luminaire shall be protected from mechanical damage by a guard or by location.
2) A short flexible drop light or luminaire shall be permitted to be used in place of the rigid luminaire in Subrule 1).

30-316 Luminaires exposed to flying objects
Where luminaires are installed in gymnasiums or similar locations where the lamps are normally exposed to damage from flying objects, the lamp shall be guarded by one of the following means:
a) metal reflectors that effectively protect the lamps;
b) metal screens; or
c) enclosures of armoured glass or suitable plastic material.

30-318 Luminaires in damp or wet locations
Δ 1) Luminaires installed in damp or wet locations shall be marked for use in such locations.
2) Luminaires suitable for use in wet locations shall be permitted to be used in damp locations as well.

30-320 Lighting equipment in damp locations or near grounded metal

1) Where luminaires are installed in damp locations or within 2.5 m vertically or 1.5 m horizontally of laundry tubs, plumbing fixtures, steam pipes, or other grounded metal work or grounded surfaces, the luminaires shall be controlled by a wall switch, except as permitted in Subrule 2).
2) Outlet-box-type luminaires marked for use in damp locations and luminaires marked for use in wet locations, with an integral switch, shall be permitted to be installed under the conditions of Subrule 1).
3) Switches (including wall switches) controlling luminaires covered by Subrules 1) and 2) shall
    a) be located not less than 1 m from a bathtub or shower stall (this distance being measured horizontally between the switch and the bathtub or shower stall, without piercing a wall, partition, or similar obstacle); or
    b) if the condition in Item a) is not practicable, be located not less than 500 mm from a bathtub or shower stall and be protected by a ground fault circuit interrupter of the Class A type.

30-322 Totally enclosed gasketted luminaires

Incandescent totally enclosed gasketted luminaires, unless marked as suitable for the purpose, shall not be mounted on a combustible ceiling.

Δ 30-324 Installation of arc lamp luminaires

1) Outdoor arc lamp luminaires, attached to a building and supplied from the interior installation, shall be suspended at least 2.5 m above ground level.
2) Indoor arc lamp luminaires shall be hung out of reach or shall be protected from mechanical damage.

Wiring of lighting equipment

30-400 Wiring of luminaires

All electrical wiring on or within a luminaire shall be
a) neatly arranged without excess wiring;
b) not exposed to mechanical damage; and
c) arranged so that it is not subjected to temperatures above those for which it is rated.

30-402 Colour coding

Notwithstanding the requirements of Sections 0, 4, and 10 with regard to the colours used for distinguishing and identifying insulated conductors, a continuous-coloured tracer in the braid of an individual braided insulated conductor shall be permitted for the supply insulated conductors of a luminaire, the colour of the tracer being black, white, and green for the ungrounded, identified, and bonding conductors respectively.

Δ 30-404 Conductor insulation

Luminaires shall be connected with conductors at least No. 18 AWG, having insulation suitable for the voltage and temperatures to which the conductors may be subjected.

30-406 Arrangement of exposed wiring on suspended luminaires

All exposed wiring shall be arranged so that neither the suspension means nor the weight of the luminaire places tension on the wiring or on the connections.

Δ 30-408 Wiring of ceiling outlet boxes

1) Branch circuit conductors having insulation suitable for 90 °C shall be used for connection of ceiling outlet boxes on which a luminaire is mounted, except for boxes in wet locations where Type NMW or NMWU cables are used.

30

2) For the purposes of compliance with this Rule, the ampacity of 90 °C insulated conductors shall be limited to the ampacity of 60 °C insulated conductors.

30-410 Wiring of show window luminaires

1) Where show window luminaires are closely spaced, they shall be permitted to be connected to an insulated conductor suitable for the purpose selected in accordance with Rule 12-402 1), with a temperature rating of not less than 125 °C.

2) The connection of show window luminaires to the insulated circuit conductors shall be in a junction box.

3) The junction box shall be maintained at a sufficient distance from the luminaire to ensure that the insulated circuit conductors are not subjected to temperatures in excess of their rating.

30-412 Tap connection conductors

No. 14 AWG copper tap connection insulated conductors shall be permitted for a single luminaire, and for luminaires mounted in a continuous row as specified in Rule 30-310 1), on a branch circuit protected by an overcurrent device rated or set at 20 A, provided that the tap connection insulated conductors

a) have an ampacity not less than the rating of the single luminaire or the luminaires mounted in a continuous row as specified in Rule 30-310 1); and

b) do not exceed 7.5 m in length.

Luminaires in buildings of residential occupancy

30-500 Lighting equipment at entrances (see Appendix G)

An exterior luminaire controlled by a wall switch located within the building shall be provided at every entrance to buildings of residential occupancy.

30-502 Luminaires in dwelling units (see Appendix G)

1) Except as provided in Subrule 2), a luminaire controlled by a wall switch shall be provided in kitchens, bedrooms, living rooms, utility rooms, laundry rooms, dining rooms, bathrooms, water closet rooms, vestibules, and hallways in dwelling units.

2) Where a receptacle controlled by a wall switch is provided in bedrooms or living rooms, such rooms shall not be required to conform to the requirements in Subrule 1).

30-504 Stairways (see Appendix G)

1) Every stairway shall be lighted.

2) Except as provided for in Subrule 3), three-way wall switches located at the head and foot of every stairway shall be provided to control at least one luminaire for stairways with four or more risers in dwelling units.

3) The stairway lighting for basements that do not contain finished space nor lead to an outside entrance or built-in garage, and that serve not more than one dwelling unit, shall be permitted to be controlled by a single switch located at the head of the stairs.

30-506 Basements (see Appendix G)

1) A luminaire shall be provided for each 30 m² or fraction thereof of floor area in unfinished basements.

2) The luminaire required in Subrule 1) that is located nearest the stairs shall be controlled by a wall switch located at the head of the stairs.

30-508 Storage rooms (see Appendix G)

A luminaire shall be provided in storage rooms.

30-510 Garages and carports (see Appendix G)

1) A luminaire shall be provided for an attached, built-in, or detached garage or carport.

2) Except as provided in Subrule 3), luminaires required in Subrule 1) shall be controlled by a wall switch near the doorway.

3) Where the luminaire required in Subrule 1) is ceiling-mounted above an area not normally occupied by a parked car or is wall-mounted, a luminaire with a built-in switch accessible to an adult of average height shall be permitted to be used.

4) Where a carport is lighted by a luminaire at the entrance to a dwelling unit, additional carport lighting shall not be required.

Lampholders

30-600 Connections to lampholders
The identified insulated conductor, if present, shall be connected to the lampholder screwshell.

30-602 Switched lampholders used on unidentified circuits
Where lampholders of the switched type are used on unidentified 2-wire circuits tapped from the ungrounded conductors of multi-wire circuits, the switching devices of the lampholders shall disconnect both conductors of the circuit simultaneously.

30-604 Luminaires with pull-type switch mechanisms
On luminaires employing pull-type switch mechanisms, the operating means shall be
a) cords made of insulating materials;
b) cords made of insulating materials or chains with links made of insulating material, connected to metal chains as close as possible to where the chains emerge from the enclosure; or
Δ c) metal chains without insulating links, provided that the lampholder does not require insulating links.

30-606 Lampholders in wet or damp locations
Where lampholders are installed in wet or damp locations, they shall be of the weatherproof type.

Δ 30-608 Pendant lampholders
1) Where pendant lampholders having permanently attached leads are used with other than festoon wiring, they shall be hung from separate stranded thermoset- or thermoplastic-insulated pendant cables that are connected directly to the circuit conductors but supported independently of them.
2) Where the pendant cables supply mogul or medium-base screwshell lampholders, they shall be not smaller than No. 14 AWG.
3) Where the pendant cables supply intermediate or candelabra-base lampholders other than Christmas-tree and decorative lighting outfits, the conductors shall be not smaller than No. 18 AWG.
4) Where the pendant cables are longer than 900 mm, they shall be twisted together.

Electric-discharge lighting systems operating at 1000 V or less

30-700 Rules for discharge lighting systems 1000 V or less
Rules 30-702 to 30-712 apply to electrical equipment used with electric-discharge lighting systems operating at 1000 V or less.

30-702 Oil-filled transformers
Transformers of the oil-filled type shall not be used.

30-704 DC equipment
Luminaires shall not be installed on a dc circuit unless they are equipped with auxiliary equipment and resistors designed for dc operation, and the luminaires are so marked.

30-706 Voltages — Dwelling units
Where equipment has an open-circuit voltage of more than 300 V, it shall not be installed in dwelling units unless the equipment is designed so that no live parts are exposed during the insertion or removal of lamps.

30

30-708 Auxiliary equipment

1) Reactors, capacitors, resistors, and other auxiliary equipment shall be
   a) enclosed within the luminaire;
   b) enclosed within an accessible, permanently installed, metal cabinet where remote from the luminaire; or
   c) of a type suitable for use without an additional enclosure.
2) Adequate provision shall be made for the dissipation of heat from enclosed auxiliary equipment and the insulated conductors supplying the auxiliary equipment.
3) The metal cabinet, if not part of the luminaire, shall be installed as close as possible to the luminaire.
4) Where display cases are not permanently installed, no part of a secondary circuit shall be included in more than one case.

30-710 Control (see Appendix B)

1) The luminaires and lamp installations shall be controlled by a switch, circuit breaker, or contactor.
Δ 2) Where a switch is used, it shall
   a) be marked for the control of electric lighting systems operating at 1000 V or less;
   b) have a current rating not less than twice the current rating of the lamps or transformers;
   c) be a manually operated general-use ac switch complying with Rule 14-510; or
   d) be a manually operated general-use 347 V ac switch complying with Rule 14-512.
3) Where a circuit breaker is used,
   a) it shall comply with the requirements of Rule 14-104; and
   b) in the case of 15 A and 20 A branch circuits at 347 V and less supplying fluorescent luminaires, the circuit breaker shall be suitable for such switching duty and shall be marked "SWD".
Δ 4) Where a contactor is used, it shall
   a) be marked for the control of electric lighting systems operating at 1000 V or less; or
   b) have a current rating of not less than twice the current rating of the lamps or transformers.

30-712 Branch circuit capacity

1) Where lighting branch circuits supply luminaires employing ballasts, transformers, or auto-transformers, the load on the branch circuits shall be computed on the basis of the total amperes of the units and not on the watts of the lamps.
2) The aggregate capacity of luminaires connected to a lighting branch circuit shall not exceed 80% of the branch circuit overcurrent protection.

Electric-discharge lighting systems operating at more than 1000 V

30-800 Rules for discharge lighting systems — More than 1000 V

Rules 30-802 to 30-822 apply to electrical equipment used with electric-discharge lighting systems operating at more than 1000 V.

30-802 Voltages — Dwelling units

Where equipment has an open-circuit voltage of more than 1000 V, it shall not be installed in dwelling units.

30-804 Control (see Appendix B)

Δ 1) The luminaires and lamp installations shall be controlled singly or in groups by an externally operated switch or circuit breaker that opens all ungrounded branch circuit conductors.
2) The switch or circuit breaker shall
   a) be installed within sight of the luminaires or lamps; or
   b) be provided with a means for locking it in the open position.
Δ 3) The switch shall
   a) be marked for the control of electric lighting systems operating at more than 1000 V;

b) have a current rating of not less than twice the current rating of the transformer or transformers controlled by it;

c) be a manually operated general-use ac switch complying with Rule 14-510; or

d) be a manually operated general-use 347 V ac switch complying with Rule 14-512.

4) The circuit breaker shall comply with the requirements of Rule 14-104.

30-806 Transformer rating

1) Every transformer and ballast shall have a secondary open-circuit voltage of not more than 15 000 V, except that every transformer and ballast of the open core-and-coil type shall have a secondary open-circuit voltage of not more than 7500 V.

2) The secondary current rating shall be not more than 240 mA, except that where the secondary open-circuit voltage exceeds 7500 V, the secondary current rating shall be not more than 120 mA.

30-808 Liquid-filled transformers

Transformers of the liquid-filled type shall not be used unless they are filled with a non-flammable liquid.

30-810 Transformers — Secondary connection

1) The high-voltage windings of transformers operating at more than 1000 V shall not be connected in series or in parallel, but where each of two transformers has one end of its high-voltage winding grounded and connected to the enclosure, the high-voltage windings shall be permitted to be connected in series to form the equivalent of a midpoint-grounded transformer.

2) The grounded end of each high-voltage winding shall be connected by an insulated stranded copper conductor not smaller than No. 14 AWG.

30-812 Location of transformers

1) Transformers operating at more than 1000 V shall be accessible for servicing or replacement.

2) The transformers shall be installed as near to the lamps as practicable.

3) The transformers shall be located so that adjacent combustible materials are not subjected to temperatures in excess of 90 °C.

30-814 Wiring method

Δ 1) The secondary cables shall be luminous-tube-sign cable rated for for the voltage of the circuit.

2) Not more than a total of 6 m of cable shall be run in a metal raceway from a transformer.

3) Not more than a total of 16 m of cable shall be run in a non-metallic raceway from a transformer.

4) The cables shall be installed in conformance with Section 34.

30-816 Transformer loading

Where the lamps are connected to a transformer, their lengths and characteristics shall not be such as to cause a condition of continuous overvoltage on the transformer.

30-818 Lamp supports

1) Lamps operating at more than 1000 V shall be supported in the manner required by Section 34.

2) The lamps shall not be installed where they are exposed to mechanical damage.

30-820 Lamp terminals and lampholders

1) Parts that must be removed for lamp replacement shall be hinged or fastened in a secure manner.

2) Lamp terminals and lampholders shall be designed so that the tubing can be replaced with the minimum exposure of bare live parts during re-lamping.

3) The designs referred to in Subrule 2) need not afford protection against "space discharge" shocks as tubes are replaced by trained maintenance staff.

30-822 Marking (see Appendix M)

Every luminaire and every secondary circuit of tubing having an open-circuit voltage of more than 1000 V shall be clearly and legibly marked in letters and figures not less than 25 mm high with the

30

words "CAUTION...V", the rated open-circuit voltage being inserted in figures in the space between the words.

Recessed luminaires (see Appendix G)

30-900 General
Rules 30-900 to 30-912 apply to the installation of luminaires recessed in cavities in ceilings or walls.

30-902 Spacings for Non-IC type luminaires
Except as provided for in Rules 30-904 and 30-908, the recessed portion of every recessed luminaire marked "Type Non-IC" shall be at least 13 mm from combustible material at every point other than the point of support, and thermal insulation shall not be installed closer than 76 mm to the luminaire.

30-904 Spacings for Non-IC — Marked spacings type luminaires
The recessed portion of every recessed luminaire marked "Type Non-IC, marked spacings" shall be installed to maintain a minimum spacing from thermal insulation and combustible material at every point other than the point of support in accordance with the manufacturer's spacings marked on the luminaire.

30-906 Luminaires designed for thermal insulation contact
The recessed portion of every recessed luminaire marked "Type IC" or "Type IC, inherently protected" shall be permitted to be in contact with combustible material or blanketed with thermal insulation.

30-908 Luminaires designed for non-combustible surfaces contact only
A recessed luminaire marked as suitable for installation on a non-combustible surface shall be installed only on a non-combustible material.

30-910 Wiring of recessed luminaires (see Appendix B)
Δ 1) The temperature rating of insulation of conductors other than branch circuit conductors used to connect recessed luminaires shall comply with the conductor temperature rating marked on the luminaire.
2) The temperature rating of insulation of the branch circuit conductors run directly to the luminaire shall be in compliance with the insulated conductor temperature rating marked on the luminaire.
3) Tap connection insulated conductors shall be installed in a raceway extending at least 450 mm but not more than 2 m from the luminaire and terminated in an outlet box conforming to Subrule 4).
4) The outlet box referred to in Subrule 3) shall be
   a) accessible as required by Rule 12-3014;
   b) located not less than 30 cm from the luminaire; and
   c) located within 35 cm from an opening intended for access.
5) Where access to the outlet box referred to in Subrule 4) is through the opening for mounting the luminaire, this opening shall not be less than a circle of 180 cm², with no dimension less than 15 cm.
6) Where the luminaire opening referred to in Subrule 5) is smaller than 15 cm in any direction, access to the outlet box referred to in Subrule 4) shall be through some other opening not less than a square or rectangle of 400 cm², with no dimension less than 20 cm.
7) A supply connection box that is an integral part of the luminaire shall
   a) be accessible in accordance with Rule 12-3014; and
   b) if access is through the opening for mounting the luminaire, meet the following requirements:
      i) the electrical components of the luminaire shall be capable of being extracted through the opening for service, and the components shall include ballasts, transformers, thermal protectors, and conductor connections in the supply connection box; and
      ii) the cover of the supply connection box shall be capable of removal by hand tool, held below the ceiling.

8) A supply connection box that is an integral part of the luminaire shall not have insulated branch circuit conductors pass directly through the junction box unless the luminaire is marked as suitable for the purpose.

30-912 Wiring of recessed fluorescent luminaires

Where a recessed fluorescent luminaire is installed in a suspended ceiling that creates a plenum or hollow space, wiring to the luminaire shall not be required to be in accordance with Rule 12-010 3), provided that

a) the luminaire is supplied by a flexible cord not exceeding 3 m in length and terminated with an attachment plug;

b) the flexible cord is rated for at least 90 °C; and

c) the flexible cord is selected in accordance with Rule 12-402 1) for
    i) hard usage where the supply voltage does not exceed 300 V; and
    ii) extra-hard usage where the supply voltage does not exceed 750 V.

Permanent outdoor floodlighting installations

30-1000 General (see Appendix B)

1) Rules 30-1002 to 30-1030 apply to permanent outdoor installations of floodlights that are mounted on poles or towers.

2) These Rules are based on the understanding that authorized persons may replace lamps but all other maintenance will be done by qualified persons.

3) Rules 30-1002 to 30-1120 cover only that portion of the installation that is outside the buildings.

30-1002 Service equipment

1) Service equipment shall comply with Section 6 for low-voltage installations, and with Section 36 for high-voltage installations.

2) Where indoor equipment is installed outdoors, it shall be installed in a weatherproof enclosure.

30-1004 Wiring methods — Underground

1) Wiring underground shall be run
    a) in rigid steel or rigid aluminum conduit;
    b) in non-metallic underground conduit;
    c) as mineral-insulated cable, aluminum-sheathed cable, or copper-sheathed cable; or
    d) as cable suitable for direct earth burial as selected in accordance with Rule 12-102 3) or, where a deviation has been allowed in accordance with Rule 2-030, for service entrance below ground as selected in accordance with Rule 12-102 3).

2) Insulated conductors in conduit shall be of types selected in accordance with Rule 12-102 3) as being suitable for use in wet locations.

3) Cables buried directly in the earth shall be installed in accordance with Rule 12-012.

4) Suitable corrosion-resistant protection shall be provided for aluminum conduit, and for aluminum-sheathed cable, copper-sheathed cable, and also for mineral-insulated cable if used where materials coming in contact with the cable may have a deteriorating effect on the sheath.

30-1006 Wiring methods on poles

Δ 1) All electrical equipment on the pole shall be controlled by a switch that can be locked in the OFF position, and each pole shall be provided with a prominent sign warning against climbing the pole if the switch is not in the OFF position, unless all conductors and live parts other than those used for pole-top wiring are guarded against accidental contact in one of the following ways:
    a) the insulated conductors are run in rigid or flexible metal conduit, as mineral-insulated cable, or up the centre of steel, aluminum, or hollow concrete poles;
    b) the insulated conductors, cables, and live parts are kept at least 1 m from the climbing ladder or climbing steps; or

30

    c)   barriers are provided between insulated conductors or live parts, or both, and the climbing ladder to reduce the likelihood of contact by the climber.

2)   Insulated conductors and cables run up the centre of poles shall be supported to prevent damage to the insulated conductors or cables inside the pole and to prevent undue strain on the insulated conductors or cables where they leave the pole.

3)   Where vertical insulated conductors, cables, and grounding conductors are within 2.5 m of locations accessible to unauthorized persons, they shall be provided with a covering that gives mechanical protection.

4)   On wood poles, for grounding conductors from lightning arresters, the protective covering specified in Subrule 3) shall be of wood moulding or other insulating material giving equivalent protection.

30-1008 Disconnecting means at individual poles

Notwithstanding Rule 14-402, a disconnecting means shall not be required adjacent to an in-line fuseholder used at individual poles, provided that

a)   the fuseholder is of the weatherproof type having load-breaking capability;

b)   the maximum number of fuseholders at any one pole is two on a single-phase system and three on a three-phase system;

Δ c)   the fuseholder is of a design and is connected such that any exposed fuse parts are retained by the load side portion of the fuseholder when it is open; and

d)   the load is connected between the live insulated conductor and the identified insulated conductor.

30-1010 Overcurrent protection of pole-top branch circuits

Notwithstanding Rule 30-104, pole-top branch circuits shall be permitted to have overcurrent protection rated or set at no more than 100 A.

30-1012 Pole-top branch circuit wiring

Pole-top branch circuit wiring, exclusive of leads provided with the floodlights to which they are connected, shall be run

a)   as lead-sheathed cable or rubber- or thermoplastic-insulated moisture-resistant types of insulated conductors installed in rigid conduit;

b)   as mineral-insulated cable, aluminum-sheathed cable, or copper-sheathed cable; or

c)   where a deviation has been allowed in accordance with Rule 2-030, as insulated or uninsulated exposed wiring, provided that

    i)   the wiring is supported on suitable insulators;

    ii)   the wiring is controlled by a switch that can be locked in the OFF position; and

Δ   iii)   the pole is provided with a prominent sign warning against climbing it unless the switch is off.

30-1014 Joints

1)   Open taps and joints shall be permitted to be made in pole-top exposed wiring, provided that the joint or tap is given insulation equivalent to that on the conductors joined.

2)   There shall be no joints or splices concealed within conduit.

30-1016 Location of transformers

Transformers shall comply with the following:

a)   if mounted on floodlight poles, all live parts shall be guarded as required by Rule 30-1006;

b)   if mounted on poles, the bottom of the transformer shall be at least 5 m above locations accessible to unauthorized persons; and

c)   if located on platforms on the ground, the transformers shall be completely enclosed to prevent access by unauthorized persons or they shall be surrounded by a protecting fence that shall comply with the requirements of Rules 26-300 to 26-324.

30-1018 Overcurrent protection of transformers

Overcurrent protection of transformers shall be in accordance with Section 26.

30-1020 Switching of floodlights
Switches controlling floodlights shall comply with the following:
a)   a switch on the primary side of a transformer shall be capable of making and interrupting the full load on the transformer;
b)   switches controlling floodlights from the secondary side of a transformer shall have a current rating not less than 125% of the current requirements of the floodlights controlled;
c)   switches shall, either by remote operation or by proper guarding, be capable of being operated without exposing the operator to danger of contact with live parts; and
d)   switches shall be capable of being locked in the OFF position.

Δ   ### 30-1022 Grounding of circuits (see Appendix B)
1)   Circuits supplying permanent outdoor floodlights shall be supplied from a solidly grounded system.
2)   Notwithstanding Subrule 1), circuits operating at voltages above 300 V between conductors shall be permitted to be supplied from an ungrounded or impedance grounded system.
3)   The grounded circuit conductor of the system referred to in Subrule 1) shall be permitted to be interconnected with the grounded circuit conductor originating at the grounded system that is established by connection to the grounding electrode.

Δ   ### 30-1024 Bonding of non-current-carrying metal parts
1)   All exposed non-current-carrying metal parts of electrical equipment and exposed metal parts of non-electrical equipment within 2.5 m of finished grade or at locations where unauthorized persons may stand shall be bonded to ground by a separate bonding conductor sized in accordance with Rule 10-614.
2)   Except for isolated metal parts, such as crossarm braces, bolts, insulator pins, and the like, all exposed non-current-carrying metal parts of electrical equipment at the pole top shall be bonded together and, if within reach of any grounded metal, shall be bonded to ground.

30-1026 Material for grounding and bonding conductors
Grounding and bonding conductors shall be of the material specified in Rules 10-112 and 10-610.

30-1028 Installation of lightning arresters
Where lightning arresters are installed, a common grounding conductor and common electrode shall be permitted to be used for grounding primary and secondary neutrals and lightning arresters.

30-1030 Climbing steps
Where it is necessary to climb the pole to replace lamps, permanent climbing steps shall be provided and the lowest permanent step shall be not less than 3.7 m above locations accessible to unauthorized persons.

Exposed wiring for permanent outdoor lighting

30-1100 General
Rules 30-1102 to 30-1120 apply to exposed wiring for permanent outdoor lighting other than floodlighting, where the circuits are run between buildings, between poles, or between buildings and poles.

30-1102 Conductors
Insulated conductors shall be stranded copper not less than No. 12 AWG, and shall be
a)   of a type suitable for exposed wiring where exposed to the weather, in accordance with Rule 12-102 3);

30

b) of the rubber-insulated type suitable for exposed wiring where exposed to the weather, in accordance with Rule 12-102 3), when lampholders of a type that punctures the insulation and makes contact with the conductors are used; or

c) of the moisture-resistant rubber-insulated type suitable for exposed wiring where exposed to the weather, in accordance with Rule 12-102 3), if cabled together and used with messenger cables.

30-1104 Use of insulators
1) Insulated conductors shall be securely attached to insulators at each end of the run if a messenger is not used and at intermediate points of support if there are any.
2) Insulators at the ends of runs shall be of the strain type unless the conductors are supported by messenger cables.
3) Split knobs shall not be used.

30-1106 Height of conductors
Insulated conductors and cables supplying lamps in parking lots, used car lots, drive-in establishments, and similar commercial areas shall be maintained such that the insulated conductors or cables themselves, or the bottom of a lamp fed from the conductors or cables, whichever is lower, shall have a clearance of not less than 4 m above grade at any point in a run except that, where a driveway or thoroughfare exists, this clearance shall be not less than 5 m.

30-1108 Spacing from combustible material
Insulated conductors and lampholders shall be maintained at a distance not less than 1 m from any combustible material, except for branch circuit insulated conductors at the point of connection to buildings or poles.

30-1110 Spacing of conductors
Insulated conductors shall be separated at least 300 mm from each other by means of insulating spacers at intervals of not more than 4.5 m unless the insulated conductors are secured to and supported by messenger cables.

30-1112 Lampholders
1) Lampholders shall be of weatherproof types.
2) Lampholders shall be of types having either
   a) permanently attached leads; or
   b) terminals of a type that puncture the insulation and make contact with the conductors.
Δ 3) Lampholders having permanently attached leads shall have the connections to the circuit conductors staggered where a cable is used.

30-1114 Protection of lampholders
Notwithstanding Rule 30-104, lampholders shall be permitted to be connected to branch circuits protected by overcurrent devices rated or set at not more than 30 A, provided that the lampholders are
a) for incandescent lamps;
b) of the unswitched type; and
c) rated not less than 660 W.

30-1116 Use of messenger cables
1) Messenger cables shall be used to support the insulated conductors
   a) if lampholders having permanently attached leads are used, and the span exceeds 12 m; and
   b) in all cases where lampholders having terminals that puncture the insulation are used.
2) Messenger cables shall be securely attached at each end of the run and shall be grounded in accordance with Section 10.
3) Insulated conductors shall be permanently attached to the messenger.

30-1118 Construction of messenger cables
1) Messenger cables shall be of galvanized steel, copper-coated steel, or stainless steel, and shall be of stranded construction with not less than seven strands.

2) Galvanized steel shall have a coating of not less than 45 g/m^2.
3) The effective ultimate strength of a messenger cable shall be not less than three times the calculated maximum working load, including loading due to ice loads and wind loads, and the individual strands shall in no case be less than
   a) 1.17 mm in diameter in the case of galvanized or copper-coated wire; or
   b) 1.11 mm in diameter in the case of stainless steel wire.

30-1120 Branch circuit loading and protection
1) Branch circuits shall be protected by overcurrent devices rated at not more than 30 A.
2) The total load on a branch circuit shall not exceed 80% of the rating or setting of the overcurrent devices.

Extra-low-voltage lighting systems

30-1200 Rules for extra-low-voltage lighting systems
Rules 30-1202 to 30-1208 apply to extra-low-voltage lighting systems.

30-1202 Sources of supply
1) Extra-low-voltage lighting systems shall be supplied from branch circuits operating at not more than 150 volts-to-ground.
Δ 2) The extra-low-voltage portion of the system shall be supplied from the secondary of an isolating transformer having no direct electrical connection between the primary and secondary windings.
3) The extra-low-voltage portion of the system shall not be grounded.

30-1204 Installation of landscape lighting systems
1) Flexible cord shall be permitted to be used on the secondary side of the transformer and be permitted to be secured to structural members and run through holes.
2) Electrical connections shall be permitted to be made without an enclosure where not exposed to mechanical damage.

30-1206 Installation of cable lighting systems
1) Cable lighting systems shall be permitted only in dry locations.
2) Cable lighting systems shall not be installed in bathrooms.
3) Cables for extra-low-voltage circuits shall be rigidly supported.
4) Cables shall not be installed in contact with combustible materials and not run through walls, ceilings, floors, or partitions.
5) Bare conductors shall not be installed less than 2.2 m from the floor.

30-1208 Installation of cabinet and undercabinet lighting systems
1) Notwithstanding Rule 12-402 3), flexible cords on the secondary side of the power supply shall be permitted to be secured to structural members of cabinets and run through cabinet holes.
2) Electrical connections shall be permitted to be made without an enclosure where they are not exposed to mechanical damage.

30

Section 32 — Fire alarm systems, smoke and carbon monoxide alarms, and fire pumps
(See Appendix G)

32-000 Scope (see Appendix B)
1) This Section applies to the installation of electrical local fire alarm systems, permanently connected carbon monoxide alarms, and fire pumps required by the *National Building Code of Canada*.
2) This Section supplements or amends the general requirements of this Code.

Fire alarm systems

32-100 Conductors
1) Except as provided by Subrule 2), conductors shall be of copper and shall have an ampacity adequate to carry the maximum current that can be provided by the circuit.
2) Optical fiber cables shall be permitted for use in data communication links between control units and transponders of a fire alarm system as described in CAN/ULC-S524.
3) Stranded conductors with more than 7 strands shall be bunch-tinned or terminated in compression connectors.
4) Conductors shall have an insulation rating not less than 300 V and shall be not smaller than
   a) No. 16 AWG for individual conductors pulled into raceways;
   b) No. 19 AWG for individual conductors laid in raceways;
   c) No. 19 AWG for an integral assembly of two or more conductors; and
   d) No. 22 AWG for an integral assembly of four or more conductors.
5) Conductors shall be suitable for the purpose and of the type selected in accordance with Rule 12-102 3), except that individual conductors smaller than No. 14 AWG copper installed in a raceway shall be equipment wire of the type selected in accordance with Rule 12-122 1).

32-102 Wiring method
1) All conductors of a fire alarm system shall be
   a) installed in metal raceway of the totally enclosed type;
   b) incorporated in a cable having a metal armour or sheath;
   c) installed in rigid non-metallic conduit; or
   d) installed in electrical non-metallic tubing, where embedded in at least 50 mm of masonry or poured concrete.
2) Notwithstanding Subrule 1), conductors installed in buildings of combustible construction in accordance with the Rules of Section 12 shall be permitted to be
   a) non-metallic-sheathed cable;
   b) fire alarm and signal cable; or
   c) installed in a totally enclosed non-metallic raceway.
3) The conductors shall be installed to be entirely independent of all other wiring and shall not enter a raceway, box, or enclosure occupied by other wiring, except as may be necessary for connection to
   a) the point of supply;
   b) a signal;
   c) an ancillary device; or
   d) a communication circuit.
4) All wiring of a communication system connected to a fire alarm system to extend the fire alarm system beyond the building shall conform to the applicable Rules of Section 60.
5) All conductors contained in the same raceway or cable shall be insulated for the highest voltage in the raceway or cable.

32-104 Equipment bonding

1) Exposed non-current-carrying metal parts of electrical equipment, including outlet boxes, conductor enclosures, raceways, and cabinets, shall be bonded to ground in accordance with Section 10.

2) Where a non-metallic wiring system is used, a bonding conductor shall be incorporated in each cable and shall be sized in accordance with Rule 10-614.

32-106 Electrical supervision

Wiring to dual terminals and dual splice leads shall be independently terminated to each terminal or splice lead.

32-108 Power supply

1) The power supply to a fire alarm system shall be provided by a separate circuit.

2) Notwithstanding Subrule 1), where a fire alarm system includes more than one control unit or transponder, the power supply to each control unit or transponder shall be permitted to be provided by a separate branch circuit.

3) Overcurrent devices and disconnecting means for the separate circuit supplying a fire alarm system shall be clearly identified as the fire alarm power supply in a permanent, conspicuous, and legible manner, and the disconnecting means shall be coloured red and be lockable in the ON position.

Smoke and carbon monoxide alarms

32-200 Installation of smoke alarms and carbon monoxide alarms in dwelling units (see Appendices B and G)

The following requirements shall apply to the installation of permanently connected smoke alarms and carbon monoxide alarms in dwelling units:

Δ a) except as permitted by Item e), smoke alarms and carbon monoxide alarms shall be supplied from a lighting circuit, or from a circuit that supplies a mix of lighting and receptacles, and in any case shall not be installed where the circuit is protected by a ground fault circuit interrupter or arc-fault circuit interrupter;

b) there shall be no disconnecting means between the smoke alarm or the carbon monoxide alarm and the overcurrent device for the branch circuit;

c) the wiring method for smoke alarms and carbon monoxide alarms, including any interconnection of units and their associated equipment, shall be in accordance with Rules 32-100 and 32-102;

d) notwithstanding Item c), where a smoke alarm or carbon monoxide alarm circuit utilizes a Class 2 power supply for the interconnection of the smoke alarms and carbon monoxide alarms and their associated equipment, Class 2 wiring methods shall be permitted in buildings of combustible construction, provided that the conductors are installed in accordance with Rules 12-506 to 12-524; and

Δ e) where a smoke alarm or a device that is a combination of a smoke alarm and a carbon monoxide alarm has an integral battery as a secondary supply source, such a smoke alarm or combination of a smoke alarm and carbon monoxide alarm shall be permitted to be connected to a circuit protected by a ground fault circuit interrupter or arc-fault circuit interrupter.

Fire pumps

32-300 Conductors (see Appendices B and G)

Conductors from the emergency power source to a fire pump shall

a) have an ampacity not less than

    i) 125% of the full load current rating of the motor, where an individual motor is provided with the fire pump; and

ii) 125% of the sum of the full load currents of the fire pump, jockey pump, and the fire pump auxiliary loads, where two or more motors are provided with the fire pump; and

b) be protected against fire exposure to provide continued operation in compliance with the *National Building Code of Canada*.

32-302 Wiring method (see Appendices B and G)

All conductors to fire pump equipment shall be

a) installed in metal raceways of the totally enclosed type;

b) incorporated in a cable, having a metal armour or sheath, of a type selected in accordance with Rule 12-102 3);

c) installed in rigid non-metallic conduit where embedded in at least 50 mm of masonry or poured concrete or installed underground; or

d) installed in electrical non-metallic tubing where embedded in at least 50 mm of masonry or poured concrete.

32-304 Service box for fire pumps (see Appendix G)

1) A separate service box conforming to Rule 32-306 shall be permitted for fire pump equipment.

2) Notwithstanding Rule 6-102 2), a service box for fire pump equipment shall be permitted to be located remote from other service boxes.

Δ **32-306 Disconnecting means and overcurrent protection** (see Appendices B and G)

1) No device capable of interrupting the fire pump circuit, other than a circuit breaker labelled in a conspicuous, legible, and permanent manner identifying it as the fire pump disconnecting means, shall be placed between

   a) the service box from the normal power supply and a fire pump controller; or

   b) the main circuit breaker of the emergency generator and a fire pump transfer switch.

2) The circuit breaker referred to in Subrule 1) shall be lockable in the closed position.

3) The circuit breaker referred to in Subrule 1) shall be permitted to be used in the separate service box described in Rule 32-304.

4) The overcurrent protective device of the circuit breaker described in Subrule 1) a) shall be set or rated to carry indefinitely the locked rotor current of the fire pump.

5) The overcurrent protective device of the circuit breaker described in Subrule 1) b) shall be set or rated at a value not less than the overcurrent protection provided integral with the fire pump transfer switch.

6) Notwithstanding Subrule 1) b), where the circuit breaker is installed in an emergency supply feeder between the emergency generator and the fire pump transfer switch, the feeder shall be permitted to bypass the generator main circuit breaker and be connected directly to the emergency generator.

32-308 Transfer switch (see Appendix G)

1) Where an on-site electrical transfer switch is used to provide emergency power supply to fire pump equipment, such a transfer switch shall be

   a) provided solely for the fire pump;

   b) located in a barriered compartment of the fire pump controller, or in a separate enclosure adjacent to the controller;

   c) labelled in a conspicuous, legible, and permanent manner identifying it as the fire pump power transfer switch; and

   d) approved for fire pump service.

2) Where more than one fire pump is provided with emergency power as described in Subrule 1), a separate transfer switch shall be provided for each fire pump.

32

32-310 Overload and overheating protection (see Appendix G)

The branch circuit conductors and control conductors or equipment of a fire pump shall not require overload or overheating protection and shall be permitted to be protected by the motor branch circuit overcurrent device(s).

32-312 Ground fault protection (see Appendices B and G)

Ground fault protection shall not be installed in a fire pump circuit.

Section 34 — Signs and outline lighting

34-000 Scope
1) This Section applies to signs and outline lighting in which the sources of light are
   a) incandescent lamps;
   b) fluorescent lamps;
   c) high-voltage luminous discharge tubes, commonly known as cold-cathode or neon tubes;
   d) high-intensity discharge lamps; and
   e) other light-emitting sources, such as LEDs.
2) This Section supplements or amends the general requirements of this Code.

34-002 Special terminology
In this Section, the following definitions shall apply:

Δ **GTO sleeving** — a flexible polymeric sleeve intended to enclose luminous tube sign GTO cable operating at not more than 7500 volts-to-ground and intended to be installed within a raceway.

Neon supply — a transformer or electronic power supply intended to operate high-voltage luminous discharge tubing.

Sign — an assembly consisting of electrical parts designed to attract attention by illumination, animation, or other electrical means, singly or in combination.

General requirements

34-100 Disconnecting means
1) Each sign and outline lighting system installation, other than the portable type, shall be provided with a disconnecting means that shall
   a) open all ungrounded conductors;
   b) be suitable for conditions of installation such as exposure to weather; and
   c) be integral with the sign or outline lighting, or be located within sight and within 9 m of the sign or outline lighting installation.
2) Notwithstanding Subrule 1) c), the disconnecting means shall be permitted to be located out of the line of sight or more than 9 m from the sign, provided that the disconnecting means is capable of being locked in the open position.

Δ ### 34-102 Rating of disconnecting means and control devices
Switches, flashers, and similar devices controlling neon supplies, transformers, and ballasts shall be either designed for the purpose or have a current rating not less than twice the current rating of the neon supply, transformer, or ballasts.

34-104 Thermal protection
Ballasts of the thermally protected type shall be required for all signs and outline lighting that employ fluorescent lamps, except where the ballasts are of the simple reactance type.

34-106 Location
1) Signs and outline lighting systems shall be located so that
   a) any person working on them is not likely to come into contact with overhead conductors;
   b) no part of the sign or outline lighting or its support will interfere with normal work operations performed on electrical and communication utility lines as defined by the utility;
   c) no part of the sign or outline lighting or its support is in such proximity to overhead conductors as to constitute a hazard; and
   d) no part of the sign or outline lighting, other than its support, is less than 2.2 m above grade.

Δ 2) Notwithstanding Subrule 1) d), free-standing signs, indoor signs, and outline lighting, including installations in show windows and similar locations, shall be permitted to be mounted with electrical components less than 2.2 m above grade where mechanical protection is provided to prevent persons or vehicles from coming into contact with the electrical components of the sign.

Δ **34-108 Supporting means**
Poles, masts, standards, or devices designed as mechanical supports or used as electrical raceways shall be suitable.

34-110 Bonding
1) All conductive non-current-carrying parts of a sign or outline lighting installation, as well as non-electrical equipment to which the sign is mounted, shall be bonded to ground in accordance with the requirements of Section 10.
2) Notwithstanding the requirements of Subrule 1), bonding shall not be required for
   a) small metal parts not exceeding 50 mm in any direction, not likely to be energized, and spaced at least 19 mm from neon tubing;
   b) metal wire-ties used to secure neon tubing supports; and
   c) subassemblies of sign or outline lighting systems supplied by a remote Class 2 power supply with an output not exceeding 30 V.

34-112 Protection of sign leads
Sign leads that pass through the surfaces or partitions of the sign structure shall be protected by non-combustible moisture-absorption-resisting bushings.

Δ **34-114 Fuseholders and flashers**
Fuseholders, flashers, etc., shall form part of an assembly or be enclosed in a suitable electrical enclosure, and shall be accessible without the necessity of removing obstructions or otherwise dismantling the sign.

Enclosures

Δ **34-200 Enclosures** (see Appendix B)
Neon supplies, switches, timers, relays, sequencing units, and other similar devices shall form part of an assembly or be enclosed in a suitable electrical enclosure.

34-202 Protection of uninsulated parts
Doors or covers accessible to unauthorized persons that give access to uninsulated parts of signs or outline lighting shall be either provided with interlock switches that, on the opening of the doors or covers, disconnect the primary circuit, or shall be fastened so that the use of other than ordinary tools will be necessary to open them.

Neon supplies

34-300 Maximum secondary voltage for neon supplies
The rated secondary open-circuit voltage of a neon supply shall not exceed 15 000 V and shall not exceed 7500 volts-to-ground.

34-302 Secondary-circuit ground fault protection
Neon supplies other than the following types shall have secondary-circuit ground fault protection:
a) transformers with isolated secondaries and with a maximum open-circuit voltage of 6000 V or less between any combination of leads or terminals; and

b) transformers with integral porcelain or glass secondary housing for neon tubing and requiring no field wiring of the secondary circuit.

34-304 Open-type neon supplies
Open-type neon supplies, such as a core-and-coil type transformer, shall be used only in dry locations.

34-306 Neon supplies for damp or wet locations
1) Neon supplies used in damp locations shall be the damp or wet type.
2) Neon supplies used in wet locations shall be the wet type.
3) Neon supplies installed in a sign body, sign enclosure, or separate enclosure shall be the damp or wet type.
4) Neon supplies installed in a location where protected from direct exposure to water and the weather by a building structure shall be the damp or wet type.

34-308 Neon supply installation
1) Neon supplies shall be installed in locations such that they are accessible and capable of being removed and replaced.
2) Where that location is in an attic, bulkhead, or similar locations, there shall be an access door not less than 900 mm × 600 mm and a passageway not less than 900 mm high by 600 mm wide, with a suitable permanent walkway not less than 300 mm wide extending from the point of entry to each component.
3) Neon supplies shall be rigidly secured to the enclosure in which they are housed in a manner to prevent rotation, and the enclosure shall be rigidly secured to structural members.

34-310 Neon supply overcurrent protection
1) Each neon supply shall be protected by an overcurrent device, rated at a maximum of 30 A, except that two or more neon supplies shall be permitted to be protected by one overcurrent device, provided that the load does not exceed that prescribed by Rule 8-104.
2) Where additional overcurrent devices for the individual protection of neon supplies in signs are used, they shall be permitted to be placed either inside or outside the sign structure.
3) Where exposed to the weather, overcurrent devices protecting neon supplies shall be of the weatherproof type.

34-312 High-voltage output connection
The high-voltage outputs of neon supplies shall not be connected in parallel nor in series with the output of any other neon supply.

Wiring methods

34-400 High-voltage wiring methods
1) High-voltage cables shall be installed in
   a) neon supply enclosures;
   b) sign enclosures;
   c) flexible metal conduit 16 trade size or larger;
   d) flexible non-metallic conduit;
   e) rigid conduit; or
   f) except for surface raceways and electrical non-metallic tubing, all other types of raceways.
Δ 2) Notwithstanding Rule 12-1302 3) c), high-voltage cables shall be permitted to be installed in liquid-tight flexible conduit 16 or larger trade size with compatible connectors in the lengths required but not exceeding that permitted by Rule 34-404.
3) In a midpoint-return connected sign, the cables from the ends of gas-tubes to the neon supply's midpoint-return shall be high-voltage cables rated for the maximum voltage in the output circuit.

4) There shall be no sharp bends in high-voltage cables and the bends shall have radii no less than specified in Table 15.

5) Where high-voltage cables are installed in non-metallic conduit, the separation of the conduit from conducting or combustible material shall be
   a) at least 38 mm for installations operating at 100 Hz or less; or
   b) at least 44 mm for installations operating at more than 100 Hz.

6) Notwithstanding Subrule 1), where cable used for high-voltage wiring of signs and outline lighting is exposed, the cable shall be
   a) run inside GTO sleeving to a point at least 50 mm inside the raceway (where a raceway is provided);
   b) spaced at least 38 mm from conducting or combustible material for installations operating at 100 Hz or less or at least 44 mm for installations operating at more than 100 Hz; and
   c) not greater than 300 mm in length.

7) Secondary wiring for field wired signs and outline lighting shall be a minimum of No. 18 AWG.

8) Only one high-voltage cable shall be installed in a conduit.

9) Where high-voltage cable enters or leaves conduit in a damp or wet location, the penetration shall be made watertight.

34-402 High-voltage cables in show windows and similar locations

Where high-voltage cables used with signs hang freely in the air and are not enclosed in raceways, as in show windows and similar locations, they shall

Δ a) be enclosed in GTO sleeving;
   b) have a separation of at least 38 mm from combustible and conducting material;
   c) be located so that they are not susceptible to mechanical damage; and
   d) not be used to support any part of the sign.

34-404 Length of high-voltage cable from neon supplies

1) The length of high-voltage cable from the high-voltage terminal of a neon supply to the first neon tube shall be
   a) not more than 6 m when the cable is installed in metal raceway; and
   b) not more than 16 m when the cable is installed in non-metallic raceway.

2) All other sections of high-voltage cable in a neon tubing circuit shall be as short as practicable.

Δ 34-406 Connections of high-voltage cables

Connections of high-voltage cables to neon tubing shall be inaccessible to unauthorized persons and made by means of

a) an electrode receptacle; or
b) a connection to the neon tube in a suitable enclosure, provided that
   i) the insulation of all cables extends not less than 100 mm beyond the raceway for damp or wet locations; or
   ii) the insulation of all cables extends not less than 65 mm beyond the raceway for dry locations.

34-408 Bonding of metal electrode assembly housing and metal parts

1) Flexible metal conduit and liquid-tight flexible metal conduit used to enclose the high-voltage cable between an electrode receptacle assembly and a neon supply or between one electrode receptacle assembly and another shall be permitted to serve as the bonding means for the metal electrode receptacle assembly, provided that the conduit terminates in a connector suitable for ensuring a secure bonding connection.

2) Where non-metallic conduit is used to enclose high-voltage cables, the bonding conductor required to bond metal electrode receptacle assemblies, metal parts of a sign, or other metal to which the sign is mounted shall be

    a)   installed exterior to the non-metallic conduit

        i)   at least 38 mm from the conduit, for installations operating at 100 Hz or less; or

        ii)   at least 44 mm from the conduit, for installations operating at more than 100 Hz; and

    b)   not smaller than No. 12 AWG.

Section 36 — High-voltage installations

General

36-000 Scope (see Appendix B)

1) This Section applies to installations operating at voltages in excess of 750 V.

2) The supply authority and the inspection department must be consulted before proceeding with any such installation.

3) This Section supplements or amends the applicable general requirements of this Code for installations operating at voltages of 750 V or less.

4) This Section does not affect construction details of factory-fabricated assemblies approved under the *Canadian Electrical Code, Part II*.

36-002 Special terminology

In this Section, the following definitions shall apply:

Boundary fence — a fence forming the boundary of a property or area, but not part of a station fence enclosure.

Ground grid conductor — the horizontally buried conductor used for interconnecting ground rods or similar equipment that forms the station ground electrode.

Maximum ground fault current — the magnitude of the greatest fault current that could flow between the grounding grid and the surrounding earth during the life of the installation.

Potential rise of ground grid — the product of the ground grid resistance and the maximum ground fault current that flows between the station ground grid and the remote earth.

Station — an assemblage of equipment at one place, including any necessary housing, for the conversion or transformation of electrical energy and for connection between two or more circuits.

Step voltage — the potential difference between two points on the earth's surface separated by a distance of one pace, assumed to be 1 m, in the direction of maximum voltage gradient.

Touch voltage — the potential difference between a grounded metal structure and a point on the earth's surface separated by a distance equal to normal maximum horizontal reach.

36-004 Guarding

Live parts of electrical equipment shall be accessible to authorized persons only.

36-006 Warning notices (see Appendices B and M)

Δ 1) A permanent, legible warning notice carrying the wording "DANGER — HIGH VOLTAGE" or "DANGER...V" shall be placed in a conspicuous position

a) at vaults, service rooms, areas, or enclosures containing electrical equipment;

b) on all high-voltage conduits and cables at points of access to the bare or insulated conductors;

c) on all cable trays containing high-voltage insulated conductors or cables, with the maximum spacing of warning notices not to exceed 10 m;

d) on exposed portions of all high-voltage cables at a spacing not to exceed 10 m; and

e) on a station fence required by Rule 26-010

    i) located immediately adjacent to the locks on all access gates;

    ii) installed at all outside corners formed by the fence perimeter; and

    iii) installed at intervals not exceeding 15 m of horizontal distance.

2) Permanent, legible signs shall be installed at isolating equipment and shall warn against operating that equipment while it is carrying current, unless the equipment is interlocked so that it cannot be operated under load.

3) Suitable warning signs shall be erected in a conspicuous place adjacent to fuses and shall warn operators not to replace fuses while the supply circuit is energized.

4) Where the possibility of feedback exists,
   a) each group-operated isolating switch or disconnecting means shall bear a warning notice to the effect that contacts on either side of the device may be energized; and
   b) a permanent, legible, single-line diagram of the station switching arrangement, clearly identifying each point of connection to the high-voltage section, shall be provided in a conspicuous location within sight of each point of connection.

5) Where metal enclosed switchgear is installed,
   a) a permanent, legible, single-line diagram of the switchgear shall be provided in a conspicuous location within sight of the switchgear, and this diagram shall clearly identify interlocks, isolation means, and all possible sources of voltage to the installation under normal or emergency conditions, including all equipment contained in each cubicle, and the marking on the switchgear shall cross-reference the diagram;
   b) permanent, legible signs shall be installed on panels or doors that give access to live parts, warning of the danger of opening them while the parts are energized;
   c) where the panel gives access only to parts that can be de-energized and visibly isolated by the supply authority, the warning shall add that access is limited to the supply authority or following an authorization of the supply authority; and
   d) notwithstanding Item a), where the equipment consists solely of a single cubicle or metal-enclosed unit substation containing only one set of high-voltage switching devices, diagrams shall not be required.

Wiring methods

36-100 Conductors (see Appendix B)
1) Bare conductors or insulated conductors not enclosed in grounded metal shall be used only
   a) outdoors;
   b) in electrical equipment vaults constructed in accordance with Rules 26-350 to 26-356;
   c) in cable trays in accordance with Subrule 2) e); or
   Δ d) in service rooms accessible only to authorized persons.

2) Except as permitted in Subrule 1) b), c), and d), insulated conductors or cables used indoors or attached to buildings outdoors shall be
   a) installed in metal conduit;
   b) installed in electrical metallic tubing;
   Δ c) installed as metal-enclosed busways;
   d) cables with a continuous metal sheath, steel wire armour, or of the interlocking armour type; or
   e) Type TC tray cable installed in cable tray in accordance with Rule 12-2202.

3) High-voltage Type TC cables shall not be installed in the same cable tray with low-voltage conductors, except where the high-voltage TC cables are separated from the low-voltage conductors by a barrier of sheet metal not less than 1.34 mm thick (No. 16 MSG).

4) The location of insulated conductors or cables encased or embedded in concrete or masonry shall be indicated by permanent markers set in the walls, floors, or ceilings at intervals of not more than 3 m.

5) Where the coverings are of a conductive nature, they shall be stripped back from the terminals sufficiently to prevent leakage of current.

6) Service conductors shall have a mechanical strength not less than that of No. 6 AWG hard drawn copper.

36-102 Radii of bends

The minimum bending radii measured at the innermost surface of the bend for permanent training of cables during installation shall be as shown in Table 15.

36-104 Shielding of thermoset insulated conductors (see Appendix B)

1) Except as permitted in Subrules 2), 3), and 4), shielding shall be provided over the thermoset insulation of each permanently installed conductor with or without a fibrous covering or non-metallic jacket, operating at circuit voltages above 2000 V phase-to-phase.

2) Shielding need not be provided for conductors having thermoset insulation where they are run underground in raceways or directly buried in the soil and operating at circuit voltages not exceeding 3000 V phase-to-phase, provided that the insulation or the non-metallic jacket, if provided, is of the ozone- and discharge-resistant type.

Δ 3) Shielding need not be provided for conductors having thermoset insulation where the circuit voltage does not exceed 5000 V phase-to-phase, where the conductors are installed on insulators and bound together, in service rooms, electrical equipment vaults, metal-enclosed switchgear assemblies, and similar permanently dry locations where the conductor run does not exceed 15 m.

4) Shielding need not be provided for conductors having thermoset insulation that are
   a) intended for operation at not more than 5000 V phase-to-phase;
   b) intended and installed for permanent duty; and
   c) provided in either single- or multi-conductor cable construction with
      i) a metal sheath;
      ii) metal armour of the interlocking type, the wire type, or the flat-tape type; or
      iii) totally enclosed metal raceways where installed above ground in dry locations.

5) Subject to Rule 10-606, metal sheaths, shielding, armour, conduit, and fittings shall be bonded together and connected to ground.

36-106 Supporting of exposed conductors

Bare conductors and insulated conductors, unless enclosed in or in contact with grounded metal, shall be mounted on suitable insulating supports capable of withstanding the short-circuit stresses liable to be imposed by the supply system.

36-108 Spacing of exposed conductors

1) Bare conductors, insulated conductors, and other bare live parts, unless enclosed in or in contact with grounded metal, other than those within or at the point of connection to apparatus or devices, shall be spaced to provide a clearance under all operating conditions, in accordance with Tables 30 and 31, between
   a) live parts of opposite polarity; and
   b) live parts and all other structural parts other than the conductor supports.

2) Where the conductors mentioned in Subrule 1) are connected to apparatus or devices having terminal spaces less than those shown in Tables 30 and 31, the conductors shall be spread out to attain the required spacings at the first point of support beyond such terminals.

36-110 Guarding of live parts and exposed conductors

1) Bare conductors, insulated conductors unless enclosed in or in contact with grounded metal, and other bare live parts shall be
   a) accessible only to authorized persons; and
   b) isolated by elevation or by barriers.

2) Where the conductors or live parts mentioned in Subrule 1) are isolated by elevation, the elevations and clearances maintained shall be as specified in Tables 32, 33, and 34, except that

   a) for voltages in excess of those specified in Tables 32, 33, and 34, the elevations and clearances maintained shall be in accordance with the requirements of CSA C22.3 No. 1; and

   b) for conductors crossing highways, railways, communication lines, and other locations not covered in this Code, the elevations and clearances maintained shall be in accordance with the requirements of CSA C22.3 No. 1 or the applicable standard, whichever are greater.

3) For a given span, the clearances specified in Table 34 shall be increased by 1% of the amount by which the span exceeds 50 m.

36-112 Terminating facilities
Suitable terminating facilities shall be provided to protect cables from harm due to moisture or mechanical damage.

36-114 Joints in sheathed cables
1) Splices or taps in sheathed cables shall have the conductor or cable covered with insulation and shall have shielding, when used, electrically and mechanically equivalent to that on the conductors or cables joined.

2) For cables having a metal or conducting sheath, provision shall be made for continuity of the sheath over the splice or tap, unless the joint is made in a suitable splicing box that maintains the continuity of the bonding path.

36-116 Elevator shafts
1) High-voltage insulated conductors or cables shall not be installed in elevator shafts.

2) The insulated conductors or cables shall be permitted to be installed in conduit embedded in the masonry walls of the hoistway, but the conduit shall be surrounded throughout the entire length of its run by not less than 50 mm of masonry or concrete.

Δ ### 36-118 Conductors over buildings
Conductors shall not be installed over buildings.

Control and protective equipment

36-200 Service equipment location
Service equipment shall be installed in a location that complies with the requirements of the supply authority and, in the case of a building, shall be at the point of service entrance.

36-202 Rating and capacity
The type and ratings of circuit breakers, fuses, and switches, including the trip settings of circuit breakers and the interrupting capacity of overcurrent devices, shall be

a) in compliance with Rule 14-012 a) and b);

b) in compliance with the requirements of the supply authority for consumer's service equipment; and

c) sized in accordance with the appropriate Rules of this Code for transformers, capacitors, motors, and other electrical equipment.

36-204 Overcurrent protection
1) Each consumer's service, operating unit of apparatus, feeder, and branch circuit shall be provided with overcurrent protection having adequate rating and interrupting capacity in all ungrounded conductors by one of the following:

   a) a circuit breaker;

b) fuses preceded by a group-operated visible break load-interrupting device capable of making and interrupting its full load rating and that may be closed with safety to the operator with a fault on the system; or

c) fuses preceded by a group-operated visible break air-break switch that is capable of interrupting the magnetizing current of the transformer installation, that may be closed with safety to the operator with a fault on the system, and that, to prevent its operation under load, is interlocked with the transformer's secondary load interrupting device.

2) Fuses shall be accessible to authorized persons only.

36-206 Indoor installation of circuit breakers, switches, and fuses

1) Circuit breakers, switches, and fuses installed indoors shall be of an enclosed type unless installed in a room of non-combustible construction.

Δ 2) In addition to the requirements of Subrule 1), dielectric liquid-filled equipment located indoors shall be installed in accordance with Rule 26-012.

36-208 Interlocking of fuse compartments

Compartments containing fuses shall have the cover (or door) interlocked with the isolating or disconnecting means so that

a) there is no access to the fuses unless the isolating or disconnecting means immediately ahead of the fuses is in the de-energized position; and

b) the switch cannot be placed in the closed position until the fuse compartment has been closed.

36-210 Protection and control of instrument transformers

1) Instrument voltage transformers shall have overcurrent protection as required by Rule 26-260.

2) A suitable disconnecting means shall be provided on the supply side of fuses used for the protection of instrument voltage transformers.

36-212 Outdoor installations

1) High-voltage switches not of the metal-enclosed type that are assembled in the field shall be spaced according to Table 35.

2) Horn-gap switches shall be mounted in a horizontal position and be capable of being locked in the open position.

3) High-voltage fuses shall be spaced according to Table 35.

36-214 Disconnecting means

1) Where insulated conductors or cables fed from a station enter a building, either

a) a load-breaking device shall be installed indoors at the entry of the insulated conductors or cables to the building; or

b) a load-breaking device at the supply station shall be capable of being tripped or operated from within the building.

2) Unless of the draw-out type, each circuit breaker and each load-break switch having contacts that are not visible for inspection in the open position shall be provided with a group-operated isolating switch on the supply side that shall be

a) provided with the means for adequate visible inspection of all contacts in both the open and closed position;

b) interlocked so that it cannot be operated under load; and

c) provided with positive position indicators.

3) Where more than one source of voltage exists in a station consisting of two or more interconnected sections operating at high voltage or where there is another possibility of feedback, a visible point of connection meeting the requirements of Subrule 2) shall be provided in all circuits where the possibility of feedback between sections exists.

Grounding and bonding

36-300 Material and minimum size of grounding conductors and ground grid conductors and connections (see Appendix B)

1) Except as provided for in Subrule 2), bare copper conductors shall be used for grounding purposes and shall be not smaller than those specified in Rules 36-302 to 36-310 and Table 51.

2) Notwithstanding the requirement of Subrule 1), a conductor other than copper shall be permitted for grounding purposes, provided that

   a) its current-carrying rating is equal to or greater than that of the copper conductor specified in Rules 36-302 to 36-310;

   b) consideration is given to galvanic action if such conductors are buried in the ground or come in contact with dissimilar metals; and

   c) the method of bolting or connecting such conductors to each other and to other surfaces is such as to maintain the required current-carrying capacity for the life of the electrode design.

36-302 Station ground electrode (see Appendix B)

1) Every outdoor station shall be grounded by means of a station ground electrode that shall meet the requirements of Rule 36-304 and shall

   a) consist of a minimum of four driven ground rods spaced at least the rod length apart and, where practicable, located adjacent to the equipment to be grounded;

   b) have the ground rods interconnected by ground grid conductors not less than No. 2/0 AWG bare copper buried to a maximum depth of 600 mm below the rough station grade and a minimum depth of 150 mm below the finished station grade; and

   c) have the station ground grid conductors specified in Item b) connected to all non-current-carrying metal parts of equipment and structures, and forming a loop around the equipment to be grounded, except that

      i) a portion of the loop shall be permitted to be omitted where an obstacle such as a wall prevents a person from standing on the corresponding side or sides of the equipment; and

      ii) loops formed by the rebar in a reinforced concrete slab shall be considered adequate when the rebar members are interconnected and reliably connected to all other parts of the station ground electrode.

2) Where a deviation has been allowed in accordance with Rule 2-030, a buried station ground electrode other than that described in Subrule 1) shall be permitted to be used.

3) Where it is not practicable to locate the station ground electrode adjacent to the station as described in Subrule 1) a), a station ground electrode that conforms to Subrule 1) a) and b) shall be permitted to be remote from the station, and

   a) two grounding conductors of a minimum of No. 2/0 AWG copper shall connect the ground electrode to the station equipment in such a way that should one grounding conductor or ground electrode be damaged, no single metal structure or equipment frame may become isolated; and

   b) in locations with system short-circuit currents exceeding 30 000 A, the grounding conductor wire size shall be increased and shall be such that it will not suffer thermal damage or be a fire hazard under the severest fault conditions occurring on the system.

4) Every indoor station shall be grounded by means of a station ground electrode

   a) in accordance with Subrule 1), 2), or 3); or

   b) if it is not practicable to ground an indoor station in accordance with Subrule 1), 2), or 3) and the indoor station receives its supply from a main station on the same property, the station equipment shall be connected to the main station ground electrode in accordance with Subrule 3).

5) All parts of the indoor station that are required to be grounded shall be connected together by copper conductors of not less than No. 2/0 AWG.

6) The reinforcing steel members to be found in building foundations and concrete platforms shall be permitted to be included as part of the station ground electrode design, provided that

   a) no insulating film separates the concrete from the surrounding soil;

   b) the maximum expected fault current magnitude and duration will not result in thermal damage to the steel members or the concrete structure;

   c) the steel members are connected to the rest of the station ground electrode with not less than two copper conductors of not less than No. 2/0 AWG in such a way that, should one grounding conductor or ground electrode be damaged, no single metal structure or equipment frame can become isolated; and

   d) the ground electrode design is based on the assumption that the concrete resistivity is greater than or equal to that of the surrounding soil.

36-304 Station ground resistance (see Appendix B)

1) The maximum permissible resistance of the station ground electrode shall be determined by the maximum available ground fault current injected into the ground by the station ground electrode or by the maximum fault current in the station, and the ground resistance shall be such that under all soil conditions that exist in practice (e.g., wet, dry, and frozen conditions), the maximum ground fault current conditions shall limit the potential rise of all parts of the station ground grid to 5000 V; however in special circumstances where this level cannot be reasonably achieved, a higher voltage up to the maximum insulation level of the communication equipment shall be permitted where a deviation has been allowed in accordance with Rule 2-030.

2) In addition to the requirements of Subrule 1), the touch and step voltage at the edge, within, and around the station grounding electrode, including all areas in which metallic structures electrically connected to the station are to be found, shall not exceed the tolerable values specified in Table 52.

3) When a station ground electrode design is selected according to the procedure specified in the Note to this Subrule in Appendix B and when it is proven that the station parameters used in the procedure are valid, this electrode design shall be deemed to meet the requirements of Subrules 1) and 2).

4) After completion of construction, the resistance of the station ground electrode at each station shall be measured, and changes shall be made if necessary to verify and ensure that the maximum permissible resistance of Subrule 1) is not exceeded.

5) Where the safety of persons depends on the integral presence of a ground surface covering layer, such as crushed rock or asphalt, the ground surface covering layer shall exist throughout the station grounding electrode area, including all areas in which metallic structures electrically connected to the station are to be found, and shall extend at least 1 m beyond the station grounding electrode area on all sides.

36-306 Station exemption

Where the phase-to-phase voltage is less than or equal to 7500 V and a ground surface covering layer with a minimum thickness of 150 mm is installed and maintained as specified in Rule 36-304 5) and it can be demonstrated that the potential rise (GPR) of a station shall not exceed the tolerable touch and step voltages specified in Table 52 during the lifetime of the station, the following exemptions shall apply:

a) no soil resistivity measurements need be made at the station site;

b) notwithstanding Rule 36-304 2), no analysis shall be required to prove that touch and step voltages within the station grounding electrode area will not exceed tolerable values; and

c) notwithstanding Rule 36-304 4), neither the resistance of the station ground electrode nor the touch voltage near the centre or corner of the ground electrode need be measured after completion of construction.

36-308 Connections to the station ground electrode (see Appendix B)

1) All non-current-carrying metal equipment and structures forming part of the station shall be grounded to the station ground electrode to prevent the buildup of dangerous potential differences between the equipment or structures and the nearby earth.

2) All metal items forming part of the station shall be connected to the station ground electrode as follows:

   a) metal structures:

      i) single columns or pedestal-type (pipe, etc.) structures shall be grounded by a grounding conductor not less than No. 2/0 AWG copper; and

      ii) single and multi-bay structures shall be bonded to ground at each column by a bonding conductor not less than No. 2/0 AWG copper;

   b) apparatus mounted on metallic or non-metallic structures:

      i) tanks or frames of transformers, generators, motors, circuit breakers, reclosers, instrument transformers, switchgear, and other equipment shall be grounded by grounding conductors of not less than No. 2/0 AWG copper;

      ii) metal bases of all gang-operated switches shall be grounded by a grounding conductor of not less than No. 2/0 AWG copper (for switch handles, see Rule 36-310); and

      iii) the grounding of metal bases of single-pole fuse cut-outs and isolating switches on wood structures shall be optional;

   c) lightning arresters:

      i) the lightning arresters shall be connected to the station ground electrode by a conductor of not less than No. 2/0 AWG copper;

      ii) lightning arrester grounding conductors shall be as short, straight, and direct as practicable; and

      iii) where lightning arresters are for the protection of high-voltage cable and cable sheath, the lightning arrester grounding conductor shall be connected to metal potheads and/or the metal sheath, armour, or shielding of all cables;

   d) a metal water main inside or adjacent to the station ground electrode area shall be grounded by at least one copper conductor of not less than No. 2/0 AWG copper, at intervals not exceeding 12 m;

   e) the non-current-carrying parts of metal equipment, such as

      i) cable sheaths, cable armour, shield, ground wires, potheads, raceways, pipe work, screen guards, and switchboards, shall be grounded by a copper conductor of not less than No. 4 AWG;

      ii) meter, instrument, and relay cases, when mounted on insulated panels, shall be grounded by a copper conductor of not less than No. 10 AWG; and

      iii) the metal frame and all exposed metal work on buildings within or forming part of the station, shall be grounded to the station ground electrode by a minimum of No. 2/0 AWG copper in at least two places and at intervals not exceeding 12 m along the building perimeter; and

   f) steel rails of railway spur tracks entering an outdoor station ground electrode area shall be connected by a copper conductor of not less than No. 2/0 AWG, with the part of the spur track located outside the station ground electrode area properly isolated from the station ground electrode or grounded, or both, in order that touch voltages along the track not exceed the tolerable values specified in Table 52.

3) Where it is proven that touch and step potentials around a building will not exceed the tolerable values specified in Table 52, no loop need be installed around the building.

4) A transmission line overhead ground wire shall be connected to the station ground electrode with a grounding conductor of not less than No. 2/0 AWG copper that, notwithstanding Rule 36-300 1), shall be permitted to be insulated.

5) A line neutral conductor on grounded neutral systems shall be connected to the station ground electrode by a grounding conductor having an ampacity not less than the neutral conductor.

6) A transformer neutral on solidly grounded neutral systems shall be connected to the station ground electrode by a copper conductor sized as follows:

    a) conductors for grounding primary and secondary neutrals shall be not less than No. 2/0 AWG and have sufficient ampacity to carry the maximum ground fault current of the transformer in accordance with Table 51, and this grounding conductor shall be in addition to the requirement of Subrule 2) b) i); and

    b) notwithstanding Item a), conductors for grounding low-voltage secondary neutrals shall be sized in accordance with Section 10, provided that the size selected is suitable for the maximum ground fault current on the transformer secondary.

7) Connections to the items referred to in Subrules 2) d), 4), and 5) shall be made through removable connectors that will permit isolation from the station ground electrode for the purpose of station ground grid resistance measurement.

36-310 Gang-operated switch handle grounds

1) The operating handle of all gang-operated switches not enclosed in metal housings shall be grounded by one of the following methods:

    a) a multi-revolution grounding device shall be connected to the station ground electrode by a conductor having a current-carrying capacity of not less than No. 2/0 AWG copper; or

    b) the operating shaft shall be grounded to the station ground electrode by a combination of extra-flexible conductor, braid, and/or stranded conductor of not less than No. 2/0 AWG copper.

2) In addition to the requirements of Subrule 1), the touch voltage shall be maintained at a tolerable level as specified in Table 52 at the location where the operator is normally standing, as follows:

    a) by the use of a metallic gradient control mat connected to the operating handle grounding conductor as required in Subrule 1) by two separate conductors, each not less than No. 2/0 AWG copper; and

    b) the gradient control mat shall

        i) be positioned so that the operator will not be required to step from the mat during the operation of the switch;

        ii) be placed on a minimum of 150 mm of crushed stone on the ground;

        iii) have dimensions approximately 1.2 m × 1.8 m; and

        iv) be permitted to be covered by a layer of crushed stone, asphalt, or concrete not exceeding 150 mm in depth.

36-312 Grounding of metallic fence enclosures of outdoor stations

1) The fence shall be located at least 1 m inside the perimeter of the station ground electrode area.

2) The station ground electrode shall be connected to the fence by a tap conductor at each end post, corner post, and gate post, and at intermediate posts at intervals not exceeding 12 m by a conductor of not less than No. 2/0 AWG copper.

3) The tap conductor at each hinge gate post shall be clamped or bonded to the gate frame by a copper braid or a flexible copper conductor of at least No. 2/0 AWG.

4) The tap conductor shall be connected to the fence post, the bottom tension wire, the fence fabric (for which the conductor may be woven in at least two places), the top rail, and each strand of

barbed wire, with the connection to the bottom tension wire, the fence fabric, and barbed wire strands made with bolted or equivalent connectors, and with the top rail connections bonded at every joint by a jumper equivalent to No. 2/0 AWG copper.

5) When there is a metal boundary fence in proximity to the station fence, the touch voltages within 1 m of all parts of the boundary fence shall not exceed the tolerable values specified in Table 52.

C22.1-18

Section 38
Elevators, dumbwaiters, material lifts, escalators, moving walks, lifts for persons with physical disabilities, and similar equipment

Section 38 — Elevators, dumbwaiters, material lifts, escalators, moving walks, lifts for persons with physical disabilities, and similar equipment

38-001 Scope (see Appendix B)
This Section applies to the installation of electrical equipment and wiring for elevators, dumbwaiters, material lifts, escalators, moving walks, lifts for persons with physical disabilities, and similar equipment, and supplements or amends the general requirements of this Code.

38-002 Special terminology (see Appendix B)
In this Section, the following definitions shall apply:

Motor controller — the operative units of the control system comprising the starter device(s) and power conversion equipment used to drive an electric motor, or the pumping unit used to power hydraulic control equipment.

Operating device — the car switch, push buttons, key or toggle switch(es), or other devices used to activate the controller.

Signal equipment — audible and visual equipment such as chimes, gongs, lights, and displays that convey information to the user.

38-003 Voltage limitations (see Appendix B)
The circuit voltage shall not exceed 300 V unless otherwise permitted in Items a) to c):
a) branch circuits to door operator controllers and door motors, and branch circuits and feeders to motor controllers, driving machine motors, machine brakes, and motor-generator sets shall have a circuit voltage not in excess of 750 V;
b) branch lighting circuits shall comply with the requirements of Section 30; and
c) branch circuits for heating and air-conditioning equipment located on the car shall not have a circuit voltage in excess of 750 V.

38-004 Live parts enclosed
All live parts of electrical apparatus in hoistways, at the landings, or in or on the cars of elevators, dumbwaiters, material lifts, and lifts for persons with physical disabilities, or in the wellways or at the landings of escalators or moving walks, shall be enclosed to protect against accidental contact.

38-005 Working clearances
1) The minimum headroom in working spaces around controllers, disconnecting means, and other electrical equipment shall be 2000 mm.
2) The working space requirements of Subrule 1) and Rule 2-308 need not apply where conditions of maintenance and supervision ensure that only authorized persons have access to such areas, and where
   a) the equipment referred to in Items i) to iv) is equipped with flexible cables to all external connections to allow its repositioning for compliance with the working space requirements of Rule 2-308:
      i) controllers and disconnecting means for dumbwaiters, escalators, moving walks, material lifts, and lifts for persons with physical disabilities installed in the same space with the driving machine;
      ii) controllers and disconnecting means for elevators, installed in the hoistway or on the car;
      iii) controllers for door operators; and
      iv) other electrical equipment installed in the hoistway or on the car;

C22.1-18

Section 38
Elevators, dumbwaiters, material lifts, escalators, moving walks, lifts for persons with
physical disabilities, and similar equipment

b) live parts of the equipment are suitably guarded, isolated, or insulated, and the equipment can be examined, adjusted, serviced, or maintained while energized without removal of this protection;

c) electrical equipment is not required to be examined, adjusted, serviced, or maintained while energized; or

d) uninsulated parts are extra-low-voltage or do not exceed 60 V dc.

38-011 Insulation and types of conductors

1) Conductors in hoistways, in or on cars or platforms, in wellways, and in machine rooms shall be selected in accordance with Rules 12-102 3), 12-122 1), 12-402 1), and 12-406 1) as applicable and shall meet the requirements of Rule 2-130.

2) The conductors to the hoistway door interlocks from the hoistway riser shall meet the requirements of Rule 2-130.

3) The voltage rating of insulation of all conductors shall be suitable for the voltage to which the conductors are subjected and shall have an insulation voltage at least equal to the maximum nominal circuit voltage applied to any conductor within the enclosure, cable, or raceway.

4) Travelling cables used as flexible connections between the car or counterweight and the raceway shall be of the types of elevator cable selected in accordance with Rule 12-406 1) or other types approved for the purpose.

38-012 Minimum size of conductors

1) In travelling cables, the minimum size of conductors shall be
   a) for lighting circuits, No. 14 AWG copper, except that smaller conductors shall be permitted to be used in parallel provided that the ampacity is equivalent to at least that of No. 14 AWG copper; and
   b) for all operating, control, signal, and extra-low-voltage lighting circuits, No. 20 AWG copper.

2) Except as specified in Subrule 1), the minimum size of conductors for operating, control, signal, and communications circuits shall be No. 26 AWG copper.

38-013 Ampacity of feeder and branch circuit conductors (see Appendices B and G)

1) With generator field control, the conductor ampacity shall be based on the nameplate current rating of the driving motor of the motor-generator set that supplies power to the driving machine motor.

2) Conductors shall have an ampacity in accordance with Items a) to d):
   a) **Conductors supplying a single motor:** Conductors supplying a single motor shall have an ampacity not less than the percentage of motor nameplate current required by Rule 28-106 and Table 27.
   b) **Conductors supplying a single motor controller:** Conductors supplying a single motor controller shall have an ampacity not less than the motor controller nameplate current rating, plus all other connected loads.
   c) **Conductors supplying a single power transformer:** Conductors supplying a single power transformer shall have an ampacity not less than the nameplate current rating of the power transformer, plus all other connected loads.
   d) **Conductors supplying more than one motor, motor controller, or power transformer:** Conductors supplying more than one motor, motor controller, or power transformer shall have an ampacity not less than the sum of the nameplate current ratings of the equipment plus all other connected loads. The ampere ratings of motors to be used in the summation shall be determined as required by Rule 28-108 and Table 62.

38-014 Feeder demand factor

Feeder conductors of lower ampacity than that required by Rule 38-013 shall be permitted subject to the requirements of Table 62.

C22.1-18

Section 38
Elevators, dumbwaiters, material lifts, escalators, moving walks, lifts for persons with
physical disabilities, and similar equipment

38-015 Motor controller rating

The motor controller rating shall comply with Rule 28-500 1), except that the rating shall be permitted to be less than the nominal rating of the driving machine motor when the controller inherently limits the available power to the motor and is marked "power limited".

38-021 Wiring methods (see Appendix B)

Elevators

1) Unless otherwise permitted in Items a) to d), conductors and optical fibers located in hoistways, machinery spaces, control spaces, in or on cars, and in machine rooms and control rooms, not including travelling cables connecting the car or counterweight and hoistway wiring, shall be installed in rigid metal conduit, electrical metallic tubing, rigid PVC conduit, or wireways, except that mineral-insulated cable, aluminum-sheathed cable, copper-sheathed cable, or armoured cable shall be permitted if not subject to mechanical damage.

Hoistways

a) In hoistways the following wiring methods shall also be permitted if not subjected to mechanical damage:

 i) flexible metal conduit or liquid-tight flexible conduit shall be permitted in hoistways between risers and limit switches, interlocks, operating devices, or similar devices;

 ii) cables used in Class 1 extra-low-voltage and Class 2 low-energy circuits, including but not limited to hoistway cable, extra-low-voltage cable, extra-low-voltage control cable, communication cable, fire alarm and signal cable, multi-conductor jacketed thermoplastic-insulated cable, and hard-usage and extra-hard-usage cables shall be permitted to be installed between risers and signal equipment and operating devices, provided that the cables are supported and protected from physical damage and are of a jacketed and flame-tested type;

 iii) flexible cords and cables that are components of approved equipment and used in extra-low-voltage circuits (30 V or less) shall be permitted in lengths not exceeding 2 m, provided that the cords and cables are supported and protected from physical damage and are of a jacketed and flame-tested type; and

 iv) flexible metal conduit, liquid-tight flexible metal conduit, liquid-tight flexible non-metallic conduit, or flexible cords and cables, or conductors grouped together and taped or corded that are part of listed equipment, a driving machine, or a driving machine brake shall be permitted in the hoistway in lengths not exceeding 2 m without being installed in a raceway and where located to be protected from physical damage and if of a flame-tested type.

Cars

b) On cars, the following wiring methods shall also be permitted:

 i) flexible metal conduit or liquid-tight flexible conduit not exceeding 2 m in length shall be permitted on cars where located to be free from oil and if securely fastened in place;

 ii) extra-hard-usage and hard-usage cords selected in accordance with Rule 12-402 1) shall be permitted as flexible connections between the fixed wiring on the car and devices on the car doors or gates, and extra-hard-usage cords only shall be permitted as flexible connections for the top-of-car operating device or the car-top work light;

 iii) cables with smaller conductors and other types and thickness of insulation and jackets than extra-hard usage or hard usage, used as flexible connections between the fixed wiring on the car and devices on the car doors or gates, shall be permitted as flexible

C22.1-18

Section 38
Elevators, dumbwaiters, material lifts, escalators, moving walks, lifts for persons with
physical disabilities, and similar equipment

connections between the fixed wiring on the car and devices on the car doors or gates, if approved for extra-hard usage or hard usage;

iv) flexible cords and cables that are components of approved equipment and used in extra-low-voltage circuits (30 V or less) shall be permitted in lengths not exceeding 2 m, provided that the cords and cables are supported and protected from physical damage and are of a jacketed and flame-tested type; and

v) flexible metal conduit, liquid-tight flexible metal conduit, liquid-tight flexible non-metallic conduit, flexible cords and cables, conductors grouped together and taped or corded that are part of listed equipment, a driving machine, or a driving machine brake shall be permitted on the car assembly in lengths not to exceed 2 m without being installed in a raceway and where located to be protected from physical damage and if of a flame-tested type.

Within machine rooms, control rooms and machinery spaces, and control spaces

c) Within machine rooms, control rooms and machinery spaces, and control spaces, the following wiring methods shall also be permitted:

i) flexible metal conduit or liquid-tight flexible conduit shall be permitted between control panels and machine motors, machine brakes, motor-generator sets, disconnecting means, or pumping unit motors and valves;

ii) where motor-generators, machine motors, or pumping unit motors and valves are located adjacent to or underneath control equipment and are provided with extra-length terminal leads, such leads shall be permitted to be extended to connect directly to controller terminal studs without regard to the current-carrying capacity requirements of Section 28, provided that the conductors are

A) not over 2 m long;

B) bound together and supported at intervals not more than 1 m; and

C) not located where they would be subject to physical damage;

iii) auxiliary gutters shall be permitted in machine and control rooms between controllers, starters, and similar apparatus; and

iv) flexible cords and cables that are components of approved equipment and used in extra-low-voltage circuits (30 V or less) shall be permitted in lengths not to exceed 2 m, provided that the cords and cables are supported and protected from physical damage and are of a jacketed and flame-tested type.

Counterweights

d) Flexible metal conduit, liquid-tight flexible conduit, flexible cords and cables, or conductors grouped together and taped or corded that are part of approved equipment, a driving machine, or a driving machine brake shall be permitted on the counterweight assembly in lengths that do not exceed 2 m without being installed in a raceway if they are located to be protected from physical damage and are of a flame-tested type.

C22.1-18

Section 38
Elevators, dumbwaiters, material lifts, escalators, moving walks, lifts for persons with
physical disabilities, and similar equipment

38

Escalators

2) Conductors and optical fibers in escalator and moving walk wellways shall be installed in rigid metal conduit, flexible metal conduit, liquid-tight flexible conduit, electrical metallic tubing, rigid PVC conduit, or wireways or shall be mineral-insulated cable, aluminum-sheathed cable, copper-sheathed cable, or armoured cable, if not subject to physical damage, unless otherwise permitted in Items a) and b):

a) cables used in Class 1 extra-low-voltage and Class 2 low-energy circuits, including extra-low-voltage cable, extra-low-voltage control cable, communication cable, fire alarm and signal cable, multi-conductor jacketed thermoplastic-insulated cable, and hard-usage and extra-hard-usage cables shall be permitted to be installed between risers and signal equipment and operating devices, provided that the cables are supported and protected from physical damage and are of a jacketed and flame-tested type; and

b) flexible cords and cables that are components of approved equipment and used in extra-low-voltage circuits (30 V or less) shall be permitted in lengths not exceeding 2 m, provided that the cords and cables are supported and protected from physical damage and are of a jacketed and flame-tested type.

Lifts for persons with physical disabilities

3) Conductors and optical fibers located in hoistways, runways, and machinery spaces and in machine and control rooms of dumbwaiters, material lifts, and lifts for persons with physical disabilities shall be installed in rigid metal conduit, electrical metallic tubing, rigid PVC conduit, or wireways; or, if not subject to physical damage, shall be mineral-insulated cable, aluminum-sheathed cable, copper-sheathed cable, armoured cable, flexible metal conduit, or liquid-tight flexible conduit, unless otherwise permitted in Items a) and b):

a) cables used in Class 1 extra-low-voltage and Class 2 low-energy circuits, including but not limited to hoistway cable, extra-low-voltage cable, extra-low-voltage control cable, communication cable, fire alarm and signal cable, multi-conductor jacketed thermoplastic-insulated cable, and hard-usage and extra-hard-usage cables shall be permitted to be installed between risers and signal equipment and operating devices, provided that the cables are supported and protected from physical damage and are of a jacketed and flame-tested type; and

b) flexible cords and cables that are components of approved equipment and used in extra-low-voltage circuits (30 V or less) shall be permitted in lengths not exceeding 2 m, provided that the cords and cables are supported and protected from physical damage and are of a jacketed and flame-tested type.

38-022 Branch circuits for car lighting, receptacles, ventilation, accessories, heating, and air conditioning

1) At least one branch circuit shall be provided solely for the car lights, receptacles, auxiliary lighting power source, accessories, and ventilation on each car.

2) Where air-conditioning and heating units are installed on the car, they shall be supplied by separate branch circuits.

3) The overcurrent device protecting each branch circuit shall be located in the machine room or control room/machinery space or control space.

38-023 Branch circuits for machine room or control room/machinery space or control space lighting and receptacle(s) (see Appendix B)

1) A separate branch circuit shall supply the machine room or control room/machinery space or control space lighting and receptacle(s).

2) Required lighting shall not be connected to the load side terminals of a ground fault circuit interrupter.

C22.1-18

Section 38
Elevators, dumbwaiters, material lifts, escalators, moving walks, lifts for persons with
physical disabilities, and similar equipment

3) A machine room or control room/machinery space or control space lighting switch shall be provided and shall be within easy reach of the point of entry.

4) At least one 125 V, single-phase, duplex receptacle, connected to a 15 A branch circuit, having a configuration in accordance with Diagram 1, shall be provided in each machine room or control room and machinery space or control space.

38-024 Branch circuit for hoistway pit lighting and receptacles (see Appendix B)

1) A separate branch circuit shall supply the hoistway pit lighting and receptacles.

2) Required lighting shall not be connected to the load side terminals of a ground fault circuit interrupter receptacle(s).

3) A lighting switch shall be provided and shall be located so as to be readily accessible from the pit access door.

4) At least one 125 V, single-phase, duplex receptacle connected to a 15 A branch circuit shall be provided in the hoistway pit.

38-025 Branch circuits for other utilization equipment

1) Separate branch circuits shall supply other utilization equipment not identified in Rules 38-022, 38-023, and 38-024, but used in conjunction with equipment identified in Rule 38-001.

2) The overcurrent devices protecting the branch circuits shall be located in the machinery room or control room/machinery space or control space.

38-032 Metal wireways and non-metallic wireways
See Rule 12-910 and Table 8.

38-033 Number of conductors in raceways
See Rule 12-910.

38-034 Supports
Supports for cables or raceways in a hoistway or in an escalator or moving walk wellway or a hoistway or runway for a material lift or lift for persons with physical disabilities shall be securely fastened to the guide rail, escalator or moving walk truss, or to the hoistway, wellway, or runway construction.

38-035 Auxiliary gutters
See Rules 12-1900, 12-1902, and 12-1904.

38-036 Grouping of conductors
Optical fiber cables, shielded cables, and conductors for operating devices, power, motor, heating, air-conditioning, operating, control, signal, telephone, fire alarm, and lighting circuits shall be permitted to be run in the same raceway system or travelling cable, provided that all conductors are insulated for the maximum voltage found in the cable or raceway system.

38-037 Wiring in hoistways, machine rooms, control rooms, and machinery spaces and control spaces
Unless a deviation has been permitted in accordance with Rule 2-030, only conductors used in connection with operation of the elevator, dumbwaiter, escalator, moving walk, material lift, or lift for persons with physical disabilities, including supply or feeder conductors, wiring for signals, hoistway fire detection, communication with the car, and for lighting and ventilating the car, shall be permitted to be installed inside hoistways, runways, machine rooms, control rooms, machinery spaces and control spaces, or escalator wellways. (See also Rule 12-014.)

38-041 Suspension of travelling cables (see Appendix B)

1) Travelling cables shall be suspended at the car and hoistway ends, or counterweight end where applicable, to reduce to a minimum the strain on the individual copper conductors.

2) Travelling cables shall be supported by one of the following means:
   a) by their steel supporting member(s);
   b) by looping the cables around supports for unsupported lengths less than 30 m; or

C22.1-18

Section 38
Elevators, dumbwaiters, material lifts, escalators, moving walks, lifts for persons with
physical disabilities, and similar equipment

c) by suspending from the supports by a means that automatically tightens around the cable when tension is increased for unsupported lengths up to 60 m.

38-042 Hazardous locations

All electrical equipment installed in hazardous locations shall comply with Section 18.

38-043 Location of and protection for cables

1) Travelling cable supports shall be located to reduce to a minimum the possibility of damage due to the cables coming in contact with the hoistway construction or equipment in the hoistway.
2) Where necessary, suitable guards shall be provided to protect the cables against damage.

38-044 Installation of travelling cables

Travelling cable to the car or counterweight shall be permitted to be installed in the hoistway and on the car and counterweight as fixed wiring without the use of conduit or other raceway, provided that it is suitably supported and protected from damage.

38-051 Disconnecting means (see Appendix B)

1) A single disconnecting means shall be provided for the opening of all ungrounded conductors of each of the following:
   a) the drive motor and its ventilation and control circuits in each elevator, escalator, dumbwaiter, or lift for persons with physical disabilities operating individually or as one of a group; and
   b) the branch circuit(s) supplying the lighting and ventilation, heating, and air conditioning in each car, and such circuit(s) shall not be controlled by the disconnecting means described in Item a).
2) Each disconnecting means shall be an externally operated fusible switch or a circuit breaker and shall be equipped with means for locking it in the open position.
3) Where circuit breakers are used as a disconnecting means, they shall not be opened automatically by a fire alarm system.
4) Means shall be provided on the switch or circuit breaker to indicate the disconnected position.
5) The disconnecting means shall be located where it is visible on entry to the machinery area and readily accessible to authorized persons.
6) When the disconnecting means required by Subrule 1) a) is not visible from, or is located more than 9 m from, the motor controller(s), an additional manually operable motor controller disconnecting switch, whose opening is not solely dependent on springs, shall
   a) be installed so that it is visible from, or adjacent to, the remote equipment;
   b) open all ungrounded conductors; and
   c) be capable of being locked in the open position.
7)
   a) Driving machines or controllers other than motor controllers not within sight of the disconnecting means shall be provided with a manually operated switch installed in the control circuit to prevent starting.
   b) The manually operated switch(es) shall be installed adjacent to this equipment.
8) Where there is more than one driving machine in a machine room, the disconnecting means shall be numbered to correspond to the identifying number of the driving machine that it controls.
9) The disconnecting means shall be provided with a sign to identify the location of the supply side overcurrent protective device.
10)
   a) No provision shall be made for automatically closing this disconnecting means.
   b) Power shall be restored only by manual means.
11) The disconnecting means serving an escalator or moving walk controller shall be installed in the same location as the controller.

C22.1-18

Section 38
Elevators, dumbwaiters, material lifts, escalators, moving walks, lifts for persons with
physical disabilities, and similar equipment

12) Where multiple driving machines are connected to a single elevator, escalator, moving walk, or pumping unit, there shall be one disconnecting means to disconnect the motor(s) and control valve operating magnets.

13) Where the driving machine of an electric elevator, dumbwaiter, material lift, or lift for persons with disabilities or the hydraulic machine of a hydraulic elevator, dumbwaiter, material lift, or lift for persons with disabilities is located in a remote machine room or remote machinery space, or the motor-generator set is located in a remote machine room or remote machinery space, a single means for disconnecting all ungrounded main power supply conductors shall be provided that is visible from the machine and capable of being locked in the open position.

38-052 Power from more than one source (see Appendix M)

1) **Single-car and multi-car installations:** On single-car and multi-car installations, equipment receiving electrical power from more than one source shall be provided with a disconnecting means, within sight of the equipment served, for each source of electrical power.

2) **Warning sign for multiple disconnecting means:** Where multiple disconnecting means are used and parts of the controllers remain energized from a source other than the one disconnected, a clearly legible warning sign reading "Warning — Parts of the controller are not de-energized by this switch" shall be mounted on or next to the disconnecting means.

3) **Interconnection of multi-car controllers:** Where interconnections between controllers are necessary for the operation of the system on multi-car installations that remain energized from a source other than the one disconnected, a warning sign in accordance with Subrule 2) shall be mounted on or next to the disconnecting means.

38-053 Car light, receptacle(s), and ventilation disconnecting means

1) Elevators, dumbwaiters, material lifts, and lifts for persons with physical disabilities shall have a single means for disconnecting all ungrounded car light, receptacle, and ventilation power supply conductors for that car.

2) The disconnecting means shall be an enclosed, externally operable fused motor-circuit switch or circuit breaker capable of being locked in the open position and shall be located in the machine room or control room for that car, unless there is no machine room or control room, in which case the disconnecting means shall be located in the same space as the disconnecting means required by Rule 38-051.

3) The disconnecting means shall be numbered to correspond to the identifying number of the car whose light source it controls.

4) The disconnecting means shall be provided with a sign to identify the location of the supply side overcurrent protective device.

38-054 Heating and air-conditioning disconnecting means

1) Elevators, dumbwaiters, material lifts, and lifts for persons with physical disabilities shall have a single means for disconnecting all ungrounded car heating and air-conditioning power supply conductors for that car.

2) The disconnecting means shall be an enclosed, externally operable fused motor-circuit switch or circuit breaker capable of being locked in the open position and shall be located in the machine room or control room for that car, unless there is no machine room, in which case the disconnecting means shall be located in the same space as the disconnecting means required by Rule 38-051.

3) The disconnecting means shall be numbered to correspond to the identifying number of the car whose heating and air-conditioning source it controls.

4) The disconnecting means shall be provided with a sign to identify the location of the supply side overcurrent protective device.

C22.1-18

Section 38
Elevators, dumbwaiters, material lifts, escalators, moving walks, lifts for persons with
physical disabilities, and similar equipment

38-055 Utilization equipment disconnecting means

1) Each branch circuit for other utilization equipment (see Rule 38-025) shall have a single means for disconnecting all ungrounded conductors.

2) The disconnecting means shall be capable of being locked in the open position and shall be located in the machine room or control room/machine space or control space.

3) Where there is more than one branch circuit for other utilization equipment, the disconnecting means shall be numbered to correspond to the identifying number of the equipment served.

4) The disconnecting means shall be provided with a sign to identify the location of the supply side overcurrent protective device.

38-061 Overcurrent protection

1) Overcurrent protection for operating and control circuits shall be provided in accordance with Section 14.

2) Overcurrent protection for signal circuits shall be provided in accordance with Section 16.

3) Class 2 extra-low-voltage, low-energy circuits shall comply with Section 16.

4) Each ac drive motor for an elevator, dumbwaiter, escalator, moving walk, material lift, or lift for persons with physical disabilities, and each ac drive motor of a motor-generator set supplying current to the machine-drive motor, shall be provided with overload protection in accordance with Rule 28-302.

5) Overload devices shall be provided for each dc machine-drive motor where
   a) the motor-generator set provides power to two or more drive motors;
   b) the capacity of the motor-generator set is such that the protection provided in accordance with Subrule 1) is inadequate; or
   c) the drive motor of a variable-voltage machine is subject to overcurrent at reduced voltage during levelling.

6) The overload devices required by Subrule 5) c) shall be permitted to be omitted where a time-delay relay is provided in the levelling circuit to disconnect the power supply at the motor-generator set within an interval that will prevent damage to motor windings.

38-062 Selective coordination

The overcurrent protection shall be coordinated with any upstream overcurrent protective device.

38-071 Guarding equipment

Elevator, dumbwaiter, escalator, moving walk, material lift, and lift for persons with physical disabilities driving machines, motor-generator sets, motor controllers, and disconnecting means shall be installed in a room or space set aside for that purpose that is secured against unauthorized access, unless otherwise permitted in Items a) to d):

a) motor controllers shall be permitted outside the spaces specified in this Rule, provided that they are in enclosures with doors or removable panels capable of being locked in the closed position, and the disconnecting means is located adjacent to or is an integral part of the motor controller;

b) motor controller enclosures for escalators or moving walks shall be permitted in the balustrade on the side away from the moving steps or treadway;

c) where provided as an integral part of the motor controller, the disconnecting means shall be operable without opening the enclosure;

d) elevators with driving machines located on the car, counterweight, or in the hoistway and driving machines for dumbwaiters, material lifts, and lifts for persons with physical disabilities shall be permitted outside the spaces specified in this Rule.

38-081 Bonding of raceways to cars

Metal raceways, armoured cable, metallic-sheathed cable, or mineral-insulated cable attached to cars shall be bonded to the metal parts of the car that they contact.

C22.1-18

Section 38
Elevators, dumbwaiters, material lifts, escalators, moving walks, lifts for persons with
physical disabilities, and similar equipment

38-082 Bonding of equipment

The frames of all motors, generators, machines, and controllers, and the metal enclosures for all electrical equipment in or on the car or in the hoistway shall be bonded to ground in accordance with Section 10.

38-083 Bonding of non-electric elevators

For elevators other than electric having any electric conductors attached to the car, the metal frame of the car, where normally accessible to persons, shall be bonded to ground in accordance with Section 10.

38-084 Bonding of escalators, moving walks, and lifts for persons with physical disabilities

Metal parts of escalators, moving walks, and lifts for persons with physical disabilities shall be bonded to ground in accordance with Section 10.

38-085 Ground fault circuit interrupter protection for personnel

1) Each 125 V, single-phase receptacle installed in pits, hoistways, elevator and enclosed vertical platform lift car tops, and escalator or moving walk wellways shall be of the Class A ground fault circuit interrupter type.

2) All 125 V, single-phase receptacles installed in machine rooms and machinery spaces shall have Class A ground fault circuit interrupter type protection.

3) A single receptacle supplying a permanently installed sump pump shall not require ground fault circuit interrupter protection.

38-091 Emergency power (see Appendix B)

1) An elevator shall be permitted to operate from an emergency power supply in the event of normal power supply failure.

2) For elevator systems that regenerate power back into a power source that is unable to absorb the regenerative power under overhauling elevator load conditions, a means shall be provided to absorb this power.

3) Other building loads, such as power and lighting, shall be permitted as the energy absorption means required in Subrule 2), provided that such loads are automatically connected to the emergency power system operating the elevators and are large enough to absorb the elevator regenerative power.

4) The disconnecting means required by Rule 38-051 shall disconnect the emergency power source and the normal power source.

5) Where an additional power source is connected to the load side of the disconnecting means, which allows automatic movement of the car or movement of the carriage controlled by users, the disconnecting means required in Rule 38-051 shall be provided with an auxiliary contact that is positively opened mechanically, the opening not being solely dependent on springs, and this contact shall cause the additional power source to be disconnected from its load when the disconnecting means is in the open position.

Section 40 — Electric cranes and hoists

40-000 Scope
This Section applies to features of the installations of electrical equipment providing circuits for electric cranes, hoists, and monorails, and supplements or amends the general requirements of this Code.

40-002 Supply conductor sizes
The size of conductors in raceways or cables supplying main contact conductors or supplying equipment directly shall be determined from Table 58.

40-004 Conductor protection
1) Conductors supplying main contact conductors shall be in rigid conduit, electrical metallic tubing, armoured cable, mineral-insulated cable, aluminum-sheathed cable, or copper-sheathed cable, except as otherwise provided for in Rule 40-018.

2) Conductors supplying the equipment directly shall comply with Subrule 1) unless a flexible connection is required, in which case an armoured or unarmoured cable, festoon cable, or flexible cord, with take-up devices where necessary to prevent damage to the cable or cord and to keep it clear of the operating floor, shall be permitted.

40-006 Overcurrent protection
Conductors supplying main contact conductors or supplying the equipment directly where there are no main contact conductors shall be provided with overcurrent protection in accordance with the requirements of Rule 28-200 for the motor load plus an allowance in accordance with Rule 14-104 for any other loads if the size of conductors has been increased to provide capacity for the other loads.

40-008 Disconnecting means
Suitable means for disconnecting all ungrounded conductors of the circuit simultaneously shall be
a) provided within sight of the main contact conductors or within sight of the equipment if there are no main contact conductors; and
b) accessible and operable from the ground or from the floor over which the equipment operates.

40-010 Main contact conductors
1) Bare main contact conductors shall have an ampacity not less than that of the conductors supplying them and, if wire is used, in no case shall these conductors be smaller than
   a) No. 4 AWG copper or No. 2 AWG aluminum if the length of contact conductor is 18 m or less; or
   b) No. 2 AWG copper or No. 1/0 AWG aluminum if the length of contact conductor is greater than 18 m, unless the intermediate insulating supports are of a clamp type capable of providing some strain relief.

2) Bare main contact conductors shall be permitted to be of hard drawn copper or aluminum wire or shall be permitted to be made of steel or other suitable metal in the form of tees, angles, T-rails, or other rigid shapes.

40-012 Spacing of main contact conductors
1) Bare main contact conductor wires shall be supported so that
   a) they are separated, centre-to-centre, as follows:
      i) not less than 150 mm for other than monorail hoists, if installed in a horizontal plane;
      ii) not less than 75 mm for monorail hoists, if installed in a horizontal plane; or
      iii) not less than 200 mm, if installed in other than a horizontal plane; and
   b) the extreme limit of displacement does not bring them within less than 38 mm of the surface wired over.

2) Rigid main contact conductors shall be supported so that there is an air space of not less than 25 mm between conductors, between conductors and adjacent collectors, and between conductors and the surface wired over.

40-014 Supporting of main contact conductors

1) Bare main contact conductor wires shall be secured at each end to strain insulators and shall be supported on insulating supports placed at intervals not exceeding 6 m except that, where building conditions make such intervals impossible, the interval between insulating supports shall be permitted to be increased to a maximum of 12 m if the separation between contact conductors is increased proportionately.

2) Rigid main contact conductors shall be secured to insulating supports spaced at intervals of not more than 80 times the vertical dimension of the conductor, but in no case shall the interval be greater than 4.5 m.

40-016 Joints in rigid contact conductors

Joints in rigid main contact conductors shall be made so as to ensure proper ampacity without overheating.

40-018 Use of track as a conductor

Monorail, tramrail, or crane runway tracks shall be permitted to be used as a main contact conductor or as a supply circuit conductor for one phase of a three-phase ac circuit if

a) the power for all phases is obtained from an isolating transformer;

b) the voltage does not exceed 300 V;

c) the rail serving as a conductor is effectively bonded to ground, preferably at the transformer, with permissive additional grounding by the fittings used for the suspension or attachment of the rail to the building structure; and

d) any joints in the rail meet the requirements of Rule 40-016.

40-020 Guarding of contact conductors (see Appendix B)

1) Contact conductors shall be guarded so that inadvertent contact cannot be made with bare current-carrying parts, or they shall be incorporated into an enclosed contact assembly.

2) Guarding of bare contact conductors shall not be required where a clearance of at least 6 m between such conductors and grade, floor, or any working surface is provided and maintained.

40-022 Contact conductors not to supply other equipment

Contact conductors shall not be used as feeders for any equipment other than that essential for the operation of the cranes, hoists, or monorails that they supply.

40-024 Bonding (see Appendix B)

1) All exposed non-current-carrying metal parts shall be bonded to ground.

2) Tracks shall be bonded to ground as required by Rule 10-700 or 40-018.

3) The flexible supply connection permitted in Rule 40-004 2) shall incorporate a bonding conductor.

Section 42 — Electric welders

General

42-000 Scope
This Section applies to the installation of electric welders and supplements or amends the general requirements of this Code.

42-002 Special terminology
In this Section, the following definitions shall apply:

Actual primary current — the current drawn from the supply circuit during each welder operation at the particular heat tap and control setting used.

Duty cycle — the ratio of the time during which the welder is loaded to the total time required for one complete operation.

Rated primary current — the kilovolt-ampere rating of the welder as shown on its nameplate, multiplied by 1000 and divided by the rated primary voltage shown on the nameplate.

42-004 Receptacles and attachment plugs
Where a welder is cord-connected, the rating of the receptacle and attachment plug shall be permitted to be less than the rating of the overcurrent devices protecting them, but not less than the ampacity of the supply cable required for the welder.

Transformer arc welders

42-006 Supply conductors
1) The insulated supply conductors for an individual transformer arc welder shall have an ampacity of not less than the value obtained by multiplying the rated primary current of that welder in amperes by a factor of
   a) 1.00, 0.95, 0.89, 0.84, 0.78, 0.71, 0.63, 0.55, or 0.45 for welders having a duty cycle of 100, 90, 80, 70, 60, 50, 40, 30, and 20% or less respectively; or
   b) 0.75 for a welder having a time rating of 1 h.
2) The insulated supply conductors for a group of transformer arc welders shall have an ampacity not less than the sum of the currents determined for each welder in the group in accordance with Subrule 1) multiplied by a demand factor of
   a) 100% of the two largest calculated currents of the welders in the group; plus
   b) 85% of the third largest calculated current of the welders in the group; plus
   c) 70% of the fourth largest calculated current of the welders in the group; plus
   d) 60% of the calculated currents of all remaining welders in the group.
3) Lower values than those given in Subrule 2) shall be permitted in cases where the work is such that a high operating duty cycle for individual welders is impossible.

42-008 Overcurrent protection for transformer arc welders
1) Each transformer arc welder shall have overcurrent protection rated or set at not more than 200% of the rated primary current of the welder, unless the overcurrent device protecting the insulated supply conductors meets this requirement.
2) Each ungrounded conductor supplying a transformer arc welder shall have overcurrent protection rated or set at not more than 200% of the allowable ampacity of the insulated conductor as specified in Table 1, 2, 3, or 4, except that the next higher rating or setting shall be permitted to be used where
   a) the nearest standard rating of the overcurrent device is less than the rating or setting otherwise required by this Rule; or

b) the rating or setting otherwise required by this Rule results in too frequent opening of the overcurrent device.

3) The maximum rating or setting of an overcurrent device protecting a feeder supplying a group of transformer arc welders shall not exceed a value calculated by determining the maximum rating or setting of overcurrent device permitted by Subrules 1) and 2) for the welder allowed the highest overcurrent protection and adding to this value the sum of ampacities as calculated by Rule 42-006 for all other welders in the group.

42-010 Disconnecting means

1) A disconnecting means shall be provided in the supply connections of each welder that is not equipped with a disconnecting means mounted as an integral part of the welder.

2) The disconnecting means shall be a switch or circuit breaker, and its rating shall be not less than necessary to accommodate overcurrent protection as specified in Rule 42-008.

Motor-generator arc welders

42-012 Conductors, protection, and control of motor-generator arc welders

1) The Rules of Sections 4 and 28 shall apply to motor-generator arc welders, except that
   a) the motors shall be permitted to be marked in amperes only; and
   b) where the controller is built in as an integral part of the motor-generator set, the controller need not be separately marked, provided that the necessary data are on the motor nameplate.

2) The insulated supply conductors for an individual motor-generator arc welder shall have an ampacity of not less than the value obtained by multiplying the rated primary current of that welder by a factor of
   a) 1.00, 0.96, 0.91, 0.86, 0.81, 0.75, 0.69, 0.62, or 0.55 for welders having a duty cycle of 100, 90, 80, 70, 60, 50, 40, 30, and 20% or less respectively; or
   b) 0.80 for a welder having a time rating of 1 h.

3) The insulated supply conductors for a group of motor-generator arc welders shall have an ampacity not less than the sum of the currents determined for each welder in the group in accordance with Subrule 2) multiplied by a demand factor of
   a) 100% of the two highest calculated currents of the welders in the group; plus
   b) 85% of the third largest calculated current of the welders in the group; plus
   c) 70% of the fourth largest calculated current of the welders in the group; plus
   d) 60% of the calculated currents for all remaining welders in the group.

4) Lower values than those given in Subrule 3) shall be permitted in cases where the work is such that a high operating duty cycle for individual welders is impossible.

Resistance welders

42-014 Supply conductors for resistance welders

The ampacity of insulated supply conductors shall be as follows:

a) where an individual seam resistance welder or an individual automatically fed resistance welder is operated at different times at different values of primary current or duty cycle, the insulated supply conductors shall have an ampacity of not less than 70% of the rated primary current of the welder;

b) where an individual manually operated non-automatic resistance welder is operated at different times at different values of primary current or duty cycle, the ampacity of the insulated supply conductors shall be not less than 50% of the rated primary current of the welder;

c) where an individual resistance welder operates at known and constant values of actual primary current and duty cycle, the insulated supply conductors shall have an ampacity of not less than the value obtained by multiplying the actual primary current by a factor of 0.71, 0.63, 0.55, 0.50, 0.45, 0.39, 0.32, 0.27, or 0.22 for duty cycles of 50, 40, 30, 25, 20, 15, 10, 7.5, and 5% or less respectively; and

d) where there is a group of resistance welders, the insulated supply conductors shall have an ampacity of not less than

    i) the sum of the values obtained from Item a), b), or c) for the largest welder in the group; and

    ii) 60% of the values obtained for all of the other welders in the group.

42-016 Overcurrent protection

1) Every resistance welder shall have overcurrent protection rated or set at not more than 300% of the rated primary current of the welder unless the overcurrent device protecting the insulated supply conductors gives equivalent protection.

2) Every ungrounded conductor of a resistance welder shall have overcurrent protection rated or set at not more than 300% of the allowable ampacity of the insulated conductor as specified in Table 1,2, 3, or 4, except that the next higher rating or setting shall be permitted to be used where

    a) the nearest standard rating of the overcurrent device is less than the rating or setting required by this Rule; or

    b) the rating or setting required by this Rule results in too frequent opening of the overcurrent device.

3) The maximum rating or setting of an overcurrent device protecting a feeder supplying a group of resistance welders shall not exceed a value calculated by determining the maximum rating or setting of overcurrent device permitted by Subrules 1) and 2) for the welder allowed the highest overcurrent protection and adding to this value the sum of ampacities as calculated by Rule 42-014 for all other welders in the group.

42-018 Control of resistance welders

Every resistance welder shall have installed in its supply circuit a switch or circuit breaker, rated at not less than the rating of the insulated conductors as determined by Rule 42-014, whereby the welder and its control equipment can be isolated from the supply circuit.

42-020 Nameplate data for resistance welders

Every resistance welder shall be provided with a nameplate giving the manufacturer's name, primary voltage, frequency, rated kilovolt amperes at 50% duty cycle, maximum and minimum open-circuit secondary voltage, short-circuit secondary current at maximum secondary voltage, and the specified throat and gap setting.

42

Section 44 — Theatre installations

Scope

44-000 Scope
This Section applies to electrical equipment and installations in buildings or parts of a building designed, intended, or used for dramatic, operatic, motion picture, or other shows, and it supplements or amends the general requirements of this Code.

General

44-100 Travelling shows
Electrical equipment used by a travelling theatrical company, circus, or other travelling show, whether or not the performance is held within a theatre, shall not be used for the initial performance of any stand until a permit has been obtained from the inspection department.

44-102 Wiring method
1) Wiring in stage and stage wing areas, orchestra pits, and projection booths shall be in rigid metal conduit, electrical metallic tubing, mineral-insulated cable, flexible metal conduit, armoured cable, lead-sheathed armoured cable, aluminum-sheathed cable, or copper-sheathed cable, except that
   a) other wiring methods shall be permitted for temporary work; and
   b) flexible cord or cable shall be permitted in accordance with other Rules in this Section.
2) Surface raceways shall not be used on the stage side of the proscenium wall.
3) Wiring in areas other than those listed in Subrule 1) shall be in accordance with the requirements of the appropriate Sections of this Code.

44-104 Number of conductors in raceways
For border or stage pocket circuits or for remote control circuits,
a) the number of conductors run in rigid metal conduit or electrical metallic tubing shall not exceed that shown in Rule 12-910; and
b) conductors run in auxiliary gutters or metal wireways shall have a total cross-sectional area not exceeding 20% of the cross-sectional area of the gutter or wireway.

44-106 Aisle lights in moving picture theatres
Circuits for aisle lights located under seats shall be permitted to supply 30 outlets, provided that the size of lamp that can be used with each outlet is limited by barriers or the equivalent to 25 W or less.

Fixed stage switchboards

44-200 Stage switchboards to be dead front
Stage switchboards shall be
a) of the dead-front type; and
b) protected above with a suitable metal guard or hood extending the full length of the board and completely covering the space between the wall and the board to protect the latter from falling objects.

44-202 Guarding stage switchboards
1) Where a stage switchboard has exposed live parts on the back of the board, it shall be enclosed by the walls of the building, by wire mesh grilles, or by other acceptable methods.
2) The entrance to the enclosures shall have a self-closing door.

44-204 Switches
Switches shall be of the enclosed type and externally operated.

44-206 Pilot lamp on switchboards
1) A pilot lamp shall be installed within every switchboard enclosure.

2) The pilot lamp shall be connected to the circuit supplying the switchboard so that the opening of the master switch does not cut off the supply to the lamp.

3) The lamp shall be on an independent circuit protected by an overcurrent device rated or set at not more than 15 A.

44-208 Fuses

Fuses on switchboards shall be

a) of either the plug or cartridge type; and

b) provided with enclosures in addition to the switchboard enclosure.

44-210 Overcurrent protection

1) All circuits leaving the switchboard shall have an overcurrent device connected in each ungrounded conductor.

2) Notwithstanding Rule 30-104, a luminaire having an input voltage of not more than 120 V nominal shall be permitted to be protected by an overcurrent device rated or set at not more than 100 A.

44-212 Dimmers

1) Dimmers shall be connected so as to be dead when their respective circuit switches are open.

2) Dimmers that do not open the circuit shall be permitted to be connected in a grounded neutral conductor.

3) The terminals of dimmers shall be enclosed.

4) Dimmer faceplates shall be arranged so that accidental contact cannot readily be made with the faceplate contacts.

44-214 Control of stage and gallery pockets

Stage and gallery pockets shall be controlled from the switchboard.

44-216 Conductors

1) Stage switchboards equipped with resistive or transformer-type dimmer switches shall be wired with conductors having insulation suitable for the temperature generated in those switchboards and in no case less than 125 °C.

2) The conductors shall have an ampacity not less than that of the switch or overcurrent device to which they are connected.

3) Holes in the metal enclosure through which conductors pass shall be bushed.

4) The strands of the conductor shall be soldered together before they are fastened under a clamp or binding screw.

5) Where a conductor of No. 8 AWG or of a larger size is connected to a terminal,
   a) it shall be soldered into a lug; or
   b) a solderless connector shall be used.

Portable switchboards on stage

44-250 Construction of portable switchboards

1) Portable switchboards shall be placed within enclosures of substantial construction, but shall be permitted to be arranged so that the enclosure is open during operation.

2) There shall be no live parts exposed within the enclosure, except those on dimmer faceplates.

44-252 Supply for portable switchboards

1) Portable switchboards shall be supplied by means of flexible cord or cable, Type S, SO, or ST, terminating within the switchboard enclosure in an externally operated, enclosed, fused master switch.

2) The master switch shall be arranged to cut off current from all apparatus within the enclosure except the pilot light.

3) The flexible cord or cable shall have sufficient ampacity to carry the total load current of the switchboard.

4) The ampere rating of the fuses of the master switch shall be not greater than the total load current of the switchboard.

Fixed stage equipment

44-300 Footlights
1) Where footlights are wired in rigid metal conduit or electrical metallic tubing, every lampholder shall be installed in an individual outlet box.
2) Where footlights are not wired in rigid metal conduit or electrical metallic tubing, the wiring shall be installed in a metal trough.

44-302 Metal work
1) The metal work for footlights, borders, proscenium sidelights, and strips shall be not less than 0.78 mm thick.
2) The metal work for bunches and portable strips shall be not less than 0.53 mm thick.

44-304 Clearances at terminals
The terminals of lampholders shall be separated from the metal of the trough by at least 13 mm.

44-306 Mechanical protection of lamps in borders, etc.
Borders, proscenium sidelights, and strips shall be constructed so that the flanges of the reflectors or other suitable guards protect the lamps from mechanical damage and from accidental contact with scenery or other combustible material.

44-308 Suspended luminaires
Borders and strips shall be suspended so as to be electrically and mechanically safe.

44-310 Connections at lampholders
Conductors shall be soldered to the terminals of lampholders unless other suitable means are provided to obtain positive and reliable connection under severe vibration.

44-312 Ventilation for mogul lampholders
Where the lighting devices are equipped with mogul lampholders, the lighting devices shall be constructed with double walls and with adequate ventilation between the walls.

44-314 Conductor insulation for field-assembled luminaires
Foot, border, proscenium, and portable strip luminaires assembled in the field shall be wired with conductors having insulation suitable for the temperature at which the conductors will be operated and in no case less than 125 °C.

44-316 Branch circuit overcurrent protection
Branch circuits for footlights, border lights, and proscenium sidelights shall have overcurrent protection in accordance with Rule 30-104.

44-318 Pendant lights rated more than 100 W
Where a pendant lighting device contains a lamp or group of lamps of more than 100 W capacity, it shall be provided with a guard of not more than 13 mm mesh arranged to prevent damage from falling glass.

44-320 Cable for border lights
1) Flexible cord or cable for border lights shall be Type S, SO, or ST.
2) The flexible cord or cable shall be fed from points on the gridiron or from other acceptable overhead points but shall not be fed from side walls.
3) The flexible cord or cable shall be arranged so that strain is taken from clamps and binding screws.
4) Where the flexible cord or cable passes through a metal or wooden enclosure, a metal bushing shall be provided to protect the cord.

5) Terminals or binding posts to which flexible cords or cables are connected inside the switchboard enclosure shall be located to permit convenient access to the cords or cables.

44-322 Wiring to arc pockets

Where the wiring to arc pockets is in rigid metal conduit or electrical metallic tubing, the end of the conduit or tubing shall be exposed at a point approximately 300 mm away from the pocket, and the wiring shall be continued in flexible metal conduit in the form of a loop at least 600 mm long, with sufficient slack to permit the raising or lowering of the box.

44-324 Receptacles in gallery pockets

At least one receptacle having a rated capacity of not less than 30 A shall be installed in the gallery of theatres in which dramatic or operatic performances are staged.

44-326 Receptacles and plugs

1) Receptacles intended for the connection of arc lamps shall
   a)   have an ampere rating not less than 35 A; and
   b)   be supplied by copper conductors not smaller than No. 6 AWG.
2) Receptacles intended for the connection of incandescent lamps shall
   a)   have an ampere rating not less than 15 A; and
   b)   be supplied by conductors not smaller than No. 12 AWG copper or No. 10 AWG aluminum.
3) Plugs for arc and incandescent receptacles shall not be interchangeable.

44-328 Curtain motors

Curtain motors shall be of the enclosed type.

44-330 Flue damper control

1) Where stage flue dampers are released by an electrical device, the circuit operating the device shall, in normal operation, be closed.
2) The circuit shall be controlled by at least two single-pole switches enclosed in metal boxes with self-closing doors without locks or latches.
3) One switch shall be placed at the electrician's station and the other at a location that is acceptable.
4) The device shall be
   a)   designed for the full voltage of the circuit to which it is connected, no resistance being inserted;
   b)   located in the loft above the scenery; and
   c)   enclosed in a suitable metal box with a tight self-closing door.

Portable stage equipment

44-350 Fixtures on scenery

1) Fixtures attached to stage scenery shall be
   a)   of the internally wired type; or
   b)   wired with flexible cord or cable suitable for hard usage as selected in accordance with Rule 12-402 1) or 12-406 1).
2) The fixtures shall be secured firmly in place.
3) The stems of the fixtures shall be carried through to the back of the scenery and shall have a suitable bushing on the end.

44-352 String or festooned lights

1) Joints in the wiring of string or festooned lights shall be staggered where practicable.
2) Where the lamps of string or festooned lights are enclosed in paper lanterns, shades, or other devices of combustible material, they shall be equipped with lamp guards.

44

44-354 Flexible conductors for portable equipment

Conductors for arc lamps, bunches, or other portable equipment shall be flexible cord of types suitable for extra-hard usage, as selected in accordance with Rule 12-402 1) or 12-406 1), but for separate miscellaneous portable devices operated under conditions where the conductors are not exposed to severe mechanical damage, flexible cord types suitable for other than hard usage, as selected in accordance with Rule 12-402 1) or 12-406 1), shall be permitted to be used.

44-356 Portable equipment for stage effects

Portable equipment for stage effects shall be of a type acceptable for the purpose and shall be located so that flames, sparks, or hot particles cannot come in contact with combustible material.

Section 46 — Emergency power supply, unit equipment, exit signs, and life safety systems

46-000 Scope (see Appendix B)
1) This Section applies to the installation, operation, and maintenance of
   a) emergency power supply and unit equipment intended to provide power to life safety systems; and
   b) emergency power supply and unit equipment intended to provide illumination of exit signs, in the event of failure of the normal supply, where the emergency power supply is required by the *National Building Code of Canada*.
2) This Section applies to the wiring between the emergency power supply and life safety systems that are required by the *National Building Code of Canada* to be provided with an emergency power supply.
3) This Section applies to the wiring of exit signs.
4) The requirements of this Section supplement or amend the general requirements of this Code.

46-002 Special terminology (see Appendix B)
In this Section, the following definitions shall apply:

Emergency power supply — emergency power, supplied by a generator, batteries, or a combination thereof, that is required by the *National Building Code of Canada*.

Life safety systems — emergency lighting and fire alarm systems that are required to be provided with an emergency power supply from batteries, generators, or a combination thereof, and electrical equipment for building services such as fire pumps, elevators, smoke-venting fans, smoke control fans, and dampers that are required to be provided with an emergency power supply by an emergency generator in conformance with the *National Building Code of Canada*.

Unit equipment — unit equipment for emergency lighting conforming to CSA C22.2 No. 141.

General

46-100 Capacity
Emergency power supply and unit equipment shall have adequate capacity and rating to ensure the satisfactory operation of all connected equipment when the principal source of power fails.

46-102 Instructions
1) Complete instructions for the operation and care of an emergency power supply or unit equipment that shall specify testing at least once every month to ensure security of operation shall be posted on the premises in a frame under glass.
2) The form of instructions and their locations shall be in compliance with the *National Building Code of Canada*.

46-104 Maintenance
Where batteries are used as a source of the emergency power supply, the batteries shall be kept
a) in proper condition; and
b) fully charged at all times.

46-106 Arrangement of lamps
1) Emergency lights shall be arranged so that the failure of any one lamp will not leave in total darkness the area normally illuminated by it.
2) No appliance or lamp, other than those required for emergency purposes, shall be supplied by the emergency circuits.

46-108 Wiring method (see Appendices B and G)
1) Except as permitted by Subrule 3), Rule 46-304 3), and Rule 46-400 2), the following insulated conductors shall be installed in accordance with Subrule 2):
    a) insulated conductors and cables required for operation of life safety systems and installed between an emergency power supply and life safety systems;
    b) insulated conductors and cables between an emergency power supply and exit signs; and
    c) insulated conductors and cables between unit equipment and remote lamps.
2) The insulated conductors described in Subrule 1) shall be
    a) installed in metal raceway of the totally enclosed type;
    b) incorporated in a cable having a metal armour or sheath;
    c) installed in rigid non-metallic conduit; or
    d) installed in electrical non-metallic tubing where embedded in at least 50 mm of masonry or poured concrete.
3) Notwithstanding Subrule 2), insulated conductors installed in buildings of combustible construction in accordance with Rules 12-506 to 12-520 shall be permitted to be
    a) run as a non-metallic-sheathed cable; or
    b) installed in a totally enclosed non-metallic raceway.
4) Insulated conductors and cables installed in accordance with Subrule 1) shall be kept entirely independent of all other insulated conductors and equipment and shall not enter a luminaire, raceway, box, cabinet, or unit equipment occupied by other insulated conductors except where necessary
    a) in transfer switches; and
    b) in exit signs and emergency lights supplied from two sources.
5) Insulated conductors and cables installed between an emergency power supply and any electrical equipment that is not defined as a "life safety system" in accordance with this Section shall not enter a luminaire, raceway, box, or cabinet occupied by insulated conductors installed as described in Subrule 1), except where necessary in busways, splitters, and other similar enclosures provided for connection to the overcurrent device for an emergency power supply described in Rule 46-208 1).

Emergency power supply

46-200 Emergency power supply (see Appendix B)
Rules 46-202 to 46-212 apply only to emergency power supply from central standby power sources.

Δ **46-202 Types of emergency power supply** (see Appendices B and G)
1) The emergency power supply shall be a standby supply consisting of
    a) a storage battery of the rechargeable type having sufficient capacity to supply and maintain at not less than 91% of full voltage the total load of the emergency circuits for the time period required by the *National Building Code of Canada*, but in no case less than 30 min, and equipped with a charging means to maintain the battery in a charged condition automatically; or
    b) a generator.
2) Automobile batteries and lead batteries not of the enclosed glass-jar type shall not be considered suitable under Subrule 1) and shall be used only where a deviation has been allowed in accordance with Rule 2-030.
3) Where a generator is used, it shall be
    a) of sufficient capacity to carry the load;

b) arranged to start automatically without failure and without undue delay upon the failure of the normal power supply to any transfer switch connected to the generator; and

c) in conformance with CSA C282.

46-204 Protection of electrical conductors and cables (see Appendices B and G)

All power, control, and communication insulated conductors and cables between an emergency generator as described in Rule 46-202 3) and electrical equipment required to be installed as a part of the emergency power supply and located outside the generator room shall be protected against fire exposure to provide continued operation in compliance with the *National Building Code of Canada*.

46-206 Control

1) An emergency power supply shall be controlled by automatic transfer equipment that actuates the emergency power supply upon failure of the normal current supply and that is accessible only to authorized persons.

Δ 2) An automatic light-actuated device shall be permitted to be used to control separately the lights located in an area that is adequately illuminated during daylight hours without the need for artificial lighting.

46-208 Overcurrent protection

1) The overcurrent device for an emergency power supply shall be coordinated with the overcurrent devices of feeders and branch circuits supplying life safety systems and other electrical equipment connected to the emergency power supply in order to provide selective operation of the branch circuit overcurrent device when a fault occurs in that branch circuit.

2) The branch circuit overcurrent devices shall be accessible only to authorized persons.

46-210 Audible and visual trouble-signal devices

1) Every emergency power supply shall be equipped with audible and visual trouble-signal devices that warn of derangement of the current source(s) and that indicate when exit signs or life safety systems are supplied from the emergency power supply.

Δ 2) Audible trouble signals shall be permitted to be connected so that
   a) they can be silenced, but a red warning or trouble light shall continue to provide the protective function; and
   b) when the system is restored to normal, the audible signal will
      i) sound, indicating the need to restore the silencing switch to its normal position; or
      ii) reset automatically so as to provide sound for any subsequent operation of the emergency power supply.

46-212 Remote lamps

Lamps shall be permitted to be mounted at some distance from the current supply that feeds them, but the voltage drop in the wiring feeding such lamps shall not exceed 5% of the applied voltage.

Unit equipment

46-300 Unit equipment (see Appendix B)

Rules 46-302 to 46-306 apply to individual unit equipment for emergency lighting only.

46-302 Mounting of equipment

Each unit equipment shall be mounted with the bottom of the enclosure not less than 2 m above the floor, wherever practicable.

46-304 Supply connections

1) Receptacles to which unit equipment is to be connected shall be not less than 2.5 m above the floor, where practicable, and shall be not more than 1.5 m from the location of the unit equipment.

2) Unit equipment shall be permanently connected to the supply if
   a) the voltage rating exceeds 250 V; or

b)   the marked input rating exceeds 24 A.
3)   Where the ratings in Subrule 2) are not exceeded, the unit equipment shall be permitted to be connected using the flexible cord and attachment plug supplied with the equipment.
4)   Unit equipment shall be installed in such a manner that it will be automatically actuated upon failure of the power supply to the normal lighting in the area covered by that unit equipment.

46-306 Remote lamps (see Appendix B)
1)   The size of insulated circuit conductors to remote lamps shall be such that the voltage drop does not exceed 5% of the marked output voltage of the unit equipment, or such other voltage drop for which the performance of unit equipment is certified when connected to the specific remote lamp being installed.
2)   Remote lamps shall be suitable for remote connection and shall be included in the list of lamps provided with the unit equipment.
3)   The number of lamps connected to a single unit equipment shall not result in a load in excess of the watts output rating marked on the equipment for the emergency period required by the *National Building Code of Canada*, and the load shall be computed from the information in the list of lamps referred to in Subrule 2).

Exit signs

46-400 Exit signs (see Appendices B and G)
1)   Where exit signs are connected to an electrical circuit, that circuit shall be used for no other purpose.
2)   Notwithstanding Subrule 1), exit signs shall be permitted to be connected to a circuit supplying emergency lighting in the area where these exit signs are installed.
3)   The exit signs referred to in Subrules 1) and 2) shall be illuminated by an emergency power supply where emergency lighting is required by the *National Building Code of Canada*.
4)   The circuitry serving luminaires used to illuminate exit signs that are not connected to an electrical circuit shall comply with Subrules 1) to 3), as required by the *National Building Code of Canada*.

Section 48 — *Deleted*

Section 50 — *Deleted*

Section 52 — Diagnostic imaging installations

52-000 Scope

1) This Section applies to the installation of X-ray and other diagnostic imaging equipment operating at any frequency and supplements or amends the general requirements of this Code.

2) Nothing in this Section shall be construed as specifying safeguards against direct, stray, or secondary radiation emitted by the equipment.

52-002 Special terminology

In this Section, the following definitions shall apply:

Long-time rating (as applied to X-ray or computerized tomography equipment) — a rating that is applicable for an operating period of 5 min or more.

Momentary rating (as applied to X-ray or computerized tomography equipment) — a rating that is applicable for an operating period of not more than 20 s.

52-004 High-voltage guarding

1) High-voltage parts shall be mounted within metal enclosures that are bonded to ground, except when installed in separate rooms or enclosures, where a suitable switch shall be
   a) provided to control the circuit supplying diagnostic imaging equipment; and
   b) arranged so that it will be in the open position except when the door of the room or enclosure is locked.

2) High-voltage parts of diagnostic imaging equipment shall be insulated from the enclosure.

3) Conductors in the high-voltage circuits shall be of the shockproof type.

4) A milliammeter, if provided, shall be
   a) connected, if practicable, in the lead that is bonded to ground; or
   b) guarded if connected in the high-voltage lead.

52-006 Connections to the supply circuit

1) Permanently connected diagnostic imaging equipment shall be connected to the power supply by means of a wiring method meeting the general requirements of this Code, except that apparatus properly supplied by branch circuits not larger than a 30 A branch circuit shall be permitted to be supplied through a suitable plug and hard-usage cable or cord.

2) Mobile diagnostic imaging equipment of any capacity shall be permitted to be connected to its power supply by suitable temporary connections and hard-usage cable or cord.

52-008 Disconnecting means

1) A disconnecting means of adequate capacity for at least 50% of the input required for the momentary rating or 100% of the input required for the long-time rating of X-ray or computerized tomography equipment, whichever is greater, shall be provided in the supply circuit.

2) A disconnecting means of adequate capacity shall be provided in a location readily accessible from the radiation control.

3) For apparatus requiring a 120 V branch circuit fused at 30 A or less, a plug and receptacle of proper size shall be permitted to serve as a disconnecting means.

52-010 Transformers and capacitors

1) Transformers and capacitors forming a part of diagnostic imaging equipment shall not be required to conform to the requirements of Section 26 of this Code.

2) Capacitors shall be provided with an automatic means for discharging and grounding the plates whenever the transformer primary is disconnected from the source of supply, unless all current-carrying parts of the capacitors and of the conductors connected with them are
   a) at least 2.5 m from the floor and inaccessible to unauthorized persons; or

52

b)   within metal enclosures that are bonded to ground or within enclosures of insulating material if within 2.5 m of the floor.

52-012 Control

1)   For stationary equipment, the low-voltage circuit of the step-up transformer shall contain an overcurrent device that
   a)   has no exposed live parts;
   b)   protects the radiographic circuit against fault conditions under all operating conditions; and
   c)   is installed as a part of, or adjacent to, the equipment.

2)   Where the design of the step-up transformer referred to in Subrule 1) is such that branch fuses having a current rating lower than the current rating of the overcurrent device are required for adequate protection for fluoroscopic and therapeutic circuits, they shall be added for protection of these circuits.

3)   For portable equipment, the requirements of Subrules 1) and 2) shall apply, but the overcurrent device shall be located in or on the equipment except that no current-limiting device shall be required when the high-voltage parts are within a single metal enclosure that is provided with a means for bonding to ground.

4)   Where more than one piece of equipment is operated from the same high-voltage circuit, each piece or group of equipment, as a unit, shall be provided with a high-voltage switch or equivalent disconnecting means.

52-014 Bonding

Non-current-carrying parts of tube stands, tables, and other apparatus shall be bonded to ground in conformity with the requirements of Section 10.

52-016 Ampacity of supply conductors and rating of overcurrent protection

1)   The ampacity of supply conductors and the rating of overcurrent protection devices shall not be less than
   a)   the long-time current rating of X-ray or computerized tomography equipment; or
   b)   50% of the maximum momentary current rating required by X-ray or computerized tomography equipment on a radiographic setting.

2)   The ampacity of conductors and the rating of overcurrent protection devices for two or more branch circuits supplying X-ray or computerized tomography units shall be not less than
   a)   the sum of the long-time current rating of all X-ray or computerized tomography units that are intended to be operated at any one time; or
   b)   the sum of 50% of the maximum momentary current rating for X-ray or computerized tomography equipment on a radiographic setting for the two largest units, plus 20% of the maximum current rating of the other units.

Section 54 — Community antenna distribution and radio and television installations

54-000 Scope
1) This Section supplements or amends the general requirements of this Code and applies to
   a) community antenna distribution;
   b) equipment for the reception of radio and television broadcast transmission; and
   c) equipment employed in the normal operation of a radio station licensed by the Government of Canada as an experimental amateur radio station.
2) This Section does not apply to equipment and antennas used for broadcast transmission and for coupling carrier current to power line conductors.
3) In Subrule 2), "broadcast" refers to one-way communication other than by community antenna distribution.

54-002 Special terminology
In this Section, the following definitions shall apply:

Cable distribution plant — a coaxial cable system with passive devices, amplifiers, or power sources, as covered by CSA C22.3 No. 1 and CSA C22.3 No. 7, that is used to deliver radio and television frequency signals and power associated with the community antenna distribution equipment.

Customer distribution circuit — a coaxial cable with passive devices, amplifiers, or power sources that is used to deliver radio and television frequency signals and power from a cable distribution plant that has current- limiting devices.

Customer service enclosure — a cabinet not accessible by the customer that is placed on the outside or inside wall of the building to house community antenna television (CATV) equipment.

Multitap — a passive device that extends radio and television frequency signals, and that may extend current limited power, from the cable distribution plant to the customer distribution circuit associated with the community antenna distribution circuit.

Power blocking device — an approved unit that is used to prevent power other than radio and television frequency signals from extending to the outgoing coaxial cable.

54-004 Community antenna distribution (see Appendix B)
1) Community antenna distribution refers to coaxial cable circuits employed to distribute radio and television frequency signals typical of a CATV system.
2) Rules 54-100 to 54-704 apply to community antenna distribution installations.

54-006 Equipment
Equipment referred to in this Section shall not require approval in accordance with Rule 2-024, except where specifically noted in this Section.

54-008 Receiving equipment and amateur transmitting equipment Rules
Rules 54-800 to 54-1006 apply to
a) radio and television receiving equipment; and
b) amateur radio transmitting equipment.

54-010 Circuits in communication cables
Community antenna distribution circuits, or their parts, that use conductors in a cable assembly with other conductors forming parts of communication circuits are, for the purposes of this Code, deemed to be communication circuits and shall conform to the applicable Rules of Section 60, except that the requirements for protectors and grounding for the coaxial cables shall meet the requirements of this Section.

54

Community antenna distribution

54-100 Conductors

1) The conductors used in community antenna distribution shall consist of coaxial cable having a central inner conductor and an outer conductive shield of circular cross-section.

2) Conductors placed within buildings shall be of approved types selected in accordance with Rule 12-102 3).

54-102 Voltage and current limitations (see Appendix B)

1) Coaxial cable shall be permitted to be used for connection between the cable distribution plant and the customer service enclosure, or between two customer service enclosures, and for providing power to associated community antenna distribution circuits, provided that the following requirements are met:

   a) for a single dwelling, the open-circuit voltage does not exceed 90 V, and the maximum current is limited to 100/V amperes, up to and including the customer service enclosure;

   b) for a building with multiple occupancies, the open-circuit voltage does not exceed 90 V, and the maximum current is limited to 10 A, up to and including the customer service enclosure;

   c) the current supply is from an approved amplifier, transformer, or other approved device having energy-limiting characteristics;

   d) the cable distribution plant complies with the applicable requirements of CSA C22.3 No. 1 and CSA C22.3 No. 7;

   e) the power does not extend beyond the customer service enclosure unless extending to another customer service enclosure, and not to the coaxial cable extending to the customer electrical equipment;

   f) the customer service enclosure is grounded and all coaxial cables entering it are bonded to ground;

   g) the customer service enclosure is provided with a lock or similar closing device and contains power blocking devices to prevent the coaxial cable to the customer electrical equipment from being energized; and

   h) all customer distribution circuits fed from a common multitap that is capable of delivering power to the customer distribution circuit are provided with power blocking devices to prevent the coaxial cable to the customer electrical equipment from being energized.

2) Coaxial cable for the connection between the customer service enclosure and a point located at least 1 m from the customer electrical equipment shall be permitted to be energized by an approved 0 to 30 V Class 2 transformer or power supply within the premises, provided that power blocking devices are installed to prevent the connection at the customer electrical equipment from being energized.

54-104 Hazardous locations

Where the circuits or equipment within the scope of this Section are installed in hazardous locations, they shall also comply with the applicable Rules of Sections 18, 20, and 24.

54-106 Inspection by an inspector

1) Community antenna distribution circuits employed by an electrical utility, or a communication utility operating within the scope of Section 60, shall not in the exercise of its function as a utility be subject to inspection by an inspector.

2) Where the community antenna distribution circuit derives power for operation from an electric supply circuit, the transformer, amplifier, or other current-limiting device used at the junction of the community antenna distribution and electric supply circuit shall be subject to inspection by an inspector.

54-108 Supports
Where conductors are attached to, or supported on, buildings, the attachment or supporting equipment shall be acceptable for the purpose.

Protection

54-200 Grounding of outer conductive shield of a coaxial cable (see Appendix B)
1) Where coaxial cable is exposed to lightning or to accidental contact with lightning arrester conductors or power conductors operating at a voltage exceeding 300 volts-to-ground, the outer conductive shield of the coaxial cable shall be grounded at the building as close to the point of cable entry as possible.
2) Where the outer conductive shield of a coaxial cable is grounded, no other protective device shall be required.
3) Grounding of a coaxial cable shield by means of a protective device shall be permitted, provided that the device does not interrupt the grounding system within the building.

54-202 Provision of protector (see Appendix B)
Where a protective device is provided, it shall be
a) approved for the purpose;
b) located in or on the building as near as practicable to the point of cable entry;
c) located external to any hazardous location as defined in Sections 18, 20, and 24, and away from the immediate vicinity of flammable or explosive materials;
d) mounted on a flame-retardant, absorption-resisting insulating base; and
e) covered if located outdoors.

Grounding

54-300 Grounding conductor
1) The grounding conductor for the outer conductive shield of a coaxial cable or the protector shall be insulated.
2) The grounding conductor shall be made of copper.
3) The grounding conductor shall be not smaller than No. 14 AWG.
4) The grounding conductor shall have an ampacity at least equal to, or greater than, that of the outer conductive sheath of the exposed coaxial cable.
5) Where two or more coaxial cables that have outer conductive shields differing in size and ampacity join at a common connection to the grounding conductor, the ampacity of the grounding conductor shall at least equal or exceed the ampacity of the largest coaxial outer conductive shield.
6) The grounding conductor shall be run from the protector or the coaxial cable shield to the grounding electrode in as straight a line as possible.
7) The grounding conductor shall be protected when exposed to mechanical damage.

54-302 Grounding electrode
1) Grounding electrodes shall conform to Rule 10-102, except that the minimum driven length of a rod electrode shall be 2 m.
2) Grounding electrodes for community antenna distribution shall be spaced and bonded with other electrodes in accordance with Rule 10-104.

54-304 Grounding electrode connection
The grounding conductor shall be attached to a grounding electrode, as required in Rule 10-118
a) directly; or
b) to a wire lead permanently connected to the ground rod electrode in a manner specified in CSA C83.

54

Conductors within buildings

54-400 Separation from other conductors

1) Conductors of community antenna distribution circuits shall be separated at least 50 mm from insulated conductors of electric lighting, power, or Class 1 circuits operating at 300 V or less, and shall be separated at least 600 mm from any insulated conductor of an electric lighting, power, or Class 1 circuit operating at more than 300 V, unless effective separation is afforded by use of the following:
   a) grounded metal raceways for the community antenna distribution circuits or for the electric lighting, power, and Class 1 circuits;
   b) grounded metal-sheathed or armoured cable for the electric lighting, power, and Class 1 conductors; or
   c) raceways of a non-metal-type as permitted in Section 12, in addition to the insulation on the community antenna distribution circuit conductors or on the electric lighting, power, and Class 1 circuit conductors.

2) Where the electric lighting or power conductors are bare, all community antenna distribution conductors in the same room or space shall be enclosed in a grounded metal raceway and no opening, such as an outlet box, shall be located within 2 m of bare conductors if up to and including 15 kV or within 3 m of bare conductors above 15 kV.

3) The conductors of a community antenna distribution circuit shall not be placed in any raceway, compartment, outlet box, junction box, or similar fitting that contains conductors of electric light, power, or Class 1 circuits, unless
   a) the conductors of the community antenna distribution circuit are separated from the electric light, power, or Class 1 circuit conductors by a barrier that conforms to Rule 12-904 2) for conductors in raceways or Rule 12-3030 1) for conductors in boxes, cabinets, and fittings; or
   b) the power or Class 1 conductors are placed solely for the purpose of supplying power to the community antenna distribution circuit.

54-402 Conductors in a vertical shaft

Conductors of a community antenna distribution circuit in a vertical shaft shall be in a totally enclosed non-combustible raceway.

54-404 Penetration of a fire separation

Conductors of a community antenna distribution circuit extending through a fire separation shall be installed so as to limit fire spread in accordance with Rule 2-128.

54-406 Community antenna distribution conductors in ducts and plenum chambers

Community antenna distribution conductors shall not be placed in ducts or plenum chambers except as permitted by Rules 2-130 and 12-010.

54-408 Raceways

Raceways shall be installed in accordance with the requirements of Section 12.

Equipment

54-500 Community antenna distribution amplifiers and other power sources

1) Amplifiers and other devices that supply current to a community antenna distribution circuit from an electric supply circuit shall be approved for the purpose.

2) Where amplifiers and other power devices are connected to an electric supply circuit and enclosed in a cabinet, the cabinet shall be positioned to be readily accessible and shall be adequately ventilated.

3) The chassis and cabinets of the community antenna distribution amplifier or other power sources, the outer conductive shield of the coaxial cables, and the metal conduit or the metal cable sheath

enclosing the electric supply conductors shall all be connected to the system ground with a minimum No. 6 AWG copper conductor.

4) Where a cabinet containing an amplifier or other power device is mounted where it is accessible to the public, it shall be provided with a lock or similar closing device.

54-502 Exposed equipment and terminations

Exposed community antenna distribution equipment and/or associated terminations shall be located in a suitable room or similar area as required by Rule 2-202, separate from electrical light or power installations, except where it is necessary to place them in a joint-use room, in which case a minimum separation of 900 mm from electrical equipment requiring adjustment and maintenance shall be provided and maintained.

54-504 Equipment grounding

Non-powered equipment and enclosures, or equipment powered exclusively by the coaxial cable, shall be considered grounded where they are effectively connected to the grounded outer conductive coaxial cable shield.

Conductors outside buildings

54-600 Overhead conductors on poles

The installation of overhead community antenna distribution conductors in proximity to power conductors on poles and in aerial spans between buildings, poles, and other structures shall conform to the provisions of the *Canadian Electrical Code, Part III*.

54-602 Overhead conductors on roofs

1) Community antenna distribution conductors passing over buildings shall be kept at least 2.5 m above any roof that can be readily walked upon.

2) Community antenna distribution conductors shall not be attached to the upper surfaces of roofs or be run within 2.5 m, measured vertically, of a roof, unless a deviation has been allowed in accordance with Rule 2-030.

3) A deviation in accordance with Rule 2-030 shall not be necessary where the building is a garage or other auxiliary building of one storey.

54-604 Conductors on buildings

1) Community antenna distribution conductors on buildings shall be separated from insulated light or power conductors not in cable or conduit by at least 300 mm, unless the conductors are permanently separated by a continuous and firmly fixed non-metal-type raceway, as permitted in Section 12, in addition to the insulation on the conductors.

2) Community antenna distribution conductors subject to accidental contact with light or power conductors operating at voltages exceeding 300 V, and attached exposed to buildings, shall be separated from combustible material by being supported on glass, porcelain, or other insulating material acceptable for the purpose, except that such separation is not required where the outer conductive sheath of the coaxial cable is grounded.

3) Community antenna distribution conductors attached to buildings shall not conflict with other communication conductors attached to the same building, and sufficient clearances shall be provided so that there will be no unnecessary interference to maintenance operations, and in no case shall the conductors, strand, or equipment of one system cause abrasion to the conductors, strand, or equipment of the other system.

54-606 Conductors entering buildings

The community antenna distribution conductors shall enter the building either through a non-combustible, non-absorptive insulating bushing, or through a metal raceway, except that the insulating bushing or raceway shall be permitted to be omitted where the entering conductors pass through masonry or are acceptable for the purpose.

54

54-608 Lightning conductors
A separation of at least 2 m shall be maintained between conductors of a community antenna distribution circuit on buildings and lightning conductors.

54-610 Swimming pools
Where conductors are installed over or adjacent to swimming pools, they shall be placed in accordance with Rules 68-054 and 68-056.

Underground circuits

54-700 Direct buried systems
Where community antenna distribution conductors are direct buried, the sheath shall be suitable for direct burial and the conductor shall be

a) installed outside the same vertical plane that contains differing underground conductors other than communication conductors, except when installed in accordance with Item f);

b) maintained at a minimum horizontal separation of 300 mm from differing underground conductors other than communication conductors, except when installed in accordance with Item f);

c) placed at a minimum depth of 600 mm, unless rock bottom is encountered at a lesser depth, in which case a minimum depth of 450 mm shall be permitted, except that for service wires under parkways and lawns the depth shall be permitted to be reduced to 450 mm;

d) placed with a layer of sand 75 mm deep, both above and below the cable, if in rocky or stony ground;

e) placed at a minimum depth of 900 mm under an area that is subject to vehicular traffic, except that the depth shall be permitted to be reduced to 600 mm provided that there is mechanical protection that consists of
    i) treated plank at least 38 mm thick or other suitable material that shall be placed over the conductor or cable after first backfilling with 75 mm of sand or earth containing no rocks or stones; or
    ii) a conduit suitable for earth burial placed to facilitate cable replacement and to minimize traffic vibration damage; and

f) equipped with a metal shield when placed in a common trench involving random separation with power supply cables or wiring operations at 750 V or less, in which case the community antenna distribution conductors shall not cross under the supply cables.

54-702 Underground raceway
Where community antenna distribution conductors are placed in underground raceway systems

a) the raceway, including laterals, shall be separated from those used for the electric power system by not less than 50 mm of concrete or 300 mm of well-tamped earth;

b) the raceway shall be located to maintain a minimum depth of 600 mm in areas subject to vehicular traffic and 450 mm in all other areas, except that where rock bottom is encountered at lesser depth the raceway shall be encased in concrete;

c) the raceway shall not terminate in the same maintenance hole, and the conductors or cable assembly shall not be placed in the same maintenance hole, used for an electric power system, unless all requirements of Clause 6 of CSA C22.3 No. 7 are adhered to;

d) the conductors shall not be placed in the same raceway containing electric lighting, power, or Class 1 circuit conductors;

e) the cable sheath shall be suitable for wet locations; and

f) raceways entering a building and forming part of an underground installation shall be sealed with a suitable compound in such a way that moisture and gas will not enter the building and shall
    i) enter the building above ground where practicable; or
    ii) be suitably drained.

54-704 Underground block distribution

Where the entire street circuit is run underground and the circuit is placed to prevent contact with electric lighting, power, or Class 1 circuits of more than 300 V, insulating bushings or raceways as specified in Rule 54-606 shall not be required where the circuit conductors enter a building.

Receiving equipment and amateur transmitting equipment

54-800 Lightning arresters for receiving stations

1) A lightning arrester shall be provided for each lead-in conductor from an outdoor antenna to a receiving station, except where such a lead-in conductor is protected by a continuous grounded metal shield between the antenna and the point of entrance to the building.

2) Lightning arresters for receiving stations shall be located outside the building or inside the building between the point of entrance of the lead-in and the radio set or transformer, and as near as practicable to the entrance of the conductors to the building.

3) Lightning arresters for receiving stations shall not be located near combustible material nor in a hazardous location.

54-802 Lightning arresters for transmitting stations

Each conductor of a lead-in to a transmitting station from an outdoor antenna shall be provided with a lightning arrester or other suitable means that will drain static charges from the antenna system, except

a) where protected by a continuous metal shield that is grounded; or

b) where the antenna is grounded.

Grounding for receiving equipment and amateur transmitting equipment

54-900 Material for grounding conductor

The grounding conductor shall be of copper, aluminum alloy, copper-clad steel, bronze, or other corrosion-resistant material unless otherwise specified.

54-902 Insulation of grounding conductor

The grounding conductor shall be permitted to be uninsulated.

54-904 Support for grounding conductor

The grounding conductor shall be securely fastened in place and shall be permitted to be directly attached to the supporting surface without the use of insulating supports.

54-906 Mechanical protection of grounding conductor

The grounding conductor shall be protected where exposed to mechanical damage.

54-908 Grounding conductor to be run in a straight line

The grounding conductor shall be run in as straight a line as is practicable from the lightning arresters or antenna mast, or both, to the grounding electrode.

54-910 Grounding electrode

The grounding conductor shall be connected to a grounding electrode as specified in Section 10.

54-912 Grounding conductors

The grounding conductor shall be permitted to be run either inside or outside the building.

54-914 Size of protective ground

The size of the protective grounding conductor for receiving and transmitting stations providing ground connection for mast and lightning arresters shall be in accordance with Section 10.

54-916 Common ground

A single grounding conductor shall be permitted to be used for both protective and operating purposes but shall be installed so that disconnection of the operating ground will not affect the protective ground circuit.

54

54-918 Equipment in hospitals

If they could become energized, the exposed non-current-carrying metal parts of radio and television equipment installed in basic, intermediate, and critical care areas of hospitals as defined in Section 24 shall also be grounded to conform with Rule 24-104 7).

54-920 Radio noise suppressors

Radio interference eliminators, interference capacitors, or radio noise suppressors connected to power supply leads shall be of a type approved for the purpose and shall not be exposed to mechanical damage.

54-922 Grounding of antennas

Masts, metal support structures, and antenna frames for receiving stations shall be grounded in accordance with Section 10.

Transmitting stations

54-1000 Enclosure of transmitters

Transmitters shall be enclosed in a metal frame or grille, or thoroughly shielded or separated from the operating space by a barrier or other equivalent means.

54-1002 Grounding of transmitters

All exposed metal parts of transmitters, including external metal handles and controls accessible to the operating personnel and accessories such as microphone stands, shall be grounded.

54-1004 Interlocks on doors of transmitters

All access doors of transmitters shall be provided with interlocks that will disconnect all voltages in excess of 250 V when any access door is opened.

54-1006 Amplifiers

Audio amplifiers that are located outside the transmitter housing shall be suitably housed and shall be located to be readily accessible and adequately ventilated.

Section 56 — Optical fiber cables

Scope

56-000 Scope
This Section applies to the installation of optical fiber cables in conjunction with electrical systems and supplements or amends the general requirements of this Code.

General

56-100 Special terminology
In this Section, the following definition shall apply:

Optical fiber cable — a cable consisting of one or more optical fibers that transmits modulated light for the purpose of control, signalling, or communications.

56-102 Types
Optical fiber cables shall be grouped into the following three types:
a) non-conductive cables that contain no metal members and no other electrically conductive materials;
b) conductive cables that contain non-current-carrying conductive members such as metal strength members, metal vapour barriers, or metal sheaths or shields; and
c) hybrid cables that contain both optical fiber cables and current-carrying electrical conductors.

56-104 Approvals
1) Optical fiber cables placed within buildings shall be of the types selected in accordance with Rule 12-102 3).
2) Optical fiber cables outside buildings shall be suitable for outdoor installation.

56-106 Acceptance of inspector
Installations of optical fiber cables by an electrical utility or a communication utility in the exercise of its function as a utility shall not be subject to the acceptance of an inspector.

Installation methods

56-200 Non-conductive optical fiber cables (see Appendix B)
1) Non-conductive optical fiber cables shall not occupy the same raceway with conductors of electric light, power, or Class 1 circuits, unless
   a) the non-conductive optical fiber cables are functionally associated with the electric light, power, or Class 1 circuit not exceeding 750 V; and
   b) the number and size of non-conductive optical fiber cables and other types of electric conductors in the raceway meet with the applicable requirements for the electrical wiring method.
2) Non-conductive optical fiber cables shall not occupy the same cabinet, panel, outlet box, or similar enclosure housing the electric terminals of an electric light, power, or Class 1 circuit, unless
   a) the non-conductive optical fiber cables are functionally associated with the electric light, power, or Class 1 circuit not exceeding 750 V, and the number and size of non-conductive optical fiber cables and other types of electric conductors in the enclosure meet with the applicable requirements for the electrical wiring method; or
   b) the non-conductive optical fiber cables are factory assembled in the enclosure.
3) Notwithstanding Subrules 1) and 2), for industrial establishments only, where conditions of maintenance and supervision ensure that only authorized persons service the installation, non-conductive optical fiber cables shall be permitted to occupy the same raceway, cabinet, panel, outlet box, or similar enclosure as electric power, control, or instrumentation cables.

56-202 Conductive optical fiber cables (see Appendix B)
1) Conductive optical fiber cables shall be permitted to occupy the same raceway with any of the following systems:
   a) Class 2 circuits in accordance with Section 16;
   b) communication circuits in accordance with Section 60; or
   c) community antenna distribution and radio and television circuits in accordance with Section 54.
2) Conductive optical fiber cables shall not occupy the same raceway, panel, cabinet, or similar enclosure housing electric light, power, or Class 1 circuits.
3) Conductive optical fiber cables shall not occupy the same cabinet, panel, outlet box, or similar enclosure housing the electrical terminals of a Class 2, communications, community antenna distribution, or radio and television circuit, unless
   a) the conductive optical fiber cables are functionally associated with the Class 2, communication, community antenna distribution, or radio and television circuit; or
   b) the conductive optical fiber cables are factory assembled in the enclosure.
4) The conductive non-current-carrying members of conductive optical fiber cables shall be grounded in accordance with Section 10.

56-204 Hybrid cables
1) Optical fibers shall be permitted within the same hybrid cable for electric light, power, or Class 1 circuit conductors not exceeding 750 V, or within the same hybrid cable for Class 2, communications, community antenna, or radio and television circuit conductors, provided that the functions of the optical fibers and the electrical conductors are associated.
2) Hybrid cables shall be classed as electrical cables in accordance with the type of electrical circuit in the conductors and shall be installed in accordance with the Code Rules applicable to the electrical circuit conductors.

56-206 Penetration of a fire separation
Optical fiber cables extending through a fire separation shall be installed to limit fire spread in accordance with Rule 2-128.

56-208 Optical fiber cables in a vertical shaft (see Appendix B)
1) Optical fiber cables in a vertical shaft shall be in a totally enclosed non-combustible raceway.
2) Notwithstanding Subrule 1), conductive and non-conductive optical fiber cables shall be permitted to be installed in a vertical shaft without a totally enclosed non-combustible raceway, provided that these cables meet the flame spread requirements of the *National Building Code of Canada* or local building legislation for buildings of non-combustible construction.

56-210 Optical fiber cables in ducts and plenum chambers
Optical fiber cables shall not be placed in ducts or plenum chambers except as permitted by Rules 2-130 and 12-010.

56-212 Raceways
Raceways shall be installed in accordance with the requirements of Section 12.

56-214 Grounding of entrance cables (see Appendix B)
Where conductive optical fiber cables are exposed to lightning or accidental contact with electrical light or power conductors, the metal members of the conductive optical fiber cable shall be grounded in the building as close as possible to the point of cable entry.

Section 58 — Passenger ropeways and similar equipment

Scope

58-000 Scope (see Appendix B)
1) This Section applies to passenger ropeways as defined in the CSA Z98 passenger ropeways standard, including
   a) tramways;
   b) chairlifts;
   c) gondolas;
   d) surface ropeways;
   e) passenger conveyors; and
   f) similar equipment.
2) This Section supplements or amends the general requirements of this Code.

General

Δ **58-002 Special terminology**
In this Section, the following definitions shall apply:

Cabin — an enclosed or semi-enclosed carrier for transporting passengers, excluding bubble chairs.

Passenger conveyor — a device using a moving flexible element to transport persons uphill for recreational or sport activities.

Station — a location at which loading and/or unloading may take place.

General requirements

58-010 Working clearances
1) The headroom in working spaces around controllers, disconnecting means, and other electric equipment shall be not less than 2.0 m.
2) Notwithstanding Subrule 1) and Rule 2-308, headroom shall be permitted to be unrestricted where
   a) conditions of maintenance and supervision ensure that only authorized persons have access to such areas;
   b) working space is kept clear of obstructions; and
   c) one or more of the following requirements is met:
      i)   live parts of the equipment are suitably guarded, isolated, or insulated, and the equipment can be examined, adjusted, serviced, or maintained while energized without removal of this protection;
      ii) a cautionary label is applied to the electric equipment advising that the electric equipment is not to be examined, adjusted, serviced, or maintained while energized; or
      iii) voltage applied to unguarded or uninsulated parts shall not exceed 30 V rms or 42 V peak.

58-012 Grounding of circuits of less than 50 V
Circuits of less than 50 volts-to-ground shall be grounded in accordance with Rule 10-206 3), except that
a) ungrounded isolated haul ropes shall be permitted for communication, control, remote control, monitoring, supervision, and signal circuits; and
b) communication, control, remote control, monitoring, supervision, and signal circuits shall be permitted to be isolated, provided that they are grounded in accordance with Rule 10-212.

58

58-014 Voltage limitations

1) Voltages for communication, control, remote control, monitoring, supervision, and signal circuits shall not exceed 48 volts-to-ground (nominal), with the exception of circuits for hand-crank-type telephone signal bells.

2) Voltages for motors, machine brakes, motor-generator sets, floodlighting, and heaters shall not exceed 750 volts-to-ground.

3) Voltages for motor control circuits shall not exceed 120 volts-to-ground.

4) Voltages for aerial conductors carried between towers that support the passenger ropeway shall not exceed 30 volts-to-ground or 42 volts-to-ground peak, with the exception of circuits for hand-crank-type telephone signal bells.

5) Voltages for all other circuits shall not exceed 300 volts-to-ground.

58-016 Luminaires on towers and stations

Passenger ropeway towers and stations shall be permitted to support luminaires for night skiing or similar floodlighting applications, provided that

a) a circuit breaker is provided at each tower or station to disconnect all ungrounded conductors to the luminaires supported by that tower or station;

b) the circuit breakers in Item a) are in lockable enclosures; and

c) circuits to luminaires are protected by a ground fault circuit interrupter(s).

Conductors

58-102 Minimum size of conductors

1) In travelling cables, the minimum size of conductors for all communication, control, remote control, monitoring, supervision, and signal circuits shall be No. 20 AWG copper.

2) Except as specified in Subrule 1), the minimum size of conductors for all communication, control, remote control, monitoring, supervision, and signal circuits shall be No. 26 AWG copper.

58-104 Grouping of conductors

1) Optical fiber cables, shielded cables, and conductors for operating devices, power, motor, heating, air conditioning, operating, signal, communication, control, safety, fire alarm, and lighting circuits shall be permitted to be run in the same raceway system or travelling cable, provided that the insulation rating for each conductor is not less than the maximum circuit voltage in the cable or raceway system.

2) Optical fiber cables, shielded cables, and conductors for operating devices, operating, signal, communication, control, safety, and fire alarm circuits shall be permitted to be run in the same aerial cable, provided that the insulation rating for each conductor is not less than the maximum circuit voltage.

3) The optical fiber cables referred to in Subrules 1) and 2) shall include conductive, non-conductive, and hybrid types.

Wiring methods

58-200 Wiring methods

1) Conductors and optical fibers located in machine rooms, control rooms, machinery spaces, control spaces, and in or on cabins, not including travelling cables connecting the movable drive carriage or movable return carriage, shall be installed in rigid metal conduit, electrical metallic tubing, rigid PVC conduit, or wireways.

2) Notwithstanding Subrule 1), the following wiring methods shall be permitted in machine rooms, control rooms, machinery spaces, control spaces, and in or on cabins:
   a) mineral-insulated cable;
   b) aluminum-sheathed cable;

c) armoured cable;

Δ d) cable tray;

e) flexible conduit or liquid-tight flexible conduit between raceways and
   i) limit switches;
   ii) interlocks;
   iii) operating devices; or
   iv) similar devices;

f) flexible conduit or liquid-tight flexible conduit between control panels and
   i) motors;
   ii) machine brakes;
   iii) motor-generator sets;
   iv) disconnecting means; or
   v) pumping unit motors and valves;

g) the following jacketed cables installed between raceways and signal equipment and between raceways and operating devices where mechanical protection is provided and where the cables are supported:
   i) cables used in Class 1 extra-low voltage and Class 2 low-energy circuits, including but not limited to travelling cables connecting the movable carriage or movable return carriage;
   ii) extra-low-voltage control cable;
   iii) communication cable;
   iv) fire alarm and signal cable;
   v) multi-conductor thermoplastic-insulated cable;
   vi) hard-usage; and
   vii) extra-hard-usage cables;

h) auxiliary gutters between controllers, starters, and similar apparatus; or

i) jacketed flexible cords and cables used in extra-low-voltage circuits (30 V or less), provided that the cords and cables are
   i) not greater than 2 m in length; and
   ii) supported and provided with mechanical protection.

58-202 Location of and protection for travelling cables

1) Travelling cable supports shall be located to minimize the possibility of damage due to the cables coming in contact with other equipment.

2) Suitable guards shall be provided to protect the travelling cables against damage.

Protection and control

58-300 Automatic restarting after shutdown (see Appendix B)

Where automatic restarting of a motor after a shutdown could cause injury to persons, the devices controlling the motor shall be arranged so that automatic restarting cannot occur.

58-302 Disconnecting means

1) A single disconnecting means shall be provided for the opening of all ungrounded conductors of the main drive motor and auxiliary drive motor and their ventilation and control circuits for each passenger ropeway or passenger conveyor.

2) The disconnecting means shall be an externally operated fusible switch or a circuit breaker and shall be capable of being locked in the open position and be clearly labelled to describe the load or loads connected.

3) The disconnecting means shall be located where it is visible on entry to the control room or machinery area and readily accessible to authorized persons.

58

4) The disconnecting means shall be provided with a sign to identify the location of the supply side overcurrent protective device.

5) No provision shall be made to automatically close the disconnecting means.

6) Where multiple driving machines or motors are connected to a single passenger ropeway or passenger conveyor, there shall be one disconnecting means to disconnect the motors and control circuits.

7) When a motor disconnecting means is provided in addition to the disconnecting means required by Subrule 1), it shall also disconnect power to the driving machine brake(s) control circuit directly or through an auxiliary contact that is positively opened mechanically, the opening not being solely dependent on springs.

58-304 Utilization equipment disconnecting means

1) Each branch circuit for utilization equipment shall have a single means for disconnecting all ungrounded conductors.

2) The disconnecting means shall be capable of being locked in the open position and shall be located in the machine room, control room, machine space, or control space.

3) The disconnecting means shall be provided with a sign to identify the location of the supply side overcurrent protective device.

58-306 Selective coordination
The overcurrent protection shall be coordinated with any upstream overcurrent protective device(s).

58-308 Ground fault circuit interrupter
Each 125 V, single-phase receptacle installed in machine rooms, control rooms, machine spaces, control spaces, and counterweight enclosures shall be protected with a ground fault circuit interrupter of the Class A type.

58-310 Motor controller rating
The motor controller rating shall comply with Rule 28-500 1), except that the rating shall be permitted to be less than the nominal rating of the drive motor when the controller inherently limits the available power to the motor and is marked "power limited".

Branch circuits

58-400 Branch circuits for machine room, control room, machinery space, or control space luminaires and receptacle(s)

1) Luminaires shall be provided in each machine room, control room, machinery space, and control space.

2) At least one 125 V, single-phase, duplex receptacle, having a configuration in accordance with Diagram 1, shall be provided in each machine room, control room, machinery space, and control space.

3) Separate branch circuits shall supply luminaires and a receptacle(s) for each machine room, control room, machinery space, or control space.

4) The luminaires required in Subrule 1) shall not be supplied from the load side of the ground fault circuit interrupters required by Rule 58-308.

5) Lighting switches shall be provided in each machine room, control room, machinery space, and control space and shall be within easy reach of the point of entry.

58-402 Branch circuit for counterweight enclosure luminaires and receptacle(s)

1) Luminaires shall be provided in counterweight buildings or rooms.

2) Where a counterweight is enclosed in a building or room, a separate branch circuit shall supply space lighting and a receptacle(s).

3) The luminaires required in Subrule 1) shall not be supplied from the load side of the ground fault circuit interrupters required by Rule 58-308.

58-404 Branch circuits for other utilization equipment

1) Separate branch circuits shall supply utilization equipment not identified in Rules 58-400 and 58-402, however used in conjunction with equipment identified in Rule 58-000.

2) The overcurrent devices protecting the branch circuits shall be located in the machinery room or control room or machinery space or control space.

Regenerative power

58-500 Regenerative power

For passenger ropeways or passenger conveyors or material ropeways that regenerate power back into a power source that is unable to absorb the regenerative power under overhauling load or braking conditions, means shall be provided to absorb this power.

58

Section 60 — Electrical communication systems

Scope

60-000 Scope (see Appendix B)
1) This Section applies to the installation of communication systems.
2) This Section supplements or amends the general requirements of this Code.

General

60-100 Special terminology
In this Section, the following definition shall apply:

Exposed plant — the circuit or any portion of it subject to lightning strikes, to voltage exceeding 300 V rms due to accidental contact with electric lighting or power conductors, to induction from power line unbalance operation or faults, and to ground potential rise.

60-102 Use of approved equipment
Electrical equipment used in the installation of a communication system shall be approved
a)   if connected to exposed plant;
b)   if the equipment is connected to a telecommunication network, unless the equipment is specifically allowed by other Rules in this Section; or
c)   if required by other Rules in this Section.

60-104 Circuits in communication cables (see Appendix B)
Radio and television circuits, remote control circuits, and fire alarm circuits or parts of this equipment shall be
a)   permitted to use conductors in a communication building entrance cable assembly having other conductors used as communication circuits;
b)   deemed to be communication circuits for those portions of circuits that use conductors within the communication building entrance cable assembly; and
c)   suitably protected at the point of interface connection with the communication cable conductors.

60-106 Hazardous locations
Where the wiring or electrical equipment within the Scope of this Section is installed in hazardous locations as defined in Section 18, 20, or 24, it shall also comply with the applicable Rules of those Sections.

60-108 Inspection by an inspector
1)   Communication circuits employed by an electrical or communication utility in the exercise of its function as a utility shall not be subject to inspection by an inspector.
2)   Where the communication circuit derives power for operation from a supply circuit, the transformer or other current-limiting device used at the junction of the communication and the supply circuit shall be subject to inspection by an inspector.

60-110 Approved transformers
Where transformers or other devices supply current to a communication circuit from an electric supply circuit, the transformers or other devices shall be of a type approved for the service.

Protection

60-200 Provision of primary protectors (see Appendix B)
1)   A primary protector shall be provided on each electrical communication circuit, except as permitted in Subrule 4).

2) The primary protector shall be located in, on, or immediately adjacent to the structure or building served and as close as practicable to the point at which the conductors enter or attach to the structure or building.

3) The primary protector shall not be located in any hazardous location as defined in Sections 18, 20, and 24, nor in the immediate vicinity of flammable or explosive materials.

4) A primary protector need not be provided if no portion of the circuit is considered exposed plant.

60-202 Primary protector requirements

1) The primary protector shall connect between each line conductor and ground and, when required by Subrule 3), have a fuse connected in series in each line conductor.

2) Fuseless primary protectors shall be permitted
   a) on circuits that enter a building in a cable with a grounded metal sheath or shield, provided that the conductors in the cable safely fuse at currents less than the ampacity of the primary protector and the primary protector grounding conductor;
   b) on circuits served by insulated conductors extending to a building from a grounded metal-sheathed or shielded cable, provided that the conductors in the cable safely fuse at currents less than the ampacity of the primary protector, the associated insulated conductors, and the primary protector grounding conductor;
   c) on circuits served by insulated conductors, extending to a building from other than grounded metal-sheathed or shielded cable, provided that
      i) the primary protector grounding conductor is grounded in conformance with Rule 60-704; and
      ii) the connections of the insulated conductors extending from the building to the exposed plant, or the conductors of the exposed plant, safely fuse at currents less than the ampacity of the primary protector, the associated insulated conductors, and the primary protector grounding conductor; or
   d) on circuits in a cable with a grounded metal sheath or shield that are subject to lightning strikes but are otherwise not exposed plant.

3) Where the requirements of Subrule 2) are not met, fused primary protectors shall be used.

4) Primary protectors having exposed live parts shall be located in a suitable room or similar area as required by Rule 2-202, separate from electrical light or power installations, except where it is necessary to place them in a joint-use room, in which case a minimum separation of 900 mm from electrical equipment requiring adjustment and maintenance shall be provided and maintained.

60-204 Protection for communication circuits in high-voltage stations (see Appendix B)

Equipment for the protection of communication circuits used for control and signalling in high-voltage stations shall be suitable for the application.

Inside conductors

60-300 Conductor installations

Rules 60-302 to 60-334 apply to the installation of inside communication conductors.

60-302 Raceways

Raceways for communication conductors shall be installed in accordance with the requirements of Section 12 and, if metal, shall be grounded in accordance with Section 10.

60-304 Insulation

Wire and cable used for communication systems shall be of approved types selected in accordance with Rule 12-102 3).

60-306 Grounding of conductors with an outer metal covering

Where a conductor or cable is equipped with an outer metal covering, the covering shall be grounded.

60

60-308 Separation from other conductors

1) The conductors of an electrical communication system in a building shall be separated at least 50 mm from any insulated conductor of a Class 1 circuit or an electric light or power system operating at 300 V or less, and shall be separated at least 600 mm from any insulated conductor or an electric light or power system operating at more than 300 V, unless
    a) one system is in grounded metal raceways, metal-sheathed cable, or grounded armoured cable;
    b) the Class 1 circuit or electric light or power system operating at 300 V or less uses a hard-usage or extra-hard-usage flexible cord selected in accordance with Rule 12-402 1); or
    c) both systems are permanently separated by a continuous, firmly fixed non-metal raceway in addition to the insulation of the conductors.

2) Where the light or power conductors are bare, all communication conductors in the same room or space shall be enclosed in a grounded metal raceway, and no opening, such as an outlet box, shall be permitted to be located within 2 m of bare conductors if up to and including 15 kV or within 3 m of bare conductors above 15 kV.

3) The conductors of an electrical communication system shall not be placed in any outlet box, junction box, raceway, or similar fitting or compartment that contains conductors of electric light or power systems or of Class 1 circuits (as defined in Rule 16-002), unless
    a) the communication conductors are separated from the other conductors by a suitable partition; or
    b) the power or Class 1 conductors are placed solely for the purpose of supplying power to the communication system or for connection to remote control equipment, except that no communication conductors installed in an outlet box, junction box, raceway, or similar fitting or compartment that contains such conductors of power or Class 1 circuits shall show a green-coloured insulation, unless such a communication conductor is completely contained within a sheathed or jacketed cable assembly throughout the length that is present in such raceways or enclosures.

4) The conductors of an electrical communication system in a building shall not be placed in a shaft with the conductors of an electric light or power system, unless
    a) the conductors of all systems are insulated and are separated by at least 50 mm; or
    b) the conductors of either system are encased in non-combustible tubing.

60-310 Penetration of a fire separation

Conductors of communication circuits extending through a fire separation shall be installed to limit fire spread in accordance with Rule 2-128.

60-312 Communication cables in hoistways

1) Special permission shall be required to install communication conductors in hoistways.
2) All conductors, except travelling cables, shall be totally enclosed in continuous metal raceway.
3) Pull boxes required for communication interconnection shall be located outside the hoistway.

60-314 Communication conductors in ducts and plenum chambers

Communication conductors shall not be placed in ducts or plenum chambers except as permitted by Rules 2-130 and 12-010.

60-316 Data processing systems

The interconnecting cables used in data processing systems shall be permitted to contain power and communication conductors where such cables are specifically approved for the purpose.

60-318 Conductors under raised floors

Conductors of communication circuits shall be permitted to be installed without additional mechanical protection under a raised floor, provided that
a) the raised floor is of suitable non-combustible construction;

b)   a minimum separation of 50 mm is provided and maintained where the conductors are used to serve data processing systems and are placed parallel to any other power supply wiring; and

c)   the conductors serve the equipment located only on the floor above the raised floor, where the space under the raised floor is used as an air plenum.

60-320 Conductors in concealed installations
Where the ends of cables or conductors are not terminated on a device, they shall be capped or taped.

60-322 Type CFC under-carpet wiring system Rules
Rules 60-324 to 60-334 apply to the installation of communication flat cable type (CFC) systems.

60-324 Use permitted
Type CFC system wiring shall be permitted to be used

a)   only under carpet squares not exceeding 750 mm, and any adhesive used shall be of the release type;

b)   as an extension of conventional wiring to serve areas or zones, and each run of wiring from the transition point shall not exceed 15 m;

c)   on hard, smooth, continuous floor surfaces made of concrete if sealed, ceramic, composition flooring, wood, or similar materials;

d)   in dry or interior damp locations; and

e)   on floors heated in excess of 30 °C only if approved and identified for that purpose.

60-326 Use prohibited
Type CFC system wiring shall not be used

a)   outdoors or in wet locations;

b)   where subject to corrosive vapours or liquids;

c)   in hazardous locations;

d)   in dwelling units;

e)   in hospitals or institutional buildings except in office areas;

f)   on walls except when entering the transition point; or

g)   under permanent-type partitions or walls.

60-328 Floor protective coverings
Type CFC system wiring shall be covered with abrasion-resistant tape, secured to the floor, so that all cables, corners, and bare conductor ends are completely covered.

60-330 Coverings
Type CFC system wiring shall be permitted to cross over or under each other, and over or under power supply Type FCC system wiring, provided that there is a layer of grounded metal shielding between the FCC and CFC system cables as required in Rule 12-820.

60-332 System height
Type CFC system wiring shall not be stacked on top of each other except as required to enter the transition point.

60-334 Grounding of shields
Type CFC system wiring equipped with a metal shield shall be grounded.

Equipment

60-400 Communication equipment in bathrooms and in areas adjacent to pools
1)   Communication equipment located in a bathroom shall be permanently fixed on the wall and shall be located so that no part can be reached or used from the bath or from the shower enclosure; however, it shall be permitted to be actuated by means of a cord with an insulating link.

2)   Communication jacks shall not be located in a bathroom.

60

3) Communication equipment located in areas adjacent to pools shall be installed in accordance with Rule 68-070.

60-402 Equipment in air ducts, plenums, or suspended ceilings (see Appendix B)

Communication equipment and terminals shall not be placed in ducts, plenums, or hollow spaces that are used to transport environmental air nor in suspended ceiling areas, except that where a duct, plenum, or hollow space is created by a suspended ceiling having lay-in panels or tiles, connecting blocks that are of a non-protective type shall be permitted to be installed if they are placed in an accessible enclosure.

60-404 Exposed equipment and terminations

Exposed communication equipment and/or associated terminations shall be located, as required by Rule 2-202, in a suitable room or similar area that is separate from electrical light or power installations, except where it is necessary to place them in a joint-use room, in which case a minimum separation of 900 mm from electrical equipment requiring adjustment and maintenance shall be provided and maintained.

60-406 Ground start circuits

Communication circuits connected to a telecommunication network and having return paths via local ground or other circuitry that similarly could present a fire hazard shall be provided with a current-limiting device installed in or adjacent to the equipment, of a type recommended by the equipment manufacturer as suitable for the application, that will limit the current under normal operating conditions and under fault conditions, to prevent fire hazards.

60-408 Communication systems in hospitals

If they could become energized, exposed non-current-carrying metal parts of communications equipment, other than telephone sets, installed in basic, intermediate, and critical care areas of hospitals as defined in Section 24, shall also be grounded to conform with Rule 24-104 7).

Outside conductors

60-500 Overhead conductors on poles

The installation of overhead communication conductors on poles in proximity with power conductors shall be established in accordance with the *Canadian Electrical Code, Part III*.

60-502 Overhead conductors on roofs

1) Communication conductors passing over buildings shall be kept at least 2.5 m above any roof that can be readily walked upon.
2) Communication conductors shall not be attached to the upper surfaces of roofs or be run within 2 m, measured vertically, of a roof unless a deviation has been allowed in accordance with Rule 2-030.
3) A deviation in accordance with Rule 2-030 shall not be necessary where the building is a garage or other auxiliary building of one storey.

60-504 Circuits requiring primary protectors

Communication circuits that require primary protectors in accordance with Rule 60-200 shall comply with Rules 60-506 to 60-514.

60-506 Wire insulation

In a communication circuit requiring a primary protector, each wire shall have rubber or thermoplastic insulation and shall

a) have a protective jacket placed over individual or groups of wires, which shall be permitted to be integral with the insulation; and
b) be suitable for the application and in accordance with the manufacturer's recommendations.

60-508 Cable insulation

1) Wires within a cable used for communication circuits requiring primary protectors shall be permitted to have paper, thermoplastic, or other suitable insulation.

2) The cable shall be of a type suitable for the application and in accordance with the manufacturer's recommendations, with
   a) a metal sheath;
   b) a composite sheath having a metal shield and overall outer protective rubber or thermoplastic jacket; or
   c) a protective rubber or thermoplastic jacket without a metal shield.

60-510 Communication conductors on buildings

1) Communication conductors on buildings shall be separated from insulated light or power conductors not in conduit by at least 300 mm unless permanently separated by a continuously and firmly fixed non-metal raceway, in addition to the insulation on the conductors.

2) Where the light or power conductors are bare, the communication conductors shall be in the lower position and, in order to provide adequate working space, the clearance given in Subrule 1) shall be increased to a minimum of 600 mm from a conductor operating at 750 V or less.

3) Communication conductors subject to accidental contact with light or power conductors operating at voltages exceeding 300 V, and attached exposed to buildings, shall be separated from combustible material by being supported on glass, porcelain, or other suitable insulating material, except that such separation shall not be required where fuses are omitted as provided for in Rule 60-202 2), or where conductors are used to extend circuits to a building from a cable having a grounded metal sheath or shield.

60-512 Communication conductors entering buildings

Where a primary protector is installed inside the building, the communication conductors shall enter the building either through a non-combustible, non-absorptive insulating bushing, or through a metal raceway, except that the insulating bushing shall be permitted to be omitted where the entering conductors
a) are in metal-sheathed or shielded cable;
b) pass through masonry;
c) are without fuses in the primary protectors as provided for in Rule 60-202 2); or
d) are used to extend circuits to a building from a cable having a grounded metal sheath or shield.

60-514 Communication conductors entering mobile homes

Communication conductors shall enter a mobile home using the facility provided for by Rule 70-106.

60-516 Lightning conductors

A separation of at least 2 m shall, where practicable, be maintained between conductors of communication circuits on buildings and lightning conductors.

60-518 Swimming pools

Where wires or cables are installed over or adjacent to swimming pools, they shall be placed in accordance with Rules 68-054 and 68-056.

Underground circuits

60-600 Direct buried systems

Where communication conductors or cable assemblies are direct buried, they shall be suitable for direct burial and the conductor or cable assembly shall
a) not be installed in the same vertical plane with other underground systems, except when installed in accordance with Item g);
b) maintain a minimum horizontal separation of 300 mm from other underground systems, except when installed in accordance with Item g);

60

c) be not less than 600 mm deep, unless rock bottom is encountered at a lesser depth, in which case a minimum depth of 450 mm shall be permitted, except that for service wires under parkways and lawns the depth shall be permitted to be reduced to 450 mm;

d) be placed with a layer of sand 75 mm deep, both above and below the cable, if in rocky or stony ground;

e) be not less than 900 mm deep under an area that is subject to vehicular traffic, except that the depth shall be permitted to be reduced to 600 mm if mechanical protection is provided that consists of
    i) treated plank at least 38 mm thick or other suitable material, which shall be placed over the conductor or cable after first backfilling with 75 mm of sand or earth containing no rocks or stones; or
    ii) a conduit suitable for earth burial placed to facilitate cable replacement and to minimize traffic vibration damage;

f) not be placed in a common trench involving random separation with power supply cables or conductors operating at over 750 V, except when the applicable requirements of CSA C22.3 No. 7 are adhered to and the operating voltage of the power supply cables or conductors does not exceed 22 kV line-to-ground; and

g) have a metal sheath when placed in a common trench involving random separation with power supply cables or conductors, in which case the communication conductor or cable assembly shall not cross under the supply cables.

60-602 Underground raceway

Where communication conductors or cable assemblies are placed in underground raceway systems

a) the raceway, including laterals, shall be separated from those used for the electric power system by not less than 50 mm of concrete or 300 mm of well-tamped earth;

b) the raceway shall be located to maintain a minimum depth of 600 mm in areas subject to vehicular traffic and 450 mm in all other areas, except that where rock bottom is encountered at a lesser depth the raceway shall be encased in concrete;

c) the raceway shall not terminate in the same maintenance hole, and the conductors or cable assembly shall not be placed in the same maintenance hole, used for the electric power system, unless all requirements of Clause 6 of CSA C22.3 No. 7 are adhered to;

d) the cables shall not be placed in the same raceway containing electric lighting or power supply cables;

e) the cables shall be suitable for wet locations; and

f) raceways entering a building and forming part of an underground installation shall be sealed with a suitable compound in such a way that moisture and gas will not enter the building and shall
    i) enter the building above ground where practicable; or
    ii) be suitably drained.

60-604 Underground block distribution

Where the entire street circuit is run underground and the part of the circuit within the block is placed so that it is not liable to contact with electric lighting or power circuits of more than 300 V

a) no primary protector shall be required as specified in Rule 60-200;

b) the insulation requirements of Rules 60-506 and 60-508 shall not apply;

c) conductors need not be placed on insulating supports as specified in Rule 60-510 3); and

d) where the conductors enter the building, no bushings shall be required as specified in Rule 60-512.

Grounding

60-700 Bonding of cable sheath (see Appendix B)
Where cables, either aerial or underground, enter buildings, the metal sheath or shield of the cable shall be bonded to ground as close as practicable to the point of entrance or shall be interrupted as close as practicable to the point of entrance by an insulating joint or equivalent device.

60-702 Cable sheath bonding conductor (see Appendix B)
The cable sheath bonding conductor required by Rule 60-700 shall have an ampacity at least equal to, or greater than, that of the outer conductive sheath of the exposed cable, except that the bonding conductor shall not be required to be larger than No. 6 AWG copper.

60-704 Primary protector grounding conductor (see Appendix B)
The grounding conductor used to ground primary protectors specified in Rule 60-202 shall be copper and shall
a) have rubber or thermoplastic insulation;
b) be not smaller than the required grounding conductor specified in Table 59;
c) be run from the primary protector to the point of connection described in Rule 60-706 in as straight a line as possible; and
d) be guarded from mechanical damage, where necessary.

60-706 Grounding electrode (see Appendix B)
1) The grounding conductor shall, wherever possible, be connected to a water pipe grounding electrode, as close to the point of entrance as possible.
2) Where the water pipe is not readily available and the grounding conductor of the power consumer's service is connected to the water pipe at the building, the primary protector grounding conductor shall be permitted to be connected to the metal conduit, service equipment enclosures, or grounding conductor of the power consumer's service.
3) In the absence of a water pipe, the communication primary protector grounding conductor shall be permitted to be connected to an effectively grounded metal structure, or to a ground rod or pipe driven into permanently damp earth, but
    a) steam, gas, and hot water pipes and lightning rod conductors shall not be used as grounding electrodes; and
    b) a driven rod or pipe used for grounding power circuits shall not be used as a communication primary protector grounding electrode unless it is connected to the grounded conductor of a multi-grounded power neutral.
4) Where a driven ground rod or pipe is used as a grounding electrode for an electrical communication system, it shall be separated by at least 2 m from any other electrode, including those used for power circuits, radio, lightning rods, or any other purpose, and shall be connected only to that of the power circuits in accordance with Rule 10-104.
5) The normal length of a driven ground rod used as the grounding electrode for a communication station primary protector is 1.5 m, but where the normal rod would not reach moist soil when installed, a rod of suitable additional length shall be used.

60-708 Grounding electrode connection
The grounding conductor shall be attached to the grounding electrode as required in Rule 10-118
a) directly; or
b) to a wire lead permanently connected to the ground rod electrode in a manner specified in CSA C83.

60-710 Bonding of electrodes
A copper conductor not smaller than No. 6 AWG shall be connected between communication and power grounding electrodes when separate grounding electrodes are required as described in Rule 60-706.

60

Section 62 — Fixed electric heating systems

Scope

62-000 Scope (see Appendix B)
1) This Section applies to
   a) fixed electric space-heating systems for heating rooms and similar areas;
   b) fixed surface heating systems; and
   c) fixed electric heating systems not covered by Item a) or b).
2) The requirements of this Section supplement or amend the general requirements of this Code.

General

62-100 General Rules
Rules 62-102 to 62-132 apply to all heating installations, except where otherwise specified.

62-102 Special terminology (see Appendix B)
In this Section, the following definitions shall apply:

Bare element water heater — a self-contained, factory-assembled water heater that heats water by direct contact with the uninsulated heating element wire.

Central unit — any electrical heating unit (or group of units assembled to form a complete unit) permanently installed in such a way that it can convey heat to rooms or areas using air, liquid, or vapour flowing through pipes or ducts; the term includes duct heaters.

Dielectric heating — the generation of heat within electrical insulating and semiconductor materials under the action of a high-frequency electric field.

Heating cable — a parallel or series heating cable.

Heating cable set — a parallel or series heating cable assembled with the associated parts necessary to connect it to a source of electrical supply.

Heating device — any form of electrical heater, including cables, fixtures, panels, and strip systems.

Heating device set — a heating device assembled with the associated parts necessary to connect it to a source of electrical supply.

Heating fixture — any heating unit (or group of units assembled so as to form a complete unit) permanently installed in such a way that it can be removed or replaced without removing or damaging any part of the building structure.

Heating panel — a rigid or non-rigid laminated plane section in which the heating element consisting of a continuously parallel resistive material, a series resistive material, or a parallel-series resistive material is embedded between or in sheets of electrical insulating material.

Heating panel set — a heating panel assembled with the associated parts necessary to connect it to a source of electrical supply.

Impedance heating — the generation of heat by means of the application of a low ac voltage across an electrically conductive object, with the resulting current directly heating that object.

Induction heating — the generation of heat by means of the application of magnetic-field-induced alternating currents to directly heat an electrically conductive object.

Infrared radiant heater — a heating device that emits heat primarily by infrared radiation.

Infrared radiant heater of the metal-sheath glowing element type — an infrared radiant heater utilizing a metal-sheathed tubular heating element operating at a temperature high enough to become visibly glowing.

Parallel heating cable — a cable incorporating heating elements connected in parallel either continuously or intermittently such that the watt density along the length of the cable is not altered by changes in the cable length.

Parallel heating cable set — a parallel heating cable assembled with the associated parts necessary to connect it to a source of electrical supply.

Sauna heater — a device that is designed for heating air and that is installed permanently in a sauna room to produce a hot atmosphere.

Series heating cable — a cable using a series resistance conductor(s).

Series heating cable set — a series heating cable assembled with the associated parts necessary to connect it to a source of electrical supply.

Skin effect trace heating — the generation of heat within a ferromagnetic envelope (heat tube) by the application of an ac voltage across an insulated conductor internally connected in series with the surrounding heat tube, with the resulting current heating the heat tube and indirectly heating an adjacent object.

Δ   **Trace heater** — see **Heating cable**.

62-104 Installation of heating devices and bonding (see Appendix B)
1)   Electric heating devices shall be assembled and installed in accordance with the manufacturer's instructions and the applicable Rules of this Section.
2)   Electrically conductive shields, braids, sheaths, and coverings, and all exposed metal surfaces of heating devices, shall be bonded to ground.

62-106 Special locations (see Appendix B)
Heating equipment that is installed in hazardous locations or subject to wet or corrosive conditions shall be marked as suitable for the particular location.

62-108 Terminal connections (see Appendix B)
1)   Connections to heating device sets shall be made in terminal fittings or boxes, and heating device sets shall be installed so that connections between circuit conductors and equipment device conductors are accessible without disturbing any part of the wiring.
2)   Where the connections described in Subrule 1) are made in terminal fittings, they shall be contained in an enclosure of non-combustible material.
3)   Where the maximum temperature at the point of connection between a branch circuit conductor and a heating device set exceeds 60 °C, the temperature rating of the conductor insulation shall meet or exceed the temperature rating specified by the manufacturer.
4)   Where a tap conductor is used to meet the requirements of Subrule 3), the length of the tap conductor shall be not less than 500 mm.

62-110 Branch circuits
1)   Branch circuit conductors used for the supply of energy to heating device sets shall
    a)   be used solely for such heating device sets; and
    b)   have an ampacity not less than that of the connected load supplied.

62

Δ 2) For the purpose of this Rule, a unit that combines heating with ventilating or lighting equipment, or both, shall be considered to be a heating device set.

Δ 3) Notwithstanding Subrule 1), where a heat lamp is not the sole source of heat, it shall be permitted to be used in a luminaire or in a box-mount-type luminaire, where the luminaire is supplied from a branch circuit installed in accordance with Rule 8-304.

62-112 Temperature of adjacent combustible materials

Heating devices shall be installed so that any adjacent combustible materials shall not be subjected to temperatures in excess of 90 °C.

62-114 Overcurrent protection and grouping (see Appendix B)

1) Every heating fixture, heating cable set, heating panel set, or parallel heating set having an input of more than 30 A shall be supplied by a branch circuit that supplies no other equipment.

2) In buildings for residential occupancy, two or more heating fixtures, heating cable sets, or heating panel sets shall be permitted to be connected to a branch circuit used for space heating, provided that the branch circuit overcurrent devices are rated or set at not more than 30 A.

3) In other than buildings for residential occupancy,
   a) two or more heating fixtures, heating cable sets, heating panel sets, or parallel heating sets shall be permitted to be grouped on a branch circuit, and the branch circuit overcurrent devices shall not be set or rated in excess of 60 A unless a deviation has been allowed in accordance with Rule 2-030 to use overcurrent devices having a higher setting or rating; and
   b) where three heating fixtures, heating cable sets, heating panel sets, or parallel heating sets are grouped on a branch circuit in a balanced three-phase arrangement, the branch circuit overcurrent devices shall be permitted to be set or rated in excess of 60 A.

4) Where two or more heating fixtures, heating cable sets, heating panel sets, or parallel heating sets are grouped on a single branch circuit, the non-heating leads of heating cable sets, heating fixtures, and taps to heating cable sets, heating fixtures, and strip systems shall
   a) have an ampacity not less than one-third the rating of the branch circuit overcurrent device; and
   b) be not more than 7.5 m in length.

5) Notwithstanding Subrule 4), where the rating or setting of the overcurrent device does not exceed the ampacity of the non-heating leads and taps to heating devices, and the non-heating leads and taps to heating devices meet the requirements of Rule 12-102 3), there shall be no length limitation as required in Subrule 4) b).

6) Where a service, feeder, or branch circuit is used solely for the supply of energy to heating device sets, the load, as determined using Rule 62-118, shall not exceed
   a) 100% of the rating or setting of the overcurrent devices protecting the service conductors, feeder conductors, or branch circuit conductors when the fused switch or circuit breaker is marked for continuous operation at 100% of the ampere rating of its overcurrent devices; or
   b) 80% of the rating or setting of the overcurrent devices protecting the service conductors, feeder conductors, or branch circuit conductors when the fused switch or circuit breaker is marked for continuous operation at 80% of the ampere rating of its overcurrent devices.

Ⓔ 7) Service, feeder, or branch circuit conductors supplying only fixed resistance heating loads shall be permitted to have an ampacity less than the rating or setting of the circuit overcurrent protection, provided that their ampacity is
   a) not less than the load; and
   b) at least 80% of the rating or setting of the circuit overcurrent protection.

8) Notwithstanding Subrule 7) b), where 125% of the allowable ampacity of a conductor does not correspond to a standard rating of the overcurrent device, the next higher standard rating shall be permitted.

62-116 Ground fault protection (see Appendix B)

1) Ground fault protection shall be provided to de-energize all normally ungrounded conductors of electric heating cable sets, heating panel sets, and fixed infrared radiant heaters of the metal-sheath glowing element type, with a ground fault setting sufficient to allow normal operation of the heater.

2) Notwithstanding Subrule 1), in industrial establishments where continued circuit operation is necessary for safe operation of equipment or processes, and conditions of maintenance and supervision ensure that only qualified persons will service the installed systems, ground fault detection shall be permitted in place of the requirements of Subrule 1).

3) Notwithstanding Subrule 1), ground fault protection shall not be required for heating cable sets and panel sets connected to a Class 1 extra-low-voltage power circuit, where
   a) the Class 1 extra-low-voltage power circuit is supplied from the secondary of an isolating transformer having no direct electrical connection between the primary and secondary windings;
   b) the isolating transformer is supplied from a branch circuit operating at not more than 150 volts-to-ground; and
   c) the Class 1 extra-low-voltage power circuit is not grounded.

62-118 Demand factors for service conductors and feeders

1) Where service conductors or feeders are used solely for the supply of energy to heating devices, they shall have an ampacity not less than the sum of the current ratings of all the devices that they supply.

2) Notwithstanding Subrule 1), where service conductors or feeders are used solely for the supply of energy to heating devices, and where the service or feeder supplies loads of a cyclic or similar nature such that the maximum connected heating load will not be operated at the same time, the ampacity of the feeder conductors shall be permitted to be based on the maximum load that may be connected at any one time.

3) Notwithstanding Subrule 1), where a heating installation in a building for residential occupancy is provided with automatic thermostatic control devices in each room or heated area, the ampacity of service conductors or feeders supplying heating devices only shall be based on the following:
   a) the first 10 kW of connected heating load at 100% demand factor; plus
   b) the balance of the connected heating load at 75% demand factor.

4) Where service conductors or feeders are used to supply an electric thermal storage heating system, duct heater, or an electric furnace, the connected heating load shall be calculated at 100% demand factor.

5) Where service conductors or feeders supply a combined load of heating and other equipment, they shall have an ampacity consisting of the following:
   a) in the case of buildings for residential occupancy, the sum of the heating load as computed by Subrules 3) and 4) plus the combined loads of other equipment with demand factors as applicable in Section 8; or
   b) in the case of other occupancies, 75% of the total connected heating load plus the combined loads of the other equipment with demand factors as applicable in Section 8 for the type of occupancy.

6) Notwithstanding Subrule 5) b), where the combined load with applicable demand factors other than heating is less than 25% of the connected heating load on a service or feeder, no demand factor shall be applicable to the heating portion of the load.

62-120 Temperature control devices

1) Temperature control devices rated to operate at line voltage shall have a current rating at least equal to the sum of the current ratings of the equipment they control.

62

2) Temperature control devices that can be turned automatically or manually to a marked OFF position and that either interrupt line current directly or control a contactor or similar device that interrupts line current shall open all ungrounded conductors of the controlled heating circuit when in the OFF position.

62-122 Construction of series heating cable sets
Series heating cable sets shall be complete assemblies, including both the heating portion and the non-heating end leads, and shall have permanent markings as required located on one or both of the non-heating leads not more than 75 mm from the supply end of a non-heating lead.

Δ 62-124 Installation of series heating cable sets
1) The heating portion of a series heating cable set shall not be shortened, and any heating cable set that does not bear its original markings shall be considered to have been shortened unless the installer can demonstrate, by instrument measurements, that the characteristics of the series heating cable set have not been altered.
2) The entire length of the heating portion, including connections to non-heating leads, shall be installed within the heating area.

62-126 Field repair, modification, or assembly of series heating cable sets (see Appendix B)
Notwithstanding Rule 62-124, at industrial establishments where conditions of maintenance and supervision ensure use by qualified persons, series heating cable sets shall be permitted to be
a) field repaired or spliced with splice kits supplied by the heating cable manufacturer, provided that the total length of the heating portion of the sets is not changed by more than 3%; and
b) field modified or field assembled with splice and termination kits supplied by the heating cable manufacturer, provided that
   i) a permanent tag with the new design information is installed;
   ii) a permanent record of the new design information is retained;
   iii) tests for insulation resistance and verification of the finished heating cable set resistance are made;
   iv) the design, or modifications to the design, are done by a qualified person and reviewed by the heating cable manufacturer; and
   v) the electrical rating is permanently marked
      A) in or on the junction box that is provided as part of the system;
      B) on the heating cable; or
      C) on a permanent tag within 75 mm of a power connection or power connection fitting.

62-128 Non-heating leads of heating device sets (see Appendix B)
1) The non-heating leads of heating device sets shall be installed in accordance with the requirements of Rule 62-104.
2) Conductors that are not an integral factory-built part of a heating device set, or factory supplied with the heating device set, shall be installed in accordance with the requirements of Section 12.
3) Where a heating device is embedded in concrete or a subfloor assembly, or under a floor covering, the non-heating leads shall be run from the junction box to the floor in a raceway.
4) Notwithstanding Subrule 3), the raceway shall be permitted to terminate no more than 50 mm from the floor where the non-heating leads are contained within a wooden base plate and effectively protected from mechanical damage.
5) Notwithstanding Subrule 3), Rules 62-124 2), and 62-214 2), the joint between the heating portion and the non-heating leads shall be permitted to be installed in the supply junction box forming part of the system, provided that the heating portion is contained within a raceway between the point where it leaves the concrete, subfloor, or non-combustible material and enters the box.

Δ **62-130 Heater controls installed in proximity to sinks, tubs, or shower stalls**
1) A manually operated control for a heating device shall be located not less than 1 m from a sink (a wash basin complete with a drainpipe), tub, or shower stall, this distance being measured horizontally between the control and the sink, tub, or shower stall without piercing a wall, partition, or similar obstacle.
2) Notwithstanding Subrule 1), a manually operated control shall be permitted to be located less than 1 m from a sink (a wash basin complete with a drainpipe) and not less than 500 mm from a tub or shower stall, provided that it is
   a) protected by a ground fault circuit interrupter of the Class A type; or
   b) supplied by an extra-low-voltage Class 2 circuit.

Δ **62-132 Heating devices installed in proximity to sinks, tubs, or shower stalls**
1) A heating device installed less than 1.8 m above the floor shall not be installed less than 1 m horizontally from a sink (a wash basin complete with a drainpipe), tub, or shower stall, this distance being measured horizontally between the heating device and the sink, tub, or shower stall without piercing a wall, partition, or similar obstacle.
2) Notwithstanding Subrule 1), a heating device shall be permitted to be installed less than 1.8 m above the floor and less than 1 m from a sink (a wash basin complete with a drainpipe), tub, or shower stall, provided that it is protected by a ground fault circuit interrupter of the Class A type.

Electric space-heating systems

62-200 Electric space heating (see Appendix B)
1) Rules 62-200 2) and 62-202 to 62-222 apply to fixed electric space-heating systems for heating rooms and similar areas.
2) Minimum clearances from electric space-heating systems shall be as specified in Table 67.

Δ **62-202 Temperature control**
Each enclosed area within which a heater is located shall have a temperature control device.

62-204 Proximity to other wiring (see Appendix B)
1) Wiring of other circuits located above heated ceilings shall be spaced not less than 50 mm above the top surface of the heating device and shall be considered as operating at an ambient temperature of 50 °C, unless
   a) thermal insulation having a minimum thickness of 50 mm is interposed between the wiring and the top surface of the heating device; or
Δ   b) the heating device is marked for a lesser clearance.
2) Wiring of other circuits located in heated concrete slabs shall be spaced not less than 50 mm from the heating device and shall be considered as operating at an ambient temperature of 40 °C.

62-206 Installation of central units
1) Central units shall be installed so that there is accessibility for repair and maintenance.
2) Central units shall be installed
Δ   a) in an area that is large compared with the physical size of the unit unless designed for installation in an alcove or closet; and
   b) to comply with the clearances from combustible materials as specified on the nameplate.
3) A single disconnecting means that simultaneously opens all ungrounded conductors supplying the controller and the central unit shall be provided.

62

4) Notwithstanding Subrule 3), where the supply to the central unit and controller require more than one circuit, the disconnecting means shall be grouped together, and signage on the central unit and controller shall indicate the need to isolate multiple circuits before working on the central unit and controller.

5) The disconnecting means required in Subrule 3) or 4) shall be located within sight of and within 9 m of
   a) the central unit and the controller; or
   b) an alcove or closet when the central unit and the controller are installed in such a space.

62-208 Location of heating cable sets and heating panel sets

Δ 1) The heating portion of heating cable sets and heating panel sets shall not penetrate or pass through walls, partitions, floors, or similar structures.

2) Heating cable sets and heating panel sets shall be permitted to be in contact with thermal insulation but shall not be run in or through thermal insulation.

62-210 Installation of heating fixtures

1) Heating fixtures shall be installed so that heat transfer shall not be obstructed by any portion of the building structure.

Δ 2) Where a heating fixture is recessed in non-combustible material in a building of concrete, masonry, or equally non-combustible construction, the non-combustible material shall be permitted to be subjected to temperatures not exceeding 150 °C, and the heating fixture shall be so marked.

3) Heating fixtures weighing more than 4.54 kg shall be installed so that the wiring connections in the outlet box or its equivalent will be accessible for inspection without removal of the heating fixture supports.

4) Where the weight of a heating fixture does not exceed 13 kg, the heating fixture shall be permitted to be supported by a wall outlet box attached directly to the building structure or by a wall outlet box attached to a bar hanger.

5) Where the weight of a heating fixture does not exceed 23 kg, the heating fixture shall be permitted to be supported by a ceiling outlet box attached directly to the building structure or by a ceiling outlet attached to a bar hanger.

6) Where the weight of a heating fixture prohibits the installation methods specified in Subrules 4) and 5), the fixture shall be supported
   a) independently of the outlet box; or
   a) by a fixture hanger provided with an integral outlet box suitable for the purpose.

7) When heating fixtures are installed less than 5.5 m above the floor in an arena, gymnasium, or similar location where they may be exposed to damage from flying objects, the fixtures shall be suitable for the application or otherwise protected from mechanical damage.

8) No heating fixture shall be used as a raceway for circuit conductors unless the fixture is marked for this use.

9) Notwithstanding Subrule 8), use of the wiring channel of a baseboard heating fixture to contain the wiring for the interconnection of adjacent baseboard heating fixtures on the same branch circuit shall be permitted if the fixture is marked for this use.

Δ 62-212 Installation of heating cable sets and heating panel sets (see Appendix B)

1) Field-made connections necessary to assemble an individual heating panel set shall be permitted to be inaccessible, provided that they are accessible before the surface finishing materials are applied and the connectors and enclosures are part of the heating panel sets.

2) Cutting, nailing, or stapling of the heating panels and heating panel sets shall be done only through the area(s) provided for this purpose.

3) Branch circuits supplying heating cable sets and heating panel sets shall be marked with a warning label supplied by the manufacturer and affixed to the panelboard by the installer, stating that the applicable surface and location supplied by the branch circuit contains energized wiring and must not be penetrated by nails, screws, or similar devices.

62-214 Installation of heating cable sets in plaster or other cementitious material

1) Heating cable sets installed in plaster or other cementitious material shall be secured in place by fastening devices that are suitable for the temperature involved and not likely to damage the heating cable.

2) The entire length of the heating portion, including the connections to the non-heating leads, shall be completely embedded in non-combustible material.

62-216 Heating cable sets and heating panel sets in gypsum board and other cementitious ceiling and wall installations (see Appendix B)

1) Heating cable sets and heating panel sets shall be installed parallel to the joists, studs, or nailing strips, with clearance not less than 13 mm on each side of the joist, stud, or nailing strip.

2) After the heating cable sets and heating panel sets are installed, the entire ceiling below the installed heating cable set or heating panel set shall be covered with gypsum board or acceptable cementitious materials not exceeding 13 mm in thickness.

Δ ### 62-218 Installation of heating cable sets and heating panel sets under floor coverings

1) Heating panel sets and heating cable sets shall be
   a) installed on floor surfaces that are smooth and flat; and
   b) completely covered by floor coverings for which the heating device is intended.

2) Type FCC non-heating leads shall be permitted to be used in dwelling units for connecting under-floor-covering heating cable sets and heating panel sets to the branch circuit.

62-220 Infrared radiant heaters of the metal-sheath glowing element type

Where multiple heaters are used on the same branch circuit, a single means of ground fault protection as described in Rule 62-116 shall be permitted to be used in the branch circuit.

62-222 Heaters for sauna rooms (see Appendix B)

1) Heaters for sauna rooms shall be marked as being suitable for the purpose.

2) Sauna heaters shall be installed in rooms that are built in accordance with the nameplate size specifications and shall be fastened securely in place to ensure that the minimum safe clearances indicated on the nameplate are not reduced.

3) Sauna heaters shall not be installed below shower heads or water spray devices.

4) Each sauna heater shall be controlled by a timed cut-off switch having a maximum time setting of 1 h, with no override feature, that, if not forming part of the sauna heater or cabinet, shall be mounted on the outside wall of the room containing the sauna heater and shall disconnect all ungrounded conductors in the circuit supplying the heater.

Electric surface heating systems

Δ ### 62-300 Electric surface heating (see Appendix B)

Rules 62-302 to 62-316 apply to fixed surface heating systems for pipe heating, melting of snow or ice on roofs or concrete or asphalt surfaces, soil heating, and similar applications.

62-302 Installation of fixtures

If located where they will be exposed to rainfall, fixtures shall be provided with a weatherproof enclosure.

62

62-304 Heating cables and heating panels installed below the heated surface (see Appendix B)

1) Heating cables and heating panels installed outdoors under the surface of driveways, sidewalks, and similar locations shall
   a) be surrounded by non-combustible material throughout their length, including the point of connection to the non-heating leads; and
   b) be embedded or covered to a depth of 50 mm minimum below the finished surface.
2) Non-metallic heating cables or heating panels installed indoors shall be not less than 25 mm from any uninsulated metal bodies located below the surface to be heated.

62-306 Heating cable sets installed on or wrapped around surfaces

1) Heating cable sets installed on or wrapped around surfaces shall be secured in place by suitable fastening devices that will not damage the heating unit and that are suitable for the temperature involved.
2) Heating cable sets wrapped over valves, equipment, or expansion joints in piping systems shall be installed in such a manner as to avoid damage when movement occurs at these areas.

62-308 Heating cable sets or heating panel sets installed on non-metallic pipes, ducts, or vessels

A heating cable set or heating panel set installed on a non-metallic pipe, duct, or vessel shall be controlled by a thermostat or other suitable temperature-limiting system so that it does not cause damage to the pipe, duct, or vessel.

62-310 Heating panel sets installed on tanks, vessels, or pipes

Heating panel sets installed on tanks, vessels, or pipes shall be secured in place by suitable fastening devices.

62-312 Caution labels

1) Pipes, vessels, or ducts with electric heating shall have a permanent, legible caution label(s) placed on the outermost surface of the thermal insulation or cladding to indicate that they are electrically traced, if the systems are not readily visible throughout the length.
2) The caution labels required by Subrule 1) shall be visible after installation and
   a) be not more than 6 m apart on pipe and ducts; or
   b) be not more than 6 m apart measured circumferentially on tanks or vessels with not less than two labels per tank or vessel.
3) Additional caution labels shall be placed in a visible location on or near associated equipment that may have to be serviced.

62-314 Skin effect trace heating (see Appendix B)

1) Skin effect trace heating shall conform to the following installation requirements:
   a) ferromagnetic envelopes, ferrous or non-ferrous metal raceways, boxes, fittings, supports, and support hardware shall be permitted to be installed in concrete or in direct contact with the earth;
   b) the ferromagnetic envelope shall be grounded at the power connection and end termination enclosure(s);
   c) the skin effect trace heating system shall be supplied from an isolating transformer;
   d) the provisions of Rule 10-206 shall not apply to the installation of skin effect trace heating systems;
   e) the secondary system of the isolating transformer referred to in Item c) shall not be grounded;
   f) parts of a skin effect trace heating system, such as the power connection, splice, or terminations for specific applications, shall be permitted to be buried, embedded, or otherwise inaccessible except for the junction box containing the connection to the distribution wiring, which shall be accessible; and

g) the provisions of Rule 12-3022 7) shall not apply to the installation of a single conductor in a ferromagnetic envelope (metal enclosure).

Δ 2) Skin effect trace heating circuits shall meet the requirements of IEEE 844.2/CSA C293.2.

Δ **62-316 Impedance heating** (see Appendix B)

Pipe, vessel, or structure impedance heating equipment and installations of it shall conform to the following:

1) Voltage applied to the pipe, vessel, or structure shall not exceed 30 V, and the supply shall be from an isolating-type transformer.

2) The extra-low-voltage heating circuit, including the conductors and the pipe, vessel, or structure, shall not be bonded to ground.

3) Pipe hangers and supports shall have electrical insulating bushings or be made of electrical insulating material.

4) Pipes, vessels, or structures shall have a minimum clearance of 100 mm from adjacent material, and from each other, except from hangers or supports.

5) Where pipes, vessels, or structures pass through walls, floors, or ceilings, they shall be isolated with electrical insulating bushings or have 100 mm of clearance as required in Subrule 4).

6) Vertical runs shall be supported every 6 m or at each floor, whichever distance is less, by electrical insulating hangers or supports, and shall be firestopped at each floor.

7) Horizontal runs shall be supported at least every 3 m.

8) Pipes, vessels, or structures that are part of the impedance heating circuit shall be electrically isolated and guarded or shielded.

9) Pipes, vessels, or structures shall be protected from mechanical damage or installed in such a manner that the building beams or framing provide mechanical protection.

10) All pipes, vessels, or structures used for conductors in the impedance heating electrical circuit shall be of the same diameter and made of the same material.

11) Electrical connection joints shall be at least as electrically conductive as the adjacent pipe, vessel, or structure, such as provided by welding or bonding.

Other heating systems

62-400 Heating cable sets and heating panel sets installed within pipes, ducts, or vessels

1) Heating cable sets and heating panel sets installed within pipes, ducts, or vessels shall be suitable for the application.

2) Where the heating cable set or heating panel set passes through the pipe, duct, or vessel, it shall pass through a suitable gland.

3) Where a metal raceway is required for the non-heating leads of a heating cable set installed in a pipe, duct, or vessel, it shall be installed so that it will not become flooded in the event of the failure of the gland required by Subrule 2).

4) A heating cable set or heating panel set installed within a non-metallic pipe, duct, or vessel shall be controlled by a thermostat or other suitable temperature-limiting system so that it does not cause damage to the pipe, duct, or vessel.

62-402 Overcurrent protection of storage-tank water heaters and conductors

Ⓔ Overcurrent protection of storage-tank water heaters and their associated service, feeder, or branch circuit conductors shall comply with Rule 62-114.

62

Δ **62-404 Infrared drying luminaires**

The following requirements shall apply to the installation of infrared drying luminaires:

a) luminaires of the medium-base type shall be permitted to be used with lamps rated at 300 W or less;

b) screwshell luminaires shall not be used with lamps rated at more than 300 W unless intended for the purpose; and

c) in industrial establishments, luminaires shall be permitted to be operated in series on circuits of more than 150 volts-to-ground where adequate spacings for the higher circuit voltage are provided.

62-406 Induction and dielectric heating (see Appendix B)

1) In circuits supplying non-motor-generator equipment, the overcurrent device shall be permitted to be rated or set at not more than 200% of the ampacity of the circuit conductors.

2) A readily accessible disconnecting means shall

 a) be provided to disconnect each heating device from its supply circuit;

 b) be rated not less than the nameplate rating of the heating device; and

 c) be located within sight and within 9 m of the heating device unless the disconnecting means can be locked in the open position.

3) A readily accessible disconnecting means having a rating in accordance with Section 28 shall be provided for each generator or group of generators at a single location.

4) The supply circuit disconnecting means shall be permitted to be used as the disconnecting means if the circuit supplies only one motor-generator, vacuum tube, or solid-state converter.

62-408 Bare element water heater (see Appendix B)

1) A bare element water heater shall be

 a) supplied from a grounded system;

 b) permanently connected to a branch circuit that supplies no other equipment; and

 c) protected by a ground fault circuit interrupter of the Class A type.

2) A bare element water heater shall not be located within 1.5 m of the point of utilization of the heated water.

Section 64 — Renewable energy systems

64-000 Scope (see Appendix B)
1)   This Section applies to the installation of renewable energy systems except where the voltage and current are limited in accordance with Rule 16-200 1) a) and b).
2)   This Section supplements or amends the general requirements of this Code.

64-002 Special terminology (see Appendix B)
In this Section, the following definitions shall apply:

AC module — a complete, environmentally protected assembly of interconnected solar cells, an inverter, and other components designed to generate ac power from sunlight.

Array — a mechanical integrated assembly of photovoltaic modules with a support structure and foundation, tracking, and other components as required to form a power-producing unit.

Auxiliary grounding electrode — a grounding electrode that augments equipment grounding and that is not required to be directly connected to the electrode(s) that makes up the grounding electrode system.

Bipolar system — a solar photovoltaic system that has two monopole photovoltaic source or output circuits, each having opposite polarity to a common reference point or centre tap.

Controller —

   Charge controller — equipment that controls dc voltage or dc current, or both, and that is used to charge a battery or other storage device.

   Diversion charge controller — equipment that regulates the charging process of a battery or other storage device by diverting energy to ballast loads or to an interconnected supply authority service.

   Diversion load controller — equipment that regulates the output of a generator by diverting energy from the generator to ballast loads or to an interconnected utility service.

   Dump load controller — equipment that regulates the output power of a micro-hydropower system by adjusting the amount of energy flowing into the ballast load to compensate for main load variations (e.g., in stand-alone systems) and prevent generator overvoltage.

Electronic governor — equipment that regulates the output power of a micro-hydropower system by adjusting power flowing into the ballast load to compensate for main load variations (used only in stand-alone systems).

Flow channel — a natural or fabricated structure, channel, or waterway creating water flow from which electric power is generated.

Fuel cell — a device that generates a dc electrical current by the electrochemical combination of a continuously supplied fuel and oxidant.

Fuel cell system — a system consisting of one or more fuel cells and associated equipment that produces usable electricity.

   Portable fuel cell system — a fuel cell power system that is not intended to be permanently fastened or otherwise secured in a specific location.

   Stationary fuel cell system — a permanently installed fuel cell power system.

64

Full load rating — the maximum power that a micro-hydropower system is designed to generate continuously.

Δ **Guy wire** — a wire rope not intended to conduct electricity that mechanically supports a wind turbine tower.

Head — the difference in elevation between two water surfaces, measured in metres.

Hydraulic turbine — equipment that converts the kinetic and potential energy of flowing water to mechanical energy.

Δ **Hydrokinetic power system** — a system operating as an interconnected or stand-alone system and consisting of one or more hydrokinetic turbines that convert the kinetic energy of flowing water into electrical energy.

Hydrokinetic turbine electrical system — all electrical equipment from the hydrokinetic turbine generator terminals to the point of distributed resource connection, including equipment for power transmission, power conditioning, energy storage, grounding, bonding, and communications.

Hydrokinetic turbine generator — all electrical equipment and circuits within the hydrokinetic turbine structure up to the hydrokinetic turbine generator terminals.

Hydrokinetic turbine generator terminal — a point(s) identified by the hydrokinetic turbine supplier at which the hydrokinetic turbine generator can be connected to the electrical power system, including connection for the purposes of transferring energy as well as communications.

Installed capacity — the maximum capacity of the generating units in a micro-hydropower or hydrokinetic power system.

Interactive system — a power production system that operates in parallel with and can deliver power to another system, such as a supply authority system.

Δ **Inverter** —

> **Combination inverter/power conditioning unit (PCU)** — equipment that is used to invert direct current into alternating current either at a fixed voltage and frequency in a stand-alone system or following an imposed waveform in an interactive system.
>
> **Interactive inverter** — an inverter whose ac output is intended for use in parallel with an electric utility or other electricity supply authority network, whether or not the inverter injects net power into the utility or supply network.
>
> **Power conditioning unit (PCU)** — equipment that is used to change voltage level or waveform or otherwise alter or regulate the output of a power source.

Inverter input circuit — the insulated conductors between
a) the inverter and the battery in stand-alone systems; or
b) the renewable energy source and the inverter.

Inverter output circuit — the insulated conductors between
a) the inverter and a panelboard for stand-alone systems; or
b) the inverter and the service equipment or another electric power production source, such as a supply authority.

Load —

    Ballast load — see **Diversion load**.

    Diversion load — a resistive device, usually consisting of water or air electric heating elements, to which energy is diverted when more energy is generated than required.

    Dump load — see **Diversion load**.

Mechanical governor — a controlling device that adjusts the flow of water through a hydraulic turbine.

Micro-hydropower system — a system with a rated output of 100 kW or less operating as an interconnected or stand-alone system and consisting of one or more hydraulic turbines that convert energy derived from flowing and falling water primarily by utilizing the available head difference.

    Battery-based micro-hydropower system — a micro-hydropower system that uses batteries for energy storage, usually in less than 5 kW capacities.

Monopole — an array or portion of an array that has two source circuit insulated conductors, one positive (+) and one negative (–).

Nacelle — the body, shell, and casing covering the gearbox, generator, blade hub, and other parts mounted on the top of the tower structure of a propeller-type wind turbine and electrically connected to the rest of the wind turbine generator electrical system after installation.

Photovoltaic combiner — an assembly of buses and connections that may contain overcurrent protective devices, control apparatus, switches, or other equipment and that connects photovoltaic source circuits or the outputs of other combiners together to create an output at higher current or higher voltage, or both.

Δ   **Photovoltaic module** — a complete, environmentally protected assembly of interconnected solar cells.

    Application Class A photovoltaic module — an unrestricted access module for use in solar photovoltaic systems operating in excess of 50 V dc or in excess of 240 W.

    Application Class B photovoltaic module — a restricted access module for use in solar photovoltaic systems where the module is inaccessible to the public.

    Application Class C photovoltaic module — a limited voltage, unrestricted access module for use in photovoltaic systems operating at 50 V dc or less and 240 W or less.

Photovoltaic output circuit — circuit insulated conductors or cables between the photovoltaic source circuit(s) and the power conditioning unit or dc utilization equipment.

Photovoltaic power source — an array or aggregate of arrays that generates dc power at system voltage and current.

Δ   **Photovoltaic recombiner** — an assembly of buses and connections that may contain overcurrent protective devices, control apparatus, switches, or other equipment and that connects outputs from photovoltaic combiners together to create an output at higher current or higher voltage, or both.

Photovoltaic source circuit — insulated conductors or cables between photovoltaic modules and from photovoltaic modules to the common connection point(s) of the dc system.

64

Point of common coupling — the point where the supply authority's system is connected to the power producer's facilities or conductors.

Point of distributed resource connection — the point where the renewable energy system is connected to a different system, and that can be the same as the point of common coupling or, in the case of a stand-alone system, the point at which the stand-alone network or load is connected to the renewable energy system.

Power conditioning unit (PCU) — see **Inverter**.

Power conditioning unit output circuit — see **Inverter output circuit**.

Power electronics input — the insulated conductors or cables between the hydrokinetic turbine terminals and the first stage of the power electronics system.

Rated power (as applied to small wind turbines) — a wind turbine's maximum power output at a wind speed of 11.0 m/s or less.

Renewable energy — energy derived from resources that are naturally replenished, such as sunlight, wind, water, tides, and geothermal heat.

Renewable energy system — a complete assembly consisting of equipment that converts renewable energy into electrical energy suitable for connection to a utilization load.

Solar cell — the basic photovoltaic device that generates electricity when exposed to light.

Solar photovoltaic system — all the components and subsystems that in combination convert solar energy into electrical energy suitable for connection to a utilization load.

Stand-alone system — a system that supplies power independently of a supply authority's electrical production and distribution network.

Δ   **Supply wiring** — the insulated conductors or cables used to connect the renewable energy system to its electrical point of delivery, which can include an alternator, integrated rectifier, controller or inverter or both, or batteries.

Tower — a pole or other structure that supports a wind turbine.

Turbine speed/load controller — equipment that adjusts the electrical load applied to the hydrokinetic turbine generator to control turbine speed.

Wind —

   Large wind system — a system consisting of one or more wind turbines with a rated power output exceeding 100 kW.

   Small wind system — a system consisting of one or more wind turbines with a rated output up to and including 100 kW.

   Wind turbine — mechanical equipment that converts the kinetic energy of wind into electrical energy and includes all electrical components and circuits within the wind turbine structure.

   Wind turbine electrical system — a system consisting of all the electrical equipment integral to the wind turbine, including the wind turbine terminals, generators, inverters, controllers, and equipment for grounding, bonding, and communications, up to the point of common coupling to the load or grid.

Wind turbine generator (WTG) — all electrical equipment and circuits within the wind turbine structure, to the point of coupling to the load or grid.

Wind turbine generator (WTG) system — a system that converts the kinetic energy of wind into electrical energy.

Wind turbine terminal — a point(s) identified by the wind turbine supplier at which the wind turbine can be connected to the power collection system, including connection for the purposes of transferring energy and communications.

General

64-050 General
A renewable energy system shall be permitted to supply a building or other structure in addition to any service(s) from another supply system(s).

64-052 Insulated conductors of different systems (see Appendix B)
Insulated conductors of renewable energy systems shall be separated from different systems in accordance with Rules 12-904 2) and 12-3030.

64-054 Common return conductor
For a renewable energy power source that has multiple supply circuit voltages and employs a common return conductor, the ampacity of the common return conductor shall not be less than the sum of the ampere ratings of the overcurrent devices of the individual supply circuits.

64-056 Bipolar systems
1) Where the sum, without consideration of polarity, of the voltages of the two monopoles of a bipolar system exceeds the voltage rating of the insulated conductors and connected equipment, the monopoles shall be physically separated, and the electrical output circuits from each monopole shall be installed in separate raceways until they are connected to the inverter.
2) The disconnecting means and overcurrent protective devices for each monopole output circuit shall be in separate enclosures.
3) Notwithstanding Subrule 2), equipment rated for the maximum voltage between circuits and containing a physical barrier separating the disconnecting means for each monopole shall be permitted to be used instead of disconnecting means in separate enclosures.
4) All insulated conductors from each separate monopole shall be routed in the same raceway.
5) Bipolar systems shall be clearly marked with a permanent, legible warning notice, indicating that the disconnection of the grounded conductor(s) may result in overvoltage on the equipment.

64-058 Overcurrent protection (see Appendix B)
1) Circuits connected to more than one electrical source shall have overcurrent devices located so as to provide overcurrent protection from all sources.
2) Overcurrent protection for a transformer with a source(s) on each side shall be provided in accordance with Section 26 by considering first one side of the transformer, then the other side of the transformer, as the primary.
Δ 3) Overcurrent devices used in any dc portion of a renewable energy power system shall be marked for the purpose.
4) Overcurrent devices such as circuit breakers, if backfed, shall be suitable for such operation.

64

64-060 Disconnecting means (see Appendix B)

1) A disconnecting means shall be provided to disconnect simultaneously all ungrounded conductors supplied from a renewable energy power supply source from all other insulated conductors in a building or other structure.

Δ 2) The disconnecting means referred to in Subrule 1) shall
   a) be capable of being energized from both sides;
   b) indicate whether it is in the open or closed position;
   c) have provision for being locked in the open position;
   d) conform to Section 14;
   e) be capable of being opened at rated load;
   f) be capable of being closed with a fault on the system; and
   g) be located within sight of and within 9 m of the equipment or be integral to the equipment.

3) Where the disconnecting means referred to in Subrule 1) is used as the service disconnecting means, it shall be suitable for service entrance equipment.

4) A disconnecting means shall be provided to disconnect equipment such as inverters, batteries, and charge controllers from all ungrounded conductors of all sources.

5) The disconnecting means required by this Rule shall not be connected in any grounded conductor if operation of that disconnecting means would cause the grounded conductor to be in an ungrounded and energized state.

6) Where the equipment is energized from more than one supply source, the disconnecting means shall comply with Rules 14-414 and 14-700.

7) Output circuits rated 48 V and greater shall have means to disable and isolate them.

8) Disconnecting means shall be provided to disconnect a fuse from all sources of supply if the fuse is energized from both directions, as required by Rule 14-402.

Δ 9) Disconnecting means provided on dc circuits shall be marked for the purpose.

10) The disconnecting means shall bear a warning to the effect that the terminals on both the line and load sides could be energized when the disconnecting means is open.

11) The disconnecting means for a hydrokinetic power system shall be permitted to be located beyond the limits defined in Subrule 2), provided that it is capable of being locked in the open position.

12) For installations with combiners, a single disconnecting means capable of being opened at the ampere rating of its photovoltaic output circuit in accordance with Rule 64-206 shall be installed for the photovoltaic output circuit as follows:
   a) for photovoltaic combiners equipped with fuses protecting photovoltaic source circuits, the disconnecting means shall be
      i) integral with the photovoltaic combiner and interlocked with the door; or
      ii) installed within 2 m of the photovoltaic combiner and interlocked with the combiner door; and
Δ b) for photovoltaic combiners equipped with circuit breakers protecting photovoltaic source circuits, the disconnecting means shall be integral with the photovoltaic combiner or located not more than 2 m from each photovoltaic combiner.

Δ 13) Notwithstanding Subrules 6) and 12), for installations with recombiners, where the recombiner is installed in excess of 7.5 m from the inverter, a single disconnecting means capable of being opened at the ampere rating of the inverter input circuit in accordance with Rule 64-206 shall be installed for the inverter input circuit as follows:
   a) for photovoltaic recombiners equipped with fuses protecting photovoltaic output circuits, the disconnecting means shall be
      i) integral with the photovoltaic recombiner and interlocked with the door; or
      ii) installed within 2 m of the photovoltaic recombiner and interlocked with the recombiner door; and

b) for photovoltaic recombiners equipped with circuit breakers protecting photovoltaic output circuits, the disconnecting means shall be
   i) integral with the photovoltaic recombiner; or
   ii) located not more than 2 m from each photovoltaic recombiner.

64-062 Wiring methods

Δ 1) Except as provided for by Rule 64-210, insulated conductors for dc renewable energy sources or supply circuits of an interactive inverter, installed inside a building or structure, shall be contained in metallic raceways, metal enclosures, or cables with a metal armour or metal sheath.

2) Wiring methods as required by Subrule 1) shall be provided from the point of penetration of the surface of the building or structure to the first readily accessible disconnecting means.

64-064 System grounding (see Appendix B)

1) AC systems shall be grounded in accordance with Rule 10-206 1).

2) For renewable energy dc supply circuits, one conductor of a 2-wire system with a system voltage of 50 V or greater shall be grounded.

3) For renewable energy dc supply circuits, the reference (centre tap) conductor of a bipolar system shall be grounded.

4) The dc supply circuits referred to in Subrules 2) and 3) shall be provided with a ground fault protection device or system that
   a) detects a ground fault;
   b) indicates that a ground fault has occurred; and
   c) interrupts the fault current by either
      i) automatically disconnecting all conductors of the dc supply circuit or of the faulted portion of the dc supply circuit; or
      ii) automatically causing the inverter or charge controller connected to the faulted circuit to cease supplying power to the output circuits.

5) The dc circuit grounding connection shall be made at any single point on the renewable energy supply circuit and shall be located as close as practicable to the supply source.

6) A renewable energy dc supply system equipped with a ground fault protection device shall be permitted to have the grounding conductor connected to the grounding electrode via the ground fault protection device.

7) Where the connection permitted in Subrule 6) is internal to the equipment equipped with a ground fault protection device, it shall not be duplicated by an external connection.

64-066 Ungrounded renewable energy power systems (see Appendix B)

Δ 1) Notwithstanding Rule 64-064, renewable energy power systems shall be permitted to operate with ungrounded source and supply circuits where the system complies with the following:
   a) all source and supply circuit conductors shall have overcurrent protection except as permitted by Rule 64-214 1);
   b) the renewable energy power source shall be labelled in a conspicuous, legible, and permanent manner with a suitable warning at each junction box, disconnecting means, and device where the ungrounded circuits can be exposed during service;
   c) inverters or charge controllers used in systems with ungrounded source and supply circuits shall be suitable for the purpose; and
   d) all ungrounded dc systems shall be provided with a ground fault protection device or system that
      i) detects a ground fault;
      ii) interrupts the fault current, if fault current can result from a single ground fault;
      iii) indicates that a ground fault has occurred; and

64

      iv)   either

          A)   automatically disconnects all conductors of the dc supply circuit or of the faulted portion of the dc supply circuit; or

          B)   automatically causes the inverter or charge controller connected to the faulted circuit to cease supplying power to inverter output circuits.

2)   Notwithstanding Subrule 1), the renewable energy power system dc circuits shall be permitted to be ungrounded where they are used with ungrounded battery systems that comply with Rule 64-800.

64-068 Grounding electrodes and grounding conductors (see Appendix B)

AC and DC renewable energy power systems required to be grounded shall be connected to a grounding conductor by one of the following means:

a)   the dc grounding conductor and ac grounding conductor shall be connected to a single electrode, with separate grounding conductors sized as required by Rule 10-114;

b)   the dc grounding conductor shall be connected to a separate electrode by

      i)   the grounding conductor connected between the identified dc grounding point and a separate dc grounding electrode; and

      ii)   bonding the dc grounding electrode to the ac grounding electrode where such bonding means is required by Rule 10-104 b); or

c)   a combined dc grounding conductor and ac equipment bonding conductor shall be

      i)   installed in accordance with Rule 10-116; and

      ii)   sized in accordance with Rule 10-114 or 10-614, whichever is larger.

64-070 Equipment bonding (see Appendix B)

The bonding connection between the grounding conductor and exposed conductive surfaces of the renewable energy source or supply circuit equipment shall be made in such a manner that disconnection or removal of the equipment will not interfere with or interrupt bonding continuity.

64-072 Marking

1)   All interactive system(s) points of interconnection with other sources shall be marked with the maximum ac output operating voltage and current.

2)   The marking referred to in Subrule 1) shall be provided at the disconnecting means for each interconnecting power source.

64-074 Warning notice and diagram (see Appendix B)

1)   Any structure or building with a renewable energy power system that is not connected to a supply service source and is a stand-alone system shall be marked in a conspicuous, legible, and permanent manner to indicate the location of the system disconnecting means and that the structure contains a stand-alone electrical power system.

2)   Buildings and structures with both a utility supply service and a renewable energy system shall, where practicable, have the disconnecting means grouped in accordance with Rule 6-102 2) or, where such an arrangement is not practicable, shall have a permanent plaque posted on or near each disconnecting means, indicating the location of all other service boxes supplying power to the building, in accordance with Rule 6-102 3).

3)   A permanent plaque or directory identifying all electrical power sources on or in the premises shall be installed at each service equipment location and at the supply authority meter location.

4)   Renewable energy power systems that store electrical energy shall be labelled in a conspicuous, legible, and permanent manner with a suitable warning sign at the location of the service disconnecting means of the premises.

64-076 Interconnections to other circuits (see Appendix B)

Where an installation is supplied from a renewable energy system that is not intended to be interconnected with a supply authority, the switching equipment controlling the systems shall be constructed or arranged so that it will be impossible to accidentally switch on power from one source before power from another has been cut off.

64-078 Loss of interactive system power (see Appendix B)

1) The renewable energy system shall
   a) be provided with a means of detecting when the electrical production and distribution network has become de-energized; and
   b) not feed the electrical production and distribution network side of the point of common coupling during this condition.
2) The renewable energy system shall remain in the state described in Subrule 1) until the normal voltage and frequency of the supply authority system have been restored.
3) A normally interactive renewable energy system shall be permitted to operate as a stand-alone system to supply loads that have been disconnected from electrical production and distribution network sources.

Inverters

64-100 Maximum circuit loading (see Appendix B)

1) The maximum current of the inverter output circuit shall be the inverter continuous output current rating.
2) The maximum current of a stand-alone inverter input circuit shall be the stand-alone continuous inverter input current rating when the inverter is producing rated power at the lowest input voltage.
3) Renewable energy system maximum current ratings shall be based on continuous operation.

64-102 Stand-alone systems (see Appendix B)

The premises wiring system and the wiring on the supply side of the building or structure disconnecting means shall comply with the applicable requirements of this Code, except as follows:

a) the ac inverter output from a stand-alone system shall be permitted to supply ac power to the building or structure disconnecting means at current levels below the rating of that disconnecting means, provided that the inverter output rating is equal to or greater than the connected load of the largest single utilization equipment connected to the system;

b) the circuit conductors between the inverter output and the building or structure disconnecting means shall be
   i) sized based on the output rating of the inverter; and
   ii) provided with overcurrent protection located at the output of the inverter, in accordance with Section 14; and

c) the inverter output of a stand-alone renewable energy system shall be permitted to supply 120 V to single-phase, 3-wire, 120/240 V service equipment or distribution panels, provided that
   i) there are no 240 V loads;
   ii) there are no multi-wire branch circuits;
   iii) the rating of the overcurrent device connected to the output of the inverter does not exceed the rating of the neutral bus in the service equipment; and
   iv) the equipment is marked in a conspicuous, legible, and permanent manner with a warning not to connect it to multi-wire branch circuits.

Δ **64-104 Interactive inverters mounted in locations that are not readily accessible**

Interactive inverters shall be permitted to be mounted on roofs or other exterior areas that are not readily accessible, provided that

a) a dc and ac disconnecting means is provided in accordance with Rule 64-060 2);

64

b)   an additional ac disconnecting means for the inverter is provided in accordance with Rule 84-020; and

c)   a diagram is installed in accordance with Rule 84-030 2).

Δ   **64-106 Connection to other sources** (see Appendix B)
Only inverters and ac modules marked as interactive shall be permitted in interactive systems.

64-108 Ampacity of neutral conductor
1)   The inverter output rating and maximum load connected between the neutral and any one ungrounded conductor shall not exceed the ampacity of the neutral conductor, where an inverter with a single-phase, 2-wire output is connected to the neutral and only one ungrounded conductor of
a)   a single-phase, 3-wire system; or
b)   a three-phase, 4-wire wye-connected system.

Δ 2)   A conductor used solely for instrumentation, voltage detection, or phase detection, and connected to a single-phase or three-phase interactive inverter, shall be
a)   permitted to be sized at less than the ampacity of the other current-carrying conductors; and
b)   in no case smaller than the bonding conductor required by Rule 10-614.

Δ   **64-110 Unbalanced interconnections** (see Appendix B)
1)   Single-phase inverters for renewable energy systems and ac modules in interactive renewable energy systems shall not be connected to three-phase systems unless the interactive system
a)   is designed such that under normal operating conditions, the resulting three-phase system voltages are balanced within the limits of supply authority requirements; and
b)   complies with Rules 84-008 and 84-018.
2)   Three-phase inverters and three-phase ac modules in interactive systems shall have all phases automatically de-energized upon loss of the system voltage in one or more phases.

Δ   **64-112 Interactive point of connection** (see Appendix B)
1)   The output of an interactive inverter or power conditioning unit shall be connected to the supply authority system in accordance with Section 84.
2)   Except as provided for in Subrule 3), the output of an interactive inverter described in this Section shall be connected to the supply side of the service disconnecting means.
3)   The output of an interactive inverter shall be permitted to be connected to the load side of the service disconnecting means of the other source(s) at any distribution equipment on the premises under the provisions of Subrule 4).
4)   Where distribution equipment such as switchboards or panelboards located on the premises is supplied simultaneously by a primary power source and one or more interactive inverters and where the distribution equipment connected as permitted by Subrule 3) is capable of supplying multiple branch circuits or feeders, or both, provisions for interconnection between the primary power supply source and the interactive inverter(s) shall comply with the following conditions:
a)   each source interconnection shall be made at a dedicated circuit breaker or fusible disconnecting means;

b) each panelboard, busbar, or conductor supplied by the multiple sources in the interactive system shall be provided with

   i) suitable warning signs adjacent to each source disconnecting means to indicate that all of the disconnecting means must be opened to ensure complete de-energization of the equipment in accordance with Rule 14-414;

   ii) the point of connection positioned at the opposite (load) end from the input feeder location or main circuit location, where the panelboard is rated less than the sum of the ampere ratings of all overcurrent devices in source circuits supplying the panelboard; and

   iii) a permanent warning label at the distribution equipment to indicate that the overcurrent device shall not be relocated;

c) notwithstanding Section 14, the sum of the ampere ratings of the overcurrent devices in source circuits supplying power to a busbar or conductor shall be permitted to exceed the busbar or conductor rating to a maximum of 120% of the rating of the busbar or conductor;

d) notwithstanding Section 14, for a dwelling unit, the sum of the ampere ratings of the overcurrent devices in source circuits supplying power to a busbar or conductor shall be permitted to exceed the busbar or conductor rating to a maximum of 125% of the rating of the busbar or conductor; and

e) except as provided for in Subrule 5), the interconnection point shall be made on the line side of all ground fault protection equipment.

5) The interconnection point described in Subrule 4) e) shall be permitted to be made on the load side of ground fault protection equipment, provided that

   a) there is ground fault protection for equipment from all ground fault current sources; and

   b) ground fault protection devices used with supplies connected to the load side terminals are suitable for back-feeding.

Solar photovoltaic systems

64-200 Marking (see Appendix B)

1) In addition to the marking requirements given in Rule 64-072, a permanent marking shall be provided at an accessible location at the disconnecting means for the photovoltaic output circuit, specifying the following:

   a) the rated operating current and voltage;

   b) the maximum photovoltaic source circuit voltage calculated in accordance with Rule 64-202 1) and 2); and

   c) the rated short-circuit current.

2) A photovoltaic system with rapid shutdown in accordance with Rule 64-218 shall be provided with a permanent marking in an accessible location at the disconnecting means for the photovoltaic output circuit stating that the photovoltaic system is equipped with rapid shutdown.

3) A warning sign for a photovoltaic system shall be in capital letters with a minimum height of 9.5 mm, in white on a red background.

64-202 Voltage of solar photovoltaic systems (see Appendix B)

1) The maximum photovoltaic source and output circuit voltage shall be the rated open-circuit voltage of the photovoltaic power source multiplied by 125%.

2) Notwithstanding Subrule 1), the maximum photovoltaic source and output circuit voltage shall be permitted to be calculated using

   a) the rated open-circuit voltage of the photovoltaic power source;

   b) the difference between 25 °C and the lowest expected daily minimum temperature; and

   c) the voltage temperature coefficient as specified by the manufacturer.

64

3) The maximum photovoltaic source and output circuit voltage shall be used to determine the voltage ratings of insulated conductors, cables, disconnects, overcurrent protection, and other equipment in photovoltaic source or output circuits.

4) The photovoltaic source and output circuits for installations in or on dwelling units shall be permitted to have a voltage not exceeding 600 V dc, provided that
   a) all energized parts in the photovoltaic source and output circuits over 150 volts-to-ground are accessible only to qualified persons;
   b) the photovoltaic source and output circuits are not connected as a bipolar system; and
   c) the insulated conductors for photovoltaic source and output circuits over 30 V located inside the building are contained in metallic raceways, metal enclosures, or cables with a metal armour or metal sheath.

Δ 5) Photovoltaic source and output circuits, and equipment connected to or within those circuits, with maximum voltages higher than 750 V dc but not exceeding 1500 V dc shall not be required to comply with Rules 36-204, 36-208, and 36-214, provided that
   a) the installation is serviced only by qualified persons;
   b) the part of the installation exceeding 750 V dc is inaccessible to the public; and
   c) enclosures in which photovoltaic source and output circuits exceeding 750 V dc are present are marked with the word "DANGER" followed by the maximum rated photovoltaic circuit voltage of the equipment.

64-204 Voltage drop
Notwithstanding the requirements of Rule 8-102, photovoltaic output circuit and photovoltaic source circuit conductors shall meet one of the following requirements:
a) the voltage drop shall be considered acceptable where the conductors are rated not less than 125% of the maximum available short-circuit current of the solar photovoltaic system;
b) the voltage drop shall not exceed 5% of the rated operating voltage;
c) the rated operating voltage drop shall not exceed the percentage calculated by multiplying 50% of the rated current of the photovoltaic source circuit under consideration divided by the rated current of the entire array connected to the power conditioning unit or directly connected loads; or
d) the resistance shall be sufficiently low to facilitate the operation of the overcurrent device protecting the circuit in the event of a short-circuit.

64-206 Ampere rating of photovoltaic source and output circuits
The ampere rating of a photovoltaic source and output circuit shall be
a) the ampere rating of the overcurrent device protecting the circuit or the ampacity of the conductors, whichever is less; and
b) not less than 125% of the rated short-circuit current of that photovoltaic source's circuit.

64-208 Photovoltaic module application class use (see Appendix B)
1) Photovoltaic modules marked with application Class A or C shall be permitted to be installed in a location accessible to the public.
2) Photovoltaic modules marked with an application Class B shall not be permitted for installations accessible to the public.

64-210 Wiring method (see Appendix B)
1) Notwithstanding Rule 12-102 3), flexible cords suitable for extra-hard usage shall be permitted for the interconnection of photovoltaic modules within an array.
Δ 2) Notwithstanding Rule 12-204 4), cables included as part of photovoltaic modules shall be permitted for the interconnection of photovoltaic modules within an array, provided that the photovoltaic source and output circuits operate at a maximum system voltage
   a) of 30 V or less; or

    b)   greater than 30 V where the array is not installed in readily accessible locations.

3)   Notwithstanding Rule 12-204, Type RPVU cables shall be permitted for the interconnection of photovoltaic modules within an array, provided that
    a)   the installation is serviced only by qualified persons; and
    b)   the installation is inaccessible to the public.

4)   Insulated conductors and cables installed in accordance with Subrules 1), 2), and 3) shall be adequately protected against mechanical damage during and after installation, and supported by straps or other devices located
    a)   within 300 mm of every box or connector; and
    b)   at intervals of not more than 1 m throughout the run.

5)   Where the dc arc-fault protection referred to in Rule 64-216 is not located at the module, photovoltaic source circuit insulated conductors and cables installed on or above a building and installed in accordance with Subrules 1), 2), and 3) shall be provided with mechanical protection in the form of an enclosed raceway or other acceptable material to protect against damage from rodents.

6)   Notwithstanding Rule 12-2202 1), 2), and 3), Type RPVU cables shall be permitted to be installed in cable tray for the interconnection of the solar photovoltaic system.

7)   Type RPV conductors installed in a raceway shall be permitted for the interconnection of the solar photovoltaic system.

8)   Cables used for solar photovoltaic installations on or above a building shall meet the flame spread requirements of the *National Building Code of Canada* or local building legislation.

9)   Types RPV insulated conductors and RPVU cables installed inside a building or structure shall be contained in a raceway.

10)   Notwithstanding Rules 12-904 and 12-3030, junction boxes, enclosures, fittings, and raceways or compartments of multiple-channel raceways shall be permitted to contain insulated conductors of a single renewable energy system that are connected to different sources of voltage where
    a)   all conductors are insulated for at least the same voltage as that of the circuit having the highest voltage; and
    b)   a suitable warning notice is placed at each enclosure and junction box giving access to the insulated conductors, indicating where multiple photovoltaic source circuits and photovoltaic output circuits are available within the junction boxes, enclosures, and raceways or compartments of a multiple-channel raceway.

64-212 Insulated conductor marking or colour coding (see Appendix B)

1)   Notwithstanding Rule 4-032, dc photovoltaic output circuit insulated conductors, and photovoltaic source circuit insulated conductors installed between a module and the power conditioning unit of the dc system, shall be coloured or coded, or both, as follows:
    a)   for a 2-wire circuit
        i)   red for positive and black for negative; or
        ii)   black insulated conductors manufactured with permanent surface printing indicating the polarity on the insulated conductor; and
    b)   for a 3-wire circuit (bipolar circuit)
        i)   white, grey, or white with a coloured stripe for the mid-wire (identified as the centre tap), red for positive, and black for negative; or
        ii)   black insulated conductors manufactured with permanent surface printing indicating the polarity on the conductor insulation.

2)   The requirements of Subrule 1) shall not be met by field marking or labelling.

3)   Notwithstanding Subrule 2), insulated conductor colour coding for multi-conductor cables required in Subrule 1) shall be permitted to be made through suitable field labelling or marking in a permanent manner.

64

4) The insulated conductor labelling and marking permitted in Subrule 3) shall

Δ   a)   be made at every point where the separate insulated conductors are rendered accessible and visible by removal of the outer jacket of the cable;

     b)   be made by painting or other suitable means; and

     c)   not render the manufacturer's numbering of the insulated conductors illegible.

Δ **64-214 Overcurrent protection for apparatus and conductors** (see Appendix B)

1) Notwithstanding Rules 64-058 1) and 64-066 1) a), individual overcurrent protection devices shall not be required where the sum of the available short-circuit current from all photovoltaic source circuits connected to the same power conditioning unit is not greater than the rated ampacity of the apparatus or conductors.

2) Where overcurrent protection is required by Rule 64-058 1) for a photovoltaic source circuit, each photovoltaic source circuit shall be protected by an individual overcurrent device rated or set at not more than the allowable ampacity of the conductors of the photovoltaic source circuit or the maximum overcurrent protection indicated on the photovoltaic module nameplate, whichever is less.

3) Where the value as specified in Subrule 2) does not correspond to the standard rating of an overcurrent device, the next higher standard rating shall be permitted.

4) Overcurrent devices for photovoltaic source circuits shall be accessible and shall be grouped where practicable.

Δ **64-216 Photovoltaic dc arc-fault circuit protection**

1) Solar photovoltaic systems with dc source circuits or output circuits, or both, and operating at a maximum system voltage of 80 V or greater, shall be protected by

     a)   a dc arc-fault circuit interrupter; or

     b)   other system equipment that provides equivalent protection.

2) The protection required in Subrule 1) shall

     a)   detect and interrupt arcing faults resulting from a failure in the intended continuity of a conductor, connection, photovoltaic module, or other system component in the dc photovoltaic source and output circuits;

     b)   not have the capability of being automatically restarted;

     c)   have annunciation, without an automatic reset, that provides a visual indication that the circuit interrupter has operated; and

     d)   disable or disconnect

         i)   inverters or charge controllers connected to the faulted circuit when the fault is detected; or

         ii)   the photovoltaic dc source circuits or dc output circuits either within the combiner, at the module junction box, or at the module cable connectors.

Δ **64-218 Photovoltaic rapid shutdown** (see Appendix B)

1) Photovoltaic rapid shutdown shall be provided for a photovoltaic system installed on or in buildings where the photovoltaic source or output circuit insulated conductors or cables installed on or in buildings are more than 1 m from a photovoltaic array.

2) Notwithstanding Subrule 1), photovoltaic rapid shutdown shall not be required for ground-mounted photovoltaic system circuits that enter a building whose sole purpose is to house photovoltaic system equipment.

3) Photovoltaic rapid shutdown shall limit photovoltaic source or output circuits located more than 1 m from the photovoltaic array to not more than 30 V within 30 s of rapid shutdown initiation.

4) A device used to initiate photovoltaic rapid shutdown shall be readily accessible and located
   a) for single dwelling units, at the supply authority meter location;
   b) for other than single dwelling units, at the consumer's service equipment or supply authority meter location, and
      i) at a permanent access to a building roof where an array(s) is installed; or
      ii) within sight and within 9 m of the array(s); and
   c) for a stand-alone system, in accordance with Items b) i) and ii).

5) The location of the device used to initiate photovoltaic rapid shutdown shall be shown on the diagram required in Rule 84-030 2).

6) A label indicating that the photovoltaic system is equipped with photovoltaic rapid shutdown shall be installed at the supply authority meter location and at the consumer's service equipment location.

Δ **64-220 Attachment plugs and similar wiring devices** (see Appendix B)

1) Attachment plugs and similar wiring devices shall be permitted to connect cables between photovoltaic modules, or between dc photovoltaic source and photovoltaic output circuits, where
   a) there are no exposed energized parts, whether the devices are connected or disconnected;
   b) the devices are polarized;
   c) the devices have a configuration that is not interchangeable with receptacles or attachment plugs of other systems on the premises;
   d) the devices are of the locking type;
   e) the devices are rated for the voltage and current of the circuit in which they are installed;
   f) the devices provide strain relief;
   g) the devices are a mated pair; and
   h) the attachment plugs and similar wiring devices are compatible with the types of cables used.

2) Where attachment plugs and similar wiring devices installed in accordance with Subrule 1) are readily accessible and are used in circuits operating at over 30 V, they shall be of a type that requires the use of a tool to open the connector.

3) Attachment plugs and similar wiring devices shall
   a) be rated for interrupting current without hazard to the operator; or
   b) be of a type that requires the use of a tool to open them and be marked "Do Not Disconnect Under Load" or "Not for Interrupting Current."

4) A single-pole attachment plug or similar wiring device designed for dc use shall be permitted to be used as a dc isolation means, provided that it complies with the requirements of Subrules 1), 2), and 3).

5) A multi-pole attachment plug or similar wiring device shall be permitted to be used as an ac isolation means, provided that it complies with the requirements of
   a) Subrule 1) a), b), c), e), f), and g); and
   b) Subrule 3).

64-222 Photovoltaic module bonding (see Appendix B)

1) Exposed, non-current-carrying metal parts of photovoltaic modules shall be bonded to ground.

2) Module bonding connections shall be as specified in the module installation manual.

Δ 3) Notwithstanding Subrule 2), bonding connectors intended for bonding photovoltaic modules and installed in accordance with the manufacturer's instructions shall be permitted to be used.

64

4) The connections to a photovoltaic module shall be arranged so that removal of a photovoltaic module from a photovoltaic source circuit does not interrupt a bonding conductor to other photovoltaic source equipment.

Small wind systems

64-300 Marking (see Appendix B)
1) A permanent marking shall be provided in accordance with Rule 2-100 at a readily accessible location at the disconnecting means for the wind turbine output circuit, specifying the following additional information:
   a) overcurrent protection values provided by the wind turbine for the stator and rotor, if applicable;
   b) short-circuit current rating (SCCR);
   c) a brief system description, including the type of generator (synchronous or induction);
   d) the rated output current; and
   e) the rated output voltage(s) at the connection to the turbine.
2) A plaque shall be installed at or adjacent to a turbine location providing instructions for disabling the turbine.

64-302 Maximum voltage (see Appendix B)
1) For wind turbines connected to single dwellings, turbine output circuits shall be permitted to have a maximum nominal voltage up to 600 V.
2) When wind turbines are connected to single dwellings, live parts in circuits over 150 volts-to-ground shall be accessible only to qualified personnel.
3) Small wind systems operating on dedicated branch or feeder circuits shall be permitted to exceed normal voltage operating ranges at the end of these circuits, provided that the voltage at any distribution equipment supplying other loads remains within normal ranges.

Δ 64-304 Insulated conductors
1) Supply wiring insulated conductors or cables from the wind turbine shall have an ampacity of not less than 125% of the maximum rated current of the generator.
2) Supply wiring insulated conductors or cables shall have a temperature rating of not less than 90 °C.

64-306 Wiring methods
1) Insulated conductors installed in raceways shall be of types specified in accordance with Rule 12-102 as suitable for use in raceways in wet locations.
2) Cables installed on the exterior of a support pole or tower structure shall be installed in one of the following ways:
   a) in rigid or flexible liquid-tight conduit;
   b) in mineral-insulated cable; or
   c) in armoured cable suitable for exposed wiring in wet locations as specified in accordance with Rule 12-102.
3) Insulated conductors and cables run up the centre of a support pole or hollow tower shall be
   a) insulated conductors as specified in Subrule 1);
   b) notwithstanding Section 12, flexible cords of the extra-hard-usage type suitable for use in wet locations in accordance with Rule 12-402; or
   c) in armoured cable suitable for exposed wiring in wet locations in accordance with Rule 12-102.
4) Insulated conductors and cables run up the centre of a support pole or hollow tower shall be supported in accordance with Rule 12-120.

5) Mechanical protection shall be provided where insulated conductors, cables, and grounding conductors are within 2.5 m of locations accessible to unauthorized persons.

6) Cables run on the outside of a support pole or tower structure shall be supported in accordance with Section 12.

64-308 Overcurrent protection for apparatus and insulated conductors (see Appendix B)

1) Notwithstanding Rules 64-058 1) and 64-066 1) a), individual overcurrent protection devices shall not be required where the available steady-state short-circuit current is not greater than the rated ampacity of the apparatus or insulated conductor.

2) Each ungrounded supply insulated conductor from the wind turbine shall be protected by an overcurrent device not exceeding 125% of the maximum rated current of the generator.

Δ 3) Notwithstanding Subrule 2), an overcurrent device shall not be required for insulated circuit conductors sized in accordance with this Rule and when the maximum currents from all sources do not exceed the allowable ampacity of the insulated conductors.

4) Notwithstanding Subrule 2), wind turbines with a maximum current of 12 A or less shall be permitted to be protected by an overcurrent device with a rating of 15 A.

5) Circuits connected to more than one electrical supply shall have overcurrent devices located so as to provide overcurrent protection from all sources.

6) Overcurrent devices for small wind turbine supply circuits shall be accessible.

7) Overcurrent protection for a power transformer shall be in accordance with Rule 64-058.

8) Notwithstanding Subrule 7), a power transformer with a full load current rating on the side connected to the inverter output that is not less than the rated continuous output current rating of the inverter shall be permitted without overcurrent protection from the inverter.

64-310 Disconnecting means (see Appendix B)

1) A disconnecting means shall be installed in each load circuit of the wind turbine.

2) Notwithstanding Subrule 1), a wind turbine that uses the turbine output circuit for regulating turbine speed shall not require a turbine output circuit disconnecting means.

3) All disconnecting means shall be rated for 125% of the full load rated current.

4) Disconnecting means shall be in accordance with Rule 84-024.

5) A disconnecting means of the lockable type shall be installed at each wind turbine and shall be labelled in a conspicuous, legible, and permanent manner identifying it as the wind turbine disconnecting means.

6) Means shall be provided to disconnect all equipment, including the power conditioning unit, from all ungrounded conductors of all sources.

7) Notwithstanding Rule 64-060 2), a disconnecting means shall be located within sight of the base of the wind turbine or be capable of being locked in the open position.

8) Notwithstanding Rule 64-060 2), the disconnecting means referred to in Subrule 1) shall be installed
   a) at a readily accessible location either on or adjacent to the turbine tower;
   b) on the outside of a building or structure or as close as practicable to the point of entrance of the system insulated conductors or cables; and
   c) not more than 9.0 m from the base of the turbine tower.

64-312 Grounding and bonding (see Appendix B)

1) Exposed non-current-carrying metal parts of towers, turbine nacelles, other metallic equipment, and insulated conductor enclosures shall be bonded to ground in accordance with Section 10 regardless of voltage.

2) Metallic towers or supporting structures shall be bonded to ground with a minimum No. 6 AWG.

3) Guy wires used to support turbine towers need not be grounded.

64

4) Towers or structures shall be grounded by means of grounding electrodes in accordance with Section 10 to limit voltages imposed by lightning.

5) Notwithstanding Subrule 4), metal towers located on steel-supported buildings shall be bonded to non-current-carrying metal parts of the building.

64-314 Receptacles for maintenance
Receptacles installed for maintenance of the wind turbine having CSA configuration 5-15R or 5-20R shall be protected by a ground fault circuit interrupter of the Class A type.

64-316 Lightning protection systems (see Appendix B)
Where auxiliary grounding conductors and grounding electrodes for a renewable energy system are used for lightning protection, the grounding conductors and grounding electrodes shall be installed in accordance with Rule 10-108 and shall be interconnected with grounding electrodes of other systems in conformance with Rule 10-104 c).

64-318 Diversion load controllers (see Appendix B)
A diversion load controller shall not use the supply authority system as a diversion load.

64-320 Surge protective devices (see Appendix B)
1) A surge protective device shall be installed between a small wind system and any loads served by the premises electrical system.

2) The surge protective device shall be permitted to be located on a dedicated branch circuit serving a small wind electric system or anywhere on the load side of the service disconnect.

Large wind systems

64-400 Marking (see Appendix B)
1) A permanent marking shall be provided at a readily accessible location at the base of the tower (entrance) of the wind turbine and shall include the following:
   a) overcurrent protection values provided by the wind turbine for the stator and rotor, if applicable;
   b) short-circuit current-interrupting capacity for stator and rotor protective devices;
   c) a brief system description, including the type of generator (synchronous or induction);
   d) rated output current;
   e) rated voltage(s) at the connection to the turbine; and
   f) a warning notice and diagram in accordance with Rule 84-030.

2) The information required to complete the electrical shock and arc flash labels, where such labels are supplied and installed by the manufacturer within a wind turbine and on the wind turbine access door, shall be field assessed and recorded on those labels.

Δ ### 64-402 Insulated conductors
1) Supply wiring insulated conductors or cables from the wind turbine shall have an ampacity of not less than 125% of the maximum rated current of the generator.

2) Supply wiring insulated conductors or cables shall have an insulation temperature rating of not less than 90 °C.

64-404 Overcurrent protection for apparatus and conductors (see Appendix B)
Δ 1) Each ungrounded supply wiring insulated conductor or cables from the wind turbine shall be protected by an overcurrent device not exceeding 125% of the maximum rated current of the generator.

2) Overcurrent devices shall be accessible.

64-406 Disconnecting means (see Appendix B)
1) A disconnecting means shall be installed in the supply conductors at the base of the tower.

2) All disconnecting means shall be rated for 125% of the maximum rated generator current.

3) Disconnecting means shall be in accordance with Rule 84-024.

4) Notwithstanding Rules 26-248 and 36-204 1), a single disconnect shall be permitted to serve as a disconnecting means for multiple transformers where mechanical interlocking is installed between the disconnecting means and the transformer access doors.

5) The disconnecting means installed in accordance with Rules 64-060 and 84-020 shall be labelled in a conspicuous, legible, and permanent manner, identifying it as the wind turbine generator system disconnecting means.

64-408 Grounding and bonding

1) Exposed non-current-carrying metal parts of towers, turbine nacelles, other equipment, and insulated conductor enclosures shall be bonded to ground in accordance with Section 10.

2) Metallic towers or supporting structures shall be bonded to ground with a minimum No. 2/0 AWG bare copper conductor.

3) Towers or structures shall be grounded by means of grounding electrodes in accordance with Section 10.

4) Grounding electrodes installed in accordance with Subrule 3) shall be interconnected in accordance with Rule 10-104.

5) Station ground electrodes shall be in accordance with Section 36 and, when installed within 2.4 m of the tower grounding electrodes, shall be interconnected with the tower grounding system with a minimum No. 2/0 AWG bare copper conductor.

64-410 Receptacles for maintenance
Receptacles installed for maintenance of the wind turbine having CSA configuration 5-15R or 5-20R shall be protected by a ground fault circuit interrupter of the Class A type.

64-412 Lightning protection systems (see Appendix B)

1) Auxiliary electrodes and grounding conductors shall be permitted to act as lightning protection system components if they meet applicable requirements.

2) If separate, the tower lightning protection system grounding electrodes shall be bonded to the tower grounding electrode system with a minimum No. 2/0 AWG bare copper conductor.

64-414 System demarcation point
A diagram shall be provided to the inspection department indicating the demarcation between customer-owned and supply authority systems.

Micro-hydropower systems

64-500 Marking (see Appendix B)
A permanent marking shall be provided in accordance with Rule 2-100 at an accessible location at the disconnecting means or the micro-hydropower system output circuit and shall include the following additional information:

a) a brief system description, including rated power and the type of generation system; and

b) rated ballast load voltage and current (if a ballast load is used).

Δ ### 64-502 Insulated conductors (see Appendix B)
Supply wiring insulated conductors or cables supplying electric power from the micro-hydropower system shall have

a) an ampacity of not less than 125% of the full load rated current of the micro-hydropower system; and

b) an insulation temperature rating of not less than 90 °C.

64

64-504 Wiring methods

1) Wiring methods in micro-hydropower systems shall comply with Section 12.
2) Wiring methods in locations where excessive moisture is likely to be present shall comply with Section 22.

64-506 Overcurrent protection for apparatus and insulated conductors

1) Notwithstanding Rules 64-058 1) and 64-066 1) a), individual overcurrent protection devices shall not be required where the available short-circuit current is not greater than the rated ampacity of the equipment or insulated conductor.
2) Overcurrent devices for micro-hydropower system source circuits shall be accessible.
3) Each ungrounded conductor supplying power to or from the micro-hydropower system shall be protected by an overcurrent device not exceeding 125% of the full load rated current of the generator.
4) Notwithstanding Subrule 3), a micro-hydropower system with a full load rated current of 12 A or less shall be permitted to be protected by an overcurrent device with a rating of 15 A.

64-508 Disconnecting means (see Appendix B)

The disconnecting means installed in accordance with Rules 64-060 and 84-020 shall be labelled in a conspicuous, legible, and permanent manner, identifying it as the micro-hydropower generator system disconnecting means.

64-510 Stand-alone systems (see Appendix B)

1) An electronic governor used to regulate the micro-hydropower system shall have a rating equal to the installed capacity unless mechanical governors of sufficient capacity are used to regulate power generation.
2) The diversion load shall be rated to a minimum of 100% of the rating of the electronic governor.
3) The identified conductor shall be rated at the same ampacity as the phase insulated conductors where an electronic governor or power converter is connected.
4) Battery-based micro-hydropower systems shall comply with Rules 64-800 to 64-814.

64-512 Grounding and bonding

All supporting structures shall be bonded to ground with a minimum No. 6 AWG.

Hydrokinetic power systems

64-600 Marking (see Appendix B)

A permanent marking shall be provided for each piece of electrical equipment in accordance with Rule 2-100 at an accessible location at the disconnecting means or the hydrokinetic turbine electrical system output circuit and shall include the following additional information:
a) a brief system description, including rated power and the type of hydrokinetic power system generation system (variable speed or fixed speed); and
b) rated diversion load voltage and current (if a diversion load is used).

64-602 Insulated conductors and cables (see Appendix B)

1) Insulated conductors and cables used to supply power generated by the hydrokinetic turbine generator shall have an ampacity of not less than 125% of the full load rated current.
2) Current calculations shall be made in accordance with Rule 8-100 except where frequencies are different from 60 Hz (e.g., in dc or hydrokinetic turbine generator conductors).
3) For cables used to transmit power from the hydrokinetic turbine generator terminals to the power electronics input, the cables shall be sized using recommended factors supplied by the manufacturer to account
   a) for the skin effect where frequencies are different from 60 Hz; and
   b) for non-unity power factors.

4) Notwithstanding Rule 8-102, a voltage drop not exceeding 10% in the conductors between the electric generator and the input of the power electronics input shall be permitted.

64-604 Stand-alone systems (see Appendix B)

1) The diversion load shall be rated to a minimum of 100% of the installed capacity of the hydrokinetic power system it protects unless otherwise specified by the hydrokinetic power system generation manufacturer.

2) Battery-based hydrokinetic power systems shall comply with Rule 64-800.

3) The neutral conductor shall be rated at the same ampacity as the phase insulated conductors in cases where an electronic governor or power converter is connected.

64-606 Overcurrent protection for apparatus and insulated conductors

1) Notwithstanding Rules 64-058 1) and 64-066 1) a), individual overcurrent protection devices shall not be required where the available steady-state short-circuit current is not greater than the rated ampacity of the apparatus or insulated conductor.

2) Each overcurrent protection device shall be either rated for, or adjusted in size for, the frequency range of the current passing through it.

3) Each ungrounded conductor supplying power to or from the hydrokinetic turbine terminals shall be protected by an overcurrent device not exceeding 125% of the full load rated current.

4) Notwithstanding Subrule 3), a hydrokinetic turbine electrical system with a full load rated current of 12 A or less shall be permitted to be protected by an overcurrent device with a rating of 15 A.

64-608 Wiring methods

1) Notwithstanding Section 12, flow-channel-based insulated conductors shall be permitted to be
   a) of the types specified in accordance with Rule 12-102 for exposed wiring in wet locations; or
   b) flexible cords of the extra-hard-usage type suitable for wet locations as specified in Rule 12-402.

2) Insulated conductors installed in raceways shall be of types specified in accordance with Rule 12-102 for use in raceways in wet locations.

3) Cables installed in the flow channel shall be installed in accordance with Section 22.

64-610 Disconnecting means (see Appendix B)

The disconnecting means installed in accordance with Rules 64-060 and 84-020 shall be labelled in a conspicuous, legible, and permanent manner, identifying it as the hydrokinetic power system generator disconnecting means.

64-612 Grounding and bonding (see Appendix B)

All non-current-carrying metal parts of the turbine, including extra-low-voltage turbines, shall be bonded to ground in accordance with Section 10.

Stationary fuel cell systems

64-700 Marking (see Appendix B)

1) A permanent marking shall be provided in accordance with Rule 2-100 at the disconnecting means, specifying the following additional information:
   a) overcurrent protection values provided by the output;
   b) short-circuit current-interrupting capacity for protective devices; and
   c) a brief system description.

2) The location of the manual fuel shut-off valve shall be marked at the location of the primary disconnecting means of the building or circuits supplied.

3) A fuel cell system that stores electrical energy shall be labelled in a conspicuous, legible, and permanent manner with a suitable warning sign at the location of the service disconnecting means of the premises.

64

64-702 Conductors

1) The rated circuit current shall be the rated current indicated on the fuel cell system nameplate(s).
2) The ampacity of the feeder or circuit insulated conductors from the fuel cell system(s) to the premises wiring system shall not be less than the greater of
    a) the nameplate(s) rated circuit current; or
    b) the rating of the fuel cell system(s) overcurrent protection device(s).

64-704 Overcurrent protection

1) If the stationary fuel cell system is provided with overcurrent protection sufficient to protect the circuit conductors that supply the load, additional circuit overcurrent devices shall not be required.
2) Overcurrent devices shall be readily accessible.

64-706 Disconnecting means (see Appendix B)

The disconnecting means installed in accordance with Rules 64-060 and 84-020 shall be labelled in a conspicuous, legible, and permanent manner, identifying it as the fuel cell system disconnecting means.

64-708 Grounding and bonding

Hydrogen and fuel containers, associated piping, flanges, and hydrogen vent systems shall be bonded to ground by means of a copper bonding conductor not smaller than No. 6 AWG except as required for cathodic protection.

64-710 Location of fuel cells (see Appendix B)

A fuel cell system(s) and associated equipment, components, and controls shall meet the following requirements:
a) stationary fuel cell systems shall be sited and installed in accordance with the manufacturer's instructions;
b) the area classification around outlets from processes or compartments that contain fuel-bearing components shall be in accordance with the manufacturer's instructions and Section 18;
c) stationary fuel cell systems shall not be located in clothes closets, bathrooms, stairways, high ambient rooms, hazardous locations, or any similar undesirable places; and
d) stationary fuel cell systems shall be marked as suitable for the particular location.

64-712 Outdoor installations

For outdoor installations, a stationary fuel cell system shall meet the following requirements:
a) the stationary fuel cell system shall be suitable for outdoor installation; and
b) security barriers, fences, landscaping, and other enclosures shall not affect the required air flow into or exhaust out of the stationary fuel cell system.

Δ ## 64-714 Indoor installations

Stationary fuel cell systems that are to be installed indoors shall be marked for indoor installation.

64-716 Electrical equipment (see Appendix B)

1) Transformers installed in rooms that contain fuel cell power systems shall be of the dry type.
2) Areas provided with mechanical ventilation required for safety during normal operation shall be interlocked to provide an alarm and shut down the fuel cell power system upon loss of ventilation.
3) Indoor installations of fuel cell power systems that are fuelled by a gas that has not been odorized shall have an automatic shut-off valve located outdoors that is interlocked with indoor combustible gas detection.
4) Where an automatic fire suppression system is provided for the fuel cell system, it shall be interconnected to shut off the fuel supply when the suppression system is activated.

Storage batteries

64-800 Installation (see Appendix B)

1) Storage batteries in a renewable energy system shall be installed in accordance with the provisions of Rule 26-500, except as otherwise required by the manufacturer.

2) The interconnected battery cells shall be considered grounded where the renewable energy power source is installed in accordance with Rule 64-064.

3) Storage batteries for dwelling units shall have the cells connected so as to operate at less than 50 V nominal.

4) Lead-acid storage batteries for dwellings shall have no more than twenty-four 2 V cells connected in series (48 V nominal).

5) Live parts of battery systems for dwelling units shall be guarded to prevent accidental contact by persons or objects, regardless of voltage or battery type.

64-802 Current-limiting overcurrent devices (see Appendix B)

A current-limiting overcurrent device shall be installed in each battery circuit where the available short-circuit current from a battery or battery bank exceeds the interrupting or withstand ratings of other equipment in that circuit.

64-804 Battery non-conductive cases and conductive racks (see Appendix B)

1) Flooded, vented, lead-acid batteries with more than twenty-four 2 V cells connected in series (more than 48 V nominal) shall not use conductive cases or be installed in conductive cases.

2) Conductive racks used to support non-conductive cases shall be permitted where no rack material or other obstacle is located within 150 mm of the tops of the non-conductive cases.

3) No conductive materials shall be located within 150 mm of the tops of the non-conductive cases.

4) The requirement specified in Subrule 1) shall not apply to any type of valve-regulated lead-acid (VRLA) battery or any other battery type that could require steel cases for proper operation.

64-806 Disconnection of series battery circuits

Battery circuits subject to field servicing, operating at more than 48 V nominal, shall

a) have provisions for disconnecting the series-connected strings; and

b) have provisions for disconnecting the grounded circuit conductor(s) in the battery electrical system for maintenance without disconnecting the grounded circuit conductor(s) for the remainder of the renewable energy electrical system.

64-808 Battery systems of more than 48 V

For renewable energy systems where the battery system consists of more than twenty-four 2 V cells connected in series (more than 48 V nominal), the battery system shall be permitted to operate with ungrounded conductors, provided that the following conditions are met:

a) the renewable energy source and output circuits comply with Rule 64-066;

b) the dc and ac load circuits are solidly grounded;

c) all main ungrounded battery input/output circuit conductors are provided with disconnecting means and overcurrent protection; and

d) a dc rated ground fault detector and indicator are installed to monitor all ungrounded conductors for ground faults in the battery bank.

Δ **64-810 Battery interconnections** (see Appendix B)

1) Flexible cables, as identified in Section 12, in sizes No. 2/0 AWG and larger shall be permitted within the battery enclosure from battery terminals to a nearby junction box.

2) Flexible cables shall also be permitted between batteries and cells within the battery enclosure.

3) Cables shall be of a type for hard-service use and identified as moisture-resistant.

64

64-812 Charge control (see Appendix B)
1)   Equipment shall be provided to control the charging process of the battery.
2)   Charge control shall not be required where the design of the renewable energy source circuit is matched to the voltage rating and charge current requirements of the interconnected battery cells and the maximum charging current multiplied by 1 h is less than 3% of the rated battery capacity.
3)   All adjusting means for control of the charging process shall be accessible only to qualified persons.

64-814 Diversion charge controller (see Appendix B)
1)   A renewable energy system employing a diversion charge controller as the sole means of regulating the charging of a battery shall be equipped with an additional, independent means to prevent overcharging of the battery.
2)   Circuits containing a dc diversion charge controller and a dc diversion load shall comply with the following:
   a)   the current rating of the diversion load shall be less than or equal to the current rating of the diversion load charge controller;
   b)   the voltage rating of the diversion load shall be greater than the maximum battery voltage;
   c)   the power rating of the diversion load shall be at least 150% of the power rating of the renewable energy system; and
   d)   the conductor ampacity and the rating of the overcurrent device for the circuit shall be at least 150% of the maximum current rating of the diversion charge controller.
Δ   3)   Renewable energy systems using interactive inverters to control battery state-of-charge by diverting excess power into the utility system shall have an additional, independent means of controlling the battery charging process for use when the utility is not present or when the primary charge controller fails or is disabled.

C22.1-18

Section 66
Amusement parks, midways, carnivals, film and TV sets, TV remote broadcasting
locations, and travelling shows

Section 66 — Amusement parks, midways, carnivals, film and TV sets, TV remote broadcasting locations, and travelling shows

Scope and application

66-000 Scope

1) This Section applies to the temporary installation of electrical equipment, using any source of electrical power, for
   a) amusement parks;
   b) midways;
   c) carnivals;
   d) fairs;
   e) film, television, and radio productions;
   f) remote broadcasting and recording locations;
   g) live performance and entertainment events;
   h) touring shows and productions;
   i) concerts;
   j) sporting events;
   k) trade shows; and
   l) similar events.

2) The installation of electrical equipment forming part of an amusement ride shall comply with CAN/CSA-Z267.

3) This Section supplements or amends the general requirements of this Code.

66-002 Special terminology

In this Section, the following definitions shall apply:

Amusement park — a tract of land used as a temporary or permanent location for amusement rides and structures.

Amusement ride — a device or combination of devices designated or intended to entertain or amuse people by physically moving them.

Concession — a structure or a combination of structures erected for the purpose of entertaining or amusing people with games or shows and for the dispensing of food, souvenirs, and tickets, by sale or for any other purpose.

General

66-100 Supporting of conductors

1) Only decorative lighting, signal, communication, and control circuits shall be supported on structures that support amusement rides.

2) The decorative lighting and control circuits of one amusement ride shall not be installed on a supporting structure of another ride.

3) Overhead conductors shall have a vertical clearance to finished grade of not less than the following:
   a) across highways, streets, lanes, and alleys: 5.5 m;
   b) across areas accessible to vehicles: 5 m; and
   c) across areas accessible to pedestrians: 3.5 m.

66

C22.1-18

Section 66
Amusement parks, midways, carnivals, film and TV sets, TV remote broadcasting
locations, and travelling shows

66-102 Protection of electrical equipment
Electrical equipment shall be protected in accordance with Rule 2-200.

Grounding

66-200 Grounding
1) The service and electrical distribution shall be grounded in accordance with Section 10.
2) Notwithstanding Rule 10-118 1) a), grounding electrodes for mobile generators shall be permitted to be connected using single-conductor, plug-in, locking-type connectors.
3) A mobile generator grounding conductor shall
   a) be dedicated to the mobile generator;
   b) be run directly, by the shortest practicable route;
   c) have no more than two sets of mated, in-line, single-pin connections, excluding the connections at the grounding electrodes and the mobile generator;
   d) not exceed 50 m in total length; and
   e) be not less than No. 4 AWG.

66-202 Equipment bonding
1) Exposed non-current-carrying metal parts of fixed electrical equipment, such as motor frames, starters, and switch boxes; parts of rides, concessions, and ticket booths; and moving electrically operated equipment, shall be bonded to ground by
   a) means of the bonding conductor in the supply cord; or
   b) connection to a separate insulated flexible copper bonding conductor, not less than No. 6 AWG, that is connected to the grounded circuit conductor at the service disconnect.
2) Cord-connected, operator-controlled remote stations shall be bonded to ground.

Services and distribution

66-300 Service equipment
1) Service equipment shall be of a size suitable for the connected load.
2) Where accessible to unauthorized persons, enclosures for service equipment shall be lockable.
3) Generators shall not be accessible to unauthorized persons.

66-302 Mounting of service equipment
Service equipment shall be mounted on a solid backing and be
a) located so as to be protected from the weather;
b) installed in a weatherproof enclosure; or
c) of weatherproof construction.

66-304 Distribution equipment
1) Each concession and ride shall be provided with a fused disconnect switch or circuit breaker.
2) Where accessible to unauthorized persons, enclosures for switches, panelboards, and splitters shall be lockable.

Wiring methods and equipment

66-400 Wiring methods
1) Except as permitted in Rules 66-450 to 66-458, wiring methods shall be in accordance with Section 12 and suitable for the condition of use.
2) Cords, cables, conduits, and other electrical equipment shall be protected from physical damage.
3) Cords shall be of the hard-usage type, in good repair, and
   a) provided with strain relief where they enter into enclosures and plug-in connectors;
   b) if exposed to the weather, be of a type suitable for outdoor use; and

C22.1-18

Section 66
Amusement parks, midways, carnivals, film and TV sets, TV remote broadcasting
locations, and travelling shows

c) where plug-in connections are used,
    i) have connectors and receptacles that are rated in amperes and designed so that differently rated devices cannot be connected together;
    ii) have the female connector attached to the load end of the cord; and
    iii) be polarized if an ac multi-conductor connector is used.

4) Notwithstanding Subrule 3) c) ii), for single-conductor cables, the grounded conductor and the bonding conductor shall be permitted to have the female half connected to the supply end of the cord.

5) With the exception of amusement parks, midways, carnivals, home shows, and tent meetings, receptacles rated 15 A, conforming to CSA configuration 5-15R rated 120 V, hospital grade, and protected by a fuse or circuit breaker rated not greater than 20 A, shall be permitted for temporary lighting installations within the Scope of this Section, where the loads are of an intermittent nature.

6) Temporary wiring for portable stage equipment shall be in accordance with Rules 44-350, 44-352, and 44-356.

66-402 Equipment

1) Lighting streamers shall be made up of extra-hard-usage outdoor flexible cord with weatherproof lampholders having either
    a) terminals of a type that puncture the insulation and make contact with the conductors; or
    b) permanently attached leads connected to the cord.

2) Fluorescent luminaires shall not be mounted end-to-end unless they are marked for that purpose.

3) Incandescent lampholders shall be of the screwshell type.

4) Notwithstanding Subrule 3), bayonet-type lampholders shall be permitted for film and TV sets and TV remotes.

5) Utilization equipment intended for use outdoors shall be suitable for the location, unless precautions are taken to protect it from inclement weather.

66-404 Receptacles

Receptacles having CSA configuration 5-15R or 5-20R installed in itinerant midways, carnivals, fairs, and festivals and intended to supply loads in outdoor or damp locations shall be protected by ground fault circuit interrupters of the Class A type.

Single-conductor cables

66-450 Single-conductor cables

Single-conductor cables shall be permitted in sizes No. 4 AWG and larger, provided that they are
a) rated for the circuit voltage and suitable for the intended application;
b) a matched set with the same length for all conductors of the circuit, including the bonding conductor; and
c) covered or guarded so as not to present a tripping hazard in pedestrian walkways or roadways.

66-452 Fault current limiting

Where the available fault current exceeds 10 000 A, systems employing single-conductor cables, except where installed as fixed wiring, shall be supplied by means of current-limiting overcurrent devices to prevent inadvertent movement of the cables.

66-454 Free air ampacity

1) Single-conductor cables shall be rated in accordance with Section 4.

2) Notwithstanding Subrule 1), for temporary installations, bundled single-conductor cables of any one circuit shall be permitted to be free air rated without correction factors if different circuits are separated by at least one cable bundle diameter.

66

C22.1-18

Section 66
Amusement parks, midways, carnivals, film and TV sets, TV remote broadcasting
locations, and travelling shows

66-456 Single-conductor cable connections

1) Connections to single-conductor cables shall not be accessible to unqualified persons.

2) Plug-in connectors for single-conductor cables shall
   a) be of a locking type;
   b) incorporate a mechanical interlock to prevent wrong connections or be colour-coded; and
   c) have all connections that are not in use covered with a seal or cap that is acceptable.

3) Single-conductor cables shall not be connected in parallel except as a means of reducing voltage drop, and cables so connected shall have overcurrent protection sized to protect the cable having the smallest ampacity as though it were used alone.

4) Tapping tees, paralleling tees, or rigid turnarounds shall
   a) not be directly connected to any single-pin plug or connector rigidly housed or mounted in a multiple-connection device;
   b) not be directly connected to a panel mount inlet or outlet or to a multiple-connection device with a cable less than 2 m in length; and
   c) be arranged so that no mechanical strain is imposed on the connection.

5) In-line single-conductor cable connections forming part of a circuit of more than 150 volts-to-ground shall be mechanically protected by enclosing the connector(s) in a lockable, non-conductive box or similar enclosure.

6) The lockable enclosure referred to in Subrule 5) shall
   a) be labelled on the outside, in a conspicuous, legible, and permanent manner, identifying the supply voltage of the circuit; and
   b) be acceptable.

7) No more than one tapping or parallel tee per conductor shall be used at any one point in a power distribution system.

Δ 8) Any distribution splitting or combining devices requiring more than two load connections per conductor shall use a single multiple-connection device at that point.

66-458 Bonding

Each circuit incorporating single-conductor cables shall include a bonding conductor that shall be run with the circuit conductors.

Motors

66-500 Motors

Motors, including protection and control, shall be installed in accordance with Section 28.

66-502 Location

Motors shall be installed only in dry locations unless they are of a type specifically marked for the location or are suitably protected.

66-504 Portable motors

Connections to portable motors shall be permitted to be made with flexible cord with a serviceability not less than Type SOW for outdoor use.

Section 68 — Pools, tubs, and spas

Scope

68-000 Scope

1) This Section applies to
   a) electrical installations and electrical equipment in or adjacent to pools; and
   b) non-electrical metal accessories in a pool or within 3 m of the inside wall of a pool.
2) A pool shall be deemed to include
   a) permanently installed and storable swimming pools;
   b) hydromassage bathtubs;
   c) spas and hot tubs;
   d) wading pools;
   e) baptismal pools;
   f) decorative pools; and
   g) splash pads.
3) This Section supplements or amends the general requirements of this Code.

General

68-050 Special terminology

In this Section, the following definitions shall apply:

Decorative pool — a pool that could be used as a wading pool, that is larger than 1.5 m in any dimension, and that is readily accessible to the public.

Dry-niche luminaire — a luminaire intended for installation in the wall of the pool in a niche that is sealed against the entry of pool water by a fixed lens.

Forming shell — a structure intended for mounting in a pool structure to support a wet-niche luminaire assembly.

Hydromassage bathtub — a permanently installed bathtub having an integral or remote water pump or air blower, and having a fill and drain water system; this term includes therapeutic pools.

Leakage current collector — a device designed to provide a path to ground for leakage current originating from devices in contact with pool water.

Permanently installed swimming pool — a pool constructed in such a manner that it cannot be disassembled for storage.

Spa or **hot tub** — a pool or tub designed for the immersion of persons in heated water circulated in a closed system incorporating a filter, heater, and pump, and with or without a motor-driven blower, but not intended to be filled and drained with each use.

Splash pad — an area designed for water play that is not intended to have standing water.

Storable swimming pool — a pool constructed in such a manner that it can be readily disassembled for storage and reassembled to its original integrity.

Wet-niche luminaire — a luminaire intended for installation in a forming shell mounted in a pool structure where the luminaire will be completely surrounded by pool water.

68-052 Electrical wiring or equipment in pool walls or water

Electrical wiring or equipment shall not be installed in the walls nor in the water of pools except as permitted by this Section.

68-054 Overhead wiring (see Appendix B)

1) No pool shall be placed under or near overhead wiring, and no overhead wiring shall be placed over or near a pool, unless the installation complies with the requirements of this Rule.

2) There shall not be any overhead wiring above the pool and other elevated surfaces associated with the pool, such as a diving structure, slide, swings, observation stand, tower, or platform, or above the adjacent area extending 5.0 m horizontally from the pool edge, except as permitted by Subrules 3) and 4).

3) Insulated communication conductors, communication antenna distribution conductors, and neutral supported cables not exceeding 750 V shall be permitted to be located over a pool and other elevated surfaces associated with the pool, or above the adjacent area extending horizontally from the pool edge, provided that there is a clearance of at least 5.0 m measured from the outer edge of the pool or from other elevated surfaces associated with the pool.

4) Conductors other than those covered by Subrule 3) and operating at not more than 50 kV phase-to-phase shall be permitted to be located over a pool and other elevated surfaces associated with the pool, or above the adjacent area extending horizontally from the pool edge, provided that there is a clearance of at least 7.5 m measured from the outer edge of the pool or from other elevated surfaces associated with the pool.

68-056 Underground wiring

The horizontal separation between the inside walls of a pool and underground conductors, except for bonding conductors or conductors supplying electrical equipment associated with the pool and protected by a Class A ground fault circuit interrupter, shall be not less than that shown in Table 61.

68-058 Bonding (see Appendix B)

1) The metal parts of the pool and of other non-electrical equipment associated with the pool, such as piping, pool reinforcing steel, ladders, diving board supports, and fences within 1.5 m of the pool, shall be bonded together and to non-current-carrying metal parts of electrical equipment such as decorative-type pool luminaires and lighting equipment not located in a forming shell, forming shells, metal screens of shields for underwater speakers, conduit, junction boxes, and the like by a copper bonding conductor.

2) Pool reinforcing steel shall be bonded with a minimum of four connections equally spaced around the perimeter.

3) Notwithstanding Subrule 2), where reinforcing steel is encapsulated with a non-conductive compound, provisions shall be made for an alternative means to eliminate voltage gradients that would otherwise be provided by unencapsulated, bonded reinforcing steel.

4) Bonding conductors for pools shall be
   a) not smaller than No. 6 AWG for permanently installed pools and for all in-ground pools; or
   Δ b) as required by Table 16 for all other pools.

5) Metal sheaths and raceways shall not be relied upon as the bonding medium, and a separate copper bonding conductor shall be used, except that a metal conduit between a forming shell and its associated junction box shall be permitted to be used as the bonding medium, provided that the forming shell and junction box are installed in the same structural section.

6) The bonding conductor from the junction box referred to in Rule 68-060 shall be run to the panelboard supplying pool electrical equipment and, if smaller than No. 6 AWG, shall be installed and mechanically protected in the same manner as the circuit conductors.

Δ 7) The bonding conductor specified in Subrule 4) shall be of copper and not smaller than that required by Table 16 except that the bonding conductor for an in-ground pool shall be not smaller than No. 6 AWG.

8) A continuous metal pool shell made up of individual panels securely bolted or welded together shall be bonded in at least one location.

68-060 Junction and deck boxes (see Appendix B)

1) Junction boxes shall be permitted to be submerged in decorative pools, provided that the boxes are marked for such usage.

2) Junction boxes installed on the supply side of conduits extending to forming shells, hereafter referred to as deck boxes, shall be specifically approved for the purpose.

3) Deck boxes shall be provided with a means for independently terminating at least three bonding conductors inside the box and one No. 6 AWG bonding conductor outside the box.

4) Deck boxes shall not contain the conductors of any circuits other than those used exclusively to supply the underwater equipment.

5) Deck boxes shall be provided with electrical continuity between every connected metal conduit and the bonding terminals by means of copper, brass, or other corrosion-resistant metal that is integral with the box.

6) Deck boxes shall be installed
   a) above the normal water level of the pool;
   b) so that the top of the box is located at or above the finished level of the pool deck;
   c) in such a manner or location that the box will not be an obstacle; and
   d) in such a manner that any water on the deck will drain away from the box.

7) Junction boxes and conduit shall be watertight and provided with a packing seal that will seal around the cord and effectively prevent water from entering the box through the conduit from the forming shell.

68-062 Transformers and transformer enclosures (see Appendix B)

1) Transformers shall not be located within 3 m of the inside wall of the pool unless suitably separated from the pool area by a fence, wall, or other permanent barrier that will make the transformer not accessible to persons using the pool area.

2) A metal shield, if provided between the primary and secondary windings of a transformer, shall be bonded to ground.

3) Audio isolation transformers shall
   a) be connected between the audio output terminals of each amplifier and any loudspeaker that is located within 3 m of the pool wall;
   b) be located in or adjacent to the amplifier with which they are used; and
   c) have an audio output voltage of not more than 75 V rms.

68-064 Receptacles

1) Receptacles shall not be located within 1.5 m of the inside walls of a pool.

2) Receptacles located between 1.5 m and 3 m of the inside walls of a pool shall be protected by a ground fault circuit interrupter of the Class A type.

3) In maintaining the dimensions referred to in this Rule, the distance to be measured shall be the shortest path that the power supply cord of an appliance connected to the receptacle would follow without piercing a building floor, wall, or ceiling.

68-066 Luminaires and lighting equipment

1) Wet-niche or submersible luminaires shall
   a) be mounted in forming shells that have provision for a suitable connection to the wiring method used;
   b) unless specifically approved and marked for submersion at a greater depth, not be submersed in the pool water at a depth of more than 600 mm, such distance being measured from the centre of the lens face of the luminaire to the normal water level; and

c)   operate with neither the supply voltage to the luminaire nor its associated ballast or transformer, if applicable, nor the secondary open-circuit voltage of the ballast or transformer exceeding 150 V during either starting or operating conditions.

2)   Notwithstanding Subrule 1) a), wet-niche or submersible luminaires installed in a decorative pool need not be mounted in a forming shell but shall have provision for a suitable connection to the wiring method used.

3)   Where dry-niche luminaires are installed to be accessible from a walkway or a service tunnel outside the walls of the pool or from a closed, drained recess in the walls of the pool, neither the supply voltage to the luminaire nor its associated ballast or transformer shall exceed 300 V during either starting or operating conditions.

4)   Dry-niche luminaires shall be accessible for maintenance
a)   from a service tunnel or walkway outside the walls of the pool; or
b)   through a handhole in the deck of the pool to a closed, drained recess in the wall of the pool.

5)   Metal parts of luminaires in contact with the pool water shall be of brass or other suitable corrosion-resistant material.

6)   Luminaires installed below, or within 3 m of, the pool surface or walls, and not suitably separated from the pool area by a fence, wall, or other permanent barrier, shall be electrically protected by a Class A ground fault circuit interrupter.

7)   Standards or supports for luminaires shall not be installed within 3 m of the inside walls of a swimming pool unless such luminaires are protected by Class A ground fault circuit interrupters.

8)   Forming shells for lamps supplied from a grounded circuit or a circuit operating at a voltage exceeding 30 V shall be metal and have provision for a threaded connection to a rigid metal conduit.

68-068 Ground fault circuit interrupters (see Appendix B)

1)   Where ground fault circuit interrupters of the Class A type are not available due to rating, the equipment shall be permitted to be provided with ground fault protection that will clear a ground fault within the time and current values specified for a Class A type ground fault circuit interrupter.

2)   Where a Class A ground fault circuit interrupter is referenced in this Section, that reference shall also apply to a device or system permitted by Subrule 1).

3)   Class A ground fault circuit interrupters shall be permanently connected.

4)   Class A ground fault circuit interrupters shall be permitted to be applied to a feeder, a branch circuit, or an individual device.

5)   A warning sign shall be located beside the switches controlling circuits electrically protected by Class A ground fault circuit interrupters, advising that the circuits have such protection and that the equipment shall be tested regularly.

6)   Class A ground fault circuit interrupters shall be installed
a)   in a location that will facilitate the testing required in Subrule 5);
b)   not closer than 3 m to the pool water except as permitted by Item c); and
c)   not closer than 3 m to the pool water in a spa or hot tub and not closer than 1.5 m to a hydromassage bathtub, unless the Class A ground fault circuit interrupter is an integral part of an approved factory-built spa, hot tub, or hydromassage bathtub or is located behind a barrier that will prevent the occupant of the pool from contacting the device.

7)   Except as permitted by Rule 68-070, the following equipment shall be protected by a Class A ground fault circuit interrupter:
a)   electrical equipment placed in the water in the pool;
b)   spas and hot tubs;
c)   audio amplifiers connected to loudspeakers in the pool water;

d) electrical equipment located within the confines of the pool walls or within 3 m of the inside walls of the pool and not suitably separated from the pool area by a fence, wall, or other permanent barrier; and

e) receptacles located in wet areas of a building, and associated with the pool, such as locker and change rooms.

68-070 Other electrical equipment

1) Loudspeakers installed beneath the pool surface shall be
   a) mounted in a recess in the wall or floor of the pool and enclosed by a separate, rigid, corrosion-resistant metal screen; and
   b) connected to their audio isolating transformers by ungrounded wiring.

2) Communication equipment installed within 3 m of the inside walls of the pool shall be
   a) permanently fixed on the wall and located so that no part is within 1.5 m of the inside walls of the pool or can be used from the pool, unless actuated by means of a cord with an insulating link; or
   b) separated from the pool area by a fence, wall, or other permanent barrier.

3) Notwithstanding Subrule 2), communication jacks shall not be installed within 3 m of the inside walls of the pool.

Permanently installed swimming pools

68-100 Wiring method

1) Rigid conduit of copper or other corrosion-resistant metal or rigid PVC conduit shall be provided between the forming shell of luminaires installed below the pool surface and the junction boxes referred to in Rule 68-060.

2) The wiring method between wet-niche luminaires and the junction boxes referred to in Rule 68-060 shall be flexible cord suitable for use in wet locations and supplied as a part of the luminaire.

3) Where Subrules 1) and 2) do not apply, any suitable wiring method specified in Section 12 shall be permitted to be used.

4) Conductors on the load side of each Class A ground fault circuit interrupter shall be kept entirely independent of all other wiring that is not protected in that way and shall not enter a luminaire, raceway, box, or cabinet occupied by other wiring except for panelboards that house the interrupters.

5) Conduits in the walls and deck of a swimming pool shall be installed so that suitable drainage is provided.

Storable swimming pools

68-200 Electrical equipment

No electrical equipment shall be located in the pool water or on the pool wall unless specifically approved for the purpose.

68-202 Pumps

1) Swimming pool pumps shall be
   a) supplied from a permanently installed receptacle located not less than 1.5 m nor more than 7.5 m from the pool wall; and
   b) protected by a Class A ground fault circuit interrupter if located within 3 m of the inside walls of the pool and not suitably separated from the pool area by a fence, wall, or other permanent barrier.

2) Swimming pool pumps located within 3 m of the pool walls shall be specifically approved for the purpose.

Hydromassage bathtubs

68-300 General
Rules 68-302 to 68-308 apply to the installation of permanently connected and cord-connected hydromassage bathtubs.

68-302 Protection
Electrical equipment forming an integral part of a hydromassage bathtub shall be protected by a ground fault circuit interrupter of the Class A type.

68-304 Control
1) A hydromassage bathtub shall be controlled by an on-off device located in accordance with Subrule 2).
2) Electric controls associated with a hydromassage bathtub shall be located behind a barrier or shall be located not less than 1 m horizontally from the wall of the hydromassage bathtub, unless they are an integral part of an approved factory-built hydromassage bathtub.

Δ ### 68-306 Receptacles for a cord-connected hydromassage bathtub (see Appendix B)
1) Where a cord-connected hydromassage bathtub is provided with one or more power supply cords, each cord and attachment plug shall be connected to a receptacle that is
   a) supplied by at least one branch circuit that supplies only receptacles described in this Rule;
   b) located at not less than 300 mm from the floor; and
   c) inaccessible to the hydromassage bathtub occupant.
2) When more than one receptacle is required to supply a cord-connected hydromassage bathtub, the receptacles shall be located in close proximity to each other.
3) Where a hydromassage bathtub is not provided with a ground fault circuit interrupter of the Class A type, each receptacle referred to in Subrule 1) shall be protected by a ground fault circuit interrupter of the Class A type.
4) An appropriate warning label shall be affixed to the receptacles specified in Subrule 1) warning against the connection of any equipment not associated with the hydromassage bathtub.

68-308 Other electric equipment
Luminaires, switches, receptacles, and other electrical equipment not directly associated with a hydromassage bathtub shall be installed in accordance with the Rules of this Code covering the installation of that equipment in bathrooms.

Spas and hot tubs

68-400 General
Rules 68-402 to 68-408 apply to the installation of spas and hot tubs.

68-402 Bonding to ground
1) Metal parts of spas and hot tubs shall be bonded together and to ground in accordance with Rule 68-058.
2) Notwithstanding Subrule 1), metal rings or bands used to secure staves of wooden hot tubs need not be bonded.

68-404 Controls and other electrical equipment (see Appendix B)
1) Controls for a spa or hot tub shall be located behind a barrier or not less than 1 m horizontally from the spa or hot tub, unless they are an integral part of an approved factory-built spa or hot tub.
2) Receptacles shall be installed in accordance with Rule 68-064.
3) Luminaires shall be installed in accordance with Rule 68-066.

4) Except for a spa or hot tub installed at a dwelling unit, an emergency shut-off switch shall be installed for each spa or hot tub that
   a) disconnects the motors supplying power to the closed water circulating systems;
   b) is independent of the controls for a spa or hot tub;
   c) is located at a point readily accessible to the users and within sight of and within 15 m of the spa or hot tub;
   d) is labelled in a conspicuous, legible, and permanent manner, identifying it as the emergency shut-off switch; and
   e) activates audible and visual trouble-signal devices that give immediate warning upon actuation of the emergency shut-off switch.

68-406 Leakage current collectors

1) Leakage current collectors shall be installed in all water inlets and all water outlets of a field-assembled spa or hot tub so that all water flows through the leakage current collectors.
2) A leakage current collector shall be
   a) a section of corrosion-resistant metal tubing at least five times as long as its diameter, provided with a corrosion-resistant lug, in a run of non-metallic pipe; or
   b) a device providing protection equal to that described in Item a) when it is an integral part of a spa or hot tub that is factory built for field installation or assembly.
3) Leakage current collectors shall be electrically insulated from the spa or hot tub and shall be bonded to the control panel or the main service ground with a copper bonding conductor.
4) Notwithstanding Subrule 1), leakage current collectors shall not be required in a system in which the only electrical component is a pump marked as an insulated wet end pump.
5) The bonding conductor for leakage current collectors shall be
   a) not smaller than that required by Table 16 where the bonding conductors are mechanically protected in the same manner as the circuit conductors; or
   b) a minimum No. 6 AWG copper conductor.

Δ

68-408 Field-assembled units (see Appendix B)

1) Spas and hot tubs field assembled with individual components shall be installed in accordance with Rules 68-402 to 68-406 and Subrules 2) and 3) of this Rule.
2) Individual components such as pumps, heaters, and blowers shall be specifically approved for use with spas or hot tubs.
3) Air blowers shall be installed above the tub rim, or other means shall be used to prevent water from contacting blower live parts.

Section 70 — Electrical requirements for factory-built relocatable structures and non-relocatable structures

Scope

70-000 Scope
1) Rules 70-100 to 70-130 apply to relocatable structures (factory-built) towable on their own chassis, for use without permanent foundations and having provision for connection to utilities, including
   a) mobile homes; and
   b) mobile commercial and industrial structures.
2) Rules 70-200 to 70-204 apply to non-relocatable structures (factory-built) for use on permanent foundations, including
   a) housing (residential); and
   b) commercial and industrial structures.
3) These Rules do not apply to recreational vehicles covered by CSA Z240 RV Series.
4) This Section supplements or amends the general requirements of this Code.

Relocatable structures

70-100 Equipment
Electrical components, including those connected in Class 1 extra-low-voltage power circuits (e.g., luminaires) and in Class 2 extra-low-voltage circuits, shall conform to the requirements of the *Canadian Electrical Code, Part II* and be suitable for the application.

70-102 Method of connection
1) Subject to the conditions of Subrule 2), the method of connection to the supply circuit shall be
   a) connection to an overhead or underground supply;
   b) a power supply cord or cord set; or
   c) a length of flexible cord, or cord or cable without an attachment plug.
2) For mobile homes, the method of connection to the power supply shall be directly to an overhead or underground supply, except where a deviation has been allowed in accordance with Rule 2-030.

70-104 Connection to an overhead or underground supply
1) Where the supply connection is directly to an overhead or underground supply, a conduit nipple or a length of rigid conduit shall be provided and shall
   a) project from the structure through the exterior wall, roof, or floor to permit attachment of a conduit fitting;
   b) have a suitable cap on the exposed end;
   c) terminate at the disconnecting means, at an intermediate box, or, for other than mobile homes, at the distribution equipment if a disconnecting means is not provided; and
   d) be of sufficient size to accommodate copper conductors of a calculated ampacity for the load involved, except
      i) where the structure is specifically designed for connection by conductors other than copper; or
      ii) as specified in Subrule 3).
2) For mobile homes, the conduit shall project so that it is readily accessible for power supply connection.
3) For mobile homes, the size of conduit shall be not less than that specified in Table 48.
4) Where it is intended or likely that the system grounding conductor be run separately, a non-metallic raceway shall be installed at the time of manufacture for this purpose.

70-106 Service for communication systems (see Appendix B)

All mobile homes shall be provided with a length of raceway, 16 trade size or larger, for use as a communication service that shall

a) project from the structure a minimum of 75 mm through the floor;

b) terminate at least 300 mm above the finished floor in a wall or partition in a standard switch or outlet box complete with cover;

c) where made of metal, be bonded to the frame of the mobile home; and

d) have a suitable cap on the exposed end of the conduit stub.

70-108 Power supply cord or cord set

1) Where a power supply cord or cord set is used except as provided for in Subrule 4), the cord shall
   a) be provided as part of the mobile structure;
   b) have an ampacity not less than the ampere rating of the attachment plug;
   c) be of the extra-hard-usage type suitable for outdoor use as selected in accordance with Rule 12-402 1) or 12-406 1);
   d) have separate identified and bonding conductors;
   e) be not less than 7.5 m in length, as measured from the attachment plug to the point of entrance to the unit;
   f) if it is a permanently connected power supply cord, terminate at the main disconnecting means in the unit or at a box in or on the unit, suitable space being provided in the unit for storage of the cord when it is not in use to protect it from damage; and
   g) have a suitable grounding-type attachment plug with an ampere rating as follows:
      i) for applications covered by Section 8, not less than that of the service conductor ampacity required in Section 8; or
      ii) for other applications, not less than that for which it is approved.

2) Bushings of rubber, unless of an oil-resistant compound, shall not be used in locations where they are exposed to mechanical damage.

3) Where a cord set is used, a male receptacle shall be provided on the unit and shall
   a) be of weatherproof construction unless adequately protected or enclosed;
   b) have a contact arrangement that will mate with the cord connector on the cord; and
   c) have a current rating not less than that of the main overcurrent protection.

4) Where provided for in Rule 70-102 2), a cord or cord set shall be permitted to be used for mobile homes, provided that it
   a) is not smaller than No. 6 AWG;
   b) has an attachment plug moulded to the cord with a configuration designated as CSA 14-50P (3-pole, 4-wire, 125/250 V, 50 A); and
   c) enters where it will not be subject to mechanical damage.

70-110 Disconnecting means and main overcurrent protection

1) Except as provided for in Subrule 2), each structure shall be provided with
   a) a service box or a combined service and distribution box located within the structure with provision for grounding the neutral;
   b) main overcurrent protection having a current rating at least equal to the minimum ampacity of the consumer's service, as determined in accordance with Section 8, but in no case less than 50 A for mobile homes and not exceeding the ampacity of the supply conductors actually used, except as permitted by Rule 14-104; and
   c) an identified conductor that shall be
      i) connected to ground within the mobile structure if a power supply cord or cord set is not provided; or
      ii) isolated from ground if a power supply cord or cord set is used.

2) For other than mobile homes, the structure shall be permitted to be provided with distribution equipment instead of the type of service equipment listed in Subrule 1) where such service equipment is provided in the supply to the unit.

70-112 Location of service or distribution equipment
Service or distribution equipment shall be
a) readily accessible;
b) not located in clothes closets unless in its own compartment, in bathrooms, in stairways, or in any similar or undesirable location;
c) located within the structure with consideration being given to the possibility of the formation of condensation;
d) located as close as practicable to the point where the supply conductors enter the structure; and
e) of the circuit-breaker type if in other than extra-low-voltage circuits and if mounted less than 1.5 m above the floor, in which case it shall be protected from mechanical damage.

70-114 Wiring methods — General
1) The wiring method shall be as specified in Section 12, except where flexible cords are permitted in Rule 70-116 or for Class 2 circuits.
2) Surfaces against which conductors are in contact shall be smooth and entirely free from sharp edges and burrs that may cause abrasion of the insulation on the conductors.
3) Where cable is required to be protected from mechanical damage by Rules 12-516, 12-616, and 12-710, plates or tubes of sheet steel of at least No. 16 MSG or the equivalent, secured in place, shall be used to protect the cable from driven nails, screws, or staples.
4) Cable run through holes in joists or studs shall be considered to be secured for the purposes of Rules 12-510 and 12-618.
5) Unless provided with insulation suitable for the highest voltage involved, insulated conductors of low-voltage and extra-low-voltage circuits shall be separated by barriers, or shall be segregated by clamping, routing, or equivalent means that will ensure permanent separation, and shall in any case be separated or segregated from bare live parts of the other circuit.
6) For the purposes of Subrule 5), the outer covering of non-metallic-sheathed cable shall be considered to be a suitable barrier.
7) Bare live parts, including terminals of electrical equipment in extra-low-voltage circuits other than Class 2 circuits, shall be enclosed in accordance with Rule 2-202 1).
8) Conductors for extra-low-voltage Class 2 circuits shall be Type LVT, low-energy safety control cable, or the equivalent, and if protected by fuses in accordance with Rule 16-200, the fuses shall not be interchangeable with those of higher ratings.

70-116 Wiring methods — Swing-out and expandable room sections
1) The means used to make electrical connections between a swing-out or expandable room section and the wiring in the main section of the structure shall be located or protected so that there is no likelihood of damage to the interconnecting means when the section is extended or retracted, or when the structure is in transit.
2) A flexible cord or power supply cable shall be used as an interconnecting means where flexibility is involved and shall
    a) be of the extra-hard-usage type;
    b) have an ampacity suitable for the connected load but in no case be smaller than No. 14 AWG;
    c) be of the outdoor type if it has thermoplastic insulation or is exposed to the weather; and
    d) incorporate a bonding conductor.
3) A plug, connector, or fitting used in conjunction with a flexible cord for electrical interconnections shall have an electrical rating suitable for the maximum connected load and, if located outside the

mobile home, shall be protected from the weather or other adverse conditions (including when the structure is in transit).

70-118 Wiring methods — Multiple-section mobile units

1) Provision shall be made for interconnection of circuits in each section of multiple-section units.
2) The means of interconnection shall be such that no bare live parts of a low-voltage circuit are exposed to accidental contact should any section be temporarily energized before the other sections are in place.

70-120 Branch circuits — Mobile homes

1) Circuits other than those referred to in Rules 26-746, 26-806, 26-808, and 62-108 supplying permanently connected appliances shall be permitted to have additional outlets, but not receptacles, provided that these outlets are for fans, stationary luminaires, or similar permanently connected appliances.
2) The outlets referred to in Subrule 1) shall be considered to have a demand of 1 A each, except where the load is known to be greater, and in no case shall the total load exceed 80% of the rating of the overcurrent device protecting the circuit.
3) Notwithstanding Rule 8-104, a circuit supplying an electric water heater having an input not more than 1500 W at 115 V or 3000 W at 230 V shall be permitted to have overcurrent protection rated or set at 15 A.
4) In determining compliance with Rule 62-110 2), fans on oil or gas heaters that are not required for the operation of the heaters, and that are rated not more than 3 A, shall not be required to be on individual branch circuits.

70-122 Receptacles, switches, and luminaires (see Appendix B)

1) In applying Rule 26-724 a), a hallway need not be considered a room.
2) Switches of the pull type, including those for fans and lights, shall conform to Rule 30-604.
3) Where a ceiling-mounted, rigid luminaire is located at a height of less than 2 m above the floor and is readily accessible, the luminaire shall be protected from mechanical damage by a guard or by location.
4) A receptacle installed on the underside of a mobile home, intended to supply a heating cable set(s) for freeze protection of plumbing pipes, shall be
   a) provided with ground fault protection in accordance with Rule 62-116 1); and
   b) labelled in a conspicuous, legible, and permanent manner, identifying it for the supply of a heating cable set(s) for plumbing pipes.

70-124 Ventilating fans used in kitchen areas

1) The motor of any fan installed in the kitchen area above or in the vicinity of cooking equipment and located in the air stream shall be of the totally enclosed type unless specifically approved for this application.
2) For the purposes of Subrule 1), the "area above or in the vicinity of cooking equipment" shall be
   a) that portion of any wall located within 1.2 m of the cooking surface, as measured from any point on the cooking surface, regardless of the height of the walls; and
   b) that portion of the ceiling defined by a rectangle having sides parallel to the edges of the cooking surface and located within 1.2 m of a vertical projection of the cooking surface, as measured from any point on this projection, regardless of the height of the ceiling.
3) For the purposes of Subrule 2), the "cooking surface" of a built-in oven shall be the area of a bottom-hinged door of a size required to close the oven opening, when such a door is in the fully opened (horizontal) position; and for a free-standing stove or range (with or without an oven) or a built-in countertop surface element unit, the "cooking surface" shall be the entire top surface of the unit, including the backsplash (if any).

4) For the purposes of Subrules 1), 2), and 3), if any full-height wall or partition is located within the space defined above, the space beyond this full height shall not be included in this restriction.

70-126 Grounding and bonding

1) All major exposed metal parts that may become energized, including the water, gas, and waste plumbing, the roof and outer metal covering, the chassis, and metal circulating air ducts, shall be in good electrical contact with one another.

2) The metal roof and exterior covering shall be considered bonded as required by Subrule 1)
   a) if the metal panels overlap one another and are securely attached to the wood or metal frame parts by metal fasteners; and
   b) if bonded to the chassis by metal fasteners or by a metal strap.

3) All exposed non-current-carrying metal parts of a swing-out or expandable room section shall be reliably bonded to the exposed non-current-carrying metal parts of the main section of the mobile unit.

4) The grounding or bonding conductors of the low-voltage wiring system other than the chassis shall not be used to carry current of any extra-low-voltage circuit.

5) Grounding and bonding connections and terminals shall be
   a) made of non-ferrous metal or plated steel;
   b) used for no other purpose than grounding or bonding except for bonding between the chassis and skin where assembly screws may be used;
   c) protected from mechanical damage; and
   d) readily accessible for inspection and maintenance.

6) Bare grounding and bonding conductors shall be located so that there is no danger of contact with live parts, but if their location or flexibility is such that separation from live parts is not ensured, they shall be insulated by taping or sleeving.

7) The major exposed metal parts described in Subrule 1) shall be bonded to ground with a bonding conductor from the metal chassis directly to
   a) the neutral terminal of the service box for structures built in conformance with Rule 70-110 1); or
   b) the bonding terminal in the distribution equipment for structures built in conformance with Rule 70-110 2).

8) The bonding conductor in Subrule 7) shall be permitted to be insulated or bare and shall be
   a) made of copper;
   b) protected from salt spray;
   c) not smaller than that specified in Table 41 where the values in the first column in Table 41 shall correspond to the rated input current of the structure;
   d) located so that it is not subject to mechanical damage; and
   e) suitably secured within 300 mm of the attachment to the chassis.

9) Bonding conductors other than those referred to in Subrule 7) shall have adequate ampacity but in no case less than that of a No. 14 AWG copper conductor.

70-128 Marking

1) Units connecting to the main power supply shall be marked in a permanent manner, in a place where the details will be readily visible, with the following information as required by Rule 2-100:
   a) manufacturer's name, trademark, trade name, or other recognized symbol of identification;
   b) model, style, or type designation;
   c) nominal voltage of the system to which the unit is to be connected (e.g., 120, 120/240, etc.);
   d) rated frequency; and
   e) rated input current in amperes.

2) For the purposes of Subrule 1) e), the rated input current in amperes shall be
    a) the ampere rating of the main overcurrent protection, if provided;
    b) the ampere rating of the distribution equipment, if no main overcurrent protection and no power supply cord are provided; or
    c) the ampere rating of the attachment plug, if provided.
3) Markings adjacent to the main and branch circuit overcurrent devices shall be provided in accordance with Rule 2-100 3).
4) For multiple-section mobile homes or structures, each section shall be suitably and permanently marked to identify the other sections to be used with it to form a single structure.
5) Unless it is otherwise clearly evident, instructions shall be provided on the main section of multiple-section mobile homes or structures to indicate the interconnections necessary to complete the installation.

70-130 Tests (see Appendix B)
1) The following tests shall be performed on the complete assembly at the factory:
    a) all circuits, including grounding or bonding circuits, shall be tested for continuity; and
    b) the insulation resistance between live parts and ground at the completion of a 1 min application of a 500 V dc test voltage shall be not less than that specified in Table 24.
2) As an alternative to the insulation resistance test specified in Subrule 1) b), an ac dielectric strength test shall be permitted to be performed, in which case an ac voltage of 900 V shall be applied for 1 min (or 1080 V for 1 s) between all live parts and non-current-carrying metal parts without breakdown occurring.
3) In performing either the insulation resistance or the dielectric strength test referred to in Subrules 1) b) and 2), the neutral shall be disconnected from ground for the test and be reconnected afterwards.

Non-relocatable structures (factory-built)

70-200 General
Rules 70-100, 70-112, 70-114, 70-118, and 70-122 to 70-130 shall also apply to non-relocatable structures.

70-202 Connection to overhead and underground supply
Provision shall be made at the factory for the electrics in the structure to be connected either to an overhead or underground power supply through conduit nipples, or the equivalent, and supports that shall be
a) of sufficient size to accommodate conductors having the minimum ampacity determined in accordance with Section 8 of this Code; and
b) limited in number to meet the limitations set out in Rules 6-102 and 6-200.

70-204 Service and distribution equipment
1) Provision shall be made at the factory for the installation either at the factory or on the job site of a service box or other service equipment in the structure that shall be
    a) in a readily accessible location within the building;
    b) as close as practicable to the point where the service conductors enter the building; and
    c) within the individual units where multiple occupancy residential condominium or row-house structures are involved or, in all other cases, in a central location accessible to all tenants.
2) Each complete structure shall be provided with distribution equipment.

Section 72 — Mobile home and recreational vehicle parks

Scope and application

72-000 Scope

1) This Section applies to services and distribution facilities for mobile home and recreational vehicle parks.
2) This Section supplements or amends the general requirements of this Code.

General

72-100 Service

Each mobile home and recreational vehicle park and/or consumer's service shall be provided with service equipment in accordance with the applicable requirements of Section 6 of this Code.

72-102 Demand factors for service and feeder conductors

1) The minimum ampacity of the consumer's service and feeder conductors for mobile home parks shall be based on the requirements of
   a) Rule 8-200 with respect to service or feeder conductors supplying an individual mobile home; and
   b) Rule 8-202 with respect to service or feeder conductors supplying more than one mobile home.
2) The minimum ampacity of the consumer's service and feeder conductors in the case of recreational vehicle parks shall be calculated on the basis of the ampere rating of the receptacles and by applying the following demand factors:
   a) 100% of the sum of the first five receptacles having the highest ampere ratings; plus
   b) 75% of the sum of the ampere ratings of the next ten receptacles having the same or next smaller ratings to those specified in Item a); plus
   c) 50% of the sum of the ampere ratings of the next ten receptacles having the same or next smaller ratings to those specified in Item b); plus
   d) 25% of the sum of the ampere ratings of the remainder of the receptacles.
3) For the purpose of Subrule 2), each duplex receptacle supplied from a multi-wire branch circuit shall be counted as two receptacles.
4) For the purpose of Subrule 2), where receptacles of different ratings are installed on one lot, the receptacle having the highest ampere rating shall serve as a basis for calculation.

72-104 Feeders

Feeders between the park consumer's service equipment and the park distribution centres shall be permitted to be installed in accordance with the applicable requirements for service conductors.

72-106 Overcurrent devices and disconnecting means for recreational vehicles

1) The branch circuit for each receptacle for a recreational vehicle lot shall be preceded by an individual overcurrent device not exceeding the rating of the receptacle involved and by a suitable disconnecting means.
2) The disconnecting means shall be accessible.

72-108 Overcurrent devices and disconnecting means for mobile homes

1) The circuit for each mobile home lot shall be preceded by an individual overcurrent device not exceeding the rating of the equipment involved and by a suitable disconnecting means.
2) All supply facilities for overcurrent devices and disconnecting means for mobile homes shall be within enclosures of weatherproof construction if installed outdoors.
3) The disconnecting means shall be accessible.

72-110 Connection facilities for recreational vehicles and mobile homes (see Appendix B)
1) Where receptacles are installed on recreational vehicle lots, they shall be of the following types:
   a) 15 A, 125 V, 2-pole, 3-wire Type 5-15R receptacle;
   b) 20 A, 125 V, 2-pole, 3-wire Type 5-20R receptacle;
   c) 30 A, 125 V, 2-pole, 3-wire Type TT-30R receptacle; or
   d) 50 A, 125/250 V, 3-pole, 4-wire Type 14-50R receptacle.
2) Each mobile home lot shall have provision for a permanent connection to the mobile unit, except that for mobile homes having main overcurrent protection of 50 A, a 50 A, 125/250 V, 3-pole, 4-wire Type 14-50R receptacle shall be permitted where a deviation has been allowed in accordance with Rule 2-030.
3) When mounted in other than a horizontal plane, receptacles shall be oriented so that the U-ground slot is uppermost.
4) The receptacle described in Subrule 1) a) or b) shall be protected by a ground fault circuit interrupter of the Class A type.

72-112 Power supply cords
1) Power supply cords shall be permitted only for the connection of recreational vehicles where the cords are not subject to severe physical abuse or extended periods of use.
2) Power supply cords or cord sets shall be permitted only for the connection of a mobile home when the lot is equipped with a 50 A, 3-pole, 4-wire Type 14-50R receptacle and a deviation has been allowed in accordance with Rule 2-030.

72

Section 74 — Airport installations

74-000 Scope
1) This Section applies to the installation of series-type constant-current circuitry supplying airport visual aid systems.
2) This Section supplements or amends the general requirements of this Code.

74-002 Special terminology
In this Section, the following definitions shall apply:

Ground counterpoise — a conductor installed over lighting cables for the purpose of interconnecting the system ground electrodes and providing lightning protection for the cables.

Mounting stake — an angle iron, section of rigid galvanized steel conduit, or other metallic post set into the ground for the purpose of supporting an elevated light fixture.

Series isolating transformer — a transformer used in airport series lighting circuits to maintain continuity of the primary circuit when the continuity of the secondary circuit is interrupted.

Transformer housing — a below-grade junction box used as a cable pulling point and to house transformers or series lighting cable splices.

74-004 Wiring methods (see Appendix B)
1) Cables for series systems shall be Type ASLC.
2) For aircraft visual aid systems on public areas of airports, or that extend beyond the airport property, the installation of buried cables shall be in accordance with the requirements of Rule 12-012.
3) For installations covered by this Section of the Code, in areas not accessible to the public, single conductors and cable assemblies shall be Type ASLC and shall be installed as follows:
   a) when installed in a raceway, be no less than 450 mm deep;
   b) when direct buried, be no less than 450 mm deep with a layer of sand or screened earth extending at least 75 mm above and below the conductors, if in rocky or stony ground; and
   c) when installed under runways, taxiways, aprons, and roads, be provided with mechanical protection in the form of rigid conduit or a system of concrete-encased underground raceways installed a minimum of 600 mm deep.
4) When installed within a concrete or asphalt surface, Type ASLC shall be installed in a raceway.
5) Series cables directly buried in a trench shall have at least
   a) 75 mm lateral separation between cables of different series circuits;
   b) 300 mm lateral separation from low-voltage and control cables;
   c) 75 mm vertical separation in crossovers on the same system; and
   d) 300 mm vertical separation from low-voltage cables crossing over, with the low-voltage cables in the upper position.
6) Each cable of a series circuit shall be identified with a cable marker indicating the circuit origin at each point where the cables are accessible, including maintenance holes, transformer housings, and similar locations.

74-006 Direct burial transformers
1) When direct buried in a trench, series isolating transformers shall be installed such that the transformer body and primary leads are at a minimum depth of 450 mm below grade.
2) The secondary conductors shall be colour-coded and one conductor shall be identified.
3) The secondary connectors shall be polarized, with the identified conductor connected to the larger pin or receptacle.
4) The identified conductor shall be grounded.

74-008 Series lighting systems
Series lighting systems shall be installed with a ground counterpoise.

74-010 Ground counterpoise
1) Ground counterpoise conductors shall be soft copper wire not smaller than No. 8 AWG and shall be
   a) solid bare wire where installed in earth; or
   b) insulated and have a green finish if installed underground in raceways.
2) The ground counterpoise when installed in earth shall be
   a) placed 75 mm above all cable in a trench;
   b) run in a zig-zag pattern when outer cables are more than 150 mm apart, crossing cables at 300 mm intervals measured along the trench;
   c) placed 75 mm over non-metallic conduit containing groups of cables; and
   d) placed under any protective covering used.
3) The counterpoise shall be connected to
   a) the mounting stake of each stake-mounted light unit;
   b) the ground terminal of each series isolating transformer;
   c) the sheath of metal-sheathed cables and the armour of armoured cables where such cables are used to supply light units;
   d) the ground electrodes at all regulators, towers, and lighting equipment that the counterpoise system serves;
   e) the ground electrode in each maintenance hole through which the counterpoise conductor passes;
   f) metallic transformer housings, lids, or covers; and
   g) non-current-carrying metallic parts of inset lights.
4) Where counterpoise conductors of different systems come together or cross each other, they shall be bonded together at those points.

Section 76 — Temporary wiring
(See Appendix G)

76-000 Scope
1) This Section of the Code applies to temporary wiring installations for buildings or projects under construction or demolition and experimental or testing facilities of a temporary nature.
2) The requirements of this Section supplement or amend the general requirements of this Code.

76-002 Conductors
1) Conductors shall be
   a) of a type in accordance with Section 12; or
   b) power supply cable or flexible cord of the outdoor type suitable for extra-hard usage as selected in accordance with Rule 12-402 1) or 12-406 1).
2) Conductors shall be insulated except as permitted by Rules 6-308, 10-112, and 10-116.
3) Service conductors shall be installed in accordance with Sections 6, 10, and 36.
4) Overhead conductors shall be aerially supported on poles or other equally substantial means with the spacing of supports not to exceed the maximum span length allowable for the type of conductors used.

76-004 Grounding and bonding
All grounding and bonding shall be in accordance with Section 10.

76-006 Service entrance equipment
Where the service equipment is installed in an outdoor location, the equipment shall
a) be accessible to authorized persons only;
b) be capable of being locked;
c) be protected against weather and mechanical damage; and
d) not exceed 200 A where mounted on a single pole.

76-008 Distribution centres
1) Distribution centres shall have a sufficient number of branch circuits and be of adequate capacity to serve the connected load without overloading any branch circuits and without violating the requirements of Section 14.
2) Distribution centres shall be installed in a weatherproof building or be of weatherproof construction.
3) Distribution centres, including portable ones, shall be mounted in an upright position.

76-010 Feeders
1) Feeders supplying distribution centres shall be installed in armoured cable or the equivalent.
2) Notwithstanding Subrule 1), feeders to portable distribution centres shall be permitted to be flexible cord or power supply cable of the outdoor type suitable for extra-hard usage as selected in accordance with Rule 12-402 1) or 12-406 1) and containing a bonding conductor.
3) Feeders shall be protected at all times from mechanical damage and protected by suitable overcurrent protective devices and controlled by suitable disconnecting means.

76-012 Branch circuits
1) Non-metallic-sheathed cable shall be permitted to be used for branch circuits, provided that it is installed in accordance with Rules 12-500 to 12-526.
2) Lighting branch circuits shall be kept entirely separate from power branch circuits.
3) The installation and type of luminaires or lampholders shall comply with Section 30.
4) Each lighting branch circuit shall be protected by a circuit breaker set in accordance with Rule 30-104 and the connected load shall not exceed 80% of the circuit breaker rating.

5) Power branch circuits shall be provided as follows:
   a) separate branch circuits sized and protected by circuit breakers in accordance with Section 28 shall be provided for motor loads exceeding that encountered from general-use hand-held tools;
   b) separate branch circuits for known loads such as electric heating shall be protected by circuit breakers set at a value so that the load connected does not exceed 80% of the rating of the breaker; and
   c) general-use receptacle power branch circuits shall be protected by a circuit breaker set at a value not exceeding the lowest rating of any receptacle connected on the branch circuit.

76-014 Interconnections
Temporary installations shall be constructed as separate installations and shall not be interconnected with any of the circuits of the permanent installations except by special permission.

76-016 Receptacles
Receptacles having CSA configuration 5-15R or 5-20R installed to provide power for buildings or projects under construction or demolition shall be protected by ground fault circuit interrupters of the Class A type.

76

Δ

Section 78 — Marine wharves, docking facilities, fixed and floating piers, and boathouses

78-000 Scope
1) This Section applies to the installation of electric equipment and wiring methods on marine wharves, fixed or floating piers, docking facilities, and boathouses that are used for the construction, repair, storage, launching, berthing, and fuelling of watercraft.
2) This Section supplements or amends the general requirements of this Code.

78-002 Special terminology
In this Section, the following definitions shall apply:

Boathouse — a building designed for storage of watercraft that is located on or adjacent to the edge of a body of water.

Docking facility — any marina, boat basin, marine terminal, or other area on navigable waters containing a single structure or a collection of related structures, such as docks, fixed or floating piers, bulkheads, breakwaters, and pilings, used for the reception, securing, and protection of boats, ships, barges, or other watercraft.

Fixed pier — a structure built on posts extending from land out over water, used as a landing place for watercraft.

Floating pier — a platform or ramp supported by pontoons, usually joined to the shore by a gangway, and that may be held in place by vertical poles or pilings embedded in the bottom of the body of water or by anchored cables.

Marine wharf — a permanent structure built along or at an angle from the shore of navigable waters so that ships can lie alongside to receive and discharge cargo and passengers.

General

78-050 Receptacles (see Appendix B)
1) All receptacles installed outdoors on fixed or floating piers, docking facilities, marine wharves, or boathouses, including receptacles intended to supply shore power to boats, shall
   a) for receptacles rated 15 A and 20 A, be of the straight blade or locking type conforming to either Diagram 1 or 2;
   b) for receptacles rated over 20 A up to and including 60 A, be of the locking type conforming to Diagram 2 or of the pin and sleeve type; or
   c) for receptacles rated over 60 A, be of the pin and sleeve type.
2) Receptacles shall be made of corrosion-resistant materials and shall be provided with weatherproof enclosures.
3) Receptacles exposed to the weather shall be installed in accordance with Rule 26-708.
4) Receptacles shall be located above the permanent or maximum normal water level so that they cannot become immersed in water and shall be protected from splashing.
5) All receptacles rated at 125 V, 15 A or 20 A installed in conformance with Subrule 1) shall be protected by a ground fault circuit interrupter of the Class A type.
6) Notwithstanding Subrule 1), receptacles of other configurations shall be permitted for connection of shore power where the receptacles specified in Subrule 1) are not suitable for the specific application.

78-052 Branch circuits and feeders (see Appendix B)

1) Each receptacle that supplies shore power to boats shall be supplied by an individual branch circuit that supplies no other equipment.

2) Ground fault protection shall be provided to de-energize all normally ungrounded conductors of each feeder for distribution equipment in or on fixed or floating piers, docking facilities, and boathouses, with the ground fault setting sufficient to allow normal operation of the distribution equipment, but in no case greater than 30 mA.

3) Branch circuits installed in or on fixed or floating piers, docking facilities, and boathouses shall not be required to have additional ground fault protection where such protection is provided in accordance with Subrule 2).

78-054 Demand factors

1) The load for each feeder and service supplying receptacles installed on fixed or floating piers, docking facilities, boathouses, or marine wharves, and intended to supply shore power to boats, shall be calculated on the basis of the ampere rating of the receptacles and by applying the following demand factors:
   a) 100% of the sum of the first four receptacles having the highest ampere ratings; plus
   b) 65% of the sum of the ampere ratings of the next 4 receptacles having the same or next smaller ratings to those specified in Item a); plus
   c) 50% of the sum of the ampere ratings of the next 5 receptacles having the same or next smaller ratings to those specified in Item b); plus
   d) 25% of the sum of the ampere ratings of the next 16 receptacles having the same or next smaller ratings to those specified in Item c); plus
   e) 20% of the sum of the ampere ratings of the next 20 receptacles having the same or next smaller ratings to those specified in Item d); plus
   f) 15% of the sum of the ampere ratings of the next 20 receptacles having the same or next smaller ratings to those specified in Item e); plus
   g) 10% of the sum of the ampere ratings of the remainder of the receptacles.

2) Where a service or feeder supplies receptacles as described in Subrule 1) plus other loads, the capacity of the insulated conductors or cables shall be calculated in accordance with Subrule 1), and the other loads shall be added in accordance with the Rules of the Code.

78-056 Wiring methods

1) The wiring method, where exposed to the weather or splashing of water or salt spray, shall be
   a) corrosion-resistant rigid metal conduit, rigid RTRC conduit, or rigid PVC conduit;
   b) mineral-insulated cable having a copper sheath;
   c) non-metallic-sheathed cable of the NMWU type;
   d) armoured cable having moisture-resistant insulation and overall corrosion protection; or
   e) metal-sheathed cable having overall corrosion protection.

2) To allow for tidal movement, or where flexibility is required, an outdoor flexible cord suitable for wet locations and at least hard usage as selected in accordance with Rule 12-402 1), or equivalent, shall be used.

3) Where flexible cables are installed as required by Subrule 2), they shall be supported at both ends by means capable of gripping the cable, except where the end of the cable is securely fastened to a structure in which relative motion will not occur.

4) Conduit, cable, and overhead wiring shall be installed to avoid mechanical damage and shall be routed to avoid conflict with other potential users of the wharf, pier, or docking facility.

5) Conduit, cable, and wiring systems shall be installed to prevent damage from wave action, ice, storm damage, and mooring hooks and lines.

6) Fastening hardware shall be galvanized steel, stainless steel, PVC-coated steel, brass, or other materials with similar corrosion-resistant properties.

78-058 Grounding and bonding

1) Grounding and bonding conductors shall
   a) be installed in accordance with Section 10;
   b) be of copper; and
   c) if installed in an area subject to splashing of salt water or salt spray, be a minimum No. 12 AWG.

2) For electrical systems on marine wharves located in areas where it is impractical to install a shore-based grounding electrode because of poor earth conductivity, an underwater grounding grid conforming to one of the following methods shall be permitted:
   a) on structures with steel piling where the piles are founded in the harbour bottom and continually immersed in salt water, it shall be permitted to ground to the piling, provided that the connections are readily accessible and the grounding conductor is mechanically protected throughout its length; or
   b) on structures that do not conform to Item a), it shall be permitted to connect the grounding conductor to a steel plate electrode, minimum 10 mm thick and 0.36 m^2 in area, and
      i) the grounding conductor shall be connected to the plate electrode using a thermit-weld connection and shall be mechanically protected to a point 2 m below the normal low tide elevation; and
      ii) the plate electrode shall be founded on the harbour bottom on the lee side of the wharf where the lee side is determined from the prevailing winds.

78-060 Wiring over and under navigable water

Wiring over and under navigable water shall not contravene the Government of Canada's *Navigation Protection Act*, R.S.C. 1985, c. N-22.

78-062 Gasoline dispensing stations

Requirements shall be in accordance with Section 20, except that when considering hazardous areas, the grade or ground level shall be the highest water surface and the specific hazardous area shall include the total tidal movement space.

78-064 Communication systems

Where communication systems and circuits are installed, they shall conform to Section 60.

Marine wharves, fixed and floating piers, and docking facilities

78-100 General

Rule 78-102 applies to electrical installations on marine wharves, fixed and floating piers, and docking facilities.

78-102 Protection of electrical equipment

1) All electrical wiring and equipment shall be located to avoid interference with docking of vessels, unloading and loading of vessels, and operation of wharf equipment and vehicular traffic.

2) Electrical equipment shall be
   a) located above the wharf, pier, or docking facility deck and protected from wave action, ice, storm damage, and mooring lines;
   b) located in such a manner as to minimize the risk of damage from wave action and splashing; and
   c) located to avoid impact from docking vessels and vehicular traffic on the wharf.

3) Receptacles, communication systems, equipment, and other electrical apparatus that may be subject to mechanical damage from boats, vehicles, or other apparatus shall be protected by

mounting the equipment in robust shrouds or kiosks constructed of metal, concrete bollards, plywood, or fibreglass, or shall be protected by other equivalent methods.

78

Section 80 — Cathodic protection

80-000 Scope (see Appendix B)
1) This Section applies to the installation of impressed current cathodic protection systems.
2) This Section supplements or amends the general requirements of this Code.

80-002 Wiring methods for dc conductors
1) DC wiring in non-hazardous areas shall conform to the requirements of Section 12 except that wiring below ground shall be permitted to be buried at a depth of not less than
   a) 450 mm; or
   b) 200 mm where installed in a raceway or where mechanical protection is provided in accordance with Rule 12-012 3).
2) DC wiring in hazardous areas shall conform to the requirements of Sections 18 and 20.
3) Notwithstanding Rule 20-004 8), underground dc wiring below a Class I area shall be permitted to be installed in accordance with Subrule 1), provided that
   a) the wiring is in threaded rigid metal conduit where it emerges from the ground; and
   b) the conduit is sealed where it emerges from the ground and at other locations as required by Rule 18-104 or 18-154.

80-004 Conductors
1) Conductors for dc cathodic protection wiring shall be not smaller than No. 12 AWG and shall be selected in accordance with Rule 12-102 3) as suitable for the conditions of use and the particular location where they are installed.
2) Notwithstanding Subrule 1), conductors smaller than No. 12 AWG shall be permitted for instrumentation and reference electrode leads.

80-006 Splices, taps, and connections (see Appendix B)
1) Splices and taps shall be permitted to be made in dc wiring below ground, provided that
   a) the splice or tap is made by welding, by a positive compression tool, by crimping and soldering, or by means of a copper, bronze, or brass cable connector; and
   b) the splice or tap is effectively sealed against moisture by taping or by some other method that is at least as effective as the original insulation of the conductor.
2) Where exposed to the weather, splices and taps in dc wiring shall be in accordance with Subrule 1).
3) Connections to piping shall be made by means of
   a) thermit welding;
   b) a clamp constructed of the same material as the piping; or
   c) a clamp constructed of material that is anodic to the piping.
4) Connections to tanks or other structures shall be made by means of a welded stud, thermit welding, or other permanent means.
5) Underground connections and connections exposed to the weather shall be sealed against moisture by the application of a material resistant to the specific corrosive environment.

80-008 Branch circuit
The branch circuit supplying the rectifier shall be
a) in accordance with the requirements of Section 12; and
b) provided solely for the cathodic protection system rectifier.

80-010 Disconnecting means
1) A separate disconnecting means shall be installed at a point readily accessible to users and within sight of and within 15 m of a rectifier unit of a cathodic protection system.

2) Notwithstanding Subrule 1), a disconnecting means integral to the rectifier unit shall be permitted to serve as the disconnecting means required in Subrule 1), provided that
   a) the disconnecting means is equipped with barriers or other suitable means to protect service personnel from live parts on the line side; and
   b) the rectifier enclosure is rendered inaccessible to unauthorized persons by a lockable cover.
3) The disconnecting means referred to in Subrule 1) shall be labelled in a conspicuous, legible, and permanent manner identifying it as the disconnecting means for a cathodic protection system.

80-012 Operating voltage
When a cathodic protection system has a maximum available voltage of more than 50 V, the voltage difference between any exposed point of the protected system or any point in the vicinity of the anodes and any point 1 m away on the earth's surface shall not exceed 10 V.

80-014 Warning signs and drawings
1) Tanks, pipes, or structures protected by a cathodic protection system shall bear a marking, either on the structure or on a tag attached to the conductor close to the connection to the structure, warning that the connection is not to be disconnected unless the power source is turned off.
2) A sign shall be placed in a conspicuous location adjacent to the disconnecting means for any electrical apparatus connected to the cathodically protected structures, advising that before equipment or piping is replaced or modified
   a) cathodic protection must be turned off; and
   b) a temporary cathodic protection bypass conductor, sized for the maximum available current, must be installed.
3) Notwithstanding Subrule 2), in a non-hazardous location the required sign shall be permitted to advise the use of a temporary conductor, sized for the maximum available current, to bypass the location where equipment or piping is to be replaced or modified, as an alternative to turning off the cathodic protection.
4) A drawing showing the location of underground wiring, polarity, and anodes shall be provided inside the rectifier cabinet or in a location near the cabinet.
5) When the immersed surfaces of a storage or process container are cathodically protected, a notice shall be placed in a conspicuous location adjacent to the entranceway, advising that the cathodic protection system must be turned off before the container is entered.

Section 82 — *Deleted*

Section 84 — Interconnection of electric power production sources

84-000 Scope (see Appendix B)

This Section applies to the installation of electric power production sources interconnected with a supply authority system and supplements or amends the general requirements of this Code.

84-002 General requirement (see Appendix B)

The interconnection arrangements shall be in accordance with the requirements of the supply authority.

84-004 Interconnection

The outputs of interconnected electric power production sources shall provide protection against back-feed into a supply authority system fault.

84-006 Synchronization

Electric power production sources shall be equipped with the necessary means to establish and maintain a synchronous condition without adverse effect on the interconnected system.

84-008 Loss of supply authority voltage (see Appendix B)

1) Unless an alternative procedure is followed in accordance with the requirements of the supply authority, electric power production sources shall, upon loss of voltage in one or more phases of the supply authority system,

   a) be automatically disconnected from all ungrounded conductors of the supply authority system that the electric power production source feeds; and

   b) not be reconnected until the normal voltage of the supply authority system is restored.

2) An inverter suitable for interconnection with electric power production sources and designed to serve as a disconnection device shall be permitted to be used to meet the requirement of Subrule 1) if approved by the supply authority.

84-010 Overcurrent protection

Equipment and conductors that are energized from both directions shall be provided with overcurrent protection from each source of supply.

84-012 Transformer overcurrent protection

Overcurrent protection for a transformer that is energized from both directions shall be provided in accordance with Section 26 by considering first one side of the transformer, then the other side of the transformer, as the primary.

84-014 System protection devices

Each interconnected electric power production source installation shall be provided with such additional devices as are necessary for system stability and equipment protection.

84-016 Ground fault protection

Ground fault protection shall be provided in accordance with Rule 14-102.

84-018 Loss of electric power production source voltage

An electric power production source shall, upon loss of voltage in one or more of its phases, automatically disconnect all phases from the interconnected system.

84-020 Disconnecting means — Electric power production source

Disconnecting means shall be provided to disconnect simultaneously all ungrounded conductors of any electric power production source of an interconnected system from all circuits supplied by the electric power production source equipment.

84-022 Disconnecting means — Supply authority system (see Appendix B)

Disconnecting means shall be provided to disconnect simultaneously all the electric power production sources from the supply authority system.

84-024 Disconnecting means — General (see Appendix B)

1) Disconnecting means shall
   a) be capable of being energized from both sides;
   b) plainly indicate whether it is in the open or closed position;
   c) have contact operation verifiable by direct visible means if required by the supply authority;
   d) have provision for being locked in the open position;
   e) conform to Sections 14, 28, and 36 if it includes an overcurrent device;
   f) be capable of being opened at rated load;
   g) be capable of being closed with safety to the operator with a fault on the system;
   h) disconnect all ungrounded conductors of the circuit simultaneously;
   i) bear a warning to the effect that inside parts can be energized when the disconnecting means is open; and
   j) be readily accessible.
2) Where a main fusible disconnecting means is used, an isolating switch shall be provided to allow the fuses to be dead during handling.

84-026 Isolating means

Means shall be provided to isolate equipment that is energized from both directions from all ungrounded conductors of each source of supply.

84-028 Grounding (see Appendix B)

1) The grounding means at the service entrance shall be permitted to serve as the grounding means for the electric power production source, and the grounding shall be in accordance with Sections 10 and 36.
2) Notwithstanding Subrule 1), a dc power source connected through a solid-state inverter shall not be grounded unless the inverter ac power is separated from the supply authority system by means of an isolating transformer.

84-030 Warning notice and diagram (see Appendix B)

1) A warning notice of an interconnected system shall be installed in a conspicuous place at the supply authority disconnecting means of Rule 84-022 and the supply authority meter location.
2) A single-line, permanent, legible diagram of the interconnected system shall be installed in a conspicuous place at the supply authority disconnecting means.

84

Section 86 — Electric vehicle charging systems

Scope

86-000 Scope

1) This Section applies to the installation of
   a) the insulated conductors and cables and the equipment external to an electric vehicle that connect it to a source of electric current by conductive or inductive means; and
   b) equipment and devices related to electric vehicle charging.
2) This Section supplements or amends the general requirements of this Code.

General

86-100 Special terminology (see Appendix B)

In this Section, the following definitions shall apply:

Electric vehicle — an automotive-type vehicle for use on public roads that
a) includes automobiles, buses, trucks, vans, low-speed vehicles, motorcycles, and similar vehicles powered by one or more electric motors that draw current from a fuel cell, photovoltaic array, rechargeable energy storage system (such as a battery or capacitor), or other source of electric current;
b) includes plug-in hybrid electric vehicles (PHEVs); and
c) excludes off-road electric vehicles, such as industrial trucks, hoists, lifts, transports, golf carts, airline ground support equipment, tractors, and mobility scooters for persons with disabilities.

Electric vehicle connector — a device that, when electrically coupled to a mating device on the electric vehicle, establishes means for power transfer and information exchange between an electric vehicle and electric vehicle supply equipment.

Δ **Electric vehicle supply equipment (EVSE)** — a complete assembly consisting of cables, connectors, devices, apparatus, and fittings installed for the purpose of power transfer and information exchange between the branch circuit and the electric vehicle.

Plug-in hybrid electric vehicle (PHEV) — a type of electric vehicle having an additional energy source for motive power.

86-102 Voltages

The nominal ac system voltages used to supply equipment covered in this Section shall not exceed 750 V.

86-104 Permanently connected and cord-connected equipment

Rules 86-300 to 86-404 apply to installation of permanently connected and cord-connected electric vehicle supply equipment.

Equipment

86-200 Warning sign

Permanent, legible signs shall be installed at the point of connection of the electric vehicle supply equipment to the branch circuit wiring, warning against operation of the equipment without sufficient ventilation as recommended by the manufacturer's installation instructions.

Control and protection

86-300 Branch circuits (see Appendix B)

1) Electric vehicle supply equipment shall be supplied by a separate branch circuit that supplies no other loads except ventilation equipment intended for use with the electric vehicle supply equipment.

Ⓔ Δ 2) Notwithstanding Subrule 1), electric vehicle supply equipment shall be permitted to be supplied from a branch circuit supplying another load(s), provided that an electric vehicle energy management system is installed in accordance with Subrule 8-106 10) or 11).

3) For the purposes of Subrule 2), the calculated demand shall be determined in accordance with Section 8.

86-302 Connected load

The total connected load of a branch circuit supplying electric vehicle supply equipment and the ventilation equipment permitted by Rule 86-300 shall be considered continuous for the purposes of Rule 8-104.

86-304 Disconnecting means

1) A separate disconnecting means shall be provided for each installation of electric vehicle supply equipment rated at 60 A or more, or more than 150 volts-to-ground.

2) The disconnecting means required in Subrule 1) shall be
   a) on the supply side of the point of connection of the electric vehicle supply equipment;
   b) located within sight of and accessible to the electric vehicle supply equipment; and
   c) capable of being locked in the open position.

86-306 Receptacles for electric vehicle supply equipment (see Appendix B)

1) Each receptacle for the purpose of electric vehicle charging shall be labelled in a conspicuous, legible, and permanent manner, identifying it as an electric vehicle supply equipment receptacle and shall be
   a) a single receptacle of CSA configuration 5-20R supplied from a 125 V branch circuit rated not less than 20 A; or
   b) of the appropriate CSA configuration in accordance with Diagram 1 or 2 when supplied from a branch circuit rated at more than 125 V or more than 20 A.

2) When the receptacle referred to in Subrule 1) a) is installed outdoors and within 2.5 m of finished grade, it shall be protected with a ground fault circuit interrupter of the Class A type.

86-308 Electric vehicle as electric power production source

Δ 1) Electric vehicle supply equipment and other parts of a system, either on board or off board the vehicle, that are identified for and intended to be interconnected to a vehicle and also serve as an optional standby system or an electric power production source or provide for bi-directional power feed shall be marked accordingly.

2) When an electric vehicle is used as described in Subrule 1), the requirements of Section 84 shall apply.

Electric vehicle supply equipment locations

86-400 Indoor charging sites (see Appendix B)

1) Indoor sites shall be permitted to include, but not be limited to, integral, attached, and detached residential garages, enclosed or underground parking structures, repair and non-repair commercial garages, agricultural buildings, and similar rooms or locations where the electric vehicle connector can couple to the electric vehicle.

2) Where the electric vehicle supply equipment requires ventilation,
   a) adequate ventilation shall be provided in each indoor charging site as specified in Rule 26-506;

b)   the electric vehicle supply equipment shall be electrically interlocked with the ventilation equipment so that the ventilation equipment operates with the electric vehicle supply equipment; and

c)   if the supply to the ventilation equipment is interrupted, the electric vehicle supply equipment shall be made inoperable.

86-402 Outdoor charging sites

Outdoor charging sites shall be permitted to include, but not be limited to, residential carports and driveways, curbsides, open parking structures, parking lots, commercial charging facilities, and similar locations.

86-404 Hazardous locations

Electric vehicle supply equipment and the supply connection to such equipment located in hazardous locations or areas shall conform to the applicable requirements of this Code.

Tables

Tables

Δ

Table 1
Allowable ampacities for single copper conductors, bare, covered, or insulated, rated not more than 5000 V and unshielded, in free air
(based on an ambient temperature of 30 °C*)
(See Rules 4-004, 4-006, 8-104, 26-142, 42-008, and
42-016 and Tables 5A, 5B, and 19.)

Size, AWG or kcmil	Allowable ampacity†					
	60 °C‡	75 °C‡	90 °C‡§	110 °C‡ See Note 3)	125 °C‡ See Note 3)	200 °C‡ See Note 3)
14**	25	30	35	40	40	50
12**	30	35	40	45	45	55
10**	40	50	55	65	65	80
8	60	70	80	90	95	115
6	80	95	105	120	130	155
4	105	125	140	160	170	205
3	120	145	165	185	195	240
2	140	170	190	215	230	280
1	165	195	220	245	265	320
0	195	230	260	290	310	375
00	220	265	300	335	355	435
000	260	310	350	390	420	510
0000	300	360	405	455	485	590
250	340	405	455	510	545	—
300	370	445	500	560	600	—
350	425	505	570	640	680	—
400	455	545	615	690	735	—
500	520	620	700	785	835	—
600	580	690	780	870	930	—
700	630	755	850	955	1020	—
750	655	785	885	990	1060	—
800	680	815	920	1030	1100	—
900	730	870	980	1100	1175	—
1000	785	935	1055	1180	1260	—
1250	890	1065	1200	1345	—	—
1500	985	1175	1325	1485	—	—
1750	1070	1280	1445	1620	—	—
2000	1160	1385	1560	1750	—	—
Col. 1	**Col. 2**	**Col. 3**	**Col. 4**	**Col. 5**	**Col. 6**	**Col. 7**

* See Table 5A for the correction factors to be applied to the values in Columns 2 to 7 for ambient temperatures over 30 °C.
† The ampacity of single-conductor aluminum-sheathed cable is based on the type of insulation used on the copper conductor.
‡ These are maximum allowable conductor temperatures for single insulated conductors run in free air and may be used in determining the ampacity of other insulated conductor types listed in Table 19 that are run in free air, as follows: From Table 19 determine the

(Continued)

Table 1 (Concluded)

maximum allowable conductor insulation temperature for that particular type, then from this Table determine the ampacity under the column of corresponding temperature rating.

§ *These ratings are based on the use of 90 °C insulation on the emerging conductors and for sealing. Where a deviation has been allowed in accordance with Rule 2-030, mineral-insulated cable may be used at a higher temperature without a decrease in the allowable ampacity, provided that the insulation, sealing material, and any jacketing material are suitable for the higher temperature.*

** *See Rule 14-104 2).*

Ⓔ **Notes:**

1) *The ratings of this Table may be applied to a conductor mounted on a plane surface of masonry, plaster, wood, or any material having a conductivity not less than 0.4 W/(m °C).*

2) *See Table 5B for correction factors where from two to four insulated conductors are present and in contact.*

3) *These ampacities apply to bare conductors or under special circumstances where the use of insulated conductors having this temperature rating is acceptable.*

Δ

Table 2
Allowable ampacities for not more than three insulated copper conductors, rated not more than 5000 V and unshielded, in raceway or cable
(based on an ambient temperature of 30 °C*)
(See Rules 4-004, 8-104, 12-3034, 26-142, 42-008, and 42-016
and Tables 5A, 5C, 19, 39, and D3.)

Size, AWG or kcmil	Allowable ampacity†,††					
	60 °C‡	75 °C‡	90 °C‡**	110 °C‡ See Note	125 °C‡ See Note	200 °C‡ See Note
14§	15	20	25	25	30	35
12§	20	25	30	30	35	40
10§	30	35	40	45	45	60
8	40	50	55	65	65	80
6	55	65	75	80	90	110
4	70	85	95	105	115	140
3	85	100	115	125	135	165
2	95	115	130	145	155	190
1	110	130	145	165	175	215
0	125	150	170	190	200	245
00	145	175	195	220	235	290
000	165	200	225	255	270	330
0000	195	230	260	290	310	380
250	215	255	290	320	345	—
300	240	285	320	360	385	—
350	260	310	350	390	420	—
400	280	335	380	425	450	—
500	320	380	430	480	510	—
600	350	420	475	530	565	—
700	385	460	520	580	620	—
750	400	475	535	600	640	—
800	410	490	555	620	660	—
900	435	520	585	655	700	—
1000	455	545	615	690	735	—
1250	495	590	665	745	—	—
1500	525	625	705	790	—	—
1750	545	650	735	820	—	—
2000	555	665	750	840	—	—
Col. 1	**Col. 2**	**Col. 3**	**Col. 4**	**Col. 5**	**Col. 6**	**Col. 7**

* *See Table 5A for the correction factors to be applied to the values in Columns 2 to 7 for ambient temperatures over 30 °C.*
† *The ampacity of aluminum-sheathed cable is based on the type of insulation used on the copper conductors.*

(Continued)

Table 2 (Concluded)

‡ *These are maximum allowable conductor temperatures for one, two, or three insulated conductors run in a raceway, or two or three insulated conductors run in a cable, and may be used in determining the ampacity of other conductor types listed in Table 19, which are so run, as follows: From Table 19 determine the maximum allowable conductor insulation temperature for that particular type, then from this Table determine the ampacity under the column of corresponding temperature rating.*
§ *See Rule 14-104 2).*

** *For mineral-insulated cables, these ratings are based on the use of 90 °C insulation on the emerging conductors and for sealing. Where a deviation has been allowed in accordance with Rule 2-030, mineral-insulated cable may be used at a higher temperature without a decrease in the allowable ampacity, provided that the insulation, sealing material, and any jacketing material are suitable for the higher temperature.*

†† *See Table 5C for the correction factors to be applied to the values in Columns 2 to 7 where there are more than three insulated conductors in a run of raceway or cable.*

Note: *These ampacities apply to bare conductors or under special circumstances where the use of insulated conductors having this temperature rating is acceptable.*

Δ
Table 3
Allowable ampacities for single aluminum conductors, bare, covered, or insulated, rated not more than 5000 V and unshielded, in free air
(based on an ambient temperature of 30 °C*)
(See Rules 4-004, 8-104, 26-142, 42-008, and 42-016 and Tables 5A, 5B, and 19.)

Size, AWG or kcmil	Allowable ampacity†					
	60 °C‡	75 °C‡	90 °C‡	110 °C‡ See Note 3)	125 °C‡ See Note 3)	200 °C‡ See Note 3)
12§	25	30	35	40	40	50
10§	35	40	45	50	55	65
8	45	55	60	70	75	90
6	65	75	85	95	100	125
4	85	100	115	125	135	165
3	95	115	130	145	155	190
2	115	135	150	170	180	220
1	130	155	175	195	210	255
0	150	180	205	225	245	295
00	175	210	235	265	285	345
000	200	240	270	305	325	395
0000	235	280	315	355	375	460
250	265	315	355	400	425	—
300	295	350	395	440	470	—
350	330	395	445	500	535	—
400	355	425	480	535	575	—
500	405	485	545	615	655	—
600	455	545	615	690	735	—
700	500	595	670	750	800	—
750	520	620	700	785	835	—
800	540	645	725	815	870	—
900	585	700	790	885	945	—
1000	630	750	845	950	1010	—
1250	715	855	965	1080	—	—
1500	795	950	1070	1200	—	—
1750	880	1050	1185	1325	—	—
2000	965	1150	1295	1455	—	—
Col. 1	Col. 2	Col. 3	Col. 4	Col. 5	Col. 6	Col. 7

* *See Table 5A for the correction factors to be applied to the values in Columns 2 to 7 for ambient temperatures over 30 °C.*

(Continued)

Table 3 (Concluded)

† *The ampacity of single-conductor aluminum-sheathed cable is based on the type of insulation used on the aluminum conductor.*

‡ *These are maximum allowable conductor temperatures for single insulated conductors run in free air and may be used in determining the ampacity of other insulated conductor types listed in Table 19 that are run in free air, as follows: From Table 19 determine the maximum allowable conductor insulation temperature for that particular type, then from this Table determine the ampacity under the column of corresponding temperature rating.*

§ *See Rule 14-104 2).*

Notes:

1)   *The ratings of this Table may be applied to a cable mounted on a plane surface of masonry, plaster, wood, or any material having a conductivity not less than 0.4 W/(m °C).*

2)   *See Table 5B for correction factors where two to four insulated conductors are present and in contact.*

3)   *These ampacities apply to bare conductors or under special circumstances where the use of insulated conductors having this temperature rating is acceptable.*

Table 4
Allowable ampacities for not more than three insulated aluminum conductors, rated not more than 5000 V and unshielded, in raceway or cable
(based on an ambient temperature of 30 °C*)
(See Rules 4-004, 8-104, 26-142, 42-008, and 42-016 and Tables 5A and 5C.)

| Size, AWG or kcmil | Allowable ampacity†§ | | | | | |
	60 °C‡	75 °C‡	90 °C‡	110 °C‡ See Note	125 °C‡ See Note	200 °C‡ See Note
12**	15	20	25	25	25	35
10**	25	30	35	40	40	50
8	35	40	45	50	55	65
6	40	50	55	65	70	80
4	55	65	75	80	90	105
3	65	75	85	95	100	125
2	75	90	100	115	120	150
1	85	100	115	125	135	165
0	100	120	135	150	160	195
00	115	135	150	170	180	220
000	130	155	175	195	210	255
0000	150	180	205	225	245	295
250	170	205	230	260	275	—
300	195	230	260	290	310	—
350	210	250	280	315	335	—
400	225	270	305	340	365	—
500	260	310	350	390	420	—
600	285	340	385	430	460	—
700	315	375	425	475	505	—
750	320	385	435	485	520	—
800	330	395	445	500	535	—
900	355	425	480	535	575	—
1000	375	445	500	560	600	—
1250	405	485	545	615	—	—
1500	435	520	585	655	—	—
1750	455	545	615	690	—	—
2000	470	560	630	710	—	—
Col. 1	**Col. 2**	**Col. 3**	**Col. 4**	**Col. 5**	**Col. 6**	**Col. 7**

* *See Table 5A for the correction factors to be applied to the values in Columns 2 to 7 for ambient temperatures over 30 °C.*

† *The ampacity of aluminum-sheathed cable is based on the type of insulation used on the aluminum conductors.*

(Continued)

Tables

Table 4 (Concluded)

‡ *These are maximum allowable conductor temperatures for one, two, or three insulated conductors run in a raceway, or two or three insulated conductors run in a cable, and may be used in determining the ampacity of other insulated conductor types listed in Table 19, which are so run, as follows: From Table 19 determine the maximum allowable conductor insulation temperature for the particular type, then from this Table determine the ampacity under the column of corresponding temperature rating.*

§ *See Table 5C for the correction factors to be applied to the values in Columns 2 to 7 where there are more than three insulated conductors in a run of raceway or cable.*

** *See Rule 14-104 2).*

Note: *These ampacities apply to bare conductors or under special circumstances where the use of insulated conductors having this temperature rating is acceptable.*

Δ

Table 5A
Correction factors applying to Tables 1, 2, 3, 4, and 60 (ampacity correction factors for ambient temperatures above 30 °C)
[See Rules 4-004 7) and 16-330 and Tables 1 to 4, 57, 58, and 60.]

Ambient temper-ature, °C	Correction factor								
	Insulation temperature rating, °C†								
	60	75	90	105*	110*	125*	150*	200*	250*
35	0.91	0.94	0.96	0.97	0.97	0.97	0.98	0.99	0.99
40	0.82	0.88	0.91	0.93	0.94	0.95	0.96	0.97	0.98
45	0.71	0.82	0.87	0.89	0.90	0.92	0.94	0.95	0.97
50	0.58	0.75	0.82	0.86	0.87	0.89	0.91	0.94	0.95
55	0.41	0.67	0.76	0.82	0.83	0.86	0.89	0.92	0.94
60	—	0.58	0.71	0.77	0.79	0.83	0.87	0.91	0.93
65	—	0.47	0.65	0.73	0.75	0.79	0.84	0.89	0.92
70	—	0.33	0.58	0.68	0.71	0.76	0.82	0.87	0.90
75	—	—	0.50	0.63	0.66	0.73	0.79	0.86	0.89
80	—	—	0.41	0.58	0.61	0.69	0.76	0.84	0.88
90	—	—	—	0.45	0.50	0.61	0.71	0.80	0.85
100	—	—	—	0.26	0.35	0.51	0.65	0.77	0.83
110	—	—	—	—	—	0.40	0.58	0.73	0.80
120	—	—	—	—	—	0.23	0.50	0.69	0.77
130	—	—	—	—	—	—	0.41	0.64	0.74
140	—	—	—	—	—	—	0.29	0.59	0.71
Col. 1	Col. 2	Col. 3	Col. 4	Col. 5	Col. 6	Col. 7	Col. 8	Col. 9	Col. 10

* *These ampacities are applicable only under special circumstances where the use of insulated conductors having this temperature rating is acceptable.*

† *The insulation temperature rating is the temperature marked on the conductor.*

Notes:

1) *These correction factors apply to Tables 1, 2, 3, 4, and 60. The correction factors in Column 2 also apply to Table 57.*

2) *The ampacity of a given conductor type at higher ambient temperatures is obtained by multiplying the appropriate value from Table 1, 2, 3, 4, or 60 by the correction factor for that higher temperature.*

Tables

Table 5B
Correction factors for Tables 1 and 3 (where from two to four single insulated conductors are present and spaced less than 25% of the largest cable diameter)
(See Rule 4-004 and Tables 1 and 3.)

Number of conductors	Correction factors
2	0.90
3	0.85
4	0.80

Notes:

1) *Where four insulated conductors form a three-phase-with-neutral system, the values for three insulated conductors shall be permitted to be used. Where three conductors form a single-phase, 3-wire system, the values for two insulated conductors shall be permitted to be used.*

2) *Where more than four insulated conductors are in contact, the ratings for conductors in raceways shall be used.*

Table 5C
Ampacity correction factors for Tables 2 and 4
(See Rule 4-004 and Tables 2 and 4.)

Number of insulated conductors	Ampacity correction factor
1–3	1.00
4–6	0.80
7–24	0.70
25–42	0.60
43 and up	0.50

Table 5D
Current rating correction factors where spacings are maintained (in ventilated and ladder-type cable trays)
(See Rule 4-004 and Table 12E.)

Number of insulated conductors or cables horizontally	1	2	3	4	5	6
Number vertically (layers)						
1	1.00	0.93	0.87	0.84	0.83	0.82
2	0.89	0.83	0.79	0.76	0.75	0.74

Table 6
Deleted

Table 6A
Maximum number of 600 V thermoset insulated conductors without a jacket, Types R90, RW75, RW90, and RPV90, of one size in trade sizes of conduit or tubing

[See Rule 12-910 5) and Appendix B.]

Δ

Conductor size, AWG or kcmil	Size of conduit or tubing																	
	16	21	27	35	41	53	63	78	91	103	116	129	155	200
14	5	11	21	33	49	89	132	200	200	200	200	200	200	200
12	3	9	16	26	37	68	101	155	200	200	200	200	200	200
10	2	6	12	19	27	50	75	114	156	200	200	200	200	200
8	1	3	6	10	15	28	41	63	87	111	144	176	200	200
6	1	2	5	7	11	20	31	47	64	82	107	131	185	200
4	1	1	3	5	8	15	22	34	46	60	77	94	134	200
3	0	1	3	4	7	12	19	29	39	50	65	80	113	200
2	0	1	2	4	5	10	15	24	33	42	55	67	95	169
1	0	1	1	3	4	8	11	18	24	31	41	50	71	126
1/0	0	1	1	1	3	6	9	15	20	26	34	42	59	105
2/0	0	0	1	1	3	5	8	12	17	22	28	35	49	88
3/0	0	0	1	1	1	4	6	10	14	18	23	29	41	73
4/0	0	0	1	1	1	3	5	8	11	15	19	24	34	60
250	0	0	1	1	1	3	4	7	9	12	16	19	27	49
300	0	0	0	1	1	2	4	6	8	10	13	17	24	42
350	0	0	0	1	1	1	3	5	7	9	12	15	21	37
400	0	0	0	1	1	1	3	4	6	8	10	13	18	33
450	0	0	0	0	1	1	2	4	5	7	9	12	17	30
500	0	0	0	0	1	1	2	3	5	6	9	11	15	27

(Continued)

Tables

Table 6A (Concluded)

Conductor size, AWG or kcmil	Size of conduit or tubing																
	16	21	27	35	41	53	63	78	91	103	116	129	155	200
600	0	0	0	0	1	1	1	3	4	5	7	8	12	22
700	0	0	0	0	0	1	1	2	3	4	6	7	11	19
750	0	0	0	0	0	1	1	2	3	4	5	7	10	18
800	0	0	0	0	0	1	1	1	3	4	5	6	9	17
900	0	0	0	0	0	1	1	1	3	3	5	6	8	15
1000	0	0	0	0	0	1	1	1	2	3	4	5	8	14
1250	0	0	0	0	0	0	1	1	1	2	3	4	6	11
1500	0	0	0	0	0	0	1	1	1	1	3	3	5	9
1750	0	0	0	0	0	0	1	1	1	1	2	3	4	8
2000	0	0	0	0	0	0	0	1	1	1	1	2	4	7

Note: This Table is not intended to be used for cables with dual insulated conductor type marking that may have a larger overall diameter.

Table 6B
Maximum number of 1000 V thermoset insulated conductors without a jacket, Types R90, RW75, RW90, and RPV90, of one size in trade sizes of conduit or tubing
[See Rule 12-910 5) and Appendix B.]

△

Conductor size, AWG or kcmil	Size of conduit or tubing																	
	16	21	27	35	41	53	63	78	91	103	116	129	155	200
14	3	7	14	22	32	59	88	134	183	200	200	200	200	200
12	2	6	11	18	26	47	70	108	147	189	200	200	200	200
10	1	4	8	14	20	37	55	83	114	146	189	200	200	200
8	1	3	6	10	15	28	41	63	87	111	144	176	200	200
6	1	1	4	6	9	17	25	38	52	67	87	106	150	200
4	0	1	3	4	6	12	18	28	39	50	64	79	112	199
3	0	1	2	4	5	10	16	24	33	43	55	68	96	170
2	0	1	1	3	5	9	13	20	28	36	47	57	82	145
1	0	1	1	1	3	6	9	14	20	25	33	40	57	101
1/0	0	0	1	1	3	5	8	12	17	21	28	34	48	86
2/0	0	0	1	1	1	4	6	10	14	18	23	29	41	73
3/0	0	0	1	1	1	3	5	8	12	15	20	24	35	62
4/0	0	0	1	1	1	3	4	7	10	13	16	20	29	52
250	0	0	0	1	1	2	4	6	8	10	14	17	24	43
300	0	0	0	1	1	1	3	5	7	9	12	14	21	37
350	0	0	0	1	1	1	3	4	6	8	10	13	18	33
400	0	0	0	0	1	1	2	4	5	7	9	11	16	29
450	0	0	0	0	1	1	1	3	5	6	8	10	15	27
500	0	0	0	0	1	1	1	3	4	6	8	9	14	25

(Continued)

Tables

Table 6B (Concluded)

Conductor size, AWG or kcmil	Size of conduit or tubing																
	16	21	27	35	41	53	63	78	91	103	116	129	155	200
600	0	0	0	0	0	1	1	3	4	5	6	8	12	21
700	0	0	0	0	0	1	1	2	3	4	6	7	10	18
750	0	0	0	0	0	1	1	1	3	4	5	7	10	17
800	0	0	0	0	0	1	1	1	3	4	5	6	9	16
900	0	0	0	0	0	1	1	1	2	3	4	6	8	15
1000	0	0	0	0	0	1	1	1	2	3	4	5	7	13
1250	0	0	0	0	0	0	1	1	1	2	3	4	6	10
1500	0	0	0	0	0	0	1	1	1	1	3	3	5	9
1750	0	0	0	0	0	0	1	1	1	1	2	3	4	8
2000	0	0	0	0	0	0	0	1	1	1	1	2	4	7

Note: This Table is not intended to be used for cables with dual insulated conductor type marking that may have a larger overall diameter.

Table 6C

Maximum number of 600 V thermoset insulated conductors with a jacket, Types RW75, RW90, R90, and RPV90, of one size in trade sizes of conduit or tubing

[See Rule 12-910 5) and Appendix B.]

Conductor size, AWG or kcmil	Size of conduit or tubing													
	16	21	27	35	41	53	63	78	91	103	116	129	155	200
14	3	7	14	22	32	59	88	134	183	200	200	200	200	200
12	2	6	11	18	26	47	70	107	146	187	200	200	200	200
10	1	4	8	14	20	37	55	83	114	146	189	200	200	200
8	1	2	5	8	12	22	33	50	68	88	113	139	196	200
6	1	1	3	5	7	14	20	31	43	55	72	88	124	200
4	0	1	2	4	5	10	16	24	33	42	55	67	95	169
3	0	1	1	3	5	9	13	21	28	37	47	58	82	146
2	0	1	1	3	4	8	11	18	24	31	41	50	71	126
1	0	0	1	1	3	5	8	12	17	21	28	34	49	87
1/0	0	0	1	1	2	4	7	10	14	18	24	29	42	75
2/0	0	0	1	1	1	4	6	9	12	16	20	25	36	64
3/0	0	0	1	1	1	3	5	7	10	13	17	21	30	54
4/0	0	0	0	1	1	2	4	6	9	11	15	18	26	46
250	0	0	0	1	1	1	3	5	6	8	11	14	19	35
300	0	0	0	0	1	1	2	4	6	7	10	12	17	31
350	0	0	0	0	1	1	2	4	5	7	9	11	15	28
400	0	0	0	0	1	1	1	3	4	6	8	10	14	25
450	0	0	0	0	1	1	1	3	4	5	7	9	13	23
500	0	0	0	0	0	1	1	3	4	5	6	8	12	21

(Continued)

△

Tables

Table 6C (Concluded)

Conductor size, AWG or kcmil	Size of conduit or tubing															
	16	21	27	35	41	53	63	78	91	103	116	129	155	200
600	0	0	0	0	0	1	1	1	3	4	5	7	9	17
700	0	0	0	0	0	1	1	1	3	3	5	6	8	15
750	0	0	0	0	0	1	1	1	2	3	4	5	8	14
800	0	0	0	0	0	1	1	1	2	3	4	5	7	14
900	0	0	0	0	0	1	1	1	1	3	4	5	7	12
1000	0	0	0	0	0	1	1	1	1	2	3	4	6	11
1250	0	0	0	0	0	0	1	1	1	1	2	3	4	8
1500	0	0	0	0	0	0	0	1	1	1	1	3	4	7
1750	0	0	0	0	0	0	0	1	1	1	1	2	3	6
2000	0	0	0	0	0	0	0	1	1	1	1	1	3	6

Note: This Table is not intended to be used for cables with dual insulated conductor type marking that may have a larger overall diameter.

Table 6D
Maximum number of underground cables, Types RWU90 (1000 V), TWU (600 V), and TWU75 (600 V), of one size in trade sizes of conduit or tubing
[See Rule 12-910 5) and Appendix B.]

Conductor size, AWG or kcmil	Size of conduit or tubing													
	16	21	27	35	41	53	63	78	91	103	116	129	155	200
14	1	5	10	16	23	42	63	96	131	168	200	200	200	200
12	1	4	8	13	19	35	52	79	108	139	180	200	200	200
10	1	3	6	10	15	28	42	64	87	112	145	177	200	200
8	1	1	4	6	9	16	24	38	51	66	86	105	148	200
6	0	1	3	5	7	13	19	30	41	52	68	83	117	200
4	0	1	1	3	5	10	15	23	31	40	52	63	90	160
3	0	1	1	3	4	8	13	20	27	35	45	55	78	139
2	0	1	1	2	4	7	11	17	23	30	39	48	68	120
1	0	1	1	1	3	5	8	13	17	22	29	36	51	90
1/0	0	0	1	1	2	4	7	11	15	19	25	31	43	77
2/0	0	0	1	1	1	4	6	9	13	16	21	26	37	66
3/0	0	0	1	1	1	3	5	8	11	14	18	22	31	56
4/0	0	0	0	1	1	3	4	6	9	11	15	18	26	47
250	0	0	0	1	1	1	3	5	7	9	12	15	21	38
300	0	0	0	1	1	1	3	4	6	8	11	13	19	34
350	0	0	0	0	1	1	2	4	6	7	9	12	17	30
400	0	0	0	0	1	1	2	3	5	6	8	10	15	27
450	0	0	0	0	1	1	1	3	4	6	8	9	14	25
500	0	0	0	0	1	1	1	3	4	5	7	9	13	23

(Continued)

Δ

Table 6D (Concluded)

Conductor size, AWG or kcmil	Size of conduit or tubing																
	16	21	27	35	41	53	63	78	91	103	116	129	155	200
600	0	0	0	0	0	1	1	2	3	4	6	7	10	18
700	0	0	0	0	0	1	1	1	3	4	5	6	9	16
750	0	0	0	0	0	1	1	1	3	3	5	6	8	15
800	0	0	0	0	0	1	1	1	2	3	4	5	8	15
900	0	0	0	0	0	1	1	1	2	3	4	5	7	13
1000	0	0	0	0	0	1	1	1	1	3	4	4	7	12
1250	0	0	0	0	0	0	1	1	1	2	3	4	5	10
1500	0	0	0	0	0	0	1	1	1	1	2	3	4	8
1750	0	0	0	0	0	0	0	1	1	1	1	3	4	7
2000	0	0	0	0	0	0	0	1	1	1	1	2	3	6

Table 6E
Maximum number of 1000 V and 2000 V thermoset cables without a jacket,
Type RPVU90, of one size in trade sizes of conduit or tubing
[See Rule 12-910 5) and Appendix B.]

Conductor size, AWG or kcmil	Size of conduit or tubing													
	16	21	27	35	41	53	63	78	91	103	116	129	155	200
14	1	5	10	16	23	42	62	95	130	167	200	200	200	200
12	1	4	8	13	19	35	52	79	108	139	180	200	200	200
10	1	3	6	10	15	28	41	63	87	111	144	176	200	200
8	1	1	4	6	9	16	24	37	51	66	85	104	148	200
6	0	1	3	5	7	13	19	30	40	52	67	83	117	200
4	0	1	1	3	5	10	15	23	31	40	52	63	90	160
3	0	1	1	3	4	8	13	20	27	35	45	55	78	139
2	0	1	1	2	4	7	11	17	23	30	39	48	68	120
1	0	1	1	1	3	5	8	13	17	22	29	36	51	90
1/0	0	0	1	1	2	4	7	11	15	19	25	31	44	78
2/0	0	0	1	1	1	4	6	9	13	16	21	26	37	66
3/0	0	0	1	1	1	3	5	8	11	14	18	22	31	56
4/0	0	0	0	1	1	3	4	6	9	12	15	19	26	47
250	0	0	0	1	1	1	3	5	7	9	12	15	22	39
300	0	0	0	1	1	1	3	4	6	8	11	13	19	34
350	0	0	0	0	1	1	2	4	5	7	9	12	17	30
400	0	0	0	0	1	1	2	3	5	6	8	10	15	27
450	0	0	0	0	1	1	1	3	4	6	8	9	14	25
500	0	0	0	0	1	1	1	3	4	5	7	9	13	23

(Continued)

Tables

Table 6E (Concluded)

Conductor size, AWG or kcmil	Size of conduit or tubing																
	16	21	27	35	41	53	63	78	91	103	116	129	155	200
600	0	0	0	0	0	1	1	2	3	4	6	7	10	18
700	0	0	0	0	0	1	1	1	3	4	5	6	9	16
750	0	0	0	0	0	1	1	1	3	3	5	6	8	15
800	0	0	0	0	0	1	1	1	2	3	4	5	8	15
900	0	0	0	0	0	1	1	1	2	3	4	5	7	13
1000	0	0	0	0	0	1	1	1	1	3	4	4	7	12
1250	0	0	0	0	0	0	1	1	1	1	3	3	5	10
1500	0	0	0	0	0	0	1	1	1	1	2	3	4	8
1750	0	0	0	0	0	0	0	1	1	1	1	3	4	7
2000	0	0	0	0	0	0	0	1	1	1	1	2	3	6

Table 6F

**Maximum number of 1000 V and 2000 V thermoset cables with a jacket,
Type RPVU90, of one size in trade sizes of conduit or tubing**

[See Rule 12-910 5) and Appendix B.]

Conductor size, AWG or kcmil	Size of conduit or tubing																
	16	21	27	35	41	53	63	78	91	103	116	129	155	200
14	1	4	7	12	17	31	47	71	97	125	162	198	200	200
12	1	3	6	10	14	27	40	61	83	107	138	169	200	200
10	1	2	5	8	12	22	33	50	68	87	113	139	196	200
8	0	1	2	4	6	11	17	26	36	46	60	73	103	184
6	0	1	1	3	5	9	14	21	29	38	49	60	85	151
4	0	1	1	2	4	7	11	17	23	30	39	48	68	120
3	0	1	1	2	3	6	10	15	21	27	34	42	60	107
2	0	0	1	1	2	5	7	12	16	21	27	33	47	83
1	0	0	1	1	1	4	6	9	12	16	21	26	37	65
1/0	0	0	1	1	1	3	5	8	11	14	18	23	32	58
2/0	0	0	1	1	1	3	4	7	9	12	16	20	28	50
3/0	0	0	0	1	1	2	4	6	8	11	14	17	24	43
4/0	0	0	0	1	1	1	3	4	6	8	11	13	19	34
250	0	0	0	0	1	1	2	4	5	7	9	11	16	28
300	0	0	0	0	1	1	1	3	5	6	8	10	14	25
350	0	0	0	0	1	1	1	3	4	5	7	9	13	23
400	0	0	0	0	0	1	1	3	4	5	6	8	11	21
450	0	0	0	0	0	1	1	2	3	4	6	7	11	19
500	0	0	0	0	0	1	1	2	3	4	5	7	10	18

(Continued)

Table 6F (Concluded)

Conductor size, AWG or kcmil	Size of conduit or tubing													
	16	21	27	35	41	53	63	78	91	103	116	129	155	200
600	0	0	0	0	0	1	1	1	2	3	4	6	8	15
700	0	0	0	0	0	1	1	1	2	3	4	5	7	13
750	0	0	0	0	0	1	1	1	1	3	4	5	7	12
800	0	0	0	0	0	1	1	1	1	3	4	4	6	12
900	0	0	0	0	0	0	1	1	1	2	3	4	6	11
1000	0	0	0	0	0	0	1	1	1	2	3	4	5	10
1250	0	0	0	0	0	0	0	1	1	1	2	3	4	7
1500	0	0	0	0	0	0	0	1	1	1	1	2	3	6
1750	0	0	0	0	0	0	0	1	1	1	1	1	3	6
2000	0	0	0	0	0	0	0	1	1	1	1	1	3	5

Table 6G

Maximum number of 2000 V thermoset insulated conductors without a jacket, Type RPV90, of one size in trade sizes of conduit or tubing

[See Rule 12-910 5) and Appendix B.]

Conductor size, AWG or kcmil	Size of conduit or tubing													
	16	21	27	35	41	53	63	78	91	103	116	129	155	200
14	1	5	10	16	23	42	62	95	130	167	200	200	200	200
12	1	4	8	13	19	35	52	79	108	139	180	200	200	200
10	1	3	6	10	15	28	41	63	87	111	144	176	200	200
8	1	1	4	7	10	19	28	43	59	75	97	119	169	200
6	1	1	3	5	8	14	22	33	46	59	76	93	132	200
4	0	1	2	4	6	11	16	25	34	44	57	70	100	178
3	0	1	1	3	5	9	14	22	30	38	50	61	86	154
2	0	1	1	3	4	8	12	19	25	33	42	52	74	131
1	0	1	1	1	3	5	8	13	18	23	30	37	52	93
1/0	0	0	1	1	2	5	7	11	15	20	26	32	45	80
2/0	0	0	1	1	1	4	6	9	13	17	22	27	38	68
3/0	0	0	1	1	1	3	5	8	11	14	18	23	32	58
4/0	0	0	0	1	1	3	4	7	9	12	16	19	27	49
250	0	0	0	1	1	1	3	5	7	10	13	15	22	39
300	0	0	0	1	1	1	3	5	6	8	11	13	19	34
350	0	0	0	0	1	1	2	4	6	7	10	12	17	31
400	0	0	0	0	1	1	2	4	5	7	9	11	15	28
450	0	0	0	0	1	1	1	3	5	6	8	10	14	25
500	0	0	0	0	1	1	1	3	4	5	7	9	13	23

(Continued)

Tables

Table 6G (Concluded)

Conductor size, AWG or kcmil	Size of conduit or tubing																	
	16	21	27	35	41	53	63	78	91	103	116	129	155	200
600	0	0	0	0	0	1	1	2	3	4	6	7	10	19
700	0	0	0	0	0	1	1	1	3	4	5	6	9	16
750	0	0	0	0	0	1	1	1	3	4	5	6	9	16
800	0	0	0	0	0	1	1	1	3	3	4	6	8	15
900	0	0	0	0	0	1	1	1	2	3	4	5	7	13
1000	0	0	0	0	0	1	1	1	1	3	4	5	7	12
1250	0	0	0	0	0	0	1	1	1	1	3	3	5	10
1500	0	0	0	0	0	0	1	1	1	1	2	3	4	8
1750	0	0	0	0	0	0	0	1	1	1	1	3	4	7
2000	0	0	0	0	0	0	0	1	1	1	1	2	3	6

Table 6H

Maximum number of 1000 V thermoset insulated conductors with a jacket, Type RPV90, of one size in trade sizes of conduit or tubing

[See Rule 12-910 5) and Appendix B.]

Conductor size, AWG or kcmil	Size of conduit or tubing													
	16	21	27	35	41	53	63	78	91	103	116	129	155	200
14	1	5	10	16	23	42	62	95	130	167	200	200	200	200
12	1	4	8	13	19	35	52	79	108	139	180	200	200	200
10	1	3	6	10	15	28	41	63	87	111	144	176	200	200
8	1	1	4	6	9	17	26	40	55	71	91	112	159	200
6	0	1	2	4	6	11	17	26	36	47	60	74	105	186
4	0	1	1	3	5	9	13	20	28	36	47	58	82	145
3	0	1	1	3	4	8	12	18	25	32	41	50	72	127
2	0	1	1	2	3	7	10	15	21	27	36	44	62	110
1	0	0	1	1	1	4	6	10	14	18	23	29	41	72
1/0	0	0	1	1	1	4	6	9	12	16	20	25	35	63
2/0	0	0	1	1	1	3	5	7	10	13	18	22	31	55
3/0	0	0	0	1	1	3	4	6	9	11	15	18	26	47
4/0	0	0	0	1	1	2	3	5	8	10	13	16	22	40
250	0	0	0	1	1	1	2	4	6	7	10	12	17	31
300	0	0	0	0	1	1	2	4	5	7	9	11	15	27
350	0	0	0	0	1	1	1	3	4	6	8	10	14	25
400	0	0	0	0	1	1	1	3	4	5	7	9	12	22
450	0	0	0	0	0	1	1	3	4	5	6	8	11	21
500	0	0	0	0	0	1	1	2	3	4	6	7	11	19

(Continued)

Table 6H (Concluded)

Conductor size, AWG or kcmil	Size of conduit or tubing													
	16	21	27	35	41	53	63	78	91	103	116	129	155	200
600	0	0	0	0	0	1	1	1	3	4	5	6	9	17
700	0	0	0	0	0	1	1	1	2	3	4	6	8	15
750	0	0	0	0	0	1	1	1	2	3	4	5	8	14
800	0	0	0	0	0	1	1	1	2	3	4	5	7	13
900	0	0	0	0	0	1	1	1	1	3	4	4	7	12
1000	0	0	0	0	0	0	1	1	1	2	3	4	6	11
1250	0	0	0	0	0	0	1	1	1	1	2	3	4	8
1500	0	0	0	0	0	0	0	1	1	1	1	2	4	7
1750	0	0	0	0	0	0	0	1	1	1	1	2	3	6
2000	0	0	0	0	0	0	0	1	1	1	1	1	3	5

Table 6I
Maximum number of 2000 V thermoset insulated conductors with a jacket, Type RPV90,
of one size in trade sizes of conduit or tubing
[See Rule 12-910 5) and Appendix B.]

Conductor size, AWG or kcmil	Size of conduit or tubing													
	16	21	27	35	41	53	63	78	91	103	116	129	155	200
14	1	4	7	12	17	31	47	71	97	125	162	198	200	200
12	1	3	6	10	14	27	40	61	83	107	138	169	200	200
10	1	1	4	6	9	17	26	40	55	71	91	112	159	200
8	0	1	3	4	7	13	19	29	40	51	67	81	116	200
6	0	1	1	4	5	10	15	24	32	42	54	66	94	167
4	0	1	1	3	4	8	12	19	25	33	43	52	74	132
3	0	1	1	2	4	7	11	16	22	29	37	46	65	116
2	0	1	1	1	3	5	8	13	17	22	29	36	51	90
1	0	0	1	1	1	4	6	9	13	17	22	27	38	68
1/0	0	0	1	1	1	3	5	8	11	15	19	23	33	59
2/0	0	0	1	1	1	3	4	7	10	13	16	20	29	52
3/0	0	0	0	1	1	2	4	6	8	11	14	17	25	44
4/0	0	0	0	1	1	1	3	5	6	8	11	13	19	35
250	0	0	0	0	1	1	2	4	5	7	9	11	16	29
300	0	0	0	0	1	1	1	3	5	6	8	10	14	26
350	0	0	0	0	1	1	1	3	4	5	7	9	13	23
400	0	0	0	0	1	1	1	3	4	5	7	8	12	21
450	0	0	0	0	0	1	1	2	3	5	6	7	11	19
500	0	0	0	0	0	1	1	2	3	4	6	7	10	18

(Continued)

Tables

Table 6I (Concluded)

Conductor size, AWG or kcmil	Size of conduit or tubing																
	16	21	27	35	41	53	63	78	91	103	116	129	155	200
600	0	0	0	0	0	1	1	1	3	3	5	6	8	15
700	0	0	0	0	0	1	1	1	2	3	4	5	7	13
750	0	0	0	0	0	1	1	1	2	3	4	5	7	13
800	0	0	0	0	0	1	1	1	1	3	4	5	7	12
900	0	0	0	0	0	0	1	1	1	2	3	4	6	11
1000	0	0	0	0	0	0	1	1	1	2	3	4	6	10
1250	0	0	0	0	0	0	0	1	1	1	2	3	4	7
1500	0	0	0	0	0	0	0	1	1	1	1	2	3	6
1750	0	0	0	0	0	0	0	1	1	1	1	1	3	6
2000	0	0	0	0	0	0	0	1	1	1	1	1	3	5

Table 6J
Maximum number of 600 V thermoplastic insulated conductors, Types TW and TW75, of one size in trade sizes of conduit or tubing
[See Rule 12-910 5) and Appendix B.]

△

Conductor size, AWG or kcmil	Size of conduit or tubing																
	16	21	27	35	41	53	63	78	91	103	116	129	155	200
14	5	11	21	33	49	89	132	200	200	200	200	200	200	200
12	3	9	16	26	37	68	101	155	200	200	200	200	200	200
10	2	6	12	19	27	50	75	114	156	200	200	200	200	200
8	1	3	6	10	15	28	41	63	87	111	144	176	200	200
6	1	1	4	6	9	17	25	38	52	67	87	106	150	200
4	0	1	3	4	6	12	18	28	39	50	64	79	112	199
3	0	1	2	4	5	10	16	24	33	43	55	68	96	170
2	0	1	1	3	5	9	13	20	28	36	47	57	82	145
1	0	1	1	1	3	6	9	14	20	25	33	40	57	101
1/0	0	0	1	1	3	5	8	12	17	21	28	34	48	86
2/0	0	0	1	1	1	4	6	10	14	18	23	29	41	73
3/0	0	0	1	1	1	3	5	8	12	15	20	24	35	62
4/0	0	0	1	1	1	3	4	7	10	13	16	20	29	52
250	0	0	0	1	1	2	3	6	8	10	13	16	23	42
300	0	0	0	1	1	1	3	5	7	9	11	14	20	36
350	0	0	0	1	1	1	3	4	6	8	10	13	18	32
400	0	0	0	0	1	1	2	4	5	7	9	11	16	29
450	0	0	0	0	1	1	1	3	5	6	8	10	15	26
500	0	0	0	0	1	1	1	3	4	6	7	9	13	24

(Continued)

Tables

Table 6J (Concluded)

Conductor size, AWG or kcmil	Size of conduit or tubing																
	16	21	27	35	41	53	63	78	91	103	116	129	155	200
600	0	0	0	0	0	1	1	2	3	5	6	7	11	19
700	0	0	0	0	0	1	1	1	3	4	5	7	9	17
750	0	0	0	0	0	1	1	1	3	4	5	6	9	16
800	0	0	0	0	0	1	1	1	3	3	5	6	8	15
900	0	0	0	0	0	1	1	1	2	3	4	5	8	14
1000	0	0	0	0	0	1	1	1	1	3	4	5	7	13
1250	0	0	0	0	0	0	1	1	1	2	3	4	5	10
1500	0	0	0	0	0	0	1	1	1	1	2	3	5	8
1750	0	0	0	0	0	0	0	1	1	1	1	3	4	7
2000	0	0	0	0	0	0	0	1	1	1	1	2	3	6

Δ

Table 6K
Maximum number of 600 V thermoplastic insulated conductors, Types TWN75 and T90 NYLON, of one size in trade sizes of conduit or tubing
[See Rule 12-910 5) and Appendix B.]

Conductor size, AWG or kcmil	Size of conduit or tubing													
	16	21	27	35	41	53	63	78	91	103	116	129	155	200
14	7	16	30	48	70	128	191	200	200	200	200	200	200	200
12	5	12	22	35	51	93	139	200	200	200	200	200	200	200
10	3	7	14	22	32	58	86	132	180	200	200	200	200	200
8	1	4	8	12	18	33	49	76	103	133	171	200	200	200
6	1	3	5	9	13	24	36	55	75	96	124	152	200	200
4	1	1	3	5	8	14	22	33	46	59	76	93	132	200
3	0	1	3	4	6	12	18	28	39	50	64	79	112	198
2	0	1	1	4	5	10	15	24	32	42	54	66	94	167
1	0	1	1	2	4	7	11	17	24	31	40	49	69	123
1/0	0	1	1	1	3	6	9	14	20	26	33	41	58	103
2/0	0	0	1	1	3	5	8	12	17	21	28	34	48	86
3/0	0	0	1	1	1	4	6	10	14	18	23	28	40	72
4/0	0	0	1	1	1	3	5	8	11	15	19	23	33	59
250	0	0	0	1	1	3	4	7	9	12	15	19	27	48
300	0	0	0	1	1	2	3	6	8	10	13	16	23	42
350	0	0	0	1	1	1	3	5	7	9	12	14	20	37
400	0	0	0	1	1	1	3	4	6	8	10	13	18	33
450	0	0	0	0	1	1	2	4	5	7	9	11	16	29
500	0	0	0	0	1	1	2	3	5	6	8	10	15	27

Tables

Table 7
Radius of conduit or tubing bends
(See Rule 12-924.)

Size of conduit or tubing	Minimum radius to centre of conduit or tubing, mm
16	102
21	114
27	146
35	184
41	210
53	241
63	267
78	330
91	381
103	406
129	610
155	762

Table 8
Maximum allowable per cent conduit and tubing fill
(See Rules 12-902, 12-910, and 38-032.)

	Maximum conduit and tubing fill, %				
	Number of conductors or multi-conductor cables				
	1	2	3	4	Over 4
Conductors or multi-conductor cables (not lead-sheathed)	53	31	40	40	40
Lead-sheathed conductor or multi-conductor cables	55	30	40	38	35

Table 9
Deleted

Table 9A
Cross-sectional areas of rigid metal conduit
(See Rule 12-910.)

Nominal conduit size	Internal diameter, mm	Cross-sectional area of rigid metal conduit, mm²							
		100%	55%	53%	40%	38%	35%	31%	30%
16	16.05	202	111	107	81	77	71	63	61
21	21.23	354	195	188	142	135	124	110	106
27	27.00	573	315	303	229	218	200	177	172
35	35.41	985	542	522	394	374	345	305	295
41	41.25	1336	735	708	535	508	468	414	401
53	52.91	2199	1209	1165	879	836	770	682	660
63	63.22	3139	1726	1664	1256	1193	1099	973	942
78	78.49	4839	2661	2564	1935	1839	1694	1500	1452
91	90.68	6458	3552	3423	2583	2454	2260	2002	1937
103	102.87	8311	4571	4405	3325	3158	2909	2576	2493
129	128.85	13 039	7172	6911	5216	4955	4564	4042	3912
155	154.76	18 811	10 346	9970	7524	7148	6584	5831	5643

Table 9B
Cross-sectional areas of flexible metal conduit
(See Rule 12-910.)

Nominal conduit size	Internal diameter, mm	Cross-sectional area of flexible metal conduit, mm²							
		100%	55%	53%	40%	38%	35%	31%	30%
12	9.52	71	39	38	28	27	25	22	21
16	15.88	198	109	105	79	75	69	61	59
21	20.62	334	184	177	134	127	117	104	100
27	25.4	507	279	269	203	193	177	157	152
35	31.75	792	435	420	317	301	277	245	238
41	38.1	1140	627	604	456	433	399	353	342
53	50.8	2027	1115	1074	811	770	709	628	608
63	63.5	3167	1742	1678	1267	1203	1108	982	950
78	76.2	4560	2508	2417	1824	1733	1596	1414	1368
91	88.9	6207	3414	3290	2483	2359	2173	1924	1862
103	101.6	8107	4459	4297	3243	3081	2838	2513	2432

Tables

Table 9C
Cross-sectional areas of rigid PVC conduit
(See Rule 12-910.)

Nominal conduit size	Internal diameter, mm	Cross-sectional area of rigid PVC conduit, mm²							
		100%	55%	53%	40%	38%	35%	31%	30%
16	14.57	167	92	88	67	63	58	52	50
21	19.77	307	169	163	123	117	107	95	92
27	25.4	507	279	269	203	193	177	157	152
35	31.75	792	435	420	317	301	277	245	238
41	38.1	1140	627	604	456	433	399	353	342
53	50.8	2027	1115	1074	811	770	709	628	608
63	61.3	2951	1623	1564	1181	1121	1033	915	885
78	76.2	4560	2508	2417	1824	1733	1596	1414	1368
91	88.4	6138	3376	3253	2455	2332	2148	1903	1841
103	100.1	7870	4328	4171	3148	2990	2754	2440	2361
129	125.85	12 439	6842	6593	4976	4727	4354	3856	3732
155	149.75	17 613	9687	9335	7045	6693	6164	5460	5284
200	199.39	31 225	17 174	16 549	12 490	11 865	10 929	9680	9367

Table 9D
Cross-sectional areas of rigid Type EB1 PVC conduit
and rigid Type DB2/ES2 PVC conduit
(See Rule 12-910.)

Nominal conduit size	Internal diameter, mm	Cross-sectional area of rigid Type EB1 PVC conduit and rigid Type DB2/ES2 PVC conduit, mm²							
		100%	55%	53%	40%	38%	35%	31%	30%
53	50.80	2027	1115	1074	811	770	709	628	608
78	76.20	4560	2508	2417	1824	1733	1596	1414	1368
91	88.40	6138	3376	3253	2455	2332	2148	1903	1841
103	100.10	7870	4328	4171	3148	2990	2754	2440	2361
116	114.30	10 261	5643	5438	4104	3899	3591	3181	3078
129	126.35	12 538	6896	6645	5015	4765	4388	3887	3762
155	149.75	17 613	9687	9335	7045	6693	6164	5460	5284

Table 9E
Cross-sectional areas of rigid RTRC conduit marked IPS
(See Rule 12-910.)

Nominal conduit size	Internal diameter, mm	Cross-sectional area of rigid RTRC conduit Type IPS, mm²							
		100%	55%	53%	40%	38%	35%	31%	30%
16	17.27	234	129	124	94	89	82	73	70
21	22.61	402	221	213	161	153	141	124	120
27	29.34	676	372	358	270	257	237	210	203
35	38.1	1140	627	604	456	433	399	353	342
41	44.2	1534	844	813	614	583	537	476	460
53	56.26	2486	1367	1318	994	945	870	771	746
63	69.6	3805	2093	2016	1522	1446	1332	1179	1141
78	84.84	5653	3109	2996	2261	2148	1979	1752	1696
103	109.72	9455	5200	5011	3782	3593	3309	2931	2836
129	136.14	14 557	8006	7715	5823	5532	5095	4513	4367
155	162.05	20 625	11 344	10 931	8250	7837	7219	6394	6187

Note: *IPS is a marking on the conduit that defines the dimensions based on outside diameters of iron pipe sizes.*

Table 9F
Cross-sectional areas of rigid RTRC conduit marked ID
(See Rule 12-910.)

Nominal conduit size	Internal diameter, mm	Cross-sectional area of rigid RTRC conduit Type ID, mm²							
		100%	55%	53%	40%	38%	35%	31%	30%
16	11.94	112	62	59	45	43	39	35	34
21	18.29	263	145	139	105	100	92	81	79
27	24.64	477	262	253	191	181	167	148	143
35	30.99	754	415	400	302	287	264	234	226
41	37.34	1095	602	580	438	416	383	339	329
53	50.29	1986	1092	1053	795	755	695	616	596
63	63.00	3117	1714	1652	1247	1185	1091	966	935
78	75.69	4500	2475	2385	1800	1710	1575	1395	1350
91	88.39	6136	3375	3252	2454	2332	2148	1902	1841
103	101.09	8026	4414	4254	3210	3050	2809	2488	2408
116	113.79	10 169	5593	5390	4068	3864	3559	3153	3051
129	126.24	12 517	6884	6634	5007	4756	4381	3880	3755

Note: *ID is a marking on the conduit that defines the dimensions based on inside diameters.*

Tables

Table 9G
Cross-sectional areas of liquid-tight flexible metal conduit
(See Rule 12-910.)

Nominal conduit size	Internal diameter, mm	Cross-sectional area of metallic liquid-tight flexible conduit, mm²							
		100%	55%	53%	40%	38%	35%	31%	30%
12	12.29	119	65	63	47	45	42	37	36
16	15.8	196	108	104	78	75	69	61	59
21	20.83	341	187	181	136	129	119	106	102
27	26.44	549	302	291	220	209	192	170	165
35	35.05	965	531	511	386	367	338	299	289
41	40.01	1257	691	666	503	478	440	390	377
53	51.31	2068	1137	1096	827	786	724	641	620
63	62.99	3116	1714	1652	1247	1184	1091	966	935
78	77.98	4776	2627	2531	1910	1815	1672	1481	1433
91	88.9	6207	3414	3290	2483	2359	2173	1924	1862
103	101.6	8107	4459	4297	3243	3081	2838	2513	2432

Table 9H
Cross-sectional areas of non-metallic liquid-tight flexible conduit
(See Rule 12-910.)

Nominal conduit size	Internal diameter, mm	Cross-sectional area of non-metallic liquid-tight flexible conduit, mm²							
		100%	55%	53%	40%	38%	35%	31%	30%
12	12.07	114	63	61	46	43	40	35	34
16	15.49	188	104	100	75	72	66	58	57
21	20.45	328	181	174	131	125	115	102	99
27	25.91	527	290	279	211	200	185	163	158
35	34.54	937	515	497	375	356	328	290	281
41	40.01	1257	691	666	503	478	440	390	377
53	51.69	2098	1154	1112	839	797	734	651	630

Table 9I
Cross-sectional areas of electrical metallic tubing
(See Rule 12-910.)

Nominal conduit size	Internal diameter, mm	Cross-sectional area of electrical metallic tubing, mm²							
		100%	55%	53%	40%	38%	35%	31%	30%
16	15.4	186	102	99	75	71	65	58	56
21	20.5	330	182	175	132	125	116	102	99
27	26.2	539	297	286	216	205	189	167	162
35	34.6	940	517	498	376	357	329	291	282
41	40.5	1288	709	683	515	490	451	399	386
53	52.1	2132	1173	1130	853	810	746	661	640
63	69.4	3783	2081	2005	1513	1437	1324	1173	1135
78	85.2	5701	3136	3022	2280	2166	1995	1767	1710
91	97.4	7451	4098	3949	2980	2831	2608	2310	2235
103	110	9503	5227	5037	3801	3611	3326	2946	2851

Δ

Table 9J
Cross-sectional areas of electrical non-metallic tubing
(See Rule 12-910.)

Nominal conduit size	Internal diameter, mm	Cross-sectional area of electrical non-metallic tubing, mm²							
		100%	55%	53%	40%	38%	35%	31%	30%
16	14.58	167	92	88	67	63	58	52	50
21	19.66	304	167	161	121	115	106	94	91
27	25.37	506	278	268	202	192	177	157	152
35	33.73	894	491	474	357	340	313	277	268
41	39.57	1230	676	652	492	467	430	381	369
53	51.18	2057	1131	1090	823	782	720	638	617
63	61.70	2990	1644	1585	1196	1136	1046	927	897

Tables

Δ

Table 9K
Cross-sectional areas of HDPE conduit Schedule 40
(See Rule 12-910.)

Nominal conduit size	Internal diameter, mm	Cross-sectional area of HDPE conduit Schedule 40, mm²							
		100%	55%	53%	40%	38%	35%	31%	30%
16	14.67	169	93	90	68	64	59	52	51
21	19.78	307	169	163	123	117	108	95	92
27	25.4	507	279	269	203	193	177	157	152
35	33.82	898	494	476	359	341	314	278	269
41	39.63	1233	678	654	493	469	432	382	370
53	51.18	2057	1131	1090	823	782	720	638	617
63	61.13	2935	1614	1556	1174	1115	1027	910	880
78	76.14	4553	2504	2413	1821	1730	1594	1411	1366
103	100.26	7895	4342	4184	3158	3000	2763	2447	2368
129	125.91	12 451	6848	6599	4980	4731	4358	3860	3735
155	151.5	18 027	9915	9554	7211	6850	6309	5588	5408
200	199.64	31 303	17 217	16 591	12 521	11 895	10 956	9704	9391

Δ

Table 9L
Cross-sectional areas of HDPE conduit Schedule 80
(See Rule 12-910.)

Nominal conduit size	Internal diameter, mm	Cross-sectional area of HDPE conduit Schedule 80, mm²							
		100%	55%	53%	40%	38%	35%	31%	30%
16	12.75	128	70	68	51	49	45	40	38
21	17.7	246	135	130	98	94	86	76	74
27	23.06	418	230	221	167	159	146	129	125
35	31.1	760	418	403	304	289	266	235	228
41	36.63	1054	580	559	422	400	369	327	316
53	47.82	1796	988	952	718	682	629	557	539
63	56.97	2549	1402	1351	1020	969	892	790	765
78	71.38	4002	2201	2121	1601	1521	1401	1241	1201
103	94.56	7023	3862	3722	2809	2669	2458	2177	2107
129	119.25	11 169	6143	5919	4468	4244	3909	3462	3351
155	142.86	16 029	8816	8495	6412	6091	5610	4969	4809

Δ

Table 9M
Cross-sectional areas of HDPE DR9 conduit
(See Rule 12-910.)

Nominal conduit size	Internal diameter, mm	Cross-sectional area of HDPE DR9 conduit, mm²							
		100%	55%	53%	40%	38%	35%	31%	30%
16	15.47	188	103	100	75	71	66	58	56
21	19.65	303	167	161	121	115	106	94	91
27	24.86	485	267	257	194	184	170	150	146
35	31.51	780	429	413	312	296	273	242	234
41	36.1	1024	563	542	409	389	358	317	307
53	45.19	1604	882	850	642	609	561	497	481
63	54.63	2344	1289	1242	938	891	820	727	703
78	66.56	3479	1914	1844	1392	1322	1218	1079	1044
103	85.36	5723	3147	3033	2289	2175	2003	1774	1717
129	105.54	8748	4812	4637	3499	3324	3062	2712	2624
155	125.63	12 396	6818	6570	4958	4710	4339	3843	3719
200	163.58	21 016	11 559	11 138	8406	7986	7356	6515	6305
275	203.84	32 634	17 949	17 296	13 054	12 401	11 422	10 117	9790
325	241.79	45 916	25 254	24 336	18 367	17 448	16 071	14 234	13 775

Δ

Table 9N
Cross-sectional areas of HDPE DR11 conduit
(See Rule 12-910.)

Nominal conduit size	Internal diameter, mm	Cross-sectional area of HDPE DR11 conduit, mm²							
		100%	55%	53%	40%	38%	35%	31%	30%
16	16.3	209	115	111	83	79	73	65	63
21	20.73	338	186	179	135	128	118	105	101
27	26.21	540	297	286	216	205	189	167	162
35	33.31	871	479	462	349	331	305	270	261
41	38.27	1150	633	610	460	437	403	357	345
53	47.91	1803	992	955	721	685	631	559	541
63	57.92	2635	1449	1396	1054	1001	922	817	790
78	70.6	3915	2153	2075	1566	1488	1370	1214	1174
103	90.52	6435	3539	3411	2574	2445	2252	1995	1931
129	111.93	9840	5412	5215	3936	3739	3444	3050	2952
155	133.22	13 939	7666	7388	5576	5297	4879	4321	4182
200	173.49	23 640	13 002	12 529	9456	8983	8274	7328	7092
275	216.19	36 708	20 189	19 455	14 683	13 949	12 848	11 379	11 012
325	256.46	51 657	28 411	27 378	20 663	19 630	18 080	16 014	15 497

Tables

Table 9O
Cross-sectional areas of HDPE DR13.5 conduit
(See Rule 12-910.)

Nominal conduit size	Internal diameter, mm	Cross-sectional area of HDPE DR13.5 conduit, mm²							
		100%	55%	53%	40%	38%	35%	31%	30%
16	17.02	228	125	121	91	86	80	71	68
21	21.63	367	202	195	147	140	129	114	110
27	27.33	587	323	311	235	223	205	182	176
35	34.73	947	521	502	379	360	332	294	284
41	39.93	1252	689	664	501	476	438	388	376
53	50.18	1978	1088	1048	791	752	692	613	593
63	60.68	2892	1591	1533	1157	1099	1012	896	868
78	73.95	4295	2362	2276	1718	1632	1503	1331	1289
103	94.83	7063	3885	3743	2825	2684	2472	2189	2119
129	117.25	10 797	5939	5723	4319	4103	3779	3347	3239
155	139.57	15 299	8415	8109	6120	5814	5355	4743	4590
200	181.74	25 941	14 268	13 749	10 377	9858	9079	8042	7782
275	226.49	40 289	22 159	21 353	16 116	15 310	14 101	12 490	12 087
325	268.66	56 689	31 179	30 045	22 675	21 542	19 841	17 573	17 007

Table 9P
Cross-sectional areas of HDPE DR15.5 conduit
(See Rule 12-910.)

Nominal conduit size	Internal diameter, mm	Cross-sectional area of HDPE DR15.5 conduit, mm²							
		100%	55%	53%	40%	38%	35%	31%	30%
16	17.43	239	131	126	95	91	84	74	72
21	22.14	385	212	204	154	146	135	119	115
27	27.97	614	338	326	246	233	215	190	184
35	35.54	992	546	526	397	377	347	308	298
41	40.85	1311	721	695	524	498	459	406	393
53	51.4	2075	1141	1100	830	788	726	643	622
63	62.24	3042	1673	1613	1217	1156	1065	943	913
78	75.85	4519	2485	2395	1807	1717	1581	1401	1356
103	97.29	7434	4089	3940	2974	2825	2602	2305	2230
129	120.29	11 364	6250	6023	4546	4318	3978	3523	3409
155	143.19	16 103	8857	8535	6441	6119	5636	4992	4831
200	186.43	27 297	15 014	14 468	10 919	10 373	9554	8462	8189
275	232.35	42 401	23 321	22 472	16 960	16 112	14 840	13 144	12 720
325	275.59	59 651	32 808	31 615	23 860	22 667	20 878	18 492	17 895

Table 10A
Dimensions of stranded insulated conductors for calculating conduit and tubing fill
(See Rule 12-910 and Appendix B.)

Conductor size, AWG or kcmil	R90XLPE*, RW75XLPE*, RW90XLPE* 600 V Class B		R90XLPE*, RW75XLPE*, RW90XLPE* 1000 V Class B		R90XLPE†, RW75XLPE†, R90EP†, RW75EP†, RW90XLPE†, RW90EP‡ 600 V Class B		TWN75, T90 NYLON Class C		TW, TW75 Class B		TWU, TWU75, RW90XLPE* Class B	
	Dia., mm	Area, mm²	Dia., mm	Area, mm²	Dia., mm	Area, mm²	Dia., mm	Area, mm²	Dia., mm	Area, mm²	Dia., mm	Area, mm²
14	3.36	8.89	4.12	13.36	4.12	13.36	2.80	6.18	3.36	8.89	4.88	18.70
12	3.84	11.61	4.60	16.65	4.60	16.75	3.28	8.47	3.84	11.61	5.36	22.56
10	4.47	15.67	5.23	21.45	5.23	21.45	4.17	13.63	4.47	15.67	5.97	27.99
8	5.99	28.17	5.99	28.17	6.75	35.77	5.49	23.66	5.99	28.17	7.76	47.29
6	6.95	37.98	7.71	46.73	8.47	56.39	6.45	32.71	7.71	46.73	8.72	59.72
4	8.17	52.46	8.93	62.67	9.69	73.79	8.23	53.23	8.93	62.67	9.95	77.76
3	8.88	61.99	9.64	73.05	10.40	85.01	8.94	62.83	9.64	73.05	10.67	89.42
2	9.70	73.85	10.46	85.88	11.22	98.82	9.76	74.77	10.46	85.88	11.48	103.5
1	11.23	99.10	12.49	122.6	13.51	143.4	11.33	100.9	12.49	122.6	13.25	137.9
1/0	12.27	118.3	13.53	143.9	14.55	166.4	12.37	120.3	13.53	143.9	14.28	160.2
2/0	13.44	141.9	14.70	169.8	15.72	194.2	13.54	144.0	14.70	169.8	15.45	187.5
3/0	14.74	170.6	16.00	201.0	17.02	227.5	14.84	172.9	16.00	201.0	16.76	220.6
4/0	16.21	206.4	17.47	239.7	18.49	268.5	16.31	209.0	17.47	239.7	18.28	262.4
250	17.90	251.8	19.17	288.5	21.21	353.2	18.04	255.7	19.43	296.4	20.20	320.5
300	19.30	292.6	20.56	332.1	22.60	401.2	19.44	296.9	20.82	340.5	21.54	364.4
350	20.53	331.0	21.79	372.9	23.83	446.0	20.67	335.6	22.05	381.9	22.81	408.6
400	21.79	373.0	23.05	417.3	25.09	494.5	21.93	377.8	23.31	426.8	24.07	455.0

(Continued)

Tables

Table 10A (Concluded)

Conductor size, AWG or kcmil	R90XLPE*, RW75XLPE*, RW90XLPE* 600 V Class B		R90XLPE*, RW75XLPE*, RW90XLPE* 1000 V Class B		R90XLPE†, RW75XLPE†, RW90EP†, RW75EP†, RW90XLPE†, RW90EP‡ 600 V Class B		TWN75, T90 NYLON Class C		TW, TW75 Class B		TWU, TWU75, RWU90XLPE* Class B	
	Dia., mm	Area, mm²	Dia., mm	Area, mm²	Dia., mm	Area, mm²	Dia., mm	Area, mm²	Dia., mm	Area, mm²	Dia., mm	Area, mm²
450	22.91	412.2	24.17	458.8	26.21	539.5	23.05	417.3	24.43	468.7	25.19	498.4
500	23.95	450.5	25.21	499.2	27.25	583.2	24.09	455.8	25.47	509.5	26.24	540.8
600	26.74	561.7	27.24	582.9	30.04	708.8	—	—	28.26	627.3	29.02	661.4
700	28.55	640.0	29.05	662.6	31.85	796.5	—	—	30.07	710.0	30.82	746.0
750	29.41	679.3	29.91	702.6	32.71	840.3	—	—	30.93	751.3	31.69	788.7
800	30.25	718.7	30.75	742.6	33.55	884.0	—	—	31.77	792.7	32.53	831.1
900	31.85	796.6	32.35	821.8	35.15	970.2	—	—	33.37	874.5	34.13	914.9
1000	33.32	872.0	33.82	898.4	36.62	1053	—	—	34.84	953.4	35.60	995.4
1250	37.56	1108	38.32	1153	42.38	1411	—	—	39.08	1200	39.08	1199
1500	40.68	1300	41.44	1349	45.50	1626	—	—	42.20	1399	42.96	1449
1750	43.58	1492	44.34	1544	48.40	1840	—	—	45.10	1598	45.86	1652
2000	46.27	1681	47.03	1737	51.09	2050	—	—	47.79	1794	48.55	1851

* Unjacketed.
† Jacketed.
‡ Includes EPCV.

Note: Aluminum conductors may not be available in the same range of sizes as copper conductors.

Table 10B
Dimensions of photovoltaic insulated conductors and cable for calculating conduit and tubing fill
(See Rule 12-910 and Appendix B.)

Conductor size, AWG or kcmil	RPV*, 600 V Class B		RPV*, 1000 V Class B		RPV*, 2000 V Class B		RPV†, 600 V Class B		RPV†, 1000 V Class B		RPV†, 2000 V Class B		RPVU*, 1000 V and 2000 V Class B		RPVU†, 1000 V and 2000 V Class B	
	Dia., mm	Area, mm²	Dia., mm	Area, mm²	Dia., mm	Area, mm²	Dia., mm	Area, mm²	Dia., mm	Area, mm²	Dia., mm	Area, mm²	Dia., mm	Area, mm²	Dia., mm	Area, mm²
14	3.37	8.92	4.13	13.40	4.89	18.78	4.13	13.40	4.89	18.78	5.65	25.07	4.89	18.78	5.65	25.07
12	3.84	11.58	4.60	16.62	5.36	22.56	4.60	16.62	5.36	22.56	6.12	29.42	5.36	22.56	6.12	29.42
10	4.47	15.69	5.23	21.48	5.99	28.18	5.23	21.48	5.99	28.18	7.51	44.30	5.99	28.18	6.75	35.78
8	5.99	28.18	5.99	28.18	7.27	41.51	7.51	44.30	7.51	44.30	8.79	60.68	7.77	47.42	9.29	67.78
6	6.95	37.94	7.71	46.69	8.23	53.20	8.47	56.35	9.23	66.91	9.75	74.66	8.73	59.86	10.25	82.52
4	8.17	52.42	8.93	62.63	9.45	70.14	9.69	73.75	10.45	85.77	10.97	94.52	9.95	77.76	11.47	103.3
3	8.88	61.93	9.64	72.99	10.16	81.07	10.40	84.95	11.16	97.82	11.68	107.1	10.66	89.25	12.18	116.5
2	9.70	73.90	10.46	85.93	10.98	94.69	11.22	98.87	11.98	112.7	13.26	138.1	11.48	103.5	13.76	148.7
1	11.23	99.05	12.49	122.5	13.01	132.9	13.51	143.4	14.77	171.3	15.29	183.6	13.25	137.9	15.53	189.4
1/0	12.25	117.9	13.51	143.4	14.03	154.6	14.53	165.8	15.79	195.8	16.31	208.9	14.27	159.9	16.55	215.1
2/0	13.42	141.4	14.68	169.3	15.20	181.5	15.70	193.6	16.96	225.9	17.48	240.0	15.44	187.2	17.72	246.6
3/0	14.74	170.6	16.00	201.1	16.52	214.3	17.02	227.5	18.28	262.4	18.80	277.6	16.76	220.6	19.04	284.7
4/0	16.21	206.4	17.47	239.7	17.99	254.2	18.49	268.5	19.75	306.4	21.29	356.0	18.23	261.0	21.53	364.1
250	17.90	251.6	19.16	288.3	19.94	312.3	21.20	353.0	22.46	396.2	23.24	424.2	20.18	319.8	23.48	433.0
300	19.30	292.6	20.56	332.0	21.34	357.7	22.60	401.1	23.86	447.1	24.64	476.8	21.58	365.8	24.88	486.2
350	20.60	333.3	21.86	375.3	22.64	402.6	23.90	448.6	25.16	497.2	25.94	528.5	22.88	411.2	26.18	538.3
400	21.79	372.9	23.05	417.3	23.83	446.0	25.09	494.4	26.35	545.3	27.13	578.1	24.07	455.0	27.37	588.4
450	22.91	412.2	24.17	458.8	24.95	488.9	26.21	539.5	27.47	592.7	28.25	626.8	25.19	498.4	28.49	637.5
500	23.95	450.5	25.21	499.2	25.99	530.5	27.25	583.2	28.51	638.4	29.29	673.8	26.23	540.4	29.53	684.9
600	26.74	561.6	27.24	582.8	28.78	650.5	30.04	708.7	30.54	732.5	32.08	808.3	29.04	662.3	32.34	821.4

(Continued)

Tables

Table 10B (Concluded)

Conductor size, AWG or kcmil	RPV*, 600 V Class B Dia., mm	RPV*, 600 V Class B Area, mm²	RPV*, 1000 V Class B Dia., mm	RPV*, 1000 V Class B Area, mm²	RPV*, 2000 V Class B Dia., mm	RPV*, 2000 V Class B Area, mm²	RPV†, 600 V Class B Dia., mm	RPV†, 600 V Class B Area, mm²	RPV†, 1000 V Class B Dia., mm	RPV†, 1000 V Class B Area, mm²	RPV†, 2000 V Class B Dia., mm	RPV†, 2000 V Class B Area, mm²	RPVU*, 1000 V and 2000 V Class B Dia., mm	RPVU*, 1000 V and 2000 V Class B Area, mm²	RPVU†, 1000 V and 2000 V Class B Dia., mm	RPVU†, 1000 V and 2000 V Class B Area, mm²
700	28.55	640.2	29.05	662.8	30.59	734.9	31.85	796.7	32.35	821.9	33.89	902.1	30.85	747.5	34.15	915.9
750	29.41	679.3	29.91	702.6	31.45	776.8	32.71	840.3	33.21	866.2	34.75	948.4	31.71	789.7	35.01	962.7
800	30.22	717.3	30.72	741.2	32.26	817.4	33.52	882.5	34.02	909.0	35.56	993.1	32.52	830.6	35.82	1008
900	31.85	796.7	32.35	821.9	33.89	902.1	35.15	970.4	35.65	998.2	37.19	1086	34.15	915.9	37.45	1102
1000	33.32	872.0	33.82	898.3	35.36	982.0	36.62	1053	37.12	1082	38.66	1174	35.62	996.5	38.92	1190
1250	37.56	1108	38.32	1153	39.86	1248	42.38	1411	43.14	1462	44.68	1568	39.86	1248	44.68	1568
1500	40.68	1300	41.44	1349	42.98	1451	45.50	1626	46.26	1681	47.80	1795	42.98	1451	47.80	1795
1750	43.58	1492	44.34	1544	45.88	1653	48.40	1840	49.16	1898	50.70	2019	45.88	1653	50.70	2019
2000	46.27	1681	47.03	1737	48.57	1853	51.09	2050	51.85	2111	53.39	2239	48.57	1853	53.39	2239

* Unjacketed.
† Jacketed.

Note: Aluminum insulated conductors and cables may not be available in the same range of sizes as copper insulated conductors and cables.

Table 10C
Dimensions of solid insulated conductors for calculating conduit and tubing fill
(See Rule 12-910 and Appendix B.)

Conductor size, AWG	R90XLPE*, RW75XLPE*, RW90XLPE*, 600 V		R90XLPE*, RW75XLPE*, RW90XLPE*, 1000 V		R90XLPE†, RW75XLPE†, R90EP†, RW75EP†, RW90XLPE†, RW90EP‡, 600 V		TWN75, T90 NYLON		TW, TW75		TWU, TWU75, RWU90XLPE*	
	Dia., mm	Area, mm²	Dia., mm	Area, mm²	Dia., mm	Area, mm²	Dia., mm	Area, mm²	Dia., mm	Area, mm²	Dia., mm	Area, mm²
14	3.15	7.78	3.91	11.99	3.91	11.99	2.59	5.26	3.15	7.78	4.67	17.11
12	3.57	10.02	4.33	14.74	4.33	14.74	3.01	7.13	3.57	10.02	5.09	20.36
10	4.11	13.25	4.87	18.61	4.87	18.61	3.81	11.39	4.11	13.25	5.63	24.88

* Unjacketed.
† Jacketed.
‡ Includes EPCV.

Note: Aluminum insulated conductors and cables may not be available in the same range of sizes as copper insulated conductors and cables.

Tables

Table 10D
Dimensions of DLO cable for calculating conduit and tubing fill
(See Rule 12-910 and Appendix B.)

Conductor size, AWG or kcmil	R90 (DLO), RW90 (DLO) Diameter, mm	Area, mm²
14	5.59	24.54
12	6.10	29.22
10	6.86	36.96
8	8.38	55.15
6	10.41	85.11
4	11.68	107.15
3	12.45	121.74
2	13.21	137.06
1	16.51	214.08
1/0	17.53	241.35
2/0	18.29	262.73
3/0	20.57	332.32
4/0	22.10	383.60
262	25.40	506.71
313	26.92	569.17
373	27.94	613.12
444	31.24	766.50
535	34.04	910.06
646	36.83	1065.35
777	38.10	1140.09
929	40.89	1313.18
1111	44.45	1551.79

                              January 2018

Δ
Table 11
Conditions of use, voltage, and temperature ratings of flexible cords, heater cords, tinsel cords, equipment wires, Christmas-tree cords, portable power cables, elevator cables, stage lighting, electric vehicle supply equipment cables, and festoon cables
(See Rules 12-010, 12-402, 12-406, and 12-122.)

Location	Use	Kind	CSA type designation	Voltage rating, V	Temperature rating, °C	Reference Notes
Dry locations only	Not for hard usage	Heat-resistant equipment wire	GTF	600	125	4
		Equipment wire	TXF, TXF-S	125	60	15
		Indoor Christmas-tree cord	PXT	125	60	—
			DPT	300	105	—
Damp (or dry) locations	Not for hard usage	Flexible cord	SV	300	60, 75, 90	16
			SVO, SVOO	300	60, 75, 90	3
			SVT	300	60, 75, 90, 105	16
			SVTO, SVTOO	300	60, 75, 90, 105	3
			SPT-1, NISPT-1	300	60, 75, 90, 105	7, 16
			SPT-2, NISPT-2	300	60, 75, 90, 105	16
			SPT-3	300	105	16
			SVE, SVEO, SVEOO, SPE-1, SPE-2, SPE-3, NISPE-1, NISPE-2	300	90, 105	3
		Heater cord	HPN	300	90, 105	3
	Not for hard usage	Tinsel cord	TPT	300	60	—
			TST	300	60	—
		Equipment wire	TEW	600	105	1, 3, 4, 11
			SIS	600	90	4, 11
			REW	300	105	1, 3, 6, 11
			REW	600	105	1, 3, 4, 6, 11
			SEWF-1	300	150	1, 5, 11
			SEW-1	300	200	1, 5, 11
			SEWF-2	600	150	4, 5, 11
			SEW-2	600	200	4, 5, 11
			TEWN	600	105	1, 3, 11
	For hard usage	Flexible cord	SJ	300	60, 75, 90, 105	10
			SJO, SJOO	300	60, 75, 90, 105	3, 10
			SJT	300	60, 75, 90, 105	10
			SJTO, SJTOO	300	60, 75, 90, 105	3, 10
			SJE, SJEO, SJEOO	300	90, 105	3, 10

(Continued)

Table 11 (Continued)

Location	Use	Kind	CSA type designation	Voltage rating, V	Temperature rating, °C	Reference Notes
	For hard usage	Heater cord	HSJ, HSJO, HSJOO	300	90, 105	3, 8, 9, 10
	For extra-hard usage	Flexible cord	S	600	60, 75, 90, 105	10
			SO, SOO	600	60, 75, 90, 105	3, 10
			ST	600	60, 75, 90, 105	10
			STO, STOO	600	60, 75, 90, 105	3, 10
			SE, SEO, SEOO	600	90, 105	3, 10
		Dryer and range cable	DRT	300	60	2
	Elevator travelling cable		E	300	60	11
			E	600	60	11
			ETT, ETP	300	60	11
			ETT, ETP	600	60	11
			EO	300	60	3, 11
			EO	600	60	3, 11
Wet (or damp or dry) locations	Not for hard usage	Outdoor Christmas-tree cord	CXWT	300	60	—
			CXWT	600	60	—
			PXWT	300	60	—
			SPT-1W	300	105	7
			SPT-2W	300	105	—
		Outdoor equipment wire	TXFW, TXFW-S	300	60	—
		Heater cord	HPNW, HSJW	300	90, 105	—
	For hard usage	Outdoor flexible cord	SJOW, SJOOW	300	60, 75, 90, 105	3
			SJTW	300	60, 75, 90, 105	—
			SJTOW, SJTOOW	300	60, 75, 90, 105	3
			SJEW, SJEOW, SJEOOW	300	90, 105	3
		Electric vehicle supply equipment cable	EVJ, EVJT	300	60, 75, 90, 105	3, 10
			EVJE	300	90, 105	3, 10
	For extra-hard usage	Outdoor flexible cord	SOOW	600	60, 75, 90, 105	3
			SOW	600	60, 75, 90, 105	3
			STW	600	60, 75, 90, 105	—
			STOW, STOOW	600	60, 75, 90, 105	—
		Electric vehicle supply equipment cable	EV, EVT	600	60, 75, 90, 105	3, 10
			EVE	600	90, 105	3, 10
			EVK, EVKT	1000	60, 75, 90, 105	3, 10
			EVKE	1000	90, 105	3, 10

(Continued)

Table 11 (Continued)

Location	Use	Kind	CSA type designation	Voltage rating, V	Temperature rating, °C	Reference Notes
		Portable power cables	W	2000	90	12, 13
			G	2000	90	12, 13
			G-GC	2000	90	12
			G-BGC	2000	90	12
			SHC-GC	2000	90	12
			SH, SHD, SHD-GC, SHD-BGC	2000, 5000, 8000, 15 000, 25 000, or 35 000	90	12
			DLO	2000	90	—
	For hard usage	Stage lighting	PPC	600	60, 75, 90, 105	13
		Festoon	Festoon	600	60, 105	14
			Festoon-outdoors	600	60, 105	14

Notes:

1) *Types REW, SEW, SEWF, TEW, and TEWN shall be permitted in raceways for Class 1 circuits in accordance with Rule 16-112 2).*

2) *Dryer and range cables are for use in household dryer and range power supply cords only. These cables are not for sale to the public for general use.*

3) *When exposed to oil, the following are limited to 60 °C, regardless of the temperature rating of the product:*
   a) *the temperature rating of the jacket of Types SVO, SVEO, SVTO, HSJO, EO, SJO, SJEO, SJTO, STO, SO, SEO, SEOW, SOW, SJOW, SJTOW, EV, EVE, EVJ, EVJE, EVJT, EVK, EVKT, EVKE and EVT;*
   b) *the insulation and jacket of Types SVOO, SVEOO, SVTOO, SJOO, SJEOO, SJTOO, STOO, SOO, SEOO, SOOW, SEOOW, SJOOW, SJEOOW, SJEOW, and SJTOOW; and*
   c) *the insulation of Type HPN and HPNW heater cord and TEWN, REW, and TEW equipment wire.*

4) *Types GTF, REW, TEW, TBS, SIS, SEWF-2, and SEW-2 may be used in raceways in accordance with Rule 30-310 2) c) ii).*

5) *Types SEWF-1 and SEWF-2 with an insulated nickel or nickel-coated copper conductor have a temperature rating of 200 °C. Types SEW-1, SEWF-1, SEW-2, and SEWF-2 with an insulated nickel or nickel-coated copper conductor may also have a temperature rating of 250 °C.*

6) *Types having cross-linked PVC insulation are surface marked with the type designation followed by (XLPVC) and types having cross-linked chlorinated polyethylene are surface marked with the type designation followed by (XLCPE).*

7) *Type SPT-1 and SPT-1W No. 20 AWG are for electric clock and decorative lighting use.*

8) *When Type HSJO heater cord is provided with 90 °C polychloroprene insulation (no asbestos insulation), the type designation "HSJO" is surface printed on the cord.*

9) *When Type HSJO heater cord is provided with 90 °C ethylene propylene rubber insulation (no asbestos insulation), the type designation "HSJO" is surface printed on the cord.*

10) *Types HSJO, SJ, SJO, SJOO, SJEO, SJEOW, SJEOO, SJT, SJTO, SJTOO, S, SO, SOO, ST, STO, STOO, EV, EVE, EVJ, EVJE, EVJT, EVK, EVKT, EVKE, and EVT flexible cords are now recognized only as components of equipment.*

11) *Suitable for use in accordance with Rule 38-011 2) when flame-retardant and moisture-resistant.*

12) *Natural rubber jackets are not suitable for use in oily environments.*

(Continued)

Tables

Table 11 (Concluded)

13) *Type PPC is single-conductor cable intended for use in temporary installations, such as portable stage lighting and outdoor functions. If multi-conductor cable is needed for the same applications, Type W or G shall be permitted to be used if ampacities are higher than those for flexible cords specified in Section 44.*

14) *Festoon cable has a flat configuration incorporating insulated power and/or control conductors and is supported by a messenger. It supplies power and control wiring for cranes and hoists, indoors or outdoors. See Rule 40-004.*

15) *Type TXF is also suitable for indoor Christmas-tree cord.*

16) *The type designation may be followed by a "-B" suffix when a decorative braid is applied over the cord.*

△

Table 12
Allowable ampacity of flexible insulated copper conductor cord and equipment wire
(based on an ambient temperature of 30 °C)
(See Rules 4-012 and 4-014.)

Allowable ampacity

| | Flexible cord | | | | | | | Electric vehicle supply equipment cable types EV††, EVE††, EVJ††, EVJE††, EVT††, EVJT††, EVK††, EVKT††, EVKE†† | | Equipment wire | | | |
| | Tinsel cord | Christmas-tree cord | | Elevator cable | Types NISPT-1, NISPT-2, SV§, SVO§, SVEO§, SVOO§, SVEOO§, SJ‡§, SJE‡§, SJEW‡§, SJO‡§, SJEO‡§, SJOO‡§, SJEOO‡§, SJOW§, SJEOW§, SJOOW§, SJEOOW§, S‡, SE‡, SEW‡, SO‡, SEO‡, SEOW‡, SOO‡, SEOO‡, SEOOW‡, SOW, SOOW, SPT-1, SPT-2, SPT-3, SVT§, SVTO§, SVTOO§, SJT‡§, SJTO‡§, SJTOO‡§, ST‡, STO‡, STOO‡, SJTW§, SJTOW§, SJTOOW§, STW, STOW, STOOW | | Types HSJ‡, HSJW‡, HSJO‡, HSJOO, HPN**, HPNW** | | | | | |
Size, AWG	Types TPT, TST	Types CXWT, PXWT, TXFW, TXFW-S, SPT-1W, SPT-2W, DPTW	Types PXT, TXF, TXF-S, DPT	Types E, EO, ETT, ETP	2 current-carrying conductors	3 current-carrying conductors*		2 current-carrying conductors	3 current-carrying conductors	Type TXF, TXF-S	Type DRT	Type TXFW, TXFW-S	Types GTF*, TEW*, SEW*, REW*, TEWN*, SEWF*, TBS*, SIS*
27	0.5	—	—	—	—	—	—	—	—	—	—	—	—
26	—	—	—	—	—	—	—	—	—	—	—	—	1
24	—	—	—	—	—	—	—	—	—	—	—	—	2
22	—	1.8†	1.8†	—	—	—	—	—	—	—	—	1.8†	3
20	—	3.6†	3.6†	—	2‡‡	—	—	—	—	2	—	3.6†	4
18	—	7	—	5	10	7	10	10	7	—	—	5	6
17	—	—	—	—	12	9	13	12	9	—	—	7	—
16	—	10	—	7	13	10	15	13	10	—	—	—	8
15	—	—	—	—	16	12	17	16	12	—	—	—	—
14	—	15	—	15	18	15	20	18	15	—	—	—	17
13	—	—	—	—	21	17	—	21	17	—	—	—	—

(Continued)

Tables

Table 12 (Continued)

| | Flexible cord | | | | | | | | | Equipment wire | | | |
| | Tinsel cord | Christmas-tree cord | | Elevator cable | Types NISPT-1, NISPT-2, SV§, SVO§, SVEO§, SVOO§, SVEOO§, SI‡§, SJE‡§, SJEW‡§, SJO‡§, SJEO‡§, SJOO‡§, SJEOO‡§, SJOW§, SJEOW§, SJEOOW§, S‡, SE‡, SEW‡, SO‡, SEO‡, SEOW‡, SOO‡, SEOO‡, SEOOW‡, SOW, SOOW, SPT-1, SPT-2, SPT-3, SVT§, SVTO§, SVTOO§, SJT‡§, SJTO‡§, SJTOO‡§, ST‡, STO‡, STOO‡, SJTW§, SJTOW§, SJTOOW§, STW, STOW, STOOW | | Types HSJ‡, HSJW‡, HSJO‡, HSJOO, HPN**, HPNW** | Electric vehicle supply equipment cable types EV††, EVE††, EVJ††, EVJE††, EVT††, EVIT††, EVK††, EVKT††, EVKE†† | | | | | |
Size, AWG	Types TPT, TST	Types CXWT, PXWT, TXFW, TXFW-S, SPT-1W, SPT-2W, DPTW	Types PXT, TXF, TXF-S, DPT	Types E, EO, ETT, ETP	2 current-carrying conductors	3 current-carrying conductors*		2 current-carrying conductors	3 current-carrying conductors	Type TXF, TXF-S	Type DRT	Type TXFW, TXFW-S	Types GTF*, TEW*, SEW*, REW*, TEWN*, SEWF*, TBS*, SIS*
12	—	20	—	20	25	20	25	25	20	—	—	—	23
11	—	—	—	—	27	23	—	27	23	—	—	—	—
10	—	—	—	25	30	25	—	30	25	—	30	—	28
9	—	—	—	—	34	29	—	34	29	—	—	—	—
8	—	—	—	35	40	35	—	40	35	—	40	—	40
6	—	—	—	45	55	45	—	55	45	—	50	—	55
4	—	—	—	60	70	60	—	70	60	—	60	—	70
3	—	—	—	—	—	—	—	—	—	—	—	—	80
2	—	—	—	80	95	80	—	95	80	—	—	—	95
1	—	—	—	—	—	—	—	150	131	—	—	—	110
1/0	—	—	—	—	—	—	—	173	151	—	—	—	125
2/0	—	—	—	—	—	—	—	199	174	—	—	—	145
3/0	—	—	—	—	—	—	—	230	201	—	—	—	165
4/0	—	—	—	—	—	—	—	265	232	—	—	—	195
250	—	—	—	—	—	—	—	296	259	—	—	—	—

(Continued)

Table 12 (Concluded)

Size, AWG	Flexible cord								Equipment wire			
	Tinsel cord — Types TPT, TST	Christmas-tree cord — Types CXWT, PXWT, TXFW, TXFW-S, SPT-1W, SPT-2W, DPTW	Christmas-tree cord — Types PXT, TXF, TXF-S, DPT	Elevator cable — Types E, EO, ETT, ETP	Types NISPT-1, NISPT-2, SV§, SVO§, SVEO§, SVOO§, SVEOO§, SI‡§, SIE‡§, SIEW‡§, SIO‡§, SIEO‡§, SIOO‡§, SIEOO‡§, SIOW§, SIEOW§, SIOOW§, SIEOOW§, S‡, SE‡, SEW‡, SO‡, SEO‡, SEOW‡, SOO‡, SEOO‡, SEOOW‡, SOW, SOOW, SPT-1, SPT-2, SPT-3, SVT§, SVTO§, SVTOO§, SJT‡§, SJTO‡§, SJTOO‡§, ST‡, STO‡, STOO‡, SJTW§, SJTOW§, SJTOOW§, STW, STOW, STOOW — 2 current-carrying conductors	... 3 current-carrying conductors*	Types HSJ‡, HSJW‡, HSJO‡, HSJOO, HPN**, HPNW**	Electric vehicle supply equipment cable types EV††, EVE††, EVJ††, EVJE††, EVT††, EVJT††, EVK††, EVKT††, EVKE†† — 2 current-carrying conductors	... 3 current-carrying conductors	Type TXF, TXF-S	Type DRT	Type TXFW, TXFW-S	Types GTF*, TEW*, SEW*, REW*, TEWN*, SEWF*, TBS*, SIS*
300	—	—	—	—	—	—	—	330	289	—	—	—	—
350	—	—	—	—	—	—	—	363	318	—	—	—	—
400	—	—	—	—	—	—	—	392	343	—	—	—	—
500	—	—	—	—	—	—	—	448	392	—	—	—	—

* The derating factors of Rule 4-012 1) b), c), d), and e) shall be applied to these values for the types listed in this Column.

† Types PXT, TXF, TXF-S, CXWT, PXWT, TXFW, and TXFW-S No. 22 AWG are suitable for 1.8 A with 3 A fuse protection, and No. 20 AWG for 3.6 A with 5 A fuse protection. SPT-1 and SPT-1W No. 20 AWG are suitable for 3.6 A with 5 A fuse protection.

‡ Types HSJ, HSJW, HSJO, SJ, SJE, SJEW, SJO, SJOO, SJT, SJTO, SJTOO, S, SE, SO, SEW, SEO, SEOW, SOO, SEOO, SEOOW, ST, STO, and STOO flexible cords are now recognized only as components of equipment.

§ Types SJ, SJE, SJEW, SJO, SJEO, SJOO, SJOW, SJEOW, SJOOW, SJEOOW, SVT, SVTO, SVTOO, SV, SVE, SVO, SVOO, SVEO, SVEOO, SJT, SJTO, SJTOO, SJTW, SJTOW, and SJTOOW No. 17 AWG are recognized with an ampacity of 12 A as a component of vacuum cleaners with retractable power supply cords.

** Types HPN and HPNW No. 17 AWG are recognized with an ampacity of 13 A.

†† The size range for Types EVJ, EVJE, and EVJT shall be 18 to 12 AWG. The size range for types EV, EVK, EVKT, EVE, EVKE, and EVT shall be 18 AWG to 500 kcmil.

‡‡ Type SPT-1 No. 20 AWG is suitable for 3.6 A with 5 A fuse protection when used as Christmas-tree cord.

Note: This Table is intended to be used in conjunction with applicable end-use product Standards to ensure selection of the proper size and type.

Tables

Table 12A
Allowable ampacities for portable insulated copper conductor power cables (amperes per insulated conductor)

(See Rule 4-034 and Tables 12B to 12D.)

Power conductor size, AWG or kcmil	Single insulated conductor					Two conductor	Three insulated conductors					Four conductor	Five conductor	Six conductor
	≤ 2 kV non-shielded	5 and 8 kV shielded	15 kV shielded	25 kV shielded	35 kV shielded	2 kV	2 kV non-shielded	2, 5, and 8 kV shielded	15 kV shielded	25 kV shielded	35 kV shielded	2 kV	2 kV	2 kV
14	—	—	—	—	—	—	—	28	—	—	—	—	—	—
12	—	—	—	—	—	42	35	35	—	—	—	31	30	28
10	—	—	—	—	—	59	49	49	—	—	—	44	42	39
8	80	—	—	—	—	74	65	65	—	—	—	59	55	53
6	105	—	—	—	—	99	87	102	—	—	—	79	75	70
4	140	—	—	—	—	130	114	134	—	—	—	102	97	91
2	190	—	—	—	—	174	152	175	180	—	—	134	128	121
1	220	248	248	244	—	202	177	202	206	210	—	157	150	142
1/0	260	286	285	280	277	234	205	232	236	240	241	182	—	—
2/0	300	329	328	322	319	271	237	267	271	274	275	211	—	—
3/0	350	380	377	371	367	313	274	307	311	315	316	243	—	—
4/0	405	440	437	428	424	361	316	353	358	360	361	280	—	—
250	455	488	484	473	468	402	352	390	395	396	397	308	—	—
300	505	546	540	528	523	449	393	438	441	441	442	341	—	—
350	570	604	597	582	576	495	433	478	482	482	483	368	—	—
400	615	656	649	629	—	535	468	517	517	517	—	392	—	—
500	700	757	746	725	718	613	536	590	590	590	591	434	—	—

(Continued)

Table 12A (Concluded)

Power conductor size, AWG or kcmil	Single insulated conductor					Two conductor	Three insulated conductors					Four conductor	Five conductor	Six conductor
	≤ 2 kV non-shielded	5 and 8 kV shielded	15 kV shielded	25 kV shielded	35 kV shielded	2 kV	2 kV non-shielded	2, 5, and 8 kV shielded	15 kV shielded	25 kV shielded	35 kV shielded	2 kV	2 kV	2 kV
750	885	—	—	—	—	—	—	735	735	—	—	2 kV	2 kV	2 kV
1000	1055	—	—	—	—	—	—	845	—	—	—	—	—	—

Notes:

1) The ampacity values are based on a single isolated cable in air at an ambient temperature of 30 °C. For cables operating at a different ambient air temperature, the ampacity shall be obtained by multiplying the appropriate value from this Table by the correction factor for that other ambient temperature, as contained in Table 12B.

2) The ampacities are based on a conductor insulation temperature of 90 °C. For conductor insulation temperatures other than 90 °C, the ampacity of a given insulated conductor type shall be obtained by multiplying the appropriate value from this Table by the correction factor for that conductor insulation temperature as contained in Table 12C.

3) When cables are used with one or more layers wound on a drum, the actual internal temperature of the cable can exceed the 90 °C rating. Thermal overheating may shorten the run life of the cable. The appropriate ampacity correction factors are shown in Table 12D.

4) For single-conductor cables with metallic shields, the ampacity values are for cables operated with an open-circuit shield.

Tables

Table 12B
Temperature correction factor
(See Tables 12A and 12E.)

Ambient air temperature, °C	Correction factor
10	1.14
20	1.07
30	1.00
40	0.91
50	0.82

Table 12C
Conductor insulation rating correction factor
(See Tables 12A and 12E.)

Insulated conductor temperature rating, °C	Correction factor
60	0.75
75	0.885
90	1.00

Table 12D
Layering correction factor
(See Table 12A.)

Number of layers of cable on drum	Correction factor
1	0.85
2	0.65
3	0.45
4	0.35

Table 12E
Allowable ampacities for Type DLO cables in a permanent installation in cable tray
[See Rules 4-006 6) and 12-406 4) and Tables 5D, 12B, and 12C.]

Size, AWG or kcmil	Ampacity, A
1/0	260
2/0	300
3/0	350
4/0	405
262	475
313	520
373	605
444	660
535	735
646	820
777	910
929	1005
1111	1110

Notes:

1) *The ampacity values are based on a single isolated cable in air at an ambient temperature of 30 °C. For cables operating at a different ambient temperature, the ampacity shall be obtained by multiplying the appropriate value from this Table by the correction factor for that ambient temperature as given in Table 12B.*

2) *The ampacity values are based on a conductor insulation temperature of 90 °C. For conductor insulation temperatures other than 90 °C, the ampacity of a given insulated conductor type shall be obtained by multiplying the appropriate value from this Table by the correction factor for that insulation conductor temperature as given in Table 12C.*

3) *When cables are used with more tray layers, the appropriate correction factors are shown in Table 5D.*

Tables

Table 13
Rating or setting of overcurrent devices protecting conductors*
(See Rules 14-104 and 28-204.)

Ampacity of conductor, A	Rating or setting permitted, A	Ampacity of conductor, A	Rating or setting permitted, A
0–15	15	111–125	125
16–20	20	126–150	150
21–25	25	151–175	175
26–30	30	176–200	200
31–35	35	201–225	225
36–40	40	226–250	250
41–45	45	251–300	300
46–50	50	301–350	350
51–60	60	351–400	400
61–70	70	401–450	450
71–80	80	451–500	500
81–90	90	501–600	600
91–100	100	601–700	700
101–110	110	701–800	800

* For general use where not otherwise specifically provided for.

Table 14
Watts per square metre and demand factors for services and feeders for various types of occupancy
(See Rules 8-002 and 8-210.)

Type of occupancy	Watts per square metre	Demand factor, %	
		Insulated service conductors or cables	Feeders
Store, restaurant	30	100	100
Office			
First 930 m²	50	90	100
All in excess of 930 m²	50	70	90
Industrial and commercial	25	100	100
Church	10	100	100
Garage	10	100	100
Storage warehouse	5	70	90
Theatre	30	75	95
Armouries and auditoriums	10	80	100
Banks	50	100	100
Barbershops and beauty parlours	30	90	100
Clubs	20	80	100
Courthouses	20	100	100
Lodges	15	80	100

Tables

Table 15
Bending radii — High-voltage cable
(See Rules 34-400 and 36-102.)

Type of cable	Cable diameter multiplying factor (see Note)		
	Up to and including 25 mm diameter	Over 25 mm diameter and up to and including 50 mm diameter	Over 50 mm diameter
Lead covered	10	12	12
Corrugated aluminum-sheathed	10	12	12
Smooth aluminum-sheathed	12	15	18
Tape shielded	12	12	12
Flat tape armoured	12	12	12
Wire armoured	12	12	12
Non-shielded	7	7	7
Wire shielded	7	7	7
Portable power cables 5 kV and less	6	6	6
Portable power cables over 5 kV	8	8	8

Note: *The bending radius is the radius measured at the innermost surface. It equals the overall diameter of the cable multiplied by the appropriate number shown in Columns 2, 3, and 4.*

Δ
Table 16
Minimum size of field-installed system bonding jumpers and bonding conductors
(See Rule 10-614.)

Ampere rating or setting of overcurrent device protecting conductor(s), equipment, etc.	Allowable ampacity of largest ungrounded conductor or group of conductors.	Minimum size of system bonding jumper and bonding conductor			
		Wire		Bus	
Not exceeding		Copper, AWG or kcmil	Aluminum, AWG or kcmil	Copper, mm²	Aluminum, mm²
20		14	12	2.0	3.5
30		12	10	3.5	5.5
60		10	8	5.5	8.5
100		8	6	8.5	10.5
200		6	4	10.5	21.0
300		4	2	21.0	26.5
400		3	1	26.5	33.5
500		2	0	33.5	42.5
600		1	00	42.5	53.5
800		0	000	53.5	67.5
1000		00	0000	67.5	84.0
1200		000	250	84.0	127.0
1600		0000	350	107.0	177.5
2000		250	400	127.5	203.0
2500		350	500	177.5	253.5
3000		400	600	203.0	355.0
4000		500	800	253.5	405.5
5000		700	1000	355.0	507.0
6000		800	1250	405.5	633.5

Table 16A
Deleted

Table 16B
Deleted

Table 17
Deleted

Δ

Ⓔ

Table 18
Equipment suitable for explosive atmospheres
(See Rules 18-090, 18-100, 18-150, 18-190, 18-200, 18-250, J18-100, J18-150, J18-200, J18-250, J18-300, and J18-350.)

Zone system			Division system	
Intrinsic safety	ia			
Intrinsically safe	Intrinsically safe, IS, I.S., Exi, Exia	Zone 0		
Encapsulation	ma			
Flameproof	da*			
Inherently safe optical radiation	op is, with Ga**			
Optical system with interlock	op sh, with Ga**			
EPL††	Ga			
Equipment suitable for use in Zone 0				
Equipment suitable for use in Class I, Division 1				Equipment suitable for use in Zone 0
Flameproof	d, db		Class I, Division 1†	
Intrinsic safety	ib			Class I, Division 1 equipment†
Increased safety	e, eb			
Pressurized enclosure	p, px, pxb, py, pyb			Intrinsically safe IS, I.S., Exi, Exia
Encapsulation	m, mb	Zone 1		
Powder filling	q, qb			
Oil immersion	o, ob			
Electrical resistance trace heating	60079-30-1, with Gb**			
Inherently safe optical radiation	op is, with Gb**			
Optical system with interlock	op sh, with Gb**			
Protected optical radiation	op pr, with Gb**			
EPL††	Gb			
Equipment suitable for use in Zone 1				
Equipment suitable for use in Class I, Division 2				Equipment suitable for use in Zone 2
Type of protection	nA, nC, nL, nR			
Pressurized enclosure	pz, pzc			Equipment suitable for use in Class I, Division 1
Intrinsic safety	ic			
Flameproof	dc			
Increased safety	ec	Zone 2	Class I, Division 2	Class I, Division 2 equipment
Oil immersion	oc			
Encapsulation	mc			Non-incendive
Electrical resistance trace heating	60079-30-1, with Gc**			Other electrical apparatus‡
Inherently safe optical radiation	op is, with Gc**			
Optical system with interlock	op sh, with Gc**			

(Continued)

Table 18 (Continued)

Zone system				Division system	
Protected optical radiation	op pr, with Gc**				
EPL††	Gc				
Other electrical apparatus‡					
Equipment suitable for use in Class II, Division 1					
Intrinsic safety	ia				
Intrinsically safe	Intrinsically safe, IS, I.S., Exi, Exia				
Protection by enclosure	ta	Zone 20			
Encapsulation	ma				
Inherently safe optical radiation	op is, with Da**				
Optical system with interlock	op sh, with Da**				
EPL††	Da				
Equipment suitable for use in Zone 20			Class II and Class III, Division 1†	Equipment suitable for use in Zone 20§	
Equipment suitable for use in Class II, Division 1					
Intrinsic safety	ib			Class II/III, Division 1 equipment	
Protection by enclosure	tb				
Pressurized enclosure	p, px, pxb, py, pyb			Intrinsically safe, IS, I.S., Exi, Exia	
Encapsulation	mb	Zone 21			
Ⓔ Electrical resistance trace heating	60079-30-1, with Db**				
Inherently safe optical radiation	op is, with Db**				
Optical system with interlock	op sh, with Db**				
Protected optical radiation	op pr, with Db**				
EPL††	Db				
Equipment suitable for use in Zone 21			Class II and Class III, Division 2	Equipment suitable for use in Zone 22§	
Equipment suitable for use in Class II, Division 2					
Intrinsic safety	ic			Equipment suitable for use in Class II/III, Division 1	
Protection by enclosure	tc				
Pressurized enclosure	pz, pzc				
Encapsulation	mc	Zone 22		Class II/III, Division 2 equipment	
Ⓔ Electrical resistance trace heating	60079-30-1, with Dc**				
Inherently safe optical radiation	op is, with Dc**			Non-incendive	
Optical system with interlock	op sh, with Dc**				
Protected optical radiation	op pr, with Dc**			Other electrical apparatus‡	
EPL††	Dc				
Other electrical apparatus‡					

Table 18 (Concluded)

* *"da" is limited to sensors of portable combustible gas detectors.*

† *Because Class I, Division 1 encompasses the equivalent of Zone 0, types of protection designed for Zone 1 are not allowed in Class I, Division 1 (e.g., an intrinsic safety ib device is not allowed in a Class I, Division 1 location). Similarly, types of protection designed for Zone 21 are not allowed in a Class II/III, Division 1 location.*

‡ *"Other electrical apparatus" means electrical apparatus complying with the requirements of a recognized Standard for industrial electrical apparatus that does not in normal service*

a)   have ignition-capable hot surfaces; or

b)   produce incendive arcs or sparks.

See Rules 18-150 2), 18-250 2), J18-150 2) and 3), and J18-250. "Other electrical apparatus" also makes reference to equipment or systems currently acceptable as alternative means of protection (see Rules 18-064, 18-068, J18-062 and J18-066).

§ *For use in Class II and Class III, such (Zone acceptable) equipment is subject to the limitation of Rules J18-054 2) or J18-054 3) respectively. Group IIIA equipment is not suitable for use in Class II locations.*

** *Equipment marked with these types of protection is available in multiple levels of protection that are not specifically identified within the Ex marking.*

†† *The EPL takes precedence over the type of protection; for example, "Ex ia Gb" is suitable for Zone 1 (not Zone 0), "Ex op is Db" is suitable for Zone 21 (not Zone 20), and "Ex 60079-30-1 Gc" is suitable for Zone 2 (not Zone 1). Selection according to the marked EPL is critical to the safe application of this equipment.*

Note: *This Table is structured to show the Zone equipment on the left side and Class/Division equipment on the right side. Zone equipment is suitable for use in Class/Division locations and vice versa. This is indicated by the phrase "Equipment suitable for use in ....". For example, in Class I, Division 1 locations, "Equipment suitable for use in Zone 0" means all equipment listed under Zone 0 can be used.*

Table 19
Conditions of use and maximum allowable insulation temperature of conductors and cables other than flexible cords, portable power cables, and equipment wires

(See Rules 12-100, 12-102, 12-302, 12-406, 12-602, 12-606, 12-902, 12-904, 12-1606, 12-2104, 12-2202, 16-330, and 22-202, Tables 1, 2, 3, 4, D1, and D3.)

Conditions of use	Trade designation	CSA type designation	Maximum allowable conductor temperature, °C	Reference Notes
For exposed wiring in dry locations only	Armoured cable	TECK90	90	8, 9
		AC90	90	8, 9, 37
		ACG90	90	8, 9, 33, 37
		ACIC	250	8, 9, 27, 28, 37
For exposed wiring in dry locations where exposed to corrosive action, if suitable for corrosive conditions encountered	Armoured cable	TECK90	90	2, 8, 9
For exposed wiring in dry locations where not exposed to mechanical damage	Non-metallic-sheathed cable	NMD90	90	20
For exposed wiring in dry locations and in Category 1 and 2 locations, where not exposed to mechanical damage	Non-metallic-sheathed cable	NMW, NMWU	60	20
For exposed wiring in dry or damp locations	Rubber (thermoset) insulated conductor	R90	90	7, 8, 9
	Thermoplastic-insulated conductor	TW	60	—
	Nylon jacketed thermoplastic-insulated conductor	T90 NYLON	90	11
	Non-metallic-sheathed cable	NMD90	90	15, 26
For exposed wiring in wet locations	Armoured cable	TECK90	90	5, 8, 9
		ACWU90	90	5, 8, 9

(Continued)

Δ

Table 19 (Continued)

Conditions of use	Trade designation	CSA type designation	Maximum allowable conductor temperature, °C	Reference Notes
	Rubber (thermoset) insulated conductor	ACGWU90	90	5, 8, 9, 33
		RW75	75	5, 8, 9
		RL90, RW90	90	5, 8, 9
	Aluminum-sheathed cable	RA75	75	5
		RA90	90	5, 8, 9
	Copper-sheathed cable	RC90	90	5, 7, 8, 9
	Mineral-insulated cable	MI, LWMI	90	5, 18
	Thermoplastic-insulated cable	TW	60	5
Ⓔ		TW75, TWN75	75	
	Non-metallic-sheathed cable	NMWU	60	5, 6, 20
For exposed wiring where subjected to the weather	Armoured cable	TECK90	90	8, 9, 30
		ACWU90	90	8, 9, 30
	Rubber (thermoset) insulated conductor	RW75	75	8, 9, 30
		R90, RW90	90	8, 9, 30
	Thermoplastic-insulated conductor	TW, TWU	60	30
Ⓔ		TW75, TWU75	75	30
	Neutral supported cable	NS75	75	30
		NS90	90	30, 31
	Non-metallic-sheathed cable	NMWU	60	6, 20, 30
For concealed wiring in dry locations only	Armoured cable	TECK90	90	8, 9

(Continued)

Table 19 (Continued)

Conditions of use	Trade designation	CSA type designation	Maximum allowable conductor temperature, °C	Reference Notes
		AC90	90	8, 9, 37
		ACG90	90	8, 9, 33, 37
		ACIC	250	8, 9, 27, 28, 37
For concealed wiring in dry and damp locations	Non-metallic-sheathed cable	NMD90	90	15, 20
For concealed wiring in dry locations and in Category 1 and 2 locations where not exposed to mechanical damage	Non-metallic-sheathed cable	NMW, NMWU	60	20
For concealed wiring in wet locations	Armoured cable	TECK90	90	5, 8, 9
		ACWU90	90	5, 8, 9
		ACGWU90	90	5, 8, 9, 33
	Non-metallic-sheathed cable	NMWU	60	5, 6, 20
	Aluminum-sheathed cable	RA75	75	5
		RA90	90	5, 8, 9
	Copper-sheathed cable	RC90	90	5, 7, 8, 9
	Mineral-insulated cable	MI, LWMI	90	5, 18
For use in raceways, except cable trays, in dry or damp locations	Rubber (thermoset) insulated conductor	R90	90	7, 8, 9, 10
	Thermoplastic-insulated conductor	TW	60	—
	Nylon jacketed thermoplastic-insulated conductor	T90 NYLON	90	11
	Solar photovoltaic conductor	RPV90	90	8, 9, 10, 34

(Continued)

Tables

Table 19 (Continued)

Conditions of use	Trade designation	CSA type designation	Maximum allowable conductor temperature, °C	Reference Notes
For use in raceways, except cable trays, in wet locations	Rubber (thermoset) insulated conductor	RW75, RWU75	75	5, 8, 9
		RW90, RWU90	90	5, 8, 9
	Thermoplastic-insulated conductor	TW, TWU	60	4, 5
		TW75, TWN75, TWU75	75	—
	Solar photovoltaic insulated conductor or cable	RPV90, RPVU90	90	5, 8, 9, 34
For use in ventilated, non-ventilated, and ladder-type cable trays in dry locations only	Armoured cable	AC90	90	8, 9, 37
		ACG90	90	8, 9, 33, 37
		TECK90	90	8, 9
		ACIC	250	8, 9, 27, 28, 29, 37
For use in ventilated, non-ventilated, and ladder-type cable trays in wet locations	Armoured cable	TECK90	90	5, 8, 9
		ACWU90	90	5, 8, 9
		ACGWU90	90	5, 8, 9, 33
	Aluminum-sheathed cable	RA75	75	5
		RA90	90	5, 8, 9
	Copper-sheathed cable	RC90	90	5, 7, 8, 9
	Mineral-insulated cable	MI, LWMI	90	5
	Rubber (thermoset) insulated lead-sheathed cable	RL90	90	5, 8, 9

(Continued)

         January 2018

Table 19 (Continued)

Conditions of use	Trade designation	CSA type designation	Maximum allowable conductor temperature, °C	Reference Notes
For use in ventilated and non-ventilated cable trays in vaults and switch rooms	Rubber (thermoset) insulated conductor	RW75	75	8, 9, 10
		RW90	90	8, 9, 10
For direct earth burial (with protection as required by inspection authority)	Armoured cable	ACWU90	90	3, 8, 9
		ACGWU90	90	3, 8, 9, 33
		TECK90	90	3, 8, 9
	Non-metallic-sheathed cable	NMWU	60	3, 20
	Rubber (thermoset) insulated cable	RWU75	75	3, 8, 9
		RL90, RWU90	90	3, 8, 9
	Aluminum-sheathed cable	RA75	75	3
		RA90	90	3, 7, 8
	Copper-sheathed cable	RC90	90	3, 7, 8, 9
	Mineral-insulated cable	MI, LWMI	90	1, 3, 18
	Thermoplastic-insulated cable	TWU	60	3, 5
		TWU75	75	3
	Airport series lighting cable	ASLC	90	19
	Tray cable	TC	90	25
	Solar photovoltaic cable	RPVU90	90	5, 8, 9, 34
For solar photovoltaic wiring	Solar photovoltaic insulated conductor or cable	RPV90, RPVU90	90	5, 8, 9, 34
For service entrance above ground	Armoured cable	AC90	90	16
		ACG90	90	16, 33

(Continued)

Tables

Table 19 (Continued)

Conditions of use	Trade designation	CSA type designation	Maximum allowable conductor temperature, °C	Reference Notes
	Aluminum-sheathed cable	ACWU90	90	—
		ACGWU90	90	33
		TECK90	90	—
	Aluminum-sheathed cable	RA75	75	—
		RA90	90	—
	Copper-sheathed cable	RC90	90	—
	Mineral-insulated cable	MI	90	1, 18
	Neutral supported cable	NS75	75	30
		NS90	90	30, 31
For service entrance below ground	Service entrance cable	USEI75	75	—
		USEI90	90	3, 8, 9
		USEB90	90	3, 8, 9, 12
	Thermoplastic-insulated wire	TWU	60	3
		TWU75	75	3
	Rubber (thermoset) insulated cable	RWU75	75	3, 8, 9
		RWU90	90	3, 8, 9
	Armoured cable	TECK90	90	—
		ACWU90	90	—
		ACGWU90	90	33
	Aluminum-sheathed cable	RA75	75	3
		RA90	90	—

(Continued)

Table 19 (Continued)

Conditions of use	Trade designation	CSA type designation	Maximum allowable conductor temperature, °C	Reference Notes
	Copper-sheathed cable	RC90	90	—
For high-voltage wiring in luminous-tube signs	Luminous-tube sign cable	GTO, GTOL	60	—
For use in raceways in hoistways	Hoistway cable	—	60	13, 14
For use in Class 2 circuits, in exposed or concealed wiring or used in raceways, in dry or damp locations	Extra-low-voltage control cable	LVT	60	—
For use in Class 2 circuits in dry locations in concealed wiring or exposed wiring where not subject to mechanical damage	Extra-low-voltage cable	ELC	60	17
For use when concealed indoors under carpet squares, in dry or damp locations	Flat conductor cable	FCC	60	—
For use in communication circuits when exposed, concealed, or used in raceways; indoors in dry or damp locations; or in ceiling air-handling plenums	Communications cable	CMP, CMR, CMG, CM, CMX, CMH, CMUC	60	21, 32
	Under-carpet communications cable			
	Cross-connect cable			
For use in fire alarm, signal, and voice communication circuits where exposed, concealed, or used in raceways, or indoors in dry or damp locations	Fire alarm and signal cable	FAS	60	22
		FAS90	90	
		FAS105	105	
		FAS200	200	
		MI		
For use in raceways including ventilated, non-ventilated, and ladder-type cable trays in wet locations and where exposed to weather	Tray cable	TC	—	23
For use in cable trays in Class I, Division 2 and Class II, Division 2 hazardous locations	Tray cable	TC	—	23

(Continued)

Tables

Table 19 (Continued)

Conditions of use	Trade designation	CSA type designation	Maximum allowable conductor temperature, °C	Reference Notes
For use in buildings in dry or damp locations, where exposed, concealed, or used in raceways including cable trays, or in plenums	Non-conductive optical fiber cable	OFNP, OFNR, OFNG, OFN, OFNH	—	24
For use in buildings in dry or damp locations, where exposed, concealed, or used in raceways including cable trays, or in plenums	Conductive optical fiber cable	OFCP, OFCR, OFCG, OFC, OFCH	—	24
For use in buildings in dry or damp locations, where exposed or concealed	Hybrid conductor cable	NMDH90	90	—
For concealed wiring used as non-heating leads on heating panels and panel sets	Thermoset insulated conductor	R90, RW90, RWU90 (XLPE, EP insulation only)	90	26
For use in ventilated, non-ventilated, and ladder-type cable trays, direct earth burial, in ceiling air-handling plenums, for exposed or concealed wiring in wet (or damp or dry) locations	Control and instrumentation cable (without armour)	CIC	250 (dry or damp locations) 90 (wet locations)	27, 29, 35
For use in ventilated, non-ventilated, and ladder-type cable trays, direct earth burial, for exposed and concealed wiring in wet (or damp or dry) locations, in ceiling air-handling plenums	Armoured control and instrumentation cable (other than steel wire armour)	ACIC	250 (dry or damp locations) 90 (wet locations)	27, 28, 29
For use in ventilated, non-ventilated, and ladder-type cable trays, direct earth burial, for exposed and concealed wiring in wet (or damp or dry) locations, in ceiling air-handling plenums	Steel wire armour control and instrumentation cable	SW-ACIC	250 (dry or damp locations) 90 (wet locations)	27, 28, 29
For use in Class 2 circuits in exposed or concealed wiring or use in raceways, in dry or damp locations	Communications cable	CMP, CMP-LP, CMR, CMR-LP, CMG, CMG-LP, CM, CM-LP, CMX,	60	21, 32, 36
	Under-carpet communications cable			
	Cross-connect cable			

(Continued)

Table 19 (Continued)

Conditions of use	Trade designation	CSA type designation	Maximum allowable conductor temperature, °C	Reference Notes
		CMX-LP, CMH, CMH-LP, CMUC, CMUC-LP		
	Golf course sprinkler system cable	GCS	60	35
	Lawn sprinkler system cable	LSS	60	35
	Low-voltage landscape lighting cable	LVLL	60	35
For use in Class 2 circuits direct earth burial only	Underground low energy circuit cable	ULEC	60	35
For use in Class 2 circuits in dry locations in concealed wiring or exposed wiring where not subject to mechanical damage	Communications cable	CMP, CMR, CMG, CM, CMX, CMH, CMUC	60	21, 32
	Under-carpet communications cable			
	Cross-connect cable			
	Golf course sprinkler system cable	GCS	60	35
	Lawn sprinkler system cable	LSS	60	35
	Low-voltage landscape lighting cable	LVLL	60	35

(Continued)

Notes:

1) *A maximum sheath temperature of 250 °C is permissible for mineral-insulated cable, provided that the temperature at the terminations does not exceed that specified in Tables 1 and 2. Any protective covering provided shall be suitable for the applicable sheath temperature.*

2) *Shall be permitted to be used where exposed to heat, grease, or corrosive fumes, if suitable for the corrosive condition.*

3) *Cable acceptable for direct earth burial shall be permitted to be used for underground services in accordance with Rule 6-300.*

Tables

Table 19 (Continued)

4) Types TW and TWU, when marked "GRI" or "GRII", are suitable for use where adverse conditions could exist, such as in oil refineries and around gasoline storage or pump areas (e.g., where subjected to alkaline conditions in the presence of petroleum solvents).

5) Types suitable for use in wet locations shall also be permitted to be used in dry or damp locations.

6) Type NMWU cable is not suitable for use in aerial spans.

7) Types having silicone rubber insulation are surface marked with the type designation followed by "silicone".

8) Types having cross-linked polyethylene insulation are surface marked with the type designation followed by "X-Link" or "XLPE", e.g., R90 (X-Link) or R90XLPE.

9) Types having insulation or a covulcanizate of ethylene and propylene with polyethylene are surface marked with the type designation followed by "EP" or "EPCV" respectively, e.g., R90 (EP).

10) Types RW75, RW90, RPV90, and RPVU90, when used under Rule 12-2202, are required to be flame tested.

11) When exposed to oil, Type T90 NYLON is limited to 60 °C.

12) Type USEB90 shall have a non-metallic jacket over a concentric neutral conductor.

13) Hoistway cables may also be provided with 90 °C insulation.

14) Except for short runs not exceeding 1.5 m in length, the parallel construction is intended for use in raceways in which the cables are laid.

15) With thermoplastic jacket in damp locations.

16) For dry locations only.

17) Type ELC cable is limited to Class 2 circuit application as per Rule 16-210.

18) Mineral-insulated cable having a stainless steel sheath requires a separate bonding conductor. See Rule 10-610 4).

19) Type ASLC is for use only in accordance with Section 74.

20) NMD90, NMW, and NMWU were previously marked NMD-7, NMW-9, and NMW-10 respectively.

21) The following cable substitutions shall be permitted:

a) Communications cables, under-carpet communications (CMUC) cables, and cross-connect cables marked CMP, CMR, CMG, CM, CMX, CMH, FT6, FT4, and FT4/IEEE 1202 have been found to meet the standard criteria for FT1.

b) Communications cables, under-carpet communications (CMUC) cables, and cross-connect cables marked CMP, CMR, CMG, and FT6 have been found to meet the standard criteria for FT4 and FT4/IEEE 1202.

c) Communications cables, under-carpet communications (CMUC) cables, and cross-connect cables marked CMP have been found to meet the standard criteria for FT6.

22) Types FAS, FAS90, FAS105, and FAS200 may be provided with mechanical protection such as interlock armour or an aluminum sheath, with or without an overall thermoplastic covering. A thermoplastic covering shall be provided over the interlock armoured cable when it is installed in a damp location.

23) The maximum allowable conductor insulation temperature for Type TC cables depends on the temperature rating, which is marked on the cable.

24) OFNP, OFNR, OFNG, OFN, OFNH, OFCP, OFCR, OFCG, OFC, and OFCH shall have a minimum cable temperature rating of 60 °C. Cables having a temperature rating greater than 60 °C shall be permitted, provided that the temperature rating is surface marked on the cable.

25) Type TC cable directly buried in the earth shall be marked as suitable for the purpose.

26) Types R90, RW90, and RWU90 are required to be marked as suitable for the use when used as non-heating leads in accordance with Section 62.

(Continued)

Table 19 (Concluded)

27) The maximum allowable conductor insulation temperature(s) for wet and/or dry locations depends on the material in the cable and is marked on the outer covering of the cable.

28) When cables are installed in Category 2 locations (see Rule 22-202), they shall be suitable for the corrosive conditions encountered.

29) Proper additional markings are needed when used on cable trays.

30) Insulated conductors and cables suitable for exposed wiring where exposed to the weather are marked as such.

31) The type designations of 90 °C rated neutral supported cables reflect their maximum temperature ratings.

32) Cables having a temperature rating greater than 60 °C shall be permitted, provided that the temperature rating is surface marked on the cable.

33) Types ACG90 and ACGWU90 include a full-size bare aluminum bonding conductor with the insulated conductors in direct intimate contact with the interlocked armour. Fittings to be used with Types ACG90 and ACGWU90 are marked accordingly, either on the fitting or on the smallest unit carton.

34) Types RPV insulated conductors and RPVU cables are available with temperature ratings in excess of 90 °C.

35) Types CIC, GCS, LSS, and LVLL are suitable for direct earth burial if marked "DIRECT BURIAL" or "DIR BUR". Type ULEC shall be used for direct burial only and is marked "DIRECT BURIAL ONLY" or "DIR-BUR ONLY".

36) Limited-power-type cables used in accordance with Rule 16-330 are marked with the suffix "-LP" and "(xx A)", where xx denotes the maximum allowable ampacity per conductor.

37) The CSA type designation may be followed with the suffix "-PCS" indicating that the cable is suitable for power, control, and signal applications. The insulated control and signal conductors are jacketed for separation from the insulated power conductors.

Tables

Table 20
Spacings for insulated conductors
(See Rules 12-204 and 12-214.)

Voltage of circuit, V	Minimum distance, mm	
	Between insulated conductors	From adjacent surfaces
0 to 300	65	13
301 to 750	100	25

Table 21
Supporting of insulated conductors in vertical runs of raceways
(See Rule 12-120.)

Conductor sizes, AWG or kcmil	Maximum distance, m	
	Copper	Aluminum
14 to 8	30	30
6 to 0	30	60
00 to 0000	24	55
250 to 350	18	40
Over 350 to 500	15	35
Over 500 to 750	12	30
Over 750	10	25

Table 22
Space for insulated conductors in boxes
(See Rule 12-3034.)

Size of conductor, AWG	Usable space required for each insulated conductor, mL
14	24.6
12	28.7
10	36.9
8	45.1
6	73.7

Table 23
Number of insulated conductors in boxes
(See Rule 12-3034.)

Box dimensions trade size		Capacity, mL (in³)	Maximum number of conductors (per AWG size)				
			14	12	10	8	6
Octagonal	4 × 1-1/2	245 (15)	10	8	6	5	3
	4 × 2-1/8	344 (21)	14	12	9	7	4
Square	4 × 1-1/2	344 (21)	14	12	9	7	4
	4 × 2-1/8	491 (30)	20	17	13	10	6
	4-11/16 × 1-1/2	491 (30)	20	17	13	10	6
	4-11/16 × 2-1/8	688 (42)	28	24	18	15	9
Round	4 × 1/2	81 (5)	3	2	2	1	1
Device	3 × 2 × 1-1/2	131 (8)	5	4	3	2	1
	3 × 2 × 2	163 (10)	6	5	4	3	2
	3 × 2 × 2-1/4	163 (10)	6	5	4	3	2
	3 × 2 × 2-1/2	204 (12.5)	8	7	5	4	2
	3 × 2 × 3	245 (15)	10	8	6	5	3
	4 × 2 × 1-1/2	147 (9)	6	5	4	3	2
	4 × 2-1/8 × 1-7/8	229 (14)	9	8	6	5	3
	4 × 2-3/8 × 1-7/8	262 (16)	10	9	7	5	3
Masonry	3-3/4 × 2 × 2-1/2	229 (14)/gang	9	8	6	5	3
	3-3/4 × 2 × 3-1/2	344 (21)/gang	14	12	9	7	4
	4 × 2-1/4 × 2-3/8	331 (20.25)/gang	13	11	9	7	4
	4 × 2-1/4 × 3-3/8	364 (22.25)/gang	14	12	9	8	4
Through box	3-3/4 × 2	3.8/mm (6/in) depth	4	3	2	2	1
Concrete ring	4	7.7/mm (12/in) depth	8	6	5	4	2
FS	1 Gang	229 (14)	9	8	6	5	3
	1 Gang tandem	557 (34)	22	19	15	12	7
	2 Gang	426 (26)	17	14	11	9	5
	3 Gang	671 (41)	27	23	18	14	9
	4 Gang	917 (56)	37	32	24	20	12
FD	1 Gang	368 (22.5)	15	12	10	8	5

(Continued)

Table 23 (Concluded)

Box dimensions trade size	Capacity, mL (in³)	Maximum number of conductors (per AWG size)				
		14	12	10	8	6
2 Gang	671 (41)	27	23	18	14	9
3 Gang	983 (60)	40	34	26	21	13
4 Gang	1392 (85)	56	48	37	30	18

Table 24
Minimum insulation resistances for installations
(See Rule 70-130.)

Installation, copper or aluminum	Insulation resistance, Ω
For circuits of No. 14 or No. 12 AWG	1 000 000
For circuits of No. 10 AWG or larger:	
25 to 50 A	250 000
51 to 100 A	100 000
101 to 200 A	50 000
201 to 400 A	25 000
401 to 800 A	12 000
Over 800 A	5 000

Note: *Where lampholders, receptacles, luminaires, baseboard heaters, or other appliances are connected to the installation or where excessive humidity exists, lower insulation resistance values may be expected.*

Table 25
Overcurrent trip coils for circuit breakers and
overload devices for protecting motors
(See Rules 14-306 and 28-304.)

For circuit protection*		For motor overload protection	
Number and location of overcurrent devices (trip coils)	**System**	**Number and location of overload devices such as trip coils, relays, or thermal cut-outs**	**Kind of motor**
3-trip coils, one in each conductor	3-wire, 3-phase ac, ungrounded or with grounded neutral	3 — one in each phase not to be connected in any neutral conductor	3-phase ac
3-trip coils, one in each phase	4-wire, 3-phase ac		
2-trip coils, one in each phase†	4-wire, 2-phase ac, ungrounded	2 — one in each phase, not to be connected in any neutral or grounded conductor	2-phase ac
2-trip coils, one in each outside conductor	3-wire, 2-phase ac		
4-trip coils, one in each ungrounded conductor	4-wire, 2-phase ac, with grounded neutral		
4-trip coils, one in each ungrounded conductor	5-wire, 2-phase ac		
2-trip coils, one in each outside conductor	3-wire, 1-phase ac or dc	1 — in any conductor except a neutral or grounded conductor	1-phase ac or dc
1-trip coil in each ungrounded conductor	2-wire ac or dc, ungrounded or with one conductor grounded‡		
2-trip coils, one in each ungrounded conductor	3-wire, 1-phase ac or dc, with grounded neutral		

* This does not preclude the use of other arrangements that will provide equivalent protection.

† For services, see Section 6.

‡ This does not preclude the use of one single-pole circuit breaker in each insulated conductor for the protection of an ungrounded 2-wire circuit.

Table 26
This Table is now Table D16

Tables

Table 27
Determining conductor sizes for motors for different requirements of service
(See Rules 28-106, 28-112, and 38-013.)

Classification of service	Percentage of nameplate current rating of motor			
	5-minute rating	15-minute rating	30- and 60-minute rating	Continuous rating
Short-time duty Operating valves, raising or lowering rolls, etc.	110	120	150	—
Intermittent duty Freight and passenger elevators, tool heads, pumps, drawbridges, turntables, etc.	85	85	90	140
Periodic duty Rolls, ore- and coal-handling machines, etc.	85	90	95	140
Varying duty	110	120	150	200

Note: *For motor-generator arc welders, see Section 42.*

Table 28
Determining conductor sizes in the secondary circuits of motors
(See Rule 28-112.)

Resistor duty classification	Duty cycles	Carrying capacity of insulated conductors in per cent of full load secondary circuit
Light starting duty	5 s on 75 s off	35
Heavy starting duty	10 s on 70 s off	45
Extra-heavy starting duty	15 s on 75 s off	55
Light intermittent duty	15 s on 45 s off	65
Medium intermittent duty	15 s on 30 s off	75
Heavy intermittent duty	15 s on 15 s off	90
Continuous duty	Continuous duty	110

Δ
Table 29
Rating or setting of overcurrent devices for the protection of motor branch circuits
(See Rules 28-200, 28-206, 28-208, and 28-308 and Table D16.)

Type of motor	Full load current, %		Maximum setting inverse-time circuit breaker
	Maximum fuse rating		
	Time-delay* fuses	Non-time-delay	
Alternating current			
Single-phase all types	175	300	250
Squirrel-cage and synchronous:			
Full-voltage, resistor and reactor starting	175	300	250
Auto-transformer and star delta starting:			
Not more than 30 A	175	250	200
More than 30 A	175	200	200
Wound rotor	150	150	150
Direct current	150	150	150

* *Includes time-delay "D" fuses referred to in Rule 14-200.*

Notes:

1) *Synchronous motors of the low-torque, low-speed type (usually 450 rpm or lower), such as those used to drive reciprocating compressors, pumps, etc., and that start up unloaded, do not require a fuse rating or circuit breaker setting in excess of 200% of full load current.*

2) *For the use of instantaneous-trip (magnetic only) circuit breakers in motor branch circuits, see Rule 28-210.*

Tables

Table 30
Minimum clearances for bus support and rigid conductors
(See Rule 36-108.)

Maximum system voltage, kV	Minimum air gap distance, mm			
	From live parts to adjacent surfaces other than insulation and bases of bare conductor supports*	Between live parts† (not centre-to-centre)		
	Indoor and outdoor	Indoor	Outdoor
Not exceeding 7.5	190	150	180
15	260	230	305
25	305	330	380
		Indoor and outdoor	
34.5	380	460	
46	460	530	
69	740	790	
120	1200	1350	
161	1560	1830	
230	2300	2670	

* *For ungrounded systems, the maximum system voltage is the phase-to-phase voltage, and for grounded systems, it is the phase-to-ground voltage.*
† *For all systems, the maximum system voltage is the phase-to-phase voltage.*

Table 31
Minimum horizontal separations of line conductors
attached to the same supporting structure
(See Rule 36-108.)

Maximum system voltage*, kV	Minimum separation of conductors for span 50 m or less†, mm
Not exceeding 5.0	300
7.5	325
15	400
25	500
34.5	600
46	700
69	950

* *For all systems, the maximum system voltage is the phase-to-phase voltage.*
† *For voltages greater than 69 kV and for spans greater than 50 m, the requirements of CSA C22.3 No. 1 shall apply.*

Table 32
Vertical isolation of unguarded live parts
(See Rule 36-110 and Appendix B.)

Maximum system voltage*, kV	Minimum separation from ground, m			
	Areas accessible to pedestrians only			
	Indoors	Outdoors		Areas likely to be travelled by vehicles
		Light snow area†	Heavy snow area†	
Not exceeding 15	2.9	3.4	4.0	4.7
25	3.2	3.7	4.3	5.2
34.5	3.2	3.7	4.3	5.2
46	3.2	3.7	4.3	5.2
69	3.5	4.0	4.6	5.5
120	4.0	4.5	5.1	6.0
161	4.4	4.9	5.5	6.4
230	4.8	5.3	5.9	6.8

* *For ungrounded systems, the maximum system voltage is the phase-to-phase voltage, and for grounded systems, it is the phase-to-ground voltage.*
† *See Appendix B.*

Note: *Radial clearances from live parts shall be maintained in accordance with this Table where conductors overhang the edge of a building or structure, including any protuberances.*

Table 33
Horizontal clearances from adjacent structures (including protuberances)*
(See Rules 26-302 and 36-110 and Appendix B.)

Maximum system voltage†, kV	Clearance, m
Not exceeding 46.0	3
69	3.7

* *See Appendix B.*
† *For ungrounded systems, the maximum system voltage is the phase-to-phase voltage, and for grounded systems, it is the phase-to-ground voltage.*

Table 34
Vertical ground clearances for open line conductors*
(See Rule 36-110 and Appendix B.)

Maximum system voltage†, kV	Minimum vertical clearances above ground, m
Not exceeding 25.0	6.1
34.5	6.7
46	7
69	7.6

* See Appendix B.

† For ungrounded systems, the maximum system voltage is the phase-to-phase voltage, and for grounded systems, it is the phase-to-ground voltage.

Table 35
Spacing for switches and fuses assembled in the field
(not of the metal-enclosed type)
(See Rule 36-212.)

Maximum system voltage*, kV	Minimum phase spacing (centre-to-centre), mm	
	Disconnect switches and fuses other than the expulsion type	Horn-gap switches and expulsion fuses
Not exceeding 7.5	460	915
15	610	915
25	760	1220
34.5	915	1520
46	1220	1830
69	1520	2130
120	2130	3050
161	2740	4270
230	3960	5500

* For all systems, the maximum system voltage is the phase-to-phase voltage.

Table 36A
Maximum allowable ampacity for aluminum conductor neutral supported cables
[See Rule 4-004 5).]

Phase conductor size, AWG or kcmil	Ampacity, A NS75		Ampacity, A NS90	
	Duplex, triplex	Quadruplex	Duplex, triplex	Quadruplex
6	80	70	95	85
4	105	95	125	110
2	140	125	165	150
1	160	145	190	170
1/0	185	165	220	200
2/0	210	190	255	230
3/0	245	220	290	265
4/0	280	255	335	305
266.8	325	290	390	355
336.4	375	335	450	410
397.5	415	370	500	455
477	460	415	560	510
500	500	450	605	555

Notes:

1) *The ampacity ratings are based on a 30 °C ambient temperature and wind velocity of 0.6 m/s and sun-radiated heat energy of 1025 W/m².*

2) *For ambient temperatures of 30 °C, 35 °C, and 40 °C, multiply the values in this Table by the corresponding correction factor of 1.0, 0.94, and 0.88, respectively.*

Tables

Table 36B
Maximum allowable ampacity for copper conductor neutral supported cables
[See Rule 4-004 5).]

Phase conductor size, AWG	Ampacity, A NS75		Ampacity, A NS90	
	Duplex, triplex	Quadruplex	Duplex, triplex	Quadruplex
6	100	90	120	110
4	135	120	155	140
2	175	160	210	190
1	205	185	240	220
1/0	235	210	280	255
2/0	270	245	325	295
3/0	310	280	370	335
4/0	360	320	430	390

Notes:

1) *The ampacity ratings are based on a 30 °C ambient temperature and wind velocity of 0.6 m/s and sun-radiated heat energy of 1025 W/m².*

2) *For ambient temperatures of 30 °C, 35 °C, and 40 °C, multiply the values in this Table by the corresponding correction factor of 1.0, 0.92, and 0.84, respectively.*

Table 37
Motor supply conductor insulation minimum temperature rating, °C
(based on an ambient temperature of 30 °C)
(See Rule 28-104.)

Motor enclosure	Insulation class rating			
	A	B	F	H
All except totally enclosed non-ventilated	75	75	90	110
Totally enclosed non-ventilated	75	90	110	110

Δ

Table 38
Electric vehicle supply equipment demand factors
(See Rules 8-202 to 8-210.)

Number of automobile spaces or stalls per feeder	Maximum load per space or stall, W	Demand factor, %
1 to 4	2000	100
	4000	100
	6000	100
	8000 or more	100
5 to 8	2000	100
	4000	100
	6000	90
	8000 or more	90
9 to 12	2000	100
	4000	90
	6000	90
	8000 or more	80
13 to 16	2000	100
	4000	90
	6000	80
	8000 or more	80
17 to 24	2000	100
	4000	90
	6000	80
	8000 or more	70
25 and over	2000	100
	4000	90
	6000	70
	8000 or more	70

Tables

Δ

Table 39
Minimum permitted size for 3-wire 120/240 V and 120/208 V service conductors for single dwellings and feeder conductors or cables supplying single dwelling units of row housing, apartment, or similar buildings and terminating on equipment having a conductor termination temperature of not less than 75 °C
[See Rule 4-004 22).]

Ⓔ

Overcurrent device rating, A	Copper [See Note 2)]		Aluminum [See Note 2)]	
	For calculated loads up to, A*	Conductor size, AWG or kcmil	For calculated loads up to, A*	Conductor size, AWG or kcmil
60	60	6	53	6
100	89	4	95	2
125	121	2	125	1/0
200	184	2/0	189	4/0
225	210	3/0	215	250
400	352	400	357	600

* *These ampacities are the ampacities given in Tables 2 and 4 for 75 °C, increased by 5%.*

Notes:

1) *This Table applies only to conductors sized for loads calculated in accordance with Rules 8-200 1) a), 8-200 2), or 8-202 1).*

2) *If the calculated load exceeds the limit shown in this Table, the next larger size insulated conductor or cable shall be used.*

Table 40
External tapered threads for rigid metal conduit
(See Rule 12-1006.)

Trade size of conduit	Number of threads per 25.4 mm	External threads	
		Length of thread	
		Minimum, mm	Maximum, mm
16	14	16.3	19.8
21	14	16.5	20.1
27	11-1/2	20.6	24.9
35	11-1/2	21.3	25.7
41	11-1/2	21.8	26.2
53	11-1/2	22.6	26.9
63	8	33.5	39.9
78	8	34.5	41.4
91	8	36.3	42.7
103	8	37.6	43.9
129	8	40.4	46.7
155	8	43.2	49.5

Table 41
Minimum size of bonding jumper for service raceways
(See Rule 70-126.)

Ampacity of largest service conductor or equivalent for multiple conductors, A	Size of bonding jumper	
	Copper wire, AWG	Aluminum wire, AWG
100 or less	8	6
200	6	4
400	4	2
600	2	0
800	0	00
1000	00	000
1200	000	0000

Table 42
Deleted

Table 43
Minimum conductor size for concrete-encased electrodes
(See Rule 10-102.)

Ampacity of largest service conductor or equivalent for multiple conductors, A	Size of bare copper conductor, AWG
165 or less	4
166–200	3
201–260	2
261–355	0
356–475	00
Over 475	000

Table 44
Three-phase ac motors
(See Rules 28-010 and 28-704.)

Three-phase	AC motor full load current, A [see Notes 1), 2), and 4)]							Synchronous type, unity power factor [see Note 3)], A				
	Induction type, squirrel-cage and wound rotor, A											
Motor rating, hp	115 V	200 V	208 V	230 V	460 V	575 V	2300 V	200 V	230 V	460 V	575 V	2300 V
1/2	4.4	2.5	2.4	2.2	1	0.9	—	—	—	—	—	—
3/4	6.4	3.7	3.5	3.2	1.4	1.3	—	—	—	—	—	—
1	8.4	4.8	4.6	4.2	1.8	1.7	—	—	—	—	—	—
1-1/2	12.0	6.9	6.6	6.0	2.6	2.4	—	—	—	—	—	—
2	13.6	7.8	7.5	6.8	3.4	2.7	—	—	—	—	—	—
3	19.2	11.0	10.6	9.6	4.8	3.9	—	—	—	—	—	—
5	30.4	17.5	16.7	15.2	7.6	6.1	—	—	—	—	—	—
7-1/2	44	25.3	24.2	22	11	9	—	—	—	—	—	—
10	56	32.2	30.8	28	14	11	—	—	—	—	—	—
15	84	48.3	46.2	42	21	17	—	—	—	—	—	—
20	108	62.1	59.4	54	27	22	—	—	—	—	—	—
25	136	78.2	74.8	68	34	27	—	62	54	27	22	—
30	160	92	88	80	40	32	—	75	65	33	26	—
40	208	120	114	104	52	41	—	99	86	43	35	—
50	260	150	143	130	65	52	—	124	108	54	44	—

(Continued)

Table 44 (Concluded)

Three-phase	AC motor full load current, A [see Notes 1), 2), and 4)]											
	Induction type, squirrel-cage and wound rotor, A							Synchronous type, unity power factor [see Note 3)], A				
Motor rating, hp	115 V	200 V	208 V	230 V	460 V	575 V	2300 V	200 V	230 V	460 V	575 V	2300 V
60	—	177	169	154	77	62	16	147	128	64	51	12
75	—	221	211	192	96	77	20	185	161	81	65	15
100	—	285	273	248	124	99	26	243	211	106	85	20
125	—	359	343	312	156	125	31	304	264	132	106	25
150	—	414	396	360	180	144	37	—	—	158	127	30
200	—	552	528	480	240	192	49	—	—	210	168	40
250	—	—	—	604	302	242	—	—	—	—	—	—
300	—	—	—	722	361	289	—	—	—	—	—	—
350	—	—	—	828	414	336	—	—	—	—	—	—
400	—	—	—	954	477	382	—	—	—	—	—	—
450	—	—	—	1030	515	412	—	—	—	—	—	—
500	—	—	—	1180	590	472	—	—	—	—	—	—

Notes:

1) These values of motor full load current are to be used as guides only. Where exact values are required (e.g., for motor protection), always use the values on the motor nameplate.

2) These values of motor full load current are for motors running at speeds typical for belted motors and motors with normal torque characteristics. Motors built for especially low speeds or high torques may require more running current, and multi-speed motors have full load current varying with speed, in which case the nameplate current ratings shall be used.

3) For 90 and 80% power factor, multiply the values in this Table by 1.1 and 1.25, respectively.

4) The voltages listed are rated motor voltages. Corresponding nominal system voltages are 120, 208, 240, 480, and 600 V. Refer to CSA CAN3-C235.

Table 45
Single-phase ac motors
(See Rules 28-010 and 28-704.)

Single-phase ac motors full load current, A
[see Notes 1) to 4)]

hp rating	115 V	230 V
1/6	4.4	2.2
1/4	5.8	2.9
1/3	7.2	3.6
1/2	9.8	4.9
3/4	13.8	6.9
1	16	8
1-1/2	20	10
2	24	12
3	34	17
5	56	28
7-1/2	80	40
10	100	50

Notes:

1) *For full load currents of 208 and 200 V motors, increase the corresponding 230 V motor full load current by 10 and 15%, respectively.*

2) *These values of motor full load current are to be used as guides only. Where exact values are required (e.g., for motor protection), always use the values on the motor nameplate.*

3) *These values of full load current are for motors running at their usual speeds and motors with normal torque characteristics. Motors built for especially low speeds or high torques may have higher full load currents, and multi-speed motors have full load current varying with speed, in which case the nameplate current ratings shall be used.*

4) *The voltages listed are rated motor voltages. Corresponding nominal system voltages are 120 and 240 V. Refer to CSA CAN3-C235.*

Table 46
This Table is now Diagram 1

Table 47
This Table is now Diagram 2

Table 48
Size of conduit for mobile homes
(See Rule 70-104.)

Rating of main overcurrent protection, A	Minimum trade size of conduit	
	Excluding system ground	Including system ground
50	27	35
60	35	35
100	35	41
150	53	53
200	53	63

Note: *These sizes are based on the use of copper conductors.*

Table 49
This Table is now Diagram 3

Table 50
Transformers rated over 750 V having primary and secondary overcurrent protection
(See Rule 26-250.)

Transformer rated impedance	Maximum setting or rating of overcurrent device as a percentage of rated current of transformer				
	Primary side		Secondary side		
	Over 750 V		Over 750 V		750 V or less
	Circuit breaker setting, %	Fuse rating, %	Circuit breaker setting, %	Fuse rating, %	Circuit breaker setting or fuse rating, %
Not more than 7.5%	600	300	300	150	250
More than 7.5% and not more than 10%	400	200	250	125	250

Table 51
Minimum size of bare copper grounding conductors
(See Rules 36-300 and 36-308 and Appendix B.)

| Maximum available short-circuit current, A | Maximum fault duration | | | |
| | 0.5 s | | 1.0 s | |
	With exothermic weld, compression or bolted joint	With brazed joint	With exothermic weld, compression or bolted joint	With brazed joint
5 000	6	5	4	3
10 000	3	2	1	1/0
15 000	1	1/0	1/0	3/0
20 000	1/0	2/0	3/0	4/0
25 000	2/0	3/0	4/0	250*
30 000	3/0	4/0	4/0	300*
35 000	4/0	250*	250*	350*
40 000	4/0	300*	300*	400*
50 000	250*	350*	350*	500*
60 000	300*	400*	500*	600*
70 000	350*	500*	500*	700*
80 000	400*	600*	600*	800*
90 000	500*	600*	700*	900*
100 000	500*	700*	700*	1000*

* *Wire size in kcmil, all others in AWG.*

Note: *Sizes are calculated in accordance with IEEE 80.*

Tables

Δ

Table 52
Tolerable touch and step voltages
(See Rules 36-304, 36-306, 36-308, 36-310, and 36-312.)

Type of ground	Soil resistivity (infinite depth), Ω•m	Fault duration, 0.5 s		Fault duration, 1.0 s	
		Step voltage, V	Touch voltage, V	Step voltage, V	Touch voltage, V
Wet organic soil	10	174	167	123	118
Moist soil	100	262	189	186	133
150 mm (3000 Ω•m) stone over moist soil	100	2458	738	1738	522
100 mm (10 000 Ω•m) unbroken asphalt over moist soil	100	6983	1869	4938	1321
Bedrock	10 000	10 007	2625	7076	1856

Notes:

1) *The step and touch voltage values given in this Table are calculated in accordance with IEEE 80 for a body weight of 50 kg.*

2) *In a typical substation installation, the entire ground surface inside the station fence is covered with 150 mm crushed stone having a minimum tested resistivity of 3000 Ω•m when wet.*

3) *Values shall not be interpolated in this Table for other soil resistivities, fault durations, or surface-layer treatments. IEEE 80 prescribes a methodology for such variations.*

Table 53
Minimum cover requirements for direct buried cables
or insulated conductors in raceways
(See Rule 12-012.)

Wiring method	Minimum cover, mm			
	Non-vehicular areas		Vehicular areas	
	750 V or less	Over 750 V	750 V or less	Over 750 V
Cable not having a metal sheath or armour	600	750	900	1000
Cable having a metal sheath or armour	450	750	600	1000
Raceway	450	750	600	1000

Note: *Minimum cover means the distance between the top surface of the conductor, cable, or raceway and the finished grade.*

Table 54
This Table is now Diagram 4

Table 55
This Table is now Diagram 5

Table 56
**Minimum working space around electrical equipment
having exposed live parts**
(See Rule 2-308.)

Nominal voltage-to-ground	Working space, m
0–750	1.0
751–2 500	1.2
2 501–9 000	1.5
9 001–25 000	1.9
25 001–46 000	2.5
46 001–69 000	3.0
Over 69 000	3.7

Tables

Table 57
Allowable ampacities for Class 2 copper conductors
(based on an ambient temperature of 30 °C†)
[See Rule 16-210 6) and Table 5A.]

Size, AWG	Single conductors in free air, A	Not more than three copper conductors in raceway or cable*, A
26	3	1
24	4	2
22	5	2.5
20	7	3.5
19	8	4
18	9	5
16	13	10
Col. 1	**Col. 2**	**Col. 3**

* *Where more than three conductors are in a raceway or cable, apply the following derating factors to Column 3:*

Conductors in raceway or cable	Derating factor
4–6	0.8
7–24	0.7
25–42	0.6
43–50	0.5

† *For ambient temperatures over 30 °C for Columns 2 and 3, apply the correction factors of Table 5A, Column 2.*

Table 58
Ampacities of up to four insulated copper conductors in raceway or cable for short-time-rated crane and hoist motors
(based on an ambient temperature of 30 °C)
(See Rule 40-002.)

Maximum operating temperature	75 °C		90 °C		110 °C	
Size, AWG or kcmil	60 minutes	30 minutes	60 minutes	30 minutes	60 minutes	30 minutes
16	10	12	—	—	—	—
14	25	26	31	32	38	40
12	30	33	36	40	45	50
10	40	43	49	52	60	65
8	55	60	63	69	73	80
6	76	86	83	94	93	105
5	85	95	95	106	109	121
4	100	117	111	130	126	147
3	120	141	131	153	145	168
2	137	160	148	173	163	190
1	143	175	158	192	177	215
0	190	233	211	259	239	294
00	222	267	245	294	275	331
000	280	341	305	372	339	413
0000	300	369	319	399	352	440
250	364	420	400	461	447	516
300	455	582	497	636	554	707
350	486	646	542	716	616	809
400	538	688	593	760	666	856
450	600	765	660	836	740	930
500	660	847	726	914	815	1004

Notes:

1) *Allowable ampacities of copper conductors used with 15 minute motors shall be the 30 minute ratings increased by 12%.*

2) *For five or more simultaneously energized power conductors in raceway or cable, the ampacity of each shall be reduced to 80% of that shown in this Table.*

3) *For conductors subject to ambient temperatures in excess of 30 °C, the derating factors in Table 5A shall apply to the ampacities shown in this Table.*

Tables

Table 59
Minimum size of protector grounding conductors for communications systems
(See Rule 60-704.)

| Size, AWG | Maximum number of protected circuits | |
	Fuseless	Fused
No. 14	1	3
No. 12	2	6
No. 10	6	7
No. 6	7 or more	8 or more

Note: *The grounding conductor between protectors shall be of at least the minimum size required in this Table for the maximum number of protected circuits.*

Table 60
Allowable ampacities for copper, eight-conductor, Class 2 power and data communication circuit cables
(based on an ambient temperature of 30 °C)

(See Rule 16-330.)

Δ

Allowable ampacity

Number of cables in one cable bundle

Size, AWG	1			2–7			8–19			20–37			38–61			62–91			92–192		
	60 °C	75 °C	90 °C	60 °C	75 °C	90 °C	60 °C	75 °C	90 °C	60 °C	75 °C	90 °C	60 °C	75 °C	90 °C	60 °C	75 °C	90 °C	60 °C	75 °C	90 °C
26	1.0	1.0	1.0	1.0	1.0	1.0	0.7	0.8	1.0	0.5	0.6	0.7	0.4	0.5	0.6	0.4	0.5	0.6	–	–	–
24	2.0	2.0	2.0	1.0	1.4	1.6	0.8	1.0	1.1	0.6	0.7	0.9	0.5	0.6	0.7	0.4	0.5	0.6	0.3	0.4	0.5
23	2.5	2.5	2.5	1.2	1.5	1.7	0.8	1.1	1.2	0.6	0.8	0.9	0.5	0.7	0.8	0.5	0.7	0.8	0.4	0.5	0.6
22	3.0	3.0	3.0	1.4	1.8	2.1	1.0	1.2	1.4	0.7	0.9	1.1	0.6	0.8	0.9	0.6	0.8	0.9	0.5	0.6	0.7

Note: Ampacities shown are for each conductor of the eight-conductor cable.

Table 61
Minimum buried cable horizontal separations from pools
(See Rule 68-056.)

Type of installation	Minimum horizontal separation, m	
	Direct buried unjacketed cable with bare neutral or cables with a semi-conducting jacket	Cables with a non-conducting jacket or conductors in non-conducting ducts
Communication conductors	1.5	1.0
Power conductors		
0–750 V	1.5	1.0
751–15 000 V	3.0	1.5
15 001–28 000 V	6.0	2.0

Notes:

1) *Voltages are phase-to-phase.*
2) *This Table is derived from CEA 266 D 991.*
3) *The separation from non-conducting ducts is measured from the nearest edge of the duct to the inside wall of the pool.*

Table 62
Feeder demand factors for elevators
[See Rules 38-013 2) and 38-014.]

Number of elevators on a single feeder	Demand factor (DF)
1	1.00
2	0.95
3	0.90
4	0.85
5	0.82
6	0.79
7	0.77
8	0.75
9	0.73
10 or more	0.72

Note: *Demand factors (DFs) are based on 50% duty (i.e., half time load, half time no load).*

Table 63
Hazardous areas for propane dispensing, container filling, and storage
(See Rule 20-034.)

Part	Location	Extent of hazardous locations*	Group IIA hazardous location
A	Storage containers other than TC/CTC/DOT cylinders and ASME vertical containers of less than 454 kg water capacity	Within 4.5 m in all directions from connections, except connections otherwise covered in this Table	Zone 2
B	Tank vehicle and tank car loading and unloading†	Within 3 m in all directions from connections regularly made or disconnected from product transfer	Zone 1
		Beyond 3 m but within 7.5 m in all directions from a point where connections are regularly made or disconnected and within the cylindrical volume between the horizontal equator of the sphere and grade (see Diagram 7)	Zone 2
C	Gauge vent openings other than those on TC/CTC/DOT cylinders and ASME vertical containers of less than 454 kg water capacity	Within 1.5 m in all directions from point of discharge	Zone 1
		Beyond 1.5 m but within 4.5 m in all directions from point of discharge	Zone 2
D	Relief device discharge other than those on CTC/DOT cylinders and ASME vertical containers of less than 454 kg water capacity	Within direct path of discharge‡	Zone 1
		Within 1.5 m in all directions from point of discharge	Zone 1
		Beyond 1.5 m but within 4.5 m in all directions from point of discharge except within the direct path of discharge	Zone 2
E	Pumps, vapour compressors, gas-air mixers, and vaporizers (other than direct-fired or indirect-fired with an attached or adjacent gas-fired heat source)	—	—
	Indoors without ventilation	Entire room and any adjacent room not separated by a gas-tight partition	Zone 1
		Within 4.5 m of the exterior side of any exterior wall or roof that is not vapour-tight or within 4.5 m of any exterior opening	Zone 2

(Continued)

Table 63 (Continued)

Part	Location	Extent of hazardous locations*	Group IIA hazardous location
	Indoors with adequate ventilation	Entire room and any adjacent room not separated by a gas-tight partition	Zone 2
	Outdoors in open air at or above grade	Within 4.5 m in all directions from this equipment and within the cylindrical volume between the horizontal equator of the sphere and grade (see Diagram 8)	Zone 2
F	Service station dispensing units	Entire space within dispenser enclosure or up to a solid partition within the enclosure at any height above the base. The space within 450 mm horizontally from the dispenser enclosure up to 1.2 m above the base or to the height of a solid partition within the enclosure. Entire pit or open space beneath the dispenser	Zone 1
		The space above a solid partition within the dispenser enclosure. The space up to 450 mm above grade within 6 m horizontally from any edge of the dispenser enclosure§	Zone 2
G	Pits or trenches containing or located beneath propane gas valves, pumps, vapour compressors, regulators, and similar equipment	—	—
	Without mechanical ventilation	Entire pit or trench	Zone 1
		Entire room and any adjacent room not separated by a gas-tight partition	Zone 2
		Within 4.5 m in all directions from a pit or trench when located outdoors	Zone 2
	With adequate mechanical ventilation	Entire pit or trench	Zone 2
		Entire room and any adjacent room not separated by a gas-tight partition	Zone 2
		Within 4.5 m in all directions from a pit or trench when located outdoors	Zone 2

(Continued)

Table 63 (Concluded)

Part	Location	Extent of hazardous locations*	Group IIA hazardous location
H	Special buildings or rooms for storage of portable containers	Entire room	Zone 2
I	Pipelines and connections containing operational bleeds, drips, vents, or drains	Within 1.5 m in all directions from point of discharge	Zone 1
		Beyond 1.5 m from point of discharge, same as Part E of this Table	See Part E
J	Container filling	—	—
	Indoors with adequate ventilation	Within 1.5 m in all directions from the dispensing hose inlet connections for product transfer	Zone 1
		Beyond 1.5 m and entire room	Zone 2
	Outdoors in open air	Within 1.5 m in all directions from the dispensing hose inlet connections for product transfer	Zone 1
		Beyond 1.5 but within 4.5 m in all directions from the dispensing hose inlet connections and within the cylindrical volume between the horizontal equator of the sphere and grade (see Diagram 9)	Zone 2
K	Outdoor storage area for portable cylinders or containers	—	—
	Aggregate storage up to and including 454 kg water capacity	Within 1.5 m in all directions from connections	Zone 2
	Aggregate storage over 454 kg water capacity	Within 4.5 m in all directions from connections	Zone 2

* The classified area shall not extend beyond an unpierced wall, roof, or solid vapour-tight partition.

† When the extent of a hazardous area is being classified, consideration shall be given to possible variations in the locating of tank cars and tank vehicles at the unloading points and the effect these variations of location may have on the point of connection.

‡ Fixed electrical equipment should not be installed in this space.

§ For pits within this area, see Part G of this Table.

Δ

Table 64
Hazardous locations at NGV fuelling facilities*
(See Rules 20-062 and J20-062.)

Location		Extent of hazardous location	Zone (Division)
Vents	Vent openings including relief valves	A distance equal to 100 vent orifice diameters, within 15° of the line of discharge of a vent opening	Zone 1 (Division 1)
		1.8 m in all directions from the vent opening (excluding the Zone 1 space)	Zone 2 (Division 2)
Compressor packages See Notes 1), 2), and 3)	Outdoors	Up to and including 3 m measured from the compressor package	Zone 2 (Division 2)
	Enclosed†	Enclosed space‡	Zone 1 (Division 1)
		Up to and including 3 m from non-gas-tight seams or openings in the enclosure	Zone 2 (Division 2)
Gas storage facilities — Storage volume up to and including 4000 L of water	Measured from opening in reservoir	2.5 m in all directions from opening§	Zone 2 (Division 2)
Gas storage facilities — Storage volume 4001 to 10 000 L of water	Measured from opening in reservoir	4 m in all directions from opening§	Zone 2 (Division 2)
Gas storage facilities — Storage volume over 10 000 L of water	Measured from opening in reservoir	10 m in all directions from opening§	Zone 2 (Division 2)
Dispenser	Slow fill	Enclosed area in direct communication with gas-carrying fittings and components	Zone 1** (Division 1)
		A radius of 1.5 m beyond the perimeter of the Zone 1 area or the dispensing point as applicable	Zone 2 (Division 2)
Dispenser	Fast fill	Enclosed area in direct communication with gas-carrying fittings and components	Zone 1** (Division 1)
		A radius of 3 m beyond the perimeter of the Zone 1 area or the dispensing point as applicable	Zone 2 (Division 2)

* *See CSA B108.*

† *A compressor shall be regarded as enclosed when it is sheltered by a building or enclosure having four sides, a roof, and limited ventilation.*

‡ *An enclosed space shall be permitted to be classified Zone 2, Group IIA or Class I, Division 2, Group D when the enclosure is provided with an exhaust fan interlocked with a gas detection system that functions to shut down the compressor and activate the exhaust fan when the concentration of gas within the building reaches 20% of the lower explosive limit. The exhaust fan shall also incorporate controls for manual operation. The gas detection system shall be maintained in accordance with the manufacturer's recommendations.*

(Continued)

Table 64 (Concluded)

§ *When a wall with a 4 h fire resistance rating is located within these distances, the distances shall be measured either around the end of the wall or over the wall, but not through it. The wall shall not be located closer than 1 m from a fuel container with up to 10 000 L in storage volume, and 1.5 m from a fuel container with a storage volume greater than 10 000 L.*

** *The space inside the dispenser enclosure shall be permitted to be classified as Zone 2 or Division 2 when the following are provided:*

a) *adequate ventilation; and*

b) *a means of limiting, to a short time, the length of time explosive concentrations of gas or vapour in the air can be present as result of abnormal operation.*

Notes:

1) *When a gas-tight wall is located within 3 m of the compressor, the distances shall be measured around the end of the wall, over the wall, or through any doors, windows, or openings in the wall.*

2) *When a gas-tight wall is located within 3 m of the enclosure, the distances shall be measured around the end of the wall, over the wall, or through any doors, windows, or openings in the wall.*

3) *Where the enclosure is designed and built to ensure that its walls and ceiling are gas tight except for required openings, the distances shall be measured from its openings.*

Table 65
Enclosure selection table for non-hazardous locations
(See Rules 2-400 and 2-402.)

Provides a degree of protection against the following environmental conditions	Enclosure type															
	Indoor use						Indoor/outdoor use								Submersible	
	1	2	5	12*	12K†	13	3	3X	3R	3RX	3S	3SX	4	4X	6	6P
Accidental contact with live parts	X	X	X	X	X	X	X	X	X	X	X	X	X	X	X	X
Falling dirt	X	X	X	X	X	X	X	X	X	X	X	X	X	X	X	X
Dripping and light splashing of non-corrosive liquids	—	X	X	X	X	X	X	X	X	X	X	X	X	X	X	X
Circulating dust, lint, fibres, and flyings	—	—	—	X	X	X	X	X	—	—	X	X	X	X	X	X
Settling dust, lint, fibres, and flyings	—	—	X	X	X	X	X	X	—	—	X	X	X	X	X	X
Hosedown and splashing water	—	—	—	—	—	—	—	—	—	—	—	—	X	X	X	X
Corrosion	—	—	—	—	—	—	—	X	—	X	—	X	—	X	—	X
Occasional temporary submersion	—	—	—	—	—	—	—	—	—	—	—	—	—	—	X	X
Occasional prolonged submersion	—	—	—	—	—	—	—	—	—	—	—	—	—	—	—	X
Oil and coolant seepage, spraying and splashing	—	—	—	—	—	X	—	—	—	—	—	—	—	—	—	—
Rain, snow, and external formation of ice‡	—	—	—	—	—	—	X	X	X	X	X	X	X	X	X	X
External formation of ice§	—	—	—	—	—	—	—	—	—	—	X	X	—	—	—	—
Wind-blown dust	—	—	—	—	—	—	X	X	—	—	X	X	X	X	X	X

* Without knockouts.
† With knockouts.
‡ The external operating mechanism(s) is not required to operate when the enclosure is ice covered.
§ The external operating mechanism(s) shall be operable when the enclosure is ice covered.

Ⓔ

Table 66
Ampacities of bare or covered conductors in free air, based on 40 °C ambient, 80 °C total conductor temperature, and 610 mm/s wind velocity
[See Rule 4-004 21).]

Copper conductors				AAC aluminum conductors			
Bare		Covered		Bare		Covered	
AWG, kcmil	Ampacity	AWG, kcmil	Ampacity	AWG, kcmil	Ampacity	AWG, kcmil	Ampacity
8	98	8	103	8	76	8	80
6	124	6	130	6	96	6	101
4	155	4	163	4	121	4	127
2	209	2	219	2	163	2	171
1/0	282	1/0	297	1/0	220	1/0	231
2/0	329	2/0	344	2/0	255	2/0	268
3/0	382	3/0	401	3/0	297	3/0	312
4/0	444	4/0	466	4/0	346	4/0	364
250	494	250	519	266.8	403	266.8	423
300	556	300	584	336.4	468	336.4	492
500	773	500	812	397.5	522	397.5	548
750	1000	750	1050	477.0	588	477.0	617
1000	1193	1000	1253	556.5	650	556.5	682
—	—	—	—	636.0	709	636.0	744
—	—	—	—	795.0	819	795.0	860
—	—	—	—	954.0	920	—	—
—	—	—	—	1033.5	968	1033.5	1017
—	—	—	—	1272	1103	1272	1201
—	—	—	—	1590	1267	1590	1381
—	—	—	—	2000	1454	2000	1527

Δ

Table 67
Clearance requirements for installed space heating systems
(See Rule 62-200.)

Heating system type and location	Minimum clearance, mm	Obstructions and protrusions
All systems, including heating fixtures; heating cable sets; heating panel sets; heating device sets	100	From protruding water pipes and fans
	200	From electrical outlets to which a luminaire or other heat-producing equipment is liable to be connected From receptacles and switches From other heating devices, unless otherwise rated
Floor systems above sub-floors, for heating cable sets or panel sets	50	From walls, partitions, and permanently fixed cabinetry
Floor systems under sub-floors, for heating cable sets or panel sets	50	Minimum air gap between bottom of subfloor and heating device sets, unless otherwise rated
Wall systems for heating cable sets or panel sets	50	Minimum air gap behind the wall surface to protect installed heating devices, unless the heating device set is protected by design from mechanical damage. From the top and side surfaces of permanently fixed cabinetry
	150	From ceiling, floor, and other wall corners
	150	From partitions, bottom surfaces of permanently fixed cabinetry, door and window frames, or other thermal obstructions, unless otherwise rated
Ceiling systems for heating cable sets or panel sets	50	From glass walls and window walls
	150	From corners, partitions, and adjacent surfaces, and not overlapping permanently fixed cabinetry or other thermal obstructions, unless otherwise rated

Table 68
Maximum insulated conductor length measured from the supply side of the consumer's service to the furthest point of utilization on a circuit using 90 °C rated copper insulated conductors at 30 °C ambient temperature for 120 V single-phase ac circuits (2-wire circuits) when used in dwelling units
(See Rule 8-102.)

Conductor size, AWG	Maximum insulated conductor length, m	
	Overcurrent protection setting/rating	
	15 A	20 A
14	38	—
12	60	50
10	96	78

Δ

Table 69
Hazardous locations at bulk storage plants
(See Rule 20-202.)

Location		Extent of hazardous location	Zone of hazardous location
Areas containing pumps, bleeders, withdrawal fittings, meters, and similar devices that are located in pipelines handling flammable liquids under pressure	Indoor areas with adequate ventilation	Within 1.5 m extending in all directions from the exterior of such devices as well as 7.5 m horizontally from any exterior surface of these devices and extending upward to 900 mm above floor or grade level	Zone 2* † ‡
	Indoor areas not having adequate ventilation	Within a 1.5 m distance extending in all directions from the exterior surface of such devices as well as 7.5 m horizontally from any surface of the device and extending upward 900 mm above floor or grade level	Zone 1† ‡
	Outdoor areas	Within a 900 mm distance extending in all directions from the exterior surface of such devices and up to 450 mm above grade level within 3 m horizontally from any surface of the devices	Zone 2
Areas where flammable liquids are transferred to individual containers	Outdoor areas or adequately ventilated indoor areas	Within 900 mm of the vent or fill opening extending in all directions	Zone 1
		Within the area between a 900 mm radius and a 1.5 m radius from the vent or fill opening extending in all directions	Zone 2
		Within a horizontal radius of 3 m from the vent or fill opening and extending to a height of 450 mm above floor or grade levels	Zone 2
	Indoor areas not having adequate ventilation	The entire indoor area	Zone 1
Outdoor areas where tank vehicles and tank cars are loaded and unloaded	Loading through an open dome or through a closed dome with atmospheric venting	Within 900 mm in all directions from the open dome or from the vent	Zone 1
		Within the area extending between a 900 mm radius and a 1.5 m radius from the open dome or from the vent	Zone 2
	Loading through a closed dome with atmospheric venting or through a closed	Within 900 mm in all directions from vents	Zone 2

(Continued)

Table 69 (Concluded)

Location		Extent of hazardous location	Zone of hazardous location
	dome with a vapour recovery system		
	Bottom loading or unloading	Within 3 m from the point of connection and extending up to 450 mm above grade	Zone 2
	Internal space of tank vehicles and tank cars	The entire internal space	Zone 0
Areas in the vicinity of above-ground tanks	Floating-roof-type tanks	The space above the roof and within the shell	Zone 1
	All types of above-ground tanks	Within 3 m in all directions from the shell, ends, and roof other than a floating roof	Zone 2
	Dikes around above-ground tanks	The area inside the dike and extending upward to the top of the dike	Zone 2
	Area around vents	Within 1.5 m in all directions from the vent opening	Zone 1
		The area between 1.5 m and 3 m of the vent opening and extending in all directions	Zone 2
	Vapour space above the liquid in a storage tank	The entire vapour space	Zone 0
Pits and depressions	Any part of a pit or depression that is not adequately ventilated and lies within a Zone 1 or Zone 2 area	The entire pit or depression	Zone 1
	Any part of a pit or depression that does not lie within a Zone 1 or Zone 2 area and contains piping, valves, or fittings for flammable gases or liquids	The entire pit or depression	Zone 2
	Any part of a pit or depression that is adequately ventilated and lies within a Zone 1 or Zone 2 area	The entire pit or depression	Zone 2
Garages where tank vehicles are stored or repaired		450 mm above floor or grade level, unless conditions warrant more severe classification or a greater extent of the hazardous area	Zone 2
Buildings such as office buildings, boiler rooms, etc.		If located outside the limits of hazardous areas and not used for handling or storage of volatile flammable liquids or containers for such liquids	Non-hazardous

* *The design of the ventilation systems shall take into account that the vapours are heavier than air.*
† *Where openings are used in outside walls, they shall be of adequate size, located at floor level, and unobstructed except by louvres or coarse screens.*
‡ *Where natural ventilation is inadequate, mechanical ventilation shall be provided.*

Diagrams

Diagrams

Diagram 1
CSA configurations for non-locking receptacles

(See Rules 26-700, 26-720, 26-744, 38-023, 58-400, 78-052, 78-102, and 86-306, Diagram 2, and Appendix B.)

Description			15 A	20 A	30 A	50 A	60 A
			Receptacle	Receptacle	Receptacle	Receptacle	Receptacle
2-pole 3-wire grounding	120 V	TT			TT-30R		
2-pole 3-wire grounding	125 V	5	5-15R	5-20R	5-30R	5-50R	
2-pole 3-wire grounding	125 V	5A		5-20RA ALTERNATE			
2-pole 3-wire grounding	*250 V	6	6-15R	6-20R	6-30R	6-50R	
2-pole 3-wire grounding	*250 V	6A		6-20RA ALTERNATE			
2-pole 3-wire grounding	277 V AC	7	7-15R	7-20R	7-30R	7-50R	
2-pole 3-wire grounding	347 V AC	24	24-15R	24-20R	24-30R	24-50R	
3-pole 4-wire grounding	125/250 V	14	14-15R	14-20R	14-30R	14-50R	14-60R
3-pole 4-wire grounding	3 ϕ 250 V	15	15-15R	15-20R	15-30R	15-50R	15-60R

* *For configurations 6-15R, 6-20R, 6-20RA, 6-30R, and 6-50R, Y denotes the identified terminal when used on circuits derived from three-phase, 4-wire 416 V circuits.*

Note: *Except as noted above, in Diagrams 1 and 2,*

a) *G represents the terminal for bonding to ground;*

b) *W represents the identified terminal; and*

c) *X, Y, and Z represent the terminals for ungrounded conductors.*

Diagram 2
CSA configurations for locking receptacles
(See Rules 12-020, 26-700, 78-052, 78-102, and 86-306, Diagram 1, and Appendix B.)

	Description		15 A Receptacle	20 A Receptacle	30 A Receptacle	50 A Receptacle	60 A Receptacle
2-pole 3-wire grounding	125 V	L5	L5-15R	L5-20R	L5-30R	L5-50R	L5-60R
	125 V	ML2	ML2-15R				
	125 V	SS1				SS1-50R	
	250 V	L6	L6-15R	L6-20R	L6-30R	L6-50R	L6-60R
	277 V AC	L7	L7-15R	L7-20R	L7-30R	L7-50R	L7-60R
	347 V AC	L24		L24-20R			
	480 V AC	L8		L8-20R	L8-30R	L8-50R	L8-60R
	600 V AC	L9		L9-20R	L9-30R	L9-50R	L9-60R
3-pole 4-wire grounding	125/250 V	L14		L14-20R	L14-30R	L14-50R	L14-60R
	125/250 V	SS2				SS2-50R	
	3 φ 250 V	L15		L15-20R	L15-30R	L15-50R	L15-60R
	3 φ 480 V	L16		L16-20R	L16-30R	L16-50R	L16-60R
	3 φ 600 V	L17			L17-30R	L17-50R	L17-60R
4-pole 5-wire grounding	3 φ 208 Y / 120 V	L21		L21-20R	L21-30R	L21-50R	L21-60R
	3 φ 480 Y / 277 V	L22		L22-20R	L22-30R	L22-50R	L22-60R
	3 φ 600 Y / 347 V	L23		L23-20R	L23-30R	L23-50R	L23-60R

Note: *In Diagrams 1 and 2,*
a) *G represents the terminal for bonding to ground;*
b) *W represents the identified terminal; and*
c) *X, Y, and Z represent the terminals for ungrounded conductors.*

Diagrams

Diagram 3
Ultimate point of conductor de-energization
(See Rule 14-102 and Appendix B.)

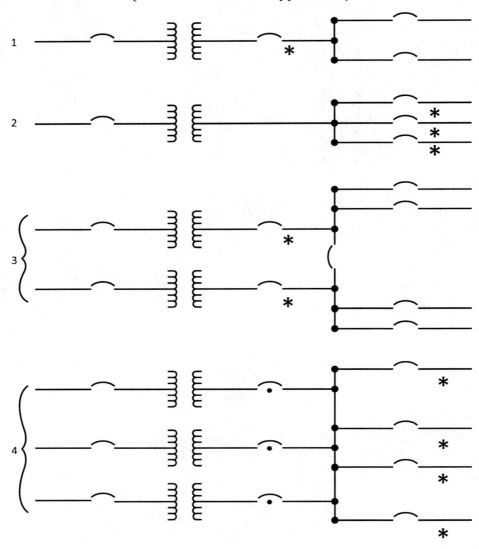

Notes:

1) The symbol ─◠─ represents a circuit breaker, a combination of circuit breaker and fuses, or a fused switch.

2) The symbol ─◠─ represents a network protector that protects against reverse current.

3) An asterisk (*) indicates the ultimate point beyond which the downstream ungrounded circuit conductors must be de-energized in the event of a ground fault in the circuit fed by such conductors.

Δ

Diagram 4
Extent of hazardous location for open-face spray booths
[See Rule 20-302 2).]

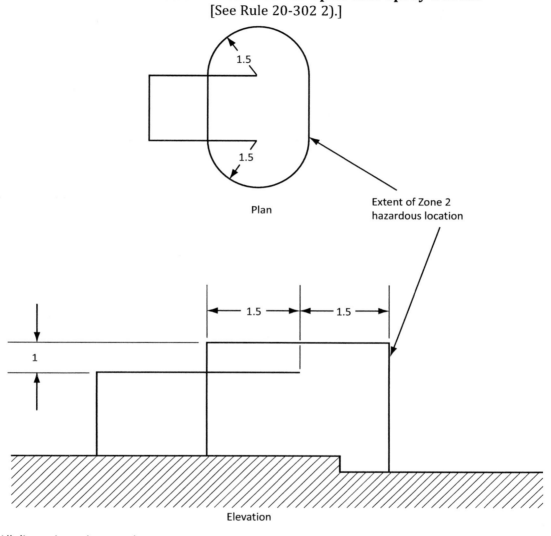

Plan

Extent of Zone 2
hazardous location

Elevation

Note: *All dimensions given are in metres.*

Diagrams

Δ

Diagram 5
Extent of hazardous location for spraying operations not conducted in spray booths
(See Rule 20-302.)

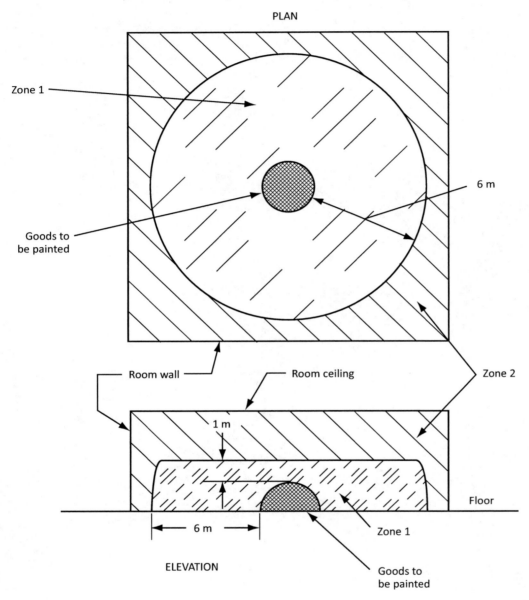

Δ

Diagram 6
Extent of hazardous location for spraying operations not conducted in spray booths — Ventilation system interlocked
[See Rule 20-302 7).]

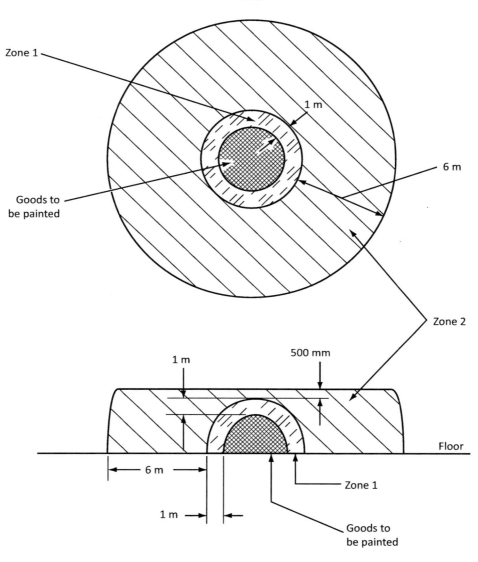

PLAN

ELEVATION

Diagrams

Diagram 7
Extent of hazardous location for tank vehicle and tank car loading and unloading
(See Part B of Table 63.)

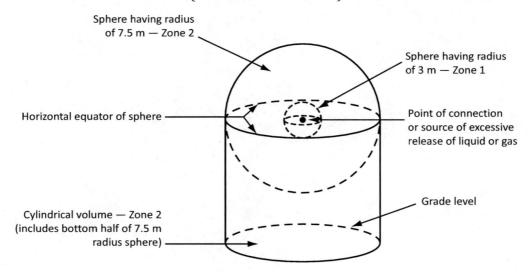

Sphere having radius of 7.5 m — Zone 2

Sphere having radius of 3 m — Zone 1

Horizontal equator of sphere

Point of connection or source of excessive release of liquid or gas

Grade level

Cylindrical volume — Zone 2 (includes bottom half of 7.5 m radius sphere)

Diagram 8
Extent of hazardous location for pumps, vapour compressors, gas-air mixers, and vaporizers outdoors in open air
(See Part E of Table 63.)

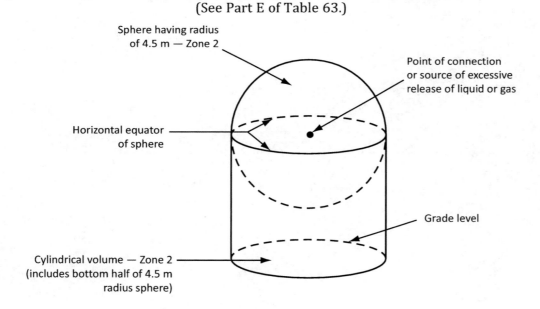

Sphere having radius of 4.5 m — Zone 2

Point of connection or source of excessive release of liquid or gas

Horizontal equator of sphere

Grade level

Cylindrical volume — Zone 2 (includes bottom half of 4.5 m radius sphere)

Diagram 9
Extent of hazardous location for container filling outdoors in open air
(See Part J of Table 63.)

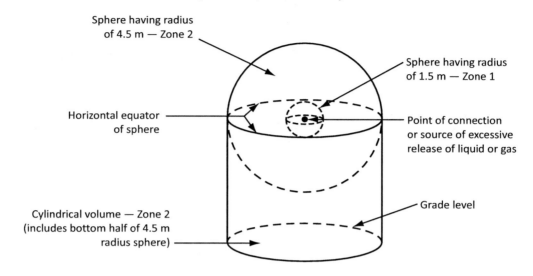

Δ

Diagram 10
Extent of hazardous location adjacent to openings in a closed spray booth or room
[See Rule 20-302 3).]

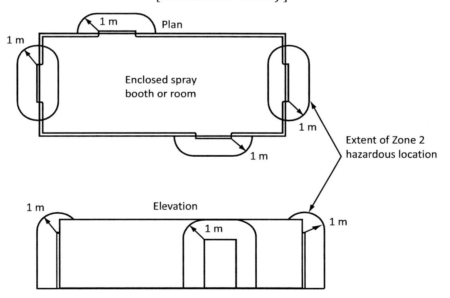

Appendix A — Safety standards for electrical equipment

Notes:
1) *This Appendix is a normative (mandatory) part of this Standard.*
2) *This Appendix lists Standards used to certify electrical equipment for the purpose of being "Approved" as defined in Section 0.*
3) *Adopted International Standards listed in this Appendix may include Canadian deviations. Compliance with these Canadian deviations is required for implementation in Canada.*
4) *CSA and other accredited Standards Development Organizations may publish new Canadian standards for electrical equipment or periodically amend or publish new editions of standards listed in this Appendix. In cases of newly published standards or where the editions listed below are amended, replaced by new editions, or superseded by another standard(s) during the life of this referencing Code, the newly published standards or newly published editions of these standards may be used for product approval purposes by accredited certification organizations.*

Annex A.1

CSA *Canadian Electrical Code, Part II* safety standards for electrical equipment

General

CAN/CSA-C22.2 No. 0-10 (R2015)	General Requirements — Canadian Electrical Code, Part II
C22.2 No. 0.1-M1985 (R2013)	General Requirements for Double-Insulated Equipment
C22.2 No. 0.2-16	Insulation Coordination
CAN/CSA-C22.2 No. 0.4-17	Bonding of Electrical Equipment
C22.2 No. 0.5-16	Threaded Conduit Entries
C22.2 No. 0.8 (R2016)	Safety Functions Incorporating Electronic Technology
C22.2 No. 0.12-M1985 (R2016)	Wiring Space and Wire Bending Space in Enclosures for Equipment Rated 750 V or Less
C22.2 No. 0.15-15	Adhesive Labels
CAN/CSA-C22.2 No. 0.17-00 (R2013)	Evaluation of Properties of Polymeric Materials
C22.2 No. 0.19-10 (R2015)	Requirements for Service Entrance Equipment
C22.2 No. 0.22-11 (R2016)	Evaluation Methods for Arc Resistance Ratings of Enclosed Electrical Equipment
C22.2 No. 0.23-15	General requirements for battery-powered appliances
CAN/CSA-C22.2 No. 60896-11:17	Stationary lead-acid batteries — Part 11: Vented types — General requirements and methods of tests
CAN/CSA-C22.2 No. 60896-21:17	Stationary lead-acid batteries — Part 21: Valve regulated types — Methods of test
CAN/CSA-C22.2 No. 60896-22:17	Stationary lead-acid batteries — Part 22: Valve regulated types — Requirements
CAN/CSA-C22.2 No. 61508-1:17	Functional safety of electrical/electronic/programmable electronic safety-related systems — Part 1: General requirements
CAN/CSA-C22.2 No. 61508-2:17	Functional safety of electrical/electronic/programmable electronic safety-related systems — Part 2: Requirements for

electrical/electronic/programmable electronic safety-related systems

CAN/CSA-C22.2 No. 61508-3:17	Functional safety of electrical/electronic/programmable electronic safety-related systems — Part 3: Software requirements
CAN/CSA-C22.2 No. 61511-1:17	Functional safety - Safety instrumented systems for the process industry sector — Part 1: Framework, definitions, system, hardware and application programming requirements
CAN/CSA-E61951-1:14	Secondary cells and batteries containing alkaline or other non-acid electrolytes — Portable sealed rechargeable single cells — Part 1: Nickel-cadmium
CAN/CSA-E61951-2:14	Secondary cells and batteries containing alkaline or other non-acid electrolytes — Portable sealed rechargeable single cells — Part 2: Nickel-metal hydride
CAN/CSA-E61959:14	Secondary cells and batteries containing alkaline or other non-acid electrolytes — Mechanical tests for sealed portable secondary cells and batteries

Wiring products

C22.2 No. 0.3-09 (R2014)	Test Methods for Electrical Wires and Cables
C22.2 No. 18.1-13	Metallic Outlet Boxes
C22.2 No. 18.2-06 (R2016)	Nonmetallic Outlet Boxes
C22.2 No. 18.3-12 (R2017)	Conduit, Tubing, and Cable Fittings
C22.2 No. 18.4-15	Hardware for the Support of Conduit, Tubing, and Cable
C22.2 No. 18.5-13	Positioning Devices
C22.2 No. 21-14	Cord Sets and Power-Supply Cords
C22.2 No. 26-13	Construction and Test of Wireways, Auxiliary Gutters, and Associated Fittings
C22.2 No. 34-M1987 (R2013)	Electrode Receptacles, Fittings, and Connectors for Gas Tubes
C22.2 No. 35-09 (R2014)	Extra-Low-Voltage Control Circuit Cable, Low-Energy Control Cable, and Extra-Low-Voltage Control Cable
C22.2 No. 38-14	Thermoset-Insulated Wires and Cables
C22.2 No. 40-M1989 (R2014)	Cutout, Junction, and Pull Boxes
C22.2 No. 41-13	Grounding and Bonding Equipment
C22.2 No. 42-10 (R2015)	General Use Receptacles, Attachment Plugs, and Similar Wiring Devices
C22.2 No. 42.1-13	Cover Plates for Flush-Mounted Wiring Devices
C22.2 No. 43-08 (R2013)	Lampholders
C22.2 No. 45.1-07 (R2017)	Electrical Rigid Metal Conduit — Steel
C22.2 No. 45.2-08 (R2013)	Electrical Rigid Metal Conduit — Aluminum, Red Brass, and Stainless Steel

Appendix A

C22.2 No. 48-15	Nonmetallic Sheathed Cable
C22.2 No. 49-14	Flexible Cords and Cables
C22.2 No. 51-14	Armoured Cables
C22.2 No. 52-15	Underground Secondary and Service-Entrance Cables
C22.2 No. 55-15	Special Use Switches
C22.2 No. 56-13	Flexible Metal Conduit and Liquid-Tight Flexible Metal Conduit
C22.2 No. 57-17	Flatiron and appliance plugs
C22.2 No. 62-93 (R2013)	Surface Raceway Systems
C22.2 No. 62.1-15	Nonmetallic Surface Raceways and Fittings
C22.2 No. 65-13	Wire Connectors
C22.2 No. 75-17	Thermoplastic Insulated Wires and Cables
C22.2 No. 79-16	Cellular Metal and Cellular Concrete Floor Raceways and Fittings
C22.2 No. 80-16	Underfloor Raceways and Fittings
C22.2 No. 82-1969 (R2013)	Tubular Support Members and Associated Fittings for Domestic and Commercial Service Masts
C22.2 No. 83-M1985 (R2013)	Electrical Metallic Tubing
C22.2 No. 83.1-07 (R2017)	Electrical Metallic Tubing — Steel
C22.2 No. 85-14	Rigid PVC Boxes and Fittings
C22.2 No. 96-17	Portable Power Cables
C22.2 No. 96.1-16	Mine Power Feeder Cables
C22.2 No. 96.2-15	Down tower power cables for wind turbine applications rated 2–35 kV
C22.2 No. 111-10 (R2015)	General-Use Snap Switches
C22.2 No. 123-16	Metal Sheathed Cables
C22.2 No. 124-16	Mineral-Insulated Cable
C22.2 No. 126.1-09 (R2014)	Metal Cable Tray Systems
CAN/CSA-C22.2 No. 126.2-02 (R2017)	Nonmetallic Cable Tray Systems
C22.2 No. 127-15	Equipment and Lead Wires
C22.2 No. 129-10 (R2014)	Neutral-Supported Cables
C22.2 No. 130-16	Requirements for Electrical Resistance Trace Heating Cables and Heating Device Sets
C22.2 No. 131-14	Type TECK 90 Cable
C22.2 No. 153-14	Electrical Quick-Connect Terminals
C22.2 No. 159-M1987 (R2014)	Attachment Plugs, Receptacles, and Similar Wiring Devices for Use in Hazardous Locations: Class I, Groups A, B, C, and D; Class II, Group G, in Coal or Coke Dust, and in Gaseous Mines

C22.2 No. 179-09 (R2014)	Airport Series Lighting Cables
C22.2 No. 182.1-17	Plugs, Receptacles, and Cable Connectors of the Pin and Sleeve Type
C22.2 No. 182.2-M1987 (R2014)	Industrial Locking Type, Special Use Attachment Plugs, Receptacles, and Connectors
C22.2 No. 182.3-16	Special Use Attachment Plugs, Receptacles, and Connectors
CAN/CSA-C22.2 No. 182.4-M90 (R2015)	Plugs, Receptacles, and Connectors for Communication Systems
C22.2 No. 182.5-14	Photovoltaic Connectors
C22.2 No. 184-15	Solid-State Lighting Controls
C22.2 No. 184.1-15	Solid-State Dimming Controls
C22.2 No. 188-13	Splicing Wire Connectors
C22.2 No. 197-M1983 (R2013)	PVC Insulating Tape
CAN/CSA-C22.2 No. 198.1-06 (R2015)	Extruded Insulating Tubing
C22.2 No. 198.2-15	Sealed Wire Connector Systems
CAN/CSA-C22.2 No. 198.3-05 (R2014)	Coated Electrical Sleeving
C22.2 No. 198.4-14	Expanded Sleeving for Wire and Cable
C22.2 No. 203-16	Modular Wiring Systems for Office Furniture
C22.2 No. 203.1-14	Manufactured Wiring Systems
C22.2 No. 203.2-14	Powered table systems for residential and commercial use
C22.2 No. 208-14	Fire Alarm and Signal Cable
C22.2 No. 210-15	Appliance Wiring Material Products
C22.2 No. 211.0-03 (R2013)	General Requirements and Methods of Testing for Nonmetallic Conduit
C22.2 No. 211.1-06 (R2016)	Rigid Types EB1 and DB2/ES2 PVC Conduit
C22.2 No. 211.2-06 (R2016)	Rigid PVC (Unplasticized) Conduit
C22.2 No. 214-17	Communications Cables
C22.2 No. 222-16	Type FCC Undercarpet Wiring System
CAN/CSA-C22.2 No. 227.1-06 (R2016)	Electrical Nonmetallic Tubing
C22.2 No. 227.2.1-14	Liquid-Tight Flexible Nonmetallic Conduit
C22.2 No. 227.3-15	Mechanical Protection Tubing (MPT) and Fittings
C22.2 No. 230-17	Tray Cables
C22.2 No. 232-17	Optical Fiber Cables
C22.2 No. 233-17	Cords and Cord Sets for Communication Systems
C22.2 No. 239-17	Control and Instrumentation Cables

Appendix A

C22.2 No. 245-15	Marine Shipboard Cable
C22.2 No. 249-96 (R2015)	Standard Tests for Determining Compatibility of Cable-Pulling Lubricants with Wire and Cable
CAN/CSA-C22.2 No. 262-04 (R2013)	Optical Fiber Cable and Communication Cable Raceway Systems
C22.2 No. 265-12 (R2017)	Out of Parameter Circuit Interrupter (OPCI)
C22.2 No. 267-16	Armoured Segmented Power and Communication Assembly (ASPCA)
C22.2 No. 271-11 (R2016)	Photovoltaic Cables
C22.2 No. 273-14	Cablebus
CAN/CSA-C22.2 No. 282-13	Plugs, Receptacles, and Couplers for Electric Vehicles
C22.2 No. 284-16	Nonindustrial photoelectric switches for lighting control
C22.2 No. 291-14	Bare and Covered Ferrules
C22.2 No. 298-16	High voltage couplers
C22.2 No. 308-14	Cord reels and multi-outlet assemblies
C22.2 No. 327-16	HDPE conduit, conductors-in-conduit, and fittings
C22.2 No. 331-17	Flat cable systems
C22.2 No. 1691-12 (R2016)	Single Pole Locking-Type Separable Connectors
C22.2 No. 2420-09 (R2014)	Belowground Reinforced Thermosetting Resin Conduit (RTRC) and Fittings
C22.2 No. 2459-08 (R2013)	Insulated Multi-pole Splicing Wire Connectors
C22.2 No. 2515-09 (R2014)	Aboveground Reinforced Thermosetting Resin Conduit (RTRC) and Fittings
C22.2 No. 2515.1-13	Supplemental Requirements for Extra Heavy Wall (XW) Reinforced Thermosetting Resin Conduit (RTRC) and Fittings
C22.2 No. 2556-15	Wire and Cable Test Methods
CAN/CSA-C22.2 No. 60320-1-11 (R2016)	Appliance Couplers for Household and Similar General Purposes — Part 1: General Requirements
CAN/CSA-C22.2 No. 61058-1-09 (R2014)	Switches for Appliances — Part 1: General Requirements
CAN/CSA-C22.2 No. 62275-16	Cable Management Systems — Cable Ties for Electrical Installations

Industrial products

C22.2 No. 4-16	Enclosed and Dead-Front Switches
C22.2 No. 5-16	Molded-Case Circuit Breakers, Molded-Case Switches, and Circuit-Breaker Enclosures
C22.2 No. 13-13	Transformers for Oil- or Gas-Burner Ignition Equipment
C22.2 No. 14-13	Industrial Control Equipment

C22.2 No. 22-M1986 (R2013)	Electrical Equipment for Flammable and Combustible Fuel Dispensers
C22.2 No. 25-1966 (R2014)	Enclosures for Use in Class II Groups E, F, and G Hazardous Locations
C22.2 No. 27-09 (R2013)	Busways
C22.2 No. 29-15	Panelboards and Enclosed Panelboards
C22.2 No. 30-M1986 (R2016)	Explosion-Proof Enclosures for Use in Class I Hazardous Locations
C22.2 No. 31-14	Switchgear Assemblies
C22.2 No. 33-M1984 (R2014)	Construction and Test of Electric Cranes and Hoists
C22.2 No. 39-13	Fuseholder Assemblies
C22.2 No. 47-13	Air-Cooled Transformers (Dry Type)
C22.2 No. 58-M1989 (R2015)	High-Voltage Isolating Switches
C22.2 No. 60-M1990 (R2016)	Arc Welding Equipment
C22.2 No. 66.1-06 (R2015)	Low Voltage Transformers — Part 1: General Requirements
C22.2 No. 66.2-06 (R2015)	Low Voltage Transformers — Part 2: General Purpose Transformers
C22.2 No. 66.3-06 (R2015)	Low Voltage Transformers — Part 3: Class 2 and Class 3 Transformers
C22.2 No. 73-1953 (R2013)	Construction and Test of Electrically Equipped Machine Tools
C22.2 No. 76-14	Splitters
C22.2 No. 77-14	Motors with Inherent Overheating Protection
C22.2 No. 88-1958 (R2013)	Construction and Test of Industrial Heating Equipment
C22.2 No. 94.1-15	Enclosures for Electrical Equipment, Non-Environmental Considerations
C22.2 No. 94.2-15	Enclosures for Electrical Equipment, Environmental Considerations
C22.2 No. 100-14	Motors and Generators
C22.2 No. 102-1958 (R2013)	Brooders and Incubators
C22.2 No. 105-1953 (R2013)	Electrical Equipment for Woodworking Machinery
C22.2 No. 106-05 (R2014)	HRC-Miscellaneous Fuses
C22.2 No. 107.1-16	Power Conversion Equipment
CAN/CSA-C22.2 No. 107.2-01 (R2016)	Battery Chargers
C22.2 No. 107.3-14	Uninterruptible Power Systems
C22.2 No. 108-14	Liquid Pumps
C22.2 No. 115-14	Meter-Mounting Devices
C22.2 No. 137-M1981 (R2014)	Electric Luminaires for Use in Hazardous Locations

Appendix A

C22.2 No. 139-13	Electrically Operated Valves
C22.2 No. 142-M1987 (R2014)	Process Control Equipment
CAN/CSA-C22.2 No. 144-M91 (R2015)	Ground Fault Circuit Interrupters
C22.2 No. 144.1-16	Ground-Fault Circuit-Interrupters
C22.2 No. 145-11 (R2015)	Electric Motors and Generators for Use in Hazardous (Classified) Locations
C22.2 No. 152-M1984 (R2016)	Combustible Gas Detection Instruments
C22.2 No. 155-M1986 (R2013)	Electric Duct Heaters
C22.2 No. 156-M1987 (R2013)	Solid-State Speed Controls
CAN/CSA-C22.2 No. 157-92 (R2016)	Intrinsically Safe and Non-Incendive Equipment for Use in Hazardous Locations
C22.2 No. 158-10 (R2014)	Terminal Blocks
C22.2 No. 160-15	Voltage and Polarity Testers
C22.2 No. 165-17	Electric Boilers
C22.2 No. 173-M1983 (R2014)	Transformers for Toy and Hobby Use
C22.2 No. 174-M1984 (R2017)	Cables and Cable Glands for Use in Hazardous Locations
C22.2 No. 177-13	Clock-Operated Switches
C22.2 No. 178.1-14	Transfer Switch Equipment
C22.2 No. 178.2-04 (R2014)	Requirements for Manually Operated Generator Transfer Panels
C22.2 No. 180-13	Series Isolating Transformers for Airport Lighting
C22.2 No. 183.1-M1982 (R2013)	Alternating-Current (AC) Electrical Installations on Boats
C22.2 No. 183.2-M1983 (R2013)	DC Electrical Installations on Boats
C22.2 No. 190-14	Capacitors for Power Factor Correction
C22.2 No. 193-M1983 (R2014)	High-Voltage Full-Load Interrupter Switches
C22.2 No. 201-M1984 (R2014)	Metal-Enclosed High Voltage Busways
C22.2 No. 204-M1984 (R2013)	Line Isolation Monitors
C22.2 No. 213-16	Non-Incendive Electrical Equipment for Use in Class I, Division 2 Hazardous Locations
CAN/CSA-C22.2 No. 223-15	Power Supplies with Extra-Low-Voltage Class 2 Outputs
C22.2 No. 229-17	Switching and Metering Centres
C22.2 No. 235-04 (R2013)	Supplementary Protectors
C22.2 No. 244-05 (R2015)	Switchboards
C22.2 No. 248.1-11 (R2016)	Low-Voltage Fuses — Part 1: General Requirements

CAN/CSA-C22.2 No. 248.2-00 (R2015)	Low-Voltage Fuses — Part 2: Class C Fuses
CAN/CSA-C22.2 No. 248.3-00 (R2015)	Low-Voltage Fuses — Part 3: Class CA and CB Fuses
CAN/CSA-C22.2 No. 248.4-00 (R2015)	Low-Voltage Fuses — Part 4: Class CC Fuses
CAN/CSA-C22.2 No. 248.5-00 (R2015)	Low-Voltage Fuses — Part 5: Class G Fuses
CAN/CSA-C22.2 No. 248.6-00 (R2015)	Low-Voltage Fuses — Part 6: Class H Non-Renewable Fuses
CAN/CSA-C22.2 No. 248.7-00 (R2015)	Low-Voltage Fuses — Part 7: Class H Renewable Fuses
C22.2 No. 248.8-11 (R2016)	Low-Voltage Fuses — Part 8: Class J Fuses
CAN/CSA-C22.2 No. 248.9-00 (R2015)	Low-Voltage Fuses — Part 9: Class K Fuses
C22.2 No. 248.10-11 (R2016)	Low-Voltage Fuses — Part 10: Class L Fuses
C22.2 No. 248.11-11 (R2016)	Low-Voltage Fuses — Part 11: Plug Fuses
C22.2 No. 248.12-11 (R2016)	Low-Voltage Fuses — Part 12: Class R Fuses
CAN/CSA-C22.2 No. 248.13-00 (R2015)	Low-Voltage Fuses — Part 13: Semiconductor Fuses
CAN/CSA-C22.2 No. 248.14-00 (R2015)	Low-Voltage Fuses — Part 14: Supplemental Fuses
CAN/CSA-C22.2 No. 248.15-00 (R2015)	Low-Voltage Fuses — Part 15: Class T Fuses
CAN/CSA-C22.2 No. 248.16-00 (R2015)	Low-Voltage Fuses — Part 16: Test Limiters
C22.2 No. 248.19-15	Fuses — Part 19: Photovoltaic fuses
C22.2 No. 253-16	Medium-voltage AC Contactors, Controllers, and Control Centres
C22.2 No. 254-05 (R2015)	Motor Control Centres
CAN/CSA-C22.2 No. 257-06 (R2015)	Interconnecting Inverter-based Micro-Distributed Resources to Distribution Systems
C22.2 No. 263-15	Fire Pump Controllers
C22.2 No. 268-16	Power circuit breakers up to 1000 Vac/1500 Vdc
C22.2 No. 269.1-17	Surge Protective Devices — Type 1 — Permanently Connected
C22.2 No. 269.2-17	Surge Protective Devices — Type 2 — Permanently Connected
C22.2 No. 269.3-17	Surge Protective Devices — Type 3 — Cord Connected, Direct Plug-in, and Receptacle Type
C22.2 No. 269.4-17	Surge protective devices — Type 4 — Component assemblies

Appendix A

C22.2 No. 269.5-17	Surge protective devices — Type 5 — Components
C22.2 No. 270-16	Arc-fault protective devices
C22.2 No. 274-17	Adjustable Speed Drives
C22.2 No. 280-16	Electric Vehicle Supply Equipment
CAN/CSA-C22.2 No. 281.1-12 (R2017)	Standard for Safety for Personnel Protection Systems for Electric Vehicle (EV) Supply Circuits: General Requirements
CAN/CSA-C22.2 No. 281.2-12 (R2017)	Standard for Safety for Personnel Protection Systems for Electric Vehicle (EV) Supply Circuits: Particular Requirements for Protection Devices for Use in Charging Systems
C22.2 No. 286-17	Industrial control panels and assemblies
C22.2 No. 295-15	Neutral grounding devices
C22.2 No. 301-16	Industrial electrical machinery
C22.2 No. 304-14	Enclosed and Dead-Front Switches for Photovoltaic Applications
C22.2 No. 305-16	Molded-case circuit breakers, molded-case switches, and circuit-breaker enclosures for use with photovoltaic (PV) systems
C22.2 No. 4248.1-17	Fuseholders — Part 1: General Requirements
CAN/CSA-C22.2 No. 4248.4-07 (R2016)	Fuseholders — Part 4: Class CC
CAN/CSA-C22.2 No. 4248.5-07 (R2016)	Fuseholders — Part 5: Class G
CAN/CSA-C22.2 No. 4248.6-07 (R2016)	Fuseholders — Part 6: Class H
CAN/CSA-C22.2 No. 4248.8-07 (R2016)	Fuseholders — Part 8: Class J
CAN/CSA-C22.2 No. 4248.9-07 (R2016)	Fuseholders — Part 9: Class K
CAN/CSA-C22.2 No. 4248.11-07 (R2016)	Fuseholders — Part 11: Type C (Edison Base) and Type S Plug Fuse
CAN/CSA-C22.2 No. 4248.12-07 (R2016)	Fuseholders — Part 12: Class R
CAN/CSA-C22.2 No. 4248.15-07 (R2016)	Fuseholders — Part 15: Class T
C22.2 No. 4248.19-15	Fuseholders — Part 19: Photovoltaic fuseholders
CAN/CSA-C22.2 No. 60079-0-15	Explosive Atmospheres — Part 0: Equipment — General Requirements
CAN/CSA-C22.2 No. 60079-1-16	Explosive Atmospheres — Part 1: Equipment Protection by Flameproof Enclosures "d"
CAN/CSA-C22.2 No. 60079-2-16	Explosive Atmospheres — Part 2: Equipment Protection by Pressurized Enclosure "p"

CAN/CSA-C22.2 No. 60079-5-16	Explosive Atmospheres — Part 5: Equipment Protection by Powder Filling "q"
CAN/CSA-C22.2 No. 60079-6-17	Explosive Atmospheres — Part 6: Equipment Protection by Liquid Immersion "o"
CAN/CSA-C22.2 No. 60079-7-16	Explosive Atmospheres — Part 7: Equipment Protection by Increased Safety "e"
CAN/CSA-C22.2 No. 60079-11-14	Explosive Atmospheres — Part 11: Equipment Protection by Intrinsic Safety "i"
CAN/CSA-C22.2 No. 60079-15-16	Explosive Atmospheres — Part 15: Equipment Protection by Type of Protection "n"
CAN/CSA-C22.2 No. 60079-18-16	Explosive Atmospheres — Part 18: Equipment Protection by Encapsulation "m"
CAN/CSA-C22.2 No. 60079-25:14	Explosive atmospheres — Part 25: Intrinsically safe electrical systems
CAN/CSA-C22.2 No. 60079-26:16	Explosive atmospheres — Part 26: Equipment with Equipment Protection Level (EPL) Ga
CAN/CSA-C22.2 No. 60079-28:16	Explosive atmospheres — Part 28: Protection of equipment and transmission systems using optical radiation
CAN/CSA-C22.2 No. 60079-29-1-17	Explosive Atmospheres — Part 29-1: Gas Detectors — Performance Requirements of Detectors for Flammable Gases
CAN/CSA-C22.2 No. 60079-29-4:16	Explosive atmospheres — Part 29-4: Gas detectors — Performance requirements of open path detectors for flammable gases
CAN/CSA-C22.2 No. 60079-30-1:17	Explosive Atmospheres — Part 30-1: Electrical Resistance Trace Heating — General and Testing Requirements
CAN/CSA-C22.2 No. 60079-31-15	Explosive Atmospheres — Part 31: Equipment Dust Ignition Protection by Enclosure "t"
CAN/CSA-C22.2 No. 60079-35-1:16	Explosive atmospheres — Part 35-1: Caplights for use in mines susceptible to firedamp — General requirements — Construction and testing in relation to the risk of explosion
CAN/CSA-C22.2 No. 60079-35-2:16	Explosive atmospheres — Part 35-2: Caplights for use in mines susceptible to firedamp — Performance and other safety-related matters
CAN/CSA-C22.2 No. 60529-16	Degrees of Protection Provided by Enclosures (IP Code)
CAN/CSA-C22.2 No. 60947-1-13	Low-Voltage Switchgear and Controlgear — Part 1: General Rules
CAN/CSA-C22.2 No. 60947-4-1-14	Low-Voltage Switchgear and Controlgear — Part 4-1: Contactors and Motor-Starters — Electromechanical Contactors and Motor-Starters
CAN/CSA-C22.2 No. 60947-4-2-14	Low-voltage Switchgear and Controlgear — Part 4-2: Contactors and Motor-Starters — AC Semiconductor Motor Controllers and Starters
CAN/CSA-C22.2 No. 60947-5-1-14	Low-voltage Switchgear and Controlgear — Part 5-1: Control Circuit Devices and Switching Elements — Electromechanical Control Circuit devices

Appendix A

CAN/CSA-C22.2 No. 60947-5-2-14	Low-voltage Switchgear and Controlgear — Part 5-2: Control Circuit Devices and Switching Elements — Proximity Switches
CAN/CSA-C22.2 No. 60947-7-1:17	Low-voltage switchgear and controlgear — Part 7-1: Ancillary equipment — Terminal blocks for copper conductors
CAN/CSA-C22.2 No. 60947-7-2:17	Low-voltage switchgear and controlgear — Part 7-2: Ancillary equipment — Protective conductor terminal blocks for copper conductors
CAN/CSA-C22.2 No. 60947-7-3:17	Low-voltage switchgear and controlgear — Part 7-3: Ancillary equipment — Safety requirements for fuse terminal blocks
CAN/CSA-C22.2 No. 61730-1:11 (R2016)	Photovoltaic (PV) Module Safety Qualification — Part 1: Requirements for Construction
CAN/CSA-C22.2 No. 61730-2:11 (R2016)	Photovoltaic (PV) Module Safety Qualification — Part 2: Requirements for Testing
CAN/CSA-E60127-6-03 (R2017)	Miniature Fuses — Part 6: Fuse-Holders for Miniature Cartridge Fuse-Links
CAN/CSA-E61131-2-06 (R2016)	Programmable controllers — Part 2: Equipment Requirements and Tests
CAN/CSA-E61496-1-04 (R2013)	Safety of Machinery — Electro-Sensitive Protective Equipment — Part 1: General Requirements and Tests
CAN/CSA-E61496-2-04 (R2013)	Safety of Machinery — Electro-Sensitive Protective Equipment — Part 2: Particular Requirements for Equipment Using Active Opto-Electronic Protective Devices (AOPDs)

Consumer and commercial products

ANSI Z83.21-2016/C22.2 No. 168-16	Commercial Dishwashers
C22.2 No. 8-13	Electromagnetic Interference (EMI) Filters
C22.2 No. 9.0-96 (R2016)	General Requirements for Luminaires
C22.2 No. 9.0S1-97 (R2016)	Supplement No. 1 to C22.2 No. 9.0-96, General Requirements for Luminaires
C22.2 No. 10-1965 (R2013)	Electric Floor Surfacing and Cleaning Machines
C22.2 No. 15-16	Electrically Heated Warming Pads
C22.2 No. 23.1-M1986 (R2013)	Electric Furnaces in Combination with Solid Fuel Fired Furnaces
C22.2 No. 24-15	Temperature-Indicating and -Regulating Equipment
C22.2 No. 37-14	Christmas Tree and Other Decorative Lighting Outfits
C22.2 No. 46-13	Electric Air-Heaters
C22.2 No. 53-1968 (R2014)	Electric Washing Machines
C22.2 No. 61-16	Household Cooking Ranges
C22.2 No. 64-10 (R2014)	Household Cooking and Liquid-Heating Appliances
C22.2 No. 68-09 (R2014)	Motor-Operated Appliances (Household and Commercial)

C22.2 No. 71.2-10 (R2015)	Electric Bench Tools
C22.2 No. 72-10 (R2014)	Heater Elements
C22.2 No. 74-16	Equipment for Use With Electric Discharge Lamps
C22.2 No. 81-14	Electric Irons
C22.2 No. 84-05 (R2015)	Incandescent Lamps
C22.2 No. 89-15	Swimming Pool Luminaires, Submersible Luminaires and Accessories
C22.2 No. 92-15	Dehumidifiers
C22.2 No. 101-17	Electrically Heated Bedding Appliances for Household Use
CAN/CSA-C22.2 No. 103-M92 (R2015)	Electric Fence Controllers
C22.2 No. 104-11 (R2015)	Humidifiers
C22.2 No. 109-17	Commercial Cooking Appliances
CAN/CSA-C22.2 No. 110-94 (R2014)	Construction and Test of Electric Storage-Tank Water Heaters
C22.2 No. 112-15	Electric Clothes Dryers
C22.2 No. 113-15	Fans and Ventilators
C22.2 No. 117-1970 (R2016)	Room Air Conditioners
C22.2 No. 120-13	Refrigeration Equipment
C22.2 No. 128-16	Vending Machines
C22.2 No. 140.2-96 (R2016)	Hermetic Refrigerant Motor-Compressors
C22.2 No. 140.3-15	Refrigerant-Containing Components for Use in Electrical Equipment
C22.2 No. 141-15	Emergency Lighting Equipment
C22.2 No. 147-15	Motor-Operated Gardening Appliances
C22.2 No. 149-1972 (R2013)	Electrically Operated Toys
C22.2 No. 150-16	Microwave Ovens
CAN/CSA-C22.2 No. 164-M91 (R2016)	Electric Sauna Heating Equipment
C22.2 No. 166-15	Stage and Studio Luminaires
C22.2 No. 167-17	Household Dishwashers
C22.2 No. 169-15	Electric Clothes Washing Machines and Extractors
C22.2 No. 187-15	Electrostatic Air Cleaners
CAN/CSA-C22.2 No. 189-M89 (R2013)	High-Voltage Insect Killers
CAN/CSA-C22.2 No. 191-M89 (R2014)	Engine Heaters and Battery Warmers

Appendix A

C22.2 No. 195-16	Motor Operated Food Processing Appliances (Household and Commercial)
C22.2 No. 205-17	Signal Equipment
C22.2 No. 206-13	Lighting Poles
C22.2 No. 207-15	Portable and Stationary Electric Signs and Displays
C22.2 No. 218.1-13	Spas, Hot Tubs, and Associated Equipment
C22.2 No. 218.2-15	Hydromassage Bathtub Appliances
C22.2 No. 221-M1986 (R2013)	Electrically Heated Hobby and Educational Type Kilns
CAN/CSA-C22.2 No. 224-M89 (R2014)	Radiant Heaters and Infrared and Ultraviolet Lamp Assemblies for Cosmetic or Hygienic Purposes in Nonmedical Applications
CAN/CSA-C22.2 No. 226-92 (R2016)	Protectors in Telecommunication Networks
C22.2 No. 236-15	Heating and Cooling Equipment
C22.2 No. 243-15	Vacuum Cleaners, Blower Cleaners, and Household Floor Finishing Machines
C22.2 No. 247-14	Operators and Systems of Doors, Grates, Draperies, and Louvres
C22.2 No. 250.0-08 (R2013)	Luminaires
C22.2 No. 250.1-16	Retrofit kits for luminaire conversion
C22.2 No. 250.4-14	Portable luminaires
C22.2 No. 250.7-07 (R2012)	Extra-Low-Voltage Landscape Lighting Systems
CAN/CSA-C22.2 No. 250.13-14	Light Emitting Diode (LED) Equipment for Lighting Applications
C22.2 No. 250.570-16	Track lighting
C22.2 No. 255-04 (R2014)	Neon Transformers and Power Supplies
C22.2 No. 256-14	Direct Plug-in Nightlights
C22.2 No. 287-16	Plumbing fittings incorporating electrical and/or electronic features
C22.2 No. 309-16	Industrial clothes dryers
C22.2 No. 1335.1-93 (R2013)	Portable Electrical Motor-Operated and Heating Appliances: General Requirements
C22.2 No. 1335.2.14-93 (R2013)	Portable Electrical Motor-Operated and Heating Appliances: Particular Requirements for Electrical Motor-Operated Kitchen Appliances
C22.2 No. 1993-17	Self-Ballasted Lamps and Lamp Adapters
CAN/CSA-C22.2 No. 60065-16	Audio, Video and Similar Electronic Apparatus — Safety Requirements
CAN/CSA-C22.2 No. 60745-1-07 (R2017)	Hand-held Motor-Operated Electric Tools — Safety — Part 1: General Requirements

CAN/CSA-C22.2 No. 60745-2-1-04 (R2013)

Hand-held Motor-Operated Electric Tools — Safety —
Part 2-1: Particular Requirements for Drills and Impact Drills

CAN/CSA-C22.2 No. 60745-2-2-04 (R2013)

Hand-held Motor-Operated Electric Tools — Safety —
Part 2-2: Particular Requirements for Screwdrivers and Impact Wrenches

CAN/CSA-C22.2 No. 60745-2-3-07 (R2017)

Hand-held Motor-Operated Electric Tools — Safety —
Part 2-3: Particular Requirements for Grinders, Polishers and Disk-Type Sanders

CAN/CSA-C22.2 No. 60745-2-4-04 (R2013)

Hand-held Motor-Operated Electric Tools — Safety —
Part 2-4: Particular Requirements for Sanders and Polishers Other Than Disk-Type

CAN/CSA-C22.2 No. 60745-2-5-12 (R2016)

Hand-held Motor-Operated Electric Tools — Safety —
Part 2-5: Particular Requirements for Circular Saws

CAN/CSA-C22.2 No. 60745-2-6-04 (R2013)

Hand-held Motor-Operated Electric Tools — Safety —
Part 2-6: Particular Requirements for Hammers

CAN/CSA-C22.2 No. 60745-2-8-04 (R2013)

Hand-held Motor-Operated Electric Tools — Safety —
Part 2-8: Particular Requirements for Shears and Nibblers

CAN/CSA-C22.2 No. 60745-2-9-04 (R2013)

Hand-held Motor-Operated Electric Tools — Safety —
Part 2-9: Particular Requirements for Tappers

CAN/CSA-C22.2 No. 60745-2-11-04 (R2013)

Hand-held Motor-Operated Electric Tools — Safety —
Part 2-11: Particular Requirements for Reciprocating Saws

CAN/CSA-C22.2 No. 60745-2-12-05 (R2014)

Hand-held Motor-Operated Electric Tools — Safety —
Part 2-12: Particular Requirements for Concrete Vibrators

CAN/CSA-C22.2 No. 60745-2-13:11 (R2016)

Hand-Held Motor-Operated Electric Tools — Safety —
Part 2-13: Particular Requirements for Chain Saws

CAN/CSA-C22.2 No. 60745-2-14-04 (R2013)

Hand-held Motor-Operated Electric Tools — Safety —
Part 2-14: Particular Requirements for Planers

CAN/CSA-C22.2 No. 60745-2-15-10 (R2015)

Hand-held Motor-Operated Electric Tools — Safety —
Part 2-15: Particular Requirements for Hedge Trimmers

CAN/CSA-C22.2 No. 60745-2-16-09 (R2014)

Hand-held Motor-Operated Electric Tools — Safety —
Part 2-16: Particular Requirements for Trackers

CAN/CSA-C22.2 No. 60745-2-17-11 (R2015)

Hand-held Motor-Operated Electric Tools — Safety —
Part 2-17: Particular Requirements for Routers and Trimmers

CAN/CSA-C22.2 No. 60745-2-18-05 (R2014)

Hand-held Motor-Operated Electric Tools — Safety —
Part 2-18: Particular Requirements for Strapping Tools

CAN/CSA-C22.2 No. 60745-2-19-05 (R2014)

Hand-held Motor-Operated Electric Tools — Safety —
Part 2-19: Particular Requirements for Jointers

CAN/CSA-C22.2 No. 60745-2-20-05 (R2014)

Hand-held Motor-Operated Electric Tools — Safety —
Part 2-20: Particular Requirements for Band Saws

CAN/CSA-C22.2 No. 60745-2-21-05 (R2014)

Hand-held Motor-Operated Electric Tools — Safety —
Part 2-21: Particular Requirements for Drain Cleaners

CAN/CSA-C22.2 No. 60745-2-22-12 (R2017)

Hand-held Motor-Operated Electric Tools — Safety —
Part 2-22: Particular Requirements for Cut-Off Machines

Appendix A

CAN/CSA-C22.2 No. 60745-2-23-13	Hand-held Motor-Operated Electric Tools — Safety — Part 2-23: Particular Requirements for Die Grinders and Small Rotary Tools
CAN/CSA-C22.2 No. 745-2-30-95 (R2014)	Safety of Portable Electric Tools — Part 2: Particular Requirements for Staplers
CAN/CSA-C22.2 No. 745-2-31-95 (R2014)	Safety of Portable Electric Tools — Part 2: Particular Requirements for Diamond Core Drills
CAN/CSA-C22.2 No. 745-2-32-95 (R2014)	Safety of Portable Electric Tools — Part 2: Particular Requirements for Magnetic Drill Presses
CAN/CSA-C22.2 No. 745-2-36-95 (R2014)	Safety of Portable Electric Tools — Part 2: Particular Requirements for Hand Motor Tools
CAN/CSA-C22.2 No. 745-4-36-95 (R2014)	Safety of Portable Battery-Operated Tools — Part 4: Particular Requirements for Hand Motor Tools
CAN/CSA-C22.2 No. 60950-1-07 (R2016)	Information Technology Equipment — Safety — Part 1: General Requirements
CAN/CSA-C22.2 No. 60950-21-03 (R2016)	Information Technology Equipment — Safety — Part 21: Remote Power Feeding
CAN/CSA-C22.2 No. 60950-22-17	Information Technology Equipment — Safety — Part 22: Equipment to be Installed Outdoors
CAN/CSA-C22.2 No. 60950-23-07 (R2016)	Information Technology Equipment — Safety — Part 23: Large Data Storage Equipment
CAN/CSA-C22.2 No. 61010-1-12 (R2017)	Safety Requirements for Electrical Equipment for Measurement, Control, and Laboratory Use — Part 1: General Requirements
CAN/CSA-C22.2 No. 61010-2-010-15	Safety Requirements for Electrical Equipment for Measurement, Control, and Laboratory Use — Part 2-010: Particular Requirements for Laboratory Equipment for the Heating of Materials
CAN/CSA-C22.2 No. 61010-2-011:17	Safety requirements for electrical equipment for measurement, control, and laboratory use — Part 2-011: Particular requirements for refrigerating equipment
CAN/CSA-C22.2 No. 61010-2-012:17	Safety requirements for electrical equipment for measurement, control and laboratory use — Part 2-012: Particular requirements for climatic and environmental testing and other temperature conditioning equipment
CAN/CSA-C22.2 No. 61010-2-020-17	Safety Requirements for Electrical Equipment for Measurement, Control, and Laboratory Use — Part 2-020: Particular Requirements for Laboratory Centrifuges
CAN/CSA-C22.2 No. 61010-2-030-12 (R2016)	Safety Requirements for Electrical Equipment for Measurement, Control, and Laboratory Use — Part 2-030: Particular Requirements for Testing and Measuring Circuits
CAN/CSA-C22.2 No. 61010-2-031-17	Safety Requirements for Electrical Equipment for Measurement, Control, and Laboratory Use — Part 031: Safety Requirements for Hand-Held Probe Assemblies for Electrical Measurement and Test

CAN/CSA-C22.2 No. 61010-2-032-14	Safety Requirements for Electrical Equipment for Measurement, Control, and Laboratory Use — Part 2-032: Particular Requirements for Hand-Held and Hand-Manipulated Current Sensors for Electrical Test and Measurement
CAN/CSA-C22.2 No. 61010-2-033:14	Safety requirements for electrical equipment for measurement, control, and laboratory use — Part 2-033: Particular requirements for hand-held multimeters and other meters, for domestic and professional use, capable of measuring mains voltage
CAN/CSA-C22.2 No. 61010-2-040-16	Safety Requirements for Electrical Equipment for Measurement, Control, and Laboratory Use — Part 2-040: Particular Requirements for Sterilizers and Washer-Disinfectors used to Treat Medical Materials
CAN/CSA-C22.2 No. 61010-2-051-15	Safety Requirements for Electrical Equipment for Measurement, Control, and Laboratory Use — Part 2-051: Particular Requirements for Laboratory Equipment for Mixing and Stirring
CAN/CSA-C22.2 No. 61010-2-061-15	Safety Requirements for Electrical Equipment for Measurement, Control, and Laboratory Use — Part 2-061: Particular Requirements for Laboratory Atomic Spectrometers with Thermal Atomization and Ionization
CAN/CSA-C22.2 No. 61010-2-081-15	Safety Requirements for Electrical Equipment for Measurement, Control, and Laboratory Use — Part 2-081: Particular Requirements for Automatic and Semi-Automatic Laboratory Equipment for Analysis and Other Purposes
CAN/CSA-C22.2 No. 61010-2-091:14	Safety requirements for electrical equipment for measurement, control, and laboratory use — Part 2-091: Particular requirements for cabinet X-ray systems
CAN/CSA-C22.2 No. 61010-2-101:15	Safety Requirements for Electrical Equipment for Measurement, Control, and Laboratory Use — Part 2-101: Particular Requirements for In Vitro Diagnostic (IVD) Medical Equipment
CAN/CSA-IEC 61010-2-201-14	Safety requirements for Electrical Equipment for Measurement, Control, and Laboratory Use — Part 2-201: Particular Requirements for Control Equipment
CAN/CSA-C22.2 No. 62368-1:14	Audio/Video, Information and Communication Technology Equipment — Part 1: Safety Requirements
CAN/CSA-E155-98 (R2017)	Glow-Starters for Fluorescent Lamps
CAN/CSA-E335-1/3E-94 (R2013)	Safety of Household and Similar Electrical Appliances — Part 1: General Requirements
CAN/CSA-C22.2 No. 60335-1-16	Household and Similar Electrical Appliances — Safety — Part 1: General Requirements
CAN/CSA-E60335-2-2-06 (R2015)	Household and Similar Electrical Appliances — Safety — Part 2-2: Particular Requirements for Vacuum Cleaners and Water-Suction Cleaning Appliances
CAN/CSA-E60335-2-3-13	Household and Similar Electrical Appliances — Safety — Part 2-3: Particular Requirements for Electric Irons

Appendix A

CAN/CSA-E60335-2-4-13	Household and Similar Electrical Appliances — Safety — Part 2-4: Particular Requirements for Spin Extractors
CAN/CSA-E60335-2-5-12	Household and Similar Electrical Appliances — Safety — Part 2-5: Particular Requirements for Dishwashers
CAN/CSA-E60335-2-6-13	Household and Similar Electrical Appliances — Safety — Part 2-6: Particular Requirements for Stationary Cooking Ranges, Hobs, Ovens and Similar Appliances
CAN/CSA-E60335-2-7-13	Household and Similar Electrical Appliances — Safety — Part 2-7: Particular Requirements for Washing Machines
CAN/CSA-C22.2 No. 60335-2-8:16	Household and similar electrical appliances — Safety — Part 2-8: Particular requirements for shavers, hair clippers and similar appliances
CAN/CSA-C22.2 No. 60335-2-9:14	Household and similar electrical appliances — Safety — Part 2-9: Particular requirements for grills, toasters and similar portable cooking appliances
CAN/CSA-E60335-2-10-15	Household and Similar Electrical Appliances — Safety — Part 2-10: Particular Requirements for Floor Treatment Machines and Wet Scrubbing Machines
CAN/CSA-E60335-2-11-13	Household and Similar Electrical Appliances — Safety — Part 2-11: Particular Requirements for Tumble Dryers
CAN/CSA-E60335-2-12-13	Household and Similar Electrical Appliances — Safety — Part 2-12: Particular Requirements for Warming Plates and Similar Appliances
CAN/CSA-E60335-2-13-13	Household and Similar Electrical Appliances — Safety — Part 2-13: Particular Requirements for Deep Fat Fryers, Frying Pans, and Similar Appliances
CAN/CSA-E60335-2-14-05 (R2013)	Household and Similar Electrical Appliances — Safety — Part 2-14: Particular Requirements for Kitchen Machines
CAN/CSA-C22.2 No. 60335-2-15:14	Household and similar electrical appliances — Safety — Part 2-15: Particular requirements for appliances for heating liquids
CAN/CSA-C22.2 No. 60335-2-16:16	Household and similar electrical appliances — Safety — Part 2-16: Particular requirements for food waste disposers
CAN/CSA-E60335-2-21-01 (R2016)	Safety of Household and Similar Electrical Appliances — Part 2-21: Particular Requirements for Storage Water Heaters
CAN/CSA-C22.2 No. 60335-2-23:15	Household and similar electrical appliances — Safety — Part 2-23: Particular requirements for appliances for skin or hair care
CAN/CSA-C22.2 No. 60335-2-24-17	Household and Similar Electrical Appliances — Safety — Part 2-24: Particular Requirements for Refrigerating Appliances, Ice-Cream Appliances, and Ice-Makers
CAN/CSA-E60335-2-25-01 (R2016)	Safety of Household and Similar Electrical Appliances — Part 2-25: Particular Requirements for Microwave Ovens
CAN/CSA-E60335-2-26-13	Household and Similar Electrical Appliances — Safety — Part 2-26: Particular Requirements for Clocks
CAN/CSA-C22.2 No. 60335-2-27:16	Household and similar electrical appliances — Safety — Part 2-27: Particular requirements for appliances for skin exposure to ultraviolet and infrared radiation

CAN/CSA-C22.2 No. 60335-2-28:16	Household and similar electrical appliances — Safety — Part 2-28: Particular requirements for sewing machines
CAN/CSA-E60335-2-29-06 (R2016)	Household and Similar Electrical Appliances — Safety — Part 2-29: Particular Requirements for Battery Chargers
CAN/CSA-E60335-2-30-13	Household and Similar Electrical Appliances — Safety — Part 2-30: Particular Requirements for Room Heaters
CAN/CSA-E60335-2-31-12	Household and Similar Electrical Appliances — Safety — Part 2-31: Particular Requirements for Range Hoods and Other Cooking Fume Extractors
CAN/CSA-E60335-2-32-01 (R2016)	Safety of Household and Similar Electrical Appliances — Part 2-32: Particular Requirements for Massage Appliances
CAN/CSA-C22.2 No. 60335-2-34-13	Safety of Household and Similar Electrical Appliances — Part 2-34: Particular Requirements for Motor-Compressors
CAN/CSA-E60335-2-35-01 (R2016)	Safety of Household and Similar Electrical Appliances — Part 2: Particular Requirements for Instantaneous Water Heaters
CAN/CSA-E60335-2-36-01 (R2016)	Safety of Household and Similar Electrical Appliances — Part 2-36: Particular Requirements for Commercial Electric Cooking Ranges, Ovens, Hobs and Hob Elements
CAN/CSA-E60335-2-37-01 (R2016)	Safety of Household and Similar Electrical Appliances — Part 2-37: Particular Requirements for Commercial Electric Deep Fat Fryers
CAN/CSA-E60335-2-38-01 (R2016)	Safety of Household and Similar Electrical Appliances — Part 2-38: Particular Requirements for Commercial Electric Griddles and Griddle Grills
CAN/CSA-E60335-2-39-01 (R2016)	Safety of Household and Similar Electrical Appliances — Part 2-39: Particular Requirements for Commercial Electric Multi-Purpose Cooking Pans
CAN/CSA-C22.2 No. 60335-2-40-17	Household and Similar Electrical Appliances — Safety — Part 2-40: Particular Requirements for Electrical Heat Pumps, Air-Conditioners and Dehumidifiers
CAN/CSA-E60335-2-41-13	Household and Similar Electrical Appliances — Safety — Part 2-41: Particular Requirements for Pumps
CAN/CSA-E60335-2-42-01 (R2016)	Safety of Household and Similar Electrical Appliances — Part 2-42: Particular Requirements for Commercial Electric Forced Convection Ovens, Steam Cookers and Steam-Convection Ovens
CAN/CSA-E60335-2-43-13	Household and Similar Electrical Appliances — Safety — Part 2-43: Particular Requirements for Clothes Dryers and Towel Rails
CAN/CSA-C22.2 No. 60335-2-44-14	Household and Similar Electrical Appliances — Safety — Part 2-44: Particular Requirements for Ironers
CAN/CSA-C22.2 No. 60335-2-45-14	Household and Similar Electrical Appliances — Safety — Part 2-45: Particular Requirements for Portable Heating Tools and Similar Appliances
CAN/CSA-E60335-2-47-01 (R2016)	Safety of Household and Similar Electrical Appliances — Part 2-47: Particular Requirements for Commercial Electric Boiling Pans

Appendix A

CAN/CSA-E60335-2-48-01 (R2016)	Safety of Household and Similar Electrical Appliances — Part 2-48: Particular Requirements for Commercial Electric Grillers and Toasters
CAN/CSA-E60335-2-49-01 (R2016)	Safety of Household and Similar Electrical Appliances — Part 2-49: Particular Requirements for Commercial Electric Hot Cupboards
CAN/CSA-E60335-2-50-01 (R2016)	Safety of Household and Similar Electrical Appliances — Part 2-50: Particular Requirements for Commercial Electric Bains-Marie
CAN/CSA-E60335-2-51-01 (R2016)	Safety of Household and Similar Electrical Appliances — Part 2: Particular Requirements for Stationary Circulation Pumps for Heating and Service Water Installations
CAN/CSA-C22.2 No. 60335-2-52-14	Household and Similar Electrical Appliances — Safety — Part 2-52: Particular Requirements for Oral Hygiene Appliances
CAN/CSA-E60335-2-53-05 (R2013)	Household and Similar Electrical Appliances — Safety — Part 2-53: Particular Requirements for Sauna Heating Appliances
CAN/CSA-E60335-2-54-01 (R2015)	Safety of Household and Similar Electrical Appliances — Part 2: Particular Requirements for Surface-Cleaning Appliances Employing Liquids
CAN/CSA-C22.2 No. 60335-2-55:15	Household and similar electrical appliances — Safety — Part 2-55: Particular requirements for electrical appliances for use with aquariums and garden ponds
CAN/CSA-C22.2 No. 60335-2-56:15	Household and similar electrical appliances — Safety — Part 2-56: Particular requirements for projectors and similar appliances
CAN/CSA-C22.2 No. 60335-2-59:16	Household and similar electrical appliances — Safety — Part 2-59: Particular requirements for insect killers
CAN/CSA-E60335-2-61-11 (R2016)	Household and Similar Electrical Appliances — Safety — Part 2-61: Particular Requirements for Thermal Storage Room Heaters
CAN/CSA-E60335-2-64-01 (R2016)	Safety of Household and Similar Electrical Appliances — Part 2: Particular Requirements for Commercial Electric Kitchen Machines
CAN/CSA-E60335-2-65-11 (R2016)	Household and Similar Electrical Appliances — Safety — Part 2-65: Particular Requirements for Air-Cleaning Appliances
CAN/CSA-E60335-2-67-01 (R2015)	Safety of Household and Similar Electrical Appliances — Part 2: Particular Requirements for Floor Treatment and Floor Cleaning Machines, for Industrial and Commercial Use
CAN/CSA-E60335-2-68-01 (R2015)	Safety of Household and Similar Electrical Appliances — Part 2: Particular Requirements for Spray Extraction Appliances, for Industrial and Commercial Use
CAN/CSA-E60335-2-69-01 (R2015)	Safety of Household and Similar Electrical Appliances — Part 2: Particular Requirements for Wet and Dry Vacuum Cleaners, Including Power Brush, for Industrial and Commercial Use
CAN/CSA-E60335-2-70-06 (R2016)	Household and Similar Electrical Appliances — Safety — Part 2-70: Particular Requirements for Milking Machines

CAN/CSA-E60335-2-76-05 (R2013)	Household and Similar Electrical Appliances — Safety — Part 2-76: Particular Requirements for Electric Fence Energizers
CAN/CSA-C22.2 No. 60335-2-78:14	Household and similar electrical appliances — Safety — Part 2-78: Particular requirements for outdoor barbecues
CAN/CSA-E60335-2-79-09 (R2013)	Household and Similar Electrical Appliances — Safety — Part 2-79: Particular Requirements for High Pressure Cleaners and Steam Cleaners
CAN/CSA-E60335-2-82-13	Household and Similar Electrical Appliances — Safety — Part 2-82: Particular Requirements for Amusement Machines and Personal Service Machines
CAN/CSA-C22.2 No. 60335-2-102:16	Household and similar electrical appliances — Safety — Part 2-102: Particular requirements for gas, oil and solid-fuel burning appliances having electrical connections
CAN/CSA-E342-1-95 (R2016)	Safety Requirements for Electric Fans and Regulators — Part 1: Fans and Regulators for Household and Similar Purposes
CAN/CSA-E60384-1-14	Fixed Capacitors for Use in Electronic Equipment — Part 1: Generic Specification
CAN/CSA-E60384-14-14	Fixed Capacitors for Use in Electronic Equipment — Part 14: Sectional Specification: Fixed Capacitors for Electromagnetic Interference Suppression and Connection to the Supply Mains
CAN/CSA-E432-1-98 (R2017)	Safety Specifications for Incandescent Lamps — Part 1: Tungsten Filament Lamps for Domestic and Similar General Lighting Purposes
CAN/CSA-E432-2-98 (R2017)	Safety Specifications for Incandescent Lamps — Part 2: Tungsten Halogen Lamps for Domestic and Similar General Lighting Purposes
CAN/CSA-E491-94 (R2013)	Safety Requirements for Electronic Flash Apparatus for Photographic Purposes
CAN/CSA-E570-98 (R2017)	Electrical Supply Track Systems for Luminaires
CAN/CSA-E60598-1-16	Luminaires — Part 1: General Requirements and Tests
CAN/CSA-E598-2-1-98 (R2017)	Luminaires — Part 2: Particular Requirements — Section 1: Fixed General-Purpose Luminaires
CAN/CSA-E598-2-2-98 (R2017)	Luminaires — Part 2: Particular Requirements — Section 2: Recessed Luminaires
CAN/CSA-E60598-2-3-98 (R2017)	Luminaires — Part 2: Particular Requirements — Section 3: Luminaires for Road and Street Lighting
CAN/CSA-E60598-2-4-98 (R2017)	Luminaires — Part 2: Particular Requirements — Section 4: Portable General-Purpose Luminaires
CAN/CSA-E60598-2-5-02 (R2016)	Luminaires — Part 2-5: Particular Requirements — Floodlights
CAN/CSA-E598-2-6-98 (R2017)	Luminaires — Part 2: Particular Requirements — Section 6: Luminaires with Built-in Transformers for Filament Lamps
CAN/CSA-E598-2-7-98 (R2017)	Luminaires — Part 2: Particular Requirements — Section 7: Portable Luminaires for Garden Use

CAN/CSA-E598-2-8-98 (R2017)	Luminaires — Part 2: Particular Requirements — Section 8: Handlamps
CAN/CSA-E598-2-9-98 (R2017)	Luminaires — Part 2: Particular Requirements — Section 9: Photo and Film Luminaires (Non-professional)
CAN/CSA-E598-2-10-98 (R2017)	Luminaires — Part 2: Particular Requirements — Section 10: Portable Child-Appealing Luminaires
CAN/CSA-E598-2-17-98 (R2017)	Luminaires — Part 2: Particular Requirements — Section 17: Luminaires for Stage Lighting, Television and Film Studios (Outdoor and Indoor)
CAN/CSA-E598-2-18-98 (R2017)	Luminaires — Part 2: Particular Requirements — Section 18: Luminaires for Swimming Pools and Similar Applications
CAN/CSA-E598-2-19-98 (R2017)	Luminaires — Part 2: Particular Requirements — Section 19: Air-Handling Luminaires (Safety Requirements)
CAN/CSA-C22.2 No. 60691:15	Thermal-links — Requirements and application guide
CAN/CSA-E60730-1-15	Automatic Electrical Controls for Household and Similar Use — Part 1: General Requirements
CAN/CSA-E730-2-1-94 (R2013)	Automatic Electrical Controls for Household and Similar Use — Part 2: Particular requirements for electrical controls for electrical household appliances
CAN/CSA-E730-2-2-94 (R2013)	Automatic Electrical Controls for Household and Similar Use — Part 2: Particular Requirements for Thermal Motor Protectors
CAN/CSA-E730-2-3-94 (R2013)	Automatic Electrical Controls for Household and Similar Use — Part 2: Particular Requirements for Thermal Protectors for Ballasts for Tubular Fluorescent Lamps
CAN/CSA-E60730-2-4-13	Automatic Electrical Controls for Household and Similar Use — Part 2-4: Particular Requirements for Thermal Motor Protectors for Motor-Compressors of Hermetic and Semi-Hermetic Type
CAN/CSA-E730-2-5-94 (R2013)	Automatic Electrical Controls for Household and Similar Use — Part 2: Particular requirements for automatic electrical burner control systems
ANSI Z21.20-2014/CAN/CSA-C22.2 No. 60730-2-5-14	Automatic Electrical Controls for Household and Similar Use — Part 2-5: Particular Requirements for Automatic Electrical Burner Control Systems
CAN/CSA-E730-2-6-94 (R2013)	Automatic Electrical Controls for Household and Similar Use — Part 2: Particular Requirements for Automatic Electrical Pressure Sensing Controls Including Mechanical Requirements
CAN/CSA-E730-2-7-94 (R2013)	Automatic Electrical Controls for Household and Similar Use — Part 2: Particular Requirements for Timers and Time Switches
CAN/CSA-E60730-2-8-17	Automatic Electrical Controls for Household and Similar Use — Part 2-8: Particular Requirements for Electrically Operated Water Valves, Including Mechanical Requirements
CAN/CSA-E60730-2-9-15	Automatic Electrical Controls for Household and Similar Use — Part 2-9: Particular Requirements for Temperature Sensing Controls

CAN/CSA-E60730-2-10-13	Automatic Electrical Controls for Household and Similar Use — Part 2-10: Particular Requirements for Motor-Starting Relays
CAN/CSA-E730-2-11-94 (R2013)	Automatic Electrical Controls for Household and Similar Use — Part 2: Particular Requirements for Energy Regulators
CAN/CSA-E730-2-12-94 (R2013)	Automatic Electrical Controls for Household and Similar Use — Part 2: Particular Requirements for Electrically Operated Door Locks
CAN/CSA-E60730-2-14-13	Automatic Electrical Controls for Household and Similar Use — Part 2-14: Particular Requirements for Electric Actuators
CAN/CSA-E60730-2-15-14	Automatic Electrical Controls for Household and Similar Use — Part 2-15: Particular Requirements for Automatic Electrical Air Flow, Water Flow and Water Level Sensing Controls
CAN/CSA-E60825-1-15	Safety of Laser Products — Part 1: Equipment Classification, Requirements and User's Guide
CAN/CSA-E920-98 (R2017)	Ballasts for Tubular Fluorescent Lamps — General and Safety Requirements
CAN/CSA-E922-98 (R2017)	Ballasts for Discharge Lamps (Excluding Tubular Fluorescent Lamps) — General Safety Requirements
CAN/CSA-E926-98 (R2017)	Auxiliaries for Lamps — Starting Devices (Other than Glow Starters) — General and Safety Requirements
CAN/CSA-E968-99 (R2013)	Self-Ballasted Lamps for General Lighting Services — Safety Requirements
CAN/CSA-E60974-1-12	Arc Welding Equipment — Part 1: Welding Power Sources
CAN/CSA-E60974-5-09 (R2013)	Arc Welding Equipment — Part 5: Wire Feeders
CAN/CSA-E60974-7-02 (R2016)	Arc Welding Equipment — Part 7: Torches
CAN/CSA-E1029-1-94 (R2013)	Safety of Transportable Motor-Operated Electric Tools — Part 1: General Requirements
CAN/CSA-E1029-2-1-94 (R2013)	Safety of Transportable Motor-Operated Electric Tools — Part 2: Particular Requirements for Circular Saws
CAN/CSA-E1029-2-2-94 (R2013)	Safety of Transportable Motor-Operated Electric Tools — Part 2: Particular Requirements for Radial Arm Saws
CAN/CSA-E1029-2-3-94 (R2013)	Safety of Transportable Motor-Operated Electric Tools — Part 2: Particular Requirements for Planers and Thicknessers
CAN/CSA-E1029-2-4-94 (R2013)	Safety of Transportable Motor-Operated Electric Tools — Part 2: Particular Requirements for Bench Grinders
CAN/CSA-E1029-2-5-94 (R2013)	Safety of Transportable Motor-Operated Electric Tools — Part 2: Particular Requirements for Band Saws
CAN/CSA-E1029-2-6-94 (R2013)	Safety of Transportable Motor-Operated Electric Tools — Part 2: Particular Requirements for Diamond Drills with Water Supply
CAN/CSA-E1029-2-7-94 (R2013)	Safety of Transportable Motor-Operated Electric Tools — Part 2: Particular Requirements for Diamond Saws with Water Supply

Appendix A

CAN/CSA-C22.2 No. 61029-2-8-06 (R2016)	Safety of Transportable Motor-Operated Electric Tools — Part 2: Particular Requirements for Single Spindle Vertical Moulders
CAN/CSA-C22.2 No. 61029-2-9-06 (R2016)	Safety of Transportable Motor-Operated Electric Tools — Part 2: Particular Requirements for Mitre Saws
CAN/CSA-C22.2 No. 61029-2-10-06 (R2016)	Safety of Transportable Motor-Operated Electric Tools — Part 2-10: Particular Requirements for Cutting-Off Grinders
CAN/CSA-E1048-98 (R2013)	Capacitors for Use in Tubular Fluorescent and Other Discharge Lamp Circuits — General and Safety Requirements
CAN/CSA-E61347-1-03 (R2013)	Lamp Controlgear — Part 1: General and Safety Requirements
CAN/CSA-E61347-2-3-03 (R2013)	Lamp Controlgear — Part 2-3: Particular Requirements for A.C. Supplied Electronic Ballasts for Fluorescent Lamps
CAN/CSA-C22.2 No. 61347-2-13:15	Lamp controlgear — Part 2-13: Particular requirements for d.c. or a.c. supplied electronic controlgear for LED modules
CAN/CSA-E61558-1-17	Safety of Power Transformers, Power Supplies, Reactors and Similar Products — Part 1: General Requirements and Tests
CAN/CSA-E61558-2-1-03 (R2017)	Safety of Power Transformers, Power Supply Units and Similar — Part 2: Particular Requirements for Separating Transformers for General Use
CAN/CSA-E61558-2-2-03 (R2017)	Safety of Power Transformers, Power Supply Units and Similar — Part 2-2: Particular Requirements for Control Transformers
CAN/CSA-E61558-2-4-03 (R2017)	Safety of Power Transformers, Power Supply Units and Similar — Part 2: Particular Requirements for Isolating Transformers for General Use
CAN/CSA-E61558-2-5-03 (R2017)	Safety of Power Transformers, Power Supply Units and Similar — Part 2-5: Particular Requirements for Shaver Transformers and Shaver Supply Units
CAN/CSA-E61558-2-6-03 (R2017)	Safety of Power Transformers, Power Supply Units and Similar — Part 2: Particular Requirements for Safety Isolating Transformers for General Use
CAN/CSA-E61558-2-13-03 (R2017)	Safety of Power Transformers, Power Supply Units and Similar Devices — Part 2-13: Particular Requirements for Auto-Transformers for General Use
CAN/CSA-E61965-04 (R2013)	Mechanical Safety of Cathode Ray Tubes
CAN/CSA-C22.2 No. 62031-13	LED Modules for General Lighting — Safety Specifications
CAN/CSA-E62133-13	Secondary Cells and Batteries Containing Alkaline or Other Non-Acid Electrolytes — Safety Requirements for Portable Sealed Secondary Cells, and for Batteries Made From Them, For use in Portable Applications
CAN/CSA-C22.2 No. 62471-12	Photobiological Safety of Lamps and Lamp Systems
CAN/CSA-C22.2 No. 62560:16	Self-ballasted LED-lamps for general lighting services by voltage > 50 V — Safety specifications
CAN/CSA-E62660-1:15	Secondary lithium-ion cells for the propulsion of electric road vehicles — Part 1: Performance testing

CAN/CSA-E62660-2:15 — Secondary lithium-ion cells for the propulsion of electric road vehicles — Part 2: Reliability and abuse testing

CAN/CSA-C22.2 No. 62841-1-15 — Electric motor-operated hand-held tools, transportable tools and lawn and garden machinery — Safety — Part 1: General requirements

CAN/CSA-C22.2 No. 62841-2-2:16 — Electric motor-operated hand-held tools, transportable tools and lawn and garden machinery — Safety — Part 2-2: Particular requirements for hand-held screwdrivers and impact wrenches

CAN/CSA-C22.2 No. 62841-2-4:15 — Electric motor-operated hand-held tools, transportable tools and lawn and garden machinery — Safety — Part 2-4: Particular requirements for hand-held sanders and polishers other than disc type

CAN/CSA-C22.2 No. 62841-2-5:16 — Electric motor-operated hand-held tools, transportable tools and lawn and garden machinery — Safety — Part 2-5: Particular requirements for hand-held circular saws

CAN/CSA-C22.2 No. 62841-2-8:16 — Electric motor-operated hand-held tools, transportable tools and lawn and garden machinery — Safety — Part 2-8: Particular requirements for hand-held shears and nibblers

CAN/CSA-C22.2 No. 62841-2-9:16 — Electric motor-operated hand-held tools, transportable tools and lawn and garden machinery — Safety — Part 2-9: Particular requirements for hand-held tappers and threaders

CAN/CSA-C22.2 No. 62841-2-11:17 — Electric motor-operated hand-held tools, transportable tools and lawn and garden machinery — Safety — Part 2-11: Particular requirements for hand-held reciprocating saws

CAN/CSA-C22.2 No. 62841-2-14:16 — Electric motor-operated hand-held tools, transportable tools and lawn and garden machinery — Safety — Part 2-14: Particular requirements for hand-held planers

CAN/CSA-C22.2 No. 62841-3-1:16 — Electric motor-operated hand-held tools, transportable tools and lawn and garden machinery — Safety — Part 3-1: Particular requirements for transportable table saws

CAN/CSA-C22.2 No. 62841-3-4:16 — Electric motor-operated hand-held tools, transportable tools and lawn and garden machinery — Safety — Part 3-4: Particular requirements for transportable bench grinders

CAN/CSA-C22.2 No. 62841-3-6:16 — Electric motor-operated hand-held tools, transportable tools and lawn and garden machinery — Safety — Part 3-6: Particular requirements for transportable diamond drills with liquid system

CAN/CSA-C22.2 No. 62841-3-9:16 — Electric motor-operated hand-held tools, transportable tools and lawn and garden machinery — Safety — Part 3-9: Particular requirements for transportable mitre saws

CAN/CSA-C22.2 No. 62841-3-10:16 — Electric motor-operated hand-held tools, transportable tools and lawn and garden machinery — Safety — Part 3-10: Particular requirements for transportable cut-off machines

Appendix A

Health care products

CAN/CSA-C22.2 No. 60601-1-14	Medical Electrical Equipment — Part 1: General Requirements for Basic Safety and Essential Performance
CAN/CSA-C22.2 No. 60601-1-2-16	Medical Electrical Equipment — Part 1-2: General Requirements for Basic Safety and Essential Performance — Collateral Standard: Electromagnetic Compatibility — Requirements and Tests
CAN/CSA-C22.2 No. 60601-1-3-09 (R2014)	Medical Electrical Equipment — Part 1-3: General Requirements for Basic Safety and Essential Performance — Collateral Standard: Radiation Protection in Diagnostic X-Ray Equipment
CAN/CSA-C22.2 No. 60601-1-6-11 (R2016)	Medical Electrical Equipment — Part 1-6: General Requirements for Basic Safety and Essential Performance — Collateral Standard: Usability
CAN/CSA-C22.2 No. 60601-1-8-08 (R2014)	Medical Electrical Equipment — Part 1-8: General Requirements for Basic Safety and Essential Performance — Collateral Standard: General Requirements, Tests and Guidance for Alarm Systems in Medical Electrical Equipment and Medical Electrical Systems
CAN/CSA-C22.2 No. 60601-1-9:15	Medical electrical equipment — Part 1-9: General requirements for basic safety and essential performance — Collateral Standard: Requirements for environmentally conscious design
CAN/CSA-C22.2 No. 60601-1-10-09 (R2014)	Medical Electrical Equipment — Part 1-10: General Requirements for Basic Safety and Essential Performance — Collateral Standard: Requirements for the Development of Physiologic Closed-Loop Controllers
CAN/CSA-C22.2 No. 60601-1-11-15	Medical Electrical Equipment — Part 1-11: General Requirements for Basic Safety and Essential Performance — Collateral Standard: Requirements for Medical Electrical Equipment and Medical Electrical Systems Used in the Home Healthcare Environment
CAN/CSA-C22.2 No. 60601-1-12:15	Medical electrical equipment — Part 1-12: General requirements for basic safety and essential performance — Collateral Standard: Requirements for medical electrical equipment and medical electrical systems intended for use in the emergency medical services environment
CAN/CSA-C22.2 No. 60601-2-1-11 (R2016)	Medical Electrical Equipment — Part 2-1: Particular Requirements for the Basic Safety and Essential Performance of Electron Accelerators in the Range 1 MeV to 50 MeV
CAN/CSA-C22.2 No. 60601-2-2-09 (R2014)	Medical Electrical Equipment — Part 2-2: Particular Requirements for the Basic Safety and Essential Performance of High Frequency Surgical Equipment and High Frequency Surgical Accessories
CAN/CSA-C22.2 No. 60601-2-3-14	Medical Electrical Equipment, Part 2-3: Particular Requirements for the Basic Safety and Essential Performance of Short-Wave Therapy Equipment

CAN/CSA-C22.2 No. 60601-2-4-12 (R2016)
Medical Electrical Equipment — Part 2-4: Particular Requirements for the Basic Safety and Essential Performance of Cardiac Defibrillators

CAN/CSA-C22.2 No. 60601-2-5-11 (R2016)
Medical Electrical Equipment — Part 2-5: Particular Requirements for the Basic Safety and Essential Performance of Ultrasonic Physiotherapy Equipment

CAN/CSA-C22.2 No. 60601-2-6-14
Medical Electrical Equipment — Part 2-6: Particular Requirements for the Basic Safety and Essential Performance of Microwave Therapy Equipment

CAN/CSA-C22.2 No. 60601-2-8-12 (R2016)
Medical Electrical Equipment — Part 2-8: Particular Requirements for the Basic Safety and Essential Performance of Therapeutic X-Ray Equipment Operating in the Range 10 kV to 1 MV

CAN/CSA-C22.2 No. 60601-2-10-14
Medical Electrical Equipment — Part 2-10: Particular Requirements for the Basic Safety and Essential Performance of Nerve and Muscle Stimulators

CAN/CSA-C22.2 No. 60601-2-11-15
Medical Electrical Equipment — Part 2-11: Particular Requirements for the Safety of Gamma Beam Therapy Equipment

CAN/CSA-C22.2 No. 60601-2-16-14
Medical Electrical Equipment — Part 2-16: Particular Requirements for the Basic Safety and Essential Performance of Haemodialysis, Haemodiafiltration and Haemofiltration Equipment

CAN/CSA-C22.2 No. 60601-2-17-15
Medical Electrical Equipment — Part 2-17: Particular Requirements for the Basic Safety and Essential Performance of Automatically-Controlled Brachytherapy Afterloading Equipment

CAN/CSA-C22.2 No. 60601-2-18-11 (R2016)
Medical Electrical Equipment — Part 2-18: Particular Requirements for the Basic Safety and Essential Performance of Endoscopic Equipment

CAN/CSA-C22.2 No. 60601-2-19-09 (R2014)
Medical Electrical Equipment — Part 2-19: Particular Requirements for the Basic Safety and Essential Performance of Infant Incubators

CAN/CSA-C22.2 No. 60601-2-20-10 (R2014)
Medical Electrical Equipment — Part 2-20: Particular Requirements for the Basic Safety and Essential Performance of Infant Transport Incubators

CAN/CSA-C22.2 No. 60601-2-21-10 (R2014)
Medical Electrical Equipment — Part 2-21: Particular Requirements for the Basic Safety and Essential Performance of Infant Radiant Warmers

CAN/CSA-C22.2 No. 60601-2-22-08 (R2014)
Medical Electrical Equipment — Part 2-22: Particular Requirements for Basic Safety and Essential Performance of Surgical, Cosmetic, Therapeutic and Diagnostic Laser Equipment

CAN/CSA-C22.2 No. 60601-2-23-12 (R2016)
Medical Electrical Equipment — Part 2-23: Particular Requirements for the Basic Safety and Essential Performance of Transcutaneous Partial Pressure Monitoring Equipment

CAN/CSA-C22.2 No. 60601-2-24-15
Medical Electrical Equipment — Part 2-24: Particular Requirements for the Basic Safety and Essential Performance of Infusion Pumps and Controllers

Appendix A

CAN/CSA-C22.2 No. 60601-2-25-12 (R2017)	Medical Electrical Equipment — Part 2-25: Particular Requirements for the Basic Safety and Essential Performance of Electrocardiographs
CAN/CSA-C22.2 No. 60601-2-26-14	Medical Electrical Equipment — Part 2-26: Particular Requirements for the Basic Safety and Essential Performance of Electroencephalographs
CAN/CSA-C22.2 No. 60601-2-27-11 (R2016)	Medical Electrical Equipment — Part 2-27: Particular Requirements for the Basic Safety and Essential Performance of Electrocardiographic Monitoring Equipment
CAN/CSA-C22.2 No. 60601-2-28-12 (R2016)	Medical Electrical Equipment, Part 2-28: Particular Requirements for the Basic Safety and Essential Performance of X-Ray Tube Assemblies for Medical Diagnosis
CAN/CSA-C22.2 No. 60601-2-29-10 (R2014)	Medical Electrical Equipment — Part 2-29: Particular Requirements for the Basic Safety and Essential Performance of Radiotherapy Simulators
CAN/CSA-C22.2 No. 60601-2-31-09 (R2014)	Medical Electrical Equipment — Part 2-31: Particular Requirements for the Basic Safety and Essential Performance of External Cardiac Pacemakers with Internal Power Source
CAN/CSA-C22.2 No. 60601-2-33-12 (R2016)	Medical Electrical Equipment — Part 2-33: Particular Requirements for the Basic Safety and Essential Performance of Magnetic Resonance Equipment for Medical Diagnosis
CAN/CSA-C22.2 No. 60601-2-34-12 (R2017)	Medical Electrical Equipment — Part 2-34: Particular Requirements for the Basic Safety and Essential Performance of Invasive Blood-Pressure Monitoring Equipment
CAN/CSA-C22.2 No. 60601-2-36-16	Medical Electrical Equipment — Part 2-36: Particular Requirements for the Basic Safety and Essential Performance of Equipment for Extracorporeally Induced Lithotripsy
CAN/CSA-C22.2 No. 60601-2-37-08 (R2014)	Medical Electrical Equipment — Part 2-37: Particular Requirements for the Basic Safety and Essential Performance of Ultrasonic Medical Diagnostic and Monitoring Equipment
CAN/CSA-C22.2 No. 60601-2-39-09 (R2014)	Medical Electrical Equipment — Part 2-39: Particular Requirements for Basic Safety and Essential Performance of Peritoneal Dialysis Equipment
CAN/CSA-C22.2 No. 60601-2-40-17	Medical Electrical Equipment — Part 2-40: Particular Requirements for the Basic Safety and Essential Performance of Electromyographs and Evoked Response Equipment
CAN/CSA-C22.2 No. 60601-2-41-11 (R2016)	Medical Electrical Equipment — Part 2-41: Particular Requirements for the Basic Safety and Essential Performance of Surgical Luminaires and Luminaires for Diagnosis
CAN/CSA-C22.2 No. 60601-2-43-11 (R2016)	Medical Electrical Equipment — Part 2-43: Particular Requirements for the Basic Safety and Essential Performance of X-Ray Equipment for Interventional Procedures
CAN/CSA-C22.2 No. 60601-2-44-10 (R2015)	Medical Electrical Equipment — Part 2-44: Particular Requirements for the Basic Safety and Essential Performance of X-Ray Equipment for Computed Tomography
CAN/CSA-C22.2 No. 60601-2-45-11 (R2016)	Medical Electrical Equipment — Part 2-45: Particular Requirements for the Basic Safety and Essential Performance

of Mammographic X-Ray Equipment and Mammographic Stereotactic Devices

CAN/CSA-C22.2 No. 60601-2-46-12 (R2016)	Medical Electrical Equipment — Part 2-46: Particular Requirements for the Basic Safety and Essential Performance of Operating Tables
CAN/CSA-C22.2 No. 60601-2-47-14	Medical Electrical Equipment — Part 2-47: Particular Requirements for the Basic Safety and Essential Performance of Ambulatory Electrocardiographic Systems
CAN/CSA-C22.2 No. 60601-2-49-11 (R2016)	Medical Electrical Equipment — Part 2-49: Particular Requirements for the Basic Safety and Essential Performance of Multifunction Patient Monitoring Equipment
CAN/CSA-C22.2 No. 60601-2-50-10 (R2014)	Medical Electrical Equipment — Part 2-50: Particular Requirements for the Basic Safety and Essential Performance of Infant Phototherapy Equipment
CAN/CSA-C22.2 No. 60601-2-52-11 (R2016)	Medical Electrical Equipment — Part 2-52: Particular Requirements for the Basic Safety and Essential Performance of Medical Beds
CAN/CSA-C22.2 No. 60601-2-54-11 (R2016)	Medical Electrical Equipment — Part 2-54: Particular Requirements for the Basic Safety and Essential Performance of X-ray Equipment for Radiography and Radioscopy
CAN/CSA-C22.2 No. 60601-2-57-11 (R2016)	Medical Electrical Equipment — Part 2-57: Particular Requirements for the Basic Safety and Essential Performance of Non-Laser Light Source Equipment Intended for Therapeutic, Diagnostic, Monitoring and Cosmetic/Aesthetic Use
CAN/CSA-C22.2 No. 60601-2-62:15	Medical electrical equipment — Part 2-62: Particular requirements for the basic safety and essential performance of high intensity therapeutic ultrasound (HITU) equipment
CAN/CSA-C22.2 No. 60601-2-63:15	Medical electrical equipment — Part 2-63: Particular requirements for the basic safety and essential performance of dental extra-oral X-ray equipment
CAN/CSA-C22.2 No. 60601-2-64:15	Medical electrical equipment — Part 2-64: Particular requirements for the basic safety and essential performance of light ion beam medical electrical equipment
CAN/CSA-C22.2 No. 60601-2-65:15	Medical electrical equipment — Part 2-65: Particular requirements for the basic safety and essential performance of dental intra-oral X-ray equipment
CAN/CSA-C22.2 No. 60601-2-66:15	Medical electrical equipment — Part 2-66: Particular requirements for the basic safety and essential performance of hearing instruments and hearing instrument systems
CAN/CSA-C22.2 No. 60601-2-68:15	Medical electrical equipment — Part 2-68: Particular requirements for the basic safety and essential performance of X-ray-based image-guided radiotherapy equipment for use with electron accelerators, light ion beam therapy equipment and radionuclide beam therapy equipment
CAN/CSA-C22.2 No. 80601-2-12-12 (R2017)	Medical Electrical Equipment — Part 2-12: Particular Requirements for the Basic Safety and Essential Performance of Critical Care Ventilators

Appendix A

CAN/CSA-C22.2 No. 80601-2-13:15	Medical electrical equipment — Part 2-13: Particular requirements for basic safety and essential performance of an anaesthetic workstation
CAN/CSA-C22.2 No. 80601-2-30-10 (R2015)	Medical Electrical Equipment — Part 2-30: Particular Requirements for the Basic Safety and Essential Performance of Automated Non-invasive Sphygmomanometers
CAN/CSA-C22.2 No. 80601-2-35-12 (R2016)	Medical Electrical Equipment — Part 2-35: Particular Requirements for the Basic Safety and Essential Performance of Heating Devices Using Blankets, Pads or Mattresses and Intended for Heating in Medical Use
CAN/CSA-C22.2 No. 80601-2-55-14	Medical Electrical Equipment — Part 2-55: Particular Requirements for the Basic Safety and Essential Performance of Respiratory Gas Monitors
CAN/CSA-C22.2 No. 80601-2-56-12 (R2016)	Medical Electrical Equipment — Part 2-56: Particular Requirements for the Basic Safety and Essential Performance of Clinical Thermometers for Body Temperature Measurement
CAN/CSA-C22.2 No. 80601-2-58-15	Medical Electrical Equipment — Part 2-58: Particular Requirements for the Basic Safety and Essential Performance of Lens Removal Devices and Vitrectomy Devices for Ophthalmic Surgery
CAN/CSA-C22.2 No. 80601-2-59-10 (R2015)	Medical Electrical Equipment — Part 2-59: Particular Requirements for the Basic Safety and Essential Performance of Screening Thermographs for Human Febrile Temperature Screening
CAN/CSA-C22.2 No. 80601-2-60:14	Medical electrical equipment — Part 2-60: Particular requirements for the basic safety and essential performance of dental equipment
CAN/CSA-C22.2 No. 80601-2-61-14	Medical Electrical Equipment — Part 2-61: Particular Requirements for the Basic Safety and Essential Performance of Pulse Oximeter Equipment
CAN/CSA-C22.2 No. 80601-2-67:17	Medical electrical equipment — Part 2-67: Particular requirements for basic safety and essential performance of oxygen conserving equipment
CAN/CSA-C22.2 No. 80601-2-69:16	Medical electrical equipment — Part 2-69: Particular requirements for basic safety and essential performance of oxygen concentrator equipment
CAN/CSA-C22.2 No. 80601-2-70:17	Medical electrical equipment — Part 2-70: Particular requirements for basic safety and essential performance of sleep apnoea breathing therapy equipment
CAN/CSA-C22.2 No. 80601-2-72:17	Medical electrical equipment — Part 2-72: Particular requirements for basic safety and essential performance of home healthcare environment ventilators for ventilator dependent patients

Renewables

| C22.2 No. 272-14 | Wind turbine electrical systems |
| C22.2 No. 290-15 | Photovoltaic combiners |

C22.2 No. 330-17	Photovoltaic rapid shutdown systems
CAN/CSA-C22.2 No. 62109-1:16	Safety of power converters for use in photovoltaic power systems — Part 1: General requirements
CAN/CSA-C22.2 No. 62109-2:16	Safety of power converters for use in photovoltaic power systems — Part 2: Particular requirements for inverters

Annex A.2
Other Canadian safety standards for electrical equipment

CAN/ULC-S304-2016	Signal Receiving Centre and Premise Burglar Alarm Control Units
ULC-S306-03	Intrusion Detection Units
ULC-S318-96 (R2016)	Power Supplies for Burglar Alarm Systems
ANSI/CAN/UL 96	Lightning Protection Components
CAN/ULC-S319-05	Electronic Access Control Systems
ANSI/CAN/UL 325	Door, Drapery, Gate, Louver, and Window Operators and Systems
CAN/ULC-S524-14-AM1	Standard for Installation of Fire Alarm Systems
CAN/ULC-S525-2016	Audible Signal Devices for Fire Alarm Systems, Including Accessories
CAN/ULC-S526-2016	Visible Signal Devices for Fire Alarm Systems, Including Accessories
CAN/ULC-S527-11 (Amd. 1, 2014)	Control Units for Fire Alarm Systems
CAN/ULC-S528-2014	Manual Stations for Fire Alarm Systems, Including Accessories Systems
ULC-S529-2016	Smoke Detectors for Fire Alarm Systems
CAN/ULC-S530-M91 (R1999)	Standard for Heat Actuated Fire Detectors for Fire Alarm Systems
CAN/ULC-S531-14	Standard for Smoke Alarms
CAN/ULC-S533-2015	Egress Door Securing and Releasing Devices
CAN/ULC-S541-2016	Speakers for Fire Alarm Systems, Including Accessories
ULC-S545-02	Standard for Residential Fire Warning Alarm Systems Control Units
CAN/ULC-S559-13	Standard for Equipment for Signal Receiving Centres & Systems
ULC-S571 (ULC/ORD-C386-90)	Flame Detectors for Fire Alarm Systems
ULC-S645-93 (R2016)	Standard for Power Roof Ventilators for Commercial and Institutional Kitchen Exhaust Systems
CAN/ULC-S646-10 (R2016)	Standard for Exhaust Hoods and Related Controls for Commercial and Institutional Kitchens
CAN/ULC-S1088-15	Standard for Temporary Lighting Strings

ANSI/CAN/UL/ULC 2271	Batteries for Use in Light Electric Vehicle (LEV) Applications
CAN/ULC-S2577-13-AM2	Standard for Suspended Ceiling Grid Low Voltage Systems and Equipment
ANSI/CAN/UL/ULC 2580	Batteries for Use in Electric Vehicles
CAN/ULC-S8752-12-AM1	Standard for Organic Light Emitting Diode (OLED) Panels
CAN/ULC-S8753-13	Standard for Field-Replaceable Light Emitting Diode (LED) Light Engines
CAN/ULC-S8754-13-AM1	Standard for Holders, Bases and Connectors for Solid-State (LED) Light Engines and Arrays
ANSI/CAN/UL 9540	Energy Storage Systems and Equipment
CAN/ULC-60839-11-1:2016	Alarm and Electronic Security Systems — Part 11-1: Electronic Access Control Systems — System and Components Requirements

Appendix B — Notes on Rules

Note: *This Appendix is an informative (non-mandatory) part of this Standard.*

The notes and illustrations in this Appendix are for information and clarification purposes only and apply to the following:

Appendix B

Section 0

Object

The safety provisions of this Code are not intended to limit installation methods to those specifically described by the Rules in this Code. The safety objectives of this Code may be met by utilizing alternative installation methods based on the fundamental safety principles of IEC 60364-1.

Such alternative methods are intended only for industrial and similar installations where objective-based installation criteria are addressed under the provisions of safety management systems or equivalent programs developed between users (industrial plants, independent power producers, etc.) and the authorities adopting and enforcing this Code.

Chapter 13 of IEC 60364-1 offers the fundamental safety principles and is included in Appendix K.

Approved

It is intended by this definition that electrical equipment installed under provisions of this Code is required to be certified to the applicable CSA product Standards as listed in Appendix A. Where such CSA Standards do not exist or are not applicable, it is intended by this definition that such electrical equipment be certified to other applicable Standards, such as ULC Standards. Code users should be aware that fire alarm system equipment is deemed to be approved when it is certified to the applicable product Standards listed in CAN/ULC-S524.

This definition is also intended to reflect the fact that equipment approval could be accomplished via a field evaluation procedure in conformance with CSA Model Code SPE-1000, where special inspection bodies are recognized by participating provincial and territorial authorities having jurisdiction. For new products that are not available at the time this Code is adopted, the authority having jurisdiction may permit the use of products that comply with the requirements set out by that jurisdiction.

Cablebus

Cablebus is ordinarily assembled at the point of installation from the components furnished or specified by the manufacturer in accordance with instructions for the specific job. This assembly is designed to carry fault current and to withstand the magnetic forces of such current.

Circuit

For the purposes of this Code, a circuit is generally considered to mean the portion of a wiring installation that is connected to the load side terminals of an ac or dc system and that forms a complete path or paths through which electrical current is normally intended to flow, including utilization equipment. For example, a cable connecting the load side terminals of a three-phase circuit breaker up to and including utilization equipment is generally considered to be a circuit, as would be a similar 3-wire single-phase installation.

Ground fault circuit interrupter, Class A (Class A GFCI)

A Class A ground fault circuit interrupter (Class A GFCI) is an interrupter that will interrupt the circuit to the load when the ground fault current is 6 mA or more, but not when the ground fault current is 4 mA* or less in a time

a) not greater than that given by the equation

$$T = \left(\frac{20}{I}\right)^{1.43}$$

where

T is in seconds; and

I is the ground fault current in rms milliamperes for fault currents between 4 mA and 260 mA; and

b) not greater than 25 ms for ground fault currents over 260 mA.

* *When the ambient air temperature is less than −5 °C or more than 40 °C, the minimum tripping current may be 3.5 mA instead of 4.*

In addition, a Class A GFCI is to be capable of interrupting the circuit to the load, in keeping with the above requirements, if the identified circuit conductor (neutral) becomes inadvertently grounded between the interrupter and the load.

The prime function of a Class A GFCI is to provide protection against hazardous electric shocks from leakage current flowing to ground from defective circuits or equipment. It does not provide protection against shock if a person makes contact with two of the circuit conductors on the load side of the GFCI.

Class A GFCIs are marked "GROUND FAULT CIRCUIT INTERRUPTER CLASS A" or with an abbreviated form such as "GFCI CL A", "GFCI A", or "CL A" where the area available for marking makes the complete text impracticable.

Ground fault detection
Ground fault detection devices (or devices and remote current sensors making up a detection system) are devices that detect a ground fault and provide an indication or alarm, or both, that a ground fault has been detected. They do not necessarily control or interrupt ground fault current and are therefore not considered a form of ground fault protection.

Ground fault protection
Ground fault detection devices that indicate a ground fault but do not control or interrupt ground fault current are not considered a form of ground fault protection.

Users of this Code should refer to *Canadian Electrical Code, Part II* Standards for design, construction, and performance requirements for each particular type of ground fault protection mandated by this Code.

Grounding conductor
It is intended that the grounding conductor will terminate on the enclosure for the service box or protective devices supplying the system in cases where the system is not grounded, and at the internal bus for the grounded conductor where the system is grounded.

Hazardous location
In this definition, "special precautions" refers to the special features of electrical equipment design, installation, and use that are intended to prevent the equipment from igniting flammable vapours, dust, fibres, or flyings. See Section 18 for more specific requirements for hazardous locations.

Ladder cable tray
Although a single-rail cable tray by definition is not a ladder cable tray, it is subject to the same performance requirements as a ladder-type cable tray in CSA C22.2 No. 126.1 (NEMA VE 1).

Mobile home
The following is the complete definition of mobile home given in CAN/CSA-Z240.0.1:

> **Mobile home** — a transportable, single- or multiple-section single family dwelling conforming to the CAN/CSA-Z240 MH Series at time of manufacture. It is ready for occupancy upon completion of set-up in accordance with required factory-recommended installation instructions.

Mobile industrial or commercial structure

Such structures are built specifically for commercial or industrial use, such as construction offices, bunkhouses, wash houses, kitchen and dining units, libraries, TV units, industrial display units, laboratory units, and medical clinics.

Neutral

By definition, a neutral conductor of a circuit requires at least three conductors in that circuit. However, in the trade, the term "neutral conductor" is commonly applied to the conductor of a 2-wire circuit that is connected to a conductor grounded at the supply end. Care should therefore be taken in the use of this term when applying the Code.

Non-combustible construction

The specific details for buildings of non-combustible construction are provided in Part 3 of the *National Building Code of Canada*.

Outdoor location

Locations that are sheltered from the weather are not considered outdoor locations.

Park model trailer

The following is the complete definition of park model trailer given in CAN/CSA-Z241:

> **Park model trailer** — a recreational vehicle unit that meets the following criteria:
> a) it is built on a single chassis mounted on wheels;
> b) it is designed to facilitate relocation from time to time;
> c) it is designed as living quarters for seasonal camping and may be connected to those utilities necessary for operation of installed fixtures and appliances; and
> d) it has a gross floor area, including lofts, not exceeding 50 m^2 when in the set-up mode, and having a width greater than 2.6 m in the transit mode.

Recreational vehicle

The following is the complete definition of recreational vehicle given in CAN/CSA-Z240.0.2 in the CAN/CSA-Z240 RV Series of Standards:

> **Recreational vehicle** — a structure designed to provide temporary living accommodation for travel, vacation, or recreational use and to be driven, towed, or transported. Except for fifth-wheel trailers, it has an overall length not exceeding 12.5 m and an overall width not exceeding 2.6 m, where the width is the sum of the distances from the vehicle centreline to the outermost projections on each side. These dimensions exclude safety-related equipment such as side safety and warning lights and entry and exit handholds. Also excluded are water spray suppression attachments, load-induced tire bulge, and equipment used to secure cargo on a vehicle. These excluded items are allowed to extend not more than 100 mm when the vehicle is folded or stowed for transit. For a fifth-wheel trailer the maximum overall length is 11.3 m taken from the rear extremity to the front of the main body, measured at the floorline. Such structures include travel trailers, slide-in campers, camping trailers, motor homes, and fifth-wheel trailers:
>
> > **Camping trailer** — a recreational vehicle built on its own chassis, having a rigid or canvas top and side walls, that may be folded or otherwise stowed for transit and that is designed to be towed behind a motor vehicle.

Fifth-wheel trailer — a recreational vehicle designed to be coupled to the towing vehicle by a fifth-wheel-type coupler, through which a substantial part of the trailer weight is supported by the towing vehicle.

Motor home — a recreational vehicle that is self-propelled. For purposes of applying the CAN/CSA-Z240 RV Series, this includes a van conversion containing at least one
a) plumbing fixture;
b) fuel-burning appliance; or
c) 120 V electrical component.

Slide-in camper — a recreational vehicle designed to be loaded onto and unloaded from the bed of a pick-up truck.

Travel trailer — a recreational vehicle designed to be towed behind a motor vehicle by means of a bumper or frame hitch.

Service box

This definition does not require that an electrically operated switch or circuit breaker be capable of being externally operable by hand to the closed position.

Supply authority

These bodies are sometimes referred to as electric utilities, wire owners, local distribution companies, municipal utilities, distributors, transmitters, etc. Some supply authorities may own and operate electrical power production facilities as part of their electrical power network operations and be deemed to be utilities by the regulatory authority having jurisdiction. Refer to Section 0, Scope, Item a) for the regulation of utilities.

System

Within this Code, the word "system" is used in many different contexts. However, within the context of electrical power distribution, a system is intended to mean an electrical installation in which the energy provided by that installation to utilization equipment is derived from a single energy source. For example, an electrical installation supplied from a transformer or bank of transformers can be considered a system; an installation supplied from a different transformer would be considered a different system.

Ventilated cable tray

Ventilated cable tray includes a cable tray of the wire mesh type.

Section 2

Rule 2-024 1)

It is intended by this Rule to emphasize that only electrical equipment approved for the application should be used under the provisions of this Code. "Approved" is a defined term that includes certification of electrical equipment to the applicable product Standards or other means that conform to the requirements of the regulatory authority.

Code users should be aware that when electrical equipment is subjected to field modification by means other than an approved field installable kit, such modification may void the original approval of the equipment. Thus, it is also intended by this Rule that upon completion of any field modification that voids the original approval of the equipment, the equipment should be made approved in accordance with provisions of the regulatory authority (i.e., in accordance with CSA Model Code SPE-1000 or other programs accepted by the participating regulatory authority).

Rule 2-026
As a condition of approval of certain types of electrical equipment, the manufacturer supplies instructions pertaining to its installation. It is of the utmost importance that the installer closely follow installation instructions supplied by the manufacturer to fulfill the terms of the approval agreement.

Rule 2-100
Evidence of approval may consist of either of the following:
a) the certification mark of the certification agency, usually in the form of a monogram or seal of that agency; or
b) the special inspection label or document of the authority having jurisdiction.

Rule 2-100 3)
The marking required by Rule 2-100 3) a) can be accomplished by labelling or directories.

The required marking provided on complex distribution systems, such as systems with multiple sources, should be supplemented with additional information such as single-line diagrams, mimic or display panels, drawing packages, etc.

The supplementary information should be readily available to persons who will operate or work on such systems.

Procedures should be in place to ensure that the required markings and supplementary information are kept up to date.

Δ Rule 2-100 4)
It is intended by this Subrule that, where Rule 8-104 5) and 6) limits the maximum continuous load to a value less than the continuous operating marking of the fused switch or circuit breaker, the following or equivalent wording be provided adjacent to the equipment nameplate:

CAUTION: The maximum continuous loading is limited to XXX amperes.

See Appendix M for a French translation of this marking.

Δ Rule 2-104 1)
It is intended by this Subrule that, when electrical equipment is marked with a short-circuit current rating or withstand rating in accordance with the equipment safety Standard listed in Appendix A, the fault current available at the equipment terminals will not exceed the short-circuit current rating or withstand rating marked on the electrical equipment.

Rule 2-106
The intent of this Rule is to prevent use of any moulded case circuit breaker and any moulded case switch that was subjected to adverse conditions, such as smoke, water, or similar environmental damage, or to the impact of faults at current levels greater than those for which the device is rated. It is intended by this Rule that a moulded case circuit breaker or moulded case switch that was subjected to these adverse conditions be permanently removed from the electrical installation and destroyed. It is not the intent to prohibit replacement and use of interchangeable trip units and field-installable accessories or reuse of a device not subjected to any of the listed adverse conditions in other electrical installations.

Rules 2-128 and 12-1602
Specific requirements pertaining to penetration of fire separations in buildings can be found in Subsections 3.1.7 and 3.1.9 of the *National Building Code of Canada* or in the appropriate provincial/territorial legislation.

Rule 2-130

The flame spread requirements for insulated conductors and cables in buildings are located in the *National Building Code of Canada* as follows:

a)   combustible building construction — Article 3.1.4.3 and Article 9.34.1.5;

b)   non-combustible building construction — Article 3.1.5.21; and

c)   plenum spaces in buildings — Article 3.6.4.3.

The markings for wires and cables meeting the flame spread requirements of the *National Building Code of Canada* (without additional fire protection) are

a)   FT1* — insulated conductors and cables that are suitable for installation in buildings of combustible construction;

b)   FT4† — insulated conductors and cables that are suitable for installation in buildings of non-combustible and combustible construction; and

c)   FT6‡ — insulated conductors and cables that are suitable for installation in

   i)   buildings of non-combustible and combustible construction; and

   ii)   spaces between a ceiling and floor, or ceiling and roof, that may be used as a plenum in buildings of combustible or non-combustible construction.

* Communication and optical fiber cables marked CMP, CMR, CMG, CM, CMX, CMH, OFNP, OFCP, OFNR, OFCR, OFNG, OFCG, OFN, OFC, OFNH, OFCH, and communication and optical fiber cables marked FT4 have been found to meet the standard criteria for FT1.

† Communication and optical fiber cables marked CMP, CMR, CMG, OFNP, OFCP, OFNR, OFCR, OFNG, and OFCG have been found to meet the standard criteria for FT4.

‡ Communication and optical fiber cables marked CMP, OFNP, and OFCP have been found to meet the standard criteria for FT6.

Insulated conductors and cables with combustible insulation, jackets, or sheaths that do not meet the above classifications but are located in

a)   totally enclosed non-combustible raceways;

b)   masonry walls;

c)   concrete slabs;

d)   a service room separated from the remainder of the building by a fire separation having not less than 1 h fire-resistance rating; or

e)   totally enclosed non-metallic raceways conforming to Rule 2-132

may be considered to comply with the *National Building Code of Canada* requirements relating to flame spread.

It is the intent of this Rule to limit flame spread and smoke propagation of cables in plenum spaces to the values specified by Article 3.6.4.3 (1) (a) of the *National Building Code of Canada*. Authorities enforcing provisions of the *National Building Code of Canada* and the *National Fire Code of Canada* in each jurisdiction should be consulted in order to determine the acceptable volume of cables in plenums for the purpose of conformance with the *National Building Code of Canada* and the *National Fire Code of Canada* requirements.

Sentence 2.4.1.1 (5) of the *National Fire Code of Canada* (2015 edition) requires that, when located in plenum chambers, abandoned optical fiber cables and electrical cables with combustible insulation, jackets, or sheaths be removed except when

a)   the cables or raceways are permanently enclosed by the structure or finish, such as inside a wall located in a plenum;

b)   the cables or raceways are not capable of being removed without disturbing the building structure or finish, such as when embedded in plaster, cement, or similar finish; or

c)   there is a risk that the removal of the cables or raceways will affect the performance of cables in use. For example, if abandoned cables are located in a cable tray together with cables in use and their removal could adversely affect the safety or performance of the cables in use, then the abandoned cables can be left in place.

Rules 2-132 and 12-1602

The flame spread requirement for totally enclosed non-metallic raceways can be found in Article 3.1.5.23 of the *National Building Code of Canada*. The *National Building Code of Canada* permits the use of totally enclosed non-metallic raceways for insulated conductors and cables in buildings required to be of non-combustible construction, provided that the totally enclosed non-metallic raceways do not exceed 175 mm in outside diameter, or equivalent cross-sectional area, and conform to the vertical flame test requirement specified in Clause 6.16 of CSA C22.2 No. 211.0. The marking on totally enclosed non-metallic raceways to indicate compliance with this flame test is "FT4".

The *National Building Code of Canada* also permits the use of totally enclosed non-metallic raceways in plenums of buildings. Where a totally enclosed non-metallic raceway is installed in a plenum of a building permitted to be of combustible construction, such a raceway should meet, as a minimum, the requirements of an FT4 rating. Where a totally enclosed non-metallic raceway is installed in a plenum of a building required to be of non-combustible construction, such a raceway should meet the requirements of an FT6 rating.

Rule 2-134

It is the intent of this Rule to protect totally enclosed non-metallic raceways as well as insulated conductors, and/or the jackets of insulated conductors, and cables against adverse effects caused by direct exposure to rays of the sun. Electrical conductors and non-metallic raceways marked for this application are suitable for installation and use for direct exposure to rays of the sun.

Insulated conductors and cables marked "SR", "Sun Res", "Sunlight Resistant", "CMX-Outdoor" (for communications cable), and outdoor cords and equipment wire listed in Table 11 for wet locations, have been found to meet the standard criteria for sunlight resistance.

Rigid RTRC conduit marked "RTRC Type AG" and totally enclosed non-metallic raceways marked "SR", "Sun Res", "Sunlight Resistant", or "Outdoor" have been found to meet the standard criteria for sunlight resistance.

Rule 2-136

When insulation resistance or dielectric strength tests are performed, precautions should be taken to ensure that voltage-sensitive devices such as ground fault circuit interrupters are not subjected to voltages that will damage the device.

Rule 2-304

Examples of tasks that are not feasible when electrical equipment has been completely disconnected are troubleshooting of control circuits, testing, and diagnostics.

It is intended by this Rule that persons performing maintenance, adjustment, servicing, or examination of energized electrical equipment adhere to all applicable safe work practices around the energized electrical equipment.

See Section 0 for the definition of **Qualified person**.

CSA Z462 provides assistance in determining severity of potential exposure, planning safe work practices, and selecting personal protective equipment (PPE) to protect against shock and arc flash hazards.

Rule 2-306

CSA Z462 provides assistance in determining the severity of potential exposure, planning safe work practices, and selecting personal protective equipment to protect against shock and arc flash hazards.

ANSI/NEMA Z535.4 provides guidelines for the design of safety signs and labels for application to products.

IEEE 1584 provides assistance in determining the arc flash hazard distance and incident energy that workers may be exposed to from electrical equipment.

Δ **Rule 2-308**
It is intended by this Rule that working space with secure footing be provided and maintained about electrical equipment such as switchboards, switchgear, panelboards, control panels, overcurrent devices, disconnecting means, motor control centres, etc.

Rule 2-310 1)
Specific requirements pertaining to unobstructed means of egress can be found in Articles 3.3.1.23 and 9.9.5.5 of the *National Building Code of Canada*.

It is intended that doors and gates in the unobstructed means of egress described in this Rule will open in the direction of exit travel. However, where the room is large relative to the required working space, the *National Building Code of Canada* may allow doors or gates located more than 7.6 m away from the working space to open in either direction. Articles 3.4.4.4 (7), 3.4.3.3, and 9.9.6.1 of the *National Building Code of Canada* should be consulted as to the limitations that any door swinging out from an electrical room may have to comply with.

Rule 2-310 2)
To obtain the required path of travel, a second exit may be required.

Rule 2-310 4)
The intent of this Subrule is to permit an occupant to open the door or gate and leave the room quickly in case of an emergency. Door hardware of the push-bar type is considered to meet the intent of this Subrule. Door hardware that is not considered to meet the intent of this Subrule includes a door or gate that

a)   requires a key to exit the room;
b)   is equipped with a door handle and one or more additional devices such as a deadbolt; or
c)   requires other special devices or specialized knowledge to exit the room.

Article 3.4.6.16 of the *National Building Code of Canada* should also be consulted regarding applicable door release hardware.

Rule 2-322
Equipment considered to have relatively high losses generally consists of generators, motors, transformers, and similar apparatus. Approximately 3.5 to 4.3 m³ of air per minute for each kilowatt of loss is normally required for ventilating 40 °C rise equipment. A value of 2.8 m³ of air per minute will have a temperature rise of approximately 18 °C when absorbing a 1 kW loss.

The temperature rise of all such equipment is based on a 40 °C ambient temperature.

Rule 2-326
The clearance distances specified in CSA B149.1 between a source of ignition and a combustible gas relief discharge device or vent are as follows:
a)   1 m for natural gas; and
b)   3 m for propane gas.

Rule 2-400
Enclosures are not intended to protect against conditions such as condensation, icing, corrosion, or contamination that may occur within the enclosure or enter via the conduit or unsealed openings.

Ingress protection (IP) describes the degree of protection an enclosure provides from ingress of water or foreign bodies. [See the ingress protection table in the Note to Rule 18-102 5)]. For further information on the IP designations, refer to CAN/CSA-C22.2 No. 60529. The IP designations are supplemental to the enclosure types specified in Rule 2-400 and Table 65. There is no direct correlation between the IP designations and enclosure types, and CAN/CSA-C22.2 No. 60529 does not cover environmental considerations such as resistance to corrosion or the effects of ultraviolet.

Section 4

△ **Rule 4-000**

Branch circuits include lighting, appliance, and power supply circuits, as well as flexible cords and equipment wires, and are subject to the requirements of this Section.

Rule 4-004

The allowable ampacities of Tables 1, 2, 3, and 4 are based on temperature alone and do not take voltage drop into consideration (see Table D3).

Rule 4-004 1) d) and 2) d)

The ampacities shown in Tables D8A to D11B have been determined using the Neher-McGrath methodology, as applied in IEEE 835, for the cable and insulated conductor arrangements shown in Diagrams D8, D9, D10, and D11.

Tables D8A to D11B are based on 90 °C. If equipment rated at 75 °C, for example, is connected, then Rule 4-006 may limit the conductor termination ampacity.

For "stacked" arrangements of two single conductors per phase in parallel (one row located vertically over another row), it is recommended that ampacities be obtained from the Detail 5 column of Table D8A (copper) or Table D8B (aluminum) for direct buried cables or from the Detail 2 column of Table D9A (copper) or Table D9B (aluminum) for cables in underground raceways.*

For single-conductor metal-armoured and metal-sheathed cables in which the sheath, armour, or bonding conductors are bonded at more than one point, the derating factors of Rule 4-008 apply, unless the ampacity has been determined by detailed calculation according to the method outlined in Rule 4-004 1) e), 1) f), 2) e), and 2) f).

It is recommended that ampacities for three single conductors per phase and for five single conductors per phase with spacings, directly buried in the earth, be selected from Table D8A (copper) or Table D8B (aluminum) for the installation configurations of Diagram D8, Detail 5 and Detail 7, respectively. It is recommended that ampacities for three single-conductor cables per phase and for five single-conductor cables per phase installed in separate underground conduits in a single bank be selected from Table D9A (copper) or Table D9B (aluminum) for the installation configurations of Diagram D9, Detail 3 and Detail 4, respectively.*

It is recommended that ampacities for three-conductor cables and for three single-conductor cables grouped, directly buried in the earth, be selected from Table D10A (copper) or Table D10B (aluminum) for installation configurations of Diagram D10, and ampacities for three-conductor cables in separate underground raceways be selected from Table D11A (copper) or Table D11B (aluminum) for installation configurations of Diagram D11.

It is recommended that ampacities for seven three-conductor cables in separate underground raceways be selected from Table D11A (copper) or Table D11B (aluminum) for installation configurations of Diagram D11, Detail 8.

It is recommended that the ampacities of groups of cables in twos, and two-conductor cables, be obtained from the ampacity Tables D10A to D11B for groups of three single-conductor cables, and three-conductor cables, for the appropriate spacings between groups and numbers of conductors in parallel.* The neutral conductor of a three-phase, 4-wire system need not be counted in the determination of ampacities.

Underground ampacities for conductor temperatures of 75 °C may be obtained by multiplying the appropriate ampacity at a 90 °C conductor temperature from Tables D8A to D11B by the derating factor 0.886.*

Ampacities for underground installations at ambient earth temperatures other than the assumed value of 20 °C may be obtained by multiplying the appropriate underground ampacity obtained from Tables D8A to D11B by the following factor:

$$\sqrt{[(90 - T_{ae}) / 70]}$$

where

T_{ae} = the new ambient temperature.*

* *Where precisely calculated values are not available.*

It is the intent of this Rule that where ampacities of underground installations of cable and insulated conductors in a raceway size 1/0 and larger are based on conditions of use other than those set out in the foregoing notes or the defined assumptions preceding them, they should be justified by precise calculation based on IEEE 835.

Where IEEE 835 is used to compute the ampacities of copper and aluminum conductors, the following data may be required by the inspection department:
a) **Cable and insulated conductors:**
   i) type of cable or insulated conductors and voltage rating;
   ii) maximum conductor temperature rating;
   iii) maximum continuous current rating; and
   iv) short-circuit rating;
b) **Equipment:**
   i) voltage and current rating;
   ii) short-circuit rating; and
   iii) type of overcurrent devices, with their characteristics;
c) **Operating conditions:**
   i) nominal voltage of the system;
   ii) highest voltage of the system;
   iii) system frequency;
   iv) type of grounding, and where the neutral is not effectively grounded, the maximum permitted duration of ground fault conditions on any one occasion;
   v) rated current for continuous operation;
   vi) load factor;
   vii) maximum currents that may flow during short-circuits between phases and to ground; and
   viii) maximum time for which short-circuit current may flow;
   Note: *The conductor heating during short-circuit is governed by the following:*

For copper: $\dfrac{I^2}{A^2}t = 0.0297 \, log_{10}\dfrac{(T_2 + 234)}{(T_1 + 234)}$

For aluminum: $\dfrac{I^2}{A^2}t = 0.0125 \, log_{10}\dfrac{(T_2 + 228)}{(T_1 + 228)}$

where

I = *short-circuit current in amperes*

A = *conductor area in circular mils*

t = *time of short-circuit in seconds*

T_1 = initial conductor temperature in degrees Celsius. (The maximum conductor insulation temperature rating is to be used.)

T_2 = final conductor temperature in degrees Celsius. (This temperature must not exceed the maximum short-circuit temperature rating of the cable or insulated conductors.)

d) **Underground raceway installation data:**
   i) length and profile of route including location of maintenance holes;
   ii) depth of duct bank;
   iii) number and geometric arrangement of the ducts if there are more than one;
   iv) spacing of the ducts;
   v) duct material including encasements;
   vi) thermal resistivity and kinds of soil along the route and whether data are based on measurement and inspection or only assumed;
   vii) maximum ground temperature if in excess of 20 °C at the duct depth; and
   viii) proximity of other current-carrying cables or insulated conductors, or other heat sources, with details;

e) **Direct burial data:**
   i) length and profile of route;
   ii) depth of burial;
   iii) spacing of cables;
   iv) thermal resistivity and kinds of soil along the route and whether data are based on measurement and inspection or only assumed;
   v) maximum ground temperature if in excess of 20 °C at burial depth; and
   vi) proximity of other current-carrying cables or other heat sources, with details;

f) **Conduit installation data:**
   i) length and profile of route;
   ii) number and geometric arrangement of conduits if there are more than one;
   iii) spacing of the conduits;
   iv) whether exposed to direct sunlight;
   v) details of ventilation for cables or insulated conductors indoors or in tunnels;
   vi) proximity of other current-carrying cables, insulated conductors, or other heat sources, with details; and
   vii) maximum air ambient temperature; and

g) **Cables in free air:**
   i) length and profile of route;
   ii) cable spacing and if spacing is maintained;
   iii) whether exposed to direct sunlight;
   iv) details of ventilation for cables indoors or in tunnels;
   v) proximity of other current-carrying cables or other heat sources, with details; and
   vi) maximum air ambient temperature.

Rules 4-004 1) g) and 2) g)

Ampacities for cables in these voltage ranges can vary substantially due to a number of factors, including configuration, construction, orientation, ambient temperature, resistivity of adjacent material, proximity to other cables, and other such criteria. It is important to note that the ampacities listed in Tables D17A to D17N are valid only for the configurations shown and the conditions specified in Table D17. A change in any one or more installation conditions or cable construction will result in a change in maximum conductor ampacity. The cable manufacturer should be consulted, where conditions or configurations differ from those shown in the D17 series of tables, to provide maximum conductor ampacity values based on Neher-McGrath methodology.

Cables described in these Rules are manufactured and certified to CAN/CSA-C68.5 and CSA C68.10.

Rule 4-004 20)
Nickel and nickel-plated conductors are recognized in CSA C22.2 No. 124.

Rule 4-004 21)
A covered conductor is a conductor encased within material of composition or thickness that is not recognized by this Code as electrical insulation. Because they are considered uninsulated conductors, covered conductors should always be treated as bare conductors for working clearances.

Δ Rule 4-004 22)
It is intended by this Subrule that the maximum calculated load from Table 39 be provided adjacent to the equipment nameplate, using the following or equivalent wording:

CAUTION: The maximum permitted loading is limited to XXX amperes.

See Appendix M for a French translation of this marking.

Rule 4-006
In accordance with CSA product Standards (e.g., CSA C22.2 No. 4 or CSA C22.2 No. 5), when equipment of 600 V or less is evaluated relative to the appropriate temperature characteristics of the terminations, conductors sized similar to those in the 75 °C column of Table 2 or 4 are used.

It is intended by this Rule that the size of conductors terminating on equipment described in Subrules 1), 2), 3), and 4) be not less than the conductor size selected for the maximum insulated conductor ampacity in the corresponding temperature column of Table 1, 2, 3, or 4.

This Rule is not intended to address conductor allowable ampacity (see Rule 4-004).

Regardless of conductor allowable ampacities determined by other Rules in this Code (for underground conductors, cables, flexible cords, portable power cables, DLO cables, and conductors with higher temperature ratings, etc.), it is intended that the minimum conductor size be based on the requirements of this Rule.

Δ Rule 4-006 3)
High-voltage equipment may be tested and rated for termination temperature at 90 °C. For high-voltage installations rated up to 5 kV, where conductors are selected in accordance with Tables 1 to 4, 12E, or D8A to D11B, or for high-voltage installations rated 5 kV to 46 kV, where insulated conductors or cables are selected in accordance with Tables D17A to D17N, the equipment manufacturer should be consulted when insulated conductors or cables are intended for termination on each specific type of high-voltage equipment.

Rules 4-006 4) and 5)
The 1.2 m length is based on test requirements from equipment Standards.

Rule 4-008
Induced voltages and sheath currents in metal sheaths and interlocked armour of single-conductor cables
When an alternating current flows in the conductor of a single-conductor metal-armoured cable, continuous or interlocked, an alternating magnetic field is created around the entire cable, which induces a voltage in the metal armour sheathing. The magnitude of the induced voltage is proportional to the magnitude of the current in the conductor and its length.

Sheath current will flow along the sheath as a result of the induced voltage, provided that the sheath circuit is completed, e.g., by grounding both ends of the sheath (or by contacts made along the sheath to the sheaths of adjacent cables or to metal building members). If the sheath circuit is not completed, no sheath current will flow. If the sheath circuit is completed, the magnitude of the sheath current is a function of the induced voltage and sheath impedance. Sheath current increases in magnitude with increased spacing between single-conductor cables and decreases with reduced spacing (within the range of typical spacings).

Sheath currents can be large and result in considerable heating of the sheath. Coupled with the heat resulting from the passage of current through the conductor, the conductor insulation will subjected to temperatures that can cause failure or a serious reduction in the life expectancy of the cable.

The phenomenon of sheath currents is common in varying degrees to single-conductor cables enclosed in ferrous metals, as in galvanized conduit, and in non-ferrous metals, such as copper, aluminum, and lead employed as cable sheaths, and will occur whether the enclosure is of the continuous tube or the spiral armoured type.

Single conductors in free air — mitigating the effects of sheath voltages and currents

For cables carrying currents up to and including 425 A, sheath losses can be reduced to tolerable levels, without the need to apply derating, by spacing cables approximately a diameter apart. This reduces the induced sheath voltage (by virtue of the three-phase field cancellation effect at close spacing). For cables carrying currents greater than 425 A, it is generally necessary to apply derating to avoid overheating of the cable unless sheath currents are eliminated. To eliminate the flow of sheath currents, it is necessary to ensure that all paths through which they may circulate are open-circuit. Cable sheaths should be grounded at the supply end only and thereafter be isolated from ground and each other. Sheath isolation may be attained by installing the cables in individual ducts of insulating material, by employing cables jacketed with PVC or other insulating material, or by mounting unjacketed cables on insulated supports. The sheath or sheaths should be isolated from any metal enclosures or other terminations at the load end that might bridge them or cause them to contact ground. The cable sheaths in such circumstances cannot be used for bonding the electrical system, and a bonding conductor of adequate size for this purpose must be provided [see Rules 10-610 5) and 10-614].

Sheath currents are allowed to flow in single-conductor mineral-insulated cables, with phase conductors grouped to minimize the flow of sheath currents [see Rule 4-004 10)] without Table 5B derating. The sheaths are bonded to ground at both ends to provide an effective equipment bonding conductor.

Single conductors — external effects

The magnetic field around a single-conductor cable or single insulated conductors can create heating in ferrous materials through which it passes, e.g., the wall of an enclosure, steel supports, connectors, glands, locknuts, or clamps that encircle a cable or insulated conductor.

There are two effects. The magnetic field causes currents to flow in the wall of the enclosure (as an example) through which a single-conductor cable or single insulated conductor passes. These are known as "eddy currents" and create heating. The other effect is that the wall itself has magnetic properties, and a magnetic field will be set up within the wall. The energy expended in setting this up causes heating in the wall known as hysteresis heating. This type of heating occurs only in ferrous materials, and only when the encircling ferrous material is in close proximity around the cable or insulated conductor.

Single insulated conductors or single-conductor cables in free air — mitigation of external effects

Cables or single insulated conductors carrying currents 200 A and less, with typical spacings in air, do not constitute a problem because of the low current levels. If the opening in an enclosure is large — e.g., coming up underneath equipment through a large opening from the floor beneath — the cancellation effect can be taken advantage of by grouping the phase conductors close together to reduce the external magnetic field to the point where there is no impact on surrounding ferrous materials that are not closely encircling the group. For all other cases, the preferred option is to cut out a section of the enclosure a little larger than the opening required for the insulated conductors or

Appendix B

cables, and replace it with a non-ferrous plate through which the single insulated conductors or cables pass.

Δ **Single conductors in underground locations**
The wider spacings generally employed with underground single-conductor cables or single insulated conductor installations, in comparison with cables in free air, can be expected to generate circulating currents of greater magnitude in metallic sheaths or armours when these are bonded together or grounded at both ends. It is necessary to correct all such installation ampacities to avoid overheating of the cable if sheath currents are not to be eliminated. If derating is the desired course, the cable manufacturer should be consulted because this factor depends on the type and size of cable and installation arrangements and could be more favourable than the factor given in Subrule 1) a).

Rule 4-018 2)
Examples of non-linear loads include dimmers, computers, microprocessors, and most other electronic loads.

Δ **Rule 4-022 2)**
Examples of manual or automatic control devices are general-use switches, motion sensors, photocells, light dimmers, or components of an energy or lighting management system.

Section 6

Rule 6-102
The supply authority should be consulted on the number and location of supply services.

Rule 6-112
Clearances for overhead conductors in this Code apply under the conditions existing at the time of installation rather than at maximum sag and are therefore greater than, but consistent with, the clearances specified in CSA C22.3 No. 1.

Δ **Rule 6-112 1)**
It is not intended by this Rule that an attachment point be provided for conductors other than supply or consumer's service conductors. Where an attachment point is provided for conductors other than supply or consumer's service conductors, the applicable provisions of Section 12, 54, or 60 should be applied.

Rule 6-112 5)
Components that meet the requirements of CSA C22.2 No. 82 include
a)   tubular support members;
b)   support clamps;
c)   roof plates;
d)   supply service attachments, e.g., racks;
e)   service entrance heads; and
f)   support member terminations (i.e., at the lower end).

As an example, a consumer service that does not exceed 200 A and 750 V, and whose supply service span length is 30 m or less, is acceptable when the maximum unguyed projection of the support member does not exceed 1.5 m, the cantilever load does not exceed 270 kg, three support clamps are used, the upper one being located at the roofline and the other two being installed on the wall of the building, a roof plate is provided to prevent entrance of moisture, the supply conductors or cables are attached on the mast to comply with Rule 6-116, and a clearance of not less than 915 mm is provided between the roof and the supply service attachment, except that the clearance may be reduced to 600 mm to the bottom of the drip loops. For a consumer service that exceeds 200 A or is over 750 V, or whose supply service span length is over 30 m, or for non-standard mast installations (multiple masts supporting each other), additional engineering provisions may be required, and consultation with the inspection department and supply authority may be necessary.

Rule 6-206 2)

The local regulatory authority may forbid the locking of service boxes in the ON position, for example, on construction sites.

Where the operating means of a service switch or circuit breaker is rendered inaccessible, it is recommended that a notice be displayed on the outside of the service box enclosure, room, or building advising of the location of the key to gain access to the service box operating means.

Δ **Rule 6-206 3)**

Enclosures suitable for use in an outdoor location must be marked accordingly. Refer to Rules 2-400 and 2-402 and Table 65.

It is intended by this Rule that enclosures not suitable for an outdoor location be provided with equivalent protection from weather.

Rule 6-402 2)

The supply authority should be consulted regarding the acceptability of installing the metering equipment on the supply side of the service box.

Section 8

Rule 8-002

Basic load

It is intended by this definition that only a typical lighting and receptacle load within an area bound by the outside dimensions of that area signifies "basic load". Such loads as outside lighting, specialty lighting (i.e., stage, show window lighting, etc.), electric space heating, or air-conditioning loads are not intended to be part of the basic load. Code users should be aware that the value of basic load for each particular building occupancy is different and is dependent on the type of occupancy from Table 14 and on load calculation requirements for residential occupancies.

Demonstrated load

The intent of this definition is to allow comparison of loads that are used in a similar fashion based on the type of fuel source for heating and cooling, type of occupancy, type of occupancy load, and type of operational requirements. It is intended by this definition that comparison may need to be made between facilities in the same geographic area and also in similar climatic conditions.

With respect to determining demonstrated load and recognition of qualified persons, Code users should be aware that it may be advisable to consult with the regulatory authority having jurisdiction.

Rule 8-102 2)

It is intended by this Subrule that, when overcurrent devices for feeders and branch circuits are selected such that their rating is greater than the ampacity of the load due to the nature of the equipment they feed (e.g., motors, transformers, and capacitors), the permitted voltage drop should be calculated on the demand load of the feeder or branch circuit and not on the overcurrent device feeding the feeder or branch circuit.

Rule 8-102 3)

Experience indicates that the voltage drop of lighting and general-use branch circuits in dwelling units will meet the requirements of Rule 8-102 1) when the insulated conductor length from the supply side of the consumer's service to the furthest point of utilization is less than or equal to the values shown in Table 68.

This Rule is not intended to apply to branch circuits for the following:
a) household appliances (e.g., refrigerators, washing machines, central vacuum systems, and other receptacles as per Rule 26-652);
Δ b) kitchen receptacles [Rule 26-654 b)];

c)   electrical heating and cooking appliances (Rule 26-744); and

d)   other specific receptacles installed in dwellings, such as those dedicated for medical devices.

Rule 8-102 1) and Table D3 are applicable to these branch circuits excluded from Rule 8-102 3), based on either the connected load, or one load equal to 80% of the rating on the overcurrent device, connected at the furthest point.

It is intended by this Subrule that when the load on a circuit or feeder is unknown, the load value used in determining the voltage drop calculation should be based on the maximum loading permissible in accordance with Rule 8-104.

Further analysis has shown that these values will not affect the operation of the branch circuit overcurrent protection.

Rules 8-104 and 62-114
When an overcurrent device is located in an assembly such as a fused switch or a panelboard, the assembly is required to be marked for continuous operation of its overcurrent devices in accordance with the requirements of CSA C22.2 No. 4 or CSA C22.2 No. 29.

Fused switches and circuit breakers not marked as suitable for continuous operation at either 80% or 100% of the rating of their overcurrent devices are considered to be suitable for continuous operation at 80%.

Δ   **Rules 8-104 5) b) and 6) b)**
It is intended that Subrule 5) b) or 6) b) be applied when the allowable ampacity of conductors is obtained from tables such as Table 1, 3, 12E, D8A, D8B, D9A, D9B, D17A, D17B, D17C, D17D, D17I, D17J, or D17M in accordance with Section 4.

Rule 8-106 9)
It is intended by this Subrule that demonstrated load data could be used for the purpose of sizing of services or feeders. It is also intended by this Subrule that the qualified person, as determined by the regulatory authority having jurisdiction, who is responsible for the design should be able, upon request, to demonstrate to the regulatory authority having jurisdiction that historical data related to actual demand substantiates the fact that this historical demand is the maximum possible demand for the specific application.

Ⓔ Δ   **Rule 8-106 10)**
It is intended by this Rule that the loads of the electric vehicle supply equipment controlled by an electric vehicle energy management system should be considered to have a demand within the maximum limits allowed by the electric vehicle energy management system.

The electric vehicle energy management system is provided with a maximum load rating, which determines the branch circuit, feeder, and service loading.

Rules 8-200 and 8-202
If more than one electric range is involved, the initial range will be provided for according to Rule 8-200 1) a) iv) or 8-202 1) a) v), and any subsequent ranges will be provided for by Rule 8-200 1) a) vii) or 8-202 1) a) vii).

Rule 8-202
See the Note to Rule 8-200.

Rule 8-208
For the purpose of this Rule, a motel unit with cooking facilities may be considered an apartment.

Δ

Section 10

Rule 10-000
It should be noted that many installations employ grounding features that are not a requirement of this Code but are designed to provide supplemental protection. As an example, the direct connection, often used in industrial applications, between a vessel or some specific electrical equipment and a ground grid is not a response to the requirements of the Code. The use of terms such as "bonding conductor" or "grounding conductor" in relation to this supplemental protection is outside the scope of the definitions for these terms given in this Code. Grounding and bonding as required by the Code are provided through grounding arrangements at the source, service, or equivalent equipment, by the bonding conductor run with the circuit conductor(s), and by the equipotential bonding of specified non-electrical conductive objects.

Rule 10-000 b)
The use of the term "bonding", as in the 10-600 series of Rules, describes a low impedance path established to facilitate the operation of the protective device(s) of a circuit during a ground fault. The term "bonding conductor" as defined in Section 0 is used throughout the Code generally to describe the ground fault current carrying function of bonding.

Rule 10-000 c)
The use of the term "bonding" with the qualifier "equipotential", as in the 10-700 series of Rules, describes the interconnection of conductive parts or objects to create equipotentiality between them. The term "equipotential bonding" is used in Section 10 to refer to the bonding of non-electrical equipment to establish equipotentiality.

Rule 10-002 d)
The primary function of bonding as described in this Item is to provide a low impedance path to facilitate the operation of protective devices under ground fault conditions. By interconnecting the non-current-carrying conductive parts of electrical equipment, bonding also establishes equipotentiality between that equipment.

Rule 10-002 e)
The primary function of equipotential bonding as described in this Item is to minimize shock hazard by creating equipotentiality of conductive objects that may become energized either directly (e.g., a damaged current-carrying conductor contacting a conductive object) or indirectly (e.g., parallel conductive paths of ground faults or stray currents).

Rule 10-004
Grounded conductor
The term "grounded conductor" is used to refer to the conductor of an electrical system that is grounded. The term can be used to refer to any of the following types of grounded conductors, distinguished by the point at which the conductor is grounded:
a) a system grounded conductor (or grounded system conductor) is grounded at the source;
b) a service grounded conductor (or grounded service conductor) is grounded at the service box; and
c) a circuit grounded conductor (or grounded circuit conductor) is the conductor of a circuit that is an extension of the system grounded conductor.

The conductor of an impedance grounded system that is grounded through an impedance may also be referred to as the grounded conductor or as the impedance grounded conductor.

Impedance system bonding jumper
This term describes the connection between the grounded side of an impedance grounding device and the non-current-carrying conductive parts of electrical system equipment.

Appendix B

Separately derived system

A separately derived system has no direct electrical connection to a supply authority system. Examples of separately derived systems include generators, batteries, converters, inverters, isolation transformers, and solar photovoltaic systems, provided that they have no direct electrical connection to a supply authority system.

The earth, metal enclosures, metal raceways, and bonding conductors may provide incidental connection between the supply authority system and the separately derived system. In addition, a common grounding electrode can be installed for multiple separately derived systems as well as a supply authority system. Two or more separately derived systems can be commonly connected either by direct connection of phase conductors and/or grounded conductors and still be separately derived if they do not connect to the corresponding conductors of a supply authority system. Where the grounded conductors of two or more separately derived systems terminate at a common tie point, the system bonding jumper and grounding conductor connections for all the systems are made at that common tie point.

Where a system has a common connection with a supply authority system, through phase conductors and/or grounded conductors, it is not a separately derived system. Examples of that are an emergency standby generator connected to building loads via a transfer switch that does not switch the grounded conductor or an interconnected power production source under the scope of Section 84. The grounding requirements for such systems are met by the grounding connection of the supply authority system to which they are conductively connected.

Solidly grounded system

A solidly grounded system is achieved when a current-carrying conductor of an electrical system is, in addition to being connected to a grounding electrode, bonded to the non-current-carrying conductive parts of the system via the system bonding jumper, thus establishing a complete low impedance circuit for mitigating ground fault currents.

System bonding jumper

This term describes the connection between the point of an electrical system to be solidly grounded and the non-current-carrying conductive parts of the electrical equipment supplied by that system to establish a complete circuit for ground fault currents. The system bonding jumper establishes a solidly grounded system and extends the bonding conductor to the grounded point of the system.

Ungrounded system

No point of an ungrounded systems is grounded; instead, the non-current-carrying conductive parts (equipment) of the ungrounded system are grounded.

Rule 10-100

The purpose of grounding is to establish equipotentiality between neighbouring exposed conductive surfaces and nearby surfaces of the earth.

Under normal operation, there should be no objectionable current flow in the grounding conductor. During a ground fault, the grounding conductor may carry a portion of the fault current as a parallel fault current path, but it is not the primary intended path.

The use of multiple grounds on a system (e.g., grounding at the transformer and again in the service equipment) may create a situation where there is an unbalanced neutral current on the grounding conductor. An objectionable current on the grounding conductor can also be caused by an accidental loosening or disconnection of the neutral conductor at a grounded main service on the line side of the system grounding connection. Any neutral current on a grounding conductor is considered objectionable. Corrective action for neutral currents on grounding conductors may require that
a)   one or more of the grounds be abandoned;

b) the location of the grounds be changed;
c) the continuity of the conductor between the grounding connections be suitably interrupted; or
d) other effective action be taken to limit the current.

Currents in a grounding conductor that are not considered objectionable are those that may occur under normal operation, such as the temporary current resulting from a ground fault or the induced current from adjacent single conductors.

Rule 10-102
Manufactured grounding electrodes are manufactured to meet the requirements of CSA C22.2 No. 41.

It is important that in-situ grounding electrodes provide a surface area contact with earth equivalent to that provided by manufactured electrodes (see CSA C22.2 No. 41). Consideration should also be given to the effects that corrosion may have on an in-situ ground electrode, affecting its durability and life expectancy. For example, the metallic reinforcement of a concrete slab, concrete piling, or concrete foundation and iron pilings in significant contact with earth at 600 mm or more below finished grade have been found to be suitable in-situ grounding electrodes; however, metallic material encapsulated with a non-conductive compound to protect it from corrosion does not meet the criteria for use as an in-situ ground electrode.

In-situ grounding electrodes may extend from the earth for some distance (e.g., steel beams in direct contact with the structural steel of a concrete foundation). To assure a permanent ground, it is intended that the grounding conductor connection be made such that there are no insulating joints or sections between the connection and the point at which the electrode contacts earth.

Rule 10-104
Grounding electrodes for signal circuits, radio, lightning protection, communication, and community antenna distribution systems are examples of multiple grounding electrodes at a building.

Rule 10-106
It is intended by this Rule that the use of railway tracks as an electrode be limited to the railway circuit and lightning arresters for the railway circuit. The grounded conductor of a railway electrical circuit may be used to ground metal conduit, the armour or sheath of armoured or metal-sheathed cable, metal raceway, and the like associated with the circuit. A separate grounding electrode conforming to Rule 10-102 is used for grounding interior wiring systems other than those supplied from the railway circuit itself.

Rule 10-108
Recommended practices for the installation of a lightning protection system, including lightning rods, interconnecting conductors, and ground electrodes, are given in CAN/CSA-B72. Other national and international industry-recognized Standards on lightning protection are also available. It should be noted that the *National Building Code of Canada* mandates the use of CAN/CSA-B72 as the Standard for lightning protection systems.

Rule 10-112
It is recognized that copper, aluminum, and copper-clad aluminum are the most common materials used for grounding conductors. Other materials may be used, such as copper-clad steel, steel-clad copper, lead-clad copper, or steel-clad aluminum. Where these alternative materials are being considered, the inspection department should be consulted to ensure that they are acceptable. Supporting information for suitability of the material and proper sizing may be required. Consideration should also be given to the compatibility of the termination methods at the electrodes, especially where they are not made of the same material.

Subrule 2) requires that consideration be given to materials subject to corrosive environments. Copper conductors in contact with aluminum are subject to galvanic action; aluminum conductors in contact with masonry or earth are subject to corrosion. Therefore, as an example, the connection of an aluminum grounding conductor to the electrode is made at some point above earth, normally at

450 mm or more. Precautions should be taken to ensure that deterioration from corrosion of the material used will have no adverse effect.

Rule 10-114

Because the primary function of the grounding conductor is to establish a common reference to earth and to create equipotentiality with earth, it is intended that the size of a grounding conductor for a solidly grounded ac system connected to a grounding electrode need not be larger than No. 6 AWG copper (4 AWG aluminum) nor larger than the system current-carrying conductor(s) of smaller systems. Where alternative materials are being considered, the authority having jurisdiction may require supporting information for proper sizing.

The grounded conductor of the system is the primary conductor between the service and the source for mitigating faults. However, a parallel fault path back to the source is also present via the grounding conductor connection at the service equipment, thus allowing the grounding conductor to carry a portion of a fault current, depending on the impedance of the grounding circuit. Because the ampacity of the grounded conductor is sized to effectively carry the fault current for the duration of a fault, the size of the grounding conductor is inconsequential in terms of its role in mitigating faults.

Rule 10-116 3)

Protection from damage is afforded by either

a)   mechanical protection, such as cable armour, conduit, tubing, or other substantive means; or

b)   location, based on an assessment that the conductor is installed in such a manner that it will not be subject to damage.

Further protection from damage is afforded by adequate securing and supporting means.

Rule 10-116 4)

When currents are imposed on the grounding conductor, the magnetic field encircling the conductor is increased by magnetic material surrounding the conductor unless the magnetic material is bonded at both ends. An increased magnetic field correspondingly increases the inductive voltage drop, thus increasing conductor impedance.

Non-magnetic material such as PVC, aluminum, and some metal alloys are not affected by the magnetic field and accordingly need not be bonded at both ends.

See Figure B10-1.

Figure B10-1
Sleeve of magnetic material over grounding conductor

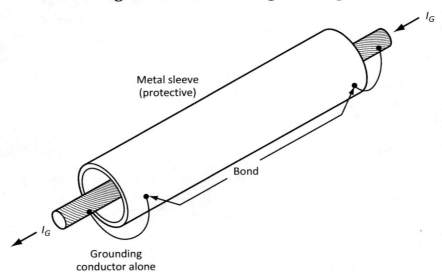

Rule 10-118

In making the connection accessible, care should be taken to avoid exposing the grounding conductor and grounding electrode connection to damage, thereby jeopardizing assurance of a permanent ground. Ensuring that the grounding conductor and ground clamp are not exposed to mechanical damage by installing them below grade may be considered an acceptable method of "protection by location". Maintaining reasonable access where practicable can be achieved by locating the connection just slightly below finished grade.

Where connection is made in a wet location or for direct earth burial, consideration should be given in accordance with other requirements of the Code to corrosion or to the use of dissimilar metals.

Rule 10-202

The common conductor of a 3-wire dc system is the conductor common to two series-connected dc sources (a bipolar system).

See Figure B10-2.

Figure B10-2
Series dc sources (bipolar)

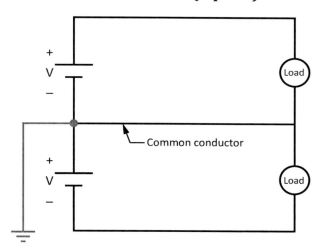

Rule 10-208
For solidly grounded ac wiring systems, common configurations for the conductor to be grounded are shown in Figure B10-3.

Figure B10-3
Common solidly grounded configurations

 Single-phase, 2-wire — one conductor (either one) referred to as the identified conductor

 Single-phase, 3-wire — the identified neutral conductor

 Multi-phase systems having one wire common to all phases — the identified neutral conductor

 Multi-phase systems having one phase grounded — the identified conductor

 Multi-phase systems in which the midpoint of one phase is used to create a single-phase 3-wire system — the identified conductor

Rule 10-210

The system bonding jumper may be a bonding screw or bonding strap supplied with the consumer's service equipment, sized in accordance with the corresponding *Canadian Electrical Code, Part II* Standard. Where the system bonding jumper provided by the manufacturer is removed or missing, a field-installed system bonding jumper is sized in accordance with Rule 10-614.

Meter mounting devices are often supplied with a termination point for a system grounded conductor (neutral) that is solidly connected to the conductive metal enclosure of the meter mounting device. This arrangement may not have been tested for suitability as a system bonding jumper and should not be used as such. If the grounding connections for a solidly grounded system are to be made at the meter mounting device, an isolated neutral bus that incorporates provision for a bonding screw, a bonding strap, or a field-installed system bonding jumper should be installed as prescribed by the manufacturer.

The term "grounded conductor" is used to refer to the conductor or point of an electrical system that is grounded.

Where the midpoint conductor (neutral) of a single-phase or multi-phase midpoint system is solidly grounded, the grounded conductor serves as the identified neutral conductor intended to carry the unbalanced load (neutral currents). The grounded conductor serves as the bonding conductor in addition to its primary function of carrying neutral currents.

A consumer's service that is supplied by the supply authority and grounded at the meter mounting device is shown in Figure B10-4.

Figure B10-4
Consumer's service grounded at the meter mounting device

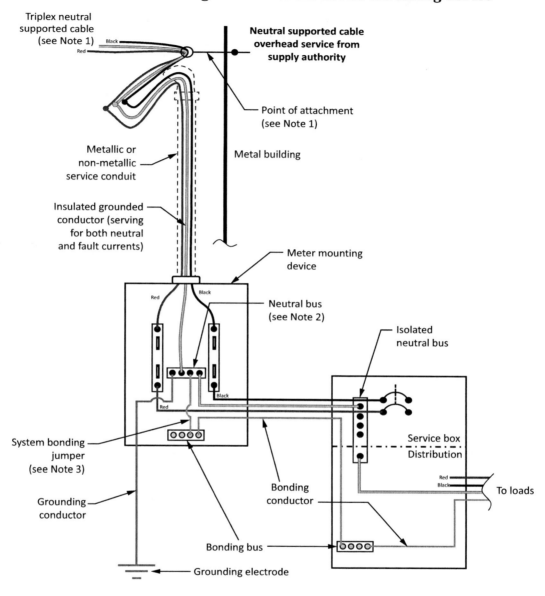

Notes:

1) *When the bare neutral of the triplex neutral supported cable is used as a neutral conductor, it is attached to an insulator at the point of support and terminations. It should not be in contact with any grounded surface [see Rule 12-318 e)].*

2) *The neutral bus in the meter mounting device may be isolated from, or solidly connected to, the enclosure, as follows:*

   a) *when it is isolated from the meter enclosure, either a factory-installed or a field-installed system bonding jumper is acceptable; or*

   b) *when it is solidly connected to the meter enclosure, the manufacturer's instructions should be consulted to determine if the solid connection to the meter enclosure is suitable as the system bonding jumper or if a field-installed system bonding jumper is required.*

3) *The system bonding jumper may be field-installed (a conductor) or factory-installed (a screw or strap).*

Where a meter-mounting device is not being used as the point for establishing the grounding connection at the consumer's service, the grounded conductor termination point of the meter mounting device is conductively isolated from the conductive metal enclosure.

A consumer's service that is supplied by the supply authority and grounded at the service box is shown in Figure B10-5.

© *2018 Canadian Standards Association*

Figure B10-5
Consumer's service grounded at the service box

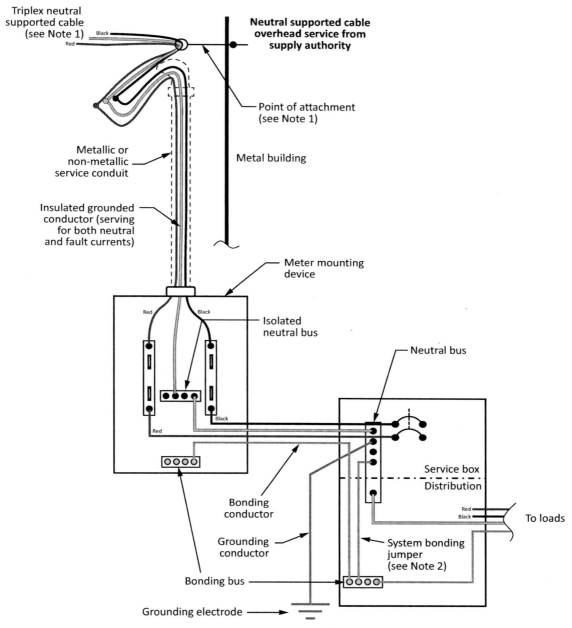

Notes:

1) *When the bare neutral of the triplex neutral supported cable is used as a neutral conductor, it is attached to an insulator at the point of support and terminations. It should not be in contact with any grounded surface [see Rule 12-318 e)].*

2) *The system bonding jumper may be field-installed (a conductor) or factory-installed (a screw or strap).*

Figure B10-6 shows an example of a three-phase, 4-wire solidly grounded ac system supplied from a supply authority.

Figure B10-6
Three-phase, 4-wire solidly grounded system, without a bonding conductor, supplied from the supply authority

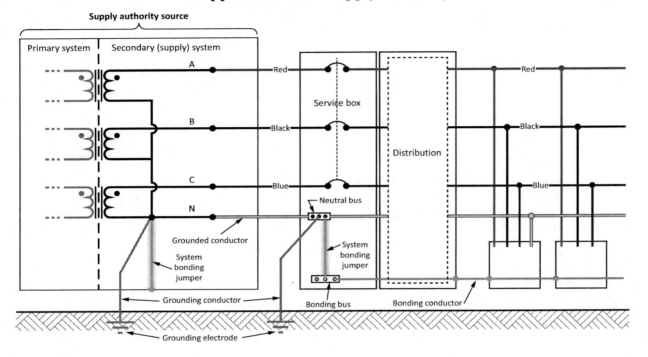

Rule 10-212
See Rule 10-004 and the Note to Rule 10-004 in this Appendix for the definition of a separately derived system.

In addition to the supply authority system supplying a facility, one or more separate systems may be installed at the facility (e.g., a generator to supply emergency power, a transformer to supply a different voltage to parts of the facility).

In a separately derived system that is required to be solidly grounded, the circuit conductors (the grounded conductor and the ungrounded conductors) of the newly established system have no direct connection to circuit conductors of the supply authority system other than those established by grounding and bonding connections. The grounded conductor of a solidly grounded separately derived system is grounded at only one point, with no connection between the grounded conductor and the non-current-carrying conductive parts of electrical equipment on the supply side or on the load side of the grounding point.

Figures B10-7 to B10-10 illustrate grounding connections permitted for a solidly grounded separately derived system, as follows:
a)   at the source of a separately derived system (see Figure B10-7);
b)   at the first switch controlling the system (see Figure B10-8);
c)   at each source of two separately derived systems supplying a transfer switch (see Figure B10-9); and
d)   at the tie point of two separately derived systems supplying a transfer switch (see Figure B10-10).

Figure B10-7
Separately derived system grounded at the source

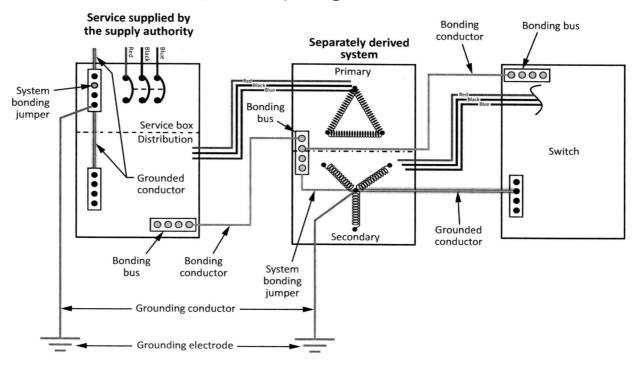

Figure B10-8
Separately derived system grounded at the first switch

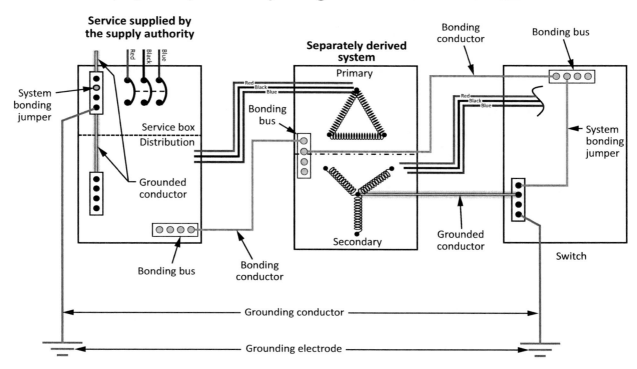

Where circuits are supplied from two separately derived systems, certain grounding arrangements may affect the operation of ground fault sensing devices. The following are some guidelines for effectively grounding two sources supplying circuits through a transfer switch:

Grounding at two sources of supply

Where two ground electrodes are used, one for each source of supply, it is good design practice to isolate the grounded conductor for each system through an extra pole at the transfer switch. This arrangement reduces the potential for nuisance tripping of ground fault sensing equipment (see Figure B10-9).

Figure B10-9
Two separately derived systems grounded at each source

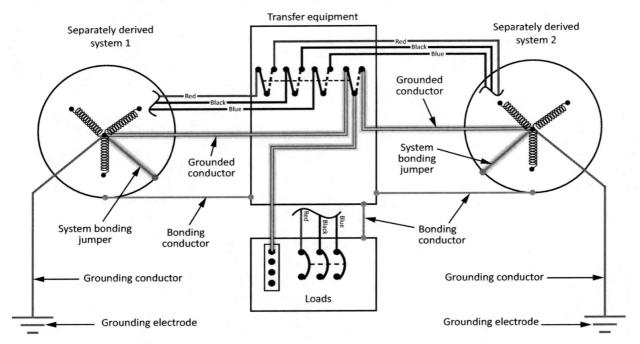

Grounding at a single point

Where a single grounding connection is made at the neutral tie point in a transfer switch, the grounded conductor is not permitted to be switched if the system bonding jumper is installed at only one point, either at the source or at the tie point. Figure B10-10 shows a circuit supplied from two separately derived systems, with the grounding connection made at the tie point with no system bonding jumper at either source.

Figure B10-10
Two separately derived systems grounded at the transfer equipment tie point

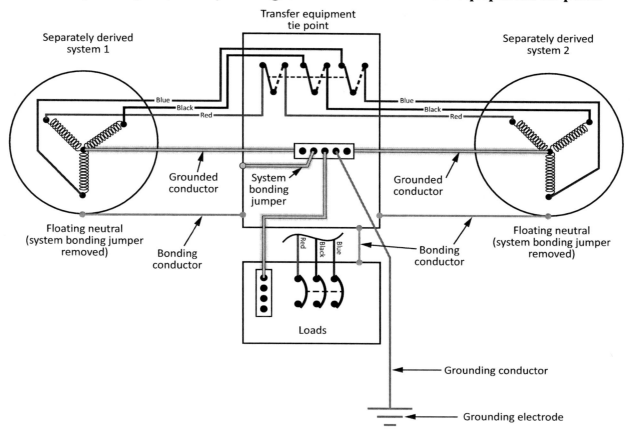

Where a circuit (including the bonding conductor) supplies the primary of a transformer, the system bonding jumper of the secondary separately derived system forms a direct connection to ground via the bonding conductor of the primary circuit. This system bonding jumper serves the two functions described in its definition:

a) it carries any fault current likely to be imposed on it; and

b) it establishes equipotentiality.

It is the latter function, establishing equipotentiality, that ensures that the non-current-carrying conductive parts of the electrical equipment are at the same potential as the grounded service or primary source. Essentially, the non-current-carrying conductive parts of the separately derived system are grounded via the primary bonding conductor. When it is required that the separately derived system (secondary of a transformer) be grounded, the system bonding jumper, by connection to the non-current-carrying conductive parts of the separately derived system, establishes a connection to a conductive body that extends the ground connection.

This applies only to situations where both the primary and the secondary of the transformer are rated 750 V or less. At higher voltages, Section 36 requires a station ground electrode to be installed. Figure B10-11 illustrates this alternative means of grounding a system operating at 750 V or less.

Figure B10-11
Grounding alternative for a separately derived system operating at 750 V or less

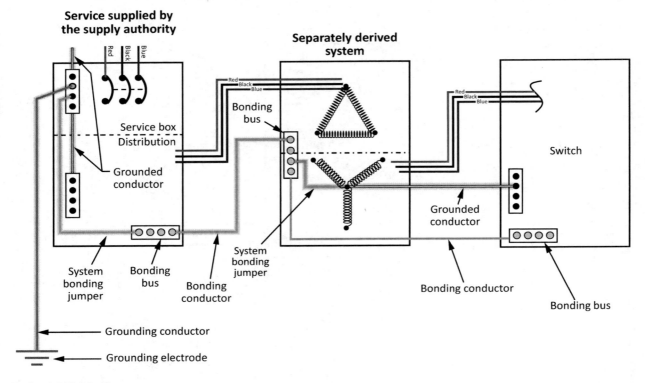

Rule 10-214 1)

CSA C22.2 No. 100 specifies the construction requirements for generators, including portable generator assemblies.

A portable generator assembly

a)   consists of a prime mover, a generator, overcurrent devices, and output receptacles that are assembled and connected on a common machine frame; and

b)   is capable of being carried or moved about by personnel.

A portable generator assembly is rated at not more than 12 kW and not more than 240 V and is intended to be used as an isolated system for the supply of cord-connected electrical equipment.

As a condition of approval of certain types of electrical equipment, such as portable generators, the manufacturer supplies instructions pertaining to its installation and operation. It is important that the end-users closely follow the instructions supplied by the manufacturer to fulfill the terms of the approval agreement.

Rule 10-214 2)

A mobile or vehicle-mounted generator that exceeds the rating of a portable generator given in CSA C22.2 No. 100 is a power source that may be connected to a fixed electrical installation

a)   to act as a stand-alone power system;

b)   to act as a standby power source via a transfer means, in parallel with one or more other power sources; or

c)   to power only equipment mounted on the vehicle.

It may be configured as a solidly grounded system, impedance grounded system, or ungrounded system. The applicable grounding requirements of Section 10 apply in each case.

When only equipment mounted on the vehicle or vehicle-mounted receptacles for accommodating attachment plugs are being powered, the generator frame or system neutral need not be connected to a grounding electrode.

Rule 10-300

Impedance grounded systems have characteristics that can be of benefit to facility owners; however, these systems rely on technology for safe and reliable operation. Special training is required to maintain these systems and, when installed, it is important that they be kept up to date.

Rule 10-302

An impedance grounding device (also known as a neutral grounding device) consists of neutral grounding resistors, single-phase neutral grounding transformers, ground fault neutralizers (resonant or Petersen coil), three-phase zig-zag transformers, or combinations of these, whose purpose is to decrease the level of ground fault current for safety (reduced arc flash), to reduce loss of production, and to mitigate equipment damage.

Other benefits of an impedance grounded system are to limit the voltage rise of the other phases so as not to exceed the line-to-line voltage and to stabilize the system voltage-to-ground both during normal operating conditions and during phase-to-ground fault conditions.

Conductors for high-voltage systems (greater than 750 V) are typically insulated for line-to-ground voltages but are labelled as if they are to be applied on line-to-line, solidly grounded systems. A fault on a single phase of an impedance grounded system causes the line-to-ground voltage on the non-faulted phase(s) to rise as high as line-to-line voltage. If this voltage is likely to be applied for longer than 1 min, the insulation of the cable should be upgraded so that it can withstand this increased voltage. Cable suppliers should be consulted to confirm if the system being designed requires 100%, 133%, or 173% insulation (or the equivalent, such as the application of 1000 V cable on 600 V impedance grounded systems).

The ground grid system of the supply authority should always be interconnected with the consumer's ground grid system. Where impedance grounding systems are installed, a grounded service conductor is not available for this purpose, and a separate conductor may have to be installed to interconnect the two ground grid systems.

For systems permitted to remain energized in accordance with Subrule 5), maintenance practices should encourage timely corrective action to avoid the consequences resulting from a second fault.

Figure B10-12 illustrates an impedance grounded system.

Figure B10-12
Impedance grounded system

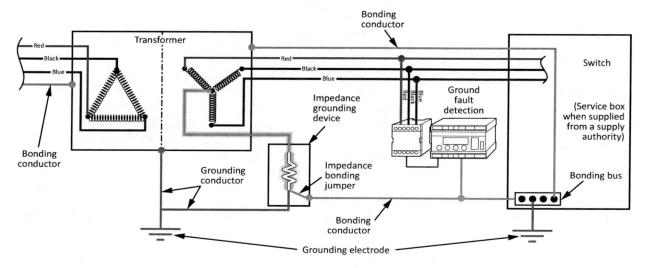

Rule 10-306

Impedance grounding devices produce heat when faults occur. To avoid overheating, follow the manufacturer's instructions regarding clearances.

The warning signs required by this Rule warn against bypassing the impedance grounding device with a direct connection from the system to the grounding electrode. It should also be noted that the source of the system may be an uninterrupted power supply (UPS) or other source, in addition to the generator and transformer.

Rule 10-308

The conductor connecting the impedance grounding device to the system source should be routed to take the shortest and most direct route. The entire impedance grounded system depends on the integrity of this conductor being free from faults or open circuits and, therefore, its routing should be designed accordingly, minimizing its length, where possible, to preserve its integrity.

Rule 10-400

Ungrounded systems have traditionally been used for an added degree of service continuity and reliability. However, a fault on one phase of a three-phase ungrounded system places a sustained increased voltage on the insulation of the ungrounded phases, which tends to reduce the life of the insulation. Although ungrounded systems are still permitted by the Code, they are increasingly being replaced by impedance grounded systems, which provide better voltage-to-ground stability.

Ungrounded systems may provide greater continuity of operations in the event of a ground fault. However, a second fault can be more catastrophic than a grounded system fault. Whenever ungrounded systems are used, it is important that qualified persons monitor the system on a regular basis for early identification of ground faults so that timely corrective action of the first ground fault can be made before a second ground fault occurs.

Rule 10-402

In an ungrounded system derived from the supply authority, the grounding connection is between the grounding electrode and the non-current-carrying conductive parts of the source equipment as well as between the grounding electrode and the non-current-carrying conductive enclosure of the service box or equivalent. For effective operation of ground fault detection when a ground fault occurs somewhere between the supply authority derived system and the grounded service equipment, there should be a conductive low impedance interconnection between the non-current-carrying parts of the source equipment and the grounded service equipment.

There may not be a service box in an ungrounded separately derived system (see Rule 10-004 and the Note to Rule 10-004 in this Appendix for the definition of a separately derived system). In such cases, the grounding conductor terminates at the equivalent supply source equipment, such as at the main switch or at the source equipment for the separately derived system.

Figure B10-13 illustrates an ungrounded system.

Figure B10-13
Ungrounded system

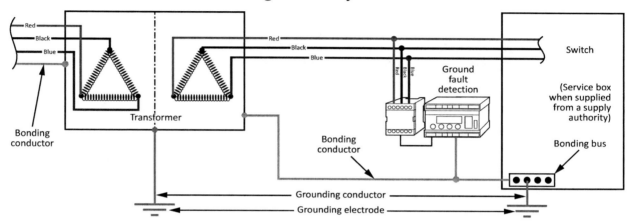

Rule 10-500
Under normal operation, there should be no objectionable current flow in a bonding conductor.

Currents in the bonding conductor that are not considered objectionable are those that may occur under normal operation, such as the temporary current resulting from a ground fault by way of capacitive or inductive coupling.

In situations such as a ground fault, the bonding conductor is designed to carry the available fault current for the time required to mitigate the fault. The equipotential bonding conductor may carry a portion of the fault current as a parallel fault current path.

See also the Note to Rule 10-100.

Rule 10-502
Locknuts, washers, drilled and tapped screws or bolts, etc., that penetrate insulating coatings do not require the coating to be removed first.

Rule 10-604
Supplementary bonding is required for service entrance equipment as the supply authority side conductors are considered unprotected. Once past the main protective devices, standard bonding methods apply.

Rule 10-606
Reducing washers are not tested for their suitability for maintaining a bonding connection. The use of reducing washers to maintain bonding continuity is a misapplication of the product in non-conformance with Rule 2-024.

Rule 10-610 2)
It is not the intent of this Rule to limit the use of cable constructions such as Type ACG90 that provide a combination of armour in contact with an internal bare conductor as the overall bonding conductor for the cable. These cable constructions rely on the use of suitable fittings designed specifically for the cable (such as press fittings) as required by Rule 10-612 1).

Rule 10-614

The principal purpose of a bonding conductor is to provide a low impedance path for fault current and facilitate the operation of overcurrent protective devices, in addition to serving as an equipotential bonding connection.

Rule 10-614 1) and 3) a)

When the system or circuit conductors on the secondary side of a transformer are protected only by the overcurrent devices on the primary side, the voltage ratio of the transformer is applied to the overcurrent device rating in applying Column 1 of Table 16.

Rule 10-614 3) b)

When the size of a circuit conductor is increased to compensate for voltage drop due to circuit length, the ampacity of that conductor exceeds that required for the connected load and the rating of the overcurrent protective device. The bonding conductor needs to be increased proportionately to minimize the impedance of the bonding path and facilitate the operation of the overcurrent device. The size of the bonding conductor is based on the circuit conductor allowable ampacity given in Column 2 of Table 16 to compensate for conductor length.

Rule 10-614 4)

When system or circuit conductors are installed in parallel in separate raceways or cables, Rule 10-602 requires a bonding conductor to be installed with each set of parallel conductors.

When the size of each field-installed bonding conductor is based on Subrule 3) a), Column 1 of Table 16 is applied by dividing the rating of the overcurrent device protecting the conductors by the number of conductors in parallel.

When Subrule 3) b) is used, the ampacity of each set of conductors in parallel in the group is applied using Column 2 of Table 16.

Rule 10-614 6)

A metal raceway approved as a bonding means and sized to contain the circuit conductors adequately serves as a bonding means for a given application.

Rule 10-614 7)

A bonding means that is integral to a cable assembly is sized based on the applicable product Standard and is of adequate size for the purposes of this Rule. See Rule 10-610 2) and 3).

Rule 10-700

This Rule applies to equipotential bonding of the conductive surfaces of non-electrical equipment, devices, and structures where the control of voltage rise is required or desired.

The equipotential bonding of these conductive pipes and systems is provided to prevent them from carrying a voltage different from the electrical system in order to control potential differences that may cause unwanted circulating currents, galvanic corrosion, or tingle voltages. Continuous water and waste water systems can, under certain circumstances, carry impressed currents from lightning strikes or faults in neighbouring buildings where conductive piping may interconnect the electrical systems of other structures that share the same water supply.

Waste water systems constructed of cast iron and rubber couplings are not considered continuous. Metallic waste water systems that used solder joints are considered continuous. The installer should verify that the system is metallic and continuous.

It should be noted that exterior gas piping systems may be required to be isolated from interior gas piping to prevent the introduction of current as well as to preserve any cathodic protection of the gas piping system. In general, this is accomplished using dielectric fittings at the demarcation between the interior and exterior gas piping system. Any conditions limiting the equipotential bonding of the exterior gas system should be verified with the local gas inspection authority.

It should also be noted that the requirement in Rule 10-700 c) to provide equipotential bonding to a metal gas piping system is not intended to apply to metal gas tubing. Attempts to bond metal gas tubing with conventional bonding means can create a hazardous situation where the tubing can be punctured by installation of the bonding means or by arcing between improperly secured bonding means during faults or lightning strikes.

Livestock are particularly sensitive to the effects of step and touch voltages. For this reason, equipotential bonding is prescribed for all conductive metal parts (e.g., metal water pipes, stanchions, water bowls or troughs, vacuum lines, and other metal objects that could become energized) accessible by livestock in a building housing livestock.

Methods to establish equipotentiality at buildings housing livestock are described in ASABE EP473.2-2001.

Low grounding electrode system resistances may reduce potential differences in livestock facilities.

Conductive materials used for equipotential bonding need not be wires and can take the form of structural steel, bus, metallic framing and support structures, conductive static mats, or the support structure of a computer room floor. Each of these materials, when adequately interconnected, form an effective equipotential plane.

The user should be aware of the effects of galvanic corrosion where dissimilar metals are joined together and ensure that the materials used are compatible or appropriately protected from corrosion at joints and connections.

Rule 10-706
Connections to non-electrical equipment may not have electrical connectors specifically constructed for the connection of electrical conductors. Conditions of use, good mechanical and electrical connection, and the atmospheric conditions or corrosive nature of the bonding location should be taken into consideration in selecting connectors and alternative connection methods.

Section 12

Rule 12-000
Reference should be made to the *National Building Code of Canada* or to appropriate sections of the provincial/territorial building codes regarding the installation and use of combustible electrical equipment such as raceways, boxes, and cables.

Δ **Rule 12-012**
Wooden planks, when buried in the ground, should be treated with a solution of pentachlorophenol or other suitable material as recommended by a manufacturer of wood preservatives. The use of creosote as a wood preservative in such installations is not recommended because it is known to damage rubber and thermoplastic insulations and acts as a catalyst in the corrosion of lead.

Rule 12-012 4)
The maximum size of sand is based on standard sieve sizes detailed in ASTM D2487.

Rule 12-012 12)
The intent of this Rule is to avoid damage to the installation during movement of the building, raceway, or cable.

Rule 12-100
Table 19 indicates the maximum allowable conductor temperature for various types of building insulated conductors and cables. Where the surface temperature and/or the temperature on the insulation of conductors, cables, or raceway systems exceeds 90 °C, such assemblies are a potential fire hazard if installed adjacent to combustible material and, in such cases, the assemblies should be relocated or supported in a manner to remove this potential hazard.

The low temperature marking on insulated conductors and cables indicates compliance with a test at that temperature, as specified in the product Standard, but does not guarantee safe installation at that temperature.

Care should be taken when installing insulated conductors and cables at low temperatures. Measures to consider include preconditioning at higher temperatures prior to installation, and avoidance of mechanical shock from dropping the insulated conductors or cable, unreeling the insulated conductors or cable too quickly, or bending sharply or quickly at bends. Manufacturers should be consulted when further information is desired.

Δ **Rule 12-102 1) and 2)**
For insulated conductors or cables without a low temperature marking, the minimum recommended handling and installation temperature is −10 °C. Where marked −25 °C or −40 °C, the minimum recommended handling and installation temperature is equivalent to that low temperature marking; however, appropriate precautions should be taken for all installations at temperatures below −10 °C.

Appropriate precautions include
a)   warming the insulated conductor or cable prior to handling and installation, in accordance with the manufacturer's instructions;
b)   minimizing flexing of the insulated conductor or cable;
c)   when flexing the insulated conductor or cable, bending the insulated conductor or cable slowly;
d)   working with an increased minimum bend radius;
e)   working with a reduced pulling speed; and
f)   applying other precautions recommended by the manufacturer.

When designing installations intended to operate continuously at a lower ambient temperature, consideration should be given to installing an insulated conductor or cable suitable for handling at that temperature.

In addition to the application of appropriate low temperature precautions, insulated conductors and cables should not be installed when the ambient temperature is lower than
a)   −40 °C when the conductor or cable is marked "−40C";
b)   −25 °C when the conductor or cable is marked "−25C";
c)   −10 °C when the conductor or cable is not marked with a lower temperature limit; or
d)   that specified by the manufacturer when conditioned, handled, and installed according to the manufacturer's instructions.

Once a conductor or cable is installed in a fixed position, it may operate safely at lower ambient temperatures. However, the manufacturer should be consulted for additional instructions for all installations when the conductors or cables will be subjected, either during or after installation, to temperatures below the limitations marked on them.

Δ **Rules 12-102 3) and 4), 12-122, 12-402, and 12-406**
When a conductor, cable, flexible cord, equipment wire, or portable power cable is being selected, it is important that it be designed for the specific application and conditions of intended use. Rule 2-024 requires conductors, cables, flexible cords, equipment wire, or portable power cables to be approved and installed for use within the design parameters for which they were manufactured and certified. Consult Table 11 or 19 as applicable and the cable manufacturer to ensure that the proper conductor, cable, flexible cord, equipment wire, or portable power cable is selected for the specific application. Limitations on the use of certain product types may be specified in other Rules of this Code.

△ **Rules 12-106, 12-904, and 12-3030**

For the application of Rules 12-106, 12-904, and 12-3030, a remote device is considered to be a device that is connected to a control circuit and is used to control or provide indication (e.g., limit switches, push buttons, thermostats, pilot lights, and alarms). Examples of equipment that are not considered remote devices are task and room luminaires, receptacles, unit equipment, heaters, etc.

Rule 12-108

The following configurations are acceptable for insulated conductors and single-conductor cables in parallel to minimize the difference in inductive reactance and the unequal division of current. Additional insulated conductors and single-conductor cables in parallel should be arranged in repetitive configurations of those illustrated. Other factors that affect load sharing and should be considered are outlined in Subrule 1).

Figure B12-1
Configurations for the installation of parallel single-conductor cables

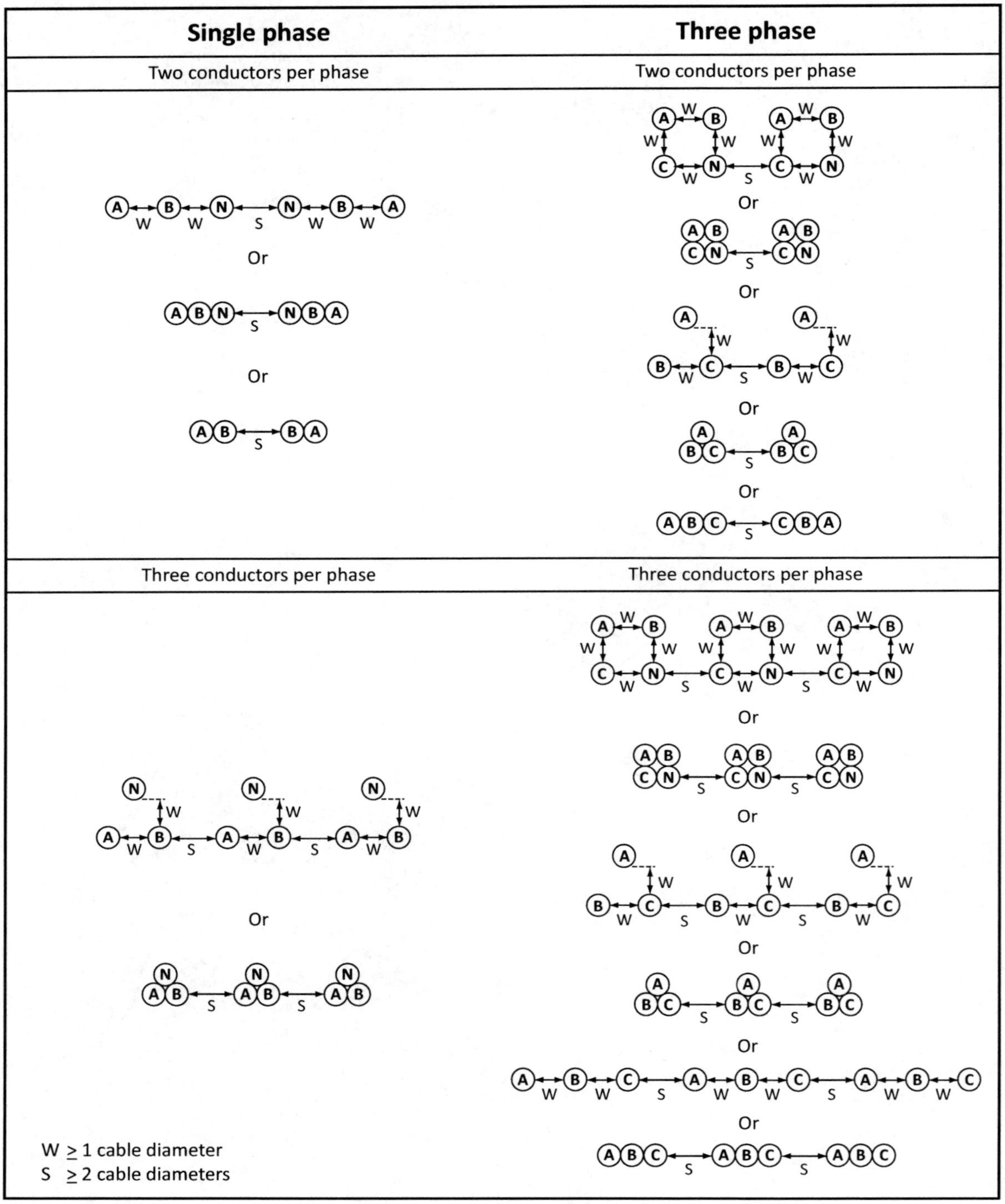

Single phase	Three phase
Two conductors per phase	Two conductors per phase
Three conductors per phase	Three conductors per phase

W ≥ 1 cable diameter
S ≥ 2 cable diameters

Note: *The configurations above may not result in equal ampacity or division of current for all cable systems (see also Rule 4-008).*

Rule 12-116
Solderless conductor connectors or their cartons are identified as follows:
a) "solid" or equivalent for conductor sizes Nos. 18, 16, and 8 AWG and larger; and
b) "stranded" or equivalent for conductor sizes Nos. 14 to 10 AWG.

If not so marked, solderless conductor connectors are suitable for connecting stranded conductors in sizes Nos. 18, 16, and 8 AWG and larger, and solid conductors in sizes Nos. 14 to 10 AWG.

A conductor connector marked as indicated in Item a) or b) of this Note is suitable for use with the marked type of construction only.

Rule 12-120 4)
The design and construction of cable types such as TECK90, RA90, RC90, AC90, and ACWU90 do not provide internal support between the sheath or armour and the internal cable assembly. Horizontal runs of TECK90, RA90, RC90, AC90, and ACWU90 that equal or exceed the vertical length, or that incorporate a bend or bends equivalent to a total of not less than 90°, reduce the strain on conductor terminations.

Δ ### Rule 12-406 4)
CSA C22.2 No. 65 requires that connectors tested for use with conductors more finely stranded than Class C indicate the conductor class or classes and the number of strands permitted. This marking may appear on the connector, a unit container, or an information sheet packed in the unit container.

Rule 12-504
The specific details for buildings of non-combustible construction are located in Part 3 of the *National Building Code of Canada* or in the appropriate provincial/territorial legislation.

Rule 12-506
Specific requirements pertaining to materials suitable as thermal barriers can be found in Article 3.1.5.11 of the *National Building Code of Canada*.

Rules 12-510, 12-706, 12-1010, 12-1308, and 12-1504
CAN/CSA-C22.2 No. 62275 recognizes six types of cable ties: Types 1, 11, 2, 21, 2S, and 21S. See Table B12-1.

Table B12-1
Cable ties

Types 1 and 11*	Approved type of cable tie but not specifically approved to provide primary support for flexible conduit, flexible tubing, or cable in accordance with this Code. Examples of uses: in approved equipment; to bundle wires for circuit identification or to maintain critical spacings in cabinets; or to otherwise provide supplemental means for routing wires, flexible conduit, flexible tubing, or cables.
Types 2 and 21*	Approved type of cable tie but not specifically approved to provide primary support for flexible conduit, flexible tubing, or cable in accordance with this Code. Examples of uses: in approved equipment; to bundle wires for circuit identification or to maintain critical spacings in cabinets; or to otherwise provide supplemental means for routing wires, flexible conduit, flexible tubing, or cables.
Type 2 also identified with AH-2	Approved type of cable tie but not specifically approved to provide primary support for flexible conduit, flexible tubing, or cable in accordance with this Code. Examples of uses: in approved equipment; to bundle wires for circuit identification or to maintain critical spacings in cabinets; or to otherwise

(Continued)

Table B12-1 (Concluded)

	provide supplemental means for routing wires, flexible conduit, flexible tubing, or cables; and suitable for use in air-handling spaces (plenums) in accordance with Rules 12-010 3), 4), and 5) and 12-020.
Types 2S and 21S*	Specifically approved to provide primary support for flexible conduit, flexible tubing, or cable in accordance with this Code.
Types 2S and 21S* also identified with AH-2	Specifically approved to provide primary support for flexible conduit, flexible tubing, or cable in accordance with this Code. Suitable for use in air-handling spaces (plenums) in accordance with Rules 12-010 3), 4), and 5) and 12-020.

* For the purposes of this Code, Type 1 is identical to Type 11, Type 2 is identical to Type 21, and Type 2S is identical to Type 21S.

Each cable tie is required to be marked with the manufacturer's or responsible vendor's name, trademark, and identifying symbol. In addition, the following markings are required to be provided on labels, packaging, or installation instructions shipped with the cable tie instructions provided with the product:

a) maximum operating temperature;
b) minimum operating temperature;
c) minimum installation temperature if lower than 0 °C (temperature at time of installation advisory only to installer for cold temperature handling);
d) minimum and maximum bundle diameter;
e) loop tensile strength; and
f) type designation.

In accordance with CAN/CSA-C22.2 No. 62275, the marking indicating the classification "Resistant to ultraviolet light" may alternatively be given as "For use outdoors" or "For use outdoors or indoors", or equivalent wording.

Rules 12-510 4), 12-3000 8), and 12-3010 7)

Rules 12-510 4), 12-3000 8), and 12-3010 7) are intended to permit the use of a self-contained device in lieu of a device box. A self-contained device is a wiring device with an integral enclosure having brackets that securely fasten the device to walls or ceilings of conventional frame construction, for use with non-metallic-sheathed cable. Self-contained devices used in dry locations are certified to CSA C22.2 No. 111 for switches and CSA C22.2 No. 42 for receptacles and are primarily used in mobile homes, recreational vehicles, manufactured buildings, and on-site frame construction.

Δ Rule 12-516

CSA C22.2 No. 18.3 provides requirements for inserts. CSA C22.2 No. 18.4 provides requirements for protector plates and cylindrical bushings.

Rule 12-602

The steel wire armour (SWA) used in cables features inherently different mechanical characteristics from conventional interlocked armour. Due to its physical structure, steel wire armour provides high tensile strength but may provide less mechanical protection than interlocked armour when, for example, subjected to puncture. The user should consider the particular application when selecting SWA for cables.

Rule 12-610 1)

The paper or plastic wrap around the cable core, directly under the armour of an armoured cable, is not considered the inner jacket referred to in Item b).

Rule 12-714
Mineral-insulated cable has a copper, aluminum, or stainless steel sheath. Box connectors suitable for use with the particular sheath material should therefore be used.

Rule 12-802
The bottom shield may or may not be incorporated as an integral part of the whole system. The top shield and the metal tape may be two separate components or may be a single integral component of the Type FCC system.

Rule 12-814
Tapes having a conductive surface in intimate electrical contact with metal shields throughout the Type FCC system are considered to be bonded when approved for the purpose.

Rule 12-902
Armoured cables intended to be pulled into conduit or tubing are subject to damage when the maximum pulling tension is exceeded or the sidewall bearing pressure is beyond the capability of the cable. Typically, the limiting factor in these installations is the sidewall bearing pressure. Cable specification data and calculation methods to determine the acceptable length of cable to be pulled into a raceway are available from cable manufacturers. Furthermore, the minimum cable bending radius must be considered. There may be different values for the minimum bending radii depending on the type of cable. The cable manufacturer should be consulted for accurate values of the minimum bending radii of specific cables.

The examples of acceptable installations described in Item 2) b) ii) are based on a maximum cable size of 1000 kcmil and a run of raceway with a 90° bend at each end, using bends with a 0.944 m radius for low-voltage cable and bends with a 1.524 m radius for high-voltage cable. Installations beyond these parameters should have calculations completed to establish acceptability.

Δ ### Rule 12-910
The maximum permitted number of insulated conductors and cables in a raceway is based on the actual measured dimensions of the raceways and the insulated conductors and cables. Where calculations of the maximum number of permitted insulated conductors and cables in a given raceway are based on supplied dimensions or product Standards, they should be validated by measuring the products concerned before installation.

The corresponding Standards for the raceways detailed in Tables 9A to 9P are as follows:

Table 9A — CSA C22.2 No. 45.1 — Rigid metal conduit

Table 9B — CSA C22.2 No. 56 — Flexible metal conduit

Table 9C — CSA C22.2 No. 211.2 — Rigid PVC conduit

Table 9D — CSA C22.2 No. 211.1 — Rigid Type EB1 PVC conduit

Table 9D — CSA C22.2 No. 211.1 — Rigid Type DB2/ES2 PVC conduit

Table 9E — CSA C22.2 No. 211.3 (withdrawn) — Rigid RTRC conduit marked IPS

Table 9F — CSA C22.2 No. 211.3 (withdrawn) — Rigid RTRC conduit marked ID

Table 9G — CSA C22.2 No. 56 — Liquid-tight flexible metal conduit

Table 9H — CSA C22.2 No. 227.2.1 — Liquid-tight flexible non-metallic conduit

Table 9I — CSA C22.2 No. 83 and CSA C22.2 No. 83.1 — Electrical metallic tubing

Table 9J — CSA C22.2 No. 227.1 — Electrical non-metallic tubing

Table 9K — CSA C22.2 No. 327 — HDPE conduit Schedule 40

Table 9L — CSA C22.2 No. 327 — HDPE conduit Schedule 80

Table 9M — CSA C22.2 No. 327 — HDPE DR9 conduit

Table 9N — CSA C22.2 No. 327 — HDPE DR11 conduit

Table 9O — CSA C22.2 No. 327 — HDPE DR13.5 conduit

Table 9P — CSA C22.2 No. 327 — HDPE DR15.5 conduit

Calculating the maximum permissible number of conductors of the same size in a given raceway provides an alternative basis for determining the maximum number of permitted conductors, provided that the dimensions of such raceways and conductors are derived from Tables 9A to 9J, 10A, and 10B. The maximum numbers of single conductors of one size permitted in a conduit or raceway as determined from Tables 6A to 6K are based on these tables, with no allowance for bare bonding or grounding conductors. The raceway types used for the calculation of Tables 6A to 6K are as follows:

Trade size 12 — Flexible metal conduit

Trade size 16 — Rigid RTRC conduit Type ID

Trade size 21 — Rigid RTRC conduit Type ID

Trade size 27 — Rigid RTRC conduit Type ID

Trade size 35 — Rigid RTRC conduit Type ID

Trade size 41 — Rigid RTRC conduit Type ID

Trade size 53 — Rigid RTRC conduit Type ID

Trade size 63 — Rigid PVC conduit

Trade size 78 — Rigid RTRC conduit Type ID

Trade size 91 — Rigid RTRC conduit Type ID

Trade size 103 — Rigid PVC conduit

Trade size 116 — Rigid RTRC conduit Type ID

Trade size 129 — Rigid PVC conduit

Trade size 155 — Rigid PVC conduit

Trade size 200 — Rigid PVC conduit

Subrule 6) does not permit Tables 6A to 6K to be used to determine the number of insulated conductors of the same size in one HDPE conduit because for each available trade size, HDPE conduit has the smallest internal diameter.

Dimensions of bare bonding or grounding conductors, such as bonding conductors that are required for some raceway installations under applicable Code Rules, may be obtained from Table D5. They should be verified by measurement before installation.

Rule 12-936
Where raceways pass across structural expansion or control joints, possible relative movement that could damage the raceway should be accommodated in the design.

Rules 12-944 and 12-3000 4)
The intent of this Rule is to protect metal raceways and boxes against corrosion in concrete slabs of unheated parkades and similar structures, where permeation of salt represents a corrosion hazard. Users of this Code should be aware that CSA S413 restricts the use of metal raceways and boxes embedded in concrete slabs where they are subject to corrosion.

Rule 12-1006
When field threading rigid metal conduit, see ANSI/ASME B1.20.1.

Rules 12-1012, 12-1118, and 12-1214
Table B12-2 provides information on the linear expansion of materials where extreme temperature changes are encountered:

Table B12-2
Coefficient of linear expansion

Coefficient of linear expansion (mm per m per °C)	
Wood	0.0050
Brick	0.0047 to 0.0090
Steel conduit	0.0114
Rigid RE conduit	0.0108 to 0.0135
Concrete	0.0144
Aluminum conduit	0.0220
PVC conduit	0.0520

Example:

> The change in length, in millimetres, of a run of rigid PVC conduit, due to the maximum expected variation in temperature, is found by multiplying the length of the run, in metres, by the maximum expected temperature change, in degrees Celsius, and by the coefficient of linear expansion.
>
> For a 20 m run of rigid PVC conduit when the minimum expected temperature is –40 °C and the maximum expected temperature is 30 °C, the change in length is
>
> 20 × (40 + 30) × 0.0520 = 73 mm

Rules 12-1104, 12-1154, and 12-1508
Tests show that 90 °C insulated conductors, continuously loaded, under conditions of 50% fill and 30 °C ambient, do not result in a temperature exceeding 75 °C. Insulated conductors having insulation ratings in excess of 90 °C may be used in PVC conduit, provided that the ampacity is derated to 90 °C.

Rule 12-1108
When bending PVC conduit, an open flame should not be used.

Rule 12-1118
Refer to the Note in this Appendix for Rules 12-1012, 12-1118, and 12-1214. In the example given, the change in length is 73 mm and therefore one or more expansion joints would be required, depending on the maximum range that a particular joint is capable of handling.

Rule 12-1150
Precautions should be taken to ensure that no pour of concrete and/or its reinforcement exerts a load on the conduit that will render the conduit unsuitable for use. Too high a pour may cause failure through collapse on overloading when the concrete is in a wet (uncured) state.

Rule 12-1154
See the Note to Rules 12-1104, 12-1154, and 12-1508.

Rule 12-1156
In general, a thermostatically controlled heat gun may be used for field bends on trade sizes up to 53 trade size. For sizes 27 to 53 trade sizes, springs or equivalent devices should be used in conjunction with the heat gun to prevent reduction of the internal diameter. For sizes larger than 53 trade size, special jigs, moulds, springs, and heating arrangements are required.

See also the Note to Rule 12-1108.

Rule 12-1158
When connecting rigid Types EB1 and DB2/ES2 PVC conduit to conduit made of materials other than PVC through the use of a taper threaded connection, it is preferable that a female threaded adapter be made from the same PVC material as the PVC conduit and the male threaded adapter be made from materials suited to the other than PVC material.

Rule 12-1204
Specific requirements pertaining to use of combustible conduit and tubing in buildings can be found in Articles 3.1.4.3, 3.1.5.15, 3.1.5.17, and 3.1.5.20 of the *National Building Code of Canada* or in the appropriate provincial/territorial legislation.

Rule 12-1214
See the Note to Rules 12-1012, 12-1118, and 12-1214.

Δ Rule 12-1254 5) b)
Horizontal directional drilling and plow-trenching installations are greatly affected by soil conditions, which vary for each installation. Soil containing sand, loose gravel, cobbles, boulders, or other obstructions induce significant crush loads on conduits; therefore, thicker walled conduit is required.

Δ Rule 12-1254 5) d)
HDPE elongates under the pull forces produced during horizontal directional drilling installations. Adequate time shall be provided before the conduit is cut to ensure that it has returned to its original, unstretched state. The elongation is greater in warm weather.

Rule 12-1508
See the Note to Rules 12-1104, 12-1154, and 12-1508.

Rule 12-1602
See the Notes to Rules 2-128 and 2-132.

Rule 12-1606
In applying this Rule, the "minimum available cross-sectional area" is the minimum cross-sectional area of the surface raceway minus the maximum cross-sectional area of any device installed in the surface raceway that projects into the surface raceway.

Rule 12-2200
Recommended installation requirements are available from the manufacturer of cable trays. Additional points to consider include the following:
a) the ideal support point for cable trays is at the one-quarter span point. Locating cable tray supports at or near the centre of a span or near cable tray joints may significantly increase the deflection of cable trays;
b) there should not be more than one joint between support points;

c)   allowance for wind and snow loading should be included within the maximum design load; and

d)   some fittings (particularly horizontal elbows) may require additional support, depending on the loading.

Rule 12-2202

Particular concerns to address when installing insulated conductors and cable in cable trays are

a)   protection by elevation or other means at traffic areas;

b)   protection from falling objects through the use of covers, shields, or other means;

c)   protection from radiant heat by heat shields, insulation, or other means;

d)   protection from people walking on insulated conductors or cables in trays by covers, guards, location, or other means; and

e)   protection from movable objects, stored goods, or other material by elevation, covers, guards, or other means.

Rule 12-2202 2)

CSA C22.2 No. 126.1 and CAN/CSA-C22.2 No. 126.2 require the marking on the cable tray to include the load/span rating of the cable tray.

Rule 12-2250

Rules 12-2250 to 12-2258 are intended to provide the electrical and mechanical requirements for installation of a metal-enclosed cablebus system.

A cablebus system includes all necessary straight sections, fittings, cable support blocks, covers, splice plates, hardware, weatherproof entrance fittings, fire stops, single insulated conductors or cables, compression lugs, termination kits, external supports, and other accessories required to form a complete system.

It is also intended by these Rules that a complete set of engineering drawings and installation drawings be made available for each system to facilitate system design, construction, and installation; to include electrical detail of the insulated conductor or cable configuration, together with enclosure dimensions; and to specify maximum allowable span support. It is also intended that each straight section and fitting be individually identified with an affixed label to correspond to an itemized list as shown on the installation drawing.

The intent of these Rules is to establish that cablebus systems are assembled at the point of installation in accordance with installation drawings provided by the manufacturer. It is also intended that cablebus representing a complete system approved for the purpose be marked as such in accordance with the product Standard.

Rule 12-2252

CSA C22.2 No. 273 defines Class A and Class B cablebus as follows:

Class A cablebus — cablebus that provides protection from contact with [insulated] conductors [or cables] by design and construction of the enclosure.

Class B cablebus — cablebus that does not provide protection from contact with [insulated] conductors [or cables] by design and construction of the enclosure.

Cablebus not marked as Class A is considered to be Class B.

Rules 12-2252 and 12-2254

It is intended by these Rules that cablebus be manufactured to be suitable for indoor and outdoor use, with load-bearing members of the cablebus system, including side rails, rungs, and splices for maximum strength and equipment bonding conductor ratings. Straight sections of enclosure are capable of supporting spans of up to 3.7 m, including an allowance for wind and snow loading, within the maximum design load. Insulated conductors are positively secured on supports spaced a maximum of

900 mm horizontally and 450 mm vertically along the length of the cablebus. Upon completion of the installation, the entire field assembly is approved as a complete system.

Δ **Rule 12-2258**
CSA C22.2 No. 273 allows optional testing for cablebus intended to be used as a bonding conductor. Cablebus meeting the bonding requirements includes the following or equivalent wording on the cablebus nameplate:

CABLEBUS ENCLOSURE HAS BEEN TESTED AS A SYSTEM BOND CONDUCTOR.

Δ **Rule 12-2300**
Refer to Section 16 for requirements for Class 2 circuits.

Δ **Rule 12-2302**
Busbar
A busbar enables connection to utilization equipment, such as sensors, actuators, audio-video devices, extra-low-voltage luminaire assemblies, and similar electrical equipment.

Δ **Rule 12-2314**
The mounting hardware to be used with extra-low-voltage suspended ceiling power distribution systems is either packaged with the system or specified in the installation instructions.

Δ **Rule 12-2316**
Connectors for use with grid bus rail, cables, and conductors are designed for use in accordance with CAN/ULC-S2577 with properties inherent in the connectors to ensure that they cannot be used in applications for which they are not designed. Refer to the manufacturer's installation and operating instructions.

Rule 12-3000
Sealing around outlet boxes and cables to provide an air barrier may be required. Requirements for air and vapour barriers are in the *National Building Code of Canada*, Subsections 9.25.3 and 9.25.4.

Rule 12-3000 9)
CSA C22.2 No. 18.1 and CSA C22.2 No. 18.2 contain provisions for construction and marking of outlet boxes intended to support a ceiling fan. Outlet boxes approved for support of a ceiling fan are marked "Acceptable for Fan Support". When outlet boxes are being installed in a ceiling where a ceiling fan may be installed, consideration should be given to installing outlet boxes approved to support ceiling fans.

Rules 12-3000 10) and 12-3002 2)
CSA C22.2 No. 18.1, CSA C22.2 No. 18.2, and CSA C22.2 No. 85 require that all floor boxes be provided with installation instructions indicating the type of floor structure with which they are intended to be installed. Floor box covers intended for use only in a floor covered with carpet or wood are marked on the product or smallest unit shipping carton "Not for use with tile covered floors", or the equivalent.

Rule 12-3016 3)
The intent of this Subrule is that the installation of an outlet box requiring a wet location cover plate will be such that the box and cover are in intimate contact and will provide a seal to prevent ingress of water into the outlet box.

Rule 12-3016 4)
The intent of this Subrule is that a flush box, cabinet, or fitting be of a type approved for the intended location of installation (e.g., a flush box installed in a masonry wall should be approved for installation in a masonry wall; or a fitting installed in a wet location should be approved for wet locations).

Ⓔ Δ **Rule 12-3030**
See the Note to Rules 12-106, 12-904, and 12-3030.

Rule 12-3032 4)
It is essential that appropriate space be provided around circuit breakers and fusible disconnect switches to allow proper dissipation of heat, in order that the specified current rating of insulated conductors and protection rating of overcurrent devices be maintained. This Subrule specifies 75% as the allowable portion of the wiring space, based on adding passive materials and 40% for current-carrying insulated conductors. Code users should note that instrument transformers, energy usage metering devices, and the associated wiring, although current-carrying, conduct only a small fraction of the current borne by the load-bearing insulated conductors in a power distribution enclosure.

Δ **Rule 12-3034 3)**
As an example, a device having a depth of 4 cm occupies a space of 128 cm³, that is, 32 cm³ × 4.

Section 14

Δ **Rule 14-000**
Other sections of this Code may provide additional protection requirements for specific circuits or for specific equipment and the associated conductors.

Rule 14-012
It is the intent of this Rule to ensure that the overcurrent protective and control devices, the total impedance, and other characteristics of the circuit to be protected are selected and coordinated so that the circuit protective devices will clear a fault without extensively damaging the electrical components of the circuit.

Interrupting ratings of overcurrent devices (circuit breakers or fuses) are 5000 A symmetrical maximum for circuit breakers rated 100 A or less and 250 V or less, and 10 000 A symmetrical maximum for circuit breakers rated above 100 A or above 250 V unless otherwise marked. The interrupting rating of fuses is 10 000 A symmetrical maximum unless otherwise marked.

Rule 14-014
A series rated system is one in which either a circuit breaker or a fuse is in series with a downstream circuit breaker that has an interrupting rating less than the fault current available at the line terminals of the upstream overcurrent device. The upstream device always has an interrupting rating at least equal to the available fault current.

This series combination is tested and approved at the higher rating in accordance with special requirements for series rated devices in the CSA Standards for the equipment involved (e.g., circuit breakers, panelboards, or metering equipment).

The tests verify that the combination acts together to safely clear a fault up to the maximum rating of the line side overcurrent device.

The downstream equipment is marked, as a part of its electrical rating, with its series rating and with the specific upstream overcurrent device required to achieve the series rating.

Where motors are connected in the system between the series connected devices, any significant motor contribution to the fault current should be considered. It is generally agreed that the contribution of asynchronous motors to the short-circuit current may be neglected if the sum of the rated currents of motors connected directly to the point between the series connected devices is 1% or less of the interrupting rating of the downstream circuit breaker. (See IEC 60781.)

Rule 14-100
This Rule applies only to conductors and cables interconnecting electrical equipment. It does not apply to overcurrent protection of electrical equipment as required by other Rules of the Code.

Rule 14-102 and Diagram 3

It is recognized that ground fault protection may be desired for circuits other than those described in this Rule.

Ground fault protective equipment at the supply will make it necessary to review the overall system for proper coordination with other overcurrent protection. Additional ground fault protective equipment may be needed on feeders and branch circuits where maximum continuity of electrical supply to the remainder of the system is required.

It should be noted that with disconnecting devices located as shown in Diagram 3, no protection is given for faults between the transformer and the disconnecting device. If this protection is required, the primary disconnecting device must be tripped.

In any ground fault protective scheme, the protective equipment should be applied to ensure that the external tripping power (if required) will be available whenever the circuit being protected is energized.

It should be noted that ground fault relays are usually factory set at the lowest current and shortest time settings available to ensure against unnecessary equipment damage during early stages of construction. These settings should be adjusted to the intended settings prior to final commissioning of the equipment.

Multi-fed installations with ties and interconnected neutrals may be grounded at more than two locations. In such cases, it will be the responsibility of the system designer to ensure that tripping occurs only on the main breaker associated with the supply affected by the ground fault (see Items 3 and 4 of Diagram 3). It is also recognized that for purposes of selectivity and continuity of service, many installations, in addition to utilizing multi-feeds for systems, also use multi-stage ground fault protection as described in Subrule 8). This results in complex schemes. In both of these special cases, the designer should be required to submit data to the inspection department showing that such considerations have been taken into account in the design of the system involved.

Δ **Rule 14-104**

When conductors are selected based on a calculated load or a known load, Table 13 is useful in selecting the appropriate rating of overcurrent device based on the installed ampacity of the conductor for the installation. Code users are reminded that the circuit loading requirements of Rule 8-104 apply. It is intended that the conductor ampacity values used in Table 13 can refer to single or multiple conductors. Table 13 is also useful in determining standard overcurrent ratings for Rules such as 14-212 b) or 26-254 3).

Δ **Rule 14-108**

Further information about assembly of circuit breaker overcurrent protection devices is provided in CSA C22.2 No. 5.

Rule 14-114

Supplementary overcurrent protectors used as components of some appliances and equipment are not suitable for the protection of branch circuit conductors.

Rule 14-204

There are two types of non-interchangeable plug fuses currently available, i.e., Types C and S as described in CAN/CSA-C22.2 No. 248.5.

Rule 14-212

The fuse "Classes" are cross-referenced to the former "Form" and "HRC" fuse designations in Table B14-1.

Table B14-1
Fuse "Classes" cross-referenced to "Form" and "HRC" fuse designations

CSA C22.2 Nos. 248.1 to 248.15, published in 1994, 1996, 2000, and 2011	CSA C22.2 No. 106-M1985, CAN/CSA-C22.2 No. 106-M92, C22.2 No. 106-05, and C22.2 No. 59.1-M1987	CSA C22.2 No. 106-1953 and Electrical Bulletin No. 832-1971
Class J	HRCI-J	HRC Form I
Class R	HRCI-R	HRC Form I
Class T	HRCI-T, HRC-T	HRC Form I
Class CA	HRCI-CA	HRC Form I
Class CB	HRCI-CB	HRC Form I
Class CC	HRCI-CC	HRC Form I
—	HRCI-Misc‡	HRC Form I
Class G*	—	—
Class K*	—	—
Class H†	—	—
Class L	HRC-L	Class L
Class C	HRCII-C	HRC Form II
—	HRCII-Misc‡	HRC Form II

* *Class G and Class K fuses did not formerly have a fuse classification.*

† *Class H fuses were formerly referred to as "standard fuses" but are now marked as "Class H" in accordance with CAN/CSA-C22.2 No. 248.6 and CAN/CSA-C22.2 No. 248.7.*

‡ *"Misc" (miscellaneous) fuse designations will remain in use for fuses that meet the requirements of CSA C22.2 No. 106 and that do not have a "Class" designation.*

Rule 14-302
The voltage ratings referred to in Item b) ii) covering single-pole circuit breakers suitable for use with handle ties appear on each breaker, e.g., 120/240 V.

Rule 14-402
A relaxation to the requirement for a disconnecting means is allowed under Subrule c) because a plug fuse can be safely handled while it is installed in a live circuit having only one ungrounded conductor.

Rule 14-508
The requirements for general use ac/dc switches are given in CSA C22.2 No. 111.

Rule 14-510
The intent of this requirement is to permit only manually operated switches that are designed, constructed, and marked in accordance with CSA C22.2 No. 111 to be used.

Table B14-2
Manually operated switches — Markings

Marking	Indication
"T"	Indicates an ac/dc switch intended for the control of tungsten-filament lamps on ac or dc circuits of 125 V maximum.
"L"	Indicates an ac/dc switch acceptable for the control of tungsten-filament lamps on ac circuits of 125 V maximum.
"AC" or "~" or frequency marking (for example, "60 Hz") or a phase marking	Indicates a general-use switch that is intended for use only on ac circuits.

Rule 14-512
The requirements for manually operated general-use 347 V ac switches are given in CSA C22.2 No. 111.

Section 16

Δ **Rule 16-000 1) e)**
Class 2 power and data communication circuits are based on the concept known as PoE (power over ethernet) introduced by the IEEE 802.3 series of Standards. These IEEE Standards originally limited the delivered power to 15.4 W. However, the limit was later increased to 25.5 W, and then two additional power types were introduced: up to 55 W (Type 3) and up to 100 W (Type 4). Type 3 and Type 4 power levels are incompatible with the Rules applicable to communication equipment given in Section 60 of this Code but are compatible with the existing requirements for Class 2 circuits in Section 16.

Δ **Rule 16-200**
A primary battery for Class 2 power sources consists of one or more cells electrically connected under the same cover, with each cell producing an electrical current by an electrochemical reaction that is not reversible, that is, non-rechargeable.

The use of the Class 2 circuits described in Subrule 1) a) to c) is highly dependent on the characteristics of the device having a Class 2 output.

Δ **Rule 16-200 4)**
It is intended by this Subrule that a device having a Class 2 output have energy-limiting characteristics that limit the output current and power to acceptable values in accordance with CSA C22.2 No. 223. This Standard allows a Class 2 power source to be inherently limited or not inherently limited. It should be noted that maximum output current and power are limited as specified in the following Standards:
a)   CAN/CSA-C22.2 No. 60950-1 for limited power supplies (LPS);
b)   CSA C22.2 No. 223 for power supplies with extra-low-voltage Class 2 outputs;
c)   CSA C22.2 No. 66.3 for Class 2 transformers;
d)   CAN/CSA-C22.2 No. 62368-1 for audio/video, information, and communication technology equipment; and
e)   CAN/CSA-C22.2 No. 250.13 for light-emitting diode (LED) equipment.

Therefore, the Class 2 circuits described in Rule 16-200 are considered safe from a fire-initiation standpoint and provide acceptable protection from electric shock. For wet locations, additional measures, such as additional voltage-level restrictions to accessible live parts, or a physical safeguard and marking may be required to provide protection from an electric shock hazard.

The Class 2 circuits described in Subrule 1) d) are also considered safe from a fire-initiation standpoint; however, due to higher voltage levels, additional safeguards should be specified to provide protection from an electric shock hazard that could be encountered.

Rule 16-210

Both LVT and ELC are approved cables for Class 2 circuit applications under the conditions outlined in Table 19. Type ELC conductors do not have an overall protective jacket and are further limited in use under this Rule to certain Class 2 circuits operating at 30 V or less, such as doorbells, intrusion devices, etc., in dwelling units in buildings of combustible construction. Type ELC is not permitted for the wiring of circuits related to fire safety, such as fire alarms or smoke alarm devices.

Rule 16-222 1) a)

With respect to the acceptance of equipment for connection to Class 2 circuits operating at not more than 42.4 V peak or dc, consideration should be given to the fact that while Class 2 circuits limit the power that can be dissipated in the circuit continuously, this power is more than sufficient to be a fire hazard if dissipated in a fault within improperly designed equipment, e.g., shorted turns in a coil.

Rule 16-222 2)

Examples of lighting products include the following:

a)   luminaires;
b)   signs;
c)   rope lights;
d)   decorative strings and outfits;
e)   illuminated novelty items; and
f)   lighting devices that incorporate light-emitting diodes (LEDs).

Δ   Rule 16-222 3) a) i), ii), and iii)

The maximum voltage between any two output terminals under any load condition, including no load, for Subrule 3), a) i), ii), and iii) is 42.4 V peak or (33 + 0.45 × the dc component voltage), up to a maximum of 60 V. This corresponds to a limit of 30 V rms for sinusoidal ac waveforms, 42.4 V peak for other waveforms, and 60 V continuous dc.

Δ   Rule 16-300

This Subsection applies to the installation of Class 2 power and data communication circuits consisting of power sourcing equipment and powered devices operating as a complete system. Examples include extra-low-voltage lighting systems, closed circuit television systems (CCTV), wireless access points (WAP), distributed antenna systems (DAS), and building automation systems (BAS).

Δ   Rule 16-310

Power sourcing equipment
Power sourcing equipment is equipment meeting the requirements of CAN/CSA-C22.2 No. 60950-1 or CAN/CSA-C22.2 No. 62368-1.

Δ   Rules 16-310 and 16-340

For the application of the definition of a Class 2 power and data communication circuit, a circuit is considered a twisted pair of insulated conductors or pair of twisted pair conductors within a common cable assembly marked as being suitable for application from power sourcing equipment to a powered device. This recognizes that more than one circuit in one cable assembly may supply one powered device.

Δ   Rule 16-330 2)

Limited power cables complying with CSA C22.2 No. 214 are suitable for carrying both power and data. Limited power cables are marked with the cable type designation, followed by "-LP" and "(x.x A)", where x.x is the current rating in amperes of each conductor in that cable.

Δ **Rule 16-330 4)**

8P8C modular jack/plug (8 position, 8 contact) connectors are commonly used in this application and are typically rated 1.3 A maximum per conductor.

Δ **Rule 16-330 9)**

Although Table 60 references conductors that have the capacity to operate at 90 °C, in accordance with IEC Standards, the connecting hardware typically used for these systems is not designed to carry any current at that temperature. It is intended by this Subrule that when the termination temperature is not marked on the equipment, the ampacity of the conductors be selected from the 60 °C column.

Section 18

Rule 18-000

Through the exercise of ingenuity in the layout of electrical installations for hazardous locations, it is frequently possible to locate much of the equipment in a reduced level of classification or in a non-hazardous location and thus to reduce the amount of special equipment required.

To assist users in the proper design and selection of equipment for electrical installations in hazardous locations, numerous reference documents are available. Table B18-1 lists commonly referenced documents.

Δ

Table B18-1
Documents applicable to hazardous locations

By function	Publisher	Reference publication
General		
• Design, installation, maintenance	API	RP 14F, *Design, Installation, and Maintenance of Electrical Systems for Fixed and Floating Offshore Petroleum Facilities for Unclassified and Class 1, Division 1 and Division 2 Locations*
• Design, installation, maintenance	API	RP 14FZ, *Design and Installation of Electrical Systems for Fixed and Floating Offshore Petroleum Facilities for Unclassified and Class I, Zone 0, Zone 1 and Zone 2 Locations*
• Design, installation, maintenance	IEC/IEEE	60079-30-2, *Explosive atmospheres — Part 30-2: Electrical resistance trace heating — Application guide for design, installation and maintenance*
• Design, equipment, installation	IEC	60079-14, *Explosive atmospheres — Part 14: Electrical installations design, selection and erection*
• Equipment, area classification	IEC	60079-20-1, *Explosive atmospheres — Part 20-1: Material characteristics for gas and vapour classification — Test methods and data*
• Equipment, area classification	ISO/IEC	FDIS 80079-20-1, *Explosive atmospheres — Part 20-1: Material characteristics for gas and vapour classification — Test methods and data*
• Equipment, area classification	ISO/IEC	80079-20-2, *Explosive atmospheres — Part 20-2: Material characteristics — Combustible dusts test methods*
Design	IEC	60079-25, *Explosive atmospheres — Part 25: Intrinsically safe electrical systems*
	ISA	TR12.2, *Intrinsically Safe System Assessment Using the Entity Concept*
	ISA	RP12.02.02, *Recommendations for the Preparation, Content, and Organization of Intrinsic Safety Control Drawings*
	NFPA	51A, *Standard for Acetylene Cylinder Charging Plants* (withdrawn)

(Continued)

Table B18-1 (Continued)

By function	Publisher	Reference publication
	NFPA	Haz 10, *Fire Protection Guide to Hazardous Materials*
	NFPA	30, *Flammable and Combustible Liquids Code*
	NFPA	61, *Standard for the Prevention of Fires and Dust Explosions in Agricultural and Food Processing Facilities*
	NFPA	68, *Standard on Explosion Protection by Deflagration Venting*
	NFPA	77, *Recommended Practice on Static Electricity*
	NFPA	484, *Standard for Combustible Metals*
	NFPA	654, *Standard for the Prevention of Fire and Dust Explosions from the Manufacturing, Processing, and Handling of Combustible Particulate Solids*
	NFPA	655, *Standard for the Prevention of Sulfur Fires and Explosions*
	NFPA	664, *Standard for the Prevention of Fires and Explosions in Wood Processing and Woodworking Facilities*
	NFPA	91, *Standard for Exhaust Systems for Air Conveying of Vapors, Gases, Mists, and Noncombustible Particulate Solids*
Area classification*	API	RP 505, *Recommended Practice for Classification of Locations for Electrical Installations at Petroleum Facilities Classified as Class I, Zone 0, Zone 1, and Zone 2*
	API	RP 500, *Recommended Practice for Classification of Locations for Electrical Installations at Petroleum Facilities Classified as Class I, Division 1 and Division 2*
	API	PUBL 4615, *Emission Factors for Oil and Gas Production Operations*
	API	PUBL 4638, *Calculation Workbook for Oil and Gas Production Equipment Fugitive Emissions*
	API	PUBL 4589, *Fugitive Hydrocarbon Emissions from Oil and Gas Production Operations*
	Energy Institute	EI 15, *Model code of safe practice Part 15: Area classification code for installations handling flammable fluids*
	IEC	60079-10-1, *Explosive atmospheres — Part 10-1: Classification of areas — Explosive gas atmospheres*
	IEC	60079-10-2, *Explosive atmospheres — Part 10-2: Classification of areas — Explosive dust atmospheres*
	ISA	12.10, *Area Classification in Hazardous (Classified) Dust Locations*
	ISA	TR12.13.01, *Flammability Characteristics of Combustible Gases and Vapors*
	NFPA	497, *Recommended Practice for the Classification of Flammable Liquids, Gases, or Vapors and of Hazardous (Classified) Locations for Electrical Installations in Chemical Process Areas*
	NFPA	499, *Recommended Practice for the Classification of Combustible Dusts and of Hazardous (Classified) Locations for Electrical Installations in Chemical Process Areas*
Equipment, equipment	IEC	60079-13, *Explosive atmospheres — Part 13: Equipment protection by pressurized room "p" and artificially ventilated room "v"*

(Continued)

Table B18-1 (Concluded)

By function	Publisher	Reference publication
selection (products)†	IEC	60079-29-2, *Explosive atmospheres — Part 29-2: Gas detectors — Selection, installation, use and maintenance of detectors for flammable gases and oxygen*
	IEC	60079-29-3, *Explosive atmospheres — Part 29-3: Gas detectors — Guidance on functional safety of fixed gas detection systems*
	IEEE	1673, *IEEE Standard for Requirements for Conduit and Cable Seals for Field Connected Wiring to Equipment in Petroleum and Chemical Industry Exposed to Pressures above Atmospheric (1.5 kPa, 0.22 psi)*
	IEEE	1349, *IEEE Guide for Application of Electric Motors in Class I, Division 2 and Class I, Zone 2 Hazardous (Classified) Locations*
	ISA	12.27.01, *Requirements for Process Sealing Between Electrical Systems and Flammable or Combustible Process Fluids*
	ISA	TR12.13.03, *Guide for Combustible Gas Detection as a Method of Protection*
	ISA	TR12.13.04, *Performance Requirements for Open Path Combustible Gas Detectors*
	ISA	12.20.01, *General Requirements for Electrical Ignition Systems for Internal Combustion Engines in Class I, Division 2 or Zone 2, Hazardous (Classified) Locations*
	ISA	TR12.21.01, *Use of Fiber Optic Systems in Class I Hazardous (Classified) Locations*
	ISA	12.01.01, *Definitions and Information Pertaining to Electrical Equipment in Hazardous (Classified) Locations*
	ISA	12.04.04, *Pressurized Enclosures*
	ISA	12.12.03, *Standard for Portable Electronic Products Suitable for Use in Class I and II, Division 2, Class I Zone 2 and Class III, Division 1 and 2 Hazardous (Classified) Locations*
	ISA	12.12.04, *Electrical Equipment in a Class I, Division 2/Zone 2 Hazardous Location*
	ISA	*Electrical Instruments in Hazardous Locations*, 4th edition, Author: Ernest Magison
	NFPA	496, *Standard for Purged and Pressurized Enclosures for Electrical Equipment*
	NFPA	505, *Fire Safety Standard for Powered Industrial Trucks Including Type Designations, Areas of Use, Conversions, Maintenance, and Operations*
Erection, verification (installation)	CSA	C22.1, *Canadian Electrical Code, Part I*
	NFPA	70, *National Electrical Code*
	ISA	RP 12.06.01, *Recommended Practice for Wiring Methods for Hazardous (Classified) Locations — Instrumentation — Part 1: Intrinsic Safety*
Operations, maintenance	IEC	60079-17, *Explosive atmospheres — Part 17: Electrical installations inspection and maintenance*
	IEC	60079-19, *Explosive atmospheres — Part 19: Equipment repair, overhaul and reclamation*

* *Area classification is a subset of design for hazardous locations.*
† *Product certification Standards are listed in Appendix A, not in this Table.*

Δ **Rules 18-000, 18-006, and 18-008**
The Zone and Division systems of area classification are deemed to provide equivalent levels of safety; however, the Code has been written to give preference to the Zone system of area classification. It is important to understand that while the Code gives preference to the Zone system of area classification, it does not give preference to the IEC type of equipment. Equipment marked for use in Class I or Class I, Division 1 will be acceptable in Zone 1 and Zone 2, and equipment marked Class I, Division 2 will be acceptable only in Zone 2. See Rules 18-100 and 18-150 and Table 18.

The Scope of this Section recognizes that there are cases where renovations or additions will occur on existing installations employing the Class/Division system of classification. It is expected that such installations will comply with the requirements for Class I installations as found in Appendix J.

Rule 18-002

Cable seal — a seal that is designed to prevent the escape of flames from an explosion-proof enclosure. Because cables are not designed to withstand the pressures of an explosion, transmission of an explosion into a cable could result in ignition of gases or vapours in the area outside the enclosure.

Combustible dust — combustible dust includes dust and grit as defined in ISO 4225. The term "solid particles" is intended to address particles in the solid phase and not the gaseous or liquid phase but does not preclude a hollow particle. See ASTM E1226 or ISO 6184-1 for procedures for determining the explosibility of dusts. Dusts are considered combustible dusts unless it has been confirmed by test in accordance with ASTM E1226 or ISO 6184-1 that they are not combustible dusts.

Combustible flyings — examples of combustible flyings include rayon, cotton (including cotton linters and cotton waste), sisal, jute, hemp, cocoa fibre, oakum, and baled waste kapok.

Conduit seal — a seal that is designed to prevent the passage of flames from one portion of the electrical installation to another through the conduit system and to minimize the passage of gases or vapours at atmospheric pressure. Unless specifically designed for the purpose, conduit seals are not intended to prevent the passage of fluids at a continuous pressure differential across the seal. Even at differences in pressure across the seal equivalent to a few centimetres of water, there may be passage of gas or vapour through the seal and/or through the insulated and bare conductors passing through the seal. Where conduit seals are exposed to continuous pressure, there may be a danger of transmission of flammable fluids to "safe areas" resulting in fire or explosions.

Δ **Hazardous location cables** — cables that are certified to CSA C22.2 No. 174 are marked "HL". Before a cable type can be submitted for testing under CSA C22.2 No. 174, it must first be approved under a CSA cable Standard, for example, CSA C22.2 No. 131. The additional tests in CSA C22.2 No. 174 ensure a more rugged cable suitable for all hazardous locations. While "HL" marked cables are suitable for use in all hazardous locations, they are not required for all hazardous locations. For example, tray cables and instrument and control cables are also suitable for use in Zones 2 and 22.

Primary seal — a seal that is typically a part of electrical devices such as pressure-, temperature-, or flow-measuring devices and devices (such as canned pumps) in which the electrical connections are immersed in the process fluids.

Secondary seal — a seal that is designed to prevent flammable process fluids from entering the electrical wiring system upon failure of a primary seal. These devices typically prevent passage of fluids at process pressure by a combination of sealing and pressure relief.

Δ **Rules 18-004, 18-006, and 18-008**
Reference material for area classification is listed in Table B18-1.

See also the Note to Rule 18-062.

Δ **Rule 18-004 2)**

If a hazard assessment determines that an area is a hazardous location, an area classification is performed. Due to the nature of hazardous locations and the risk of fire and explosions associated with them, involvement by various individuals who understand the relevance and significance of the properties of the hazardous locations identified in Subrule 1), are knowledgeable in the appropriate classification Standards/guidelines, and who are familiar with the process and equipment, is essential to ensure that appropriate measures are taken to mitigate the hazard. For a small or simple facility, this may involve a single discipline, whereas for a large or complex facility, it may involve more than one discipline, such as electrical, mechanical, process, safety, and operations specialists.

Documentation is an essential element in area classifications and may include items such as drawings, studies and calculations, reports, and operating descriptions. This documentation should be maintained and updated over the life of the facility. Appendix L contains more details on area classification guidelines.

Δ **Rule 18-004 3)**

Hazardous location classification documentation is authenticated by the person taking responsibility for the classification. The person taking responsibility is normally an engineering professional or other individual permitted to practise engineering.

Δ **Rule 18-006**

Zone 0 area classifications

Typical situations leading to a Zone 0 area classification are
a) the interiors of storage tanks that are vented to atmosphere and that contain flammable liquids stored above their flash point;
b) enclosed sumps containing flammable liquids stored above their flash point continuously or for long periods; and
c) the area immediately around atmospheric vents that are venting from a Zone 0 hazardous area.

Zone 1 area classifications

Typical situations leading to a Zone 1 area classification are
a) inadequately ventilated buildings or enclosures;
b) adequately ventilated buildings or enclosures, such as remote unattended and unmonitored facilities, that have insufficient means of limiting the duration of explosive gas atmospheres when they do occur; and
c) enclosed sumps containing flammable liquids stored above their flash point during normal operation.

Zone 2 area classifications

Typical situations leading to a Zone 2 area classification are
a) areas where flammable volatile liquids, flammable gases, or vapours are handled, processed, or used, but in which liquids, gases, or vapours are normally confined within closed containers or closed systems from which they can escape only as a result of accidental rupture or breakdown of the containers or systems or the abnormal operation of the equipment by which the liquids or gases are handled, processed, or used;
b) adequately ventilated buildings that have means of ensuring that the length of time during which abnormal operation resulting in the occurrence of explosive gas atmospheres can exist will be limited to a "short time"; and
c) most outdoor areas, except those around open vents, or open vessels or sumps containing flammable liquids.

API RP 505 defines "adequate ventilation" as "ventilation (natural or artificial) that is sufficient to prevent the accumulation of significant quantities of vapour-air or gas-air mixtures in concentrations above 25% of their lower flammable limit, LFL". Annex B of API RP 505 outlines a method for calculating the ventilation requirements for enclosed areas based on fugitive emissions.

Industry documents such as API RP 505 provide guidance on how industry interprets a "short time".

Flammable mists may form or be present at the same time as flammable gas or vapour. In such cases, the strict application of the details in the classification Standards referenced might not be appropriate. Flammable mists can also form when liquids not considered to be a hazard due to their high flash point are released under pressure. In these cases, the classifications and details in the Standards referenced do not apply. Information on flammable mists can be found in industry Standards such as IEC 60079-10-1.

Rule 18-008
Readily ignitable fibres and flyings include rayon, cotton (including cotton linters and cotton waste), sisal or henequen, istle, jute, hemp, tow, cocoa fibre, oakum, baled waste kapok, Spanish moss, excelsior, and other materials of similar nature.

Rule 18-010
Maintaining electrical installation safety in hazardous locations is dependent on a regimen of regular maintenance that will ensure that the electrical installation continues to provide safety throughout its life. Maintenance personnel are cautioned that modifications to original equipment or substitution of original components may void certification. In addition to the manufacturer's instructions, the following documents may be used to guide owners and operators of hazardous locations in developing appropriate maintenance procedures:
a) IEC 60079-17, *Explosive atmospheres — Part 17: Electrical installations inspection and maintenance*;
b) IEC 60300 series of Standards, *Dependability management*;
c) IEEE 902, *IEEE Guide for Maintenance, Operation, and Safety of Industrial and Commercial Power Systems*; and
d) NFPA 70B, *Recommended Practice for Electrical Equipment Maintenance*.

Ⓔ Δ **Rule 18-050**
At present, the marking requirements of Zone-based Standards and Division-based Standards differ concerning the gas groups for which equipment is certified.

With Zone-based Standards, equipment marked IIB is also suitable for applications requiring Group IIA equipment. Similarly, equipment that is marked IIC is also suitable for applications requiring Group IIB or IIA equipment.

Equipment marked in accordance with Division-based Standards bears the mark of each Group for which it is suitable, e.g., equipment that is suitable for Groups B, C, and D is marked to indicate such by including all three Groups.

Rules 18-102 7), 18-152 8), 18-192 5), 18-202 6), and 18-252 5) indicate that equipment suitable for Division-classified hazardous locations described in Annex J18 is also suitable for use in Zone-classified hazardous locations.

Table 18 provides a summary of what equipment types are suitable for installation in the various hazardous locations.

Δ **Rules 18-050 and 18-064**
It should be noted that battery-operated and self-generating equipment is not excluded from the Rules of Section 18, regardless of the voltage involved. Examples of such equipment are flashlights,

transceivers, paging receivers, tape recorders, combustible gas detectors, vibration monitors, tachometers, battery- or voice-powered telephones, and portable test equipment that may be carried into or located within a hazardous area. Such equipment may be eligible for approval under CAN/CSA-C22.2 No. 157 or CAN/CSA-C22.2 No. 60079-11.

Where general-purpose enclosures are used for such equipment and the Rules of this Section require hazardous location equipment, the electrical equipment is required to be intrinsic safety or intrinsically safe in accordance with Rule 18-064 and marked in accordance with the appropriate *Canadian Electrical Code, Part II* Standards.

In cases where the Rules of this Section permit general-purpose enclosures with the qualification that acceptable non-incendive circuits are incorporated, the electrical equipment should be approved as such and marked in accordance with Rule 18-052.

The users of this Code should recognize that the Class/Zone system of classification uses a method to identify gas groups that is different from that used by the Class/Division system.

Table B18-2 illustrates the correspondence between the two systems.

Table B18-2
Temperature and gas groups

Atmosphere		CAS reference number	Relative vapour density (air = 1)	Flash point, °C	Autoignition temperature, °C	Division-based gas group	Zone-based gas group
Typical North American name	**Synonyms [see Note 1)]**						
acetylene	ethine ethyne	74-86-2	0.90	gas	305	A	IIC
butadiene	1,3-butadiene biethylene bivinyl divinyl erythrene vinylethylene	106-99-0	1.87	gas	420	B	IIB
hydrogen		1333-74-0	0.07	gas	560	B	IIC
propylene oxide	2-methyloxirane 1,2-epoxypropane	75-56-9	2.00	−37	430	B	IIB
acetaldehyde	ethanal acetic aldehyde ethyl aldehyde	75-07-0	1.52	−38	155	C	IIA
cyclopropane	trimethylene	75-19-4	1.45	gas	500	D	IIA
diethyl ether	1,1'-oxybisethane diethyl oxide ethyl ether ethyl oxide ether	60-29-7	2.55	− 45	175	C	IIB
ethylene	ethene	74-85-1	0.97	gas	440	C	IIB
hydrogen sulphide	hydrosulfuric acid sewer gas sulfuretted hydrogen	7783-06-4	1.19	gas	260	C	IIB
unsymmetrical dimethyl hydrazine	N,N-Dimethyl-hydrazine UDMH 1,1-dimethyl hydrazine	57-14-7	2.07	−18	240	C	IIB

(Continued)

Table B18-2 (Continued)

Atmosphere							
Typical North American name	Synonyms [see Note 1)]	CAS reference number	Relative vapour density (air = 1)	Flash point, °C	Autoignition temperature, °C	Division-based gas group	Zone-based gas group
acetone	2-propanone dimethyl ketone	67-64-1	2.00	< −20	539	D	IIA
acrylonitrile	2-propenenitrile cyanoethylene propenenitrile vinyl cyanide VCN	107-13-1	1.83	−5	480	D	IIB
alcohol (see ethanol)							
ammonia	anhydrous ammonia	7664-41-7	0.59	gas	630	D	IIA
benzene	phenyl hydride	71-43-2	2.70	−11	498	D	IIA
benzine (see petroleum naphtha)							
benzol (see benzene)							
butane	butyl hydride diethyl methylethylmethane	106-97-8	2.05	gas	372	D	IIA
1-butanol	butan-1-ol n-Butyl alcohol n-Butanol Butyl alcohol Hydroxybutane n-Propyl carbinol	71-36-3	2.55	36	343	D	IIA
2-butanol	butan-2-ol sec-Butyl alcohol Butylene hydrate 2-Hydroxybutane Methyl ethyl carbinol	78-92-2	2.55	36	406	D	IIA
butyl acetate	Acetic acid n-butyl ester n-Butyl ester of acetic acid Butyl ethanoate	123-86-4	4.01	22	390	D	IIA
isobutyl acetate		110-19-0		18	421 [Note 2)]	D	IIA
ethane		74-84-0	1.04	−29	515	D	IIA
ethanol	ethyl alcohol alcohol	64-17-5	1.59	13	400	D	IIB
ethyl acetate	Acetic acid ethyl ester Ethyl ethanoate	141-78-6	3.04	−4	470	D	IIA
ethylene dichloride	1,2-Dichloroethane Ethylene chloride	107-06-2	3.42	13	438	D	IIA
gasoline	motor fuel petrol	86290-81-5, 8006-61-9 [Note 4)]	3.0	−46	280	D	IIA
heptanes (mixed isomers)	n-heptane	142-82-5	3.46	−7	204	D	IIA

(Continued)

Table B18-2 (Continued)

Atmosphere		CAS reference number	Relative vapour density (air = 1)	Flash point, °C	Autoignition temperature, °C	Division-based gas group	Zone-based gas group
Typical North American name	Synonyms [see Note 1)]						
hexanes (mixed isomers)	n-hexane	110-54-3	2.97	−22	225	D	IIA
isoprene		78-79-5	2.35	−54	220 [Note 2)]	D	IIA
methane	natural gas [(Note 3)]	74-82-8	0.55	gas	600	D	IIA
methanol	methyl alcohol carbinol	67-56-1	1.11	9	440	D	IIA
isoamyl alcohol	3-methylbutan-1-ol	123-51-3	3.03	42	339	D	IIA
methyl ethyl ketone	butanone 2-butanone ethyl methyl ketone methyl acetone	78-93-3	2.48	−10	404	D	IIB
methyl isobutyl ketone	4-methylpentan-2-one hexone isopropylacetone	108-10-1	3.45	16	475	D	IIA
isobutyl alcohol	iso-butanol iso-propylcarbinol iso-butyl alcohol	78-83-1	2.55	28	408	D	IIA
tertiary butyl alcohol	2-methyl-2-propanol tert-butanol	75-65-0	2.6	11	478 [Note 2)]	D	IIA
naphtha (see petroleum naphtha)							
natural gas (see methane)							
petroleum naphtha	naphtha	64742-95-6			290 [Note 2)]	D	IIA
octanes	n-octane	111-65-9	3.93	13	206	D	IIA
pentanes (mixed isomers)	n-pentane	109-66-0	2.48	−40	243	D	IIA
1-pentanol	pentan-1-ol n-amyl alcohol n-butyl carbinol n-pentyl alcohol n-pentanol	71-41-0	3.03	42	320	D	IIA
propane	dimethyl methane propyl hydride	74-98-6	1.56	gas	450	D	IIA
propyl alcohol	1-propanol propan-1-ol	71-23-8	2.07	15	385	D	IIB
isopropyl alcohol	propan-2-ol 2-propanol dimethyl carbinol isopropanol	67-63-0	2.07	12	399	D	IIA
propene	methylethylene propylene	115-07-1	1.50	gas	455	D	IIA

(Continued)

Table B18-2 (Concluded)

Atmosphere		CAS reference number	Relative vapour density (air = 1)	Flash point, °C	Autoignition temperature, °C	Division-based gas group	Zone-based gas group
Typical North American name	Synonyms [see Note 1)]						
styrene	ethenylbenzene vinylbenzene phenylethylene styrol	100-42-5	3.6	30	490	D	IIA
toluene	methyl benzene methyl benzol phenyl methane	108-88-3	3.2	4	530	D	IIA
vinyl acetate	acetic acid ethenyl ester 1-acetoxyethylene	108-05-4	3.0	−7	385	D	IIA
vinyl chloride	chloroethylene chloroethane vinyl chloride	75-01-4	2.15	gas	415	D	IIA
xylenes	1,4-dimethyl benzene p-xylene p-Xyol	106-42-3	3.66	25	535	D	IIA

Notes:

1) *Most of the values in this Table have been obtained from IEC 60079-20-1,* Explosive atmospheres — Part 20-1: Material characteristics for gas and vapour classification — Test methods and data, *Edition 1.0, 2010-01. In many cases, the name used in the IEC Standard differs from the name typically used in North America for the same substance. In fact, chemicals may have several different names. The CAS numbering system referenced in this Table is a well-known method of uniquely identifying chemicals and is a required feature of MSDS documentation. Further information on the CAS numbering system may be found at www.cas.org.*

2) *This substance is not listed in IEC 60079-20-1.*

3) *Natural gas is classified as Group IIA, provided that it does not contain more than 25% (by volume) of hydrogen.*

4) *Gasoline is identified under several CAS numbers.*

Δ **Rule 18-050, 18-052, and 18-054**

Explosion protected equipment has the following markings:

a) the letters "Ex";

b) the symbol(s) to indicate the type(s) of protection used;

Note: *For electrical resistance trace heating, the type of protection is designated as "60079-30-1", which is the product certification Standard number. The IEC allows an Ex marking to be the Standard number where the existing types of protection do not fit the equipment. In addition, the ambient temperature markings in CAN/CSA-C22.2 No. 60079-0 do not apply to trace heating; however, the minimum installation temperature is marked.*

c) the group as specified in Rule 18-050 2) or 18-050 6);

d) the maximum surface temperature rating;

e) the equipment protection level (EPL) Ga, Gb, Gc, Da, Db, or Dc as appropriate; and

f) the certificate number as specified in CAN/CSA-C22.2 No. 60079-0.

See the Note to Rules 18-090, 18-100, and 18-150 for additional information on markings.

The maximum surface temperature rating for equipment suitable for Zones 0, 1, or 2 is marked in degrees Celsius or a temperature code, or both, to indicate the maximum surface temperature. See Table B18-3.

Table B18-3
Maximum surface temperature ratings for equipment suitable for Zones 0, 1, or 2

Temperature code	Maximum surface temperature, °C
T1	450
T2	300
(T2A)	280
(T2B)	260
(T2C)	230
(T2D)	215
T3	200
(T3A)	180
(T3B)	165
(T3C)	160
T4	135
(T4A)	120
T5	100
T6	85

Note: *The bracketed temperature codes are for Canada only; they are not included in the IEC Standards.*

The maximum surface temperature rating of equipment is based on a 40 °C ambient temperature, except that if the equipment is rated for a higher ambient temperature, it is marked as such.

The maximum surface temperature rating for equipment suitable for Zones 20, 21, or 22 is marked in degrees Celsius, preceded by a "T".

Equipment suitable for Division classified hazardous locations has markings as stated in Appendix J, Rule J18-052, and the associated Annex JB Notes.

Some equipment permitted for use in Zone 2 hazardous locations is not marked to indicate suitability for Zone 2 because it is not specifically designed for use in hazardous locations [e.g., motors and generators for Zone 2 that do not incorporate arcing, sparking, or heat-producing components. See Rule 18-150 2) e)].

The *Canadian Electrical Code, Part II* product Standards for Ex equipment certification require that a certificate number be marked on the equipment. The format of the certificate number is the name or mark of the certificate issuer and the certificate reference in the following form: the last two figures of the year of issue of the certificate, followed by "CA", followed by the certificate number.

Where the certificate number includes an "X" suffix, it indicates that there are "Specific Conditions of Use" detailed on the certificate that are to be taken into account during the selection and installation of the equipment. For example, "CSA15CA1000X" identifies the 1000th certificate issued by CSA and the year of issue as 2015 and indicates that there are specific conditions of use for the product. As an alternative to the "X" marking, an advisory marking or a reference to a specific instruction document containing the detailed information may appear on the equipment.

Where the certificate number includes a "U" suffix, it indicates that the product is an "Ex Component" and is incomplete and not suitable for installation without further evaluation or certification. For example, "QPS15CA0100U" identifies the 100th certificate issued by QPS and the year of issue as 2015 and indicates that that the product is incomplete and not suitable for installation without further evaluation or certification.

Exposure of hazardous locations equipment to ambient temperatures that are outside the intended ambient temperature range of the equipment can affect the explosion protection features of such equipment. Some equipment may be marked with a safe ambient temperature range in accordance with the relevant *Canadian Electrical Code, Part II* product Standards, but other equipment may not have such markings.

Hazardous locations equipment subjected to ambient temperature conditions exceeding the design maximum ambient temperature can result in the equipment operating at a temperature in excess of the maximum (surface) temperature marked on the nameplate of the equipment, possibly exceeding maximum internal operating temperature limits as well as the temperature limits stated in Rule 18-054.

Hazardous locations equipment subjected to ambient temperature conditions that are colder than the design low ambient temperature can result in the equipment being subjected to excessive explosion pressures due to higher gas densities at low temperatures. Cold temperatures also affect the brittleness of materials, which can also compromise the explosion protection integrity of the equipment.

Note that ambient temperatures marked on equipment apply to explosion protection safety only. Equipment performance is not considered.

Where an ambient temperature range is not indicated on equipment, the default temperatures are as follows:
a)   for products marked "Ex", the design ambient temperature range is (−20 °C ≤ ambient ≤ 40 °C); and
b)   for products marked Class I, II, or III, Division 1 or 2, the design ambient temperature range is (−50 °C ≤ ambient ≤ 40 °C).

Rule 18-050 5)
One common example combines these Group markings with the equipment marked "IIB + H2". This equipment is suitable for applications requiring Group IIA equipment, Group IIB equipment, or equipment for hydrogen atmospheres.

Electrical equipment marked Group II is to be installed as if it were Group IIC.

Rule 18-052
A typical example of equipment marking is as follows:

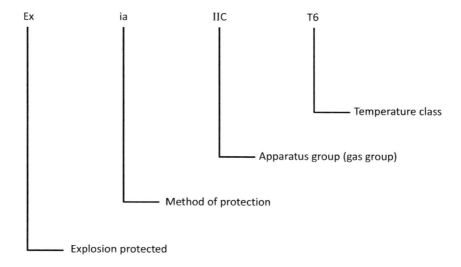

January 2018

The users of this Code are reminded that, in all cases, the identifying mark of an accredited certification organization is required as well as the marking requirements of this Section.

Equipment marked for Class I but not marked with a Division is suitable for both Zones 1 and 2.

Rules 18-052, 18-090, 18-100, and 18-150

The 2011 edition of CAN/CSA-C22.2 No. 60079-0 [adopted IEC 60079-0 (fifth edition, 2007-10)] introduces "equipment protection levels" (EPLs) as a required marking on hazardous location electrical equipment certified to the IEC 60079 series of Standards. This marking will appear on new electrical equipment approved under the adopted 60079 series of Standards. For older equipment, in stock or in the field, that does not include the EPL marking, suitability for the intended zone will continue to be determined by the types of protection. EPLs will enable users to identify the zone(s) in which the IEC 60079 type of hazardous location electrical equipment can be used, without having to identify the zone by the types of protection used.

EPLs provide an indication of the suitability of electrical equipment for each zone. Further information on EPLs can be found in CAN/CSA-C22.2 No. 60079-0. See Table B18-4 for the acceptable EPLs for Zones 0, 1, and 2.

Table B18-4
Acceptable equipment protection levels for Zones 0, 1, and 2

Zone	Acceptable equipment protection level
Zone 0	Ga
Zone 1	Ga or Gb
Zone 2	Ga, Gb, or Gc

Δ Rules 18-054 and 18-150

Equipment of the heat-producing type is currently required by product Standards to have a temperature code (T-Code) or maximum temperature marking if its temperature exceeds 100 °C. However, for equipment manufactured prior to the T-Code requirement (prior to 1972) and electrical equipment such as motors applied in accordance with Rule 18-150, there may be no such marking. Therefore, the suitability of older hazardous locations equipment of the heat-producing type and motors applied in accordance with Rule 18-150 should be reviewed in the context of Rule 18-054 before such equipment is installed in a hazardous location. For the purpose of Rule 18-150, equipment such as boxes, terminals, fittings, and resistance temperature detectors (RTDs) are not considered to be heat-producing devices.

Determination of the maximum surface temperatures for Rule 18-054 is set by the area classification for the location in which the equipment is installed. This is normally based on the minimum ignition temperature of the flammable or combustible substances that may be released into the atmosphere in that location. The temperature markings on electrical equipment are in accordance with the requirements in the *Canadian Electrical Code, Part II* product Standards, which set the specifications determining where surface temperature measurements are to be taken. For equipment suitable for Zones 0, 1, or 2, this applies to both external and, where gases can reach an internal surface, internal temperatures. For example, type of protection nR applies only to external temperatures because the design of this equipment prevents gases from reaching internal surfaces. For equipment suitable for Zones 20, 21, or 22, this applies to external surfaces only. The design of equipment for explosive dust atmospheres, with gasketing and other features to prevent ingress of dusts, is such that the only concern for ignition is on the exterior of the equipment. Therefore, the maximum surface temperature requirement for dusts applies to the external surfaces of the equipment only.

Rule 18-060

For the purposes of this Rule, metal-covered cable includes cable with a metal sheath or with a metal armour of the interlocking type, the wire type, or the flat-tape type, or with metal shielding.

Rule 18-060 1)

Suitable lightning protective devices should include primary devices and also secondary devices if overhead secondary lines exceed 90 m in length or if the secondary is ungrounded.

Interconnection of all grounds should include grounds for primary and secondary lightning protective devices, secondary system grounds, if any, and grounds of conduit and equipment of the interior wiring system.

Rule 18-060 2) b)

Where single-conductor metal-covered or armoured cables with jackets are used in hazardous locations, the armour must be grounded in the hazardous location only to prevent circulating currents. As a result, there will be a standing voltage on the metal covering in the non-hazardous location area. There is, therefore, a need to properly isolate the armour in the non-hazardous area to ensure that circulating currents will not occur.

Rule 18-062

To meet the intent of the Rule for effectively maintaining a protective gas pressure, the following references for pressurization are recommended:

a) CAN/CSA-C22.2 No. 60079-2, *Explosive atmospheres — Part 2: Equipment protection by pressurized enclosure "p"*;

b) NFPA 496, *Standard for Purged and Pressurized Enclosures for Electrical Equipment*; and

c) IEC 60079-13, *Explosive atmospheres — Part 13: Equipment protection by pressurized room "p"*.

Δ Rule 18-064

See the Note to Rules 18-050 and 18-064.

When reference is made to intrinsically safe systems, including equipment, wiring, and installation, the term used is "intrinsically safe". When reference is made to product certification and markings, the terms used are

a) intrinsic safety "ia", "ib", or "ic" for Zone hazardous locations; or

b) intrinsically safe "Exi", "Exia", "Intrinsically Safe", "IS", or "I.S." for Class I, II, or III hazardous locations.

Non-hazardous location wiring methods can be used for intrinsically safe and non-incendive field wiring circuits, with the additional restrictions stated in this Rule. This applies to the selection of wiring materials such as cable, conduit, raceways, fittings, and junction boxes, as set out in the other Rules of this Code.

Non-incendive field wiring circuits are energy-limited under normal operating conditions and are intended for use in Class I, Division 2 hazardous locations. Non-incendive field wiring circuits provide the same level of protection as "nL" or "ic" and are therefore suitable for installation in Zone 2 and Zone 22 hazardous locations. For additional information on non-incendive systems, see Annexes J18 and JB.

Δ Rule 18-064 1) and 2)

The descriptive system document is necessary to ensure that all aspects of the intrinsically safe or non-incendive field wiring installation are addressed and documented. See Appendix F for additional information regarding descriptive system documents.

Δ Rule 18-064 5)

Intrinsically safe and non-incendive field wiring systems are not required to prevent the transmission of an explosion and therefore the only concern is the transmission of flammable fluids. Migration of flammable fluids at atmospheric pressure can be prevented by the use of conduit and cable seals. Other alternatives for cables include the use of a compound such as silicone rubber applied around the end of the connector to prevent flammable fluids from entering the end of the cable. Where the flammable fluids could be operating at pressures above atmospheric pressure, the provisions of Rule 18-070 should be applied.

Δ **Rule 18-068**

The definition of lower and upper explosive limits (LELs and UELs) in Rule 18-002 has been changed to lower and upper flammable limits (LFLs and UFLs) and, therefore, has been revised in this Rule. Flammable limits are material properties that are covered in documents such as IEC 60079-20-1. Explosive limits depend on installation factors such as enclosure geometry or igniter location and generally fall within a narrower range than flammable limits. Therefore, flammable limits are now used because they are fixed values, define a wider range than explosive limits, are harmonized with IEC area classification Standards.

Note: *Combustible gas detectors read LFL even though the scale may be marked as LEL.*

It is intended that this Rule be used only where suitable equipment meeting the requirements of Rule 18-100 or 18-150 (whichever is applicable) is not available. In the context of this Rule, "available" means that equipment certified for use in a specific application is available on the market. It is not intended to refer to situations where certified equipment is available on the market, but the owner or the installer does not happen to possess it. For example, Class I, Division 1 ignition systems for internal combustion engines are not available on the market; only Class I, Division 2 ignition systems are available. Therefore, ignition systems rated for Class I, Division 2 are currently the only hazardous location ignition systems that are available and could possibly be used in Zone 1 locations.

"Normal operation" in Item b) of this Rule means a piece of electrical equipment does not produce arcs, sparks, or hot surfaces while being used in accordance with its design. For example, standard wall outlets and standard plugs (i.e., outlets and plugs not certified for use in a hazardous location) are designed to allow the plug to be inserted and withdrawn under load as a part of their normal operation. Because this could create an incendive spark, standard wall outlets and plugs do not meet the intent of Item b). Similarly, although a standard wall switch may be operated infrequently, operation of the switch is part of its normal operation and will produce an incendive spark, thus making it unsuitable for use under this Rule.

In many situations, proper area classification eliminates the need to use this Rule. This Rule should not be used to compensate for improper area classification.

When this Rule is used, the gas detection system should consist of an adequate number of sensors to ensure the sensing of flammable gases or vapours in all areas where they may accumulate.

Electrical equipment that is suitable for non-hazardous locations and that has unprotected arcing, sparking, or heat-producing components must not be installed in a Zone 2 location. Arcing, sparking, or heat-producing components may be protected by encapsulating, hermetically sealing, or sealing by other means such as restricted breathing.

Before applying this Rule, the user should fully understand the risks associated with such an installation. When this Rule is being applied, it remains the responsibility of the owner of the facility, or agents of the owner, to ensure that the resulting installation is safe. Simply complying with the requirements of this Rule may not ensure a safe installation in all situations.

Rule 18-070

ANSI/ISA 12.27.01 provides construction, performance, and marking requirements for the process seals incorporated into process-connected electrical equipment. Equipment containing a primary seal that complies with this Standard is eligible to include either the "Single Seal" or "Dual Seal" designation in the nameplate markings. These markings indicate that the electrical equipment is designed to prevent the migration of flammable fluid through the equipment into the wiring system when the equipment is operated at or lower than its rated pressure. Devices certified as conforming to ANSI/ISA 12.27.01 and marked either "Single Seal" or "Dual Seal" meet the intent of Subrule 1) a).

Where devices containing primary seals are not marked to indicate conformance with ANSI/ISA 12.27.01, other means may be used to prevent fluid migration though the wiring system. This may include the use of suitable barriers located between the primary seal and the wiring system, such as secondary seals or short lengths of mineral-insulated (MI) cable. Where secondary seals are installed, examples of design features that make the occurrence of primary seal failure obvious are vents, drains, visible rupture or leakage, audible whistles, or electronic monitoring. The intent of making the primary seal failure obvious is to prevent continuous pressure on the secondary seal and the possibility of an eventual secondary seal failure, as well as to protect personnel working on the device. Alternatively, where means to relieve pressure on a secondary seal is not provided, a cautionary label should be provided to warn personnel that the enclosure may contain flammable fluid under pressure.

Engineering considerations may lead to the conclusion that the probability of leakage from a specific installation will be negligible. Acceptable factors such as an extensive history of safe operation with similar installations, or the use of a primary seal with a pressure rating well in excess of the maximum process operating pressure, may be considered.

Δ **Rules 18-090, 18-100, and 18-150**

The equipment protection level (EPL) marked on equipment takes precedence over the type(s) of explosion protection marked on it and may, to account for other aspects of the equipment, such as material limitations, be more restrictive than what is normally applied for a specific type of protection. To take the marking Ex ia IIC T4 Gb as an example: ia would normally be acceptable in Zone 0; however, the equipment was constructed with a greater aluminum content than the product Standards permit and, therefore, EPL Gb indicates that the equipment is restricted to a Zone 1 area.

For Zone 0, CAN/CSA-C22.2 No. 60079-26 provides for an alternative to meeting equipment protection level (EPL) Ga where two types of protection suitable for Zone 1 (EPL Gb) would be permitted. In this case, the equipment is marked with the two types of protection connected by a "+", for example, Ex db +eb IIB T4 Ga.

In some cases, equipment may be installed on the boundary of Zone 0 and Zone 1 and may have two types of protection, with the appropriate type of protection for each side of the boundary identified and connected by a "/". For example, an intrinsic safety device installed on the wall of a flammable liquid storage tank (Zone 0 inside) having a flameproof termination compartment on the tank exterior (Zone 1) would be marked Ex ia/db IIB T4 Ga/Gb. Equipment with a "/" marking is accompanied by instructions for the user, specifying features and limitations of the separation element between the Ga and Gb equipment sections.

CAN/CSA-C22.2 No. 60079-28 describes four possible methods of ignition of an explosive atmosphere and focuses on two of them: absorption of optical radiation by particles or surfaces causing heating and laser breakdown of gases, both of which can cause ignition. The Standard provides for three methods of protection:

a) inherently safe optical radiation "op is": visible or infrared radiation that is incapable of producing sufficient energy to ignite an explosive atmosphere;

b) protected optical radiation "op pr": visible or infrared radiation that is confined inside a medium, such as optical fiber, where there is no escape from the confinement; and

c) optical system with interlock "op sh": visible or infrared radiation confined inside a medium, such as optical fiber, that has an interlock cut-off if the confinement fails.

Other, supporting equipment also requires certification in accordance with other Standards, resulting in additional markings. The following are some marking examples:

Ex d [op is IIA T3 Ga] IIB T4 Gb — protected by a flameproof enclosure and allowed into a Zone 1 area with gas group IIB and a T4 code; the optical system can transmit into a Zone 0 area with gas group IIA and a T3 T-code.

[Ex op is IIB T4] — equipment cannot be in a hazardous location but can transmit into a hazardous location with a IIB gas group and T4 T-code.

Ex mb op is IIC T4 Gb — equipment with an optical source, type of protection "op is", protected by encapsulation "m".

T-coding and gas groups are normally independent of each other, but with optical radiation, this is not the case because of the particular causes of ignition by lasers and the use of other, supporting equipment. In addition, equipment may have more than one T-code or EPL for different parts of the equipment. Therefore, attention must be paid to gas grouping, T-codes, and EPLs in applying optical equipment.

See Table 18 for equipment and types of protection permitted in the three Zones. Other equipment may be permitted by specific Rules (e.g., fuses in Rule 18-150).

Δ **Rule 18-092**
Zone 0 wiring methods other than intrinsically safe are not provided for because equipment intended for installation in Zone 0 will include the necessary wiring instructions. In many cases, such wiring is not needed as the Zone 0 equipment is installed at the Zone 0 boundary, with the equipment connections not located in Zone 0.

For specific requirements and information regarding intrinsically safe wiring in Zone 0 locations, see Rule 18-064 and the Note to Rules 18-050 and 18-064.

Δ **Rule 18-100**
Equipment marked for Class I, Division 1 is suitable for use in Zone 1 and Zone 2.

Δ **Rules 18-100 and 18-150**
The following briefly explains the various types of protection used in the Zone system. For further information, see the applicable *Canadian Electrical Code, Part II* Standards.
a) **Intrinsic safety (ib, ic):** a type of protection based on the limitation of electrical energy to levels where any open spark or thermal effect occurring in equipment or interconnecting wiring that may occur in normal use, or under fault conditions likely to occur in practice, is incapable of causing an ignition. The use of intrinsic safety equipment in a hazardous location also requires that associated wiring and equipment, which is not necessarily located in a hazardous area, be assessed as part of any intrinsically safe system. The primary difference between equipment marked Ex ib and Ex ic is that equipment marked Ex ib must continue to provide explosion protection after a fault has been applied.
    Note: *For Zone 0 areas, equipment marked Ex ia must continue to provide explosion protection after two such faults have been applied (see CAN/CSA-C22.2 No. 60079-11).*
b) **Flameproof (d):** a type of protection of electrical apparatus in which the enclosure will withstand, without suffering damage and without causing ignition, an internal explosion of a flammable mixture that has penetrated into the interior through any joints or structural openings in the enclosure of an external explosive atmosphere consisting of one or more of the gases or vapours for which it is designed (see CAN/CSA-C22.2 No. 60079-1).
c) **Increased safety (e):** a type of protection by which additional measures are applied to an electrical apparatus to give increased security against the possibility of excessive temperatures and of the occurrence of arcs and sparks during the service life of the apparatus. It applies only to an

electrical apparatus no parts of which produce arcs or sparks or exceed the limiting temperature in normal service (see CAN/CSA-C22.2 No. 60079-7).

d) **Oil immersion (o):** a type of protection in which electrical apparatus is made safe by oil immersion in the sense that an explosive atmosphere above the oil or outside the enclosure will not be ignited (see CAN/CSA-C22.2 No. 60079-6).

e) **Pressurized enclosure (p):** a type of protection using the pressure of a protective gas to prevent the ingress of an explosive atmosphere into a space that may contain a source of ignition and, where necessary, using continuous dilution of an atmosphere within a space that contains a source of emission of gas that may form an explosive atmosphere (see CAN/CSA-C22.2 No. 60079-2).

f) **Powder filling (q):** a type of protection in which the enclosure of electrical apparatus is filled with a mass of granular material such that, if an arc occurs, the arc will not be liable to ignite the outer flammable atmosphere (see CAN/CSA-C22.2 No. 60079-5).

g) **Encapsulation (m):** a type of protection in which parts that could ignite an explosive atmosphere by either sparking or heating are enclosed in a compound in such a way that this explosive atmosphere cannot be ignited (see CAN/CSA-C22.2 No. 60079-18).

h) **Non-sparking, restricted breathing, etc. (n):** a type of protection applied to an electrical apparatus such that, in normal operation, the apparatus is not capable of igniting a surrounding explosive atmosphere, and a fault capable of causing ignition is not likely to occur (see CAN/CSA-C22.2 No. 60079-15).

Note: *Type of protection "n" includes a number of means of providing protection. In addition to non-sparking, component parts of apparatus that in normal operation arc, spark, or produce surface temperatures of 85 °C or greater may be protected by one of the following:*
a) *enclosed break devices;*
b) *non-incendive components;*
c) *hermetically sealed devices;*
d) *sealed devices;*
e) *energy-limited apparatus and circuits; or*
f) *restricted breathing enclosures.*
Some of these methods are similar to methods previously allowed in Class I, Division 2 locations. To better understand the various methods allowed under type of protection "n", refer to CAN/CSA-C22.2 No. 60079-15.

i) **Electrical resistance trace heating (60079-30-1):** a type of protection applied to trace heating that limits the surface temperature of the heater to below that which could cause ignition of an explosive atmosphere (see CAN/CSA-C22.2 No. 60079-30-1).

j) **Optical (op is, op pr, op sh):** see the Note to Rules 18-090, 18-100, and 18-150 for a description of optical types of protection.

Δ **Rules 18-102, 18-104, 18-152 1) b), 18-192 1) b), 18-202 1) b), and 18-252 1) b)**
Cables meeting the requirements of CSA C22.2 No. 174 are acceptable for use in hazardous locations and are marked "HL".

Cables marked for use in hazardous locations are suitable for all locations, but the termination fittings must be suitable for the particular hazardous location. For example, in a Zone 1 or Zone 2 hazardous location, a termination fitting entering an enclosure required to be explosion-proof or flameproof must be a sealing-type termination fitting, whereas a termination fitting entering an enclosure not required to be explosion-proof or flameproof in a Zone 2 hazardous location is not required to be marked for use in Zone 2 hazardous locations. It is intended that termination fittings in all hazardous locations be compatible with the degree of protection and the explosion protection provided by the enclosure they enter. In general, the minimum requirement will be weatherproof termination fittings.

For the application of Section 18, rigid metal couplings are not considered fittings. The CSA Standard for rigid metal conduit and couplings is CSA C22.2 No. 45.1. This Standard does not require hazardous location markings. Certified rigid metal conduit and couplings are suitable for hazardous locations without specific area classification marking.

Rules 18-102 3) a) and 18-152 3) a)

Where tapered threads are used, the requirement to have 4-1/2 fully engaged threads (i.e., threads done up tight) is critical for the following reasons:

a)   When the threads are not fully engaged, the flame path is compromised, making it possible for an explosion occurring within the conduit system to be transmitted to the area outside the conduit.

b)   If there are not 4-1/2 fully engaged threads, the flame path may be too short to cool the gases resulting from an internal explosion to a temperature below that which could ignite gas in the surrounding area.

c)   Because the conduit forms a bonding path to ground, not making the conduit tight introduces resistance into the flame path and, if a fault occurs, arcing at the interface may result.

While it may not always be possible to install certain fittings without backing off, it is important to ensure that the connection is as tight as possible. Properly made conduit connections are critical to the safety of hazardous location wiring systems.

Rules 18-102 3) b) and 18-152 3) b)

Tolerance 6g/6H is defined by ISO 965-1.

Δ   Rule 18-102 4)

It is recognized that electrical equipment that has been certified to IEC-based Canadian Standards (IEC Standards adapted for use as Canadian Standards) may have conduit or cable entries with threads that are either tapered or straight, complying with ISO (International Organization for Standardization) Standards. Subrule 4) requires that appropriate adapters be used to ensure an effective connection to this equipment where thread forms differ between the equipment and the wiring method.

ISO 965, Parts 1 and 3, may be used for guidance in understanding ISO threads.

Rule 18-102 5)

The type of protection "increased safety" incorporates protection from ingress of water or foreign bodies. CAN/CSA-C22.2 No. 60079-7 requires that enclosures containing bare conductive parts provide at least degree of protection IP54 (see Table B18-5) and that enclosures containing only insulated conductive parts provide at least degree of protection IP44. It is important that conduit and cable entries maintain at least the degree of protection provided by the enclosure by the use of devices such as gaskets and sealing lock nuts. Increased safety enclosures should restrict easy entry of gases or vapours in order to minimize the entry of gases or vapours from short-term releases.

Ingress protection (IP) describes the degree of protection an enclosure provides. The first number of the IP designation describes the degree of protection against physical contact (i.e., fingers, tools, dust, etc.) with internal parts; the second number designates the IP against liquids. For example, an IP54 rating requires an enclosure to be dust-protected and protected against water splashing from any direction. While the minimum requirement for an increased safety enclosure is IP44 or IP54 as stated in the previous paragraph, typically most increased safety enclosures meet IP65 or IP66 rating.

For further information on the IEC IP designations, refer to CAN/CSA-C22.2 No. 60529.

Table B18-5
Ingress protection

Protection against contact and solid objects		Protection against liquids	
Number	**Description**	**Number**	**Description**
0	No protection	0	No protection
1	Objects greater than 50 mm	1	Vertically dripping water
2	Objects greater than 12 mm	2	Dripping water when tilted up to 15°
3	Objects greater than 2.5 mm	3	Spraying water at an angle up to 60°
4	Objects greater than 1 mm	4	Splashing water from any direction
5	Dust-protected	5	Low-pressure water jets
6	Dust-tight	6	Strong jets of water
		7	The effects of immersion to a depth of 1 m
		8	Submersion

Δ **Rules 18-104 and 18-154**

Seals are provided in conduit or cable systems to prevent the passage of gases, vapours, or flames from one portion of the electrical installation to another through the system.

Passage of gases, vapours, or flames through mineral-insulated cable is inherently prevented by the construction of the cable, but sealing compound is used in cable glands to exclude moisture and other fluids from the cable insulation and is required to be of a type intended for the conditions of use.

Cables and flexible cords are not tested to determine their ability to resist internal explosions. Therefore, regardless of size, each cable must be sealed at the point of entry into any enclosure that is required to be explosion-proof.

Some designs of cable glands incorporate an integral seal, and these are marked "SL" to indicate that the seal is provided by the cable gland. Cable glands of this type are identified with the class designation. Designs requiring a field- or factory-installed sealing fitting have the group designation marked on this component.

The appropriate sealing characteristics may be achieved by different means; therefore, the manufacturer's instructions should be followed.

Sealing of insulated and bare conductors in the conduit, or in most cables, requires that the sealing compound completely surround each individual insulated and bare conductor to ensure that the seal performs its intended function. In certain constructions of cables, specifically those containing bundles of shielded pairs, triads, or quads, removal of the shielding or overall covering from the bundles negates the purpose for which the shielding was provided. Testing of this type of cable now includes testing for flame propagation along the length of the individual subassemblies of the cable.

The letters A, B, C, or D, or a combination of them, may be added to signify the group(s) for which the cable has been tested, for example,

a) the marking "HL-CD" indicates that the cable has been tested for flame propagation for gas groups C and D; and

b) the marking "TC-BCD" indicates that the cable has been tested for flame propagation for gas groups B, C, and D.

See also Table B18-2.

Rule 18-104 2)

Reducers may have one side larger than the trade size of the conduit where the entry to the explosion-proof or flameproof enclosure is larger than the trade size of the conduit.

Δ Rules 18-104 2) and 18-154 2)

Conduit fittings for use in Zone 1 or Zone 2 locations and similar to the "L", "T", or "Cross" type are not usually classed as enclosures when not larger than the trade size of the conduit.

Rule 18-104 4)

It is important to follow the manufacturer's instructions closely; otherwise, seals will not function properly to prevent the transmission of an explosion beyond the seal. Improper sealing has been the primary factor in a number of explosions resulting in loss of life and/or major equipment damage. Users are reminded that only the sealing compound specified in the instructions may be used in a seal. Use of other manufacturers' compounds in a seal may compromise the integrity of the installation.

Δ Rule 18-104 4) a)

Motors and generators for use in Zone 1 locations may be required to have a seal provided by the manufacturer between the main motor or generator enclosure and the enclosure for the conduit entry (connection box). Therefore, a marking regarding provision of the seal may or may not appear on this particular class of product.

Cable glands with integral seals are marked "SL".

The term "accessible" as used in this Item is in accordance with the Code definition in Section 0 for **Accessible (as applied to wiring methods)**.

Rules 18-106 and 18-150 2) e)

Sections 7.2 and 11.3 of IEC 60079-14 (edition 4.0, 2007-12) are included here for the convenience of designers and users. For additional information on design and installation requirements of increased safety motors, consult the following:

a) IEC 60079-14, *Explosive atmospheres — Part 14: Electrical installations design, selection and erection*; and

b) CAN/CSA-C22.2 No. 60079-7, *Explosive atmospheres — Part 7: Equipment protection by increased safety "e"*.

The following extracts from IEC 60079-14 outline additional requirements for the application of type of protection "e" (increased safety) motors in Class I, Zone 1 hazardous locations.

11.3 Cage induction motors

11.3.1 Mains-operated

In order to meet the requirements of item (a) of 7.2, inverse-time delay overload protective devices shall be such that not only is the motor current monitored, but the stalled motor will also be disconnected within the time t_E stated on the marking plate. The current-time characteristic curves giving the delay time of the overload relay or release as a function of the ratio of the starting current to the rated current shall be held by the user.

The curves will indicate the value of the delay time from the cold state related to an ambient temperature of 20 °C and for a range of starting current ratios (I_A / I_N) of at least 3 to 8. The tripping time of the protective devices shall be equal to these values of delay ±20 %.

The properties of delta wound machines in the case of the loss of one phase should be specifically addressed. Unlike star wound machines, the loss of one phase may not be detected, particularly if it occurs during operation. The effect will be current imbalance in the lines feeding the machine and increased heating of the motor. A delta wound motor with a low torque load during start-up might also be able to start under this winding failure condition and therefore the fault may exist undetected for long periods. Therefore, for delta wound machines, phase imbalance protection shall be provided which will detect machine imbalances before they can give rise to excessive heating effects.

In general, motors designed for continuous operation, involving easy and infrequent starts which do not produce appreciable additional heating, are acceptable with inverse-time delay overload protection. Motors designed for arduous starting conditions or which are to be started frequently are acceptable only when suitable protective devices ensure that the limiting temperature is not exceeded.

Arduous starting conditions are considered to exist if an inverse-time delay overload protective device, correctly selected as above, disconnects the motor before it reaches its rated speed. Generally, this will happen if the total starting time exceeds 1.7 t_E.

NOTE 1 Operation
Where the duty of the motor is not S1 (continuous operation at constant load), the user should obtain the appropriate parameters for the determination of suitability given a definition of operation.

NOTE 2 Starting
It is preferred that the direct on-line starting time for the motor is less than the t_E time so that the motor protection device does not trip the motor during start-up. Where the starting time exceeds 80% of the t_E time, the limitations associated with starting whilst maintaining operation within the machine instruction manual should be ascertained from the motor manufacturer.

As the voltage dips during a direct on-line start, the starting current decreases and the run-up time increases. Although these effects may tend to cancel out for small voltage dips, for voltages less than 85% of U_N during startup, the motor manufacturer should declare the associated limitations on start-up.

Motors may be limited by the manufacturer to a fixed number of start attempts.

NOTE 3 Protection relay
The protection relay for machines in accordance with type of protection 'e' should, in addition to the requirements of Clause 7:
a)   monitor the current in each phase;
b)   provide close overload protection to the fully loaded condition of the motor.

Inverse-time delay overload protection relays may be acceptable for machines of duty type S1 which have easy and infrequent starts. Where the starting duty is arduous or starting is required frequently, the protection device should be selected so that it ensures limiting temperatures are not exceeded under the declared operational parameters of the machine. Where the starting time exceeds 1.7t_E, an inverse-time relay would be expected to trip the machine during start-up.

Under some circumstances, e.g., for duty types other than S1, the motor may be certified with the temperature detection and protection. If this is the case, the t_E time may not be identified.

11.3.2 Winding temperature sensors
In order to meet the requirements of 7.2(b), winding temperature sensors associated with protective devices shall be adequate for the thermal protection of the machine even when the machine is stalled.

The use of embedded temperature sensors to control the limiting temperature of the machine is only permitted if such use is specified in the machine documentation.

NOTE The type of built-in temperature sensors and associated protective device will be identified on the machine.

11.3.3 Machines with rated voltage greater than 1 kV

Machines with a rated voltage exceeding 1 kV shall be selected taking into account the 'Potential stator winding discharge risk assessment — Ignition risk factors' (see Annex E). If the total sum of the risk factors is greater than 6, then anti-condensation space heaters shall be employed, and special measures shall be applied to ensure that the enclosure does not contain an explosive gas atmosphere at the time of starting.

NOTE 1 If the machine is intended to operate under 'special measures', the certificate will have the symbol 'X' in accordance with IEC 60079-0.

NOTE 2 Special measures may include pre-start ventilation, the application of fixed gas detection inside the machine or other methods specified in manufacturer's instructions.

NOTE 3 In the table in Annex E, the reference to 'Time between detailed inspections' is intended to reflect the interval between cleaning of the stator windings. It should read 'Time between major overhauls (disassembly and cleaning where necessary)' as a detailed inspection in accordance with IEC 60079-17 would not normally require the stator winding to be examined.

11.3.4 Motors with converter supply

Motors supplied at varying frequency and voltage by a converter shall have been type tested for this duty as a unit in association with the converter and the protective device.

11.3.5 Reduced-voltage starting (soft starting)

Motors with a soft start supply require either:
a)   the motor has been tested as a unit in association with the soft start device specified in the descriptive documents and with the protective device provided; or
b)   the motor has not been tested as a unit in association with the soft start device. In this case, means (or equipment) for direct temperature control by embedded temperature sensors specified in the motor documentation, other effective measures for limiting the temperature of the motor shall be provided or the speed control device ensures that the motor run up is such that the temperature is not exceeded. The effectiveness of the temperature control or proper run up shall be verified and documented. The action of the protective device shall be to cause the motor to be disconnected.

NOTE 1 It is considered that soft starting is used for a short time period.

NOTE 2 When using a soft start device with high-frequency pulses in the output, care should be taken to ensure that any overvoltage spikes and higher temperatures which may be produced in the terminal box are taken into consideration.

7.2 Rotating electrical machines

Rotating electrical machinery shall additionally be protected against overload unless it can withstand continuously the starting current at rated voltage and frequency or, in the case of generators, the short-circuit current, without inadmissible heating. The overload protective device shall be:
a)   a current-dependent, time lag protective device monitoring all three phases, set at not more than the rated current of the machine, which will operate in 2 h or less at 1.20 times the set current and will not operate within 2 h at 1.05 times the set current; or

b) a device for direct temperature control by embedded temperature sensors; or

c) another equivalent device.

Δ **Rules 18-106 and 28-314**

Users are cautioned that combining a variable frequency drive (VFD) with a motor may increase the operating temperature of the motor as a result of the harmonics produced by the drive. This may cause the motor temperature to exceed its temperature code rating. This is of particular concern where the operating temperature of the motor is close to the ignition temperature of hazardous materials that may be in the area. Because of the generally lower ignition temperatures associated with dust materials, it will be of particular concern in explosive dust atmospheres. It remains the responsibility of the user to ensure that the operating temperature of the motor, in combination with the drive, is below the minimum ignition temperature of the hazardous material in the area. The motor manufacturer should be consulted where necessary. The following are some references that may assist the user in determining the suitability of an installation:

a) API RP 2216, *Ignition Risk of Hydrocarbon Liquids and Vapors by Hot Surfaces in the Open Air*; and

b) IEEE Paper No. PCIC-97-04, "Flammable Vapor Ignition Initiated by Hot Rotor Surfaces Within an Induction Motor — Reality or Not?".

Rule 18-150

Equipment marked Class I, Division 2 is suitable only for Zone 2. See the Note to Rule 18-100.

Rule 18-150 2) c) ii)

The equipment referred to in this Item includes service and branch circuit switches and circuit breakers; motor controllers, including push buttons, pilot switches, relays, and motor-overload protective devices; and switches and circuit breakers for the control of lighting and appliance circuits. Oil-immersed circuit breakers and controllers of the ordinary general-use type may not confine completely the arc produced in the interruption of heavy overloads, and specific approval for locations of this Class and Division is therefore necessary.

Rule 18-150 2) c) iv)

A group of three fuses protecting an ungrounded three-phase circuit and a single fuse protecting the ungrounded conductor of an identified 2-wire single-phase circuit would each be considered a set of fuses.

Δ **Rule 18-150 2) e)**

See the Note to Rules 18-106 and 18-150 2) e).

Rotating electrical machines of the open or non-explosion-proof type do not have a certification Standard for Class I, Division 2; however, there are types of protection that can be used for certifying these machines for use in Zone 2 locations. This Rule provides the criteria for applying, in Zone 2, rotating electrical machines that do not have a certification suitable for Zone 2 or Division 2. Refer to IEEE 1349 for more detailed information on applying these rotating electrical machines in Zone 2 locations.

Δ **Rule 18-150 3)**

These heaters are not marked for use in hazardous locations. They are considered suitable on the basis that they are contained within the motor or generator and are therefore mechanically protected, do not use temperature controls (to eliminate heater temperature runaway in the event of a controls failure), and are non-ignition-capable under normal operating conditions.

Example of a motor heater nameplate

Motor space heater
Rated voltage: _____ V
Phase: _____
Rated current: _____ A, or Power: _____ W
Maximum surface temperature: _____ °C, or
Temperature code: _____

Rule 18-152 1) b)
See the Notes to Rule 18-102.

Δ **Rules 18-152 1) h), 18-192 3) a), 18-202 4) a), and 18-252 1) h)**
Liquid-tight flexible metal conduit and associated connectors intended for use in hazardous locations are marked "HEAVY DUTY" or "HD".

Δ **Rule 18-152 7)**
Cable glands should be compatible with the degree of ingress protection and explosion protection provided by the enclosure on which they are installed.

For example, to maintain the protection of an enclosure required to be explosion-proof, a sealing-type gland marked for the location should be used. Where unarmoured cables must enter an enclosure required to be explosion-proof, a combination of a sealing fitting marked for the location and a non-sealing cable gland may be used.

Where equipment normally considered suitable for use in ordinary locations is acceptable in Zone 2 locations, such as terminal boxes and motors, ordinary location cable glands that maintain the degree of protection of the enclosure may be used. Similarly, where purged enclosures are used in Zone 1 and Zone 2 locations, ordinary location cable glands that maintain the degree of protection of the enclosure may be used.

Where equipment is specifically designed for use in Zone 2 locations, such as "Ex nX", ordinary location cable glands that maintain the degree of protection of the enclosure may be used. One means of achieving equivalent protection would be to use a cable gland with the same or better IP rating as the enclosure (for ingress protection designations, see Table B18-5). If the gland does not have an IP rating, other ratings, such as weatherproof, may be matched to the enclosure rating.

Rule 18-154
See the Note to Rules 18-104 and 18-154.

Δ **Rule 18-154 1) c)**
This Item allows the seal at the boundary between an outdoor Zone 2 location and an outdoor non-hazardous location to be located further than 300 mm from the boundary of the Zone 2 location, provided that it is located on the conduit prior to its entering an enclosure or a building. Because gas is present in Zone 2 locations only for short periods, it is unlikely that gas or vapour could be released through conduit couplings at sufficiently high rates to form an explosive gas atmosphere in outdoor areas. However, the seal must be located on the conduit before it enters an enclosure or a building because, depending on the ventilation rate, gas transmitted through the conduit may build up to flammable concentrations.

Rule 18-154 2)
See the Note to Rules 18-104 2) and 18-154 2).

Δ **Rules 18-190 and 18-200**
The equipment protection level (EPL) marked on equipment takes precedence over the type(s) of explosion protection marked on it and may, to account for other aspects of the equipment, such as material limitations, be more restrictive than that normally applied for a specific type of protection. To take the marking Ex ia Db as an example: ia would normally be acceptable in Zone 20; however, the equipment was constructed with a greater aluminum content than the product Standards permit and, therefore, EPL Db indicates that the equipment is restricted to a Zone 21 area.

Rule 18-192 1) b)
See the Note to Rule 18-102.

Section 20

Rule 20-004
For the purposes of Subrules 6) and 7), buildings such as kiosks, in which electrical equipment such as cash registers and/or self-service console controls are located, are considered to be buildings not suitably cut off.

Rule 20-030
Information on the non-electrical aspects of propane tank systems, refill centres, and filling plants may be found in CSA B149.2.

Rule 20-060
Information on the non-electrical aspects of compressed natural gas (NGV) refuelling stations and NGV storage facilities may be found in CSA B149.1.

Rule 20-100
This Rule applies to areas where vehicles that use fuels classified as flammable liquids are repaired or serviced. It does not apply to areas where vehicles burning combustible liquids such as diesel fuel are repaired or serviced. Table B20-1 lists the flash points of combustible and flammable liquids as determined by the methods specified in NFPA 30.

Table B20-1
Flash points of combustible and flammable liquids
determined in accordance with NFPA 30

Liquid classification	Closed-cup flash point
Flammable liquid (Class I liquid)*	Less than 37.8 °C
Combustible liquid (Class II liquid)	Not less than 37.8 °C and less than 60 °C
Combustible liquid (Class IIIA liquid)	Not less than 60 °C and less than 93 °C
Combustible liquid (Class IIIB liquid)	Not less than 93 °C

* Class I liquids are further subdivided into Classes IA, IB, and IC.

Flash point is typically used to determine if the possibility of a liquid being released into the air requires the area to be classified as a hazardous location. If a liquid is stored or used in an area at temperatures below its flash point, the area may be classified as a non-hazardous area.

Section 22

Rule 22-002
Examples of some, but not all, of the occupancies in which Category 1 or Category 2 locations may be encountered are listed in Table B22-1.

Table B22-1
Examples of Category 1 and Category 2 locations

Category 1

Basements (other than in residential occupancies)	Dye works
Bathhouses	Ice cream plants
Bottling works	Ice plants
Breweries	Laundries (commercial)
Canneries	Stables for cattle only
Cold storage plants	Stables for horses in rural farm areas
Dairies (commercial and farm)	

Category 2

Abattoirs	Metal refineries
Casing rooms	Potato storage facilities
Chemical works (some)	Pulp mills
Fertilizer rooms	Railway roundhouses
Glue houses	Stables for horses
Hide cellars	Sugar mills
Meat-packing plants	Tanneries

Rule 22-100
Circuit breakers located in a Category 2 location have experienced nuisance tripping due to internal corrosion and may not operate as designed in all cases if located in a corrosive environment.

Rule 22-204
Farm buildings that are of weathertight construction and that are not Category 1 or Category 2 locations can be considered dry locations (e.g., machinery warehouses).

Additional information on the ventilation of buildings housing livestock and poultry can be found in the *National Farm Building Code of Canada*.

Rule 22-204 5)
Non-metallic-sheathed cable is not approved for installation in a continuous raceway system.

Rule 22-704
Sewage lift and treatment plants
Sewage lift and treatment plants produce a combination of conditions that may require specialized attention to the electrical installation. Abnormal hazardous conditions can occur due to the buildup of methane gas and spills of chemicals, gasoline, or other volatile liquids into the sewer system. Reference material for hazardous area classification can be found in NFPA 820. Wet well areas normally contain an atmosphere of high humidity and corrosive hydrogen sulphide vapours.

An extreme hazard to personnel working in wet wells is the presence of sewer gas (hydrogen sulphide). This gas is treacherous because the ability to sense it by smell is quickly lost. If workers ignore the first notice of the gas, their senses will give them no further warning. If the concentration is high enough, loss of consciousness and death can result.

Before work in wet well locations begins, the air in the wet well area should be purged, and ventilation with fresh air should be maintained while work continues in the area.

Section 24

△ Rule 24-000

This Section consolidates requirements that arise from electrical safety considerations applicable to specific areas in health care facilities.

Code users should consult CSA Z32 for further information regarding electrical safety and essential electrical systems in health care facilities. CSA Z32 contains provisions that are supplementary to the installation requirements specified in Sections 24 and 52 of this Code. These provisions include, for example, the arrangement of normal and emergency power supply, classification of patient care areas, classification of loads and branches of an essential electrical system, arrangements of normal and emergency power supply sources for the loads of an essential electrical system, and the minimum number of receptacles per patient care environment.

The content of this Section reflects the changing nature of health care. Procedures once reserved for hospitals are now performed in medical clinics. As such, this Section applies to patient care areas in all health care facilities, and its requirements are based on the care area (e.g., basic, intermediate, or critical). This approach is consistent with the provisions of CSA Z32.

Rule 24-002
Hazard index

The hazard index with one isolated conductor connected to ground is not necessarily the same as the hazard index with the other isolated conductor connected to ground; of the two, the greater hazard index governs.

Patient care environment

The patient care environment is a zone fixed to the patient bed, table, or other supporting mechanism and does not move with the patient as the patient moves through the health care facility or room.

Rule 24-100

Users of this Code should also consult CSA Z32, as it recommends additional precautions to take in the design, construction, use, and maintenance of electrical systems in such areas.

It is highly desirable that the intended use of all patient care areas be designated by the health care facility's administration in a manner that may be readily understood by the facility's staff.

Rules 24-102 and 24-106

Basic care areas should not, even in long-term facilities, be considered residential occupancies that are governed by general Rules such as 26-710 and 26-726. Users of this Code should be aware that the need for circuits and receptacles in patient care areas is frequently greater than in most other locations. Users are directed to CSA Z32 for recommendations regarding the minimum number of receptacles and circuits normally required in the various patient care areas.

Rule 24-102 3)

This Subrule is not intended to restrict the number of patient care environments served by a branch circuit. Users of this Code should consider the nature of the care area (e.g., basic, intermediate, or critical), Table 6 of CSA Z32, and the voltage drop requirements of Rule 8-102. It is the intent that receptacles supplied by the branch circuit supply only medical electrical equipment. The actual use of the receptacle by health care facility staff within the patient care environment is beyond the scope of this Subrule. The word "load" within this Subrule is intended to refer exclusively to permanently connected medical electrical equipment or receptacles intended for medical electrical equipment.

Δ **Rule 24-102 4)**
It is the intent of this Subrule to permit branch circuits to supply loads between two patient care environments within the same patient care area.

Δ **Rule 24-102 5)**
As indicated by Subrule 24-302 1), it is the responsibility of the health care facility administration to designate which circuits, if any, are essential. Certain types of health care facilities (outpatient clinics, doctors' and dental offices, massage therapy offices, group homes, etc.) may not have a designated essential electrical system. The intent of this Subrule is to make provision for such situations.

Rule 24-102 7)
It is intended by this Subrule that a branch circuit that supplies the receptacles and permanently connected electrical equipment constituting loads of an essential electrical system as described in Rule 24-300 not be permitted to supply other receptacles (such as housekeeping receptacles, etc.) that are not required to be a part of the essential electrical system.

Loads constituting an essential electrical system of a health care facility are described in Clause 6 and Table 6 of CSA Z32.

Rules 24-104 1) and 24-112
The object of these Rules is to limit the voltage difference in the vicinity of the patient and thus to minimize the risk of electric shock. The adequacy of the installation may be verified by test in accordance with the procedure outlined in CSA Z32. It is important to note the specifications of the measurement instrument.

Bonding to ground in patient care areas must accomplish two functions:
a)   limit the voltage that occurs on exposed metal parts in the event of a fault in the electrical insulation of the wiring system or of a utilization device; and
b)   eliminate small but potentially hazardous voltage differences that might otherwise exist between grounded points in the vicinity of the patient.

To enable the integrity of the bonding conductor to be checked, the conductor should not be permitted to make intermediate contact with grounded metal, as would be the case in metal conduit and in some armoured cables.

Δ **Rule 24-104 1) b)**
The bare bonding conductor of a Type AC90 cable is not considered suitable for the purpose.

Rules 24-104 2) and 24-112
It is intended that the bonding methods specified by these Rules may be mixed, i.e., some bonding conductors for an area may be terminated at a grounding bus, and others may be terminated at the panelboard. In some situations, "daisy chaining" of bonding conductors from outlet to outlet may prove to be more effective than installing a separate conductor from each outlet to a common point.

Rule 24-104 5)
This Subrule is not intended to isolate the three-phase equipment bonding conductor from other equipment within the patient care environment.

Rule 24-104 8)
This Subrule is intended to require that all exposed metal parts of non-electrical equipment located within a patient care environment that could become energized during a single fault condition be bonded to ground. Examples of such equipment are metal parts of medical gas equipment, metal parts of support arms or consoles installed in a patient care environment, etc.

It is not intended by this Subrule that metal parts of portable non-electrical equipment or metal parts of the building structure and miscellaneous small conductive parts (e.g., metal door frames, window frames, and soap dishes) be bonded to ground.

Δ **Rule 24-104 9)**

It is intended by this Subrule that the bonding of general-type recessed and surface-mounted luminaires located more than 2.3 m above floor level and their associated switches located outside a patient care environment, not be required to meet the bonding provisions of Section 24, but such luminaires and switches must comply with the general bonding requirements of Section 10.

The relaxation provided by this Subrule is not intended for lighting equipment that may extend into the patient care environment, such as surgical lights, stem-mounted examination light fixtures, ceiling-mounted fixtures with a hinged and framed lens, etc., that are used for patient care as loads of the essential electrical system.

Δ **Rule 24-106 1)**

The extent of each type of patient care area is described in CSA Z32. Table 5 of CSA Z32 (reproduced below) identifies the minimum number and general arrangement of receptacles in patient care areas, based on the level of patient care.

Table 5 from CSA Z32
Minimum number of receptacles required

	Housekeeping		Electric bed (if applicable)		Patient care	
	No. of receptacles per room	Type of branch circuits	No. of receptacles per bed	No. of branch circuits per bed*	No. of duplex receptacles per patient care environment. See Note 2)	No. of branch circuits per patient care environment†
Basic care area	1 duplex	Shared	1	0.5	3	1
Intermediate care areas	1 duplex	Shared	1	0.5	4	1.5
Critical care areas (intensive care units, cardiac care units, and intensive care nurseries)	As required	Shared	1	0.5	8	4
Operating rooms	—	—	—	—	14 in total, located as follows: 6 on the walls and 8 on ceiling or floor-mounted service units, at a minimum of 2 locations	7

* *0.5 means one circuit shared by two beds.*
† *1.5 means one dedicated circuit plus one circuit shared by two patient care environments.*

Notes:
1) *Consideration should be given to supplying some receptacles from a different source so that a failure of one system will not deprive an entire area of electrical power.*
2) *The prescribed number of patient care receptacles per patient care environment should be located within the patient care environment unless it is not practical for the intended application.*

Rule 24-106 3)

Rule 26-704 requires that receptacles installed within 1.5 m of wash basins, bathtubs, or shower stalls be protected by a ground fault circuit interrupter of the Class A type.

Rules 24-106 3) and 24-114
The intent of these Rules is to provide protection against electric shock hazard when personal grooming appliances are being used. See also the Note to Rules 24-102 and 24-106.

Rule 24-106 5)
It is not intended by this Subrule to mandate installation of hospital-grade receptacles in bathrooms or washrooms within a patient care area.

Rule 24-106 6)
CSA Z32 identifies receptacles and other loads that should be connected to the circuits in essential electrical systems (i.e., those listed in Table 6 of CSA Z32 and considered essential for the life, safety, and care of the patient and the effective operation of the health care facility during an interruption of the normal electrical supply for any reason).

Rule 24-110
In intermediate and critical care areas, either grounded or isolated systems may be used. Users of this Code should consult CSA Z32 regarding the relative merits of each system.

Rule 24-112
See the Notes to Rule 24-104.

Rule 24-114
See the Notes to Rule 24-106.

Rule 24-116
Areas subject to standing fluids on the floor or drenching of the work area can create a condition where a patient or staff member can become a path for ground fault current under fault conditions.

Routine housekeeping procedures and incidental spillage of liquids are not intended to be considered for the purpose of this Rule.

Use of receptacles protected by a ground fault circuit interrupter of a Class A type is intended for those wet locations within a patient care area where interruption of power to the receptacles by actuation of a ground fault circuit interrupter is deemed to be acceptable in accordance with the provisions of CSA Z32.

These receptacles are intended to be supplied by an isolated system where such power interruption to the receptacles is not acceptable in accordance with CSA Z32.

Rules 24-200, 24-202 2), and 24-204 7)
Users of this Code should recognize that while fixed luminaires and medical electrical equipment, permanently connected or otherwise, identified in these Rules may physically be located outside the patient care environment, they nonetheless serve the patient care environment.

Rule 24-204 6)
Users of this Code should refer to CSA Z32 regarding methods for verifying the impedance-to-ground of an isolated system.

Rule 24-206
It is imperative that the impedance-to-ground of individually isolated branch circuits be tested at regular intervals, and that maintenance procedures be instituted for the system and the equipment connected to it as necessary to limit the hazard index to 2 mA.

Δ Rule 24-208
Three-phase isolated systems should be subjected to a periodic test of the impedance-to-ground of the system, together with any connected load, unless an isolation-sensing device (e.g., an isolation monitor) is used.

Rule 24-300

Users of this Code are directed to CSA Z32, which makes further recommendations regarding the design, installation, use, and maintenance of these systems.

Rule 24-302

CSA Z32 provides advice as to what loads should be supplied by the vital, delayed vital, or conditional branch of an essential electrical system.

Rule 24-304

The intent of the requirement that transfer switches be mechanically held is to ensure that, once the essential system has been connected to the emergency supply, it will not be disconnected until the normal supply has been restored.

Section 26

Rule 26-004

Electrical equipment certified after September 30, 1986 is acceptable for mounting directly over combustible surfaces without additional protection unless it bears a cautionary marking requiring additional protection. Equipment certified prior to that date is not required to carry the cautionary marking.

Rule 26-008

The intent of this Rule is to protect electrical apparatus within ventilated enclosures from the direct spray from sprinkler heads. The intent of the Rule is considered to be met when

a) water following a direct line-of-sight path from the sprinkler head cannot strike live parts within the enclosure through ventilation openings in the sides and tops of electrical equipment; and

b) water accumulating on the top of the equipment cannot flow into the interior through significant openings. Examples of significant openings are ventilation openings, openings around bus duct, and dry-type armoured cable connectors. Bolts and seams are not considered to be significant openings.

The intent of this Rule can also be met through use of weatherproof equipment.

Rule 26-012

Dielectric liquid-filled circuit breakers or switches should have their vents piped directly to an outside area in accordance with the manufacturer's instructions or recommendations.

Construction criteria for service rooms are provided in Articles 3.6.2.1 and 9.10.10.3 of the *National Building Code of Canada*. Where a service room is required by this Code, it must be separated from the remainder of the building by a fire separation having a 1 h fire-resistance rating, unless the service room is sprinklered.

Ⓔ **Rule 26-012 2)**

Figure B26-1
Separation of liquid-filled equipment, indoors, exclusive
of installations in electrical equipment vaults

Total amount of liquid at location, L	Radius, m		
	Open floor location, R_a	Against wall location, R_b	Corner location, R_c
5	0.36	0.51	0.72
15	0.63	0.88	1.25
30	0.88	1.25	1.77
45	1.08	1.53	2.17
60	1.25	1.77	2.50
75	1.40	1.98	2.80

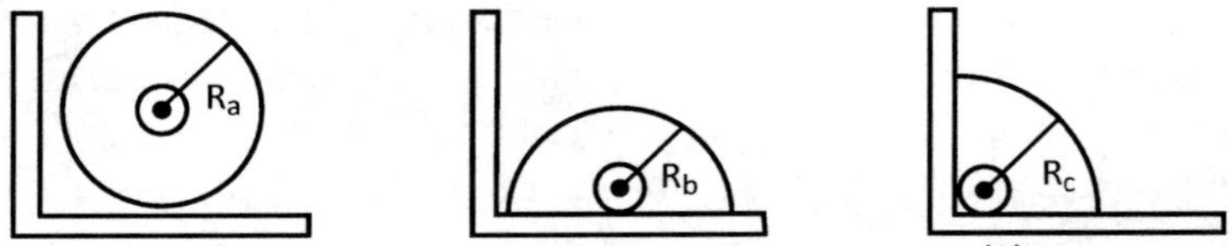

(1) Open floor   (2) Against wall   (3) In corner

Radius is calculated from formula $R_a = \sqrt{\dfrac{area}{\pi}} = \sqrt{\dfrac{0.08184 \times litres}{\pi}}$

Similarly $R_b = \sqrt{\dfrac{0.16388 \times litres}{\pi}}$ and $R_c = \sqrt{\dfrac{0.32738 \times litres}{\pi}}$

Note: *Radii are to be measured from the centre of the liquid-filled container.*

Example: Two pieces of equipment, each containing 75 L of liquid, one installed in a corner and the other along the wall as shown, must have the centre points of the containers at least 2.80 + 1.98 = 4.78 m apart.

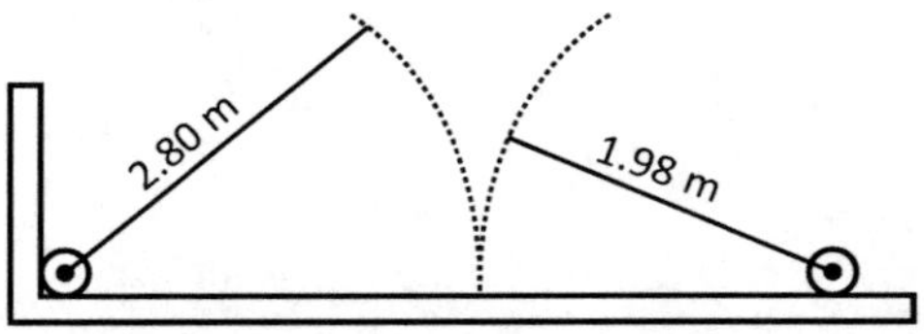

Rule 26-014 3)
The normal enclosure for the equipment is not to be considered as the barrier referred to in this Subrule.

Rule 26-210
In addition to the circuit overcurrent protection provided by this Rule, overcurrent protection should be provided for the capacitors to protect them against bursting if a unit becomes defective.

Where capacitors for power factor correction are assembled in the field to form banks or groups of banks, the manufacturer's instructions with respect to proper application and connection should be obtained in order to ensure that such overcurrent protection is properly provided.

Generally, individual capacitor fusing or the single fusing of a capacitor bank is used. It becomes an application engineering problem and involves the coordination of the time-current (i.e., blowing) characteristics of the fuse with those of the container with respect to bursting caused by the generation of gas pressure under fault conditions. The selection of the fuse also requires consideration to be given to the available fault current of the circuit and to proper connection of the capacitors in the circuit (i.e., whether parallel, series-parallel, Y-connected with a floating neutral, etc.). Improper capacitor connections can also cause overvoltage on adjacent units upon failure of a unit.

Δ **Rule 26-240 1) b)**
The associated equipment of a unit substation, each contained in an enclosure designed and constructed to restrict access to live parts, is deemed to comply with the requirements of Rule 26-014 4) a).

Rule 26-244 2)
For the purposes of this Rule, a non-propagating liquid is one that when subjected to a source of ignition may burn, but the flame will not spread from the source of ignition. The flash point of a liquid is the minimum temperature at which the liquid gives off sufficient vapour to form an ignitable mixture with air near the surface of the liquid or within the test vessel used.

Rule 26-254
Selection of overcurrent devices with a rating too low for the primary of a dry-type transformer can result in unintended operation when the transformer is being energized (such as might occur after a power outage). To avoid such operation, the overcurrent device should be able to carry
a)   12 times the transformer rated primary full load current for 0.1 s; and
b)   25 times the transformer rated primary full load current for 0.01 s.

Δ **Rule 26-256 4)**
Rule 26-256 1) and 2) mandates that the ampacity of primary and secondary conductors for transformers be not smaller than 125% of the respective primary or secondary currents. It is intended by Subrule 4) that if the primary overcurrent protection does not exceed 125% of the primary rated current for dry transformers, such overcurrent protective devices will adequately protect transformers and primary and secondary conductors, and that the fundamental provision of Rule 14-104 will be met.

The intent of Subrule 4) is to clarify that when the transformer circuit is protected by overcurrent devices in accordance with Rule 26-250 1) or 2) or Rule 26-254 3), such overcurrent protection may not be adequate for the purpose of Rules 14-100 and 14-104 (and of Table 13, where use of Table 13 is applicable).

Rule 26-258
The intent of this requirement is to provide for coordination between loads connected to a transformer secondary and the rating of the transformer circuit (i.e., rating of the transformer overcurrent device and ampacity of transformer conductors). Compliance with this requirement allows the proper selection of the minimum acceptable conductor size under the applicable provisions of Rule 26-256 and selection of the transformer overcurrent device under the applicable requirements of Rules 26-250 to 26-254.

Because selection criteria for the overcurrent devices and conductors are based on the rated (primary or secondary) current of the transformer, the actual calculated load connected to the transformer may not necessarily fully correlate with the transformer rated primary and secondary currents, in which case the intent of this requirement could be met by increasing the rating of the overcurrent device under the relaxation permitted by Rule 26-254 3). This Rule would also have to be considered when conductor size is permitted to be reduced under the provisions of Rule 26-256 3).

Rule 26-260 1)

The purpose of installing primary fuses between power lines and instrument voltage transformers is to protect the power system from possible destructive power arc-over due to breakdown of the major insulation of the transformers. Such fuses must have adequate interrupting capacity for the power system to which they are connected, either self-contained or in conjunction with suitable current-limiting resistors.

Rule 26-260 3) c)

The reference in this Item to primary terminals outside the enclosure being common to both voltage transformers and current transformers includes the "centre" (common) phase primary terminals of open-delta-connected voltage transformers and the primary grounded neutral terminal.

Rule 26-266

The neutral current to a zero sequence filter is three times the phase current.

Installation of a zero sequence filter can increase the single phase-to-ground fault current to 1.5 times the available phase-to-phase fault current.

Rule 26-354

Construction requirements for electrical equipment vaults are found in Article 3.6.2.7 of the *National Building Code of Canada*.

It is recommended, wherever practicable, that vaults be located where they can be ventilated directly from and to an outside area without the use of flues or ducts. In order to minimize the possible explosion hazard from gases that might seep into a vault, vaults should be located remote from points where gas, sewer, water, and other pipelines and conduits enter the building. It is also recommended that they not be located adjacent or close to vertical openings such as elevator shafts.

Rule 26-364

Because nitrocellulose film is known to be subject to exothermic decomposition, which may result in the generation of combustible and usually poisonous gases, these requirements are necessary to retard the possible migration of such gases, as well as to prevent the spread of fire or heated gases to other vaults through raceways. For additional information, refer to NFPA 40.

Rule 26-420

Low-voltage surge protective devices (SPDs) or transient voltage surge suppressors are surge suppression products designed for repeated suppression of transient voltage surges on 50 and 60 Hz power circuits not exceeding 750 V. IEEE C62.41.1 and C62.41.2 describe three general categories of operating environment for surge protective devices. The three system exposure environments are Category A, Category B, and Category C. Surge rating for Category A is intended for outlets and long branch circuits that exceed 10 m in length from Category B or 20 m in length from Category C. Surge rating for Category B is intended for feeders and short branch circuits, distribution panels, heavy appliance outlets with short connections to the service entrance, and lighting systems in large buildings. Surge rating for Category C is intended for outdoor and service entrance installations, service drops from a pole to a building, and underground lines to a well pump. The CSA C22.2 No. 269 series of Standards covers five types of surge protective devices as described in Table B26-1.

Δ

Table B26-1
Surge protective devices

Type of surge protective device (SPD)	Intended application and environment
1	• Permanently connected between the secondary of the service transformer and the line side of the service equipment overcurrent device, as well as the load side, including watt-hour meter socket enclosures, and intended to be installed without an external overcurrent protective device • Categories A, B, and C exposure environments
2	• Permanently connected on the load side of the service equipment overcurrent device • Categories A and B exposure environments
3	• Cord-connected or direct plug-in type incorporating Type 3 SPDs • Receptacles* incorporating Type 3 SPDs connected at a minimum conductor or cable length of 10 m from the electrical service panel to the point of utilization • Category A* exposure environments
4	• A component assembly forming part of a Type 1, 2, or 3 SPD • Not intended for field installation independent of a Type 1, 2, or 3 SPD
5	• A discrete component such as a metal oxide varistor (MOV), gas tube, or avalanche diode • Not intended for field installation

* Receptacle-type Type 3 surge protective devices that have been subjected to the nominal discharge current test in CSA C22.2 No. 269.3 are suitable for use in Category B exposure environments and for permanent connection on the load side of the service equipment overcurrent device.

Rule 26-506
Sufficient ventilation should be provided to prevent the hydrogen gas from building up to a level of 2% by volume in the room air at any time.

When batteries are operated in constant-voltage-float service and the float voltage is maintained at appropriate levels, generation of gas is very slight.

The rate of ventilation required to maintain the volume of hydrogen gas below the 2% level in a battery room may be calculated in accordance with IEEE 484.

As an example, the volume of hydrogen gas generated daily by a 60 cell, 840 ampere-hour lead calcium grid battery charging at 2.2 V per cell is determined as follows:

Total m³/min of hydrogen gas = number of cells × gas generation rate of battery type in m³/min × float current in amperes × minutes/day.

$$\text{Volume of gas production} = 60 \text{ cells} \times 7.6 \times 10^{-6} \frac{m^3}{min} \times \frac{0.006 \text{ A}}{100 \text{ A.H.}} \times 840 \text{ A.H.} \times \frac{60 \text{ min}}{h} \times \frac{24 \text{ h}}{day}$$

$$= \frac{0.03309 \text{ m}^3 \text{ gas}}{day}$$

For a room volume of 30 m³, the total volume of gas that should be allowed to accumulate in this room is 30 m³ × 2% = 0.6 m³.

Therefore, to meet this 2% maximum level, one air change is required for each

$$\frac{0.6 \text{ m}^3}{0.03309 \text{ m}^3 \frac{gas}{day}} = 18 \text{ days}$$

However, a minimum of one to four air changes per hour in the battery room is recommended to prevent pockets of hydrogen gas from accumulating and to ensure the comfort of the maintenance personnel.

Rule 26-506 2)

The freezing point of the electrolyte used in a lead-acid battery is −15 °C for a specific gravity of 1.150, −20 °C for a specific gravity of 1.175, and −27 °C for a specific gravity of 1.200. The freezing point will be higher if the battery is completely discharged. Therefore, batteries should not be located in areas where the temperature is likely to fall below −7 °C.

Rule 26-602

Where in dwelling units, the branch circuit breakers are equipped with ground fault circuit interrupters of the Class A type, panelboards containing these circuit breakers should be provided with a self-adhesive label indicating the test procedure for the ground fault circuit interrupter and a chart for recording the tests.

Rule 26-656 1) and 2)

The intent of these Subrules is to provide both series (also called low-level) and parallel (also called high-level) arc-fault protection downstream from the panelboard through the entire branch circuit wiring, including cord sets and power supply cords connected to the outlets.

Considering that the outlet branch-circuit-type arc-fault circuit interrupter does not provide upstream parallel arc-fault protection, Rule 26-656 2) b) requires mechanical protection for the portion of the branch circuit between the branch circuit overcurrent device and the first outlet. The mechanical protection minimizes the risk of direct contact with and damage to the cable that could cause ignition due to an arc and spread of the flame should ignition occur.

Ⓔ Δ **Rule 26-656 3)**

The intent of this Subrule can be met by installing
a)   a combination-type arc-fault circuit interrupter located at the origin of the branch circuit; or
b)   an outlet branch-circuit-type arc-fault circuit interrupter at the first added receptacle or upstream from the added receptacle.

Rule 26-700 and Diagrams 1 and 2

The configurations of Diagrams 1 and 2 are all of the grounding type. With two exceptions (5-20RA and 6-20RA), these configurations are identical to those similarly designated in the United States, dimensional details of which are given in ANSI/NEMA WD 6.

The CSA 5-20RA and 6-20RA configurations differ from those in the United States in that they will not accept a 15 A attachment plug of the same voltage rating. Receptacles of the CSA 5-20R and 6-20R configurations are intended to accommodate both 15 A and 20 A rated attachment plugs.

Δ **Rule 26-702 2)**

Receptacles can be protected by a Class A ground fault circuit interrupter that is
a)   an integral part of the receptacle; or
b)   incorporated in an upstream receptacle, dead-front device, or circuit breaker.

Δ **Rule 26-704**
The term "sink" is intended to include kitchen sinks, bar sinks, laundry sinks, utility room sinks, wash basins, etc., that are connected to a plumbing drain pipe. It is not intended to include portable wash basins.

It is not intended that the 1.5 m dimension be extended through a wall opening that is fitted with a door. Where a room combines a wash basin or shower/bathing facilities with an area serving another purpose, such as an ensuite bathroom in a bedroom, requirements for receptacles located in such rooms or areas should be considered similar to the requirements for receptacles located in bathrooms and washrooms.

The requirement for Class A ground fault circuit interrupter protection is not intended to apply to receptacles supplying appliances located behind such appliances as washers, dryers, fridges, ranges, built-in microwaves, and other similar appliances, provided that those receptacles, by virtue of their location, are rendered essentially inaccessible for use for other portable appliances.

Rule 26-706
This Rule requires that only receptacles that are designed, constructed, and marked as tamper-resistant receptacles, "TAMPER RESISTANT" or "TR", in accordance with CSA C22.2 No. 42, be used in the locations designated in Subrule 1).

The intent of the Rule is to protect children from shock if they tamper with receptacles accessible to them. For those situations where the receptacle is inaccessible, a non-tamper-resistant receptacle may be used. Examples of such situations where the receptacle is inaccessible are microwaves in cabinets, refrigerators, freezers, washing machines, those located in an attic or crawl space, or those installed above 2 m from the floor or finished grade.

Rule 26-706 1) a)
It is intended by this Rule that unless otherwise designated by an authority having jurisdiction for child care facilities, a child care facility is considered to be an area designed to provide care to persons 7 years of age or less.

Δ **Rule 26-708**
The Standard for wet location cover plates is CSA C22.2 No. 42.1.

The cover plates required for the receptacle configurations identified in Rule 26-708 2) are designed to be suitable for use in wet locations whether or not a plug is inserted into the receptacle, i.e., tested for resistance to moisture both with a plug inserted and without a plug inserted into the receptacle. These plates are required to be marked "Wet Locations" with the marking being visible after installation.

Other wet location cover plates suitable for use in wet locations only when the plug is removed, i.e., tested for resistance to moisture only without a plug inserted into the receptacle, may be used with other receptacle configurations not identified in Rule 26-708 2) and are required to be marked "Wet Location Only When Cover Closed", or the equivalent, with the marking being visible after installation.

Δ **Rule 26-708 2) and 3)**
It is intended by Rule 26-708 3) b) to recognize the protection provided by soffits, overhanging balconies, canopies, marquees, roofed open porches, and similar architectural elements from precipitation that may drip, splash, or flow on or against receptacles located outdoors, thus reducing the environmental protection requirement to damp locations. To determine if a receptacle location is damp, not wet, a zone defined in its borders by a 45° line from the roof edge and a horizontal line at

least 1 m off finished grade or floor level is conceptualized as shown in Figure B26-2. Subrules 26-708 2) and 3) are intended to apply to outlets in the areas identified in Figure B26-2 as follows:

a) Area 1 — An "in-use" cover that is marked "Extra-duty" and is suitable for wet locations is required. A cover marked "Wet Location Only When Cover Closed", not of the "in-use" type, is permitted for receptacles facing downward 45° or less.

b) Area 2 — A cover marked "Wet Location Only When Cover Closed", not of the "in-use" type, is permitted.

When a plug is inserted into the receptacle, a wet location cover plate marked "Extra Duty" provides the intended protection only when the cover is closed. For this reason, an "Extra Duty" wet location cover plate may also be marked "Wet Location Only When Cover Closed". Covers of wet location cover plates that are not marked "Extra Duty" (formerly referred to as weatherproof cover plates) cannot be closed when a plug is inserted into the receptacle; consequently, cover plates that are not marked "Extra Duty" should be installed only in damp or dry locations such as described in Rule 26-708 3) a) and b).

Δ

Figure B26-2
Covers for receptacles located outdoors

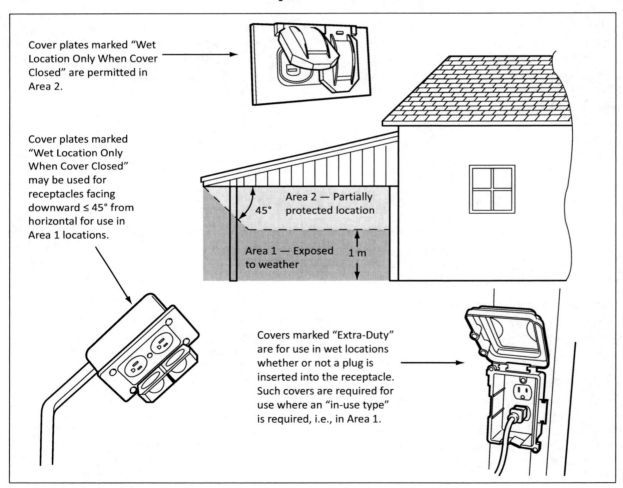

Cover plates marked "Wet Location Only When Cover Closed" are permitted in Area 2.

Cover plates marked "Wet Location Only When Cover Closed" may be used for receptacles facing downward ≤ 45° from horizontal for use in Area 1 locations.

Area 2 — Partially protected location

45°

Area 1 — Exposed to weather

1 m

Covers marked "Extra-Duty" are for use in wet locations whether or not a plug is inserted into the receptacle. Such covers are required for use where an "in-use type" is required, i.e., in Area 1.

Rule 26-710

The minimum distance of 7.5 m is intended to ensure that a standard 10 m long extension cord will reach the rooftop equipment. The minimum 750 mm clearance from the finished roof is intended to ensure that the receptacle remains visible in the event of snow buildup.

Some maintenance procedures may require that receptacles with a higher current or voltage rating be provided in addition to that specified in the Rule.

Rule 26-720 l)

For the purposes of this Subrule, the installation of the duct should be considered complete when enough duct has been installed to allow identification of the central vacuum unit location.

Rule 26-720 n)

It is intended by this requirement to recognize a need for additional electric vehicle charging infrastructure in residential occupancies only in those cases where such electric vehicle charging infrastructure is mandated by the provincial/territorial building codes or local building or zoning regulations.

Users of this Code should consult local building or zoning bylaws for electric vehicle charging infrastructure requirements and for the number of dedicated receptacles for electric vehicle charging equipment required as a percentage of the total parking spaces for cars in a residential occupancy.

Rule 26-722

It is the intent of this Subrule that all receptacles of residential occupancies installed outdoors and within 2.5 m of finished grade be protected by a Class A ground fault circuit interrupter. This includes receptacles located on buildings or structures associated with the residential occupancy, such as garages, carports, sheds, and receptacles on posts or fences, etc.

While its use is not precluded in such applications, this Rule is not intended to apply to receptacles located in parking lots of apartments that are installed solely for use as automobile heater receptacles.

Rule 26-724 a)

In laying out the location of receptacle outlets in residential premises, consideration should be given to the placement of electric baseboard heaters, hot air registers, and hot water or steam registers to avoid having cords pass over hot or conductive surfaces wherever possible.

Rule 26-724 d) iv) and v)

It is intended by these Items that a continuous counter surface is one that is not interrupted by sinks, ranges, and other built-in equipment.

Rule 26-724 d) v)

A peninsular countertop is measured from the connecting edge.

Rule 26-726 a)

For single dwellings of the detached, semi-detached, and row housing types, it is recommended that outdoor receptacles be placed at both the front and rear of the house and that these be controlled by a switch located inside the house.

Δ **Rule 26-744 10)**

Some permanently connected appliances are provided with multiple points of supply as permitted by the applicable safety Standard for electrical equipment and are marked accordingly.

Rule 26-804

The following are excerpts from CSA C22.2 No. 3:

> **4.8.5** The nominal supply voltage of a safety control circuit shall not exceed 120 V.

4.8.6 A safety control circuit intended to be supplied by a nominal 120 V branch circuit shall comply with the following:

a) the circuit shall not be grounded within the equipment;

b) the ungrounded conductor shall have an overcurrent protection device rated at not more than 125% of the current drawn by the circuit, except that this value may be increased because of inrush currents and ambient temperatures. These requirements shall apply only where the maximum current to the appliance exceeds 12 A and the safety controls are in series with the total load they control.

4.8.7 A safety control circuit supplied other than as specified in Clause 4.8.6, such as one supplied by a battery or a transformer, shall comply with the following:

a) it shall be a 2-wire circuit not exceeding 120 V;

b) one side of the circuit shall be grounded;

c) except for the condition specified in Item d), the ungrounded conductor shall have an overcurrent protection device rated at not more than 125% of the current drawn by the circuit, except that for circuits drawing currents up to and including 2 A the protection shall be rated at not more than 200%. These values may be increased because of inrush currents and ambient temperatures; and

d) a safety control circuit supplied by a Class 2 transformer shall not require overcurrent protection.

4.8.8 A safety control shall interrupt the current in the ungrounded conductor of the circuit between the overcurrent protection and the load.

4.8.9 Except for multiphase loads and circuits in which the load to be controlled exceeds the contact rating of the safety control*, safety controls that open an electrical circuit to the burner or to the shut-off device shall directly open the circuit regardless of whether the switching mechanism is integral with, or remote from, the sensing element.

* In these instances, the safety control may interrupt the coil circuit of a magnetic relay or contactor, which in turn directly opens the circuit to the burner or shut-off device.

The purpose of this requirement is to minimize the interposing of other controls in the safety control circuit, the failure of which might create an unsafe condition that the safety control is intended to prevent.

Rule 26-806 1)
Subrule 1) is intended to apply only to central heating equipment that does not use electricity as the source of heat. It is not intended to apply to electrical components of non-electric heating equipment such as water heaters, fireplace inserts, room heaters, or other similar auxiliary heating equipment that has electric auto-ignition, controls, or blower motors rated not more than 1/8 hp.

Section 28

Example to determine motor insulated conductors and protection
The following is a sample calculation for determining copper conductor size and overcurrent and overload protection for one 100 hp, one 30 hp, and two 7-1/2 hp motors, 575 V, three-phase, at full-voltage start.

Conductors
It is necessary to determine the motor full load currents, preferably from the motor nameplate, or from Table 44. Conductor sizes for the individual motors (see Rule 28-106 and Table 2) are as follows:

	100 hp	**30 hp**	**7-1/2 hp**
Full load current (from Table 44)	99 A	32 A	9 A
125% calculation	124 A	40 A	11 A
From Table 2			
75 °C insulated conductors	No. 1	No. 8	No. 14
90 °C insulated conductors	No. 1	No. 8	No. 14

Feeder insulated conductor ampacity [see Rule 28-108 1) a)]
Insulated conductor ampacity is calculated as 125% of 99 A plus 32 A plus 2 times 9 A equals 174 A for the four motors. Conductor size from Table 2 is No. 4/0 AWG for 60 °C insulated conductors and No. 2/0 AWG for 75 or 90 °C insulated conductors.

Protection
Overload protection
The maximum allowable setting of overload devices is determined from Rule 28-306. Assuming a 1.15 service factor, the ratings are 123.8 A for the 100 hp motor, 40 A for the 30 hp motor, and 11.3 A for the 7-1/2 hp motors.

Overcurrent protection
Branch circuit overcurrent protection for each motor is determined by using Rule 28-200. For the purpose of the motors described, use Rule 28-200 a) and Table 29. Listed below are actual currents with the standard size protector shown in brackets.

	100 hp	**30 hp**	**7-1/2 hp**
Time-delay fuse	99 × 175% = 174 A (150)	32 × 175% = 56 A (50)	9 × 175% = 15.8 A (15)
Non-time-delay fuse	99 × 300% = 297 A (250)	32 × 300% = 96 A (90)	9 × 300% = 27.0 A (25)
Δ Inverse-time circuit breaker	99 × 250% = 248 A (225)	32 × 250% = 80 A (80)	9 × 250% = 22.5 A (20)

Note that Table D16 may be used to select the size of overcurrent devices in accordance with Rule 28-200, where the full load current rating of the motor is shown in the Table.

Feeder overcurrent protection
The maximum allowable feeder overcurrent protection for motors is determined from Rule 28-204.

Using Rule 28-204 1), the ratings are as shown below, with the standard size shown in parentheses:

Time-delay fuse	174 + 32 + 9 + 9 = 224 A (200)
Non-time-delay fuse	297 + 32 + 9 + 9 = 347 A (300)
Inverse-time circuit breaker	248 + 32 + 9 + 9 = 298 A (250)

Figure B28-1
Circuits, control, and protective devices for motors

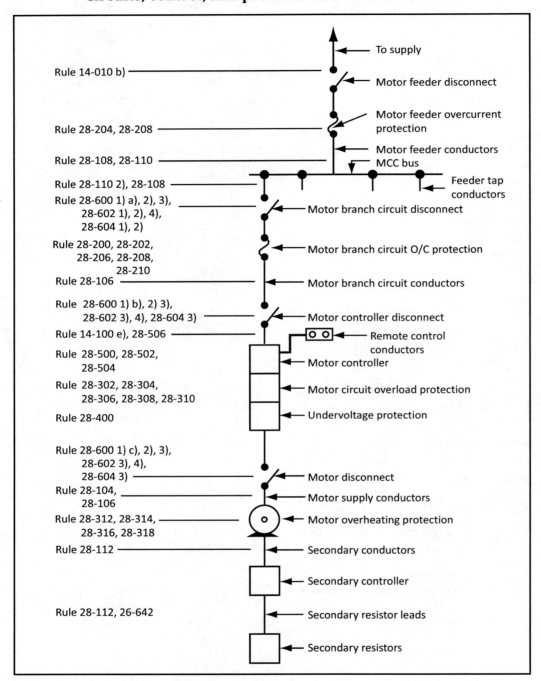

Rule 28-100

Where a motor is supplied by rigid conduit and is provided with noise or vibration damping, a flexible fitting installed between the motor terminal enclosure and the conduit will prevent damage to the conduit system due to vibration.

Δ **Rule 28-104**
Rule 4-006 does not apply to conductors terminating on motors because Rule 28-104 3) allows sizing of conductors for Class A motors based on a 90 °C conductor insulation rating. However, the Code user should be aware that the conductor termination temperature requirements of Rule 4-006 do apply to conductors that are terminated on supply or control equipment.

Rule 28-200 2) e)
In CSA C22.2 No. 14, a motor controller having non-replaceable or integral discriminating overload and short-circuit current sensors, and provided with one or more sets of contacts where the contacts cannot be isolated for separate testing, is considered to be a self-protected combination motor controller.

Rule 28-210
Instantaneous-trip circuit breakers are a magnetic-only trip device without time delay that may be provided with a dampening means to accommodate the transient motor inrush current.

Rule 28-210 a)
The intent of this Item is to allow an increase in the trip setting above 1300% for motors with high locked rotor currents that will trip on the asymmetrical inrush at the 1300% rating. For example, a motor with 800% locked rotor current would result in a trip setting of up to 1720% of full load current. Higher locked rotor currents are common in energy-efficient motors.

Rule 28-212
Power electronic devices such as adjustable speed drives (ASDs), variable frequency drives (VFDs), or solid-state contactors may be additionally protected by semiconductor fuses. These power electronic controllers are required to be approved with such fuses mounted integral to the device. Semiconductor fuses are components recognized in accordance with CAN/CSA-C22.2 No. 248.13 and provide short-circuit protection but may not provide overload protection.

Rule 28-304
There are several conditions that may create current imbalance in three-phase motor circuits of sufficient magnitude to overload one or more phase insulated conductors of the circuit. When the overload occurs in only one of the three insulated conductors, a current-sensitive element is necessary in each insulated conductor of the circuit to protect the motor against burnout, since two such elements will not protect it if the overload is in the third or unprotected insulated conductor. Among the conditions that may create this situation are

a)   single phasing in the primary of wye-delta or delta-wye connected transformers feeding the motors;

b)   a single-phase load taken from the same circuit that feeds the motor, where one of the phases feeding the single-phase load is open;

c)   a single-phase load fed from the same feeder that serves the motor, where the line drop is not negligible. No single-phase condition is necessary in this case to create current imbalance that may overload one phase of the motor; and

d)   a large and a small motor fed from the same feeder, in which single phasing occurs. The small motor may be damaged, since it attempts to act as a phase converter to maintain current balance in the larger motor.

Rule 28-306
The manufacturer's instructions should be consulted to determine how to match the trip setting or rating information to the motor full load current rating.

Rule 28-308 c)
The intent of this Item is to allow motors that are designed, constructed, certified to CSA C22.2 No. 77, and marked as impedance "ZP" and thermally "TP" protected motors to be installed without the overload protection that is required by Rule 28-300.

Rule 28-314
See the Note to Rules 18-106 and 28-314.

Rule 28-316
The abbreviations "TP" and "ZP" may be used for marking "Thermally Protected" and "Impedance Protected", respectively, on motors having less than 100 W input.

Rule 28-400
Upon the inspection of an installation, if it is the opinion of an inspector that automatic restarting of such motor-operated machinery as saws, routers, millers, wood and metal turning lathes, conveyors, or other moving machinery would create a hazard on return of voltage after stopping due to failure of voltage, the motor control device will be required to provide low-voltage protection.

Rule 28-602
A motor branch circuit disconnecting means is required to be located in close proximity to the branch circuit overcurrent device(s); therefore, the use of fused motor-circuit switches or circuit breakers is obvious. Unfused motor-circuit switches, moulded case switches, and instantaneous-trip circuit interrupters, etc., are often used in certain switchgear and control gear, along with a separate overcurrent or overload device(s), to meet this requirement.

Rule 28-602 1) d)
An approved combination motor controller, including a self-protected control device, is a type of equivalent device that is suitable for use as the motor branch circuit disconnecting means.

Rule 28-602 3) b)
The use of a manually operated across-the-line type of motor controller that serves as both a starter and disconnecting means is limited by Rule 28-602 3) b) to the following:

a) the manual across-the-line controller is part of an approved combination controller, motor control unit, or controller that also includes the overcurrent protection as required by Rules 28-200 and 28-202; or

b) the manual across-the-line controller is used on the load side of the branch circuit overcurrent protection.

A manual motor starter marked "Suitable for Motor Disconnect" is certified for use with overcurrent protection on the line side of the switch. Contact welding or other damage may result when overcurrent protection, located on the load side of the motor starter, opens (interrupts a fault current). Overcurrent devices, including those that may be integral to the equipment, are not intended to be installed on the load side of a manual motor starter that is marked "Suitable for Motor Disconnect".

Rule 28-900
The intent of this Rule is to provide disconnecting means that will completely disconnect a generator from all circuits supplied by the generator. It is not intended by this requirement to mandate installation of such disconnecting means if provided with a generator constructed in conformance with CSA C22.2 No. 100 or when the generator is part of an emergency power supply system conforming to CSA C282.

CSA C282 requires a disconnecting means and overcurrent protection for an emergency generator.

Section 30

Rule 30-002
Cabinet lighting system
The intent of this definition is to describe a complete, extra-low-voltage cabinet lighting system that is packaged by the manufacturer and intended for installation in accordance with the manufacturer's instructions.

Convertible luminaire
The following is the definition of a convertible luminaire as provided in CSA C22.2 No. 250.0:

> **Convertible luminaire** — a recessed luminaire that can be converted by the installer from a Type Non-IC to a Type IC or from a Type IC to a Type Non-IC recessed luminaire.

Undercabinet lighting system

The intent of this definition is to describe a complete, extra-low-voltage undercabinet lighting system that is packaged by the manufacturer and intended for installation in accordance with the manufacturer's instructions.

Rule 30-104

In the application of this Rule, mogul base includes Edison screw, end prong, extended end prong, side prong, bipost, and prefocus.

Rules 30-710 and 30-804

Manually operated general-use 347 V ac switches can be identified by their 347 V rating and the marking "AC ONLY". Those intended for use in a box are not interchangeable in their mounting centres with switches of other types. Boxes having mounting centres spaced 89.7 mm are required.

Rule 30-710 4) a)

Suitable markings meeting the intent of this Rule are "Electric-Discharge Lamp Control", where the contactor rating is expressed in amperes, or "HP", where the contactor rating is expressed in horsepower.

Where the contactor rating is expressed in horsepower, conversion to amperes can be effected by referring to the appropriate table in CSA C22.2 No. 14, the product Standard for contactors.

Rule 30-910 1)

Examples of insulated conductors other than insulated branch circuit conductors are

a)   through insulated conductors that pass directly through the supply junction box to feed other luminaires down the line; and

b)   remote ballast secondary circuit insulated conductors.

Rule 30-1000

Clause 15.1 of CSA C22.3 No. 7 addresses the grounding of poles under the authority of electric and communication utilities.

Δ   **Rules 30-1022 and 30-1024**

It is intended by these Rules that when a solidly grounded system is established at the secondary of transformer 2 (see Figure B30-1) to supply a floodlight circuit in accordance with Subrule 3) of Rule 30-1022, grounding of the solidly grounded system can be made by interconnection between the grounded circuit conductor of this system and the grounded circuit conductor at the primary of transformer 2, provided that the primary circuit grounded conductor is connected to ground at the supply transformer (transformer 1) where the solidly grounded system has been established.

Δ

Figure B30-1
Bonding and grounding — Permanent outdoor floodlighting installations

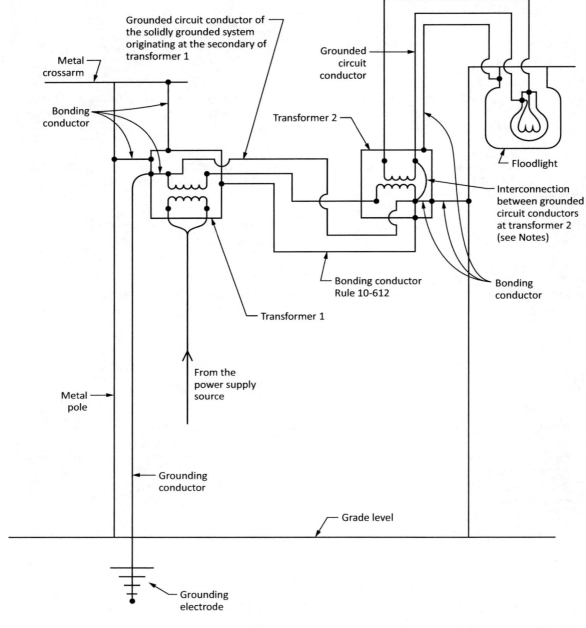

Notes:

1) *The primary of transformer 2 is supplied from the solidly grounded system derived at transformer 1.*

2) *The secondary of transformer 2 is a solidly grounded system established by interconnection with the solidly grounded system at transformer 1.*

Section 32

Rule 32-000
For further information pertaining to the installation of fire alarm systems, reference should be made to CAN/ULC-S524.

It is essential that fire alarm systems be maintained in an operating condition at all times. The inspection, maintenance, and testing procedures are detailed in the *National Fire Code of Canada* or the appropriate provincial fire code.

For further information pertaining to the installation of fire pumps, reference should be made to NFPA 20.

Rule 32-200
The intent of this Rule is to provide requirements for permanently connected smoke alarms and carbon monoxide alarms.

While the *National Building Code of Canada* requires that smoke alarms be permanently connected to an electrical circuit, it recognizes that a carbon monoxide alarm may be permanently connected to the electrical circuit or be supplied from batteries.

It is also the intent that 120 V smoke alarms conforming to CAN/ULC-S531 or 120 V carbon monoxide alarms conforming to CSA 6.19 be installed on a branch circuit that supplies lighting or a mix of lighting and receptacles in each dwelling unit and in each sleeping room that is not within a dwelling unit.

Rule 32-200 a)
It is not intended by this Rule to allow smoke alarms or carbon monoxide alarms to be installed in a branch circuit supplying receptacles only.

Δ **Rule 32-300**
The intent of this Rule is to protect the feeder conductors between a fire pump and an emergency power source from fire damage.

The *National Building Code of Canada* requires that conductors supplying life and fire safety equipment be protected against exposure to fire to ensure continued operation of this equipment for a period not less than 1 h.

NFPA 20 also mandates protection of circuits feeding fire pumps against possible damage by fire.

Specific requirements pertaining to the protection of conductors against exposure to fire can be found in Article 3.2.7.10 of the *National Building Code of Canada* or in the appropriate provincial/territorial legislation.

Rule 32-302
Consideration should be given to the location, routing, and design of wiring to minimize hazards that might cause failure due to explosions, floods, fires, icing, vandalism, and other adverse external conditions that might impair the function of a fire pump.

Δ **Rule 32-306**
The intent of this Rule is to allow only a circuit breaker lockable in the closed position and identified as the fire pump disconnecting means to be installed upstream from the fire pump controller in a normal power supply circuit, or upstream from the fire pump transfer switch in an emergency power supply circuit. This Rule also allows for the possibility of this circuit breaker being used in the fire pump service box described in Rule 32-304.

This Rule requires that an overcurrent protective device for a fire pump be set to enable uninterrupted operation under fire pump starting conditions. Such overcurrent protective devices are installed upstream from the fire pump controller or the fire pump transfer switch and must have this capability whether they form part of the normal power supply feeder or the emergency power supply feeder.

Fire pump locked rotor currents are typically not less than 500% of the full load current, and fire pump suppliers should be consulted to determine the specific locked rotor current of a fire pump selected for a specific installation. The overcurrent device settings described in Subrule 4) should be able to carry the locked rotor current indefinitely, as required by NFPA 20. The overcurrent device settings described in Subrule 5) should be coordinated with the integral overcurrent protection of the fire pump controller or the transfer switch in such a manner that upstream overcurrent devices will not disconnect the circuit prior to the operation of the controller/fire pump transfer switch overcurrent protection.

The intent of Subrule 6) is to recognize that NFPA 20 allows for the generator main circuit breaker to be bypassed by a direct connection between the emergency supply feeder and the fire pump transfer switch. This permission removes the requirement for coordination between the generator main circuit breaker and the fire pump feeder circuit breaker as required by Rule 46-208 1).

It should also be noted that NFPA 20 requires that the circuit breaker in the controller or in the transfer switch must have an instantaneous-trip setting of not more than 20 times the full load current. NFPA 20 also requires that the overcurrent device in a fire pump controller or in a fire pump transfer switch must carry a minimum of 300% of the fire pump full load current for a period of 8 to 20 s.

Rule 32-312
For the purpose of this Rule, a fire pump circuit is defined as the circuit supplied from the emergency power source referred to in Rule 32-300, or the circuit supplied from a separate service box for fire pump equipment in accordance with Rule 32-304.

Section 34

Rule 34-200
The enclosure should be constructed to prevent the emission of flames or any burning or ignited material. Openings for ventilation should be arranged to be at least 100 mm from live parts.

Metal sign enclosures should be not less than 0.68 mm thick (22 MSG). At the point where it is intended that the supply connections be made, the sign enclosure should be not less than 1.34 mm thick (16 MSG). Each enclosure housing a neon supply, transformer, or other components should be marked in accordance with the requirements of Section 2.

For neon supplies, the enclosure volume should be three times the volume of the transformer and/or internal box.

Section 36

Rule 36-000 4)
Gas-filled high-voltage switchgear and control gear enclosures may not be subject to regulation or inspection by local boiler and pressure vessel authorities. Equipment owners and electrical inspectors should be cognizant of such circumstances and take the necessary precautions to ensure the installation of safe and reliable equipment. Compliance with the following manufacturing Standards for the design, construction, testing, inspection, and certification of enclosures is recommended:

CAN/CSA-C50052, *Cast Aluminium Alloy Enclosures for Gas-Filled High-Voltage Switchgear and Controlgear* (adopted EN 50052 (1986) with Canadian deviations);

CAN/CSA-C50064, *Wrought Aluminium and Aluminium Alloy Enclosures for Gas-Filled High-Voltage Switchgear and Controlgear* (adopted EN 50064 (1989) with Canadian deviations);

CAN/CSA-C50068, *Wrought Steel Enclosures for Gas-Filled High-Voltage Switchgear and Controlgear* (adopted EN 50068 (1991) with Canadian deviations);

CAN/CSA-C50069, *Welded Composite Enclosures of Cast and Wrought Aluminium Alloys for Gas-Filled High-Voltage Switchgear and Controlgear* (adopted EN 50069 (1991) with Canadian deviations);

CAN/CSA-C50089, *Cast Resin Partitions for Metal-Enclosed Gas-Filled High-Voltage Switchgear and Controlgear* (adopted EN 50089 (1992) with Canadian deviations);

CAN/CSA-C62155, *Hollow Pressurized and Unpressurized Ceramic and Glass Insulators for Use in Electrical Equipment with Rated Voltages Greater Than 1000 V* (adopted CEI/IEC 62155 (2003) with Canadian deviations).

Rule 36-006 1)

For a small access gate intended for foot traffic, a warning notice should typically be mounted on the gate. For a large vehicle access gate that may remain open for periods of time during construction work, consideration should be given to mounting the warning notice on the station fence adjacent to the gate lock for improved visibility under all situations.

Rule 36-100 4)

The marking must be designed to draw attention to the location and nature of the embedded equipment; it also must be indelible and easily legible through the use of such materials as metal markers and dye markings.

Rule 36-104

Any fabric tape, semi-conducting or otherwise, over the insulation should be removed completely with the metal shielding and the surface of the insulation thoroughly cleaned to remove any current-carrying residue. At all terminations and joints, stress cones should be made and adequate leakage distance provided from bare live parts. Electrical continuity of the metal shielding should be maintained across insulated joints.

Grounding should be effected at several convenient points if possible. The manufacturer's instructions and kits, if necessary, should be made available with each order of shielded cable to ensure proper installation.

Rules 36-300 and 36-308 and Table 51

The conductor sizes shown in Table 51 are the minimum required to prevent conductor damage due to heating of the conductor.

Precautions should be taken where other factors are to be considered, particularly the intended application and class of use. Reference to IEEE 80, IEEE 837, and CSA C22.2 No. 41 may be necessary to select appropriate devices and material. Special attention should be paid to downleads, as they may be subjected to the total fault current passed into the grid.

Rule 36-302 1) a)

Grounding rods are manufactured and certified to CSA C22.2 No. 41. It is intended by this Item that the designer of the station ground electrode will verify for each installation that the selected diameter and length of the ground rod are sufficient in order to comply with Rule 36-304.

The diameter may vary depending on the material chosen. The minimum diameter and length values should be used in preference to nominal values in the validation of compliance.

Δ Rule 36-302 2)

Any station grounding system that has been designed in a manner other than as required by these Rules should be documented and signed by an engineer in addition to being subject to acceptance in accordance with Rule 2-030.

Rule 36-302 6)

IEEE 80 should be consulted for conductor sizing to prevent thermal damage to the rebar during fault conditions.

Rule 36-304 3)
The procedure specified in this Subrule for a station ground electrode design can be found in CEA 249 D 541.

Rule 36-308
See the Note to Rule 36-300.

Rule 36-308 6)
For solidly grounded systems, the size of the transformer secondary grounding conductor should be not less than No. 2/0 AWG. Where a neutral resistance or impedance grounding device is used, grounding conductors may be sized in accordance with Rule 10-308.

Section 38

Rule 38-001
For further information, see
a)   ASME A17.1/CSA B44, *Safety Code for Elevators and Escalators*;
b)   CSA B44.1/ASME A17.5, *Elevator and Escalator Electrical Equipment*;
c)   CSA B355, *Lifts for Persons With Physical Disabilities*; and
d)   CAN/CSA-B613 (withdrawn), *Private Residence Lifts for Persons With Physical Disabilities*.

Rule 38-002
The control system hardware is permitted to be located in a single enclosure or a combination of enclosures, including the separate functions of motor control, motion control, and operational control.

Rule 38-003
See CSA B44.1/ASME A17.5 for voltage limitations within equipment.

Rule 38-013
The heating of conductors depends on rms current values, which, with generator field control, are reflected by the nameplate current rating of the motor-generator driving motor rather than by the rating of the driving machine motor, which represents actual but short-time and intermittent full load current values.

Rule 38-013 2) a)
Driving machine motor currents, or those of similar functions, are permitted to exceed the nameplate value, but since they are inherently intermittent duty, and the heating of the motor and conductors is dependent on the rms current value, conductors are sized for duty cycle service as required by Rule 28-106 and Table 27.

Rule 38-013 2) b)
The motor controller nameplate current rating is permitted to be derived based on the rms value of the motor current using an intermittent duty cycle and other control system loads, if applicable.

Rule 38-013 2) c)
The nameplate current rating of a power transformer supplying a motor controller reflects the nameplate current rating of the motor controller at line voltage (transformer primary).

Rule 38-021 1) a) ii), 2) a), and 3) a)
Only electrical protective devices as required by ASME A17.1/CSA B44 and CSA B355 are recognized as devices that can introduce a direct life hazard. (See Rule 16-010.)

If a life hazard can occur, Class 2 cables are not permitted. Cables suitable for Class 1 extra-low-voltage circuits are permitted, such as communication cable, fire alarm and signal cable, multi-conductor jacketed thermoplastic-insulated cable, and hard-usage and extra-hard-usage cable (see Table 19).

Rule 38-023
See ASME A17.1/CSA B44 and CSA B355 for illumination levels.

It is not intended that devices that have machine or control spaces incorporated within the equipment, e.g., stair chairlifts that have the machine built into the chair housing, need to have separate lighting and receptacles within that space (housing).

Rule 38-024
See ASME A17.1/CSA B44 for illumination levels.

Rule 38-041
Unsupported length for the hoistway suspension means is the length of cable measured from the point of suspension in the hoistway to the bottom of the loop, with the elevator car located at the bottom landing. Unsupported length for the car suspension means is the length of cable measured from the point of suspension on the car to the bottom of the loop, with the elevator car located at the top landing.

Rule 38-051
In order to completely isolate all control conductors in the circuits to a machine operating as one of a group, it is necessary to disconnect all the selector or programming circuitry, thereby taking all the other cars out of service. Not only is it impractical to shut down all cars in order to service one, it is often necessary to locate troubles by checking the performance of components with the controller energized. Where undue shock hazards might exist, the enforcing authority may require the provision of cautions or warning labels pertaining thereto.

Rule 38-091 1)
The elevator must operate on such emergency power in accordance with the emergency power system requirements of ASME A17.1/CSA B44. For additional information, see ASME A17.1/CSA B44, Section 2.27.2.

Section 40

Rule 40-020 2)
An access catwalk, designed for crane operators and maintenance trades personnel to access a crane for operation, maintenance, and repair, is considered a working surface.

Rule 40-024 1)
In the case of equipment supplied by contact conductors, metal-to-metal contact between wheels and tracks may constitute effective grounding when a low impedance grounding path is ensured. Where local conditions, such as paint or other insulating material, prevent reliable metal-to-metal contact between wheels and tracks, a separate bonding conductor must be provided for bonding to ground.

Section 46

Rule 46-000
This Section is intended to apply to the installation, operation, and maintenance of emergency power supplies, such as batteries or generators, that are required by the *National Building Code of Canada* to provide emergency power for the operation of life safety systems.

This Section is also intended to govern wiring methods between the emergency power supply and emergency lights, exits signs, or life safety systems where the emergency power supply, emergency lights, exit signs, or life safety systems are mandated by the *National Building Code of Canada*.

This Section is not intended to prohibit connection of loads other than the *National Building Code of Canada* required emergency lights, exit signs, or life safety systems to the emergency power system mandated by the *National Building Code of Canada*, provided that all applicable requirements for wiring methods described in this Section are met.

Rule 46-002

The intent of this Rule is to correlate the special terminology of this Section with the descriptions in the *National Building Code of Canada* of an emergency power supply and life safety systems (see Subsection 3.2.7 of the *National Building Code of Canada*).

Rule 46-108

Reference should be made to the *National Building Code of Canada* or the appropriate sections of the provincial building codes to obtain additional requirements for the fire protection of electrical insulated conductors and cables used in conjunction with emergency equipment (see Section 3.2.6 of the *National Building Code of Canada*).

Rule 46-108 4)

The intent of this Subrule is to keep the wiring between the *National Building Code of Canada* required emergency power supply and the *National Building Code of Canada* required electrically connected exit signs or life safety systems entirely independent of all other wiring, including wiring to other loads that are connected to the emergency power supply.

Rule 46-108 5)

The intent of this Subrule is to keep the wiring between the *National Building Code of Canada* required emergency power supply and life safety systems entirely independent of all wiring to other loads that are connected to the emergency power supply, except where necessary in enclosures for splitters that are provided for connection between the emergency power supply overcurrent device and

a) a separate disconnecting means and overcurrent device for a feeder supplying a transfer switch for equipment that does not fall within the definition of "life safety systems" in this Section;

b) a separate circuit breaker for a feeder supplying a fire pump transfer switch in conformance with Rules 32-306 4) and 32-308; and

c) except for a fire pump circuit breaker, a separate disconnecting means and the overcurrent device for a feeder supplying a transfer switch for equipment that falls within the definition of "life safety systems" in this Section. See Figure B46-1.

Figure B46-1

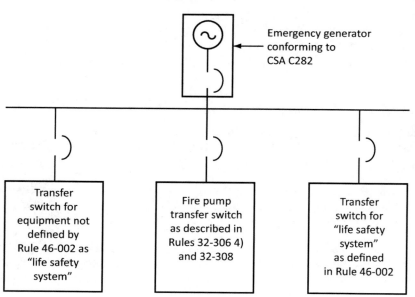

Emergency generator conforming to CSA C282

Transfer switch for equipment not defined by Rule 46-002 as "life safety system"

Fire pump transfer switch as described in Rules 32-306 4) and 32-308

Transfer switch for "life safety system" as defined in Rule 46-002

Rule 46-200

For additional requirements regarding the location and fire protection of emergency power supplies, reference should be made to Sections 3.2.7 and 3.6.2 of the *National Building Code of Canada* or to the appropriate provincial/territorial legislation.

Δ **Rule 46-202**

It is intended by this Rule that when batteries are used as an emergency power supply source for emergency lighting or for internally illuminated exit signs, a central power system conforming to CSA C22.2 No. 141 should be used.

Rule 46-204

The intent of this Rule is to protect electrical conductors and cables between an emergency generator and associated electrical equipment, such as the transfer switch(es), bypass switch(es), engine control panel, etc., required to be installed as a part of the emergency power supply and located outside the generator room against exposure to fire for a period not less than 1 h. The *National Building Code of Canada* requires that electrical conductors and cables supplying life and fire safety equipment be protected against such exposure. CSA C282 also mandates protection of circuits interconnecting field-installed equipment forming part of an emergency generator against possible damage by fire.

The following examples illustrate acceptable methods for achieving this protection:

a) using mineral-insulated cables conforming to fire rating requirements as specified in Clause 6.3 of CSA C22.2 No. 124 or other cables that comply with the ULC S139 circuit integrity test and are marked "S139" and "2 h CIR";

b) embedding the raceway containing conductors between an emergency generator and associated equipment in concrete with a thickness sufficient to provide protection of electrical conductors from fire exposure for a period of at least 1 h in compliance with the *National Building Code of Canada*; or

c) installing the raceway containing insulated conductors between an emergency generator and associated equipment in a shaft enclosure or service space of at least 1 h fire resistance construction.

Rule 46-300

CSA C22.2 No. 141 defines unit equipment for emergency lighting as follows:

Unit equipment for emergency lighting means equipment that

a) is intended to provide automatically, in response to a failure of the power supply to which it is connected, a specified light output and a specified amount of power for illumination purposes, for a specified period of time, but in any case not less than 30 min;

b) comprises in a unit construction
   i)   a storage battery;
   ii) a charging means to maintain the battery in a charged condition;
   iii) lamps or output terminals to which specifically listed lamps can be connected;
   iv) a means to energize the lamps when the normal power supply fails and to de-energize the lamps when the normal power supply is restored; and
   v)   a means to indicate and test the operating condition of the equipment;

c) is designed for use in applications in which the provision of emergency illumination is required by a governmental or other agency having jurisdiction; and

d) has a maximum capacity of 1.44 kW.

Unit equipment certified to CSA C22.2 No. 141 is required to be marked in accordance with Clause 6.9 of that Standard with the following or equivalent wording:

CSA C22.2 No. 141, EMERGENCY LIGHTING EQUIPMENT

and

CSA C22.2 n° 141, APPAREIL D'ÉCLAIRAGE DE SECOURS

Unit equipment is not to be confused with other emergency lighting equipment certified by CSA as emergency lighting units. Such emergency lighting units do not bear the above marking but are marked "ELECTRICAL ONLY" and "CERTIFIÉ DU POINT DE VUE ÉLECTRIQUE SEULEMENT", adjacent to the CSA mark.

Rule 46-306 1)
Where approved unit equipment includes a list of lamps suitable for remote installations, the requirements of CSA C22.2 No. 141 take into account a voltage drop of 5% in the remote lamp's circuit unless the list specifies that certain lamps conform to the requirements with a greater voltage drop.

Table D4 can be used to determine approximate permissible circuit lengths.

Rule 46-306 2)
The requirements of CSA C22.2 No. 141 are designed to ensure that any lamps forming part of the equipment, or specified in a list provided with the equipment as suitable for remote connection, will not exhibit an undue diminution of light intensity during the emergency period.

Rule 46-400
This Rule applies to exit signs containing electrically connected luminaires (internally illuminated exit signs) and to luminaires used to illuminate exit signs not directly connected to an electrical circuit (externally illuminated exit signs). It is intended by this Rule that each electrically connected exit sign represents approved electrical equipment conforming to CSA C22.2 No. 141.

It is also intended by this Rule that where an externally illuminated exit sign is installed in accordance with Article 3.4.5.1 of the *National Building Code of Canada*, circuitry serving lighting used to illuminate such externally illuminated exit signs is installed in compliance with Subrules 1) and 3).

Rule 46-400 2)
The circuit supplying emergency lighting could be ac or dc. The *National Building Code of Canada* requires that exit signs be illuminated continuously. Caution should be taken to ensure that a circuit supplying both emergency lighting and exit signs is not controlled by a switch, time clock, or other means.

Section 54

Rule 54-004
A community antenna distribution system consists of a coaxial cable wiring system for the purpose of distributing radio and television frequency signals to and within premises. This distribution system is commonly known as a community antenna television or cable TV (CATV) system. Where other than a coaxial cable wiring system is employed, the requirements of Section 56 or 60 prevail.

Rule 54-102
Figure B54-1 illustrates typical installations covered by this Rule.

Figure B54-1
Rule 54-102 — Typical installations

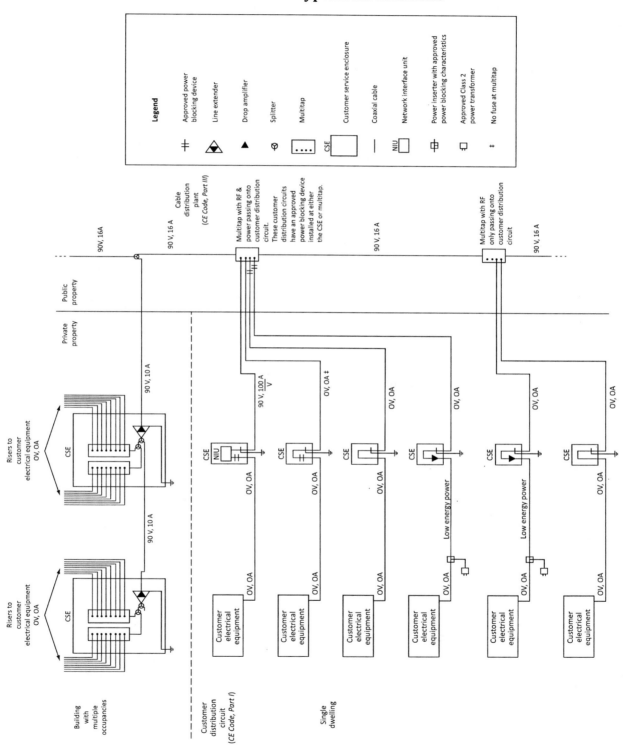

Appendix B

Rule 54-200 1)

The point at which the exposed conductors enter a building is considered to be the point of emergence through an exterior wall, a concrete floor slab, or from a totally enclosed non-combustible entrance raceway.

Rule 54-202 b)

The point of cable entry into a building is considered to be the point of emergence through an exterior wall, through a concrete floor slab, or from a totally enclosed non-combustible entrance raceway.

Section 56

Rules 56-200 1) and 56-202 1)

The intent of Rules 56-200 1) and 56-202 1) is to allow installation of non-conductive and conductive optical fiber cables in raceways, including cable trays, provided that the other requirements in Section 56 are met and such cables are listed in Table 19.

Rule 56-208

Where hybrid cables are installed in a vertical shaft, they should be located in a totally enclosed non-combustible raceway, as these cables are classed as electrical cables in conformance with Rule 56-204 2).

Conductive and non-conductive cables should be allowed to be installed in a vertical shaft of a building of combustible or non-combustible construction without a totally enclosed non-combustible raceway, provided that these cables will meet the flame spread requirements for buildings of non-combustible construction. CSA marking for wires and cables meeting the flame spread requirements for the *National Building Code of Canada* for installation in buildings of non-combustible construction is FT4.

Rule 56-214

The point at which the exposed conductive optical fiber cables enter a building is considered to be the point of emergence through an exterior wall, through a concrete floor slab, or from a totally enclosed non-combustible entrance raceway.

Section 58

Rule 58-000

For further information, consult the following:
a)   CSA Z98, *Passenger Ropeways and Passenger Conveyors*;
b)   ANSI B77.1, *Passenger Ropeways — Aerial Tramways, Aerial Lifts, Surface Lifts, Tows and Conveyors — Safety Standard*; and
c)   CSA C22.3 No. 1, *Overhead Systems*.

Rule 58-300

See Rules 28-312 and 28-400.

Section 60

Rule 60-000

Communication circuits are designed primarily to carry information or signals in the form of audio, video, or data and may also transmit signals for supervision and control. Generally these circuits operate within the line-to-ground current and voltage limitations established for Class 2 circuits as described in Rule 16-200.

Rule 60-104

A communication building entrance cable is deemed to be the cable that enters into a building to provide the main incoming communication circuits from other external buildings, telephone central offices, or similar locations, and that terminates at the point of building entrance (see the Note to Rule 60-700 for point of entrance).

Rule 60-200 2)

The point at which the exposed conductors enter a building is considered to be the point of emergence through an exterior wall, through a concrete floor slab, or from a totally enclosed non-combustible entrance raceway.

Rule 60-204

These circuits are subject to high ground potential rises and/or electromagnetic induction from faults of high-voltage power lines terminating at the power station. This could cause extraneous cable stresses and transfer of ground potential rises and propagation of hazardous electrical surges to equipment or personnel. ANSI/IEEE 487 should be used as the reference in providing protection for communication circuits in high-voltage stations.

Rule 60-402

Connecting blocks of a non-protective type are deemed to be those that provide for an electrical connection only and that do not provide protection as required by Rules 60-200 and 60-202.

Rule 60-700

The point of cable entry into a building is considered to be the point of emergence through an exterior wall, through a concrete floor slab, or from a totally enclosed non-combustible entrance raceway.

Rule 60-702

It is the intent of this Rule that where a conductor is installed to exclusively bond to ground the entrance cable sheath, the maximum required size is No. 6 AWG copper. However, where the conductor will also function as a common bonding conductor for other equipment, a larger gauge size may be required.

Rule 60-704 c)

The wave front of a lightning surge has a rise time in the order of microseconds and is approximated by equivalent frequencies between 25 and 250 kHz. As a result, the self-impedance of the grounding conductor to the wave front of a lightning surge is very significant. For this reason it is paramount to keep the length of the grounding conductor as short as practicable to guarantee the effectiveness of the protector. As a guideline, it is suggested that the length of the grounding conductor be limited to 6 m maximum.

Rule 60-706

It is intended that the grounding electrode for power circuits be the common point of any multi-bonding with other grounding electrodes.

Section 62

Rule 62-000
Space heating

Space heating is the application of any fixed heater technology that results in adding heat to an enclosed space or room. This is normally for increasing the comfort of persons or animals but could include storage spaces or rooms where it is important to keep stored material above a certain temperature. Some examples of space heating are

a)   central heating units;

b)   baseboard heaters;

c)   radiant heaters;

d)   wall and ceiling heaters; and

e)   floor warming heaters (the primary purpose of a floor warming heater may be for comfort of persons walking on the floor, but such heaters also add heat to the room)

Note: *Many heater technologies add heat to a room by convection, conduction, and radiation.*

Surface heating

Surface heating is the application of fixed heater technology that results in increasing the temperature of a surface. Some examples of surface heating are

a)   pipe heating;

b)   storage tank or vessel heating; and

c)   snow and/or ice melting on or embedded in a surface, such as on roofs and gutters or embedded in concrete, asphalt or soil, and similar applications.

Other heating systems

Other heating systems are applications of fixed heaters that are not space or surface heating systems. Some examples of these systems are

a)   pipe internal heaters, often referred to as "gut" heating;

b)   immersion heaters; and

c)   hot water tanks.

Δ   **Rule 62-102**

The term "heating cable" is being replaced in product Standards and International Standards (CSA, IEEE, IEC) with "trace heater".

Dielectric heating

The operating principle behind dielectric heating is that when an insulating material is placed within a high-frequency electrical field, molecules are excited by the alternating electric field, causing heating within the material. The frequency applied is generally between 1 and 300 MHz, and depends on the material to be heated. This is sometimes called capacitive or radio frequency (RF) heating.

Impedance heating

The operating principle behind impedance heating is that an applied ac voltage on an electrically conductive object to be heated will generate a current in that object, resulting in direct Joule (I^2R, sometimes called resistive or ohmic) heating within the object itself. There is also some additional heat generated due to impedance effects of eddy currents and hysteresis losses.

Note: *Impedance heating was called pipeline resistance heating in previous editions of this Code.*

Induction heating

The operating principle behind induction heating is that a coil of conductors surrounding an electrically conductive object or running parallel to it creates magnetic-flux-induced currents in that object and results in direct Joule (I^2R, sometimes called resistive or ohmic) heating of the object itself. Eddy currents and hysteresis losses will add to the heat generated. Induction heating is generally applied at line frequencies for surface heating of pipelines and vessels (see Rule 62-300), and at higher frequencies for heating objects and materials, e.g., in aluminum smelting or induction welding (see Rules 62-400 to 62-408).

Skin effect trace heating

The operating principle behind skin effect trace heating is that an applied ac voltage will generate a current in a conductor that returns along the inner skin of a surrounding ferromagnetic envelope (heat tube). The concentration of the return current on the inner surface of the heat tube is due to the magnetic field associated with the current flow through the inner conductor. This has the effect of increasing the electrical resistance of the heat tube, thereby creating direct Joule (I^2R, sometimes called resistive or ohmic) heating.

Table B62-1
Usage marking of heating devices and cross-references to Table 60 of the *Canadian Electrical Code, Part I* (18th edition, 1998) — Heating cable set type designations and applications

Usage marking and usage		Weather resistance	Wet location applications	Wet location under pressure	Previous type designations and applications
No usage mark or G	General use	No	No	No	1A — Ceiling 1B — Floor embedded in concrete (if dry location) 3A, 3C, 5A — Dry and damp location external pipe or vessel tracing
S	With weather resistance	Yes	No	No	All applications where a degree of weather resistance is required, including damp locations. (No previous equivalent.)
W	With wet rating	No	Yes	No	2A — Soil heating 2B — Snow melting and floor embedded in concrete (wet location) 2C — Animal pens 2D — Pool decks 3B, 3D, 5B — Wet location pipe and vessel surface heating 4A, 4B — Pipe interior heating systems (unpressurized applications)
P	With wet/ pressure test	No	Yes	Yes	4A, 4B — Pipe interior heating systems
WS	With wet test and weather resistance	Yes	Yes	No	2E — Roof de-icing
PS	With wet/ pressure test and weather resistance	Yes	Yes	Yes	4A, 4B — Pipe interior heating systems
X*	Specially investigated heating device or heating device set	—	—	—	e.g., 2C — Animal pens 4A, 4B — Pipe interior heating in potable water applications where mechanical abuse is very unlikely, allowing for lower mechanical test levels

* X indicates additional requirements and/or exemptions for specific applications. The manufacturer's instructions must include a complete explanation of these additional requirements or exemptions.

Rules 62-102 and 62-116
For fixed infrared radiant heaters of the metal-sheath glowing element type, CSA C22.2 No. 46 requires that a specific marking be used. Clause 6.1.24 of CSA C22.2 No. 46 reads as follows:

When permanently connected radiant-type heaters employ a metal-sheathed heater element, and the visible portion of the element attains a temperature of at least 650 °C under normal operating conditions, the heaters shall be permanently marked with the following or equivalent:

CAUTION: METAL-SHEATH ELEMENT-TYPE RADIANT HEATER. CONNECT ONLY TO A CIRCUIT PROTECTED BY SUITABLE GROUND-FAULT PROTECTION.

and

ATTENTION : RADIATEUR À UNITÉ DE CHAUFFE SOUS GAINE MÉTALLIQUE. RACCORDER UNIQUEMENT À UN CIRCUIT PROTÉGÉ PAR UN DISJONCTEUR APPROPRIÉ.

Rule 62-104 1)
Manufacturers' instructions are incorporated into the *Canadian Electrical Code, Part II* certification process for heating equipment and form an important part of the overall safety of the final installation.

Δ Rule 62-106
The purpose of this Rule is to ensure that heating devices are marked for the environment for which they are installed. Wet conditions include areas where heating devices are installed in concrete slabs or other masonry in direct contact with moist earth, or in slabs complete with drains such as showers, where measures to isolate the area from moisture have not been installed. Concrete floors exposed to periodic hosing down or rain (such as might occur at loading docks) should be considered wet locations.

Rule 62-108 4)
Where a tap conductor is installed to ensure that the conductor terminating to a heating device set meets the conductor temperature rating specified by the manufacturer, the tap conductor needs to be of a sufficient length to dissipate the heat generated by the heating device.

Rule 62-114
See the Note to Rules 8-104 and 62-114.

Rule 62-116 1)
The intent of the "ground fault setting sufficient to allow normal operation of the heater" is that the setting should be as low as practical to allow start-up and running of the heater without nuisance trips, yet still providing ground fault protection for the equipment and supply conductors. For many systems, this would be a fixed trip 30 mA ground fault protection device. For higher leakage current circuits, the trip level for adjustable devices is typically set at 30 mA above any inherent capacitive leakage current. If a fixed trip ground fault protection device is to be used, it should be selected to meet this intent.

Rule 62-126
Splicing, modification, or assembly of series heat tracing cables in the field should be done only by trained personnel. Design of series heat tracing cables should be done by persons qualified to do so. This Rule recognizes the ability of a qualified person, using the manufacturer's design tools, to do similar design to that normally done by the manufacturer. Owners of industrial establishments are responsible for ensuring that persons undertaking work outlined in this Rule are properly qualified.

Rule 62-128
Subrule 2) requires that Section 12 be followed for conductors used as non-heating leads that are not factory built or factory supplied.

The intent of Subrule 4) is to allow a small gap from the end of the raceway to the wooden base plate, as it is impractical to terminate the raceway at the wooden base plate or to continue it through the wooden base plate.

Δ Rules 62-200 2) and 62-212
The following table (reproduced from CSA C22.2 No. 130) provides maximum temperatures for different materials and lists sources of these data. It forms the basis for the clearance limits specified in Table 67.

Δ

Table E.1 from CSA C22.2 No. 130
Maximum temperatures as applicable

Location		Maximum temperature, °C
1	At any point on or within a supply terminal box	Manufacturer's declared maximum temperature of the supply terminal box and connected branch circuit wiring
2	On heating device envelope or overall sheath	Manufacturer's declared maximum temperature of the material
3	On combustible material	90 °C, in accordance with CE Code, Section 62
4	On non-combustible materials other than concrete	Manufacturer's declared maximum temperature of the heating device or the material, whichever is lower
5	On or in concrete	150 °C, in accordance with CE Code, Section 62
6	On non-metallic enclosures	Manufacturer's declared maximum temperature of the material
7	On the exposed surface of floor covering	43 °C, in accordance with ASTM C1055
8	On the exposed surface of wall covering below 1.8 m	43 °C, in accordance with ASTM C1055
9	On the exposed surface of gypsum wall covering above 1.8 m	52 °C, in accordance with ASTM C1055, IEC Guide 117, and CAN/CSA-C22.2 No. 61010-1
10	On the exposed surface of gypsum ceiling covering	52 °C, in accordance with ASTM C1055, IEC Guide 117, and CAN/CSA-C22.2 No. 61010-1
11	On non-heating leads/ trace heater and terminations or trace heater	Manufacturer's declared maximum temperature of the component

Figures B62-1 to B62-5 provide examples of heater minimum installation clearance distances to clarify the requirements specified in Table 67.

Appendix B

Figure B62-1

Table 67 clearances — Elevated ceiling heating arrangement

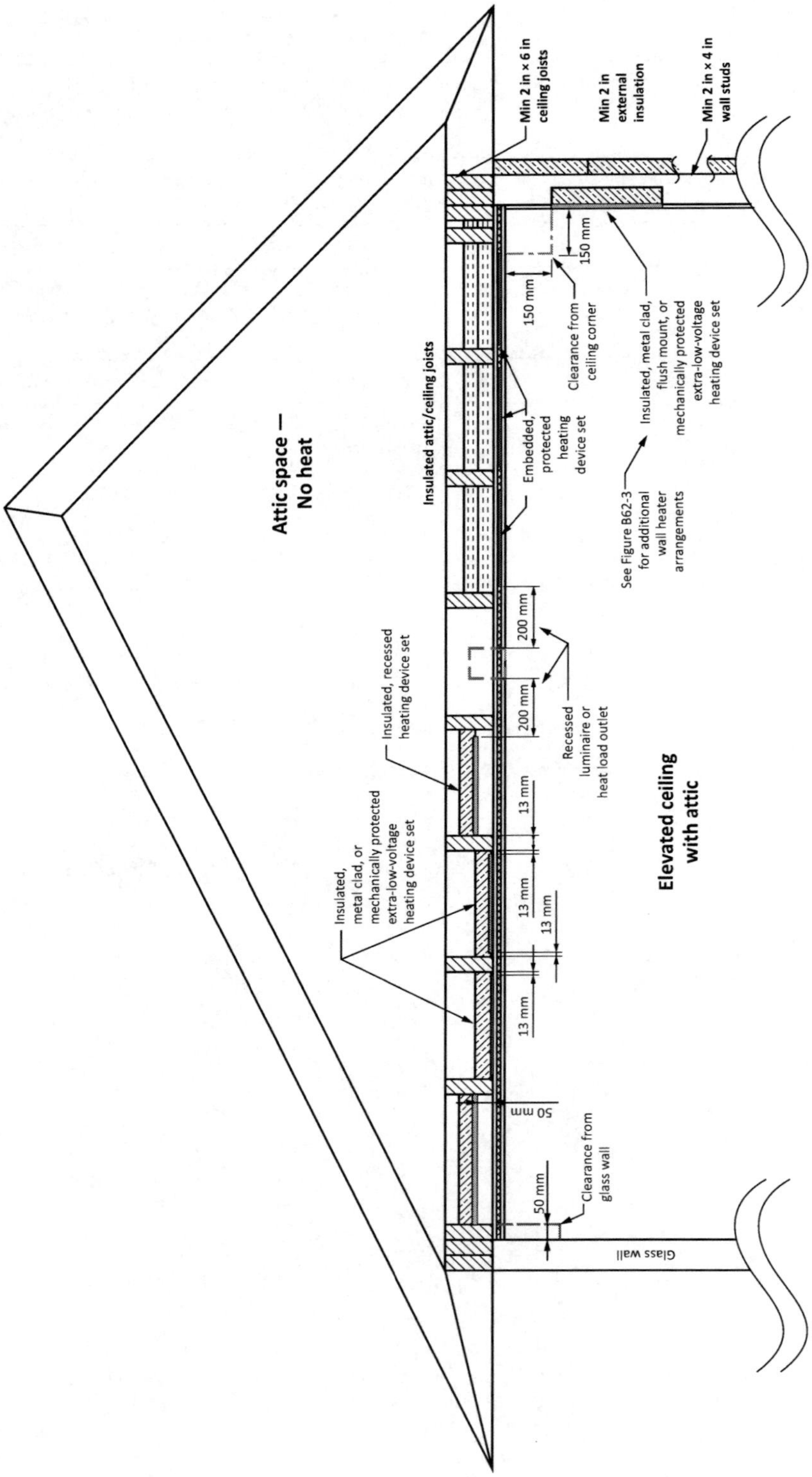

Appendix B

Figure B62-2

Table 67 clearances — Vaulted ceiling heating arrangement

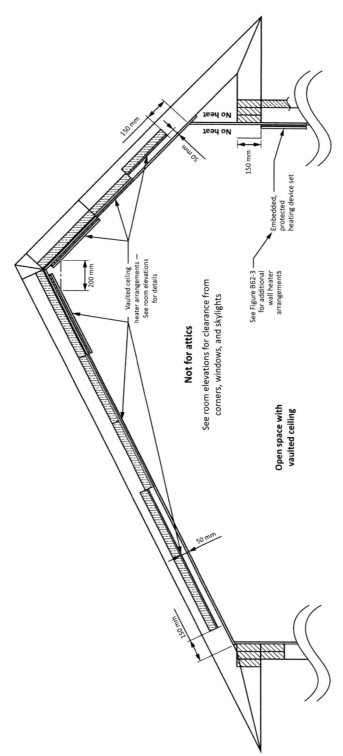

Figure B62-3
Table 67 clearances — Elevated floor and wall heating arrangements

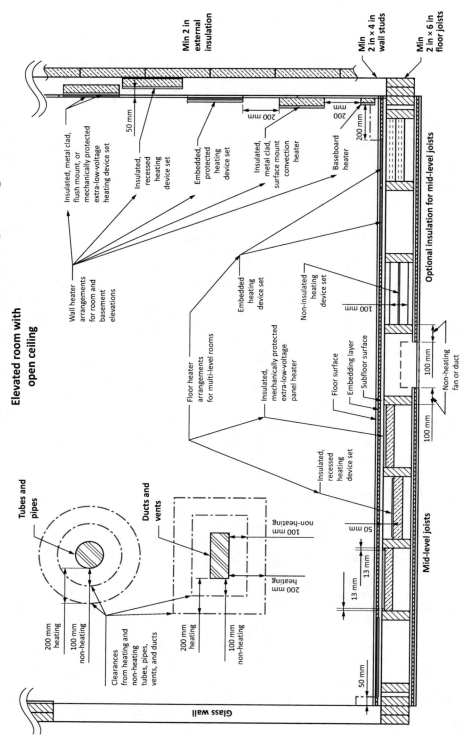

Figure B62-4
Table 67 clearances — Main elevation — Floor, wall, and ceiling heating arrangements

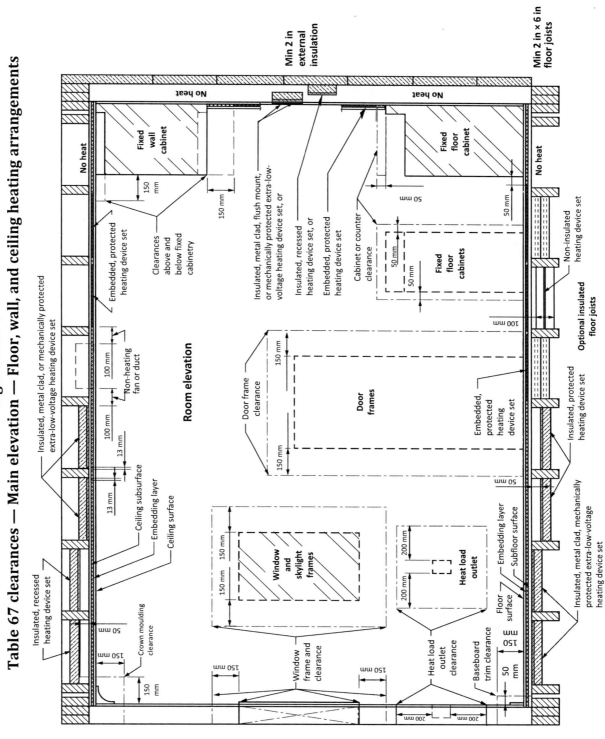

Figure B62-5
Table 67 clearances — Basement and suspended ceiling heating arrangements

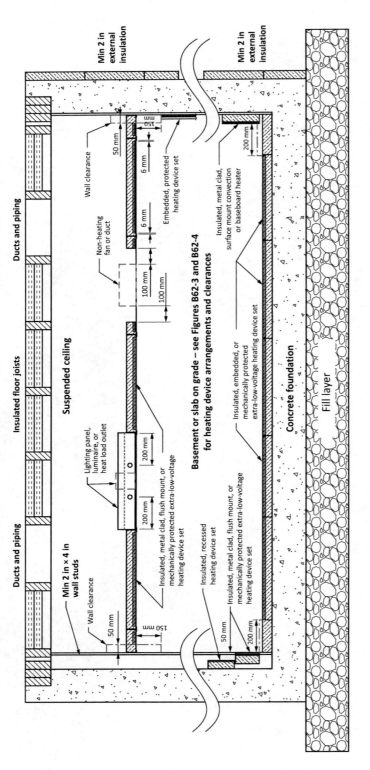

Rule 62-204

Heating cables embedded in concrete or in plaster attached to the concrete have about the same effect on temperatures within the concrete; therefore, Item b) applies in either case.

Rule 62-212

See the Note to Rules 62-200 2) and 62-212.

Rule 62-216 1)

The 13 mm clearance is to prevent mechanical damage of the heating device during installation of the gypsum board and other cementitious material.

Rule 62-222

Sauna heaters should be secured in place to ensure that the minimum clearances specified on the nameplate are not reduced. If the heater is provided with legs, they should not be removed in favour of other supports. Covering combustible surfaces with non-combustible material, such as metal tile or asbestos board, does not ensure safety from fire.

Sauna heaters marked "FOR INSTALLATION ON CONCRETE FLOORS ONLY" should not be installed on combustible floors, even if the floor is covered with ceramic tile, asbestos board, or other non-combustible material.

Equipment or material of other than an electrical nature should not be installed or placed in proximity to electrical equipment or in a manner that may create a dangerous condition. Benches, shelves, guardrails, and other structures or obstructions should not be placed closer to the heating unit than is permitted for the clearances specified on the nameplate.

To properly control the maximum temperature in the room, the heat sensor for the temperature control should be located near the heater. A timer should be installed to turn off the heater after a predetermined or preset time.

Δ **Rule 62-300**

Some surface heating devices may be used in space heating applications. For example, CSA C22.2 No. 130, which covers surface heating devices, recognizes that some surface heaters may be used for space heating.

Rule 62-304

For the purposes of Item a), mechanical protection of the heater cable that exits the medium may include metallic or non-metallic conduit. It is recommended that heating cables and heating panels installed outdoors under the surface of driveways, sidewalks, and similar locations
a)   not have spacing between adjacent heating cable runs less than 25 mm on centres;
b)   be installed so that adjacent runs of heating cable are spaced between 25 mm and 200 mm apart to provide for even heating;
c)   be secured in place by frames, spreaders, or other means while being embedded or covered, to prevent damage to the heaters;
d)   be installed on an appropriate substrate to support maximum load without crumbling, settling, or extensive movement to prevent cracking or breaking of the heating cable or panel; and
e)   not be installed where they cross expansion joints unless provision is made for expansion and contraction.

It is recommended that when heating cables are embedded in asphalt, they be rated at not more than 82 W/m to prevent softening or warping of the asphalt and, where no curbs are provided, that they be installed 300 mm or more from the edge of the driveway.

Δ **Rule 62-314**

This Rule covers skin effect trace heating system technology, which is typically used for pipe, vessel, equipment, and structure heating. Skin effect trace heating is a special form of heating in which a single insulated conductor is run inside a ferromagnetic envelope (heat tube or enclosure).

Because the conductor is part of a certified system, it does not need to meet the requirements of Table 19 or the ampacity requirements of Rule 4-004.

The skin effect conductor is connected to the envelope at one end (the far end) and a source of ac power is connected between the insulated skin effect conductor and the envelope at the other end (the supply end). Current flows from the power source through the insulated skin effect conductor to the far end and returns through the envelope. Figure B62-6 illustrates the basic system.

Δ
Figure B62-6
Typical skin effect trace heating system

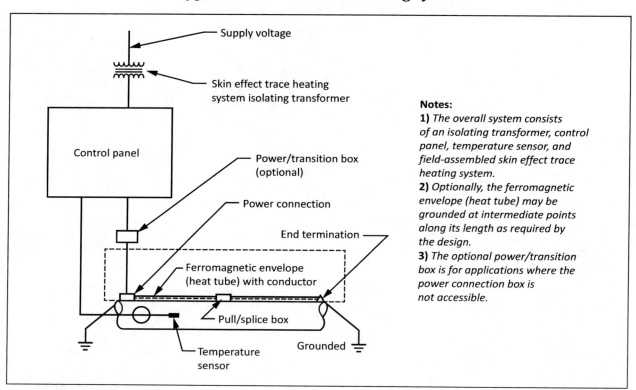

In skin effect trace heating, heat is generated in the ferromagnetic envelope (or heat tube) wall by the I^2R loss of the return current flow in the envelope (heat tube) and by hysteresis and eddy currents induced by the alternating magnetic field around the insulated conductor. Additional heat is produced by the I^2R loss in the insulated conductor.

The inductive interaction between the current in the insulated skin effect conductor and the return current in the envelope (heat tube) causes the current in the envelope (heat tube) to concentrate at its inner surface (skin).

Maximum current limitations for insulated skin effect conductors are based on the insulated skin effect conductor operating temperature calculated values established by the manufacturer and usually verified by a third-party certification body.

All components should be properly protected from corrosion with coatings or materials suitable for the location. Skin effect trace heating systems include overcurrent devices upstream and downstream of the supply transformer. In addition, trace heating system current monitoring is recommended.

In Rule 62-314 1) b), the exterior surface of the ferromagnetic envelope does not see any ac voltage from the skin effect circuit due to the magnetic interaction between the skin effect conductor and the ferromagnetic envelope. However, grounding of the envelope is an additional safety measure to ensure that, under all fault conditions, there will be no shock voltage imparted on the protected equipment. If the protected equipment, such as a pipeline, is buried in the ground, it may be protected by a cathodic protection system. In this case, the cathodic protection system design should take into consideration the presence of an ac ground on the skin effect system.

In Subrule 2), the reference is made to IEEE 844.2/CSA C293.2, which is the application guide for design, equipment selection, and installation. IEEE 844.1/CSA C22.2 No. 293.1 is the Part II certification standard, providing construction and performance requirements for skin effect trace heating systems. These systems are custom engineered for each application, needing the combination of design, equipment selection, system certification, installation and operating information, to enable initial safe initial installation and long term operations. This is provided by the use of the certification standard and the companion application guide.

Δ **Rule 62-316**
This Rule covers impedance heating system technology. Impedance heating is a special form of heating in which an alternating current is passed directly through the object to be heated in order to raise its temperature. See Figure B62-7.

Impedance heating systems should be properly designed, installed, and maintained in order to ensure safe operation. These systems are normally supplied with sufficient documentation to ensure safe installation and operation throughout the system's working life. For additional guidance on the application of these systems, refer to IEEE 844.

Δ

Figure B62-7
Typical impedance heating system

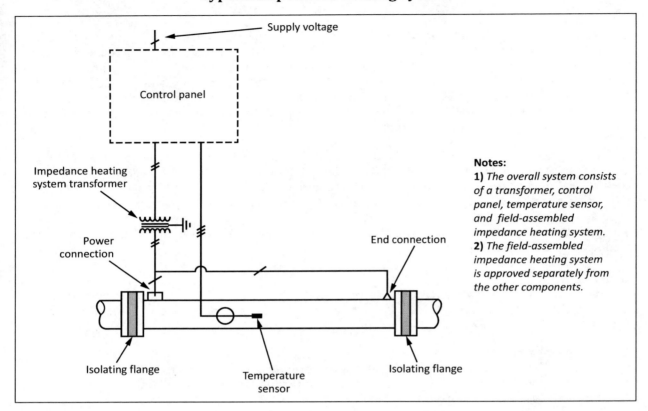

Supply voltage

Control panel

Impedance heating
system transformer

Power
connection

End connection

Isolating flange

Temperature
sensor

Isolating flange

Notes:
1) *The overall system consists of a transformer, control panel, temperature sensor, and field-assembled impedance heating system.*
2) *The field-assembled impedance heating system is approved separately from the other components.*

Rule 62-406
This Rule does not apply to induction heaters for surface heating of pipes and vessels.

Rule 62-408
CSA C22.2 No. 64 requires that bare element water heaters be marked "BARE ELEMENT WATER HEATER" and "CHAUFFE-EAU À ÉLÉMENT NU". The requirements for bare element water heaters in CSA C22.2 No. 64 apply to permanently connected heaters and do not apply to cord-connected equipment.

Section 64

Δ **Rule 64-000**

Figures B64-1 and B64-2 illustrate typical renewable energy systems and the various terms and circuits referenced in this Section.

Figure B64-1
Typical renewable energy system

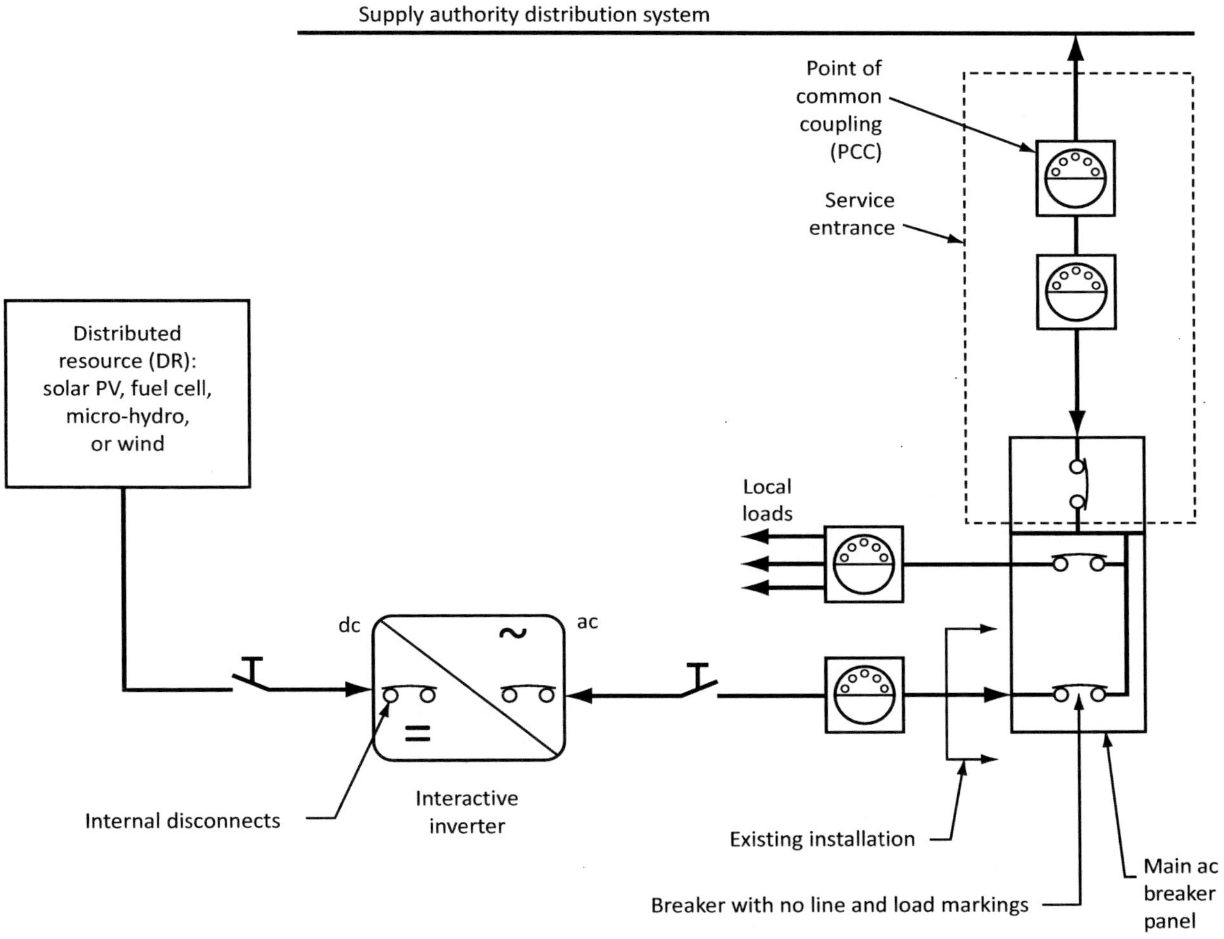

Figure B64-2
Typical renewable energy system with storage

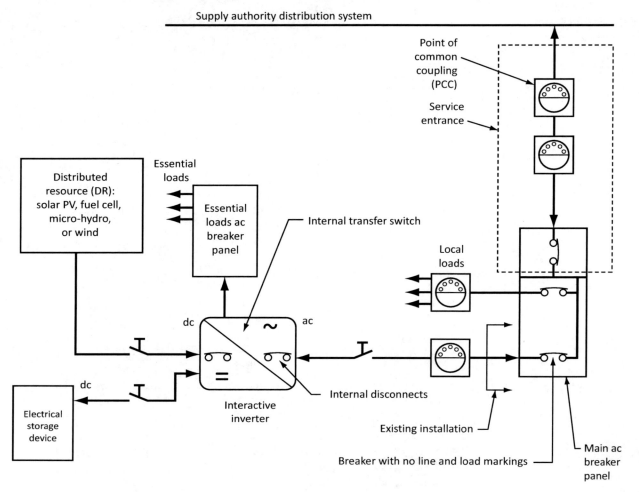

The use of renewable energy systems as stand-alone or interactive power supply systems has steadily increased as the technology and availability of renewable energy equipment have evolved. Section 64 covers stand-alone and interactive renewable energy systems.

The rising demand for electrical power has led to the development of power sources that are viable alternatives to or can be interconnected with electric utility distribution systems.

For additional information, see CAN/CSA-C22.2 No. 257.

Small stationary power systems, with less than 10 kW net electrical output, are intended for power supply or combined heat and power production primarily for residential applications, such as single homes or clusters of homes, and commercial occupancies, such as small stores, warehouses, small and medium enterprises, and small and medium industry. Small stationary power plants are equipped with a control system enabling at least fully automatic and unattended emergency shutdown. Fully automatic operation, including regular start-up and shutdown procedures, are not required.

Medium-sized stationary power systems, operating from 10 kW up to 500 kW net electrical output, are intended for power supply or combined heat and power production in the medium power range. Typical applications are big office buildings, supermarkets, cold stores, and industrial and municipal applications and installations for decentralized combined heat and power production. Medium-sized stationary power systems are usually equipped with a fully automated control system, including start-up, shutdown, and emergency shutdown procedures.

Large stationary power systems, operating at more than 500 kW net electrical output, are intended for power supply or combined heat and power production primarily for industrial, municipal, and commercial applications. Large stationary power systems should be operated by a master control unit that uses electrical and/or thermal requirements from a grid or stand-alone distribution network for control purposes and that can be superseded by safeguard personnel. These safeguard personnel should be trained to react to hazards and be prepared to interact with the automatic control system.

Rule 64-002
Figures B64-3 to B64-5 illustrate typical solar photovoltaic systems, showing the various terms and circuits referenced.

Different inverters may require different photovoltaic array and wiring configurations. These configurations may be divided into two groups:

a) a floating array (as shown in the illustration of an interconnected system in Figure B64-4) that requires a 2-pole disconnect switch; and

b) a grounded array that requires a single-pole disconnect switch, except for a 3-wire neutral-grounded array that requires a 2-pole disconnect switch to interrupt both ungrounded conductors.

Figure B64-3
Stand-alone system

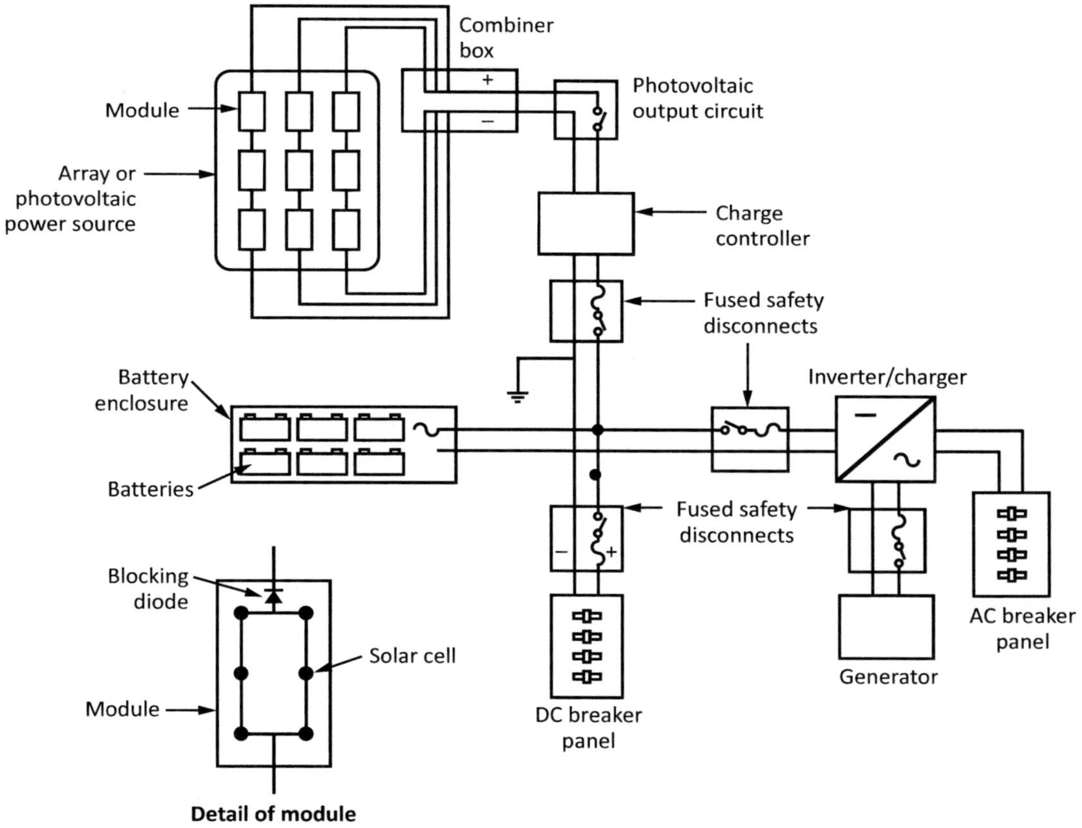

Figure B64-4
Interconnected system

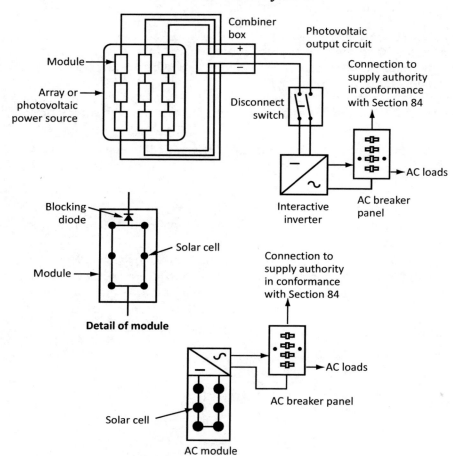

Combiner box

Photovoltaic output circuit

Module

Array or photovoltaic power source

\+

\−

Connection to supply authority in conformance with Section 84

Disconnect switch

AC loads

AC breaker panel

Interactive inverter

Blocking diode

Solar cell

Module

Detail of module

Connection to supply authority in conformance with Section 84

AC loads

AC breaker panel

Solar cell

AC module

January 2018

Figure B64-5
Large interconnected system

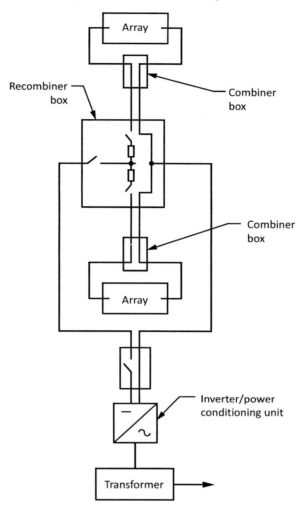

AC module

AC modules do not provide access to the photovoltaic output circuit that is internally connected to the power conditioning unit. The output of an ac module is then referenced as the power conditioning unit output.

Fuel cell systems

Fuel cell systems generate dc electrical current through a chemical reaction in which fuel such as natural gas or liquefied petroleum gas is consumed. In contrast to internal combustion prime movers, the fuel gas is consumed through an electrochemical process rather than a combustion process. A power inverter converts the direct current to alternating current. The installation requirements of Section 64 allow power derived from fuel cells to be safely delivered into residential and light commercial occupancies, either as the sole source of electrical power or as a source integrated with a utility or other power source.

Full load rating

This is the maximum power that the hydraulic turbine is able to generate at design head and flow.

Hydrokinetic power system

Hydrokinetic power systems include river energy converters and tidal energy converters.

Δ **Inverter**

Inverters that are connected to the grid may incorporate a power conditioning unit (PCU) that improves power quality in order to deliver voltage at a proper level and with proper characteristics. Users of this Code should refer to CSA C22.2 No. 107.1, Clause 14, which provides additional information on the requirements for interactive inverters.

Micro-hydropower systems

Micro-hydropower systems convert the potential energy in flowing and falling water into electricity by means of a waterwheel or hydraulic turbine. A typical system has the following components: a water intake or weir, canal, forebay tank, penstock, and powerhouse and tailrace.

Δ **Photovoltaic combiner**

This is a general term that applies to both photovoltaic combiners and photovoltaic recombiners. It is used where there is no need to make a distinction between the two.

Δ **Photovoltaic recombiner**

This term is specific to photovoltaic recombiners and is used where the requirements for a photovoltaic recombiner differ from those for a photovoltaic combiner.

Point of common coupling

See Figure B64-6.

Figure B64-6

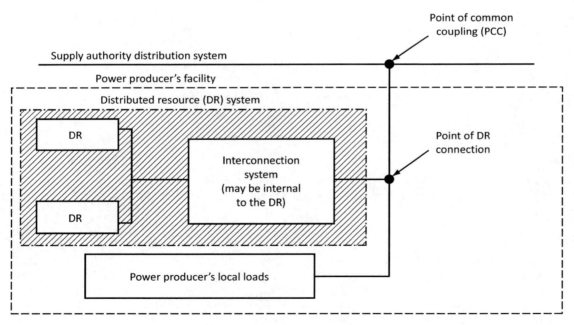

Renewable energy systems

Renewable energy systems may be stand-alone or interactive with other electrical power production sources and may be with or without electrical energy storage such as batteries.

Rule 64-052
For the purpose of this Rule, multiple inverters and associated components connected to the same renewable energy source are considered as one power generation source, and associated wiring may be contained in the same raceway.

Δ **Rule 64-058 3)**
DC fault currents are considerably harder to interrupt than ac faults. Overcurrent devices marked only for ac use should not be used in dc circuits. Equipment acceptable in dc systems, such as automotive, marine, and telecommunications applications, is not suitable for use in permanent renewable energy systems meeting the requirements of this Code.

Rule 64-058 4)
Circuit breakers that are marked "Line" and "Load" have been evaluated for connection only in the direction marked. Circuit breakers without "Line" and "Load" have been evaluated for connection in both directions.

Rule 64-060
Because photovoltaic modules are energized while exposed to light, the installation, replacement, or servicing of array components while the photovoltaic modules are irradiated may expose persons to the hazard of electric shock.

It is intended that means will be provided to isolate and disable portions of an array or photovoltaic module that may require servicing. An opaque covering is an acceptable means of disabling the array.

Rule 64-060 8)
The required disconnecting means is to ensure complete isolation when fuses that could be energized from both sides are being removed.

Rule 64-060 10)
It is intended by this Subrule that the following or equivalent wording should be provided on or adjacent to the disconnecting means:

WARNING: ELECTRIC SHOCK HAZARD. DO NOT TOUCH TERMINALS. TERMINALS ON BOTH THE LINE AND LOAD SIDES MAY BE ENERGIZED IN THE OPEN POSITION.

See Appendix M for a French translation of this marking.

Rule 64-060 12)
The intent of this Rule is to have a disconnecting means for the output circuit of a photovoltaic combiner capable of making and interrupting its full load rating and that may be opened with safety to the operator with a fault on the system.

Rule 64-064
Inverters used in renewable energy power systems usually contain a transformer that isolates the dc grounded circuit conductor from the ac grounded circuit conductor. This isolation necessitates that both a dc and ac grounding system be installed. The two grounding systems are bonded together or have a common grounding electrode so that all ac and dc grounded circuit conductors and equipment grounding conductors have the same near-zero potential to earth.

Rule 64-064 6)
A renewable energy dc supply system equipped with a ground fault protection device is permitted to have the required grounded conductor connected to the ground via the ground fault protection device. Where this connection is internal to the ground fault equipment, it is not duplicated by an external connection.

Rule 64-066 1) b)
It is intended by this Item that the following or equivalent wording should be provided on or adjacent to the disconnecting means:

WARNING: ELECTRIC SHOCK HAZARD. THE CONDUCTORS OF THIS RENEWABLE ENERGY POWER SYSTEM ARE UNGROUNDED AND MAY BE ENERGIZED.

See Appendix M for a French translation of this marking.

Rule 64-066 1) d) ii)
In an ungrounded dc system, a single ground fault will cause current to flow if there is another connection to ground in the system and if there is no isolation between the grounding point and the ground fault. For example, fault current will flow in a system in which a non-isolated inverter is connected to a grounded ac system with a ground fault on the dc supply circuit.

Rules 64-068 and 64-070
See Figure B64-7.

Figure B64-7

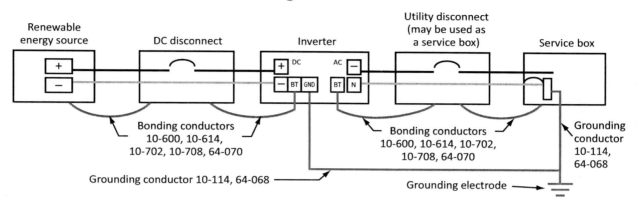

Rule 64-068 a) Grounding electrode requirements

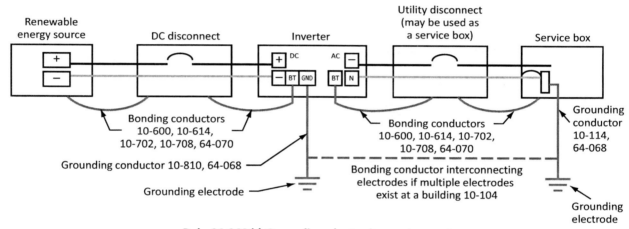

Rule 64-068 b) Grounding electrode requirements

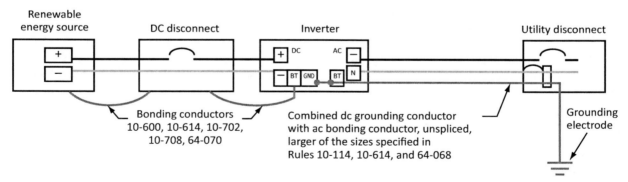

Rule 64-068 c) Grounding electrode requirements

Legend
BT — equipment bonding terminals
GND — DC grounding electrode terminal

Rules 64-070 and 64-612

Equipment bonding is required even in extra-low-voltage (12 and 24 V) systems not otherwise required to have a system ground. A grounding electrode must be added to an ungrounded system to accommodate equipment bonding. To maintain the shortest electrical time constant in each dc circuit, the equipment bonding conductor should be routed as close as possible to the circuit conductors. This facilitates the operation of overcurrent devices.

In many renewable energy systems, the bonding connection between the grounding conductor and exposed conductive surfaces is located in the inverter or a dc power centre that may require removal for service. In order to prevent shock and fire hazards, it is important that the bonding continuity be maintained even when the equipment is removed.

Additional information regarding the grounding and bonding requirements for offshore hydrokinetic systems may be found in IEEE 45.

Rule 64-074 4)

It is intended by this Subrule that the following or equivalent wording should be provided on or adjacent to the disconnecting means:

WARNING: RENEWABLE ENERGY SYSTEM CONTAINS ELECTRICAL ENERGY STORAGE DEVICES.

See Appendix M for a French translation of this marking.

Rule 64-076

For the type of connection described in this Rule, the switching equipment ensures isolation because the system is a non-grid-interactive renewable energy system and does not export any power to the supply system.

Rule 64-078 2)

To ensure system stability of the grid and the restoration of normal voltage and frequency, the supply authority may specify a delay period.

Δ Rule 64-100

Both stand-alone and interactive inverters are power-limited devices. Output circuits connected to these devices are sized on the continuous rated outputs of these devices and are not based on load calculations or battery banks, if any. Some inverters may have specifications listing sustained maximum output currents, and the higher of this number or the rated output should be used.

Rule 64-102 a)

A stand-alone residential or commercial renewable energy installation may have an ac output and be connected to a building electrical system in compliance with all the Rules of this Code. Even though such an installation may have service entrance equipment rated at 100 or 200 A at 120/240 V, there is no requirement that the renewable energy source provide either the rated full current or the dual voltages of the service equipment. While safety requirements mandate full compliance with this Code, a renewable energy installation is usually designed so that the actual ac demands on the system are sized to the output rating of the renewable energy system.

Rule 64-102 c) ii)

Multi-wire branch circuits are common in one- and two-family dwelling units. When these multi-wire branch circuits are connected to a normal 120/240 V ac service, the currents in the neutral conductors of the circuits (typically Nos. 14 to 3 AWG) subtract or are, at most, no larger than the rating of the branch circuit overcurrent device. When these electrical systems are connected to a single 120 V renewable energy power system inverter by paralleling the two ungrounded conductors in the service entrance load centre, the currents in the neutral conductor for each multi-wire branch circuit add rather than subtract. The currents in the neutral conductors may be as high as twice the rating of the branch circuit overcurrent device. With this configuration, neutral conductor overloading is possible.

Rule 64-102 c) iv)

It is intended by this Item that the following or equivalent wording should be provided on or adjacent to the disconnecting means:

WARNING: SINGLE 120 V SUPPLY. DO NOT CONNECT MULTI-WIRE BRANCH CIRCUITS.

See Appendix M for a French translation of this marking.

Δ **Rule 64-106**

An inverter or an ac module in an interactive renewable energy system should automatically de-energize its output to the connected electrical production and distribution network upon loss of voltage in that system and should remain in that state until the electrical production and distribution network voltage has been restored. A renewable energy system that is normally interactive may be permitted to operate as a stand-alone system to supply loads that have been disconnected from an electrical production and distribution network source.

Marking requirements for interactive inverters are given in CSA C22.2 No. 107.1 and CAN/CSA-C22.2 No. 62109.

Δ **Rule 64-110**

Supply authority standards typically specify voltage balance requirements. The voltage unbalance limit usually allowed in accordance with supply authority requirements is approximately 2 to 3%. For interactive single-phase inverters, unbalanced voltages can be minimized by the same methods that are used for single-phase loads on a three-phase power system. See ANSI/C84.1-2011.

Rule 64-112 4) b) iii)

It is intended by this Item that the following or equivalent wording should be provided on or adjacent to the disconnecting means:

WARNING: INVERTER OUTPUT CONNECTION. DO NOT RELOCATE THIS OVERCURRENT DEVICE.

See Appendix M for a French translation of this marking.

Rule 64-112 5)

Load side connection of energy sources to commonly available ac ground fault circuit interrupters and ac equipment ground fault protection circuit breakers may result in back-feed currents from the renewable energy system output. Tests have shown that back-feed currents through these devices may damage them and prevent operation.

Rules 64-200 and 64-218

When a reflecting system is used for irradiance enhancement, increased levels of output power may result. Marking of equipment should indicate the increased levels when such equipment is used.

Δ **Rule 64-200 2)**

It is intended by this Subrule that the following or equivalent wording should be provided on or adjacent to the disconnecting means for the photovoltaic output circuit:

PHOTOVOLTAIC SYSTEM EQUIPPED WITH RAPID SHUTDOWN.

See Appendix M for a French translation of this marking.

△ **Rule 64-200 2) and 3)**

Figure B64-8
Label for photovoltaic systems that shut down the conductors leaving the array only

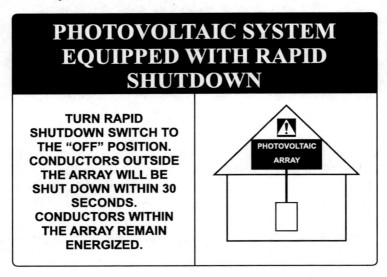

PHOTOVOLTAIC SYSTEM EQUIPPED WITH RAPID SHUTDOWN

TURN RAPID SHUTDOWN SWITCH TO THE "OFF" POSITION. CONDUCTORS OUTSIDE THE ARRAY WILL BE SHUT DOWN WITHIN 30 SECONDS. CONDUCTORS WITHIN THE ARRAY REMAIN ENERGIZED.

PHOTOVOLTAIC ARRAY

Rule 64-202 1)
The 125% factor specified by Rule 64-202 is the temperature adjustment factor. The rating of photovoltaic modules is based on the standard test conditions (an irradiance of 1000 W/m² and an ambient temperature of 25 °C). The voltage produced by the module increases as the temperature decreases. The 125% factor is based on a minimum module temperature of − 40 °C.

Rule 64-202 2)
The lowest daily minimum temperature described in this Subrule is available from Environment Canada, "Canadian Climate Normals". Using the manufacturer's temperature coefficient, the maximum photovoltaic source circuit and output circuit voltage may be calculated using the following formula:

$V_{MPC} = V_{OC} \times [1 + (T_M − 25) \times T_K]$
where

T_M = lowest daily minimum temperature in degrees Celsius

T_K = temperature coefficient in per cent per degree Celsius

V_{OC} = rated open-circuit voltage of the photovoltaic power source in volts

V_{MPC} = maximum photovoltaic source circuit and output circuit voltage in volts

Example:

A solar photovoltaic system is installed in a geographic location where the lowest daily minimum temperature (T_M) is −18 °C. According to the manufacturer's data, the temperature coefficient (T_K) is −0.25%/°C and the rated open-circuit voltage (V_{OC}) is 92 V.

$V_{MPC} = 92$ V $\times \{1 + [(−18$ °C $− 25$ °C$) \times −0.25\%/$°C$]\}$

$V_{MPC} = 92$ V $\times [1 + (− 43 \times −0.0025)]$

$V_{MPC} = 92$ V $\times 1.1075$

$V_{MPC} = 101.89$ V

Δ **Rule 64-202 5) c)**

"DANGER 1500 V dc" (see Appendix M for a French translation of this marking) is an example of the marking required by Subrule 5) c) for a system operating at a 1500 V dc maximum photovoltaic circuit voltage.

Photovoltaic source and output circuits and equipment connected to or within those circuits are considered inaccessible where they are located within a fenced enclosure in accordance with Rule 26-300, guarded by locked doors, elevated 3 m or more above grade level or above any surface that a person can stand on, or where access is restricted by other effective means.

Δ **Rule 64-208**

For the application of this Rule, photovoltaic modules are considered inaccessible to the public where they are located within a fenced enclosure in accordance with Rule 26-300, guarded by locked doors, elevated 3 m or more above grade level or above any surface that a person can stand on, or where access is restricted by other effective means.

For the application of this Rule, modules without an application class marking are considered to be application Class A.

Δ **Rule 64-210**

Most photovoltaic modules do not have provision for attaching raceways. These circuits may have to be made not readily accessible by physical barriers such as metal screening, elevation, or fencing.

Photovoltaic modules operate at elevated temperatures when exposed to high ambient temperatures and to bright sunlight. These temperatures may routinely exceed 70 °C in many locations. Module interconnection insulated conductors and cables are available with insulation rated for wet locations and a temperature rating of 90 °C or greater.

Rule 64-210 4)

The intent of Subrule 4) is to protect solar photovoltaic cable from mechanical damage, including rubbing on surfaces such as roofing and array structures.

Rule 64-210 5)

The intent of Subrule 5) is to provide protection against damage from rodents by enclosing the photovoltaic source circuit insulated conductors and cables in material such as expanded metal, solid metal, and screening.

Δ **Rule 64-210 8)**

Type RPVU cable with FT1 markings is suitable for installation on buildings.

Rule 64-212

CSA C22.2 No. 271 requires the positive or negative identification on RPV or RPVU multi-conductor cables to be "+/-", "pos/neg", or "positive/negative". Single-conductor cables are permitted to be marked in the same manner.

Rule 64-214 1)

Where there is no back-feed from a battery or inverter, the maximum short-circuit current that can flow in any of the photovoltaic source circuits is the sum of the short-circuit current ratings of all the other photovoltaic source circuits connected in parallel.

Example of a calculation where the short-circuit current ratings of all photovoltaic source circuits are equal:

Maximum photovoltaic source circuit short-circuit current = (the sum of the short-circuit current for all photovoltaic source circuits connected in parallel) minus (the short-circuit current for one of the photovoltaic source circuits)

Δ **Rule 64-218**
The requirements for a photovoltaic rapid shutdown system are given in CSA C22.2 No. 330.

Rule 64-218 3)
The intent of Subrule 3) is to limit photovoltaic source or output circuits to not more than 30 V within 30 s of rapid shutdown initiation, where the voltage and power are measured between any two photovoltaic source or output circuit conductors, and between any photovoltaic source or output circuit conductors and ground.

Δ **Rule 64-220**
Photovoltaic connectors of the sleeve- and pin-type are approved for use as a mated pair only, i.e., the connectors are certified as a pair.

Each connector manufacturer uses materials and procedures to manufacture their connectors in a proprietary manner. Although the connectors may look electrically and mechanically compatible, there is no evaluation to ensure that the production process of one manufacturer will result in its connectors being compatible with another's.

Rule 64-222
CAN/CSA-C22.2 No. 61730-1 requires all conductive parts of a module that are accessible during normal use to be bonded together and the method of bonding to be detailed in the installation manual. During the approval process, all components, such as bonding clips, brackets, hardware, lugs, etc., used for bonding are tested in accordance with CAN/CSA-C22.2 No. 61730-2.

Rules 64-300 1) c), 64-400 1) c), 64-500 a), 64-600 a), and 64-700 1) c)
A brief system description typically includes a single-line diagram to identify components of the interconnected system, including switching arrangements, interlocks, isolation points, and their relative locations. See Figures B64-1 and B64-2 in the Note to Rule 64-000 for diagrams of interconnected renewable energy systems.

Rule 64-300 2)
Some wind turbines rely on the connection from the alternator to a remote controller for speed regulation. Opening turbine output circuit insulated conductors may cause mechanical damage to a turbine and create excessive voltages that could damage equipment or expose persons to electric shock.

Open-circuiting, short-circuiting, or mechanical brakes are used to disable a turbine for installation and service.

Rule 64-302 3)
Wind turbines may use the electric grid to dump energy from short-term wind gusts. Normal operating voltages are defined in CSA CAN3-C235.

Rule 64-308 3)
Possible back-feed of current from any source of supply, including a supply through an inverter to the wind turbine output circuit, is a consideration in determining whether adequate overcurrent protection from all sources is provided. Some small wind systems rely on the turbine output circuit to regulate turbine speed. Inverters may also operate in reverse for turbine start-up or speed control. In systems of these types, the manufacturer's instructions should be followed.

Rule 64-310 1)
The disconnecting means need not be suitable for use as service equipment unless used as service entrance equipment.

Rule 64-310 5)
It is intended by this Subrule that the following or equivalent wording should be provided on or adjacent to the disconnecting means:

WIND TURBINE GENERATOR SYSTEM DISCONNECT SWITCH.

Rule 64-312 1)
Attached metal parts, such as turbine blades and tails, that have no source of electrical energization need not be grounded.

Rule 64-312 3)
Guy wires supporting towers that are adequately grounded are not likely to become energized and are therefore not subject to the requirements of Section 10. Grounding of metallic guy wires may be required by lightning codes.

Rule 64-316
Refer to CAN/CSA-B72 and CAN/CSA-IEC 61400-24.

Rule 64-318
A small wind system employing a diversion load controller as the primary means of regulating the speed of a wind turbine rotor is equipped with an additional, independent means to prevent overspeed operation.

Rule 64-320
Some small wind turbines are equipped with integral surge devices.

Rule 64-400 2)
CSA C22.2 No. 272 requires the working space in wind turbines to meet the requirements of Rules 2-308 and 2-310. The Standard permits the working space to be reduced when electrical shock and arc flash information is field assessed and recorded on the information labels supplied and installed by the manufacturer.

Rule 64-404
In larger interconnected installations, additional devices are sometimes necessary to ensure stability and the adequacy of the electrical equipment protection. For example, ferroresonance can produce very high voltages in transformers with a wye-delta connection, requiring a surge arrester or high-speed overvoltage relay or both. Other types of protection (e.g., loss of excitation protection and over-excitation protection) are sometimes required to ensure the stability of the supply authority system in the interests of public safety and equipment protection. This Rule requires that interconnected installations be properly protected so that system stability is ensured and the electrical equipment operates safely. The protection depends on the size and type of the interconnected generation equipment.

Rule 64-406
In a consumer-owned interconnected power generation system, multiple sources can feed into a system fault or feed a portion of the supply authority system. If a disconnecting means is opened for some reason (e.g., as a result of a temporary fault or during a maintenance procedure) and isolates a portion of the supply authority system, the interconnected electric power generation system can continue to feed the load to the open disconnecting means, endangering personnel who expect the line to be de-energized when the disconnecting means is open. If the supply authority disconnection means is closed while the isolated section is still energized, the system will likely be out of phase. This can cause severe damage to the wind turbine generator and other electrical equipment.

After the clearance of a fault, the supply authority equipment sometimes recloses automatically to avoid a long interruption due to a temporary fault. When the supply authority equipment recloses, the interconnected source must be out of service. Protection of the interconnected wind turbine generator must be in effect before this automatic reclosing, and the automatic reclosing time must be long enough to allow the interconnected source to be disconnected from the supply authority system. Since there is often more than one automatic reclosing, it is important to wait until the normal voltage of the supply authority is restored before reconnecting the interconnected source.

The requirements for the separation of the interconnected wind turbine generators from the supply authority system depend on the type and size of the interconnected source. For example, line-commutated inverters and induction generators are not usually capable of supplying load in isolation from the power system because they need the supply authority voltage to operate. In the case of self-commutated inverters and synchronous generation, under- or over-voltage relays, under- or over-frequency relays, or more sophisticated protection may be required, depending on the size of the interconnected source.

Rule 64-406 1)
The disconnecting means need not be suitable for use as service equipment unless the grounded circuit conductor is grounded at the switch. The disconnecting means may be located either outside at the base of the tower or inside the tower as close as practicable to where the supply insulated conductors or cables enter.

Rule 64-406 5)
It is intended by this Subrule that the following or equivalent wording be provided on or adjacent to the disconnecting means:

WIND TURBINE GENERATOR SYSTEM DISCONNECT SWITCH.

Rule 64-412
When installing lightning protection systems, installers should refer to the manufacturer's recommendations or applicable Standards (e.g., CAN/CSA-B72, CAN/CSA-IEC 61400-24).

Rule 64-500
See also IEEE P1020 and NRCan's *Micro-Hydropower Systems: A Buyer's Guide*.

Rule 64-502 a)
The rating of the generator is normally oversized to meet other electrical and mechanical safety requirements; therefore, the nameplate rating of the generator does not necessarily represent the full load current of the system. The capacity of the hydraulic turbine to generate power should be taken into account when sizing the insulated supply conductors or cables.

Rule 64-508
It is intended by this Rule that the following or equivalent wording should be provided on or adjacent to the disconnecting means:

MICRO-HYDROPOWER SYSTEM GENERATOR DISCONNECT SWITCH.

Rule 64-510 1)
The rating of the electronic governor may vary if it is used in combination with a mechanical governor.

Rules 64-510 3) and 64-604 3)
In order to compensate for non-sinusoidal current or harmonics generated as a result of power electronic switching, the neutral conductor must be rated at the same ampacity as the phase supply conductors.

Rule 64-602 4)
For general, stand-alone, or grid-tie systems, the conductors between the electric generator and the input of the power conditioning unit may be permitted a voltage drop as high as 10%.

Rule 64-610
It is intended by this Rule that the following or equivalent wording should be provided on or adjacent to the disconnecting means:

HYDROKINETIC POWER SYSTEM GENERATOR DISCONNECT SWITCH.

Rule 64-612
In offshore installations, there is no connection to the earth's true ground. For an offshore structure, the ground is created by the contact of the structure with the water. Non-metallic structures should include a metallic ground plate, which becomes the zero potential reference on the structure. All structural parts connected to the ground plate are considered to be part of the ground plane. This results in the whole structure being grounded. Connection to the ground plane should be accomplished

such that the surface does not become a current-carrying conductor. All metal parts should be solidly connected to the ground plane.

Rule 64-700 3)

It is intended by this Subrule that the following or equivalent wording be provided on or adjacent to the disconnecting means:

WARNING: THIS DISCONNECTING MEANS DOES NOT CONTROL THE ELECTRICAL ENERGY STORAGE DEVICES.

See Appendix M for a French translation of this marking.

Rule 64-706

It is intended by this Rule that the following or equivalent wording be provided on or adjacent to the disconnecting means:

STATIONARY FUEL CELL SYSTEM DISCONNECT SWITCH.

Rule 64-710

Fuel cells should be considered fuel-burning equipment and be installed in accordance with the *National Building Code of Canada*. Hydrogen-fuelled systems should be installed in accordance with CAN/BNQ 1784-000.

Rule 64-716 2)

Ventilation systems should be designed to provide a negative or neutral pressure, with respect to the building, in the room where the fuel cell power system is located.

Rule 64-716 3)

Typically, hydrogen is not odorized.

Rule 64-800 5)

Batteries in renewable energy systems are subject to extensive charge/discharge cycles and typically require frequent maintenance (e.g., checking electrolyte, cleaning connections). At any voltage, a primary safety concern in battery systems is that a fault (e.g., caused by a metal tool dropped onto a terminal) might result in a fire or explosion. The best method for reducing this hazard is to ensure that battery systems are guarded, as defined in Section 2.

Rule 64-802

Large banks of storage batteries can deliver significant amounts of short-circuit current. As a result, installers are reminded to ensure that the circuit overcurrent protective devices are selected and coordinated so that the devices will clear a fault without extensively damaging the electrical components of the circuit.

Rule 64-804

Grounded metal trays and cases or containers in flooded, lead-acid battery systems operating over 48 V nominal have been shown to be a contributing factor in ground faults. Non-conductive racks, trays, and cases minimize this problem.

Δ **Rule 64-810**

Battery plates and terminals are frequently constructed of relatively soft lead and lead alloys encased in plastics that are sealed with asphalt. Large-size, low-stranding stiff copper conductors attached to these components can cause them to be distorted. The use of flexible cables reduces such distortions. Cables with the appropriate physical and chemical-resistant properties should be used. Flexible building-wire-type cables are available and are suitable for this use. This Code does not permit welding and battery cables to be used for this purpose.

Rule 64-812

Certain battery types, such as valve-regulated lead-acid or nickel-cadmium, can experience thermal failure when overcharged.

Charge control is not required where the design of the renewable energy source circuit is matched to the voltage rating and charge current requirements of the interconnected battery cells, and the maximum charging current multiplied by 1 h is less than 3% of the rated battery capacity expressed in ampere-hours or as recommended by the battery manufacturer.

Rule 64-814

If any portion of a diversion charge control system fails, the batteries may be overcharged, creating a potentially hazardous condition. A second, independent charge control method (usually a series regulator) and robust diversion controller circuits minimize potential problems.

Rule 64-814 3)

An interconnected utility service is not to be considered a reliable diversion load.

Section 68

Rule 68-054

Figure B68-1 illustrates the minimum clearances for conductors over swimming pools. No conductors are permitted under any circumstances in the area under Line 1. In the area above Line 1, insulated communication conductors and neutral supported cables operating at 750 V or less may be permitted [see Subrules 2) and 3)]. Any other conductors operating at not more than 50 kV are permitted above the area outlined by Line 2 [see Subrules 2) and 4)].

Figure B68-1
Minimum clearances for conductors over swimming pools

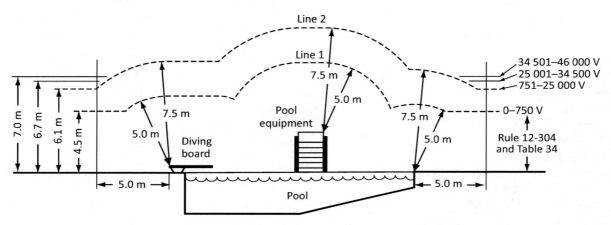

Note: *Clearances shown beyond 5 m from the pool edge are found in Rule 12-304 and Table 34.*

Rule 68-058 1)

This Subrule is intended to establish an effective equipotential plane by bonding together metal parts of the pool and non-electrical equipment associated with the pool. A panelboard supplying pool electrical equipment need only be connected to this equipotential plane as detailed in Subrule 6).

If there is no electrical equipment associated with the pool in the pool vicinity, it is intended that the bonding conductor required by Subrule 1) need only interconnect the metal parts identified in that Subrule.

Rule 68-058 3)

Where reinforcing steel encapsulated with a non-conductive compound (epoxy-coated rebar) is used in the construction of a pool, an alternative means to eliminate voltage gradients could be a loop around the pool of a minimum No. 6 copper conductor installed below normal water level.

Rule 68-060 6)
The deck in the vicinity of the deck box may be sloped up to the top of the deck box from the normal deck level.

If a deck box is located so that the top of the box is above the finished level of the pool deck, the box should not be located in a walkway unless afforded additional protection such as by location under diving boards, adjacent to fixed structures, or in similar areas.

Rule 68-062 3)
Audio isolation transformers should

a)   have either the primary and secondary windings wound on separate bobbins on the core legs or a grounded metal shield between the primary and secondary windings; and

b)   withstand a 60 Hz test voltage of 2500 V applied between the primary and secondary windings for a period of 1 min without breakdown.

Microphones used in the vicinity of pools and baptismal fonts must have audio isolation transformers and cables with ungrounded conductors installed between them and any mixer, pre-amplifier, amplifier, or like equipment.

Rule 68-068 6)
The 1.5 m separation is intended to prevent the occupant of the pool from resetting the ground fault circuit interrupter. This separation should be the shortest unobstructed distance, which need not follow a straight line.

Rule 68-068 7) b)
CSA C22.2 No. 218.1 requires that all spas and hot tubs be provided with ground fault circuit interrupters of the Class A type as part of the equipment or that the equipment be marked with the following or equivalent caution:

CAUTION: CONNECT ONLY TO A CIRCUIT PROTECTED BY A CLASS A GROUND FAULT CIRCUIT INTERRUPTER

and

ATTENTION : CONNECTER UNIQUEMENT À UN CIRCUIT PROTÉGÉ PAR UN DISJONCTEUR DIFFÉRENTIEL DE CLASSE A.

Rule 68-306 4)
The warning label to be affixed to the receptacle for the cord-connected hydromassage bathtub is intended to warn against and prevent the connection of any other equipment to the receptacle.

Rule 68-404 4)
The intent of Subrule 4) is to provide protection against entrapment hazards associated with spas and hot tubs located in any occupancy except a dwelling unit, by installing an emergency shut-off switch within sight and 15 m of the spa or hot tub. It is also intended that such a switch be located at least 1 m horizontally from the spa or hot tub, as specified in Subrule 1). It is intended by this requirement that an emergency shut-off switch required to activate the audible and visual trouble-signal devices may be assembled and interconnected with these devices in the field, and it may be provided by an inline-operated device or a remote control circuit that causes the pump circuit to open.

Rule 68-408 3)
An inverted U-shaped pipe installed in the air pipe so that the bottom of the top loop of the pipe is not less than 300 mm above the tub rim is considered an acceptable means to prevent water from contacting blower live parts.

Section 70

Rule 70-106
The conduit service facility that must be provided for the main communication entrance service into a mobile home is usually located in the living room, main hallway, or kitchen area. An additional conduit service facility should be provided wherever an extension communication outlet is to be installed, such as in the master bedroom. If the conduit service facility is to be used for both telephone and cable television services, the minimum conduit size should be 21 trade size inside diameter.

Rule 70-122 1)
In applying Rule 26-724 a) for this Subrule, it is not necessary to include in the linear measurements the space occupied by standard door openings, closets, or cupboards that have been designed to render the wall space unusable for electrical equipment.

Rule 70-122 4)
The intent of this Subrule is to ensure that receptacles that are mounted on the underside of trailers to supply power to heating cable sets for freeze protection of plumbing pipes on trailers are provided with ground fault protection and that they are properly identified for that use. Heating cable sets (particularly the self-limiting type) without ground fault protection have caused numerous fires on trailers.

Rule 70-130
When insulation resistance or ac dielectric strength tests are performed, precautions should be taken to ensure that voltage-sensitive devices such as ground fault circuit interrupters are not subjected to voltages that will damage the device.

Section 72

Rule 72-110
The 5-15R, 5-20R, and 14-50R receptacle configurations referred to in Subrules 1) a), 1) b), and 1) d) are shown in Diagram 1.

Section 74

Rule 74-004 3)
Because there are many variables in the structural design of airport runways, taxiways, and aprons depending on the required design strength of the surface material, and to ensure that the installation of a conduit within the surface material will not result in damage to the runway, taxiway, or apron, this Subrule intends that such an installation be designed by a civil engineer in accordance with good engineering practice and that the design be acceptable to the airport authorities.

Section 78

Δ Rule 78-050 2)
Receptacles resistant to condensing marine humidity are typically of industrial specification, constructed using copper-rich metallic alloys for both electrical components and for mounting means, whether nickel plated or not. Steel, plated or not, other than stainless steel, is usually not used. Receptacles complying with the ASTM B117 500 h salt spray (fog) test with no visible corrosion are deemed to meet the requirement.

To minimize deterioration due to marine environmental conditions, the following materials have been found to be generally acceptable:
a)   copper-free aluminum with aluminum or stainless steel hardware;
b)   fibreglass with stainless steel hardware;
c)   epoxy-coated rigid steel threaded conduit;
d)   PVC-coated rigid steel threaded conduit;

e) 19 mm plywood, either penta-treated or painted with two coats of marine grade paint and used with galvanized or stainless steel hardware;

f) rigid PVC boxes and enclosures with stainless steel hardware; or

g) hot-dipped galvanized structural steel.

Δ **Rule 78-052 2) and 3)**

It is the intent of Rule 78-052 2) to ensure that ground fault protection is provided for branch circuits and feeder circuits installed in or on fixed or floating piers, docking facilities, and boathouses, with a setting low enough for safe operation but not exceeding 30 mA. There may be instances where the panelboard or distribution equipment supplying power to the branch circuit is installed in a location that is not in or on the fixed or floating pier, docking facility, or boathouse. In such cases, Rule 78-052 3) requires additional ground fault protection to be installed at the branch circuit level, thus fulfilling the requirements of Rule 78-052 2).

Section 80

Rule 80-000

This Section has the following objectives:

a) to recognize that cathodic protection systems have to be installed using wiring methods that may not be consistent with those of other Sections of the Code;

b) to address the electrical safety of the cathodic protection systems and not their efficacy.

NACE International Standards are recommended as guides to the design, materials specifications, installation, and operation of cathodic protection systems.

Rule 80-006

Care should be taken to select clamps that maintain a secure electrical connection and that will be anodic to the material being protected when in the presence of an electrolyte, so that the clamp will not itself corrode the material if the connection becomes wet.

When welding to oil or gas piping, reference should be made to CAN/CSA-Z662.

Section 84

Δ **Rule 84-000**

Where power-generating equipment such as photovoltaic arrays, fuel cells, micro-turbines, etc., supplies power through an inverter, the output of the inverter is considered to be the electric power production source.

Rule 84-002

The consumer electric power generator owner should consult with the supply authority before planning the interconnection.

The interconnection arrangements should not adversely affect the safety of the supply authority system.

When interconnected with a supply authority electric system, the output of the electric power production source should not adversely affect the voltage, frequency, or wave shape of the system to which it is connected.

Rule 84-008

Where the utility loses one phase of a three-phase system, some transformer configurations allow a voltage to continue to be present on all phases, and the voltage drop is often not high enough to cause the electric power production source to shut down. Because the electric power production source continues to detect a voltage within tolerance on all phases, it is not expected that the electric power production source is shut down.

The words "disconnected" and "disconnection" in the context of this Rule do not necessarily mean "disconnecting means" as used elsewhere in the Code.

Rule 84-022

The supply authority disconnecting means is intended to allow the supply authority a single point of access to simultaneously isolate one or more electric power production sources on the premises. The main service box, or the equivalent, is normally used to provide this function.

Δ Rule 84-024

In some circumstances, the supply authority may use the provisions of Rule 84-002 to require that the disconnecting means have "contact operation verifiable by direct visible means". This is a common worker-safety feature used by supply authority workers to provide added assurance that the circuit is open before work is initiated.

Where inverters are used for interconnection, the anti-islanding feature automatically isolates the generation equipment from the supply authority upon loss of supply authority voltage, so that having "contact operation verifiable by visible means" may not be required. CSA C22.2 No. 107.1, Clause 14, applies to interactive inverters and requires the inverter to automatically cease to deliver ac power to the utility in accordance with an anti-islanding test, within the time specified and after the output voltage and frequency of the utility source are adjusted to each condition. Utility abandonment of the interface disconnect switch would require the utility to rely entirely on the inverter to be fail-safe under normal operation and component fault mode re-energizing a dead utility bus. A small generator can magnetize a single-phase distribution transformer when the transformer is disconnected from the primary conductor.

Rule 84-028 2)

The isolating transformer referred to can be remote from or integral to the inverter.

Rule 84-030

The single-line diagram should identify related components of the interconnected system, including switching arrangements, interlocks, isolation points, and their relative locations. See Figure B64-4 in the Note to Rule 64-002 for an illustration of an interconnected photovoltaic system.

Section 86

Rule 86-100
Electric vehicle

A "low speed vehicle" or LSV is a class of vehicle described as a small four-wheeled electric vehicle that can attain a maximum speed of 40 km/h in a distance of 1.6 km. An LSV is designed for use in controlled areas. There is a maximum weight limit and a requirement that the LSV not use fuel as an on-board source of energy.

Electric vehicle supply equipment

The primary function of electric vehicle supply equipment is to transfer power for electric vehicle charging by means (e.g., ac, dc, conductive, or wireless) appropriate for the specific electric vehicle to which it is connected.

Rule 86-300 2) and 3)

These requirements are intended to recognize the use of load management systems, from the simplest manual load transfer type to the automated type, for use with electric vehicle supply equipment and other loads.

Rule 86-306 1) b)

It is intended by this requirement that, when a connector is used with an attachment plug other than CSA configuration 5-20P, this connector be a universal plug compatible with the receptacles of the appropriate CSA configuration as specified in Diagram 1 or 2.

Rule 86-400

It is the intent of this Rule to provide ventilation with electric vehicle supply equipment unless the equipment is marked for use with electric vehicles not requiring ventilation, or where the manufacturer's installation instructions specify that ventilation is not required. When ventilation is being designed for indoor charging sites where vented storage batteries are used, both supply and mechanical exhaust equipment should be installed and located to intake from, and vent directly to, the outdoors.

See the Note to Rule 26-506 for similar considerations.

Tables

Tables 6A to 6K

The calculated values in Tables 6A to 6K are based on conventional concentric stranded conductors as detailed in Tables 10A and 10B.

The calculated values in these Tables are based on raceways selected from Tables 9A to 9J with the smallest cross-sectional area. Raceways of the same nominal size may have different dimensions, and it may, therefore, be permissible to exceed the values in Tables 6A and 6B.

Some raceways are required to contain a separate bonding or grounding conductor. No allowance is made for extra conductors in Tables 6A to 6K.

Tables 10A, 10B, 10C, and 10D

The diameters of the insulated conductors are calculated based on the nominal diameter of the conductors for a given class and the nominal thickness of the insulation for the conductor or cable type. Classes of stranding other than those identified in Tables 10A and 10B are permitted and will result in different diameters for the same gauge of conductor. Use of higher class stranding could result in the acceptable conduit fill being exceeded.

Table 32

A light snow area is considered to be an area in which the mean annual recorded depth of snow is 500 mm or less. This information for any area in Canada can be obtained from the following:

a)   Meteorological Service of Canada, Environment Canada; and

b)   *Atlas of Canada*, published by Natural Resources Canada.

Tables 33 and 34

The spacings and clearances shown in these tables differ intentionally from those found in CSA C22.3 No. 1, as explained in Clause 5.2.1 of that Standard:

5.2.1 Construction and day-to-day clearances

The clearances specified in Clause 5 for wires and conductors are minimum values related to maximum specified loads and service conditions and represent design limits rather than clearances for construction or day-to-day operation. Clearances under day-to-day conditions are greater than the minimum clearances specified in Clause 5 when loads and service conditions are less severe than specified maximum conditions. Clearances provided at the time of construction shall by design be sufficiently greater than the minimum clearances specified in Clause 5 to ensure that the actual clearances under maximum specified loads and service conditions meet minimum clearance requirements.

Note: *Clearances specified in the* Canadian Electrical Code, Part I, *apply at the time of installation rather than under specified maximum conditions and are therefore larger than those specified in the* Canadian Electrical Code, Part III, *for the reasons explained in this Clause.*

Table 51

See the Note to Rules 36-300 and 36-308 and Table 51:

Diagrams

Diagrams 1 and 2
See the Note to Rule 26-700.

Diagram 3
See the Note to Rule 14-102 and Diagram 3.

C22.1-18

Appendix C
The Technical Committee on the Canadian
Electrical Code, Part I — Organization and rules of procedure

Appendix C — The Technical Committee on the *Canadian Electrical Code, Part I* — Organization and rules of procedure

Note: *This Appendix is a normative (mandatory) part of this Standard.*

C1 General

C1.1
The Technical Committee on the *Canadian Electrical Code, Part I* (hereafter called the Committee on Part I) shall operate under the authority of the Strategic Steering Committee on Requirements for Electrical Safety and in accordance with *CSA Policy governing standardization — Code of good practice for standardization* and *CSA Directives and guidelines governing standardization*.

C1.2
The Committee on Part I shall be responsible for the development of the *Canadian Electrical Code, Part I* (hereafter called the *CE Code, Part I*), which shall consist of safety Standards for the installation and maintenance of electrical equipment.

C2 Committee on Part I

C2.1 Terms of reference
The Committee on Part I shall be responsible for
a) establishing Committees and Subcommittees, appointing a Chair and Vice-Chair, and establishing the terms of reference for them;
b) planning, programming, coordinating, and monitoring the activities of Committees and Subcommittees;
c) recommending adoption of amendments to the *CE Code, Part I*;
d) determining the form and arrangement of the *CE Code, Part I*;
e) interpreting the *CE Code, Part I*;
f) all policy matters related to the *CE Code, Part I*;
g) setting up procedures that will facilitate feedback to the Committee on Part I from regulatory authorities, CSA, industry, users, and others; and
h) establishing and maintaining liaison with the Canadian Advisory Council on Electrical Safety, the Technical Committee on the *CE Code, Part II*, other Strategic Steering Committees, and national and international organizations responsible for safety Standards for the installation and maintenance of electrical equipment.

C2.2 Structure

C2.2.1
The Committee on Part I shall consist of
a) members as specified in Clause C2.3;
b) a Chair and Vice-Chair appointed from the members, each of whom shall serve, subject to the approval of the Strategic Steering Committee on Requirements for Electrical Safety, a term of 3 years and shall be eligible for reappointment;
c) an Executive Committee;
d) Subcommittees; and
e) a Project Manager (nonvoting) appointed by CSA.

C2.2.2
Chairs of Subcommittees, if they are not voting members of the Committee on Part I, shall be recorded as ex officio, nonvoting members of the Committee on Part I.

C22.1-18

Appendix C
The Technical Committee on the Canadian
Electrical Code, Part I — Organization and rules of procedure

C2.3 Members

C2.3.1 Matrix

C2.3.1.1 General

The Committee on Part I shall be composed of not more than 41 voting members, representing the following interests:

	Range	
	Minimum	**Maximum**
Regulatory authority	11	16
Owner/Operator/Producer	9	14
General interest	9	14

The Committee shall also include associate, liaison, and ex officio members (nonvoting) as required.

C2.3.1.2 Regulatory authorities

The regulatory authorities shall be selected from the various provincial, territorial, and municipal electrical inspection authorities.

C2.3.1.3 Owners/Operators/Producers

The Owner/Operator/Producer representatives shall be selected from groups with national stature representing the viewpoints of
a) electrical equipment manufacturers;
b) electrical installation designers and installers; and
c) electrical installation users.

C2.3.1.4 General interest representatives

The general interest representatives shall be selected from groups with national stature representing the viewpoints of
a) fire chiefs;
b) electric utilities;
c) committees responsible for related electrical Codes and Standards;
d) fire insurers;
e) labour;
f) issuers of building Codes; and
g) educators.

C2.3.2

Members shall be nominated by the interest or organization that they represent, and their appointment shall be subject to the approval of the Executive Committee or the Chair, in concurrence with the Project Manager.

C2.3.3

Members shall participate actively in the work of the Committee on Part I, attend meetings, accept the Chair of Section Subcommittees, and participate in Subcommittee work.

C2.3.4 Termination of membership

In consultation with the Project Manager and after enquiry, the Chair of the Committee on Part I (on behalf of the Executive Committee) should recommend that a TC member be removed from the Committee if the member has failed to
a) attend three consecutive meetings;
b) respond to three consecutive letter ballots; or
c) be actively and effectively involved in the work and responsibilities of the Committee.

Appendix C
The Technical Committee on the Canadian
C22.1-18
Electrical Code, Part I — Organization and rules of procedure

Notice of pending termination should be sent to that member by CSA staff. Subsequent failure to comply with the requirements should result in termination as directed by the Vice-President or Program Director, Standards Development.

C2.3.5

The Executive Committee shall recommend the removal of a member after consultation with the nominating interest and the Project Manager.

C2.4 Meetings

C2.4.1

The Committee on Part I shall meet at least once a year.

C2.4.2

Notices and agendas of meetings shall be sent at least 4 weeks in advance of the meeting date.

C2.4.3

One half of the total membership shall constitute a quorum. Proxies shall not be included. Alternates shall be included.

C2.4.4

Voting by proxy shall be permitted for the Committee on Part I, provided that notice of the proxy is filed with the Chair prior to the meeting.

C2.4.5

An absent member may, with the approval of the Chair, be represented at a meeting by an alternate who may vote in that member's stead.

C2.4.6

In the event of a lack of quorum, or if desired by those at a meeting where a quorum is present, the vote shall be taken by a letter ballot at a later date. To be valid, a ballot shall be returned within 30 days.

C3 Regulatory authority committee

C3.1 Terms of reference

The Regulatory Authority Committee shall be responsible for advising the Committee on Part I when the language of an amendment is deemed unacceptable from an enforcement or legal standpoint.

C3.2

The Regulatory Authority Committee shall consist of

a)   the regulatory authorities' representatives who are members of the Committee on Part I;

b)   a Chair and Vice-Chair appointed from the members of the Regulatory Authority Committee; and

c)   a Project Manager (nonvoting) provided by CSA.

C3.3

The voting members of the Regulatory Authority Committee shall consist of the provincial and territorial inspection authority representatives who are members of the Committee on Part I.

C3.4

The Regulatory Authority Committee shall have the authority, within its terms of reference, to agree or disagree with the proposed amendments to the *CE Code, Part I*. Its terms of reference shall not give it the authority to amend the *CE Code, Part I*. (See Clause C7.2.1.3.)

C3.5 Legal amendments

C3.5.1

A legal amendment changes

a)   the words but not the intent of Rules in one or more Sections of the Code; or

b)   the administrative Rules in Section 2 or the Scope of Section 0 affecting regulatory implementation of the Code.

C22.1-18

Appendix C
The Technical Committee on the Canadian
Electrical Code, Part I — Organization and rules of procedure

A legal amendment is initiated by a member of the Regulatory Authority Committee.

C3.5.2
The Regulatory Authority Committee may act as the Section Subcommittee for legal amendments.

C3.5.3
The Chair of the Regulatory Authority Committee may appoint a member of the Regulatory Authority Committee to act as the Chair of the Subcommittee for purposes of achieving consensus, preparing a Subcommittee report, or resolving negative Part I ballots.

C3.5.4
While the Regulatory Authority Committee is acting as a Subcommittee for a legal amendment, the voting process in Clause C7.2 does not necessarily apply.

C3.5.5
After a report has been submitted to the Committee on Part I, it will be sent to each affected Part I Subcommittee for a minimum of one month and a maximum of two months to identify and report on those Rules where the proposed legal amendment may have changed the intent.

C3.5.6
The report, as revised by the Regulatory Authority Committee (in its role as a Subcommittee) due to comments from the affected *CE Code, Part I* Subcommittees, will then be processed as any other Subcommittee report and submitted for Part I letter ballot in accordance with Clause C7.1.2.

C3.6 Editorial changes

C3.6.1
An editorial change is one that revises the words of a Rule or a portion of an Appendix to improve clarity of expression without changing the intent of the original wording or affecting the safety or cost of an installation.

C3.6.2
The Regulatory Authority Committee may act as the Section Subcommittee for editorial amendments.

C3.6.3
The Regulatory Authority Committee may appoint a working group(s) to review particular Rules and prepare recommendations.

C3.6.4
Editorial changes shall be voted on following the process described in Clauses C7.2.2 and C7.2.3.

C3.6.5
Chairs of the Part I Section Subcommittee responsible for the Rules under discussion will be advised when there is to be a Regulatory Authority Committee ballot. Any negative comment shall be treated as a negative vote by a Regulatory Authority Committee member.

C4 Executive Committee

C4.1 Terms of reference
The Executive Committee shall
a)   act in an advisory capacity to the Committee on Part I on administrative matters;
b)   assist the Chair in monitoring the rate of progress of the Subcommittees and be ready to offer administrative assistance in the event of delays;
c)   assist the Chair in the appointment or replacement of Subcommittee Chairs;
d)   recommend to the Committee on Part I any proposed changes that it deems necessary in procedures, operation, or policy of the Committee on Part I;
e)   work with CSA staff to implement any changes in procedures or operations that have been approved by the Committee on Part I;

Appendix C
The Technical Committee on the Canadian
C22.1-18
Electrical Code, Part I — Organization and rules of procedure

Appendix C

f) make recommendations to the Committee on Part I on
   i) requests for membership on the Committee on Part I; and
   ii) replacements of members of the Committee on Part I; and
g) periodically review the matrix of the Committee on Part I and make recommendations to that Committee.

C4.2 Membership
1) The members of the Executive Committee shall be members of the Committee on Part I and shall consist of the following:
   a) the Chair and Vice-Chair of the Committee on Part I (who shall be Chair and Vice-Chair, respectively, of the Executive Committee);
   b) two representatives from each of the regulatory authority, owner/operator/producer, and general interest categories who shall be elected by the Committee on Part I; and
   c) a Project Manager (nonvoting) provided by CSA.
Δ 2) The immediate Past Chair and Past Vice-Chair of the Committee on Part I shall be invited to be members of the Executive Committee.

C5 Section Subcommittees

C5.1 Terms of reference
Subcommittees shall be responsible for the preparation, amendment, and interpretation of the Sections assigned to them by the Committee on Part I.

Δ C5.2 Structure
The Executive Committee shall appoint a Chair and a Vice-Chair of each Subcommittee. The Chair of a Subcommittee shall be a member of the Committee on Part I and may be a voting or nonvoting member (see Clause C2.2.2). The Vice-Chair of the Subcommittee shall act as the Subcommittee Chair in the absence of the Chair.

C5.3 Members

C5.3.1
The Chair of a Subcommittee shall appoint the Subcommittee members. Requests for membership on Subcommittees shall be directed through the Project Manager of the Committee on Part I, who shall coordinate such requests with the Subcommittee Chair.

C5.3.2
It is recommended that representation on Section Subcommittees be chosen from among the following categories, in accordance with the major interests of the Subcommittee:
a) inspection authorities;
b) manufacturers of electrical equipment;
c) employers;
d) employees;
e) consultants;
f) utilities;
g) testing laboratories, underwriters, or fire marshals;
h) primary and secondary industries;
i) corresponding Code-making panels of the *National Electrical Code*; and
j) users.

C5.3.3
It is further recommended that
a) Subcommittees for the General Sections (Sections 0 to 16 and 26) be composed of not more than 12 members;

Appendix C
The Technical Committee on the Canadian
C22.1-18   *Electrical Code, Part I — Organization and rules of procedure*

b)   Subcommittees for the other Sections (Sections 18 to 24 and 28 to 86) be composed of not more than 8 members;

c)   at the discretion of the Subcommittee Chair, the number of members be increased if further representation is required;

d)   at least one member of a Subcommittee in addition to the Chair be from the Committee on Part I;

e)   75% of a Subcommittee membership be non-Part I members with not more than one-third of the membership from any one category;

f)   if practicable, the Subcommittee membership be balanced in representation from the various geographical areas of Canada; and

g)   requests for representation from categories such as manufacturers, electrical contractors, consultants, and utilities be directed to the organization if such exists.

C5.3.4
Subcommittees should consult with individuals or organizations outside the membership of the Subcommittee or the Committee on Part I when specific data or information may be required. Experts on specific subjects may be asked to attend meetings of the Subcommittee or to submit special data or information to the Subcommittee for its use.

C5.3.5
The Subcommittee Chair may set up task groups to study and report on specific problems. Task groups may include individuals with expertise not available within the Subcommittee.

C5.3.6
Members of a Subcommittee shall be provided with the names and addresses of the other members of the Subcommittee.

Δ   ### C5.3.7
The Subcommittee Chair should review periodically the performance of each member of the Subcommittee and, with the concurrence of the Project Manager, decide on any changes to the Subcommittee membership. Consideration should be given to the calibre of responses to correspondence, promptness in responding to requests for comment, and attendance at meetings.

C5.3.8
Members of Section Subcommittees who are not members of the Committee on Part I should be advised by the Project Manager about the action taken by the Committee on Part I.

C5.3.9
Members of the Subcommittee should review, on a continuing basis, the Section of the Code for which they are responsible and should propose amendments where necessary.

C5.4 Subcommittee operation

C5.4.1
After receiving a proposal from the Project Manager of the Committee on Part I, the Subcommittee Chair shall review the proposal and shall submit it to the Subcommittee members (see Annex C).

C5.4.2
Meetings shall be held as necessary.

C5.4.3
The Project Manager shall forward public review comments to the Subcommittee for consideration (see Clause C6.4).

Appendix C
The Technical Committee on the Canadian
Electrical Code, Part I — Organization and rules of procedure

C22.1-18

C5.4.4

Decisions at meetings or through correspondence shall be based on the consensus principle.

Note: *As defined in the* CSA Directives, *CSA-SDP-2.1, consensus in standardization practice is achieved when substantial agreement is achieved. Consensus implies much more than a simple majority, but not necessarily unanimity.*

C5.4.5

The Subcommittee Chair shall report the Subcommittee's recommendation on the proposal to the Project Manager of the Committee on Part I.

Δ **C5.4.6**

A Subcommittee recommendation should be submitted to the Project Manager of the Committee on Part I within a period not exceeding 12 months from the date that the original proposal was received, in accordance with Clause C5.4.1.

C5.4.7

Subcommittee reports should be presented in the standard format (see Annex A) and should include, in addition to the proposal, the name and affiliation of the submitter, the reason for the proposal, a summary of the Subcommittee's deliberations, and the Subcommittee's recommendation.

C5.4.8

The summary of the Subcommittee's deliberations should include the comments of any members who may not be in agreement with the Subcommittee's recommendation.

C5.4.9

If the proposed amendment could affect a product, the Subcommittee report to the Committee on Part I shall include a recommendation that the Technical Committee on the pertinent Standard(s) of the *CE Code, Part II* be advised.

C5.4.10

If the Subcommittee report recommends removal of a product design requirement, the Subcommittee report shall state whether or not the particular requirement is included in applicable equipment Standards.

C5.4.11

The Project Manager shall submit the Subcommittee report to the Committee on Part I for letter ballot in accordance with Clause C7.1.2. The report shall not be submitted for ballot until the public review period has ended.

C5.4.12

The submitter of a proposal that has been sent to the Subcommittee in accordance with Clause C5.4.1 has the right to withdraw the proposal at any time before the Subcommittee's recommendation is sent to the Committee on Part I for approval.

C5.4.13

If the submitter of a proposal requests its withdrawal after the Subcommittee recommendation has been sent to the Committee on Part I for approval, the withdrawal is subject to the approval of the Subcommittee.

Where the Subcommittee agrees not to take sponsorship of a proposal withdrawn by the original submitter, the subject shall be closed.

C6 Requests for amendments to the *CE Code, Part I* — General

C6.1

A request for an amendment to the *CE Code, Part I* may be submitted to the Project Manager of the Committee on Part I by any person, organization, or committee (see Annex B).

Appendix C
The Technical Committee on the Canadian
Electrical Code, Part I — Organization and rules of procedure

C22.1-18

C6.2

A request for an amendment to the Code shall include a specifically worded proposal, reasons for the proposal, and supporting data. The wording to be added, changed, or deleted shall be submitted in such a way that the intent is clear. An unclear proposal may be returned to the submitter by the Project Manager after consultation with the Section Chair and the Chair of the Committee on Part I.

C6.3

If the request for amendment is of a horizontal nature that proposes similar changes to two or more Sections of the Code, it shall be submitted for public review in accordance with Clause C6.4 b) and submitted to the Executive Committee for preparation of a report and recommendation either to proceed with the request or to reject it. The recommendation shall be processed in accordance with Clause C7. If a recommendation to proceed is approved, or a recommendation to reject is not approved, the Project Manager shall assign a subject number to each Section-specific part of the request for amendment and process it in accordance with Clause C6.4.

C6.4

The Project Manager shall assign the request a subject number and submit it

a) to the Chair of the appropriate Section Subcommittee for the preparation of a report and recommendation by the Subcommittee (see Clause C5.4);

b) for 60 day public review; and

c) to the Technical Committee on the Application of Electricity in Health Care for a 30 day review if the request affects Section 24 or 52.

C6.5

If the report on the assigned subject is not completed by the Section Subcommittee in accordance with Clause C5.4.5, the subject may be closed on the recommendation of the Chair of the Committee on Part I.

C6.6

If the proposed change affects new products, the Project Manager shall request that the appropriate Subcommittee Chair give priority to these proposed amendments. As soon as the Subcommittee report is received from the Section Subcommittee, it shall be forwarded by the Project Manager to the Committee on Part I for 30 day ballot.

Δ ### C6.7

Proposals shall be permitted to provide for temporary suspension of amendments to the *CE Code, Part I* Rules until such time that necessary changes to a product Standard(s) are in force. The Subcommittee Chair, in consultation with the Project Manager and the Regulatory Authority Committee Chair, shall determine when such suspended subjects are to be released and put into effect. The Project Manager shall maintain a current list of all such suspended subjects on agendas for review at the regular meetings of the Committee on Part I, the Regulatory Authority Committee, and the Part I Executive Committee.

C7 Approval of amendments to the *CE Code, Part I*

C7.1 Approval by the Committee on Part I

C7.1.1 General

C7.1.1.1

The Chair and Vice-Chair shall be entitled to vote.

C7.1.1.2

If the recommendation is approved and the resulting Rule amendment affects a Standard under the *CE Code, Part II*, the Project Manager of the Committee on Part I shall inform the relevant Part II Technical Committee Chair and Project Manager that a modification of the Standard is required,

Appendix C
The Technical Committee on the Canadian
C22.1-18   *Electrical Code, Part I — Organization and rules of procedure*

Appendix C

emphasizing that the Committee on Part I requires an answer within 8 months regarding the action to be taken.

C7.1.1.3
In approving amendments to the *CE Code, Part I*, the Committee attests that
a) the amendment satisfies the intent;
b) the amendment has been subjected to proper procedures; and
c) as far as it is aware, the amendment does not conflict with other amendments, with published CSA Standards, or with National Standards of Canada.

C7.1.1.4
In addition to the criteria given in Clause C7.1.1.3, members may vote on the technical adequacy of an amendment. Any points raised by the members shall be dealt with by the appropriate Section Subcommittee.

C7.1.2 Approval by letter ballot

C7.1.2.1
The Subcommittee report and recommendation shall be submitted to the Committee on Part I for letter ballot approval, unless otherwise authorized by the Chair of the Committee on Part I. To be valid, a ballot shall be returned within 30 days.

C7.1.2.2
If there are no negative votes, the recommendation shall be considered approved, provided that more than 50% of the total voting membership voted affirmative.

C7.1.2.3
Disposition of negative votes shall be in accordance with Clause C7.3.

C7.1.2.4
If a member of the Regulatory Authority Committee submits a negative vote for regulatory reasons, it shall be indicated as such and shall be accompanied by a revised amendment carrying the same intent regarding safety and technical requirements.

C7.1.2.5
If the recommendation is not approved, the subject shall be included in the agenda of the next meeting, when it shall either be returned to the Subcommittee or closed.

C7.1.3 Approval at a meeting

C7.1.3.1
Meetings shall be conducted in accordance with the procedures in the CSA Directives, CSA-SDP-2.2, Clause 7.3.9, "Rules of procedure for conducting a meeting".

C7.1.3.2
The Subcommittee's recommendations on motions or on an amendment or interpretation shall be considered approved, provided that more than 50% of the total voting membership voted affirmative and that at least two-thirds of the votes cast are affirmative.

C7.1.3.3
When a subject is placed on the floor, the Chair should allow a general discussion of it prior to a motion being made.

C7.1.3.4
If the Section Subcommittee's recommendation is to reject the submitter's proposal and the Committee on Part I rejects the Section Subcommittee's recommendation, the Committee on Part I shall return the proposal to the Section Subcommittee for further review of the reasons for rejection provided by the Committee on Part I.

C22.1-18

Appendix C
The Technical Committee on the Canadian
Electrical Code, Part I — Organization and rules of procedure

C7.1.3.5

If the Section Subcommittee's recommendation is either to accept the proposal as submitted or to accept the proposal with amendment and the Committee on Part I rejects that recommendation, the Committee on Part I shall

a) accept a motion to close the subject; or

b) accept a motion to return the subject to the Subcommittee for further review.

C7.1.3.6

Amendments to a motion cannot be accepted if they have the effect of defeating the main motion.

C7.1.3.7

When a motion to close the subject is passed by the Committee on Part I, the submitter shall be informed by the Project Manager of the Committee on Part I of the proposal's rejection, with the reasons for rejection, unless the submitter is also a member of the Committee on Part I. The matter may be resubmitted after a period of 6 months.

C7.2 Approval of subjects by the regulatory authority committee

C7.2.1 General

C7.2.1.1

The Chair and Vice-Chair shall be entitled to vote.

C7.2.1.2

If at the Committee on Part I stage, no voting member of the Regulatory Authority Committee has voted negative as a Part I member for reasons concerning the suitability of the amendment for use in a regulation and the subject is approved by that Committee, no further vote is necessary in the Regulatory Authority Committee.

C7.2.1.3

If the Regulatory Authority Committee disagrees with the proposed amendment accepted by the Committee on Part I, the Regulatory Authority Committee shall submit a revised amendment carrying the same intent in terms of safety and technical requirements to the Section Subcommittee for further consideration.

C7.2.1.4

A revised amendment from the Section Subcommittee shall be proposed to the Committee on Part I by letter ballot or by a recorded vote at a meeting.

C7.2.2 Approval by letter ballot

C7.2.2.1

Proposals for amendment as submitted by the Committee on Part I shall be distributed for letter ballot approval. To be valid, a ballot shall be returned within 30 days.

C7.2.2.2

If there are no negative votes, the recommendation shall be considered approved, provided that more than 50% of the total voting membership voted affirmative.

C7.2.2.3

If there are any negative votes that cannot be resolved by the Chair of the Regulatory Authority Committee, the subject shall be included in the agenda of the next meeting of the Regulatory Authority Committee for the purpose of resolution.

C7.2.3 Approval at a meeting

C7.2.3.1

Letter ballots referred to a meeting shall be reconsidered and an open vote taken. The amendment shall be considered approved, provided that more than 50% of the total voting membership voted affirmative and that at least two-thirds of the votes cast are affirmative.

Appendix C
The Technical Committee on the Canadian
C22.1-18
Electrical Code, Part I — Organization and rules of procedure

C7.2.3.2
Subjects that have not been submitted for letter ballot may be considered at a meeting, provided that all voting members present are agreeable or that the subject has been placed on the agenda and no objection is registered.

C7.3 Consideration of negative votes

The Chair of the Committee on Part I shall consult with the Chair of the Section Subcommittee and CSA staff, and one or more of the following courses of action shall be taken, as appropriate:

a) an attempt shall be made to resolve each negative vote by editorial changes or explanation and thereby have the negative vote withdrawn;

b) a negative vote may be ruled non-germane if
   i) the negative vote is not accompanied by supporting comments;
   ii) the negative vote and supporting comments are not considered to conform to the criteria outlined in Clauses C7.1.1.3 and C7.1.1.4; or
   iii) the negative vote and supporting reasons are not considered relevant to the items being balloted;

c) a negative vote may be ruled non-persuasive if the particular reasons for the vote have been previously discussed and rejected by the Section Subcommittee*;

   * In such instances, this decision should be supported by Subcommittee records.

d) if the reasons for the negative vote are considered by the Subcommittee Chair to be of a valid, technical nature not previously discussed or not adequately addressed by the Section Subcommittee,
   i) the negative vote shall be referred to the Section Subcommittee for further deliberation;
   ii) the Committee on Part I shall be notified accordingly; and
   iii) the Section Subcommittee Chair shall submit to the Project Manager a new Subcommittee report for re-balloting by the Committee on Part I or shall refer the new Subcommittee report to the next meeting of the Committee on Part I;

e) if the reasons for the negative vote are considered by the Subcommittee Chair to be non-germane or non-persuasive, the negative vote shall be referred to the next meeting of the Committee on Part I, except that the Section Subcommittee Chair shall be permitted to act on the negative vote in accordance with Item d); or

f) a negative vote shall be referred to the next meeting of the Committee on Part I (see Clause C7.1.3) if the vote has not been disposed of under Items a), b), c), d), or e).

C8 Approval of other subjects

Voting on other motions shall comply with Clause C7.1.3.2.

C9 Interpretation of the *CE Code, Part I*

C9.1
Interpretation of the *CE Code, Part I* shall be a function of the Committee on Part I in accordance with Clauses C9.2 to C9.13.

C9.2
Requests for interpretation shall be submitted in writing to the Project Manager of the Committee on Part I in the form of a question that can be answered by a categoric "yes" or "no".

C9.3
The request shall make specific reference to the relevant Rule or Rules and shall provide an explanation of circumstances surrounding the actual field situation.

C22.1-18

Appendix C
The Technical Committee on the Canadian
Electrical Code, Part I — Organization and rules of procedure

C9.4
Requests for interpretation shall not be accepted for
a)   the degree and extent of a hazardous location area;
b)   the suitability of isolation or guarding; or
c)   items that involve an intimate knowledge of the installation rather than the meaning of the Rule.

C9.5
The request for an interpretation shall be referred to the appropriate Section Subcommittee.

Δ   **C9.6**
The Project Manager and, if necessary, the Section Subcommittee Chair shall review the request for interpretation to ensure that it is clear, unambiguous, and in compliance with Clauses C9.2 and C9.3.

Δ   **C9.7**
Where changes are required to a request for interpretation in order for it to comply with Clauses C9.2 and C9.3, the request shall be referred back to the submitter, identifying why the request does not comply with the requirements.

C9.8
Interpretations shall be based on the literal text and not on the intent.

C9.9
The Section Subcommittee shall present a recommended interpretation to the Committee on Part I for vote. Voting shall be in accordance with Clause C7.1.

C9.10
The results of the letter ballot shall be made known by the Project Manager to the submitter and to the Committee on Part I.

C9.11
Interpretations shall be published on the Current Standards Activities page at standardsactivities.csa.ca.

C9.12
When an interpretation of a Rule has been adopted by the Committee on Part I in accordance with Clause C9.9,
a)   the responsible Subcommittee Chair shall ensure that an appropriate proposal for a new subject is made promptly to the Subcommittee of a new subject in accordance with Clause C6.1 to reword the subject Rule in a way that removes ambiguity of meaning; and
b)   subject to Clause C9.13, the interpretation shall be published in Appendix I and the Rule shall reference the Appendix if the rewording of the Rule has not been approved by the cut-off date for that edition.

C9.13
Where rewording of the Rule as described in Clause C9.12 b) has not been approved in time for the next edition, the Committee on Part I may, at the final meeting prior to publication of the next edition, vote to withhold publication of the related interpretation in Appendix I. The motion to withhold publication shall be considered approved if more than 50% of the total voting membership vote affirmative and at least two-thirds of the votes cast are affirmative.

C10 Appeals

C10.1
Any Committee member or individual who believes that this CSA Standard is being prepared under procedures that do not conform to the *CSA Policy governing standardization — Code of good practice for standardization*, the *CSA Directives and guidelines governing standardization*, and these Rules of

Appendix C
The Technical Committee on the Canadian
C22.1-18   *Electrical Code, Part I — Organization and rules of procedure*

Appendix C

Procedures may appeal to the Strategic Steering Committee on Requirements for Electrical Safety for a review of the project.

C10.2
Appeals shall be based on procedural matters and not on technical considerations.

C10.3
Application for appeal shall not necessarily be considered cause for delaying the development or publication of this Standard.

C10.4
All appeals shall be submitted in writing to the Secretary of the Strategic Steering Committee on Requirements for Electrical Safety.

C10.5
The Secretary of the Strategic Steering Committee on Requirements for Electrical Safety shall notify the appellant of the decision of the Strategic Steering Committee on Requirements for Electrical Safety and shall refer the decision to the appropriate CSA staff for implementation.

C11 Code format and Rule terminology

C11.1
Because the *CE Code, Part I* may be adopted as a regulatory document, it is important that all Rules, Subrules, and Items be stated in mandatory language in accordance with CSA guidelines. In this respect, the verb form "shall" must be used rather than "is to be", "are to be", "will be", "should be", etc. or as "shall not" if the negative is required. Requirements shall be stated in the positive rather than the negative.

C11.2
The term "may" shall not be used in a permissive sense because it may indicate to the user or the enforcer of the Code that the permissive idea may or may not be acceptable to the enforcer. The term "shall be permitted" shall be used because it indicates definitely that the enforcer has no alternative but to allow the easement.

C11.3
Recommendations or explanatory notes shall not be included in the text of the Code, but they may be included in an Appendix and shall be written in a permissive, not mandatory, manner.

C11.4
Each Section should be assigned an even number, the odd numbers being reserved for new Sections pending their inclusion in the next edition of the *CE Code, Part I*. The title shall be descriptive of the contents of the Section.

C11.5
Rules and Subrules should occur in a logical sequence. Where the Section is not a General Section, the first Rule should contain a statement that the Section supplements and/or amends the general requirements of the Code.

C11.6
Where reference is made to a Subrule or Item in the same Rule, only the Subrule number and/or Item letter and the word "Subrule" and/or "Item" need be mentioned. If the reference is to another Rule or Section, then the Rule number and the word "Rule" shall be stated.

C11.7
Each Rule of a Section shall be provided with a title or caption following the Rule number that indicates the contents of the Rule.

C11.8
Each Rule should be assigned an even number, the odd numbers being reserved for new Rules pending their inclusion in the next edition of the *CE Code, Part I*.

C22.1-18

Appendix C
The Technical Committee on the Canadian
Electrical Code, Part I — Organization and rules of procedure

C11.9
References to other Codes or Standards shall be to a specific edition of the referenced Code or Standard rather than to the latest edition, except for Standards forming part of the *CE Code, Part II*.

Δ ### C11.10
The term "ampacity", as defined in Section 0, applies to the current-carrying capacity of bare or insulated conductors only and shall not be used in relation to switches, panels, motors, etc.

C11.11
Maximum and minimum limits shall be expressed in the following ways as appropriate:
a)   "...shall not exceed...volts-to-ground...";
b)   "...shall have a clearance of not less than...between conductors..."; and
c)   "...shall be supported at intervals not exceeding...".

C11.12
The term "voltage" shall be used instead of the term "potential".

C11.13
The term "damage" should be used to describe damage to equipment or property. It should not be used to describe injury to persons.

C11.14
The term "injury" should be used to describe injury to persons. It should not be used to describe damage to equipment or property.

Δ ### C11.15
The term "approved" as defined in Section 0 and described in Rule 2-024 applies to all electrical equipment and shall not be used outside Section 0 and Rule 2-024. Where additional emphasis is required to describe equipment acceptability, a note with a reference to the product Standard shall be included in Appendix B.

C11.16
The term "acceptable" should be used to describe equipment that is not required to be approved.

C11.17
Use of the term "acceptable" in the dictionary sense is permissible, and the attributes that are important in deciding on acceptance should be included in the wording (e.g., "acceptable in terms of clearance, ruggedness, separation from..., colour, legibility, location, etc.").

C11.18
In the technical sections of the Code, the phrase "acceptable to (x)" shall not be used (where x may stand for the electrical inspector, the building inspector, or the supply authority).

C11.19
Where one wishes to indicate that the supply authority has to agree, the phrase "in accordance with the requirements of the supply authority" shall be used.

C11.20
Standard terms have been established by usage or practice and shall be used in preference to similar terms that do not have such wide or established recognition. Some examples are
a)   "authority having jurisdiction";
b)   "disconnecting means" (not "disconnection means");
c)   "ducts" (only for air-handling purposes; not as raceways);
d)   "electric" (as applied to equipment);
e)   "electrical" (as applied to requirements, Standards, or Codes);
f)   "equipment" (both singular and plural);

Appendix C
The Technical Committee on the Canadian
C22.1-18
Electrical Code, Part I — Organization and rules of procedure

g) "metal" (not "metallic", in general);
h) "metallic" (only where directly related to material using this term, e.g., electrical metallic tubing or non-metallic-sheathed cable);
i) "not exceeding" instead of "not more than";
j) "not less than"; and
k) "provided with mechanical protection" instead of "protection against mechanical damage".

C11.21
Terms such as "adequate", "adjacent", "reasonable", "near to", "large", "small", "high", "low", etc., shall be replaced by more definitive terms.

C11.22
The following terms shall not be used:
a) "fire-resistant";
b) "fireproof";
c) "flame-retarding"; and
d) "that will (not) burn in air".

C11.23
Numbers shall be used to express values and shall be expressed as numerals instead of as words, except at the beginning of a sentence or where two numbers in sequence would be confusing. Words shall be used to express a quantity of items.

C11.24
There shall be only one sentence per Rule, per Subrule, or per Item.

C11.25
The following is a list of standardized comments that Subcommittees may wish to use in reports:
a) Accept:
     i) Acceptance is unconditional; or
     ii) Acceptance is conditional on acceptance by the Subcommittee or Committee on Section _____ or Standard _____;
b) Hold pending:
     i) Submission of further supporting data;
     ii) Further study;
     iii) Receipt of fact-finding report; or
     iv) Receipt of the findings of a Task Group;
c) Reject:
     i) The supporting comment does not justify the proposed amendment or addition;
     ii) See the Subcommittee or Committee on Part I action on Subject No. _____;
     iii) The Subcommittee agrees with the intent of the proposal. However, please note the intent of the action taken on Subject No. _____;
     iv) No additional clarification would be achieved by this proposal;
     v) The present wording adequately represents the intent;
     vi) The supporting data are not consistent with the proposal;
     vii) The supporting comment is not persuasive as to the necessity;
     viii) The supporting data are not adequate;
     ix) The Subcommittee disagrees with the supporting data;
     x) The proposal is already adequately covered by ...;
     xi) The extension of the coverage as proposed is not appropriate at this time;
     xii) Safety is not enhanced by the proposal;
     xiii) The intent of the proposal is not specific or definite;

Appendix C

Appendix C
The Technical Committee on the Canadian
C22.1-18 *Electrical Code, Part I — Organization and rules of procedure*

xiv) The proposal is primarily a design consideration and adds nothing to the safety of the product involved or the method;

xv) The proposal covers a method or practice that is not prohibited by the present Code and thus is not necessary;

xvi) The proposal is beyond the scope of the Code; or

xvii) Deletion of the present requirement as suggested by the proposal is not desirable because ....

C11.26

Rules dealing with flammability limits for wiring systems in a building shall be contained in the *National Building Code of Canada* in liaison with the Committee on Part I, and Rules accomplishing these limits shall be contained in the *CE Code, Part I*, in liaison with the *National Building Code of Canada* Committees.

C11.27

Where *National Building Code of Canada* requirements are referenced in the *CE Code, Part I*, informational notes concerning those requirements should be contained in Appendix B, and the *National Building Code of Canada* article or sentence number should be listed in Appendix G.

C11.28

Where reference is made to the Building Code, the phrase "the *National Building Code of Canada*" shall be used (e.g., "in accordance with the *National Building Code of Canada*").

C11.29

Except for the last Item, each Item in a listing shall end with a semicolon. The penultimate Subrule or Item shall end with either an "and" or an "or".

C11.30

Where it is necessary to include messages or warnings in the Code, the content of those messages or warnings shall be included in the Code, but specific wordings shall be avoided.

Δ
C12 Inclusion of reference Standards in Appendix A

C12.1

Following the issuance of a notice of intent (NOI), the Standards Development Organization (SDO) developing a new Standard, new edition, or amendment to an existing Standard that is being proposed for reference in Appendix A shall provide the Standard designation, title, and scope to the Project Manager of the Committee on Part I for distribution to the Committee.

Note: *The Standards Council of Canada's (SCC) Centralized Notification System (CNS) is a centralized, transparent notification system for notices of intent (NOIs) for new Standards development. The system allows SCC-accredited SDOs and members of the public to be informed of new work in Canadian Standards development; it also allows SCC-accredited SDOs to raise and resolve potential duplication of Standards and effort. The CNS is updated weekly.*

C12.2

When changes to the requirements in the *CE Code, Part I* are necessary due to

a) the inclusion in Appendix A of
   i) a new Standard;
   ii) a new edition of a Standard; or
   iii) an amendment to a Standard; or
b) withdrawal from Appendix A of an existing Standard

a proposal for an amendment to the *CE Code, Part I* in accordance with Clause C6 shall be submitted by the SDO responsible or any other party.

Note: *See Item 6 in Annex D of this Appendix.*

C12.3

With respect to proposals submitted in accordance with Clause C12.2, the Project Manager of the Committee on Part I shall communicate decisions of the Committee to the SDO developing the Standard.

Appendix C
The Technical Committee on the Canadian
C22.1-18
Electrical Code, Part I — Organization and rules of procedure

C12.4

Upon publishing the new Standard, new edition, or amendment, or upon the reaffirmation or withdrawal of an existing Standard, the SDO responsible shall submit a completed Appendix A declaration checklist (see Annex D) to the Project Manager of the Committee on Part I.

C12.5

The Project Manager of the Committee on Part I shall

a)   inform the Committee on the Part I and the SDO responsible of the acceptance of the request submitted in accordance with Clause C12.4; or

b)   return the Appendix A declaration checklist to the SDO responsible indicating items requiring additional action, and inform the Committee on Part I that this has been done.

C12.6

A subject may be opened to appeal any decision made in accordance with Clause C12.5 for consideration by the Committee on Part I.

C12.7

The necessary changes to requirements in the *CE Code, Part I* as described in Clause C12.2 shall be incorporated into the *CE Code, Part I* at the time the Standard is referenced in or withdrawn from Appendix A.

Note: *Annex E illustrates the process detailed in Clauses C12.1 to C12.7.*

Appendix C

C22.1-18

Appendix C
The Technical Committee on the Canadian
Electrical Code, Part I — Organization and rules of procedure

Annex A
Standard format for subcommittee reports

CSA Group **Toronto, Ontario** **Section Subcommittee Report**		
SUBJECT NO.	**TITLE:**	**CHAIR:** **DATE:**

Submitted by: Date:

Affiliation:

Request or proposal:

Reason for request or proposal:

Supporting information:

Summary of Subcommittee deliberations:

Subcommittee recommendation:

Appendix C
The Technical Committee on the Canadian
C22.1-18   *Electrical Code, Part I — Organization and rules of procedure*

Annex B
Request for an amendment to the *Canadian Electrical Code, Part I*

Notes:

1)   *This Annex contains the suggested form to be used when requesting a change to the CE Code, Part I.
See Clause C6.*

2)   *An electronic version of this form is available for download from www.csagroup.org/cecodechanges.*

TO: The Project Manager of the Committee on Part I

FROM:

AFFILIATION:

DATE:

RE: Request for an Amendment to Rule(s):

Primary reasons for request (mark with an "x"):

☐   **Improve safety**

☐   **Address new technology**

☐   **Correlate with electrical product Standard requirements**

☐   **Correlate with other relevant Standards***

☐   **Clarify existing wording**

**Relevant Standards include the National Electrical Code, the National Building Code of Canada,
CSA C22.3 No. 1, CSA Z32, CSA C282, etc.*

Request (specifically worded):

Reasons for request:

Supporting information:

Notice: *By submitting this proposal (the "Proposal") to CSA Group, you assign all right, title and interest in the copyright to the
Proposal to CSA Group, and you waive all moral rights associated with the Proposal. By submitting this Proposal to CSA Group, you
represent and warrant that the Proposal does not contain any content that you do not have a right to transmit and assign under any
law or under contractual or fiduciary relationships (such as inside information, proprietary and confidential information learned or
disclosed as part of employment relationships or under nondisclosure agreements); or any content that infringes any patent, trademark,
trade secret, copyright or other proprietary rights) of any party, and acknowledge that CSA Group is relying on this representation
and warranty.*

Appendix C

C22.1-18

Appendix C
The Technical Committee on the Canadian
Electrical Code, Part I — Organization and rules of procedure

Annex C
Guide to Subcommittee chairs for evaluation of proposals submitted in accordance with Clause C5.4.1 and for evaluation of Subcommittee reports required in accordance with Clause C5.4.5

Note: *This Annex contains the suggested criteria for evaluating the feasibility of proposals for Code amendments and of reports provided by the Subcommittee on these proposals.*

1) The following are the basic principles for evaluating the submitted proposals. When a request is made to amend the Code, the following general criteria should be considered:
   a) improvements to safety;
   b) clarification of the existing wording;
   c) correlation with product Standards requirements;
   d) technological changes; and
   e) correlation with the *National Electrical Code, National Building Code of Canada*, and other relevant CSA, NFPA, or ULC Standards (CAN/CSA-B72, CSA C22.3 No. 1, CSA C22.3 No. 7, CSA C282, CSA Z32, NFPA 20, CAN/ULC-S524, etc.).

2) The Section Subcommittee that will be deliberating the proposed Code amendment should consider the following measurement points before accepting the submission for deliberation by the Subcommittee:
   a) Does the subject have relevance to the Code?
   b) Are the reasons and supporting information that are required to be submitted with the proposal deemed sufficient to meet all applied measurement points? (Frivolous proposals should not be accepted.)
   c) Does the subject try to do what has already been attempted? It may be necessary to research the topic to find out if it has been dealt with in previous years. If the issue was dealt with at a previous time, it should not be handled again unless there is reason to do so.
   d) For a proposed definition, does the term actually appear in the Code? Is a definition really required or is the terminology used in a dictionary sufficient? Is the definition necessary only in one Section of the Code or should it be in Section 0 (General Section)?
   e) Is it a safety issue? The CE Code is a safety Standard for installation and maintenance only, so convenience or other issues should not qualify for inclusion.
   f) Is the proposal technically sound?
   g) Is the proposal dealing with a very prescriptive method that would exclude other methods of achieving the same desired goal?
   h) Is it consistent with the language of the Code?
   i) Is this Rule enforceable (i.e., it is written in unambiguous language, using indisputable criteria)?
      Note: *The Code user must also be able to determine compliance from a visual inspection of the installation on site and without the use of supplementary information or judgment. Rules that, in their wording, require a great deal of judgment on the part of the reader may not be consistently enforced and are a source of conflict and frustration to users of the Code.*
   j) Is this proposal consistent with the *National Electrical Code*? If it is not, there should be sufficient reasons provided by the submitter.
   k) Is the proposal in conflict with other CSA Standards (i.e., the *CE Code, Part II* Standards) or other Canadian safety Standards for electrical equipment?
      Note: *The* CE Code, Part I *is not supposed to include* CE Code, Part II *(product design and construction) or other Canadian safety Standards for electrical equipment requirements, unless it is as an interim measure and is substantiated accordingly.*

Appendix C
The Technical Committee on the Canadian
C22.1-18   *Electrical Code, Part I — Organization and rules of procedure*

l)   Is the proposal in conflict with other relevant Codes, such as the *National Building Code of Canada*? Is the proposal in conflict with industry-specific Codes such as NFPA Codes that deal with specific occupancies, hazardous locations, Codes of practice (e.g., API), *CE Code, Part III* Standards, etc.?

m)   If accepted, would this proposal have an impact on already certified products (i.e., would the existing products have to be recertified to meet this new requirement, and is such an approach justifiable)?

n)   Does the subject impact on other Sections, Tables, and Appendices of the Code? If so, have the potential consequences been reviewed?

o)   Does the document style conform with CSA editorial requirements (CSA Guidelines)?

Δ   p)   Does the proposal introduce amendments that will require new product Standards or changes to existing product Standards? If so, consideration should be given to including a statement in the proposal that the amendments, if approved, should be suspended until such time that the product requirements are in effect.

3)   The following are the basic principles for evaluating the Subcommittee recommendation before reporting it to the Committee on Part I:

a)   Is the Subcommittee recommendation understandable and readable?

b)   Has the length of the Subcommittee recommendation been reduced to the absolute minimum necessary to convey the intent? It should be noted that the members of the Committee on Part I may not have the time to review long subjects when they come in the form of the Subcommittee recommendation. A suitable one-page summary should be made, especially for lengthy proposals. This would enable members of the Committee on Part I (who are not necessarily technical experts in the specific subject area) to understand the key issues, recommendations, and impacts of the proposal.

c)   Has the Subcommittee recommendation expanded to include issues other than that which the original proposal intended to cover? If so, is this expansion of the subject matter justifiable (i.e., it was discussed with the submitter and it is accepted by the submitter) or should it be more appropriately covered by a new subject?

d)   Does the Subcommittee recommendation address the issues of the original proposal and satisfy the submitter's intent or does it digress?

Appendix C
The Technical Committee on the Canadian
C22.1-18   *Electrical Code, Part I — Organization and rules of procedure*

Δ

Annex D
Appendix A declaration checklist
(See Clauses C12.2, C12.4, and C12.5)

Annex D — Declaration Checklist for Appendix A

1. Standard designation: _____

2. Standard title: _____

3. Type of Standard (new edition, new Standard, amendment, reaffirmation, withdrawal): _____

4. Publication date: _____

5. Scope: _____

6. Compatibility with the *CE Code, Part I*:

    a) The Standard makes reference to the *CE Code, Part I* and contains a statement that the product is intended to be installed in compliance with the *CE Code, Part I*: Yes ☐ No ☐

    b) The Standard is compatible with the *CE Code, Part I* Rules: Yes ☐ No ☐

    c) The terms used in the Standard are compatible with the definitions in the *CE Code, Part I*: Yes ☐ No ☐

    d) Changes to requirements in the *CE Code, Part I* are necessary as a result of the development of this Standard: Yes ☐, continue below. No ☐, go to Item 7.

    e) The proposal has been developed and approved (see Clause C12.7): Yes ☐

7. Compatibility with existing documents used to approve electrical equipment [*CE Code, Part II*, other Canadian electrical safety Standards, and Other Recognized Documents (ORDs)], including

    a) Compliance with horizontal Standards: The Standard complies with and/or references the horizontal requirements of CSA C22.2 No. 0 and other applicable C22.2 No. 0 Series horizontal Standards (see Appendix A, Annex A.1, "General")?

    b) Absence of conflict with other requirements, such as the *CE Code, Part II*, other Canadian electrical safety Standards for electrical products, and ORDs?

        Yes ☐ No ☐

Declared and submitted on behalf of: _____
Signed: _____
Name and Title: _____
Date: _____

C22.1-18

Appendix C
The Technical Committee on the Canadian
Electrical Code, Part I — Organization and rules of procedure

Δ

Annex E
Process for inclusion of reference Standards in Appendix A

Notes:
1) *This flow chart describes the process for submitting proposals for the inclusion of an electrical safety Standard in Appendix A of the* CE Code, Part I.
2) *The following abbreviations are used in this flow chart:*
   a) *Committee — the Committee on Part I;*
   b) *Part I PM — the Project Manager of the Committee on Part I; and*
   c) *SDO — Standards development organization.*

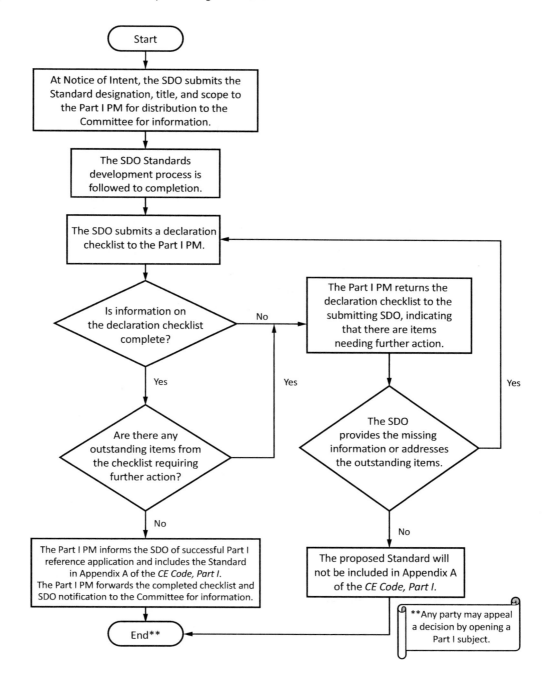

Appendix D — Tabulated general information

Note: *This Appendix is an informative (non-mandatory) part of this Standard.*

Δ

Table D1
Type designations, voltage ratings, and construction of insulated conductors and cables other than flexible cords

Note: *These data are subject to frequent revision and in cases where any doubt exists, the latest edition of the appropriate Standard of the Canadian Electrical Code, Part II, or appropriate laboratory requirements should be consulted.*

Trade designation (CSA Standard)	CSA type designation	Voltage rating	Number of circuit insulated conductors	Size range, AWG or kcmil	Insulation	Covering on each insulated conductor	Outer covering	Reference Notes
Armoured cable (C22.2 No. 51)	AC90	600, 1000, and 2000	1 or more	14 to 2000	Cross-linked polyethylene	None or thermoset or thermoplastic	Interlocking metal armour	1, 8, 10, 25
	ACWU90						Interlocking metal armour and flame-tested thermoplastic	
	ACG90	600	2 or more	14 to 6			Interlocking metal armour	
	ACGWU90						Interlocking metal armour and flame-tested thermoplastic	
Armoured cable (C22.2 No. 131)	TECK90	600, 1000, and 5000	1	6 to 2000	Cross-linked polyethylene		Thermoset or thermoplastic jacket and interlocking metal armour with or without thermoplastic or thermoset covering overall	8, 10, 14
					Ethylene propylene rubber			8, 14, 17
			2 or more	14 to 2000	Cross-linked polyethylene			1, 8, 10
					Ethylene propylene rubber			1, 8, 17
Non-metallic-sheathed cable	NMD90	300	2, 3, or 4	14 to 2	90 °C heat-resistant thermoplastic	Nylon sheath	Thermoplastic	1, 28, 31 / 28

(Continued)

Appendix D

Table D1 (Continued)

Trade designation (CSA Standard)	CSA type designation	Voltage rating	Number of circuit insulated conductors	Size range, AWG or kcmil	Insulation	Covering on each insulated conductor	Outer covering	Reference Notes
(C22.2 No. 48)					Cross-linked polyethylene	None		31
	NMWU				Moisture-resistant thermoplastic			1
	NMDH90		2, 3, or 4 (plus control and bonding conductors)	14 to 10	90 °C heat-resistant thermoplastic	None	With or without metallic shield; thermoplastic jacket	1
					Cross-linked polyethylene			
Thermoset insulated wires and cables (C22.2 No. 38)	RW75, R90, RW90	600, 1000, and 2000	1	14 to 2000	Cross-linked polyethylene	None or thermoplastic or thermoset	None	1, 10
			2 or more				Thermoplastic or thermoset	1, 8, 10, 11
			1		Ethylene propylene rubber	Thermoplastic or thermoset	Thermoplastic or thermoset	1, 8, 17
			2 or more				Thermoplastic or thermoset	1, 8, 11, 17
			1		EPCV	None or thermoplastic or thermoset	Thermoplastic or thermoset	1, 37
			2 or more				Thermoplastic or thermoset	1, 8, 11, 37
		5000	1	8 to 2000	Cross-linked polyethylene	None or thermoplastic or thermoset	None	5, 10
			2 or more				Thermoplastic or thermoset	5, 8, 10, 11
			1		Ethylene propylene rubber	Thermoplastic or thermoset	Thermoplastic or thermoset	5, 8, 17
			2 or more				Thermoplastic or thermoset	5, 8, 11, 17

(Continued)

Table D1 (Continued)

Trade designation (CSA Standard)	CSA type designation	Voltage rating	Number of circuit insulated conductors	Size range, AWG or kcmil	Insulation	Covering on each insulated conductor	Outer covering	Reference Notes
			1		EPCV	None or thermoplastic or thermoset	Thermoplastic or thermoset	5, 37
			2 or more					5, 8, 37
	RWU75 and RWU90	1000	1	14 to 2000	Cross-linked polyethylene	None or thermoplastic or thermoset	None	1, 8, 10
					Ethylene propylene rubber	Thermoplastic or thermoset		1, 8, 17
					EPCV	Thermoplastic or thermoset		1, 8, 37
	SIS	600	1	14 to 4/0	Cross-linked polyethylene, EPCV, chlorosulfonated polyethylene, chlorinated polyethylene	None	None	1, 7
Aluminum-sheathed cables (C22.2 No. 123)	RA90	600 and 1000	1	14 to 2000	Cross-linked polyethylene	None or thermoplastic or thermoset	Aluminum or aluminum with thermoplastic covering	1, 8
			2 or more					1, 8, 10, 11
			1		Ethylene propylene rubber	Thermoplastic or thermoset		1, 8, 17
			2 or more					1, 8, 11, 17
		5000	1	8 to 2000	Cross-linked polyethylene	None or thermoplastic or thermoset		5, 8
			2 or more					5, 8, 10, 11

(Continued)

Appendix D

Table D1 (Continued)

Trade designation (CSA Standard)	CSA type designation	Voltage rating	Number of circuit insulated conductors	Size range, AWG or kcmil	Insulation	Covering on each insulated conductor	Outer covering	Reference Notes
			1		Ethylene propylene rubber	Thermoplastic or thermoset		5, 8, 17
			2 or more					5, 8, 11, 17
Copper-sheathed cables (C22.2 No. 123)	RC90	600 and 1000	1	14 to 2000	Silicone	None or thermoplastic or thermoset	Copper or copper with thermoplastic or thermoset covering	1, 8, 18
			2 or more					
		5000	1	8 to 2000	Silicone	None or thermoplastic or thermoset		5, 8, 18
			2 or more					
Mineral-insulated cable (C22.2 No. 124)	MI and SSMI	600	7 to 12	18 to 8	Magnesium oxide or silicon dioxide	None	Copper or stainless steel	—
			4	18 to 6				
			5	18 to 4 (nickel only)				
			3	18 to 3				
			2	18 to 1				
			1	18 to 1000 for copper and clad copper				
				18 to 1 if nickel				
	LWMI and SSLWMI	300	1 to 12	18 to 8 copper or clad copper or nickel				22
		600	7 to 12	18 to 8				

(Continued)

Table D1 (Continued)

Trade designation (CSA Standard)	CSA type designation	Voltage rating	Number of circuit insulated conductors	Size range, AWG or kcmil	Insulation	Covering on each insulated conductor	Outer covering	Reference Notes
			4	18 to 6				
			5	18 to 4 (nickel only)				
			3	18 to 3				
			2	18 to 1				
			1	18 to 1000 for copper and clad copper				
				18 to 1 for nickel				
Thermoplastic cable (C22.2 No. 75)	TW, TWU, TW75, and TWU75	600	1	14 to 2000	Moisture-resistant flame-tested thermoplastic	None or nylon	None	1, 12
	TWN75 and T90 Nylon			14 to 1000	Heat- and moisture-resistant flame-tested thermoplastic	Nylon / None		12
Neutral supported cable (C22.2 No. 129)	NS 75 / NS 90	600	2, 3, 4, or 5	8 to 4/0 copper, 6 to 500 kcmil aluminum (minimum size of neutral	Polyethylene or cross-linked polyethylene, with bare or insulated neutral	None or flame-tested polyvinyl chloride	None	16

(Continued)

Appendix D

Table D1 (Continued)

Trade designation (CSA Standard)	CSA type designation	Voltage rating	Number of circuit insulated conductors	Size range, AWG or kcmil	Insulation	Covering on each insulated conductor	Outer covering	Reference Notes
Service entrance cable (C22.2 No. 52)	USEI75	600	2, 3, or 4	8 copper, 6 aluminum)	Polyethylene	Polyvinyl chloride		2, 10, 17
				6 to 1000 kcmil	Cross-linked polyethylene			
	USEI90				Ethylene propylene rubber			
	USEB90				Cross-linked polyethylene			
					Ethylene propylene rubber			
Luminous tube sign and oil burner ignition cable (C22.2 No. 127)	GTO-5	5000	1	18 to 10	Rubber or polyethylene	Thermoplastic or thermoset jacket	Flame and moisture resistant braid in lieu of jacket	3
	GTO-10	10 000						
	GTO-15	15 000						
Ignition cable (C22.2 No. 127)	ICS	10 000	1	18 to 10 (125 °C rated) 16 or 20 (150 °C rated)	Silicone rubber	Moisture-resistant braid and silicone rubber	None	7
Extra-low-voltage	LVT	30	2 or more	22 to 16	Thermoplastic	Flame-tested thermoplastic	Optional metallic armour	9, 32

(Continued)

Table D1 (Continued)

Trade designation (CSA Standard)	CSA type designation	Voltage rating	Number of circuit insulated conductors	Size range, AWG or kcmil	Insulation	Covering on each insulated conductor	Outer covering	Reference Notes
control circuit cable (C22.2 No. 35)								
Low-energy control circuit cable (C22.2 No. 35)	Low-energy control cable		2 or 3	18	Thermoplastic	None	None	13
Extra-low-voltage control cable (C22.2 No. 35)	ELC	30	1 or more	26 to 16	Thermoplastic			—
Golf course sprinkler systems (C22.2 No. 35)	GCS	30	1 or more	20 to 2	Thermoplastic	Optional thermoplastic or thermoset jackets		
Lawn sprinkler systems (C22.2 No. 35)	LSS	30						
Low-voltage landscape lighting (C22.2 No. 35)	LVLL	30	1 and 2- or 3-conductor parallel	18 to 8				
Underground low-energy circuits (C22.2 No. 35)	ULEC	30	1 and 2- or 3-conductor parallel	18 to 8				
Thermoset insulated	REW	300	1	26 to 10	Flame-tested cross-linked	None	None	7, 19

(Continued)

Appendix D

Table D1 (Continued)

Trade designation (CSA Standard)	CSA type designation	Voltage rating	Number of circuit insulated conductors	Size range, AWG or kcmil	Insulation	Covering on each insulated conductor	Outer covering	Reference Notes
equipment wire (C22.2 No. 127)		600		24 to 4/0	PVC or flame-tested cross-linked chlorinated polyethylene			4, 7, 19
		300	2 or more	26 to 10	Flame-tested cross-linked PVC	None or shield	Shield and flame-tested cross-linked PVC insulating covering	7, 19, 20
		600		24 to 4/0				
Thermoplastic-insulated equipment wire (C22.2 No. 127)	TEWN	600	1	18 and 16	Flame-tested thermoplastic	Extruded nylon		4, 7
	TEW	300	2 or more	26 to 16	Flame-tested thermoplastic	None	None	7, 20
	TEW	600	2 or more	26 to 4/0		None	None	4, 7, 20
	TXF	125	1	22 to 20		None	None	7
	TXFW	300		22 to 16		None		7
	GTF	600		18 to 10		Lacquered glass braid		4, 7
Silicone rubber insulated equipment wire (C22.2 No. 127)	SEW-1	300	1	22 to 16	Silicone rubber	Glass-braid-treated	None	7
	SEWF-1		2 or more					
	SEW-2	600	1	22 to 4/0				
			2 or more					
	SEWF-2	600	1	22 to 6	Silicone rubber	Glass-braid-treated		
			2 or more					
Insulated conductors	RR-64	600	1	28 to 14	Cross-linked PVC	None	None or shield with or without	19, 26, 33
			2 or more					

(Continued)

Table D1 (Continued)

Trade designation (CSA Standard)	CSA type designation	Voltage rating	Number of circuit insulated conductors	Size range, AWG or kcmil	Insulation	Covering on each insulated conductor	Outer covering	Reference Notes
for power-operated electronic devices (C22.2 No. 127)	RR-32	1400	1	28 to 10			thermoplastic insulating covering	
			2 or more					
	RR-64	600	2 up to 7	28 to 10		None or shield	Shield and cross-linked PVC insulating covering	20, 26, 33
	RR-32	1400		24 to 10				
	RR-64	600	1	28 to 14	Cross-linked chlorinated polyethylene	None	None	19, 26, 33
	RR-32	1400		24 to 10				
	TRSR-64	600		28 to 14	Semi-rigid PVC	None or extruded nylon	None or shield with or without thermoplastic insulating covering	26, 33
	TR-64	600	2 or more		Thermoplastic			20, 26, 33
	TR-32	1400	1	24 to 10		None or shield		
			2 or more					
			2 up to 7					
	Twin lead	—	2	24 to 20	Flame-tested polyethylene	None	None or thermoplastic covering	29
					Polyvinyl chloride			30
	TTR	600	1	26 to 14	Thermoplastic	Cotton, or rayon-braid-treated, or nylon	None	7, 26, 33
	TV-6	6000 (dc)	1	24 minimum	Flame-tested polyethylene, cross-linked low-density polyethylene,	None or PVC, cross-linked low-density polyethylene, cross-linked	None or shield with 2 kV dc PVC insulating covering	7, 34
	TV-10	10 000 (dc)						
	TV-15	15 000 (dc)						

(Continued)

Appendix D

Table D1 (Continued)

Trade designation (CSA Standard)	CSA type designation	Voltage rating	Number of circuit insulated conductors	Size range, AWG or kcmil	Insulation	Covering on each insulated conductor	Outer covering	Reference Notes
	TV-20	20 000 (dc)			cross-linked high-density polyethylene, cross-linked PVC, silicone rubber, fluorinated ethylene propylene	high-density polyethylene		
	TV-30	30 000 (dc)						
	TV-40	40 000 (dc)						
	TV-50	50 000 (dc)						
Arc-welding cable (C22.2 No. 96)	Arc-welding cable	(See Note 6)	1	8 to 300	Rubber or flame-tested polychloroprene covering	None	None or shield with 2 kV dc PVC insulating covering	5
Coil-lead wire (C22.2 No. 127)	CL901	600	1	22 to 500	Polychloroprene			4, 7
	CL902	300		22 to 500				
	CL903	600		22 to 500				
	CL904	600		22 to 500	PVC			
	CL905	600		22 to 4/0	Ethylene propylene rubber			
	CL906	300		22 to 500	Ethylene propylene rubber/ chlorosulfonyl polyethylene			
	CL907	600		22 to 500				
	CL908	600		22 to 500	Chlorinated polyethylene			
	CL909	300		22 to 500				

(Continued)

Table D1 (Continued)

Trade designation (CSA Standard)	CSA type designation	Voltage rating	Number of circuit insulated conductors	Size range, AWG or kcmil	Insulation	Covering on each insulated conductor	Outer covering	Reference Notes
	CL1051	300		22 to 16	PVC			
	CL1052	300		22 to 500	Chlorinated PE or chlorosulfonyl polyethylene			
	CL1053	600		22 to 500				
	CL1054	300		22 to 14	Cross-linked PE or ethylene propylene rubber			
	CL1055	600		22 to 4/0	Ethylene propylene rubber			
	CL1056	300		22 to 14	Thermoplastic elastomer			
	CL1151	300		22 to 500	Chlorosulfon-yl polyethylene			
	CL1152	600		22 to 500				
	CL1251	600		22 to 500	Cross-linked polyethylene			
	CL1252	300		22 to 16				
	CL1253	600		22 to 500	Thermoplastic elastomer			
	CL1254	600		22 to 4/0	Ethylene propylene rubber			
	CL1255	600		22 to 12				
	CL1501	600		22 to 500	Silicone			
	CL1502	600		22 to 500	Ethylene propylene			
	CL1503	600		22 to 500				

(Continued)

Appendix D

Table D1 (Continued)

Trade designation (CSA Standard)	CSA type designation	Voltage rating	Number of circuit insulated conductors	Size range, AWG or kcmil	Insulation	Covering on each insulated conductor	Outer covering	Reference Notes
					rubber or cross-linked polyethylene			
	CL1504	300		24 to 10	Silicone or ethylenetetrafluoroethylene			
	CL1505	600		24 to 14	Ethylenetetrafluoroethylene			
	CL2001	600		22 to 500	Silicone			
	CL2002	300		24 to 10	Silicone or ethylenetetrafluoroethylene			
	CL2003	600		24 to 14	Ethylenetetrafluoroethylene			
	CL2501	300		32 to 10	Polytetrafluoroethylene			
	CL2502	600		26 to 4/0				
	CL2503	300		32 to 10	Perfluoroalkoxy			
	CL2504	600		32 to 4/0				
Pendant weatherproof lampholder lead wire (C22.2 No. 127)	TLW	600	1	14	Flame-tested thermoplastic			7
Hoistway cable	—	600	2 to 4	18 to 12	Flame-tested thermoplastic		None	

(Continued)

January 2018

Table D1 (Continued)

Trade designation (CSA Standard)	CSA type designation	Voltage rating	Number of circuit insulated conductors	Size range, AWG or kcmil	Insulation	Covering on each insulated conductor	Outer covering	Reference Notes
(C22.2 No. 49)			parallel construction				None or PVC jacket	
		300	2 to 75 twisted construction					
			2 to 75 twisted construction	20 to 12				
Airport series lighting cable (C22.2 No. 179)	ASLC	5000	1	8, 6, or 4	Cross-linked polyethylene		None	
Communications cable (C22.2 No. 214)	CMP	300	30 to 6	1 or multiple conductor or multiple coaxial	Thermoplastic	None	Thermoplastic jacket with or without a metal sheath or braid	38
	CMR							
	CMG							
	CM							
	Cross-connect							
	CMX and CMUC							
	CMH							
Fire alarm and signal cable (C22.2 No. 208)	FAS	300	1 or more	26 to 10	Thermoplastic	None	None or thermoplastic or thermoset jacket, or interlocking metal armour or aluminum metallic sheath with or	—
	FAS 90				Thermoplastic or thermoset			
	FAS 105				Thermoplastic			
	FAS 150				Thermoset			

(Continued)

Appendix D

Table D1 (Continued)

Trade designation (CSA Standard)	CSA type designation	Voltage rating	Number of circuit insulated conductors	Size range, AWG or kcmil	Insulation	Covering on each insulated conductor	Outer covering	Reference Notes
	FAS 200				Thermoplastic or thermoset		without overall thermoplastic covering	
Control and instrumentation cables (C22.2 No. 239)	CIC and ACIC	150 and 300	2 or more subassemblies	26 to 14	Thermoplastic or thermoset	Thermoplastic or thermoset	Metallic outer covering on ACIC	
		600 and 1000		18 to 4/0				

Notes:

1) No. 14 AWG for insulated copper conductors; No. 12 AWG for insulated aluminum conductors.

2) USEI75 and USEI90 PVC jacketed individual insulated conductors are twisted together without overall cable jacket.

3) For Type GTO cable, the maximum voltage rating shall be designated as follows:

   a) GTO-5 — for use at not more than 5000 V;

   b) GTO-10 — for use at not more than 10 000 V; and

   c) GTO-15 — for use at not more than 15 000 V.

4) When used in applications where the current is limited or controlled, or both, by means of a ballast, resistor, transformer, etc., the following types of wire may be operated at the voltages shown below:

   a) Types GTF, REW rated at 600 V; TEW; TEWN, CL904, CL1251, CL1501, CL1502, and CL2001 — 1000 V;

   b) Types CL901, CL903, CL905, CL907, CL908, CL911, CL1053, and CL1152 — 750 V; and

   c) Types CL902, CL906, CL909, CL910, CL1051, CL1052, CL1054, CL1151, and CL1252 — 600 V.

5) No. 8 AWG minimum for insulated copper conductors; No. 6 AWG minimum for insulated aluminum conductors.

6) Arc-welding cables are intended only for use with electric welders having an open-circuit secondary voltage of 100 V or less.

7) See Table 19 for maximum allowable conductor temperatures for all wire types except the following:

   a) Types TXF, TXFW, TLW, and arc-welding cable — 60 °C;

   b) Types TV-6, TV-10, TV-15, TV-20, TV-30, TV-40, and TV-50

      — with flame-tested polyethylene — 80, 90, or 105 °C;

      — with cross-linked low-density polyethylene — 80, 90, 105, or 125 °C;

      — with cross-linked high-density polyethylene — 90 or 105 °C;

      — with cross-linked polyvinyl chloride — 80, 90, or 105 °C;

      — with silicone rubber — 150 or 200 °C; and

(Continued)

Table D1 (Continued)

— with fluorinated ethylene propylene — 150 °C;

c) Types RR-64, RR-32, TR-64, TR-32, TRB-64, TRB-32, TTR, CL901, CL902, CL903, CL904, CL905, CL906, CL907, CL908, CL909, CL910, and CL911 — 90 °C, except Type TR-64 may also have a maximum allowable temperature of 105 °C;

d) Types REW, TEW, TEWN, CL1051, CL1052, CL1053, CL1054, and low-energy control cable — 105 °C;

e) Type SIS — 90 °C;

f) Types CL1151 and CL1152 — 115 °C;

g) Types CL1251, GTF, and CL1252 — 125 °C;

h) Types CL1501, ICS, SEWF-1, and SEWF-2 — 150 °C, except Types SEWF-1 and SEWF-2 with an insulated nickel-coated copper or nickel conductor — 200 °C;

i) Types CL2001, SEW-1, and SEW-2 — 200 °C;

j) Types CL1501, CL1502, ICS, SEWF-1, and SEWF-2 — 150 °C, except Types SEWF-1 and SEWF-2 with an insulated nickel-coated copper conductor — 200 °C;

k) Type SEWF-1 with an insulated nickel conductor — 200 °C or 250 °C and Type SEWF-2 with an insulated nickel conductor — 200 °C;

l) Types CL2001 and SEW-2 — 200 °C; and

m) Type SEW-1 with an insulated copper or nickel-coated copper conductor — 200 °C, and with an insulated nickel conductor — 200 °C or 250 °C.

8) Thermoset coverings include polychloroprene and chlorosulfonyl polyethylene where applicable.

9) Type LVT may be provided with an overall armour consisting of a single layer of a closely wound, D-shaped, soft aluminum conductor.

10) Conductors having cross-linked polyethylene insulation are surface marked with the type designation followed by "XLPE".

11) For 2-conductor parallel construction, the maximum size is No. 6 AWG.

12) When provided with a nylon jacket, Types TW and TWU are also approved for use where adverse conditions can exist, such as in oil refineries and around gasoline storage or pump areas (e.g., where they are subjected to alkaline conditions in the presence of petroleum solvents), and are limited to sizes No. 14 to 1000 kcmil in copper only.

13) For operation at 30 V or less, low-energy control cable is suitable for Class 1 remote control, signal, and extra-low-voltage power circuits, and Class 2 remote control, signal, and low-energy power circuits, in accordance with Section 16.

14) No. 6 AWG minimum for insulated copper conductors; No. 4 AWG minimum for insulated aluminum conductors.

15) A nickel-plated iron conductor may be used as an alternative to copper or nickel conductors.

16) In 5-conductor neutral supported cable, the fifth insulated conductor is to control or supply power to an auxiliary device, e.g., a water heater, street light, etc. The fifth insulated conductor is No. 10 AWG minimum for copper or No. 8 AWG minimum for aluminum.

17) Conductors having ethylene propylene rubber insulation are surface marked with the type designation followed by "EP".

18) Conductors having silicone rubber insulation are surface marked with the type designation followed by "Silicone".

19) Cross-linked PVC insulation is surface marked (XLPVC) and cross-linked chlorinated polyethylene is surface marked (XLCPE).

20) The 2-conductor type may be of parallel or twisted construction.

21) Nickel-coated copper or nickel alloy conductors may be used as an alternative to copper or nickel conductors. Where nickel alloy is employed for the conductor, the suffix letters "NA" shall be added to the type designation.

22) The voltage rating is ink printed on the surface of the copper sheath of 300 V Type LWMI cables.

(Continued)

Appendix D

Table D1 (Concluded)

23) Conductors are of stranded silver-coated copper.

24) Conductors are of stranded nickel-coated copper.

25) Single-conductor armoured cables in sizes No. 4 AWG and smaller, and single-conductor armoured cables without a concentric grounding conductor in sizes larger than No. 4 AWG, are intended for use as grounding conductors only, and the covering over the insulation, or the insulation where a covering is not provided, is coloured green. Single-conductor armoured cables with a concentric bonding conductor are not intended for use as bonding conductors, and the insulation and the covering over the insulation, or the insulation where a covering is not provided, are not coloured green.

26) These voltages are peak values.

27) When Type CL1251 wire is provided with gasoline vapour-resistant insulation, it is surface marked "Gasoline Vapour-Resistant".

28) When Type NMD90 is provided with nylon sheaths over the insulated conductors, "NMD90 NYLON" is marked on the surface of the jacket.

29) Polyethylene insulated non-jacketed twin lead with 15 mil average thickness over the conductors is surface marked "TWIN LEAD-64 80C PE" and with 30 mil average thickness over the conductors is surface marked "TWIN LEAD-32 80C PE"; polyethylene insulated jacketed twin lead is surfaced marked "TWIN LEAD 80C".

30) PVC insulated twin lead with 15 mil average thickness over the conductors is surface marked "TWIN LEAD-64 90C PVC" and PVC insulated twin lead with 30 mil average thickness over the conductors is surface marked "TWIN LEAD-32 90C PVC".

31) Type NMD90 with cross-linked polyethylene insulation is surface marked on the jacket "NMD90 XLPE".

32) Type LVT is surface marked on the jacket "LVT".

33) Peak voltage rating is as assigned by CSA C22.2 No. 1.

34) The shield and PVC jacket are recognized only over Types TV-20, TV-30, and TV-40 with cross-linked high-density polyethylene insulation and PVC jacket over Types TV-6, TV-10, TV-15, TV-20, TV-30, TV-40, and TV-50 with cross-linked PVC insulation.

35) Airport series lighting cable is surface marked "ASLC 5000 V".

36) CFC cables that are used to electrically connect communications equipment to a telecommunications network shall be not smaller than No. 26 AWG copper. Cables with insulated conductors of No. 28 and No. 30 AWG copper shall be permitted for other types of communication applications.

37) Conductors having EPCV insulation are surface marked with the type designation, followed by "EPCV".

38) For coaxial cable only, the conductor may consist of copper, copper-clad steel, or copper-clad aluminium.

Table D2
DC motors

Motor rating, hp	DC full load current rating, A [see Notes 1) and 2)]		
	120 V	240 V	500 V
1/4	2.9	1.5	—
1/3	3.6	1.8	—
1/2	5.2	2.6	—
3/4	7.4	3.7	1.8
1	9.4	4.7	2.3
1-1/2	13.2	6.6	3.2
2	17	8.5	4.1
3	25	12.5	6.0
5	40	20	9.7
7-1/2	58	29	14
10	76	38	18
15	110	55	26
20	145	72	35
25	179	89	43
30	212	106	51
40	280	140	68
50	349	174	84
60	418	209	101
75	518	259	124
100	—	343	165
125	—	426	205
150	—	507	243
200	—	675	324

Notes:

1) *These values of full load current are for motors running at the moderate base speeds usual for belted motors and motors with normal torque characteristics. Motors built for especially low speeds may require more running current, in which case the nameplate current rating should be used.*

2) *These values of full load current are to be used as guides only. When exact values are required (e.g., for motor protection), always use the values on the motor nameplate.*

Table D3
Distance to centre of distribution for a 1% drop in voltage on nominal 120 V, 2-conductor copper circuits
(See Appendix B Note to Rule 4-004.)

| Current, A | Insulated copper conductor size, AWG | | | | | | | | | | | | | | |
	18	16	14	12	10	8	6	4	3	2	1	1/0	2/0	3/0	4/0
	Distance to centre of distribution measured along the insulated conductor run, m (calculated for conductor insulation temperature of 60 °C)														
1.00	24.2	38.5	61.4												
1.25	19.4	30.8	49.1												
1.6	15.1	24.1	38.4	61.0											
2.0	12.1	19.3	30.7	48.8											
2.5	9.7	15.4	24.6	39.0	62										
3.2	7.6	12.0	19.2	30.5	48.5										
4.0	6.1	9.6	15.3	24.4	38.8	61.7									
5.0	4.8	7.7	12.3	19.5	31.0	49.3									
6.3	3.8	6.1	9.7	15.5	24.6	39.1	62.2								
8.0	3.0	4.8	7.7	12.2	19.4	30.8	49.0								
10.0	2.4	3.9	6.1	9.8	15.5	24.7	39.2	62.4							
12.5		3.1	4.9	7.8	12.4	19.7	31.4	49.9	62.9						
16		2.4	3.8	6.1	9.7	15.4	24.5	39.0	49.1	62.0					
20			3.1	4.9	7.8	12.3	19.6	31.2	39.3	49.6	62.5				
25				3.9	6.2	9.9	15.7	24.9	31.4	39.7	50.0	63.1			
32					4.8	7.7	12.2	19.6	24.6	31.0	39.1	49.3	62.1		
40					3.9	6.2	9.8	15.6	19.7	24.8	31.3	39.4	49.7	62.7	
50						4.9	7.8	12.5	15.7	19.8	25.0	31.5	39.8	50.1	63.2
63						3.9	6.2	9.9	12.5	15.7	19.8	25.0	31.6	39.8	50.2
80						3.1	4.9	7.8	9.8	12.4	15.6	19.7	24.8	31.3	39.5
100							3.9	6.2	7.9	9.9	12.5	15.8	19.9	25.1	31.6
125								5.0	6.3	7.9	10.0	12.6	15.9	20.1	25.3
160									4.9	6.2	7.8	9.9	12.4	15.7	19.8
200										5.0	6.3	7.9	9.9	12.5	15.8
250												6.3	8.0	10.0	12.6
320													6.2	7.8	9.9

Notes:

1) *Table D3 is calculated for copper conductor sizes No. 18 AWG to No. 4/0 AWG and, for each size specified, gives the approximate distance in metres to the centre of distribution measured along the insulated conductor run for a 1% drop in voltage at a given current, with the conductor at a temperature of 60 °C. Inductive reactance has not been included because it is a function of conductor size and spacing.*

(Continued)

Table D3 (Concluded)

2) The distances for a 3% or 5% voltage drop are 3 or 5 times those for a 1% voltage drop.

3) Because the distances in Table D3 are based on conductor resistances at 60 °C, these distances must be multiplied by the correction factors below according to the temperature rating of the conductor insulation used and the percentage load with respect to the allowable ampacity. Where the calculation and the allowable ampacity fall between two columns, the factor in the higher percentage column shall be used.

Rated conductor insulation temperature	Distance correction factor						
	Percentage of allowable ampacity						
	100	90	80	70	60	50	40
60 °C	1.00	1.02	1.04	1.06	1.07	1.09	1.10
75 °C	0.96	1.00	1.00	1.03	1.06	1.07	1.09
85–90 °C	0.91	0.95	1.00	1.00	1.04	1.06	1.08
110 °C	0.85	0.90	0.95	1.00	1.02	1.05	1.07
125 °C	0.82	0.87	0.92	0.97	1.00	1.04	1.07
200 °C	0.68	0.76	0.83	0.90	0.96	1.00	1.04

4) For other nominal voltages, multiply the distances in metres by the other nominal voltage (in volts) and divide by 120.

5) Aluminum conductors have equivalent resistance per unit length to copper conductors that are smaller in area by two AWG sizes. Table D3 may be used for aluminum conductors because of this relationship, i.e., for No. 6 AWG aluminum, use the distances listed for No. 8 AWG copper in Table D3. Similarly, for No. 2/0 AWG aluminum, use the distances for No. 1 AWG copper.

6) The distances and currents listed in Table D3 follow a pattern. When the current, for any conductor size, is increased by a factor of 10, the corresponding distance decreases by a factor of 10. This relationship can be used when no value is shown in the table. In that case, look at a current 10 times larger. The distance to the centre of distribution is then 10 times larger than the listed value.

7) For multi-conductor cables, ensure that the wire size obtained from this Table is suitable for the ampacity from Table 2 or 4 and Rule 4-004.

8) For currents intermediate to listed values, use the next highest current value.

9) Example of the use of this Table:

Consider a 2-insulated conductor circuit of No. 12 AWG copper NMD90 carrying 16 A at nominal 240 V under a maximum ambient temperature of 30 °C.

The maximum run distance from the centre of distribution to the load without exceeding a 3% voltage drop is as follows:

Maximum run length for No. 12 AWG, 16 A, 1% voltage drop at nominal 120 V from this Table is 6.1 m. Distance correction factor to be used is as follows:

From Table 2, allowable ampacity for 2-insulated conductor No. 12 AWG NMD90 (90 °C rating per Table 19) is 30 A. The given current is 16 A or 53% (16/30) of the allowable ampacity.

The distance correction factor to be used, from Note 3), 85–90 °C row, 60% column, is 1.04.

The maximum run length is:

$$6.1 \text{ m} \times 3(\%) \times 1.04 \times \frac{240 \text{ V}}{120 \text{ V}} = 38 \text{ m}$$

If the distance is between 38 and 60.5 m, a larger size of conductor is required, e.g., No. 10 AWG (40 A allowable ampacity).

$$9.7 \text{ m} \times 3(\%) \times 1.08 \times \frac{240 \text{ V}}{120 \text{ V}} = 62.9 \text{ m}$$

Appendix D

Table D4
Copper conductor sizes for 5% drop in voltage on 6 V — Two conductors
[See Appendix B Note to Rule 46-306 1).]

Current, A	One-way distance from power source measured along the conductor, m (calculated for conductor temperature of 20 °C)				
	No. 12 AWG	No. 10 AWG	No. 8 AWG	No. 6 AWG	No. 4 AWG
2-1/2	11.5	18.3	28.5	49.4	72.2
4-1/4	6.8	10.8	16.8	26.7	42.5
7	4.1	6.5	10.2	16.2	25.8
10	2.9	4.6	7.1	11.3	18.0
12	2.4	3.8	5.9	9.5	15.0
15	1.9	3.1	4.8	7.6	12.0
20	1.4	2.3	3.6	5.7	9.0

Note: *Acceptable one-way distance in metres (L) for a selected conductor wire size may be calculated using the following formula where one or all of the actual current (I), the actual voltage (V), and the actual voltage drop permitted (P) differ from Table D4:*

$$L = \frac{V}{6} \times \frac{P}{5} \times \frac{I_t}{I} \times L_t$$

where

I_t = *current shown in Table D4 closest to the actual current (I)*

L_t = *one-way distance in metres shown in Table D4 corresponding to the conductor size used for the value I_t selected*

Example: System characteristics

V = 12 V

P = 7%

I = 3 A

Wire size = No. 12 AWG

Values of I_t and L_t to be used in the calculation are

I_t = 2.5 A

L_t = 11.5 m

$L = \frac{12}{6} \times \frac{7}{5} \times \frac{2.5}{3} \times 11.5 = 26.8\ m$

Table D5
Strandings for building insulated conductors and cables
(See Appendix B Note to Rule 12-910.)

Nominal Conductor size, AWG or kcmil	Conductor area, mm²	Standard*			Flexible			Extra flexible		
		Number of conductors†	Diameter, mm	Occupied area‡, mm²	Number of conductors	Diameter, mm	Occupied area‡, mm²	Number of conductors	Diameter, mm	Occupied area‡, mm²
14	2.08	7	1.84	2.74	19	1.87	2.74	37	1.87	2.74
12	3.31	7	2.32	4.34	19	2.35	4.34	37	2.35	4.34
10	5.26	7	2.95	6.94	19	2.97	6.94	37	2.97	6.94
8	8.37	7	3.71	11.1	19	3.76	11.1	37	3.76	11.1
6	13.3	7	4.67	17.5	19	4.72	17.5	37	4.72	17.5
4	21.2	7	5.89	28.0	19	5.97	28.0	37	5.99	28.2
3	26.7	7	6.60	35.0	19	6.68	35.0	37	6.71	35.3
2	33.6	7	7.42	44.4	19	7.52	44.4	37	7.54	44.7
1	42.4	19	8.43	56.2	37	8.46	56.2	61	8.46	56.2
1/0	53.5	19	9.47	70.9	37	9.50	70.9	61	9.53	71.3
2/0	67.4	19	10.6	89.4	37	10.7	89.4	61	10.7	89.8
3/0	85.0	19	11.9	112	37	12.0	112	61	12.0	113
4/0	107	19	13.4	142	37	13.4	142	61	13.5	142
250	127	37	14.6	168	61	14.6	168	91	14.7	169
300	152	37	16.0	202	61	16.0	202	91	16.1	202
350	177	37	17.3	236	61	17.3	236	91	17.3	236
400	203	37	18.5	269	61	18.5	269	91	18.5	270
450	228	37	19.6	280	61	19.6	280	91	19.7	304

(Continued)

Appendix D

Table D5 (Concluded)

Nominal		Standard*			Flexible			Extra flexible		
Conductor size, AWG or kcmil	Conductor area, mm²	Number of conductors†	Diameter, mm	Occupied area‡, mm²	Number of conductors	Diameter, mm	Occupied area‡, mm²	Number of conductors	Diameter, mm	Occupied area‡, mm²
500	253	37	20.7	337	61	20.7	337	91	20.7	337
550	279	61	21.7	370	91	21.7	370	127	21.7	371
600	304	61	22.7	405	91	22.7	405	127	22.7	405
650	329	61	23.6	438	91	23.6	438	127	23.6	438
700	355	61	24.5	472	91	24.5	472	127	24.5	472
750	380	61	25.3	506	91	25.4	506	127	25.4	506
800	405	61	26.2	540	91	26.2	540	127	26.2	541
900	456	61	27.8	606	91	27.8	606	127	27.8	608
1000	507	61	29.3	674	91	29.3	674	127	29.3	675
1250	633	91	32.7	843	127	32.8	843	169	32.8	843
1500	760	91	35.9	1010	127	35.9	1010	169	35.9	1010
1750	887	127	38.8	1180	169	38.8	1180	217	38.8	1180
2000	1010	127	41.5	1350	169	41.5	1350	217	41.5	1350

* Compact conductor diameters of equivalent cross-sectional area are reduced by up to 10% of the dimension indicated. Compressed conductor diameters of equivalent cross-sectional area are reduced by 2% of the dimension indicated.

† The number of conductors indicated may be reduced by one in each layer.

‡ Area of circumscribing circle; use for conduit space calculations.

Table D6
Recommended* tightening torques for wire-binding screws, connectors with slotted screws, and connectors for external drive wrenches
(See Table D7.)

Type of connection	Wire size, AWG or kcmil	Tightening torque, N•m
Wire-binding screws	14–10	1.4
Connectors with slotted screws (slot width — 1.2 mm or less and slot length — 6.4 mm or less)	30–10	2.3
	8	2.8
	6–4	4.0
	3	4.0
	2	4.5
Connectors with slotted screws (slot width over 1.2 mm and slot length over 6.4 mm)	30–10	4.0
	8	4.5
	6–4	5.1
	3	5.6
	2	5.6
	1	5.6
	1/0–2/0	5.6
	3/0–4/0	5.6
	250–350	5.6
	400	5.6
	500	5.6
	600–750	5.6
	800–1000	5.6
Connectors for hexagonal head — External drive wrench (split-bolt connectors)	30–10	9.0
	8	9.0
	6–4	18.6
	3	31.1
	2	31.1
	1	31.1
	1/0–2/0	43.5
	3/0–4/0	56.5
	250–350	73.4
	400	93.2
	500	93.2

(Continued)

Appendix D

Table D6 (Concluded)

Type of connection	Wire size, AWG or kcmil	Tightening torque, N•m
	600–750	113.0
	800–1000	124.3
	1250–2000	124.3
Connectors for hexagonal head — External drive wrench (other connectors)	30–10	8.5
	8	8.5
	6–4	12.4
	3	16.9
	2	16.9
	1	16.9
	1/0–2/0	20.3
	3/0–4/0	28.2
	250–350	36.7
	400	36.7
	500	42.4
	600–750	42.4
	800–1000	56.5
	1250–2000	67.8

* *For proper termination of conductors, it is very important that field connections be properly tightened. In the absence of manufacturer's instructions on the equipment, the torque values given in Tables D6 and D7 are recommended. Because it is normal for some relaxation to occur in service, checking torque values some time after installation is not a reliable means of determining the values of torque applied at installation.*

Note: *The values in this Table are correlated for consistency with the harmonized Standard CSA C22.2 No. 65.*

Table D7
Recommended* tightening torques
(See Table D6.)

Usage	Connection type and size	Tightening torque, N•m
Screws with recessed allen or square drives	**Socket (across flats) mm (inches)**	
	3.2 (1/8)	5.1
	4.0 (5/32)	11.3
	4.8 (3/16)	13.6
	5.6 (7/32)	16.9
	6.4 (1/4)	22.6
	7.9 (5/16)	31.1
	9.5 (3/8)	42.4
	12.7 (1/2)	56.5
	14.3 (9/16)	67.8
Connecting hardware	**Screw or bolt metric (SAE)**	
	No. 8 or smaller	2
	No. 10	3
	M6 (1/4)	8
	5/16	15
	M10 (3/8)	26
	7/16	41
	M12 (1/2)	54
	9/16, 5/8, or larger	75
	Slot width of screw less than 1.2 mm (3/64 inch) — Slot length mm (inches)	
Slotted head screws smaller than No. 10 intended for use with No. 8 AWG or smaller conductors	< 4 (< 5/32)	7
	4 (5/32)	7
	4.8 (3/16)	7
	5.6 (7/32)	7
	6.4 (1/4)	9

(Continued)

Table D7 (Concluded)

Usage	Connection type and size	Tightening torque, N•m
	Slot width of screw 1.2 mm (3/64 inch) and larger — Slot length mm (inches)	
	< 4 (< 5/32)	9
	4 (5/32)	12
	4.8 (3/16)	12
	5.6 (7/32)	12
	6.4 (1/4)	12
	7.1 (9/32)	15
	> 7.1 (> 9/32)	20

* *For proper termination of conductors, it is very important that field connections be properly tightened. In the absence of manufacturer's instructions on the equipment, the torque values given in Tables D6 and D7 are recommended. Because it is normal for some relaxation to occur in service, checking torque values some time after installation is not a reliable means of determining the values of torque applied at installation.*

Note: *The values in this Table are correlated for consistency with the harmonized Standard CSA C22.2 No. 65.*

Diagram D8
Installation configurations — Direct buried

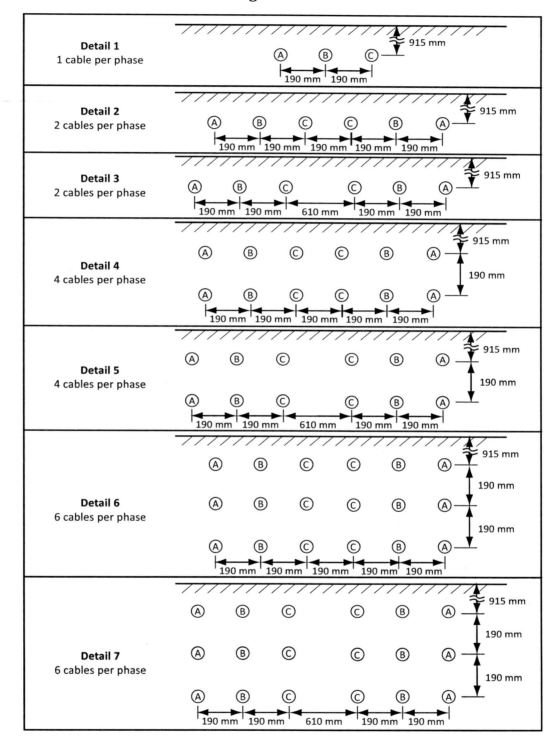

Appendix D

Δ

Table D8A
Allowable insulated copper conductor ampacities for cables rated not more than 5000 V and unshielded for the installation configurations of Diagram D8
(See Rule 4-004.)

Size, AWG or kcmil	1/Phase Detail 1	2/Phase Detail 2	2/Phase Detail 3	4/Phase Detail 4	4/Phase Detail 5	6/Phase Detail 6	6/Phase Detail 7
1/0	315	269	288	204	221	171	186
2/0	357	304	326	230	249	192	209
3/0	405	343	369	259	281	217	236
4/0	458	388	418	292	317	244	265
250	499	422	454	317	344	265	289
300	550	464	500	348	378	291	317
350	597	503	543	376	409	314	342
400	642	540	582	403	439	336	366
500	721	605	654	451	491	375	409
600	790	662	716	493	536	410	447
750	885	740	801	549	598	457	498
900	972	810	877	599	653	498	543
1000	1020	850	921	629	686	522	570
1250	1132	941	1020	694	757	576	629
1500	1227	1017	1104	749	817	621	678
1750	1308	1083	1176	796	869	659	720
2000	1376	1138	1236	835	911	691	755

Notes:

1) *This Table provides the allowable ampacities for 90 °C rated single copper conductor cables with spacings directly buried in earth.*

2) *Underground ampacities for an insulated conductor or cable temperature of 75 °C may be obtained by multiplying the appropriate allowable ampacity at 90 °C conductor insulation temperature by the derating factor 0.886.*

3) *See Rule 4-006 for equipment termination temperature requirements.*

Δ
Table D8B
Allowable insulated aluminum conductor ampacities for cables rated not more than 5000 V and unshielded for the installation configurations of Diagram D8
(See Rule 4-004.)

Size, AWG or kcmil	1/Phase Detail 1	2/Phase Detail 2	2/Phase Detail 3	4/Phase Detail 4	4/Phase Detail 5	6/Phase Detail 6	6/Phase Detail 7
1/0	244	208	223	158	172	133	144
2/0	276	236	253	179	194	150	163
3/0	313	266	286	201	218	169	183
4/0	356	302	325	227	247	190	207
250	387	328	353	247	268	206	225
300	427	361	389	271	294	226	247
350	464	391	422	293	319	245	267
400	498	420	453	314	342	262	286
500	561	472	509	352	383	293	320
600	617	518	559	386	420	321	350
750	694	581	628	432	470	359	392
900	764	638	691	473	515	393	429
1000	807	673	729	498	543	414	452
1250	906	753	817	556	606	461	503
1500	992	822	893	605	661	502	548
1750	1068	884	960	649	709	538	588
2000	1134	937	1018	687	751	569	622

Notes:

1) *This Table provides the allowable ampacities for 90 °C rated single aluminum conductor cables with spacings directly buried in earth.*

2) *Underground ampacities for an insulated conductor or cable temperature of 75 °C may be obtained by multiplying the appropriate allowable ampacity at 90 °C conductor insulation temperature by the derating factor 0.886.*

3) *See Rule 4-006 for equipment termination temperature requirements.*

Appendix D

Diagram D9
Installation configurations — Conduit or raceway

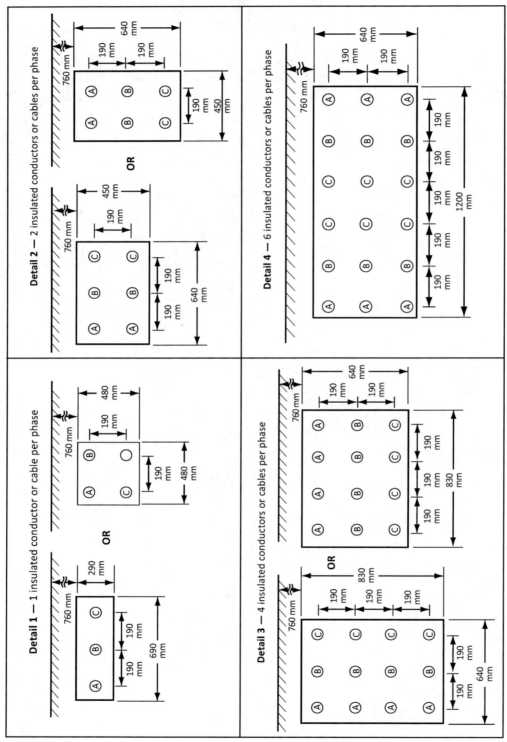

Δ

Table D9A
Allowable insulated copper conductor ampacities for insulated conductors or cables rated not more than 5000 V and unshielded for the installation configurations of Diagram D9
(See Rule 4-004.)

Size, AWG or kcmil	1/Phase Detail 1	2/Phase Detail 2	4/Phase Detail 3	6/Phase Detail 4
1/0	258	221	181	165
2/0	293	250	205	186
3/0	333	283	231	210
4/0	378	321	261	237
250	414	351	285	258
300	458	387	313	284
350	499	420	339	307
400	537	451	364	329
500	607	507	408	369
600	669	558	447	404
750	754	626	500	451
900	832	687	547	492
1000	875	722	574	517
1250	978	803	635	572
1500	1065	870	687	617
1750	1140	928	731	656
2000	1203	976	767	689

Notes:

1) *This Table provides the allowable ampacities for 90 °C rated single copper conductor cables with spacings installed in non-metallic underground raceways.*

2) *Underground ampacities for an insulated conductor or cable temperature of 75 °C may be obtained by multiplying the appropriate allowable ampacity at 90 °C conductor insulation temperature by the derating factor 0.886.*

3) *See Rule 4-006 for equipment termination temperature requirements.*

Appendix D

Δ

Table D9B
Allowable insulated aluminum conductor ampacities for insulated conductors or cables rated not more than 5000 V and unshielded for the installation configurations of Diagram D9

(See Rule 4-004.)

Size, AWG or kcmil	1/Phase Detail 1	2/Phase Detail 2	4/Phase Detail 3	6/Phase Detail 4
1/0	199	171	141	128
2/0	226	194	159	145
3/0	257	219	179	163
4/0	293	249	203	184
250	321	272	221	201
300	355	300	243	221
350	386	326	264	239
400	416	351	283	256
500	471	395	318	288
600	521	435	350	316
750	590	491	392	354
900	652	540	431	388
1000	690	570	454	409
1250	783	643	509	458
1500	861	703	555	499
1750	930	757	596	536
2000	991	804	632	567

Notes:

1) *This Table provides the allowable ampacities for 90 °C rated single aluminum conductor cables with spacings installed in non-metallic underground raceways.*

2) *Underground ampacities for an insulated conductor or cable temperature of 75 °C may be obtained by multiplying the appropriate allowable ampacity at 90 °C conductor insulation temperature by the derating factor 0.886.*

3) *See Rule 4-006 for equipment termination temperature requirements.*

Diagram D10
Installation configurations — Direct buried

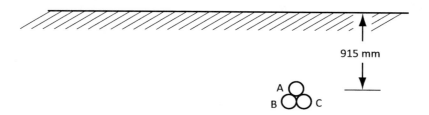

Detail 1
1 cable per phase

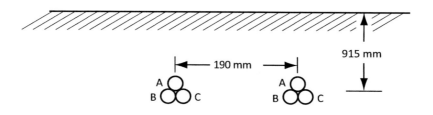

Detail 2
2 cables per phase

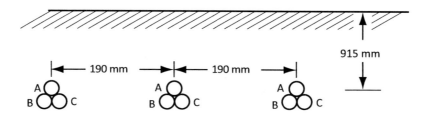

Detail 3
3 cables per phase

(Continued)

Diagram D10 (Concluded)

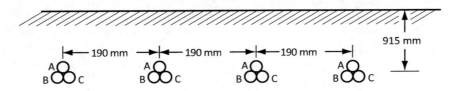

Detail 4
4 cables per phase

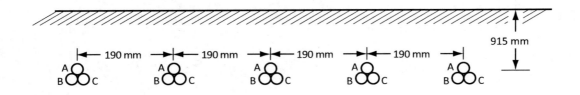

Detail 5
5 cables per phase

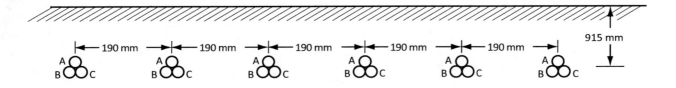

Detail 6
6 cables per phase

Δ

Table D10A
Allowable insulated copper conductor ampacities for cables rated not more than 5000 V and unshielded for the installation configurations of Diagram D10
(See Rule 4-004.)

Size, AWG or kcmil	1/Phase Detail 1	2/Phase Detail 2	3/Phase Detail 3	4/Phase Detail 4	5/Phase Detail 5	6/Phase Detail 6
1/0	262	221	195	181	170	163
2/0	298	250	220	205	192	184
3/0	337	282	248	230	216	207
4/0	382	319	280	260	244	233
250	418	348	306	283	265	253
300	462	382	336	310	291	278
350	500	413	362	335	314	300
400	538	443	388	358	336	320
500	602	494	432	398	373	356
600	658	538	470	433	405	387
750	731	595	518	478	447	426
900	795	643	560	515	481	458
1000	827	669	582	535	500	476
1250	907	728	632	581	542	516
1500	966	772	670	615	574	546
1750	1017	809	702	643	600	571
2000	1060	840	728	667	622	591

Notes:

1) *This Table provides the allowable ampacities for 90 °C rated copper conductor cables containing not more than three current-carrying conductors or three single copper current-carrying conductors in contact, directly buried in earth.*

2) *Underground ampacities for an insulated conductor or cable temperature of 75 °C may be obtained by multiplying the appropriate allowable ampacity at 90 °C conductor insulation temperature by the derating factor 0.886.*

3) *See Rule 4-006 for equipment termination temperature requirements.*

Δ

Table D10B
Allowable insulated aluminum conductor ampacities for cables rated not more than 5000 V and unshielded for the installation configurations of Diagram D10
(See Rule 4-004.)

Size, AWG or kcmil	1/Phase Detail 1	2/Phase Detail 2	3/Phase Detail 3	4/Phase Detail 4	5/Phase Detail 5	6/Phase Detail 6
1/0	203	172	152	141	132	127
2/0	230	193	171	159	149	143
3/0	261	219	193	179	168	161
4/0	298	249	219	203	190	182
250	324	270	238	220	207	197
300	359	298	262	242	227	217
350	390	323	284	262	246	235
400	419	347	304	281	263	251
500	473	389	340	314	294	281
600	522	428	374	345	323	308
750	586	478	417	384	359	342
900	643	522	455	418	391	373
1000	677	548	477	439	410	391
1250	757	608	528	485	453	431
1500	819	655	568	521	487	463
1750	873	695	602	552	515	490
2000	917	727	630	577	538	512

Notes:

1) *This Table provides the allowable ampacities for 90 °C rated aluminum conductor cables containing not more than three current-carrying conductors or three single aluminum current-carrying conductors in contact, directly buried in earth.*

2) *Underground ampacities for an insulated conductor or cable temperature of 75 °C may be obtained by multiplying the appropriate allowable ampacity at 90 °C conductor insulation temperature by the derating factor 0.886.*

3) *See Rule 4-006 for equipment termination temperature requirements.*

Diagram D11
Installation configurations — Conduit or raceway

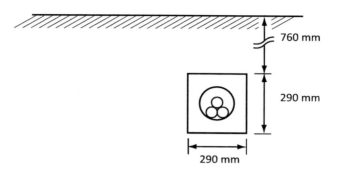

Detail 1 — 1 insulated conductor or cable per phase

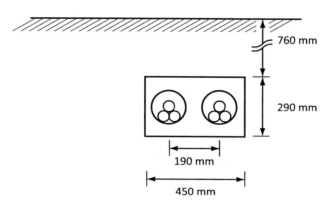

Detail 2 — 2 insulated conductors or cables per phase

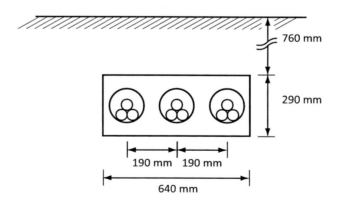

Detail 3 — 3 insulated conductors or cables per phase

(Continued)

Diagram D11 (Continued)

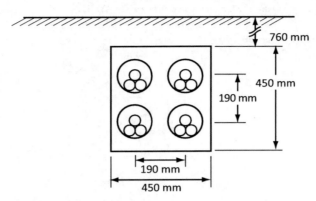

Detail 4 — 4 insulated conductors or cables per phase

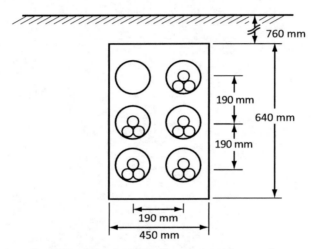

Detail 5 — 5 insulated conductors or cables per phase

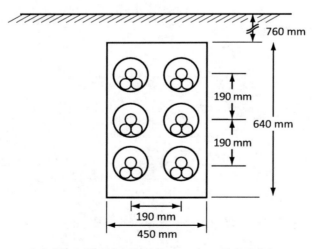

Detail 6 — 6 insulated conductors or cables per phase

(Continued)

Diagram D11 (Concluded)

Detail 7 — *(This detail intentionally left blank)*

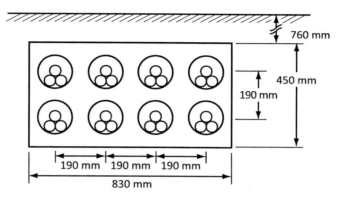

760 mm

450 mm

190 mm

190 mm 190 mm 190 mm

830 mm

Detail 8 — 8 insulated conductors or cables per phase

Appendix D

Δ

Table D11A
Allowable insulated copper conductor ampacities for insulated conductors or cables rated not more than 5000 V and unshielded for the installation configurations of Diagram D11

(See Rule 4-004.)

Size, AWG or kcmil	1/Phase Detail 1	2/Phase Detail 2	3/Phase Detail 3	4/Phase Detail 4	5/Phase Detail 5	6/Phase Detail 6	8/Phase Detail 8
1/0	205	185	169	158	147	139	130
2/0	233	210	192	179	166	157	147
3/0	266	239	218	202	188	178	166
4/0	303	271	247	229	212	201	187
250	335	298	271	251	232	219	204
300	370	329	298	276	255	241	224
350	403	357	323	299	276	261	242
400	434	384	347	320	295	279	259
500	489	430	388	357	329	310	288
600	539	472	424	390	359	339	314
750	601	524	470	431	397	374	346
900	655	569	509	466	428	403	373
1000	683	593	530	485	445	419	388
1250	752	649	578	528	484	455	421
1500	804	691	614	561	513	482	445
1750	847	726	644	587	537	504	466
2000	901	744	659	601	549	515	476

Notes:

1) *This Table provides the allowable ampacities for 90 °C rated copper conductor cables containing not more than three current-carrying conductors or three single copper current-carrying conductors in contact, installed in underground raceway.*

2) *Underground ampacities for an insulated conductor or cable temperature of 75 °C may be obtained by multiplying the appropriate allowable ampacity at 90 °C conductor insulation temperature by the derating factor 0.886.*

3) *See Rule 4-006 for equipment termination temperature requirements.*

Δ

Table D11B
Allowable insulated aluminum conductor ampacities for insulated conductors or cables rated not more than 5000 V and unshielded for the installation configurations of Diagram D11

(See Rule 4-004.)

Size, AWG or kcmil	1/Phase Detail 1	2/Phase Detail 2	3/Phase Detail 3	4/Phase Detail 4	5/Phase Detail 5	6/Phase Detail 6	8/Phase Detail 8
1/0	157	143	131	122	114	108	101
2/0	179	162	148	138	129	122	114
3/0	205	184	168	157	146	138	129
4/0	235	210	192	178	165	156	146
250	258	231	210	195	180	171	159
300	286	255	232	215	199	188	175
350	312	278	252	233	215	204	189
400	337	299	271	250	231	218	203
500	382	337	305	281	259	245	227
600	424	373	336	309	285	269	249
750	478	419	376	346	318	300	278
900	527	459	412	378	347	327	303
1000	555	483	433	397	364	343	318
1250	626	541	482	441	404	380	351
1500	679	585	520	475	435	409	377
1750	724	621	552	503	461	432	399
2000	777	646	573	522	477	448	413

Notes:

1) *This Table provides the allowable ampacities for 90 °C rated aluminum conductor cables containing not more than three current-carrying conductors or three single aluminum current-carrying conductors in contact, installed in underground raceway.*

2) *Underground ampacities for an insulated conductor or cable temperature of 75 °C may be obtained by multiplying the appropriate allowable ampacity at 90 °C conductor insulation temperature by the derating factor 0.886.*

3) *See Rule 4-006 for equipment termination temperature requirements.*

Table D12A
Deleted

Table D12B
Deleted

Table D13A
Deleted

Table D13B
Deleted

Table D14A
Deleted

Table D14B
Deleted

Table D15A
Deleted

Table D15B
Deleted

Δ

Table D16

Sizes of conductors, fuse ratings, and circuit breaker settings for motor overload protection and motor circuit overcurrent protection

(See Rules 28-106, 28-200, and 28-208.)

Note: *This Table is based on Table 29 and a room temperature of 30 °C.*

| Full load current rating of motor, A | Minimum allowable ampacity of insulated conductor, A | Overcurrent protection maximum allowable rating of fuses and maximum allowable setting for inverse-time circuit breakers for motor circuits | | | | | | | | |
| | | Single-phase — All types and squirrel-cage and synchronous (full-voltage, resistor and reactor starting) | | | Squirrel-cage and synchronous (auto-transformer and star delta starting) | | | DC or wound rotor AC | | |
		Non-time-delay fuses, A	Time-delay* fuses, A	Circuit breaker, A	Non-time-delay fuses, A	Time-delay* fuses, A	Circuit breaker, A	Non-time-delay fuses, A	Time-delay* fuses, A	Circuit breaker, A
1	1.25	15	15	15	15	15	15	15	15	15
2	2.50	15	15	15	15	15	15	15	15	15
3	3.80	15	15	15	15	15	15	15	15	15
4	5.00	15	15	15	15	15	15	15	15	15
5	6.25	15	15	15	15	15	15	15	15	15
6	7.50	15	15	15	15	15	15	15	15	15
7	8.75	20	15	15	15	15	15	15	15	15
8	10.00	20	15	20	20	15	15	15	15	15
9	11.25	25	15	20	20	15	15	15	15	15
10	12.50	30	15	25	25	15	20	15	15	15
11	13.75	30	15	25	25	15	20	15	15	15
12	15.00	35	20	30	30	20	20	15	15	15

(Continued)

Appendix D

Table D16 (Continued)

Overcurrent protection maximum allowable rating of fuses and maximum allowable setting for inverse-time circuit breakers for motor circuits

Full load current rating of motor, A	Minimum allowable ampacity of insulated conductor, A	Single-phase — All types and squirrel-cage and synchronous (full-voltage, resistor and reactor starting)			Squirrel-cage and synchronous (auto-transformer and star delta starting)			DC or wound rotor AC		
		Non-time-delay fuses, A	Time-delay* fuses, A	Circuit breaker, A	Non-time-delay fuses, A	Time-delay* fuses, A	Circuit breaker, A	Non-time-delay fuses, A	Time-delay* fuses, A	Circuit breaker, A
13	16.25	35	20	30	30	25	20	15	15	15
14	17.50	40	20	35	35	25	20	20	20	20
15	18.75	45	25	35	35	25	30	20	20	20
16	20.00	45	25	40	40	25	30	20	20	20
17	21.3	50	25	40	40	25	30	25	25	25
18	22.5	50	30	45	45	35	30	25	25	25
19	23.8	50	30	45	45	35	30	25	25	25
20	25.0	60	35	50	50	35	40	30	30	30
22	27.5	60	35	50	50	35	40	30	30	30
24	30.0	70	40	60	60	45	40	35	35	35
26	32.5	70	45	60	60	45	50	35	35	35
28	35.0	80	45	70	70	45	50	40	40	40
30	37.5	90	50	70	70	50	60	45	45	45
32	40.0	90	50	80	60	50	60	45	45	45
34	42.5	100	50	80	60	50	60	50	50	50
36	45.0	100	60	90	70	60	70	50	50	50

(Continued)

Table D16 (Continued)

Full load current rating of motor, A	Minimum allowable ampacity of insulated conductor, A	Overcurrent protection maximum allowable rating of fuses and maximum allowable setting for inverse-time circuit breakers for motor circuits								
		Single-phase — All types and squirrel-cage and synchronous (full-voltage, resistor and reactor starting)			Squirrel-cage and synchronous (auto-transformer and star delta starting)			DC or wound rotor AC		
		Non-time-delay fuses, A	Time-delay* fuses, A	Circuit breaker, A	Non-time-delay fuses, A	Time-delay* fuses, A	Circuit breaker, A	Non-time-delay fuses, A	Time-delay* fuses, A	Circuit breaker, A
38	47.5	110	60	90	70	60	70	50	50	50
40	50.0	110	70	100	80	80	70	60	60	60
42	52.5	125	70	100	80	80	70	60	60	60
44	55.0	125	70	110	80	80	70	60	60	60
46	57.5	125	80	110	90	90	70	60	60	60
48	60.0	125	80	110	90	90	70	70	70	70
50	62.5	150	80	125	100	90	100	70	70	70
52	65.0	150	90	125	100	90	100	70	70	70
54	67.5	150	90	125	100	90	100	80	80	80
56	70.0	150	90	125	110	110	100	80	80	80
58	72.5	150	100	125	110	110	100	80	80	80
60	75.0	175	100	150	110	110	100	90	90	90
62	77.5	175	100	150	110	110	100	90	90	90
64	80.0	175	110	150	125	110	125	90	90	90
66	82.5	175	110	150	125	110	125	90	90	90
68	85.0	200	110	150	125	110	125	100	100	100

(Continued)

Appendix D

Table D16 (Continued)

Overcurrent protection maximum allowable rating of fuses and maximum allowable setting for inverse-time circuit breakers for motor circuits

Full load current rating of motor, A	Minimum allowable ampacity of insulated conductor, A	Single-phase — All types and squirrel-cage and synchronous (full-voltage, resistor and reactor starting)			Squirrel-cage and synchronous (auto-transformer and star delta starting)			DC or wound rotor AC		
		Non-time-delay fuses, A	Time-delay* fuses, A	Circuit breaker, A	Non-time-delay fuses, A	Time-delay* fuses, A	Circuit breaker, A	Non-time-delay fuses, A	Time-delay* fuses, A	Circuit breaker, A
70	87.5	200	110	175	125	110	125	100	100	100
72	90.0	200	125	175	125	125	125	100	100	100
74	92.5	200	125	175	125	125	125	110	110	110
76	95.0	225	125	175	150	125	150	110	110	110
78	97.5	225	125	175	150	125	150	110	110	110
80	100.0	225	125	200	150	125	150	110	110	110
82	102.5	225	125	200	150	125	150	110	110	110
84	105.0	250	125	200	150	125	150	125	125	125
86	107.5	250	150	200	150	150	150	125	125	125
88	110.0	250	150	200	175	150	175	125	125	125
90	112.5	250	150	225	175	150	175	125	125	125
92	115.0	250	150	225	175	150	175	125	125	125
94	117.5	250	150	225	175	150	175	125	125	125
96	120.0	250	150	225	175	150	175	125	125	125
98	122.5	250	150	225	175	150	175	125	125	125
100	125.0	300	175	250	200	175	200	150	150	150

(Continued)

Table D16 (Continued)

Overcurrent protection maximum allowable rating of fuses and maximum allowable setting for inverse-time circuit breakers for motor circuits

Full load current rating of motor, A	Minimum allowable ampacity of insulated conductor, A	Single-phase — All types and squirrel-cage and synchronous (full-voltage, resistor and reactor starting)			Squirrel-cage and synchronous (auto-transformer and star delta starting)			DC or wound rotor AC		
		Non-time-delay fuses, A	Time-delay* fuses, A	Circuit breaker, A	Non-time-delay fuses, A	Time-delay* fuses, A	Circuit breaker, A	Non-time-delay fuses, A	Time-delay* fuses, A	Circuit breaker, A
105	131.3	300	175	250	200	175	200	150	150	150
110	137.5	300	175	250	200	175	200	150	150	150
115	143.8	300	200	250	225	200	225	150	150	150
120	150.0	350	200	300	225	200	225	175	175	175
125	156.3	350	200	300	250	200	250	175	175	175
130	162.5	350	225	300	250	225	250	175	175	175
135	168.8	400	225	300	250	225	250	200	200	200
140	175.0	400	225	350	250	225	250	200	200	200
145	181.3	400	250	350	250	250	250	200	200	200
150	187.5	450	250	350	300	250	300	225	225	225
155	193.8	450	250	350	300	250	300	225	225	225
160	200.0	450	250	400	300	250	300	225	225	225
165	206.3	450	250	400	300	250	300	225	225	225
170	212.5	500	250	400	300	250	300	250	250	250
175	218.8	500	300	400	350	300	350	250	250	250
180	225.0	500	300	450	350	300	350	250	250	250

(Continued)

Appendix D

Table D16 (Continued)

Overcurrent protection maximum allowable rating of fuses and maximum allowable setting for inverse-time circuit breakers for motor circuits

Full load current rating of motor, A	Minimum allowable ampacity of insulated conductor, A	Single-phase — All types and squirrel-cage and synchronous (full-voltage, resistor and reactor starting)			Squirrel-cage and synchronous (auto-transformer and star delta starting)			DC or wound rotor AC		
		Non-time-delay fuses, A	Time-delay* fuses, A	Circuit breaker, A	Non-time-delay fuses, A	Time-delay* fuses, A	Circuit breaker, A	Non-time-delay fuses, A	Time-delay* fuses, A	Circuit breaker, A
185	231.3	500	300	450	350	300	350	250	250	250
190	237.5	500	300	450	350	300	350	250	250	250
195	243.8	500	300	450	350	300	350	250	250	250
200	250.0	600	350	500	400	350	400	300	300	300
210	262.5	600	350	500	400	350	400	300	300	300
220	275.0	600	350	500	400	350	400	300	300	300
230	287.5	600	400	500	450	450	400	300	300	300
240	300.0		400		450	450	400	350	350	350
250	312.5		400		500	450	500	350	350	350
260	325.0		450	600	500	450	500	350	350	350
270	337.5		450	600	500	450	500	400	400	400
280	350.0		450		500	450	500	400	400	400
290	362.5		500		600	500	500	400	400	400
300	375.0		500		600	500	600	450	450	450
320	400		500		600	500	600	450	450	450
340	425		500		600	500	600	500	500	500

(Continued)

© 2018 Canadian Standards Association

January 2018

Table D16 (Concluded)

Overcurrent protection maximum allowable rating of fuses and maximum allowable setting for inverse-time circuit breakers for motor circuits

Full load current rating of motor, A	Minimum allowable ampacity of insulated conductor, A	Single-phase — All types and squirrel-cage and synchronous (full-voltage, resistor and reactor starting)			Squirrel-cage and synchronous (auto-transformer and star delta starting)			DC or wound rotor AC		
		Non-time-delay fuses, A	Time-delay* fuses, A	Circuit breaker, A	Non-time-delay fuses, A	Time-delay* fuses, A	Circuit breaker, A	Non-time-delay fuses, A	Time-delay* fuses, A	Circuit breaker, A
360	450		600			600		500	500	500
380	475					600		500	500	500
400	500							600	600	600
420	525							600	600	600
440	550							600	600	600
460	575							600	600	600
480	600									
500	625									

* *Includes time-delay "D" fuses referred to in Rule 14-200.*

Note: *For overload protection, refer to Rule 28-306 and the motor nameplate data.*

Appendix D

Table D17 series
Ampacities for shielded cables rated 5 kV to 46 kV
Index

Table	Configurations	Page
D17	Conditions applicable to all configurations	788
D17A	Allowable ampacities for three single-conductor shielded cables, direct buried 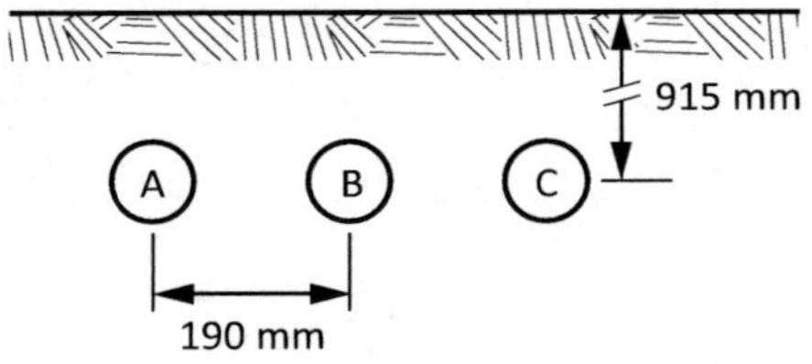	790

Diagram 17A

915 mm

190 mm

Table	Configurations	Page
D17B	Allowable ampacities for two sets of three single shielded conductor cables, direct buried (two insulated conductors per phase) 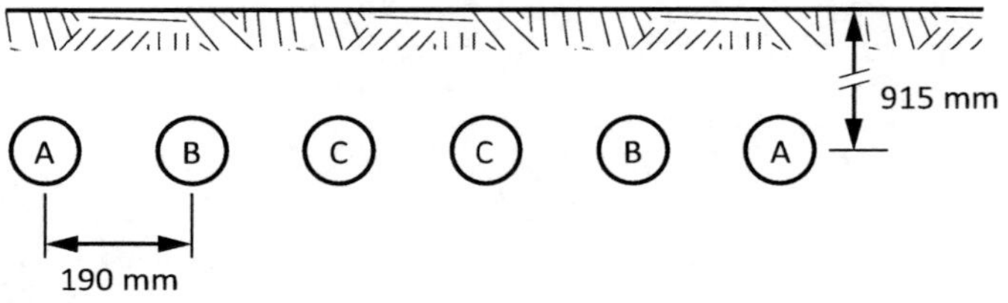	791

Diagram 17B

915 mm

190 mm

Table	Configurations	Page
D17C	Allowable ampacities for three single shielded insulated conductors or single-conductor cables in buried conduit 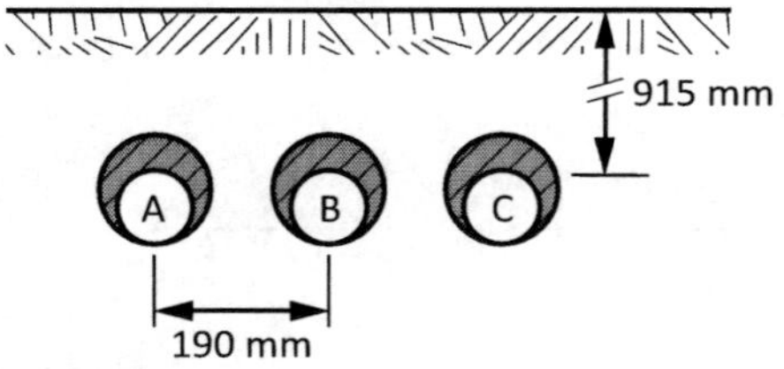	792

Diagram 17C

915 mm

190 mm

Table	Configurations	Page
D17D	Allowable ampacities for two sets of three single shielded insulated conductors or single-conductor cables in buried conduit (two insulated conductors per phase) 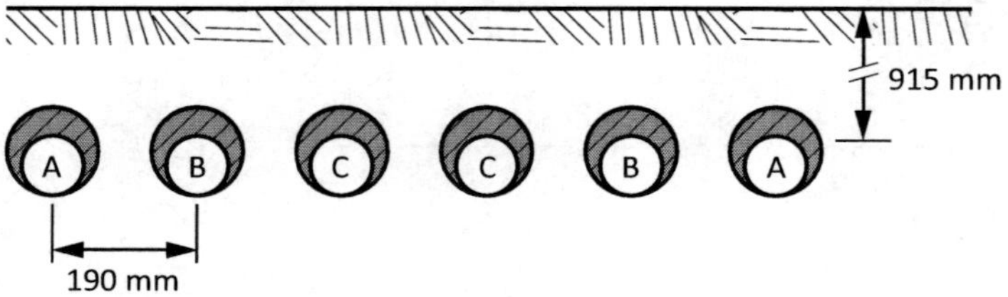	793

Diagram 17D

915 mm

190 mm

Table	Configurations	Page
D17E	Allowable ampacities for 3-conductor shielded cable or three single shielded conductor cables in contact, direct buried	794
	Diagram 17E	
D17F	Allowable ampacities for two 3-conductor shielded cables or two sets of three single shielded conductor cables in contact, direct buried (two insulated conductors per phase)	795
	Diagram 17F	
D17G	Allowable ampacities for 3-conductor shielded cable or three single shielded conductor cables in contact in buried conduit	796
	Diagram 17G	
D17H	Allowable ampacities for two 3-conductor shielded cables or two sets of three single shielded conductor cables in contact in buried conduit (two insulated conductors per phase)	797
	Diagram 17H	

Appendix D

Table	Configurations	Page
D17I	Allowable ampacities for three single shielded insulated conductors or single-conductor cables in a concrete-encased duct bank	*798*
D17J	Allowable ampacities for two sets of three single shielded insulated conductors or single-conductor cables in a concrete-encased duct bank (two insulated conductors per phase)	*799*
D17K	Allowable ampacities for 3-conductor shielded cable or three single shielded conductor cables in contact in a concrete-encased duct bank	*800*

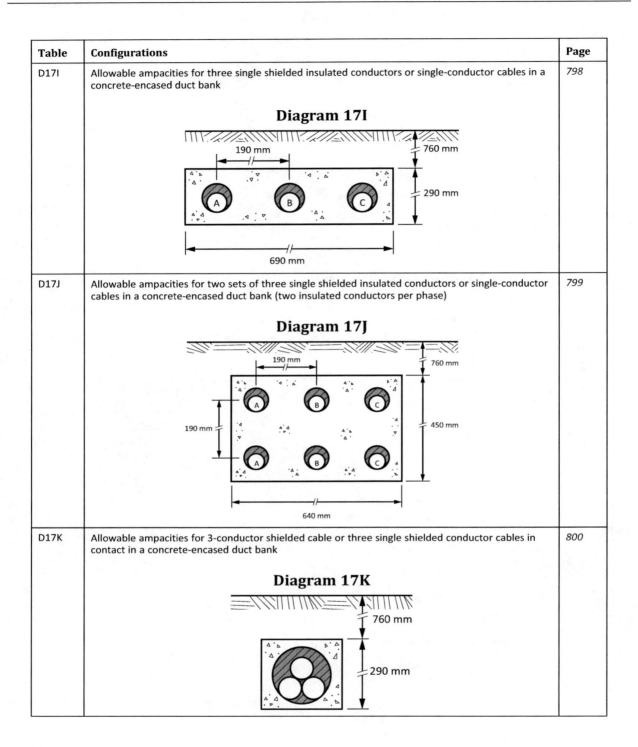

Table	Configurations	Page
D17L	Allowable ampacities for two 3-conductor shielded cables or two sets of three single shielded conductor cables in contact in a concrete-encased duct bank (two insulated conductors per phase) **Diagram 17L** 	801
D17M	Allowable ampacities for three single shielded conductor cables on ladder or ventilated cable tray **Diagram 17M** **Note:** D = diameter of one conductor.	802
D17N	Allowable ampacities for 3-conductor shielded cable or three single shielded conductor cables in contact on ladder or ventilated cable tray **Diagram 17N** **Note:** Cables are in contact or spaced less than one diameter apart.	804

Appendix D

Δ

Table D17
Conditions of use for Tables D17A to D17N*††
(See Rule 4-004.)

Item	Characteristic	Condition
1	Load factor	100%
2	Earth (backfill) thermal resistivity	90 °C•cm/W
3	Concrete thermal resistivity	60 °C•cm/W
4	Ambient earth temperature	20 °C
5	Ambient air temperature	40 °C
6	Maximum conductor temperature	90 °C
7	Conductor insulation level	100% or 133%
8	Insulated conductor or cable shield, ground conductors, and armour bonding†	Both ends of each run
9	Minimum separation from any other adjacent installation‡	3 m
10	Number of circuits	1
11	Number of single-conductor cables per phase	1 or 2
12	Number of phases	3
13	Maximum load variation between phases	10%
14	Maximum concealed vertical distance at each end of the run§	2 m
15	Armour material	Aluminum, galvanized steel, or steel wire
16	Bedding material for direct buried cables	Sand
17	Height above sea level	300 m
18	Latitude**	45 to 49°

* It is important to note that the ampacities listed in Tables D17A to D17N are valid only for the configurations shown and the conditions specified in Table D17. A change in any one or more installation conditions or cable construction will result in a change in maximum insulated conductor ampacity.

† It is assumed that insulated conductor shields, ground conductors, and armour (if present) are grounded at more than one point. The ampacities in the D17 series of Tables have been adjusted to take into consideration the heating due to shield, ground conductor, and armour circulating currents.

‡ This minimum separation does not apply to sets of cable run in parallel for the same circuit.

§ The maximum concealed vertical distance is intended to be the maximum transition distance from an underground installation to a pad-mounted (not pole- or building-mounted) device, such as a transformer or switchgear, where the cables are shaded from direct sunlight and the raceway is ventilated both top and bottom for air to circulate freely. Pole risers and other vertical runs have not been considered in these calculations and may be a limiting factor for maximum insulated conductor ampacity.

** This characteristic is applicable only to Tables D17M and D17N for cables exposed to direct sunlight in an outdoor location (not shaded).

(Continued)

Table D17 (Concluded)

†† *Underground ampacities for an insulated conductor or cable temperature of 75 °C may be obtained by multiplying the appropriate allowable ampacity at 90 °C conductor insulation temperature by the termination temperature correction factor 0.886. [See Rule 4-006 3) for equipment termination temperature requirements.]*

Appendix D

Δ

Table D17A
Allowable ampacities for three single-conductor shielded cables, direct buried as shown in Diagram D17A

Diagram D17A

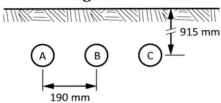

Size, AWG or kcmil	Concentric ground wire or concentric neutral wire size	Allowable ampacity			
		5 kV to 15 kV		25 kV to 46 kV	
		Copper	Aluminum	Copper	Aluminum
2	Full	221	176	—	—
1	Full	247	198	244	194
1/0	Full	275	223	272	219
2/0	Full	306	250	303	246
3/0	Full	335	278	333	275
4/0	Full	369	309	367	305
250	1/3	412	347	411	343
350	1/3	456	402	459	399
500	1/3	497	451	499	451
750	1/3	551	500	557	505
1000	1/3	—	539	—	544
1000	1/6	596	—	608	—

Note: *For buried installations, the values shown may be limited by the maximum earth interface temperature due to soil moisture migration. Knowledge of local soil conditions is necessary for the determination of the earth interface temperature to be used. Typical values are between 50 °C and 60 °C, which experience has shown to be satisfactory for most types of soils.*

Δ

Table D17B
Allowable ampacities for two sets of three single shielded conductor cables, direct buried (two insulated conductors per phase) as shown in Diagram D17B

Diagram D17B

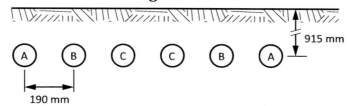

190 mm

915 mm

Size, AWG or kcmil	Concentric ground wire or concentric neutral wire size	Allowable ampacity			
		5 kV to 15 kV		25 kV to 46 kV	
		Copper	Aluminum	Copper	Aluminum
2	Full	191	153	—	—
1	Full	213	171	211	169
1/0	Full	236	192	230	190
2/0	Full	261	214	260	212
3/0	Full	287	237	286	235
4/0	Full	316	262	316	261
250	1/3	348	293	348	292
350	1/3	388	336	390	336
500	1/3	428	380	431	380
750	1/3	480	428	485	432
1000	1/3	—	466	—	472
1000	1/6	517	—	528	—

Note: *For buried installations, the values shown may be limited by the maximum earth interface temperature due to soil moisture migration. Knowledge of local soil conditions is necessary for the determination of the earth interface temperature to be used. Typical values are between 50 °C and 60 °C, which experience has shown to be satisfactory for most types of soils.*

Appendix D

Δ

Table D17C
Allowable ampacities for three single shielded insulated conductors or single-conductor cables in buried conduit as shown in Diagram D17C

Diagram D17C

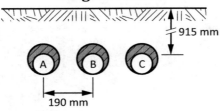

Size, AWG or kcmil	Concentric ground wire or concentric neutral wire size	Allowable ampacity			
		5 kV to 15 kV		25 kV to 46 kV	
		Copper	Aluminum	Copper	Aluminum
2	Full	186	148	—	—
1	Full	207	167	208	166
1/0	Full	228	187	230	187
2/0	Full	252	210	254	210
3/0	Full	276	232	278	233
4/0	Full	303	255	306	257
250	1/3	339	290	344	291
350	1/3	375	332	383	336
500	1/3	407	372	417	378
750	1/3	456	415	471	428
1000	1/3	—	453	—	462
1000	1/6	500	—	514	—

Notes:

1) *For buried installations, the values shown may be limited by the maximum earth interface temperature due to soil moisture migration. Knowledge of local soil conditions is necessary for the determination of the earth interface temperature to be used. Typical values are between 50 °C and 60 °C, which experience has shown to be satisfactory for most types of soils.*

2) *Conduit size is calculated based on 53% fill for a single conductor in conduit.*

3) *Conductor spacing is the centre-to-centre conduit or conductor spacing, typically 190 mm. For conduits larger than 103 mm, use an edge-to-edge conduit spacing of 50 mm.*

Δ

Table D17D
Allowable ampacities for two sets of three single shielded insulated conductors or single-conductor cables in buried conduit (two insulated conductors per phase) as shown in Diagram D17D

Diagram D17D

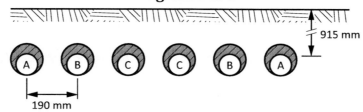

Size, AWG or kcmil	Concentric ground wire or concentric neutral wire size	Allowable ampacity			
		5 kV to 15 kV		25 kV to 46 kV	
		Copper	Aluminum	Copper	Aluminum
2	Full	167	134	—	—
1	Full	186	150	186	149
1/0	Full	205	167	206	168
2/0	Full	227	187	229	187
3/0	Full	250	207	254	208
4/0	Full	276	229	279	230
250	1/3	303	256	307	258
350	1/3	339	294	345	297
500	1/3	372	333	380	337
750	1/3	414	377	426	387
1000	1/3	—	410	—	418
1000	1/6	452	—	464	—

Notes:

1) *For buried installations, the values shown may be limited by the maximum earth interface temperature due to soil moisture migration. Knowledge of local soil conditions is necessary for the determination of the earth interface temperature to be used. Typical values are between 50 °C and 60 °C, which experience has shown to be satisfactory for most types of soils.*

2) *Conduit size is calculated based on 53% fill for a single conductor in conduit.*

3) *Conductor spacing is the centre-to-centre conduit or conductor spacing, typically 190 mm. For conduits larger than 103 mm, use an edge-to-edge conduit spacing of 50 mm.*

Appendix D

Δ

Table D17E
Allowable ampacities for 3-conductor shielded cable or three single shielded conductor cables in contact, direct buried as shown in Diagram D17E1 or D17E2

Diagram D17E1

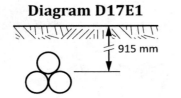

Diagram D17E2

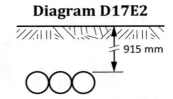

Size, AWG or kcmil	Concentric ground wire or concentric neutral wire size	Allowable ampacity			
		5 kV to 15 kV		25 kV to 46 kV	
		Copper	Aluminum	Copper	Aluminum
2	Full	201	157	—	—
1	Full	228	178	226	177
1/0	Full	257	202	256	200
2/0	Full	292	229	290	228
3/0	Full	330	260	327	258
4/0	Full	372	294	369	292
250	1/3	410	323	408	321
350	1/3	487	386	485	385
500	1/3	573	465	571	462
750	1/3	668	563	670	562
1000	1/3	—	638	—	638
1000	1/6	772	—	776	—

Note: *For buried installations, the values shown may be limited by the maximum earth interface temperature due to soil moisture migration. Knowledge of local soil conditions is necessary for the determination of the earth interface temperature to be used. Typical values are between 50 °C and 60 °C, which experience has shown to be satisfactory for most types of soils.*

Δ

Table D17F
Allowable ampacities for two 3-conductor shielded cables or two sets of three single shielded conductor cables in contact, direct buried (two insulated conductors per phase) as shown in Diagram D17F1 or D17F2

Diagram D17F1

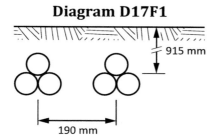

Diagram D17F2

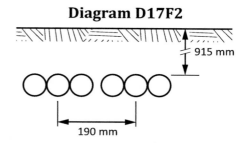

Size, AWG or kcmil	Concentric ground wire or concentric neutral wire size	Allowable ampacity			
		5 kV to 15 kV		25 kV to 46 kV	
		Copper	Aluminum	Copper	Aluminum
2	Full	170	133	—	—
1	Full	193	150	191	150
1/0	Full	217	170	216	169
2/0	Full	245	192	244	191
3/0	Full	275	217	274	216
4/0	Full	309	245	307	243
250	1/3	341	269	339	267
350	1/3	401	319	400	318
500	1/3	469	381	467	379
750	1/3	540	457	541	456
1000	1/3	—	512	—	513
1000	1/6	621	—	624	—

Note: *For buried installations, the values shown may be limited by the maximum earth interface temperature due to soil moisture migration. Knowledge of local soil conditions is necessary for the determination of the earth interface temperature to be used. Typical values are between 50 °C and 60 °C, which experience has shown to be satisfactory for most types of soils.*

Δ

Table D17G
Allowable ampacities for 3-conductor shielded cable or three single shielded conductor cables in contact in buried conduit as shown in Diagram D17G

Diagram D17G

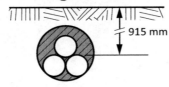

915 mm

Size, AWG or kcmil	Concentric ground wire or concentric neutral wire size	Allowable ampacity			
		5 kV to 15 kV		25 kV to 46 kV	
		Copper	Aluminum	Copper	Aluminum
2	Full	161	126	—	—
1	Full	182	144	188	147
1/0	Full	206	162	212	166
2/0	Full	239	188	241	189
3/0	Full	270	213	271	214
4/0	Full	305	240	306	242
250	1/3	336	264	338	266
350	1/3	399	317	410	325
500	1/3	480	389	482	390
750	1/3	560	472	575	483
1000	1/3	—	544	—	548
1000	1/6	659	—	666	—

Notes:

1) *For buried installations, the values shown may be limited by the maximum earth interface temperature due to soil moisture migration. Knowledge of local soil conditions is necessary for the determination of the earth interface temperature to be used. Typical values are between 50 °C and 60 °C, which experience has shown to be satisfactory for most types of soils.*

2) *Conduit size is calculated based on 40% fill for three conductors in conduit.*

Δ

Table D17H
Allowable ampacities for two 3-conductor shielded cables or two sets of three single shielded conductor cables in contact in buried conduit (two insulated conductors per phase) as shown in Diagram D17H

Diagram D17H

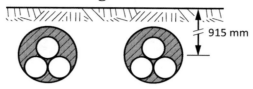

915 mm

Size, AWG or kcmil	Concentric ground wire or concentric neutral wire size	Allowable ampacity			
		5 kV to 15 kV		25 kV to 46 kV	
		Copper	Aluminum	Copper	Aluminum
2	Full	145	113	—	—
1	Full	164	128	168	131
1/0	Full	185	145	189	148
2/0	Full	213	167	214	168
3/0	Full	239	189	240	190
4/0	Full	269	213	270	214
250	1/3	296	234	298	235
350	1/3	351	278	358	284
500	1/3	417	338	418	340
750	1/3	483	408	493	416
1000	1/3	—	465	—	468
1000	1/6	564	—	569	—

Notes:

1) *For buried installations, the values shown may be limited by the maximum earth interface temperature due to soil moisture migration. Knowledge of local soil conditions is necessary for the determination of the earth interface temperature to be used. Typical values are between 50 °C and 60 °C, which experience has shown to be satisfactory for most types of soils.*

2) *Conduit size is calculated based on 40% fill for three conductors in conduit.*

3) *Conductor spacing is the centre-to-centre conduit or conductor spacing, typically 190 mm. For conduits larger than 103 mm, use an edge-to-edge conduit spacing of 50 mm.*

Appendix D

Table D17I
Allowable ampacities for three single shielded insulated conductors or single-conductor cables in a concrete-encased duct bank as shown in Diagram D17I

Diagram D17I

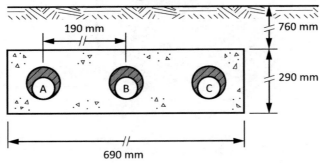

Size, AWG or kcmil	Concentric ground wire or concentric neutral wire size	Allowable ampacity			
		5 kV to 15 kV		25 kV to 46 kV	
		Copper	Aluminum	Copper	Aluminum
2	Full	189	151	—	—
1	Full	210	170	211	169
1/0	Full	232	190	234	190
2/0	Full	256	213	258	213
3/0	Full	280	235	283	236
4/0	Full	308	259	311	261
250	1/3	344	294	349	296
350	1/3	381	337	392	344
500	1/3	414	378	427	387
750	1/3	468	425	477	434
1000	1/3	—	481	—	469
1000	1/6	507	—	522	—

Notes:

1) *For buried installations, the values shown may be limited by the maximum earth interface temperature due to soil moisture migration. Knowledge of local soil conditions is necessary for the determination of the earth interface temperature to be used. Typical values are between 50 °C and 60 °C, which experience has shown to be satisfactory for most types of soils.*

2) *Conduit size is calculated based on 53% fill for a single conductor in conduit.*

3) *Conductor spacing is the centre-to-centre conduit or conductor spacing, typically 190 mm. For conduits larger than 103 mm, use an edge-to-edge conduit spacing of 50 mm.*

Δ

Table D17J
Allowable ampacities for two sets of three single shielded insulated conductors or single-conductor cables in a concrete-encased duct bank (two insulated conductors per phase) as shown in Diagram D17J

Diagram D17J

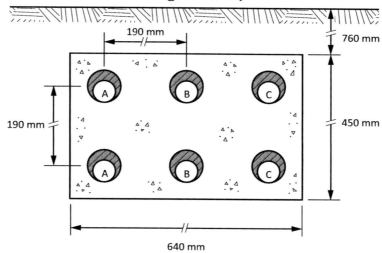

Size, AWG or kcmil	Concentric ground wire or concentric neutral wire size	Allowable ampacity			
		5 kV to 15 kV		25 kV to 46 kV	
		Copper	Aluminum	Copper	Aluminum
2	Full	165	131	—	—
1	Full	182	147	183	147
1/0	Full	200	165	202	165
2/0	Full	220	183	222	184
3/0	Full	240	202	242	203
4/0	Full	263	222	265	223
250	1/3	293	252	298	253
350	1/3	323	287	331	292
500	1/3	348	319J	357	326
750	1/3	388	354	395	361
1000	1/3	—	380	—	387
1000	1/6	419	—	430	—

Notes:

1) *For buried installations, the values shown may be limited by the maximum earth interface temperature due to soil moisture migration. Knowledge of local soil conditions is necessary for the determination of the earth*

(Continued)

Appendix D

Table D17J (Concluded)

interface temperature to be used. Typical values are between 50 °C and 60 °C, which experience has shown to be satisfactory for most types of soils.

2) *Conduit size is calculated based on 53% fill for a single conductor in conduit.*

3) *Conductor spacing is the centre-to-centre conduit or conductor spacing, typically 190 mm. For conduits larger than 103 mm, use an edge-to-edge conduit spacing of 50 mm.*

Δ

Table D17K
Allowable ampacities for 3-conductor shielded cable or three single shielded conductor cables in contact in a concrete-encased duct bank as shown in Diagram D17K

Diagram D17K

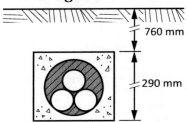

Size, AWG or kcmil	Concentric ground wire or concentric neutral wire size	Allowable ampacity			
		5 kV to 15 kV		25 kV to 46 kV	
		Copper	Aluminum	Copper	Aluminum
2	Full	165	129	—	—
1	Full	187	146	192	150
1/0	Full	211	166	217	170
2/0	Full	244	192	246	193
3/0	Full	275	217	277	219
4/0	Full	311	246	313	247
250	1/3	343	270	346	272
350	1/3	409	324	418	331
500	1/3	490	396	492	398
750	1/3	572	483	586	492
1000	1/3	—	555	—	558
1000	1/6	671	—	679	—

Notes:

1) *For buried installations, the values shown may be limited by the maximum earth interface temperature due to soil moisture migration. Knowledge of local soil conditions is necessary for the determination of the earth*

(Continued)

Table D17K (Concluded)

interface temperature to be used. Typical values are between 50 °C and 60 °C, which experience has shown to be satisfactory for most types of soils.

2) *Conduit size is calculated based on 40% fill for three conductors in conduit.*

Δ

Table D17L
Allowable ampacities for two 3-conductor shielded cables or two sets of three single shielded conductor cables in contact in a concrete-encased duct bank (two insulated conductors per phase) as shown in Diagram D17L

Diagram D17L

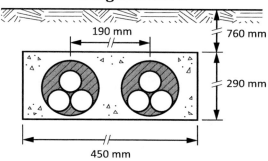

Size, AWG or kcmil	Concentric ground wire or concentric neutral wire size	Allowable ampacity			
		5 kV to 15 kV		25 kV to 46 kV	
		Copper	Aluminum	Copper	Aluminum
2	Full	148	116	—	—
1	Full	167	131	171	134
1/0	Full	189	148	193	151
2/0	Full	217	170	218	171
3/0	Full	244	193	245	194
4/0	Full	275	217	276	218
250	1/3	303	238	304	240
350	1/3	358	284	365	289
500	1/3	425	345	426	346
750	1/3	492	416	506	426
1000	1/3	—	478	—	480
1000	1/6	578	—	584	—

Notes:

1) *For buried installations, the values shown may be limited by the maximum earth interface temperature due to soil moisture migration. Knowledge of local soil conditions is necessary for the determination of the earth*

(Continued)

Table D17L (Concluded)

interface temperature to be used. Typical values are between 50 °C and 60 °C, which experience has shown to be satisfactory for most types of soils.

2) *Conduit size is calculated based on 40% fill for three conductors in conduit.*

3) *Conductor spacing is the centre-to-centre conduit or conductor spacing, typically 190 mm. For conduits larger than 103 mm, use an edge-to-edge conduit spacing of 50 mm.*

Δ

Table D17M
Allowable ampacities for three single shielded conductor cables on ladder or ventilated cable tray as shown in Diagram D17M

Diagram D17M

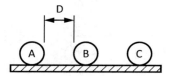

Note: *D = diameter of one conductor.*

Size, AWG or kcmil	Concentric ground wire or concentric neutral wire size	Allowable ampacity — Indoor installation*			
		5 kV to 15 kV		25 kV to 46 kV	
		Copper	Aluminum	Copper	Aluminum
2	Full	215	169	—	—
1	Full	245	194	245	193
1/0	Full	278	222	278	221
2/0	Full	317	255	316	253
3/0	Full	357	290	356	288
4/0	Full	404	329	403	327
250	1/3	456	370	455	367
350	1/3	537	446	537	443
500	1/3	616	533	616	529
750	1/3	706	631	716	633
1000	1/3	—	707	—	711
1000	1/6	813	—	825	—

(Continued)

Table D17M (Concluded)

Size, AWG or kcmil	Concentric ground wire or concentric neutral wire size	Allowable ampacity — Outdoor installation†			
		5 kV to 15 kV		25 kV to 46 kV	
		Copper	Aluminum	Copper	Aluminum
2	Full	198	156	—	—
1	Full	225	178	223	176
1/0	Full	255	203	254	201
2/0	Full	291	233	289	231
3/0	Full	327	266	325	263
4/0	Full	373	301	368	298
250	1/3	417	339	415	335
350	1/3	491	407	489	403
500	1/3	562	487	560	481
750	1/3	642	575	650	575
1000	1/3	—	643	—	645
1000	1/6	740	—	749	—

* *Indoor installation ampacities assume no exposure to the sun and no wind.*
† *Outdoor installation ampacities assume exposure to the sun and no wind.*

Appendix D

Δ

Table D17N
Allowable ampacities for 3-conductor shielded cable or three single shielded conductor cables in contact on ladder or ventilated cable tray as shown in Diagram D17N1 or D17N2

Diagram D17N1

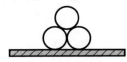

Diagram D17N2

Note: *Cables are in contact or spaced less than one diameter apart.*

Size, AWG or kcmil	Concentric ground wire or concentric neutral wire size	Allowable ampacity — Indoor installation*			
		5 kV to 15 kV		25 kV to 46 kV	
		Copper	Aluminum	Copper	Aluminum
2	Full	172	135	—	—
1	Full	197	154	202	158
1/0	Full	225	176	231	181
2/0	Full	260	204	265	208
3/0	Full	297	234	303	239
4/0	Full	342	268	348	273
250	1/3	376	296	384	302
350	1/3	460	363	468	368
500	1/3	556	447	565	454
750	1/3	678	566	691	573
1000	1/3	—	661	—	669
1000	1/6	798	—	813	—

Size, AWG or kcmil	Concentric ground wire or concentric neutral wire size	Allowable ampacity — Outdoor installation†			
		5 kV to 15 kV		25 kV to 46 kV	
		Copper	Aluminum	Copper	Aluminum
2	Full	141	110	—	—
1	Full	161	126	164	128
1/0	Full	184	144	187	147
2/0	Full	212	167	215	169

(Continued)

Table D17N (Concluded)

Size, AWG or kcmil	Concentric ground wire or concentric neutral wire size	Allowable ampacity — Outdoor installation†			
		5 kV to 15 kV		25 kV to 46 kV	
		Copper	Aluminum	Copper	Aluminum
3/0	Full	242	191	245	193
4/0	Full	278	218	281	221
250	1/3	306	241	310	244
350	1/3	373	294	377	297
500	1/3	450	361	454	365
750	1/3	545	455	552	458
1000	1/3	—	529	—	533
1000	1/6	640	—	648	—

* *Indoor installation ampacities assume no exposure to the sun and no wind.*

† *Outdoor installation ampacities assume exposure to the sun and no wind.*

Appendix D

Appendix E — Dust-free rooms
(See Rules in Appendix J for Class II and Class III hazardous locations)

Note: *This Appendix is an informative (non-mandatory) part of this Standard.*

E1 Introduction

This Appendix covers recommended practices for the housing of electrical equipment. With respect to actual constructional requirements, it is not practical to cover all materials and methods that are or may become available and, therefore, any specific details mentioned in this Appendix are to be considered examples rather than specific requirements. The *National Building Code of Canada* or any other building code that may be in force in any particular locality should take precedence over this Appendix and should be consulted in this respect.

E2 Scope

This Appendix applies to the construction of dust-free rooms built adjacent to or as part of buildings that, by the nature of their use or occupancy, are subject to accumulations of dusts that may create a fire or explosion hazard or that may be detrimental to the proper operation of electrical equipment not provided with dust-tight enclosures.

E3 Definition

The following definition applies in this Appendix:

Dust-free room — a room, building, or other area, of a size that permits the entrance of persons for operation and maintenance purposes and constructed so that the quantity of dust that can enter will not create a hazardous condition.

E4 Use

E4.1
Dust-free rooms are intended to be used to house electrical equipment except equipment required by this Code to be installed in vaults.

E4.2
Dust-free rooms should not be used for any manufacturing, processing, maintenance, storage, or other purposes except those that may be essential for the proper operation and maintenance of the electrical equipment that they house.

E5 Enclosing of electrical equipment

E5.1
Electrical equipment in dust-free rooms need not be of types approved for Class II locations.

E5.2
Where access to the dust-free room by unauthorized persons is permitted, the electrical equipment should be enclosed, guarded, protected, etc. as required by this Code for ordinary locations.

E5.3
Where access is to authorized persons only, enclosures may be omitted as provided for by this Code (e.g., Section 26).

E6 Materials and methods of construction

Materials used for the construction of dust-free rooms and the method of construction should fulfill the following conditions:

a) the enclosure of the room should be as impervious to the passage of dust from outside the room as is practicable;

b) the various components, walls, floors, ceilings, etc. should be capable of safely supporting the live and dead loads (including impact) to which they are liable to be subjected;

c) there should be no likelihood that dust passages will be created due to shrinkage, breaking, or cracking;

d) the completed structure should have a fire resistance rating of 1 h or better;

e) in buildings constructed of non-combustible materials, the rooms should also be constructed of non-combustible material, but in other buildings, the rooms may be constructed of combustible materials with non-combustible facing on at least the inner surfaces; and

f) if it is necessary that shafts or other rotating or sliding members be used to connect equipment outside the room with that inside, suitable means such as seals, gaskets, baffles, etc. should be provided to prevent passage of dust through the necessary openings.

E7 Floors

Some acceptable floor constructions are as follows:

a) solid concrete slab of minimum thickness 75 mm and reinforced as necessary; or

b) steel joists with welded plate metal floor or concrete slabs of minimum thickness 50 mm over the joists and 22 mm Portland cement plaster on metal lath under them.

Wherever necessary, floors should be surfaced with insulating material to prevent shock hazard.

E8 Walls

Some acceptable wall constructions are as follows, and it is to be noted that lath and plaster on both sides must have other construction built into the wall to ensure continuance of the dust-free features, and plywood joints must be backed by studding:

a) monolithic concrete of minimum thickness 100 mm reinforced as necessary;

b) built-up masonry consisting of
   i) solid bricks of minimum thickness 95 mm;
   ii) hollow tile of minimum thickness 75 mm if plastered both sides, and 150 mm if not plastered; or
   iii) hollow concrete or cinder concrete block of minimum thickness 125 mm if plastered both sides, and 200 mm if not plastered; or

c) stud construction of 50 mm if of metal or 100 mm if of wood, faced on the outside with metal or perforated gypsum lath with 19 mm gypsum or 22 mm Portland cement plaster, faced on the inside with
   i) metal-faced laminated wood;
   ii) laminated wood with 19 mm gypsum or 22 mm Portland cement plaster on metal or perforated gypsum lath;
   iii) laminated wood with fire-resisting non-metallic facing; or
   iv) sheet metal equivalent to 1.69 mm (No. 14 MSG) steel with welded or riveted locked-seam joints secured to metal studs by welding or by self-locking screws.

E9 Ceilings

Ceilings, if load-bearing, should have the same construction as floors, but if non-load-bearing, may be constructed similarly to walls with wood joists, if used, of greater depth in accordance with the span.

E10 Cubicle construction

E10.1
Where the room is constructed as a free-standing cubicle with walls and ceiling not forming a part of and spaced away from the structure of the building proper, the walls and ceiling may be of sheet steel not less than 1.69 mm (No. 14 MSG) thick, suitably joined and reinforced as may be necessary.

E10.2
If the floor is elevated above the floor of the building proper, it may be constructed in accordance with Clause E7 and the plaster may be omitted.

E11 Doors

E11.1
Doors giving access to the room from dusty locations should be
a)   either metal-clad or hollow metal and weatherstripped or otherwise arranged to prevent dust leakage at the edges of frames and sills; and
b)   equipped with self-closers.

E11.2
If operation of the electrical equipment requires entry to the room from dusty locations, two hinged doors with a 1.5 m vestibule between them should be provided, but where entry is necessary for maintenance only, single doors may be used.

E11.3
Doors giving access to the room from a dust-free atmosphere may be of ordinary types.

E11.4
If more than one point of access to a room is provided, all but the principal one should be either securely locked or other adequate means should be used to prevent unauthorized traffic through the room.

E11.5
All doors should be provided with means whereby they can be readily unlocked and opened from the inside without the use of a removable key.

E12 Windows

E12.1
Windows facing dusty locations should have a fixed metal sash and wired glass.

E12.2
Windows in exterior walls may be arranged for opening if it is reasonably certain that the surrounding exterior area will remain sufficiently dust-free.

E13 Ventilation

E13.1
Ventilation by clean air should be adequate for the dissipation of heat from the electrical apparatus installed.

E13.2
If ventilation is by means of forced air circulation, the air should be forced into the room rather than exhausted out of it.

E13.3
It is recommended that the air in the room be kept at a pressure slightly above atmospheric, which will tend to blow any dust out of the room rather than have it sucked in.

E13.4
The amount of ventilating air required is difficult to specify in an empirical value because it depends on
a)   the size of the room;
b)   the dissipating ability of walls and ceilings;
c)   the amount and nature of the electrical equipment; and
d)   the temperature of the incoming air.

E13.5
The cooling effect may be obtained by radiation alone (if the area is sufficient), by ventilation alone, or by a combination of both.

Appendix E

Appendix F
Engineering guidelines for preparing descriptive system documents for intrinsically
safe electrical systems and non-incendive field wiring circuits

C22.1-18

Δ   # Appendix F — Engineering guidelines for preparing descriptive system documents for intrinsically safe electrical systems and non-incendive field wiring circuits
(See Rules 18-002, 18-064, J18-002, and J18-064)

Note: *This Appendix is an informative (non-mandatory) part of this Standard.*

F1 Scope

This Appendix provides guidance for the development of descriptive system documents required for the installation and verification of intrinsically safe electrical systems and non-incendive field wiring circuits. It is to be used in conjunction with the reference publications listed in Section F9 of this Appendix.

F2 Intent

Intrinsically safe electrical systems and non-incendive field wiring circuits ensure a high level of safety in hazardous locations when equipment is properly selected, installed, and maintained. To ensure the safety of such systems, qualified persons should be provided with sufficient information for installation, verification, and maintenance. This information is provided in a descriptive system document, which is integral to the safety of the installation.

F3 Definitions

Note: *See Rule 18-002 for definitions of **Intrinsically safe circuit**, **Intrinsically safe electrical system**, and **Non-incendive field wiring circuit**.*

The following definitions apply in this Appendix:

Associated apparatus — electrical equipment that contains both intrinsically safe circuits and non-intrinsically safe circuits and is constructed so that the non-intrinsically safe circuits cannot adversely affect the intrinsically safe circuits. Associated apparatus may be
a)   equipment additionally protected by a type of protection suitable for use in a given explosive atmosphere; or
b)   equipment not protected by a type of protection suitable for use in an explosive atmosphere and therefore not to be used in an explosive atmosphere.

Associated non-incendive field wiring apparatus — electrical equipment in which the circuits are not necessarily non-incendive themselves but that affects the energy in non-incendive field wiring circuits and is relied upon to maintain non-incendive energy levels. Associated non-incendive field wiring apparatus may be
a)   equipment that has an alternative type of protection suitable for use in a given hazardous location; or
b)   equipment not protected by an alternative type of protection suitable for use in a hazardous location and therefore not to be used in a hazardous location.

Control drawing — a drawing or other document that is prepared by the manufacturer of the intrinsically safe apparatus, associated apparatus, non-incendive field wiring apparatus, or the associated non-incendive field wiring. A control drawing details the electrical parameters governing interconnections to other circuits or apparatus.

Intrinsically safe apparatus — electrical equipment in which all the circuits are intrinsically safe circuits.

Appendix F
C22.1-18   *Engineering guidelines for preparing descriptive system documents for intrinsically*
                                                safe electrical systems and non-incendive field wiring circuits

Simple apparatus —

a)   an electrical component or combination of components of simple construction with well-defined electrical parameters that does not generate more than 1.5 V, 100 mA, and 25 mW; or

b)   a passive component that does not dissipate more than 1.3 W and is compatible with the intrinsic safety of the circuit in which it is used.

F4 Technology overview

F4.1 General

Intrinsically safe electrical systems are designed to limit the electrical and thermal energy in a circuit to a level below what is required to ignite an explosive gas or dust atmosphere. A circuit design should take into account potential energy that may be present in field devices and interconnecting wiring as well as fault conditions specified on the basis of the hazardous location where the field device could be installed so that the overall energy limitations of the system are respected. The application of intrinsically safe electrical systems technology is generally limited to low-powered instrumentation circuits.

Intrinsically safe electrical systems and non-incendive field wiring circuits are similar in design and application. The provisions of this Appendix that apply to intrinsically safe electrical systems also apply to non-incendive field wiring circuits.

F4.2 Design, application, and installation

F4.2.1

Intrinsically safe circuits vary widely in design, application, and installation requirements. A circuit typically consists of three components:

a)   a field device installed in a hazardous location (the field device may be a simple apparatus or an intrinsically safe apparatus);

b)   a barrier device (an associated apparatus); and

c)   the interconnecting wiring.

F4.2.2

Intrinsically safe circuits fall into two categories:

a)   circuits for which the manufacturer designs and markets the intrinsically safe field device, the associated equipment, and the interconnecting wiring as a complete system; or

b)   circuits for which the designer selects an intrinsically safe field device and matches its electrical parameters (commonly known as entity parameters) to the associated equipment and the interconnecting wiring.

F4.2.3

Field devices that do not store or generate sufficient energy to be a factor in the design of an intrinsically safe circuit are considered simple apparatus. A simple apparatus does not require a hazardous location certification when it is protected by an associated apparatus. Examples of simple apparatus include switches, terminals, terminal boxes, light-emitting diodes (LEDs), resistance temperature detectors (RTDs), thermocouples, and photocells that do not generate more than 1.5 V, 100 mA, and 25 mW.

F4.2.4

Field devices that do not meet the criteria for simple apparatus are considered intrinsically safe apparatus. A control drawing issued by the manufacturer of the intrinsically safe apparatus or by a certification agency is supplied with the device. The control drawing sets out the entity parameters of the device, which define the maximum voltage, current, inductance, and capacitance that may be attached to the device for the purposes of a safe installation. Examples of intrinsically safe apparatus include instrument transmitters, transducers, and solenoids.

C22.1-18

Appendix F
Engineering guidelines for preparing descriptive system documents for intrinsically
safe electrical systems and non-incendive field wiring circuits

F4.2.5

Associated apparatus (e.g., barrier devices) are designed to serve as an interface between intrinsically safe circuit devices and a non-intrinsically safe circuit and to limit the energy in the intrinsically safe circuit. The technology employed may consist of a Zener barrier, galvanic isolation, and/or power-limiting communication bus technology. A control drawing issued by the manufacturer of the associated apparatus or by a certification agency is supplied with the associated apparatus. The control drawing sets out the electrical parameters of the associated apparatus, which define its capacity to protect a field device and associated wiring.

F4.2.6

The cumulative energy-storing effect of distributed inductance and capacitance in the field wiring should be considered in the design of an intrinsically safe electrical system. Inductance and capacitance values for the wire can be obtained from the wire manufacturer, which allows the electrical parameters of the wiring for the application to be calculated based on the length of the wire.

F4.2.7

The designer of the intrinsically safe electrical system selects appropriate equipment and documents the interconnection requirements in a descriptive system document, taking into account the entity parameters given in the control drawings. The descriptive system document is intended to facilitate the safe installation, verification, and maintenance of the intrinsically safe electrical system.

F4.2.8

The following publications are useful references for determining the interconnection requirements for intrinsically safe circuits:

a)   ISA TR12.2 outlines a method of matching the entity parameters of intrinsically safe field devices with the parameters of associated equipment and interconnecting wiring. This publication is useful for assessing relatively simple intrinsically safe circuits.

b)   CAN/CSA-C22.2 No. 60079-25 applies to all aspects of intrinsically safe design, including bonding and grounding. This publication outlines procedures for the design and assessment of all types of intrinsically safe circuits, including more complex circuit designs incorporating multiple field devices and sources of power.

F4.2.9

Intrinsically safe electrical systems and non-incendive field wiring circuits are suitable for use in hazardous locations as shown in the following table:

Equipment	Suitable for use in
Intrinsically safe apparatus and associated apparatus marked "Intrinsically Safe", "IS", "I.S.", "Ex i", or "Ex ia"	All hazardous locations
Intrinsically safe equipment marked "Ex ib"	Zones 1 and 2, Zones 21 and 22, and Class I, Division 2 hazardous locations
Intrinsically safe equipment marked "Ex ic"	Zone 2, Zone 22, and Classes I, II, and III, Division 2 hazardous locations
Non-incendive field wiring apparatus and associated apparatus	Zone 2, Zone 22, and Classes I, II, and III, Division 2 hazardous locations

F5 Descriptive system documents

The minimum information to be included in a descriptive system document is as follows:

a)   a block diagram of the system, listing all the items of apparatus in it, including simple apparatus and interconnecting wiring;

C22.1-18

Appendix F
Engineering guidelines for preparing descriptive system documents for intrinsically
safe electrical systems and non-incendive field wiring circuits

b) a statement of the group subdivision as follows:
   i) for explosive gas atmospheres:
      A) Zone system of classification: Group IIA, IIB, or IIC and Zone 0, 1, or 2, as applicable; or
      B) Division system of classification: Class I, Group A, B, C, or D and Division 1 or 2, as applicable; and
   ii) for explosive dust atmospheres:
      A) Zone system of classification: Group IIIA, IIIB, or IIIC and Zone 20, 21, or 22, as applicable; or
      B) Division system of classification: Class II, Group E, F, or G, Class III, and Division 1 or 2, as applicable;
c) the level of protection for each part of the system, as follows:
   i) Type i;
   ii) Ex ia;
   iii) Ex ib;
   iv) Ex ic; or
   v) non-incendive (Ex nL);
d) the temperature class or maximum surface temperature of the equipment, in accordance with Rule 18-054;
e) the ambient temperature range if components will be subject to temperatures outside the operating temperature range of −20 °C to 40 °C;
f) entity parameters of all intrinsically safe apparatus;
g) entity parameters of associated apparatus, where applicable;
h) identification of simple apparatus in the circuit;
i) evaluation of the entity parameters for a safe installation;
j) electrical parameters for the interconnecting wiring or specification of the type of cable to be used, including the maximum length permitted and the justification for its use;
k) details of grounding and bonding requirements, clearly indicating which point or points of the system are intended to be connected to the plant reference potential and any special requirements for such a bond; bonding of cable screens should also be indicated;
l) when surge protection devices are used, identification of the manufacturer and model number (the capacitance and inductance of the surge suppression devices must be considered in the assessment of the intrinsically safe electrical system); and
m) reference to a manufacturer's or certification agency's control drawing(s), where applicable.

The content of a descriptive system document may be presented in table format or in the context of a drawing. Examples of drawings are provided in CAN/CSA-C22.2 No. 60079-25 and ISA RP12.02.02.

F6 Engineering authentication

When an engineer is involved, all descriptive system documents and supporting calculations should be traceable to a registered professional engineer working under a permit to practice, or the system should be certified by an accredited certification organization. Traceability and authentication requirements are governed by the particular jurisdiction, but typically this means that drawings and reports are
a) signed and stamped; or
b) signed with the title "P. Eng." (or equivalent).

F7 Documentation and records

Descriptive system documents and supporting calculations should be maintained on file with the owner/operator of the facility for the life of the facility. These records should be accessible, upon request, by installers, inspectors, and operations, safety, and maintenance personnel.

Appendix F

C22.1-18

Appendix F
Engineering guidelines for preparing descriptive system documents for intrinsically
safe electrical systems and non-incendive field wiring circuits

F8 Management of change

A management-of-change process should be put in place to ensure that descriptive system documents remain valid throughout the life of the facility.

F9 Selected reference publications

The following reference publications provide additional guidance on the design, application, and documentation of intrinsically safe electrical systems and non-incendive field wiring circuits.

CSA Group

C22.2 No. 213, *Nonincendive electrical equipment for use in Class I and II, Division 2 and Class III, Divisions 1 and 2 hazardous (classified) locations*

CAN/CSA-C22.2 No. 60079-11, *Explosive atmospheres — Part 11: Equipment protection by intrinsic safety "i"*

CAN/CSA-C22.2 No. 60079-25, *Explosive atmospheres — Part 25: Intrinsically safe electrical systems*

IEC (International Electrotechnical Commission)

60079-14, *Explosive atmospheres — Part 14: Electrical installations design, selection and erection*

ISA (International Society of Automation)

RP12.02.02, *Recommendations for the Preparation, Content, and Organization of Intrinsic Safety Control Drawings*

TR12.2, *Intrinsically Safe System Assessment Using the Entity Concept*

ANSI/ISA (American National Standards Institute/International Society of Automation)

RP12.06.01, *Recommended Practice for Wiring Methods for Hazardous (Classified) Locations — Instrumentation — Part 1: Intrinsic Safety*

Appendix G — Electrical installations of fire protection systems

Note: *This Appendix is an informative (non-mandatory) part of this Standard.*

G1 Introduction

G1.1
This Appendix lists requirements related to electrical installations that are not governed by Rules of the *Canadian Electrical Code, Part I* but are required by the *National Building Code of Canada*.

G1.2
References listed in this Appendix are associated with electrical installations that are a part of the fire protection requirements contained in the *National Building Code of Canada*.

G2 Application

G2.1
The intent of this Appendix is to advise *Canadian Electrical Code, Part I* users of performance requirements for electrically connected fire-protective equipment required by the *National Building Code of Canada*.

G2.2
Special fire protection requirements, such as use of thermal insulation, fire spread, flame spread requirements for electrical wiring and cables, flame-spread requirements for combustible raceways, and construction of electrical equipment vaults are covered by this Code (e.g., Rules 2-126, 2-128, 2-130, 2-132, 26-354, etc.).

G2.3
Provincial and municipal building codes may deviate from the *National Building Code of Canada*, and users of this list should also check those codes.

Δ

G3 *Canadian Electrical Code* reference to the *National Building Code of Canada* — 2015 edition

CE Code Sections and Rules	NBCC Sections, Articles, and Sentences (unless otherwise stated, references refer to Division B of the NBCC)
Section 0	1.4.1.2. of Division A Defined terms
Section 0	1.5.1.1. of Division A Application of referenced documents
Section 0	1.3.1. and Table 1.3.1.2., Effective date and edition of referenced documents (e.g., NFPA 96, CAN/ULC-S524, etc.)
Section 0	3.6.1.2. and 9.34.1.1., Electrical facilities — general
Section 0	3.1.6.6., Automatic emergency generator for emergency air supply in air supported structures
Section 0	3.1.6.7., Electrical systems and equipment in tents and air supporting structures
Rule 2-122	3.8.3.8., Mounting height of electrical controls in barrier-free areas
Rule 2-128	3.1.9.1.(1) and (2), Fire stopping of service penetrations through fire-rated assemblies or fire separations
Rule 2-128	3.1.9.3., Penetration of fire-rated assemblies or fire separations by wires, cables, boxes, and raceways

Rule 2-128	3.1.13.4., Flame-spread rating for combustible light diffusers and lenses
Rule 2-128	9.10.9.6., Electrical wiring and boxes and penetrating a fire separation
Rule 2-130	3.1.4.3.(1) and 9.34.1.5., Wires and cables in combustible buildings
Rule 2-130	3.1.5.21.(1), Wires and cables in noncombustible buildings
Rule 2-130	3.1.5.18.(2) and (3), Wires and cables within plenums of noncombustible buildings or wiring and cables that extend from plenums
Rule 2-130	3.4.4.4.(1)(b), Restrictions on wiring and raceways penetrating an exit enclosure
Rule 2-130	3.6.4.3.(1), Equipment and wiring within plenums
Rule 2-132	3.1.5.23., Combustible raceways in noncombustible buildings
Rule 2-132	3.1.5.21.(3), Combustible raceways within plenums of noncombustible buildings
Rule 2-310	3.3.1.23., Obstructions
Rule 2-310	9.9.5.5., Obstructions in means of egress
Rule 2-314	3.8.3.8., Mounting height of electrical controls in barrier-free areas
Rule 6-206	3.6.1.2. and 9.34.1., Electrical facilities — general
Rule 10-108	3.6.1.3., Lightning protection systems
Rule 12-506 5)	3.1.5.12., Combustible interior finishes 9.21.5., Clearance from combustible construction
Rules 12-506 to 12-518	9.23.5., Drilling and notching in plates, studs, trusses, and framing members
Rule 20-102 and Annex J20	6.3.1.4., Ventilation requirement for storage garages
Rule 26-012	3.6.2.1.(6) and 9.10.10.3., Construction of service room required by *Canadian Electrical Code, Part I*
Rule 26-012	3.6.2.1., Service rooms containing electrical and other types of service equipment
Rules 26-012 and 26-354	3.6.2.7., Electrical equipment vaults
Section 26	3.8.2.7., Power-operated barrier-free doors
Section 26	3.8.2.9., Assistive listening device systems
Section 26	3.8.3.8., Location of controls in barrier-free areas
Rule 26-600	9.34.1., Electrical facilities — general
Section 26	6.2.1.5., Installation standard of heating, ventilating, and air-conditioning equipment
Section 26	6.3.2.13.(2), Electrical control of electrostatic-type air filters
Section 28	6.3.2.8. and 9.32.3.8.(3), Interlock requirements, make-up air systems, and exhaust systems
Rule 30-900	3.2.7.2. and 9.34.1.4., Recessed luminaires

Section 32	3.2.4.17., Alert and alarm signals in a fire alarm system
Section 32	3.2.4.18., Audibility of a fire alarm system
Section 32	3.2.4.19., Visual signal devices in a fire alarm system
Section 32	3.2.4.21., Residential fire warning systems
Section 32	3.2.4.22., Voice communication systems
Section 32	3.2.4.10.(2), Standpipe valve supervision
Section 32	3.2.5.14., Supervision of sprinklers installed in service spaces
Section 32	3.2.5.16.(2), Electrical remote release of locked fire extinguisher cabinets in B1 occupancies
Rules 32-300 and 62-300	3.2.5.17., Protection from freezing of fire protection system
Rules 32-300 to 32-312	3.2.5.18., Fire pumps
Section 32	3.2.6.2.(5) and (6), and 3.2.6.6.(1), Control of air-moving fans in high buildings
Section 32	3.2.6.4., Emergency operation of elevators
Section 32	3.2.6.7., Central alarm and control facility
Section 32	3.2.6.8., Voice communication system
Section 32	3.2.6.9., Testing of smoke control and smoke venting systems
Sections 32 and 46	3.2.7.8., Emergency power for fire alarm systems
Sections 32, 38, and 46	3.2.7.10., Protection of electrical conductors
Sections 32 and 46	3.2.8.7.(2), Electrical control of a mechanical exhaust system required in a building having interconnected floor spaces
Sections 32 and 46	3.2.1.1.(8)., Audible signal devices and emergency lighting in service spaces
Section 32	3.3.2.14., Control and operation of fire protection systems for theatrical stages (deluge system, fire curtains, and ventilation)
Section 32	3.3.5.7.(4)(c), Restrictions on use of hold-open devices on doors between storage garages and specific occupancies
Sections 32 and 46	3.4.6.16.(4) and (5), Release of electromagnetic locks on exit doors
Section 32	3.2.4.8.(2)., Reference to NFPA 96 for commercial cooking ventilation equipment (interconnection with fire alarm system, etc.)
Section 32	9.10.8.2., Supervision of sprinklers used in lieu of roof fire-resistance rating
Section 32	6.9.2.2., Requirement for smoke detectors in circulating air handling systems
Section 32	9.10.9.15.(2) and (3), Supervision of sprinklers used in lieu of public corridor fire separation
Section 32	9.10.13.11., Hold-open devices on doors in fire separations
Section 32	9.10.18.1., Continuity of fire alarm system
Section 32	9.10.18.2., Where fire alarm required

Section 32	9.10.18.3., Fire alarm system design and installation requirements
Section 32	9.10.18.4., Heat and smoke detectors
Section 32	9.10.18.5., Duct-type smoke detectors
Section 32	9.10.18.6., Fire alarm system for portions of buildings separated from remainder of building
Section 32	9.10.18.7., Shutdown of central vacuum on fire alarm system activation
Section 32	9.10.18.8., Fire alarm system in storage garages
Section 38	3.1.5.22., Combustible travelling cables for elevators
Section 38	3.3.1.7.(1), Protection of conductors for elevator used in barrier-free floor area
Section 38	3.2.4.14., Alternate floor recall for elevators
Section 38	3.2.6.4., Emergency operation of elevators
Section 38	3.5.1., Vertical transportation
Section 38	3.8.3.7., Elevators in barrier-free areas
Rule 46-202 3)	3.2.6.6., Use of building exhaust system to vent smoke from sprinklered floor areas
Rule 46-400	3.4.5., Exit signs
Rule 46-400	9.9.11.3., Exit signs
Section 46	3.2.7.3., Emergency lighting, where required
Section 46	3.2.7.4., Power supply for emergency lighting, time (duration) requirements
Section 46	3.2.7.5., Emergency power supply installation, general
Section 46	3.2.7.6., Emergency power supply installation for health care facilities
Section 46	3.2.7.9., Emergency power supply for building services (elevators, fire pumps, fans, etc.)
Section 46	3.3.1.13.(6) and (9), Electrical operation of locked egress doors serving contained-use area or impeded egress zone
Section 46	3.3.1.24., Exit signs in service spaces
Section 46	3.3.3.7.(4)(c), Electrical release of doors in contained-use area
Section 46	3.4.4.4.(1)(b), Electrical conductors and raceways in exits
Section 46	3.4.6.14.(2), Electrical release of a sliding door used as an exit door
Section 46	3.4.6.16.(4) and (5), Installation of electromagnetic locks
Rule 46-202 3)	3.6.2.8., Emergency power installations
Section 46	9.9.12.3., Emergency lighting
Section 46	9.34.3., Emergency lighting

Sections 32 and 46   3.2.9.1. and 9.10.1.2., Integrated fire protection and life safety systems

Section 76   5.6.1.9.(3) of the *National Fire Code of Canada*, 2015, Temporary electrical installations on construction and demolition sites

△ # Appendix H — Combustible gas detection equipment for use in explosive gas atmospheres

(See Rules 18-068 and J18-066)

Note: *This Appendix is an informative (non-mandatory) part of this Standard.*

H1 Introduction

H1.1 General
Combustible gas detection is frequently used to monitor flammable gas or vapour concentrations in enclosed spaces. Combustible gas detectors may be portable hand-held devices or equipment permanently installed in a hazardous location.

H1.2 Portable combustible gas detectors
Portable combustible gas detectors can be used to

a) provide advance warning to personnel when flammable gas or vapour concentrations in the air reach unsafe levels;

b) identify locations and prompt corrective action in process buildings where pockets of flammable gas or vapour could persist in normal operation; and

c) monitor potential sources of release where hot work is in progress.

H1.3 Permanently installed combustible gas detectors
Permanently installed combustible gas detectors can be used to

a) meet the requirements of Rule 18-068 allowing for the use of equipment not rated for the particular hazardous area;

b) verify that the design of ventilation systems is such that fugitive emissions will be diluted to safe concentrations as prescribed in API RP 500, API RP 505, and IEC 60079-10-1;

c) monitor the normal operation of process equipment to ensure that it is operating within its design parameters. Small but measurable increases in the background concentration of flammable materials in an enclosed space can provide an early indication of a potential problem with the process that, if not corrected, could lead to a major containment failure resulting in large releases of flammable material, which could in turn require total shutdown of the process; and

d) detect failures in process equipment that could result in large releases of flammable material, necessitating prompt operator intervention or automated shutdown.

H1.4
Combustible gas detection equipment should never be used as a substitute for safe electrical design. Because such devices may not perform as intended, as a result of poor maintenance, adverse conditions (sensor poisoning), or deliberate tampering, they should be used only where installation, operation, and maintenance are performed by qualified personnel in accordance with the gas detection equipment manufacturer's recommendations and/or recognized industry standards.

H2 General

H2.1
This Appendix applies to combustible gas detection equipment consisting of permanently installed point detectors of the stationary type certified to the requirements of CAN/CSA-C22.2 No. 60079-29-1. Open path (line-of-sight) gas detectors are not suitable for use with Rules 18-068 and J18-066 because they do not provide information sufficient for remedial action about the percentage of the lower flammable limit (% LFL) of gas concentration at a specific location along the sight path. Open path detectors provide an average measurement over the complete sight path.

H2.2
Gas detection equipment is certified for the designated gas group to be encountered and calibrated specifically for the gas or vapour to be detected. If more than one gas or vapour could be present, the

gas detector should be capable of detecting all gases and vapours that could be encountered, with a direct reading for the gas that gives the lowest response. Since combustible gas detectors are able to provide correct readings only for the gas or vapour for which they have been calibrated, a correction factor is applied for an accurate reading of other gases or vapours. The manufacturer's instruction manual typically provides such correction factors for specific gases or vapours when standard calibration gases are used.

H2.3

Combustible gas detection equipment is certified in accordance with CAN/CSA-C22.2 No. 60079-29-1 for its ability to function satisfactorily within certain environmental parameters involving temperature, humidity, air velocity, and vibration. Reference should be made to these Standards to determine if the expected environmental operating conditions of the gas detection equipment application in question fall within the parameters specified in the product Standards. Equipment applications involving environmental conditions outside the specified parameters should be given special consideration. In addition, for the continued satisfactory performance of gas detection equipment under various environmental operating conditions, consideration should be given to environmental factors such as the following:

a) **Temperature** — The manufacturer's data should be consulted to ensure that the gas detector instrument sensor and controller are suitable for the temperature range of the application. Operating the equipment outside the manufacturer's specified operating range can result in a slow or erroneous response to a release of flammable gas or vapour.

b) **Airborne particles** — Airborne particles, such as dust, fibres, and aerosols, can affect the diffusion of the atmosphere to the sensing element of combustible gas detection equipment. Sensors should be adequately guarded against particle contamination through proper maintenance based on operating experience. The provision of contaminant-excluding hardware and the orientation and location of sensing elements can also help to minimize such effects. Similar consideration should be given to protecting sensors from the effects of rain, ice, and snow.

c) **Contaminants** — The gas sensing element of catalytic sensor combustible gas detection equipment may be susceptible to desensitization by certain airborne compounds, such as silicone, silanes, halogenated compounds, etc., as listed in the manufacturer's instruction manual. The possible effect of such exposure should be considered when such compounds are used in the vicinity of catalytic sensor combustible gas sensors. Where such compounds are integral to the process in the area monitored, point-type infrared sensor gas detection equipment may be more appropriate.

d) **Corrosive compounds** — For satisfactory operation of combustible gas detection equipment, the presence of corrosive compounds in the area monitored should be taken into consideration both for material compatibility and for compatibility with any gases that could be generated as a result of chemical reactions involving such corrosive compounds.

H3 Application recommendations

H3.1

Provided that combustible gas detection is used as a means of equipment protection, Rules 18-068 and J18-066 permit the installation of

a) equipment suitable for non-hazardous locations in Zone 2 (Class I, Division 2) locations; and

b) equipment suitable for Zone 2 (Class I, Division 2) locations in Zone 1 (Class I, Division 1) locations.

Equipment for ordinary (non-hazardous) locations can be ignition capable. If the equipment incorporates components that arc or spark in normal operation or operate at surface temperatures above the auto-ignition temperature defined for a given hazardous location, the use of combustible gas detection as a means of equipment protection is not appropriate. The provisions in Rules 18-068 and J18-066 are based on the following conditions: that the equipment, during its normal operation, does not produce arcs, sparks, or hot surfaces capable of igniting an explosive gas atmosphere and that no suitable equipment certified for the designated hazardous location is available. The provisions are not intended to be applied as an alternative to using properly certified equipment in a hazardous location. See the Appendix B Notes to Section 18 and the Annex JB Notes to Annex J18 for further guidance on the application and intent of the Rules related to gas detection.

H3.2

Where equipment is installed in accordance with Rule 18-068 or J18-066, consideration should be given to the consequences of disconnecting power to the equipment being protected. The equipment should be capable of being switched off at any time, without warning and without causing any personnel or operational safety hazards. Essential services such as lighting, instruments required for the safe operation of the process, and the gas detection equipment itself must be certified for the designated hazardous area classification.

H3.3

It may be necessary to use combustible gas detection equipment in enclosed locations designated Zone 2 (Class I, Division 2) to ensure the integrity of the designated classification. Locations designated Zone 2 (Class I, Division 2) require two conditions to be met: first, that it is not likely that an explosive gas atmosphere will exist in normal operation and, secondly, that if an explosive gas atmosphere does occur, it will exist for a short time only (see Rules 18-002 and J18-004). The primary purpose of combustible gas detection equipment in such applications is to activate an alarm when abnormally high concentrations of flammable gas or vapour are present so that steps can be taken to ensure that they will be eliminated within the "short time" requirement in the Zone 2 (Class I, Division 2) definition. The generally accepted rule of thumb for the "short time" requirement for Zone 2 (Class I, Division 2) locations is that an explosive gas atmosphere will be present in an area a total of 10 h or less per year (see API RP 505).

H3.4

Enclosed facilities that are not monitored on a continuous basis may require some means of ensuring that the "short time" criterion is met. This is to prevent the possibility of an undetected flammable gas release persisting longer than the 10 h per year industry standard. The use of gas detection equipment in such situations is highly recommended.

H3.5

The application of combustible gas detection equipment by itself does not designate an enclosed location Zone 2 (Class I, Division 2). An appropriate ventilation design is also required. For additional information on the ventilation design of enclosed classified locations, see the selected references listed in Appendix L, Clause L14.2.

H3.6

Additional considerations related to alarm response time apply to remote, unmanned facilities. If an operator cannot respond to an alarm within the "short time" required for the Zone 2 (Class I, Division 2) designation, an enclosed location in such facilities should be classified Zone 1 (Class I, Division 1), not Zone 2 (Class I, Division 2).

H4 Installation recommendations

H4.1

Consideration should be given to the following factors when locating remote detector heads (sensors):
a)   the density of the gases or vapours to be detected (in relation to air);
b)   the locations of the potential gas or vapour sources and the hazardous area classification for which the equipment is certified;
c)   provision for extra (i.e., redundant) detector heads;
d)   the effects of ventilation systems on the flow of hazardous gases or vapours from the hazardous location and the possibility of gas or vapour concentration gradients in the hazardous location;
e)   adverse environments at detector locations; and
f)   accessibility for calibration and maintenance.

H4.2
Audible and visual alarms distinguishable from any other alarms should be installed locally and repeated at central control locations to warn those in the area protected by the detectors and those approaching the area that a potential hazard exists.

H4.3
Gas detection equipment should be calibrated in accordance with the manufacturer's instructions or IEC 60079-29-2.

Δ

Appendix I — Interpretations
(See Clauses C9.12 b) and C9.13)

Notes:
1) *This Appendix is an informative (non-mandatory) part of this Standard.*
2) *Committee interpretations of the* Canadian Electrical Code, Part I, *are available on the* Current Standards Activities *page at standardsactivities.csa.ca.*
3) *The interpretations in this Appendix are based on Rules in the 2015 Code. Rule numbering and content in the 2018 Code may differ from the 2015 edition.*

Rule 2-314

Question: Is a receptacle that complies with Rule 26-704 and that is supplied as an integral part of a rooftop unit considered to meet the requirements of Rule 2-314?

Answer: Yes.

Rule 6-212(1)

Question: With respect to Rule 6-212(1), is it permitted to make the water bond and/or gas bond connection in the main disconnect area of a combination breaker panel?

Answer: No.

Rule 8-106(4)

Question: Are the electric space-heating and air-conditioning loads referred to in Rule 8-106(4) required to be installed so that only one can be operated at any one time if only the greater load is used to calculate the demand ampacity?

Answer: No.

Rules 18-104(2) and 18-154(2)

Question: With respect to Rules 18-104(2) and 18-154(2), is it intended that an LBY elbow conduit fitting be permitted to be installed between the conduit seal and an explosion-proof enclosure in a Zone 1 or 2 location?

Answer: Yes.

Rules 18-154(1)(b) and J18-154(1)(b)

Question: With respect to Rules 18-154(1)(b) and J18-154(1)(b), is an RTRC XW coupling viewed in the same manner as a rigid steel coupling?

Answer: Yes.

Rule 26-724

Question: Where a branch circuit originates from a panelboard within a dwelling unit and feeds receptacles (rated 125 V, 20 A or less) that are associated with but outside the dwelling unit (such as in a yard, accessory building, or detached garage), does that branch circuit require arc-fault circuit interrupter (AFCI) protection as described in Rule 26-724(f) and (g)?

Answer: No.

Rule 26-724

Question: Where a feeder originates from a panelboard within a dwelling unit and runs to a subpanel in a location associated with but outside the dwelling unit (such as in an accessory building or detached

Appendix I

garage), are receptacles (rated 125 V, 20 A or less) located outside the dwelling unit and fed from that subpanel required to have arc-fault circuit interrupter (AFCI) protection as described in Rule 26-724(f) and (g)?

Answer: No.

Rule 26-724(f)

Question: Does Rule 26-724(f) apply to an existing branch circuit in which one or more existing receptacles are to be replaced?

Answer: No.

Rule 28-204(2)

Question: When increasing the overcurrent protection of a feeder supplying a group of motors to allow for simultaneous starting in accordance with Rule 28-204(2), after performing the calculation outlined in Rule 28-204(2), should we then add the sum of the full load current ratings of all the other motors that will be in operation at the same time?

Answer: Yes.

Rule 70-000

Question: Are industrial skids covered by the Scope of Section 70?

Answer: Yes.

C22.1-18

Appendix J
Rules and Notes to Rules for installations using the
Class and Division system of classification

Appendix J — Rules and Notes to Rules for installations using the Class and Division system of classification

Δ **Notes:**
1) *The Introduction and Annexes J18, J20, JD, and JT of this Appendix are normative (mandatory) for installations that use the Division system of hazardous location classification. Rules 18-000 4) and 20-000 3) require that the Rules in these Annexes be applied to Class/Division installations as provided for by Rules 18-000 3) and 20-000 2).*

2) *Annex JB consists of notes and illustrations for information and clarification purposes only and is informative (non-mandatory).*

Δ

Contents

J1 Introduction

As indicated in Section 18, new installations in Class I hazardous locations now employ the Zone system of classification. For existing installations, it is left to the discretion of the user/owner whether to reclassify these facilities to the Zone system or continue using the Division system of classification. For installations that continue using the Division system of classification, the Rules in Annexes J18 and J20 shall apply.

Appendix J

C22.1-18

Appendix J
Rules and Notes to Rules for installations using the
Class and Division system of classification

Annex J18
Hazardous locations classified using the Division system

Scope and introduction

J18-000 Scope (see Annex JB)
1)   This Section constitutes an Annex to this Code and applies to Class I, II, and III hazardous locations in which electrical equipment and wiring are subject to the conditions outlined in this Section.
2)   This Annex supplements or amends the general requirements of this Code.

J18-002 Special terminology (see Annex JB)
In this Section, the following definitions shall apply:

Cable gland — a device or combination of devices intended to provide a means of entry for a cable or flexible cord into an enclosure situated in a hazardous location and that also provides strain relief and shall be permitted to provide sealing characteristics where required, either by an integral means or when combined with a separate sealing fitting.

Cable seal — a seal that is installed at a cable termination to prevent the release of an explosion from an explosion-proof enclosure and that minimizes the passage of gases or vapours at atmospheric pressure.

Class I location — a location where flammable gases or vapours are or may be present in the air in quantities sufficient to produce explosive gas atmospheres.

Class II location — a location that is hazardous because of the presence of combustible or electrically conductive combustible dusts.

Class III location — a location that is hazardous because of the presence of easily ignitable fibres or flyings, but in which such fibres or flyings are not likely to be in suspension in air in quantities sufficient to produce ignitable mixtures.

Conduit seal — a seal that is installed in a conduit to prevent the passage of an explosion from one portion of the conduit system to another and that minimizes the passage of gases or vapours at atmospheric pressure.

Degree of protection — the measures applied to the enclosures of electrical apparatus to ensure
a)   the protection of persons against contact with live or moving parts inside the enclosure and protection of apparatus against the ingress of solid foreign bodies; and
b)   the protection of apparatus against ingress of liquids.

Δ **Descriptive system document** (see Appendix F) — a document in which the items of electrical apparatus, their electrical parameters, and those of the interconnecting wiring are specified.

Dust — generic term including both combustible dust and combustible flyings.

  Combustible dust — dust particles that are 500 μm or smaller (material passing a No. 35 standard sieve as defined in ASTM E11) and present a fire or explosion hazard when dispersed and ignited in air.

    Conductive dust — combustible metal dust.

    Non-conductive dust — combustible dust other than combustible metal dust.

Appendix J
Rules and Notes to Rules for installations using the
Class and Division system of classification

C22.1-18

Combustible flyings — solid particles, including fibres, greater than 500 μm in nominal size that may be suspended in air and can settle out of the atmosphere under their own weight.

Δ **Explosive gas atmosphere** — a mixture with air, under atmospheric conditions, of flammable substances in the form of gas or vapour that, after ignition, permits self-sustaining flame propagation.

Δ **Flammable limits** — the lower and upper percentage by volume of concentration of flammable gas or vapour in air that will form an ignitable mixture.

> **LFL** — lower flammable limit.

> **UFL** — upper flammable limit.

Fluid — a substance in the form of gas, vapour, or liquid.

Δ **Intrinsically safe circuit** — a circuit in which any spark or thermal effect produced under prescribed conditions, which include normal operation and specified fault conditions, is not capable of causing ignition of a given explosive atmosphere.

Δ **Intrinsically safe electrical system** — an assembly of interconnected items of electrical equipment, described in a descriptive system document, in which the circuits or parts of circuits intended to be used in a hazardous location are intrinsically safe.

Δ **Non-incendive field wiring circuit** — a circuit, described in a descriptive system document, in which any spark or thermal effect that may occur under normal operating conditions or due to opening, shorting, or grounding of field wiring is not capable of causing an ignition of the prescribed flammable gas or vapour.

Normal operation — the situation in which the plant or equipment is operating within its design parameters.

Primary seal — a seal that isolates process fluids from an electrical system and that has one side of the seal in contact with the process fluid.

Protective gas — the gas used to maintain pressurization or to dilute a flammable gas or vapour.

Secondary seal — a seal that is designed to prevent the passage of process fluids at the pressure it will be subjected to upon failure of the primary seal.

Type of protection — a defined method to reduce the risk of ignition of explosive gas atmospheres.

J18-004 Division of Class I locations (see Annex JB and Appendix L)
Class I locations shall be further divided into two Divisions based on frequency of occurrence and duration of an explosive gas atmosphere as follows:
a) Division 1, consisting of Class I locations in which explosive gas atmospheres are likely to be present continuously, intermittently, or periodically during normal operation; and
b) Division 2, consisting of Class I locations in which
  i)   explosive gas atmospheres are not likely to occur in normal operation and, if they do occur, they will exist for a short time only; or
  ii) the location is adjacent to a Class I, Division 1 location from which explosive gas atmospheres could be communicated, unless such communication is prevented by adequate positive-pressure ventilation from a source of clean air, and effective safeguards against ventilation failure are provided.

Appendix J

C22.1-18

Appendix J
Rules and Notes to Rules for installations using the
Class and Division system of classification

J18-006 Division of Class II locations (see Annex JB and Appendix L)

Class II locations shall be further divided into two Divisions as follows:

a) Division 1, consisting of Class II locations in which

    i) combustible dust is or may be in suspension in air continuously, intermittently, or periodically under normal operating conditions, in quantities sufficient to produce explosive or ignitable mixtures;

    ii) the abnormal operation or failure of equipment might

        A) cause explosive or ignitable mixtures to be produced; and

        B) provide a source of ignition through simultaneous failure of electrical equipment, operation of protection devices, or from other causes; or

    iii) combustible dusts having the property of conducting electricity may be present; and

b) Division 2, consisting of Class II locations in which

    i) combustible dust may be in suspension in the air as a result of infrequent malfunctioning of handling or processing equipment, but such dust would be present in quantities insufficient to

        A) interfere with the normal operation of electrical or other equipment; and

        B) produce explosive or ignitable mixtures, except for short periods of time; or

    ii) combustible dust accumulations on, in, or in the vicinity of the electrical equipment may be sufficient to interfere with the safe dissipation of heat from electrical equipment or may be ignitable by abnormal operation or failure of electrical equipment.

J18-008 Division of Class III locations (see Annex JB and Appendix L)

Class III locations shall be further divided into two Divisions as follows:

a) Division 1, consisting of Class III locations in which readily ignitable fibres or materials producing combustible flyings are handled, manufactured, or used; and

b) Division 2, consisting of Class III locations in which readily ignitable fibres other than those in process of manufacture are stored or handled.

J18-010 Maintenance (see Annex JB)

Special precautions shall be observed as follows:

a) unauthorized repairs or alterations shall not be made to live equipment; and

b) electrical equipment shall be maintained in its original safe condition.

General

J18-050 Electrical equipment (see Annex JB)

Δ 1) Where electrical equipment is required by this Section to be marked for the class of location, it shall also be marked for use with the specific material that will be present.

Δ 2) For Class I, Division 1 or 2 equipment, the specific gas shall be permitted to be marked in accordance with one or more of the following atmospheric group designations:

    a) Group A, consisting of atmospheres containing acetylene;

    b) Group B, consisting of atmospheres containing butadiene, ethylene oxide, hydrogen (or gases or vapours equivalent in hazard to hydrogen, such as manufactured gas), or propylene oxide;

    c) Group C, consisting of atmospheres containing acetaldehyde, cyclopropane, diethyl ether, ethylene, hydrogen sulphide, or unsymmetrical dimethyl hydrazine (UDMH), or other gases or vapours of equivalent hazard; or

    d) Group D, consisting of atmospheres containing acetone, acrylonitrile, alcohol, ammonia, benzine, benzol, butane, ethylene dichloride, gasoline, hexane, isoprene, lacquer solvent vapours, naphtha, natural gas, propane, propylene, styrene, vinyl acetate, vinyl chloride, xylenes, or other gases or vapours of equivalent hazard.

Appendix J
Rules and Notes to Rules for installations using the
Class and Division system of classification

C22.1-18

3) Notwithstanding Subrule 2) b), where the atmosphere contains
   a) butadiene, Group D equipment shall be permitted to be used if such equipment is isolated in accordance with Rule J18-108 1) by sealing all conduit 16 trade size or larger; or
   b) ethylene oxide or propylene oxide, Group C equipment shall be permitted to be used if such equipment is isolated in accordance with Rule J18-108 1) by sealing all conduit 16 trade size or larger.

Δ 4) For equipment marked for Class II locations, markings for the specific dust shall be permitted to be indicated by one or more of the following atmospheric group designations:
   a) Group E, consisting of atmospheres containing combustible metal dust, including aluminum, magnesium, and their commercial alloys, and other metals of similarly hazardous characteristics;
   b) Group F, consisting of atmospheres containing carbon black, coal, or coke dust; or
   c) Group G, consisting of atmospheres containing flour, starch, or grain dust, and other dusts of similarly hazardous characteristics.

Δ **J18-052 Marking** (see Annex JB)
Electrical equipment installed in Class I, II, or III hazardous locations shall have markings that are suitable for the Class and Division in which the equipment is installed.

Δ **J18-054 Temperature** (see Annex JB)
1) In Class I locations, the maximum surface temperature rating marked on equipment shall not exceed the minimum ignition temperature determined for the hazardous location in which the equipment is installed.
2) In Class II locations, the maximum surface temperature rating marked on equipment shall not exceed the lower of the dust cloud or dust layer ignition temperature determined for the hazardous location in which the equipment is installed.
3) In Class II locations, for organic dusts that may dehydrate or carbonize, the maximum surface temperature rating marked on equipment shall not exceed the lower of 165 °C or the dust layer or dust cloud ignition temperature determined for the hazardous location in which the equipment is installed.
4) In Class III locations, the maximum surface temperature rating marked on equipment shall not exceed 165 °C for equipment that is not subject to overloading and 120 °C for equipment (such as motors or power transformers) that may be overloaded.
5) Equipment installed in accordance with Rule J18-150 2) or 3) shall have surface temperatures at any point on the equipment that may be exposed to an explosive gas atmosphere that do not exceed the minimum ignition temperature determined for the hazardous location in which the equipment is installed.
6) If no maximum surface temperature rating is marked on Class I or Class II equipment marked for the Class and Group, the maximum surface temperature rating shall be deemed to be 100 °C.

J18-056 Rooms, sections, or areas
Each room, section, or area, including motor and generator rooms and rooms for the enclosure of control equipment, shall be considered a separate location for the purpose of determining the classification of the hazard.

J18-058 Equipment rooms
1) Where walls, partitions, floors, or ceilings are used to form hazard-free rooms or sections, they shall be
   a) of substantial construction;

Appendix J

C22.1-18

Appendix J
Rules and Notes to Rules for installations using the
Class and Division system of classification

b)   built of or lined with non-combustible material; and

c)   such that the rooms or sections will remain free from hazards.

2)   Where a non-hazardous location within a building communicates with a Class I, Division 2 location, the locations shall be separated by close-fitting, self-closing, approved fire doors.

3)   For communication from a Class I, Division 1 location, the provisions of Rule J18-004 b) ii) shall apply.

J18-060 Metal-covered cable (see Annex JB)

1)   Where exposed overhead conductors supply mineral-insulated cable in a hazardous location, surge arresters shall be installed to limit the surge voltage on the cable to 5 kV.

2)   Where single-conductor metal-covered cable is used in hazardous locations, it shall be installed so as to prevent sparking between cable sheaths or between cable sheaths and metal bonded to ground, and the cables in the circuit shall

a)   be clipped or strapped together in a manner that will ensure good electrical contact between metal coverings, at intervals of not more than 1.8 m, and the metal coverings shall be bonded to ground; or

b)   have the metal coverings continuously covered with insulating material and bonded to ground at the point of termination in the hazardous location only.

Δ   **J18-062 Pressurized equipment or rooms** (see Annex JB)

Electrical equipment and associated wiring in Class I locations shall be permitted to be located in enclosures or rooms constructed and arranged so that a protective gas pressure is effectively maintained, in which case the provisions of Rules J18-100 to J18-160 shall not be required.

Δ   **J18-064 Intrinsically safe and non-incendive electrical equipment and wiring** (see Annex JB and Appendix F)

1)   Where an intrinsically safe electrical system or non-incendive field wiring circuit is installed in a hazardous location, a descriptive system document shall be provided.

2)   Intrinsically safe electrical systems and non-incendive field wiring circuits shall be installed in accordance with the descriptive system document.

3)   Except as permitted by Subrule 4), no raceway, compartment, enclosure, outlet, junction box, or similar fitting, excluding cable tray, shall contain insulated conductors of intrinsically safe or non-incendive field wiring circuits and insulated conductors of any other circuit unless the conductors are separated by

a)   not less than 50 mm;

b)   the metal armour or sheath of cable assemblies;

c)   a grounded metal barrier not less than 1.34 mm (No. 16 MSG) thick; or

d)   a non-metallic insulating material not less than 1.5 mm in thickness.

4)   Insulated conductors of different intrinsically safe or non-incendive field wiring circuits shall be permitted in the same raceway, compartment, outlet, junction box, or multi-conductor cable, provided that

a)   the insulated conductors of each circuit are within grounded electrically conductive shields, braids, or sheaths; or

b)   the insulated conductors of each circuit have insulation with a minimum thickness of 0.25 mm.

5)   Raceways or cable systems for intrinsically safe and non-incendive wiring and equipment in explosive atmospheres shall be installed to minimize migration of flammable fluids to other locations.

Appendix J
Rules and Notes to Rules for installations using the
Class and Division system of classification

C22.1-18

6) All apparatus forming part of an intrinsically safe or non-incendive system shall be identified as being part of an intrinsically safe or non-incendive system.

7) Intrinsically safe and non-incendive field wiring circuits shall be identified at terminal and junction locations.

8) Wiring methods for intrinsically safe and or non-incendive field wiring circuits shall be
   a) identified with permanently affixed labels; or
   b) colour coded light blue where no other cables or insulated conductors colored light blue are used.

J18-066 **Combustible gas detection** (see Annex JB and Appendix H)

Electrical equipment suitable for non-hazardous locations shall be permitted to be installed in a Class I, Division 2 hazardous location, and electrical equipment suitable for Class I, Division 2 hazardous locations shall be permitted to be installed in a Class I, Division 1 hazardous location, provided that

a) no specific equipment suitable for the purpose is available;

b) the equipment, during its normal operation, does not produce arcs, sparks, or hot surfaces capable of igniting an explosive gas atmosphere; and

Δ c) the location is continuously monitored by a combustible gas detection system that will
   i) activate an alarm when the gas concentration reaches 20% of the lower flammable limit;
   ii) activate ventilating equipment or other means designed to prevent the concentration of gas from reaching the lower flammable limit when the gas concentration reaches 20% of the lower flammable limit, where such ventilating equipment or other means is provided;
   iii) automatically de-energize the electrical equipment being protected when the gas concentration reaches 40% of the lower flammable limit, where the ventilating equipment or other means referred to in Item ii) is provided;
   iv) automatically de-energize the electrical equipment being protected when the gas concentration reaches 20% of the lower flammable limit, where the ventilating equipment or other means referred to in Item ii) cannot be provided; and
   v) automatically de-energize the electrical equipment being protected upon failure of the gas detection instrument.

J18-068 **Flammable fluid seals** (see Annex JB)

1) Electrical equipment with a primary seal in contact with flammable fluids shall be
   a) constructed or installed so as to prevent migration of flammable fluid through the wiring system; and
   b) used at pressures lower than the marked maximum working pressure (MWP).

2) Where Subrule 1) is met through the installation of secondary seals, the possibility of primary seal failure shall be indicated by
   a) design features that will make the occurrence of a primary seal failure obvious; or
   b) acceptable marking means indicating that the enclosure may contain flammable fluid under pressure.

J18-070 **Bonding in hazardous locations**

1) Exposed non-current-carrying metal parts of electrical equipment, including the frames or metal exteriors of motors, fixed or portable luminaires or other utilization equipment, luminaires, cabinets, cases, and conduit, shall be bonded to ground using
   a) bonding conductors sized in accordance with Rule 10-614; or
   b) rigid metal conduit with threaded couplings and threaded bosses on enclosures with joints made up tight.

2) Notwithstanding Subrule 1), where raceways or cables incorporate an internal bonding conductor, box connectors with standard locknuts shall be permitted to bond the metallic armour or raceway.

Appendix J

C22.1-18

Appendix J
Rules and Notes to Rules for installations using the
Class and Division system of classification

J18-072 Uninsulated exposed parts

There shall be no uninsulated exposed parts of an electrical installation or of electrical equipment such as conductors, buses, terminals, or components unless

a) they operate at less than 30 V (15 V in wet locations) and are additionally protected by a type of protection suitable for the location; or

b) as provided for in Rule J18-324 for electric cranes, hoists, and similar equipment in a Class III location.

Class I locations

Installations in Class I, Division 1 locations

Δ **J18-100 Equipment in Class I, Division 1 locations** (see Annex JB)

Equipment installed in a Class I, Division 1 location shall be in accordance with Table 18.

J18-102 Transformers and capacitors, Class I, Division 1

1) Transformers and electrical capacitors that contain a liquid that will burn shall be installed in electrical equipment vaults in accordance with Rules 26-350 to 26-356, and the following shall apply:

a) there shall be no door or other connecting opening between the vault and the hazardous area;

b) the vault shall be ventilated to ensure the continuous removal of hazardous gases or vapours;

c) vent openings or vent ducts shall lead to a safe location outside the building containing the vault;

d) vent openings and vent ducts shall be of sufficient area to relieve pressure caused by explosions within the vault; and

e) every portion of a vent duct within the building shall be constructed of reinforced concrete.

2) Transformers and electrical capacitors that do not contain a liquid that will burn shall be

a) installed in electrical equipment vaults conforming to Subrule 1); or

b) in compliance with Rule J18-100.

J18-104 Meters, instruments, and relays, Class I, Division 1

1) Where practicable, meters, instruments, and relays, including kilowatt-hour meters, instrument transformers, and resistors, rectifiers, and thermionic tubes, shall be located outside the hazardous location.

2) Where it is not practicable to install meters, instruments, and relays outside Class I, Division 1 locations, they shall comply with the requirements of Rule J18-100.

Δ **J18-106 Wiring methods, Class I, Division 1** (see Annex JB)

1) The wiring method shall be threaded rigid metal conduit or hazardous location cables with associated cable glands that comply with the requirements of Rule J18-100.

2) Explosion-proof boxes, fittings, and joints shall be threaded for connection to conduit and cable glands.

3) Threaded joints shall have at least five fully engaged threads, and running threads shall not be used.

4) Cables shall be installed and supported so as to avoid tensile stress at the cable glands.

5) Where it is necessary to use flexible connections at motor terminals and similar places, flexible fittings of the explosion-proof type shall be used.

6) Notwithstanding Subrules 1) to 5), intrinsically safe equipment and associated circuits designed and installed as intrinsically safe "i" or "ia" shall be permitted as specified in Rule J18-064.

Appendix J
Rules and Notes to Rules for installations using the
Class and Division system of classification

C22.1-18

J18-108 Sealing, Class I, Division 1 (see Annex JB)
1) Conduit seals shall be provided in conduit systems where
   a) the conduit enters an explosion-proof enclosure containing devices that may produce arcs, sparks, or high temperatures, and shall be located as close as practicable to the enclosure, or as marked on the enclosure, but not farther than 450 mm from the enclosure;
   b) the conduit is 53 trade size or larger and enters an explosion-proof enclosure housing terminals, splices, or taps, and shall be located no further than 450 mm from the enclosure;
   c) the conduit leaves the Class I, Division 1 location with no box, coupling, or fitting in the conduit run between the seal and the point at which the conduit leaves the location, except that a rigid unbroken conduit that passes completely through a Class I, Division 1 area, with no fittings less than 300 mm beyond each boundary, need not be sealed, provided that the termination points of the unbroken conduit are in non-hazardous areas; or
   d) the conduit enters an enclosure that is not required to be explosion-proof, except that a seal is not required where an unbroken and continuous run of conduit connects two enclosures that are not required to be explosion-proof.
2) Only explosion-proof unions, couplings, reducers, and elbows that are not larger than the trade size of the conduit shall be permitted between the sealing fitting and an explosion-proof enclosure.
3) Cable seals shall be provided in a cable system where
   a) the cable enters an enclosure required to be explosion-proof; or
   b) the cable first terminates after entering the Division 1 area.
4) Where secondary seals, cable seals, or conduit seals are required, they shall conform to the following:
   a) the seal shall be made
      i) in a field-installed sealing fitting or cable gland that is accessible and complies with the requirements of Rule J18-100; or
      ii) in a sealing fitting provided as part of an enclosure, and where the seal is factory made, the enclosure shall be marked to indicate that such a seal is provided;
   b) splices and taps shall not be made in fittings intended only for sealing with compound, nor shall other fittings in which splices or taps are made be filled with compound;
   c) where there is a probability that liquid or other condensed vapour may be trapped within enclosures for control equipment or at any point in the raceway system, means shall be provided to prevent accumulation or to permit periodic draining of such liquid or condensed vapour; and
   d) where there is a probability that liquid or condensed vapour may accumulate within motors or generators, joints and conduit systems shall be arranged to minimize entrance of liquid, but if means to prevent accumulation or to permit periodic draining are judged necessary, such means shall be provided at the time of manufacture and shall be deemed an integral part of the machine.
5) Runs of cables, each having a continuous sheath, either metal or non-metal, shall be permitted to pass through a Class I, Division 1 location without seals.
6) Cables that do not have a continuous sheath, either metal or non-metal, shall be sealed at the boundary of the Division 1 location.

J18-110 Switches, motor controllers, circuit breakers, and fuses, Class I, Division 1
Switches, motor controllers, circuit breakers, and fuses, including push buttons, relays, and similar devices, shall be provided with enclosures, and the enclosure in each case, together with the enclosed apparatus, shall be a complete assembly and shall comply with the requirements of Rule J18-100.

Appendix J

C22.1-18

Appendix J
Rules and Notes to Rules for installations using the
Class and Division system of classification

J18-112 Control transformers and resistors, Class I, Division 1

Transformers, impedance coils, and resistors used as or in conjunction with control equipment for motors, generators, and appliances, and the switching mechanism, if any, associated with them, shall comply with the requirements of Rule J18-100.

J18-114 Motors and generators, Class I, Division 1 (see Annex JB)

Motors, generators, and other rotating electrical machines shall comply with the requirements of Rule J18-100.

J18-116 Ignition systems for gas turbines, Class I, Division 1 (see Annex JB)

Ignition systems for gas turbines shall comply with the requirements of Rule J18-100.

Δ J18-118 Luminaires, Class I, Division 1

1) Luminaires and portable lighting shall be complete assemblies marked for use in Class I locations and shall be clearly marked to indicate the maximum wattage of lamps for which they are approved.
2) Luminaires intended for portable use shall be complete assemblies for that use.
3) Each luminaire shall be protected against physical damage by a suitable guard or by location.
4) Pendant luminaires shall be
   a) suspended by and supplied through threaded rigid conduit stems, and threaded joints shall be provided with set screws or other effective means to prevent loosening; and
   b) for stems longer than 300 mm, provided with
      i) permanent and effective bracing against lateral displacement at a level not more than 300 mm above the lower end of the stem; or
      ii) flexibility in the form of a fitting or flexible connector in compliance with the requirements of Rule J18-100 and situated not more than 300 mm from the point of attachment to the supporting box or fitting.
5) Luminaires shall be supported by boxes, box assemblies, and fittings in accordance with the requirements of Rule J18-100.

J18-120 Utilization equipment, fixed and portable, Class I, Division 1

1) Utilization equipment, fixed and portable, including electrically heated and motor-driven equipment, shall comply with the requirements of Rule J18-100.
2) Ground fault protection shall be provided to de-energize all normally ungrounded conductors of an electric heat tracing cable set, with the ground fault trip setting adjusted to allow normal operation of the heater.

Δ J18-122 Flexible cords, Class I, Division 1

1) Flexible cords shall be permitted to be used only for connection between a portable lamp, or other portable utilization equipment, and the fixed portion of its supply circuit and, where used, shall
   a) be of the extra-hard-usage type;
   b) contain, in addition to the insulated conductors of the circuit, a bonding conductor; and
   c) be provided with glands marked for the class and group where the flexible cord enters a box, fitting, or enclosure of the explosion-proof type.
2) Flexible cord shall also be permitted for that portion of the circuit where fixed wiring methods cannot provide the necessary degree of movement for fixed and mobile electrical utilization equipment and, where used, shall
   a) meet all the requirements of Subrule 1); and
   b) be protected from damage by location or by a suitable guard.

Appendix J
Rules and Notes to Rules for installations using the
Class and Division system of classification

C22.1-18

J18-124 Receptacles and attachment plugs, Class I, Division 1

Receptacles and attachment plugs shall be of the type providing for connection to the bonding conductor of the flexible cord and shall comply with the requirements of Rule J18-100.

Δ **J18-126 Conductor insulation, Class I, Division 1**

Where condensed vapours or liquids may collect on or come in contact with the insulation on conductors, such insulation shall be of a type intended for use under such conditions, or the insulation shall be protected by a sheath of lead or by other means intended for the purpose.

J18-128 Signal, alarm, remote control, and communication systems, Class I, Division 1

Signal, alarm, remote control, and communication systems shall conform to the following:

a) all apparatus and equipment shall comply with the requirements of Rule J18-100; and

b) all wiring shall comply with Rules J18-106 and J18-108.

Installations in Class I, Division 2 locations

J18-150 Equipment in Class I, Division 2 locations (see Annex JB)

Δ 1) Equipment installed in a Class I, Division 2 location shall be in accordance with Table 18.

Δ 2) Notwithstanding Subrule 1) and Rule J18-052, the following shall be permitted:

    a) transformers, capacitors, solenoids, and other windings that do not incorporate sliding or make-and-break contacts, heat-producing resistance devices, and arcing or spark-producing components;

    b) conduit and cables as specified in Rule J18-152 1);

    c) non-explosion-proof or non-flameproof enclosures housing

        i) non-arcing connections and connecting devices such as joints, splices, terminals, and terminal blocks;

        ii) switches, controllers, and circuit breakers meeting the requirements of Subrule 1);

        iii) unfused isolating switches that are interlocked with their associated current-interrupting devices such that they cannot be opened under load; or

        iv) not more than

Δ   A) ten sets of enclosed fuses; or

            B) ten circuit breakers that are not used as switches for the normal operation of the lamps for the protection of a branch circuit or a feeder circuit that supplies fixed lighting;

    d) for the protection of motors, appliances, and luminaires,

        i) a standard plug or cartridge fuse, provided that it is placed within an explosion-proof or flameproof enclosure;

        ii) a fuse installed within a non-explosion-proof or non-flameproof enclosure, provided that the operating element of the fuse is

            A) immersed in oil or other suitable liquid; or

            B) enclosed within a hermetically sealed chamber; or

        iii) a fuse installed within a non-explosion-proof or non-flameproof enclosure, provided that the fuse is

            A) a non-indicating, filled, current-limiting type; or

            B) an indicating, filled, current-limiting type, constructed in a manner that the blown fuse indication does not cause the fuse body to be penetrated; or

    e) motors, generators, and other rotating electrical machines of the open or non-explosion-proof type that

        i) except as permitted by Subrule 3), do not incorporate arcing, sparking, or heat-producing components; or

C22.1-18

Appendix J
Rules and Notes to Rules for installations using the
Class and Division system of classification

Δ   ii)   incorporate arcing, sparking, or heat-producing components that comply with the requirements of Rule J18-100.

3)   The machines referred to in Subrule 2) e) i) shall be permitted to contain anti-condensation heaters suitable for non-hazardous locations, provided that they

    a)   do not use arcing or sparking components;

    b)   do not use temperature-limiting controls;

    c)   comply with the requirements of Rule J18-054 under normal operating conditions; and

Δ   d)   are marked on a separate nameplate on the machine with

        i)   the maximum surface temperature of the heater in degrees Celsius; or

        ii)   a temperature code that indicates the maximum surface temperature.

Δ   **J18-152 Wiring methods, Class I, Division 2** (see Annex JB)

1)   The wiring method shall be

    a)   threaded metal conduit;

    b)   hazardous location cables;

    c)   Type TC cable, installed in cable tray in accordance with Rule 12-2202;

    d)   armoured cable with overall non-metallic jacket, such as TECK90, ACWU90, copper-sheathed RC90, or aluminum sheath RA90;

    e)   control and instrumentation cables with an interlocking metallic armour and a continuous jacket in control circuits (Type ACIC);

    f)   Type CIC cable (non-armoured control and instrumentation cable) installed in cable tray in accordance with the installation requirements of Rule 12-2202 2), where

        i)   the voltage rating of the cable is not less than 300 V;

        ii)   the circuit voltage is 150 V or less; and

        iii)   the circuit current is 5 A or less;

    g)   rigid RTRC conduit Type XW, provided that

        i)   associated boxes, fittings, and joints are marked with the suffix "–XW"; and

        ii)   installation is performed in industrial establishments that are not accessible to the public and where only qualified persons service the installation;

    h)   intrinsically safe or non-incendive wiring circuits installed in accordance with Rule J18-064; or

    i)   liquid-tight flexible metal conduit and connectors, marked for heavy duty.

2)   Explosion-proof or flameproof boxes, fittings, and joints shall be threaded for connection to conduit and cable glands.

3)   Threaded joints that are required to be explosion-proof or flameproof shall be permitted to be either tapered or straight and shall comply with the following:

    a)   tapered threads shall have at least five fully engaged threads, and running threads shall not be used;

    b)   where straight threads are used in Groups IIA and IIB atmospheres, they shall have at least five fully engaged threads; and

    c)   where straight threads are used in Group IIC atmospheres, they shall have at least eight fully engaged threads.

4)   Where thread forms differ between the equipment and the wiring system, adapters in accordance with Rule J18-150 shall be used.

5)   Cables shall be installed and supported so as to avoid tensile stress at the cable glands.

6)   Boxes, fittings, and joints need not be explosion-proof or flameproof, except as required by the Rules in this Section.

Appendix J
Rules and Notes to Rules for installations using the
Class and Division system of classification

C22.1-18

7) Cable glands shall be compatible with the degree of ingress protection and explosion protection provided by the enclosure that the cable enters, where the area classification and environmental conditions require these degrees of protection.

J18-154 Sealing, Class I, Division 2 (see Annex JB)
1) Conduit seals shall be provided in a conduit system where
   a) the conduit enters an enclosure that is required to be explosion-proof or flameproof and shall be located as close as practicable to the enclosure, or as marked on the enclosure, but not farther than 450 mm from the enclosure;
   b) the conduit leaves the Class I, Division 2 location with no box, coupling, or fitting in the conduit run between the seal and the point at which the conduit leaves the location, except that a rigid unbroken conduit that passes completely through a Class I, Division 2 area, with no fittings less than 300 mm beyond each boundary, need not be sealed, provided that the termination points of the unbroken conduit are in non-hazardous areas; or
   c) the conduit leaves a Class I, Division 2 location outdoors, in which case the seal shall be permitted to be located more than 300 mm beyond the Class I, Division 2 boundary, provided that it is located on the conduit before the conduit enters an enclosure or building.
2) Only explosion-proof unions, couplings, reducers, and elbows that are not larger than the trade size of the conduit shall be permitted between the sealing fitting and an explosion-proof or flameproof enclosure.
3) Cable seals shall be provided in a cable system where
   a) the cable enters an enclosure required to be explosion-proof or flameproof; or
   b) the cable enters an enclosure not required to be explosion-proof or flameproof, and the other end of the cable terminates in a non-hazardous location in which a negative atmospheric pressure greater than 0.2 kPa exists.
4) Where a run of conduit enters an enclosure that is required to be explosion-proof or flameproof, every part of the conduit from the seal to that enclosure shall comply with Rule J18-106.
5) Runs of cables, each having a continuous sheath, either metal or non-metal, shall be permitted to pass through a Class I, Division 2 location without seals.
6) Cables that do not have a continuous sheath, either metal or non-metal, shall be sealed at the boundary of the Division 2 location.
7) Where seals are required, Rule J18-108 4) shall apply.

J18-156 Luminaires and portable lamps, Class I, Division 2
1) Luminaires shall be protected from physical damage by suitable guards or by location.
Δ 2) Pendant luminaires shall be suspended by threaded rigid conduit stems or by other means as specified by the manufacturer.
3) Where pendant luminaires are suspended by threaded rigid conduit stems longer than 300 mm, they shall be provided with
   a) permanent and effective bracing against lateral displacement at a level not more than 300 mm above the lower end of the stem; or
   b) flexibility in the form of a fitting or flexible connector suitable for the purpose and for the location not more than 300 mm from the point of attachment to the supporting box or fitting.
4) Portable lamps shall comply with Rule J18-118 1) and 2).

J18-158 Electrically heated utilization equipment, fixed and portable, Class I, Division 2
Electrically heated utilization equipment, whether fixed or portable, shall comply with the requirements of Rule J18-100.

Appendix J

C22.1-18

Appendix J
Rules and Notes to Rules for installations using the
Class and Division system of classification

J18-160 Flexible cords, Class I, Division 2

1) Flexible cords shall be permitted to be used for connection between permanently mounted luminaires, portable lamps, or other portable utilization equipment and the fixed portion of supply circuits and, where used, shall
   a) be of the extra-hard-usage type;
   b) contain, in addition to the insulated conductors of the circuit, a bonding conductor; and
   c) be provided with a sealing gland where the flexible cord enters a fitting or an enclosure that is required to be explosion-proof.
2) Flexible cord shall also be permitted for that portion of the circuit where fixed wiring methods cannot provide the necessary degree of movement for fixed and mobile electrical utilization equipment and, where used, shall
   a) meet all the requirements of Subrule 1); and
   b) be protected from damage by location or by a suitable guard.

Class II locations

Installations in Class II, Division 1 locations (see Appendix E)

Δ **J18-200 Equipment in Class II, Division 1 hazardous locations**
Equipment installed in a Class II, Division 1 location shall be in accordance with Table 18.

J18-202 Transformers and capacitors, Class II, Division 1

1) Transformers and electrical capacitors that contain a liquid that will burn shall be installed in electrical equipment vaults in accordance with Rules 26-350 to 26-356, and the following shall apply:
   a) doors or other openings communicating with the hazardous area shall have self-closing fire doors on both sides of the wall, and the doors shall be carefully fitted and provided with suitable seals (such as weatherstripping) to minimize the entrance of dust into the vault;
   b) vent openings and ducts shall communicate only with the air outside the building; and
   c) suitable pressure relief openings communicating only with the air outside the building shall be provided.
2) Transformers and electrical capacitors that do not contain a liquid that will burn shall be
   a) installed in electrical equipment vaults conforming to Subrule 1); or
Δ   b) marked for use in Class II locations as a complete assembly, including terminal connections.
3) No transformer or capacitor shall be installed in a location where dust from magnesium, aluminum, aluminum bronze powders, or other metals of similarly hazardous characteristics may be present.

Δ **J18-204 Wiring methods, Class II, Division 1** (see Annex JB)

1) The wiring method shall be
   a) threaded rigid metal conduit; or
   b) hazardous location cables.
2) Boxes, fittings, and joints shall be threaded for connection to conduit or cable glands, and boxes and fittings shall be marked for use in Class II locations.
3) Cables shall be installed and supported so as to avoid tensile stress at the cable glands.
4) Where flexible connections are necessary, they shall be provided by
   a) flexible connection fittings marked for use in the location;
   b) liquid-tight flexible metal conduit and connectors, marked for heavy duty; or
   c) extra-hard-usage flexible cord and cable glands marked for use in the location.

Appendix J
Rules and Notes to Rules for installations using the
Class and Division system of classification

C22.1-18

5) Where flexible connections are subject to oil or other corrosive conditions, the insulation of the conductors shall be of a type for the condition of use or shall be protected by means of a suitable sheath.

J18-206 Sealing, Class II, Division 1

Where a raceway provides communication between an enclosure that is required to be dust-tight and one that is not, the entrance of dust into the dust-tight enclosure through the raceway shall be prevented by

a) a permanent and effective seal;

b) a horizontal section not less than 3 m long in the raceway; or

c) a vertical section of raceway not less than 1.5 m long and extending downward from the dust-tight enclosure.

Δ ### J18-208 Switches, controllers, circuit breakers, and fuses, Class II, Division 1

Switches, motor controllers, circuit breakers, and fuses, including push buttons, relays, and similar devices, shall be provided with a dust-tight enclosure marked for use in Class II locations.

Δ ### J18-210 Control transformers and resistors, Class II, Division 1

Transformers, impedance coils, and resistors used as or in conjunction with control equipment for motors, generators, or electric appliances, and the overcurrent devices or switching mechanisms, if any, associated with them, shall be provided with a dust-tight enclosure marked for use in Class II locations.

Δ ### J18-212 Motors and generators, Class II, Division 1 (see Annex JB)

Motors, generators, and other rotating electrical machines shall be marked for use in Class II locations.

J18-214 Ventilating pipes, Class II, Division 1 (see Annex JB)

1) Every vent pipe for a motor, generator, or other rotating electrical machine or for enclosures for electrical apparatus or equipment shall
   a) be of metal not less than 0.52 mm (No. 24 MSG) thick or of an equally substantial non-combustible material;
   b) lead directly to a source of clean air outside a building;
   c) be screened at the outer end to prevent the entrance of small animals or birds; and
   d) be protected against mechanical damage and corrosion.

2) Every vent pipe and its connection to a motor or to a dust-tight enclosure for other equipment or apparatus shall be dust-tight throughout its entire length.

3) The seams and joints of every metal vent pipe shall be
   a) riveted and soldered;
   b) bolted and soldered;
   c) welded; or
   d) rendered dust-tight by some other equally effective means.

4) No exhaust pipe shall discharge inside a building.

Δ ### J18-216 Utilization equipment, fixed and portable, Class II, Division 1

Utilization equipment, fixed and portable, including electrically heated and motor-driven equipment shall be marked for use in Class II locations.

Appendix J

C22.1-18

Appendix J
Rules and Notes to Rules for installations using the
Class and Division system of classification

Δ   **J18-218 Luminaires, Class II, Division 1**
1) Luminaires and portable lighting shall be complete assemblies marked for use in Class II locations and shall be clearly marked to indicate the maximum wattage of lamps for which they are approved.
2) Luminaires intended for portable use shall be complete assemblies for that purpose.
3) Each luminaire shall be protected against physical damage by a suitable guard or by location.
4) Pendant luminaires shall be
   a) suspended by threaded rigid conduit stems or chains with approved fittings or by other approved means that do not include a flexible cord as the supporting medium, and threaded joints shall be provided with set screws or other effective means to prevent loosening;
   b) where suspended by threaded rigid conduit stems longer than 300 mm, provided with
      i) permanent and effective bracing against lateral displacement at a level not more than 300 mm above the lower end of the stem; or
      ii) flexibility in the form of a fitting or flexible connector suitable for the purpose and for the location not more than 300 mm from the point of attachment to the supporting box or fitting; and
   c) where wiring between an outlet box or fitting and the luminaire is not enclosed in conduit, provided with a flexible cord approved for extra-hard usage and suitable seals where the cord enters the luminaire and the outlet box or fitting.
5) Luminaires shall be supported by boxes, box assemblies, and fittings that are intended for the purpose and for Class II locations.

J18-220 Flexible cords, Class II, Division 1
Flexible cords used shall
a) be of a type approved for extra-hard usage;
b) contain a bonding conductor in addition to the insulated conductors of the circuit; and
c) be provided with glands approved for the class and group to prevent the entrance of dust at the point where the cord enters a box or fitting that is required by this Section to be dust-tight.

J18-222 Receptacles and attachment plugs, Class II, Division 1
Receptacles and attachment plugs shall be approved for Class II locations.

J18-224 Signal, alarm, remote control, and communication systems, meters, instruments, and relays, Class II, Division 1
Signal, alarm, remote control, and communication systems, meters, instruments, and relays shall conform to the following:
Δ   a) all apparatus and equipment shall be provided with enclosures marked for use in Class II locations, except that
      i) devices that carry or interrupt only a voice current shall not be required to be provided with such enclosures; and
      ii) current-breaking contacts that are immersed in oil or enclosed in a chamber sealed against the entrance of dust shall be permitted to be provided with a general-purpose enclosure if the prevailing dust is electrically non-conductive; and
   b) all wiring shall comply with Rules J18-204 and J18-206.

J18-226 Other equipment
Equipment providing EPL Da shall be permitted in a Class II, Division 1 location for the same explosive dust atmosphere and with a suitable temperature class.

C22.1-18

Appendix J
Rules and Notes to Rules for installations using the
Class and Division system of classification

Installations in Class II, Division 2 locations (see Appendix E)

Δ **J18-250 Equipment in Class II, Division 2 hazardous locations**
Equipment installed in a Class II, Division 2 location shall be in accordance with Table 18.

J18-252 Transformers and capacitors, Class II, Division 2
1) Transformers and electrical capacitors that contain a liquid that will burn shall be installed in electrical equipment vaults in accordance with Rules 26-350 to 26-356.
2) Transformers and electrical capacitors that contain a liquid that will not burn shall be
   a) installed in electrical equipment vaults in accordance with Rules 26-350 to 26-356; or
Δ b) marked for use in Class II locations.
3) Dry-core transformers installed in Class II, Division 2 locations shall
   a) be installed in electrical equipment vaults in accordance with Rules 26-350 to 26-356; or
   b) have their windings and terminal connections enclosed in tight housings without ventilating or other openings and operate at not more than 750 V.

J18-254 Wiring methods, Class II, Division 2 (see Annex JB)
1) The wiring method shall be
   a) threaded metal conduit;
Δ b) hazardous location cables;
   c) Type TC cable installed in cable tray in accordance with Rule 12-2202 and enclosed in rigid conduit or another acceptable wiring method wherever it leaves the cable tray;
   d) armoured cable with overall non-metallic jacket, such as TECK90, ACWU90, copper-sheathed RC90, or aluminum-sheathed RA90;
   e) control and instrumentation cables with an interlocking metallic armour and a continuous jacket in control circuits (Type ACIC);
   f) Type CIC cable (non-armoured control and instrumentation cable) installed in cable tray in accordance with the installation requirements of Rule 12-2202 2), where
      i) the voltage rating of the cable is not less than 300 V;
      ii) the circuit voltage is 150 V or less; and
      iii) the circuit current is 5 A or less;
   g) rigid RTRC conduit Type XW, provided that
Δ   i) associated boxes, fittings, and joints are marked with the suffix "–XW"; and
      ii) installation is performed in industrial establishments that are not accessible to the public and where only qualified persons service the installation; or
Δ h) liquid-tight flexible metal conduit and connectors, marked for heavy duty.
2) Boxes and fittings in which taps, joints, or terminal connections are made shall be either an Enclosure Type 4 or 5, or
   a) be provided with telescoping or close-fitting covers or with other effective means to prevent the escape of sparks or burning material; and
   b) have no openings, such as holes for attachment screws, through which, after installation, sparks or burning material might escape, or through which exterior accumulations of dust or adjacent combustible material might be ignited.
3) Cables shall be installed and supported so as to avoid tensile stress at the cable glands.
Δ 4) Where it is necessary to use flexible connections, the provisions of Rule J18-204 4) a) and c) and 5) shall apply.

J18-256 Sealing, Class II, Division 2
Sealing of raceways shall conform to Rule J18-206.

Appendix J

Appendix J
Rules and Notes to Rules for installations using the
Class and Division system of classification

C22.1-18

J18-258 Switches, controllers, circuit breakers, and fuses, Class II, Division 2

Enclosures for switches, motor controllers, circuit breakers, and fuses, including push buttons, relays, and similar devices, shall be either an Enclosure Type 4 or 5, or

a) be provided with telescoping or close-fitting covers or with other effective means to prevent the escape of sparks or burning material; and

b) have no openings, such as holes for attachment screws, through which, after installation, sparks or burning material might escape, or through which exterior accumulations of dust or adjacent combustible material might be ignited.

J18-260 Control transformers and resistors, Class II, Division 2

1) Switching mechanisms, including overcurrent devices, used in conjunction with control transformers, impedance coils, and resistors shall be provided with enclosures conforming to Rule J18-258.

2) Where not located in the same enclosure with switching mechanisms, control transformers and impedance coils shall be provided with tight housings without ventilating openings.

Δ 3) Resistors and resistance devices shall have dust-tight enclosures marked for use in Class II locations, except that where the maximum normal operating temperature of the resistor will not exceed 120 °C, non-adjustable resistors and resistors that are part of an automatically timed starting sequence may have enclosures conforming to Subrule 2).

J18-262 Motors and generators, Class II, Division 2 (see Annex JB)

1) Except as provided for in Subrule 2), motors, generators, and other rotating electrical machinery shall be

Δ   a) marked for use in Class II or Class II, Division 2 locations; or

    b) ordinary totally enclosed pipe-ventilated or totally enclosed fan-cooled, subject to the following:

        i)   equipped with integral overheating protection in accordance with Rule 28-314; and

        ii) if drain holes or other openings are provided, they shall be closed with threaded plugs.

2) Where accumulations of non-conductive, non-abrasive combustible dust are or will be moderate and if machines can be easily reached for routine cleaning and maintenance, the following shall be permitted to be installed:

    a) standard open-type machines without sliding contacts, centrifugal or other types of switching mechanisms (including motor overcurrent, overload, and overtemperature devices), or integral resistance devices;

    b) standard open-type machines with such contacts, switching mechanisms, or resistance devices enclosed within dust-tight housings without ventilating or other openings; and

    c) self-cleaning textile motors of the squirrel-cage type.

J18-264 Ventilation pipes, Class II, Division 2 (see Annex JB)

1) Vent pipes for motors, generators, or other rotating electrical machinery, or for enclosures for electrical apparatus or equipment, shall conform to Rule J18-214 1).

2) Vent pipes and their connections shall be sufficiently tight to prevent the entrance of appreciable quantities of dust into the ventilated equipment or enclosure, and to prevent the escape of sparks, flame, or burning material that might ignite accumulations of dust or combustible material in the vicinity.

3) Where metal vent pipes are used, lock seams and riveted or welded joints shall be permitted to be used and, where some flexibility is necessary, for example at connections to motors, tight-fitting slip joints shall be permitted to be used.

J18-266 Utilization equipment, fixed and portable, Class II, Division 2

Δ 1) Electrically heated utilization equipment, whether fixed or portable, shall be marked for use in Class II locations.

Appendix J
Rules and Notes to Rules for installations using the
Class and Division system of classification

C22.1-18

2) Motors of motor-driven utilization equipment shall conform to Rule J18-262.
3) The enclosure for switches, circuit breakers, and fuses shall conform to Rule J18-258.
4) Transformers, impedance coils, and resistors forming part of or used in connection with utilization equipment shall conform to Rule J18-260 2) and 3).
5) Where portable utilization equipment is permitted to be used in Class II, Division 1 locations and in Class II, Division 2 locations, it shall conform to Rule J18-216.

Δ **J18-268 Luminaires, Class II, Division 2**
1) Lighting equipment shall conform to the following:
  a) portable lamps shall be complete assemblies marked for use in Class II locations and shall be clearly marked to indicate the maximum wattage of lamps with which they are permitted to be used; and
  b) luminaires shall
    i) be protected from physical damage by suitable guards or by location;
    ii) provide enclosures for lamps and lampholders that shall be designed to minimize the deposit of dust on lamps and to prevent the escape of sparks, burning material, or hot metal; and
    iii) be clearly marked to indicate the maximum wattage of lamps for which they are permitted to be used without exceeding the marked maximum surface temperature or temperature code.
2) Pendant luminaires shall be
  a) suspended by threaded rigid conduit stems or chains with fittings or other means marked for use in Class II locations that do not include flexible cord as the supporting medium;
  b) where suspended by threaded rigid conduit stems longer than 300 mm, provided with
    i) permanent and effective bracing against lateral displacement at a level not more than 300 mm above the lower end of the stem; or
    ii) flexibility in the form of a fitting or flexible connector suitable for the purpose and for the location not more than 300 mm from the point of attachment to the supporting box or fitting; and
  c) where wiring between an outlet box or fitting and the luminaire is not enclosed in conduit, provided with an extra-hard-usage flexible cord.
3) Luminaires shall be supported by boxes, box assemblies, or fittings designed for the purpose.
4) Starting and control equipment for mercury vapour and fluorescent lamps shall conform to Rule J18-260.

J18-270 Flexible cords, Class II, Division 2
Flexible cords shall conform to Rule J18-220.

J18-272 Receptacles and attachment plugs, Class II, Division 2
Receptacles and attachment plugs shall be
a) of a polarized type that affords automatic connection to the bonding conductor of the flexible supply cord; and
b) designed so that the connection to the supply circuit cannot be made or broken while live parts are exposed.

J18-274 Signal, alarm, remote control, and communication systems, meters, instruments, and relays, Class II, Division 2
Signal, alarm, remote control, and communications systems, meters, instruments, and relays shall conform to the following:
a) contacts that interrupt other than voice currents shall be enclosed in conformity with Rule J18-258;

Appendix J

C22.1-18

Appendix J
Rules and Notes to Rules for installations using the
Class and Division system of classification

b) the windings and terminal connections of transformers and choke coils that may carry other than voice currents shall be provided with tight enclosures without ventilating openings; and

Δ c) resistors, resistance devices, thermionic tubes, and rectifiers that may carry other than voice currents shall be provided with Class II dust-tight enclosures, except that where the maximum normal operating temperature of thermionic tubes, non-adjustable resistors, or rectifiers will not exceed 120 °C, such devices shall be permitted to have tight enclosures without ventilating openings.

J18-276 Other equipment
Equipment providing EPL Da, Db, or Dc shall be permitted in a Class II, Division 2 location for the same explosive dust atmosphere and with a suitable temperature class.

Class III locations

Installations in Class III, Division 1 locations (see Appendix E)

Δ ### J18-300 Equipment in Class III, Division 1 hazardous locations
Equipment installed in a Class III, Division 1 location shall be in accordance with Table 18.

J18-302 Transformers and capacitors, Class III, Division 1
Transformers and electrical capacitors shall conform to Rule J18-252.

J18-304 Wiring methods, Class III, Division 1 (see Annex JB)
Δ 1) The wiring method shall be
   a) threaded rigid metal conduit;
   b) hazardous location cables;
   c) electrical metallic tubing;
   d) armoured cable with overall jacket, such as TECK90, ACWU90, copper-sheathed RC90, or aluminum-sheathed RA90;
   e) control and instrumentation cables with an interlocking metallic armour and a continuous jacket in control circuits (Type ACIC); or
   f) liquid-tight flexible metal conduit and connectors, marked for heavy duty.
2) Boxes and fittings in which taps, joints, or terminal connections are made shall be either an Enclosure Type 5 or shall
   a) be provided with telescoping or close-fitting covers or with other effective means to prevent the escape of sparks or burning material; and
   b) have no openings, such as holes for attachment screws, through which, after installation, sparks or burning material might escape, or through which adjacent combustible material might be ignited.
3) Cables shall be installed and supported so as to avoid tensile stress at the cable glands.
Δ 4) Where it is necessary to use flexible connections, the provisions of Rule J18-204 4) a) and c) and 5) shall apply.

J18-306 Switches, controllers, circuit breakers, and fuses, Class III, Division 1
Enclosures for switches, motor controllers, circuit breakers, and fuses, including push buttons, relays, and similar devices, shall be either an Enclosure Type 5 or shall be tight enclosures designed to minimize entrance of fibres and flyings, and shall
a) be provided with telescoping or close-fitting covers or with other effective means to prevent the escape of sparks or burning material; and
b) have no openings, such as holes for attachment screws, through which, after installation, sparks or burning material might escape, or through which exterior accumulations of fibres or flyings or adjacent combustible material might be ignited.

Appendix J
Rules and Notes to Rules for installations using the
Class and Division system of classification

C22.1-18

J18-308 Control transformers and resistors, Class III, Division 1

Transformers, impedance coils, and resistors used as or in conjunction with control equipment for motors, generators, and appliances shall conform to Rule J18-260, with the exception that, when these devices are in the same enclosure with switching devices of such control equipment and are used only for starting or short-time duty, the enclosure shall conform to the requirements of Rule J18-306.

J18-310 Motors and generators, Class III, Division 1 (see Annex JB)

1) Except as provided for in Subrule 2), motors, generators, and other rotating electrical machinery shall be
   a) totally enclosed non-ventilated;
   b) totally enclosed pipe-ventilated; or
   c) totally enclosed fan-cooled.
2) Where only moderate accumulations of lint and flyings are likely to collect on, or in the vicinity of, a rotating electrical machine and the machine is readily accessible for routine cleaning and maintenance, it shall be permissible to install the following in the location:
   a) standard open-type machines without sliding contacts or centrifugal or other types of switching mechanisms, including motor overload devices;
   b) standard open-type machines that have contacts, switching mechanisms, or resistance devices enclosed within tight housings without ventilating or other openings; or
   c) self-cleaning textile motors of the squirrel-cage type.
3) Motors, generators, or other rotating electrical machinery of the partially enclosed or splash-proof type shall not be installed in Class III locations.

J18-312 Ventilating pipes, Class III, Division 1 (see Annex JB)

1) Vent pipes for motors, generators, or other rotating electrical machinery or for enclosures for electrical apparatus or equipment shall conform to Rule J18-214 1).
2) Vent pipes and their connections shall be sufficiently tight to prevent the entrance of appreciable quantities of fibres or flyings into the ventilated equipment or enclosure, and to prevent the escape of sparks, flame, or burning material that might ignite accumulations of fibres or flyings or combustible material in the vicinity.
3) Where metal vent pipes are used, lock seams and riveted or welded joints shall be permitted to be used and, where some flexibility is necessary, tight-fitting slip joints shall be permitted to be used.

J18-314 Utilization equipment, fixed and portable, Class III, Division 1

Δ 1) Electrically heated utilization equipment, whether fixed or portable, shall be marked for use in Class III locations.
2) Motors of motor-driven utilization equipment shall conform to Rule J18-310.
3) The enclosures for switches, motor controllers, circuit breakers, and fuses shall conform to Rule J18-306.

J18-316 Luminaires, Class III, Division 1

1) Lighting equipment shall conform to the following:
   a) portable lamps shall
      i) be equipped with handles;
      ii) be protected with substantial guards;
      iii) have lampholders of the unswitched type with no exposed metal parts and without provision for receiving attachment plugs; and
      iv) in all other aspects comply with Item b); and
   b) luminaires shall
      i) provide enclosures for lamps and lampholders that shall be designed to minimize entrance of fibres and flyings and to prevent the escape of sparks, burning material, or hot metal; and

C22.1-18

Appendix J
Rules and Notes to Rules for installations using the
Class and Division system of classification

    ii)   be clearly marked to indicate the maximum wattage lamp that is permitted to be used without exceeding a maximum exposed surface temperature of 165 °C under normal conditions of use.

2) Luminaires that may be exposed to physical damage shall be protected by a suitable guard.

3) Pendant luminaires shall comply with Rule J18-268 2).

Δ 4) Luminaires shall be supported by boxes, box assemblies, or fittings designed for the purpose.

5) Starting and control equipment for mercury vapour and fluorescent lamps shall comply with Rule J18-308.

J18-318 Flexible cords, Class III, Division 1
Flexible cords shall comply with Rule J18-220.

J18-320 Receptacles and attachment plugs, Class III, Division 1
Receptacles and attachment plugs shall comply with Rule J18-272.

J18-322 Signal, alarm, remote control, and communication systems, Class III, Division 1
Signal, alarm, remote control, and communication systems shall comply with Rule J18-274.

J18-324 Electric cranes, hoists, and similar equipment, Class III, Division 1
Where installed for operation over combustible fibres or accumulations of flyings, travelling cranes and hoists for material handling, travelling cleaners for textile machinery, and similar equipment shall conform to the following:

a) the power supply to contact conductors shall be isolated from all other systems, ungrounded, and equipped with
    i)   recording ground detection that will give an alarm and will automatically de-energize the contact conductors in case of a fault to ground; or
    ii)   ground fault detection that will give a visual and audible alarm and maintain the alarm as long as power is supplied to the system and the ground fault remains;

b) contact conductors shall be located or guarded so as to be inaccessible to other than authorized persons and shall be protected against accidental contact with foreign objects;

c) current collectors shall conform to the following:
    i)   they shall be arranged or guarded to confine normal sparking and to prevent escape of sparks or hot particles;
    ii)   to reduce sparking, two or more separate surfaces of contact shall be provided for each contact conductor; and
    iii)   reliable means shall be provided to keep contact conductors and current collectors free of accumulations of lint or flyings; and

d) control equipment shall comply with Rules J18-306 and J18-308.

J18-326 Storage-battery charging equipment, Class III, Division 1
Storage-battery charging equipment shall be located in separate rooms built or lined with substantial non-combustible materials constructed so as to adequately exclude flyings or lint and shall be well ventilated.

J18-328 Other equipment
Equipment providing EPL Da shall be permitted in a Class III, Division 1 location with a temperature class not greater than T120 °C for equipment that may be overloaded and not greater than T165 °C for equipment not subject to overloading.

Installations in Class III, Division 2 locations (see Appendix E)

Δ ### J18-350 Equipment in Class III, Division 2 hazardous locations
Equipment installed in a Class III, Division 2 location shall be in accordance with Table 18.

Appendix J
Rules and Notes to Rules for installations using the
Class and Division system of classification

C22.1-18

J18-352 Transformers and capacitors, Class III, Division 2
Transformers and capacitors shall conform to Rule J18-252.

J18-354 Wiring method, Class III, Division 2 (see Annex JB)
The wiring method shall be
a)   threaded rigid metal conduit;
Δ   b)   hazardous location cables;
c)   electrical metallic tubing;
d)   armoured cable with overall jacket, such as TECK90, ACWU90, copper-sheathed RC90, or aluminum-sheathed RA90;
e)   control and instrumentation cables with an interlocking metallic armour and a continuous jacket in control circuits (Type ACIC);
f)   Type TC cable installed in cable tray in accordance with Rule 12-2202;
g)   Type CIC cable (non-armoured control and instrumentation cable) installed in cable tray in accordance with the installation requirements of Rule 12-2202 2), where
   i)   the voltage rating of the cable is not less than 300 V;
   ii)   the circuit voltage is 150 V or less; and
   iii) the circuit current is 5 A or less; or
Δ   h)   liquid-tight flexible metal conduit and connectors, marked for heavy duty.

J18-356 Switches, controllers, circuit breakers, and fuses, Class III, Division 2
Enclosures for switches, motor controllers, circuit breakers, and fuses shall conform to Rule J18-306.

J18-358 Control transformers and resistors, Class III, Division 2
Transformers, impedance coils, and resistors used as or in conjunction with control equipment for motors, generators, and appliances shall conform to Rule J18-308.

J18-360 Motors and generators, Class III, Division 2 (see Annex JB)
Motors, generators, and other rotating machinery shall conform to Rule J18-310.

J18-362 Ventilating pipes, Class III, Division 2 (see Annex JB)
Ventilating pipes shall conform to Rule J18-214 1).

J18-364 Utilization equipment, fixed and portable, Class III, Division 2
Fixed or portable utilization equipment shall conform to Rule J18-314.

J18-366 Luminaires, Class III, Division 2
Luminaires shall conform to Rule J18-316.

J18-368 Flexible cords, Class III, Division 2
Flexible cords shall conform to Rule J18-220.

J18-370 Receptacles and attachment plugs, Class III, Division 2
Receptacles and attachment plugs shall conform to Rule J18-272.

J18-372 Signal, alarm, remote control, and communication systems, Class III, Division 2
Signal, alarm, remote control, and communication systems shall conform to Rule J18-274.

J18-374 Electric cranes, hoists, and similar equipment, Class III, Division 2
Electric cranes, hoists, and similar equipment shall be installed as prescribed by Rule J18-324.

J18-376 Storage-battery charging equipment, Class III, Division 2
Storage-battery charging equipment shall be located in rooms conforming to Rule J18-326.

J18-378 Other equipment
Equipment providing EPL Da, Db, or Dc shall be permitted in a Class III, Division 2 location with a temperature class not greater than T120 °C for equipment that may be overloaded and not greater than T165 °C for equipment not subject to overloading.

C22.1-18

Appendix J
Rules and Notes to Rules for installations using the
Class and Division system of classification

Annex J20
Flammable liquid and gasoline dispensing, service stations, garages, bulk storage plants, finishing processes, and aircraft hangars

J20-000 Scope (see Appendix G)

1) This Section constitutes an Annex to this Code and supplements or amends the general requirements of this Code and applies to installations as follows:
   a) gasoline dispensing and service stations — Rules J20-002 to J20-014;
   b) propane dispensing, container filling, and storage — Rules J20-030 to J20-042;
   c) compressed natural gas refuelling stations, compressors, and storage facilities — Rules J20-060 to J20-070;
   d) commercial repair garages — Rules J20-100 to J20-112;
   e) bulk storage plants — Rules J20-200 to J20-212;
   f) finishing processes — Rules J20-300 to J20-314; and
   g) aircraft hangars — Rules J20-400 to J20-422.

2) The definitions stated in Rule J18-002 shall also apply to Annex J20.

Gasoline dispensing and service stations

J20-002 General

1) Rules J20-004 to J20-014 apply to electrical apparatus and wiring installed in gasoline dispensing and service stations, and other locations where gasoline or other similar volatile flammable liquids are dispensed or transferred to the fuel tanks of self-propelled vehicles.

2) Other areas used as lubritoriums, service rooms, repair rooms, offices, salesrooms, compressor rooms, and similar locations shall conform to Rules J20-100 to J20-112 with respect to electrical wiring and equipment.

J20-004 Hazardous areas (see Annex JB)

1) Except as provided for in Subrule 3), the space within a dispenser enclosure up to 1.2 m vertically above its base, including the space below the dispenser that may contain electrical wiring and equipment, shall be considered a Class I, Division 1 location.

2) The space within a nozzle boot of a dispenser shall be considered a Class I, Division 1 location.

3) The space within a dispenser enclosure above the Class I, Division 1 location as specified in Subrule 1) or spaces within a dispenser enclosure isolated from the Division 1 location by a solid vapour-tight partition or by a solid nozzle boot but not completely surrounded by a Division 1 location shall be considered a Class I, Division 2 location.

4) The space within 450 mm horizontally from the Division 1 location within the dispenser enclosure as specified in Subrule 1) shall be considered a Class I, Division 1 location.

5) The space outside the dispenser within 450 mm horizontally from the opening of a solid nozzle boot located above the vapour-tight partition shall be considered a Class I, Division 2 location, except that the classified area need not be extended beyond the plane in which the boot is located.

6) In an outside location, any area beyond the Class I, Division 1 area (and in buildings not suitably cut off) within 6 m horizontally from the exterior enclosure of any dispenser shall be considered a Class I, Division 2 location that extends to a level 450 mm above driveway or ground level.

7) In an outside location, any area beyond the Class I, Division 1 location (and in buildings not suitably cut off) within 3 m horizontally from any tank fill-pipe shall be considered a Class I, Division 2 location extending upward to a level 450 mm above driveway or ground level.

Appendix J
Rules and Notes to Rules for installations using the
Class and Division system of classification

C22.1-18

8) Electrical wiring and equipment, any portion of which is below the surface of areas defined as Class I, Division 1 or Division 2 in Subrule 1), 4), 6), or 7) shall be considered to be within a Class I, Division 1 location that extends at least to the point of emergence above grade.

9) Areas within the vicinity of tank vent pipes shall be classified as follows:

a) the spherical volume within a 900 mm radius from the point of discharge of any tank vent pipe shall be considered a Class I, Division 1 location and the volume between the 900 mm radius and the 1.5 m radius from the point of discharge of a vent shall be considered a Class I, Division 2 location;

b) for any vent that does not discharge upward, the cylindrical volume below both the Division 1 and Division 2 locations extending to the ground shall be considered a Class I, Division 2 location; and

c) the hazardous area shall not be considered to extend beyond an unpierced wall.

10) Areas within lubrication rooms shall be classified as follows:

a) the area within any pit or space below grade or floor level in a lubrication room shall be considered a Class I, Division 1 location, unless the pit or space below grade is beyond the hazardous areas specified in Subrules 6), 7), and 9), in which case the pit or space below grade shall be considered a Class I, Division 2 location;

b) notwithstanding Item a), for each floor below grade that is located beyond the hazardous area specified in Subrules 6), 7), and 9) and where adequate mechanical ventilation is provided, a Class I, Division 2 location shall extend up to a level of only 50 mm above each such floor; and

c) the area within the entire lubrication room up to 50 mm above the floor or grade, whichever is higher, and the area within 900 mm measured in any direction from the dispensing point of a hand-operated unit dispensing volatile flammable liquids shall be considered a Class I, Division 2 location.

J20-006 Wiring and equipment within hazardous areas

1) Electrical wiring and equipment within the hazardous areas defined in Rule J20-004 shall conform to Annex J18 requirements.

2) Where dispensers are supplied by rigid metal conduit, a union and a flexible fitting shall be installed between the conduit and the dispenser junction box in addition to any sealing fittings required by Annex J18.

3) The flexible metal fitting required by Subrule 2) shall be installed in a manner that allows for relative movement of the conduit and the dispenser.

Δ 4) Where dispensers are supplied by a cable, provision shall be made to separate the cable from the dispenser junction box without rendering ineffective the explosion-proof cable seal.

J20-008 Wiring and equipment above hazardous areas

Wiring and equipment above hazardous areas shall conform to Rules J20-106 and J20-110.

J20-010 Circuit disconnects

Each circuit leading to or through a dispensing pump shall be provided with a switching means that will simultaneously disconnect all ungrounded conductors of the circuit from the source of supply.

J20-012 Sealing

1) Seals as required by Annex J18 shall be provided in each conduit run entering or leaving a dispenser or any cavities or enclosures in direct communication with a dispenser.

2) Additional seals shall be provided in conformance with Rules J18-108 and J18-154, and the requirements of Rules J18-108 1) c) and J18-154 1) b) shall include horizontal and vertical boundaries.

J20-014 Bonding

All non-current-carrying metal parts of dispensing pumps, metal raceways, and other electrical equipment shall be bonded to ground in accordance with Section 10.

Appendix J

C22.1-18

Appendix J
Rules and Notes to Rules for installations using the
Class and Division system of classification

Propane dispensing, container filling, and storage

J20-030 Scope (see Annex JB)
Rules J20-032 to J20-042 apply to locations where propane is dispensed or transferred to the fuel tanks of self-propelled vehicles or to portable containers and to locations where propane is stored or transferred from rail cars or tanker vehicles to storage containers.

J20-032 Special terminology
In this Subsection, the following definitions shall apply:

Container refill centre — a facility such as a propane service station that is open to the public and at which propane is dispensed into containers or the fuel tanks of motor vehicles and that consists of propane storage containers, piping, and pertinent equipment, including pumps and dispensing devices.

Filling plant — a facility such as a bulk propane plant, the primary purpose of which is the distribution of propane, that receives propane in tank car or truck transport for storage and/or distribution in portable containers or tank trucks, that has bulk storage, and that usually has container-filling and truck-loading facilities on the premises.

Propane — any material that is composed predominantly of the following hydrocarbons either by themselves or as mixtures: propane, propylene, butane (normal butane or iso-butane), and butylene.

J20-034 Hazardous areas
In container refill centres and in filling plants, the hazardous areas shall be classified as listed in Table JT-63.

J20-036 Wiring and equipment in hazardous areas
1) All electrical wiring and equipment in the hazardous areas referred to in Rule J20-034 shall conform to the requirements of Annex J18.
2) Where dispensing devices are supplied by rigid metal conduit, the requirements of Rule J20-006 2) and 3) shall be met.

J20-038 Sealing
1) Seals shall be installed as required by Annex J18, and the requirements shall be applied to horizontal as well as vertical boundaries of the defined hazardous locations.
2) Seals for dispensing devices shall be provided as required by Rule J20-012.

J20-040 Circuit disconnects
Each circuit leading to or through a propane dispensing device or pump shall be provided with a switching means that will disconnect simultaneously all ungrounded conductors of the circuit from the source of supply.

J20-042 Bonding
All non-current-carrying metal parts of equipment and raceways shall be bonded to ground in accordance with Section 10.

Compressed natural gas refuelling stations, compressors, and storage facilities

J20-060 Scope (see Annex JB)
1) Rules J20-062 to J20-070 apply to locations where compressed natural gas is dispensed to the fuel tanks of self-propelled vehicles and to associated compressors and storage facilities.
2) The Rules in this Subsection do not apply to vehicle refuelling appliances installed in accordance with CSA B149.1 that do not have storage facilities.

Appendix J
Rules and Notes to Rules for installations using the
Class and Division system of classification

C22.1-18

J20-062 Hazardous areas

Compressed natural gas refuelling stations, compressors, and storage facilities shall be classified as shown in Table 64.

J20-064 Wiring and equipment in hazardous areas

1) All electrical wiring and equipment in the hazardous areas defined in Rule J20-062 shall comply with the requirements of Annex J18.

2) Where dispensing devices are supplied by rigid metal conduit, the requirements of Rule J20-006 2) and 3) shall be met.

J20-066 Sealing

1) Seals shall be installed as required by Annex J18, and the requirements shall be applied to horizontal as well as vertical boundaries of the defined hazardous locations.

2) Seals for dispensing devices shall be provided as required by Rule J20-012.

J20-068 Circuit disconnects

Each circuit leading to a compressor or a dispensing device shall be provided with a switching means that will disconnect simultaneously all ungrounded conductors of the circuit from the source of supply.

J20-070 Bonding

All non-current-carrying metal parts of equipment and raceways shall be bonded to ground in accordance with Section 10.

Commercial repair garages

J20-100 Scope (see Annex JB)

Rules J20-102 to J20-112 apply to commercial garages where vehicles powered by gasoline, propane, or other flammable fuels are serviced or repaired.

J20-102 Hazardous areas

1) For each floor at or above grade, the entire area up to a level 50 mm above the floor shall be considered a Class I, Division 2 location except that adjacent areas shall not be classified as hazardous locations, provided that they are
   a) elevated from a service and repair area by at least 50 mm; or
   b) separated from a service and repair area by tight-fitting barriers such as curbs, ramps, or partitions at least 50 mm high.

2) For each floor below grade, the entire area up to a level 50 mm above the bottom of outside doors or other openings that are at, or above, grade level shall be considered a Class I, Division 2 location, except that where adequate mechanical ventilation is provided, the hazardous location shall extend up to a level of only 50 mm above each such floor.

3) Any pit or depression below floor level shall be considered a Class I, Division 2 location that extends up to 50 mm above the floor level.

J20-104 Wiring and equipment in hazardous areas

Within hazardous areas as defined in Rule J20-102, wiring and equipment shall conform to the applicable requirements of Annex J18.

J20-106 Wiring above hazardous areas

1) All fixed wiring above hazardous areas shall be in accordance with Section 12 and suitable for the type of building and occupancy.

2) For pendants, flexible cord of the hard-usage type shall be used.

3) For connection of portable lamps, portable motors, or other portable utilization equipment, flexible cord of the hard-usage type shall be used.

Appendix J

C22.1-18

Appendix J
Rules and Notes to Rules for installations using the
Class and Division system of classification

J20-108 Sealing

1) Seals shall be installed as required by Annex J18, and the requirements of Rule J18-154 1) b) shall include horizontal and vertical boundaries.

2) Raceways embedded in a masonry floor or buried beneath a floor shall be considered to be within the hazardous area above the floor if any connections or extensions lead into or through such an area.

J20-110 Equipment above hazardous areas

1) Fixed equipment that is less than 3.6 m above floor level and that may produce arcs, sparks, or particles of hot metal, such as cut-outs, switches, charging panels, generators, motors, or other equipment (excluding receptacles, lamps, and lampholders) having make-and-break or sliding contacts, shall be of the totally enclosed type or constructed to prevent escape of sparks or hot metal particles.

2) Permanently installed luminaires that are located over lanes through which vehicles are commonly driven shall be permitted to be suitable for non-hazardous locations and shall be
   a) located not less than 3.6 m above floor level; or
   b) protected from mechanical damage by a guard or by location.

3) Portable lamps shall comply with the following:
   a) they shall be of the totally enclosed gasketted type, equipped with a handle, lampholder, hook, and substantial guard attached to the lampholder or handle, and all exterior surfaces that may come in contact with battery terminals, wiring terminals, or other objects shall be of non-conducting materials or shall be effectively protected with an insulating jacket;
   b) the lampholders shall be of the unswitched type; and
   c) they shall not be provided with receptacles for attachment plugs.

J20-112 Battery charging equipment

Battery chargers and their control equipment, and batteries being charged, shall not be located within the hazardous areas classified in Rule J20-102.

Bulk storage plants

J20-200 Scope

Rules J20-202 to J20-212 apply to locations where gasoline or other similar volatile flammable liquids are stored in tanks having an aggregate capacity of one carload or more, and from which such products are distributed (usually by tank truck).

Δ ## J20-202 Hazardous areas

Hazardous locations at bulk storage plants shall be classified as shown in Table JT-69.

J20-204 Wiring and equipment in hazardous areas

All electrical wiring and equipment in the hazardous areas defined in Rule J20-202 shall conform to the requirements of Annex J18.

J20-206 Wiring and equipment above hazardous areas

1) Wiring installed above a hazardous location shall conform to the requirements of Section 12 and be suitable for the type of building and the occupancy.

2) Fixed equipment that may produce arcs, sparks, or particles of hot metal, such as lamps and lampholders, cut-outs, switches, receptacles, motors, or other equipment having make-and-break or sliding contacts, shall be of the totally enclosed type or constructed to prevent the escape of sparks or hot metal particles.

3) Portable lamps or utilization equipment and the flexible cords supplying them shall conform to the requirements of Annex J18 for the class of location above which they are connected or used.

C22.1-18

Appendix J
Rules and Notes to Rules for installations using the
Class and Division system of classification

J20-208 Sealing
1) Seals shall be installed in accordance with Annex J18 and shall be applied to horizontal as well as vertical boundaries of the defined hazardous locations.
2) Buried raceways under defined hazardous areas shall be considered to be within such areas.

J20-210 Gasoline dispensing
Where gasoline dispensing is carried on in conjunction with bulk station operations, the applicable provisions of Rules J20-002 to J20-014 shall apply.

J20-212 Bonding
All non-current-carrying metal parts of equipment and raceways shall be bonded to ground in accordance with Section 10.

Finishing processes

J20-300 Scope
Rules J20-302 to J20-314 apply where paints, lacquers, or other flammable finishes are regularly or frequently applied by spraying, dipping, brushing, or other means, and where volatile flammable solvents or thinners are used, or where readily ignitable deposits or residues from such paints, lacquers, or finishes may occur.

J20-302 Hazardous locations
1) The following areas shall be considered Class I, Division 1 locations:
   a) the interiors of spray booths and their exhaust ducts;
   b) all space within 6 m horizontally in any direction, extending to a height of 1 m above the goods to be painted, from spraying operations more extensive than touch-up spraying and not conducted within a spray booth and as otherwise shown in Diagram JD-5;
   c) all space within 6 m horizontally in any direction from dip tanks and their drain boards, with the space extending to a height of 1 m above the dip tank and drain board; and
   d) all other spaces where hazardous concentrations of flammable vapours are likely to occur.
2) For spraying operations within an open-face spray booth, the extent of the Class I, Division 2 location shall extend not less than 1.5 m from the open face of the spray booth, and as otherwise shown in Diagram JD-4.
3) For spraying operations confined within a closed spray booth or room, or for rooms where hazardous concentrations of flammable vapours are likely to occur, such as paint mixing rooms, the space within 1 m in all directions from any openings in the booth or room shall be considered a Class I, Division 2 location, and as otherwise shown in Diagram JD-10.
4) All space within the room but beyond the limits for Class I, Division 1 as classified in Subrule 1) for extensive open spraying, and as otherwise shown in Diagram JD-5 for dip tanks and drain boards and for other hazardous operations, shall be considered Class I, Division 2 locations.
5) Adjacent areas that are cut off from the defined hazardous area by tight partitions without communicating openings, and within which hazardous vapours are not likely to be released, shall be permitted to be classed as non-hazardous.
Δ 6) Drying and baking areas provided with positive mechanical ventilation to prevent formation of flammable concentrations of vapours and provided with effective interlocks to de-energize all electrical equipment not meeting the requirements for the classified area in case the ventilating equipment is inoperative shall be permitted to be classed as non-hazardous.
7) Notwithstanding the requirements of Subrule 1) b), where adequate mechanical ventilation with effective interlocks is provided at floor level and as otherwise shown in Diagram JD-6,
   a) the space within 1 m horizontally in any direction from the goods to be painted and such space extending to a height of 1 m above the goods to be painted shall be considered a Class I, Division 1 location; and

Appendix J

Appendix J
Rules and Notes to Rules for installations using the
Class and Division system of classification

C22.1-18

b) all space between a 1 m and a 1.5 m distance above the goods to be painted and all space within 6 m horizontally in any direction beyond the limits for a Class I, Division 1 location shall be considered a Class I, Division 2 location.

8) Notwithstanding the requirements of Subrule 2), where a baffle of sheet metal of not less than No. 18 MSG is installed vertically above the front face of an open-face spray booth to a height of 1 m or to the ceiling, whichever is less, and extending back on the side edges a distance of 1.5 m, the space behind this baffle shall be considered a non-hazardous location.

9) Notwithstanding the requirements of Subrule 3), where a baffle of sheet metal of not less than No. 18 MSG is installed vertically above an opening in a closed spray booth or room to a height of 1 m or to the ceiling, whichever is less, and extends horizontally a distance of 1 m beyond each side of the opening, the space behind the baffle shall be considered a non-hazardous location.

J20-304 Ventilation and spraying equipment interlock

The spraying equipment for a spray booth shall be interlocked with the spray booth ventilation system so that the spraying equipment is made inoperable when the ventilation system is not in operation.

J20-306 Wiring and equipment in hazardous areas

1) All electrical wiring and equipment within the hazardous areas as defined in Rule J20-302 shall conform to the requirements of Annex J18.

Δ 2) Unless designed for use in areas with readily ignitable deposits and in flammable vapour locations, no electrical equipment shall be installed or used where it may be subject to a hazardous accumulation of readily ignitable deposits or residue.

3) Illumination of readily ignitable areas through panels of glass or other transparent or translucent materials shall be permitted only where
   a) fixed lighting units are used as the source of illumination;
   b) the panel is non-combustible and effectively isolates the hazardous area from the area in which the lighting unit is located;
   c) the panel is of such a material or is protected so that breakage will be unlikely; and
   d) the arrangement is such that normal accumulations of hazardous residue on the surface of the panel will not be raised to a dangerous temperature by radiation or conduction from the source of illumination.

4) Portable electric lamps or other utilization equipment shall
   a) not be used within a hazardous area during operation of the finishing process; and
Δ   b) meet the requirements for the classified area when used during cleaning or repairing operations.

5) Notwithstanding Subrule 2),
   a) totally enclosed and gasketted lighting shall be permitted to be used on the ceiling of a spray room where adequate and positive mechanical ventilation is provided; and
   b) infrared paint drying units shall be permitted to be utilized in a spray room if the controls are interlocked with those of the spraying equipment so that both operations cannot be performed simultaneously, and if portable, the paint drying unit shall not be brought into the spray room until spraying operations have ceased.

J20-308 Fixed electrostatic equipment

Electrostatic spraying and detearing equipment shall conform to the following:

Δ a) no transformers, power packs, control apparatus, or other electrical portions of the equipment except high-voltage grids and their connections shall be installed in any of the hazardous areas defined in Rule J20-302, unless they meet the requirements for the classified area;
b) high-voltage grids or electrodes shall be
   i) located in suitable non-combustible booths or enclosures provided with adequate mechanical ventilation;

Appendix J
Rules and Notes to Rules for installations using the
Class and Division system of classification

C22.1-18

  ii) rigidly supported and of substantial construction; and

  iii) effectively insulated from ground by means of nonporous, non-combustible insulators;

c) high-voltage leads shall be

  i) effectively and permanently supported on suitable insulators;

  ii) effectively guarded against accidental contact or grounding; and

  iii) provided with automatic means for discharging any residual charge to ground when the supply voltage is interrupted;

d) where goods are being processed

  i) they shall be supported on conveyors in such a manner that the minimum clearance between goods and high-voltage grids or conductors cannot be less than twice the sparking distance; and

  ii) a conspicuous sign indicating the sparking distance shall be permanently posted near the equipment;

e) automatic controls shall be provided that will operate without time delay to disconnect the power supply and to signal the operator in case of

  i) stoppage of ventilating fans;

  ii) failure of ventilating equipment;

  iii) stoppage of the conveyor carrying goods through the high-voltage field;

  iv) occurrence of a ground or of an imminent ground at any point on the high-voltage system; or

  v) reduction of clearance below that specified in Item d); and

f) adequate fencing, railings, or guards that are electrically conducting and effectively bonded to ground shall be provided for safe isolation of the process, and signs shall be permanently posted designating the process as dangerous because of high voltage.

J20-310 Electrostatic hand spraying equipment

Electrostatic hand spray apparatus and devices used with them shall conform to the following:

a) the high-voltage circuits shall be intrinsically safe and not produce a spark of sufficient intensity to ignite any vapour-air mixtures, nor result in appreciable shock hazard upon coming in contact with a grounded object;

b) the electrostatically charged exposed elements of the hand gun shall be capable of being energized only by a switch that also controls the paint supply;

c) transformers, power packs, control apparatus, and all other electrical portions of the equipment, with the exception of the hand gun itself and its connections to the power supply, shall be located outside the hazardous area;

d) the handle of the spray gun shall be bonded to ground by a metallic connection and be constructed so that the operator in normal operating position is in intimate electrical contact with the handle in order to prevent buildup of a static charge on the operator's body;

e) all electrically conductive objects in the spraying area shall be bonded to ground and the equipment shall carry a prominent, permanently installed warning regarding the necessity for this bonding feature;

f) precautions shall be taken to ensure that objects being painted are maintained in metallic contact with the conveyor or other grounded support, and these precautions shall include the following:

  i) hooks shall be regularly cleaned;

  ii) areas of contact shall be sharp points or knife edges; and

  iii) points of support of the object shall be concealed from random spray where feasible, and where the objects being sprayed are supported from a conveyor, the point of attachment to the conveyor shall be located so as not to collect spray material during normal operation; and

g) the spraying operation shall take place within a spray area that is adequately ventilated to remove solvent vapours released from the operation, and the electrical equipment shall be interlocked

C22.1-18

Appendix J
Rules and Notes to Rules for installations using the
Class and Division system of classification

with the ventilation of the spraying area so that the equipment cannot be operated unless the ventilation system is in operation.

J20-312 Wiring and equipment above hazardous areas

1) All fixed wiring above hazardous areas shall conform to Section 12.

2) Equipment that may produce arcs, sparks, or particles of hot metal, such as lamps and lampholders for fixed lighting, cut-outs, switches, receptacles, motors, or other equipment having make-and-break or sliding contacts, where installed above a hazardous area or above an area where freshly finished goods are handled, shall be of the totally enclosed type or constructed to prevent the escape of sparks or hot metal particles.

J20-314 Bonding

All metal raceways and all non-current-carrying metal portions of fixed or portable equipment, regardless of voltage, shall be bonded to ground in accordance with Section 10.

Aircraft hangars

J20-400 Scope

Rules J20-402 to J20-422 apply to locations used for storage or servicing of aircraft in which gasoline, jet fuels, or other volatile flammable liquids, or flammable gases, are used, but shall not include those locations used exclusively for aircraft that have never contained such liquids or gases, or that have been drained and properly purged.

J20-402 Hazardous areas

1) Any pit or depression below the level of the hangar floor shall be considered a Class I, Division 1 location that shall extend up to the floor level.

2) The entire area of the hangar, including any adjacent and communicating areas not suitably cut off from the hangar, shall be considered a Class I, Division 2 location up to a level 450 mm above the floor.

3) The area within 1.5 m horizontally from aircraft power plants, aircraft fuel tanks, or aircraft structures containing fuel shall be considered a Class I, Division 2 location that extends upward from the floor to a level 1.5 m above the upper surface of wings and of engine enclosures.

4) Adjacent areas in which hazardous vapours are not likely to be released, such as stock rooms, electrical control rooms, and other similar locations, shall be permitted to be classed as non-hazardous when adequately ventilated and when effectively cut off from the hangar itself in accordance with Rule J18-058.

J20-404 Wiring and equipment in hazardous areas

1) All fixed and portable wiring and equipment that is or may be installed or operated within any of the hazardous locations defined in Rule J20-402 shall conform to the requirements of Annex J18.

2) All wiring installed in or under the hangar floor shall conform to the requirements for Class I, Division 1 locations.

3) Wiring systems installed in pits, or other spaces in or under the hangar floor, shall be provided with adequate drainage and shall not be placed in the same compartment with any other service except piped compressed air.

4) Attachment plugs and receptacles in hazardous locations shall be explosion-proof or shall be designed so that they cannot be energized while the connections are being made or broken.

J20-406 Wiring not within hazardous areas

1) All fixed wiring in a hangar not within a hazardous area as defined in Rule J20-402 shall be installed in metal raceways or shall be armoured cable, Type MI cable, aluminum-sheathed cable, or copper-sheathed cable, except that wiring in a non-hazardous location as set out in Rule J20-402 4) shall be permitted to be of any type recognized in Section 12 as suitable for the type of building and the occupancy.

Appendix J
Rules and Notes to Rules for installations using the
Class and Division system of classification

C22.1-18

2) For pendants, flexible cord of the hard-usage type and containing a separate bonding conductor shall be used.

Δ 3) For portable utilization equipment and lamps, flexible cord of the hard-usage type and containing a separate bonding conductor shall be used.

4) Suitable means shall be provided for maintaining continuity and adequacy of the bonding between the fixed wiring system and the non-current-carrying metal portions of pendant luminaires, portable lamps, and other portable utilization equipment.

J20-408 Equipment not within hazardous areas

1) In locations other than those described in Rule J20-402, equipment that is less than 3 m above wings and engine enclosures of aircraft and that may produce arcs, sparks, or particles of hot metal, such as lamps and lampholders or fixed lighting, cut-outs, switches, receptacles, charging panels, generators, motors, or other equipment having make-and-break or sliding contacts, shall be of a totally enclosed type or constructed to prevent the escape of sparks or hot metal particles, except that equipment in areas described in Rule J20-402 4) shall be permitted to be of the general-purpose type.

2) Lampholders of metal shell, fibre-lined types shall not be used for fixed lighting.

3) Portable lamps that are used within a hangar shall comply with Rule J18-118.

4) Portable utilization equipment that is, or may be, used within a hangar shall be of a type suitable for use in Class I, Division 2 locations.

J20-410 Stanchions, rostrums, and docks

1) Electric wiring, outlets, and equipment, including lamps on, or attached to, stanchions, rostrums, or docks that are located, or likely to be located, in a hazardous area as defined in Rule J20-402 3), shall conform to the requirements for Class I, Division 2 locations.

2) Where stanchions, rostrums, and docks are not located, or are not likely to be located, in a hazardous area as defined in Rule J20-402 3), wiring and equipment shall conform to Rules J20-406 and J20-408, except for the following:
   a) receptacles and attachment plugs shall be of the locking type that will not break apart readily; and
   b) wiring and equipment not more than 450 mm above the floor in any position shall conform to Subrule 1).

3) Mobile stanchions with electrical equipment conforming to Subrule 2) shall carry at least one permanently affixed warning sign stating that the stanchions are to be kept 1.5 m clear of aircraft engines and fuel tank areas.

J20-412 Sealing

1) Seals shall be installed in accordance with Annex J18 and shall apply to horizontal as well as to vertical boundaries of the defined hazardous areas.

2) Raceways embedded in a masonry floor or buried beneath a floor shall be considered to be within the hazardous area above the floor when any connections or extensions lead into or through the hazardous area.

J20-414 Aircraft electrical systems

Aircraft electrical systems shall be de-energized when the aircraft is stored in a hangar and, whenever possible, while the aircraft is undergoing maintenance.

J20-416 Aircraft battery charging and equipment

1) Aircraft batteries shall not be charged when installed in an aircraft located inside or partially inside a hangar.

2) Battery chargers and their control equipment shall not be located or operated within any of the hazardous areas defined in Rule J20-402 but shall be permitted to be located or operated in a separate building or in an area complying with Rule J20-402 4).

Appendix J

C22.1-18

Appendix J
Rules and Notes to Rules for installations using the
Class and Division system of classification

3) Mobile chargers shall carry at least one permanently affixed warning sign stating that the chargers must be kept 1.5 m clear of aircraft engines and fuel tank areas.

4) Tables, racks, trays, and wiring shall not be located within a hazardous area and shall conform to the provisions of Section 26 pertaining to storage batteries.

J20-418 External power sources for energizing aircraft

1) Aircraft energizers shall be designed and mounted so that all electrical equipment and fixed wiring will be at least 450 mm above floor level and shall not be operated in a hazardous area as defined in Rule J20-402 3).

2) Mobile energizers shall carry at least one permanently affixed sign stating that the energizer be kept 1.5 m clear of aircraft engines and fuel tank areas.

3) Aircraft energizers shall be equipped with polarized external power plugs and with automatic controls to isolate the ground power unit electrically from the aircraft in case excessive voltage is generated by the ground power unit.

4) Flexible cords for aircraft energizers and ground support equipment shall be of the extra-hard-usage type and shall include a bonding conductor.

J20-420 Mobile servicing equipment with electrical components

1) Mobile servicing equipment, such as vacuum cleaners, air compressors, and air movers, etc., having electrical wiring and equipment not suitable for Class I, Division 2 locations shall
   a) be designed and mounted so that all such wiring and equipment will be at least 450 mm above the floor;
   b) not be operated within the hazardous areas defined in Rule J20-402 3); and
   c) carry at least one permanently affixed warning sign stating that the equipment be kept 1.5 m clear of aircraft engines and fuel tank areas.

2) Flexible cords used for mobile equipment shall be of the extra-hard-usage type and shall include a bonding conductor.

3) Attachment plugs and receptacles shall provide for the connection of the bonding conductor to the raceway system.

4) Equipment shall not be operated in areas where maintenance operations likely to release hazardous vapours are in progress, unless the equipment is at least suitable for use in a Class I, Division 2 location.

J20-422 Bonding

All metal raceways and all non-current-carrying metal portions of fixed or portable equipment, regardless of voltage, shall be bonded to ground in accordance with Section 10.

C22.1-18

Appendix J
Rules and Notes to Rules for installations using the
Class and Division system of classification

Annex JB
Notes to Rules for Annexes J18 and J20

Δ **Rule J18-000**

Through the exercise of ingenuity in the layout of electrical installations for hazardous locations, it is frequently possible to locate much of the equipment in a reduced level of classification or in a non-hazardous area and thus to reduce the amount of special equipment required.

To assist users in the proper design and selection of equipment for electrical installations in hazardous locations, numerous reference documents are available. See Table B18-1 for a list of the commonly referenced documents.

Rule J18-002

Cable seal — a seal that is designed to prevent the escape of flames from an explosion-proof enclosure. Because cables are not designed to withstand the pressures of an explosion, transmission of an explosion into a cable could result in ignition of gases or vapours in the area outside the enclosure.

Conduit seal — a seal that is designed to prevent the passage of flames from one portion of the electrical installation to another through the conduit system and to minimize the passage of gases or vapours at atmospheric pressure. Unless specifically designed for the purpose, conduit seals are not intended to prevent the passage of fluids at a continuous pressure differential across the seal. Even at differences in pressure across the seal equivalent to a few inches of water, there may be passage of gas or vapour through the seal and/or through the conductors passing through the seal. Where conduit seals are exposed to continuous pressure, there may be a danger of transmission of flammable fluids to "safe areas" resulting in fire or explosions.

Primary seal — a seal that is typically a part of electrical devices such as pressure-, temperature-, or flow-measuring devices and devices (such as canned pumps) in which the electrical connections are immersed in the process fluids.

Secondary seal — a seal that is designed to prevent flammable process fluids from entering the electrical wiring system upon failure of a primary seal. These devices typically prevent passage of fluids at process pressure by a combination of sealing and pressure relief.

Δ **Rules J18-004, J18-006, and J18-008**

Reference material for area classification is listed in Table B18-1.

See also the Note to Rule J18-062 in this Annex.

Δ **Rule J18-004**
Division 1 area classifications
Typical situations leading to a Division 1 area classification are
a) the interiors of storage tanks that are vented to atmosphere and that contain flammable liquids stored above their flash point;
b) enclosed sumps containing flammable liquids stored above their flash point during normal operation;
c) the area immediately around atmospheric vents;
d) inadequately ventilated buildings or enclosures; and
e) adequately ventilated buildings or enclosures, such as remote unattended and unmonitored facilities, that have insufficient means of limiting the duration of explosive gas atmospheres when they do occur.

© 2018 Canadian Standards Association

Appendix J

C22.1-18

Appendix J
Rules and Notes to Rules for installations using the
Class and Division system of classification

Division 2 area classifications

Typical situations leading to a Division 2 area classification are

a) areas where flammable volatile liquids, flammable gases, or vapours are handled, processed, or used, but in which liquids, gases, or vapours are normally confined within closed containers or closed systems from which they can escape only as a result of accidental rupture or breakdown of the containers or systems or the abnormal operation of the equipment by which the liquids or gases are handled, processed, or used;

b) adequately ventilated buildings that have means of ensuring that the length of time during which abnormal operation resulting in the occurrence of explosive gas atmospheres can exist will be limited to a "short time"; and

c) most outdoor areas except those around open vents, or open vessels or sumps containing flammable liquids.

API RP 500 defines "adequate ventilation" as "ventilation (natural or artificial) that is sufficient to prevent the accumulation of significant quantities of vapour-air or gas-air mixtures in concentrations above 25% of their lower flammable limit, LFL". Annex B of API RP 500 outlines a method for calculating the ventilation requirements for enclosed areas based on fugitive emissions.

Industry documents such as API RP 505 provide guidance on how industry interprets a "short time".

Flammable mists may form or be present at the same time as flammable gas or vapour. In such cases, the strict application of the details in the classification Standards referenced might not be appropriate. Flammable mists can also form when liquids not considered to be a hazard due to their high flash point are released under pressure. In these cases, the classifications and details in the Standards referenced do not apply. Information on flammable mists can be found in industry Standards such as IEC 60079-10-1.

Rule J18-006

Class II, Division 1 locations usually include the working areas of grain-handling and storage plants; rooms containing grinders or pulverizers, cleaners, graders, scalpers, open conveyors or spouts, open bins or hoppers, mixers or blenders, automatic or hopper scales, packing machinery, elevator heads and boots, stock distributors, dust and stock collectors (except all-metal collectors vented to the outside), and all similar dust-producing machinery and equipment in grain processing plants, starch plants, sugar pulverizing plants, malting plants, hay grinding plants, and other occupancies of similar nature; coal pulverizing plants (except where the pulverizing equipment is essentially dust-tight); all working areas where metal dusts and powders are produced, processed, handled, packed, or stored (except in tight containers); and all other similar locations where combustible dust may, under normal operating conditions, be present in the air in quantities sufficient to produce explosive or ignitable mixtures.

Combustible dusts that are electrically non-conducting will include dusts produced in the handling and processing of grain and grain products, pulverized sugar and cocoa, dried egg and milk powders, pulverized spices, starch and pastes, potato and wood flour, oil meal from beans and seeds, dried hay, and other organic materials that may produce combustible dusts when processed or handled. Only Group E dusts are considered electrically conductive for the purposes of classification. Metallic dusts of magnesium, aluminum, and aluminum bronze are particularly hazardous, and every precaution should be taken to avoid ignition and explosion.

Class II, Division 2 locations include those in which dangerous concentrations of suspended dust are not likely, but where dust accumulation might form on, in, or in the vicinity of electrical equipment, and include rooms and areas containing only closed spouting and conveyors, closed bins or hoppers, or machines and equipment from which appreciable quantities of dust might escape only under abnormal conditions; rooms or areas adjacent to Class II, Division 1 locations and into which explosive or ignitable concentrations of suspended dust might be communicated only under abnormal operating conditions; rooms or areas where the formulation of explosive or ignitable concentrations of suspended dust is

Appendix J
Rules and Notes to Rules for installations using the
Class and Division system of classification

C22.1-18

prevented by the operation of effective dust control equipment; warehouses and shipping rooms in which dust-producing materials are stored or handled only in bags or containers; and other similar locations.

There are many dusts, such as fine sulphur dust, that cannot be equated specifically to dusts mentioned above, and in a number of cases further information may be obtained by reference to Standards included in the NFPA *National Fire Codes*; for example, NFPA 655 gives information on prevention of sulphur fires and explosions and makes reference to electrical wiring and equipment.

Rule J18-008

Class III, Division 1 locations include parts of rayon, cotton, and other textile mills; combustible fibre manufacturing and processing plants; cotton gins and cotton-seed mills; flax processing plants; clothing manufacturing plants; woodworking plants; and establishments and industries involving similar hazardous processes or conditions.

Readily ignitable fibres and flyings include rayon, cotton (including cotton linters and cotton waste), sisal or henequen, istle, jute, hemp, tow, cocoa fibre, oakum, baled waste kapok, Spanish moss, excelsior, and other materials of similar nature.

Rule J18-010

Maintaining electrical installation safety in hazardous locations is dependent on a regimen of regular maintenance that will ensure that the electrical installation continues to provide safety throughout its life. Maintenance personnel are cautioned that modifications to original equipment or substitution of original components may void certification. In addition to the manufacturer's instructions, the following documents may be used to guide owners and operators of hazardous locations in developing appropriate maintenance procedures:

a)   IEC 60079-17, *Explosive atmospheres — Part 17: Electrical installations inspection and maintenance*;

b)   IEC 60300 series of Standards, *Dependability management*;

c)   IEEE 902, *IEEE Guide for Maintenance, Operation, and Safety of Industrial and Commercial Power Systems*; and

d)   NFPA 70B, *Recommended Practice for Electrical Equipment Maintenance*.

Δ   **Rules J18-050 and J18-064**

Table 18 provides a summary of what equipment types are suitable for installation in the various hazardous locations.

It should be noted that battery-operated and self-generating equipment is not excluded from the Rules of Annex J18, regardless of the voltage involved. Examples of such equipment are flashlights, transceivers, paging receivers, tape recorders, combustion gas detectors, vibration monitors, tachometers, battery- or voice-powered telephones, and portable test equipment that may be carried into or located within a hazardous area. Such equipment may be eligible for approval under CAN/CSA-C22.2 No. 157.

Where general-purpose enclosures are used for such equipment and the Rules of Annex J18 require the equipment to be specifically approved for the hazardous location, the electrical equipment is required to be approved for the location as intrinsically safe in accordance with Rule J18-064 and marked in accordance with Rule J18-052.

In cases where the Rules of Annex J18 permit general-purpose enclosures with the qualification that acceptable non-incendive circuits be incorporated, the electrical equipment should be approved as such and marked in accordance with Rule J18-052.

Appendix J

Appendix J
Rules and Notes to Rules for installations using the
Class and Division system of classification

C22.1-18

Rule J18-050 2) a)
Information on classification of areas (as well as ventilation requirements) in plants engaged in the generation and compression of acetylene and in the charging of acetylene cylinders may be found in NFPA 51A.

Rule J18-050 2) d)
Information on classification of areas for refrigeration systems utilizing flammable gases (including ammonia) may be found in CSA B52.

Δ ### Rule J18-052
Electrical equipment certified for Class I, II, or III hazardous locations has the following markings:
- For Class I or II, Division 1 or 2 locations, the equipment is marked with the Class and Group described in Rules J18-050 and J18-052 or with the Class and specific gas or vapour for which it is certified.
- For Class I, Division 2 only, the equipment may be marked as Class I, Division 2.
- For Class II and III locations, the equipment is marked as Class II and/or III, and for Class II, also for the group or specific dust for which it is certified.
- For Class I or II locations, the equipment is marked with the maximum surface temperature in degrees Celsius or one of the temperature codes given in Table JB-1.

Table JB-1
Maximum surface temperature ratings for equipment suitable for
Class I or Class II locations

Temperature code	Maximum surface temperature, °C
T1	450
T2	300
(T2A)	280
(T2B)	260
(T2C)	230
(T2D)	215
T3	200
(T3A)	180
(T3B)	165
(T3C)	160
T4	135
(T4A)	120
T5	100
T6	85

Note: *The temperature codes in parentheses are for Canada only; they are not included in the IEC Standards.*

The maximum surface temperature rating of equipment is based on a 40 °C ambient temperature, except that if the equipment is rated for a higher ambient temperature, it is marked as such.

Equipment marked for Class I but not marked with a Division is suitable for both Divisions 1 and 2.

Appendix J
Rules and Notes to Rules for installations using the
Class and Division system of classification

C22.1-18

Where equipment is certified to the 60079 series of Standards, it will be marked with one or more "Types of Protection", as indicated in Table 18.

The mark includes the letters "Ex" to indicate that the equipment is "explosion protected", followed by one or more of the symbols.

Where equipment uses more than one type of protection, each type of protection is shown. For example, equipment suitable for Zone 1 with flameproof "d" components and increased safety "e" terminals is marked with "Ex db eb". Refer to Table 18, and the Note to Rule 18-052 in Appendix B for more information.

Exposure of hazardous locations equipment to ambient temperatures that are outside the intended ambient temperature range of the equipment can affect the explosion protection features of such equipment. Some equipment may be marked with a safe ambient temperature range in accordance with the relevant *Canadian Electrical Code, Part II* product Standards, but other equipment may not have such markings.

Hazardous locations equipment subjected to ambient temperature conditions exceeding the design maximum ambient temperature can result in the equipment operating at a temperature in excess of the maximum (surface) temperature marked on the nameplate of the equipment, possibly exceeding maximum internal operating temperature limits as well as the temperature limits stated in Rule 18-054.

Hazardous locations equipment subjected to ambient temperature conditions that are colder than the design low ambient temperature can result in the equipment being subjected to excessive explosion pressures due to higher gas densities at low temperatures. Cold temperatures also affect the brittleness of materials, which can also compromise the explosion protection integrity of the equipment.

Note that ambient temperatures marked on equipment apply to explosion protection safety only. Equipment performance is not considered.

Where an ambient temperature range is not indicated on equipment, the default temperatures are as follows:
a)   for products marked "Ex", the design ambient temperature range is (−20 °C ≤ ambient ≤ 40 °C); and
b)   for products marked Class I, II, or III, Division 1 or 2, the design ambient temperature range is (−50 °C ≤ ambient ≤ 40 °C).

Δ   **Rules J18-052, J18-100, and J18-150**
The 2011 edition of CAN/CSA-C22.2 No. 60079-0 [adopted IEC 60079-0 (fifth edition, 2007-10)] introduces "equipment protection levels" (EPLs) as a required marking on hazardous location electrical equipment certified to the IEC 60079 series of Standards. This marking will appear on new electrical equipment that is designed in accordance with the adopted 60079 series of Standards. For older equipment, in stock or in the field, that does not include the EPL marking, suitability for the intended zone will continue to be determined by the types of protection. EPLs will enable users to identify the zone(s) in which the IEC 60079 type of hazardous location electrical equipment can be used, without having to identify the zone by the types of protection used.

EPLs provide an indication of the suitability of electrical equipment for each zone. Further information on EPLs can be found in CAN/CSA-C22.2 No. 60079-0. Table JB-2 shows the acceptable EPLs for Divisions 1 and 2.

Appendix J

C22.1-18

Appendix J
Rules and Notes to Rules for installations using the
Class and Division system of classification

Table JB-2
Acceptable equipment protection levels for Divisions 1 and 2

Class I Division	Equipment protection level
Division 1	Ga
Division 2	Ga, Gb, or Gc

Δ **Rules J18-052 and J18-054**

Some equipment permitted for use in Division 2 hazardous locations is not marked to indicate the class and group because it is not specifically designed for hazardous locations [e.g., motors and generators for Class I, Division 2 that do not incorporate spark-producing components or integral resistance devices. See Rule J18-150 2) e)].

Table JB-3
Temperature and gas groups

Atmosphere		CAS reference number	Relative vapour density (air = 1)	Flash point, °C	Autoignition temperature, °C	Division-based gas group	Zone-based gas group
Typical North American name	**Synonyms [see Note 1)]**						
acetylene	ethine ethyne	74-86-2	0.90	gas	305	A	IIC
butadiene	1,3-butadiene biethylene bivinyl divinyl erythrene vinylethylene	106-99-0	1.87	gas	420	B	IIB
hydrogen		1333-74-0	0.07	gas	560	B	IIC
propylene oxide	2-methyloxirane 1,2-epoxypropane	75-56-9	2.00	−37	430	B	IIB
acetaldehyde	ethanal acetic aldehyde ethyl aldehyde	75-07-0	1.52	−38	155	C	IIA
cyclopropane	trimethylene	75-19-4	1.45	gas	500	D	IIA
diethyl ether	1,1′-oxybisethane diethyl oxide ethyl ether ethyl oxide ether	60-29-7	2.55	− 45	175	C	IIB
ethylene	ethene	74-85-1	0.97	gas	440	C	IIB
hydrogen sulphide	hydrosulfuric acid sewer gas sulfuretted hydrogen	7783-06-4	1.19	gas	260	C	IIB
unsymmetrical dimethyl hydrazine	N,N-Dimethyl-hydrazine UDMH 1,1-dimethyl hydrazine	57-14-7	2.07	−18	240	C	IIB
acetone	2-propanone dimethyl ketone	67-64-1	2.00	< −20	539	D	IIA

(Continued)

C22.1-18

Appendix J
Rules and Notes to Rules for installations using the
Class and Division system of classification

Table JB-3 (Continued)

Atmosphere		CAS reference number	Relative vapour density (air = 1)	Flash point, °C	Autoignition temperature, °C	Division-based gas group	Zone-based gas group
Typical North American name	Synonyms [see Note 1)]						
acrylonitrile	2-propenenitrile cyanoethylene propenenitrile vinyl cyanide VCN	107-13-1	1.83	−5	480	D	IIB
alcohol (see ethanol)							
ammonia	anhydrous ammonia	7664-41-7	0.59	gas	630	D	IIA
benzene	phenyl hydride	71-43-2	2.70	−11	498	D	IIA
benzine (see petroleum naphtha)							
benzol (see benzene)							
butane	butyl hydride diethyl methylethylmethane	106-97-8	2.05	gas	372	D	IIA
1-butanol	butan-1-ol n-Butyl alcohol n-Butanol Butyl alcohol Hydroxybutane n-Propyl carbinol	71-36-3	2.55	36	343	D	IIA
2-butanol	butan-2-ol sec-Butyl alcohol Butylene hydrate 2-Hydroxybutane Methyl ethyl carbinol	78-92-2	2.55	36	406	D	IIA
butyl acetate	Acetic acid n-butyl ester n-Butyl ester of acetic acid Butyl ethanoate	123-86-4	4.01	22	390	D	IIA
isobutyl acetate		110-19-0		18	421 [Note 2)]	D	IIA
ethane		74-84-0	1.04	−29	515	D	IIA
ethanol	ethyl alcohol alcohol	64-17-5	1.59	13	400	D	IIB
ethyl acetate	Acetic acid ethyl ester Ethyl ethanoate	141-78-6	3.04	−4	470	D	IIA
ethylene dichloride	1,2-Dichloroethane Ethylene chloride	107-06-2	3.42	13	438	D	IIA
gasoline	motor fuel petrol	86290-81-5, 8006-61-9 [Note 4)]	3.0	−46	280	D	IIA
heptanes (mixed isomers)	n-heptane	142-82-5	3.46	−7	204	D	IIA
hexanes (mixed isomers)	n-hexane	110-54-3	2.97	−22	225	D	IIA

(Continued)

C22.1-18

Appendix J
Rules and Notes to Rules for installations using the
Class and Division system of classification

Table JB-3 (Continued)

Atmosphere		CAS reference number	Relative vapour density (air = 1)	Flash point, °C	Autoignition temperature, °C	Division-based gas group	Zone-based gas group
Typical North American name	**Synonyms [see Note 1)]**						
isoprene		78-79-5	2.35	−54	220 [Note 2)]	D	IIA
methane	natural gas [(Note 3)]	74-82-8	0.55	gas	600	D	IIA
methanol	methyl alcohol carbinol	67-56-1	1.11	9	440	D	IIA
isoamyl alcohol	3-methylbutan-1-ol	123-51-3	3.03	42	339	D	IIA
methyl ethyl ketone	butanone 2-butanone ethyl methyl ketone methyl acetone	78-93-3	2.48	−10	404	D	IIB
methyl isobutyl ketone	4-methylpentan-2-one hexone isopropylacetone	108-10-1	3.45	16	475	D	IIA
isobutyl alcohol	iso-butanol iso-propylcarbinol iso-butyl alcohol	78-83-1	2.55	28	408	D	IIA
tertiary butyl alcohol	2-methyl-2-propanol tert-butanol	75-65-0	2.6	11	478 [Note 2)]	D	IIA
naphtha (see petroleum naphtha)							
natural gas (see methane)							
petroleum naphtha	naphtha	64742-95-6			290 [Note 2)]	D	IIA
octanes	n-octane	111-65-9	3.93	13	206	D	IIA
pentanes (mixed isomers)	n-pentane	109-66-0	2.48	−40	243	D	IIA
1-pentanol	pentan-1-ol n-amyl alcohol n-butyl carbinol n-pentyl alcohol n-pentanol	71-41-0	3.03	42	320	D	IIA
propane	dimethyl methane propyl hydride	74-98-6	1.56	gas	450	D	IIA
propyl alcohol	1-propanol propan-1-ol	71-23-8	2.07	15	385	D	IIB
isopropyl alcohol	propan-2-ol 2-propanol dimethyl carbinol isopropanol	67-63-0	2.07	12	399	D	IIA
propene	methylethylene propylene	115-07-1	1.50	gas	455	D	IIA
styrene	ethenylbenzene vinylbenzene phenylethylene	100-42-5	3.6	30	490	D	IIA

(Continued)

C22.1-18

Appendix J
Rules and Notes to Rules for installations using the
Class and Division system of classification

Table JB-3 (Concluded)

Atmosphere		CAS reference number	Relative vapour density (air = 1)	Flash point, °C	Autoignition temperature, °C	Division-based gas group	Zone-based gas group
Typical North American name	Synonyms [see Note 1)]						
	styrol						
toluene	methyl benzene methyl benzol phenyl methane	108-88-3	3.2	4	530	D	IIA
vinyl acetate	acetic acid ethenyl ester 1-acetoxyethylene	108-05-4	3.0	−7	385	D	IIA
vinyl chloride	chloroethylene chloroethane vinyl chloride	75-01-4	2.15	gas	415	D	IIA
xylenes	1,4-dimethyl benzene p-xylene p-Xyol	106-42-3	3.66	25	535	D	IIA

Notes:

1) *Most of the values in this Table have been obtained from IEC 60079-20-1,* Explosive atmospheres — Part 20-1: Material characteristics for gas and vapour classification — Test methods and data, *Edition 1.0, 2010-01. In many cases, the name used in the IEC Standard differs from the name typically used in North America for the same substance. In fact, chemicals may have several different names. The CAS numbering system referenced in this table is a well-known method of uniquely identifying chemicals and is a required feature of MSDS documentation. Further information on the CAS numbering system may be found at www.cas.org.*

2) *This substance is not listed in IEC 60079-20-1.*

3) *Natural gas is classified as Group IIA, provided that it does not contain more than 25% (by volume) of hydrogen.*

4) *Gasoline is identified under several CAS numbers.*

△ **Rules J18-054 and J18-150**

Equipment of the heat-producing type is currently required by product Standards to have a temperature code (T-Code) marking if its temperature exceeds 100 °C. However, for equipment manufactured prior to the T-Code requirement and motors applied in accordance with Rule J18-150, there may be no such marking. Therefore, the suitability of older hazardous locations equipment of the heat-producing type and motors applied in accordance with Rule J18-150 should be reviewed prior to being installed in a hazardous location to ensure compliance with Rule J18-054. For the purpose of these Rules, equipment such as boxes, terminals, fittings, and resistance temperature detectors (RTDs) are not considered to be heat-producing devices.

Determination of the maximum surface temperatures for Rule J18-054 is set by the area classification for the location in which the equipment is installed. This is normally based on the minimum ignition temperature of the flammable or combustible substances that may be released into the atmosphere in that location. The temperature markings on electrical equipment are in accordance with the requirements in the *Canadian Electrical Code, Part II* product Standards, which set the specifications determining where surface temperature measurements are taken. For equipment suitable for Class I areas, this applies to both external and, where gases can reach an internal surface, internal temperatures. For equipment suitable for Class II and III areas, this applies to external surfaces only. The design of equipment for explosive dust atmospheres, with gasketing and other features to prevent ingress of dusts, is such that the only concern for ignition is on the exterior of the equipment. Therefore, the maximum surface temperature requirement for dusts applies to the external surfaces of the equipment only.

Appendix J

C22.1-18

Appendix J
Rules and Notes to Rules for installations using the
Class and Division system of classification

Rule J18-060

For the purpose of this Rule, metal-covered cable includes a cable with a metal sheath or with a metal armour of the interlocking type, the insulated conductor type, or the flat-tape type or with metal shielding.

Rule J18-060 1)

Suitable lightning protective devices should include primary devices and also secondary devices if overhead secondary lines exceed 90 m in length or if the secondary is ungrounded.

Interconnection of all grounds should include grounds for primary and secondary lightning protective devices, secondary system grounds, if any, and grounds of conduit and equipment of the interior wiring system.

Rule J18-060 2) b)

Where single-conductor metal-covered or armoured cables with jackets are used in hazardous locations, the armour must be grounded in only the hazardous location to prevent circulating currents. As a result, there will be a standing voltage on the metal covering in the non-hazardous location area. There is, therefore, a need to properly isolate the armour in the non-hazardous area to ensure that circulating currents will not occur.

Rule J18-062

To meet the intent of this Rule for effectively maintaining a protective gas pressure, the following references for pressurization are recommended:

a)   CAN/CSA-C22.2 No. 60079-2, *Explosive atmospheres — Part 2: Equipment protection by pressurized enclosure "p"*;

b)   NFPA 496, *Standard for Purged and Pressurized Enclosures for Electrical Equipment*; and

c)   IEC 60079-13, *Explosive atmospheres — Part 13: Equipment protection by pressurized room "p"*.

Δ   Rule J18-064

See the Note to Rules J18-050 and J18-064.

When reference is made to intrinsically safe systems, including equipment, wiring, and installation, the term used is "intrinsically safe". When reference is made to product certification and markings, the terms used are

a)   intrinsic safety "ia", "ib", or "ic" for Zone hazardous locations; or

b)   intrinsically safe "Exi", "Exia", "Intrinsically Safe", "IS", or "I.S." for Class I, II, or III hazardous locations.

Non-incendive terminology may be used to describe non-incendive components, circuits, equipment, and wiring. Non-incendive components and circuits are typically integral to non-incendive equipment, which is designed to prevent the ignition of the flammable atmospheres under normal operation. Non-incendive components are used where the energy in the circuit is ignition capable but ignition of the flammable atmosphere is prevented by one or more of the following technologies:

a)   incorporating non-ignition-capable components;

b)   hermetically sealing ignition-capable components; and

c)   incorporating enclosed break device technology similar in design to a flameproof enclosure.

Non-incendive circuits within the equipment prevent the ignition of the flammable atmosphere by limiting the energy within the circuit to a level below the energy required to ignite a flammable material. Non-incendive equipment may also be designated to have non-incendive wiring circuits. Non-incendive wiring circuits are designed to be connected to other equipment or to associated non-incendive wiring apparatus as specified by the manufacturer's control drawing and the descriptive system document. A non-incendive wiring circuit is considered to provide the same level of protection as a field wiring circuit with methods of protection "nL" or "ic". Non-incendive equipment that does not have designated non-incendive wiring circuits should be installed using the standard wiring methods

Appendix J
Rules and Notes to Rules for installations using the
Class and Division system of classification

C22.1-18

and sealing for the applicable location. For additional information related to the application of non-incendive components, circuits, equipment, and wiring, refer to CSA C22.2 No. 213.

Δ **Rule J18-064 1) and 2)**

The descriptive system document is necessary to ensure that all aspects of the intrinsically safe or non-incendive wiring installation are addressed and documented. See Appendix F for additional information regarding descriptive system documents.

Δ **Rule J18-066**

The definition of lower and upper explosive limits (LELs and UELs) in Rule J18-002 has been changed to lower and upper flammable limits (LFLs and UFLs) and, therefore, has been revised in this Rule. Flammable limits are material properties that are covered in documents such as IEC 60079-20-1. Explosive limits depend on installation factors such as enclosure geometry or igniter location and generally fall within a narrower range than flammable limits. Therefore, flammable limits are now used because they are fixed values, define a wider range than explosive limits, and are harmonized with IEC area classification Standards.

Note: *Combustible gas detectors read LFL even though the scale may be marked as LEL.*

It is intended that this Rule be used only where suitable equipment, certified for use in the hazardous location, is not available. For example, Class I, Division 1 ignition systems for internal combustion engines are not available; only Class I, Division 2 ignition systems are available. Therefore, ignition systems rated for Class I, Division 2 are currently the only hazardous location ignition systems that are available and could possibly be used in Class I, Division 1 locations.

In many situations, proper area classification eliminates the need to use this Rule. This Rule should not be used to compensate for improper area classification.

When this Rule is used, the gas detection system should consist of an adequate number of sensors to ensure the sensing of flammable gases or vapours in all areas where they may accumulate.

Electrical equipment suitable for non-hazardous locations and having unprotected arcing, sparking, or heat-producing components must not be installed in a Division 2 location. Arcing, sparking, or heat-producing components may be protected by encapsulating, hermetically sealing, or sealing by other means such as restricted breathing.

Before applying this Rule, the user should fully understand the risks associated with such an installation. When this Rule is being applied, it remains the responsibility of the owner of the facility, or agents of the owner, to ensure that the resulting installation is safe. Simply complying with the requirements of this Rule may not ensure a safe installation in all situations.

Rule J18-068

ANSI/ISA 12.27.01 provides construction, performance, and marking requirements for the process seals incorporated into process-connected electrical equipment. Equipment containing a primary seal that complies with this Standard is eligible to include either the "Single Seal" or "Dual Seal" designation in the nameplate markings. These markings indicate that the electrical equipment is designed to prevent the migration of flammable fluid through the equipment into the wiring system when the equipment is operated at or lower than its rated pressure. Devices certified as conforming to ANSI/ISA 12.27.01 and marked either "Single Seal" or "Dual Seal" meet the intent of Subrule 1) a).

Where devices containing primary seals are not marked to indicate conformance with ANSI/ISA 12.27.01, other means may be used to prevent fluid migration though the wiring system. This may include the use of suitable barriers located between the primary seal and the wiring system, such as secondary seals or short lengths of mineral-insulated (MI) cable. Where secondary seals are installed, examples of design features that make the occurrence of primary seal failure obvious are vents, drains, visible rupture or leakage, audible whistles, or electronic monitoring. The intent of making the primary

C22.1-18

Appendix J
Rules and Notes to Rules for installations using the
Class and Division system of classification

seal failure obvious is to prevent continuous pressure on the secondary seal and the possibility of an eventual secondary seal failure, as well as to protect personnel working on the device. Alternatively, where means to relieve pressure on a secondary seal is not provided, a cautionary label should be provided to warn personnel that the enclosure may contain flammable fluid under pressure.

Engineering considerations may lead to the conclusion that the probability of leakage from a specific installation will be negligible. Acceptable factors such as an extensive history of safe operation with similar installations, or the use of a primary seal with a pressure rating well in excess of the maximum process operating pressure, may be considered.

Δ **Rule J18-100**
Electrical equipment marked with a type of protection (e.g., flameproof "d") is not suitable for use in Class I, Division 1 locations unless also marked with the "Class" of location.

Δ **Rules J18-106, J18-108, J18-152, J18-204 1) b), J18-254 1) b), J18-304, and J18-354**
Cables meeting the requirements of CSA C22.2 No. 174 are acceptable for use in hazardous locations and are marked "HL".

Cables marked for use in hazardous locations are suitable for all locations, but the termination fittings must be designed for the particular hazardous location. For example, in a Class I, Zone 1 or 2 hazardous location, a termination fitting entering an enclosure required to be explosion-proof or flameproof must be a sealing-type termination fitting, whereas a termination fitting entering an enclosure not required to be explosion-proof or flameproof in a Class I, Zone 2 hazardous location is not required to be marked for use in Class I, Zone 2 hazardous areas. It is intended that termination fittings in all hazardous areas be compatible with the degree of protection and the explosion protection provided by the enclosure they enter. In general, the minimum requirement will be weatherproof termination fittings.

For the application of Annex J18, rigid metal couplings are not considered fittings. The CSA Standard for rigid metal conduit and couplings is CSA C22.2 No. 45.1. This Standard does not require hazardous location markings. Certified rigid metal conduit and couplings are suitable for hazardous locations without specific area classification marking.

Rule J18-106 3)
Where tapered threads are used, the requirement to have five fully engaged threads (i.e., threads done up tight) is critical for three reasons:
a) When the threads are not fully engaged, the flame path is compromised, making it possible for an explosion occurring within the conduit system to be transmitted to the area outside the conduit.
b) If there are not five fully engaged threads, the flame path may be too short to cool the gases resulting from an internal explosion to a temperature below that which could ignite gas in the surrounding area.
c) Because the conduit forms a bonding path to ground, not making the conduit tight will introduce resistance into the flame path and, if a fault occurs, arcing at the interface may result.

While it may not always be possible to install certain fittings without backing off, it is important to ensure that the connection is as tight as possible. Properly made conduit connections are critical to the safety of hazardous location wiring systems.

Δ **Rules J18-108 and J18-154**
Seals are provided in conduit or cable systems to prevent the passage of gases, vapours, or flames from one portion of the electrical installation to another through the system.

Passage of gases, vapours, or flames through mineral-insulated cable is inherently prevented by the construction of the cable, but sealing compound is used in cable glands to exclude moisture and other fluids from the cable insulation and is required to be of a type intended for the conditions of use.

C22.1-18

Appendix J
Rules and Notes to Rules for installations using the
Class and Division system of classification

Sealing of conductors in the conduit, or in most cables, requires that the sealing compound completely surround each individual insulated conductor to ensure that the seal performs its intended function. In certain constructions of cables, specifically those that contain bundles of shielded pairs, triads, or quads, removal of the shielding or overall covering from the bundles negates the purpose for which the shielding was provided. Testing of this type of cable now includes testing for flame propagation along the length of the individual subassemblies of the cable.

The letters A, B, C, or D, or a combination of them, may be added to signify the group(s) for which the cable has been tested, for example,

a)   the marking "HL-CD" indicates that the cable has been tested for flame propagation for gas groups C and D; and

b)   the marking "TC-BCD" indicates that the cable has been tested for flame propagation for gas groups B, C, and D.

See also Table JB-3.

Seals are not required for intrinsically safe equipment and wiring systems to prevent the transmission of an explosion; however, the use of seals for conduit and cable systems is still necessary to prevent the migration of the flammable atmosphere from one zone of a hazardous location to another or from a hazardous to non-hazardous location.

Rule J18-108 1) d)

Seals are required on conduit systems where a conduit enters an enclosure not required to be explosion-proof or flameproof (typically a type "e" enclosure) because the conduit system is required to be maintained as an explosion-proof or flameproof wiring system in a Class I, Zone 1 hazardous location. The conduit entry into a type "e" enclosure must also meet the ingress protection rating of the enclosure.

Δ Rules J18-108 2) and J18-154 2)

Conduit fittings for use in Class I locations and similar to the "L", "T", or "Cross" type are not usually classed as enclosures when not larger than the trade size of the conduit.

Reducers may have one side larger than the trade size of the conduit where the entry to the explosion-proof or flameproof enclosure is larger than the trade size of the conduit.

Rules J18-108 3) a) and J18-154 3) a)

Cables and flexible cords are not tested to determine their ability to resist internal explosions. Therefore, regardless of size, each cable must be sealed at the point of entry into any enclosure that is required to be explosion-proof.

Some designs of cable glands incorporate an integral seal and these are marked "SL" to indicate that the seal is provided by the cable gland. Cable glands of this type are identified with the class designation. Designs requiring a field- or factory-installed sealing fitting have the group designation marked on this component.

Because the appropriate sealing characteristics may be achieved by different means, the manufacturer's instructions should be followed.

Δ Rule J18-108 4)

It is important to follow the manufacturer's instructions; otherwise, seals will not function properly to prevent the transmission of an explosion beyond the seal. Improper sealing has been the primary factor in a number of explosions, resulting in loss of life and/or major equipment damage. Users are reminded that only the sealing compound specified in the instructions may be used in a seal. Use of other manufacturers' compounds in a seal may compromise the integrity of the installation.

Appendix J

C22.1-18

Appendix J
Rules and Notes to Rules for installations using the
Class and Division system of classification

Seals used for intrinsically safe equipment and wiring systems are not required to be explosion-proof but should be identified for the purpose of minimizing the passage of gases, vapours, or dusts under normal operating conditions.

Δ **Rule J18-108 4) a) ii)**

All Class I motors and generators are required to have a seal provided by the manufacturer between the main motor or generator enclosure and the enclosure for the conduit entry (connection box). A marking regarding the seal being provided is therefore not necessary on this particular class of product.

For cables, compliance with Subrule 4) can be accomplished by
a) a Class I hazardous location cable gland used with the appropriate cable type(s) and a field-installed sealing fitting;
b) a Class I hazardous location cable gland used with the appropriate cable type(s) with an integral seal; or
c) a cable gland used with appropriate cable types and with an enclosure provided with sealing as specified in Subrule 4).

Cable glands with integral seals are marked "SL".

Rule J18-114 and J18-150

Users are cautioned that combining a variable frequency drive (VFD) with a motor may increase the operating temperature of the motor as a result of the harmonics produced by the drive. This may cause the motor temperature to exceed its temperature code rating. This is of particular concern where the operating temperature of the motor is close to the ignition temperature of hazardous materials that may be in the area. Because of the generally lower ignition temperatures associated with Class II materials, it will be of particular concern in Class II areas. It remains the responsibility of the user to ensure that the operating temperature of the motor, in combination with the drive, is below the minimum ignition temperature of the hazardous material in the area. The motor manufacturer should be consulted where necessary. The following are some references that may assist the user in determining the suitability of an installation:
a) API RP 2216, *Ignition Risk of Hydrocarbon Liquids and Vapors by Hot Surfaces in the Open Air*; and
b) IEEE Paper No. PCIC-97-04, "Flammable Vapor Ignition Initiated By Hot Rotor Surfaces Within an Induction Motor — Reality or Not?".

Rule J18-116

Gas turbines in hazardous locations also need safeguards against potential hazards from other than electrical ignition systems, such as exhaust and fuel systems. The complete engine assembly should be investigated for its suitability in Class I, Division 1 hazardous locations.

Rule J18-150

Equipment marked Class I, Division 2 is suitable only for Division 2.

Rule J18-150 2) c) ii)

The equipment referred to in this Item includes service and branch circuit switches and circuit breakers; motor controllers, including push buttons, pilot switches, relays, and motor-overload protective devices; and switches and circuit breakers for the control of lighting and appliance circuits. Oil-immersed circuit breakers and controllers of the ordinary general-use type may not confine completely the arc produced in the interruption of heavy overloads, and specific approval for locations of this Class and Division is therefore necessary.

Rule J18-150 2) c) iv)

A group of three fuses protecting an ungrounded three-phase circuit and a single fuse protecting the ungrounded conductor of an identified 2-wire single-phase circuit are each considered a set of fuses.

Δ **Rule J18-150 2) e)**

See the Note to Rule J18-114.

Appendix J
Rules and Notes to Rules for installations using the
Class and Division system of classification

C22.1-18

Rotating electrical machines of the open or non-explosion-proof type do not have a certification Standard for Class I, Division 2. This Rule provides the criteria for applying, in Division 2, rotating electrical machines that do not have a certification suitable for Division 2. Refer to IEEE 1349 for more detailed information on applying these rotating electrical machines in Class I, Division 2 locations.

Δ Rule J18-150 3)

These heaters may not be designed for hazardous locations. They are considered suitable on the basis that they are contained within the motor or generator and are therefore mechanically protected, do not use temperature controls (to eliminate heater temperature runaway in the event of a controls failure), and are non-ignition-capable under normal operating conditions.

Example of a motor heater nameplate

Motor space heater
Rated voltage: _____ V
Phase: _____
Rated current: _____ A, or Power: _____ W
Maximum surface temperature: _____ °C, or
Temperature code: _____

Rule J18-152

See the Note to Rule J18-106.

Δ Rules J18-152 1) i), J18-204 4) b), J18-254 1) h), J18-304 1) f), and J18-354 h)

Liquid-tight flexible metal conduit and associated connectors intended for use in hazardous locations are marked "HEAVY DUTY" or "HD".

Δ Rule J18-152 7)

Cable glands should be compatible with the degree of ingress protection and explosion protection provided by the enclosure on which they are installed.

For example, to maintain the protection of an enclosure required to be explosion-proof, a sealing-type gland marked for the location should be used. Where unarmoured cables must enter an enclosure required to be explosion-proof, a combination of a sealing fitting marked for the location and a non-sealing cable gland may be used.

Where equipment normally considered suitable for use in ordinary locations is acceptable in Division 2 locations, such as terminal boxes and motors, ordinary location cable glands that maintain the degree of protection of the enclosure may be used. Similarly, where purged enclosures are used in Division 1 and Division 2 locations, ordinary location cable glands that maintain the degree of protection of the enclosure may be used.

Where equipment is specifically designed for use in Division 2 locations, ordinary location cable glands that maintain the degree of protection of the enclosure may be used. One means of achieving equivalent protection is the use of a cable gland with the same or better IP rating as the enclosure (see Table B18-5). If the gland does not have an IP rating, other ratings, such as weatherproof, may be matched to the enclosure rating.

Δ Rule J18-154 1) c)

This Rule allows the seal at the boundary between an outdoor Class I, Division 2 location and an outdoor non-hazardous location to be located farther than 300 mm from the boundary of the Class I,

Appendix J

C22.1-18

Appendix J
Rules and Notes to Rules for installations using the
Class and Division system of classification

Division 2 location, provided that it is located on the conduit prior to it entering an enclosure or a building. Because gas is present in Class I, Division 2 locations only for short periods, it is unlikely that gas or vapour could be released through conduit couplings at sufficiently high rates to form an explosive gas atmosphere in outdoor areas. However, the seal must be located on the conduit before it enters an enclosure or a building because, depending on the ventilation rate, gas transmitted through the conduit may build up to flammable concentrations.

Rule J18-154 2)
See the Note to Rule J18-108 2).

Rule J18-154 3) a)
See the Note to Rule J18-108 3) a).

Rule J18-204 1) b)
See the Note to Rule J18-106.

Rules J18-212, J18-214, J18-262, J18-264, J18-310, J18-312, J18-360, and J18-362
Because overheated windings of large pipe-ventilated motors (or fire in these motors) are not readily detected by odour or smoke, it is advisable, especially in the case of buildings not provided with automatic sprinklers, to take the following precautions:
a) if ventilation air is supplied from a separate source, an air-pressure-operated switch should supervise the supply of air and be arranged to shut down the pipe-ventilated motor in case of air failure;
b) an automatic fire detector should be placed at the air discharge end of the pipe-ventilated motor and be arranged to shut down the motor if overheating or fire should occur;
c) a port with a self-closing shutter should be provided at the motor air intake end to facilitate discharge into the motor frame of a fire extinction medium;
d) to complement Item c), fire dampers fitted with fusible links should be provided for the air intake and discharge ends of the motor to confine fire and the fire extinction medium to the motor frame;
e) intake and discharge ducts should be carefully installed with respect to combustible construction or storage and should not pierce firewalls, fire partitions, floors, or ceilings unless provided with automatic fire shutters or dampers where they pierce the fire section or division of the building (see NFPA 91); and
f) intake and discharge ducts should be kept clear of accumulation of combustible lint or dust.

Rule J18-254
See the Note to Rule J18-106.

Rule J18-262
See the Note to Rule J18-212.

Rule J18-262 2)
It is the responsibility of the owner of the facility to demonstrate to the authority having jurisdiction that the conditions outlined in the Rule will exist. Accumulations of the dust can be considered to be moderate if the colour of a surface is visible through the dust layer.

Rule J18-264
See the Note to Rule J18-212.

Rule J18-304
See the Note to Rule J18-106.

Rule J18-310
See the Note to Rule J18-212.

Rule J18-312
See the Note to Rule J18-212.

Appendix J
Rules and Notes to Rules for installations using the
Class and Division system of classification

C22.1-18

Rule J18-354
See the Note to Rule J18-106.

Rule J18-360
See the Note to Rule J18-212.

Rule J18-362
See the Note to Rule J18-212.

Rule J20-004
For the purposes of Subrules 6) and 7), buildings such as kiosks, in which electrical equipment such as cash registers and/or self-service console controls are located, are considered to be buildings not suitably cut off.

Rule J20-030
Information on the non-electrical aspects of propane tank systems, refill centres, and filling plants may be found in CSA B149.2.

Rule J20-060
Information on the non-electrical aspects of compressed natural gas (NGV) refuelling stations and NGV storage facilities may be found in CSA B149.1.

Rule J20-100
This Rule applies to areas where vehicles that use fuels classified as flammable liquids are repaired or serviced. It does not apply to areas where vehicles burning combustible liquids such as diesel fuel are repaired or serviced. Table JB-4 lists the flash points of combustible and flammable liquids as determined by the methods specified in NFPA 30:

Table JB-4
Flash points of combustible and flammable liquids determined in accordance with NFPA 30

Liquid classification	Closed-cup flash point
Flammable liquid (Class I liquid)*	Less than 37.8 °C
Combustible liquid (Class II liquid)	Not less than 37.8 °C and less than 60 °C
Combustible liquid (Class IIIA liquid)	Not less than 60 °C and less than 93 °C
Combustible liquid (Class IIIB liquid)	Not less than 93 °C

* Class I liquids are further subdivided into Classes IA, IB, and IC.

Flash point is typically used to determine if the possibility of a liquid being released into the air requires the area to be classified as a hazardous location. If a liquid is stored or used in an area at temperatures below its flash point, the area may be classified as a non-hazardous area.

Appendix J

C22.1-18

Appendix J
Rules and Notes to Rules for installations using the
Class and Division system of classification

Annex JD
Diagrams for Annex J20

Diagram JD-4
Extent of hazardous location for open-face spray booths
[See Rule J20-302 2).]

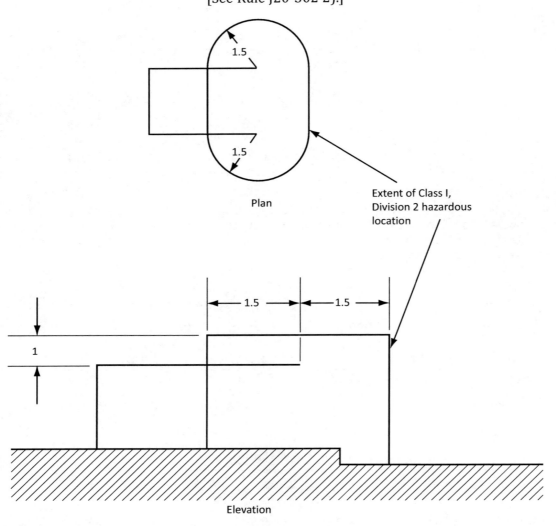

Plan

Extent of Class I,
Division 2 hazardous
location

Elevation

Note: *All dimensions given are in metres.*

Appendix J
Rules and Notes to Rules for installations using the
Class and Division system of classification

C22.1-18

Diagram JD-5
Extent of hazardous location for spraying operations not conducted in spray booths
[See Rules J20-302 1) b) and J20-302 4).]

PLAN

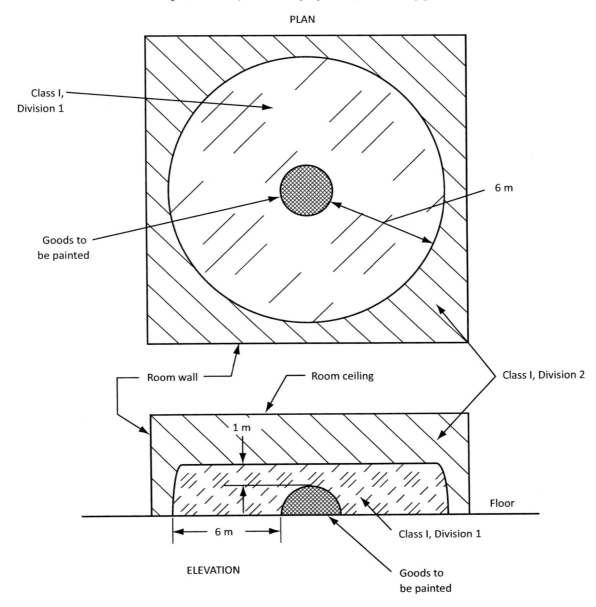

ELEVATION

Appendix J

C22.1-18

Appendix J
Rules and Notes to Rules for installations using the
Class and Division system of classification

Diagram JD-6
Extent of hazardous location for spraying operations not conducted in spray booths — Ventilation system interlocked
[See Rule J20-302 7).]

PLAN

Class I, Division 1

1 m

Goods to be painted

6 m

Class I, Division 2

500 mm

1 m

6 m

1 m

Class I, Division 1

Goods to be painted

Floor

ELEVATION

C22.1-18

Appendix J
Rules and Notes to Rules for installations using the
Class and Division system of classification

Diagram JD-7
Extent of hazardous location for tank vehicle and tank car loading and unloading
(See Part B of Table JT-63.)

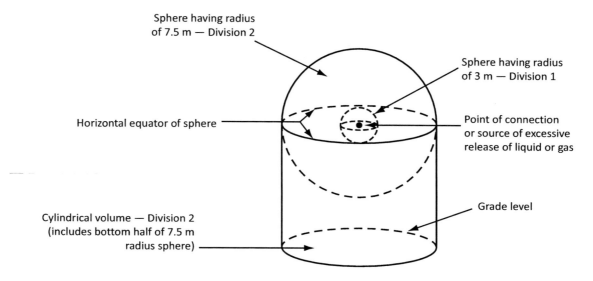

Diagram JD-8
Extent of hazardous location for pumps, vapour compressors, gas-air mixers, and vaporizers outdoors in open air
(See Part E of Table JT-63.)

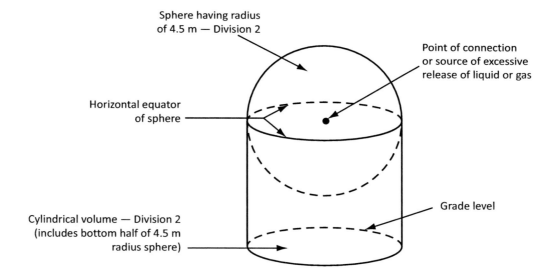

C22.1-18

Appendix J
Rules and Notes to Rules for installations using the
Class and Division system of classification

Diagram JD-9
Extent of hazardous location for container filling outdoors in open air
(See Part J of Table JT-63.)

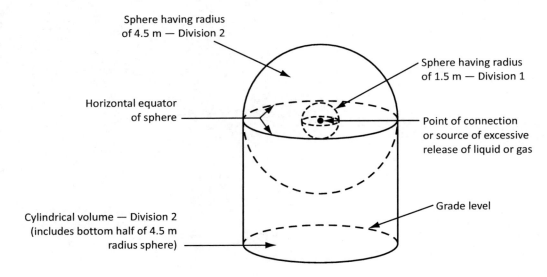

Sphere having radius of 4.5 m — Division 2

Sphere having radius of 1.5 m — Division 1

Horizontal equator of sphere

Point of connection or source of excessive release of liquid or gas

Grade level

Cylindrical volume — Division 2 (includes bottom half of 4.5 m radius sphere)

Diagram JD-10
Extent of hazardous location adjacent to openings in a closed spray booth or room
[See Rule J20-302 3).]

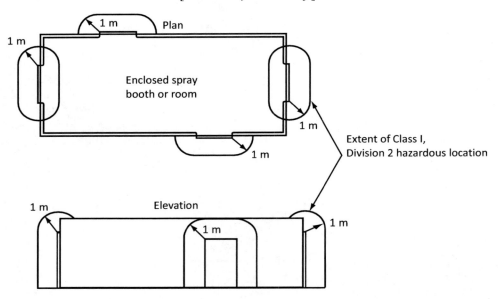

1 m — Plan

1 m

Enclosed spray booth or room

1 m

1 m

Extent of Class I, Division 2 hazardous location

1 m — Elevation

1 m

1 m

Appendix J
C22.1-18
Rules and Notes to Rules for installations using the
Class and Division system of classification

Annex JT
Tables for Annex J20

Table JT-63
Hazardous areas for propane dispensing, container filling, and storage
(See Rule J20-034.)

Part	Location	Extent of hazardous locations*	Division of Class I, Group D hazardous location
A	Storage containers other than CTC/DOT cylinders and ASME vertical containers of less than 454 kg water capacity	Within 4.5 m in all directions from connections, except connections otherwise covered in this Table	Division 2
B	Tank vehicle and tank car loading and unloading†	Within 3 m in all directions from connections regularly made or disconnected from product transfer	Division 1
		Beyond 3 m but within 7.5 m in all directions from a point where connections are regularly made or disconnected and within the cylindrical volume between the horizontal equator of the sphere and grade (see Diagram JD-7)	Division 2
C	Gauge vent openings other than those on CTC/DOT cylinders and ASME vertical containers of less than 454 kg water capacity	Within 1.5 m in all directions from point of discharge	Division 1
		Beyond 1.5 m but within 4.5 m in all directions from point of discharge	Division 2
D	Relief device discharge other than those on CTC/DOT cylinders and ASME vertical containers of less than 454 kg water capacity	Within direct path of discharge‡	Division 1
		Within 1.5 m in all directions from point of discharge	Division 1
		Beyond 1.5 m but within 4.5 m in all directions from point of discharge, except within the direct path of discharge	Division 2
E	Pumps, vapour compressors, gas-air mixers, and vaporizers (other than direct-fired or indirect-fired with an attached or adjacent gas-fired heat source)	Entire room and any adjacent room not separated by a gas-tight partition	Division 1
	Indoors without ventilation	Within 4.5 m of the exterior side of any exterior wall or roof that is not vapour-tight or within 4.5 m of any exterior opening	Division 2

(Continued)

Appendix J

C22.1-18

Appendix J
Rules and Notes to Rules for installations using the
Class and Division system of classification

Table JT-63 (Continued)

Part	Location	Extent of hazardous locations*	Division of Class I, Group D hazardous location
	Indoors with adequate ventilation	Entire room and any adjacent room not separated by a gas-tight partition	Division 2
	Outdoors in open air at or above grade	Within 4.5 m in all directions from this equipment and within the cylindrical volume between the horizontal equator of the sphere and grade (see Diagram JD-8)	Division 2
F	Service station dispensing units	Entire space within dispenser enclosure or up to a solid partition within the enclosure at any height above the base. The space within 450 mm horizontally from the dispenser enclosure up to 1.2 m above the base or to the height of a solid partition within the enclosure. Entire pit or open space beneath the dispenser	Division 1
		The space above a solid partition within the dispenser enclosure. The space up to 450 mm above grade within 6 m horizontally from any edge of the dispenser enclosure§	Division 2
G	Pits or trenches containing or located beneath propane gas valves, pumps, vapour compressors, regulators, and similar equipment	Entire pit or trench	Division 1
		Entire room and any adjacent room not separated by a gas-tight partition	Division 2
	Without mechanical ventilation	Within 4.5 m in all directions from a pit or trench when located outdoors	Division 2
	With adequate mechanical ventilation	Entire pit or trench	Division 2
		Entire room and any adjacent room not separated by a gas-tight partition	Division 2
		Within 4.5 m in all directions from a pit or trench when located outdoors	Division 2
H	Special buildings or rooms for storage of portable containers	Entire room	Division 2

(Continued)

Appendix J
Rules and Notes to Rules for installations using the
Class and Division system of classification

C22.1-18

Table JT-63 (Concluded)

Part	Location	Extent of hazardous locations*	Division of Class I, Group D hazardous location
I	Pipelines and connections containing operational bleeds, drips, vents, or drains	Within 1.5 m in all directions from point of discharge	Division 1
		Beyond 1.5 m from point of discharge, same as Part E of this Table	See Part E
J	Container filling: Indoors with adequate ventilation	Within 1.5 m in all directions from the dispensing hose inlet connections for product transfer	Division 1
		Beyond 1.5 m and entire room	Division 2
	Container filling: Outdoors in open air	Within 1.5 m in all directions from the dispensing hose inlet connections for product transfer	Division 1
		Beyond 1.5 m but within 4.5 m in all directions from the dispensing hose inlet connections and within the cylindrical volume between the horizontal equator of the sphere and grade (see Diagram JD-9)	Division 2
K	Outdoor storage area for portable cylinders or containers Aggregate storage up to and including 454 kg water capacity	Within 1.5 m in all directions from connections	Division 2
	Aggregate storage over 454 kg water capacity	Within 4.5 m in all directions from connections	Division 2

* The classified area shall not extend beyond an unpierced wall, roof, or solid vapour-tight partition.
† When the extent of a hazardous area is being classified, consideration shall be given to possible variations in the locating of tank cars and tank vehicles at the unloading points and the effect these variations in location may have on the point of connection.
‡ Fixed electrical equipment should not be installed in this space.
§ For pits within this area, see Part G of this Table.

C22.1-18

Appendix J
Rules and Notes to Rules for installations using the
Class and Division system of classification

Δ

Table JT-69
Hazardous locations at bulk storage plants
(See Rule J20-202.)

Location		Extent of hazardous location	Class of hazardous location
Areas containing pumps, bleeders, withdrawal fittings, meters, and similar devices that are located in pipelines handling flammable liquids under pressure	Indoor areas with adequate ventilation	Within 1.5 m extending in all directions from the exterior of such devices as well as 7.5 m horizontally from any exterior surface of these devices and extending upward to 900 mm above floor or grade level	Class 1, Division 2*†‡
	Indoor areas not having adequate ventilation	Within a 1.5 m distance extending in all directions from the exterior surface of such devices as well as 7.5 m horizontally from any surface of the device and extending upward 900 mm above floor or grade level	Class 1, Division 1†‡
	Outdoor areas	Within a 900 mm distance extending in all directions from the exterior surface of such devices and up to 450 mm above grade level within 3 m horizontally from any surface of the devices	Class 1, Division 2
Areas where flammable liquids are transferred to individual containers	Outdoor areas or adequately ventilated indoor areas	Within 900 mm of the vent or fill opening extending in all directions	Class 1, Division 1
		Within the area between a 900 mm radius and a 1.5 m radius from the vent or fill opening extending in all directions	Class 1, Division 2
		Within a horizontal radius of 3 m from the vent or fill opening and extending to a height of 450 mm above floor or grade levels	Class 1, Division 2
	Indoor areas not having adequate ventilation	The entire indoor area	Class 1, Division 1
Outdoor areas where tank vehicles and tank cars are loaded and unloaded	Loading through an open dome or through a closed dome with atmospheric venting	Within 900 mm in all directions from the open dome or from the vent	Class 1, Division 1
		Within the area extending between a 900 mm radius and a 1.5 m radius from the open dome or from the vent	Class 1, Division 2
	Loading through a closed dome with atmospheric venting or through a closed	Within 900 mm in all directions from vents	Class 1, Division 2

(Continued)

January 2018

Appendix J
Rules and Notes to Rules for installations using the
Class and Division system of classification

C22.1-18

Table JT-69 (Concluded)

Location		Extent of hazardous location	Class of hazardous location
	dome with a vapour recovery system		
	Bottom loading or unloading	Within 3 m from the point of connection and extending up to 450 mm above grade	Class 1, Division 2
	Internal space of tank vehicles and tank cars	The entire internal space	Class 1, Division 1
Areas in the vicinity of above-ground tanks	Floating-roof-type tanks	The space above the roof and within the shell	Class 1, Division 1
	All types of above-ground tanks	Within 3 m in all directions from the shell, ends, and roof other than a floating roof	Class 1, Division 2
	Dikes around above-ground tanks	The area inside the dike and extending upward to the top of the dike	Class 1, Division 2
	Area around vents	Within 1.5 m in all directions from the vent opening	Class 1, Division 1
		The area between 1.5 m and 3 m of the vent opening and extending in all directions	Class 1, Division 2
	Vapour space above the liquid in a storage tank	The entire vapour space	Class 1, Division 1
Pits and depressions	Any part of a pit or depression that is not adequately ventilated and lies within a Zone 1 or Zone 2 area	The entire pit or depression	Class 1, Division 1
	Any part of a pit or depression that does not lie within a Zone 1 or Zone 2 area and contains piping, valves, or fittings for flammable gases or liquids	The entire pit or depression	Class 1, Division 2
	Any part of a pit or depression that is adequately ventilated and lies within a Zone 1 or Zone 2 area	The entire pit or depression	Class 1, Division 2
Garages where tank vehicles are stored or repaired		450 mm above floor or grade level, unless conditions warrant more severe classification or a greater extent of the hazardous area	Class 1, Division 2
Buildings such as office buildings, boiler rooms, etc.		If located outside the limits of hazardous areas and not used for handling or storage of volatile flammable liquids or containers for such liquids	Non-hazardous

* *The design of the ventilation systems shall take into account that the vapours are heavier than air.*
† *Where openings are used in outside walls, they shall be of adequate size, located at floor level, and unobstructed except by louvres or coarse screens.*
‡ *Where natural ventilation is inadequate, mechanical ventilation shall be provided.*

Appendix J

Appendix K — Extract from IEC 60364-1

Chapter 13

Notes:
1) *This Appendix is an informative (non-mandatory) part of this Standard.*
2) *This extract is reprinted from IEC 60364-1 with permission.*

13 Fundamental principles

Notes:
1) *Where countries not yet having national regulations for electrical installations deem it necessary to establish legal requirements for this purpose, it is recommended that such requirements be limited to fundamental principles which are not subject to frequent modification on account of technical development. The contents of Clause 13 may be used as a basis for such legislation.*
2) *This clause contains basic requirements. In other parts of this standard (see Table A.2), more detailed requirements may be given.*

131 Protection for safety

131.1 General

The requirements stated in 131.2 to 131.7 are intended to provide for the safety of persons, livestock and property against dangers and damage which may arise in the reasonable use of electrical installations. The requirements to provide for the safety of livestock are applicable in locations intended for them.

Note: *In electrical installations, the following hazards may arise:*
— *shock currents;*
— *excessive temperatures likely to cause burns, fires and other injurious effects;*
— *ignition of a potentially explosive atmosphere;*
— *undervoltages, overvoltages and electromagnetic influences likely to cause or result in injury or damage;*
— *power supply interruptions and/or interruption of safety services;*
— *arcing, likely to cause blinding effects, excessive pressure, and/or toxic gases;*
— *mechanical movement of electrically activated equipment.*

131.2 Protection against electric shock

131.2.1 Basic protection (protection against direct contact)

Note: *For low-voltage installations, systems and equipment, basic protection generally corresponds to protection against direct contact.*

Protection shall be provided against dangers that may arise from contact with live parts of the installation by persons or livestock.

This protection can be achieved by one of the following methods:

— preventing a current from passing through the body of any person or any livestock;

— limiting the current which can pass through a body to a non-hazardous value.

131.2.2 Fault protection (protection against indirect contact)

Note: *For low-voltage installations, systems and equipment, fault protection generally corresponds to protection against indirect contact, mainly with regard to failure of basic insulation.*

Protection shall be provided against dangers that may arise from contact with exposed-conductive-parts of the installation by persons or livestock.

This protection can be achieved by one of the following methods:

— preventing a current resulting from a fault from passing through the body of any person or any livestock;

— limiting the magnitude of a current resulting from a fault, which can pass through a body, to a non-hazardous value;

— limiting the duration of a current resulting from a fault, which can pass through a body, to a non-hazardous time period.

131.3 Protection against thermal effects

The electrical installation shall be so arranged to minimize the risk of damage or ignition of flammable materials due to high temperature or electric arc. In addition, during normal operation of the electrical equipment, there shall be no risk of persons or livestock suffering burns.

131.4 Protection against overcurrent

Persons and livestock shall be protected against injury and property shall be protected against damage due to excessive temperatures or electromechanical stresses caused by any overcurrents likely to arise in conductors.

Protection can be achieved by limiting the overcurrent to a safe value or duration.

131.5 Protection against fault currents

Conductors, other than live conductors, and any other parts intended to carry a fault current shall be capable of carrying that current without attaining an excessive temperature. Electrical equipment, including conductors shall be provided with mechanical protection against electromechanical stresses of fault currents as necessary to prevent injury or damage to persons, livestock or property.

Live conductors shall be protected against overcurrents arising from faults by the methods in 131.4.

Note: *Particular attention should be given to PE conductor and earthing conductor currents.*

131.6 Protection against voltage disturbances and measures against electromagnetic influences

131.6.1 Persons and livestock shall be protected against injury and property shall be protected against any harmful effects as a consequence of a fault between live parts of circuits supplied at different voltages.

131.6.2 Persons and livestock shall be protected against injury and property shall be protected against damage as a consequence of overvoltages such as those originating from atmospheric events or from switching.

Note: *For protection against direct lightning strikes, see IEC 62305 series.*

131.6.3 Persons and livestock shall be protected against injury and property shall be protected against damage as a consequence of undervoltage and any subsequent voltage recovery.

131.6.4 The installation shall have an adequate level of immunity against electromagnetic disturbances so as to function correctly in the specified environment. The installation design shall take into consideration the anticipated electromagnetic emissions, generated by the installation or the installed equipment, which shall be suitable for the current-using equipment used with, or connected to, the installation.

Appendix K

131.7 Protection against power supply interruption

Where danger or damage is expected to arise due to an interruption of supply, suitable provisions shall be made in the installation or installed equipment.

132 Design

132.1 General

For the design of the electrical installation, the following factors shall be taken into account to provide

— the protection of persons, livestock and property in accordance with Clause 131;

— the proper functioning of the electrical installation for the intended use.

The information required as a basis for design is listed in 132.2 to 132.5. The requirements with which the design shall comply are stated in 132.6 to 132.12.

132.2 Characteristics of available supply or supplies

When designing electrical installations in accordance with IEC 60364 series it is necessary to know the characteristics of the supply. Relevant information from the network operator is necessary to design a safe installation according to IEC 60364 series. The characteristics of the power supply should be included in the documentation to show conformity with IEC 60364 series. If the network operator changes the characteristics of the power supply this may affect the safety of the installation.

132.2.1 Nature of current: a.c. and/or d.c.

132.2.2 Function of conductors:

— for a.c.: line conductor(s);
          neutral conductor;
          protective conductor.

— for d.c.: line conductor(s);
          midpoint conductor;
          protective conductor.

Note: *The function of some conductors may be combined in a single conductor.*

132.2.3 Values and tolerances:

— voltage and voltage tolerances;

— voltage interruptions, voltage fluctuations and voltage dips;

— frequency and frequency tolerances;

— maximum current allowable;

— earth fault loop impedance upstream of the origin of the installation;

— prospective short-circuit currents.

For standard voltages and frequencies, see IEC 60038.

132.2.4 Protective provisions inherent in the supply, for example, system earthing or midpoint earthing.

132.2.5 Particular requirements of the supply undertaking.

132.3 Nature of demand

The number and type of circuits required for lighting, heating, power, control, signalling, information and communication technology, etc. shall be determined by

— location of points of power demand;

— loads to be expected on the various circuits;

— daily and yearly variation of demand;

— any special conditions such as harmonics;

— requirements for control, signalling, information and communication technology, etc;

— anticipated future demand if specified.

132.4 Electric supply systems for safety services or standby electric supply systems

— Source of supply (nature, characteristics).

— Circuits to be supplied by the electric source for safety services or the standby electrical source.

132.5 Environmental conditions

The design of the electrical installation shall take into account the environmental conditions to which it will be subjected, see IEC 60364-5-51 and IEC 60721.

132.6 Cross-sectional area of conductors

The cross-sectional area of conductors shall be determined for both normal operating conditions and for fault conditions according to
a)   their admissible maximum temperature;
b)   the admissible voltage drop;
c)   the electromechanical stresses likely to occur due to earth fault and short-circuit currents;
d)   other mechanical stresses to which the conductors can be subjected;
e)   the maximum impedance with respect to the functioning of the protection against fault currents;
f)   the method of installation.

Note: *The items listed above concern primarily the safety of electrical installations. Cross-sectional areas greater than those required for safety may be desirable for economic operation.*

132.7 Type of wiring and methods of installation

For the choice of the type of wiring and the methods of installation the following shall be taken into account:

— the nature of the locations;

— the nature of the walls or other parts of the building supporting the wiring;

— accessibility of wiring to persons and livestock;

— voltage;

— the electromagnetic stresses likely to occur due to earth fault and short-circuit currents;

— electromagnetic interference;

— other stresses to which the wiring can be subjected during the erection of the electrical installation or in service.

132.8 Protective equipment

The characteristics of protective equipment shall be determined with respect to their function which may be, for example, protection against the effects of

— overcurrent (overload, short-circuit);

— earth fault current;

— overvoltage;

— undervoltage and no voltage.

The protective devices shall operate at values of current, voltage and time which are suitably related to the characteristics of the circuits and to the possibilities of danger.

132.9 Emergency control

Where, in case of danger, there is the necessity for the immediate interruption of supply, an interrupting device shall be installed in such a way that it can be easily recognized and effectively and rapidly operated.

132.10 Disconnecting devices

Disconnecting devices shall be provided so as to permit switching and/or isolation of the electrical installation, circuits or individual items of apparatus as required for operation, inspection and fault detection, testing, maintenance and repair.

132.11 Prevention of mutual detrimental influence

The electrical installation shall be arranged in such a way that no mutual detrimental influence will occur between electrical installations and non-electrical installations.

132.12 Accessibility of electrical equipment

The electrical equipment shall be arranged so as to afford as may be necessary:

— sufficient space for the initial installation and later replacement of individual items of electrical equipment;

— accessibility for operation, inspection and fault detection, testing, maintenance and repair.

132.13 Documentation for the electrical installation

Every electrical installation shall be provided with appropriate documentation.

133 Selection of electrical equipment

133.1 General

Every item of electrical equipment used in electrical installations shall comply with such IEC standards as are appropriate. In the absence of an IEC standard the equipment shall comply with the appropriate national standards. Where there are no applicable standards, the item of equipment concerned shall be selected by special agreement between the person specifying the installation and the installer.

133.2 Characteristics

Every item of electrical equipment selected shall have suitable characteristics appropriate to the values and conditions on which the design of the electrical installation (see Clause 132) is based and shall, in particular, fulfil the following requirements.

133.2.1 Voltage

Electrical equipment shall be suitable with respect to the maximum steady-state voltage (r.m.s. value for a.c.) likely to be applied, as well as overvoltages likely to occur.

Note: *For certain equipment, it may be necessary to take account of the lowest voltage likely to occur.*

133.2.2 Current

All electrical equipment shall be selected with respect to the maximum steady-state current (r.m.s. value for a.c.) which it has to carry in normal service, and with respect to the current likely to be carried in abnormal conditions and the period (for example, operating time of protective devices, if any) during which it may be expected to flow.

133.2.3 Frequency

If frequency has an influence on the characteristics of electrical equipment, the rated frequency of the equipment shall correspond to the frequency likely to occur in the circuit.

133.2.4 Load factor

All electrical equipment which is selected on the basis of its power characteristics shall be suitable for the duty demanded of the equipment taking into account the design service conditions, see IEV 691-10-02.

133.3 Conditions of installation

All electrical equipment shall be selected so as to withstand safely the stresses and the environmental conditions (see 132.5) characteristic of its location and to which it may be subjected. If, however, an item of equipment does not have by design the properties corresponding to its location, it may be used on condition that adequate additional protection is provided as part of the completed electrical installation.

133.4 Prevention of harmful effects

All electrical equipment shall be selected so that it will not cause harmful effects on other equipment or impair the supply during normal service including switching operations. In this context, the factors which can have an influence include, for example:

— power factor;

— inrush current;

— asymmetrical load;

— harmonics;

— transient overvoltages generated by equipment in the installation.

134 Erection and verification of electrical installations

134.1 Erection

134.1.1 Good workmanship by competent persons and proper materials shall be used in the erection of the electrical installation. Electrical equipment shall be installed in accordance with the instructions provided by the manufacturer of the equipment.

134.1.2 The characteristics of the electrical equipment, as determined in accordance with Clause 133, shall not be impaired during erection.

134.1.3 Conductors shall be identified in accordance with IEC 60446. Where identification of terminals is necessary, they shall be identified in accordance with IEC 60445.

134.1.4 Connections between conductors and between conductors and other electrical equipment shall be made in such a way that safe and reliable contact is ensured.

134.1.5 All electrical equipment shall be installed in such a manner that the designed heat dissipation conditions are not impaired.

134.1.6 All electrical equipment likely to cause high temperatures or electric arcs shall be placed or guarded so as to minimize the risk of ignition of flammable materials. Where the temperature of any exposed parts of electrical equipment is likely to cause injury to persons, those parts shall be so located or guarded as to prevent accidental contact therewith.

134.1.7 Where necessary for safety purposes, suitable warning signs and/or notices shall be provided.

134.1.8 Where an installation is erected by using new materials, inventions or methods leading to deviations from the rules of IEC 60364 series, the resulting degree of safety of the installation shall not be less than that obtained by compliance with IEC 60364 series.

134.1.9 In the case of an addition or alteration to an existing installation, it shall be determined that the rating and condition of existing equipment, which will have to carry any additional load, is adequate for the altered circumstances. Furthermore, the earthing and bonding arrangements, if necessary for the protective measure applied for the safety of the addition or alteration, shall be adequate.

134.2 Initial verification
Electrical installations shall be verified before being placed in service and after any important modification to confirm proper execution of the work in accordance with this standard.

134.3 Periodic verification
It is recommended that every electrical installation is subjected to periodic verification.

C22.1-18

Appendix L
Engineering guidelines for determining
hazardous area classifications

Appendix L

Appendix L — Engineering guidelines for determining hazardous area classifications

Note: *This Appendix is an informative (non-mandatory) part of this Standard.*

L1 Scope

This Appendix provides guidance for the determination of hazardous areas in facilities where explosive atmospheres can occur.

Explosive gas atmospheres can exist in the exploration for and production and transportation of crude oil, natural gas, and related hydrocarbons and in other facilities such as petrochemical plants, refineries, and distilleries.

Explosive dust atmospheres can exist in a variety of industries, including food, plastics, lumber, rubber, furniture, textiles, pharmaceuticals, and dyes, and in coal, metals, and fossil fuel generation.

Area classification codes, standards, and recommended practices do not address catastrophic release situations [see API RP 505 1.2.1(b)]. Other procedures and response plans should be put in place by facility operators to address these possibilities.

Note: *This Appendix is not intended as a mandatory code for developing area classifications.*

L2 Intent

The intent of this Appendix is to provide an overview of the most common considerations that should be addressed in performing an area classification. This Appendix is also intended to promote awareness of the various industry codes, standards, and recommended practices that can be used as resources in performing area classification studies. These references provide extensive information applicable to conditions commonly encountered in many types of facilities in Canadian industries where explosive atmospheres can be present. Proper application of these codes, standards, and recommended practices in any given situation requires knowledge and experience.

L3 Stakeholders

This Appendix is focused on engineering and design requirements essential for proper area classification but also identifies requirements that affect other stakeholders, such as original equipment manufacturers, installers, inspectors, and operations, safety, and maintenance personnel. There are also other stakeholders, such as insurers or regulatory representatives responsible for worker safety or code enforcement, who may be impacted by an area classification or require access to documentation related to it.

L4 Factors used to determine an area classification

Electrical designs and installations in hazardous locations are based on the area classifications for a facility. The factors to be taken into account in defining an area classification include the following:

Δ a) the characteristics of the fluids being handled (e.g., chemical and physical properties such as flash point, molar composition, liquid density, vapour specific gravity, lower flammable limit (LFL), upper flammable limit (UFL), mole weight);

b) operating pressures, temperatures, flow rates, and volumes;

c) the design and maintenance of the compression, pumping, piping, valve, and containment systems for handling the fluids;

d) the minimum explosible concentration of dusts;

e) dust confinement systems;

f) housekeeping and humidity;

g) building design and dimensions;

h) heating and ventilation systems in buildings;

i) the site layout and proximity to other structures;

j) the type of safety systems available (e.g., gas detection);

C22.1-18

Appendix L
Engineering guidelines for determining
hazardous area classifications

k)   outdoor terrain and topographical features (e.g., berms, low spots, slopes, vegetation);

l)   local temperature and wind conditions;

m)   the remoteness of an installation (i.e., the capacity to detect and/or respond to a release through on-site personnel or remote monitoring);

n)   operating and maintenance practices and training;

o)   the operating, maintenance, and failure history of the facility; and

p)   facility modifications resulting from site operations or maintenance that could impact the area classification boundaries.

L5 Multidisciplinary involvement

Many of the factors given as examples in Clause L4 are best understood by disciplines other than electrical engineers and designers. These disciplines may include

a)   process engineers;

b)   heating and ventilation engineers;

c)   air quality scientists or engineers;

d)   operations specialists;

e)   fire and safety specialists;

f)   maintenance personnel; and

g)   instrumentation engineers.

Decisions about the involvement of personnel from various disciplines, and the timing and level of that involvement, should be based on corporate policies and/or made by engineering staff, based on the scope and complexity of the project. The individual leading the area classification study should be knowledgeable and competent in the principles of area classification.

L6 Responsibility for training and competence

The engineering profession is responsible for determining what levels of competence are required for a given discipline or activity. There is currently no regulated certification requirement verifying competence for an engineer in order to perform an area classification study. There is, nonetheless, a professional responsibility on the part of the practising engineer to be knowledgeable and competent in practising the profession, hence in performing an area classification study.

The following are various approaches that can be taken to develop competence in performing area classification studies:

a)   taking industry-sponsored training on area classification techniques;

b)   certification to IECEx OD 504, *IEC System for Certification to Standards relating to Equipment for Use in Explosive Atmospheres (IECEx System) — IECEx Scheme for Certification of Personnel Competence for Explosive Atmospheres — Specification for Units of Competence Assessment Outcomes*;

c)   participation in codes and standards development organizations (SDOs);

d)   mentorship by more experienced engineers;

e)   familiarization with codes and standards;

f)   on-the-job performance of area classification studies (under appropriate supervision), starting with simple installations and moving towards more complex installations;

g)   reviewing existing area classification studies;

h)   reviewing incident and failure histories;

i)   participating in investigations and corrective or remedial projects; and

j)   developing and delivering area classification training programs.

L7 Engineering authentication

Where an engineer is involved, all area classification drawings and studies should be traceable to a registered professional engineer working under a permit to practise. Traceability and authentication

C22.1-18

Appendix L
Engineering guidelines for determining
hazardous area classifications

Appendix L

requirements are governed by the respective jurisdiction, but typically this means that drawings and reports are signed and stamped, or signed with the title P. Eng. (or equivalent).

L8 Engineering quality controls

In addition to competency and training of the individual professional engineer, the engineering project structure should also include peer or supervisory reviews of area classification documents.

L9 Documentation and records

Area classification drawings and supporting studies should be maintained on file with the owner/ operator of the facility for the life of the facility and any additional legally required time period thereafter. The professional engineer and/or engineering company that prepared the reports and drawings should also maintain those records in accordance with any regulatory and/or contractually required time periods. These records should be accessible, upon request, by any affected stakeholder.

In order to ensure accessibility and facilitate retrieval, all relevant information should be recorded on the area classification drawing itself (e.g., results of fugitive emissions studies with date or revision number, minimum ventilation rates, rationales, process conditions, and any other important comments). See also Clause L12.

Company-specific operating and safety procedures may require on-site access to, or posting of, area classification drawings for convenient reference. Such drawings should, therefore, be well organized, uncluttered, and easy to understand.

L10 Management of change

Area classification studies and drawings are based on certain assumptions and conditions. If process or operating conditions change (e.g., as a result of plant expansions, equipment relocations, changes in inlet or process streams, changes in operating pressures, changes in operating procedures, alteration of building ventilation, or changes in site grading), or if conditions are not maintained (e.g., gas detection is not kept in proper working order), then the area classification may be rendered invalid. Depending upon the exact nature of the changes, this may lead to an unsafe condition. A management-of-change process should be put in place to ensure that the area classification remains valid and is adhered to at all times throughout the life of a facility.

A management-of-change process may require changes such as the following:
a)   revisions to area classification studies and drawings;
b)   modifications of designs and installations; and
c)   changes to procedures.

All documentation sets should be updated, and all stakeholders should be notified of the changes and potential impacts.

Appropriate engineering review and sign-off should be part of a management-of-change process. Engineering accountability is present not only for the initial project design, but also throughout the life of a facility.

L11 Communication responsibilities

As noted, area classification studies are based on various conditions and assumptions that must be valid if the determination of area classification is to be valid. At the outset of a project, the engineer responsible should communicate these conditions and assumptions to all parties (e.g., construction, inspection, operating, and maintenance personnel) responsible for ensuring that these requirements are met during the initial installation and throughout the life of the facility. The following are examples of methods of communication and design approaches:
a)   including area classification studies in project data books;
b)   including appropriate notes on drawings;
c)   holding training sessions;
d)   requiring various warning signs in and around classified areas;

Appendix L
Engineering guidelines for determining
hazardous area classifications

C22.1-18

e)   requiring the posting of area classification drawings and/or studies that present key information;

f)   requiring classification signs for building interiors;

g)   requiring fencing or barriers to restrict access to the site;

h)   requiring equipment that will help to ensure conformance (e.g., travel stops on the louvres of dust collection or confinement systems); and

i)   mandatory housekeeping procedures.

L12 Drawing requirements

L12.1 General

Area classification drawing sets typically consist of combinations of site plans, elevation or sectional views, details, and clarifying notes. The drawings show the indoor and outdoor zone classifications in and around a facility, using standard cross-hatching. There are usually installation details for specific equipment configurations, and some aspects of the facility may have to be represented in greater detail (e.g., process or instrumentation vents, pig traps, or dust collection or confinement systems). See API RP 500 and RP 505 for examples of area classification drawings.

Key area classification supporting information, assumptions, and conditions included on drawings should be presented in an orderly and concise manner so that the drawings remain clear and can be readily understood. One approach that can be used to accomplish this is to put essential information on the drawings, along with references to more detailed information to be found in other documents. See Clauses L12.2 and L12.3 for examples of the types of information that may be appropriate.

Engineered drawings may be either typical drawings or site-specific custom drawings, depending on the complexity of the situation. For simple installations, such as stand-alone pumpjacks or wellheads, typical drawings from company standards may be used, rather than individual site-specific drawings for each small facility. Typical drawings should be used only when they accurately represent the installation. Complex facilities typically have site-specific engineering drawing sets.

L12.2 Basic information

Drawings should include the following types of basic information:

a)   area classification information, such as classes, zones, groupings, and maximum allowable surface operating temperatures for electrical equipment;

b)   legends explaining the various cross-hatchings used on the diagrams (based on IEC recommendations);

c)   diagrams showing the extent of the various zones;

d)   assumptions, notes, and conditions;

e)   site locations, professional engineering stamps, and other title block information; and

f)   bar scales embedded in the drawing that automatically scale with the drawing when it is printed out on different sizes of paper.

L12.3 Supporting information, assumptions, and conditions

Key supporting information, assumptions, and conditions may include documentation of the following, as appropriate:

a)   references to file numbers, dates, and authors' names for supporting area classification studies;

Δ b)   reference to documentation on composition and physical property parameters of process fluids (e.g., mole weight, relative density, lower flammable limit, upper flammable limit, auto-ignition temperatures, volume or molar compositions);

c)   operating conditions such as pressures, flow rates, or volumes (these may be specific point values or ranges if the area classification was performed for a range of conditions);

d)   calculation methods (e.g., API RP 505, Appendix B) with supporting data and assumptions;

e)   hydrocarbon leakage rates (including references used);

f)   fresh air introduction rates;

g)   safety factors assumed;

C22.1-18

Appendix L
Engineering guidelines for determining
hazardous area classifications

Appendix L

h)   internal and external ambient temperatures (point or range values);

i)   minimum natural or forced ventilation rates;

j)   louvre sizing and/or travel stop settings;

k)   text and layout for warning signs or labels;

l)   combustible gas detection provisions, including requirements for sensors, locations, and alarm and shutdown actions;

   Note: *Some of this information may be communicated in shutdown keys.*

m)   vapour-tight sealing requirements for walls or other barriers;

n)   purging and/or pressurization requirements; and

o)   warnings to review and update studies and drawings when conditions deviate from those specified.

L13 Inspection requirements

Field and shop inspectors should be provided with the engineered area classification studies and drawings applicable to the facility to be inspected.

L14 Selected references and information sources

L14.1 General

There are numerous references and information sources that can be used in preparing an area classification. Clauses L14.2 and L14.3 list some of the most commonly used resources, with notes where applicable about the information that can be obtained from them.

L14.2 Selected references

CSA Group

C22.1, *Canadian Electrical Code, Part I*

   The *CE Code, Part I*, particularly Section 18 and Appendices B, F, H, and J, provides formal definitions for area classification and requirements for wiring methods and equipment.

PLUS 2203, *Guide for the Design, Testing, Construction, and Installation of Equipment in Explosive Atmospheres* by John A. Bossert, 3rd edition, 2001 (withdrawn)

API (American Petroleum Institute)

RP 505, *Recommended Practice for Classification of Locations for Electrical Installations at Petroleum Facilities Classified as Class 1, Zone 0, Zone 1, and Zone 2*

   API RP 505 contains numerous examples of typical area classifications for oil and gas facilities, based on actual cases. It also contains a fugitive emissions study calculation method in Appendix B and a point source approach in Appendix D. Appendix E provides a classification procedure, with simple questions to guide the performance of area classifications. API RP 500, *Recommended Practice for Classification of Locations for Electrical Installations at Petroleum Facilities Classified as Class I, Division 1 and Division 2* is the companion document for the North American Division system.

4615, *Emission Factors for Oil and Gas Production Operations*

   API 4615 provides field measured and statistically classified emissions factors.

4638, *Calculation Workbook for Oil and Gas Production Equipment Fugitive Emissions*

   API 4638 contains several examples of fugitive emissions calculations.

Energy Institute

EI 15, *Model code of safe practice Part 15: Area classification code for installations handling flammable fluids*

   This Model code provides information on the point source concept and how to use it. It also presents several examples of both onshore and offshore installations. Supporting documents to this Code provide detailed calculation information and risk assessment methodologies.

C22.1-18

Appendix L
Engineering guidelines for determining
hazardous area classifications

IEC (International Electrotechnical Commission)

60079-10-1, *Explosive atmospheres — Part 10-1: Classification of areas — Explosive gas atmospheres*
    This Standard provides definitions of many area classification terms that are used in other codes
    and standards; an area classification method/process that factors in the grade of the release and
    ventilation; calculation examples, sample area classification diagrams, and a data collection table;
    and a means of estimating hypothetical volumes for quick checks of emission propagation distances.

60079-10-2, *Explosive atmospheres — Part 10-2: Classification of areas — Explosive dust atmospheres*

60079-20-1, *Explosive atmospheres — Part 20-1: Material characteristics for gas and vapour classification — Test methods and data*
    This Standard applies to the use of electrical apparatus. It provides a complete set of material
    properties and is intended for area classification purposes.

60079-20-2, *Explosive atmospheres — Part 20-2: Material characteristics — Combustible dusts test methods* (withdrawn)

ANSI/ISA (American National Standards Institute/International Society of Automation)

60079-10-1 (12.24.01), *Explosive Atmospheres — Part 10-1: Classification of areas — Explosive gas atmospheres*
    ANSI/ISA-60079-10-1 (12.24.01) is an adoption with modifications of IEC 60079-10-1 and
    incorporates the use of gas detection as a means of classifying indoor areas as Class I, Zone 2.

NFPA (National Fire Protection Association)

HAZ 10, *Fire Protection Guide to Hazardous Materials*
    HAZ 10 provides up-to-date facts on all types of chemicals and NFPA 30/OSHA classifications for
    flammable and combustible liquids.

61, *Standard for the Prevention of Fires and Dust Explosions in Agricultural and Food Processing Facilities*

68, *Standard on Explosion Protection by Deflagration Venting*

77, *Recommended Practice on Static Electricity*

484, *Standard for Combustible Metals*

497, *Recommended Practice for the Classification of Flammable Liquids, Gases, or Vapors and of Hazardous (Classified) Locations for Electrical Installations in Chemical Process Areas*
    NFPA 497 is applicable primarily to chemical facilities. However, it does contain an extensive list of
    flammable and combustible materials and their physical properties that may be useful in performing
    area classification studies.

654, *Standard for the Prevention of Fire and Dust Explosions from the Manufacturing, Processing, and Handling of Combustible Particulate Solids*

655, *Standard for Prevention of Sulfur Fires and Explosions*

664, *Standard for the Prevention of Fires and Explosions in Wood Processing and Woodworking Facilities*

Other publications

Province of Alberta, *Electrical STANDATA*

C22.1-18

Appendix L
Engineering guidelines for determining
hazardous area classifications

Appendix L

Alberta *Electrical STANDATA* provides interpretations and clarifications on various subjects related to area classification; other provinces may have equivalent advisory systems.

Magison, Ernest. *Electrical Instruments in Hazardous Locations*, 4th edition. ISA, 2007

L14.3 Other sources of information

Useful information applicable to area classification studies can also be obtained from the following sources:

a) Occupational health and safety (OHS) codes: Various provinces have OHS codes with safety requirements that may apply to the design, operation, or maintenance of installations in hazardous locations.

b) Canadian product standards for equipment certification (e.g., the *Canadian Electrical Code, Part II*): Canadian product certification standards provide technical requirements for equipment certification for hazardous locations, using various protection methods. These standards also provide marking information.

c) Corporate drawing details, standards, guidelines, and best practices: Industry documents contain various approaches, requirements, and details used by a specific corporation. Such documents must meet minimum regulatory requirements.

d) Manufacturer and vendor sources: Manufacturers and vendors provide guides and reference information that is useful for area classification, design, installation, and maintenance as well as for training and educating personnel.

e) Technical papers: The IEEE IAS Petroleum and Chemical Industry Committee (PCIC) and other organizations produce many technical papers every year, addressing numerous area classification issues.

Δ

Appendix M — Translated caution and warning markings

Notes:
1) *This Appendix is an informative (non-mandatory) part of this Standard.*
2) *This Appendix lists French translations for caution and warning markings.*

Rule	English	French
12-2208 4)	INTERLOCKING METAL ARMOUR CABLES OR CONTINUOUS METAL SHEATH CABLES ONLY	CÂBLES SOUS ARMURE MÉTALLIQUE ARTICULÉE OU GAINE MÉTALLIQUE CONTINUE UNIQUEMENT
30-822	CAUTION ... V	ATTENTION ... V
36-006 1)	DANGER — HIGH VOLTAGE DANGER ... V	DANGER — HAUTE TENSION DANGER ... V
38-052 2)	Warning — Parts of the controller are not de-energized by this switch	Mise en garde — Certaines parties de ce contrôleur ne sont pas mises hors tension par ce sectionneur

Appendix B Notes	English	French
Rule 2-100 4)	CAUTION: The maximum continuous loading is limited to XXX amperes.	ATTENTION : La charge continue maximale est limitée à XXX ampères.
Rule 4-004 22)	CAUTION: The maximum permitted loading is limited to XXX amperes.	ATTENTION : La charge admissible maximale est limitée à XXX ampères.
Rule 64-060 10)	WARNING: ELECTRIC SHOCK HAZARD. DO NOT TOUCH TERMINALS. TERMINALS ON BOTH THE LINE AND LOAD SIDES MAY BE ENERGIZED IN THE OPEN POSITION.	AVERTISSEMENT : RISQUE DE CHOC ÉLECTRIQUE. NE PAS TOUCHER LES BORNES. LES BORNES DES DEUX CÔTÉS (SECTEUR ET CHARGE) PEUVENT ÊTRE SOUS TENSION EN POSITION OUVERTE.
Rule 64-066 1) b)	WARNING: ELECTRIC SHOCK HAZARD. THE CONDUCTORS OF THIS RENEWABLE ENERGY POWER SYSTEM ARE UNGROUNDED AND MAY BE ENERGIZED.	AVERTISSEMENT : RISQUE DE CHOC ÉLECTRIQUE. LES CONDUCTEURS DE CE SYSTÈME À ÉNERGIE RENOUVELABLE NE SONT PAS MIS À LA TERRE ET POURRAIENT ÊTRE SOUS TENSION.
Rule 64-074 4)	WARNING: RENEWABLE ENERGY SYSTEM CONTAINS ELECTRICAL ENERGY STORAGE DEVICES.	AVERTISSEMENT : CE SYSTÈME À ÉNERGIE RENOUVELABLE CONTIENT DES ACCUMULATEURS D'ÉNERGIE ÉLECTRIQUE.
Rule 64-102 c) iv)	WARNING: SINGLE 120 V SUPPLY. DO NOT CONNECT MULTI-WIRE BRANCH CIRCUITS.	AVERTISSEMENT : ALIMENTATION 120 V. NE PAS RACCORDER DE CIRCUITS DE DÉRIVATION MULTIFILAIRES.
Rule 64-112 4) b) iii)	WARNING: INVERTER OUTPUT CONNECTION. DO NOT RELOCATE THIS OVERCURRENT DEVICE.	AVERTISSEMENT : RACCORDEMENT À LA SORTIE DE L'ONDULEUR. NE PAS DÉPLACER CE DISPOSITIF DE PROTECTION CONTRE LES SURINTENSITÉS.

Appendix B Notes	English	French
Rule 64-200 2)	PHOTOVOLTAIC SYSTEM EQUIPPED WITH RAPID SHUTDOWN.	SYSTÈME PHOTOVOLTAÏQUE ÉQUIPÉ D'UN DISPOSITIF DE FERMETURE RAPIDE.
Rule 64-202 5)	DANGER 1500 V dc	DANGER 1500 V c.c.
Rule 64-700 3)	WARNING: THIS DISCONNECTING MEANS DOES NOT CONTROL THE ELECTRICAL ENERGY STORAGE DEVICES.	AVERTISSEMENT : CE DISPOSITIF DE SECTIONNEMENT NE COMMANDE PAS LES ACCUMULATEURS D'ÉNERGIE ÉLECTRIQUE.

Appendix M

Index

Ⓔ

A

AFCI *See* Arc-fault circuit interrupters
Accessibility
    boxes 12-3014
    disconnecting means 28-604
    maintenance 2-314
    overcurrent devices 6-206, 14-106
Air conditioners *See* Hermetic type equipment
Aircraft hangars 20-400
Air ducts and plenums, conductors in 12-010, 16-220, 54-406, 56-210, 60-314, 60-402, Table 19
Airport installations Section 74
Amateur radio installations Section 54
Amendments to the Code Appendix C6, C7
Ampacity
    conductors 4-004, 4-034, 16-210, Tables 1, 2, 3, 4, 12, 12A, 57, 66, D8A to D11B
        for hermetic equipment 28-706
        for motors 28-104 to 28-112
    correction factors Tables 5A, 5B, 5C, 5D
    neutral supported cable 4-004, Tables 36A, 36B
    portable power cables Table 12A
    underground conductors 4-004, 8-104
Amplifiers for transmitters 54-1006
Amusement parks Section 66
Anchors in concrete or masonry 2-114
Antenna, community distribution Section 54
Antennas, grounding of 54-922
Appliances, non-portable 26-740 to 26-750
Application Class A photovoltaic module 64-002, 64-208
Application Class B photovoltaic module 64-002, 64-208
Application Class C photovoltaic module 64-002, 64-208

Ⓔ Arc-fault circuit interrupters 26-656, 32-200
        combination-type 26-650, 26-656
        outlet branch-circuit-type 26-650, 26-656

Ⓔ Arc-fault protection 26-650, 26-656, 64-210, 64-216
Arc flash protection 2-306
Arresters, lightning 26-400 to 26-410, 30-1028, 54-800, 54-802
Authority for Rules 2-000
Auto-transformers 26-264
Auxiliary gutters 12-1900 to 12-1904
    supports for 12-1902

B

Ballast load 64-002, 64-500
Barbed wire 26-306
Bare or covered conductor ampacities Table 66

Index

C

Index

Index

Index

Index

Index

Ground fault circuit interrupters 2-138, 24-116, 26-700, 26-720, 26-956, 30-320, 32-200, 32-312, 38-085, 62-130, 62-132, 68-056, 68-064, 68-066, 68-068, 68-100, 68-202, 68-302, 70-122, 72-110, 76-016, 78-102
Ground fault detection 10-400
Ground fault protection 14-102, 32-312, 62-116, 84-016
Ground fault protection location 14-102, Diagram 3
Grounding
    cable trays 12-2208
    capacitors 26-206
    circuits 30-1022
    communication systems 60-700 to 60-710
    community antenna distribution systems 54-200, 54-300 to 54-304
    connections
        for alternating current systems 10-210
    cranes and hoists 40-024
    diagnostic imaging equipment 52-014
    electrode connections 54-304
    electrodes 10-102, 54-302
    electrodes, interconnection of 10-104, 10-108, 54-302, 60-708
    elevator equipment 38-081, 38-082
    equipment 10-600, 32-104, 34-110, 52-014, 54-302, 54-504, 54-900 to 54-922, 68-402
    fences 36-312
    high-voltage 36-300 to 36-312
    lighting equipment 30-112
    methods for luminaires 30-1022 to 30-1026
    non-electrical equipment 10-700, 68-058
    objectives 10-002
    patient care environments Section 24
    pools 68-058
    radio and television stations 54-900 to 54-922
    separately derived systems 10-212
    signs 34-110
    systems 10-200, 10-206, 10-212, 10-214, 10-300
    transmitters 54-1002
Grounding of antennas 54-922
Grounding and bonding conductor
    connections 10-118, 10-204, 10-210, 10-212, 10-214, 10-402, 10-600
    installation 10-116, 10-610, 10-612
    sizes 10-114, 10-614, 36-300, 36-308, Tables 16, 41, 43
Grounding and bonding conductors 10-112, 10-610
    objectionable current over 10-100
Guarding
    bare live parts 2-202
    capacitors 26-204
    contact conductors 40-020
    high-voltage parts on diagnostic imaging equipment 52-004
    live parts 36-110
    motors 28-012, 28-014
Gutters, auxiliary *See* Auxiliary gutters

H

Hangars, aircraft 20-400 to 20-422
Hazardous areas
    natural gas
        division system Annex J20-062
        zone system 20-062
    propane
        division system Annex J20-034
        zone system 20-034
Hazardous locations Section 18
    cables in 18-060
    Class II J18-202 to J18-276
    Class III J18-302 to J18-378
    communication circuits in 60-106
    division system Appendix J
    equipment protection level 18-052, 18-100, 18-150, Appendix J
    flexible cords in 18-110, 18-158, 18-196, J18-220, J18-270, J18-318, J18-368
    luminaires in 18-108, 18-156, J18-218, J18-268, J18-316, J18-366
    marking for 18-052
    seals in 18-104, 18-154, 18-194, 18-254, J18-206, J18-256
    separation of 18-058
    surge protection for 18-060
    switches in 18-150, J18-208, J18-258, J18-306, J18-356
    transformers in 18-150, J18-202, J18-252, J18-302, J18-352
    wiring methods in 18-102, 18-152, 18-192, 18-202, 18-252, J18-204, J18-254, J18-304, J18-354
    zones Section 18, Section 20
    zone system 18-006, 18-100 to 18-158
HDPE
    conduit 12-1250
    conductors in conduit 12-1250
Healthcare facility administration 24-002
Health care facilities, patient care environments Section 24
Heating
    cable set 62-122 to 62-128, 62-214 to 62-218, 62-306 to 62-312
    central units 62-206
    equipment 26-800
    fixture installation 62-302
    in concrete 62-304
    installation 62-124, 62-308, 62-400
    panels and heating panel sets, installation of Section 62
    pipeline resistance 62-316
    skin effect 62-104, 62-314, 64-602
    space Section 62
    surface Section 62, 62-300
    temperature control 62-120, 62-202
    terminal connections 62-108
Height of luminaires 30-314
Hermetic equipment
    control of 28-712

Index

Index

Index

Ⓔ

Index

Index

Index

Index